THE MODERN LIBRARY
of the World's Best Books

>>>>>>>>>>>>>>>>>>>>>>>>>>>>>>>>>>>>>>

SELECTED WRITINGS
OF
THOMAS DE QUINCEY

The publishers will be pleased to send, upon request, an illustrated folder setting forth the purpose and scope of THE MODERN LIBRARY, *and listing each volume in the series. Every reader will find titles he has been looking for, handsomely printed, in definitive editions, and at an unusually low price.*

SELECTED WRITINGS
OF
Thomas De Quincey

Selected and Edited,
with an Introduction by
PHILIP VAN DOREN STERN

THE MODERN LIBRARY
NEW YORK

FIRST *Modern Library* GIANT EDITION

1949

THE MODERN LIBRARY

IS PUBLISHED BY

RANDOM HOUSE, INC.

BENNETT A. CERF · DONALD S. KLOPFER · ROBERT K. HAAS

Manufactured in the United States of America

Printed by Parkway Printing Company   *Bound by H. Wolff*

TABLE OF CONTENTS

v

INTRODUCTION

THERE are two ways to look back upon time long past. One of them—the most usual—is to fling yourself into the midst of some remote era, catch time by the forelock as it passes, and try to go forward with it in the regular chronological way. This method, although firmly established by convention, is actually an artificial one. It is not, as the least examination will show, the way we look upon our own lives. We do not, for instance, begin at the beginning with our own birth—a momentous occasion about which we universally remember nothing at all—nor do we, in our recollections, progress in an orderly manner through childhood and adolescence until we can finally catch up with ourselves as we are today. We begin rather with *now* and look back at this morning's breakfast; we remember yesterday already rather vaguely; last week is mixed up with other weeks about which we cannot be quite sure; last month is incredibly remote; and last year is neither farther nor nearer to us than the year before or five years before that—everything in the more distant past is equally unreal and fictitious, except that as we go farther and farther back towards earliest childhood, our memories become so isolated that it is difficult for us to prove to ourselves in any cold and demonstrably factual way that we ever began at all.

If we apply this same common-sense method to the life of any other person we can at once realize how absurd it is to begin by saying, for instance, that Thomas De Quincey was born in Manchester, on the fifteenth of August, 1785. Of what earthly interest to us is it that a child was born to a certain obscure Thomas Quincey,[1] middle-class merchant who had some slight pretence to culture in that he had written a book of English travels and possessed a dilettant knowledge of painting? Doubtless there were hundreds of children born into the world on that day, some few of them probably in the city of Manchester itself. They have all of them perished. They are utterly forgotten, gone into that vast charnel house of the undistinguished dead about whom it can only be said that they too once lived and rejoiced for a little while under the sun.

Our interest in Thomas De Quincey begins not with his birth, when he had yet to prove himself worthy of interest, but with his death, when he had already done so. The day of his death is nearer to us in point of time; we can, without too much effort, creep back through the veins of our fathers to our grandfathers (or great-grandfathers if necessary) to an early morning in December, 1859, when Thomas De Quincey, wasted and aged, but with a full life behind him, lay dying in a rented room at 42, Lothian Street, Edinburgh.

The little tired man who was so quietly breathing his life away had made a curious name for himself. He had been known to magazine readers throughout the world as the English Opium-Eater, and there was about him that aura of the mysterious which is associated with those who have dared to explore the farthest depths of the human mind with the aid of the strange oriental drug. A painter of the romantic school, depicting his deathbed, would have peopled the air with phantoms, misshapen and horrible images from the mythology of the East and "unutterable slimy things from the Nilotic mud." And there would be faces there,

[1] De Quincey's father called himself plain Thomas Quincey. The "De" was assumed by the family after his death in 1793.

pale and delirium-haunted, drawn with suffering, and dragged up from the dark and rain-swept streets of a London that had already ceased to exist.

These were the images of his dreams. His life, except for the one remarkable period described in the *Confessions*, had been rather uneventful, haunted by the very real spectres of poverty and hunger and by the omnipresent police officers hounding him endlessly for unpaid debts.

The last nine years had been relatively peaceful. Scattered around him in the room where he lay dying were the manuscripts and proofs from which he was building the collected edition of his far-scattered works. Nearly all of his writings had appeared first in magazine form for the very good reason that in this way it was possible, by writing comparatively short pieces, to obtain some money quickly. And there was a never-ending need for money with eight small children crying for food. His books (he had once owned five thousand) had long since been sold to feed the hungry mouths. When he says, as he often does, "I write this without books for reference," he means just that. His books were gone and it was impossible for him to venture out to borrow from friends. He was afraid of being picked up by some watchful officer of the law. He had several times taken refuge in the debtors' sanctuary of Holyrood, but finally even that had been closed to him, for he had incurred debts within the actual confines of the sanctuary itself.[1]

Poverty and debt had plagued his life for thirty years and he had been tortured since early childhood by illness. A list of his ailments reads like the index to a

[1] It has been estimated that De Quincey's income from writing did not average more than £150 a year. He received some money from his mother and his uncle but his total income was simply not large enough for the needs of his family.

treatise on pathology. As a child he had shown a tendency to tuberculosis; at the age of nineteen he had been driven to the use of opium as a respite from rheumatic pain; his eyes had never been good and at times he feared that he would lose his sight; fever and delirium held him in their grip for months on end; he suffered the agonies of erysipelas and gout; and—worst of all—he felt, on several occasions, that he was entering the soul-shaking realm of *Mater Tenebrarum*, mother of lunacies, that he describes so vividly in "Levana and Our Ladies of Sorrow."

He had lived like a recluse, solitary and shy. The amazing range of his writing reflects the range of a mind that had sampled everything and travelled everywhere—in books. Actually, he had never been out of the British Isles although he had planned to settle in the Canadian woods, to go to Germany, to France, to Spain. . . .

Those who knew him in his later years speak invariably of the little man's gentle manners, of his beautifully modulated voice, and, above all, of his conversational ability. Words flowed from him naturally; his sentences, elaborate and complex, came with the ease that only a life-long acquaintanceship with fine prose could establish. They speak too of the eccentricities of his old age. He drank up the contents of old medicine bottles in the hope that the composite mixture would have a salutary effect; he stored his tattered manuscripts in a tin bath and he carried with him a pocket brush so he could dust them off before handing them to the printer. He was always plagued by fire—it burned up his precious papers, and once, as he sat reading too near a lamp, his hair began to blaze. He casually brushed away the flames and continued with his book. He was oblivious of such external things as money or clothes; his mind lived within itself, dwelling in a country of its own where such things as time and the elements were unimportant.

He had come to Edinburgh in 1828, drawn there by the opportunity of supplying articles for *Blackwood's Magazine*. He hated the whole business of writing. He would have preferred to live the life of a scholar, drinking in knowledge rather than having to make the effort of giving it out. He was thirty-six when his first writings of any importance appeared and he had been driven to the work by the need for money. He loved to plan vast and grandiose works. He had wanted to spend his life compiling one great opus which was to have been entitled *De Emendatione Humani Intellectûs*. He never began it. At the age of seventy he wished to undertake the writing of a history of England to be published in twelve volumes. His very practical publisher held him to the task of preparing the collected edition of his works instead, but he continued to toy with the idea for some years. His letters are studded with reference to work projected, but never begun or finished.

Compared with men like Chatterton or Otway or Keats he had been fortunate. His first published work had brought him instant success—fame if not fortune. The *Confessions of an English Opium-Eater*, written hastily for *The London Magazine*, where they appeared in the autumn of 1821, immediately established the reputation of their anonymous author. Taylor and Hessey, the publishers, brought the *Confessions* out in book form and sold several editions. De Quincey received a present of £20 for the book—he had no legal rights in its profits.

Shortly after the *Confessions* appeared in *The London Magazine*, De Quincey returned to the Lake country where his wife and family had recently moved to a cottage in Fox Ghyll, a few miles from Grasmere. A new phase was beginning in his life—a phase of long-continued poverty and the necessity to struggle against it. When he had first taken up residence in Westmorland in 1809, he was still young; he was a bachelor possessed of a comfortable income and a large library of books—and the opium habit was still a pleasant novelty. He had taken over Dove Cottage in Grasmere, which the Wordsworth family had just vacated, and Wordsworth and Coleridge were still the idols of his hero-worshipping youth.

His marriage in 1817 to Margaret Simpson, three months after the birth of their illegitimate son, had outraged the righteous mind of Wordsworth who was still trying to forget the unacknowledged daughter he had brought into the world in France during the early days of the Revolution. And Wordsworth followed the traditional course of the radical who turns reactionary —he disapproved of De Quincey not only on moral grounds, but for social reasons as well. The Simpson family was of native Westmorland origin; the father was a dalesman—his daughter obviously was not suited to be the wife of a gentleman or to associate on terms of equality with people like the Wordsworths, who were shocked by the rising wave of democracy that was threatening their own country. De Quincey, in his writings, speaks of his estrangement from Wordsworth. He gives many reasons for it, but he does not mention his own marriage directly as one of them. Letters of the Wordsworth family, however, leave no doubt on the subject.

The early years of his marriage to Margaret must have been almost intolerable for her. It was fortunate that she came of good sturdy country stock—a more neurotic woman would surely have broken down under the fearful strain. There is no doubt that she made a good wife for the highly strung and eccentric De

Quincey. Few women could have stood all that she did, and even she, after years of deprivation and anxiety, became ill and melancholy, and in 1830 she threatened to kill herself.[1]

In 1818, De Quincey had permitted himself to sink into one of the deepest opium-drugged periods of his life. His young wife, terrified, would watch by his bedside as the agonized man tossed restlessly about in his hideous dreams. "I heard gentle voices speaking to me," he says, " (I hear everything when I am sleeping) ; and I instantly awoke; it was broad noon; and my children were standing, hat in hand, at my bedside; come to show me their coloured shoes, or new frocks or to let me see them dressed for going out. . . . So awful was the transition . . . that I wept, and I could not forbear it, as I kissed their faces."

He was brought back to everyday existence from his opium dreams by two things, both of them political and economic in their nature. One was his great interest in David Ricardo's book on political economy; the other was the opportunity of becoming editor of the local Tory paper, *The Westmorland Gazette*. He was not a good editor but it is worth noting that the interest in murder and horror which later served to inspire the famous "On Murder Considered as One of the Fine Arts" was prefigured in those days by his filling the paper with long and detailed accounts of sensational murder trials.

The years he spent in Dove Cottage ("cottage immortal in my remembrance!") were surely the happiest in all his troubled career. He had come to Westmorland to be in the company of the men he revered most, and for a while at least, that land of glorious lakes and mountains must have been a paradise to him.

When he arrived in Grasmere for the first time, he

[1] She died in 1837 of typhus fever.

was still a student at Oxford. It was only three years since he had made his first visit to that mysterious apothecary's shop near the stately Pantheon to buy opium. And he was still close to the vivid recollection of a July morning in the year 1802, when he had run away from the Manchester Grammar School, equipped only with a parcel of clothes and two books—an English poet and the plays of Euripides. He had spent the summer tramping in Wales, sleeping in the open and living with the country people. The autumn of that year had seen him in London, destitute and lonely. This was the period described in the *Confessions*, the period when he lived in an empty house in Greek Street, and Ann of Oxford Street became his companion in misery.

This winter in London, at the age of seventeen, when he was on his own and for the first time in his life experienced hunger and cold, left a profound impression on him. The things he saw and went through in that dark city were to haunt him for the rest of his life. The memory of them occurs and recurs in his dreams and in his writings as a foreboding leitmotiv. And yet what actually happened we do not know. What he writes about openly is not enough to explain his sheer terror of their remembrance. There must have been other, more hidden and more dreadful things that he never mentioned. He hints as much.

We have one invaluable record of him at this period. In the spring of 1803, freshly returned from his London adventure, he was at Everton. From April 28 to June 24 he kept a diary which has recently been discovered and published.[1] There is no doubt that this diary was a strictly private record intended only for

[1] *A Diary of Thomas De Quincey for 1803*, edited by Horace A. Eaton. Noel Douglas, London. Payson and Clarke, New York. 1927.

its author's own eyes. It contains certain passages—in Greek—that have to do with intimate physiological functions. It is a document that reveals the inner workings of De Quincey's mind during its most formative stage, but it contains not one single reference to the harrowing London experiences he had just gone through. He evidently wished to shut them out of his mind.

He was a precocious boy, as the diary shows. He was extraordinarily proficient in Greek even in a day when the classical languages were still the major part of every gentleman's education. And it was this very precocity that made him impatient with the routine work at school. He wanted to enter Oxford, for which he felt himself fully prepared; his mother and his guardians insisted that he stay at the Manchester Grammar School. He ran away and spent his *Wanderjahr* in Wales and in London as we have seen.

There is no doubt that his life was shaped by the lack of understanding that his mother displayed. She was a cold and ultra-religious person with an over-developed sense of duty. And she was, as De Quincey's account of her shows, more interested in her rapidly changed residences (she had a passion for building and remodelling) and in her progress in evangelical society than she was in her children. Her husband had left her a considerable amount of money. She devoted more of it to her experiments in domestic architecture than she did to the education of her sons. Thomas was not the only one who fled from a school that he disliked—his brother Richard ran away to sea and died there.

De Quincey gives us an intimate glimpse of his own childhood years in the papers entitled *Autobiographic Sketches*. He was a highly imaginative child, profoundly stirred by the mysteries of death. When he was five years old his sister Jane died. A year later

Elizabeth followed her. He crept into the room where
the dead child lay in a warm flood of summer sunlight.
The full realization of death rushed in upon him. "Life
is finished! Finished it is!" he kept saying. Then when
he was eight, he saw his father brought home from the
West Indies to die. De Quincey's dedication to the
altars of Our Ladies of Sorrow began early. He was to
live under their awful dominion until they had indeed
"plagued his heart until they had unfolded the capacities of his spirit."

We have now, by the devious method of attempting
to recapture time past, arrived very near to that initial
moment when the puny cries of a newborn infant heralded the entry of Thomas De Quincey into his troubled life. And we have the advantage of being able to
take leave of him in his birth-chamber with all his long
life before him—as we can omnisciently foresee—
rather than to have to part with him in the customary
manner, at his graveside, like mourners standing in
the rain.

He had spent his life in a welter of old papers.
Around him always were books, proofs, and manuscripts—some of them stained to this day with the
purple ring left by a glass of laudanum. He had shut
himself off from the world, so that the swift and
astounding changes taking place in his generation
reached him only at second hand, filtered through a
screen of printed symbols. He had been born into the
eighteenth century at a time when its glories were fading. He knew that the age of elegance was over, and
that there was nothing to be gained from carrying on
its already obsolete literary and artistic forms. The
rhymed couplet had gone with the rapier into oblivion.

His life was to mark the transition from a world
of stage-coaches and candle-light, to a world of

steam-engines and electricity. In the year of his birth the courts of Europe were shocked by the Affair of the Diamond Necklace that threatened the rule of Louis XVI and Marie Antoinette; in the year of his death, the citadels of orthodoxy were shaken by the publication of Darwin's *Origin of Species*. But this isolated scholar never understood that the very structure of civilization was being altered; never became fully aware of the effect that this alteration was having on the minds and characters of his fellow men. He had seen the huge spinning-mills spring up in his native city of Manchester to bring ruin to the household weavers of the countryside. He had heard the deep sullen rumblings of Watt's new engines, but he was deaf to their significance.

He had grown up in an era of revolution. He had been educated during the years when the armies of Napoleon were conquering the strongholds of European feudalism. But to De Quincey's insular mind, Bonaparte was only a bloodthirsty monster who might invade the peaceful shores of England. He disliked everything French, and to him revolution was a French disease which should be rigorously quarantined. He never experienced the revolutionary ardour that dominated the youth of Wordsworth and Coleridge, nor did he, of course, have to suffer their disillusionment. He was professedly a Tory and he preserved throughout his life a complacent belief in aristocratic institutions. He was passionately interested in the science of political economy but he never comprehended the political and economic actualities of his own times.

But if he was a Tory in politics he was at least sympathetic to radical ideas in literature. He was one of the first in all England to be drawn to the new poetry of Wordsworth and Coleridge. He was opposed to the forces that had moulded their poetic ideals, but he greeted enthusiastically these writers who were attempting to express in everyday language the rhythm of contemporary life. In his own work, however, he did not follow their lead. He drew upon the writings of past centuries for the influences which shaped his style, and his subject matter was a strange mixture of intimate self-analysis and historical pedantry.

Yet he was in every way a romantic; he helped to introduce the romantic literature of Germany to England; he was powerfully influenced by the imaginative prose of Jean Paul Richter; and he was unusually well read in the philosophy that constituted the ideational foundation of romanticism.

It is not difficult to understand why he was so unclearly oriented. Romanticism itself was a curious product of contradictory tendencies. Basically it was the artistic expression of the mighty forces that were reshaping the world. (In this phase it was as revolutionary as the Phrygian cap, and it represented a progressive movement in the development of society.) Yet it contained within itself a reactionary element— a nostalgic and backward-looking gesture toward the glories of the feudal past. In its highest form this fond look backwards was expressed in the transcendental mysticism of Blake, Coleridge, and Keats. For more popular consumption there were the historical romances of Sir Walter Scott and, on an even lower plane, the tales of Monk Lewis and Mrs. Radcliffe with their ancient castles haunted by ghosts in clanking chains, their pale knights in armour, and their inevitable maidens in distress.

This spiritual dichotomy in the romantic movement was reflected in many of the writers themselves. Wordsworth, perhaps, was the most characteristic example of it. He had gone to France to become an ardent participant in the Revolution; but the actuality

of what he saw there turned him bitterly against ideas
that were even faintly liberal. Coleridge's was a more
complex case. He had shared Wordsworth's revolutionary views, but even as a youth his mind was heavily
overlaid with a mysticism that had its origins firmly
rooted in the past. Some writers, of course, remained
always consistent in their political attitudes. Hazlitt
was ever the radical who admired Napoleon; Scott was
born a Tory, and his deep-seated hatred of democracy
forced him to take refuge in the imaginary splendours
of the age of chivalry. De Quincey was thoroughly reactionary in his politics; he was an author of Gothic
fiction that dealt almost exclusively with the feudal
past; yet, strangely enough, he was a radical of a peculiarly intransigent nature in his approach to imaginative writing. He broke the conventional restrictions of
British reserve in writing the *Confessions*, and he was
one of the pioneers who brought to English prose the
new element of subjectivity that was to be so important
in the literature of the next century.

English literature, like most other literatures, had
made the earliest progress in poetry. Prose had been
much slower in its development. During the sixteenth
and seventeenth centuries, prose had been used largely
for formal thought, for the expression of religious or
philosophical ideas, or for purely polemical purposes.
The novel began as an objective account of human experience, yet even in its earliest stages it pointed the
tendencies toward subjectivity. (Crusoe's mental re-
actions to the discovery of a mysterious footprint in
the sand of his desert island perhaps mark the initial
appearance of this new element in the English novel.)
During the eighteenth century the novel became freer
in form, more sensitive to the expression of personality.
Laurence Sterne was able to use it as an amorphous
and plastic vehicle for his own charming and utterly

disorderly mind. And in another field of prose writing, that of biography, that strange and much-snubbed little innovator, James Boswell, studied the character of one of his contemporaries so closely that he was able to immortalize him as a living figure whom we can almost see and hear.

But the strange and secret workings of the human mind, with its irrational and jumbled associations, its dark upsurgings from the primitive world of lust and murderous hatred, and its shadowy dream life, still offered fresh territory for literary exploration. Rousseau had poured out the story of his life's intimacies, but he had actually revealed very little about his inner self—what he had told was startling and unusual enough, but nearly all of it was concerned with external things.

The instant success of the *Confessions of an English Opium-Eater* indicated that the public was more than ready for subjectivity in writing. Like Rousseau, although without his all-embracing frankness, De Quincey took the reader into his confidence and exposed even the less admirable side of his own character. But he went beyond Rousseau by leading the reader into the innermost recesses of his subconscious mind where his opium dreams in all their terrible magnificence held sway.

All this was novel and thrilling to the romantic mind, for the romantic was an individualist who was interested primarily in himself. And in the new society that was rising to power [1] the individualist was being given a tremendous prominence, since anyone, in

[1]This new culture, founded on a machine economy under middle-class dominance, made its greatest contribution to literature in introspective writing, and introspective writing has faithfully recorded the development of bourgeois culture from its earliest beginnings to its climactic peak. It is significant that

theory at least, was now to be able to make his way in the world, regardless of his birth or ancestry.

It is in this field of personal writing that De Quincey did his finest work. The *Confessions*, together with the *Suspiria de Profundis*, the *Autobiographic Sketches*, and the *Reminiscences* of Wordsworth, Coleridge, Southey, and Lamb, constitute a body of literature which has permanent value. The hundreds of scattered essays on history, philology, politics, and theology have been superseded by more modern work. De Quincey originated the famous distinction between the literature of knowledge and the literature of power [1] and his own works have demonstrated its validity.

As a writer of fiction he was a failure. He lacked the peculiar kind of inventive power needed to create character and devise original plots. He could put down on paper an amazingly accurate portrait of someone he had seen and known (he makes Wordsworth a living figure, and the description of his first meeting with Charles Lamb is vividly realistic), but he always had to have the living model in mind before he could make the portrait. He possessed a fine narrative power (see the "Revolt of the Tartars" and the magnificent last paper of "On Murder Considered as One of the Fine Arts"), but in these he had the advantage of being able to work with actual historical material. Even his taste in fiction was not good. He had an unfortunate predilection for German romantic tales and for the

in our own time, when this culture is in a period of decadence, the brilliant colours of its decomposition have been described by the great authors of its silver age—Joyce, Proust, and T. S. Eliot—in a final burst of tortured introspective writing that is sometimes incomprehensible in its complete surrender to subjectivity.

[1] The idea was probably first conceived during his conversations with Coleridge. The essay outlining the distinction is reproduced in the text of the present volume.

sentimental-horror writing of the Mrs. Radcliffe
school. He was blind to the merits of the English novel
even in its greatest period of development under
Thackeray, Dickens, and the Brontës. He preferred
the now-forgotten romances of Harriet Lee to the
vigorous work of Smollett and Fielding, which to him
was disgusting and vicious because it depicted realis-
tically a society that he considered lacking in moral
virtue.

But if he lacked the faculty of being able to create
seeming images of flesh and blood, it was certainly because of no inherent lack of imaginative power. This
power in him was vast and terrible. He drew his material from that inexhaustible reservoir—the subconscious mind; he perceived the richness that lay concealed there; and at times his writing shuttles curiously
between the levels of wakeful objectivity and the dark
reaches of that hinterland which only the sleep-
drugged brain can traverse.

He was always an avowed believer in the intuitive.
He wanted to go beyond the concrete phenomena of
physical existence to the shadowy domain of noumenal
substance. He was interested in the way the mind
worked at moments of fearful stress—at the instant
before death, or at that frightful pitch when it is ready
to kill. His preoccupation with murder was no superficial thing. It was surely not brought about, as has
been suggested, merely as a reaction from the uneventful nature of his own sequestered life. (According to
this specious reasoning every clerk and scholar should
be a devotee of murder.) His interest in violent death
and horror was more likely due to his own deeply introspective nature which was forever turning to the
secret springs of human action that have their sources
in the inexplicable mysteries of birth and death. And
then, too, the age in which he lived was one that would

engender in a sensitive mind a consciousness of fleshly corruption and a realization of mankind's subjection to pain.

He lived in an age of violence and terror; the chaos of revolution and the bitterness of black reaction reigned alternately in Europe. It was a time for despair —but it was also a time for hope. The people had progressed far beyond their ancestors' unquestioning resignation to oppression. During De Quincey's lifetime the ancient English laws which inflicted capital punishment for trivial offences were repealed because it became almost impossible to find a jury that would convict a prisoner under them. The terrible conditions that had prevailed in prisons and insane asylums were ameliorated because the public conscience could no longer tolerate them. Men were beginning to realize that the brutal and casual infliction of pain and death no longer had to be taken for granted as a necessary evil in human society. It was a world that was filled with suffering, but people were at least beginning to rebel against their burden of agony, and, more important still, they were beginning to understand that their lives on this earth could be made more endurable.

The sensitive mind of the artist was acutely aware of the oppression that ruled the world, but it was morbidly attracted by the idea of inflicted pain and death (witness *Los Desastres de la guerra* of Goya), even though it condemned the torturers and the murderers. De Quincey, in the first two papers in "On Murder Considered as One of the Fine Arts," plays with the subject of murder, treating the idea facetiously; in the Postscript he tells the stories of two actual murders, and in this encounter with reality, his whole attitude changes. There is very little levity in the Postscript. It is a grim and fearful description of terror let loose at night. Death is no longer a dancing skeleton, but a sombre figure that stalks his prey with an implacable and bloody lust.

It was in this world which lies between twilight and darkness that De Quincey was most at home. To him even the simplicities of daily existence had about them a quality of strangeness. His reaction to things was never the usual one of matter-of-fact people. He saw London, not as a sprawling and industrial metropolis emerging from the provincial elegance of the eighteenth century, but as a vast nation, a conglomeration of peoples living in misery and luxury, where the slow sullen rhythm of life was made up from the heartbeats of mankind in travail. Its narrow sinister streets haunted his dreams, and again and again he would find himself back among the terraces of Oxford Street, pacing its nightly silences with the forlorn figure of Ann at his side. Even the solid and substantial reality of an English mail-coach took on in his mind a symbolic meaning. It was more than a method of transportation; it was a part of the nervous system of a great country, and its swift passage through town and village spread across the nation the tidings of defeat and victory, of dissolution and progress. And in its terrible flight it carried with it a shrouded coachman who took the place of the sleeping driver to send the flying hoofs of its horses into a rhythm that pounded out a song of death.

The writing produced by this dark and brooding mind called for a style that was founded in the vivid realization of sensual experience and in the capture of transubstantial awareness. The age had favoured the growth of an experimental technique in the handling of English prose. The rise to power of a stratum of society numerically greater than the narrow circle of aristocracy that had been the literary audience of the past, brought into existence a new reading public. It may be charged that this public lacked culture and discrimination, and that at its worst it was eager only for the romances of Sir Walter Scott and the tales of the ancient-castle school, but it was at least a public which was interested in the substance of what a writer had to say rather than in how well he abided by the established rules of a stultified and formal literary technique. It was a public that brought prose writing down from the abstractions of theological and philosophical thought to the level of contemporary human intercourse. It made prose the vehicle for the expression of common ideas that had to do with people and their way of living; it brought into being a type of writing that was concerned with concrete things—how they looked and smelled and felt.

The romantic dichotomy, however, was expressed in style as well as in subject. Prose was not only hard and real but mystical and imaginative. In the early years of the nineteenth century the tendency toward concreteness and informality was only foreshadowed. It was not to reach its full development until some years later in the hands of Dickens and Thackeray and Trollope. De Quincey indicated the trend toward realism in the style he used for the *Autobiographic Sketches* and the *Reminiscences*, but his own tastes ran in the other direction. The style for which he became famous was based on the grandiloquent prose of the seventeenth century, particularly as seen in the writings of Milton, Sir Thomas Browne, Jeremy Taylor, and the translators of the King James Bible.

It is significant that one of the dominating passions of De Quincey's life was music. He was strongly ear-minded rather than eye-minded. He was only mildly interested in the art of painting which meant so much to Lamb and Hazlitt. He speaks of spending opium-drugged nights at the opera listening in a melomanic rapture to Grassini; his dreams were filled with the mighty paeans of a superterrestrial organ. He was offended by the very presence of a book bearing on its backbone the harsh title *Burke's Works*. When he wrote, he sounded every syllable in his ear before putting it down on paper, and he built his single sentences and paragraphs on the complex and developmental patterns of a fugue.

Unfortunately he lacked the architectural sense of construction and proportion that a good musician must have. His writing is almost never soundly planned and it is never developed in an orderly and logical way. He strays from the main theme into all sorts of hopeless blind alleys. A word will set him off; its mention recalls associations in his brain that he cannot resist; sometimes he wanders even from his own wanderings into a morass of irrelevancies. This is the most serious of his faults;[1] his others may have some excuse in that they are founded on tendencies which were common in his time. He is often sentimental; he is inclined to be pedantic, and he is occasionally heavily and unwarrantably facetious when dealing with subjects that obviously do not permit the intrusion of ill-considered humour.

Much of his bad writing was unquestionably caused by the conditions under which he worked. As a writer for the periodicals, he had to supply a continual stream of copy to the printer. Often he was sick and miserable. Opium, too, had its deadening effects on the creative faculties, and his brain sometimes would simply refuse to function under the constant pressure. As a result, his work is uneven to a degree almost unparalleled in

---

[1] In the present edition, De Quincey's erratic divagations will be found to be less prevalent than in the original text of his writings. Lack of space has compelled the editor to excise many irrelevant passages.

literature. The best of it is difficult to match in any language; the worst is dangerously close to hack journalism.

It has often been maintained, especially by people ignorant of De Quincey's character and unfamiliar with any great body of his writings, that his work is the result of opium-eating, and that he owes the particular grandeur of his style and imagery to the effects of the drug on his imagination. Opium, however, cannot bring up out of the mind anything that is not already there. De Quincey says of the dreaming faculty: "He whose talk is of oxen will probably dream of oxen; and the condition of human life which yokes so vast a majority to a daily experience incompatible with much elevation of thought sometimes neutralizes the tone of grandeur in the reproductive faculty of dreaming, even for those whose minds are populous with solemn imagery. Habitually to dream magnificently, a man must have a constitutional determination to reverie." There can be no doubt that his was a mind innately endowed with imaginative splendour. His childhood was rich with the wonder of life, and his adolescence was climaxed by a premature encounter with the nocturnal world of London that was forever to remain seared into his memory. Opium needed to serve only as a key to release into consciousness the secret images of his brain.

Opium played its part in his life, but much of its influence was malign. It furthered the growth of his all too ready habit of procrastination, and it slowed down his literary output. It brought him fame as an author but it also was responsible for the distorted estimation of his character that his contemporaries established—an estimation that has unfortunately persisted to this day.

De Quincey was not at all the strange and perverted creature the popular mind supposes him to have been.[1] He had nothing in common with the Huysmans-Baudelaire school of writing with which he is sometimes mistakenly associated—in fact its subtly veiled eroticism would have horrified him.

De Quincey, like Poe, whose life paralleled his in many ways, was destined to have a greater following in other lands than in his own country. The *Confessions* were translated into French by the youthful Alfred de Musset who was compelled by his publisher to add an absurd ending to the original work. Baudelaire unquestionably owes much to the Opium-Eater, and Berlioz, in another field of artistic expression, derived the inspiration for his *Symphonie fantastique* from the *Confessions*.

The actual part that De Quincey played in the literary movement of his day was not a very active one so far as his influence on other English writers is concerned. He managed to come in contact with most of the great literary figures of his time but they made a deeper impression on him than he did on them. He has left us full-length portraits of Coleridge, Wordsworth, Lamb, and Southey. They in turn have given us nothing about him except what occurs casually in letters or in passing references. He was an unobtrusive figure, and his writings, which appeared almost exclusively in the impermanent form of periodical contributions, led his contemporaries to underestimate him as a man of letters. In the last decade of his life, when his work was gathered into the more

[1] There could hardly be more outrageous perversions of the truth than certain editions of the *Confessions* which have been published with illustrations showing De Quincey as a gaunt, wild-eyed drug fiend against a background of silly "modernistic" symbols. Such work is more expressive of the artist's poverty of conception than it is of the rich imagery of De Quincey's dreams.

respectable form of a collected edition, the great men of his youth were all dead, and time remained only for first-hand accounts of him from minor writers like Harriet Martineau, John R. Findlay, and James Hogg. By then he was an old man whose eccentricities were more apparent than his genius.

The records of great men are all too often unduly weighted by the memorabilia of their declining years when their greatness has been firmly established. With De Quincey we are more fortunate, for he has left us a wealth of autobiographical material that is concerned with his youth. We can relive with him the life of a child in the days when "Dr. Johnson had only just ceased to be a living author"; we are permitted to jog along in the family carriage behind a postilion; we can visit the night-bound purlieus of Oxford Street, forever haunted for readers of De Quincey by the pathetic ghost of Ann; and we can go down with victory on a coach carrying the Royal English Mail—and a diminutive Oxford undergraduate. These are the years that were filled with colour—they are suffused with the heady air of morning. And the memory that most of us are likely to cherish of this odd little figure, who made for himself an enduring niche in the history of our literature, is not of the wraithlike creature of the grey Edinburgh years, but of a youth who set out one bright morning to meet the vicissitudes of this world, armed only with "a parcel . . . a favorite English poet . . . and a small duodecimo volume containing about nine plays of Euripides."

PHILIP VAN DOREN STERN

1785   AUGUST 15. Thomas De Quincey born in Manchester.

1791   Family moves to new Greenhay house near Manchester.

1793   JULY 18. His father, Thomas Quincey, dies.

1793–96 Tutored by his guardian, the Reverend Samuel Hall.

1796   AUGUST 15. Greenhay is sold. The family moves to Bath.

NOVEMBER 6. Enters Bath Grammar School.

1799   FEBRUARY. Accidentally struck on head by master's cane; leaves Bath Grammar School.

AUTUMN. Enters Winkfield Academy.

1800   JULY. Joins young Lord Westport at Eton to travel with him to Ireland. They enter London and shortly afterwards meet George III. They arrive in Ireland in time to be present at the ceremonies in the House of Lords when the Irish House is dissolved and the Union Act passed.

NOVEMBER 9. Enters Manchester Grammar School.

1801   Spends summer in Everton.

1802   JULY. Runs away from Manchester Grammar School. Goes to his mother's house in Chester. Given an allowance of one guinea a week. Starts on a walking trip through Wales.

NOVEMBER. Goes to London. Lives in lodgings in great poverty for nearly two

27

months. Then takes refuge in the Greek Street house of Brunnell. The Ann of Oxford Street episode.

1803   MARCH. A reconciliation is effected with his family and guardians. He returns to Chester.

APRIL 28 to JUNE 24. This period covered in detail in the Everton Diary (published in 1927).

MAY 31. Writes to Wordsworth.

AUGUST 2. Leaves Everton and returns to Chester.

DECEMBER 17. Enters Worcester College, Oxford.

1804   AUTUMN. First takes opium.

First meets Charles Lamb.

1807   SUMMER. Meets Coleridge.

Through Joseph Cottle he arranges to make a present of £300 anonymously to Coleridge.

NOVEMBER. He volunteers to accompany Coleridge's wife and children to the Lake country. On November 4 they arrive in Grasmere and he first meets Wordsworth.

NOVEMBER 14. Returns to Oxford. Spends most of the winter in London in company with Coleridge.

1808   MAY. Leaves Oxford abruptly in the midst of an examination.

NOVEMBER. With the Wordsworths in Grasmere.

1809   FEBRUARY 20. Leaves Grasmere to go to London in order to see Wordsworth's *Convention of Cintra* pamphlet through the press.

MAY 18. The edition is finally printed.

JULY to OCTOBER. In Wrington at his mother's house (Westhay).

OCTOBER 21. Arrives in Grasmere to take up permanent residence in Dove Cottage (November 18).

1812 JUNE 12. He is entered in the Middle Temple. Studies Law intermittently until 1815.

JUNE. Death of little Kate Wordsworth.

1815 Visits Edinburgh with John Wilson.

1816 NOVEMBER 15. An illegitimate son, William, is born to him by Margaret Simpson, daughter of a local dalesman.

1817 FEBRUARY 15. Marries Margaret Simpson. The opium habit, which has been growing on him for the last four years, now reaches its height.

1818 Becomes interested in Political Economy.

JULY 11. Assumes editorship of *The Westmorland Gazette*.

1819 NOVEMBER 5. Resigns from editorship of the *Gazette*.

1820 DECEMBER. Goes to Edinburgh to write for *Blackwood's Magazine*. Plans to do the *Opium-Eater*, among other things, for it but quarrels with William Blackwood. Returns to Grasmere.

1821 SPRING. Moves his household to Fox Ghyll.

JUNE. Goes to London. Thomas Noon Talfourd introduces him to Messrs. Taylor and Hessey, proprietors of *The London Magazine*.

SEPTEMBER. *Confessions of an English Opium-Eater* appears in *The London Magazine;* the first part in the September issue; the second in October.

1822–24 Publishes twenty-two articles in *The London Magazine*.

1822 AUGUST. The *Confessions* published in book form.

DECEMBER 9. Goes to London. In ill health and in debt (he was given £20 but he received no legal rights in the *Confessions* as a book), he writes articles frantically in order to raise money.

1823 AUGUST. Returns to Westmorland. "I have been obliged to sacrifice my wife's watch and . . . jewellery."

1824 SUMMER. Goes to London.

1825 JANUARY. Taylor and Hessey sell *The London Magazine*.

JULY. Returns to Westmorland without any literary connexions.

1826 Begins to write for *Blackwood's*.

1828 AUTUMN. Moves to Edinburgh with his family.

1830 NOVEMBER. His wife threatens to commit suicide.

Debts and suits for their collection continue.

1832 *Klosterheim* published in book form.

1833 Takes sanctuary in Holyrood to escape imprisonment for debt.

1834 JULY 25. Coleridge dies.

SEPTEMBER 16. William Blackwood dies. De Quincey loses his connexion with *Blackwood's* but continues to contribute to *Tait's Edinburgh Magazine* which had printed two of his articles in 1833. The Autobiographical Sketches are published.

DECEMBER 24. Lamb dies.

1835 MAY 25. Family moves to Caroline Cottage near Portobello.

Death of William, his eldest son.

1836   NOVEMBER 24. Takes refuge in Holyrood
        again.

1837   AUGUST 7. His wife dies.

        NOVEMBER. His debts in Holyrood itself
        have grown so pressing that he loses the
        right of sanctuary there. He goes into
        hiding in Edinburgh, rapidly changing
        lodgings.

        During this year he is actually arrested for
        debt. Adam Black, the publisher, sees
        him being taken to gaol. He obtains De
        Quincey's release by paying £30 on con-
        dition that he write two articles on
        Shakespeare and Pope for the seventh
        edition of the *Encyclopædia Britannica*.

1838   SEPTEMBER. At this time his family is re-
        duced to such a state of want that they are
        enabled to have only one meal a day. His
        youngest daughter (aged 5) cries day and
        night for more food.

1840   AUTUMN. His family moves to Lasswade,
        seven miles from Edinburgh.

1841   SPRING. De Quincey leaves Edinburgh and
        goes to Glasgow.

        Fever and, later, erysipelas set in. For the
        next several years he is hardly ever free
        from sickness.

1842   AUGUST 27. His son, Horatio, dies in China
        where he had gone as a soldier.

1843   JUNE. Leaves Glasgow and joins his family
        at Lasswade.

1844   During this year the opium habit has him
        again enchained in misery.

1845   MARCH. Returns to Edinburgh in better
        health.

1846   JANUARY 8. His mother dies at the age of
        ninety-three, and leaves him a small in-
        come.

        DECEMBER. Goes again to Glasgow.

1847   NOVEMBER. Returns to Lasswade.

1850   APRIL 23. Wordsworth dies.

        Starts to contribute to *Hogg's Weekly In-
        structor*.

1851   The first volume of the American edition of
        his collected works appears, published by
        Ticknor and Fields, Boston. (Completed
        in 1859 in twenty-two volumes.)

1853   Hogg issues the first volume of the English
        Collective Edition under the title *Selec-
        tions Grave and Gay, from Writings Pub-
        lished and Unpublished* by Thomas De
        Quincey. De Quincey spends the last
        years of his life rewriting and editing
        his work for this edition. (Completed
        1860 in fourteen volumes.)

1854   APRIL 2. John Wilson dies.

        JUNE. Moves to 42, Lothian Street, Edin-
        burgh.

1855   Dorothy Wordsworth dies.

1856   SPRING and SUMMER. Revises completely
        the *Confessions* for Hogg's Collective Edi-
        tion.

1857   JULY 21. Goes to Ireland to visit his daugh-
        ter Margaret. Returns to Edinburgh in
        August.

1859   DECEMBER 8. Dies in Edinburgh.

THE complete works of Thomas De Quincey, in
their most compact form, make a formidable array
of seventeen volumes. The editor of the present edition has had the unenviable task of selecting from this
huge mass of material the equivalent of about one-
eighth of the entirety for reprinting here.

Much of De Quincey's work is of little interest to
the modern reader. The writings on political economy
are now only museum pieces; the theological work
has slight value to the lay reader; much of the historical work seems outmoded and it is often rendered
obsolete by more recent findings; and the heavy and
stilted fiction can be eliminated easily. It has been
more difficult, however, to omit certain essays, particularly those on literary theory and criticism, but
lack of space has made their excision imperative. Lack
of space has also made it necessary to delete some of
the divagations for which De Quincey is notorious,
but the editor hopefully believes that most readers are
likely to dispense with them gladly.

The arrangement of material follows in a general
way that which De Quincey used in compiling his own
Collective Edition. The present volume starts with the
Autobiographic Sketches which trace De Quincey's
growth from early childhood to the time he entered
Oxford. At the end of the essay on the Manchester
Grammar School, the reader who wishes to follow a
chronological sequence should turn aside to read the
Confessions. No purpose would have been served by
inserting the *Confessions* into the text at this point
since they are concerned not only with a description

of De Quincey's famous excursion into Wales and London in 1802, but with the effect that opium had on his whole life. Putting the *Confessions* at the end of all the autobiographical material permits the logical placing of the *Suspiria* (which were intended as an appendage to the *Confessions*), and enables the dream-like essay "The English Mail-Coach" to follow in consistent order. "On Murder Considered as One of the Fine Arts," with its Postscript that is a conscious nightmare of horror, then falls into its natural position, with the brief "On the Knocking at the Gate in Macbeth" as a sort of philosophical postlude. The last three essays in the book form no part of this organizational scheme, so, reasonably enough, they have been placed at the end.

The basic text used is the fourteen-volume collection edited by David Masson and published in Edinburgh by Adam and Charles Black in 1889–90. The Masson edition was based on De Quincey's own Collective Edition, published in 1853–60, and consequently, in most cases, reproduces the text as emended by De Quincey at that time, rather than in the original form in which it first appeared in various periodicals. The date given at the head of each article, however, refers to the time of first publication, even in cases where De Quincey has completely rewritten and considerably altered the article for the Collective Edition.

The last two *Suspiria* are from *The Posthumous Works of Thomas De Quincey*, edited by A. H. Japp and published in London by William Heinemann in 1891–93.

The *Confessions* have been reproduced (with the excision of a very few irrelevant passages) from the revised version of 1856 which De Quincey expanded to three times the length of the original edition of 1822. It has often been said that the first short version is the better one as an integrated work of art. There is a great deal of truth in this, and De Quincey himself was not unaware of it. Nevertheless it has seemed advisable to furnish the reader with the longer form which contains much valuable autobiographical information.

Any selection and arrangement of material is certain to meet with objection. The editor can only plead that he has attempted to give to the reader who wishes to gain an appreciative understanding of the work of the English Opium-Eater an extensive portion of the entire body of his writings, and he feels secure in believing that no one can take exception to what he has included. Those students of De Quincey who may be sorry to see some favourite essay of theirs omitted can be certain that the editor has already anticipated them in his own regret.

And finally he wishes to express his gratitude to Mr. Saxe Commins and to Mr. Wallace Brockway for their encouragement and assistance in the preparation of this work. They have been, of course, in no way responsible for any errors of omission or commission. All those must be on the editor's own head.

P. V. D. S.

PART ONE

AUTOBIOGRAPHIC SKETCHES

PARENTAGE AND THE PATERNAL HOME

(First published in *Tait's Magazine*, February, 1834)

MY FATHER was a plain and unpretending man, who began life with what is considered in England (or *was* considered) a small fortune, viz., six thousand pounds. I once heard a young banker in Liverpool, with the general assent of those who heard him, fix upon that identical sum of six thousand pounds as exemplifying, for the standard of English life, the absolute *ideal* of a dangerous inheritance; just too little, as he said, to promise comfort or *real* independence, and yet large enough to operate as a temptation to indolence. Six thousand pounds, therefore, he considered in the light of a snare to a young man, and almost as a malicious bequest. On the other hand, Ludlow, the regicide, who, as the son of an English baronet, and as ex-commander-in-chief of the Parliament cavalry, etc., knew well what belonged to elegant and luxurious life, records it as his opinion of an Englishman who had sheltered him from state blood-hounds, that in possessing an annual revenue of £100, he enjoyed all the solid comforts of this life—neither himself rapacious of his neighbour's goods, nor rich enough in his own person to offer a mark to the rapacity of others. This was in 1660, when the expenses of living in England were not so widely removed, *æquatis æquandis*, from the common average of this day; both scales being far below that of the long war-period which followed the French Revolution.

What in one man, however, is wise moderation, may happen in another, differently circumstanced, to be positive injustice, or sordid inaptitude to aspire. At, or about, his twenty-sixth year, my father married; and it is probable that the pretensions of my mother, which were, in some respects, more elevated than his own, might concur with his own activity of mind to break the temptation, if for him any temptation had ever existed, to a life of obscure repose. This small fortune, in a country so expensive as England, did not promise to his wife the style of living to which she had been accustomed. Every man wishes for his wife what, on his own account, he might readily dispense with. Partly, therefore, with a view to what he would consider as her reasonable expectations, he entered into trade as an Irish and a West Indian merchant. But there is no doubt that, even apart from consideration for his wife, the general tone of feeling in English society, which stamps a kind of disreputableness on the avowed intention to *do nothing*, would, at any rate, have sent him into some mode of active life. In saying that he was a *West Indian* merchant, I must be careful to acquit his memory of any connexion with the slave trade, by which so many fortunes were made at that era in Liverpool, Glasgow, etc. Whatever may be thought of *slavery* itself as modified in the British colonies, or of the remedies attempted for that evil by modern statesmanship; of the kidnapping, murdering *slave-trade*, there cannot be two opinions; and my father, though connected with the West Indian trade in all honourable branches, was so far from lending himself even by a *passive* concurrence to this most memorable abomination, that he was one of those conscientious protestors who, throughout England, for a long period after the first publication [1] of Clarkson's

---

[1] Writing where I have no books, like Salmasius, I make all my references to a forty years' course of reading, by memory. In *every* case except where I make a formal citation marked as such, this is to be understood.

famous Essay, and the evidence delivered before the
House of Commons, strictly abstained from the use of
sugar in his own family.

Meantime, as respected some paramount feelings of
my after life, I drew from both parents, and the several
aspects of their characters, great advantages. Each,
in a different sense, was a high-toned moralist; and my
mother had a separate advantage, as compared with
persons of that rank, in high-bred and polished manners. Every man has his own standard of a *summum
bonum*, as exemplified in the arrangements of life.
For my own part, without troubling others as to my
peculiar likings and dislikings, in points which illustrate nothing—I shall acknowledge frankly that in
every scheme of social happiness I could ever frame,
the spirit of *manners* entered largely as an indispensable element. The Italian ideal of their own language, as a spoken one, is expressed thus—*Lingua
Toscana in bocca Romana:* there must be two elements
—the Florentine choice of words, and the Florentine
idiom, concurring with the Roman pronunciation.
Parodying this, I would express my conception of a
society (suppose a household) entirely well constituted, and fitted to yield the greatest amount of lasting pleasure, in these terms—the morals of the middle
classes of England, combined with the manners of the
highest; or, more pointedly, by the morals of the gentry, with the manners of the nobility. Manners more
noble, or more polished than the manners of the English nobility, I cannot imagine; nor, on the other hand,
a morality which is built less upon the mere amiableness of quick sensibilities, or more entirely upon massy
substructions of principle and conscience, than the
morality of the British middle classes. Books, literature, institutions of police, facts innumerable, within
my own experience, and open to all the world, can be

brought to bear with a world of evidence upon this subject. I am aware of the anger which I shall rouse in many minds by both doctrines; but I am not disposed to concede any point of what to me appears the truth, either to general misanthropy and cynicism, to political prejudices, or to anti-national feeling. Such notices as have occurred to me on these subjects, within my personal experience, I shall bring forward as they happen to arise. Let them be met and opposed as they shall deserve. Morals are sturdy things, and not so much liable to erroneous valuation. But the fugitive, volatile, imponderable essences which concern the spirit of manners, are really not susceptible of any just or intelligible treatment by mere words and distinctions, unless in so far as they are assisted and interpreted by continual illustrations from absolute experience. Meantime, the reader will not accuse me of an aristocratic feeling, now that he understands what it is that I admire in the aristocracy, and with what limitation. It is my infirmity, if the reader chooses so to consider it, that I cannot frame an ideal of society, happily constituted, without including, as a foremost element, and possibly in an undue balance, certain refinements in the spirit of manners, which, to many excellent people, hardly exist at all as objects of conscious regard. In the same spirit, but without acknowledging the least effeminacy, even in the excess to which I carry it, far better and more cheerfully I could dispense with some part of the downright necessaries of life, than with certain circumstances of elegance and propriety in the daily habits of using them.

With these feelings, and, if the reader chooses, these infirmities, I was placed in a singularly fortunate position. My father, as I have said, had no brilliant qualities: but the moral integrity which I have attributed to his class was so peculiarly expressed in *him*,

that in my early life, and for many years after his
death, I occasionally met strangers who would say to
me, almost in the same form of words, (so essential was
their harmony as to the thing)—"Sir, I knew your
father: he was the most upright man I ever met with
in my life." Nobody, that I remember, praised him under the notion of a clever man, or a man of talent. Yet
that he was so in some subordinate sense is probable,
both from his success as a man of business, and more
unequivocally in other ways. He wrote a book [1]: and,
though not a book of much pretension in its subject,
yet in those days to have written a book at all was
creditable to a man's activity of mind, and to his
strength of character, in acting without a precedent.
In the execution, this book was really respectable. As
to the subject, it was a sketch of a tour in the midland
counties of England, in one octavo volume. The plan
upon which it was constructed made it tolerably miscellaneous; for throughout the tour a double purpose
was kept before the reader—viz., of attention to the
Fine Arts, in a general account of the paintings and
statues in the principal mansions lying near the line
of his route; and, secondly, of attention to the Mechanic Arts, as displayed in the canals, manufactories,
etc., then rising everywhere into activity, and quickened into a hastier development by Arkwright and the
Peels in one direction, and, in another, by Brindley,
the engineer, under the patronage of the Duke of
Bridgewater. This Duke, by the way, was guided by
an accident of life, concurring with his own disposition, and his gloomy sensibility to the wrong or the
indignity he had suffered, into those ascetic habits
which left his income disposable for canals, and for the
patronizing of Brindley. He had been jilted: and in

[1] *A Short Tour in the Midland Counties of England,* anon.,
London, 1775.—ED.

consequence he became a woman-hater—a misogy-
nist—as bitter as Euripides. On seeing a woman approaching, he would "quarter," and zig-zag to any
extent, rather than face her. Being, by this accident of
his life, released from the expenses of a ducal establishment, he was the better able to create that immense
wealth which afterwards yielded vast estates to the
then Marquis of Stafford, to the Earl of Bridgewater,
etc. In its outline and conception, my father's book
was exactly what is so much wanted at this time for
the whole island, and was some years ago pointed out
by the *Quarterly Review* as a *desideratum* not easily
supplied—viz., a guide to the whole wealth of art,
above ground and below, which, in this land of ours,
every square mile crowds upon the notice of strangers.
In the style of its execution, and the alternate treatment of the mechanic arts and the fine arts, the work
resembles the well-known tours of Arthur Young,
which blended rural industry with picture galleries;
excepting only that in my father's I remember no
politics, perhaps because it was written before the
French Revolution. Partly, perhaps, it might be a
cause, and partly an effect, of this attention paid by
my father to the galleries of art in the aristocratic
mansions that throughout the principal rooms of his
own house there were scattered a small collection of
paintings by old Italian masters. I mention this fact,
not as a circumstance of exclusive elegance belonging
to my father's establishment, but for the very opposite
reason, as belonging very generally to my father's
class. Many of them possessed collections much finer
than his; and I remember that two of the few visits on
which, when a child, I was allowed to accompany my
mother, were expressly to see a picture-gallery, belonging to a merchant, not much wealthier than my
father. In reality, I cannot say anything more to the

honour of this mercantile class than the fact that, being a wealthy class, and living with a free and liberal expenditure, they applied a very considerable proportion of this expenditure to intellectual pleasures—to pictures, very commonly, as I have mentioned—to liberal society—and, in a large measure, to books.

Yet, whilst the whole body of the merchants in the place lived in a style which, for its mixed liberality and elegance, resembled that of Venetian merchants, there was little about themselves or their establishments of *external* splendour—that is, in features which met the public eye. According to the manners of their country, the internal economy of their establishments erred by too much profusion. They had too many servants; and those servants were maintained in a style of luxury and comfort not often matched in the mansions of the nobility. On the other hand, none of these were kept for show or ostentation; and, accordingly, it was not very common to find servants in livery. The women had their fixed and appropriate duties; but the men acted in mixed capacities. Carriages were not very commonly kept; even where from one to two thousand a year might be spent. There was in this town a good deal of society; somewhat better in an intellectual sense than such as is merely literary; for that is, of all societies, the feeblest. From the clergymen, the medical body, and the merchants, was supported a Philosophical Society, who regularly published their Transactions. And some of the members were of a rank in science to correspond with D'Alembert, and others of the leading Parisian wits and literati. Yet so little even here did mere outside splendour and imposing names avail against the palpable evidence of things—against mother-wit and natural robustness of intellect—that the particular physician who chiefly corresponded with the Encyclopœdists, spite of his Buffon, his Diderot, his D'Alembert, by whom, in fact, he swore, and whose frothy letters he kept like amulets in his pocket-book, ranked in general esteem as no better than one of the sons of the feeble; and the treason went so far as sometimes to comprehend his correspondents—the great men of the Academy—in the same derogatory estimate; and, in reality, their printed letters are evidences enough that no great wrong was done them—being generally vapid, and as much inferior to Gray's letters, recently made popular by Mason's life, as these again are, in spirit, and *naïveté*—not to Cowper's only, but to many an unknown woman's in every night of the year— little thought of perhaps by her correspondent, and destined pretty certainly to oblivion.

One word only I shall add, descriptive of my father's library; because in describing his, I describe those of all his class. It was very extensive; comprehending the whole general literature both of England and Scotland for the preceding generation. It was impossible to name a book in the classes of history, biography, voyages and travels, belles lettres, or popular divinity, which was wanting. And to these was added a pretty complete body of local tours (such as Pennant's) and topography; many of which last, being illustrated extensively with plates, were fixed for ever in the recollections of children. But one thing was noticeable—all the books were English. There was no affectation, either in my father or mother, of decorating their tables with foreign books, not better than thousands of corresponding books in their mother idiom; or of painfully spelling out the contents, obscurely and doubtfully, as must always happen when people have not a familiar *oral* acquaintance with the whole force and value of a language. How often, upon the table of a modern *littérateur*, languid, perhaps, and dyspeptic,

so as to be in no condition for enjoying anything, do
we see books lying in six or eight different languages,
not one of which he has mastered in a degree putting
him really and unaffectedly in possession of its idiomatic wealth, or really and seriously in a condition to
seek his unaffected pleasures in that language. Besides,
what reason has any man looking only for *enjoyment*
to import exotic luxuries, until he has a little exhausted
those which are native to the soil? Are Abana and
Pharpar, rivers of Damascus, better indeed than all
the waters of Israel? True it is, there are different
reasons for learning a language; and with some I have
here nothing to do. But where the luxuries of literature are the things sought, I can understand why a
Dane should learn English; because his native literature is not wide, nor very original; and the best modern
writers of his country have a trick of writing in German, with a view to a larger audience. Even a Spaniard,
or a Portuguese, might, with much good sense, acquire
at some pains the English or the German; because his
own literature, with a few splendid jewels, is not
mounted in all departments equally well. But is it for
those who have fed on the gifts of Ceres to discard
them for acorns? This is to reverse the old mythological
history of human progress. Now, for example, one of
the richest departments in English literature happens
to be its drama, from the reign of Elizabeth to the
Parliamentary War. Such another exhibition of human life under a most picturesque form of manners
and a stage of society so rich in original portraiture,
and in strength of character, has not existed elsewhere,
nor is ever likely to revolve upon ourselves. The tragic
drama of Greece is the only section of literature having a corresponding interest or value. Well; few
readers are now much acquainted with this section of
literature; even the powerful sketches of Beaumont

and Fletcher, who, in their comic delineations, approach to Shakespeare, lie covered with dust; and yet, whilst these things are, some twenty years ago we all saw the arid sterilities of Alfieri promoted to a place in every young lady's boudoir. It is true that, in this particular instance, the undue honour paid to this lifeless painter of life and this undramatic dramatist was owing to the accident of his memoirs having been just then published; and true also it is that the insipid dramas, unable to sustain themselves, have long since sunk back into oblivion. But other writers, not better, are still succeeding; as must ever be the case with readers not sufficiently masters of a language to bring the true pretensions of a work to any test of *feeling*, and who are for ever mistaking for some pleasure conferred by the writer what is in fact the pleasure [1] naturally attached to the sense of a difficulty overcome.

Not only were there in my father's library no books except English; but even amongst those there were none connected with the Black Letter literature; none in fact, of any kind which presupposed study and labour for their enjoyment. It was a poor library, on this account, for a scholar or a man of research. Its use and purpose was mere enjoyment, instant amusement, without effort or affectation; but still liberal and intellectual. Living in the country, as most of his order did, my father could not look to a theatre for his evening pleasures—or to any public resort. To a theatre he went only when he took his family; and that might be once in five years. Books, gardens on a large scale, and a greenhouse, were the means generally relied on for daily pleasure. The last, in particular, was so commonly attached to a house that it formed a

---

[1] There can be no doubt that this particular mistake has been a chief cause of the vastly exaggerated appreciation of much that is mediocre in Greek literature.

principal room in the country-house, with the modest
name of *The Farm*, in which I passed my infancy; it
was *the* principal room, as to dimensions, in a spacious
house which my father built for himself; and was not
wanting, on some scale or other, in any one house of
those which I most visited when a school-boy.

I may finish my portrait of my father and his class
by saying that Cowper was the poet whom they generally most valued; but Dr. Johnson, who had only
just ceased to be a living author, was looked up to with
considerable reverence, upon mixed feelings: partly
for his courage, his sturdy and uncomplying morality,
and, according to *his* views, for his general love of
truth; and (as usual) for his diction amongst all who
loved the stately, the processional, the artificial, and
even the inflated—with the usual dissent on the part
of all who were more open to the natural graces of
mother English and idiomatic liveliness. Finally, I
may add that there was too little music in those houses
in those days; and that the reverence paid to learning
—to scholastic erudition, I mean—was disproportionate and excessive. Not having had the advantages of a
college education themselves, my father and his class
looked up with too much admiration to those who had;
ascribing to them, with a natural modesty, a superiority greatly beyond the fact; and, not allowing
themselves to see that business, and the practice of
life, had given to themselves countervailing advantages; nor discerning that too often the scholar had
become dull and comatose over his books; whilst the
activity of trade, and the strife of practical business,
had sharpened their own judgements, set an edge upon
their understandings, and increased the mobility of
their general powers. As to the general esteem for
Cowper, that was inevitable: his picture of an English
rural fire-side, with its long winter evening, the sofa

wheeled round to the fire, the massy draperies depending from the windows, the tea-table with its "bub-
bling and loud-hissing urn," the newspaper and the
long debate—Pitt and Fox ruling the senate, and
Erskine the bar—all this held up a mere mirror to
that particular period and their own particular houses;
whilst the character of his rural scenery was exactly
the same in Cowper's experience of England as in their
own. So that, in all these features, they recognized
their countryman and their contemporary, who saw
things from the same station as themselves; whilst his
moral denunciations upon all great public questions
then afloat were cast in the very same mould of conscientious principle as their own. In saying *that*, I
mean upon all questions where the moral bearings of
the case (as in the slave-trade, *lettres de cachet*, etc.)
were open to no doubt. They all agreed in being very
solicitous in a point which evidently gives no concern
at all to a Frenchman, viz. that in her public and
foreign acts their country should be in the right. In
other respects, upon politics, there were great differences of opinion, especially throughout the American
War, until the French Revolution began to change its
first features of promise. After *that*, a great monotony
of opinion prevailed for many years amongst all of
that class.

THE AFFLICTION OF CHILDHOOD

(First published in *Blackwood's Magazine*, 1845)

ABOUT the close of my sixth year, suddenly the first
chapter of my life came to a violent termination;
that chapter which, even within the gates of recovered
Paradise, might merit a remembrance. "*Life is Fin-*

ished!" was the secret misgiving of my heart; for the
heart of infancy is as apprehensive as that of maturest
wisdom in relation to any capital wound inflicted on
the happiness. *"Life is Finished! Finished it is!"* was
the hidden meaning that, half-unconsciously to myself,
lurked within my sighs; and, as bells heard from a
distance on a summer evening seem charged at times
with an articulate form of words, some monitory message, that rolls round unceasingly, even so for me
some noiseless and subterraneous voice seemed to
chant continually a secret word, made audible only to
my own heart——that "now is the blossoming of life
withered for ever." Not that such words formed themselves vocally within my ear, or issued audibly from
my lips: but such a whisper stole silently to my heart.
Yet in what sense could *that* be true? For an infant
not more than six years old, was it possible that the
promises of life had been really blighted? or its golden
pleasures exhausted? Had I seen Rome? Had I read
Milton? Had I heard Mozart? No. St. Peter's, the
Paradise Lost, the divine melodies of *Don Giovanni,*
all alike were as yet unrevealed to me, and not more
through the accidents of my position than through the
necessity of my yet imperfect sensibilities. Raptures
there might be in arrear; but raptures are modes of
troubled pleasure. The peace, the rest, the central security which belong to love that is past all understanding
——these could return no more. Such a love, so unfathomable——such a peace, so unvexed by storms, or the
fear of storms——had brooded over those four latter
years of my infancy, which brought me into special
relations to my eldest sister; she being at this period
three years older than myself. The circumstances
which attended the sudden dissolution of this most
tender connexion I will here rehearse. And, that I
may do so more intelligibly, I will first describe that

serene and sequestered position which we occupied in life.[1]

Any expression of personal vanity, intruding upon impassioned records, is fatal to their effect—as being incompatible with that absorption of spirit and that self-oblivion in which only deep passion originates, or can find a genial home. It would, therefore, to myself be exceedingly painful that even a shadow, or so much as a *seeming* expression of that tendency, should creep into these reminiscences. And yet, on the other hand, it is so impossible, without laying an injurious restraint upon the natural movement of such a narrative, to prevent oblique gleams reaching the reader from such circumstances of luxury or aristocratic elegance as surrounded my childhood, that on all accounts I think it better to tell him, from the first, with the simplicity of truth, in what order of society my family moved at the time from which this preliminary nar-

[1] As occasions arise in these *Sketches*, when, merely for the purposes of intelligibility, it becomes requisite to call into notice such personal distinctions in my family as otherwise might be unimportant, I here record the entire list of my brothers and sisters, according to their order of succession; and Miltonically I include myself; having surely as much logical right to count myself in the series of my own brothers as Milton could have to pronounce Adam the goodliest of his own sons. First and last, we counted as eight children—viz., four brothers and four sisters, though never counting more than six living at once—viz., 1. *William*, older than myself by more than five years; 2. *Elizabeth*; 3. *Jane*, who died in her fourth year; 4. *Mary*; 5. myself, certainly not the goodliest man of men born since my brothers; 6. *Richard*, known to us all by the household name of *Pink*, who in his after years tilted up and down what might then be called his Britannic Majesty's Oceans (viz., the Atlantic and Pacific) in the quality of midshipman, until Waterloo in one day put an extinguisher on that whole generation of midshipmen, by extinguishing all further call for their services; 7, a second *Jane*; 8. *Henry*, a posthumous child, who belonged to Brasenose College, Oxford, and died about his twenty-sixth year.

rative is dated. Otherwise it might happen that, merely by reporting faithfully the facts of this early experience, I could hardly prevent the reader from receiving an impression as of some higher rank than did really belong to my family. And this impression might seem to have been designedly insinuated by myself.

My father was a merchant; not in the sense of Scotland, where it means a retail dealer, one, for instance, who sells groceries in a cellar, but in the English sense, a sense rigorously exclusive; that is, he was a man engaged in *foreign* commerce, and no other; therefore, in *wholesale* commerce, and no other—which last limitation of the idea is important, because it brings him within the benefit of Cicero's condescending distinction [1]—as one who ought to be despised certainly, but not too intensely to be despised even by a Roman senator. He—this imperfectly despicable man—died at an early age, and very soon after the incidents recorded in this chapter, leaving to his family, then consisting of a wife and six children, an unburdened estate producing exactly £1600 a-year. Naturally, therefore, at the date of my narrative—whilst he was still living—he had an income very much larger, from the addition of current commercial profits. Now, to any man who is acquainted with commercial life as it exists in England, it will readily occur, that in an opulent English family of that class—opulent, though not emphatically *rich* in a mercantile estimate—the domestic economy is pretty sure to move upon a scale of liberality altogether unknown amongst the corresponding orders in foreign nations. The establishment of servants, for instance, in such houses, measured even *numerically* against

[1] Cicero, in a well-known passage of his *Ethics*, speaks of trade as irredeemably base, if petty, but as not so absolutely felonious if wholesale.

those establishments in other nations, would somewhat
surprise the foreign appraiser, simply as interpreting
the relative station in society occupied by the English
merchant. But this same establishment, when measured by the quality and amount of the provision
made for its comfort, and even elegant accommodation, would fill him with twofold astonishment, as
interpreting equally the social valuation of the English merchant and also the social valuation of the
English servant: for, in the truest sense, England is
the paradise of household servants. Liberal house-
keeping, in fact, as extending itself to the meanest
servants, and the disdain of petty parsimonies, are
peculiar to England. And in this respect the families
of English merchants, as a class, far outrun the scale
of expenditure prevalent, not only amongst the corresponding bodies of continental nations, but even
amongst the poorer sections of our own nobility—
though confessedly the most splendid in Europe; a
fact which, since the period of my infancy, I have had
many personal opportunities for verifying both in
England and in Ireland. From this peculiar anomaly,
affecting the domestic economy of English merchants,
there arises a disturbance upon the usual scale for
measuring the relations of rank. The equation, so to
speak, between rank and the ordinary expressions of
rank, which usually runs parallel to the graduations
of expenditure, is here interrupted and confounded,
so that one rank would be collected from the name of
the occupation, and another rank, much higher, from
the splendour of the domestic *ménage*. I warn the
reader, therefore (or, rather, my explanation has already warned him), that he is not to infer, from any
casual indications of luxury or elegance, a corresponding elevation of rank.

We, the children of the house, stood, in fact, upon

the very happiest tier in the social scaffolding for all good influences. The prayer of Agar—"Give me neither poverty nor riches"—was realized for us. That blessing we had, being neither too high nor too low. High enough we were to see models of good manners, of self-respect, and of simple dignity; obscure enough to be left in the sweetest of solitudes. Amply furnished with all the nobler benefits of wealth, with *extra* means of health, of intellectual culture, and of elegant enjoyment, on the other hand, we knew nothing of its social distinctions. Not depressed by the consciousness of privations too sordid, not tempted into restlessness by the consciousness of privileges too aspiring, we had no motives for shame, we had none for pride. Grateful, also, to this hour I am that, amidst luxuries in all things else, we were trained to a Spartan simplicity of diet—that we fared, in fact, very much less sumptuously than the servants. And if (after the model of the Emperor Marcus Aurelius) I should return thanks to Providence for all the separate blessings of my early situation, these four I would single out as worthy of special commemoration—that I lived in a rustic solitude; that this solitude was in England; that my infant feelings were moulded by the gentlest of sisters, and not by horrid, pugilistic brothers; finally, that I and they were dutiful and loving members of a pure, holy, and magnificent church.

The earliest incidents in my life which left stings in my memory so as to be remembered at this day were two, and both before I could have completed my second year; namely, first, a remarkable dream of terrific grandeur about a favourite nurse, which is interesting to myself for this reason—that it demonstrates my dreaming tendencies to have been constitutional, and not dependent upon laudanum [1]; and, secondly, the fact of having connected a profound sense of pathos with the reappearance, very early in the spring, of some crocuses. This I mention as inexplicable; for such annual resurrections of plants and flowers affect us only as memorials, or suggestions of some higher change, and therefore in connexion with the idea of death; yet of death I could, at that time, have had no experience whatever.

This, however, I was speedily to acquire. My two eldest sisters—eldest of three *then* living, and also elder than myself—were summoned to an early death. The first who died was Jane, about two years older than myself. She was three and a half, I one and a half, more or less by some trifle that I do not recollect. But death was then scarcely intelligible to me, and I could not so properly be said to suffer sorrow as a sad perplexity. There was another death in the house about the same time—viz., of a maternal grandmother; but, as she had come to us for the express purpose of dying in her daughter's society, and from illness had lived perfectly secluded, our nursery circle knew her but little, and were certainly more affected by the death (which I witnessed) of a beautiful bird—viz., a kingfisher, which had been injured by an accident. With my sister Jane's death (though otherwise, as I have said, less sorrowful than perplexing) there was, however, connected an incident which made a most fearful impression upon myself, deepening my tendencies to

---

[1] It is true that in those days *paregoric elixir* was occasionally given to children in colds; and in this medicine there is a small proportion of laudanum. But no medicine was ever administered to any member of our nursery except under medical sanction; and this, assuredly, would not have been obtained to the exhibition of laudanum in a case such as mine. For I was not more than twenty-one months old; at which age the action of opium is capricious, and therefore perilous.

thoughtfulness and abstraction beyond what would seem credible for my years. If there was one thing in this world from which, more than from any other, nature had forced me to revolt, it was brutality and violence. Now, a whisper arose in the family that a female servant, who by accident was drawn off from her proper duties to attend my sister Jane for a day or two, had on one occasion treated her harshly, if not brutally; and as this ill-treatment happened within three or four days of her death, so that the occasion of it must have been some fretfulness in the poor child caused by her sufferings, naturally there was a sense of awe and indignation diffused through the family. I believe the story never reached my mother, and possibly it was exaggerated; but upon me the effect was terrific. I did not often see the person charged with this cruelty; but, when I did, my eyes sought the ground; nor could I have borne to look her in the face; not, however, in any spirit that could be called anger. The feeling which fell upon me was a shuddering horror, as upon a first glimpse of the truth that I was in a world of evil and strife. Though born in a large town (the town of Manchester, even then among the largest of the island), I had passed the whole of my childhood, except for the few earliest weeks, in a rural seclusion. With three innocent little sisters for playmates, sleeping always amongst them, and shut up for ever in a silent garden from all knowledge of poverty, or oppression, or outrage, I had not suspected until this moment the true complexion of the world in which myself and my sisters were living. Henceforward the character of my thoughts changed greatly; for so *representative* are some acts, that one single case of the class is sufficient to throw open before you the whole theatre of possibilities in that direction. I never heard that the woman accused of this cruelty took it at all to heart, even after the event which so immediately succeeded had reflected upon it a more painful emphasis. But for myself, that incident had a lasting revolutionary power in colouring my estimate of life.

So passed away from earth one of those three sisters that made up my nursery playmates; and so did my acquaintance (if such it could be called) commence with mortality. Yet, in fact, I knew little more of mortality than that Jane had disappeared. She had gone away; but, perhaps, she would come back. Happy interval of heaven-born ignorance! Gracious immunity of infancy from sorrow disproportioned to its strength! I was sad for Jane's absence. But still in my heart I trusted that she would come again. Summer and winter came again—crocuses and roses; why not little Jane?

Thus easily was healed, then, the first wound in my infant heart. Not so the second. For thou, dear, noble Elizabeth, around whose ample brow, as often as thy sweet countenance rises upon the darkness, I fancy a *tiara* of light or a gleaming *aureola* [1] in token of thy premature intellectual grandeur—thou whose head, for its superb developments, was the astonishment of science [2]—thou next, but after an interval of

---

[1] "*Aureola*": The *aureola* is the name given in the *Legends of the Christian Saints* to that golden diadem or circlet of supernatural light (that *glory*, as it is commonly called in English) which, amongst the great masters of painting in Italy, surrounded the heads of Christ and of distinguished saints.

[2] "*The astonishment of science*": Her medical attendants were Dr. Percival, a well-known literary physician, who had been a correspondent of Condorcet, D'Alembert, etc., and Mr. Charles White, the most distinguished surgeon at that time in the North of England. It was he who pronounced her head to be the finest in its development of any that he had ever seen—an assertion which, to my own knowledge, he repeated in after years, and with enthusiasm. That he had some acquaintance

happy years, thou also wert summoned away from our nursery; and the night which for me gathered upon that event ran after my steps far into life; and perhaps at this day I resemble little for good or for ill that which else I should have been. Pillar of fire that didst go before me to guide and to quicken—pillar of darkness, when thy countenance was turned away to God, that didst too truly reveal to my dawning fears the secret shadow of death, by what mysterious gravitation was it that *my* heart had been drawn to thine? Could a child, six years old, place any special value upon intellectual forwardness? Serene and capacious as my sister's mind appeared to me upon after review, was *that* a charm for stealing away the heart of an infant? Oh no! I think of it *now* with interest, because it lends, in a stranger's ear, some justification to the excess of my fondness. But then it was lost upon me; or, if not lost, was perceived only through its effects. Hadst thou been an idiot, my sister, not the less I must have loved thee, having that capacious heart—overflowing, even as mine overflowed, with tenderness, strung, even as mine was strung, by the necessity of

with the subject may be presumed from this, that, at so early a stage of such inquiries, he had published a work on human craniology, supported by measurements of heads selected from all varieties of the human species. Meantime, as it would grieve me that any trait of what might seem vanity should creep into this record, I will admit that my sister died of hydrocephalus; and it has been often supposed that the premature expansion of the intellect in cases of that class is altogether morbid—forced on, in fact, by the mere stimulation of the disease. I would, however, suggest, as a possibility, the very opposite order of relation between the disease and the intellectual manifestations. Not the disease may always have caused the preternatural growth of the intellect; but, inversely, this growth of the intellect coming on spontaneously, and outrunning the capacities of the physical structure, may have caused the disease.

loving and being loved. This it was which crowned thee with beauty and power:

> *Love, the holy sense,*
> *Best gift of God, in thee was most intense.*

That lamp of Paradise was, for myself, kindled by reflection from the living light which burned so steadfastly in thee; and never but to thee, never again since *thy* departure, had I power or temptation, courage or desire, to utter the feelings which possessed me. For I was the shyest of children; and, at all stages of life, a natural sense of personal dignity held me back from exposing the least ray of feelings which I was not encouraged *wholly* to reveal.

It is needless to pursue, circumstantially, the course of that sickness which carried off my leader and companion. She (according to my recollection at this moment) was just as near to nine years as I to six. And perhaps this natural precedency in authority of years and judgement, united to the tender humility with which she declined to assert it, had been amongst the fascinations of her presence. It was upon a Sunday evening, if such conjectures can be trusted, that the spark of fatal fire fell upon that train of predispositions to a brain complaint which had hitherto slumbered within her. She had been permitted to drink tea at the house of a labouring man, the father of a favourite female servant. The sun had set when she returned, in the company of this servant, through meadows reeking with exhalations after a fervent day. From that day she sickened. In such circumstances, a child, as young as myself, feels no anxieties. Looking upon medical men as people privileged, and naturally commissioned, to make war upon pain and sickness, I never had a misgiving about the result. I grieved, indeed, that my

sister should lie in bed; I grieved still more to hear
her moan. But all this appeared to me no more than
as a night of trouble, on which the dawn would soon
arise. O! moment of darkness and delirium, when the
elder nurse awakened me from that delusion, and
launched God's thunderbolt at my heart in the assurance that my sister MUST die. Rightly it is said of
utter, utter misery, that it "cannot be *remembered*." [1]
Itself, as a rememberable thing, is swallowed up in its
own chaos. Blank anarchy and confusion of mind fell
upon me. Deaf and blind I was, as I reeled under the
revelation. I wish not to recall the circumstances of
that time, when *my* agony was at its height, and hers,
in another sense, was approaching. Enough it is to
say, that all was soon over; and the morning of that
day had at last arrived which looked down upon her
innocent face, sleeping the sleep from which there is
no awaking, and upon me sorrowing the sorrow for
which there is no consolation.

On the day after my sister's death, whilst the sweet
temple of her brain was yet unviolated by human
scrutiny, I formed my own scheme for seeing her once
more. Not for the world would I have made this known,
nor have suffered a witness to accompany me. I had
never heard of feelings that take the name of "sentimental," nor dreamed of such a possibility. But grief,
even in a child, hates the light, and shrinks from
human eyes. The house was large enough to have two
staircases; and by one of these I knew that about mid-
day, when all would be quiet (for the servants dined
at one o'clock), I could steal up into her chamber. I
imagine that it was about an hour after high noon
when I reached the chamber-door; it was locked but

[1] *I stood in unimaginable trance*
And agony which cannot be remember'd
Speech of Alhadra, in Coleridge's *Remorse.*

the key was not taken away. Entering, I closed the door so softly, that, although it opened upon a hall which ascended through all the storeys, no echo ran along the silent walls. Then, turning round, I sought my sister's face. But the bed had been moved, and the back was now turned towards myself. Nothing met my eyes but one large window, wide open, through which the sun of midsummer at mid-day was showering down torrents of splendour. The weather was dry, the sky was cloudless, the blue depths seemed the express types of infinity; and it was not possible for eye to behold, or for heart to conceive, any symbols more pathetic of life and the glory of life.

From the gorgeous sunlight I turned round to the corpse. There lay the sweet childish figure; there the angel face; and, as people usually fancy, it was said in the house that no features had suffered any change. Had they not? The forehead, indeed—the serene and noble forehead—*that* might be the same; but the frozen eyelids, the darkness that seemed to steal from beneath them, the marble lips, the stiffening hands, laid palm to palm, as if repeating the supplications of closing anguish—could these be mistaken for life? Had it been so, wherefore did I not spring to those heavenly lips with tears and never-ending kisses? But so it was *not*. I stood checked for a moment; awe, not fear, fell upon me; and, whilst I stood, a solemn wind began to blow—the saddest that ear ever heard. It was a wind that might have swept the fields of mortality for a thousand centuries. Many times since, upon summer days, when the sun is about the hottest, I have remarked the same wind arising and uttering the same hollow, solemn, Memnonian,[1] but saintly swell: it is in this world the one great audible symbol of eternity.

[1] *"Memnonian"*: For the sake of many readers, whose hearts may go along earnestly with a record of infant sorrow, but whose course of life has not allowed them much leisure for

And three times in my life have I happened to hear the same sound in the same circumstances—viz., when standing between an open window and a dead body on a summer day.

study, I pause to explain—that the head of Memnon, in the British Museum, that sublime head which wears upon its lips a smile co-extensive with all time and all space, an Æonian smile of gracious love and Panlike mystery, the most diffusive and pathetically divine that the hand of man has created, is represented on the authority of ancient traditions to have uttered at sunrise, or soon after, as the sun's rays had accumulated heat enough to rarefy the air within certain cavities in the bust, a solemn and dirge-like series of intonations; the simple explanation being, in its general outline, this—that sonorous currents of air were produced by causing chambers of cold and heavy air to press upon other collections of air, warmed, and therefore rarefied, and therefore yielding readily to the pressure of heavier air. Currents being thus established, by artificial arrangements of tubes, a certain succession of notes could be concerted and sustained. Near the Red Sea lies a chain of sand hills, which, by a natural system of grooves inosculating with each other, become vocal under changing circumstances in the position of the sun, etc. I knew a boy who, upon observing steadily, and reflecting upon a phenomenon that met him in his daily experience—viz., that tubes, through which a stream of water was passing, gave out a very different sound according to the varying slenderness or fulness of the current—devised an instrument that yielded a rude hydraulic gamut of sounds; and, indeed, upon this simple phenomenon is founded the use and power of the stethoscope. For exactly as a thin thread of water, trickling through a leaden tube, yields a stridulous and plaintive sound compared with the full volume of sound corresponding to the full volume of water—on parity of principles, nobody will doubt that the current of blood pouring through the tubes of the human frame will utter to the learned ear, when armed with the stethoscope, an elaborate gamut or compass of music, recording the ravages of disease, or the glorious plenitudes of health, as faithfully as the cavities within this ancient Memnonian bust reported this mighty event of sunrise to the rejoicing world of light and life—or, again, under the sad passion of the dying day, uttered the sweet requiem that belonged to its departure.

Instantly, when my ear caught this vast Æolian intonation, when my eye filled with the golden fulness of life, the pomps of the heavens above, or the glory of the flowers below, and turning when it settled upon the frost which overspread my sister's face, instantly a trance fell upon me. A vault seemed to open in the zenith of the far blue sky, a shaft which ran up for ever. I, in spirit, rose as if on billows that also ran up the shaft for ever; and the billows seemed to pursue the throne of God; but *that* also ran before us and fled away continually. The flight and the pursuit seemed to go on for ever and ever. Frost gathering frost, some Sarsar wind of death, seemed to repel me; some mighty relation between God and death dimly struggled to evolve itself from the dreadful antagonism between them; shadowy meanings even yet continue to exercise and torment, in dreams, the deciphering oracle within me. I slept——for how long I cannot say; slowly I recovered my self-possession; and, when I woke, found myself standing, as before, close to my sister's bed.

I have reason to believe that a *very* long interval had elapsed during this wandering or suspension of my perfect mind. When I returned to myself, there was a foot (or I fancied so) on the stairs. I was alarmed; for, if anybody had detected me, means would have been taken to prevent my coming again. Hastily, therefore, I kissed the lips that I should kiss no more, and slunk, like a guilty thing, with stealthy steps from the room. Thus perished the vision, loveliest amongst all the shows which earth has revealed to me; thus mutilated was the parting which should have lasted for ever; tainted thus with fear was that farewell sacred to love and grief, to perfect love and to grief that could not be healed.

O Ahasuerus, everlasting Jew![1] fable or not a fable, thou, when first starting on thy endless pilgrimage of woe—thou, when first flying through the gates of Jerusalem, and vainly yearning to leave the pursuing curse behind thee—couldst not more certainly in the words of Christ have read thy doom of endless sorrow, than I when passing for ever from my sister's room. The worm was at my heart; and, I may say, the worm that could not die. Man is doubtless *one* by some subtle *nexus*, some system of links, that we cannot perceive, extending from the new-born infant to the superannuated dotard: but, as regards many affections and passions incident to his nature at different stages, he is *not* one, but an intermitting creature, ending and beginning anew; the unity of man, in this respect, is co-extensive only with the particular stage to which the passion belongs. Some passions, as that of sexual love, are celestial by one-half of their origin, animal and earthly by the other half. These will not survive their own appropriate stage. But love, which is *altogether* holy, like that between two children, is privileged to revisit by glimpses the silence and the darkness of declining years; and, possibly, this final experience in my sister's bedroom, or some other in which her innocence was concerned, may rise again for me to illuminate the clouds of death.

On the day following this which I have recorded, came a body of medical men to examine the brain, and the particular nature of the complaint; for in some of its symptoms it had shown perplexing anomalies. An hour after the strangers had withdrawn, I crept again to the room; but the door was now locked, the key had been taken away—and I was shut out for ever.

[1] *"Everlasting Jew"*: *der ewige Jude*—which is the common German expression for "The Wandering Jew," and sublimer even than our own.

Then came the funeral. I, in the ceremonial character of *mourner*, was carried thither. I was put into a carriage with some gentlemen whom I did not know. They were kind and attentive to me; but naturally they talked of things disconnected with the occasion, and their conversation was a torment. At the church, I was told to hold a white handkerchief to my eyes. Empty hypocrisy! What need had *he* of masks or mockeries, whose heart died within him at every word that was uttered? During that part of the service which passed within the church, I made an effort to attend; but I sank back continually into my own solitary darkness, and I heard little consciously, except some fugitive strains from the sublime chapter of St. Paul, which in England is always read at burials.[1]

Lastly came that magnificent liturgical service which the English Church performs at the side of the grave; for this church does not forsake her dead so long as they continue in the upper air, but waits for her last "sweet and solemn farewell" [2] at the side of the grave. There is exposed once again, and for the last time, the coffin. All eyes survey the record of name, of sex, of age, and the day of departure from earth—records how shadowy! and dropped into darkness as messages addressed to worms. Almost at the very last comes the symbolic ritual, tearing and shattering the heart with volleying discharge, peal after peal, from the fine artillery of woe. The coffin is lowered into its home; it has disappeared from all eyes

---

[1] First Epistle to Corinthians, chap. xv., beginning at verse 20.

[2] This beautiful expression, I am pretty certain, must belong to Mrs. Trollope; I read it, probably, in a tale of hers connected with the backwoods of America, where the absence of such a farewell must unspeakably aggravate the gloom at any rate belonging to a household separation of that eternal character occurring amongst the shadows of those mighty forests.

but those that look down into the abyss of the grave.
The sacristan stands ready, with his shovel of earth
and stones. The priest's voice is heard once more—
earth to earth—and immediately the dread rattle
ascends from the lid of the coffin; *ashes to ashes*—and
again the killing sound is heard; *dust to dust*—and
the farewell volley announces that the grave, the
coffin, the face are sealed up for ever and ever.

Grief! thou art classed amongst the depressing passions. And true it is that thou humblest to the dust,
but also thou exaltest to the clouds. Thou shakest as
with ague, but also thou steadiest like frost. Thou
sickenest the heart, but also thou healest its infirmities. Among the very foremost of mine was morbid
sensibility to shame. And, ten years afterwards, I used
to throw my self-reproaches with regard to that infirmity into this shape—viz., that if I were summoned
to seek aid for a perishing fellow-creature, and that I
could obtain that aid only by facing a vast company
of critical or sneering faces, I might, perhaps, shrink
basely from the duty. It is true that no such case had
ever actually occurred; so that it was a mere romance
of casuistry to tax myself with cowardice so shocking.
But to feel a doubt was to feel condemnation; and the
crime that *might* have been, was in my eyes the crime
that *had* been. Now, however, all was changed; and,
for anything which regarded my sister's memory, in
one hour I received a new heart. Once in Westmorland I saw a case resembling it. I saw a ewe suddenly
put off and abjure her own nature, in a service of
love—yes, slough it as completely as ever serpent
sloughed his skin. Her lamb had fallen into a deep
trench, from which all escape was hopeless without
the aid of man. And to a man she advanced, bleating
clamorously, until he followed her and rescued her
beloved. Not less was the change in myself. Fifty thou-

sand sneering faces would not have troubled me *now* in any office of tenderness to my sister's memory. Ten legions would not have repelled me from seeking her, if there had been a chance that she could be found. Mockery! it was lost upon me. Laughter! I valued it not. And when I was taunted insultingly with "my girlish tears," that word *"girlish"* had no sting for me, except as a verbal echo to the one eternal thought of my heart—that a girl was the sweetest thing which I, in my short life, had known—that a girl it was who had crowned the earth with beauty, and had opened to my thirst fountains of pure celestial love, from which, in this world, I was to drink no more.

Now began to unfold themselves the consolations of solitude, those consolations which only I was destined to taste; now, therefore, began to open upon me those fascinations of solitude, which, when acting as a co-agency with unresisted grief, end in the paradoxical result of making out of grief itself a luxury; such a luxury as finally becomes a snare, overhanging life itself, and the energies of life, with growing menaces. All deep feelings of a *chronic* class agree in this, that they seek for solitude, and are fed by solitude. Deep grief, deep love, how naturally do these ally themselves with religious feeling! and all three—love, grief, religion—are haunters of solitary places. Love, grief, and the mystery of devotion—what were these without solitude? All day long, when it was not impossible for me to do so, I sought the most silent and sequestered nooks in the grounds about the house, or in the neighbouring fields. The awful stillness oftentimes of summer noons, when no winds were abroad, the appealing silence of grey or misty afternoons— these were fascinations as of witchcraft. Into the woods, into the desert air, I gazed, as if some comfort lay hid in *them*. I wearied the heavens with my inquest of beseeching looks. Obstinately I tormented the blue depths with my scrutiny, sweeping them for ever with my eyes, and searching them for one angelic face that might, perhaps, have permission to reveal itself for a moment.

At this time, and under this impulse of rapacious grief, that grasped at what it could not obtain, the faculty of shaping images in the distance out of slight elements, and grouping them after the yearnings of the heart, grew upon me in morbid excess. And I recall at the present moment one instance of that sort, which may show how merely shadows, or a gleam of bright-ness, or nothing at all, could furnish a sufficient basis for this creative faculty.

On Sunday mornings I went with the rest of my family to church: it was a church on the ancient model of England, having aisles, galleries,[1] organ, all things ancient and venerable, and the proportions majestic. Here, whilst the congregation knelt through the long litany, as often as we came to that passage, so beau-tiful amongst many that are so, where God is suppli-cated on behalf of "all sick persons and young chil-dren," and that he would "show his pity upon all prisoners and captives," I wept in secret; and raising my streaming eyes to the upper windows of the gal-leries, saw, on days when the sun was shining, a spec-tacle as affecting as ever prophet can have beheld. The *sides* of the windows were rich with storied glass; through the deep purples and crimsons streamed the golden light; emblazonries of heavenly illumination (from the sun) mingling with the earthly emblazon-

[1] *"Galleries"*: These, though condemned on some grounds by the restorers of authentic church architecture, have, never-theless, this one advantage—that, when the *height* of a church is that dimension which most of all expresses its sacred char-acter, galleries expound and interpret that height.

ries (from art and its gorgeous colouring) of what is grandest in man. *There* were the apostles that had trampled upon earth, and the glories of earth, out of celestial love to man. *There* were the martyrs that had borne witness to the truth through flames, through torments, and through armies of fierce, insulting faces. *There* were the saints who, under intolerable pangs, had glorified God by meek submission to his will. And all the time, whilst this tumult of sublime memorials held on as the deep chords from some accompaniment in the bass, I saw through the wide central field of the window, where the glass was *un*coloured, white, fleecy clouds sailing over the azure depths of the sky; were it but a fragment or a hint of such a cloud, immediately under the flash of my sorrow-haunted eye, it grew and shaped itself into visions of beds with white lawny curtains; and in the beds lay sick children, dying children, that were tossing in anguish, and weeping clamorously for death. God, for some mysterious reason, could not suddenly release them from their pain; but he suffered the beds, as it seemed, to rise slowly through the clouds; slowly the beds ascended into the chambers of the air; slowly also his arms descended from the heavens, that he and his young children, whom in Palestine, once and for ever, he had blessed, though they *must* pass slowly through the dreadful chasm of separation, might yet meet the sooner. These visions were self-sustained. These visions needed not that any sound should speak to me, or music mould my feelings. The hint from the litany, the fragment from the clouds—those and the storied windows were sufficient. But not the less the blare of the tumultuous organ wrought its own separate creations. And oftentimes in anthems, when the mighty instrument threw its vast columns of sound, fierce yet melodious, over the voices of the choir—high in arches, when it seemed to rise, surmounting and overriding the strife of the vocal parts, and gathering by strong coercion the total storm into unity—sometimes I seemed to rise and walk triumphantly upon those clouds which, but a moment before, I had looked up to as mementos of prostrate sorrow; yes, sometimes under the transfigurations of music, felt of grief itself as of a fiery chariot for mounting victoriously above the causes of grief.

God speaks to children, also, in dreams, and by the oracles that lurk in darkness. But in solitude, above all things, when made vocal to the meditative heart by the truths and services of a national church, God holds with children "communion undisturbed." Solitude, though it may be silent as light, is, like light, the mightiest of agencies; for solitude is essential to man. All men come into this world *alone;* all leave it *alone.* Even a little child has a dread, whispering consciousness, that, if he should be summoned to travel into God's presence, no gentle nurse will be allowed to lead him by the hand, nor mother to carry him in her arms, nor little sister to share his trepidations. King and priest, warrior and maiden, philosopher and child, all must walk those mighty galleries alone. The solitude, therefore, which in this world appals or fascinates a child's heart, is but the echo of a far deeper solitude, through which already he has passed, and of another solitude, deeper still, through which he *has* to pass: reflex of one solitude—prefiguration of another.

Oh, burden of solitude, that cleavest to man through every stage of his being! in his birth, which *has* been —in his life, which *is*—in his death, which *shall* be— mighty and essential solitude! that wast, and art, and art to be; thou broodest, like the Spirit of God moving upon the surface of the deeps, over every heart that sleeps in the nurseries of Christendom. Like the vast laboratory of the air, which, seeming to be nothing, or less than the shadow of a shade, hides within itself the principles of all things, solitude for the meditating child is the Agrippa's mirror of the unseen universe. Deep is the solitude of millions who, with hearts welling forth love, have none to love them. Deep is the solitude of those who, under secret griefs, have none to pity them. Deep is the solitude of those who, fighting with doubts or darkness, have none to counsel them. But deeper than the deepest of these solitudes is that which broods over childhood under the passion of sorrow—bringing before it, at intervals, the final solitude which watches for it, and is waiting for it within the gates of death. Oh, mighty and essential solitude, that wast, and art, and art to be! thy kingdom is made perfect in the grave; but even over those that keep watch outside the grave, like myself, an infant of six years old, thou stretchest out a sceptre of fascination.

DREAM-ECHOES OF THESE INFANT EXPERIENCES

(First published in *Blackwood's Magazine*, 1845)

[*Notice to the Reader*. The sun, in rising or setting, would produce little effect if he were defrauded of his rays, and their infinite reverberations. "Seen through a fog," says Sara Coleridge, the noble daughter of Samuel Taylor Coleridge, "the golden, beaming sun looks like a dull orange, or a red billiard ball."—*Introd. to Biog. Lit.*, p. clxii. And upon this same analogy, psychological experiences of deep suffering or joy first attain their entire fulness of expression when they are reverberated from dreams. The reader must therefore suppose me at Oxford [1804]; more than twelve years are gone by; I am in the glory of youth: but I have now first tampered with opium; and now first the agitations of my childhood reopened in strength; now first they swept in upon the brain with power and the grandeur of recovered life.]

ONCE again, after twelve years' interval, the nursery of my childhood expanded before me: my sister was moaning in bed; and I was beginning to be restless with fears not intelligible to myself. Once again the elder nurse, but now dilated to colossal proportions, stood as upon some Grecian stage with her uplifted hand, and, like the superb Medea towering amongst her children in the nursery at Corinth,[1] smote me senseless to the ground. Again I am in the chamber with my sister's corpse, again the pomps of life rise up in silence, the glory of summer, the Syrian sunlights, the frost of death. Dream forms itself mysteriously within dream; within these Oxford dreams remoulds itself continually the trance in my sister's chamber— the blue heavens, the everlasting vault, the soaring billows, the throne steeped in the thought (but not the sight) of *"Who* might sit thereon"; the flight, the pursuit, the irrecoverable steps of my return to earth. Once more the funeral procession gathers; the priest in his white surplice stands waiting with a book by the side of an open grave; the sacristan is waiting with his shovel; the coffin has sunk; the *dust to dust* has descended. Again I was in the church on a heavenly Sunday morning. The golden sunlight of God slept amongst the heads of his apostles, his martyrs, his saints; the fragment from the litany, the fragment from the clouds, awoke again the lawny beds that went up to scale the heavens—awoke again the shadowy arms that moved downward to meet them. Once again arose the swell of the anthem, the burst of the Hallelujah chorus, the storm, the trampling movement of the choral passion, the agitation of my own trembling sympathy, the tumult of the choir, the wrath of the organ. Once more I, that wallowed in the dust, became he that rose up to the clouds. And now all was bound

[1] Euripides.

up into unity; the first state and the last were melted into each other as in some sunny, glorifying haze. For high in heaven hovered a gleaming host of faces, veiled with wings, around the pillows of the dying children. And such beings sympathize equally with sorrow that grovels, and with sorrow that soars. Such beings pity alike the children that are languishing in death, and the children that live only to languish in tears.

INTRODUCTION TO THE WORLD OF STRIFE

(First published in *Hogg's Instructor*, 1851–52)

SO, THEN, one chapter in my life had finished. Already, before the completion of my sixth year, this first chapter had run its circle, had rendered up its music to the final chord—might seem even, like ripe fruit from a tree, to have detached itself for ever from all the rest of the arras that was shaping itself within my loom of life. No Eden of lakes and forest-lawns, such as the *mirage* suddenly evokes in Arabian sands—no pageant of air-built battlements and towers, that ever burned in dream-like silence amongst the vapours of summer sunsets, mocking and repeating with celestial pencil "the fuming vanities of earth"—could leave behind it the mixed impression of so much truth combined with so much absolute delusion. Truest of all things it seemed by the excess of that happiness which it had sustained: most fraudulent it seemed of all things, when looked back upon as some mysterious parenthesis in the current of life, "self-withdrawn into a wondrous depth," hurrying as if with headlong malice to extinction, and alienated by *every* feature from the new aspects of life that seemed to await me.

Were it not in the bitter corrosion of heart that I was called upon to face, I should have carried over to the present no connecting link whatever from the past. Mere reality in this fretting it was, and the undeniableness of its too potent remembrances, that forbade me to regard this burnt-out inaugural chapter of my life as no chapter at all, but a pure exhalation of dreams. Misery is a guarantee of truth too substantial to be refused: else, by its determinate evanescence, the total experience would have worn the character of a fantastic illusion.

Well it was for me at this period, if well it were for me to live at all, that from any continued contemplation of my misery I was forced to wean myself, and suddenly to assume the harness of life. Else, under the morbid languishing of grief, and of what the Romans called *desiderium* (the yearning too obstinate after one irrecoverable face), too probably I should have pined away into an early grave. Harsh was my awaking; but the rough febrifuge which this awaking administered broke the strength of my sickly reveries through a period of more than two years; by which time, under the natural expansion of my bodily strength, the danger had passed over.

I have rendered solemn thanks for having been trained amongst the gentlest of sisters, and not under "horrid pugilistic brothers." Meantime, one such brother I had [William]: senior by much to myself, and the stormiest of his class; him I will immediately present to the reader; for up to this point of my narrative he may be described as a stranger even to myself. Odd as it sounds, I had at this time both a brother and a father, neither of whom would have been able to challenge me as a relative, nor I *him*, had we happened to meet on the public roads.

In my father's case, this arose from the accident of

his having lived abroad for a space that, measured against *my* life, was a very long one. First, he lived for months in Portugal, at Lisbon, and at Cintra; next in Madeira; then in the West Indies; sometimes in Jamaica, sometimes in St. Kitt's; courting the supposed benefit of hot climates in his complaint of pulmonary consumption. He had, indeed, repeatedly returned to England, and met my mother at watering-places on the south coast of Devonshire, etc. But I, as a younger child, had not been one of the party selected for such excursions from home. And now, at last, when all had proved unavailing, he was coming home to die amongst his family, in his thirty-ninth year. My mother had gone to await his arrival at the port (whatever port) to which the West India packet should bring him; and amongst the deepest recollections which I connect with that period, is one derived from the night of his arrival at Greenhay.

It was a summer evening of unusual solemnity. The servants, and four of us children, were gathered for hours, on the lawn before the house, listening for the sound of wheels. Sunset came—nine, ten, eleven o'clock, and nearly another hour had passed—without a warning sound; for Greenhay, being so solitary a house, formed a *terminus ad quem*, beyond which was nothing but a cluster of cottages, composing the little hamlet of Greenhill; so that any sound of wheels coming from the winding lane which then connected us with the Rusholme Road carried with it, of necessity, a warning summons to prepare for visitors at Greenhay. No such summons had yet reached us; it was nearly midnight; and, for the last time, it was determined that we should move in a body out of the grounds, on the chance of meeting the travelling party, if, at so late an hour, it could yet be expected to arrive. In fact, to our general surprise, we met it almost im-

mediately, but coming at so slow a pace, that the fall
of the horses' feet was not audible until we were close
upon them. I mention the case for the sake of the
undying impressions which connected themselves with
the circumstances. The first notice of the approach
was the sudden emerging of horses' heads from the
deep gloom of the shady lane; the next was the mass
of white pillows against which the dying patient was
reclining. The hearse-like pace at which the carriage
moved recalled the overwhelming spectacle of that
funeral which had so lately formed part in the most
memorable event of my life. But these elements of
awe, that might at any rate have struck forcibly upon
the mind of a child, were for me, in my condition of
morbid nervousness, raised into abiding grandeur by
the antecedent experiences of that particular summer
night. The listening for hours to the sounds from
horses' hoofs upon distant roads, rising and falling,
caught and lost, upon the gentle undulation of such
fitful airs as might be stirring—the peculiar solemnity of the hours succeeding to sunset—the glory of
the dying day—the gorgeousness which, by description, so well I knew of sunset in those West Indian
islands from which my father was returning—the
knowledge that he returned only to die—the almighty
pomp in which this great idea of Death apparelled
itself to my young sorrowing heart—the corresponding pomp in which the antagonistic idea, not less mysterious, of life, rose, as if on wings, amidst tropic
glories and floral pageantries, that seemed even *more*
solemn and pathetic than the vapoury plumes and
trophies of mortality—all this chorus of restless images, or of suggestive thoughts, gave to my father's
return, which else had been fitted only to interpose
one transitory red-letter day in the calendar of a child,
the shadowy power of an ineffaceable agency among

my dreams. This, indeed, was the one sole memorial
which restores my father's image to me as a personal
reality. Otherwise, he would have been for me a bare
nominis umbra. He languished, indeed, for weeks
upon a sofa; and during that interval, it happened
naturally, from my repose of manners, that I was a
privileged visitor to him throughout his waking hours.
I was also present at his bedside in the closing hour of
his life, which exhaled quietly, amidst snatches of
delirious conversation with some imaginary visitors.

My brother was a stranger from causes quite as
little to be foreseen, but seeming quite as natural after
they had really occurred. In an early stage of his
career, he had been found wholly unmanageable. His
genius for mischief amounted to inspiration: it was a
divine *afflatus* which drove him in that direction; and
such was his capacity for riding in whirlwinds and
directing storms, that he made it his trade to create
them, as a νεφεληγερετα Ζευς, a cloud-compelling
Jove, in order that he *might* direct them. For this,
and other reasons, he had been sent to the Grammar
School of Louth, in Lincolnshire—one of those many
old classic institutions which form the peculiar [1] glory
of England. To box, and to box under the severest restraint of honourable laws, was in those days a mere
necessity of schoolboy life at *public* schools; and hence
the superior manliness, generosity, and self-control,
of those generally who had benefited by such discipline

---

[1] *"Peculiar"*: viz., as *endowed* foundations to which those
resort who are rich and pay, and those also who, being poor,
cannot pay, or cannot pay so much. This most honourable distinction amongst the services of England from ancient times
to the interests of education—a service absolutely unap-
proached by any one nation of Christendom—is amongst the
foremost cases of that remarkable class which make England,
while often the most aristocratic, yet also, for many noble
purposes, the most democratic of lands.

——so systematically hostile to all meanness, pusillanim-
ity, or indirectness. Cowper, in his "Tyrocinium," is
far from doing justice to our great public schools.
Himself disqualified, by delicacy of temperament, for
reaping the benefits from such a warfare, and having
suffered too much in his own Westminster experience,
he could not judge them from an impartial station;
but I, though ill enough adapted to an atmosphere so
stormy, yet having tried both classes of schools, public
and private, am compelled in mere conscience to give
my vote (and if I had a thousand votes, to give *all* my
votes) for the former.

Fresh from such a training as this, and at a time
when his additional five or six years availed nearly to
make *his* age the double of mine, my brother very
naturally despised me; and, from his exceeding frankness, he took no pains to conceal that he did. Why
should he? Who was it that could have a right to feel
aggrieved by his contempt? Who, if not myself? But
it happened, on the contrary, that I had a perfect craze
for being despised. I doted on it; and considered contempt a sort of luxury that I was in continual fear
of losing. Why not? Wherefore should any rational
person shrink from contempt, if it happen to form
the tenure by which he holds his repose in life?
The cases, which are cited from comedy, of such a
yearning after contempt, stand upon a footing altogether different: *there* the contempt is wooed as a
serviceable ally and tool of religious hypocrisy. But,
to me, at that era of life, it formed the main guarantee
of an unmolested repose: and security there was not,
on any lower terms, for the *latentis semita vitæ*. The
slightest approach to any favourable construction of
my intellectual pretensions alarmed me beyond measure; because it pledged me in a manner with the hearer
to support this first attempt by a second, by a third,

by a fourth—O heavens! there is no saying how far
the horrid man might go in his unreasonable demands
upon me. I groaned under the weight of his expectations; and, if I laid but the first round of such a staircase, why, then, I saw in vision a vast Jacob's ladder
towering upwards to the clouds, mile after mile,
league after league; and myself running up and down
this ladder, like any fatigue party of Irish hodmen, to
the top of any Babel which my wretched admirer
might choose to build. But I nipped the abominable
system of extortion in the very bud, by refusing to
take the first step. The man could have no pretence,
you know, for expecting me to climb the third or
fourth round, when I had seemed quite unequal to the
first. Professing the most absolute bankruptcy from
the very beginning, giving the man no sort of hope
that I would pay even one farthing in the pound, I
never could be made miserable by unknown responsibilities.

Still, with all this passion for being despised, which
was so essential to my peace of mind, I found at times
an altitude—a starry altitude—in the station of contempt for me assumed by my brother that nettled me.
Sometimes, indeed, the mere necessities of dispute
carried me, before I was aware of my own imprudence,
so far up the staircase of Babel, that my brother was
shaken for a moment in the infinity of his contempt:
and, before long, when my superiority in some bookish
accomplishments displayed itself, by results that could
not be entirely dissembled, mere foolish human nature
forced me into some trifle of exultation at these retributory triumphs. But more often I was disposed
to grieve over them. They tended to shake that solid
foundation of utter despicableness upon which I relied
so much for my freedom from anxiety; and, therefore,
upon the whole, it was satisfactory to my mind that

my brother's opinion of me, after any little transient
oscillation, gravitated determinately back towards that
settled contempt which had been the result of his
original inquest. The pillars of Hercules upon which
rested the vast edifice of his scorn were these two—
first, my physics: he denounced me for effeminacy;
second, he assumed, and even postulated as a *datum*,
which I myself could never have the face to refuse,
my general idiocy. Physically, therefore, and intellectually, he looked upon me as below notice; but,
morally, he assured me that he would give me a written character of the very best description, whenever I
chose to apply for it. "You're honest," he said; "you're
willing, though lazy; you *would* pull, if you had the
strength of a flea; and, though a monstrous coward,
you don't run away." My own demurs to these harsh
judgements were not so many as they might have been.
The idiocy I confessed; because, though positive that
I was not uniformly an idiot, I felt inclined to think
that, in a majority of cases, I really *was;* and there
were more reasons for thinking so than the reader is
yet aware of. But, as to the effeminacy, I denied it
in toto; and with good reason, as will be seen. Neither
did my brother pretend to have any experimental
proofs of it. The ground he went upon was a mere *à
priori* one—viz., that I had always been tied to the
apron-string of women or girls; which amounted at
most to this—that, by training and the natural tendency of circumstances, I *ought* to be effeminate: that
is, there was reason to expect beforehand that I *should*
be so; but, then, the more merit in me, if, in spite of
such reasonable presumptions, I really were *not*. In
fact, my brother soon learned, by a daily experience,
how entirely he might depend upon me for carrying
out the most audacious of his own warlike plans; such
plans it is true that I abominated; but *that* made no

difference in the fidelity with which I tried to fulfil them.

This eldest brother of mine was in all respects a remarkable boy. Haughty he was, aspiring, immeasurably active; fertile in resources as Robinson Crusoe; but also full of quarrel as it is possible to imagine; and, in default of any other opponent, he would have fastened a quarrel upon his own shadow for presuming to run before him when going westwards in the morning, whereas, in all reason, a shadow, like a dutiful child, ought to keep deferentially in rear of that majestic substance which is the author of its existence. Books he detested, one and all, excepting only such as he happened to write himself. And these were not a few. On all subjects known to man, from the Thirtynine Articles of our English Church, down to pyrotechnics, legerdemain, magic, both black and white, thaumaturgy, and necromancy, he favoured the world (which world was the nursery where I lived amongst my sisters) with his select opinions. On this last subject especially—of necromancy—he was very great; witness his profound work, though but a fragment, and, unfortunately, long since departed to the bosom of Cinderella, entitled, "How to raise a Ghost; and when you've got him down, how to keep him down." To which work he assured us, that some most learned and enormous man, whose name was a foot and a-half long, had promised him an appendix; which appendix treated of the Red Sea and Solomon's signet-ring; with forms of *mittimus* for ghosts that might be refractory; and probably a riot act, for any *émeute* amongst ghosts inclined to raise barricades; since he often thrilled our young hearts by supposing the case (not at all unlikely, he affirmed), that a federation, a solemn league and conspiracy, might take place amongst the infinite generations of ghosts against the

single generation of men at any one time composing
the garrison of earth. The Roman phrase for expressing that a man had died—viz., "*Abiit ad plures*" (He
has gone over to the majority) —my brother explained
to us; and we easily comprehended that any one generation of the living human race, even if combined,
and acting in concert, must be in a frightful minority,
by comparison with all the incalculable generations
that had trod this earth before us. The Parliament of
living men, Lords and Commons united, what a miserable array against the Upper and Lower House composing the Parliament of ghosts! Perhaps the Pre-
Adamites would constitute one wing in such a ghostly
army. My brother, dying in his sixteenth year, was
far enough from seeing or foreseeing Waterloo; else
he might have illustrated this dreadful duel of the
living human race with its ghostly predecessors, by
the awful apparition which at three o'clock in the
afternoon, on the 18th of June, 1815, the mighty contest at Waterloo must have assumed to eyes that
watched over the trembling interests of man. The
English army, about that time in the great agony of
its strife, was thrown into squares; and under that
arrangement, which condensed and contracted its apparent numbers within a few black geometrical dia-
grams, how frightfully narrow—how spectral did its
slender quadrangles appear at a distance, to any
philosophic spectators that knew the amount of human
interests confided to that army, and the hopes for
Christendom that even were trembling in the balance!
Such a disproportion, it seems, might exist, in the
case of a ghostly war, between the harvest of possible
results and the slender band of reapers that were to
gather it. And there was even a worse peril than any
analogous one that has been *proved* to exist at Waterloo. A British surgeon, indeed, in a work of two octavo

volumes, has endeavoured to show that a conspiracy
was traced at Waterloo, between two or three foreign
regiments, for kindling a panic in the heat of the
battle, by flight, and by a sustained blowing up of
tumbrils, under the miserable purpose of shaking the
British steadiness. But the evidences are not clear;
whereas my brother insisted that the presence of sham
men, distributed extensively amongst the human race,
and meditating treason against us all, had been demonstrated to the satisfaction of all true philosophers.
Who were these shams and make-believe men? They
were, in fact, people that had been dead for centuries,
but that, for reasons best known to themselves, had
returned to this upper earth, walked about amongst
us, and were undistinguishable, except by the most
learned of necromancers, from authentic men of flesh
and blood. I mention this for the sake of illustrating
the fact, of which the reader will find a singular instance in the foot-note attached, that the same crazes
are everlastingly revolving upon men.[1]

This hypothesis, however, like a thousand others,
when it happened that they engaged no durable sympathy from his nursery audience, he did not pursue.
For some time he turned his thoughts to philosophy,

---

[1] Five years ago, during the carnival of universal anarchy
equally amongst doers and thinkers, a closely-printed pamphlet
was published with this title, *A New Revelation; or the Communion of the Incarnate Dead with the Unconscious Living.
Important Fact, without trifling Fiction by* HIM. I have not
the pleasure of knowing HIM; but certainly I must concede to
HIM, that he writes like a man of extreme sobriety, upon his
extravagant theme. He is angry with Swedenborg, as might
be expected, for his chimeras; some of which, however, of
late years have signally altered their aspect; but as to HIM,
there is no chance that he should be occupied with chimeras,
because (p. 6) "he has met with some who have acknowledged
the fact of their having come from the dead"—*habes con-*

and read lectures to us every night upon some branch
or other of physics. This undertaking arose upon some
one of us envying or admiring flies for their power of
walking upon the ceiling. "Pooh!" he said, "they are
imposters; they pretend to do it, but they can't do it
as it ought to be done. Ah! you should see *me* standing
upright on the ceiling, with my head downwards, for
half-an-hour together, meditating profoundly." My
sister Mary remarked that we should all be very glad
to see him in that position. "If that's the case," he
replied, "it's very well that all is ready, except as to a
strap or two." Being an excellent skater, he had first
imagined that, if held up until he had started, he might
then, by taking a bold sweep ahead, keep himself in
position through the continued impetus of skating. But
this he found not to answer; because, as he observed,
"the friction was too retarding from the plaster of
Paris; but the case would be very different if the ceiling were coated with ice." As it was *not*, he changed
his plan. The true secret, he now discovered, was this:
he would consider himself in the light of a humming-
top; he would make an apparatus (and he made it)
for having himself launched, like a top, upon the
ceiling, and regularly spun. Then the vertiginous motion of the human top would overpower the force of

fitentem reum. Few, however, are endowed with so much candour; and, in particular, for the honour of literature, it grieves
me to find, by p. 10, that the largest number of these shams,
and perhaps the most uncandid, are to be looked for amongst
"publishers and printers," of whom, it seems, "the great
majority" are mere forgeries; a very few speak frankly about
the matter, and say they don't care who knows it, which, to
my thinking, is impudence; but by far the larger section dog-
gedly deny it, and call a policeman, if you persist in charging
them with being shams. Some differences there are between
my brother and HIM, but in the great outline of their views
they coincide.

gravitation. He should, of course, spin upon his own
axis, and sleep upon his own axis—perhaps he might
even dream upon it; and he laughed at "those scoundrels, the flies," that never improved in their pretended
art, nor made anything of it. The principle was now
discovered; "and, of course," he said, "if a man can
keep it up for five minutes, what's to hinder him from
doing so for five months?" "Certainly, nothing that
I can think of," was the reply of my sister, whose
scepticism, in fact, had not settled upon the five
months, but altogether upon the five minutes. The
apparatus for spinning him, however, perhaps from
its complexity, would not work; a fact evidently owing
to the stupidity of the gardener. On reconsidering the
subject, he announced, to the disappointment of some
amongst us, that, although the physical discovery was
now complete, he saw a moral difficulty. It was not a
humming-top that was required, but a *peg*-top. Now,
this, in order to keep up the *vertigo* at full stretch,
without which, to a certainty, gravitation would prove
too much for him, needed to be whipped incessantly.
But that was precisely what a gentleman ought not
to tolerate; to be scourged unintermittingly on the
legs by any grub of a gardener, unless it were Father
Adam himself, was a thing he could not bring his mind
to face. However, as some compensation, he proposed
to improve the art of flying, which was, as everybody
must acknowledge, in a condition disgraceful to civilized society. As he had made many a fire balloon, and
had succeeded in some attempts at bringing down cats
by *parachutes*, it was not very difficult to fly downwards from moderate elevations. But, as he was reproached by my sister for never flying back again,
which, however, was a far different thing, and not
even attempted by the philosopher in *Rasselas* (for

Revocare gradum, et superas *evadere ad auras,*
Hic labor, hoc opus est) ,

he refused, under such poor encouragement, to try his
winged parachutes any more, either "aloft or alow,"
till he had thoroughly studied Bishop Wilkins [1] on
the art of translating right reverend gentlemen to the
moon; and, in the meantime, he resumed his general
lectures on physics. From these, however, he was
speedily driven, or one might say shelled out, by a
concerted assault of my sister Mary's. He had been in
the habit of lowering the pitch of his lectures with
ostentatious condescension to the presumed level of
our poor understandings. This superciliousness annoyed my sister; and accordingly, with the help of
two young female visitors, and my next younger
brother [Richard]—in subsequent times a little middy
on board many a ship of H.M., and the most predes-
tined rebel upon earth against all assumptions, small
or great, of superiority—she arranged a mutiny, that
had the unexpected effect of suddenly extinguishing
the lectures for ever. He had happened to say, what
was no unusual thing with him, that he flattered himself he had made the point under discussion tolerably

[1] *"Bishop Wilkins"*: Dr. W., Bishop of Chester, in the reign
of Charles II, notoriously wrote a book on the possibility of
a voyage to the moon, which, in a bishop, would be called a
translation to the moon, and perhaps it was *his* name in combination with *his* book that suggested the *Adventures of Peter
Wilkins*. It is unfair, however, to mention him in connexion
with that single one of his works which announces an extravagant purpose. He was really a scientific man, and already
in the time of Cromwell (about 1656) had projected that
Royal Society of London which was afterwards realized and
presided over by Isaac Barrow and Isaac Newton. He was also
a learned man, but still with a vein of romance about him, as
may be seen in his most elaborate work—*The Essay towards a
Philosophic or Universal Language.*

clear; "clear," he added, bowing round the half-circle
of us, the audience, "to the meanest of capacities"; and
then he repeated, sonorously, "clear to the most ex-
cruciatingly mean of capacities." Upon which a voice,
a female voice—but whose voice, in the tumult that
followed, I did not distinguish—retorted, "No, you
haven't; it's as dark as sin"; and then, without a moment's interval, a second voice exclaimed, "Dark as
night"; then came my younger brother's insurrectionary yell, "Dark as midnight"; then another female voice chimed in melodiously, "Dark as pitch";
and so the peal continued to come round like a catch,
the whole being so well concerted, and the rolling
fire so well sustained, that it was impossible to make
head against it; whilst the abruptness of the interruption gave to it the protecting character of an oral
"round-robin," it being impossible to challenge any
one in particular as the ringleader. Burke's phrase of
"the swinish multitude," applied to mobs, was then
in everybody's mouth; and, accordingly, after my
brother had recovered from his first astonishment at
this audacious mutiny, he made us several sweeping
bows, that looked very much like tentative rehearsals
of a sweeping *fusillade*, and then addressed us in a very
brief speech, of which we could distinguish the words
pearls and *swinish multitude*, but uttered in a very
low key, perhaps out of some lurking consideration
for the two young strangers. We all laughed in chorus
at this parting salute; my brother himself condescended at last to join us; but there ended the course
of lectures on natural philosophy.

As it was impossible, however, that he should remain quiet, he announced to us, that for the rest of
his life he meant to dedicate himself to the intense
cultivation of the tragic drama. He got to work instantly; and very soon he had composed the first act

of his *Sultan Selim;* but, in defiance of the metre, he soon changed the title to *Sultan Amurath*, considering *that* a much fiercer name, more bewhiskered and be-turbaned. It was no part of his intention that we should sit lolling on chairs like ladies and gentlemen that had paid opera prices for private boxes. He expected every one of us, he said, to pull an oar. We were to *act* the tragedy. But, in fact, we had many oars to pull. There were so many characters, that each of us took four at the least, and the future middy had six. He, this wicked little middy,[1] caused the greatest affliction to Sultan Amurath, forcing him to order the amputation of his head six several times (that is, once in every one of his six parts) during the first act. In reality, the sultan, though otherwise a decent man, was too bloody. What by the bowstring, and what by the scimitar, he had so thinned the population with which he commenced business, that scarcely any of the characters remained alive at the end of act the first. Sultan Amurath found himself in an awkward situation. Large arrears of work remained, and hardly anybody to do it but the sultan himself. In composing act the second, the author had to proceed like Deucalion and Pyrrha, and to create an entirely new generation. Apparently this young generation, that ought to have been so good, took no warning by what had happened to their ancestors in act the first; one must conclude that they were quite as wicked, since the poor sultan had found himself reduced to order them all for exe-

[1] *"Middy"*: I call him so simply to avoid confusion, and by way of anticipation; else he was too young at this time to serve in the navy. Afterwards he did so for many years, and saw every variety of service in every class of ships belonging to our navy. At one time, when yet a boy, he was captured by pirates, and compelled to sail with them; and the end of his adventurous career was, that for many a year he has been lying at the bottom of the Atlantic.

cution in the course of this act the second. To the brazen age had succeeded an iron age; and the prospects were becoming sadder and sadder as the tragedy advanced. But here the author began to hesitate. He felt it hard to resist the instinct of carnage. And was it right to do so? Which of the felons whom he had cut off prematurely could pretend that a court of appeal would have reversed his sentence? But the consequences were distressing. A new set of characters in every act brought with it the necessity of a new plot; for people could not succeed to the arrears of old actions, or inherit ancient motives, like a landed estate. Five crops, in fact, must be taken off the ground in each separate tragedy, amounting, in short, to five tragedies involved in one.

Such, according to the rapid sketch which at this moment my memory furnishes, was the brother who now first laid open to me the gates of war. The occasion was this. He had resented, with a shower of stones, an affront offered to us by an individual boy, belonging to a cotton factory; for more than two years afterwards this became the *teterrima causa* of a skirmish or a battle as often as we passed the factory; and, unfortunately, *that* was twice a-day on every day, except Sunday. Our situation in respect to the enemy was as follows: Greenhay, a country-house, newly built by my father, at that time was a clear mile from the outskirts of Manchester; but in after years, Manchester, throwing out the *tentacula* of its vast expansions, absolutely enveloped Greenhay; and, for anything I know, the grounds and gardens which then insulated the house may have long disappeared. Being a modest mansion, which (including hot walls, offices, and gardener's house) had cost only six thousand pounds, I do not know how it should have risen to the distinction of giving name to a region of that great town; how-

ever, it *has* done so [1]; and at this time, therefore, after
changes so great, it will be difficult for the *habitué* of
that region to understand how my brother and myself
could have a solitary road to traverse between Greenhay and Princess Street, then the termination, on that
side, of Manchester. But so it was. Oxford *Street*, like
its namesake in London, was then called the Oxford
Road; and during the currency of our acquaintance
with it, arose the first three houses in its neighbourhood; of which the third was built for the Rev. S. H.,
one of our guardians, for whom his friends had also
built the church of St. Peter's—not a bowshot from
the house. At present, however, he resided in Salford,
nearly two miles from Greenhay; and to him we went
over daily, for the benefit of his classical instructions.
One sole cotton factory had then risen along the line
of Oxford Street; and this was close to a bridge, which
also was a new creation; for previously all passengers
to Manchester went round by Garrat. This factory
became to us the *officina gentium*, from which
swarmed forth those Goths and Vandals that continually threatened our steps; and this bridge became
the eternal arena of combat, we taking good care to
be on the right side of the bridge for retreat—*i.e.,* on
the town side, or the country side, accordingly as we
were going out in the morning, or returning in the
afternoon. Stones were the implements of warfare;
and by continual practice both parties became expert
in throwing them.

The origin of the feud it is scarcely requisite to rehearse, since the particular accident which began it

[1] "Greenheys," with a slight variation in the spelling, is the
name given to that district, of which Greenhay formed the
original nucleus. Probably, it was the solitary situation of the
house which (failing any other grounds of denomination)
raised it to this privilege.

was not the true efficient cause of our long warfare, but simply the casual occasion. The cause lay in our aristocratic dress. As children of an opulent family, where all provisions were liberal, and all appointments elegant, we were uniformly well-dressed; and, in particular, we wore trousers (at that time unheard of, except among sailors), and we also wore Hessian boots—a crime that could not be forgiven in the Lancashire of that day, because it expressed the double offence of being aristocratic and being outlandish. We were aristocrats, and it was vain to deny it; could we deny our boots? whilst our antagonists, if not absolutely *sansculottes*, were slovenly and forlorn in their dress, often unwashed, with hair totally neglected, and always covered with flakes of cotton. Jacobins they were not, as regarded any sympathy with the Jacobinism that then desolated France; for, on the contrary, they detested everything French, and answered with brotherly signals to the cry of "Church and King," or "King and Constitution." But, for all that, as they were perfectly independent, getting very high wages, and these wages in a mode of industry that was then taking vast strides ahead, they contrived to reconcile this patriotic anti-Jacobinism with a personal Jacobinism of that sort which is native to the heart of man, who is by natural impulse (and not without a root of nobility, though also of base envy) impatient of inequality, and submits to it only through a sense of its necessity, or under a long experience of its benefits.

It was on an early day of our new *tyrocinium*, or perhaps on the very first, that, as we passed the bridge, a boy happening to issue from the factory sang out to us, derisively, "Holloa, Bucks!" In this the reader may fail to perceive any atrocious insult commensurate to the long war which followed. But the reader is wrong.

The word *"dandies,"* [1] which was what the villain meant, had not then been born, so that he could not have called us by that name, unless through the spirit of prophecy. *Buck* was the nearest word at hand in his Manchester vocabulary; he gave all he could, and let us dream the rest. But in the next moment he discovered our boots, and he consummated his crime by saluting us as "Boots! boots!" My brother made a dead stop, surveyed him with intense disdain, and bade him draw near, that he might "give his flesh to the fowls of the air." The boy declined to accept this liberal invitation, and conveyed his answer by a most contemptuous and plebeian gesture,[2] upon which my brother drove him in with a shower of stones.

During this inaugural flourish of hostilities, I, for my part, remained inactive, and therefore apparently neutral. But this was the last time that I did so: for the moment, indeed, I was taken by surprise. To be called a *buck* by one that had it in his choice to have called me a coward, a thief, or a murderer, struck me as a most pardonable offence; and as to *boots*, that rested upon a flagrant fact that could not be denied; so that at first I was green enough to regard the boy as very considerate and indulgent. But my brother soon rectified my views; or, if any doubts remained, he impressed me, at least, with a sense of my paramount duty to himself, which was threefold. First, it seems that I owed military allegiance to *him*, as my commander-in-chief, whenever we "took the field"; sec-

[1] This word, however, exists in *Jack-a-dandy*—a very old English word. But what does *that* mean?

[2] Precisely, however, the same gesture, plebeian as it was, by which the English commandant at Heligoland replied to the Danes when civilly inviting him to surrender. Southey it was, on the authority of Lieutenant Southey, his brother, who communicated to me this anecdote.

ondly, by the law of nations, I, being a cadet of my house, owed suit and service to him who was its head; and he assured me, that twice in a year, on *my* birthday and on *his*, he had a right, strictly speaking, to make me lie down, and to set his foot upon my neck; lastly, by a law not so rigorous, but valid amongst gentlemen—viz., "by the *comity* of nations"—it seems I owed eternal deference to one so much older than myself, so much wiser, stronger, braver, more beautiful, and more swift of foot. Something like all this in tendency I had already believed, though I had not so minutely investigated the modes and grounds of my duty. By temperament, and through natural dedication to despondency, I felt resting upon me always too deep and gloomy a sense of obscure duties attached to life, that I never *should* be able to fulfil; a burden which I could not carry, and which yet I did not know how to throw off. Glad, therefore, I was to find the whole tremendous weight of obligations—the law and the prophets—all crowded into this one pocket command, "Thou shalt obey thy brother as God's vicar upon earth." For now, if by any future stone levelled at him who had called me a "buck," I should chance to draw blood—perhaps I might not have committed so serious a trespass on any rights which he could plead: but if I *had* (for on this subject my convictions were still cloudy), at any rate the duty I might have violated in regard to this general brother, in right of Adam, was cancelled when it came into collision with my paramount duty to this liege brother of my own individual house.

From this day, therefore, I obeyed all my brother's military commands with the utmost docility; and happy it made me that every sort of doubt, or question, or opening for demur, was swallowed up in the unity of this one papal principle, discovered by my brother

—viz., that all rights and duties of casuistry were transferred from me to himself. *His* was the judgement —*his* was the responsibility; and to me belonged only the sublime obligation of unconditional faith in *him*. That faith I realized. It is true that he taxed me at times, in his reports of particular fights, with "horrible cowardice," and even with a "cowardice that seemed inexplicable, except on the supposition of treachery." But this was only a *façon de parler* with him: the idea of secret perfidy, that was constantly moving under-ground, gave an interest to the progress of the war, which else tended to the monotonous. It was a dramatic artifice for sustaining the interest, where the incidents might happen to be too slightly diversified. But that he did not believe his own charges was clear, because he never repeated them in his *General History of the Campaigns*, which was a *résumé*, or recapitulating digest, of his daily reports.

We fought every day; and, generally speaking, *twice* every day; and the result was pretty uniform— viz., that my brother and I terminated the battle by insisting upon our undoubted right to run away. *Magna Charta*, I should fancy, secures that great right to every man; else, surely, it is sadly defective. But out of this catastrophe to most of our skirmishes, and to all our pitched battles except one, grew a standing schism between my brother and myself. My unlimited obedience had respect to action, but not to opinion. Loyalty to my brother did not rest upon hypocrisy; because I was faithful, it did not follow that I must be false in relation to his capricious opinions. And these opinions sometimes took the shape of acts. Twice, at the least, in every week, but sometimes every night, my brother insisted on singing "Te Deum" for supposed victories he had won; and he insisted also on my bearing a part in these "Te Deums."

Now, as I knew of no such victories, but resolutely asserted the truth—viz., that we ran away—a slight jar was thus given to the else triumphal effect of these musical ovations. Once having uttered my protest, however, willingly I gave my aid to the chanting; for I loved unspeakably the grand and varied system of chanting in the Romish and English Churches. And, looking back at this day to the ineffable benefits which I derived from the church of my childhood, I account among the very greatest those which reached me through the various chants connected with the "O, Jubilate," the "Magnificat," the "Te Deum," the "Benedicite," etc. Through these chants it was that the sorrow which laid waste my infancy, and the devotion which nature had made a necessity of my being, were profoundly interfused: the sorrow gave reality and depth to the devotion; the devotion gave grandeur and idealization to the sorrow. Neither was my love for chanting altogether without knowledge. A son of my reverend guardian, much older than myself, who possessed a singular faculty of producing a sort of organ accompaniment with one-half of his mouth, whilst he sang with the other half, had given me some instructions in the art of chanting: and, as to my brother, he, the hundred-handed Briareus, could do all things; of course, therefore, he could chant.

Once having begun, it followed naturally that the war should deepen in bitterness. Wounds that wrote memorials in the flesh, insults that rankled in the heart—these were not features of the case likely to be forgotten by our enemies, and far less by my fiery brother. I, for my part, entered not into any of the passions that war may be supposed to kindle, except only the chronic passion of anxiety. *Fear* it was not; for experience had taught me that, under the random firing of our undisciplined enemies, the chances were

not many of being wounded. But the uncertainties of
the war; the doubts in every separate action whether
I could keep up the requisite connexion with my
brother; and, in case I could not, the utter darkness
that surrounded my fate; whether, as a trophy won
from Israel, I should be dedicated to the service of
some Manchester Dagon, or pass through fire to Moloch; all these contingencies, for me that had no friend
to consult, ran too violently into the master-current
of my constitutional despondency, ever to give way under any casual elation of success. Success, however, we
really had at times; in slight skirmishes pretty often;
and once, at least, as the reader will find to his mortification, if he is wicked enough to take the side of the
Philistines, a most smashing victory in a pitched battle. But even then, and whilst the hurrahs were yet
ascending from our jubilating lips, the freezing remembrance came back to my heart of that deadly depression which, duly at the coming round of the morning and evening watches, travelled with me like my
shadow on our approach to the memorable bridge. A
bridge of sighs [1] too surely it was for me; and even for
my brother it formed an object of fierce yet anxious

[1] *"Bridge of Sighs"*: Two men of memorable genius, Hood
last, and Lord Byron by many years previously, have so appropriated this phrase, and re-issued it as English currency, that
many readers suppose it to be theirs. But the genealogies of
fine expressions should be more carefully preserved. The expression belongs originally to Venice. This *jus postliminii* becomes of real importance in many cases, but especially in the
case of Shakespeare. Could one have believed it possible beforehand? And yet it is a fact that he is made to seem a robber
of the lowest order, by mere dint of suffering robbery. Purely
through their own jewelly splendour have many hundreds of
his phrases forced themselves into usage so general, under
the vulgar infirmity of seeking to strengthen weak prose by
shreds of poetic quotation, that at length the majority of care-

jealousy, that he could not always disguise, as we first
came in sight of it: for, if it happened to be occupied
in strength, there was an end of all hope that we could
attempt the passage; and *that* was a fortunate solution
of the difficulty, as it imposed no evil beyond a circuit;
which, at least, was safe, if the world should choose to
call it inglorious. Even this shade of ignomiy, however, my brother contrived to colour favourably, by
calling us—that is, me and himself—"a corps of observation"; and he condescendingly explained to me,
that, although making "a lateral movement," he had
his eye upon the enemy, and "might yet come round
upon his left flank in a way that wouldn't, perhaps,
prove very agreeable." This, from the nature of the
ground, never happened. We crossed the river at Garrat, out of sight from the enemy's position; and, on
our return in the evening, when we reached that point
of our route from which the retreat was secure to
Greenhay, we took such revenge for the morning insult as might belong to extra liberality in our stone

less readers come to look upon these phrases as belonging to
the language, and traceable to no distinct proprietor any more
than proverbs: and thus, on afterwards observing them in
Shakespeare, they regard him in the light of one accepting
alms (like so many meaner persons) from the common treasury of the universal mind, on which treasury, meantime, he
had himself conferred these phrases as original donations of
his own. Many expressions in the *Paradise Lost*, in *Il Penseroso*,
and in *L'Allegro*, are in the same predicament. And thus the
almost incredible case is realized which I have described—
viz., that simply by having suffered a robbery through two
centuries (for the first attempt at plundering Milton was made
upon his juvenile poems), have Shakespeare and Milton come
to be taxed as robbers. N.B. In speaking of Hood as having
appropriated the phrase *Bridge of Sighs*, I would not be understood to represent him as by possibility aiming at any concealment. He was far above such a meanness by his nobility
of heart, as he was raised above all need for it by the overflowing opulence of his genius.

donations. On this line of policy there was, therefore, no cause for anxiety; but the common case was, that the numbers might not be such as to justify this caution, and yet quite enough for mischief. To my brother, however, stung and carried headlong into hostility by the martial instincts of his nature, the uneasiness of doubt or insecurity was swallowed up by his joy in the anticipation of victory, or even of contest; whilst to myself, whose exultation was purely official and ceremonial, as due by loyalty from a cadet to the head of his house, no such compensation existed. The enemy was no enemy in *my* eyes; his affronts were but retaliations; and his insults were so inapplicable to my unworthy self, being of a calibre exclusively meant for the use of my brother, that from me they recoiled, one and all, as cannon-shot from cotton bags.

The ordinary course of our day's warfare was this: between nine and ten in the morning occurred our first transit, and consequently our earliest opportunity for doing business. But at this time the great sublunary interest of breakfast, which swallowed up all nobler considerations of glory and ambition, occupied the work-people of the factory (or what in the pedantic diction of this day are termed the "operatives"), so that very seldom any serious business was transacted. Without any formal armistice, the paramount convenience of such an arrangement silently secured its own recognition. Notice there needed none of truce, when the one side yearned for breakfast, and the other for a respite; the groups, therefore, on or about the bridge, if any at all, were loose in their array, and careless. We passed through them rapidly, and, on my part, uneasily; exchanging a few snarls, perhaps, but seldom or ever snapping at each other. The tameness was almost shocking of those who, in the afternoon,

would inevitably resume their natural characters of
tiger-cats and wolves. Sometimes, however, my brother
felt it to be a duty that we should fight in the morning;
particularly when any expression of public joy for a
victory—bells ringing in the distance—or when a
royal birth-day, or some traditional commemoration
of ancient feuds (such as the 5th of November), irritated his martial propensities. Some of these, being
religious festivals, seemed to require of us an *extra*
homage, for which we knew not how to find any natural or significant expression, except through sharp
discharges of stones, that being a language older than
Hebrew or Sanskrit, and universally intelligible. But,
excepting these high days of religious solemnity, when
a man is called upon to show that he is not a Pagan or
a miscreant in the eldest of senses, by thumping, or
trying to thump, somebody who is accused or accusable
of being heterodox, the great ceremony of breakfast
was allowed to sanctify the hour. Some natural growls
we uttered, but hushed them soon, regardless

> *Of the sweeping whirlpool's sway,*
> *That, hush'd in grim repose, look'd for his eve-*
> *ning prey.*

That came but too surely. Yes, evening never forgot
to come; this odious necessity of fighting never missed
its road back, or fell asleep, or loitered by the way,
more than a bill of exchange, or a tertian fever. Five
times a-week (Saturday sometimes, and Sunday always, were days of rest) the same scene rehearsed itself in pretty nearly the same succession of circumstances. Between four and five o'clock we had crossed
the bridge to the safe, or Greenhay, side; then we
paused, and waited for the enemy. Sooner or later a

bell rang, and from the smoky hive issued the hornets
that night and day stung incurably my peace of mind.
The order and procession of the incidents after this
were odiously monotonous. My brother occupied the
main high-road, precisely at the point where a very
gentle rise of the ground attained its summit; for the
bridge lay in a slight valley; and the main military
position was fifty or eighty yards above the bridge;
then—but having first examined my pockets, in order
to be sure that my stock of ammunition—stones, fragments of slate, with a reasonable proportion of brickbats—was all correct and ready for action—he detached me about forty yards to the right, my orders
being invariable, and liable to no doubts or "quib-
bling." Detestable in *my* ears was that word *"quib-
bling,"* by which, for a thousand years, if the war had
happened to last so long, he would have fastened upon
me the imputation of meaning, or wishing, at least, to
do what he called "pettifogulizing"—that is, to plead
some distinction, or verbal demur, in bar of my orders,
under some colourable pretence that, according to
their literal construction, they really did not admit of
being fulfilled, or perhaps that they admitted it too
much as being capable of fulfilment in two senses,
either of them a practical sense. True it was that my
eye was preternaturally keen for flaws of language,
not from pedantic exaction of superfluous accuracy,
but, on the contrary, from too conscientious a wish to
escape the mistakes which language not rigorous is
apt to occasion. So far from seeking to "pettifogulize"
—*i.e.*, to find evasions for any purpose in a trickster's
minute tortuosities of construction—exactly in the opposite direction, from mere excess of sincerity, most
unwillingly I found, in almost everybody's words, an
unintentional opening left for double interpretations.

Undesigned equivocation prevails everywhere [1]; and it is not the cavilling hair-splitter, but, on the contrary, the single-eyed servant of truth, that is most likely to insist upon the limitation of expressions too wide or too vague, and upon the decisive election between meanings potentially double. Not in order to resist or evade my brother's directions, but for the very opposite purpose—viz., that I might fulfil them to the letter—thus and no otherwise it happened that I showed so much scrupulosity about the exact value and position of his words, as finally to draw upon myself the vexatious reproach of being habitually a "pettifogulizer."

Meantime, our campaigning continued to rage. Overtures of pacification were never mentioned on either side. And I, for *my* part, with the passions only of peace at my heart, did the works of war faithfully, and with distinction. I presume so, at least, from the results. It is true I was continually falling into treason, without exactly knowing how I got into it, or how I got out of it. My brother also, it is true, sometimes assured me that he could, according to the rigour of martial justice, have me hanged on the first tree we passed; to which my prosaic answer had been, that of trees there *were* none in Oxford Street— (which, in imitation of Von Troil's famous chapter on the snakes

[1] Geometry (it has been said) would not evade disputation, if a man could find his interest in disputing it: such is the spirit of cavil. But I, upon a very opposite ground, assert that there is not one page of prose that could be selected from the best writer in the English language (far less in the German), which, upon a sufficient interest arising, would not furnish matter, simply through its defects in precision, for a suit in Chancery. Chancery suits do not arise, it is true, because the doubtful expressions do not touch any interest of property; but what *does* arise is this—that something more valuable than a pecuniary interest is continually suffering—viz., the interests of truth.

of Lapland, the reader may accept, if he pleases, as a complete course of lectures on the "dendrology" of Oxford Street) —but, notwithstanding such little stumblings in my career, I continued to ascend in the service; and I am sure it will gratify my friendly readers to hear, that, before my eighth birth-day, I was promoted to the rank of major-general. Over this sunshine, however, soon swept a train of clouds. Three times I was taken prisoner; and with different results. The first time I was carried to the rear, and not molested in any way. Finding myself thus ignominiously neglected, I watched my opportunity; and, by making a wide circuit, easily effected my escape. In the next case, a brief council was held over me; but I was not allowed to hear the deliberations; the result only being communicated to me—which result consisted in a message not very complimentary to my brother, and a small present of kicks to myself. This present was paid down without any discount, by means of a general subscription amongst the party surrounding me—that party, luckily, not being very numerous; besides which, I must, in honesty, acknowledge myself, generally speaking, indebted to their forbearance. They were not disposed to be too hard upon me. But, at the same time, they clearly did not think it right that I should escape altogether from tasting the calamities of war. And this translated the estimate of my guilt from the public jurisdiction to that of the individual, sometimes capricious and harsh, and carrying out the public award by means of legs that ranged through all gradations of weight and agility. One kick differed exceedingly from another kick in dynamic value; and, in some cases, this difference was so distressingly conspicuous, as to imply special malice, unworthy, I conceive, of all generous soldiership.

On returning to our own frontiers, I had an oppor-

tunity of displaying my exemplary greenness. That
message to my brother, with all its *virus* of insolence,
I repeated as faithfully for the spirit, and as literally
for the expressions, as my memory allowed me to do:
and in that troublesome effort, simpleton that I was,
fancied myself exhibiting a soldier's loyalty to his
commanding officer. My brother thought otherwise:
he was more angry with me than with the enemy. I
ought, he said, to have refused all participation in such
sansculottes' insolence; to carry it, was to acknowledge
it as fit to be carried. One grows wiser every day; and
on this particular day I made a resolution that, if again
made prisoner, I would bring no more "jaw" (so my
brother called it) from the Philistines. If these people
would send "jaw," I settled that, henceforwards, it
must go through the post-office.

In my former captures, there had been nothing special or worthy of commemoration in the circumstances. Neither was there in the third, excepting that,
by accident, in the second stage of the case, I was delivered over to the custody of young women and girls;
whereas the ordinary course would have thrown me
upon the vigilant attentions (relieved from monotony
by the experimental kicks) of boys. So far, the change
was very much for the better. I had a feeling myself,
on first being presented to my new young mistresses,
of a distressing sort. Having always, up to the completion of my sixth year, been a privileged pet, and
almost, I might say, ranking amongst the sanctities of
the household, with all its female sections, whether
young or old (an advantage which I owed originally
to a long illness, an ague, stretching over two entire
years of my infancy), naturally I had learned to appreciate the indulgent tenderness of women; and my
heart thrilled with love and gratitude, as often as they
took me up into their arms and kissed me. Here it

would have been as everywhere else; but, unfortunately, my introduction to these young women was in the very worst of characters. I had been taken in arms —in arms against their own brothers, cousins, sweethearts, and on pretexts too frivolous to mention. If asked the question, it would be found that I should not myself deny the fact of being at war with their whole order. What was the meaning of *that?* What was it to which war pledged a man? It pledged him, in case of opportunity, to burn, ravage, and depopulate the houses and lands of the enemy; which enemy was these fair girls. The warrior stood committed to universal destruction. Neither sex nor age; neither the smiles of unoffending infancy nor the grey hairs of the venerable patriarch; neither the sanctity of the matron nor the loveliness of the youthful bride, would confer any privilege with the warrior, consequently not with me.

Many other hideous features in the military character will be found in books innumerable—levelled at those who make war, and therefore at myself. And it appears finally by these books—that, as one of my ordinary practices, I make a wilderness, and call it a pacification; that I hold it a duty to put people to the sword; which done, to plough up the foundations of their hearths and altars, and then to sow the ground with salt.

All this was passing through my brain, when suddenly one young woman snatched me up in her arms, and kissed me; from *her*, I was passed round to others of the party, who all in turn caressed me, with no allusion to that warlike mission, against them and theirs, which only had procured me the honour of an introduction to themselves in the character of captive. The too palpable fact that I was not the person meant by nature to exterminate their families, or to make wildernesses and call them pacifications, had withdrawn from their minds the counter fact—that, whatever had been my performances, my intentions had been hostile, and that in such a character only I could have become their prisoner. Not only did these young people kiss me, but I (seeing no military reason against it) kissed *them*. Really, if young women will insist on kissing major-generals, they must expect that the generals will retaliate. One only of the crowd adverted to the character in which I came before them: to be a lawful prisoner, it struck her too logical mind that I must have been caught in some aggressive practices. "Think," she said, "of this little dog fighting, and fighting our Jack." "But," said another, in a propitiatory tone, "perhaps he'll not do so any more." I was touched by the kindness of her suggestion, and the sweet, merciful sound of that same *"Not do so any more,"* which really was prompted, I fear, much more by that charity in her which hopeth all things, than by any signs of amendment in myself. Well was it for me that no time was allowed for investigation into my morals by point-blank questions as to my future intentions. In which case it would have appeared too undeniably, that the same sad necessity which had planted me hitherto in a position of hostility to their estimable families, would continue to persecute me; and that, on the very next day, duty to my brother, howsoever it might struggle with gratitude to themselves, would range me in martial attitude, with a pocketful of stones, meant, alas! for the exclusive use of their respectable kinsmen. Whilst I was preparing myself, however, for this painful exposition, my female friends observed issuing from the factory a crowd of boys not likely at all to improve my prospects. Instantly setting me down on my feet, they formed a sort of *cordon sanitaire* behind me, by stretching out their petticoats

or aprons, as in dancing, so as to touch: and then, crying out, "Now, little dog, run for thy life," prepared
themselves (I doubt not) for rescuing me, should my
re-capture be effected.

But this was *not* effected, although attempted with
an energy that alarmed me, and even perplexed me
with a vague thought (far too ambitious for my years)
that one or two of the pursuing party might be possessed by some demon of jealousy, as eyewitnesses to
my revelling amongst the lips of that fair girlish bevy,
kissing and being kissed, loving and being loved; in
which case, from all that ever I had read about jealousy (and I had read a great deal— viz., *Othello*, and
Collins's "Ode to the Passions"), I was satisfied that,
if again captured, I had very little chance for my life.
That jealousy was a green-eyed monster, nobody
could know better than *I* did. "Oh, my lord, beware of
jealousy!" Yes; and my lord couldn't possibly have
more reason for bewaring of it than myself; indeed,
well it would have been had his lordship run away
from all the ministers of jealousy—Iago, Cassio, and
embroidered handkerchiefs—at the same pace of six
miles an hour which kept me ahead of my infuriated
pursuers. Ah, that maniac, white as a leper with flakes
of cotton, can I ever forget him, *him* that ran so far in
advance of his party? What passion, but jealousy,
could have sustained him in so hot a chase? There
were some lovely girls in the fair company that had
so condescendingly caressed me; but, doubtless, upon
that sweet creature his love must have settled, who
suggested, in her soft, relenting voice, a penitence in
me that, alas! had not dawned, saying, "*Yes; but perhaps he will not do so any more.*" Thinking, as I ran,
of her beauty, I felt that this jealous demoniac must
fancy himself justified in committing seven times
seven murders upon me, if he should have it in his

power. But, thank heaven, if jealousy can run six miles an hour, there are other passions, as for instance panic, that can run, upon occasion, six and a-half; so, as I had the start of him (you know, reader), and not a very short start—thanks be to the expanded petticoats of my dear female friends!—naturally it happened that the green-eyed monster came in second best. Time luckily was precious with *him;* and, accordingly, when he had chased me into the by-road leading down to Greenhay, he turned back. For the moment, therefore, I found myself suddenly released from danger. But this counted for nothing. The same scene would probably revolve upon me continually; and, on the next rehearsal, Green-eyes might have better luck. It saddened me, besides, to find myself under the political necessity of numbering amongst the Philistines, and as daughters of Gath, so many kind-hearted girls, whom, by personal proof, I knew to be such. In the profoundest sense I was unhappy; and not from any momentary accident of distress, but from deep glimpses which now, and heretofore, had opened themselves, as occasions arose, into the inevitable conflicts of life. One of the saddest among such conflicts is the necessity, wheresoever it occurs, of adopting—though the heart should disown—the enmities of one's own family, or country, or religious sect. In forms how afflicting must that necessity have sometimes occurred during the Parliamentary War! And, in after years, amongst our beautiful old English metrical romances, I found the same impassioned complaint uttered by a knight, Sir Ywain, as early as A.D. 1240—

> *But now, where'er I stray or go,*
> *My heart* SHE *has that is my foe!*

I knew—I anticipated to a certainty—that my brother

would not hear of any merit belonging to the factory population whom every day we had to meet in battle; on the contrary, even submission on *their* part, and willingness to walk penitentially through the *Furcæ Caudinæ*, would hardly have satisfied his sense of their criminality. Often, indeed, as we came in view of the factory, he would shake his fist at it, and say, in a ferocious tone of voice, "*Delenda est Carthago!*" And certainly, I thought to myself, it must be admitted by everybody, that the factory people are inexcusable in raising a rebellion against my brother. But still rebels were men, and sometimes were women; and rebels that stretch out their petticoats like fans for the sake of screening one from the hot pursuit of enemies with fiery eyes (green or otherwise) really are not the sort of people that one wishes to hate.

Homewards, therefore, I drew in sadness, and little doubting that *hereafter* I might have verbal feuds with my brother on behalf of my fair friends, but not dreaming how much displeasure I had already incurred by my treasonable collusion with their caresses. That part of the affair he had seen with his own eyes, from his position on the field; and then it was that he left me indignantly to my fate, which, by my first reception, it was easy to see would not prove very gloomy. When I came into our own study, I found him engaged in preparing a *bulletin* (which word was just then travelling into universal use), reporting briefly the events of the day. The art of drawing, as I shall again have occasion to mention, was amongst his foremost accomplishments; and round the margin of the bulletin ran a black border, ornamented with cypress, and other funereal emblems. When finished, it was carried into the room of Mrs. Evans. This Mrs. Evans was an important person in our affairs. My mother, who never chose to have any direct commu-

nication with her servants, always had a housekeeper
for the regulation of all domestic business; and the
housekeeper for some years was this Mrs. Evans. Into
her private parlour, where she sat aloof from the under servants, my brother and I had the *entrée* at all
times, but upon very different terms of acceptance: he
as a favourite of the first class; *I*, by sufferance, as a
sort of gloomy shadow that ran after *his* person, and
could not well be shut out if *he* were let in. Him she
admired in the very highest degree; myself, on the
contrary, she detested—which made me unhappy. But
then, in some measure, she made amends for this, by
despising me in extremity; and for *that* I was truly
thankful—I need not say *why*, as the reader already
knows. Why she detested me, so far as I know, arose in
part out of my thoughtfulness indisposed to garrulity,
and in part out of my savage, Orson-like sincerity. I
had a great deal to say, but then I could say it only to
a very few people, amongst whom Mrs. Evans was certainly not one; and when I *did* say anything, I fear
that dire ignorance prevented my laying the proper
restraints upon my too liberal candour; and *that* could
not prove acceptable to one who thought nothing of
working for any purpose, or for no purpose, by petty
tricks, or even falsehoods—all which I held in stern
abhorrence, that I was at no pains to conceal. The
bulletin on this occasion, garnished with its pageantry
of woe, cypress wreaths, and arms reversed, was read
aloud to Mrs. Evans, indirectly therefore to me. It
communicated, with Spartan brevity, the sad intelligence (but not sad to Mrs. E.), "that the major-
general had for ever disgraced himself, by submitting
to the —— caresses of the enemy." I leave a blank
for the epithet affixed to "caresses," not because there
was any blank, but, on the contrary, because my
brother's wrath had boiled over in such a hubble-

bubble of epithets, some only half erased, some doubtfully erased, that it was impossible, out of the various
readings, to pick out the true classical text. "Infa-
famous," "disgusting," and "odious," struggled for
precedency; and *infamous* they might be; but on the
other affixes I held my own private opinions. For some
days, my brother's displeasure continued to roll in reverberating thunders; but at length it growled itself to
rest; and at last he descended to mild expostulations
with me, showing clearly, in a series of general orders,
what frightful consequences must ensue, if major-
generals (as a general principle) should allow themselves to be kissed by the enemy.

About this time, my brother began to issue, instead
of occasional bulletins, through which hitherto he had
breathed his opinions into the ear of the public (viz., of
Mrs. Evans) , a regular gazette, which, in imitation of
the *London Gazette,* was published twice a-week. I
suppose that no creature ever led such a life as *I* did in
that gazette. Run up to the giddiest heights of promotion on one day, for merits which I could not myself discern, in a week or two I was brought to a
court-martial for offences equally obscure. I was cash-
iered; I was restored "on the intercession of a distinguished lady" (Mrs. Evans, to wit) ; I was threatened with being drummed out of the army, to the
music of the "Rogue's March"; and then, in the midst
of all this misery and degradation, upon the discovery
of some supposed energy that I had manifested, I was
decorated with the Order of the Bath. My reading had
been extensive enough to give me some vague aerial
sense of the honour involved in such a decoration,
whilst I was profoundly ignorant of the channels
through which it could reach an individual, and of the
sole fountain from which it could flow. But, in this
enormity of disproportion between the cause and the

effect, between the agency and the result, I saw nothing
more astonishing than I had seen in many other cases
confessedly true. Thousands of vast effects, by all that
I had heard, linked themselves to causes apparently
trivial. The dreadful taint of scrofula, according to
the belief of all Christendom, fled at the simple touch
of a Stuart sovereign [1]: no miracle in the Bible, from
Jordan or from Bethesda, could be more sudden, or
more astoundingly victorious. By my own experience,
again, I knew that a *styan* (as it is called) upon the
eyelid could be easily reduced, though not instantaneously, by the slight application of any golden
trinket. Warts upon the fingers of children I had myself known to vanish under the *verbal* charm of a gipsy
woman, without any medicinal application whatever.
And I well knew, that almost all nations believed in
the dreadful mystery of the *evil eye;* some requiring,
as a condition of the evil agency, the co-presence of
malice in the agent; but others, as appeared from my
father's Portuguese recollections, ascribing the same
horrid power to the eye of certain select persons, even
though innocent of all malignant purpose, and absolutely unconscious of their own fatal gift, until awakened to it by the results. Why, therefore, should there
be anything to shock, or even to surprise, in the power
claimed by my brother, as an attribute inalienable
from primogeniture in certain select families, of con-

[1] "*Of a Stuart sovereign*": and by no means of a Stuart
only. Queen Anne, the last Stuart who sat on the British
throne, was the last of *our* princes who touched for the *king's
evil* (as scrofula was generally called until lately); but the
Bourbon Houses, on the thrones of France, Spain, and Naples,
as well as the House of Savoy, claimed and exercised the same
supernatural privilege down to a much later period than the
year 1714—the last of Queen Anne: according to their own
and the popular faith, they could have cleansed Naaman the
Syrian, and Gehazi too.

ferring knightly honours? The red riband of the Bath
he certainly *did* confer upon me; and once, in a paroxysm of imprudent liberality, he promised me at the
end of certain months, supposing that I swerved from
my duty by no atrocious delinquency, the Garter itself.
This, I knew, was a far loftier distinction than the
Bath. Even then it was so; and since those days it has
become much more so; because the long roll of martial
services in the great war with Napoleon compelled
our government greatly to widen the basis of the Bath.
This promise was never fulfilled; but not for any want
of clamorous persecution on my part addressed to my
brother's wearied ear, and somewhat callous sense of
honour. Every fortnight or so, I took care that he
should receive a "refresher," as lawyers call it—a new
and revised brief—memorializing my pretensions.
These it was my brother's policy to parry, by alleged
instances of recent misconduct on my part. But all such
offences, I insisted, were thoroughly washed away by
subsequent services in moments of peril, such as he
himself could not always deny. In reality, I believe his
real motive for withholding the Garter was that he had
nothing better to bestow upon himself.

"Now, look here," he would say, appealing to Mrs.
Evans; "I suppose there's a matter of half-a-dozen
kings on the Continent that would consent to lose
three of their fingers, if by such a sacrifice they could
purchase the blue riband; and here is this little scamp,
conceiting himself entitled to it before he has finished
two campaigns." But I was not the person to be beaten
off in this fashion. I took my stand upon the promise.
A promise *was* a promise, even if made to a scamp;
and then, besides——but there I hesitated; awful
thoughts interposed to check me; else I wished to suggest that, perhaps, some two or three among that half-
dozen kings might also be scamps. However, I reduced

the case to this plain dilemma: These six kings had
received a promise, or they had not. If they had not,
my case was better than theirs; if they *had*, then, said I,
"all seven of us"——I was going to add, "are sailing
in the same boat," or something to that effect, though
not so picturesquely expressed; but I was interrupted
by his deadly frown at my audacity in thus linking
myself on as a seventh to this *attelage* of kings; and
that such an absolute grub should dream of ranking as
one in a bright pleiad of pretenders to the Garter. I
had not particularly thought of that; but, now that
such a demur was offered to my consideration, I
thought of reminding him that, in a certain shadowy
sense, I also might presume to class myself as a king
—the meaning of which was this: Both my brother
and myself, for the sake of varying our intellectual
amusements, occupied ourselves at times in governing
imaginary kingdoms. I do not mention this as anything unusual; it is a common resource of mental
activity and of aspiring energies amongst boys. Hartley Coleridge, for example, had a kingdom which he
governed for many years; whether well or ill, is more
than I can say. Kindly, I am sure, he would govern it;
but, unless a machine had been invented for enabling
him to write without effort (as was really done for
our Fourth George during the pressure of illness), I
fear that the public service must have languished de-
plorably for want of the royal signature. In sailing
past his own dominions, what dolorous outcries would
have saluted him from the shore—"Holloa, royal sir!
here's the deuce to pay: a perfect lock there is, as tight
as locked jaw, upon the course of our public business;
throats there are to be cut, from the product of ten jail-
deliveries, and nobody dares to cut them, for want of
the proper warrant; archbishoprics there are to be
filled, and, because they are *not* filled, the whole nation

is running helter-skelter into heresy—and all in consequence of your majesty's sacred laziness." *Our* governments were less remissly administered; since each of us, by continued reports of improvements and gracious concessions to the folly or the weakness of our subjects, stimulated the zeal of his rival. And here, at least, there seemed to be no reason why I should come into collision with my brother. At any rate, I took pains *not* to do so. But all was in vain. My destiny was, to live in one eternal element of feud.

My own kingdom was an island called Gombroon. But in what parallel of north or south latitude it lay, I concealed for a time as rigorously as ancient Rome through every century concealed her real name.[1] The object in this provisional concealment was, to regulate the position of my own territory by that of my brother's; for I was determined to place a monstrous world of waters between us, as the only chance (and a very poor one it proved) for compelling my brother to keep the peace. At length, for some reason unknown to me, and much to my astonishment, he located his capital city in the high latitude of 65 deg. north. That fact being once published and settled, instantly I smacked my little kingdom of Gombroon down into the tropics, 10 deg., I think, south of the line. Now, at least, I was on the right side of the hedge, or so I flattered myself; for it struck me that my brother never would degrade himself by fitting out a costly

[1] One reason, I believe, why it was held a point of wisdom, in ancient days, that the metropolis of a warlike state should have a secret name hidden from the world, lay in the Pagan practice of *evocation*, applied to the tutelary deities of such a state. These deities might be lured by certain rites and briberies into a transfer of their favours to the besieging army. But, in order to make such an evocation effectual, it was necessary to know the original and secret name of the beleaguered city: and this, therefore, was religiously concealed.

nautical expedition against poor little Gombroon; and
how else could he get at me? Surely the very fiend himself, if he happened to be in a high arctic latitude,
would not indulge his malice so far as to follow its
trail into the Tropic of Capricorn. And what was to
be got by such a freak? There was no Golden Fleece
in Gombroon. If the fiend or my brother fancied *that*,
for once they were in the wrong box; and there was
no variety of vegetable produce, for I never denied
that the poor little island was only 270 miles in circuit. Think, then, of sailing through 75 deg. of latitude
only to crack such a miserable little filbert as that.
But my brother stunned me by explaining that, although his capital lay in lat. 65 deg. N., not the less
his dominions swept southwards through a matter of
80 or 90 deg.; and, as to the Tropic of Capricorn, much
of it was his own private property. I was aghast at
hearing *that*. It seemed that vast horns and promon-
tories ran down from all parts of his dominions towards
any country whatsoever, in either hemisphere—empire, or republic; monarchy, polyarchy, or anarchy—
that he might have reasons for assaulting.

Here in one moment vanished all that I had relied
on for protection: distance I had relied on, and suddenly I was found in close neighbourhood to my most
formidable enemy. Poverty I had relied on, and *that*
was not denied; he granted the poverty, but it was
dependent on the barbarism of the Gombroonians. It
seems that in the central forests of Gombroonia there
were diamond mines, which my people, from their
low condition of civilization, did not value, nor had
any means of working. Farewell, therefore, on *my*
side, to all hopes of enduring peace, for here was established, in legal phrase, *a lien* for ever upon my
island, and not upon its margin, but its very centre,
in favour of any invaders, better able than the natives

to make its treasures available. For, of old, it was an article in my brother's code of morals—that, supposing a contest between any two parties, of which one possessed an article, whilst the other was better able to use it, the rightful property vested in the latter. As if you met a man with a musket, then you might justly challenge him to a trial in the art of making gunpowder; which if you *could* make, and he could *not*, in that case the musket was *de jure* yours. For what shadow of a right had the fellow to a noble instrument which he could not "maintain" in a serviceable condition, and "feed" with its daily rations of powder and shot? Still, it may be fancied that, since all the relations between us as independent sovereigns (whether of war, or peace, or treaty) rested upon our own representations and official reports, it was surely within my competence to deny or qualify, as much as within his to assert. But, in reality, the *law* of the contest between us, as suggested by some instinct of propriety in my own mind, would not allow me to proceed in such a method. What he said was like a move at chess or draughts, which it was childish to dispute. The move being made, my business was—to face it, to parry it, to evade it, and, if I could, to overthrow it. I proceeded as a lawyer who moves as long as he can, not by blank denial of facts (or *coming to an issue*), but by *demurring* (*i.e.*, admitting the allegations of fact, or otherwise interpreting their construction). It was the understood necessity of the case, that I must passively accept my brother's statements so far as regarded their verbal expression; and, if I would extricate my poor islanders from their troubles, it must be by some distinction or evasion lying *within* this expression, or not blankly contradicting it.

"How, and to what extent," my brother asked, "did I raise taxes upon my subjects?" My first impulse was to say, that I did not tax them at all, for I had a perfect horror of doing so; but prudence would not allow of my saying *that;* because it was too probable he would demand to know how, in that case, I maintained a standing army; and if I once allowed it to be supposed that I had none, there was an end for ever to the independence of my people. Poor things! they would have been invaded and dragooned in a month. I took some days, therefore, to consider that point, but at last replied, that my people, being maritime, supported themselves mainly by a herring fishery, from which I deducted a part of the produce, and afterwards sold it for manure to neighbouring nations. This last hint I borrowed from the conversation of a stranger who happened to dine one day at Greenhay, and mentioned that in Devonshire, or at least on the western coast of that country, near Ilfracombe, upon any excessive take of herrings, beyond what the markets could absorb, the surplus was applied to the land as a valuable dressing. It might be inferred from this account, however, that the arts must be in a languishing state, amongst a people that did not understand the process of salting fish; and my brother observed derisively, much to my grief, that a wretched ichthyophagous people must make shocking soldiers, weak as water, and liable to be knocked over like nine-pins; whereas, in *his* army, not a man ever ate herrings, pilchards, mackerels, or, in fact, condescended to anything worse than sirloins of beef.

At every step I had to contend for the honour and independence of my islanders; so that early I came to understand the weight of Shakespeare's sentiment—

Uneasy lies the head that wears a crown!

Oh, reader, do not laugh! I lived for ever under the

terror of two separate wars in two separate worlds:
one against the factory boys, in a real world of flesh
and blood, of stones and brickbats, of flight and pursuit, that were anything but figurative; the other in
a world purely aerial, where all the combats and the
sufferings were absolute moonshine. And yet the
simple truth is—that, for anxiety and distress of mind,
the reality (which almost every morning's light
brought round) was as nothing in comparison of that
dream-kingdom which rose like a vapour from my
own brain, and which apparently by the *fiat* of my
will could be for ever dissolved. Ah! but no; I had contracted obligations to Gombroon; I had submitted my
conscience to a yoke; and in secret truth my will had
no such autocratic power. Long contemplation of a
shadow, earnest study for the welfare of that shadow,
sympathy with the wounded sensibilities of that
shadow under accumulated wrongs, these bitter experiences, nursed by brooding thought, had gradually
frozen that shadow into a rigour of reality far denser
than the material realities of brass or granite. Who
builds the most durable dwellings? asks the labourer
in *Hamlet;* and the answer is, The gravedigger. He
builds for corruption; and yet *his* tenements are in-
corruptible: "the houses which *he* makes last to dooms-
day." [1] Who is it that seeks for concealment? Let him
hide himself [2] in the unsearchable chambers of light—

[1] *Hamlet*, Act v. scene 1.

[2] *"Hide himself in—light":* The greatest scholar, by far,
that this island ever produced (viz., Richard Bentley) published (as is well known) a 4to volume that in some respects
is the very worst 4to now extant in the world—viz., a critical
edition of the *Paradise Lost*. I observe, in the *Edinburgh Review* (July, 1851, No. 191, p. 15), that a learned critic supposes Bentley to have meant this edition as a "practical jest."
Not at all. Neither could the critic have fancied such a possibility, if he had taken the trouble (which *I* did many a year

of light which at noonday, more effectually than any gloom, conceals the very brightest stars, rather than in labyrinths of darkness the thickest. What criminal is that who wishes to abscond from public justice? Let him hurry into the frantic publicities of London, and by no means into the quiet privacies of the country. So, and upon the analogy of these cases, we may understand that, to make a strife overwhelming by a thou-

back) to examine it. A jest-book it certainly is, and the most prosperous of jest-books, but undoubtedly never meant for such by the author. A man whose lips are livid with anger does not jest, and does not understand jesting. Still, the Edinburgh Reviewer is right about the proper functions of the book, though wrong about the intentions of the author. The fact is, the man was maniacally in error, and always in error, as regarded the ultimate or poetic truth of Milton; but, as regarded truth reputed and truth *apparent*, he often had the air of being furiously in the right; an example of which I will cite. Milton, in the First Book of the *Paradise Lost*, had said—

> That from the secret top
> Of Oreb or of Sinai didst inspire;

upon which Bentley comments in effect thus: "How!—the exposed summit of a mountain *secret?* Why, it's like Charing Cross—always the least secret place in the whole county." So one might fancy: since the summit of a mountain, like Plinlimmon or Cader Idris in Wales, like Skiddaw or Helvellyn in England, constitutes a central object of attention and gaze for the whole circumjacent district, measured by a radius sometimes of 15 to 20 miles. Upon this consideration, Bentley instructs us to substitute as the true reading—"That on the *sacred* top," &c. Meantime, an actual experiment will demonstrate that there is no place so absolutely secret and hidden as the exposed summit of a mountain, 3500 feet high, in respect to an eye stationed in the valley immediately below. A whole party of men, women, horses, and even tents, looked at under those circumstances, is absolutely invisible unless by the aid of glasses: and it becomes evident that a murder might be committed on the bare open summit of such a mountain with more assurance of absolute secrecy than anywhere else in the whole surrounding district.

sandfold to the feelings, it must not deal with gross
material interests, but with such as rise into the world
of dreams, and act upon the nerves through spiritual,
and not through fleshly, torments. Mine, in the present case, rose suddenly, like a rocket, into their meridian altitude, by means of a hint furnished to my
brother from a Scottish advocate's reveries.

This advocate, who by his writings became the remote cause of so much affliction to my childhood, and
struck a blow at the dignity of Gombroon that neither
my brother nor all the forces of Tigrosylvania (my
brother's kingdom) ever could have devised, was the
celebrated James Burnett, better known to the English
public by his judicial title of Lord Monboddo.

To the majority of readers, meantime, at this day,
Lord M. is memorable chiefly for his craze about the
degeneracy of us poor moderns, when compared with
the men of Pagan antiquity; which craze itself might
possibly not have been generally known, except in
connexion with the little skirmish between him and
Dr. Johnson, noticed in Boswell's account of the Doctor's Scottish tour. "Ah, doctor," said Lord M., upon
some casual suggestion of that topic, "poor creatures
are we of this eighteenth century; our fathers were
better men than we!" "Oh no, my lord," was Johnson's
reply; "we are quite as strong as our forefathers, and a
great deal wiser!" Such a craze, however, is too widely
diffused, and falls in with too obstinate a preconception [1] in the human race, which has in every age hypo-

---

[1] *"Too obstinate a preconception"*: Until the birth of geol-
ogy, and of fossil palæontology, concurring with vast strides
ahead in the science of comparative anatomy, it is a well-
established fact, that oftentimes the most scientific museum
admitted as genuine fragments of the human osteology what
in fact belonged to the gigantic brutes of our earth in her earliest stages of development. This mistake would go some way
in accounting for the absurd disposition in all generations to

chondriacally regarded itself as under some fatal
necessity of dwindling, much to have challenged public
attention. As real paradoxes (spite of the idle meaning
attached usually to the word *paradox*) have often no
falsehood in them, so here, on the contrary, was a
falsehood which had in it nothing paradoxical. It con-
tradicted all the indications of history and experience,
which uniformly had pointed in the very opposite
direction; and so far it ought to have been paradoxical
(that is, revolting to popular opinion) ; but was *not*

view themselves as abridged editions of their forefathers.
Added to which, as a separate cause of error, there can be little doubt, that intermingled with the human race there has at
most periods of the world been a separate and Titanic race,
such as the Anakim amongst the peoples of Palestine, the
Cyclopean race diffused over the Mediterranean in the elder
ages of Greece, and certain tribes amongst the Alps, known to
Evelyn in his youth (about Cromwell's time) by an unpleasant travelling experience. These gigantic races, however, were
no arguments for a degeneration amongst the rest of mankind.
They were evidently a variety of man, co-existent with the ordinary races, but liable to be absorbed and gradually lost by
intermarriage amongst other tribes of the ordinary standard. Occasional exhumations of such Titan skeletons would
strengthen the common prejudice. They would be taken not
for a local variety, but for an antediluvian or prehistoric type,
from which the present races of man had arisen by gradual
degeneration.

These cases of actual but misinterpreted experience, at the
same time that they naturally must tend to fortify the popular
prejudice, would also, by accounting for it, and engrafting it
upon a reasonable origin, so far tend to take from it the reproach of a prejudice. Though erroneous, it would yet seem to
us, in looking back upon it, a rational and even an inevitable
opinion, having such plausible grounds to stand upon; plausible, I mean, until science and accurate examination of the
several cases had begun to read them into a different construction. Yet, on the other hand, in spite of any colourable excuses
that may be pleaded for this prejudice, it is pretty plain that,
after all, there is in human nature a deep-laid predisposition to
an obstinate craze of this nature. Else why is it that, in every

so; for it fell in with prevailing opinions, with the oldest, blindest, and most inveterate of human super- stitions. If extravagant, yet to the multitude it did not *seem* extravagant. So natural a craze, therefore, how- ever baseless, would never have carried Lord Mon- boddo's name into that meteoric notoriety and atmos- phere of astonishment which soon invested it in England. And, in that case, my childhood would have escaped the deadliest blight of mortification and de- spondency that could have been incident to a most

age alike, men have asserted or even assumed the downward tendency of the human race in all that regards *moral* qualities. For the *physical* degeneration of man there really were some apparent (though erroneous) arguments; but for the moral degeneration, no argument at all, small or great. Yet, a big- otry of belief in this idle notion has always prevailed amongst moralists, Pagan alike and Christian. Horace, for example, in- forms us that

> *Aetas parentum, pejor avis, tulit*
> *Nos nequiores—mox daturos*
> *Progeniem vitiosiorem.*

The last generation was worse, it seems, than the penultimate, as the present is worse than the last. We, however, of the pres- ent, bad as we may be, shall be kept in countenance by the coming generation, which will prove much worse than our- selves. On the same precedent, all the sermons through the three last centuries, if traced back through decennial periods, so as to form thirty successive strata, will be found regularly claiming the precedency in wickedness for the immediate pe- riod of the writer. Upon which theories, as men ought physi- cally to have dwindled long ago into pigmies, so, on the other hand, morally they must by this time have left Sodom and Gomorrah far behind. What a strange animal must man upon this scheme offer to our contemplation; shrinking in size, by graduated process, through every century, until at last he would not rise an inch from the ground; and, on the other hand, as regards villainy, towering ever more and more up to the heavens. What a dwarf! what a giant! Why, the very crows would combine to destroy such a little monster.

morbid temperament concurring with a situation of visionary (yes! if you please, of fantastic) but still of most real distress.

How much it would have astonished Lord Monboddo to find himself made answerable—virtually made answerable, by the evidence of secret tears—for the misery of an unknown child in Lancashire. Yet night and day these silent memorials of suffering were accusing him as the founder of a wound that could not be healed. It happened that the several volumes of his work lay for weeks in the study of our tutor. Chance directed the eye of my brother, one day, upon that part of the work in which Lord M. unfolds his hypothesis that originally the human race had been a variety of the ape. On which hypothesis, by the way, Dr. Adam Clarke's substitution of *ape* for *serpent*, in translating the word *nachash* (the brute tempter of Eve), would have fallen to the ground, since this would simply have been the case of one human being tempting another. It followed inevitably, according to Lord M., however painful it might be to human dignity, that, in this their early stage of brutality, men must have had tails. My brother mused upon this reverie, and, in a few days, published an extract from some scoundrel's travels in Gombroon, according to which the Gombroonians had not yet emerged from this early condition of apedom. They, it seems, were still *homines caudati*. Overwhelming to me and stunning was the ignominy of this horrible discovery. Lord M. had not overlooked the natural question, In what way did men get rid of their tails! To speak the truth, they never *would* have got rid of them had they continued to run wild; but growing civilization introduced arts, and the arts introduced sedentary habits. By these it was, by the mere necessity of continually sitting down, that men gradually wore off their tails!

Well, and what should hinder the Gombroonians from sitting down? *Their* tailors and shoemakers would and could, I hope, sit down, as well as those of Tigrosylvania. Why not? Ay, but my brother had insisted already that they *had* no tailors, that they *had* no shoemakers; which, *then*, I did not care much about, as it merely put back the clock of our history—throwing us into an earlier, and therefore, perhaps, into a more warlike stage of society. But, as the case stood now, this want of tailors, &c., showed clearly that the process of sitting down, so essential to the ennobling of the race, had not commenced. My brother, with an air of consolation, suggested that I might even now, without an hour's delay, compel the whole nation to sit down for six hours a-day, which would always "make a beginning." But the truth would remain as before—viz., that I was the king of a people that had tails; and the slow, slow process by which, in a course of many centuries, their posterity might rub them off, a hope of vintages never to be enjoyed by any generations that are yet heaving in sight—*that* was to me the worst form of despair.

Still there was one resource: if I "didn't like it"— meaning the state of things in Gombroon—I might "abdicate." Yes, I knew *that*. I might abdicate; and, once having cut the connexion between myself and the poor abject islanders, I might seem to have no further interest in the degradation that affected them. After such a disruption between us, what was it to me if they had even three tails apiece? Ah, *that* was fine talking; but this connexion with my poor subjects had grown up so slowly and so genially, in the midst of struggles so constant against the encroachments of my brother and his rascally people; we had suffered so much together; and the filaments connecting them with my heart were so aerially fine and fantastic, but

for that reason so inseverable, that I abated nothing
of my anxiety on their account; making this difference
only in my legislation and administrative cares, that
I pursued them more in a spirit of despondency, and
retreated more shyly from communicating them. It
was in vain that my brother counselled me to dress my
people in the Roman toga, as the best means of concealing their ignominious appendages: if he meant
this as comfort, it was none to me; the disgrace lay
in the fact, not in its publication.

From this deep degradation of myself and my people, I was drawn off at intervals to contemplate a
different mode of degradation affecting two persons,
twin sisters, whom I saw intermittingly; sometimes
once a-week, sometimes frequently on each separate
day. You have heard, reader, of pariahs. The pathos
of that great idea possibly never reached you. Did it
ever strike you how far that idea had extended? Do
not fancy it peculiar to Hindostan. Before Delhi was,
before Agra, or Lahore, might the pariah say, I was.
The most interesting, if only as the most mysterious,
race of ancient days, the Pelasgi, that overspread, in
early times of Greece, the total Mediterranean—a
race distinguished for beauty and for intellect, and
sorrowful beyond all power of man to read the cause
that could lie deep enough for so imperishable an impression—*they* were pariahs. The Jews that, in the
twenty-eighth chapter of Deuteronomy, were cursed
in a certain contingency with a sublimer curse than
ever rang through the passionate wrath of prophecy,
and that afterwards, in Jerusalem, cursed themselves,
voluntarily taking on their own heads, and on the
heads of their children's children for ever and ever,
the guilt of innocent blood—*they* are pariahs to this
hour. Yet for *them* there has ever shone a sullen light
of hope. The gipsies, for whom no conscious or ac-

knowledged hope burns through the mighty darkness that surrounds them—they are pariahs of pariahs. Lepers were a race of mediæval pariahs, rejected of men, that now have gone to rest. But travel into the forests of the Pyrenees, and there you will find their modern representatives in the Cagots. Are these Pyrenean Cagots Pagans? Not at all. They are good Christians. Wherefore, then, that low door in the Pyrenean churches, through which the Cagots are forced to enter, and which, obliging them to stoop almost to the ground, is a perpetual memento of their degradation? Wherefore is it that men of pure Spanish blood will hold no intercourse with the Cagot? Wherefore is it that even the shadow of a Cagot, if it falls across a fountain, is held to have polluted that fountain? All this points to some dreadful taint of guilt, real or imputed, in ages far remote.[1]

But in ages far nearer to ourselves, nay, in our own generation, and our own land, are many pariahs, sitting amongst us all, nay, oftentimes sitting (yet not recognized for what they really are) at good men's tables. How general is that sensuous dulness, that

[1] The name and history of the Pyrenean Cagots are equally obscure. Some have supposed that, during the period of the Gothic warfare with the Moors, the Cagots were a Christian tribe that betrayed the Christian cause and interests at a critical moment. But all is conjecture. As to the name, Southey has somewhere offered a possible interpretation of it; but it struck me as far from felicitous, and not what might have been expected from Southey, whose vast historical research and commanding talent should naturally have unlocked this most mysterious of modern secrets, if any unlocking does yet lie within the resources of human skill and combining power, now that so many ages divide us from the original steps of the case. I may here mention, as a fact accidentally made known to myself, and apparently not known to Southey, that the Cagots, under a name very slightly altered, are found in France also, as well as Spain; and in provinces of France that have no connexion at all with Spain.

deafness of the heart, which the Scriptures attribute
to human beings! "Having ears, they hear not; and,
seeing, they do not understand." In the very act of
facing or touching a dreadful object, they will utterly
deny its existence. Men say to me daily, when I ask
them, in passing, "Anything in this morning's paper?"
"Oh no, nothing at all." And, as I never had any
other answer, I am bound to suppose that there never
was anything in a daily newspaper; and, therefore,
that the horrible burden of misery and of change which
a century accumulates as its *facit* or total result, has
not been distributed at all amongst its thirty-six thousand five hundred and twenty-five days: every day,
it seems, was separately a blank day, yielding absolutely nothing—what children call a deaf nut, offering
no kernel; and yet the total product has caused angels
to weep and tremble. Meantime, when I come to look
at the newspaper with my own eyes, I am astonished
at the misreport of my informants. Were there no
other section in it than simply that allotted to the
police reports, oftentimes I stand aghast at the revelations there made of human life and the human heart—
at its colossal guilt, and its colossal misery; at the suffering which oftentimes throws its shadow over palaces, and the grandeur of mute endurance which
sometimes glorifies a cottage. Here transpires the
dreadful truth of what is going on for ever under the
thick curtains of domestic life, close behind us, and
before us, and all around us. Newspapers are evanescent, and are too rapidly recurrent, and people see
nothing great in what is familiar, nor can ever be
trained to read the silent and the shadowy in what,
for the moment, is covered with the babbling garrulity
of daylight. I suppose now that, in the next generation
after that which is here concerned, had any neighbour of our tutor been questioned on the subject of a

domestic tragedy, which travelled through its natural stages in a leisurely way, and under the eyes of good Dr. S——, he would have replied, "Tragedy! oh, sir, nothing of the kind! You have been misled; the gentleman must lie under a mistake: perhaps it was in the next street." No, it was *not* in the next street; and the gentleman does not lie under a mistake, or, in fact, lie at all. The simple truth is, blind old neighbour, that you, being rarely in the house, and, *when* there, only in one particular room, saw no more of what was hourly going on, than if you had been residing with the Sultan of Bokhara.

But I, a child between seven and eight years old, had access everywhere. I was privileged, and had the *entrée* even of the female apartments; one consequence of which was, that I put *this* and *that* together. A number of syllables, that each for itself separately might have meant nothing at all, did yet, when put together, through weeks and months, read for *my* eyes into sentences as deadly and significant as *Tekel*, *upharsin*. And another consequence was, that being, on account of my age, nobody at all, or very near it, I sometimes witnessed things that perhaps it had not been meant for anybody to witness, or perhaps some half-conscious negligence overlooked my presence. "Saw things! What was it now? Was it a man at midnight, with a dark lantern and a six-barrel revolver?" No, *that* was not in the least like what I saw: it was a great deal more like what I will endeavour to describe.

Imagine two young girls, of what exact age I really do not know, but apparently from twelve to fourteen, twins, remarkably plain in person and features, unhealthy, and obscurely reputed to be idiots. Whether they really were such was more than I knew, or could devise any plan for learning. Without dreaming of anything unkind or uncourteous, my original impulse

had been to say, "If you please, are you idiots?" But I
felt that such a question had an air of coarseness about
it, though, for my own part, I had long reconciled
myself to being called an idiot by my brother. There
was, however, a further difficulty: breathed as a
gentle, murmuring whisper, the question might possibly be reconciled to an indulgent ear as confidential
and tender. Even to take a liberty with those you
love, is to show your trust in their affection; but, alas!
these poor girls were deaf; and to have shouted out,
"Are you idiots, if you please?" in a voice that would
have rung down three flights of stairs, promised (as
I felt, without exactly seeing why) a dreadful exaggeration to whatever incivility might, at any rate,
attach to the question; and some *did* attach, that was
clear even if warbled through an air of Cherubini's,
and accompanied on the flute. Perhaps they were *not*
idiots, and only seemed to be such from the slowness
of apprehension naturally connected with deafness.
That I saw them but seldom, arose from their peculiar
position in the family. Their father had no private
fortune; his income from the church was very slender;
and, though considerably increased by the allowance
made for us, his two pupils, still, in a great town, and
with so large a family, it left him little room for luxuries. Consequently, he never had more than two servants, and at times only one. Upon this plea rose the
scheme of the mother for employing these two young
girls in menial offices of the household economy. One
reason for that was, that she thus indulged her dislike
for them, which she took no pains to conceal; and thus,
also, she withdrew them from the notice of strangers.
In this way, it happened that I saw them myself but
at uncertain intervals. Gradually, however, I came to
be aware of their forlorn condition, to pity them, and
to love them. The poor twins were undoubtedly plain,

to the degree which is called, by unfeeling people, ugliness. They were also deaf, as I have said, and they were scrofulous; one of them was disfigured by the small-pox; they had glimmering eyes, red, like the eyes of ferrets, and scarcely half-open; and they did not walk so much as stumble along. There, you have the worst of them. Now, hear something on the other side. What first won my pity was, their affection for each other, united to their constant sadness; secondly, a notion which had crept into my head, probably derived from something said in my presence by elder people, that they were destined to an early death; and, lastly, the incessant persecutions of their mother. This lady belonged, by birth, to a more elevated rank than that of her husband, and she was remarkably well-bred as regarded her manners. But she had probably a weak understanding: she was shrewish in her temper; was a severe economist; a merciless exactor of what she viewed as duty; and, in persecuting her two unhappy daughters, though she yielded blindly to her unconscious dislike of them, as creatures that disgraced her, she was not aware, perhaps, of ever having put forth more expressions of anger and severity than were absolutely required to rouse the constitutional torpor of her daughters' nature; and where disgust has once rooted itself, and been habitually expressed in tones of harshness, the mere sight of the hateful object mechanically calls forth the eternal tones of anger, without distinct consciousness or separate intention in the speaker. Loud speaking, besides, or even shouting, was required by the deafness of the two girls. From anger so constantly discharging its thunders, naturally they did not show open signs of recoiling; but that they felt it deeply, may be presumed from their sensibility to kindness. My own experience showed *that;* for, as often as I met them, we exchanged kisses; and my wish had always been to beg them, if they really *were* idiots, not to mind it, since I should not like them the less on that account. This wish of mine never came to utterance; but not the less they were aware, by my manner of salutation, that one person at least, amongst those who might be considered strangers, did not find anything repulsive about them; and the pleasure they felt was expressed broadly upon their kindly faces.

Such was the outline of their position; and, that being explained, what I saw was simply this; it composed a silent and symbolic scene, a momentary interlude in dumb show, which interpreted itself and settled for ever in my recollection, as if it had prophesied and interpreted the event which soon followed. They were resting from toil, and both sitting down. This had lasted for perhaps ten or fifteen minutes. Suddenly from below-stairs the voice of angry summons rang up to their ears. Both rose in an instant, as if the echoing scourge of some avenging Tisiphone were uplifted above their heads; both opened their arms; flung them round each other's necks; and then, unclasping them, parted to their separate labours. This was my last rememberable interview with the two sisters; in a week both were corpses. They had died, I believe, of scarlatina, and very nearly at the same moment.

But surely it was no matter for grief, that the two scrofulous idiots were dead and buried. Oh no! Call them idiots at your pleasure, serfs, or slaves, strulbrugs [1] or pariahs—*their* case was certainly not wors-

[1] *"Strulbrugs":* Hardly *strulbrugs,* will be the thought of the learned reader, who knows that *young* women could not be strulbrugs; since the true strulbrug was one who, from base fear of dying, had lingered on into an old age omnivorous of every genial or vital impulse. The strulbrug of Swift (and Swift, being his horrid creator, ought to understand his own horrid creation) was a wreck, a shell, that had been burned

ened by being booked for places in the grave. Idiocy,
for anything I know, may, in that vast kingdom, enjoy
a natural precedency; scrofula and leprosy may have
some mystic privilege in a coffin; and the pariahs of
the upper earth may form the aristocracy of the dead.
That the idiots, real or reputed, were at rest—that their
warfare was accomplished—might, if a man happened
to know enough, be interpreted as a glorious festival.
The sisters were seen no more upon staircases or in
bedrooms, and deadly silence had succeeded to the
sound of continual uproars. Memorials of *them* were
none surviving on earth. Not *they* it was that furnished mementos of themselves. The mother it was,
the father it was—that mother who by persecution
had avenged the wounds offered to her pride; that
father who had tolerated this persecution—she it was,
he it was, that by the altered glances of her haunted

hollow, and cancered by the fierce furnace of life. His clock-
work was gone, or carious; only some miserable fragment of
a pendulum continued to oscillate paralytically from mere incapacity of anything so abrupt, and therefore so vigorous, as
a decided HALT! However, the use of this dreadful word may
be reasonably extended to the young who happen to have become essentially old in misery. Intensity of a suffering existence may compensate the want of extension; and a boundless
depth of misery may be a transformed expression for a boundless duration of misery. The most aged person, to all appearance, that ever came under my eyes, was an infant—hardly
eight months old. He was the illegitimate son of a poor idiot
girl, who had herself been shamefully ill-treated; and the poor
infant, falling under the care of an enraged grandmother,
who felt herself at once burdened and disgraced, was certainly
not better treated. He was dying, when I saw him, of a lingering malady, with features expressive of frantic misery; and it
seemed to me that he looked at least three centuries old. One
might have fancied him one of Swift's strulbrugs, that,
through long attenuation and decay, had dwindled back into
infancy, with one organ only left perfect—the organ of fear
and misery.

eye, that by the altered character of his else stationary habits, had revived for *me* a spectacle, once real, of visionary twin sisters, moving for ever up and down the stairs——sisters, patient, humble, silent, that snatched convulsively at a loving smile, or loving gesture, from a child, as at some message of remembrance from God, whispering to them, "You are not forgotten"——sisters born apparently for the single purpose of suffering, whose trials, it is true, were over, and could not be repeated, but (alas for her who had been their cause!) could not be recalled. Her face grew thin, her eye sunken and hollow, after the death of her daughters; and, meeting her on the staircase, I sometimes fancied that she did not see *me* so much as something beyond me. Did any misfortune befall her after this double funeral? Did the Nemesis that waits upon the sighs of children pursue her steps? Not apparently: externally, things went well; her sons were reasonably prosperous; her handsome daughter——for she had a more youthful daughter, who really *was* handsome——continued to improve in personal attractions; and some years after, I have heard, she married happily. But from herself, so long as I continued to know her, the altered character of countenance did not depart, nor the gloomy eye, that seemed to converse with secret and visionary objects.

This result from the irrevocable past was not altogether confined to herself. It is one evil attached to chronic and domestic oppression, that it draws into its vortex, as unwilling, or even as loathing, co-operators, others who either see but partially the wrong they are abetting, or, in cases where they *do* see it, are unable to make head against it, through the inertia of their own nature, or through the coercion of circumstances. Too clearly, by the restless irritation of his manner for some time after the children's death, their father testified, in a language not fully, perhaps, perceived by himself, or meant to be understood by others, that to his inner conscience he also was not clear of blame. Had he then in any degree sanctioned the injustice which sometimes he must have witnessed? Far from it: he had been roused from his habitual indolence into energetic expressions of anger: he had put an end to the wrong, when it came openly before him: I had myself heard him say on many occasions, with patriarchal fervour, "Woman, they are your children, and God made them. Show mercy to *them*, as you expect it for yourself." But he must have been aware, that, for any three instances of tyrannical usage that fell under his notice, at least five hundred would escape it. That was the sting of the case—that was its poisonous aggravation. But with a nature that sought for peace before all things, in this very worst of its aggravations was found a morbid cure—the effectual temptation to wilful blindness and forgetfulness. The sting became the palliation of the wrong, and the poison became its anodyne. For together with the five hundred hidden wrongs, arose the necessity that they *must* be hidden. Could he be pinned on, morning, noon, and night, to his wife's apron? And if not, what else should he do by angry interferences at chance times, than add special vindictive impulses to those of general irritation and dislike? Some truth there was in this, it cannot be denied: innumerable cases arise, in which a man the most just is obliged, in some imperfect sense, to connive at injustice; his chance experience must convince him that injustice is continually going on; and yet, in any attempt to intercept it or to check it, he is met and baffled by the insuperable obstacles of household necessities. Dr. S——, therefore, surrendered himself, as under a coercion that was *none* of his creating, to a passive acquiescence and a blindness that soothed his constitutional indolence; and he reconciled his feelings to a tyranny which he tolerated, under some self-flattering idea of submitting with resignation to a calamity that he suffered.

Some years after this, I read the *Agamemnon* of Æschylus; and then, in the prophetic horror with which Cassandra surveys the regal abode in Mycenæ, destined to be the scene of murders so memorable through the long traditions of the Grecian stage, murders that, many centuries after all the parties to them—perpetrators, sufferers, avengers—had become dust and ashes, kindled again into mighty life through a thousand years upon the vast theatres of Athens and Rome, I retraced the horrors, not prophetic but memorial, with which I myself had invested that humble dwelling of Dr. S——; and read again, repeated in visionary proportions, the sufferings which there had darkened the days of people known to myself through two distinct successions—not, as was natural to expect, of parents first, and then of children, but inversely of children and parents. Manchester was not Mycenæ. No, but by many degrees nobler. In some of the features most favourable to tragic effects, it was so; and wanted only those idealizing advantages for withdrawing mean details which are in the gift of distance and hazy antiquity. Even at that day Manchester was far larger, teeming with more and with stronger hearts; and it contained a population the most energetic even in the *modern* world—how much more so, therefore, by comparison with any race in *ancient* Greece, inevitably rendered effeminate by dependence too generally upon slaves. Add to this superior energy in Lancashire, the immeasurably profounder feelings generated by the mysteries which stand behind Christianity, as compared with the shallow mysteries that stood behind Paganism, and it would be easy to draw the inference, that, in the capacity for the infinite and the impassioned, for horror and for pathos, Mycenæ could have had no pretensions to measure herself against Manchester. Not that I had drawn such an inference myself. Why should I? there being nothing to suggest the points in which the two cities differed, but only the single one in which they agreed—viz., the dusky veil that overshadowed in both the noonday tragedies haunting their household recesses; which veil was raised only to the gifted eyes of a Cassandra, or to eyes that, like my own, had experimentally become acquainted with them as facts. Pitiably mean is he that measures the relations of such cases by the scenical apparatus of purple and gold. That which never *has* been apparelled in royal robes, and hung with theatrical jewels, is but suffering from an accidental fraud, having the same right to them that any similar misery can have, or calamity upon an equal scale. These proportions are best measured from the fathoming ground of a real uncounterfeit sympathy.

I have mentioned already that we had four male guardians (a fifth being my mother). These four were B., E., G., and H. The two consonants, B. and G., gave us little trouble. G., the wisest of the whole band, lived at a distance of more than one hundred miles: him, therefore, we rarely saw; but B., living within four miles of Greenhay, washed his hands of us, by inviting us, every now and then, to spend a few days at his house.

At this house, which stood in the country, there was a family of amiable children, who were more skilfully trained in their musical studies than at that day was usual. They sang the old English glees and madrigals, and correctly enough for me, who, having, even at that childish age, a preternatural sensibility

to music, had also, as may be supposed, the most entire want of musical knowledge. No blunders could
do much to mar *my* pleasure. There first I heard the
concertos of Corelli; but also, which far more profoundly affected me, a few selections from Jomelli
and Cimarosa. With Handel I had long been familiar,
for the famous chorus-singers of Lancashire sang continually at churches the most effective parts from his
chief oratorios. Mozart was yet to come; for, except
perhaps at the opera in London, even at this time his
music was most imperfectly diffused through England.
But, above all, a thing which to my dying day I
could never forget, at the house of this guardian I
heard sung a long canon of Cherubini's. Forty years
later, I heard it again, and better sung; but at that
time I needed nothing better. It was sung by four male
voices, and rose into a region of thrilling passion, such
as my heart had always dimly craved and hungered
after, but which now first interpreted itself, as a
physical possibility, to my ear.

My brother did not share my inexpressible delight;
his taste ran in a different channel; and the arrangements of the house did not meet his approbation; particularly this, that either Mrs. B. herself, or else the
governess, was always present when the young ladies
joined our society, which my brother considered particularly vulgar; since natural propriety and decorum
should have whispered to an old lady that a young
gentleman might have "things" to say to her daughters which he could not possibly intend for the general
ear of eavesdroppers—things tending to the confidential or the sentimental, which none but a shameless old
lady would seek to participate; by that means compelling a young man to talk as loud as if he were
addressing a mob at Charing Cross, or reading the
Riot Act. There were other out-of-door amusements,

amongst which a swing—which I mention for the sake
of illustrating the passive obedience which my brother
levied upon me, either through my conscience, as
mastered by his doctrine of primogeniture, or, as in
this case, through my sensibility to shame under his
taunts of cowardice. It was a most ambitious swing,
ascending to a height beyond any that I have since
seen in fairs or public gardens. Horror was at my
heart regularly as the swing reached its most aerial
altitude; for the oily, swallow-like fluency of the
swoop downwards threatened always to make me sick,
in which case it is probable that I must have relaxed
my hold of the ropes, and have been projected, with
fatal violence, to the ground. But, in defiance of all
this miserable panic, I continued to swing whenever
he tauntingly invited me. It was well that my brother's
path in life soon ceased to coincide with my own; else
I should infallibly have broken my neck in confronting perils which brought me neither honour nor profit,
and in accepting defiances which, issue how they
might, won self-reproach from myself, and sometimes
a gaiety of derision from *him*. One only of these defiances I declined. There was a horse of this same
guardian B.'s, who always, after listening to Cherubini's music, grew irritable to excess; and, if anybody
mounted him, would seek relief to his wounded feelings in kicking, more or less violently, for an hour.
This habit endeared him to my brother, who acknowledged to a propensity of the same amiable kind; protesting that an abstract desire of kicking seized him
always after hearing good performers on particular
instruments, especially the bagpipes. Of kicking? But
of kicking what or *whom?* I fear of kicking the venerable public collectively, creditors without exception,
but also as many of the debtors as might be found at
large; doctors of medicine more especially, but with

no absolute immunity for the majority of their patients; Jacobins, but not the less Anti-Jacobins; every
Calvinist, which seems reasonable; but then also,
which is intolerable, every Arminian. Is philosophy
able to account for this morbid affection, and particularly when it takes the restricted form (as sometimes it does, in the bagpipe case) of seeking furiously
to kick the piper, instead of paying him? In this case,
my brother was urgent with me to mount *en croupe*
behind himself. But, weak as I usually was, this proposal I resisted as an immediate suggestion of the
fiend; for I had heard, and have since known proofs
of it, that a horse, when he is ingeniously vicious,
sometimes has the power, in lashing out, of curving
round his hoofs, so as to lodge them, by way of in-
dorsement, in the small of his rider's back; and, of
course, he would have an advantage for such a purpose,
in the case of a rider sitting on the crupper. That sole
invitation I persisted in declining.

A young gentleman had joined us as a fellow-student
under the care of our tutor. He was an only son; indeed, the only child of an amiable widow, whose love
and hopes all centred in *him*. He was destined to
inherit several separate estates, and a great deal had
been done to spoil him by indulgent aunts; but his
good natural disposition defeated all these efforts; and,
upon joining us, he proved to be a very amiable boy,
clever, quick at learning, and abundantly courageous.
In the summer months, his mother usually took a
house out in the country, sometimes on one side of
Manchester, sometimes on another. At these rusticat-
ing seasons, he had often much further to come than
ourselves, and on that account he rode on horseback.
Generally it was a fierce mountain-pony that he rode;
and it was worth while to cultivate the pony's acquaintance, for the sake of understanding the extent

to which the fiend can sometimes incarnate himself
in a horse. I do not trouble the reader with any account
of his tricks, and drolleries, and scoundrelisms; but
this I may mention, that he had the propensity ascribed many centuries ago to the Scandinavian horses
for sharing and practically asserting his share in the
angry passions of a battle. He would fight, or attempt
to fight, on his rider's side, by biting, rearing, and
suddenly wheeling round, for the purpose of lashing
out when he found himself within kicking range.[1]
This little monster was coal-black; and, in virtue of
his carcass, would not have seemed very formidable;
but his head made amends—it was the head of a buffalo, or of a bison, and his vast jungle of mane was
the mane of a lion. His eyes, by reason of this intolerable and unshorn mane, one did not often see, except
as lights that sparkled in the rear of a thicket; but,
once seen, they were not easily forgotten, for their
malignity was diabolic. A few miles more or less being
a matter of indifference to one who was so well
mounted, O. would sometimes ride out with us to the
field of battle; and, by manœuvring so as to menace
the enemy on the flanks, in skirmishes he did good
service. But at length came a day of pitched battle.
The enemy had mustered in unusual strength, and
would certainly have accomplished the usual result
of putting us to flight with more than usual ease, but,
under the turn which things took, their very numbers
aided their overthrow, by deepening their confusion.
O. had, on this occasion, accompanied us; and, as he
had hitherto taken no very decisive part in the war,
confining himself to distant "demonstrations," the
enemy did not much regard his presence in the field.

[1] This was a manœuvre regularly taught to the Austrian cavalry in the middle of the last century, as a ready way of opening the doors of cottages.

This carelessness threw them into a dense mass, upon which my brother's rapid eye saw instantly the opportunity offered for operating most effectually by a charge. O. saw it too; and happening to have his spurs on, he complied cheerfully with my brother's suggestion. He had the advantage of a slight descent: the wicked poney went down "with a will": his echoing hoofs drew the general gaze upon him: his head, his leonine mane, his diabolic eyes, did the rest; and in a moment the whole hostile array had broken, and was in rapid flight across the brick-fields. I leave the reader to judge whether "Te Deum" would be sung on that night. A Gazette Extraordinary was issued; and my brother had really some reason for his assertion, "that in conscience he could not think of comparing Cannæ to this smashing defeat"; since at Cannæ many brave men had refused to fly—the consul himself, Terentius Varro, amongst them; but, in the present rout, there was no Terentius Varro—*everybody* fled.

The victory, indeed, considered in itself, was complete. But it had consequences which we had not looked for. In the ardour of our conflict, neither my brother nor myself had remarked a stout, square-built man, mounted on an uneasy horse, who sat quietly in his saddle as spectator of the battle, and, in fact, as the sole non-combatant present. This man, however, had been observed by O., both before and after his own brilliant charge; and, by the description, there could be no doubt that it had been our guardian B., as also, by the description of the horse, we could as little doubt that he had been mounted on Cherubini. My brother's commentary was in a tone of bitter complaint, that so noble an opportunity should have been lost for strengthening O.'s charge. But the consequences of this incident were graver than we anticipated. A general board of our guardians, vowels and consonants, was summoned to investigate the matter. The origin of the feud, or "war," as my brother called it, was inquired into. As well might the war of Troy or the purser's accounts from the Argonautic expedition have been overhauled. Ancient night and chaos had closed over the "incunabula belli"; and that point was given up in despair. But what hindered a general pacification, no matter in how many wrongs the original dispute had arisen? Who stopped the way which led to peace? Not we, was our firm declaration; we were most pacifically inclined, and ever had been; we were, in fact, little saints. But the enemy could not be brought to any terms of accommodation. "That we will try," said the vowel amongst our guardians, Mr. E. He, being a magistrate, had naturally some weight with the proprietors of the cotton factory. The foremen of the several floors were summoned, and gave it as their humble opinion that we, the aristocratic party in the war, were as bad as the *sansculottes*— "not a pin to choose between us." Well, but no matter for the past: could any plan be devised for a pacific future? Not easily. The work-people were so thoroughly independent of their employers, and so careless of their displeasure, that finally this only settlement was available, as wearing any promise of permanence —viz., that we should alter our hours, so as not to come into collision with the exits or returns of the boys.

Under this arrangement, a sort of hollow armistice prevailed for some time; but it was beginning to give way, when suddenly an internal change in our own home put an end to the war for ever. My brother, amongst his many accomplishments, was distinguished for his skill in drawing. Some of his sketches had been shown to Mr. de Loutherbourg, an academician well

known in those days, esteemed even in these days, after
he has been dead for forty or fifty years, and personally
a distinguished favourite with the king (George III).
He pronounced a very flattering opinion upon my
brother's promise of excellence. This being known, a
fee of a thousand guineas was offered to Mr. L. by the
guardians; and finally that gentleman took charge of
my brother as a pupil. Now, therefore, my brother,
King of Tigrosylvania, scourge of Gombroon, separated from me; and, as it turned out, for ever. I never
saw him again; and, at Mr. de L.'s house in Hammer-
smith, before he had completed his sixteenth year, he
died of typhus fever. And thus it happened that a little
gold-dust skilfully applied put an end to wars that
else threatened to extend into a Carthaginian length.
In one week's time

> *Hi motus animorum atque hæc certamina tanta*
> *Pulveris exigui jactu compressa quiêrunt.*

*   *   *

Here I had terminated this chapter—as at a natural
pause, which, whilst shutting out for ever my eldest
brother from the reader's sight and from my own,
necessarily at the same moment worked a permanent
revolution in the character of my daily life. Two such
changes, and both so abrupt, indicated imperiously
the close of one era and the opening of another. The
advantages, indeed, which my brother had over me
in years, in physical activities of every kind, in decision of purpose, and in energy of will—all which
advantages, besides, borrowed a ratification from an
obscure sense, on my part, of duty as incident to what
seemed an appointment of Providence—inevitably *had*
controlled, and for years to come *would have* controlled, the free spontaneous movements of a contem-

plative dreamer like myself. Consequently, this separation, which proved an eternal one, and contributed
to deepen my constitutional propensity to gloomy
meditation, had for me (partly on that account, but
much more through the sudden birth of perfect independence which so unexpectedly it opened) the value
of a revolutionary experience. A new date, a new
starting-point, a redemption (as it might be called)
into the golden sleep of halcyon quiet, after everlasting storms, suddenly dawned upon me; and not as
any casual intercalation of holidays that would come
to an end—but, for anything that appeared to the
contrary, as the perpetual tenor of my future career.
No longer was the factory a Carthage for me: if any
obdurate old Cato there were who found his amusement in denouncing it with a daily *"Delenda est,"*
take notice (I said silently to myself), that I acknowledge no such tiger for a friend of mine. Never more
was the bridge across the Irwell a bridge of sighs for
me. And the meanest of the factory population—
thanks be to their discrimination—despised my pretensions too entirely to waste a thought or a menace
upon a cipher so abject.

This change, therefore, being so sudden and so total,
ought to signalize itself externally by a commensurate
break in the narrative. A new chapter, at the least,
with a huge interspace of blank white paper, or even
a new book, ought rightfully to solemnize so profound
a revolution. And virtually it shall. But, according to
the general agreement of antiquity, it is not felt as at
all disturbing to the unity of that event which winds
up the Iliad—viz., the death of Hector—that Homer
expands it circumstantially into the whole ceremonial
of his funeral obsequies: and upon that same principle
I, when looking back to this abrupt close of all connexion with my brother—whether in my character

of major-general, or of potentate trembling daily for
my people—am reminded that the very last morning
of this connexion had its own separate distinction from
all other mornings, in a way that entitles it to its own
separate share in the general commemoration. A
shadow fell upon this particular morning as from a
cloud of danger that lingered for a moment over our
heads, might seem even to muse and hesitate, and then
sullenly passed away into distant quarters. It is noticeable that a danger which approaches, but wheels away
—which threatens, but finally forbears to strike—is
more interesting by much on a distant retrospect than
the danger which accomplishes its mission. The Alpine
precipice, down which many pilgrims have fallen, is
passed without much attention; but that precipice,
within one inch of which a traveller has passed unconsciously in the dark, first tracing his peril along the
snowy margin on the next morning, becomes invested
with an attraction of horror for all who hear the story.
The dignity of mortal danger ever after consecrates
the spot; and, in this particular case which I am now
recalling, the remembrance of such a danger consecrates the day.

That day was amongst the most splendid in a splendid June: it was, to borrow the line of Wordsworth,

One of those heavenly days which cannot die:

and, early as it was at that moment, we children, all
six of us that then survived, were already abroad upon
the lawn. There were two lawns at Greenhay in the
shrubbery that invested three sides of the house: one
of these, which ran along one side of the house, extended to a little bridge traversed by the gates of entrance. The central gate admitted carriages: on each
side of this was a smaller gate for foot passengers; and,

in a family containing so many as six children, it may
be supposed that often enough one or other of the
gates was open; which, most fortunately, on this day
was not the case. Along the margin of this side-lawn
ran a little brook, which had been raised to a uniform
level, and kept up by means of a weir at the point
where it quitted the premises; after which it resumed
its natural character of wildness, as it trotted on to
the little hamlet of Greenhill. This brook my brother
was at one time disposed to treat as Remus treated the
infant walls of Rome; but, on maturer thoughts, having built a fleet of rafts, he treated it more respectfully; and this morning, as will be seen, the breadth
of the little brook did us "yeoman's service." Me at
one time he had meant to put on board this fleet, as his
man Friday; and I had a fair prospect of first entering
life in the respectable character of supercargo. But it
happened that the current carried his rafts and himself over the weir; which, he assured us, was no accident, but a lesson by way of practice in the art of
contending with the rapids of the St. Lawrence and
other Canadian streams. However, as the danger had
been considerable, he was prohibited from trying such
experiments with me. On the centre of the lawn stood
my eldest surviving sister, Mary, and my brother
William. Round *him*, attracted (as ever) by his inexhaustible opulence of thought and fun, stood, laughing and dancing, my youngest sister, a second Jane,
and my youngest brother Henry, a posthumous child,
feeble, and in his nurse's arms, but on this morning
showing signs of unusual animation and of sympathy
with the glorious promise of the young June day.
Whirling round on his heel, at a little distance, and
utterly abstracted from all around him, my next
brother, Richard, he that had caused so much affliction
by his incorrigible morals to the Sultan Amurath,

pursued his own solitary thoughts—whatever those
might be. And, finally, as regards myself, it happened
that I was standing close to the edge of the brook,
looking back at intervals to the group of five children
and two nursemaids who occupied the centre of the
lawn; time, about an hour before *our* breakfast, or
about two hours before the world's breakfast—*i.e.*, a
little after seven—when as yet in shady parts of the
grounds the dazzling jewellery of the early dews had
not entirely exhaled. So standing, and so occupied,
suddenly we were alarmed by shouts as of some great
mob manifestly in rapid motion, and probably, at this
instant, taking the right-angled turn into the lane
connecting Greenhay with the Oxford Road. The
shouts indicated hostile and headlong pursuit: within
one minute, another right-angled turn in the lane
itself brought the uproar fully upon the ear; and it
became evident that some imminent danger—of what
nature it was impossible to guess—must be hastily
nearing us. We were all rooted to the spot; and all
turned anxiously to the gates, which happily seemed
to be closed. Had this been otherwise, we should have
had no time to apply any remedy whatever, and the
consequences must probably have involved us all. In
a few seconds, a powerful dog, not much above a furlong ahead of his pursuers, wheeled into sight. We all
saw him pause at the gates; but, finding no ready
access through the iron lattice-work that protected the
side battlements of the little bridge, and the pursuit
being so hot, he resumed his course along the outer
margin of the brook. Coming opposite to myself, he
made a dead stop. I had thus an opportunity of looking
him steadily in the face; which I did, without more
fear than belonged naturally to a case of so much
hurry, and to me, in particular, of mystery. I had
never heard of hydrophobia. But, necessarily connect-

ing the furious pursuit with the dog that now gazed at me from the opposite side of the water, and, feeling obliged to presume that he had made an assault upon somebody or other, I looked searchingly into his eyes, and observed that they seemed glazed, and as if in a dreamy state, but at the same time suffused with some watery discharge, while his mouth was covered with masses of white foam. He looked most earnestly at myself and the group beyond me; but he made no effort whatever to cross the brook, and apparently had not the energy to attempt it by a flying leap. My brother William, who did not in the least suspect the real danger, invited the dog to try his chance in a leap—assuring him that, if he succeeded, he would knight him on the spot. The temptation of a knight-hood, however, did not prove sufficient. A very few seconds brought his pursuers within sight; and steadily, without sound or gesture of any kind, he resumed his flight in the only direction open to him—viz., by a field-path across stiles to Greenhill. Half-an-hour later he would have met a bevy of children going to a dame's school, or carrying milk to rustic neighbours. As it was, the early morning kept the road clear in front. But behind immense was the body of agitated pursuers. Leading the chase, came, probably, half a troop of light cavalry, all on foot, nearly all in their stable dresses, and armed generally with pitchforks, though some eight or ten carried carbines. Half-mingled with these, and very little in the rear, succeeded a vast miscellaneous mob, that had gathered on the chase as it hurried through the purlieus of Deansgate, and all that populous suburb of Manchester. From some of these, who halted to recover breath, we obtained an explanation of the affair.

About a mile and a-half from Greenhay stood some horse-barracks, occupied usually by an entire regi-

ment of cavalry. A large dog——one of a multitude that
haunted the barracks——had for some days manifested
an increasing sullenness, snapping occasionally at
dogs and horses, but finally at men. Upon this he had
been tied up; but in some way he had this morning
liberated himself: two troop horses he had immediately bitten; and had made attacks upon several of the
men, who fortunately parried these attacks by means
of the pitchforks standing ready to their hands. On
this evidence, coupled with the knowledge of his previous illness, he was summarily condemned as mad; and
the general pursuit commenced, which brought all
parties (hunters and game) sweeping so wildly past
the quiet grounds of Greenhay. The sequel of the
affair was this: none of the carbineers succeeded in
getting a shot at the dog; in consequence of which,
the chase lasted for seventeen miles nominally; but,
allowing for all the doublings and headings-back of
the dog, by computation for about twenty-four: and
finally, in a state of utter exhaustion, he was run into,
and killed, somewhere in Cheshire. Of the two horses
whom he had bitten, both treated alike, one died in a
state of furious hydrophobia some two months later,
but the other (though the more seriously wounded of
the two) manifested no symptoms whatever of constitutional derangement. And thus it happened that
for me this general event of separation from my eldest
brother, and the particular morning on which it occurred, were each for itself separately and equally
memorable. Freedom won and death escaped, almost
in the same hour——freedom from a yoke of such secret
and fretful annoyance as none could measure but
myself——and death probably through the fiercest of
torments; these double cases of deliverance, so sudden
and so *unlooked for*, signalized, by what heraldically
might have been described as a two-headed memorial,

the establishment of an *epoch* in my life. Not only was the Chapter of INFANCY thus solemnly finished for ever, and the record closed; but—which cannot often happen—the chapter was closed pompously and conspicuously, by what the early printers through the fifteen and sixteenth centuries would have called a bright and illuminated Colophon.

I AM INTRODUCED TO THE WARFARE
OF A PUBLIC SCHOOL

(First published in *Tait's Magazine*, February, 1834)

FOUR years after my father's death, it began to be perceived that there was no purpose to be answered in any longer keeping up the costly establishment of Greenhay. A head-gardener, besides labourers equal to at least two more, were required for the grounds and gardens. And no motive existed any longer for being near to a great trading town, so long after the commercial connexion with it had ceased. Bath seemed, on all accounts, the natural station for a person in my mother's situation; and thither, accordingly, she went. I, who had been placed under the tuition of one of my guardians, remained some time longer under his care. I was then transferred to Bath. During this interval the sale of the house and grounds took place. It may illustrate the subject of *guardianship*, and the ordinary execution of its duties, to mention the result. The year was in itself a year of great depression, and every way unfavourable to such a transaction; and the particular night for which the sale had been fixed turned out remarkably wet; yet no attempt was made to postpone it, and it proceeded. Originally the house and grounds had cost about £6000. I have heard that only one offer was made—viz., of £2500. Be that as it may, for the sum of £2500 it was sold; and I have been often assured that, by waiting a few years, four to six times that sum might have been obtained with ease. This is not improbable, as the house was then out in the country; but since then the town of Manchester has gathered round it and enveloped it. Meantime, my guardians were all men of honour and integrity; but their hands were filled with their own affairs. One (my tutor) was a clergyman, rector of a church, and having his parish, his large family, and three pupils to attend. He was, besides, a very sedentary and indolent man, loving books—hating business. Another was a merchant. A third was a country magistrate, overladen with official business: him we rarely saw. Finally, the fourth was a banker in a distant county, having more knowledge of the world, more energy, and more practical wisdom, than all the rest united, but too remote for interfering effectually.

Reflecting upon the evils which befell me, and the gross mismanagement, under my guardians, of my small fortune, and that of my brothers and sisters, it has often occurred to me that so important an office, which, from the time of Demosthenes, has been proverbially mal-administered, ought to be put upon a new footing, plainly guarded by a few obvious provisions. As under the Roman laws, for a long period, the guardian should be made responsible in law, and should give security from the first for the due performance of his duties. But, to give him a motive for doing this, of course he must be paid. With the new obligations and liabilities will commence commensurate emoluments. If a child is made a ward in Chancery, its property is managed expensively, but always advantageously. Some great change is imperatively called for: no duty in the whole compass of human life being so scandalously neglected as this.

In my twelfth year it was that first of all I entered upon the arena of a great public school—viz., the Grammar School [1] of Bath, over which at that time presided a most accomplished Etonian—Mr. (or was he as yet Doctor?) Morgan. If he was not, I am sure he ought to have been; and, with the reader's concur-

---

[1] *"Grammar School":* By the way, as the grammar-schools of England are amongst her most eminent distinctions, and, with submission to the innumerable wretches (gentlemen, I should say) that hate England "worse than toad or asp," have never been rivalled by any corresponding institutions in other lands, I may as well take this opportunity of explaining the word *grammar,* which most people misapprehend. Men suppose a grammar-school to mean a school where they teach grammar. But this is not the true meaning, and tends to calumniate such schools, by ignoring their highest functions. Limiting by a false limitation the earliest object contemplated by such schools, they obtain a plausible pretext for representing all beyond grammar as something extraneous and casual that did not enter into the original or normal conception of the founders, and that may therefore have been due to alien suggestion. But now, when Suetonius writes a little book bearing this title, *De Illustribus Grammaticis,* what does he mean? What is it that he promises? A memoir upon the eminent *grammarians* of Rome? Not at all, but a memoir upon the distinguished *literati* of Rome. *Grammatica* does certainly mean sometimes grammar; but it is also the best Latin word for literature. A *grammaticus* is what the French express by the word *littérateur.* We unfortunately have no corresponding term in English: a *man of letters* is our awkward periphrasis in the singular (too apt, as our jest-books remind us, to suggest the postman); whilst in the plural we resort to the Latin word *literati.* The school which professes to teach *grammatica* professes, therefore, the culture of literature in the widest and most liberal extent, and is opposed *generically* to schools for teaching mechanic arts; and, within its own *sub-genus* of schools dedicated to liberal objects, is opposed to schools for teaching mathematics, or, more widely, to schools for teaching science.

rence, will therefore create him a doctor on the spot. Every man has reason to rejoice who enjoys the advantage of a public training. I condemned, and *do* condemn, the practice of sending out into such stormy exposures those who are as yet too young, too dependent on female gentleness, and endowed with sensibilities originally too exquisite for such a warfare. But at nine or ten the masculine energies of the character are beginning to develop themselves; or, if not, no discipline will better aid in their development than the bracing intercourse of a great English classical school. Even the selfish are *there* forced into accommodating themselves to a public standard of generosity; and the effeminate into conforming to a rule of manliness. I was myself at two public schools, and I think with gratitude of the benefits which I reaped from both; as also I think with gratitude of that guardian in whose quiet household I learned Latin so effectually. But the small private schools, of which I had opportunities for gathering some brief experience —schools containing thirty to forty boys—were models of ignoble manners as regarded part of the juniors, and of favouritism as regarded the masters. Nowhere is the sublimity of public justice so broadly exemplified as in an English public school on the old Edward the Sixth or Elizabeth foundation. There is not in the universe such an Areopagus for fair play, and abhorrence of all crooked ways, as an English mob, or one of the time-honoured English "foundation" schools. But my own first introduction to such an establishment was under peculiar and contradictory circumstances. When my "rating," or graduation in the school was to be settled, naturally my altitude (to speak astronomically) was taken by my proficiency in Greek. But here I had no advantage over others of my age. My guardian was a feeble Grecian, and had

not excited my ambition; so that I could barely con-
strue books as easy as the Greek Testament and the
Iliad. This was considered quite well enough for my
age; but still it caused me to be placed under the care
of Mr. Wilkins, the second master out of four, and
not under Dr. Morgan himself.

Within one month, however, my talent for Latin
verses, which had by this time gathered strength and
expansion, became known. Suddenly I was honoured
as never was man or boy since Mordecai the Jew.
Without any colourable relation to the doctor's jurisdiction, I was now weekly paraded for distinction at
the supreme tribunal of the school; out of which, at
first, grew nothing but a sunshine of approbation
delightful to my heart. Within six weeks all this had
changed. The approbation, indeed, continued, and the
public expression of it. Neither would there, in the
ordinary course, have been any painful reaction from
jealousy or fretful resistance to the soundness of my
pretensions; since it was sufficiently known to such
of my schoolfellows as stood on my own level in the
school, that I, who had no male relatives but military
men, and those in India, could not have benefited by
any clandestine aid. But, unhappily, Dr. Morgan was
at that time dissatisfied with some points in the progress of his head class; and, as it soon appeared, was
continually throwing in their teeth the brilliancy of
my verses at eleven or twelve, by comparison with
theirs at seventeen, eighteen, and even nineteen. I had
observed him sometimes pointing to myself, and was
perplexed at seeing this gesture followed by gloomy
looks, and what French reporters call "sensation," in
these young men, whom naturally I viewed with awe
as my leaders—boys that were called young men, men
that were reading Sophocles (a name that carried with
it the sound of something seraphic to my ears), and

who never had vouchsafed to waste a word on such a
child as myself. The day was come, however, when
all that would be changed. One of these leaders strode
up to me in the public playground; and, delivering a
blow on my shoulder, which was not intended to hurt
me, but as a mere formula of introduction, asked me,
"What the devil I meant by bolting out of the course,
and annoying other people in that manner? Were
'other people' to have no rest for me and my verses,
which, after all, were horribly bad?" There might
have been some difficulty in returning an answer to
this address, but none was required. I was briefly admonished to see that I wrote worse for the future, or
else——— At this *aposiopesis* I looked inquiringly at
the speaker, and he filled up the chasm by saying, that
he would "annihilate" me. Could any person fail to
be aghast at such a demand? I was to write worse than
my own standard, which, by his account of my verses,
must be difficult; and I was to write worse than himself, which might be impossible. My feelings revolted
against so arrogant a demand, unless it had been far
otherwise expressed; if death on the spot had awaited
me, I could not have controlled myself; and, on the
next occasion for sending up verses to the headmaster,
so far from attending to the orders issued, I double-
shotted my guns; double applause descended on myself; but I remarked, with some awe, though not re-
penting of what I had done, that double confusion
seemed to agitate the ranks of my enemies. Amongst
them, loomed out in the distance my "annihilating"
friend, who shook his huge fist at me, but with something like a grim smile about his eyes. He took an early
opportunity of paying his respects to me again, saying,
"You little devil, do you call this writing your worst?"
—"No," I replied; "I call it writing my best."
    The annihilator, as it turned out, was really a good-

natured young man; but he was on the wing for Cambridge; and with the rest, or some of them, I continued to wage war for more than a year. And yet, for a word spoken with kindness, how readily I would have resigned (had it been altogether at my own choice to do so) the peacock's feather in my cap as the merest of baubles. Undoubtedly, praise sounded sweet in *my* ears also; but that was nothing by comparison with what stood on the other side. I detested distinctions that were connected with mortification to others; and, even if I could have got over *that*, the eternal feud fretted and tormented my nature. Love, that once in childhood had been so mere a necessity to me, *that* had long been a reflected ray from a departed sunset. But peace, and freedom from strife, if love were no longer possible (as so rarely it is in this world), was the clamorous necessity of my nature. To contend with somebody was still my fate; how to escape the contention I could not see; and yet, for itself, and for the deadly passions into which it forced me, I hated and loathed it more than death. It added to the distraction and internal feud of my mind, that I could not *altogether* condemn the upper boys. I was made a handle of humiliation to them. And, in the meantime, if I had an undeniable advantage in one solitary accomplishment, which is still a matter of accident, or sometimes of peculiar direction given to the taste, they, on the other hand, had a great advantage over me in the more elaborate difficulties of Greek, and of choral Greek poetry. I could not altogether wonder at their hatred of myself. Yet still, as they had chosen to adopt this mode of conflict with me, I did not feel that I had any choice but to resist. The contest was terminated for me by my removal from the school, in consequence of a very threatening illness affecting my head; but it lasted more than a year, and it did not close before several among my public enemies had become my private friends. They were much older, but they invited me to the houses of their friends, and showed me a respect which affected me—this respect having more reference, apparently, to the firmness I had exhibited, than to any splendour in my verses. And, indeed, these had rather drooped, from a natural accident: several persons of my own class had formed the practice of asking me to write verses for *them*. I could not refuse. But, as the subjects given out were the same for the entire class, it was not possible to take so many crops off the ground, without starving the quality of all.

The most interesting public event which, during my stay at this school, at all connected itself with Bath, and, indeed, with the school itself, was the sudden escape of Sir Sidney Smith from the prison of the Temple in Paris. The mode of his escape was as striking as its time was critical. Having accidentally thrown a ball beyond the prison bounds in playing at tennis, or some such game, Sir Sidney was surprised to observe that the ball thrown back was not the same. Fortunately, he had the presence of mind to dissemble his sudden surprise. He retired, examined the ball, found it stuffed with letters; and, in the same way, he subsequently conducted a long correspondence, and arranged the whole circumstances of his escape; which, remarkably enough, was accomplished exactly eight days before the sailing of Napoleon with the Egyptian expedition; so that Sir Sidney was just in time to confront, and utterly to defeat, Napoleon in the breach of Acre. But for Sir Sidney, Bonaparte would have overrun Syria, *that* is certain. What would have followed from that event is a far more obscure problem.

Sir Sidney Smith, I must explain to readers of this generation, and Sir Edward Pellew (afterwards Lord

Exmouth), figured as the two [1] Paladins of the first war with revolutionary France. Rarely were these two names mentioned but in connexion with some splendid, prosperous, and unequal contest. Hence the whole nation was saddened by the account of Sir Sidney's capture; and this must be understood, in order to make the joy of his sudden return perfectly intelligible. Not even a rumour of Sir Sidney's escape had or could have run before him; for, at the moment of reaching the coast of England, he had started with post-horses to Bath. It was about dusk when he arrived; the postilions were directed to the square in which his mother lived; in a few minutes he was in his mother's arms; and in fifty minutes more the news had flown to the remotest suburb of the city. The agitation of Bath on this occasion was indescribable. All the troops of the line then quartered in that city, and a whole regiment of volunteers, immediately got under arms, and marched to the quarter in which Sir Sidney lived. The small square overflowed with the soldiery; Sir Sidney went out, and was immediately lost to us, who were watching for him, in the closing ranks of the troops.

Next morning, however, I, my younger brother, and a schoolfellow of my own age, called formally upon the naval hero. *Why*, I know not, unless as *alumni* of the school at which Sir Sidney Smith had received his own education. We were admitted without question or demur; and I may record it as an amiable trait in Sir Sidney, that he received us then with great kindness,

[1] To *them* in the next stage of the war succeeded Sir Michael Seymour, and Lord Cochrane (the present earl of Dundonald), and Lord Camelford. The two last were the regular fire-eaters of the day. Sir Horatio Nelson, being already an admiral, was no longer looked to for insulated exploits of brilliant adventure; his name was now connected with larger and combined attacks, less dashing and adventurous, because including heavier responsibilities.

and took us down with him to the pump-room. Considering, however, that we must have been most afflicting bores to Sir Sidney—a fact which no self-esteem could even then disguise from us—it puzzled me at first to understand the principle of his conduct. Having already done more than enough in courteous acknowledgement of our fraternal claims as fellow-students at the Bath Grammar School, why should he think it necessary to burden himself further with our worshipful society? I found out the secret, and will explain it. A very slight attention to Sir Sidney's deportment in public revealed to me that he was morbidly afflicted with nervous sensibility, and with *mauvaise honte*. He that had faced so cheerfully crowds of hostile and threatening eyes, could not support without trepidation those gentle eyes, beaming with gracious admiration, of his fair young countrywomen. By accident, at that moment Sir Sidney had no acquaintances in Bath, a fact which is not at all to be wondered at. Living so much abroad and at sea, an English sailor, of whatever rank, has few opportunities for making friends at home. And yet there was a necessity that Sir Sidney should gratify the public interest, so warmly expressed, by presenting himself somewhere or other to the public eye. But how trying a service to the most practised and otherwise most callous veteran on such an occasion —that he should step forward, saying in effect—"So you are wanting to see me; well, then, here I am; come and look at me!" Put it into what language you please, such a summons was written on all faces, and countersigned by his worship the mayor, who began to whisper insinuations of riots if Sir Sidney did not comply. Yet, if he *did*, inevitably his own act of obedience to the public pleasure took the shape of an ostentatious self-parading under the construction of those numerous persons who knew nothing of the public importunity,

or of Sir Sidney's unaffected and even morbid reluctance to obtrude himself upon the public eye. The
thing was unavoidable; and the sole palliation that it
admitted was, to break the concentration of the public
gaze, by associating Sir Sidney with some alien group,
no matter of what cattle. Such a group would relieve
both parties—gazer and gazee—from too distressing a
consciousness of the little business on which they had
met. We, the schoolboys, being three, intercepted and
absorbed part of the enemy's fire; and, by furnishing
Sir Sidney with real *bona fide* matter of conversation,
we released him from the most distressing part of his
sufferings—viz., the passive and silent acquiescence in
his own apotheosis—holding a lighted candle, as it
were, to the glorification of his own shrine. With our
help, he weathered the storm of homage silently ascending. And we, in fact, whilst seeming to ourselves
too undeniably a triad of bores, turned out the most
serviceable allies that Sir Sidney ever had by land or
sea, until several moons later, when he formed the invaluable acquaintance of the Syrian "butcher"—viz.,
Djezzar, the pacha of Acre.

I record this little trait of Sir Sidney's constitutional
temperament, and the little service through which I
and my two comrades contributed materially to his relief, as an illustration of that infirmity which besieges
the nervous system of our nation. It is a sensitiveness
which sometimes amounts to lunacy, and sometimes
even tempts to suicide. It is a mistake, however, to suppose this morbid affection unknown to Frenchmen, or
unknown to men of the world. I have myself known it
to exist in both, and particularly in a man that might
be said to live in the street, such was the American pub-
licity which circumstances threw around his life; and
so far were his habits of life removed from reserve, or
from any predisposition to gloom. And at this moment

I recall a remarkable illustration of what I am saying,
communicated by Wordsworth's accomplished friend,
Sir George Beaumont. To *him* I had been sketching
the distressing sensitiveness of Sir Sidney pretty much
as I have sketched it to the reader; and how he, the
man that on the breach at Acre valued not the eye of
Jew, Christian, or Turk, shrank back—*me ipso teste*—
from the gentle, though eager—from the admiring,
yet affectionate—glances of three very young ladies,
in Gay Street, Bath, the oldest (I should say) not more
than seventeen. Upon which Sir George mentioned, as
a parallel experience of his own, that Mr. Canning, being ceremoniously introduced to himself (Sir George),
about the time when he had reached the meridian of
his fame as an orator, and should therefore have become *blasé* to the extremity of being absolutely seared
and case-hardened against all impressions whatever appealing to his vanity or egotism, did absolutely (*credite
posteri!*) blush like any roseate girl of fifteen.

Sir Sidney was at that time slender and thin; having
an appearance of emaciation, as though he had suffered hardships and ill-treatment; which, however, I
do not remember to have heard. Meantime, his appearance, connected with his recent history, made him a
very interesting person to women; and to this hour it
remains a mystery with me why and how it came about
that in every distribution of honours Sir Sidney Smith
was overlooked. In the Mediterranean he made many
enemies, especially amongst those of his own profession, who used to speak of him as far too fine a gentleman, and above his calling. Certain it is, that he liked
better to be doing business on shore, as at Acre, although he commanded a fine 80-gun ship, the *Tiger*.
But, however that may have been, his services, whether
classed as military or naval, were memorably splendid.
And, at that time, his connexion, of whatsoever na-

ture, with the late Queen Caroline had not occurred. So that altogether, to me, his case is inexplicable.

From the Bath Grammar School I was removed in consequence of an accident, by which at first it was supposed that my skull had been fractured; and the surgeon who attended me at one time talked of trepanning.[1] This was an awful word: but at present I doubt whether in reality anything very serious had happened. In fact, I was always under a nervous panic for my head; and certainly exaggerated my internal feelings without meaning to do so, and this misled the medical attendants. During a long illness which succeeded, my mother, amongst other books past all counting, read to me, in Hoole's translation, the whole of the *Orlando Furioso;* meaning by the *whole* the entire twenty-four books into which Hoole had condensed the original forty-six of Ariosto; and, from my own experience at that time, I am disposed to think that the homeliness of this version is an advantage, from not calling off the attention at all from the narration to the narrator. At this time also I first read the *Paradise Lost;* but, oddly enough, in the edition of Bentley, that great παραδιορθωτης (or pseudo-restorer of the text). At the close of my illness, the head-master called upon my mother, in company with his son-in-law, Mr. Wilkins, as did a certain Irish Colonel Bowes, who had sons at the school, requesting earnestly, in terms most flattering to myself, that I might be suffered to remain there. But it illustrates my mother's moral austerity that she was shocked at my hearing compliments to my own merits, and was altogether disturbed at what doubtless these gentlemen expected to see received with maternal pride. She declined to let me continue at the

[1] He was accidentally hit on the head with a cane by one of the undermasters who was attempting to strike another boy. —ED.

Bath School; and I went to another, at Winkfield, in the County of Wilts, of which the chief recommendation lay in the religious character of the master.

I ENTER THE WORLD

(First published in *Tait's Magazine*, March, 1834)

YES, at this stage of my life—viz., in my fifteenth year—and from this sequestered school, ankle-deep I first stepped into the world. At Winkfield I had stayed about a year, or not much more, when I received a letter from a young friend of my own age, Lord Westport,[1] the son of Lord Altamont, inviting me to accompany him to Ireland for the ensuing summer and autumn. This invitation was repeated by his tutor; and my mother, after some consideration, allowed me to accept it.

In the spring of 1800, accordingly, I went up to Eton, for the purpose of joining my friend. Here I several times visited the gardens of the Queen's villa at Frogmore; and, privileged by my young friend's introduction, I had opportunities of seeing and hearing the Queen and all the Princesses; which at that time was a novelty in my life, naturally a good deal prized. Lord Westport's mother had been, before her marriage, Lady Louisa Howe, daughter to the great admiral, Earl Howe, and intimately known to the Royal Family, who, on her account, took a continual and especial notice of her son.

On one of these occasions I had the honour of a brief

[1] My acquaintance with Lord Westport was of some years' standing. My father, whose commercial interests led him often to Ireland, had many friends there. One of these was a country gentleman connected with the west; and at his house I first met Lord Westport.

interview with the King. Madame de Campan mentions, as an amusing incident in her early life, though
terrific at the time, and overwhelming to her sense of
shame, that not long after her establishment at Ver-
sailles, in the service of some one amongst the daughters of Louis XV, having as yet never seen the King,
she was one day suddenly introduced to his particular
notice, under the following circumstances: The time
was morning; the young lady was not fifteen: her spirits were as the spirits of a fawn in May; her *tour* of
duty for the day was either not come, or was gone;
and, finding herself alone in a spacious room, what
more reasonable thing could she do than amuse herself
with *making cheeses;* that is, whirling round, according to a fashion practised by young ladies both in
France and England, and pirouetting until the petti-
coat is inflated like a balloon, and then sinking into a
curtsy. Mademoiselle was very solemnly rising from
one of these curtsys, in the centre of her collapsing
petticoats, when a slight noise alarmed her. Jealous of
intruding eyes, yet not dreading more than a servant
at worst, she turned; and, oh heavens! whom should
she behold but his most Christian Majesty advancing
upon her, with a brilliant suite of gentlemen, young
and old, equipped for the chase, who had been all silent
spectators of her performances! From the king to the
last of the train, all bowed to her, and all laughed
without restraint, as they passed the abashed amateur
of cheesemaking. But she, to speak Homerically,
wished in that hour that the earth might gape and
cover her confusion. Lord Westport and I were about
the age of mademoiselle, and not much more decorously engaged, when a turn brought us full in view of
a royal party coming along one of the walks at Frogmore. We were, in fact, theorizing and practically
commenting on the art of throwing stones. Boys have

a peculiar contempt for female attempts in that way.
For, besides that girls fling wide of the mark, with a
certainty that might have won the applause of Gale-
rius,[1] there is a peculiar sling and rotary motion of the
arm in launching a stone, which no girl even *can* attain. From ancient practice, I was somewhat of a proficient in this art, and was discussing the philosophy of
female failures, illustrating my doctrines with pebbles,
as the case happened to demand; whilst Lord Westport
was practising on the peculiar whirl of the wrist with
a shilling; when suddenly he turned the head of the
coin towards me with a significant glance, and in a
low voice he muttered some words, of which I caught
"*Grace of God,*" "*France and Ireland,*" "*Defender of
the Faith, and so forth.*" This solemn recitation of the
legend on the coin was meant as a fanciful way of ap-
prising me that the King was approaching; for Lord
Westport had himself lost somewhat of the awe natural
to a young person in a first situation of this nature,
through his frequent admissions to the royal presence.
For my own part, I was as yet a stranger even to the
King's person. I had, indeed, seen most or all the
Princesses in the way I have mentioned above; and occasionally, in the streets of Windsor, the sudden disappearance of all hats from all heads had admonished
me that some royal personage or other was then traversing (or, if not traversing, was crossing) the street;
but either his majesty had never been of the party, or,
from distance, I had failed to distinguish him. Now,
for the first time, I was meeting him nearly face to

[1] "Sir," said that Emperor to a soldier who had missed the
target in succession I know not how many times (suppose we
say fifteen), "allow me to offer my congratulations on the
truly admirable skill you have shown in keeping clear of the
mark. Not to have hit once in so many trials argues the most
splendid talents for missing."

face; for, though the walk we occupied was not that
in which the royal party were moving, it ran so near it,
and was connected by so many cross-walks at short intervals, that it was a matter of necessity for us, as we
were now observed, to go and present ourselves. What
happened was pretty nearly as follows: The King, having first spoken with great kindness to my companion,
inquiring circumstantially about his mother and
grandmother, as persons particularly well known to
himself, then turned his eye upon me. My name, it
seems, had been communicated to him; he did not,
therefore, inquire about that. Was I of Eton? this was
his first question. I replied that I was not, but hoped I
should be. Had I a father living? I had not: my father
had been dead about eight years. "But you have a
mother?" I had. "And she thinks of sending you to
Eton?" I answered that she had expressed such an intention in my hearing; but I was not sure whether *that*
might not be in order to waive an argument with the
person to whom she spoke, who happened to have been
an Etonian. "Oh, but all people think highly of Eton;
everybody praises Eton. Your mother does right to inquire; there can be no harm in that; but the more she
inquires, the more she will be satisfied—that I can answer for."

Next came a question which had been suggested by
my name. Had my family come into England with the
Huguenots at the Revocation of the Edict of Nantes?
This was a tender point with me: of all things, I could
not endure to be supposed of French descent; yet it was
a vexation I had constantly to face, as most people supposed that my name argued a French origin; whereas
a Norman origin argued pretty certainly an origin *not*
French. I replied, with some haste, "Please your majesty, the family has been in England since the Conquest." It is probable that I coloured, or showed some

mark of discomposure, with which, however, the King
was not displeased, for he smiled, and said, "How do
you know that?" Here I was at a loss for a moment
how to answer; for I was sensible that it did not become me to occupy the King's attention with any long
stories or traditions about a subject so unimportant as
my own family; and yet it was necessary that I should
say something, unless I would be thought to have denied my Huguenot descent upon no reason or authority. After a moment's hesitation, I said in effect, that
the family from which I traced my descent had certainly been a great and leading one at the era of the
Barons' Wars, as also in one at least of the Crusades;
and that I had myself seen many notices of this family,
not only in books of heraldry, &c., but in the very earliest of all English books. "And what book was that?"
"Robert of Gloucester's *Metrical Chronicle*, which I
understood, from internal evidence, to have been written about 1280." The King smiled again, and said, "I
know, I know." But what it was that he knew, long
afterwards puzzled me to conjecture. I now imagine,
however, that he meant to claim a knowledge of the
book I referred to, a thing which at that time I thought
improbable, supposing the King's acquaintance with
literature not to be very extensive, nor likely to have
comprehended any knowledge at all of the black-letter
period. But in this belief I was greatly mistaken, as I
was afterwards fully convinced by the best evidence
from various quarters. That library of 120,000 volumes which George IV presented to the nation, and
which has since gone to swell the collection at the British Museum, had been formed (as I was often assured
by persons to whom the whole history of the library,
and its growth from small rudiments, was familiarly
known) under the direct personal superintendence of
George III. It was a favourite and pet creation; and

his care extended even to the dressing of the books in appropriate bindings, and (as one man told me) to their *health;* explaining himself to mean, that in any case where a book was worm-eaten, or touched, however slightly, with the worm, the King was anxious to prevent the injury from extending, or from infecting others by close neighbourhood; for it is supposed by many that such injuries spread rapidly in favourable situations. One of my informants was a German bookbinder of great respectability, settled in London, and for many years employed by the Admiralty as a confidential binder of records or journals containing secrets of office, &c. Through this connexion he had been recommended to the service of his majesty, whom he used to see continually in the course of his attendance at Buckingham House, where the books were deposited. This artist had (originally in the way of his trade) become well acquainted with the money value of English books; and that knowledge cannot be acquired without some concurrent knowledge of their subject and their kind of merit. Accordingly, he was tolerably well qualified to estimate any man's attainments as a reading man; and from him I received such circumstantial accounts of many conversations he had held with the King, evidently reported with entire good faith and simplicity, that I cannot doubt the fact of his majesty's very general acquaintance with English literature. Not a day passed, whenever the King happened to be at Buckingham House, without his coming into the binding-room, and minutely inspecting the progress of the binder and his allies—the gilders, toolers, &c. From the outside of the book the transition was natural to its value in the scale of bibliography; and in that way my informant had ascertained that the King was well acquainted, not only with Robert of Gloucester, but with all the other early chronicles,

published by Hearne, and, in fact, possessed that entire series which rose at one period to so enormous a
price. From this person I learned afterwards that the
King prided himself especially upon his early folios of
Shakespeare; that is to say, not merely upon the excellence of the individual copies in a bibliographical
sense, as "*tall* copies," and having large margins, &c.,
but chiefly from their value, in relation to the most
authentic basis for the text of the poet. And thus it appears that at least two of our kings, Charles I and
George III, have made it their pride to profess a reverential esteem for Shakespeare. This bookbinder added
his attestation to the truth (or to the generally reputed
truth) of a story which I had heard from other authority—viz., that the librarian, or, if not officially the
librarian, at least the chief director in everything relating to the books, was an illegitimate son of Frederick,
Prince of Wales (son to George II), and therefore
half-brother of the king. His own taste and inclinations, it seemed, concurred with his brother's wishes
in keeping him in a subordinate rank and an obscure
station; in which, however, he enjoyed affluence without anxiety, or trouble, or courtly envy, and the luxury, which he most valued, of a superb library. He
lived and died, I have heard, as plain Mr. Barnard.

During the whole dialogue, I did not even once remark that hesitation and iteration of words generally
attributed to George III; indeed, *so* generally, that it
must often have existed; but, in this case, I suppose that
the brevity of his sentences operated to deliver him
from any embarrassment of utterance, such as might
have attended longer and more complex sentences,
where some anxiety was natural to overtake the
thoughts as they arose. When we observed that the
King had paused in his stream of questions, which
succeeded rapidly to each other, we understood it as a

signal of dismissal; and, making a profound obeisance, we retired backwards a few steps. His majesty smiled in a very gracious manner, waved his hand towards us, and said something (I do not know what) in a peculiarly kind accent; he then turned round, and the whole party along with him; which set us at liberty without impropriety to turn to the right-about ourselves, and make our egress from the gardens.

THE NATION OF LONDON

(First published in *Tait's Magazine*, March, 1834)

IT WAS a most heavenly day in May of this year (1800) when I first beheld and first entered this mighty wilderness, the city—no! not the city, but the nation—of London. Often since then, at distances of two and three hundred miles or more from this colossal emporium of men, wealth, arts, and intellectual power, have I felt the sublime expression of her enormous magnitude in one simple form of ordinary occurrence —viz., in the vast droves of cattle, suppose upon the great north roads, all with their heads directed to London, and expounding the size of the attracting body, together with the force of its attractive power, by the never-ending succession of these droves, and the remoteness from the capital of the lines upon which they were moving. A suction so powerful, felt along radii so vast, and a consciousness, at the same time, that upon other radii still more vast, both by land and by sea, the same suction is operating, night and day, summer and winter, and hurrying for ever into one centre the infinite means needed for her infinite purposes, and the endless tributes to the skill or to the luxury of her endless population, crowds the imagination with a pomp to which there is nothing corresponding upon this planet, either amongst the things that have been, or the things that are. Or, if any exception there is, it must be sought in ancient Rome. We, upon this occasion, were in an open carriage, and, chiefly (as I imagine) to avoid the dust, we approached London by rural lanes, where any such could be found, or, at least, along by-roads, quiet and shady, collateral to the main roads. In that mode of approach, we missed some features of the sublimity belonging to any of the common approaches upon a main road; we missed the whirl and the uproar, the tumult and the agitation, which continually thicken and thicken throughout the last dozen miles before you reach the suburbs. Already at three stages' distance (say, forty miles from London), upon some of the greatest roads, the dim presentiment of some vast capital reaches you obscurely, and like a misgiving. This blind sympathy with a mighty but unseen object, some vast magnetic range of Alps, in your neighbourhood, continues to increase, you know not how. Arrived at the last station for changing horses—Barnet, suppose, on one of the north roads, or Hounslow on the western—you no longer think (as in all other places) of naming the next stage; nobody says, on pulling up, "Horses on to London"; that would sound ridiculous; one mighty idea broods over all minds, making it impossible to suppose any other destination. Launched upon this final stage, you soon begin to feel yourself entering the stream as it were of a Norwegian *mælstrom;* and the stream at length becomes the rush of a cataract. Finally, for miles before you reach a suburb of London such as Islington, for instance, a last great sign and augury of the immensity which belongs to the coming metropolis forces itself upon the dullest observer, in the growing sense of his own utter insignificance. Everywhere else in England, you yourself, horses, carriage, attendants (if you travel with any), are regarded with attention, perhaps even curiosity: at all events you are seen. But, after passing the final post-house on every avenue to London, for the latter ten or twelve miles, you become aware that you are no longer noticed: nobody sees you; nobody hears you; nobody regards you; you do not even regard yourself. In fact, how should you at the moment of first ascertaining your own total unimportance in the sum of things—a poor shivering unit in the aggregate of human life? Now, for the first time, whatever manner of man you were or seemed to be at starting, squire or "squireen," lord or lordling, and however related to that city, hamlet, or solitary house, from which yesterday or today you slipped your cable—beyond disguise you find yourself but one wave in a total Atlantic, one plant (and a parasitical plant besides, needing alien props) in a forest of America.

These are feelings which do not belong by preference to thoughtful people—far less to people merely sentimental. No man ever was left to himself for the first time in the streets, as yet unknown, of London, but he must have been saddened and mortified, perhaps terrified, by the sense of desertion and utter loneliness which belong to his situation. No loneliness can be like that which weighs upon the heart in the centre of faces never-ending, without voice or utterance for him; eyes innumerable, that have "no speculation" in their orbs which *he* can understand; and hurrying figures of men and women weaving to and fro, with no apparent purposes intelligible to a stranger, seeming like a mask of maniacs, or, oftentimes, like a pageant of phantoms. The great length of the streets in many quarters of London; the continual opening of transient glimpses into other vistas equally far-stretching, going off at right angles to the one which you are traversing; and

the murky atmosphere which, settling upon the remoter end of every long avenue, wraps its termination
in gloom and uncertainty; all these are circumstances
aiding that sense of vastness and illimitable proportions which for ever brood over the aspect of London
in its interior. Much of the feeling which belongs to
the outside of London, in its approaches for the last
few miles, I had lost, in consequence of the stealthy
route of by-roads, lying near Uxbridge and Watford,
through which we crept into the suburbs. But, for that
reason, the more abrupt and startling had been the effect of emerging somewhere into the Edgeware Road,
and soon afterwards into the very streets of London itself—though *what* streets, or even what quarter of
London, is now totally obliterated from my mind, having perhaps never been comprehended. All that I remember is one monotonous awe and blind sense of mysterious grandeur and Babylonian confusion, which
seemed to pursue and to invest the whole equipage
of human life, as we moved for nearly two hours [1]
through streets; sometimes brought to anchor for ten
minutes or more, by what is technically called a "lock"
—that is, a line of carriages of every description inextricably massed and obstructing each other, far as
the eye could stretch; and then, as if under an en-
chanter's rod, the "lock" seemed to thaw; motion
spread with the fluent race of light or sound through
the whole icebound mass, until the subtle influence
reached *us* also; who were again absorbed into the
great rush of flying carriages; or, at times, we turned
off into some less tumultuous street, but of the same

[1] *"Two hours"*: This slow progress must, however, in part
be ascribed to Mr. Grace's non-acquaintance with the roads,
both town and rural, along the whole line of our progress
from Uxbridge.

mile-long character; and finally, drawing up about
noon, we alighted at some place, which is as little
within my distinct remembrance as the route by which
we reached it.

For what had we come? To see London. And what
were the limits within which we proposed to crowd
that little feat? At five o'clock we were to dine at
Porters, a seat of Lord Westport's grandfather; and,
from the distance, it was necessary that we should
leave London at half-past three; so that a little more
than three hours were all we had for London. Our
charioteer, my friend's tutor, was summoned away
from us on business until that hour; and we were left,
therefore, entirely to ourselves and to our own skill in
turning the time to the best account, for contriving
(if such a thing were possible) to do something or
other which, by any fiction of courtesy, or constructively, so as to satisfy a lawyer, or in a sense sufficient
to win a wager, might be taken and received for having "seen London."

What could be done? We sat down, I remember, in
a mood of despondency, to consider. The spectacles
were too many by thousands; *inopes nos copia fecit;*
our very wealth made us poor; and the choice was distracted. But which of them all could be thought general or representative enough to stand for the universe
of London? We could not traverse the whole circumference of this mighty orb; that was clear; and, therefore, the next best thing was to place ourselves as much
as possible in some relation to the spectacles of London,
which might answer to the centre. Yet how? That
sounded well and metaphysical; but what did it mean
if acted upon? What was the centre of London for
any purpose whatever—latitudinarian or longitudi-
narian—literary, social, or mercantile—geographical,

astronomical, or (as Mrs. Malaprop kindly suggests) diabolical? Apparently that we should stay at our inn: for in that way we seemed best to distribute our presence equally amongst all—viz., by going to none in particular.

In debating the matter, we lost half-an-hour; but at length we reduced the question to a choice between Westminster Abbey and St. Paul's Cathedral. I know not that we could have chosen better. The rival edifices, as we understood from the waiter, were about equidistant from our own station; but, being too remote from each other to allow of our seeing both, "we tossed up," to settle the question between the elder lady and the younger. "Heads" came up, which stood for the Abbey. But, as neither of us was quite satisfied with this decision, we agreed to make another appeal to the wisdom of chance, second thoughts being best. This time the Cathedral turned up; and so it came to pass that, with us, the having *seen London* meant having seen St. Paul's.

The first view of St. Paul's, it may be supposed, overwhelmed us with awe; and I did not at that time imagine that the sense of magnitude could be more deeply impressed. One thing interrupted our pleasure. The superb objects of curiosity within the Cathedral were shown for separate fees. There were seven, I think; and any one could be seen independently of the rest for a few pence. The whole amount was a trifle; fourteenpence, I think; but we were followed by a sort of persecution—"Would we not see the bell?"— "Would we not see the model?"—"Surely we would not go away without visiting the Whispering Gallery?" solicitations which troubled the silence and sanctity of the place, and must tease others as it then teased us, who wished to contemplate in quiet this great monument of the national grandeur, which was at that very time [1] beginning to take a station also in the land as a depository for the dust of her heroes. What struck us most in the whole *interior* of the pile was the view taken from the spot immediately under the dome, being, in fact, the very same which, five years afterwards, received the remains of Lord Nelson. In one of the aisles going off from this centre, we saw the flags of France, Spain, and Holland, the whole trophies of the war, swinging pompously, and expanding their massy draperies, slowly and heavily, in the upper gloom, as they were swept at intervals by currents of air. At this moment we were provoked by the showman at our elbow renewing his vile iteration of "Twopence, gentlemen; no more than twopence for each"; and so on until we left the place. The same complaint has often been made as to Westminster Abbey. Where the wrong lies, or where it commences, I know not. Certainly I nor any man can have a right to expect that the poor men who attended us should give up their time for nothing, or even to be angry with them for a sort of persecution, on the degree of which possibly might depend the comfort of their own families. Thoughts of famishing children at home leave little room for nice regards of delicacy abroad. The individuals, therefore, might or might not be blameable. But in any case the system is palpably wrong. The nation is entitled to a free enjoyment of its own public monuments: not free only in the sense of being gratuitous, but free also from the molestation of *showmen*, with their imperfect knowledge and their vulgar sentiment.

Yet, after all, what is this system of restriction and annoyance, compared with that which operates on the

[1] Already monuments had been voted by the House of Commons in this cathedral, and I am not sure but they were nearly completed, to two captains who had fallen at the Nile.

use of the national libraries; or *that*, again, to the system of exclusion from some of these, where an absolute interdict lies upon any use at all of that which is confessedly national property? Books and MSS., which were collected originally, and formally bequeathed to the public, under the generous and noble idea of giving to future generations advantages which the collector had himself not enjoyed, and liberating them from obstacles in the pursuit of knowledge which experience had bitterly imprinted upon his own mind, are at this day locked up as absolutely against me, you, or anybody, as collections confessedly private. Nay, far more so; for most private collectors of eminence (as the late Mr. Heber, for instance) have been distinguished for liberality in lending the rarest of their books to those who knew how to use them with effect. But, in the cases I now contemplate, the whole funds for supporting the proper offices attached to a library, such as librarians, sub-librarians, &c., which of themselves (and without the express verbal evidence of the founder's will) presume a *public* in the daily use of the books, else they are superfluous, have been applied to the creation of lazy sinecures in behalf of persons expressly charged with the care of shutting out the public. Therefore, it is true they are *not* sinecures: for that one care, vigilantly to keep out the public, they do take upon themselves; and why? A man loving books, like myself, might suppose that their motive was the ungenerous one of keeping the books to themselves. Far from it. In several instances, they will as little use the books as suffer them to be used. And thus the whole plans and cares of the good (weighing his motives, I will say of the *pious*) founder have terminated in locking up and sequestering a large collection of books, some being great rarities, in situations where they are not accessible. Had he bequeathed them to the cata-

combs of Paris or of Naples, he could not have better
provided for their virtual extinction. I ask, does no
action at common law lie against the promoters of
such enormous abuses? Oh, thou fervent reformer—
whose fatal tread he that puts his ear to the ground
may hear at a distance coming onwards upon *every*
road—if too surely thou wilt work for me and others
irreparable wrong and suffering, work also for us a
little good; this way turn the great hurricanes and
levanters of thy wrath; winnow me this chaff; and let
us enter at last the garners of pure wheat laid up in
elder days for our benefit, and which for two centuries
have been closed against our use!

London we left in haste, to keep an engagement of
some standing at the Earl Howe's, my friend's grandfather. This great admiral, who had filled so large a
station in the public eye, being the earliest among the
naval heroes of England in the first war of the Revolution, and the only one of noble birth, I should have
been delighted to see; St. Paul's, and its naval monuments to Captain Riou and Captain —— together with
its floating pageantries of conquered flags, having
awakened within me, in a form of peculiar solemnity,
those patriotic remembrances of past glories which all
boys feel so much more vividly than men can do, in
whom the sensibility to such impressions is blunted.
Lord Howe, however, I was not destined to see; he had
died about a year before. Another death there had
been, and very recently, in the family, and under circumstances peculiarly startling; and the spirits of the
whole house were painfully depressed by that event at
the time of our visit. One of the daughters, a younger
sister of my friend's mother, had been engaged for
some time to a Scottish nobleman, the Earl of Morton,
much esteemed by the Royal Family. The day was at
length fixed for the marriage; and about a fortnight

before that day arrived, some particular dress or ornament was brought to Porters, in which it was designed
that the bride should appear at the altar. The fashion
as to this point has often varied; but at that time I believe the custom was for bridal parties to be in full
dress. The lady, when the dress arrived, was, to all appearance, in good health; but, by one of those unaccountable misgivings which are on record in so many
well-attested cases (as that, for example, of Andrew
Marvell's father), she said, after gazing for a minute
or two at the beautiful dress, firmly and pointedly,
"So, then, *that* is my wedding-dress; and it is expected
that I shall wear it on the 17th; but I shall *not;* I
shall never wear it. On Thursday the 17th I shall be
dressed in a shroud!" All present were shocked at such
a declaration, which the solemnity of the lady's manner made it impossible to receive as a jest. The countess, her mother, even reproved her with some severity
for the words, as an expression of distrust in the goodness of God. The bride-elect made no answer, but by
sighing heavily. Within a fortnight all happened, to
the letter, as she had predicted. She was taken suddenly
ill; she died about three days before the marriage-
day; and was finally dressed in her shroud, according
to the natural course of the funeral arrangements, on
the morning that was to have been the wedding festival.

Lord Morton, the nobleman thus suddenly and
remarkably bereaved of his bride, was the only gentleman who appeared at the dinner table. He took a
particular interest in literature; and it was, in fact,
through *his* kindness that, for the first time in my life,
I found myself somewhat in the situation of a *"lion."*
The occasion of Lord Morton's flattering notice was
a particular copy of verses which had gained for me
a public distinction; not, however, I must own, a very

brilliant one; the prize awarded to me being not the
first, nor even the second—what on the Continent is
called the *accessit*—it was simply the third: and that
fact, stated nakedly, might have left it doubtful
whether I were to be considered in the light of one
honoured or of one stigmatized. However, the judges
in this case, with more honesty, or more self-distrust,
than belongs to most adjudications of the kind, had
printed the first three of the successful essays. Consequently, it was left open to each of the less successful
candidates to benefit by any difference of taste amongst
their several friends; and *my* friends in particular,
with the single and singular exception of my mother,
who always thought her own children inferior to other
people's, had generally assigned the palm to myself.
Lord Morton protested loudly that the case admitted
of no doubt; that gross injustice had been done me;
and, as the ladies of the family were much influenced
by his opinion, I thus came, not only to wear the laurel
in their estimation, but also with the advantageous
addition of having suffered some injustice. I was not
only a victor, but a victor in misfortune.

At this moment, looking back from a distance of
fifty years upon those trifles, it may well be supposed
that I do not attach so much importance to the subject
of my fugitive honours as to have any very decided
opinion one way or the other upon my own proportion
of merit. I do not even recollect the major part of the
verses: that which I *do* recollect inclines me to think
that, in the structure of the metre, and in the choice of
the expressions, I had some advantage over my competitors, though otherwise, perhaps, my verses were
less finished; Lord Morton might, therefore, in a partial sense, have been just as well as kind. But, little as
that may seem likely, even then, and at the moment
of reaping some advantage from my honours, which

gave me a consideration with the family I was amongst
such as I could not else have had, most unaffectedly I
doubted in my own mind whether I were really entitled to the praises which I received. My own verses
had not at all satisfied myself; and, though I felt elated
by the notice they had gained me, and gratified by the
generosity of the earl in taking my part so warmly, I
was so more in a spirit of sympathy with the kindness
thus manifested in my behalf, and with the consequent
kindness which it procured me from others, than from
any incitement or support which it gave to my intellectual pride. In fact, whatever estimate I might make
of those intellectual gifts which I believed or which I
knew myself to possess, I was inclined, even in those
days, to doubt whether my natural vocation lay towards
poetry. Well, indeed, I knew, and I know that, had I
chosen to enlist amongst the *soi-disant* poets of the
day—amongst those, I mean, who by mere force of
talent and mimetic skill contrive to sustain the part of
poet in a scenical sense, and with a scenical effect—I
also could have won such laurels as are won by such
merit; I also could have taken and sustained a place
taliter qualiter amongst the poets of the time. Why
not then? Simply because I knew that me, as them,
would await the certain destiny in reversion of resign-
ing that place in the next generation to some younger
candidate having equal or greater skill in appropriating the vague sentiments and old traditionary language of passion spread through books, but having also
the advantage of novelty, and of a closer adaptation
to the prevailing taste of the day. Even at that early
age I was keenly alive, if not so keenly as at this moment, to the fact that by far the larger proportion of
what is received in every age for poetry, and for a
season usurps that consecrated name, is *not* the spontaneous overflow of real unaffected passion, deep, and

at the same time original, and also forced into public manifestation of itself from the necessity which cleaves to all passion alike of seeking external sympathy: this it is *not;* but a counterfeit assumption of such passion, according to the more or less accurate skill of the writer in distinguishing the key of passion suited to the particular age; and a concurrent assumption of the language of passion according to his more or less skill in separating the spurious from the native and legitimate diction of genuine emotion. Rarely, indeed, are the reputed poets of any age men who groan, like prophets, under the burden of a message which they have to deliver, and *must* deliver, of a mission which they *must* discharge. Generally—nay, with much fewer exceptions, perhaps, than would be readily believed—they are merely simulators of the part they sustain; speaking not out of the abundance of their own hearts, but by skill and artifice assuming or personating emotions at second-hand; and the whole is a business of talent (sometimes even of great talent), but not of original power, of genius, or authentic inspiration.

From Porters, after a few days' visit, we returned to Eton. Her Majesty about this time gave some splendid fêtes at Frogmore, to one or two of which she had directed that we should be invited. The invitation was, of course, on my friend's account; but Her Majesty had condescended to direct that I, as his visitor, should be specially included. Lord Westport, young as he was, had become tolerably indifferent about such things; but to me such a scene was a novelty; and, on that account, it was settled we should go as early as was permissible. We *did* go: and I was not sorry to have had the gratification of witnessing (if it were but for once or twice) the splendours of a royal party. But, after the first edge of expectation was taken off, after the vague uncertainties of rustic ignorance had given place to absolute realities, and the eye had become a little familiar with the flashing of the jewellery, I began to suffer under the constraints incident to a young person in such a situation—the situation, namely, of sedentary passiveness, where one is acted upon, but does not act. The music, in fact, was all that continued to delight me; and, but for *that*, I believe I should have had some difficulty in avoiding so monstrous an indecorum as yawning. I revise this faulty expression, however, on the spot: not the music only it was, but the music combined with the dancing, that so deeply impressed me. The ball-room—a temporary erection, with something of the character of a pavilion about it—wore an elegant and festal air; the part allotted to the dancers being fenced off by a gilded lattice-work, and ornamented beautifully from the upper part with drooping festoons of flowers. But all the luxury that spoke to the eye merely faded at once by the side of impassioned dancing, sustained by impassioned music. Of all the scenes which this world offers, none is to me so profoundly interesting, none (I say it deliberately) so affecting, as the spectacle of men and women floating through the mazes of a dance; under these conditions, however, that the music shall be rich, resonant, and festal, the execution of the dancers perfect, and the dance itself of a character to admit of free, fluent, and *continuous* motion. But this last condition will be sought vainly in the quadrilles, &c., which have for so many years banished the truly beautiful *country-dances* native to England. Those whose taste and sensibility were so defective as to substitute for the *beautiful* in dancing the merely *difficult*, were sure, in the end, to transfer the depravations of this art from the opera-house to the floors of private ball-rooms. The tendencies even then were in that

direction: but as yet they had not attained their final
stage: and the English country-dance was still in estimation at the courts of princes. Now, of all dances,
this is the only one, as a class, of which you can truly
describe the motion to be *continuous*—that is, not
interrupted or fitful, but unfolding its fine mazes with
the equability of light in its diffusion through free
space. And wherever the music happens to be not of
a light, trivial character, but charged with the spirit
of festal pleasure, and the performers in the dance so
far skilful as to betray no awkwardness verging on the
ludicrous, I believe that many people feel as I feel in
such circumstances—viz., derive from the spectacle
the very grandest form of passionate sadness which can
belong to any spectacle whatsoever. *Sadness* is not the
exact word; nor is there *any* word in any language
(because none in the finest languages) which exactly
expresses the state; since it is not a depressing, but a
most elevating state to which I allude. And, certainly,
it is easy to understand, that many states of pleasure,
and in particular the highest, are the most of all removed from merriment. The day on which a Roman
triumphed was the most gladsome day of his existence;
it was the crown and consummation of his prosperity;
yet assuredly it was also to him the most solemn of his
days. Festal music, of a rich and passionate character,
is the most remote of any from vulgar hilarity. Its
very gladness and pomp is impregnated with sadness;
but sadness of a grand and aspiring order. Let, for instance (since without individual illustrations there is
the greatest risk of being misunderstood), any person
of musical sensibility listen to the exquisite music composed by Beethoven, as an opening for Bürger's *Lenore*,
the running idea of which is the triumphal return of
a crusading host, decorated with laurels and with
palms, within the gates of their native city; and then

say whether the presiding feeling, in the midst of this
tumultuous festivity, be not, by infinite degrees, transcendent to anything so vulgar as hilarity. In fact,
laughter itself is of all things the most equivocal—as
the organ of the ludicrous, laughter is allied to the
trivial and the mean; as the organ of joy, it is allied
to the passionate and the noble. From all which the
reader may comprehend, if he should not happen experimentally to have felt, that a spectacle of young
men and women *flowing* through the mazes of an intricate dance under a full volume of music, taken with
all the circumstantial adjuncts of such a scene in rich
men's halls—the blaze of lights and jewels, the life,
the motion, the sea-like undulation of heads, the inter-
weaving of the figures, the ανακυκλησις or self-revolv-
ing, both of the dance and the music, "never ending,
still beginning," and the continual regeneration of
order from a system of motions which for ever touch
the very brink of confusion—that such a spectacle,
with such circumstances, may happen to be capable
of exciting and sustaining the very grandest emotions
of philosophic melancholy to which the human spirit
is open. The reason is, in part, that such a scene presents a sort of mask of human life, with its whole
equipage of pomps and glories, its luxury of sight and
sound, its hours of golden youth, and the interminable
revolution of ages hurrying after ages, and one generation treading upon the flying footsteps of another;
whilst all the while the overruling music attempers
the mind to the spectacle, the subject to the object, the
beholder to the vision. And although this is known to
be but one phasis of life—of life culminating and in
ascent—yet the other (and repulsive) phasis is concealed upon the hidden or averted side of the golden
arras, known but not felt: or is seen but dimly in the

rear, crowding into indistinct proportions. The effect
of the music is to place the mind in a state of elective
attraction for everything in harmony with its own
prevailing key.

This pleasure, as always on similar occasions, I had
at present; but naturally in a degree corresponding to
the circumstances of *royal* splendour through which
the scene revolved; and, if I have spent rather more
words than should reasonably have been requisite in
describing any obvious state of emotion, it is not because, in itself, it is either vague or doubtful, but
because it is difficult, without calling upon a reader
for a little reflection, to convince him that there is not
something paradoxical in the assertion, that joy and
festal pleasure, of the highest kind, are liable to a
natural combination with solemnity, or even with
melancholy the most profound. Yet, to speak in the
mere simplicity of truth, so mysterious is human nature, and so little to be read by him who runs, that
almost every weighty aspect of truth upon that theme
will be found at first sight to be startling, or sometimes paradoxical. And so little need is there for chasing or courting paradox, that, on the contrary, he who
is faithful to his own experiences will find all his
efforts little enough to keep down the paradoxical air
besieging much of what he *knows* to be the truth. No
man needs to *search* for paradox in this world of ours.
Let him simply confine himself to the truth, and he
will find paradox growing everywhere under his hands
as rank as weeds. For new truths of importance are
rarely agreeable to any preconceived theories—that is,
cannot be explained by these theories; which are insufficient, therefore, even where they are true. And
universally it must be borne in mind—that not *that*
is paradox which, seeming to be true, is upon exami-

nation false, but that which, seeming to be false, may upon examination be found true.[1]

The pleasure of which I have been speaking belongs to all such scenes; but on this particular occasion there was also something more. To see persons in "the body" of whom you have been reading in newspapers from the very earliest of your reading days—those, who have hitherto been great *ideas* in your childish thoughts, to see and to hear moving and talking as carnal existences amongst other human beings—had, for the first half-hour or so, a singular and strange effect. But this naturally waned rapidly, after it had once begun to wane. And when these first startling impressions of novelty had worn off, it must be confessed that the peculiar circumstances attaching to a royal ball were not favourable to its joyousness or genial spirit of enjoyment. I am not going to repay Her Majesty's condescension so ill, or so much to abuse the privileges of a guest, as to draw upon my recollections of what passed for the materials of a cynical critique. Everything was done, I doubt not, which court etiquette permitted, to thaw those ungenial restraints which gave to the whole too much of a ceremonial and official character, and to each actor in the scene gave too much of the air belonging to one who is discharging a duty, and to the youngest even among the principal personages concerned gave an apparent anxiety and jealousy of manner—jealousy, I mean, not of others, but a prudential jealousy of his own possible oversights or trespasses.

[1] And therefore it was with strict propriety that Boyle, anxious to fix public attention upon some truths of hydrostatics, published them avowedly as *paradoxes*. According to the false popular notion of what it is that constitutes a paradox, Boyle should be taken to mean that these hydrostatic theorems were fallacies. But far from it. Boyle solicits attention to these propositions—not as seeming to be true and turning out false; but, reversely, as wearing an air of falsehood and turning out true.

In fact, a great personage bearing a state character
cannot be regarded, nor regard himself, with the perfect freedom which belongs to social intercourse; no,
nor ought to be. It is not rank alone which is here
concerned: that, as being his own, he might lay aside
for an hour or two; but he bears a representative character also. He has not his own rank only, but the rank
of others, to protect: he (supposing him the sovereign,
or a prince near to the succession) embodies and im-
personates the majesty of a great people; and this character, were you ever so much encouraged to do so, you,
the ἰδιώτης, the *lay* spectator or "assister," neither
could nor ought to dismiss from your thoughts. Besides
all which, it must be acknowledged, that to see brothers
dancing with sisters—as too often occurred in those
dances to which the princesses were parties—disturbed
the appropriate interest of the scene, being irreconcil-
able with the allusive meaning of dancing in general,
and laid a weight upon its gaiety which no condescensions from the highest quarter could remove. This
infelicitous arrangement forced the thoughts of all
present upon the exalted rank of the parties which
could dictate and exact so unusual an assortment. And
that rank, again, it presented to us under one of its
least happy aspects; as insulating a blooming young
woman amidst the choir of her co-evals, and surrounding her with dreadful solitude amidst a vast crowd of
the young, the brave, the beautiful, and the accomplished.

Meantime, as respected myself individually, I had
reason to be grateful: every kindness and attention
were shown to me. My invitation I was sensible that
I owed entirely to my noble friend. But, *having* been
invited, I felt assured, from what passed, that it was
meant and provided that I should not, by any possibility, be suffered to think myself overlooked. Lord

Westport and I communicated our thoughts occasionally by means of a language which we, in those days,
found useful enough at times, and which bore the
name of *Ziph*. The language and the name were both
derived (that is, were *immediately* so derived; for *remotely* the Ziph language may ascend to Nineveh)
from Winchester. Dr. Mapleton, a physician in Bath,
who attended me in concert with Mr. Grant, an eminent surgeon, during the nondescript malady of the
head, happened to have had three sons at Winchester;
and his reason for removing them is worth mentioning,
as it illustrates the well-known system of *fagging*.
One or more of them showed to the quick medical eye
of Dr. Mapleton symptoms of declining health; and,
upon cross-questioning, he found that, being (as juniors) *fags* (that is, bondsmen by old prescription) to
appointed seniors, they were under the necessity of
going out nightly into the town, for the purpose of
executing commissions; but this was not easy, as all
the regular outlets were closed at an early hour. In
such a dilemma, any route, that was barely practicable
at whatever risk, must be traversed by the loyal fag;
and it so happened that none of any kind remained
open or accessible, except one; and this one communication happened to have escaped suspicion, simply because it lay through a succession of temples and sewers
sacred to the goddesses Cloacina and Scavengerina.
That of itself was not so extraordinary a fact: the
wonder lay in the number—viz., seventeen. Such were
the actual amount of sacred edifices, which, through
all their dust, and garbage, and mephitic morasses,
these miserable vassals had to thread all *but* every
night of the week. Dr. Mapleton, when he had made
this discovery, ceased to wonder at the medical symptoms; and, as *faggery* was an abuse too venerable and
sacred to be touched by profane hands, he lodged no

idle complaints, but simply removed his sons to a
school where the Serbonian bogs of the subterraneous
goddess might not intersect the nocturnal line of march
so *very* often. One day, during the worst of my illness,
when the kind-hearted doctor was attempting to amuse
me with this anecdote, and asking me whether I
thought Hannibal would have attempted his march
over the Little St. Bernard, supposing that he and the
elephant which he rode had been summoned to explore
a route through seventeen similar nuisances, he went
on to mention the one sole accomplishment which his
sons had imported from Winchester. This was the
Ziph language, communicated at Winchester to any
aspirant for a fixed fee of one half-guinea, but which
the doctor then communicated to me—as I do now to
the reader—*gratis*. I make a present of this language
without fee, or price, or entrance-money, to my honoured reader; and let him understand that it is undoubtedly a bequest of elder times. Perhaps it may be
co-eval with the Pyramids. For in the famous *Essay
on a Philosophical Character* (I forget whether *that* is
the exact title), a large folio written by the ingenious
Dr. Wilkins, bishop of Chester, and published early in
the reign of Charles II, a folio which I, in youthful
days, not only read but studied, this language is recorded and accurately described amongst many other
modes of cryptical communication, oral and visual,
spoken, written, or symbolic. And, as the bishop does
not speak of it as at all a *recent* invention, it may probably at that time have been regarded as an antique device for conducting a conversation in secrecy amongst
bystanders; and this advantage it has, that it is applicable to all languages alike; nor can it possibly be
penetrated by one not initiated in the mystery. The
secret is this (and the grandeur of simplicity at any
rate it has)—repeat the vowel or diphthong of every

syllable, prefixing to the vowel so repeated the letter G. Thus, for example: Shall we go away in an hour? Three hours we have already stayed. This in Ziph becomes: *Shagall wege gogo agawaygay igin agan hougour? Threegee hougours wege hagave agalreageadygy stagayed.*[1] It must not be supposed that Ziph proceeds slowly. A very little practice gives the greatest fluency; so that even now, though certainly I cannot have practised it for fifty years, my power of speaking the Ziph remains unimpaired. I forget whether in the Bishop of Chester's account of this cryptical language the consonant intercalated be G or not. Evidently any consonant will answer the purpose. F or L would be softer, and so far better.

In this learned tongue it was that my friend and I communicated our feelings; and having stayed nearly four hours, a time quite sufficient to express a proper sense of the honour, we departed; and, on emerging into the open high-road, we threw up our hats and huzzaed, meaning no sort of disrespect, but from uncontrollable pleasure in recovered liberty.

Soon after this we left Eton for Ireland. Our first destination being Dublin, of course we went by Holyhead. The route at that time, from Southern England to Dublin, did not (as in elder and in later days) go round by Chester. A few miles after leaving Shrewsbury, somewhere about Oswestry, it entered North Wales; a stage farther brought us to the celebrated vale of Llangollen; and, on reaching the approach to this about sunset on a beautiful evening of June, I first found myself amongst the mountains; a feature

---

[1] One omission occurs to me on reviewing this account of the Ziph—which is, that I should have directed the accent to be placed on the intercalated syllable: thus *ship* becomes *shigip*, with the emphasis on *gip*; *run* becomes *rugún*, &c.

in natural scenery for which, from my earliest days, it was not extravagant to say that I had hungered and thirsted. In no one expectation of my life have I been less disappointed; and I may add, that no one enjoyment has less decayed or palled upon my continued experience. A mountainous region, with a slender population, and *that* of a simple pastoral character; behold my chief conditions of a pleasant permanent dwelling-place! But, thus far I have altered, that *now* I should greatly prefer forest scenery—such as the New Forest, or the Forest of Dean in Gloucestershire. The mountains of Wales range at about the same elevation as those of Northern England; three thousand and four to six hundred feet being the extreme limit which they reach. Generally speaking, their forms are less picturesque individually, and they are less happily grouped than their English brethren. I have since also been made sensible by Wordsworth of one grievous defect in the structure of the Welsh valleys; too generally they take the *basin* shape—the level area at their foot does not detach itself with sufficient precision from the declivities that surround them. Of this, however, I was not aware at the time of first seeing Wales; although the striking effect from the *opposite* form the Cumberland and Westmorland valleys, which almost universally present a flat area at the base of the surrounding hills, level, to use Wordsworth's expression, *"as the floor of a temple,"* would, at any rate, have arrested my eye, as a circumstance of impressive beauty, even though the want of such a feature might not, in any case, have affected me as a fault. As something that had a positive value, this characteristic of the Cumbrian valleys had fixed my attention, but not as any telling point of contrast against the Cambrian valleys. No faults, however, at that early age disturbed my pleasure, except that, after one whole day's travel-

ling (for so long it cost us between Llangollen and
Holyhead), the want of water struck me upon review
as painfully remarkable. From Conway to Bangor
(seventeen miles), we were often in sight of the sea;
but fresh water we had seen hardly any; no lake, no
stream much beyond a brook. This is certainly a conspicuous defect in North Wales, considered as a region
of fine scenery. The few lakes I have since become
acquainted with, as that near Bala, near Beddkelert,
and beyond Machynleth, are not attractive either in
their forms or in their accompaniments: the Bala Lake
being meagre and insipid: the others as it were unfinished, and unaccompanied with their furniture of
wood.

At the *Head* (to call it by its common colloquial
name) we were detained a few days in those unsteam-
ing times by foul winds. Our time, however, thanks
to the hospitality of a certain Captain Skinner on that
station, did not hang heavy on our hands, though we
were imprisoned, as it were, on a dull rock; for Holyhead itself is a little island of rock, an insulated dependency of Anglesea; which, again, is a little insulated dependency of North Wales. The packets on this
station were at that time lucrative commands; and
they were given to post-captains in the navy. Captain
Skinner was celebrated for his convivial talents; he
did the honours of the place in a hospitable style; daily
asked us to dine with him, and seemed as inexhaustible
in his wit as in his hospitality.

This answered one purpose, at least, of special convenience to our party at that moment: it kept us from
all necessity of meeting each other during the day,
except under circumstances where we escaped the necessity of any familiar communication. Why that
should have become desirable arose upon the following
mysterious change of relations between ourselves and

the Rev. Mr. Grace, Lord Westport's tutor. On the
last day of our journey, Mr. Grace, who had accompanied us thus far, but now at Holyhead was to leave
us, suddenly took offence (or, at least, then first
showed his offence) at something we had said, done,
or omitted, and never spoke one syllable to either of
us again. Being both of us amiably disposed, and incapable of having seriously meditated either word or
deed likely to wound any person's feelings, we were
much hurt at the time, and often retraced the little
incidents upon the road, to discover, if possible, what
it was that had laid us open to misconstruction. But
it remained to both of us a lasting mystery. This tutor
was an Irishman, of Trinity College, Dublin; and, I
believe, of considerable pretensions as a scholar; but,
being reserved and haughty, or else presuming in us
a knowledge of our offence, which we really had not,
he gave us no opening for any explanation. To the
last moment, however, he manifested a punctilious
regard to the duties of his charge. He accompanied us
in our boat, on a dark and gusty night, to the packet,
which lay a little out at sea. He saw us on board; and
then, standing up for one moment, he said, "Is all
right on deck?"—"All right, sir," sang out the ship's
steward.—"Have you, Lord Westport, got your boat-
cloak with you?"—"Yes, sir."—"Then pull away,
boatmen." We listened for a time to the measured beat
of his retreating oars, marvelling more and more at
the atrocious nature of our crime which could thus
avail to intercept even his last adieus. I, for my part,
never saw him again; nor, as I have reason to think,
did Lord Westport. Neither did we ever unravel the
mystery.

As if to irritate our curiosity still more, Lord Westport showed me a torn fragment of paper in his tutor's
handwriting, which, together with others, had been

thrown (as he believed) purposely in his way. If he
was right in that belief, it appeared that he had missed
the particular fragment which was designed to raise
the veil upon our guilt; for the one he produced contained exactly these words—"With respect to your
ladyship's anxiety to know how far the acquaintance
with Mr. de Q. is likely to be of service to your son, I
think I may now venture to say that——" There the
sibylline fragment ended; nor could we torture it
into any further revelation. However, both of us saw
the propriety of not ourselves practising any mystery,
nor giving any advantage to Mr. Grace by imperfect
communications; and accordingly, on the day after
we reached Dublin, we addressed a circumstantial account of our journey and our little mystery to Lady
Altamont in England; for to her it was clear that the
tutor had confided his mysterious wrongs. Her ladyship answered with kindness; but did not throw any
light on the problem which exercised at once our memories, our skill in conjectural interpretation, and our
sincere regrets. Lord Westport and I regretted much
that there had not been a wider margin attached to
the fragment of Mr. Grace's letter to Lady Altamont;
in which case, as I could readily have mimicked his
style of writing, it would have been easy for me to
fill up thus: "With respect to your ladyship's anxiety,
&c., I think I may now venture to say that, if the solar
system were searched, there could not be found a companion more serviceable to your son than Mr. de Q.
He speaks the Ziph most beautifully. He writes it, I
am told, classically. And if there were a Ziph nation
as well as a Ziph language, I am satisfied that he would
very soon be at the head of it; as he already is, beyond
all competition, at the head of the Ziph literature."
Lady Altamont, on receiving this, would infallibly
have supposed him mad; she would have written so to

all her Irish friends, and would have commended the
poor gentleman to the care of his nearest kinsmen;
and thus we should have had some little indemnification for the annoyance he had caused us. I mention this
trifle, simply because, trifle as it is, it involved a mystery, and furnishes an occasion for glancing at that
topic. Mysteries as deep, with results a little more
important and foundations a little sounder, have many
times crossed me in life; one, for instance, I recollect
at this moment, known pretty extensively to the neighbourhood in which it occurred. It was in the county of
S———. A lady married, and married well, as was
thought. About twelve months afterwards, she returned alone in a post-chaise to her father's house;
paid, and herself dismissed, the postilion at the gate;
entered the house; ascended to the room in which she
had passed her youth, and known in the family by her
name; took possession of it again; intimated by signs,
and by one short letter at her first arrival, what she
would require; lived for nearly twenty years in this
state of *La Trappe* seclusion and silence; nor ever, to
the hour of her death, explained what circumstances
had dissolved the supposed happy connexion she had
formed, or what had become of her husband. Her looks
and gestures were of a nature to repress all questions
in the spirit of mere curiosity; and the spirit of affection naturally respected a secret which was guarded
so severely. This might be supposed a Spanish tale;
yet in happened in England, and in a pretty populous
neighbourhood. The romances which occur in real
life are too often connected with circumstances of
criminality in some one among the parties concerned;
on that account, more than any other, they are often
suppressed; else, judging by the number which have
fallen within my own knowledge, they must be of
more frequent occurrence than is usually supposed.

Among such romances, those cases, perhaps, form an unusual proportion in which young, innocent, and high-minded persons have made a sudden discovery of some great profligacy or deep unworthiness in the person to whom they had surrendered their entire affections. That shock, more than any other, is capable of blighting, in our hour, the whole after existence, and sometimes of at once overthrowing the balance of life or of reason. Instances I have known of both; and such afflictions are the less open to any alleviation, that sometimes they are of a nature so delicate as to preclude all confidential communication of them to another; and sometimes it would be even dangerous, in a legal sense, to communicate them.

A sort of adventure occurred, and not of a kind pleasant to recall, even on this short voyage. The passage to Dublin from the Head is about sixty miles, I believe; yet, from baffling winds, it cost us upwards of thirty hours. On the second day, going upon deck, we found that our only fellow-passenger of note was a woman of rank, celebrated for her beauty; and not undeservedly; for a lovely creature she was. The body of her travelling coach had been, as usual, unslung from the "carriage" (by which is technically meant the wheels and the perch), and placed upon deck. This she used as a place of retreat from the sun during the day, and as a resting-place at night. For want of more interesting companions, she invited us, during the day, into her coach; and we taxed our abilities to make ourselves as entertaining as we could; for we were greatly fascinated by the lady's beauty. The second night proved very sultry; and Lord Westport and myself, suffering from the oppression of the cabir, left our berths, and lay, wrapped up in cloaks, upon deck. Having talked for some hours, we were both on the point of falling asleep, when a stealthy tread near our heads

awoke us. It was starlight; and we traced between
ourselves and the sky the outline of a man's figure.
Lying upon a mass of tarpaulins, we were ourselves
undistinguishable, and the figure moved in the direction of the coach. Our first thought was to raise an
alarm, scarcely doubting that the purpose of the man
was to rob the unprotected lady of her watch or purse.
But, to our astonishment, we saw the coach-door silently swing open under a touch from *within*. All was
as silent as a dream; the figure entered, the door closed,
and we were left to interpret the case as we might.
Strange it was that this lady could permit herself to
calculate upon absolute concealment in such circumstances. We recollected afterwards to have heard some
indistinct rumour buzzed about the packet on the day
preceding, that a gentleman, and some even spoke of
him by name as a Colonel ——, for some unknown
purpose, was concealed in the steerage of the packet.
And other appearances indicated that the affair was
not entirely a secret even amongst the lady's servants.
To both of *us* the story proclaimed a moral already
sufficiently current—viz., that women of the highest
and the very lowest rank are alike thrown too much
into situations of danger and temptation. I might mention some additional circumstances of criminal aggravation in this lady's case; but, as they would tend to
point out the real person to those acquainted with her
history, I shall forbear. She has since made a noise in
the world, and has maintained, I believe, a tolerably
fair reputation. Soon after sunrise the next morning,
a heavenly morning of June, we dropped our anchor
in the famous bay of Dublin. There was a dead calm:
the sea was like a lake; and, as we were some miles
from the Pigeon-House, a boat was manned to put us
on shore. The lovely lady, unaware that we were
parties to her guilty secret, went with us, accompanied

by her numerous attendants, and looking as beautiful,
and hardly less innocent than an angel. Long afterwards, Lord Westport and I met her, hanging upon
the arm of her husband, a manly and good-natured
man, of polished manners, to whom she introduced us:
for she voluntarily challenged us as her fellow-voy-
agers, and, I suppose, had no suspicion which pointed
in our direction. She even joined her husband in cordially pressing us to visit them at their magnificent
chateau. Upon us, meantime, whatever might be *her*
levity, the secret of which accident had put us in possession pressed with a weight of awe; we shuddered
at our own discovery; and we both agreed to drop no
hint of it in any direction.[1]

[1] Lord Westport's age at that time was the same as my own
—that is, we both wanted a few months of being fifteen. But
I had the advantage, perhaps, in thoughtfulness and observation of life. Being thoroughly free, however, from opinion-
ativeness, Lord Westport readily came over to any views of
mine for which I could show sufficient grounds. And on this
occasion I found no difficulty in convincing him—that honour
and fidelity did not form sufficient guarantees for the custody
of secrets. Presence of mind so as to revive one's obligations
in time, tenacity of recollection, and vigilance over one's own
momentary slips of tongue, so as to keep watch over indirect
disclosures, are also requisite. And at that time I had an instance within my own remembrance where a secret had been
betrayed by a person of undoubted honour, but most inad-
vertently betrayed, and in pure oblivion of his engagement to
silence. Indeed, unless where the secret is of a nature to affect
some person's life, I do not believe that most people would
remember beyond a period of two years the most solemn obligations to secrecy. After a lapse of time, varying of course
with the person, the substance of the secret will remain upon
the mind: but how he came by the secret, or under what circumstances, he will very probably have forgotten. It is unsafe
to rely upon the most religious or sacramental obligation to
secrecy, unless, together with the secret, you could transfer
also a magic ring that should, by a growing pressure or punc-
ture, *sting* a man into timely alarm and warning.

Landing about three miles from Dublin (according to my present remembrance, at Dunleary), we were not long in reaching Sackville Street.

DUBLIN

(First published in *Tait's Magazine*, April, 1834)

IN SACKVILLE STREET stood the town-house of Lord Altamont; and here, in the breakfast-room, we found the earl seated. Long and intimately as I had known Lord Westport, it so happened that I had never seen his father, who had, indeed, of late almost pledged himself to a continued residence in Ireland by his own patriotic earnestness as an agricultural improver; whilst for his son, under the difficulties and delays at that time of all travelling, any residence whatever in England seemed preferable, but especially a residence with his mother amongst the relatives of his distinguished English grandfather, and in such close neighbourhood to Eton. Lord Altamont once told me, that the journey outward and inward between Eton and Westport, taking into account all the unavoidable deviations from the direct route, in compliance with the claims of kinship, &c. (a case which in Ireland forced a traveller often into a perpetual zig-zag), counted up to something more than a thousand miles. That is, in effect, when valued in loss of time, and allowance being made for the want of *continuity* in those parts of the travelling system that did not accurately dovetail into each other, not less than one entire fortnight must be annually sunk upon a labour that yielded no commensurate fruit. Hence the long three-years interval which had separated father and son: and hence my own nervous apprehension, as we were rac-

ing through the suburbs of Dublin, that I should unavoidably lay a freezing restraint upon that re-union
to which, after such a separation, both father and son
must have looked forward with anticipation so anxious.
Such cases of unintentional intrusion are at times inevitable; but, even to the least sensitive, they are always distressing; most of all they are so to the intruder,
who in fact feels himself in the odd position of a criminal without a crime. He is in the situation of one who
might have happened to be chased by a Bengal tiger
(or, say that the tiger were a sheriff's-officer) into the
very centre of the Eleusinian mysteries. Do not tease
me, my reader, by alleging that there were no sheriff's-
officers at Athens or Eleusis. Not many, I admit: but
perhaps quite as many as there were of Bengal tigers.
In such a case, under whatever compulsion, the man
has violated a holy seclusion. He has seen that which
he ought *not* to have seen; and he is viewed with horror
by the privileged spectators. Should he plead that this
was his misfortune, and not his fault, the answer
would be—"True: it was your misfortune; we know
it; and it is *our* misfortune to be under the necessity
of hating you for it." But there was no cause for
similar fears at present: so uniformly considerate in
his kindness was Lord Altamont. It is true, that Lord
Westport, as an only child, and a child to be proud of
—for he was at that time rather handsome, and con-
ciliated general goodwill by his engaging manners—
was viewed by his father with an anxiety of love that
sometimes became almost painful to witness. But this
natural self-surrender to a first involuntary emotion
Lord Altamont did not suffer to usurp any such lengthened expression as might too painfully have reminded
me of being "one too many." One solitary half-minute
being paid down as a tribute to the sanctities of the
case, his next care was to withdraw me, the stranger,

from any oppressive feeling of strangership. And accordingly, so far from realizing the sense of being an
intruder, in one minute, under his courteous welcome,
I had come to feel that, as the companion of his one
darling upon earth, me also he comprehended within
his paternal regards.

It must have been nine o'clock precisely when we
entered the breakfast-room. So much I know by an
à priori argument, and could wish, therefore, that it
had been scientifically important to know it—as important, for instance, as to know the occultation of a
star or the transit of Venus to a second. For the urn
was at that moment placed on the table; and though
Ireland, as a whole, is privileged to be irregular, yet
such was our Sackville Street regularity, that not so
much nine o'clock announced this periodic event, as
inversely this event announced nine o'clock. And I
used to affirm, however shocking it might sound to
poor threadbare metaphysicians, incapable of transcendental truths, that not nine o'clock was the cause
of revealing the breakfast urn, but, on the contrary,
that the revelation of the breakfast urn was the true
and secret cause of nine o'clock—a phenomenon which
otherwise no candid reader will pretend that he can
satisfactorily account for, often as he has known it to
come round. The urn was already throwing up its column of fuming mist; and the breakfast-table was
covered with June flowers sent by a lady on the chance
of Lord Westport's arrival. It was clear, therefore, that
we were expected; but so we had been for three or
four days previously; and it illustrates the enormous
uncertainties of travelling at this closing era of the
eighteenth century, that for three or four days more
we should have been expected without the least anxiety,
in case anything had occurred to detain us on the road.
In fact, the possibility of a Holyhead packet being lost

had no place in the catalogue of adverse contingencies
—not even when calculated by mothers. To come by
way of Liverpool or Parkgate, was not without grounds
of reasonable fear: I myself had lost acquaintances
(schoolboys) on each of those lines of transit. Neither
Bristol nor Milford Haven was entirely cloudless in
reputation. But from Holyhead only one packet had
ever been lost; and that was in the days of Queen Anne,
when I have good reason to think that a villain was
on board who hated the Duke of Marlborough: so that
this one exceptional case, far from being looked upon
as a public calamity, would, of course, be received
thankfully, as cleansing the nation from a scamp.

   Ireland was still smoking with the embers of rebellion; and Lord Cornwallis, who had been sent expressly to extinguish it, and had won the reputation
of having fulfilled this mission with energy and success, was then the Lord-Lieutenant; and at that moment he was regarded with more interest than any
other public man. Accordingly I was not sorry when,
two mornings after our arrival, Lord Altamont said
to us at breakfast, "Now, if you wish to see what I call
a great man, go with me this morning, and you shall
see Lord Cornwallis; for that man who has given peace
both to the East and to the West—taming a tiger in
the Mysore that hated England as much as Hannibal
hated Rome, and in Ireland pulling up by the roots a
French invasion, combined with an Irish insurrection
—will always for me rank as a great man." We willingly accompanied the earl to the Phœnix Park, where
the Lord-Lieutenant was then residing, and were
privately presented to him. I had seen an engraving
(celebrated, I believe, in its day) of Lord Cornwallis
receiving the young Mysore princes as hostages at
Seringapatam; and I knew the outline of his public
services. This gave me an additional interest in seeing

him: but I was disappointed to find no traces in his manner of the energy and activity I presumed him to possess; he seemed, on the contrary, slow or even heavy, but benevolent and considerate in a degree which won the confidence at once. Him we saw often; for Lord Altamont took us with him wherever and whenever we wished; and me in particular (to whom the Irish leaders of society were as yet entirely unknown by sight) it gratified highly to see persons of historical names—names, I mean, historically connected with the great events of Elizabeth's or Cromwell's era— attending at the Phœnix Park. But the persons whom I remember most distinctly of all whom I was then in the habit of seeing, were Lord Clare, the Chancellor, the late Lord Londonderry (then Castlereagh), at that time the Irish Chancellor of the Exchequer, and the Speaker of the House of Commons (Mr. Foster, since, I believe, created Lord Oriel). With the Speaker, indeed, Lord Altamont had more intimate grounds of connexion than with any other public man; both being devoted to the encouragement and personal superintendence of great agricultural improvements. Both were bent on introducing, through models diffused extensively on their own estates, English husbandry, English improved breeds of cattle, and, where *that* was possible, English capital and skill, into the rural economy of Ireland.

Amongst the splendid spectacles which I witnessed, as the *most* splendid I may mention an Installation of the Knights of St. Patrick. There were six knights installed on this occasion, one of the six being Lord Altamont. He had, no doubt, received his riband as a reward for his parliamentary votes, and especially in the matter of the Union; yet, from all his conversation upon that question, and from the general conscientiousness of his private life, I am convinced that he

acted all along upon patriotic motives, and in obedience to his real views (whether right or wrong) of
the Irish interests. One chief reason, indeed, which
detained us in Dublin, was the necessity of staying for
this particular Installation. At one time, Lord Altamont had designed to take his son and myself for the
two esquires who attend the new-made knight, according to the ritual of this ceremony; but that plan was
laid aside, on learning that the other five knights were
to be attended by adults; and thus, from being par-
takers as actors, my friend and I became simple spectators of this splendid scene, which took place in the
Cathedral of St. Patrick. So easily does mere external
pomp slip out of the memory, as to all its circumstantial items, leaving behind nothing beyond the general
impression, that at this moment I remember no one
incident of the whole ceremonial, except that some
foolish person laughed aloud as the knights went up
with their offerings to the altar; the object of this unfeeling laughter being apparently Lord Altamont,
who happened to be lame—a singular instance of levity to exhibit within the walls of such a building, and
at the most solemn part of such a ceremony, which to
my mind had a threefold grandeur: first, as *symbolic*
and shadowy; secondly, as representing the interlac-
ings of chivalry with religion in the highest aspirations
of both; thirdly, as *national*—placing the heraldries
and military pomps of a people, so memorably faithful to St. Peter's chair, at the foot of the altar. Lord
Westport and I sat with Lord and Lady Castlereagh.
They were both young at this time, and both wore an
impressive appearance of youthful happiness; neither,
happily for their peace of mind, able to pierce that
cloud of years, not much more than twenty, which
divided them from the day destined in one hour to
wreck the happiness of both. We had met both on other

occasions; and their conversation, through the course
of that day's pomps, was the most interesting circumstance to me, and the one which I remember with
most distinctness of all that belonged to the Installation. By the way, one morning, on occasion of some
conversation arising about Irish bulls, I made an
agreement with Lord Altamont to note down in a
memorandum-book everything throughout my stay
in Ireland which, to my feeling as an Englishman,
should seem to be, or should approach to, a bull. And
this day, at dinner, I reported from Lady Castlereagh's
conversation what struck me as such. Lord Altamont
laughed, and said, "My dear child, I am sorry that it
should so happen, for it is bad to stumble at the beginning: your bull is certainly a bull [1]; but *as* certainly
Lady Castlereagh is your countrywoman, and not an
Irishwoman at all." Lady Castlereagh, it seems, was a
daughter of Lord Buckinghamshire; and her maiden
name was Lady Emily Hobart.

One other public scene there was about this time in
Dublin, to the eye less captivating, but far more so in
a moral sense; more significant practically, more burdened with hope and with fear. This was the final

[1] The idea of a *bull* is even yet undefined; which is most
extraordinary, considering that Miss Edgeworth has applied
all her tact and illustrative power to furnish the *matter* for
such a definition; and Coleridge all his philosophic subtlety
(but in this instance, I think, with a most infelicitous result)
to furnish its *form*. But both have been too fastidious in their
admission of bulls. Thus, for example, Miss Edgeworth re-
jects, as no true bull, the common Joe Miller story, that, upon
two Irishmen reaching Barnet, and being told that it was still
twelve miles to London, one of them remarked, "Ah! just six
miles *apace*." This, says Miss E., is no bull, but a sentimental
remark on the maxim that friendship divides our pains. Nothing of the kind: Miss Edgeworth cannot have understood it.
The bull is a true representative and exemplary specimen of
the *genus*.

ratification of the bill which united Ireland to Great Britain. I do not know that any one public act, or celebration, or solemnity, in my time, did, or could, so much engage my profoundest sympathies. Wordsworth's fine sonnet on the extinction of the Venetian Republic had not then been published, else the last two lines would have expressed my feelings. After admitting that changes had taken place in Venice which in a manner challenged and presumed this last and mortal change, the poet goes on to say that all this long preparation for the event could not break the shock of it. Venice, it is true, had become a shade; but, after all,

> *Men are we, and must grieve when even the shade*
> *Of that which once was great has pass'd away.*

But here the previous circumstances were far different from those of Venice. *There* we saw a superannuated and paralytic state, sinking at any rate into the grave, and yielding, to the touch of military violence, that only which a brief lapse of years must otherwise have yielded to internal decay. *Here,* on the contrary, we saw a young eagle, rising into power, and robbed prematurely of her natural honours, only because she did not comprehend their value, or because at this great crisis she had no champion. Ireland, in a political sense, was surely then in her youth, considering the prodigious developments she has since experienced in population, and in resources of all kinds.

This great day of UNION had been long looked forward to by me: with some mixed feelings also by my young friend, for he had an Irish heart, and was jealous of whatever appeared to touch the banner of Ireland. But it was not for him to say anything which should seem to impeach his father's patriotism in voting for the Union, and promoting it through his bor-

ough influence. Yet oftentimes it seemed to me, when
I introduced the subject, and sought to learn from Lord
Altamont the main grounds which had reconciled him
and other men, anxious for the welfare of Ireland, to
a measure which at least robbed her of some splendour,
and, above all, robbed her of a name and place amongst
the independent states of Europe—that neither father
nor son was likely to be displeased should some great
popular violence put force upon the recorded will of
Parliament, and compel the two Houses to perpetuate
themselves. Dolorous they must of course have looked,
in mere consistency; but I fancied that internally they
would have laughed.

Lord Westport and I were determined to lose no
part of the scene, and we went down with Lord Altamont to the House. It was about the middle of the day,
and a great mob filled the whole space about the two
Houses. As Lord Altamont's coach drew up to the steps
of that splendid edifice, we heard a prodigious hissing
and hooting; and I was really agitated to think that
Lord Altamont, whom I loved and respected, would
probably have to make his way through a tempest of
public wrath—a situation more terrific to him than to
others, from his embarrassed walking. I found, however, that I might have spared my anxiety; the subject
of commotion was, simply, that Major Sirr, or Major
Swan, I forget which (both being so celebrated in those
days for their energy as leaders of the police), had
detected a person in the act of mistaking some other
man's pocket-handkerchief for his own—a most natural mistake, I should fancy, where people stood
crowded together so thickly. No storm of any kind
awaited us, and yet at that moment there was no other
arrival to divide the public attention; for, in order that
we might see everything from first to last, we were
amongst the very earliest parties. Neither did our party

escape under any mistake of the crowd: silence had
succeeded to the uproar caused by the tender meeting
between the thief and the major; and a man, who stood
in a conspicuous situation, proclaimd aloud to those
below him the name or title of members as they drove
up. "That," said he, "is the Earl of Altamont; the
lame gentleman, I mean." Perhaps, however, his
knowledge did not extend so far as to the politics of a
nobleman who had taken no violent or factious part in
public affairs. At least the dreaded insults did not follow, or only in the very feeblest manifestations. We
entered; and, by way of seeing everything, we went
even to the robing-room. The man who presented his
robes to Lord Altamont seemed to me, of all whom I
saw on that day, the one who wore the face of deepest
depression. But, whether this indicated the loss of a
lucrative situation, or was really disinterested sorrow,
growing out of a patriotic trouble at the knowledge
that he was now officiating for the last time, I could
not guess. The House of Lords, decorated (if I remember) with hangings representing the battle of the
Boyne, was nearly empty when we entered—an accident which furnished to Lord Altamont the opportunity required for explaining to us the whole course
and ceremonial of public business on ordinary occasions.

Gradually the House filled: beautiful women sat
intermingled amongst the peers; and, in one party of
these, surrounded by a bevy of admirers, we saw our
fair but frail enchantress of the packet. She, on her
part, saw and recognized us by an affable nod; no stain
upon her cheek, indicating that she suspected to what
extent she was indebted to our discretion; for it is a
'roof of the unaffected sorrow and the solemn awe
which oppressed us both, that we had not mentioned,
even to Lord Altamont, nor ever *did* mention, the scene

which chance had revealed to us. Next came a stir
within the house, and an uproar resounding from without, which announced the arrival of his Excellency.
Entering the house, he also, like the other peers,
wheeled round to the throne, and made to that mysterious seat a profound homage. Then commenced the
public business, in which, if I recollect, the Chancellor
played the most conspicuous part—that Chancellor
(Lord Clare) of whom it was affirmed in those days,
by a political opponent, that he might swim in the
innocent blood which he had caused to be shed. But
nautical men, I suspect, would have demurred to that
estimate. Then were summoned to the bar—summoned
for the last time—the gentlemen of the House of Commons; in the van of whom, and drawing all eyes upon
himself, stood Lord Castlereagh. Then came the recitation of many acts passed during the session, and the
sounding ratification, the jovian

Annuit et nutu totum tremefecit Olympum,

contained in the *Soit fait comme il est desiré*, or the
more peremptory *Le Roi le veut.* At which point in
the order of succession came the royal assent to the
Union Bill, I cannot distinctly recollect. But one thing
I *do* recollect—that no audible expression, no buzz,
nor murmur, nor *susurrus* even, testified the feelings
which, doubtless, lay rankling in many bosoms. Setting apart all public or patriotic considerations, even
then I said to myself, as I surveyed the whole assem-
blage of ermined peers, "How is it, and by what unaccountable magic, that William Pitt can have prevailed on all these hereditary legislators and heads of
patrician houses to renounce so easily, with nothing
worth the name of a struggle, and no reward worth
the name of an indemnification, the very brightest

jewel in their coronets? This morning they all rose from their couches Peers of Parliament, individual pillars of the realm, indispensable parties to every law that could pass. Tomorrow they will be nobody—men of straw—*terræ filii*. What madness has persuaded them to part with their birthright, and to cashier themselves and their children for ever into mere titular Lords?"

As to the Commoners at the bar, *their* case was different: they had no life estate at all events in their honours; and they might have the same chance for entering the Imperial Parliament amongst the hundred Irish members, as for re-entering a native Parliament. Neither, again, amongst the peers was the case always equal. Several of the higher had English titles, which would, at any rate, open the central Parliament to their ambition. That privilege, in particular, attached to Lord Altamont. And he, in any case, from his large property, was tolerably sure of finding his way thither (as in fact for the rest of his life he *did*) amongst the twenty-eight Representative Peers. The wonder was in the case of petty and obscure lords, who had no weight personally, and none in right of their estates. Of these men, as they were notoriously not enriched by Mr. Pitt, as the distribution of honours was not very large, and as no honour could countervail the one they lost—I could not, and cannot, fathom the policy. Thus much I am sure of—that, had such a measure been proposed by a political speculator previously to Queen Anne's reign, he would have been scouted as a dreamer and a visionary, who calculated upon men being generally somewhat worse than Esau—viz., giving up their birthrights, and *without* the mess of pottage. However, on this memorable day, thus it was the Union was ratified; the bill received the royal assent without a muttering, or a whispering, or the protest-

ing echo of a sigh. Perhaps there might be a little
pause—a silence like that which follows an earthquake; but there was no plain-spoken Lord Belhaven,
as on the corresponding occasion in Edinburgh, to fill
up the silence with, "So, there's an end of an auld
sang!" All was or looked courtly, and free from vulgar
emotion. One person only I remarked whose features
were suddenly illuminated by a smile, a sarcastic smile,
as I read it; which, however, might be all a fancy. It
was Lord Castlereagh; who, at the moment when the
irrevocable words were pronounced, looked with a
penetrating glance amongst a party of ladies. His own
wife was one of that party; but I did not discover the
particular object on whom his smile had settled. After
this I had no leisure to be interested in anything which
followed. "You are all," thought I to myself, "a pack
of vagabonds henceforward, and interlopers, with actually no more right to be here than myself. I am an
intruder; so are you." Apparently they thought so
themselves; for, soon after this solemn *fiat* of Jove had
gone forth, their lordships, having no farther title to
their robes (for which I could not help wishing that
a party of Jewish old-clothesmen would at this moment have appeared and made a loud bidding), made
what haste they could to lay them aside for ever. The
House dispersed much more rapidly than it had assembled. Major Sirr was found outside, just where we left
him, laying down the law (as before) about pocket-
handkerchiefs to old and young practitioners; and all
parties adjourned to find what consolation they might
in the great evening event of dinner.

Thus we were set at liberty from Dublin. Parlia-
ments, and installations, and masked balls, with all
other secondary splendours in celebration of primary
splendours, reflex glories that reverberated original
glories, at length had ceased to shine upon the Irish

metropolis. The "season," as it is called in great cities, was over; unfortunately the last season that was ever destined to illuminate the society or to stimulate the domestic trade of Dublin. It began to be thought scandalous to be found in town: *nobody*, in fact, remained, except some two hundred thousand people, who never did, nor ever would, wear ermine; and in all Ireland there remained nothing at all to attract, except *that* which no king, and no two Houses, can by any conspiracy abolish—viz., the beauty of her most verdant scenery. I speak of that part which chiefly it is that I know—the scenery of the west—Connaught beyond other provinces, and, in Connaught, Mayo beyond other counties. There it was, and in the county next adjoining, that Lord Altamont's large estates were situated; the family mansion and beautiful park being in Mayo. Thither, as nothing else now remained to divert us from what, in fact, we had thirsted for throughout the heats of summer, and throughout the magnificences of the capital, at length we set off by movements as slow and circuitous as those of any royal *progress* in the reign of Elizabeth. Making but short journeys on each day, and resting always at the house of some private friend, I thus obtained an opportunity of seeing the old Irish nobility and gentry more extensively, and on a more intimate footing, than I had hoped for. No experience of this kind, throughout my whole life, so much interested me. In a little work, not much known, of Suetonius, the most interesting record which survives of the early Roman literature, it comes out incidentally that many books, many idioms, and verbal peculiarities belonging to the primitive ages of Roman culture, were to be found still lingering in the old Roman settlements, both Gaulish and Spanish, long after they had become obsolete (and sometimes unintelligible) in Rome. From the tardiness and the difficulty of communication, the want of newspapers, &c., it followed, naturally enough, that the distant provincial towns, though not without their own separate literature and their own literary professors, were always two or three generations in the rear of the metropolis; and thus it happened that, about the time of Augustus, there were some grammatici in Rome, answering to our black-letter critics, who sought the material of their researches in Boulogne (*Gessoriacum*), in Arles (*Arelata*), or in Marseilles (*Massilia*). Now, the old Irish nobility—that part, I mean, which might be called the rural nobility—stood in the same relation to English manners and customs. Here might be found old rambling houses, in the style of antique English manorial chateaux, ill planned, perhaps, as regarded convenience and economy, with long rambling galleries, and windows innumerable, that evidently had never looked for that severe audit to which they were afterwards summoned by William Pitt; but displaying, in the dwelling-rooms, a comfort and "cosiness," combined with magnificence, not always so effectually attained in modern times. Here were old libraries, old butlers, and old customs, that seemed all alike to belong to the era of Cromwell, or even an earlier era than his; whilst the ancient names, to one who had some acquaintance with the great events of Irish history, often strengthened the illusion. Not that I could pretend to be familiar with Irish history *as* Irish; but, as a conspicuous chapter in the difficult policy of Queen Elizabeth, of Charles I., and of Cromwell, nobody who had read the English history could be a stranger to the O'Neils, the O'Donnells, the Ormonds (*i.e.*, the Butlers), the Inchiquins, or the De Burghs, and many scores beside. I soon found, in fact, that the aristocracy of Ireland might be divided into two great sections: the native Irish—territorial fix-tures, so powerfully described by Maturin; and those, on the other hand, who spent so much of their time and revenues at Bath, Cheltenham, Weymouth, London, &c., as to have become almost entirely English. It was the former whom we chiefly visited; and I remarked that, in the midst of hospitality the most unbounded, and the amplest comfort, some of these were conspicuously in the rear of the English commercial gentry, as to modern refinements of luxury. There was at the same time an apparent strength of character, as if formed amidst turbulent scenes, and a raciness of manner, which were fitted to interest a stranger profoundly, and to impress themselves on his recollection.

TRAVELLING IN ENGLAND IN THE OLD DAYS

(First published in *Tait's Magazine*, December, 1834)

IT WAS late in October, or early in November, that I quitted Connaught with Lord Westport; and very slowly, making many leisurely deviations from the direct route, travelled back to Dublin. Thence, after some little stay, we recrossed St. George's Channel; landed at Holyhead; and then, by exactly the same route as we had pursued in early June, we posted through Bangor, Conway, Llanrwst, Llangollen, until once again we found ourselves in England; and, as a matter of course, making for Birmingham. But why making for Birmingham? Simply because Birmingham, under the old dynasty of stage-coaches and post-chaises, was the centre of our travelling system, and held in England something of that rank which the golden milestone of Rome held in the Italian peninsula.

At Birmingham it was (which I, like myriads beside, had traversed a score of times, without ever yet

having visited it as a *terminus ad quem*) that I parted
with my friend Lord Westport. *His* route lay through
Oxford; and stopping, therefore, no longer than was
necessary to harness fresh horses—an operation, however, which was seldom accomplished in less than
half-an-hour at that era—he went on directly to Strat-
ford. My own destination was yet doubtful. I had been
directed, in Dublin, to inquire at the Birmingham
Post-office for a letter which would guide my motions.
There, accordingly, upon sending for it, lay the expected letter from my mother; from which I learned
that my sister was visiting at Laxton, in Northamptonshire, the seat of an old friend, to which I also had an
invitation. My route to this lay through Stamford.
Thither I could not go by a stage-coach until the following day; and of necessity I prepared to make the
most of my present day in gloomy, noisy, and, at that
time, dirty Birmingham.

Being left therefore alone for the whole of a rainy
day in Birmingham, and Birmingham being as yet
the centre of our travelling system, I cannot do better
than spend my Birmingham day in reviewing the most
lively of its reminiscences.

The revolution in the whole apparatus, means,
machinery, and dependencies of that system—a revolution begun, carried through, and perfected within
the period of my own personal experience—merits a
word or two of illustration in the most cursory memoirs that profess any attention at all to the shifting
scenery and moving forces of the age, whether manifested in great effects or in little. And these particular
effects, though little when regarded in their separate
details, are *not* little in their final amount. On the contrary, I have always maintained, that under a representative government, where the great cities of the

empire must naturally have the power, each in its proportion, of reacting upon the capital and the councils of the nation in so conspicuous a way, there is a result waiting on the final improvements of the arts of travelling, and of transmitting intelligence with velocity, such as cannot be properly appreciated in the absence of all historical experience. Conceive a state of communication between the centre and the extremities of a great people, kept up with a uniformity of reciprocation so exquisite, as to imitate the flowing and ebbing of the sea, or the systole and diastole of the human heart; day and night, waking and sleeping, not succeeding to each other with more absolute certainty than the acts of the metropolis and the controlling notice of the provinces, whether in the way of support or of resistance. Action and reaction from every point of the compass being thus perfect and instantaneous, we should then first begin to understand, in a practical sense, what is meant by the unity of a political body, and we should approach to a more adequate appreciation of the powers which are latent in organization. For it must be considered that hitherto, under the most complex organization, and that which has best attained its purposes, the national will has never been able to express itself upon one in a thousand of the public acts, simply because the national voice was lost in the distance, and could not collect itself through the time and the space rapidly enough to connect itself immediately with the evanescent measure of the moment. But, as the system of intercourse is gradually expanding, these bars of space and time are in the same degree contracting, until finally we may expect them altogether to vanish: and then every part of the empire will react upon the whole with the power, life, and effect of immediate conference amongst parties brought face to face. Then first will be seen a political system truly *organic*—*i.e.*, in which each acts upon all, and all react upon each: and a new earth will arise from the indirect agency of this merely physical revolution. Already, in this paragraph, written twenty years ago, a prefiguring instinct spoke within me of some great secret yet to come in the art of distant communication. At present I am content to regard the electric telegraph as the oracular response to that prefiguration. But I still look for some higher and transcendent response.

The reader whose birth attaches him to this present generation, having known only macadamized roads, cannot easily bring before his imagination the antique and almost aboriginal state of things which marked our travelling system down to the end of the eighteenth century, and nearly through the first decennium of the present. A very few lines will suffice for some broad notices of our condition, in this respect, through the last two centuries. In the Parliamentary War (1642–46), it is an interesting fact, but at the same time calculated to mislead the incautious reader, that some officers of distinction, on both sides, brought close carriages to head-quarters; and sometimes they went even upon the field of battle in these carriages, not mounting on horseback until the preparations were beginning for some important manœuvre, or for a general movement. The same thing had been done throughout the Thirty Years' War, both by the Bavarian, Imperial, and afterwards by the Swedish officers of rank. And it marks the great diffusion of these luxuries about this era, that, on occasion of the re-instalment of two princes of Mecklenburg, who had been violently dispossessed by Wallenstein, upwards of eighty coaches mustered at a short notice, partly from the territorial nobility, partly from the camp. Precisely, however, at military head-quarters, and on the route of an army, carriages of this description were an available and a most useful means of transport. Cumbrous and unwieldy they were, as we know by pictures, and they could not have been otherwise, for they were built to meet the roads. Carriages of our present light and *reedy* (almost, one might say, *corky*) construction would, on the roads of Germany or of England in that age, have foundered within the first two hours. To our ancestors, such carriages would have seemed playthings for children. Cumbrous as the carriages of that day were, they could not be more so than artillery or baggage waggons : where these could go, coaches could go. So that, in the march of an army, there was a perpetual guarantee to those who had coaches for the possibility of their transit. And hence, and not because the roads were at all better than they have been generally described in those days, we are to explain the fact, that both in the royal camp, in Lord Manchester's, and afterwards in General Fairfax's and Cromwell's, coaches were an ordinary part of the camp equipage. The roads, meantime, were as they have been described —viz., ditches, morasses, and sometimes channels for the course of small brooks. Nor did they improve, except for short reaches, and under peculiar local advantages, throughout that century.

Spite of the roads, however, public carriages began to pierce England, in various lines, from the era of 1660. Circumstantial notices of these may be found in Lord Auckland's (Sir Frederick Eden's) large work on the Poor-Laws. That to York, for example (two hundred miles), took a fortnight in the journey, or about fourteen miles a-day. But Chamberlayne, who had a personal knowledge of these public carriages, says enough to show that, if slow, they were cheap; half-a-crown being the usual rate for fifteen miles (*i.e.*, 2d. a mile). Public conveyances, multiplying rapidly, could not but diffuse a general call for improved roads; improved both in dimensions and also in the art of construction. For it is observable that, so early as Queen Elizabeth's days, England, the most equestrian of nations, already presented to its inhabitants a general system of decent bridle-roads. Even at this day, it is doubtful whether any man, taking all hindrances into account, and having laid no previous relays of horses, could much exceed the exploit of [Sir Robert] Cary (afterwards Lord Monmouth), a younger son of the first Lord Hunsden, a cousin of Queen Elizabeth. Yet we must not forget that the particular road concerned in this exploit was the Great North Road (as it is still called by way of distinction), lying through Doncaster and York, between the northern and southern capitals of the island. But roads less frequented were tolerable as bridle-roads; whilst all alike, having been originally laid down with no view to the broad and ample coaches, from 1570 to 1700, scratched the panels on each side as they crept along. Even in the nineteenth century, I have known a case in the sequestered district of Egremont in Cumberland, where a post-chaise, of the common narrow dimensions, was obliged to retrace its route of fourteen miles on coming to a bridge built in some remote age, when as yet post-chaises were neither known nor anticipated, and, unfortunately, too narrow by three or four inches.

In all the provinces of England, when the soil was deep and adhesive, a worse evil beset the stately equipage. An Italian of rank, who has left a record of his perilous adventure, visited, or attempted to visit, Petworth, near London (then a seat of the Percys, now of Lord Egremont), about the year 1685. I forget how many times he was overturned within one particular stretch of five miles; but I remember that it was a subject of gratitude (and, upon meditating a return

by the same route, a subject of pleasing hope) to dwell
upon the soft lying which was to be found in that good-
natured morass. Yet this was, doubtless, a pet road
(sinful punster! dream not that I glance at *Pet*worth),
and an improved road. Such as this, I have good reason
to think, were most of the roads in England, unless
upon the rocky strata which stretch northwards from
Derbyshire to Cumberland and Northumberland. The
public carriages were the first harbingers of a change
for the better; as these grew and prospered, slender
lines of improvement began to vein and streak the
map. And Parliament began to show their zeal, though
not always a corresponding knowledge, by legislating
backwards and forwards on the breadth of waggon
wheel-tires, etc. But not until our cotton system began
to put forth blossoms, not until our trade and our
steam-engines began to stimulate the coal mines,
which in *their* turn stimulated *them*, did any great
energy apply itself to our roads.

In my childhood, standing with one or two of my
brothers and sisters at the front windows of my
mother's carriage, I remember one unvarying set of
images before us. The postilion (for so were all carriages then driven) was employed not by fits and starts,
but always and eternally, in *quartering*—*i.e.*, in crossing from side to side—according to the casualties of
the ground. Before you stretched a wintry length of
lane, with ruts deep enough to fracture the leg of a
horse, filled to the brim with standing pools of rain
water; and the collateral chambers of these ruts kept
from becoming confluent by thin ridges, such as the
Romans called *liræ*, to maintain the footing upon
which *liræ*, so as not to swerve (or, as the Romans
would say, *delirare*), was a trial of some skill both for
the horses and their postilion. It was, indeed, next to
impossible for any horse, on such a narrow crust of

separation, not to grow *delirious* in the Roman meta-
phor; and the nervous anxiety which haunted me
when a child was much fed by this very image so often
before my eye, and the sympathy with which I followed the motion of the docile creature's legs. Go to
sleep at the beginning of a stage, and the last thing
you saw——wake up, and the first thing you saw——was
the line of wintry pools, the poor off-horse planting
his steps with care, and the cautious postilion gently
applying his spur, whilst manœuvring across this system of grooves with some sort of science that looked
like a gipsy's palmistry; so equally unintelligible to
me were his motions, in what he sought and in what
he avoided.

Whilst reverting to these remembrances of my childhood, I may add, by way of illustration, and at the
risk of gossiping, which, after all, is not the worst of
things, a brief notice of my very first journey. I might
be then seven years old. A young gentleman, the son of
a wealthy banker, had to return home for the Christmas holidays to a town in Lincolnshire, distant from
the public school where he was pursuing his education
about a hundred miles. The school was in the neighbourhood of Greenhay, my father's house. There were
at that time no coaches in that direction; now (1833)
there are many every day. The young gentleman advertised for a person to share the expense of a post-
chaise. By accident, I had an invitation of some standing to the same town, where I happened to have some
female relatives of mature age, besides some youthful
cousins. The two travellers elect soon heard of each
other, and the arrangement was easily completed. It
was my earliest migration from the paternal roof; and
the anxieties of pleasure, too tumultuous, with some
slight sense of undefined fears, combined to agitate
my childish feelings. I had a vague slight apprehen-

sion of my fellow-traveller, whom I had **never** seen,
and whom my nursery-maid, when dressing me, had
described in no very amiable colours. But a good deal
more I thought of Sherwood Forest (the forest of
Robin Hood), which, as I had been told, we should
cross after the night set in. At six o'clock I descended,
and not, as usual, to the children's room, but, on this
special morning of my life, to a room called the breakfast-room; where I found a blazing fire, candles
lighted, and the whole breakfast equipage, as if for
my mother, set out, to my astonishment, for no greater
personage than myself. The scene being in England,
and on a December morning, I need scarcely say that
it rained; the rain beat violently against the windows;
the wind raved; and an aged servant, who did the
honours of the breakfast-table, pressed me urgently to
eat. I need not say that I had no appetite: the fulness
of my heart, both from busy anticipation, and from
the parting which was at hand, had made me incapable of any other thought or attention but such as
pointed to the coming journey. All circumstances in
travelling, all scenes and situations of a representative
and recurring character, are indescribably affecting,
connected, as they have been, in so many myriads of
minds, more especially in a land which is sending off
for ever its flowers and blossoms to a clime so remote
as that of India, with heartrending separations, and
with farewells never to be repeated. But, amongst
them all, none cleaves to my own feelings more in-
delibly, from having repeatedly been concerned, either
as witness or as a principal party in its little drama,
than the early breakfast on a wintry morning long
before the darkness has given way, when the golden
blaze of the hearth, and the bright glitter of candles,
with female ministrations of gentleness more touching
than on common occasions, all conspire to rekindle, as

it were for a farewell gleam, the holy memorials of household affections.

Years that seem innumerable have passed since that December morning in my own life to which I am now recurring; and yet, even to this moment, I recollect the audible throbbing of heart, the leap and rushing of blood, which suddenly surprised me during a deep lull of the wind, when the aged attendant said, without hurry or agitation, but with something of a solemn tone, "That is the sound of wheels. I hear the chaise. Mr. H—— will be here directly." The road ran, for some distance, by a course pretty nearly equi-distant from the house, so that the groaning of the wheels continued to catch the ear, as it swelled upon the wind, for some time without much alteration. At length a right-angled turn brought the road continually and rapidly nearer to the gates of the grounds, which had purposely been thrown open. At this point, however, a long career of raving arose; all other sounds were lost; and for some time I began to think we had been mistaken, when suddenly the loud tramping of horses' feet, as they whirled up the sweep below the windows, followed by a peal long and loud upon the bell, announced, beyond question, the summons for my departure. The door being thrown open, steps were heard loud and fast; and in the next moment, ushered by a servant, stalked forward, booted and fully equipped, my travelling companion—if such a word can at all express the relation between the arrogant young blood, just fresh from assuming the *toga virilis*, and a modest child of profound sensibilities, but shy and reserved beyond even English reserve. The aged servant, with apparently constrained civility, presented my mother's compliments to him, with a request that he would take breakfast. This he hastily and rather peremptorily declined. Me, however, he condescended to notice with an approving nod, slightly inquiring if I were the young gentleman who shared his post-chaise. But, without allowing time for an answer, and striking his boot impatiently with a riding-whip, he hoped I was ready. "Not until he has gone up to my mistress," replied my old protectress, in a tone of some asperity. Thither I ascended. What counsels and directions I might happen to receive at the maternal toilet, naturally I have forgotten. The most memorable circumstance to me was, that I, who had never till that time possessed the least or most contemptible coin, received, in a network purse, six glittering guineas, with instructions to put three immediately into Mr. H——'s hands, and the others when he should call for them.

The rest of my mother's counsels, if deep, were not long; she, who had always something of a Roman firmness, shed more milk of roses, I believe, upon my cheeks than tears; and why not? What should there be to *her* corresponding to an ignorant child's sense of pathos, in a little journey of about a hundred miles? Outside her door, however, there awaited me some silly creatures, women, of course, old and young, from the nursery and the kitchen, who gave, and who received, those fervent kisses which wait only upon love without awe and without disguise. Heavens! what rosaries might be strung for the memory of sweet female kisses, given without check or art, before one is of an age to value them! And again, how sweet is the touch of female hands as they array one for a journey! If anything needs fastening, whether by pinning, tying, or any other contrivance, how perfect is one's confidence in female skill; as if, by mere virtue of her sex and feminine instinct, a woman could not possibly fail to know the best and readiest way of adjusting every case that could arise in dress. Mine was hastily completed amongst them; each had a pin to draw from her bosom, in order to put something to rights about my throat or hands; and a chorus of "God bless hims!" was arising, when, from below, young Mephistopheles murmured an impatient groan, and perhaps the horses snorted. I found myself lifted into the chaise: counsels about the night and the cold flowing in upon me, to which Mephistopheles listened with derision or astonishment. I and he had each our separate corner; and, except to request that I would draw up one of the glasses, I do not think he condescended to address one word to me until dusk, when we found ourselves rattling into Chesterfield, having barely accomplished four stages, or forty or forty-two miles, in about nine hours. This, except on the Bath or great North roads, may be taken as a standard amount of performance, in 1794 (the year I am recording), and even ten years later.[1] In these present hurrying and tumultuous days, whether time is really of more value, I cannot say; but all people on the establishment of inns are required to suppose it of the most awful value. Now-a-days (1833), no sooner have the horses stopped at the gateway of a posting-house, than a summons is passed down to the stables; and in less than one minute, upon a great road, the horses next in rotation, always ready harnessed when expecting to come on duty, are heard trotting down the yard. "Putting to," and transferring the luggage (supposing your conveyance a common post-chaise), once a work of at least thirty minutes, is now easily accomplished in three. And scarcely have you paid the ex-postilion before his successor is mounted; the ostler is standing ready with the steps

[1] It appears, however, from the Life of Hume by my distinguished friend Mr. Hill Burton, that already, in the middle of the last century, the historian accomplished without difficulty six miles an hour with only a pair of horses. But this, it should be observed, was on the great North road.

in his hands to receive his invariable sixpence; the door
is closed; the representative waiter bows his acknowledgement for the house, and you are off at a pace never
less than ten miles an hour; the total detention at each
stage not averaging above four minutes. Then (*i.e.*,
at the latter end of the eighteenth and beginning of
the nineteenth century), half-an-hour was the minimum of time spent at each change of horses. Your
arrival produced a great bustle of unloading and un-
harnessing; as a matter of course, you alighted and
went into the inn; if you sallied out to report progress,
after waiting twenty minutes, no signs appeared of
any stir about the stables. The most choleric person
could not much expedite preparations, which loitered
not so much from any indolence in the attendants, as
from faulty arrangements and total defect of forecasting. The pace was such as the roads of that day
allowed; never so much as six miles an hour, except
upon a very great road; and then only by extra payment to the driver. Yet, even under this comparatively
miserable system, how superior was England, as a
land for the traveller, to all the rest of the world, Sweden only excepted! Bad as were the roads, and defective
as were all the arrangements, still you had these advantages: no town so insignficant, no posting-house
so solitary, but that at all seasons, except a contested
election, it could furnish horses without delay, and
without licence to distress the neighbouring farmers.
On the worst road, and on a winter's day, with no more
than a single pair of horses, you generally made out
sixty miles; even if it were necessary to travel through
the night, you could continue to make way, although
more slowly; and finally, if you were of a temper to
brook delay, and did not exact from all persons the
haste or energy of Hotspurs, the whole system in those
days was full of respectability and luxurious ease, and

well fitted to renew the image of the home you had left, if not in its elegancies, yet in all its substantial comforts. What cosy old parlours in those days! low-roofed, glowing with ample fires, and fenced from the blasts of doors by screens, whose foldings were or seemed to be infinite! What motherly landladies! won, how readily, to kindness the most lavish, by the mere attractions of simplicity and youthful innocence, and finding so much interest in the bare circumstance of being a traveller at a childish age! Then what bloom-ing young handmaidens; how different from the know-ing and worldly demireps of modern high-roads! And sometimes grey-headed, faithful waiters, how sincere and how attentive, by comparison with their flippant successors, the eternal "Coming, sir, coming," of our improved generation.

Such an honest, old butler-looking servant waited on us during dinner at Chesterfield, carving for me, and urging me to eat. Even Mephistopheles found his pride relax under the influence of wine; and, when loosened from this restraint, his kindness was not de-ficient. To me he showed it in pressing wine upon me, without stint or measure. The elegancies which he had observed in such parts of my mother's establishment as could be supposed to meet his eye on so hasty a visit had impressed him perhaps favourably towards my-self: and could I have a little altered my age, or dis-missed my excessive reserve, I doubt not that he would have admitted me, in default of a more suitable com-rade, to his entire confidence for the rest of the road. Dinner finished, and myself at least, for the first time in my childish life, somewhat perhaps overcharged with wine, the bill was called for, the waiter paid in the lavish style of antique England, and we heard our chaise drawing up under the gateway——the invariable custom of those days——by which you were spared the trouble of going into the street; stepping from the hall of the inn right into your carriage.

I had been kept back for a minute or so by the land-lady and her attendant nymphs, to be dressed and kissed; and, on seating myself in the chaise, which was well lighted with lamps, I found my lordly young principal in conversation with the landlord, first, upon the price of oats—which youthful horsemen always affect to inquire after with interest—but, secondly, upon a topic more immediately at his heart—viz., the reputation of the road. At that time of day, when gold had not yet disappeared from the circulation, no travel-ler carried any other sort of money about him; and there was consequently a rich encouragement to high-waymen, which vanished almost entirely with Mr. Pitt's act of 1797 for restricting cash payments. Prop-erty which could be identified and traced was a perilous sort of plunder; and from that time the free-trade of the road almost perished as a regular occupation. At this period it did certainly maintain a languishing existence; here and there it might have a casual run of success: and, as these local ebbs and flows were con-tinually shifting, perhaps, after all, the trade might lie amongst a small number of hands.

Universally, however, the landlords showed some shrewdness, or even sagacity, in qualifying, according to the circumstances of the inquirer, the sort of credit which they allowed to the exaggerated ill fame of the roads. Returning on this very road, some months after, with a timid female relative, who put her questions with undisguised and distressing alarm, the very same people, one and all, assured her that the danger was next to nothing. Not so at present: rightly presuming that a haughty cavalier of eighteen, flushed with wine and youthful blood, would listen with disgust to a pic-ture too amiable and pacific of the roads before him,

Mr. Spread-Eagle replied with the air of one who knew more than he altogether liked to tell, and, looking suspiciously amongst the strange faces lit up by the light of the carriage lamps—"Why, sir, there have been ugly stories afloat; I cannot deny it: and sometimes, you know, sir"—winking sagaciously, to which a knowing nod of assent was returned—"it may not be quite safe to tell all one knows. But you can understand me. The forest, you are well aware, sir, *is* the forest: it never was much to be trusted, by all accounts, in my father's time, and I suppose will not be better in mine. But you must keep a sharp look-out: and, Tom," speaking to the postilion, "mind, when you pass the third gate, to go pretty smartly by the thicket." Tom replied in a tone of importance to this professional appeal. General valedictions were exchanged, the landlord bowed, and we moved off for the forest.

Mephistopheles had his travelling case of pistols. These he began now to examine; for some times, said he, I have known such a trick as drawing the charge whilst one happened to be taking a glass of wine. Wine had unlocked his heart—the prospect of the forest and the advancing night excited him—and even of such a child as myself he was now disposed to make a confidant. "Did you observe," said he, "that ill-looking fellow, as big as a camel, who stood on the landlord's left hand?"—Was it the man, I asked timidly, who seemed by his dress to be a farmer?—"Farmer, you call him! Ah! my young friend, that shows your little knowledge of the world. He is a scoundrel, the bloodiest of scoundrels. And so I trust to convince him before many hours are gone over our heads." Whilst saying this, he employed himself in priming his pistols; then, after a pause, he went on thus:—"No, my young friend, this alone shows his base purposes—his calling himself a farmer. Farmer he is not, but a desperate highwayman, of which I have full proof. I watched his malicious glances, whilst the landlord was talking; and I could swear to his traitorous intentions." So speaking, he threw anxious glances on each side as we continued to advance: we were both somewhat excited; he by the spirit of adventure, I by sympathy with him—and both by wine. The wine, however, soon applied a remedy to its own delusions; six miles from the town we had left, both of us were in a bad condition for resisting highwaymen with effect—being fast asleep. Suddenly a most abrupt halt awoke us —Mephistopheles felt for his pistols—the door flew open, and the lights of the assembled group announced to us that we had reached Mansfield. That night we went on to Newark, at which place about forty miles of our journey remained. This distance we performed, of course, on the following day, between breakfast and dinner. But it serves strikingly to illustrate the state of roads in England, whenever your affairs led you into districts a little retired from the capital routes of the public travelling, that, for one twenty-mile stage —viz., from Newark to Sleaford—they refused to take us forward with less than four horses. This was neither a fraud, as our eyes soon convinced us (for even four horses could scarcely extricate the chaise from the deep sloughs which occasionally seamed the road through tracts of two or three miles in succession), nor was it an accident of the weather. In all seasons the same demand was enforced, as my female protectress found in conducting me back at a fine season of the year, and had always found in traversing the same route.

It was not until after the year 1815 that the main improvement took place in the English travelling system, so far as regarded speed. It is, in reality, to Mr. Macadam that we owe it. All the roads in England, within a few years, were remodelled, and upon prin-

ciples of Roman science. From mere beds of torrents
and systems of ruts, they were raised universally to
the condition and appearance of gravel walks in private
parks or shrubberies. The average rate of velocity was,
in consequence, exactly doubled—ten miles an hour
being now generally accomplished, instead of five. And
at the moment when all further improvement upon
this system had become hopeless, a new prospect was
suddenly opened to us by railroads; which again, considering how much they have already exceeded the
maximum of possibility as laid down by all engineers
during the progress of the Manchester and Liverpool
line, may soon give way to new modes of locomotion
still more astonishing to our preconceptions.

One point of refinement, as regards the comfort of
travellers, remains to be mentioned, in which the improvement began a good deal earlier, perhaps by ten
years, than in the construction of the roads. Luxurious
as was the system of English travelling at all periods,
after the general establishment of post-chaises, it must
be granted that, in the circumstance of cleanliness,
there was far from being that attention, or that provision for the traveller's comfort, which might have been
anticipated from the general habits of the country. I,
at all periods of my life a great traveller, was witness
to the first steps and the whole struggle of this revolution. Maréchal Saxe professed always to look under his
bed, applying his caution chiefly to the attempts of
robbers. Now, if at the greatest inns of England you
had, in the days I speak of, adopted this maréchal's
policy of reconnoitring, what would you have seen?
Beyond a doubt, you would have seen what, upon all
principles of seniority, was entitled to your veneration
—viz., a dense accumulation of dust far older than
yourself. A foreign author made some experiments
upon the deposition of dust, and the rate of its accumu-

lation, in a room left wholly undisturbed. If I recollect, a century would produce a stratum about half-an-inch in depth. Upon this principle, I conjecture that much dust which I have seen in inns, during the first four or five years of the present century, must have belonged to the reign of George II.

It was, however, upon travellers by coaches that the full oppression of the old vicious system operated. The elder Scaliger mentions, as a characteristic of the English in his day (about 1530), a horror of cold water; in which, however, there must have been some mistake.[1] Nowhere could he and his foreign companions obtain the luxury of cold water for washing their hands either before or after dinner. One day he and his party dined with the Lord Chancellor; and now, thought he, for very shame they will allow us some means of purification. Not at all: the Chancellor viewed this outlandish novelty with the same jealousy as others. However, on the earnest petition of Scaliger, he made an order that a basin or other vessel of cold water should be produced. His household bowed to this judgement, and a slop-basin was cautiously introduced. "What!" said Scaliger, "only one, and we so many?" Even that one contained but a tea-cupful of water; but the great scholar soon found that he must be thankful for what he had got. It had cost the whole strength of the English Chancery to produce that single cup of water; and, for that day, no man in his senses could look for a second. Pretty much the same struggle, and

[1] *"Some mistake"*: The mistake was possibly this: what little water for ablution, and what little rags called towels, a foreigner ever sees at home, will at least be always within reach, from the continental practice of using the bedroom for the sitting-room. But in England our plentiful means of ablution are kept in the background. Scaliger should have asked for a bedroom: the surprise was possibly—not at his wanting water, but at his wanting it in a dining-room.

for the same cheap reform, commenced about the year
1805–6. Post-chaise travellers could, of course, have
what they liked, and generally they asked for a bedroom. It is of coach travellers I speak. And the particular innovation in question commenced, as was
natural, with the mail-coach, which, from the much
higher scale of its fares, commanded a much more select class of company.

I was a party to the very earliest attempts at breaking ground in this alarming revolution. Well do I
remember the astonishment of some waiters, the indignation of others, the sympathetic uproars which
spread to the bar, to the kitchen, and even to the
stables, at the first opening of our extravagant demands. Sometimes even the landlady thought the case
worthy of her interference, and came forward to re-
monstrate with us upon our unheard-of conduct. But
gradually we made way. Like Scaliger, at first we got
but one basin amongst us, and that one was brought
into the breakfast-room; but scarcely had two years
revolved, before we began to see four, and all appurtenances, arranged duly in correspondence to the number of inside passengers by the mail: and, as outside
travelling was continually gaining ground amongst
the wealthier classes, more comprehensive arrangements were often made: though, even to this day, so
much influence survives from the original aristocratic
principle upon which public carriages were constructed, that on the mail-coaches there still prevails
the most scandalous inattention to the comfort, and
even to the security, of the outside passengers; a slip-
pery glazed roof frequently makes the sitting a matter
of effort and anxiety, whilst the little iron side-rail of
four inches in height serves no one purpose but that of
bruising the thigh. Concurrently with these reforms
in the system of personal cleanliness, others were si-

lently making way through all departments of the household economy. Dust from the reign of George II became scarcer; gradually it came to bear an antiquarian value: basins lost their grim appearance, and looked as clean as in gentlemen's houses. And at length the whole system was so thoroughly ventilated and purified, that all good inns, nay, generally speaking, even second-rate inns, at this day, reflect the best features, as to cleanliness and neatness, of well-managed private establishments.

MY BROTHER PINK

(First published in *Tait's Magazine*, March, 1838)

MY NEXT brother,[1] younger by about four years than myself (he, in fact, that caused so much affliction to the Sultan Amurath), was a boy of exquisite and delicate beauty—delicate, that is, in respect to its feminine elegance and bloom; for else (as regards constitution) he turned out remarkably robust. In such excess did his beauty flourish during childhood that those who remember him and myself at the public school at Bath will also remember the ludicrous molestation in the streets (for to him it *was* molestation) which it entailed upon him—ladies stopping continually to kiss him.

In 1800 my visit to Ireland, and visits to other places subsequently, separated me from him for above a year. In 1801, we were at very different schools: I in the highest class of a great public school—he at a very sequestered parsonage on a wild moor (Horwich Moor) in Lancashire. This situation, probably, fed and cherished his melancholy habits; for he had no

[1] Richard.

society except that of a younger brother, who would
give him no disturbance at all. The development of
our national resources had not yet gone so far as absolutely to exterminate from the map of England everything like a heath, a breezy down, or even a village
common. Heaths were yet to be found in England, not
so spacious, indeed, as the *landes* of France, but equally
wild and romantic. In such a situation my brother
lived, and under the tuition of a clergyman, retired in
his habits, and even ascetic, but gentle in his manners.
To that I can speak myself; for in the winter of 1801
I dined with him, and I found that his yoke was, indeed, a mild one; since, even to my youngest brother
Henry, a headstrong child of seven, he used no stronger
remonstrance, in urging him to some essential point
of duty, than *"Do be persuaded, sir."* On another occasion I, accompanied by a friend, slept at Mr. J.'s: we
were accidentally detained there through the greater
part of the following day by snow; and, to the inexpressible surprise of my companion, a mercantile man
from Manchester, for a considerable time after breakfast the reverend gentleman persisted in pursuing my
brother from room to room, and at last from the
ground-floor up to the attics, holding a book open
(which turned out to be a Latin grammar); each of
them (pursuer and pursued) moving at a tolerably
slow pace: my brother Henry silent; but Mr. J., with
a voice of adjuration, solemn and even sad, yet kind
and conciliatory, singing out at intervals, "Do be persuaded, sir!" "It is *your* welfare I seek!" "Let your
own interest, sir, plead in this matter between us!"
And so the chase continued, ascending and descending,
up to the very garrets, down to the very cellars, then
steadily revolving from front to rear of the house; but
finally with no result at all. The spectacle reminded
me of a groom attempting to catch a coy pony by

holding out a sieve containing, or pretending to contain, a bribe of oats. Mrs. J., the reverend gentleman's wife, assured us that the same process went on at intervals throughout the week; and in any case it was clearly good as a mode of exercise. Now, such a master, though little adapted for the headstrong Henry, was the very person for the thoughtful and too sensitive Richard. Search the island through, there could not have been found another situation so suitable to my brother's wayward and haughty nature. The clergyman was learned, quiet, absorbed in his studies; humble and modest beyond the proprieties of his situation, and treating my brother in all points as a companion: whilst, on the other hand, my brother was not the person to forget the respect due, by a triple title, to a clergyman, a scholar, and his own preceptor—one, besides, who so little thought of exacting it. How happy might all parties have been—what suffering, what danger, what years of miserable anxiety, might have been spared to all who were interested—had the guardians and executors of my father's will thought fit to "let *well* alone!" But, "*per star meglio*," [1] they chose to remove my brother from this gentle recluse, to an active bustling man of the world, the very anti-pole in character.

What might be the pretensions of this gentleman to scholarship, I never had any means of judging; and, considering that he must now (if living at all), at a distance of thirty-six years, be grey-headed, I shall respect his age so far as to suppress his name. He was of a class now annually declining (and I hope rapidly) to extinction. Thanks be to God, in this point at least, for the dignity of human nature, that, amongst the

[1] From the well-known Italian epitaph—"*Stava bene: ma, per star meglio, sto qui*"—I was well; but, because I would be better than well, I am—where you see.

many, many cases of reform destined eventually to turn out chimerical, this one, at least, never can be defeated, injured, or eclipsed. As man grows more intellectual, the power of managing him by his intellect and his moral nature, in utter contempt of all appeals to his mere animal instincts of pain, must go on *pari passu*. And, if a "Te Deum," or an "O, Jubilate!" were to be celebrated by all nations and languages for any one advance and absolute conquest over wrong and error won by human nature in our times—yes, not excepting

The bloody writing by all nations torn—

the abolition of the commerce in slaves—to my thinking, that festival should be for the mighty progress made towards the suppression of brutal, bestial modes of punishment. Nay, I may call them worse than bestial; for a man of any goodness of nature does not willingly or needlessly resort to the spur or the lash with his horse or with his hound.

This schoolmaster had very different views of man and his nature. He not only thought that physical coercion was the one sole engine by which man could be managed, but, on the principle of that common maxim which declares that, when two schoolboys meet, with powers at all near to a balance, no peace can be expected between them until it is fairly settled *which* is the master—on that same principle, he fancied that no pupil could adequately or proportionably reverence his master, until he had settled the precise proportion of superiority in animal powers by which his master was in advance of himself. Strength of blows only could ascertain *that:* and, as he was not very nice about creating his opportunities, as he plunged at once *"in medias res,"* and more especially when he saw or suspected any rebellious tendencies, he soon picked a quarrel with my unfortunate brother. Not, be it observed, that he much cared for a well-looking or respectable quarrel. No. I have been assured that, even when the most fawning obsequiousness had appealed to his clemency, in the person of some timorous newcomer, appalled by the reports he had heard—even in such cases (deeming it wise to impress, from the beginning, a salutary awe of his Jovian thunders), he made a practice of doing thus: He would speak loud, utter some order, not very clearly, perhaps, as respected the sound, but with *perfect* perplexity as regarded the sense, to the timid, sensitive boy upon whom he intended to fix a charge of disobedience. "Sir, if you please, what was it that you said?"—"What was it that I said? What! playing upon my words? Chopping logic? Strip, sir; strip this instant." Thenceforward this timid boy became a serviceable instrument in his equipage. Not only was he a proof, even without co-operation on the master's part, that extreme cases of submission could not insure mercy, but also he, this boy, in his own person, breathed forth, at intervals, a dim sense of awe and worship—the religion of fear— towards the grim Moloch of the scene. Hence, as by electrical conductors, was conveyed throughout every region of the establishment a tremulous sensibility that vibrated towards the centre.

Meantime, my brother Richard, in an evil hour, having been removed from that most quiet of human sanctuaries, having forfeited that peace which possibly he was never to retrieve, fell (as I have said) into the power of this Moloch. And this Moloch upon him illustrated the laws of his establishment: him also, the gentle, the beautiful, but also the proud, the haughty, he beat, kicked, trampled on!

In two hours from that time, my brother was on

the road to Liverpool. Painfully he made out his way, having not much money, and with a sense of total abandonment which made him feel that all he might have would prove little enough for his purposes.

My brother went to an inn, after his long, long journey to Liverpool, foot-sore (for he had walked through four days, and, from ignorance of the world, combined with excessive shyness—oh! how shy do people become from pride!—had not profited by those well-known incidents upon English high-roads—return post-chaises, stage-coaches, led horses, or wag-gons)—foot-sore, and eager for sleep. Sleep, supper, breakfast in the morning—all these he had; so far his slender finances reached; and for these he paid the treacherous landlord: who then proposed to him that they should take a walk out together, by way of look-ing at the public buildings and the docks. It seems the man had noticed my brother's beauty, some circum-stances about his dress inconsistent with his mode of travelling, and also his style of conversation. Accord-ingly, he wiled him along from street to street, until they reached the Town Hall. "Here *seems* to be a fine building," said this Jesuitical guide, as if it had been some new Pompeii—some Luxor or Palmyra that he had unexpectedly lit upon amongst the undiscovered parts of Liverpool—"here seems to be a fine building; shall we go in and ask leave to look at it?" My brother, thinking less of the spectacle than the spectator, whom, in a wilderness of man, naturally he wished to make his friend, consented readily. In they went; and, by the merest accident, Mr. Mayor and the town-council were then sitting. To them the insidious landlord com-municated privately an account of his suspicions. He himself conducted my brother, under pretence of dis-covering the best station for picturesque purposes, to the particular box for prisoners at the bar. This was

not suspected by the poor boy, not even when Mr.
Mayor began to question him. He still thought it an
accident, though doubtless he blushed excessively on
being questioned, and questioned so impertinently, in
public. The object of the mayor and of other Liverpool
gentlemen then present was, to ascertain my brother's
real rank and family: for he persisted in representing
himself as a poor wandering boy. Various means were
vainly tried to elicit this information; until at length
—like the wily Ulysses, who mixed with his pedlar's
budget of female ornaments and attire a few arms, by
way of tempting Achilles to a self-detection in the
court of Lycomedes—one gentleman counselled the
mayor to send for a Greek Testament. This was done;
the Testament was presented open at St. John's Gospel
to my brother, and he was requested to say whether
he knew in what language that book was written; or
whether, perhaps, he could furnish them with a translation from the page before him. Richard, in his confusion, did not read the meaning of this appeal, and
fell into the snare: construed a few verses; and immediately was consigned to the care of a gentleman, who
won from him by kindness what he had refused to im-
portunities or menaces. His family he confessed at
once, but not his school. An express was therefore forwarded from Liverpool to our nearest male relative—
a military man, then by accident on leave of absence
from India. He came over, took my brother back (looking upon the whole as a boyish frolic of no permanent
importance), made some stipulations in his behalf for
indemnity from punishment, and immediately returned home. Left to himself, the grim tyrant of the
school easily evaded the stipulations, and repeated his
brutalities more fiercely than before—now acting in
the double spirit of tyranny and revenge.

In a few hours, my brother was again on the road

to Liverpool. But not on this occasion did he resort to any inn, or visit any treacherous hunter of the picturesque. He offered himself to no temptations now, nor to any risks. Right onwards he went to the docks, addressed himself to a grave, elderly master of a trading vessel, bound upon a distant voyage, and instantly procured an engagement. The skipper was a good and sensible man, and (as it turned out) a sailor accomplished in all parts of his profession. The ship which he commanded was a South Sea whaler, belonging to Lord Grenville—whether lying at Liverpool or in the Thames at that moment, I am not sure. However, they soon afterwards sailed.

For somewhat less than three years, my brother continued under the care of this good man, who was interested by his appearance, and by some resemblance which he fancied in his features to a son whom he had lost. Fortunate, indeed, for the poor boy was this interval of fatherly superintendence; for, under this captain, he was not only preserved from the perils which afterwards besieged him, until his years had made him more capable of confronting them; but also he had thus an opportunity, which he improved to the utmost, of making himself acquainted with the two separate branches of his profession—navigation and seamanship, qualifications which are not very often united.

After the death of this captain, my brother ran through many wild adventures; until at length, after a severe action fought off the coast of Peru, the armed merchantman in which he then served was captured by pirates. Most of the crew were massacred. My brother, on account of the important services he could render, was spared; and with these pirates, cruising under a black flag, and perpetrating unnumbered atrocities, he was obliged to sail for the next two years;

nor could he in all that period find any opportunity for effecting his escape.

During this long expatriation, let any thoughtful reader imagine the perils of every sort which besieged one so young, so inexperienced, so sensitive, and so haughty; perils to his life (but these, it was the very expression of his unhappy situation, were the perils least to be mourned for) ; perils to his good name, going the length of absolute infamy—since, if the piratical ship had been captured by a British man-of-war, he might have found it impossible to clear himself of a voluntary participation in the bloody actions of his shipmates; and, on the other hand (a case equally probable in the regions which they frequented) , supposing him to have been captured by a Spanish *guarda costa*, he would scarcely have been able, from his ignorance of the Spanish language, to draw even a momentary attention to the special circumstances of his own situation; he would have been involved in the general presumptions of the case, and would have been executed in a summary way, upon the *prima facie* evidence against him, that he did not appear to be in the condition of a prisoner; and, if his name had ever again reached his country, it would have been in some sad list of ruffians, murderers, traitors to their country; and even these titles, as if not enough in themselves, aggravated by the name of pirate, which at once includes them all, and surpasses them all. These were perils sufficiently distressing at any rate; but last of all came others even more appalling—the perils of moral contamination, in that excess which might be looked for from such associates: not, be it recollected, a few wild notions or lawless principles adopted into his creed of practical ethics, but that brutal transfiguration of the entire character which occurs, for instance, in the case of the young gipsy son of Effie Deans; a change making it impossible to rely upon the very holiest instincts of the moral nature, and consigning its victim to hopeless reprobation. Murder itself might have lost its horrors to one who must have been but too familiar with the spectacle of massacre by wholesale upon unresisting crews, upon passengers enfeebled by sickness, or upon sequestered villagers, roused from their slumbers by the glare of conflagration, reflected from gleaming cutlasses, and from the faces of demons. But, in my brother's case, all the adverse chances, overwhelming as they seemed, were turned aside by some good angel; all had failed to harm him; and from the fiery furnace he came out unsinged.

I have said that he would not have appeared to any capturing ship as standing in the situation of prisoner amongst the pirates, nor was he such in the sense of being confined. He moved about, when on board ship, in freedom; but he was watched, never trusted on shore, unless under very peculiar circumstances; and tolerated at all only because one accomplishment made him indispensable to the prosperity of the ship. Amongst the various parts of nautical skill communicated to my brother by his first fatherly captain was the management of chronometers. Several had been captured, some of the highest value, in the many prizes, European or American. My brother happened to be perfect in the skill of managing them; and, fortunately for him, no other person amongst them had that skill, even in its lowest degree. To this one qualification, therefore (and ultimately to this only), he was indebted for both safety and freedom; since, though he might have been spared in the first moments of carnage from other considerations, there is little doubt that, in some one of the innumerable brawls which followed through the years of his captivity, he would have fallen a sacrifice to hasty impulses of anger or wantonness, had not his safety been made an object of interest and vigilance to those in command, and to all who assumed any care for the general welfare. Much, therefore, it was that he owed to this accomplishment. Still, there is no good thing without its alloy; and this great blessing brought along with it something worse than a dull duty—the necessity, in fact, of facing fears and trials to which the sailor's heart is pre-eminently sensible. It is well known that the whole family of sailors *is* superstitious. My brother, poor Pink (this was an old household name which he retained amongst us from an incident of his childhood), was so in an immoderate degree. Being a great reader he was pretty well aware how general was the ridicule attached in our times to the subject of ghosts. But this—nor the reverence he yielded otherwise to some of those writers who had joined in that ridicule—any more had unsettled his faith in their existence, than the submission of a sailor in a religious sense to his spiritual counsellor, upon the false and fraudulent pleasures of luxury, can ever disturb his remembrance of the virtues lodged in rum or tobacco. His own unconquerable, unanswerable experience, the blank realities of pleasure and pain, put to flight all arguments whatsoever that anchor only in his understanding. Pink used, in arguing the case with me, to admit that ghosts might be questionable realities in our hemisphere, but "it's a different thing to the *suthard* of the line." And then he would go on to tell me of his own fearful experience; in particular, of one many times renewed, and investigated to no purpose by parties of men communicating from a distance upon a system of concerted signals, in one of the Galápagos Islands. These islands, which were visited, and I think described, by Dampier—and therefore must have been an asylum to the Buccaneers and Flibustiers in the latter part of the seventeenth century—were so still to their more desperate successors, the Pirates, at the beginning of the nineteenth; and for the same reason—the facilities they offer (rare in those seas) for procuring wood and water. Hither, then, the black flag often resorted; and here, amidst these romantic solitudes, islands untenanted by man—oftentimes it lay furled up for weeks together; rapine and murder had rest for a season; and the bloody cutlass slept within its scabbard. When this happened, and when it became known beforehand that it *would* happen, a tent was pitched on shore for my brother, and the chronometers were transported thither for the period of their stay.

The island selected for this purpose, amongst the many equally open to their choice, might, according to circumstances, be that which offered the best anchorage, or that from which the re-embarkation was easiest, or that which allowed the readiest access to wood and water. But, for some or all of these advantages, the particular island most generally honoured by the piratical custom and "good-will" was one known to American navigators as "The Woodcutter's Island." There was some old tradition—and I know not but it was a tradition dating from the times of Dampier—that a Spaniard or an Indian settler in this island (relying, perhaps, too entirely upon the protection of perfect solitude) had been murdered in pure wantonness by some of the lawless rovers who frequented this solitary archipelago. Whether it were from some peculiar atrocity of bad faith in the act, or from the sanctity of the man, or the deep solitude of the island, or with a view to the peculiar edification of mariners in these semi-Christian seas—so, however, it was, and attested by generations of sea-vagabonds (for most of the armed roamers in these ocean Zaaras at one time were of a suspicious order), that every night, duly as the sun went down, and the twilight began to

prevail, a sound arose——audible to other islands, and
to every ship lying quietly at anchor in that neighbourhood——of a woodcutter's axe. Sturdy were the
blows, and steady the succession in which they followed: some even fancied they could hear that sort of
groaning respiration which is made by men who use
an axe, or by those who in towns ply the "three-man
beetle" of Falstaff, as paviors; echoes they certainly
heard of every blow, from the profound woods and
the sylvan precipices on the margin of the shores;
which, however, should rather indicate that the sounds
were *not* supernatural, since, if a visual object, falling
under hyper-physical or cata-physical laws, loses its
shadow, by parity of argument, an audible object, in
the same circumstances, should lose its echo. But this
was the story; and amongst sailors there is as little variety of versions in telling any true sea-story as there
is in a log-book, or in *The Flying Dutchman: literatim*
fidelity is, with a sailor, a point at once of religious
faith and worldly honour. The close of the story was——
that after, suppose, ten or twelve minutes of hacking
and hewing, a horrid crash was heard, announcing
that the tree, if tree it were, that never yet was made
visible to daylight search, had yielded to the old woodman's persecution. It was exactly the crash, so familiar
to many ears on board the neighbouring vessels, which
expresses the harsh tearing asunder of the fibres caused
by the weight of the trunk in falling; beginning
slowly, increasing rapidly, and terminating in one
rush of rending. This over——one tree felled "towards
his winter store"——there was an interval: man must
have rest; and the old woodman, after working for
more than a century, must want repose. Time enough
to begin again after a quarter-of-an-hour's relaxation.
Sure enough, in that space of time again began, in the
words of Comus, "the wonted roar amid the woods."

Again the blows become quicker, as the catastrophe drew nearer; again the final crash resounded; and again the mighty echoes travelled through the solitary forests, and were taken up by all the islands near and far, like Joanna's laugh amongst the Westmorland hills, to the astonishment of the silent ocean. Yet, wherefore should the ocean be astonished—he that had heard this nightly tumult, by all accounts, for more than a century?

My brother, however, poor Pink, *was* astonished, in good earnest, being, in that respect, of the *genus attonitorum;* and as often as the gentlemen pirates steered their course for the Galápagos, he would sink in spirit before the trials he might be summoned to face. No second person was ever put on shore with Pink, lest poor Pink and he might become jovial over the liquor, and the chronometers be broken or neglected; for a considerable quantity of spirits was necessarily landed, as well as of provisions, because sometimes a sudden change of weather, or the sudden appearance of a suspicious sail, might draw the ship off the island for a fortnight. My brother could have pleaded his fears without shame; but he had a character to maintain with the sailors: he was respected equally for his seamanship and his shipmanship. The sailors, looking to Pink's double skill, and to his experience on shore (more astonishing than all beside, being experience gathered amongst ghosts), expressed an admiration which, to one who was also a sailor, had too genial a sound to be sacrificed, if it could be maintained at any price. Therefore it was that Pink still clung, in spite of his terrors, to his shore appointment. But hard was his trial; and many a time has he described to me one effect of it, when too long continued, or combined with darkness too intense. The woodcutter would begin his operations soon after the sun had set; but uniformly, at that time, his noise was less. Three hours after sunset it had increased; and generally at midnight it was greatest, but not always. Sometimes the case varied thus far: that it greatly increased towards three or four o'clock in the morning; and, as the sound grew louder, and thereby seemed to draw nearer, poor Pink's ghostly panic grew insupportable; and he absolutely crept from his pavilion, and its luxurious comforts, to a point of rock—a promontory—about half-a-mile off, from which he could see the ship. The mere sight of a human abode, though an abode of ruffians, comforted his panic. With the approach of daylight, the mysterious sounds ceased.

* * *

With respect to Pink's yearning for England, that had been partially gratified in some part of his long exile: twice, as we learned long afterwards, he had landed in England; but such was his haughty adherence to his purpose, and such his consequent terror of being discovered and reclaimed by his guardians, that he never attempted to communicate with any of his brothers or sisters. There he was wrong; me they should have cut to pieces before I would have betrayed him. I, like him, had been an obstinate recusant to what I viewed as unjust pretensions of authority; and, having been the first to raise the standard of revolt, had been taxed by my guardians with having seduced Pink by my example. But that was untrue; Pink acted for himself. However, he could know little of all this; and he traversed England twice, without making an overture towards any communication with his friends. Two circumstances of these journeys he used to mention: both were from the port of London (for he never contemplated London but as a port) to Liverpool; or, thus far I may be wrong, that one of the two might be (in the return order) from Liverpool to London. On the first of these journeys, his route lay through Coventry; on the other, through Oxford and Birmingham. In neither case had he started with much money; and he was going to have retired from the coach at the place of supping on the first night (the journey then occupying two entire days and two entire nights), when the passengers insisted on paying for him: that was a tribute to his beauty—not yet extinct. He mentioned this part of his adventures somewhat shyly, whilst going over them with a sailor's literal accuracy; though, as a record belonging to what he viewed as childish years, he had ceased to care about it.

On the other journey, his experience was different, but equally testified to the spirit of kindness that is everywhere abroad. He had no money, on this occasion, that could purchase even a momentary lift by a stage-coach: as a pedestrian he had travelled down to Oxford, occupying two days in the fifty-four or fifty-six miles which then measured the road from London, and sleeping in a farmer's barn, without leave asked. Wearied and depressed in spirits, he had reached Oxford, hopeless of any aid, and with a deadly shame at the thought of asking it. But, somewhere in the High Street—and, according to his very accurate sailor's description of that noble street, it must have been about the entrance of All Souls' College—he met a gentleman, a gownsman, who (at the very moment of turning into the college gate) looked at Pink earnestly, and then gave him a guinea, saying at the time, "I know what it is to be in your situation. You are a schoolboy, and you have run away from your school. Well, I was once in your situation, and I pity you." The kind gownsman, who wore a velvet cap with a silk gown, and must therefore have been what in Oxford is called a gentleman commoner, gave him an address at some college or other (Magdalen, he fancied, in after years), where he instructed him to call before he quitted Oxford. Had Pink done this, and had he frankly communicated his whole story, very probably he would have received, not assistance merely, but the best advice for guiding his future motions. His reason for not keeping the appointment was simply that he was nervously shy; and, above all things, jealous of being entrapped by insidious kindness into revelations that might prove dangerously circumstantial. Oxford had a mayor; Oxford had a corporation; Oxford had Greek Testaments past all counting; and so, remembering past experiences, Pink held it to be the wisest counsel that he should pursue his route on foot to Liverpool. That guinea, however, he used to say, saved him from despair.

One circumstance affected me in this part of Pink's story. I was a student in Oxford at that time. By comparing dates, there was no doubt whatever that I, who held my guardians in abhorrence, and above all things admired my brother for his conduct, might have rescued him at this point of his youthful trials, four years before the fortunate catastrophe of his case, from the calamities which awaited him. This is felt generally to be the most distressing form of human blindness—the case when accident brings two fraternal hearts, yearning for re-union, into almost touching neighbourhood, and then in a moment after, by the difference, perhaps, of three inches in space, or three seconds in time, will separate them again, unconscious of their brief neighbourhood, perhaps for ever. In the present case, however, it may be doubted whether this unconscious rencounter and unconscious parting in Oxford ought to be viewed as a misfortune. Pink, it is true, endured years of suffering, four at least, that might have been saved by this seasonable rencounter; but, on the other hand, by travelling through his misfortunes with unabated spirit, and to their natural end, he won experience and distinctions that else he would have missed. His further history was briefly this:

Somewhere in the river of Plata, he had effected his escape from the pirates; and a long time after, in 1807, I believe (I write without books to consult), he joined the storming party of the English at Montevideo. Here he happened fortunately to fall under the eye of Sir Home Popham; and Sir Home forthwith rated my brother as a midshipman on board his own ship, which was at that time, I think, a fifty-gun ship—the *Diadem*. Thus, by merits of the most appropriate kind, and without one particle of interest, my brother passed into the royal navy. His nautical accomplishments were now of the utmost importance to him; and, as often as he shifted his ship, which (to say the truth) was far too often—for his temper was fickle and delighting in change—so often these accomplishments were made the basis of very earnest eulogy. I have read a vast heap of certificates vouching for Pink's qualifications as a sailor, in the highest terms, and from several of the most distinguished officers in the service. Early in his career as a midshipman, he suffered a mortifying interruption of the active life which had long since become essential to his comfort. He had contrived to get appointed on board a fire-ship, the *Prometheus* (chiefly with a wish to enlarge his experience by this variety of naval warfare), at the time of the last Copenhagen expedition, and he obtained his wish; for the *Prometheus* had a very distinguished station assigned her on the great night of bombardment; and from her decks, I believe, was made almost the first effectual trial of the Congreve rockets. Soon after the Danish capital had fallen, and whilst the *Prome-*

theus was still cruising in the Baltic, Pink, in company with the purser of his ship, landed on the coast of Jutland, for the purpose of a morning's sporting. It seems strange that this should have been allowed upon a hostile shore; and, perhaps, it was *not* allowed, but might have been a thoughtless abuse of some other mission shorewards. So it was, unfortunately; and one at least of the two sailors had reason to rue the sporting of that day for eighteen long months of captivity. They were perfectly unacquainted with the localities, but conceived themselves able at any time to make good their retreat to the boat, by means of fleet heels, and arms sufficient to deal with any opposition of the sort they apprehended. Venturing, however, too far into the country, they became suddenly aware of certain sentinels, posted expressly for the benefit of chance English visitors. These men did not pursue, but they did worse, for they fired signal shots; and, by the time our two thoughtless Jack-tars had reached the shore, they saw a detachment of Danish cavalry trotting their horses pretty coolly down in a direction for the boat. Feeling confident of their power to keep ahead of the pursuit, the sailors amused themselves with various sallies of nautical wit; and Pink, in particular, was just telling them to present his dutiful respects to the Crown Prince, and assure him that, but for this lubberly interruption, he trusted to have improved his royal dinner by a brace of birds, when——oh, sight of blank confusion!——all at once they became aware that between themselves and their boat lay a perfect network of streams, deep watery holes, requiring both time and local knowledge to unravel. The purser hit upon a course which enabled him to regain the boat; but I am not sure whether he also was not captured. Poor Pink *was* at all events; and, through seventeen or eighteen months, bewailed this boyish

imprudence. At the end of that time there was an exchange of prisoners; and he was again serving on
board various and splendid frigates. Wyborg in Jutland was the seat of his Danish captivity; and such
was the amiableness of the Danish character, that, except for the loss of his time to one who was aspiring to
distinction and professional honour, none of the prisoners who were on parole could have had much reason
for complaint. The street mob, excusably irritated
with England at that time (for, without entering on
the question of right, or of expedience, as regarded that
war, it is notorious that such arguments as we had for
our unannounced hostilities could not be pleaded
openly by the English Cabinet, for fear of compromis-
ing our private friend and informant, the King of
Sweden) —the mob, therefore, were rough in their
treatment of the British prisoners; at night, they
would pelt them with stones; and here and there some
honest burgher, who might have suffered grievously
in his property, or in the person of his nearest friends,
by the ruin inflicted upon the Danish commercial shipping, or by the dreadful havoc made in Zealand, would
show something of the same bitter spirit. But the great
body of the richer and more educated inhabitants
showed the most hospitable attention to all who justified that sort of notice by their conduct. And their remembrance of these English friendships was not fugitive; for, through long years after my brother's death,
I used to receive letters, written in the Danish (a language which I had attained in the course of my studies, and which I have since endeavoured to turn to account in a public journal for some useful purposes of
research), from young men as well as women in Jutland; letters couched in the most friendly terms, and
recalling to his remembrance scenes and incidents
which sufficiently proved the terms of fraternal affec-

tion upon which he had lived amongst these public enemies; and some of them I have preserved to this day, as memorials that do honour, on different considerations, to both parties alike.

PREMATURE MANHOOD
(First published in *Tait's Magazine*, August, 1834)

I AM now returning into the main current of my narrative, although I may need to linger for a moment upon a past anecdote. I have mentioned already that, on inquiring at the Birmingham Post-office for a letter addressed to myself, I found one directing me to join my sister Mary at Laxton, a seat of Lord Carbery's in Northamptonshire, and giving me to understand, that, during my residence at this place, some fixed resolution would be taken and announced to me in regard to the future disposal of my time, during the two or three years before I should be old enough on the English system for matriculating at Oxford or Cambridge. In the poor countries of Europe, where they cannot afford double sets of scholastic establishments—having, therefore, no splendid schools, such as are, in fact, peculiar to England—they are compelled to throw the duties of such schools upon their universities; and consequently you see boys of thirteen and fourteen, or even younger, crowding such institutions, which, in fact, they ruin for all higher functions. But England, whose regal establishments of both classes emancipate her from this dependency, sends her young men to college not until they have ceased to be boys— not earlier, therefore, than eighteen.

But when, by what test, by what indication, does manhood commence? Physically by one criterion, legally by another, morally by a third, intellectually by a fourth—and all indefinite. Equator, absolute equator, there is none. Between the two spheres of youth and age, perfect and imperfect manhood, as in all analogous cases, there is no strict line of bisection. The change is a large process, accomplished within a large and corresponding space; having, perhaps, some central or equatorial line, but lying, like that of our earth, between certain tropics, or limits widely separated. This *intertropical* region may, and generally does, cover a number of years; and, therefore, it is hard to say, even for an assigned case, by any tolerable approximation, at what precise era it would be reasonable to describe the individual as having ceased to be a boy, and as having attained his inauguration as a man.

How, under so variable a standard, both natural and conventional, of everything almost that can be received for a test or a presumption of manhood, shall we seize upon any characteristic feature, sufficiently universal to serve a *practical* use, as a criterion of the transition from the childish mind to the dignity (relative dignity, at least) of that mind which belongs to conscious maturity? One such criterion, and one only, as I believe, there is—all others are variable and uncertain. It lies in the reverential feeling, sometimes suddenly developed, towards woman, and the idea of woman. From that moment when women cease to be regarded with carelessness, and when the ideal of womanhood, in its total pomp of loveliness and purity, dawns like some vast aurora upon the mind, boyhood has ended; childish thoughts and inclinations have passed away for ever; and the gravity of manhood, with the self-respecting views of manhood, have commenced.

> *Mentemque priorem*
> *Expulit, atque hominem toto sibi cedere jussit*
> *Pectore.*—LUCAN.

These feelings, no doubt, depend for their development in part upon physical causes; but they are also determined by the many retarding or accelerating forces enveloped in circumstances of position, and sometimes in pure accident.

For myself, I remember most distinctly the very day—the scene, and its accidents—when that mysterious awe fell upon me which belongs to woman in her ideal portrait: and from that hour a profounder gravity coloured all my thoughts, and a "beauty still more beauteous" was lit up for me in this agitating world. Lord Westport and myself had been on a visit to a noble family about fifty miles from Dublin; and we were returning from Tullamore by a public passage-boat on the splendid canal which connects that place with the metropolis. To avoid attracting an unpleasant attention to ourselves in public situations, I observed a rule of never addressing Lord Westport by his title: but it so happened that the canal carried us along the margin of an estate belonging to the Earl (now Marquis) of Westmeath; and on turning an angle we came suddenly in view of this nobleman taking his morning lounge in the sun. Somewhat loftily he reconnoitred the miscellaneous party of clean and unclean beasts crowded on the deck of our ark, ourselves amongst the number, whom he challenged gaily as young acquaintances from Dublin; and my friend he saluted more than once as "My Lord." This accident made known to the assembled mob of our fellow-travellers Lord Westport's rank, and led to a scene rather too broadly exposing the spirit of this world. Herded together on the deck (or roof of that den denominated the "*state-cabin*") stood a party of young ladies, headed by their governess. In the cabin below was mamma, who as yet had not condescended to illuminate our circle, for she was an awful personage—a wit, a bluestocking (I call

her by the name then current), and a leader of *ton* in
Dublin and Belfast. The fact, however, that a young
lord, and one of great expectations, was on board
brought her up. A short cross-examination of Lord
Westport's French valet had confirmed the flying report, and at the same time (I suppose) put her in possession of my defect in all those advantages of title,
fortune, and expectation which so brilliantly distinguished my friend. Her admiration of him, and her
contempt for myself, were equally undisguised. And
in the ring which she soon cleared out for public exhibition, she made us both fully sensible of the very
equitable stations which she assigned to us in her regard. She was neither very brilliant nor altogether a
pretender, but might be described as a showy woman,
of slight but popular accomplishments. Any woman,
however, has the advantage of possessing the ear of
any company: and a woman of forty, with such tact
and experience as she will naturally have gathered in a
talking practice of such duration, can find little difficulty in mortifying a boy, or sometimes, perhaps, in
tempting him to unfortunate sallies of irritation. Me,
it was clear, that she viewed in the light of a humble
friend, or what is known in fashionable life by the humiliating name of a "toad-eater." Lord Westport, full
of generosity in what regarded his own pretensions,
and who never had violated the perfect equality which
reigned in our deportment to each other, coloured with
as much confusion as myself at her coarse insinuations.
And, in reality, our ages scarcely allowed of that relation which she supposed to exist between us. Possibly,
she did *not* suppose it: but it is essential to the wit and
the display of some people that it should have a foundation in malice. A victim and a sacrifice are indispensable conditions in every exhibition. In such a case,
my natural sense of justice would generally have

armed me a hundredfold for retaliation; but at present
—chiefly, perhaps, because I had no effectual ally, and
could count upon no sympathy in my audience—I was
mortified beyond the power of retort, and became a
passive butt to the lady's stinging contumely, and the
arrowy sleet of her gay rhetoric. The narrow bounds
of our deck made it not easy to get beyond talking-
range; and thus it happened that for two hours I stood
the worst of this bright lady's feud. At length the tables turned.

Two ladies appeared slowly ascending from the
cabin, both in deepest mourning, but else as different
in aspect as summer and winter. The elder was the
Countess of Errol, then mourning an affliction which
had laid her life desolate, and admitted of no human
consolation. Heavier grief—grief more self-occupied
and deaf to all voice of sympathy—I have not happened to witness. She seemed scarcely aware of our
presence, except it were by placing herself as far as
was possible from the annoyance of our odious conversation. The circumstances of her loss are now forgotten; at that time they were known to a large circle in
Bath and London, and I violate no confidence in reviewing them. Lord Errol had been privately intrusted
by Mr. Pitt with an official secret—viz. the outline
and principal details of a foreign expedition; in which,
according to Mr. Pitt's original purpose, his lordship
was to have held a high command. In a moment of intoxication, the earl confided this secret to some false
friend, who published the communication and its author. Upon this, the unhappy nobleman, under too
keen a sense of wounded honour, and perhaps with an
exaggerated notion of the evils attached to his indiscretion, destroyed himself. Months had passed since
that calamity, when we met his widow; but time appeared to have done nothing in mitigating her sorrow.

The younger lady, on the other hand, who was Lady Errol's sister —— Heavens! what a spirit of joy and festal pleasure radiated from her eyes, her step, her voice, her manner! She was Irish, and the very impersonation of innocent gaiety, such as we find oftener, perhaps, amongst Irish women than those of any other country. Mourning, I have said, she wore; from sisterly consideration, the deepest mourning: that sole expression there was about her of gloom or solemn feeling—

> *But all things else about her drawn*
> *From May-time and the cheerful dawn.*

Odious bluestocking [1] of Belfast and Dublin! as some

[1] I have sometimes had occasion to remark, as a noticeable phenomenon of our present times, that the order of ladies called *Bluestockings,* by way of reproach, has become totally extinct amongst us, except only here and there, with superannuated clingers to obsolete remembrances. The reason of this change is interesting; and I do not scruple to call it honourable to our intellectual progress. In the last (but still more in the penultimate) generation, any tincture of literature, of liberal curiosity about science, or of ennobling interest in books, carried with it an air of something unsexual, mannish, and (as it was treated by the sycophantish satirists that for ever humour the prevailing folly) of something ludicrous. This mode of treatment was possible so long as the literary class of ladies formed a feeble minority. But now, when two vast peoples, English and American, counting between them forty-nine millions, when the leaders of transcendent civilization (to say nothing of Germany and France), behold their entire educated class, male and female alike, calling out, not for *Panem et Circenses* (Give us this day our daily bread and our games of the circus), but for *Panem et Literas* (Give us this day our daily bread and literature), the universality of the call has swept away the very name of *Bluestocking;* the very possibility of the ridicule has been undermined by stern realities; and the verbal expression of the reproach is fast becoming not simply obsolete, but even unintelligible to our juniors. By the way, the origin of this term *Bluestocking* has

would call you, how I hated you up to that moment! half-an-hour after, how grateful I felt for the hostility which had procured me such an alliance. One minute sufficed to put the quick-witted young Irishwoman in possession of our little drama, and the several parts we were playing. To look was to understand, to wish was to execute, with this ardent child of nature. Like Spenser's Bradamant, with martial scorn she couched her lance on the side of the party suffering wrong. Her rank, as sister-in-law to the Constable of Scotland, gave her some advantage for winning a favourable au-

never been satisfactorily accounted for; unless the reader should incline to think *my* account satisfactory. I incline to that opinion myself. Dr. Bisset (in his *Life of Burke*) traces it idly to a *sobriquet* imposed by Mrs. Montagu, and the literary ladies of her circle, upon a certain obscure Dr. Stillingfleet, who was the sole masculine assistant at their literary sittings in Portman Square, and chose, upon some inexplicable craze, to wear blue stockings. The translation, however, of this name from the doctor's legs to the ladies' legs is still unsolved. That great *hiatus* needs filling up. I, therefore, whether erroneously or not, in reviewing a German historical work of some pretensions, where this problem emerges, rejected the Portman Square doctor altogether, and traced the term to an old Oxford statute—one of the many which meddle with dress, and which charges it as a point of conscience upon loyal scholastic students that they shall wear cerulean socks. Such socks, therefore, indicated scholasticism: worn by females, they would indicate a self-dedication to what for them would be regarded as pedantic studies. But, says an objector, no rational female *would* wear cerulean socks. Perhaps not, female taste being too good. But, as such socks would symbolize such a profession of pedantry, so, inversely, any profession of pedantry, by whatever signs expressed, would be symbolized reproachfully by the imputation of wearing cerulean socks. It classed a woman in effect as a scholastic pedant. Now, however, when the vast diffusion of literature as a sort of daily bread has made all ridicule of female literary culture not less ridiculous than would be the attempt to ridicule that same daily bread, the whole phenomenon, thing and word, substance and shadow, is melting away from amongst us.

dience; and, throwing her ægis over me, she extended
that benefit to myself. Road was now made perforce
for me also; my replies were no longer stifled in noise
and laughter. Personalities were banished; literature
was extensively discussed; and that is a subject which,
offering little room to argument, offers the widest to
eloquent display. I had immense reading; vast command of words, which somewhat diminished as ideas
and doubts multiplied; and, speaking no longer to a
deaf audience, but to a generous and indulgent protectress, I threw out, as from a cornucopia, my illustrative details and recollections; trivial enough, perhaps, as I might now think, but the more intelligible to
my present circle. It might seem too much the case of
a storm in a slop-basin, if I were to spend any words
upon the revolution which ensued. Suffice it that I remained the lion of that company which had previously
been most insultingly facetious at my expense; and the
intellectual lady finally declared the air of the deck
unpleasant.

Never, until this hour, had I thought of women as
objects of a possible interest, or of a reverential love. I
had known them either in their infirmities and their
unamiable aspects, or else in those sterner relations
which made them objects of ungenial and uncompan-
ionable feelings. Now first it struck me that life might
owe half its attractions and all its graces to female
companionship. Gazing, perhaps, with too earnest an
admiration at this generous and spirited young daughter of Ireland, and in that way making her those acknowledgements for her goodness which I could not
properly clothe in words, I was roused to a sense of my
indecorum by seeing her suddenly blush. I believe that
Miss Bl—— interpreted my admiration rightly; for
she was not offended; but, on the contrary, for the rest
of the day, when not attending to her sister, conversed

almost exclusively, and in a confidential way, with Lord Westport and myself. The whole, in fact, of this conversation must have convinced her that I, mere boy as I was (viz., about fifteen), could not have presumed to direct my admiration to *her*, a fine young woman of twenty, in any other character than that of a generous champion, and a very adroit mistress in the dazzling fence of colloquial skirmish. My admiration had, in reality, been addressed to her moral qualities, her enthusiasm, her spirit, and her generosity. Yet that blush, evanescent as it was—the mere possibility that I, so very a child, should have called up the most transitory sense of bashfulness or confusion upon any female cheek, first—and suddenly as with a flash of lightning penetrating some utter darkness—illuminated to my own startled consciousness, never again to be obscured, the pure and powerful ideal of womanhood and womanly excellence. This was, in a proper sense, a *revelation;* it fixed a great era of change in my life; and, this new-born idea being agreeable to the uniform tendencies of my own nature—that is, lofty and aspiring—it governed my life with great power, and with most salutary effects. Ever after, throughout the period of youth, I was jealous of my own demeanour, reserved and awestruck in the presence of women; reverencing, often, not so much *them*, as my own ideal of woman latent in them. For I carried about with me the idea, to which often I seemed to see an approximation, of

> *A perfect woman, nobly plann'd,*
> *To warn, to comfort, to command.*

And from this day I was an altered creature, never again relapsing into the careless, irreflective mind of childhood.

For what purpose have I repeated this story? The

reader may, perhaps, suppose it introductory to some
tale of boyish romantic passion for some female idol
clothed with imaginary perfections. But in that case
he will be mistaken. Nothing of the kind was possible
to me. I was pre-occupied by other passions. Under the
disease—for disease it was—which at that time mastered me, one solitary desire, one frenzy, one demoniac
fascination stronger than the fascinations of calenture,
brooded over me as the moon over the tides—forcing
me day and night into speculations upon great intellectual problems, many times beyond my strength, as
indeed often beyond all human strength, but not the
less provoking me to pursue them. As a prophet in days
of old had no power to resist the voice which, from
hidden worlds, called him to a mission, sometimes,
perhaps, revolting to his human sensibilities—as he
must deliver, was under a coercion to deliver, the burning word that spoke within his heart; or as a ship on
the Indian Ocean cannot seek rest by anchoring, but
must run before the wrath of the monsoon; such in its
fury, such in its unrelentingness, was the persecution
that overmastered me. School tasks under these circumstances, it may well be supposed, had become a
torment to me. For a long time they had lost even that
slight power of stimulation which belongs to the irritation of difficulty. Easy and simple they had now
become as the elementary lessons of childhood. Not
that it is possible for Greek studies, if pursued with
unflinching sincerity, ever to fall so far into the rear
as a *palæstra* for exercising both strength and skill;
but, in a school where the exercises are pursued in common by large classes, the burden must be adapted to
the powers of the weakest, and not of the strongest.
And, apart from that objection, at this period, the
hasty unfolding of far different intellectual interests
than such as belong to mere literature had, for a time,

dimmed in my eyes the lustre of classical studies, pursued at whatsoever depth, and on whatsoever scale. For more than a year, everything connected with schools and the business of schools had been growing more and more hateful to me. At first, however, my disgust had been merely the disgust of weariness and pride. But now, at this crisis (for crisis it was virtually to me), when a premature development of my whole mind was rushing in like a cataract, forcing channels for itself and for the new tastes which it introduced, my disgust was no longer simply intellectual, but had deepened into a *moral* sense as of some inner dignity continually violated. Once the petty round of school tasks had been felt as a molestation; but now, at last, as a degradation. Constant conversation with grown-up men for the last half-year, and upon topics oftentimes of the gravest order—the responsibility that had always in some slight degree settled upon myself since I had become the eldest surviving son of my family, but of late much more so when circumstances had thrown me as an English stranger upon the society of distinguished Irishmen—more, however, than all beside, the inevitable rebound and counter-growth of internal dignity from the everlasting commerce with lofty speculations: these agencies in constant operation had embittered my school disgust, until it was travelling fast into a mania. Precisely at this culminating point of my self-conflict did that scene occur which I have described with Miss Bl———. In that hour another element, which assuredly was not wanted, fell into the seething cauldron of new-born impulses that, like the magic cauldron of Medea, was now transforming me into a new creature. Then first and suddenly I brought powerfully before myself the change which was worked in the aspects of society by the presence of woman—woman pure, thoughtful, noble, coming before me as a Pandora crowned with perfections. Right over against this ennobling spectacle, with equal suddenness, I placed the odious spectacle of schoolboy society —no matter in what region of the earth; schoolboy society, so frivolous in the matter of its disputes, often so brutal in the manner; so childish, and yet so remote from simplicity; so foolishly careless, and yet so revoltingly selfish; dedicated ostensibly to learning, and yet beyond any section of human beings so conspicuously ignorant. Was it indeed *that* heavenly, which I was soon to exchange for *this* earthly? It seemed to me, when contemplating the possibility that I could yet have nearly three years to pass in such society as this, that I heard some irresistible voice saying: Lay aside thy fleshly robes of humanity, and enter for a season into some brutal incarnation.

But what connexion had this painful prospect with Laxton! Why should it press upon my anxieties in approaching that mansion, more than it had done at Westport? Naturally enough, in part, because every day brought me nearer to the horror from which I recoiled: my return to England would recall the attention of my guardians to the question, which as yet had slumbered; and the knowledge that I had reached Northamptonshire would precipitate their decision. Obscurely, besides, through a hint which had reached me, I guessed what this decision was likely to be, and it took the very worst shape it could have taken. All this increased my agitation from hour to hour. But all this was quickened and barbed by the certainty of so immediately meeting Lady Carbery. To her it was, and to her only, that I could look for any useful advice, or any effectual aid. She over my mother, as in turn my mother over *her*, exercised considerable influence; whilst my mother's power was very seldom disturbed by the other guardians. The mistress of Laxton it was,

therefore, whose opinion upon the case would virtually
be decisive; since, if *she* saw no reasonable encouragement to any contest with my guardians, I felt too
surely that my own uncountenanced and unaided energies drooped too much for such an effort. Who Lady
Carbery was, I will explain in my next chapter, entitled *Laxton*. Meantime, to me individually, she was
the one sole friend that ever I could regard as entirely
fulfilling the offices of an honourable friendship. She
had known me from infancy: when I was in my first
year of life, she—an orphan and a great heiress—was
in her tenth or eleventh; and, on her occasional visits to
"the Farm" (a rustic old house, then occupied by my
father), I, a household pet, suffering under an ague,
which lasted from my first year to my third, naturally
fell into her hands as a sort of superior toy, a toy that
could breathe and talk. Every year our intimacy had
been renewed, until her marriage interrupted it. But,
after no very long interval, when my mother had
transferred her household to Bath, in that city we frequently met again; Lord Carbery liking Bath for itself,
as well as for its easy connexion with London, whilst
Lady Carbery's health was supposed to benefit by the
waters. Her understanding was justly reputed a fine
one; but, in general, it was calculated to win respect
rather than love, for it was masculine and austere,
with very little toleration for sentiment or romance.
But to myself she had always been indulgently kind;
I was protected in her regard, beyond anybody's power
to dislodge me, by her childish remembrances; and of
late years she had begun to entertain the highest opinion of my intellectual promises. Whatever *could* be
done to assist my views, I most certainly might count
upon her doing; that is to say, within the limits of her
conscientious judgement upon the propriety of my own
plans. Having, besides, so much more knowledge of

the world than myself, she might see cause to dissent
widely from my own view of what was expedient as
well as what was right; in which case I was well assured that, in the midst of kindness and unaffected
sympathy, she would firmly adhere to the views of
my guardians. In any circumstances she would have
done so. But at present a new element had begun to
mix with the ordinary influences which governed her
estimates of things: she had, as I knew from my sister's report, become religious; and her new opinions
were of a gloomy cast—Calvinistic, in fact, and tending to what is *now* technically known in England as
"Low Church," or "Evangelical Christianity." These
views, being adopted in a great measure from my
mother, were naturally the same as my mother's; so
that I could form some guess as to the general spirit, if
not the exact direction, in which her counsels would
flow. It is singular that, until this time, I had never
regarded Lady Carbery under any relation whatever
to female intellectual society. My early childish knowledge of her had shut out that mode of viewing her.
But now, suddenly, under the new-born sympathies
awakened by the scene with Miss Bl——, I became
aware of the distinguished place she was qualified to
fill in such society. In that Eden—for such it had now
consciously become to me—I had no necessity to cultivate an interest or solicit an admission; already,
through Lady Carbery's too flattering estimate of my
own pretensions, and through old childish memories,
I held the most distinguished place. This Eden she it
was that lighted up suddenly to my new-born powers
of appreciation, in all its dreadful points of contrast
with the killing society of schoolboys. She it was, fitted
to be the glory of such an Eden, who probably would
assist in banishing me for the present to the wilderness outside. My distress of mind was inexpressible.

And, in the midst of glittering saloons, at times also in the midst of society the most fascinating, I—contemplating the idea of that gloomy academic dungeon to which for three long years I anticipated too certainly a sentence of exile—felt very much as in the middle ages must have felt some victim of evil destiny, inheritor of a false fleeting prosperity, that suddenly in a moment of time, by signs blazing out past all concealment on his forehead, was detected as a leper, and in that character, as a public nuisance and universal horror, was summoned instantly to withdraw from society—prince or peasant, was indulged with no time for preparation or evasion—and, from the midst of any society, the sweetest or the most dazzling, was driven violently to take up his abode amidst the sorrow-haunted chambers of a lazar-house.

LAXTON, NORTHAMPTONSHIRE

(First published in the Collective Edition of De Quincey's works, vol. II, 1854)

MY ROUTE, after parting from Lord Westport at Birmingham, lay (as perhaps I mentioned before) through Stamford to Laxton, the Northamptonshire seat of Lord Carbery. From Stamford, which I had reached by some intolerable old coach, such as in those days too commonly abused the patience and long-suffering of Young England, I took a post-chaise to Laxton. The distance was but nine miles, and the postilion drove well; so that I could not really have been long upon the road; and yet, from gloomy rumination upon the unhappy destination which I believed myself approaching within three or four months, never had I weathered a journey that seemed to me so long and

dreary. As I alighted on the steps at Laxton, the first
dinner-bell rang; and I was hurrying to my toilet,
when my sister Mary, who had met me in the portico,
begged me first of all to come into Lady Carbery's
dressing-room, her ladyship having something special
to communicate, which related (as I understood her)
to one Simon. "What Simon? Simon Peter?" O no,
you irreverent boy; no Simon at all with an S, but
Cymon with a C—Dryden's Cymon—

That whistled as he went for want of thought.

This one indication was a key to the whole explanation
that followed. The sole visitors, it seemed, at that time
to Laxton, beside my sister and myself, were Lord and
Lady Massey. They were understood to be domesticated at Laxton for a very long stay. In reality, my
own private construction of the case (though unauthorized by anything ever hinted to me by Lady Carbery) was that Lord Massey might probably be under
some cloud of pecuniary embarrassments, such as suggested prudentially an absence from Ireland. Meantime, what was it that made him an object of peculiar
interest to Lady Carbery? It was the singular revolution which in one whom all his friends looked upon
as sold to constitutional torpor, suddenly and beyond
all hope, had kindled a new and nobler life. Occupied
originally by no shadow of any earthly interest, killed
by *ennui*, all at once Lord Massey had fallen passionately in love with a fair young countrywoman, well
connected, but bringing him no fortune (I report only
from hearsay), and endowing him simply with the
priceless blessing of her own womanly charms, her
delightful society, and her sweet Irish style of innocent gaiety. No transformation, that ever legends or
romances had reported, was more memorable. Lapse

of time (for Lord Massey had now been married three
or four years), and deep seclusion from general society,
had done nothing apparently to lower the tone of his
happiness. The expression of this happiness was noiseless and unobtrusive; no marks were there of vulgar
uxoriousness—nothing that could provoke the sneer
of the worldling; but not the less so entirely had the
society of his young wife created a new principle of
life within him, and evoked some nature hitherto
slumbering, and which, no doubt, would else have continued to slumber till his death, that at moments when
he believed himself unobserved he still wore the aspect
of an impassioned lover.

> He beheld
> A vision, and adored the thing he saw.
> Arabian fiction never fill'd the world
> With half the wonders that were wrought for him.
> Earth breathed in one great presence of the spring—
> Her chamber window did surpass in glory
> The portals of the dawn.

And in no case was it more literally realized, as daily
almost I witnessed, that

> All Paradise
> Could, by the simple opening of a door,
> Let itself in upon him.

For never did the drawing-room door open, and suddenly disclose the beautiful figure of Lady Massey,
than a mighty cloud seemed to roll away from the
young Irishman's brow. At this time it happened, and
indeed it often happened, that Lord Carbery was absent in Ireland. It was probable, therefore, that during
the long couple of hours through which the custom of

those times bound a man to the dinner-table after the disappearance of the ladies, his time would hang heavily on his hands. To me, therefore, Lady Carbery looked, having first put me in possession of the case, for assistance to her hospitality, under the difficulties I have stated. She thoroughly loved Lady Massey, as, indeed, nobody could help doing; and for *her* sake, had there been no separate interest surrounding the young lord, it would have been most painful to her that, through Lord Carbery's absence, a periodic tedium should oppress her guest at that precise season of the day which traditionally dedicated itself to genial enjoyment. Glad, therefore, she was that an ally had come at last to Laxton, who might arm her purposes of hospitality with some powers of self-fulfilment. And yet, for a service of that nature, could she reasonably rely upon me? Odious is the hobble-de-hoy to the mature young man. Generally speaking, that cannot be denied. But in me, though naturally the shyest of human beings, intense commerce with men of every rank, from the highest to the lowest, had availed to dissipate all arrears of *mauvaise honte;* I could talk upon innumerable subjects; and, as the readiest means of entering immediately upon business, I was fresh from Ireland—knew multitudes of those whom Lord Massey either knew or felt an interest in—and, at that happy period of life, found it easy, with three or four glasses of wine, to call back the golden spirits which were now so often deserting me. Renovated, meantime, by a hot bath, I was ready at the second summons of the dinner-bell, and descended, a new creature, to the drawing-room. Here I was presented to the noble lord and his wife. Lord Massey was in figure shortish, but broad and stout, and wore an amiable expression of face. That I could execute Lady Carbery's commission, I felt satisfied at once. And, accordingly,

when the ladies had retired from the dining-room, I
found an easy opening, in various circumstances
connected with the Laxton stables, for introducing
naturally a picturesque and contrasting sketch of
the stud and the stables at Westport. The stables,
and everything connected with the stables, at Laxton,
were magnificent; in fact, far out of symmetry with
the house, which at that time was elegant and comfortable, but not splendid. As usual in English establishments, all the appointments were complete, and
carried to the same point of exquisite finish. The stud
of hunters was first-rate and extensive; and the whole
scene, at closing the stables for the night, was so splendidly arranged and illuminated that Lady Carbery
would take all her visitors once or twice a week to
admire it. On the other hand, at Westport you might
fancy yourself overlooking the establishment of some
Albanian pacha. Crowds of irregular helpers and
grooms, many of them totally unrecognized by Lord
Altamont, some half-countenanced by this or that
upper servant, some doubtfully tolerated, some *not*
tolerated but nevertheless slipping in by postern-doors
when the enemy had withdrawn, made up a strange
mob as regarded the human element in this establishment. And Dean Browne regularly asserted that five
out of six amongst these helpers he himself could swear
to as active boys from Vinegar Hill. Trivial enough,
meantime, in our eyes, was any little matter of rebellion that they might have upon their consciences. High
treason we willingly winked at. But what we could
not wink at was the systematic treason which they
committed against our comfort—viz., by teaching our
horses all imaginable tricks, and training them up in
the way along which they should *not* go, so that when
they were old they were very little likely to depart
from it. Such a set of restive, hard-mouthed wretches

as Lord Westport and I daily had to bestride, no tongue could describe.

From these wild, Tartar-like stables of Connaught, how vast was the transition to that perfection of elegance and of adaptation between means and ends that reigned from centre to circumference through the stables at Laxton! *I*, as it happened, could report to Lord Massey their earlier condition; he to me could report their immediate changes. I won him easily to an interest in my own Irish experiences, so fresh, and in parts so grotesque, wilder also by much in Connaught than in Lord Massey's county of Limerick; whilst he (without affecting any delight in the hunting systems of Northamptonshire and Leicestershire) yet took pleasure in explaining to me those characteristic features of the English midland hunting, as centralized at Melton, which even then gave to it the supreme rank for brilliancy and unity of effect amongst all varieties of the chase.

Horses had formed the natural and introductory topic of conversation between us. What we severally knew of Ireland, though in different quarters—what we both knew of Laxton—the barbaric splendour and the civilized splendour, had naturally an interest for us both in their contrasts (at one time so picturesque, at another so grotesque), which illuminated our separate recollections. But my quick instinct soon made me aware that a jealousy was gathering in Lord Massey's mind around such a topic, as though too ostentatiously levelled to his particular knowledge, or to his *animal* condition of taste. But easily I slipped off into another key. At Laxton, it happened that the library was excellent. Founded by whom, I never heard : but certainly, when used by a systematic reader, it showed itself to have been systematically collected; it stretched pretty equally through two centuries—

viz., from about 1600 to 1800—and might perhaps amount to 17,000 volumes. Lord Massey was far from illiterate: and his interest in books was unaffected, if limited and too often interrupted by defective knowledge. The library was dispersed through six or seven small rooms, lying between the drawing-room in one wing and the dining-room in the opposite wing. This dispersion, however, already furnished the ground of a rude classification. In some one of these rooms was Lord Massey always to be found, from the forenoon to the evening. And was it any fault of *his*, that his daughter, little Grace, about two years old, pursued him down from her nursery every morning, and insisted upon seeing innumerable pictures, lurking (as she had discovered) in many different recesses of the library? More and more from this quarter it was that we drew the materials of our daily after-dinner conversation. One great discouragement arises commonly to the student, where the particular library in which he reads has been so disordinately collected that he cannot *pursue* a subject once started. Now, at Laxton, the books had been so judiciously brought together, so many hooks and eyes connected them, that the whole library formed what one might call a series of *strata*, naturally allied, through which you might quarry your way consecutively for many months. On rainy days, and often enough one had occasion to say through rainy weeks, what a delightful resource did this library prove to both of us! And one day it occurred to us that, whereas the stables and the library were both jewels of attraction, the latter had been by much the least costly. Pretty often I have found, when any opening has existed for making the computation, that, in a library containing a fair proportion of books illustrated with plates, about ten shillings a volume might be taken as expressing, upon a sufficiently large num-

ber of volumes, small and great, the fair average cost
of the whole. On this basis, the library at Laxton
would have cost less than £9000. On the other hand,
35 horses (hunters, racers, roadsters, carriage-horses,
&c.) might have cost about £8000, or a little more.
But the library entailed no permanent cost beyond the
annual loss of interest: the books did not eat, and required no aid from veterinary surgeons: whereas, for
the horses, not only such ministrations were intermittingly required, but a costly permanent establishment
of grooms and helpers. Lord Carbery, who had received an elaborate Etonian education, was even more
earnestly a student than his friend Lord Massey, who
had probably been educated at home under a private
tutor. He read everything connected with general
politics (meaning by *general* not personal politics)
and with social philosophy. At Laxton, indeed, it was
that I first saw Godwin's *Political Justice;* not the second and emasculated edition in *octavo,* but the original
quarto edition, with all its virus as yet undiluted of
raw anti-social Jacobinism.

At Laxton it was that I first saw the entire aggregate labours, brigaded, as it were, and paraded as if
for martial review, of that most industrious benefactor
to the early stages of our English historical literature,
Thomas Hearne. Three hundred guineas, I believe,
had been the price paid cheerfully at one time for a
complete set of Hearne. At Laxton, also, it was that
first I saw the total array of works edited by Dr. Birch.
It was a complete *armilustrium,* a *recognitio,* or mustering, as it were, not of pompous Prætorian cohorts,
or unique guardsmen, but of the yeomanry, the militia,
or what, under the old form of expression, you might
regard as the *trained bands* of our literature—the fund
from which ultimately, or in the last resort, students
look for the materials of our vast and myriad-faced

literature. A French author of eminence, fifty years
back, having occasion to speak of our English literature collectively, in reference to the one point of its
variety, being also a man of honour, and disdaining
that sort of patriotism which sacrifices the truth to
nationality, speaks of our pretensions in these words:
*Les Anglois qui ont une littérature infiniment plus
variée que la nôtre.* This fact is a feature in our national pretensions that could ever have been regarded
doubtfully merely through insufficient knowledge.
Dr. Johnson, indeed, made it the distinguishing merit
of the French, that they "have a book upon every subject." But Dr. Johnson was not only capricious as regards temper and variable humours, but as regards
the inequality of his knowledge. Incoherent and unsystematic was Dr. Johnson's information in most
cases. Hence his extravagant misappraisement of
Knolles, the Turkish historian, which is exposed so
severely by Spittler, the German, who, again, is himself miserably superficial in his analysis of English
History. Hence the feeble credulity which Dr. Johnson showed with respect to the forgery of De Foe
(under the masque of Captain Carleton) upon the
Catalonian campaign of Lord Peterborough. But it
is singular that a literature so unrivalled as ours in
its compass and variety should not have produced any,
even the shallowest, manual of itself. And thus it happens, for example, that writers so laborious and serviceable as Birch are in any popular sense scarcely
known. I showed to Lord Massey, among others of his
works, that which relates to Lord Worcester's (*i.e.*,
Lord Glamorgan's) negotiations with the Papal nun-
cio in Ireland about the year 1644, &c. Connected
with these negotiations were many names amongst
Lord Massey's own ancestors; so that here he suddenly alighted upon a fund of archæologic memora-

bilia, connecting what interested him as an Irishman in general with what most interested him as the head of a particular family. It is remarkable, also, as an indication of the *general* nobility and elevation which had accompanied the revolution in his life, that, concurrently with the constitutional torpor previously besetting him, had melted away the intellectual torpor under which he had found books until recently of little practical value. Lady Carbery had herself told me that the two revolutions went on simultaneously. He began to take an interest in literature when life itself unfolded a new interest, under the companionship of his youthful wife.

Meantime Lord Massey was reached by reports both through Lady Carbery and myself of something which interested him more profoundly than all earthly records of horsemanship, or any conceivable questions connected with books. Lady Carbery, with a view to the amusement of Lady Massey and my sister, for both of whom youth and previous seclusion had created a natural interest in all such scenes, accepted two or three times in every week dinner invitations to all the families on her visiting list, and lying within her winter circle, which was measured by a radius of about seventeen miles. For, dreadful as were the roads in those days, when the Bath, the Bristol, or the Dover mail was equally perplexed oftentimes to accomplish Mr. Palmer's rate of seven miles an hour, a distance of seventeen was yet easily accomplished in 100 minutes by the powerful Laxton horses. Magnificent was the Laxton turn-out; and in the roomy travelling-coach of Lady Carbery, made large enough to receive upon occasion even a bed, it would have been an idle scruple to fear the crowding a party which mustered only three besides myself: for Lord Massey uniformly declined joining us—in which I believe that he was right. A schoolboy like myself had fortunately no dignity to lose. But Lord Massey, a needy Irish peer (or, strictly speaking, since the Union no peer at all, though still a hereditary lord), was bound to be trebly vigilant over his surviving honours. This he owed to his country as well as to his family. He recoiled from what he figured to himself (but too often falsely figured) as the haughty and disdainful English nobility —all so rich, all so polished in manner, all so punctiliously correct in the ritual of *bienséance*. Lord Carbery might face them gaily and boldly; for *he* was rich, and, although possessing Irish estates and an Irish mansion, was a thorough Englishman by education and early association. "But I," said Lord Massey, "had a careless Irish education, and am never quite sure that I may not be trespassing on some mysterious law of English good-breeding." In vain I suggested to him, that most of what passed amongst foreigners and amongst Irishmen for English *hauteur* was pure reserve, which, among all people that were bound over by the inevitable restraints of their rank (imposing, it must be remembered, jealous duties as well as privileges), was sure to become the operative feeling. I contended, that in the English situation there was no escaping this English reserve, except by great impudence and defective sensibility; and that, if examined, reserve was the truest expression of respect towards those who were its objects. In vain did Lady Carbery back me in this representation. He stood firm, and never once accompanied us to any dinner party. Northamptonshire, I know not why, is (or then was) more thickly sown with aristocratic families than any in the kingdom. Many elegant and pretty women there naturally were in these parties; but undoubtedly our two Laxton baronesses shone advantageously amongst them. A boy like myself could lay no restraint upon the after-dinner feelings of the gentlemen; and almost uniformly I heard such verdicts passed upon the personal attractions of both, but especially Lady Massey, as tended greatly to soothe the feelings of Lord Massey. It is singular that Lady Massey universally carried off the palm of unlimited homage. Lady Carbery was a regular beauty, and publicly known for such; both were fine figures, and apparently not older than twenty-six; but in her Irish friend people felt something more thoroughly artless and feminine—for the masculine understanding of Lady Carbery in some way communicated its commanding expression to her deportment. I reported to Lord Massey, in terms of unexceptionable decorum, those flattering expressions of homage which sometimes, from the lips of young men partially under the influence of wine, had taken a form somewhat too enthusiastic for literal repetition to a chivalrous and adoring husband.

From the first I had been aware, on this visit to Laxton, that Lady Carbery had changed, and was changing. She had become religious, so much I knew from my sister's letters. And, in fact, this change had been due to her intercourse with my mother. But, in reality, her premature disgust with the world would at any rate have made her such; and, had any mode of monastic life existed for Protestants, I believe that she would before this have entered it, supposing Lord Carbery to have consented. People generally would have stated the case most erroneously; they would have said that she was sinking into gloom under religious influences; whereas the very contrary was the truth—viz., that, having sunk into gloomy discontent with life, and its miserable performances as contrasted with its promises, she sought relief and support to her wounded feelings from religion.

Our authorized translators of the Bible in the Shakespearian age were not in any exquisite sense learned men; they were very able men, and in a better sense able than if they had been philologically profound scholars, which at that time, from the imperfect culture of philology, they could not easily have been; men they were whom religious feeling guided correctly in choosing their expressions, and with whom the state of the language in some respects co-operated, by furnishing a diction more homely, fervent, and pathetic, than would now be available. For *their* apostolic functions, English was the language most in demand. But in polemic or controversial cases Greek is indispensable. She resolved, therefore, immediately on my suggesting it, that she would learn Greek; or, at least, that limited form of Greek which was required for the New Testament. In the language of Terence, *dictum factum*—no sooner said than done. On the very next morning we all rode in to Stamford, our nearest town for such a purpose, and astounded the bookseller's apprentice by ordering four copies of the Clarendon Press *Greek Testament*, three copies of Parkhurst's *Greek and English Lexicon*, and three copies of some grammar, but *what* I have now forgotten. The books were to come down by the mail-coach without delay. Consequently, we were soon at work. Lady Massey and my sister, not being sustained by the same interest as Lady Carbery, eventually relaxed in their attention. But Lady Carbery was quite in earnest, and very soon became expert in the original language of the New Testament.

I wished much that she should have gone on to the study of Herodotus. And I described to her the situation of the vivacious and mercurial Athenian, in the early period of Pericles, as repeating in its main features, for the great advantage of that Grecian Froissart, the situation of Adam during his earliest hours in Paradise, himself being the describer to the affable archangel. The same genial climate there was; the same luxuriation of nature in her early prime; the same ignorance of his own origin in the tenant of this lovely scenery; and the same eager desire to learn it. The very truth, and mere facts of history, reaching Herodotus through such a haze of remote abstraction, and suffering a sort of refraction at each translation from atmosphere to atmosphere, whilst continually the uninteresting parts dropped away as the whole moved onwards, unavoidably assumed the attractions of romance. And thus it has happened, that the air of marvellousness, which seems connected with the choice and preferences of Herodotus, is in reality the natural gift of his position. Culling from a field of many nations and many generations, reasonably he preferred such narratives as, though possible enough, wore the colouring of romance. Without any violation of the truth, the mere extent of his field as to space and time gave him great advantages for the wild and the marvellous. Meantime this purpose of ours with regard to Herodotus was defeated. Whilst we were making preparations for it, suddenly one morning from his Limerick estate of Carass returned Lord Carbery. And, by accident, his welcome was a rough one; for, happening to find Lady Carbery in the breakfast-room, and naturally throwing his arm about her neck to kiss her, "Ruffian," a monster of a Newfoundland dog, singularly beautiful in his colouring, and almost as powerful as a leopard, flew at him vindictively as at a stranger committing an assault, and his mistress had great difficulty in calling him off. Lord Carbery smiled a little at our Greek studies; and, in turn, made *us* smile, who knew the original object of these studies, when he suggested mildly that three or four books of the Iliad would have been as easily mastered, and might have more fully rewarded our trouble. I contented myself with replying (for I knew how little Lady Carbery would have liked to plead the *religious* motive to her husband) that Parkhurst (and there was at that time no other Greek-*English* Lexicon) would not have been available for Homer; neither, it is true, would he have been more available for Herodotus. But, considering the simplicity and uniformity of style in both these authors, I had formed a plan (not very hard of execution) for interleaving Parkhurst with such additional words as might have been easily mustered from the special dictionaries (Græco-Latin) dedicated separately to the service of the historian and of the poet. I do not believe that more than 1500 *extra* words would have been required; and these, entered at the rate of twenty per hour, would have occupied only ten days, for seven and a half hours each. However, from one cause or other, this plan was never brought to bear. The preliminary labour upon the lexicon always enforced a delay; and any delay, in such case, makes an opening for the irruption of a thousand unforeseen hindrances, that finally cause the whole plan to droop insensibly. The time came at last for leaving Laxton, and I did not see Lady Carbery again for nearly an entire year.

In passing through the park-gates of Laxton, on my departure northward, powerfully, and as if "with the might of waters," my mind turned round to contemplate that strange enlargement of my experience which had happened to me within the last three months. I had seen, and become familiarly acquainted with, a young man, who had in a manner died to every object around him, had died an intellectual death, and suddenly had been called back to life and real happiness——had been, in effect, raised from the dead——by the accident of meeting a congenial female companion. But, secondly, that very lady from whose lips I first heard this remarkable case of blight and restoration, had herself passed through an equal though not a similar blight, and was now seeking earnestly, though with what success I could never estimate, some similar restoration to some new mode of hopeful existence, through intercourse with religious philosophy. What vast revolutions (vast for the individual) within how narrow a circle! What blindness to approaching catastrophes, in the midst of what nearness to the light! And for myself, whom accident had made the silent observer of these changes, was it not likely enough that I also was rushing forward to court and woo some frantic mode of evading an endurance that by patience might have been borne, or by thoughtfulness might have been disarmed? Misgivingly I went forwards, feeling for ever that, through clouds of thick darkness, I was continually nearing a danger, or was myself perhaps wilfully provoking a trial, before which my constitutional despondency would cause me to lie down without a struggle.

THE MANCHESTER GRAMMAR SCHOOL

(First published in the Collective Edition of De Quincey's works, vol. II, 1854)

To TEACH is to learn: according to an old experience, it is the very best mode of learning—the surest, and the shortest. And hence, perhaps, it may be, that in the middle ages by the monkish word *scholaris* was meant indifferently he that learned and he that taught. Never in any equal number of months had my understanding so much expanded as during this visit to

Laxton. The incessant demand made upon me by Lady
Carbery for solutions of the many difficulties besetting
the study of divinity and the Greek Testament, or for
such approximations to solutions as my resources would
furnish, forced me into a preternatural tension of all
the faculties applicable to that purpose. Lady Carbery
insisted upon calling me her "Admirable Crichton";
and it was in vain that I demurred to this honorary
title upon two grounds: first, as being one towards
which I had no natural aptitudes or predisposing advantages; secondly (which made her stare), as carrying with it no real or enviable distinction. The splendour supposed to be connected with the attainments
of Crichton I protested against as altogether imaginary. How far that person really had the accomplishments ascribed to him, I waived as a question not
worth investigating. My objection commenced at an
earlier point: real or not real, the accomplishments
were, as I insisted, vulgar and trivial. Vulgar, that is,
when put forward as exponents or adequate expressions of intellectual grandeur. The whole rested on a
misconception; the limitary idea of knowledge was
confounded with the infinite idea of power. To have
a quickness in copying or mimicking other men, and
in learning to do dexterously what *they* did clumsily,
ostentatiously to keep glittering before men's eyes a
thaumaturgic versatility, such as that of a rope-
dancer or of an Indian juggler, in petty accomplishments, was a mode of the very vulgarest ambition:
one effort of productive power, a little book, for instance, which should impress or should agitate several
successive generations of men, even though far below
the higher efforts of human creative art—as, for example, the *De Imitatione Christi*, or the *Pilgrim's
Progress*, or *Robinson Crusoe*, or *The Vicar of Wakefield*—was worth any conceivable amount of attain-

ments when rated as an evidence of anything that
could justly denominate a man "admirable." One
felicitous ballad of forty lines might have enthroned
Crichton as really admirable, whilst the pretensions
actually put forward on his behalf simply install him
as a cleverish or dexterous ape. However, as Lady Carbery did not forego her purpose of causing me to shine
under every angle, it would have been ungrateful in
me to refuse my co-operation with her plans, however
little they might wear a face of promise. Accordingly
I surrendered myself for two hours daily to the lessons
in horsemanship of a principal groom who ranked as
a first-rate rough-rider; and I gathered manifold experiences amongst the horses—so different from the
wild, hard-mouthed horses at Westport, that were
often vicious, and sometimes trained to vice. Here,
though spirited, the horses were pretty generally gentle, and all had been regularly broke. My education
was not entirely neglected even as regarded sports-
manship, that great branch of philosophy being confided to one of the keepers, who was very attentive to
me, in deference to the interest in myself expressed by
his idolized mistress, but otherwise regarded me probably as an object of mysterious curiosity rather than of
a sublunary hope.

Equally, in fact, as regarded my physics and my
metaphysics—in short, upon all lines of advance that
interested my ambition—I was going rapidly ahead.
And, speaking seriously, in what regarded my intellectual expansion, never before or since had I been so
distinctly made aware of it. No longer did it seem to
move upon the hour-hand, whose advance, though
certain, is yet a pure matter of inference, but upon the
seconds-hand, which *visibly* comes on at a trotting
pace. Everything prospered, except my own present
happiness, and the possibility of any happiness for

some years to come. About two months after leaving
Laxton, my fate in the worst shape I had anticipated
was solemnly and definitively settled. My guardians
agreed that the most prudent course, with a view to
my pecuniary interests, was to place me at the Manchester Grammar School; not with a view to further
improvement in my classical knowledge, though the
head-master was a sound scholar, but simply with a
view to one of the school *exhibitions*.[1] Amongst the
countless establishments, scattered all over England
by the noble munificence of Englishmen and English-
women in past generations, for connecting the provincial towns with the two royal universities of the land,
this Manchester school was one: in addition to other
great local advantages (viz., *inter alia*, a fine old library and an ecclesiastical foundation, which in this
present generation has furnished the materials for a
bishopric of Manchester, with its deanery and chapter), this noble foundation secured a number of exhibitions at Brasenose College, Oxford, to those pupils
of the school who should study at Manchester for three
consecutive years. The pecuniary amount of these exhibitions has since then increased considerably through
the accumulation of funds which the commercial character of that great city had caused to be neglected. At
that time I believe each exhibition yielded about forty
guineas a year, and was legally tenable for seven successive years. Now, to me this would have offered a
most seasonable advantage, had it been resorted to
some two years earlier. My small patrimonial inheritance gave to me, as it did to each of my four brothers,

---

[1] "*Exhibitions*": This is the technical name in many cases,
corresponding to the *bursæ* or *bursaries* of the Continent;
from which word *bursæ* is derived, I believe, the German
term *Bursch*; that is, a bursarius, or student who lives at college upon the salary allowed by such a bursary.

exactly £150 a year; and to each of my sisters exactly
£100 a year. The Manchester exhibition of forty
guineas a year would have raised this income for seven
years to a sum close upon £200 a year. But at present
I was half-way on the road to the completion of my
sixteenth year. Commencing my period of pupilage
from that time, I should not have finished it until I
had travelled half-way through my nineteenth year.
And the specific evil that already weighed upon me
with a sickening oppression was the premature expansion of my mind, and, as a foremost consequence, in-
tolerance of boyish society. I ought to have entered
upon my *triennium* of schoolboy servitude at the age
of thirteen. As things were, a delay with which I had
nothing to do myself, this and the native character of
my mind had thrown the whole arrangement awry.
For the better half of the three years I endured it
patiently. But it had at length begun to eat more cor-
rosively into my peace of mind than ever I had anticipated.

Precisely at the worst crisis of this intolerable darkness (for such, without exaggeration, it was in its effects upon my spirits) arose, and for five or six months
steadily continued, a consolation of that nature which
hardly in dreams I could have anticipated. For even
in dreams would it have seemed reasonable or natural
that Laxton, with its entire society, should transfer
itself to Manchester? Some mighty Caliph, or lamp-
bearing Aladdin, might have worked such marvels;
but else who, or by what machinery? Nevertheless,
without either Caliph or Aladdin, and by the most
natural of mere human agencies, this change was suddenly accomplished.

Mr. White, whom I have already had occasion to
mention, was in those days the most eminent surgeon
by much in the North of England. He had by one

whole generation run before the phrenologists and
craniologists—having already measured innumerable
skulls amongst the omnigenous seafaring population
of Liverpool, illustrating all the races of men; and
was in society a most urbane and pleasant companion.
On my mother's suggestion, he had been summoned
to Laxton, in the hope that he might mitigate the torments of Mrs. Schreiber's [1] malady. If I am right in
supposing *that* to have been cancer, I presume that he
could not have added much to the prescriptions of the
local doctor.

What might be the quality or the extent of that relief with which Mr. White was able to crown the
expectations of poor Mrs. Schreiber, I do not know;
but that the relief could not have been imaginary is
certain, for he was earnestly invited to repeat his visits,
costly as unavoidably they were. Mrs. Schreiber did
not reside at Laxton. Tenderly as she loved Lady Carbery, it did not seem consistent with her dignity that
she should take a station that might have been grossly
misinterpreted; and accordingly she bought or hired
a miniature kind of villa, called *Tixover*, distant about
four miles from Laxton. A residence in such a house,
so sad and silent at this period of affliction for its mistress, would have offered too cheerless a life to Mr.
White. He took up his abode, therefore, at Laxton
during his earliest visit; and this happened to coincide
with that particular visit of my own during which I
was initiating Lady Carbery into the mysteries of New
Testament Greek. Already as an infant I had known
Mr. White; but now, when daily riding over to Tixover in company, and daily meeting at breakfast and
dinner, we became intimate. Greatly I profited by this
intimacy; and some part of my pleasure in the Laxton

[1] Lady Carbery's guardian.—ED.

plan of migration to Manchester was drawn from the
prospect of renewing it. Such a migration was suggested by Mr. White himself; and fortunately he *could*
suggest it without even the appearance of any mercenary views. His interest lay the other way. The large
special retainer, which it was felt but reasonable to
pay him under circumstances so peculiar, naturally
disturbed Mr. White; whilst the benefits of visits so
discontinuous became more and more doubtful. He
proposed it, therefore, as a measure of prudence, that
Mrs. Schreiber should take up her abode in Manchester. This counsel was adopted; and the entire Laxton
party in one week struck their Northamptonshire tents,
dived as it were into momentary darkness by a loitering journey of stages, short and few, out of consideration for the invalid, and rose again in the gloomy
streets of Manchester.

No great city (which technically it then was not.
but simply a town or large village) could present so
repulsive an exterior as the Manchester of that day.
Lodgings of *any* sort could with difficulty be obtained,
and at last only by breaking up the party. The poor
suffering lady, with her two friends, Lady Carbery and
my mother, hired one house, Lord and Lady Massey
another, and two others were occupied by attendants
—all the servants, except one lady's-maid, being every
night separated by a quarter of a mile from their mistresses. To me, however, all these discomforts were
scarcely apparent, in the prodigious revolution for the
better which was now impressed upon the tenor of
my daily life. I lived in the house of the head-master;
but every night I had leave to adjourn for four or five
hours to the drawing-room of Lady Carbery. Her
anxiety about Mrs. Schreiber would not allow of her
going abroad into society, unless upon the rarest occasions. And I, on my part, was too happy in her con-

versation—so bold, so novel, and so earnest—voluntarily to have missed any one hour of it.

Mr. White possessed a museum—formed chiefly by
himself, and originally, perhaps, directed simply to
professional objects, such as would have little chance
for engaging the attention of females. But surgeons
and speculative physicians, beyond all other classes of
intellectual men, cultivate the most enlarged and liberal curiosity; so that Mr. White's museum furnished
attractions to an unusually large variety of tastes. I
had myself already seen it; and it struck me that Mr.
White would be gratified if Lady Carbery would herself ask to see it; which accordingly she did; and thus
at once removed the painful feeling that he might be
extorting from her an expression of interest in his collection which she did not really feel.

Amongst the objects which gave a scientific interest
to the collection, naturally I have forgotten one and
all. Nothing survives, except the *humanities* of the
collection; and amongst these, two only I will molest
the reader by noticing. One of the two was a *mummy;*
the other was a *skeleton.* I, that had previously seen
the museum, warned Lady Carbery of both; but much
it mortified us, that only the skeleton was shown. Perhaps the mummy was too closely connected with the
personal history of Mr. White for exhibition to strangers! it was that of a lady who had been attended
medically for some years by Mr. White, and had owed
much alleviation of her sufferings to his inventive skill.
She had therefore felt herself called upon to memo-
rialize her gratitude by a very large bequest, not less
(I have heard) than £25,000; but with this condition
annexed to the gift—that she should be embalmed as
perfectly as the resources in that art of London and
Paris could accomplish, and that once a year Mr.
White, accompanied by two witnesses of credit, should

withdraw the veil from her face. The lady was placed
in a common English clock-case, having the usual glass
face: but a veil of white velvet obscured from all profane eyes the silent features behind. The clock I had
myself seen, when a child, and had gazed upon it with
inexpressible awe. But naturally, on my report of the
case, the whole of our party were devoured by a curiosity to see the departed fair one. Had Mr. White, indeed, furnished us with the key of the museum, leaving us to our own discretion, but restricting us only
(like a cruel Bluebeard) from looking into any ante-
room, great is my fear that the perfidious question
would have arisen amongst us—what o'clock it was?
and all possible anterooms would have given way to
the just fury of our passions. I submitted to Lady Carbery, as a liberty which might be excused by the torrid
extremity of our thirst after knowledge, that she (as
our leader) should throw out some angling question
moving in the line of our desires; upon which hint Mr.
White, if he had any touch of indulgence to human
infirmity—unless Mount Caucasus were his mother,
and a she-wolf his nurse—would surely relent, and
act as his conscience must suggest. But Lady Carbery
reminded me of the three Calendars in the *Arabian
Nights*, and argued that, as the ladies of Bagdad were
justified in calling upon a body of porters to kick those
gentlemen into the street, being people who had abused
the indulgences of hospitality, much more might Mr.
White do so with us; for the Calendars were the children of kings (Shahzades), which we were not; and
had found their curiosity far more furiously irritated:
in fact, Zobeide had no right to trifle with any man's
curiosity in that ferocious extent; and a counter-right
arose, as any chancery of human nature would have
ruled, to demand a solution of what had been so mali-
ciously arranged towards an anguish of insupportable

temptation. Thus, however, it happened that the mummy, who left such valuable legacies, and founded such bilious fevers of curiosity, was not seen by us; nor even the miserable clock-case.

The mummy, therefore, was not seen; but the skeleton *was*. Who was he? It is not every day that one makes the acquaintance of a skeleton; and with regard to such a thing—thing, shall one say, or person?— there is a favourable presumption from beforehand; which is this: As he is of no use, neither profitable nor ornamental, to any person whatever, absolutely *de trop* in good society, what but distinguished merit of some kind or other could induce any man to interfere with that gravitating tendency that by an eternal *nisus* is pulling him below ground? Lodgings are dear in England. True it is that, according to the vile usage on the Continent, one room serves a skeleton for bedroom and sitting-room; neither is his expense heavy, as regards wax-lights, fire, or "bif-steck." But still, even a skeleton is chargeable; and, if any dispute should arise about his maintenance, the parish will do nothing. Mr. White's skeleton, therefore, being costly, was presumably meritorious, before we had seen him or heard a word in his behalf. It was, in fact, the skeleton of an eminent robber, or perhaps of a murderer. But I, for my part, reserved a faint right of suspense. And, as to the profession of robber in those days exercised on the roads of England, it was a liberal profession, which required more accomplishments than either the bar or the pulpit; from the beginning it presumed a most bountiful endowment of heroic qualifications—strength, health, agility, and exquisite horsemanship, intrepidity of the first order, presence of mind, courtesy, and a general ambidexterity of powers for facing all accidents, and for turning to a good account all unlooked-for contingencies. The finest men

in England, physically speaking, throughout the eighteenth century, the very noblest specimens of man,
considered as an animal, were beyond a doubt the
mounted robbers who cultivated their profession on
the great leading roads—viz., on the road from London to York (technically known as "the Great North
Road") ; on the road west to Bath, and thence to
Exeter and Plymouth; north-westwards from London
to Oxford, and thence to Chester; eastwards to Tun-
bridge; southwards by east to Dover; then inclining
westwards to Portsmouth; more so still, through Salisbury to Dorsetshire and Wilts. These great roads were
farmed out as so many Roman provinces amongst
proconsuls. Yes, but with a difference, you will say,
in respect of moral principles. Certainly with a difference: for the English highwayman had a sort of
conscience for gala-days, which could not often be
said of the Roman governor or procurator.

At this moment we see that the opening for the
forger of banknotes is brilliant; but practically it
languishes, as being too brilliant: it demands an array
of talent for engraving, &c., which, wherever it exists,
is sufficient to carry a man forward upon principles
reputed honourable. Why then should *he* court danger
and disreputability? But in that century the special
talents which led to distinction upon the high road had
oftentimes no career open to them elsewhere. The
mounted robber on the highways of England, in an
age when all gentlemen travelled with firearms, lived
in an element of danger and adventurous gallantry;
which, even from those who could least allow him any
portion of their esteem, extorted sometimes a good
deal of their unwilling admiration. By the necessities
of the case, he brought into his perilous profession
some brilliant qualities—intrepidity, address, promp-
titude of decision; and if to these he added courtesy,

and a spirit (native or adopted) of forbearing generosity, he seemed almost a man that merited public encouragement: since very plausibly it might be argued that his profession was sure to exist; that, if he were removed, a successor would inevitably arise, and that successor might or might *not* carry the same liberal and humanizing temper into his practice. The man whose skeleton was now before us had ranked amongst the most chivalrous of his order, and was regarded by some people as vindicating the national honour in a point where not very long before it had suffered a transient eclipse. In the preceding generation, it had been felt as throwing a shade of disgrace over the public honour, that the championship of England upon the high road fell for a time into French hands: upon French prowess rested the burden of English honour, or, in Gallic phrase, of English *glory*. Claude Duval, a Frenchman of undeniable courage, handsome, and noted for his chivalrous devotion to women, had been honoured, on his condemnation to the gallows, by the tears of many ladies who attended his trial, and by their sympathizing visits during his imprisonment.

But the robber represented by the skeleton in Mr. White's museum (whom let us call X, since his true name has perished), added to the same heroic qualities a person far more superb. Still it was a dreadful drawback from his pretensions, if he had really practised as a murderer. Upon what ground did that suspicion arise? In candour (for candour is due even to a skeleton) it ought to be mentioned that the charge, if it amounted to so much, arose with a lady from some part of Cheshire—the district of Knutsford, I believe— but, wherever it was, in the same district, during the latter part of his career, had resided our X. At first he was not suspected even as a robber—as yet not so much as suspected of being suspicious: in a simple rustic neighbourhood, amongst good-natured peasants, for a long time he was regarded with simple curiosity, rather than suspicion; and even the curiosity pointed to his horse more than to himself. The robber had made himself popular amongst the kind-hearted rustics by his general courtesy. Courtesy and the spirit of neighbourliness go a great way amongst country people; and the worst construction of the case was, that he might be an embarrassed gentleman from Manchester or Liverpool, hiding himself from his creditors, who are notoriously a very immoral class of people. At length, however, a violent suspicion broke loose against him; for it was ascertained that on certain nights, when perhaps he had *extra* motives for concealing the fact of having been abroad, he drew woollen stockings over his horse's feet, with the purpose of deadening the sound in riding up a brick-paved entry, common to his own stable and that of a respectable neighbour. Thus far there was a reasonable foundation laid for suspicion: but suspicion of what? Because a man attends to the darning of his horse's stockings, why must he be meditating murder? The fact is—and known from the very first to a select party of amateurs— that X, our superb-looking skeleton, *did*, about three o'clock on a rainy Wednesday morning, in the dead of winter, ride silently out of Knutsford; and about forty-eight hours afterwards, on a rainy Friday, silently and softly did that same superb blood-horse, carrying that same blood-man—viz., our friend the superb skeleton—pace up the quiet brick entry, in a neat pair of socks, on his return.

During that interval of forty-eight hours, an atrocious murder was committed in the ancient city of Bristol. By whom? That question is to this day unanswered. The scene of it was a house on the west side

of the College Green; which is in fact that same quadrangle, planted with trees, and having on its southern
side the Bristol Cathedral, up and down which, early
in the reign of George III, Chatterton walked in
jubilant spirits with fair young women of Bristol; up
and down which, some thirty years later, Robert
Southey and S. T. C. walked with young Bristol belles
from a later generation. The subjects of the murder
were an elderly lady, bearing some such name as Rus-
borough, and her female servant. Mystery there was
none as to the motive of the murder—manifestly it
was a hoard of money that had attracted the assassin:
but there was great perplexity as to the agent or agents
concerned in the atrocious act, and as to the mode by
which an entrance, under the known precautions of
the lady, could have been effected. Because a thor-
oughbred horse could easily have accomplished the
distance to and fro (say 300 miles) within the forty-
eight hours, and because the two extreme dates of this
forty-eight hours' absence tallied with the requisitions
of the Bristol tragedy, it did not follow that X must
have had a hand in it. And yet, had these coincidences
then been observed, they would certainly—now that
strong suspicions had been directed to the man from
the extraordinary character of his nocturnal precautions—not have passed without investigation. But the
remoteness of Bristol, and the rarity of newspapers in
those days, caused these indications to pass unnoticed.
Bristol knew of no such Knutsford highwayman;
Knutsford knew of no such Bristol murder. It is singular enough that these earlier grounds of suspicion
against X were not viewed as such by anybody, until
they came to be combined with another and final
ground. Then the presumptions seemed conclusive.
But by that time X himself had been executed for a
robbery, had been manufactured into a skeleton by

the famous surgeon, Cruickshank, assisted by Mr.
White and other pupils. All interest in the case had
subsided in Knutsford that could now have cleared up
the case satisfactorily: and thus it happened that to
this day the riddle, which was read pretty decisively
in a northern county, still remains a riddle in the
south. When I saw the College Green house in 1809–
1810, it was apparently empty, and, as I was told, had
always been empty since the murder: forty years had
not cicatrized the bloody remembrance; and, to this
day, perhaps, it remains amongst the gloomy traditions of Bristol.

But whether the Bristol house has or has not shaken
off that odour of blood which offended the nostrils of
tenants, it is, I believe, certain that the city annals
have not shaken off the mystery: which yet to certain
people in Knutsford, as I have said, and to us the spectators of the skeleton, immediately upon hearing one
damning fact from the lips of Mr. White, seemed to
melt away and evaporate as convincingly as if we had
heard the explanation issuing in the terms of a confession from the mouth of the skeleton itself. What,
then, *was* the fact? With pain, and reluctantly, we
felt its force, as we looked at the royal skeleton, and
reflected on the many evidences which he had given
of courage, and perhaps of other noble qualities. The
ugly fact was this: In a few weeks after the College
Green tragedy, Knutsford, and the whole neighbourhood as far as Warrington (the half-way town between
Liverpool and Manchester), were deluged with gold
and silver coins, moidores and dollars, from the Spanish mint of Mexico, &c. These, during the frequent
scarcities of English silver currency, were notoriously
current in England. Now, it is an unhappy fact, and
subsequently became known to the Bristol and London
police, that a considerable part of poor Mrs. Rusbor-

ough's treasure lay in such coins, gold and silver, from
the Spanish colonial mints.

Lady Carbery at this period made an effort to teach
me Hebrew, by way of repaying in *kind* my pains in
teaching Greek to *her*. Where, and upon what motive,
she had herself begun to learn Hebrew, I forget: but
in Manchester she had resumed this study with energy
on a casual impulse derived from a certain Dr. Bailey,
a clergyman of this city who had published a Hebrew
Grammar. The doctor was the most unworldly and
guileless of men. Lady Carbery wished naturally to
testify her gratitude for his services by various splendid presents: but nothing would the good doctor accept,
unless it assumed a shape that might be available for
the service of the paupers amongst his congregation.
The Hebrew studies, however, notwithstanding the
personal assistance which we drew from the kindness
of Dr. Bailey, languished. One day, in a pause of languor amongst these arid Hebrew studies, I read to her
with a beating heart "The Ancient Mariner." It had
been first published in 1798; and about this time
(1801) was republished the first *two*-volume edition
of *The Lyrical Ballads*. Well I knew Lady Carbery's
constitutional inaptitude for poetry; and not for the
world would I have sought sympathy from her or from
anybody else upon that part of the L. B. which belonged to Wordsworth. But I fancied that the wildness
of this tale, and the triple majesties of Solitude, of
Mist, and of the Ancient Unknown Sea, might have
won her into relenting; and, in fact, she listened with
gravity and deep attention. But, on reviewing afterwards in conversation such passages as she happened
to remember, she laughed at the finest parts, and
shocked me by calling the mariner himself "an old
quiz"; protesting that the latter part of his homily to
the wedding-guest clearly pointed him out as the very

man meant by Providence for a stipendiary curate to the good Dr. Bailey in his overcrowded church. With an albatross perched on his shoulder, and who might be introduced to the congregation as the immediate organ of his conversion, and supported by the droning of a bassoon, she represented the mariner lecturing to advantage in English; the doctor overhead in the pulpit enforcing it in Hebrew. Angry I was, though forced to laugh. But of what use is anger or argument in a duel with female criticism? Our ponderous masculine wits are no match for the mercurial fancy of women. Once, however, I had a triumph: to my great surprise, one day, she suddenly repeated by heart, to Dr. Bailey, the beautiful passage:

It ceased, yet still the sails made on, &c.,

asking what he thought of *that?* As it happened, the simple childlike doctor had more sensibility than herself; for, though he had never in his whole homely life read more of poetry than he had drunk of Tokay or Constantia—in fact, had scarcely heard tell of any poetry but Watts's Hymns—he seemed petrified: and at last, with a deep sigh, as if recovering from the spasms of a new birth, said, "I never heard anything so beautiful in my whole life."

During the long stay of the Laxton party in Manchester occurred a Christmas; and at Christmas—that is, at the approach of this great Christian festival—so properly substituted in England for the Pagan festival of January and the New Year, there was, according to ancient usage, on the breaking up for the holidays at the Grammar School, a solemn celebration of the season by public speeches. Among the six speakers, I, of course (as one of the three boys who composed the head class), held a distinguished place; and it followed, also as a matter of course, that all my friends congregated on this occasion to do me honour. What I had to recite was a copy of Latin verses (Alcaics) on the recent conquest of Malta. *Melite Britannis Subacta*—this was the title of my worshipful nonsense. The whole strength of the Laxton party had mustered on this occasion. Lady Carbery made a point of bringing in her party every creature whom she could influence. And, probably, there were in that crowded audience many old Manchester friends of my father, loving his memory, and thinking to honour it by kindness to his son. Furious, at any rate, was the applause which greeted me: furious was my own disgust. Frantic were the clamours as I concluded my nonsense: frantic was my inner sense of shame at the childish exhibition to which, unavoidably, I was making myself a party. Lady Carbery had, at first, directed towards me occasional glances, expressing a comic sympathy with the thoughts which she supposed to be occupying my mind. But these glances ceased; and I was recalled, by the gloomy sadness in her altered countenance, to some sense of my own extravagant and disproportionate frenzy on this occasion: from the indulgent kindness with which she honoured me, her countenance on this occasion became a mirror to my own. At night she assured me, when talking over the case, that she had never witnessed an expression of such settled misery, and also (so she fancied) of misanthropy, as that which darkened my countenance in those moments of apparent public triumph, no matter how trivial the occasion, and amidst an uproar of friendly felicitation. I look back to that state of mind as almost a criminal reproach to myself, if it were not for the facts of the case. But, in excuse for myself, this fact, above all others, ought to be mentioned—that, over and above the killing oppression to my too sensitive system of the monotonous school tasks, and the ruinous want of exercise, I had fallen under medical advice the most misleading that it is possible to imagine. The physician and the surgeon of my family were men too eminent, it seemed to me, and, consequently, with time too notoriously bearing a high pecuniary value, for any schoolboy to detain them with complaints. Under these circumstances, I threw myself for aid, in a case so simple that any clever boy in a druggist's shop would have known how to treat it, upon the advice of an old, old apothecary, who had full authority from my guardian to run up a most furious account against me for medicine. This being the regular mode of payment, inevitably, and unconsciously, he was biased to a mode of treatment—viz., by drastic medicines varied without end—which fearfully exasperated the complaint. This complaint, as I now know, was the simplest possible derangement of the liver, a torpor in its action that might have been put to rights in three days. In fact, one week's pedestrian travelling amongst the Caernarvonshire mountains effected a revolution in my health such as left me nothing to complain of.

Some months after this, the Laxton party quitted Manchester, having no further motive for staying. Mrs. Schreiber was now confessedly dying; medical skill could do no more for her; and, this being so, there was no reason why she should continue to exchange her own quiet little Rutlandshire cottage for the discomforts of smoky lodgings. Lady Carbery retired like some golden pageant amongst the clouds; thick darkness succeeded; the ancient torpor re-established itself; and my health grew distressingly worse. Then it was, after dreadful self-conflicts, that I took the unhappy resolution of which the results are recorded in the *Opium Confessions*. At this point, the reader must understand, comes in that chapter of my life; and, for all

which concerns that delirious period, I refer him to
those *Confessions*. Some anxiety I had on leaving Manchester, lest my mother should suffer too much from
this rash step; and on that impulse I altered the direction of my wanderings; not going (as I had originally
planned) to the English Lakes, but making first of all
for St. John's Priory, Chester, at that time my mother's
residence. There I found my maternal uncle, Captain
Penson, of the Bengal establishment, just recently
come home on a two years' leave of absence; and there
I had an interview with my mother. By a temporary
arrangement I received a weekly allowance, which
would have enabled me to live in *any* district of Wales,
either North or South; for Wales, both North and
South, is (or at any rate *was*) a land of exemplary
cheapness. For instance, at Talyllyn, in Merionethshire, or anywhere off the line of tourists, I and a lieutenant in our English navy paid sixpence uniformly
for a handsome dinner; sixpence, I mean, apiece. But
two months later came a golden blockhead, who instructed the people that it was "sinful" to charge less
than three shillings. In Wales, meantime, I suffered
grievously from want of books; and, fancying, in my
profound ignorance of the world, that I could borrow
money upon my own expectations, or, at least, that I
could do so with the joint security of Lord Westport
(now Earl of Altamont, upon his father's elevation to
the Marquisate of Sligo), or (failing *that*) with the
security of his amiable and friendly cousin, the Earl of
Desart, I had the unpardonable folly to quit the deep
tranquillities of North Wales, for the uproars, and perils, and the certain miseries of London. I had borrowed
ten guineas from Lady Carbery; and at that time,
when my purpose was known to nobody, I might have
borrowed any sum I pleased. But I could never again
avail myself of that resource, because I must have

given some address, in order to insure the receipt of
Lady Carbery's answer; and in that case, so sternly
conscientious was she that, under the notion of saving
me from ruin, my address would have been immediately communicated to my guardians, and by them
would have been confided to the unrivalled detective
talents, in those days, of Townsend, or some other Bow
Street officer.[1]

THE PRIORY, CHESTER

(First published in the Collective Edition of De Quincey's
works, vol. II, 1854)

THAT episode, or impassioned parenthesis, in my life
which is comprehended in the *Confessions of an
Opium-Eater* had finished: suppose it over and gone,
and once more, after the storms of London, suppose me
resting from my dreadful remembrances in the deep
monastic tranquillity of St. John's Priory; and just
then, by accident, with no associates except my mother
and my uncle.

In 1800-1801, my mother had become dissatisfied
with Bath as a residence; and, being free from all ties
connecting her with any one county of England rather
than another, she resolved to traverse the most attractive parts of the island, and upon personal inspection
to select a home; not a ready-built home, but the
ground on which she might herself create one; for it
happened that amongst the few infirmities besetting
my mother's habits and constitution of mind was the
costly one of seeking her chief intellectual excitement
in architectural creations. She individually might be

[1] The reader who wishes to follow the strict chronological
development of De Quincey's autobiography, should at this
point turn to the *Confessions of an English Opium-Eater*.
—ED.

said to have built Greenhay; since to *her* views of domestic elegance and propriety my father had resigned *almost* everything. This was her *coup d'essai;* secondly, she built the complement to the Priory in Cheshire, which cost about £1000; thirdly, Westhay, in Somersetshire, about twelve miles from Bristol, which, including the land attached to the house, cost £12,500 —not including subsequent additions; but this was built at the cost of my uncle; finally, Weston Lea, close to Bath, which, being designed simply for herself in old age, with a moderate establishment of four servants (and some reasonable provision of accommodations for a few visitors), cost originally, I believe, not more than £1000—excluding, however, the cost of all after alterations. It may serve to show how inevitably an amateur architect, without professional aid and counsel, will be defrauded, that the first of these houses, which cost £6000, sold for no more than £2500, and the third for no more than £5000. The person who superintended the workmen, and had the whole practical management of one amongst these four houses, was a common builder, without capital or education, and the greatest knave that personally I have known. It may illustrate the way in which lady architects, without professional aid, are and ever will be defrauded, that, after all was finished, and the entire woodwork was to be measured and valued, each party, of course, needing to be represented by a professional agent, naturally the knavish builder was ready at earliest dawn with *his* agent; but, as regarded my mother's interest, the task of engaging such an agent had been confided to a neighbouring clergyman, "evangelical," of course, and a humble sycophant of Hannah More, but otherwise the most helpless of human beings —baptized or infidel. He contented himself with instructing a young gentleman, aged about fifteen, to take his pony and ride over to a distant cathedral town, which was honoured by the abode of a virtuous though drunken surveyor. This respectable drunkard he was to engage, and also with obvious discretion to fee, beforehand. All which was done: the drunken surveyor had a sort of fits, it was understood, that always towards sunset inclined him to assume the horizontal posture. Fortunately, however, for that part of mankind whom circumstances had brought under the necessity of communicating with him, these fits were intermitting; so that, for instance, in the present case, upon a severe call arising for his pocketing the fee of ten guineas, he astonished his whole household by suddenly standing bolt upright as stiff as a poker; his sister remarking to the young gentleman that he (the visitor) was in luck that evening: it wasn't everybody that could get that length in dealing with Mr. X. O. However, it is distressing to relate that the fits immediately returned; and, with that degree of exasperation which made it dangerous to suggest the idea of a receipt; since that must have required the vertical attitude. Whether that attitude ever was recovered by the unfortunate gentleman, I do not know. Forty-and-four years have passed since then. Almost everybody connected with the case has had time to assume permanently the horizontal posture: viz., that knave of a builder, whose knaveries (gilded by that morning sun of June) were controlled by nobody—that sycophantish parson—that young gentleman of fifteen (now, alas! fifty-nine), who must long since have sown his wild oats—that unhappy pony of eighteen (now, alas! sixty-two, if living; ah! venerable pony, that must (or mustest) now require thy oats to be boiled)—in short, one and all of these venerabilities—knaves, ponies, drunkards, receipts—have descended, I believe, to chaos or to Hades, with hardly one exception. Chancery itself, though somewhat of an Indian juggler, could not play with such aerial balls as these.

On what ground it was that my mother quarrelled with the advantages of Bath, so many and so conspicuous, I cannot guess. At that time—viz., the opening of the nineteenth century—the old traditionary custom of the place had established for young and old the luxury of sedan-chairs. Nine-tenths, at least, of the colds and catarrhs, those initial stages of all pulmonary complaints (the capital scourge of England), are caught in the transit between the door of a carriage and the genial atmosphere of the drawing-room. By a sedan-chair all this danger was evaded; your two chairmen marched right into the hall: the hall-door was closed; and not until then was the roof and the door of your chair opened: the translation was—from one room to another. To my mother, and many in her situation, the sedan-chair recommended itself also by advantages of another class. Immediately on coming to Bath, her carriage was "laid up in ordinary." The trifling rent of a coach-house, some slight annual repairs, and the tax, composed the whole annual cost. At that time, and throughout the war, the usual estimate for the cost of a close carriage in London was £320: since, in order to have the certain services of two horses, it was indispensable to keep three. Add to this the coachman, the wear-and-tear of harness, and the duty; and, even in Bath, a cheaper place than London, you could not accomplish the total service under £270. Now, except the duty, all this expense was at once superseded by the sedan-chair—rarely costing you above ten shillings a week—i.e., twenty-five guineas a year, and liberating you from all care or anxiety. The duty on four wheels, it is true, was suddenly exalted by Mr. Pitt's triple assessment from twelve guineas to thirty-six: but what a trifle by comparison with the cost of horses and coachman! And then, no demands for money were ever met so cheerfully by my mother as those which went to support Mr. Pitt's policy against Jacobinism and Regicide. At present, after five years' sinecure existence, unless on the rare summons of a journey, this dormant carriage was suddenly undocked, and put into commission. Taking with her two servants, and one of my sisters, my mother now entered upon a *periplus*, or systematic circumnavigation of all England; and in England only, through the admirable machinery matured for such a purpose—viz., inns, innkeepers, servants, horses, all first-rate of their class—it was possible to pursue such a scheme in the midst of domestic comfort. My mother's resolution was to see all England with her own eyes, and to judge for herself upon the qualifications of each county, each town (not being a bustling seat of commerce), and each village (having any advantages of scenery), for contributing the main elements towards a home that might justify her in building a house. The qualifications insisted on were these five—good medical advice somewhere in the neighbourhood; first-rate means of education; elegant (or what most people might think aristocratic) society; agreeable scenery: and so far the difficulty was not insuperable in the way of finding all the four advantages concentrated. But my mother insisted on a fifth, which in those days insured the instant shipwreck of the entire scheme: this was a Church of England parish clergyman, who was to be strictly orthodox, faithful to the articles of our English Church, yet to these articles as interpreted by evangelical divinity. My mother's views were precisely those of her friend Mrs. Hannah More, of Wilberforce, of Henry Thornton, of Zachary Macaulay (father of the historian), and generally of those who were then known amongst sneerers as "the Clapham saints." This one requisition it was on which the scheme foundered. And the fact merits recording, as an exposition of the broad religious difference between the England of that day and of this. At present, no difficulty would be found as to this fifth requisition. "Evangelical" clergymen are now sown broadcast; at that period, there were not, on an average, above six or eight in each of the fifty-two counties.

The conditions, as a whole, were in fact incapable of being realized; where two or three were attained, three or two failed. It was too much to exact so many advantages from any one place, unless London; or really, if any other place could be looked to with hope in such a chase, that place was Bath—the very city my mother was preparing to leave. Yet, had this been otherwise, and the prospect of success more promising, I have not a doubt that the pretty gem which suddenly was offered at a price unintelligibly low in the ancient city of Chester would have availed (as instantly it *did* avail, and perhaps ought to have availed) in obscuring those five conditions, of which else each separately for itself had seemed a *conditio sine quâ non*. This gem was an ancient house, on a miniature scale, called the *Priory;* and, until the dissolution of religious houses in the earlier half of the sixteenth century, had formed part of the Priory attached to the ancient Church (still flourishing) of St. John's. Towards the end of the sixteenth, and through the first quarter of the seventeenth century, this Priory had been in the occupation of Sir Robert Cotton, the antiquary, the friend of Ben Jonson, of Coke, of Selden, &c., and advantageously known as one of those who applied his legal and historical knowledge to the bending back into constitutional moulds of those despotic twists which new interests and false counsels had developed in the Tudor and Stuart dynasties. It was an exceedingly pretty place: and the kitchen, upon the ground storey, which had a

noble groined ceiling of stone, indicated, by its disproportionate scale, the magnitude of the establishment
to which once it had ministered. Attached to this
splendid kitchen were tributary offices, &c. On the
upper storey were exactly five rooms—viz., a servants'
dormitory, meant in Sir Robert's day for two beds [1] at
the least, and a servants' sitting-room. These were shut
off into a separate section, with a little staircase (like
a ship's companion-ladder) and a little lobby of its
own. But the principal section on this upper storey had
been dedicated to the use of Sir Robert, and consisted
of a pretty old hall, lighted by an old monastic-painted
window in the door of entrance; secondly, a rather elegant dining-room; thirdly, a bedroom. The glory of
the house internally lay in the monastic kitchen, and,
secondly, in what a Frenchman would have called,
properly, Sir Robert's own *apartment* of three rooms;
but, thirdly and chiefly, in a pile of ruined archways,
most picturesque, so far as they went, but so small that
Drury Lane could easily have found room for them on
its stage. These stood in the miniature pleasure-
ground, and were constantly resorted to by artists for
specimens of architectural decays, or of nature working for the concealment of such decays by her ordinary
processes of gorgeous floral vegetation. Ten rooms
there may have been in the Priory, as offered to my
mother for less than £500. A drawing-room, bedrooms, dressing-rooms, &c., making about ten more,
were added by my mother for a sum under £1000. The
same miniature scale was observed in all these additions. And, as the Priory was not within the walls of

[1] The contrivance amongst our ancestors, even at haughty
Cambridge and haughtier Oxford, was, that one bed rising
six inches from the floor ran (in the day-time) under a loftier
bed; it ran upon castors or little wheels. The learned word
for a little wheel is *trochlea;* from which Grecian and Latin
term comes the English word *truckle*-bed.

the city, whilst the river Dee, flowing immediately below, secured it from annoyance on one side, and the church, with its adjacent churchyard, insulated it from the tumults of life on all the other sides, an atmosphere of conventual stillness and tranquillity brooded over it and all around it for ever.

Such was the house, such was the society, in which I now found myself; and upon the whole I might describe myself as being, according to the modern phrase, "in a false position." I had, for instance, a vast superiority, as was to have been expected, in bookish attainments, and in adroitness of logic; whilst, on the other hand, I was ridiculously shortsighted or blind in all fields of ordinary human experience. It must not be supposed that I regarded my own particular points of superiority, or that I used them with any vanity or view to present advantages. On the contrary, I sickened over them, and laboured to defeat them. But in vain I sowed errors in my premises, or planted absurdities in my assumptions. Vainly I tried such blunders, as putting four terms into a syllogism, which, as all the world knows, ought to run on three; a tripod it ought to be, by all rules known to man, and, behold, I forced it to become a quadruped. Upon my uncle's military haste and tumultuous energy in pressing his opinions, all such delicate refinements were absolutely thrown away. With disgust *I* saw, with disgust *he* saw, that too apparently the advantage lay with me in the result; and, whilst I worked like a dragon to place myself in the wrong, some fiend apparently so counterworked me that eternally I was reminded of the Manx halfpennies, which lately I had continually seen current in North Wales, bearing for their heraldic distinction three human legs in armour, but so placed in relation to each other, that always one leg is vertical and mounting guard on behalf of the other two, which, therefore, are enabled to sprawl aloft in the air—in fact, to be as absurdly negligent as they choose, relying upon their vigilant brother below, and upon the written legend or motto, STABIT QUOCUNQUE JECERIS (Stand it will upright, though you should fling it in any conceivable direction).

What gave another feature of distraction and incoherency to my position was, that I still occupied the position of a reputed boy, nay, a child, in the estimate of my audience, and of a child in disgrace. Time enough had not passed since my elopement from school to win for me, in minds so fresh from that remembrance, a station of purification and assoilment. Oxford might avail to assoil me, and to throw into a distant retrospect my boyish trespasses; but as yet Oxford had not arrived. I committed, besides, a great fault in taking often a tone of mock seriousness, when the detection of the playful extravagance was left to the discernment or quick sympathy of the hearer; and I was blind to the fact, that neither my mother nor my uncle was distinguished by any natural liveliness of vision for the comic, or any toleration for the extravagant.

But altogether serious were the disputes upon India —a topic on separate grounds equally interesting to us all, as the mightiest of English colonies, and the superbest monument of demoniac English energy, revealing itself in such men as Clive, Hastings, and soon after in the two Wellesleys. To my mother, as the grave of one brother, as the home of another, and as a new centre from which Christianity (she hoped) would mount like an eagle—for just about that time the Bible Society was preparing its initial movements: whilst to my uncle India appeared as the *arena* upon which his activities were yet to find their adequate career. With respect to the Christianization of India, my uncle assumed a hope which he did not really feel; and in another point, more trying to himself personally, he had soon an opportunity for showing the sincerity of this deference to his spiritual-minded sister. For, very soon after his return to India, he received a civil appointment (*Superintendent of Military Buildings in Bengal*), highly lucrative; and the more so, as it could be held conjointly with his military rank; but a good deal of its pecuniary advantages was said to lie in fees, or perquisites, privately offered, but perfectly regular and official, which my mother (misunderstanding the Indian system) chose to call "bribes." A very ugly word was *that;* but I argued that even at home, even in the courts at Westminster, in the very fountains of justice, private fees constituted one part of the salaries —a fair and official part, so long as Parliament had not made such fees illegal by commuting them for known and fixed equivalents. It was mere ignorance of India, as I dutifully insisted against "Mamma," that could confound these regular oriental "nuzzers" with the clandestine wages of corruption.

Suddenly, however, our Indian discussions were brought to a close by the following incident: My uncle had brought with him to England some Arabian horses, and amongst them a beautiful young Persian mare, called Sumroo, the gentlest of her race. Sumroo it was that he happened to be riding, upon a frosty day. Unused to ice, she came down with him, and broke his right leg. This accident laid him up for a month, during which my mother and I read to him by turns. One book, which one day fell to my share by accident, was De Foe's *Memoirs of a Cavalier*. This book attempts to give a picture of the Parliamentary War, but in some places an unfair, and everywhere a most superficial account. I said so: and my uncle, who had an old craze in behalf of the book, opposed me with asperity; and in the course of what he said, under some movement of ill temper, he asked me, in a way which I felt to be taunting, how I could consent to waste my time as I did. Without any answering warmth, I explained that my guardians, having quarrelled with me, would not grant for my use anything beyond my school allowance of £100 per annum. But was it not possible that even this sum might by economy be made to meet the necessities of the case? I replied that, from what I had heard, very probably it was. Would I undertake an Oxford life upon such terms? Most gladly, I said. Upon that opening, he spoke to my mother; and the result was that, within seven days from the above conversation, I found myself entering that time-honoured University.

OXFORD

(First published in *Tait's Magazine, February,* 1835)

IT WAS in winter, and in the wintry weather of the year 1803, that I first entered Oxford with a view to its vast means of education, or rather with a view to its vast advantages for study. A ludicrous story is told of a young candidate for clerical orders—that, being asked by the bishop's chaplain if he had ever "been to Oxford," as a colloquial expression for having had an academic education, he replied, "No: but he had twice been to Abingdon": Abingdon being only seven miles distant. In the same sense I might say that once before I had been at Oxford: but *that* was as a transient visitor with Lord Westport, when we were both children. Now, on the contrary, I approached these venerable towers in the character of a student, and with the purpose of a long connexion; personally interested in the constitution of the University, and obscurely anticipating that in this city, or at least during the period of my nominal attachment to this academic body, the remoter parts of my future life would unfold before me. All hearts were at this time occupied with the public interests of the country. The "sorrow of the time" was ripening to a second harvest. Napoleon had commenced his Vandal, or rather Hunnish war with Britain, in the spring of this year, about eight months before; and profound public interest it was, into which the very coldest hearts entered, that a little divided with me the else monopolizing awe attached to the solemn act of launching myself upon the world. That expression may seem too strong as applied to one who had already been for many months a houseless wanderer in Wales, and a solitary roamer in the streets of London. But in those situations, it must be remembered, I was an unknown, unacknowledged vagrant; and without money I could hardly run much risk, except of breaking my neck. The perils, the pains, the pleasures, or the obligations, of the world, scarcely exist in a proper sense for him who has no funds. Perfect weakness is often secure: it is by imperfect power, turned against its master, that men are snared and decoyed. Here in Oxford I should be called upon to commence a sort of establishment upon the splendid English scale; here I should share in many duties and responsibilities, and should become henceforth an object of notice to a large society. Now first becoming separately and individually answerable for my conduct, and no longer absorbed into the general unit of a family, I felt myself, for the first time, burthened with the anxieties of a man, and a member of the world.

Oxford, ancient Mother! hoary with ancestral honours, time-honoured, and, haply, it may be, time-shattered power—I owe thee nothing! Of thy vast riches I took not a shilling, though living amongst multitudes who owed to thee their daily bread. Not the less I owe thee justice; for that is a universal debt. And at

this moment, when I see thee called to thy audit by unjust and malicious accusers—men with the hearts of
inquisitors and the purposes of robbers—I feel towards
thee something of filial reverence and duty. However,
I mean not to speak as an advocate, but as a conscientious witness in the simplicity of truth; feeling neither
hope nor fear of a personal nature, without fee, and
without favour.

For my part, though neither giving nor accepting
invitations for the first two years of my residence,
never but once had I reason to complain of a sneer, or
indeed any allusion whatever to habits which might be
understood to express poverty. Perhaps even then I had
no reason to complain, for my own conduct in that instance was unwise; and the allusion, though a personality, and so far ill-bred, might be meant in real kindness. The case was this: I neglected my dress in one
point habitually; that is, I wore clothes until they were
threadbare—partly in the belief that my gown would
conceal their main defects, but much more from carelessness and indisposition to spend upon a tailor what I
had destined for a bookseller. At length, an official person, of some weight in the college, sent me a message
on the subject through a friend. It was couched in these
terms: That, let a man possess what talents or accomplishments he might, it was not possible for him to
maintain his proper station in the public respect,
amongst so many servants and people servile to external impressions, without some regard to the elegance
of his dress. A reproof so courteously prefaced I could
not take offence at; and at that time I resolved to spend
some cost upon decorating my person. But always it
happened that some book, or set of books—that passion
being absolutely endless, and inexorable as the grave
—stepped between me and my intentions; until one
day, upon arranging my toilet hastily before dinner, I

suddenly made the discovery that I had no waistcoat (or *vest*, as it is now called, through conceit or provincialism) which was not torn or otherwise dilapidated; whereupon, buttoning up my coat to the throat, and drawing my gown as close about me as possible, I went into the public "hall" (so is called in Oxford the public eating-room) with no misgiving. However, I was detected; for a grave man, with a superlatively grave countenance, who happened on that day to sit next me, but whom I did not personally know, addressing his friend sitting opposite, begged to know if he had seen the last Gazette, because he understood that it contained an Order in Council laying an interdict upon the future use of waistcoats. His friend replied, with the same perfect gravity, that it was a great satisfaction to his mind that his Majesty's Government should have issued so sensible an order; which he trusted would be soon followed up by an interdict on breeches, they being still more disagreeable to pay for. This said, without the movement on either side of a single muscle, the two gentlemen passed to other subjects; and I inferred, upon the whole, that, having detected my manœuvre, they wished to put me on my guard in the only way open to them. At any rate, this was the sole personality, or equivocal allusion of any sort, which ever met my ear during the years that I asserted my right to be as poor as I chose. And, certainly, my censors were right, whatever were the temper in which they spoke, kind or unkind; for a little extra care in the use of clothes will always, under almost any extremity of poverty, pay for so much extra cost as is essential to neatness and decorum, if not even to elegance. They were right, and I was wrong, in a point which cannot be neglected with impunity.

But, to enter upon my own history, and my sketch of Oxford life. Late on a winter's night, in the latter

half of December, 1803, when a snow-storm, and a
heavy one, was already gathering in the air, a lazy
Birmingham coach, moving at four and a half miles an
hour, brought me through the long northern suburb of
Oxford, to a shabby coach-inn, situated in the Corn
Market. Business was out of the question at that hour.
. . . On the next morning, I assembled a small council
of friends to assist me in determining at which of the
various separate societies I should enter, and whether
as a "commoner," or as a "gentleman commoner." Under the first question was couched the following latitude of choice: I give the names of the colleges, and the
numerical account of their numbers, as it stood in January 1832; for this will express, as well as the list of
that day (which I do not accurately know), the *proportions* of importance amongst them.

		Members
1. University College	. . . . .	207
2. Balliol "	. . . . .	257
3. Merton "	. . . . .	124
4. Exeter "	. . . . .	299
5. Oriel "	. . . . .	293
6. Queen's "	. . . . .	351
7. New "	. . . . .	157
8. Lincoln "	. . . . .	141
9. All Souls' "	. . . .	98
10. Magdalene "	. . . .	165
11. Brasenose "	. . . . .	418
12. Corpus Christi "	. . . . .	127
13. Christ Church "	. . . . .	949
14. Trinity "	. . . . .	259
15. St. John's "	. . . .	218
16. Jesus "	. . . . .	167
17. Wadham "	. . . . .	217
18. Pembroke "	. . . . .	189
19. Worcester "	. . . . .	231

Then, besides these colleges, five *Halls*, as they are
technically called (the term *Hall* implying chiefly
that they are societies not endowed, or not endowed
with fellowships as the colleges are), namely:

		Members
1. St. Mary Hall	. . . . . .	83
2. Magdalen "	. . . . .	178
3. New Inn "	. . . . .	10
4. St. Alban "	. . . . .	41
5. St. Edmund "	. . . . .	96

Such being the names, and general proportions on
the scale of local importance, attached to the different
communities, next comes the very natural question,
What are the chief determining motives for guiding
the selection amongst them? These I shall state. First
of all, a man not otherwise interested in the several advantages of the colleges has, however, in all probability, some choice between a small society and a large
one; and thus far a mere ocular inspection of the list
will serve to fix his preference. For my part, supposing
other things equal, I greatly preferred the most populous college, as being that in which any single member, who might have reasons for standing aloof from
the general habits of expense, of intervisiting, &c.,
would have the best chance of escaping a jealous notice. However, amongst those "other things" which I
presumed equal, one held a high place in my estimation, which a little inquiry showed to be very far from
equal. All the colleges have chapels, but all have not
organs; nor, amongst those which have, is the same
large use made of the organ. Some preserve the full
cathedral service; others do not. Christ Church, meantime, fulfilled *all* conditions: for the chapel here happens to be the cathedral of the diocese; the service,

therefore, is full and ceremonial; the college, also, is far the most splendid, both in numbers, rank, wealth, and influence. Hither I resolved to go; and immediately I prepared to call on the head.

The "head," as he is called generically, of an Oxford college (his *specific* appellation varies almost with every college—principal, provost, master, rector, warden, &c.), is a greater man than the uninitiated suppose. His situation is generally felt as conferring a degree of rank not much less than episcopal; and, in fact, the head of Brasenose at that time, who happened to be the Bishop of Bangor, was not held to rank much above his brothers in office. Such being the rank of heads generally, *à fortiori*, that of Christ Church was to be had in reverence; and this I knew. He is always, *ex officio*, dean of the diocese; and, in his quality of college head, he only, of all deans that ever were heard of, is uniformly considered a greater man than his own diocesan. But it happened that the present dean had even higher titles to consideration. Dr. Cyril Jackson had been tutor to the Prince of Wales (George IV); he had repeatedly refused a bishopric; and *that*, perhaps, is entitled to place a man one degree above him who has accepted one. He was also supposed to have made a bishop, and afterwards, at least, it is certain that he made his own brother a bishop. All things weighed, Dr. Cyril Jackson seemed so very great a personage that I now felt the value of my long intercourse with great dons in giving me confidence to face a lion of this magnitude.

Those who know Oxford are aware of the peculiar feelings which have gathered about the name and pretensions of Christ Church; feelings of superiority and leadership in the members of that college, and often enough of defiance and jealousy on the part of other colleges. Hence it happens that you rarely find your-

self in a shop, or other place of public resort, with a
Christ-Church man, but he takes occasion, if young
and frivolous, to talk loudly of the Dean, as an indirect
expression of his own connexion with this splendid college; the title of *Dean* being exclusively attached to
the headship of Christ Church. The Dean, as may be
supposed, partakes in this superior dignity of his
"House"; he is officially brought into connexion with
all orders of the British aristocracy—often with royal
personages; and with the younger branches of the aristocracy his office places him in a relation of authority
and guardianship—exercised, however, through inferior ministry, and seldom by direct personal interference. The reader must understand that, with rare exceptions, all the princes and nobles of Great Britain
who choose to benefit by an academic education resort
either to Christ Church College in Oxford, or to Trinity College in Cambridge: these are the alternatives.
Naturally enough, my young friends were somewhat
startled at my determination to call upon so great a
man; a letter, they fancied, would be a better mode of
application. I, however, who did not adopt the doctrine
that no man is a hero to his valet, was of opinion that
very few men indeed are heroes to themselves. The
cloud of external pomp, which invests them to the eyes
of the *attoniti*, cannot exist to their own; they do not,
like Kehama entering the eight gates of Padalon at
once, meet and contemplate their own grandeurs; but,
more or less, are conscious of acting a part. I did not,
therefore, feel the tremor which was expected of a
novice, on being ushered into so solemn a presence.

The Dean was sitting in a spacious library or study,
elegantly, if not luxuriously, furnished. Footmen, stationed as repeaters, as if at some fashionable rout, gave
a momentary importance to my unimportant self, by
the thundering tone of their annunciations. All the

machinery of aristocratic life seemed indeed to in-
trench this great Don's approaches; and I was really
surprised that so very great a man should condescend
to rise on my entrance. But I soon found that, if the
Dean's station and relation to the higher orders had
made him lofty, those same relations had given a peculiar suavity to his manners. Here, indeed, as on other
occasions, I noticed the essential misconception, as to
the demeanour of men of rank, which prevails amongst
those who have no personal access to their presence. In
the fabulous pictures of novels (such novels as once
abounded), and in newspaper reports of conversations,
real or pretended, between the King and inferior persons, we often find the writer expressing *his* sense of
aristocratic assumption, by making the King address
people without their titles. The Duke of Wellington,
for instance, or Lord Liverpool, figures usually, in
such scenes, as "Wellington," or "Arthur," and as
"Liverpool." Now, as to the private talk of George IV
in such cases, I do not pretend to depose; but, speaking
generally, I may say that the practice of the highest
classes takes the very opposite course. Nowhere is a
man so sure of his titles or official distinctions as
amongst *them;* for it is upon giving to every man the
very extreme punctilio of his known or supposed
claims that they rely for the due observance of their
own. Neglecting no form of courtesy suited to the case,
they seek, in this way, to remind men unceasingly of
what they expect; and the result is what I represent—
that people in the highest stations, and such as bring
them continually into contact with inferiors, are, of
all people, the least addicted to insolence or defect of
courtesy. Uniform suavity of manner is indeed rarely
found *except* in men of high rank. Doubtless this may
arise upon a motive of self-interest, jealous of giving
the least opening or invitation to the retorts of ill-

temper or low breeding. But, whatever be its origin, such I believe to be the fact. In a very long conversation of a general nature upon the course of my studies, and the present direction of my reading, Dr. Cyril Jackson treated me just as he would have done his equal in station and in age. Coming, at length, to the particular purpose of my visit at this time to himself, he assumed a little more of his official stateliness. He condescended to say that it would have given him pleasure to reckon me amongst his flock; "But, sir," he said, in a tone of some sharpness, "your guardians have acted improperly. It was their duty to have given me at least one year's notice of their intention to place you at Christ Church. At present I have not a dog-kennel in my college untenanted." Upon this, I observed that nothing remained for me to do but to apologize for having occupied so much of his time; that, for myself, I now first heard of this preliminary application; and that, as to my guardians, I was bound to acquit them of all oversight in this instance, they being no parties to my present scheme. The Dean expressed his astonishment at this statement. I, on my part, was just then making my parting bows, and had reached the door, when a gesture of the Dean's, courteously waving me back to the sofa I had quitted, invited me to resume my explanations; and I had a conviction at the moment that the interview would have terminated in the Dean's suspending his standing rule in my favour. But, just at that moment, the thundering heralds of the Dean's hall announced some man of high rank: the sovereign of Christ Church seemed distressed for a moment; but then, recollecting himself, bowed in a way to indicate that I was dismissed. And thus it happened that I did not become a member of Christ Church.

A few days passed in thoughtless indecision. At the end of that time, a trivial difficulty arose to settle my determination. I had brought about fifty guineas to Oxford; but the expenses of an Oxford inn, with almost daily entertainments to young friends, had made such inroads upon this sum, that, after allowing for the contingencies incident to a college initiation, enough would not remain to meet the usual demand for what is called "caution money." This is a small sum, properly enough demanded of every student, when matriculated, as a pledge for meeting any loss from unsettled arrears, such as his sudden death or his unannounced departure might else continually be inflicting upon his college. By releasing the college, therefore, from all necessity for degrading vigilance or persecution, this demand does, in effect, operate beneficially to the feelings of all parties. In most colleges it amounts to twenty-five pounds: in one only it was considerably less. And this trifling consideration it was, concurring with a reputation *at that time* for relaxed discipline, which finally determined me in preferring Worcester College to all others. This college had the capital disadvantage, in my eyes, that its chapel possessed no organ, and no musical service. But any other choice would have driven me to an instant call for more money—a measure which, as too flagrantly in contradiction to the whole terms on which I had volunteered to undertake an Oxford life, I could not find nerves to face.

There was one reason why I sought solitude at that early age, and sought it in a morbid excess, which must naturally have conferred upon my character some degree of that interest which belongs to all extremes. My eye had been couched into a secondary power of vision, by misery, by solitude, by sympathy with life in all its modes, by experience too early won, and by the sense of danger critically escaped. Suppose the case of a man suspended by some colossal arm over an unfathomed abyss—suspended, but finally and slowly withdrawn —it is probable that he would not smile for years. That was my case: for I have not mentioned in the *Opium Confessions* a thousandth part of the sufferings I underwent in London and in Wales; partly because the misery was too monotonous, and, in that respect, unfitted for description; but still more because there is a mysterious sensibility connected with real suffering, which recoils from circumstantial rehearsal or delineation, as from violation offered to something sacred, and which is, or should be, dedicated to privacy. Grief does not parade its pangs, nor the anguish of despairing hunger willingly count again its groans or its humiliations. Hence it was that Ledyard, the traveller, speaking of his Russian experiences, used to say that some of his miseries were such that he never *would* reveal them. Besides all which, I really was not at liberty to speak, without many reserves, on this chapter of my life, at a period (1821) not twenty years removed from the actual occurrences, unless I desired to court the risk of crossing at every step the existing law of libel, so full of snares and man-traps, to the careless equally with the conscientious writer. This is a consideration which some of my critics have lost sight of in a degree which surprises me. One, for example, puts it to his readers whether any house such as I describe as the abode of my money-lending friend could exist "*in* Oxford-street"; and, at the same time, he states, as circumstances drawn from my description, but, in fact, pure coinages of his own, certain romantic impossibilities, which, doubtless, could as little attach to a house in Oxford-street as they could to a house in any other quarter of London. Meantime, I had sufficiently indicated that, whatsoever street *was* concerned in that affair, Oxford-street was *not:* and it is remarkable

enough, as illustrating this amiable reviewer's veracity, that no one street in London was absolutely ex-
cluded *but* one, and that one, Oxford-street. For I happened to mention that, on such a day (my birth-day),
I had turned aside *from* Oxford-street to look at the
house in question. I will now add that this house was
in Greek-street: so much it may be safe to say. But
every candid reader will see that both prudential restraints, and also disinterested regard to the feelings of
possibly amiable descendants from a vicious man,
would operate with any thoughtful writer, in such a
case, to impose reserve upon his pen. Had my guardians, had my money-lending friend of Jewry, and others
concerned in my memoirs, been so many shadows, bodiless abstractions, and without earthly connexions, I
might readily have given my own names to my own
creations, and have treated them as unceremoniously
as I pleased. Not so under the real circumstances of the
case. My chief guardian, for instance, though obstinate to a degree which risked the happiness and the life
of his ward, was an upright man otherwise; and his
children are entitled to value his memory. Again, my
Greek-street τραπεξίτης, the "*fœnerator Alpheus*,"
who delighted to reap where he had not sown, and too
often (I fear) allowed himself in practices which not
impossibly have long since been found to qualify him
for distant climates and "Botanic" regions—even he,
though I might truly describe him as a mere highwayman whenever he happened to be aware that I had received a friendly loan, yet, like other highwaymen of
repute, and "gentle thieves," was not inexorable to
the petitions of his victim: he would sometimes toss
back what was required for some instant necessity of
the road; and at *his* breakfast-table it was, after all, as
elsewhere recorded, that I contrived to support life;
barely, indeed, and most slenderly, but still with the

final result of escaping absolute starvation. With that
recollection before me, I could not allow myself to
probe his frailties too severely, had it even been certainly safe to do so. But enough; the reader will understand that a year spent either in the valleys of Wales,
or upon the streets of London, by a wanderer too often
houseless in both situations, might naturally have peopled the mind of one constitutionally disposed to solemn contemplations with memorials of human sorrow
and strife too profound to pass away for years.

Thus, then, it was. Past experience of a very peculiar kind, the agitations of many lives crowded into the
compass of a year or two, in combination with a peculiar structure of mind, offered one explanation of the
very remarkable and unsocial habits which I adopted
at college; but there was another not less powerful, and
not less unusual. In stating this, I shall seem, to some
persons, covertly designing an affront to Oxford. But
that is far from my intention. It is noways peculiar to
Oxford, but will, doubtless, be found in every University throughout the world, that the younger part of
the members—the undergraduates, I mean, generally,
whose chief business must have lain amongst the great
writers of Greece and Rome—cannot have found leisure to cultivate extensively their own domestic literature. Not so much that time will have been wanting;
but that the whole energy of the mind, and the main
course of the subsidiary studies and researches, will
naturally have been directed to those difficult languages amongst which lie their daily tasks. I make it
no subject of complaint or scorn, therefore, but simply
state it as a fact, that few or none of the Oxford undergraduates, with whom parity of standing threw me
into collision at my first outset, knew anything at all of
English Literature. The *Spectator* seemed to me the
only English book of a classical rank which they had

read; and even this less for its inimitable delicacy, humour, and refined pleasantry in dealing with manners and characters, than for its insipid and meagre essays, ethical or critical. This was no fault of theirs: they had been sent to the book chiefly as a subject for Latin translations, or of other exercises; and, in such a view, the vague generalities of superficial morality were more useful and more manageable than sketches of manner or character, steeped in national peculiarities. To translate the terms of Whig politics into classical Latin would be as difficult as it might be for a Whig himself to give a consistent account of those politics from the year 1688. Natural, however, and excusable, as this ignorance might be, to myself it was intolerable and incomprehensible. Already, at fifteen, I had made myself familiar with the great English poets. About sixteen, or not long after, my interest in the story of Chatterton had carried me over the whole ground of the Rowley controversy; and that controversy, by a necessary consequence, had so familiarized me with the "Black Letter" that I had begun to find an unaffected pleasure in the ancient English metrical romances; and in Chaucer, though acquainted as yet only with part of his works, I had perceived and had felt profoundly those divine qualities which, even at this day, are so languidly acknowledged by his unjust countrymen. With this knowledge, and this enthusiastic knowledge of the elder poets——of those most remote from easy access——I could not well be a stranger in other walks of our literature, more on a level with the general taste, and nearer to modern diction, and, therefore, more extensively multiplied by the press. Yet, after all——as one proof how much more commanding is that part of a literature which speaks to the elementary affections of men than that which is founded on the mutable aspects of manners——it is a fact that, even in our elaborate system of society, where an undue value is unavoidably given to the whole science of social intercourse, and a continual irritation applied to the sensibilities which point in that direction, still, under all these advantages, Pope himself is less read, less quoted, less thought of, than the elder and graver section of our literature. It is a great calamity for an author such as Pope, that, generally speaking, it requires so much experience of life to enjoy his peculiar felicities as must argue an age likely to have impaired the general capacity for enjoyment. For my part, I had myself a very slender acquaintance with this chapter of our literature; and what little I had was generally, at that period of my life, as with most men it continues to be to the end of life, a reflex knowledge, acquired through those pleasant miscellanies, half gossip, half criticism—such as Warton's *Essay on Pope*, Boswell's *Johnson*, Mathias's *Pursuits of Literature*, and many scores besides of the same indeterminate class: a class, however, which do a real service to literature, by diffusing an indirect knowledge of fine writers in their most effective passages, where else, in a direct shape, it would often never extend.

In some parts, then, having even a profound knowledge of our literature, in all parts having some, I felt it to be impossible that I should familiarly associate with those who had none at all; not so much as a mere historical knowledge of the literature in its capital names and their chronological succession. Do I mention this in disparagement of Oxford? By no means. Among the undergraduates of higher standing, and occasionally, perhaps, of my own, I have since learned that many might have been found eminently accomplished in this particular. But seniors do not seek after juniors; they must be sought; and, with my previous bias to solitude, a bias equally composed of impulses and motives, I had no disposition to take trouble in seeking any man for any purpose.

But, on this subject, a fact still remains to be told, of which I am justly proud; and it will serve, beyond anything else that I can say, to measure the degree of my intellectual development. On coming to Oxford, I had taken up one position in advance of my age by full thirty years: that appreciation of Wordsworth, which it has taken full thirty years to establish amongst the public, I had already made, and had made operative to my own intellectual culture, in the same year when I clandestinely quitted school. Already, in 1802, I had addressed a letter of fervent admiration to Mr. Wordsworth. I did not send it until the spring of 1803; and, from misdirection, it did not come into his hands for some months. But I had an answer from Mr. Wordsworth before I was eighteen; and that my letter was thought to express the homage of an enlightened admirer may be inferred from the fact that his answer was long and full. On this anecdote I do not mean to dwell; but I cannot allow the reader to overlook the circumstances of the case. At this day [1835] it is true, no journal can be taken up which does not habitually speak of Mr. Wordsworth as of *a* great, if not *the* great, poet of the age. Mr. Bulwer, living in the intensest pressure of the world, and though recoiling continually from the judgements of the world, yet never in any violent degree ascribes to Mr. Wordsworth (in his *England and the English*, p. 308) "an influence of a more noble and purely intellectual character than *any* writer of our age or nation has exercised." Such is the opinion held of this great poet in 1835; but what were those of 1805–15—nay, of 1825? For twenty years after the date of that letter to Mr. Wordsworth above referred to, language was exhausted, ingenuity was put on the rack, in the search after images and expres-

sions vile enough, insolent enough, to convey the unutterable contempt avowed for all that he had written
by the fashionable critics. One critic—who still, I believe, edits a rather popular journal, and who belongs
to that class, feeble, fluttering, ingenious, who make it
their highest ambition not to lead, but, with a slave's
adulation, to obey and to follow all the caprices of the
public mind—described Mr. Wordsworth as resembling, in the quality of his mind, an old nurse babbling in her paralytic dotage to sucking babies. If this
insult was peculiarly felt by Mr. Wordsworth, it was
on a consideration of the unusual imbecility of him
who offered it, and not because in itself it was baser or
more insolent than the language held by the majority
of journalists who then echoed the public voice. *Blackwood's Magazine* (1817) first accustomed the public
ear to the language of admiration coupled with the
name of Wordsworth. This began with Professor Wilson; and well I remember—nay, the proofs are still
easy to hunt up—that, for eight or ten years, this singularity of opinion, having no countenance from other
journals, was treated as a whim, a paradox, a bold extravagance, of the *Blackwood* critics. Mr. Wordsworth's neighbours in Westmorland, who had (generally speaking) a profound contempt for him, used to
rebut the testimony of *Blackwood* by one constant reply—"Ay, *Blackwood* praises Wordsworth, but who
else praises him?" In short, up to 1820, the name of
Wordsworth was trampled under foot; from 1820 to
1830, it was militant; from 1830 to 1835, it has been
triumphant. In 1803, when I entered at Oxford, that
name was absolutely unknown; and the finger of
scorn, pointed at it in 1802 by the first or second number of the *Edinburgh Review*, failed to reach its mark
from absolute defect of knowledge in the public mind.
Some fifty besides myself knew who was meant by

"that poet who had cautioned his friend against grow-ing double," &c.; to all others it was a profound secret.

These things must be known and understood prop-erly to value the prophetic eye and the intrepidity of two persons, like Professor Wilson and myself, who, in 1802–3, attached themselves to a banner not yet raised and planted; who outran, in fact, their contemporaries by one entire generation, and did *that* about 1802 which the rest of the world are doing in chorus about 1832.

Professor Wilson's period at Oxford exactly coin-cided with my own; yet, in that large world, we never met. I know, therefore, but little of his policy in re-gard to such opinions or feelings as tended to dissoci-ate him from the mass of his coevals. This only I know, that he lived as it were in public, and must, therefore, I presume, have practised a studied reserve as to his deepest admirations; and, perhaps, at that day (1803–8) the occasions would be rare in which much dissimulation would be needed. Until Lord Byron had begun to pilfer from Wordsworth and to abuse him, al-lusions to Wordsworth were not frequent in conversa-tions; and it was chiefly on occasions of some question arising about poetry in general, or about the poets of the day, that it became difficult to dissemble. For my part, hating the necessity for dissimulation as much as the dissimulation itself, I drew from this peculiarity also of my own mind a fresh reinforcement of my other motives for sequestering myself; and, for the first two years of my residence in Oxford, I compute that I did not utter one hundred words.

I remember distinctly the first (which happened also to be the last) conversation that I ever held with my tutor. It consisted of three sentences, two of which fell to his share, one to mine. On a fine morning, he met me in the Quadrangle, and, having then no guess of the nature of my pretensions, he determined (I suppose) to probe them. Accordingly, he asked me, "What I had been lately reading?" Now, the fact was that I, at that time immersed in metaphysics, had really been reading and studying very closely the *Parmenides*, of which obscure work some Oxford man, early in the last century, published a separate edition. Yet, so profound was the benignity of my nature that, in those days, I could not bear to witness, far less to cause, the least pain or mortification to any human being. I recoiled, indeed, from the society of most men, but not with any feelings of dislike. On the contrary, in order that I *might* like all men, I wished to associate with none. Now, then, to have mentioned the *Parmenides* to one who, fifty thousand to one, was a perfect stranger to its whole drift and purpose, looked too *méchant*, too like a trick of malice, in an age when such reading was so very unusual. I felt that it would be taken for an express stratagem for stopping my tutor's mouth. All this passing rapidly through my mind, I replied, without hesitation, that I had been reading Paley. My tutor's rejoinder I have never forgotten: "Ah! an excellent author; excellent for his matter; only you must be on your guard as to his style; he is very vicious *there*." Such was the colloquy; we bowed, parted, and never more (I apprehend) exchanged one word. Now, trivial and trite as this comment on Paley may appear to the reader, it struck me forcibly that more falsehood, or more absolute falsehood, or more direct inversion of the truth, could not, by any artifice or ingenuity, have been crowded into one short sentence. Paley, as a philosopher, is a jest, the disgrace of the age; and, as regards the two Universities, and the enormous responsibility they undertake for the books which they sanction by their official examinations for degrees, the name of Paley is their great opprobrium.

But, on the other hand, for style, Paley is a master. Homely, racy, vernacular English, the rustic vigour of a style which intentionally forgoes the graces of polish on the one hand, and of scholastic precision on the other—that quality of merit has never been attained in a degree so eminent. This first interchange of thought upon a topic of literature did not tend to slacken my previous disposition to retreat into solitude; a solitude, however, which at no time was tainted with either the moroseness or the pride of a cynic.

PART TWO

LITERARY REMINISCENCES:
FROM THE AUTOBIOGRAPHY
OF AN ENGLISH OPIUM-EATER

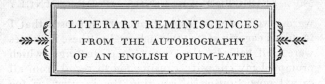
SAMUEL TAYLOR COLERIDGE

(First published in *Tait's Magazine*, 1834–5)

IT WAS, I think, in the month of August, but certainly in the summer season, and certainly in the year 1807, that I first saw this illustrious man. My knowledge of him as a man of most original genius began about the year 1799. A little before that time Wordsworth had published the first edition (in a single volume) of the *Lyrical Ballads*, and into this had been introduced Mr. Coleridge's poem of the "Ancient Mariner," as the contribution of an anonymous friend. It would be directing the reader's attention too much to myself if I were to linger upon this, the greatest event in the unfolding of my own mind. Let me say, in one word, that, at a period when neither the one nor the other writer was valued by the public—both having a long warfare to accomplish of contumely and ridicule before they could rise into their present estimation— I found in these poems "the ray of a new morning," and an absolute revelation of untrodden worlds teeming with power and beauty as yet unsuspected amongst men. I may here mention that, precisely at the same time, Professor Wilson, entirely unconnected with myself, and not even known to me until ten years later, received the same startling and profound impressions from the same volume. With feelings of reverential interest, so early and so deep, pointing to-

wards two contemporaries, it may be supposed that I
inquired eagerly after their names. But these inquiries
were self-baffled; the same deep feelings which
prompted my curiosity causing me to recoil from all
casual opportunities of pushing the inquiry, as too
generally lying amongst those who gave no sign of
participating in my feelings; and, extravagant as this
may seem, I revolted with as much hatred from cou-
pling my question with any occasion of insult to the
persons whom it respected as a primitive Christian
from throwing frankincense upon the altars of Cæsar,
or a lover from giving up the name of his beloved to
the coarse license of a Bacchanalian party. It is laughable to record for how long a period my curiosity in
this particular was thus self-defeated. Two years
passed before I ascertained the two names. Mr. Wordsworth published *his* in the second and enlarged edition
of the poems; and for Mr. Coleridge's I was "indebted" to a private source; but I discharged that debt
ill, for I quarrelled with my informant for what I considered his profane way of dealing with a subject so
hallowed in my own thoughts. After this I searched,
east and west, north and south, for all known works or
fragments of the same authors. I had read, therefore, as
respects Mr. Coleridge, the "Allegory" which he contributed to Mr. Southey's *Joan of Arc*. I had read his
fine Ode entitled "France," his "Ode to the Duchess of
Devonshire," and various other contributions, more or
less interesting, to the two volumes of the *Anthology*
published at Bristol, about 1799–1800, by Mr.
Southey; and, finally, I had, of course, read the small
volume of poems published under his own name.
These, however, as a juvenile and immature collection, made expressly with a view to pecuniary profit,
and therefore courting expansion at any cost of critical discretion, had in general greatly disappointed me.

Meantime, it had crowned the interest which to me invested his name, that about the year 1804 or 1805 I had been informed by a gentleman from the English Lakes, who knew him as a neighbour, that he had for some time applied his whole mind to metaphysics and psychology—which happened to be my own absorbing pursuit. From 1803 to 1808, I was a student at Oxford; and, on the first occasion when I could conveniently have sought for a personal knowledge of one whom I contemplated with so much admiration, I was met by a painful assurance that he had quitted England, and was then residing at Malta, in the quality of secretary to the Governor. I began to inquire about the best route to Malta; but, as any route at that time promised an inside place in a French prison, I reconciled myself to waiting; and at last, happening to visit the Bristol Hotwells in the summer of 1807, I had the pleasure to hear that Coleridge was not only once more upon English ground, but within forty and odd miles of my own station. In that same hour I bent my way to the south; and, before evening, reaching a ferry on the river Bridgewater, at a village called, I think, Stogursey (*i.e.*, Stoke de Courcy, by way of distinction from some other Stoke), I crossed it, and a few miles farther attained my object—viz., the little town of Nether Stowey, amongst the Quantock Hills. Here I had been assured that I should find Mr. Coleridge, at the house of his old friend Mr. Poole. On presenting myself, however, to that gentleman, I found that Coleridge was absent at Lord Egmont's, an elder brother (by the father's side) of Mr. Perceval, the Prime Minister, assassinated five years later; and, as it was doubtful whether he might not then be on the wing to another friend's in the town of Bridgewater, I consented willingly, until his motions should be ascertained, to stay a day or two with this Mr. Poole.

Two or three days had slipped away in waiting for
Coleridge's re-appearance at Nether Stowey, when suddenly Lord Egmont called upon Mr. Poole, with a present for Coleridge: it was a canister of peculiarly fine
snuff, which Coleridge now took profusely. Lord Egmont, on this occasion, spoke of Coleridge in the terms
of excessive admiration, and urged Mr. Poole to put
him upon undertaking some great monumental work,
that might furnish a sufficient arena for the display of
his various and rare accomplishments; for his multiform erudition on the one hand, for his splendid power
of theorizing and combining large and remote notices
of facts on the other. And he suggested, judiciously
enough, as one theme which offered a field at once
large enough and indefinite enough to suit a mind that
could not show its full compass of power unless upon
very plastic materials—a History of Christianity, in
its progress and in its chief divarications into Church
and Sect, with a continual reference to the relations
subsisting between Christianity and the current philosophy; their occasional connexions or approaches,
and their constant mutual repulsions. "But, at any
rate, let him do something," said Lord Egmont; "for
at present he talks very much like an angel, and does
nothing at all." Lord Egmont I understood from everybody to be a truly good and benevolent man; and on
this occasion he spoke with an earnestness which
agreed with my previous impression. Coleridge, he
said, was now in the prime of his powers—uniting
something of youthful vigour with sufficient experience of life; having the benefit, beside, of vast meditation, and of reading unusually discursive. No man had
ever been better qualified to revive the heroic period of
literature in England, and to give a character of weight
to the philosophic erudition of the country upon the
Continent. "And what a pity," he added, "if this man

were, after all, to vanish like an apparition, and you, I, and a few others, who have witnessed his grand *bravuras* of display, were to have the usual fortune of ghost-seers, in meeting no credit for any statements that we might vouch on his behalf!"

On this occasion we learned, for the first time, that Lord Egmont's carriage had, some days before, conveyed Coleridge to Bridgewater, with a purpose of staying one single day at that place, and then returning to Mr. Poole's. From the sort of laugh with which Lord Egmont taxed his own simplicity, in having confided at all in the stability of any Coleridgian plan, I now gathered that procrastination in excess was, or had become, a marking feature in Coleridge's daily life. Nobody who knew him ever thought of depending on any appointment he might make: spite of his uniformly honourable intentions, nobody attached any weight to his assurances *in re futura:* those who asked him to dinner or any other party, as a matter of course, sent a carriage for him, and went personally or by proxy to fetch him; and, as to letters, unless the address were in some female hand that commanded his affectionate esteem, he tossed them all into one general *dead-letter bureau*, and rarely, I believe, opened them at all. Bourrienne mentions a mode of abridging the trouble attached to a very extensive correspondence, by which infinite labour was saved to himself, and to Napoleon, when First Consul. Nine out of ten letters, supposing them letters of business with official applications of a special kind, he contends, answer themselves: in other words, time alone must soon produce events which virtually contain the answer. On this principle the letters were opened periodically, after intervals, suppose, of six weeks; and, at the end of that time, it was found that not many remained to require any further more particular answer. Coleridge's plan, however, was shorter: he opened none, I understood, and answered none. At least such was his habit at that time. But, on that same day, all this, which I heard now for the first time, and with much concern, was fully explained; for already he was under the full dominion of opium, as he himself revealed to me, and with a deep expression of horror at the hideous bondage, in a private walk of some length which I took with him about sunset.

Lord Egmont's information, and the knowledge now gained of Coleridge's habits, making it very uncertain when I might see him in my present hospitable quarters, I immediately took my leave of Mr. Poole, and went over to Bridgewater. I had received directions for finding out the house where Coleridge was visiting; and, in riding down a main street of Bridgewater, I noticed a gateway corresponding to the description given me. Under this was standing, and gazing about him, a man whom I will describe. In height he might seem to be about five feet eight (he was, in reality, about an inch and a-half taller, but his figure was of an order which drowns the height) ; his person was broad and full, and tended even to corpulence; his complexion was fair, though not what painters technically style fair, because it was associated with black hair; his eyes were large, and soft in their expression; and it was from the peculiar appearance of haze or dreaminess which mixed with their light that I recognized my object. This was Coleridge. I examined him steadfastly for a minute or more; and it struck me that he saw neither myself nor any other object in the street. He was in a deep reverie; for I had dismounted, made two or three trifling arrangements at an inn-door, and advanced close to him, before he had apparently become conscious of my presence. The sound of my voice, announcing my own name, first awoke him; he started,

and for a moment seemed at a loss to understand my
purpose or his own situation; for he repeated rapidly
a number of words which had no relation to either of
us. There was no *mauvaise honte* in his manner, but
simple perplexity, and an apparent difficulty in recovering his position amongst daylight realities. This little
scene over, he received me with a kindness of manner
so marked that it might be called gracious. The hospitable family with whom he was domesticated were
distinguished for their amiable manners and enlightened understandings: they were descendants from
Chubb, the philosophic writer, and bore the same name.
For Coleridge they all testified deep affection and esteem—sentiments in which the whole town of Bridgewater seemed to share; for in the evening, when the
heat of the day had declined, I walked out with him;
and rarely, perhaps never, have I seen a person so much
interrupted in one hour's space as Coleridge, on this
occasion, by the courteous attentions of young and old.

All the people of station and weight in the place, and
apparently all the ladies, were abroad to enjoy the
lovely summer evening; and not a party passed without some mark of smiling recognition, and the majority stopping to make personal inquiries about his
health, and to express their anxiety that he should
make a lengthened stay amongst them. Certain I am,
from the lively esteem expressed towards Coleridge at
this time by the people of Bridgewater, that a very
large subscription might, in that town, have been
raised to support him amongst them, in the character
of a lecturer, or philosophical professor.

Coleridge led me to a drawing-room, rang the bell
for refreshments, and omitted no point of a courteous
reception. He told me that there would be a very large
dinner party on that day, which, perhaps, might be
disagreeable to a perfect stranger; but, if not, he could

assure me of a most hospitable welcome from the family. I was too anxious to see him under all aspects to think of declining this invitation. That point being settled, Coleridge, like some great river, the Orellana, or the St. Lawrence, that, having been checked and fretted by rocks or thwarting islands, suddenly recovers its volume of waters and its mighty music, swept at once, as if returning to his natural business, into a continuous strain of eloquent dissertation, certainly the most novel, the most finely illustrated, and traversing the most spacious fields of thought by transitions the most just and logical, that it was possible to conceive. What I mean by saying that his transitions were "just" is by way of contradistinction to that mode of conversation which courts variety through links of *verbal* connexions. Coleridge, to many people, and often I have heard the complaint, seemed to wander; and he seemed then to wander the most when, in fact, his resistance to the wandering instinct was greatest— viz., when the compass and huge circuit by which his illustrations moved travelled farthest into remote regions before they began to revolve. Long before this coming round commenced most people had lost him, and naturally enough supposed that he had lost himself. They continued to admire the separate beauty of the thoughts, but did not see their relations to the dominant theme. Had the conversation been thrown upon paper, it might have been easy to trace the continuity of the links; just as in Bishop Berkeley's *Siris*,[1] from a pedestal so low and abject, so culinary, as Tar Water, the method of preparing it, and its medicinal effects, the dissertation ascends, like Jacob's ladder, by just gradations, into the Heaven of Heavens and the

---

[1] *Seiris* ought to have been the title—*i.e.* Σειρις, a chain. From this defect in the orthography, I did not in my boyish days perceive, nor could obtain any light upon, its meaning.

thrones of the Trinity. But Heaven is there connected
with earth by the Homeric chain of gold; and, being
subject to steady examination, it is easy to trace the
links; whereas, in conversation, the loss of a single
word may cause the whole cohesion to disappear from
view. However, I can assert, upon my long and intimate knowledge of Coleridge's mind, that logic the
most severe was as inalienable from his modes of thinking as grammar from his language.

For about three hours he had continued to talk,
and in the course of this performance he had delivered many most striking aphorisms, embalming more
weight of truth, and separately more deserving to be
themselves embalmed, than would easily be found in a
month's course of select reading. In the midst of our
conversation, if that can be called conversation which
I so seldom sought to interrupt, and which did not often
leave openings for contribution, the door opened, and
a lady entered. She was in person full and rather below
the common height; whilst her face showed to my eye
some prettiness of rather a commonplace order. Coleridge paused upon her entrance; his features, however,
announced no particular complacency, and did not re-
lax into a smile. In a frigid tone he said, whilst turning
to me, "Mrs. Coleridge"; in some slight way he then
presented me to her: I bowed; and the lady almost immediately retired. From this short but ungenial scene,
I gathered, what I afterward learned redundantly, that
Coleridge's marriage had not been a very happy one.
But let not the reader misunderstand me. Never was
there a baser insinuation, viler in the motive, or more
ignoble in the manner, than that passage in some lam-
poon of Lord Byron's, where, by way of vengeance on
Mr. Southey (who was the sole delinquent), he described both him and Coleridge as having married "two
milliners from Bath." Everybody knows what is *meant*

to be conveyed in that expression, though it would be hard, indeed, if, even at Bath, there should be any class under such a fatal curse, condemned so irretrievably, and so hopelessly prejudged, that ignominy must, at any rate, attach, in virtue of a mere name or designation, to the mode by which they gained their daily bread, or possibly supported the declining years of a parent. However, in this case, the whole sting of the libel was a pure falsehood of Lord Byron's. Bath was not the native city, nor at any time the residence, of the ladies in question, but Bristol. As to the other word, "*milliners*," that is not worth inquiring about. Whether they, or any one of their family, ever *did* exercise this profession, I do not know; they were, at all events, too young, when removed by marriage from Bristol, to have been much tainted by the worldly feelings which may beset such a mode of life. But, what is more to the purpose, I heard, at this time, in Bristol, from Mr. Cottle, the author, a man of high principle, as also from his accomplished sisters—from the ladies, again, who had succeeded Mrs. Hannah More in her school, and who enjoyed her entire confidence—that the whole family of four or five sisters had maintained an irreproachable character, though naturally exposed, by their personal attractions, to some peril, and to the malevolence of envy. This declaration, which I could strengthen by other testimony equally disinterested, if it were at all necessary, I owe to truth; and I must also add, upon a knowledge more personal, that Mrs. Coleridge was, in all circumstances of her married life, a virtuous wife and a conscientious mother; and, as a mother, she showed at times a most meritorious energy. In particular, I remember that, wishing her daughter to acquire the Italian language, and having in her retirement at Keswick no means of obtaining a master, she set to work resolutely, under Mr. Southey's guidance, to learn the language herself, at a time of life when such attainments are not made with ease or pleasure. She became mistress of the language in a very respectable extent, and then communicated her new accomplishment to her most interesting daughter.

I go on, therefore, to say, that Coleridge afterwards made me, as doubtless some others, a confidant in this particular. What he had to complain of was simply incompatibility of temper and disposition. Wanting all cordial admiration, or indeed comprehension, of her husband's intellectual powers, Mrs. Coleridge wanted the original basis for affectionate patience and candour. Hearing from everybody that Coleridge was a man of most extraordinary endowments, and attaching little weight, perhaps, to the distinction between popular talents and such as by their very nature are doomed to a slower progress in the public esteem, she naturally looked to see, at least, an ordinary measure of worldly consequence attend upon their exercise. Now, had Coleridge been as persevering and punctual as the great mass of professional men, and had he given no reason to throw the *onus* of the different result upon his own different habits, in that case this result might, possibly and eventually, have been set down to the peculiar constitution of his powers, and their essential mal-adaptation to the English market. But, this trial having never fairly been made, it was natural to impute his non-success exclusively to his own irregular application, and to his carelessness in forming judicious connexions. In circumstances such as these, however, no matter how caused or how palliated, was laid a sure ground of discontent and fretfulness in any woman's mind, not unusually indulgent or unusually magnanimous. Coleridge, besides, assured me that his marriage was not his own deliberate act, but was in a manner forced upon his sense of honour by the scrupulous Southey, who insisted that he had gone too far in his attentions to Miss Fricker for any honourable retreat. On the other hand, a neutral spectator of the parties protested to me, that, if ever in his life he had seen a man under deep fascination, and what he would have called desperately in love, Coleridge, in relation to Miss F., was that man. Be that as it might, circumstances occurred soon after the marriage which placed all the parties in a trying situation for their candour and good temper. I had a full outline of the situation from two of those who were chiefly interested, and a partial one from a third: nor can it be denied that all the parties offended in point of prudence. A young lady became a neighbour, and a daily companion of Coleridge's walks, whom I will not describe more particularly than by saying that intellectually she was very much superior to Mrs. Coleridge. That superiority alone, when made conspicuous by its effects in winning Coleridge's regard and society, could not but be deeply mortifying to a young wife. However, it was moderated to her feelings by two considerations: 1. That the young lady was much too kind-hearted to have designed any annoyance in this triumph, or to express any exultation; 2. That no shadow of suspicion settled upon the moral conduct or motives of either party: the young lady was always attended by her brother; she had no personal charms; and it was manifest that mere intellectual sympathies, in reference to literature and natural scenery, had associated them in their daily walks.

Still, it is a bitter trial to a young married woman to sustain any sort of competition with a female of her own age for any part of her husband's regard, or any share of his company. Mrs. Coleridge, not having the same relish for long walks or rural scenery, and their residence being, at this time, in a very sequestered village, was condemned to a daily renewal of this trial.

Accidents of another kind embittered it still further: often it would happen that the walking party returned drenched with rain; in which case, the young lady, with a laughing gaiety, and evidently unconscious of any liberty that she was taking, or any wound that she was inflicting, would run up to Mrs. Coleridge's wardrobe, array herself, without leave asked, in Mrs. Coleridge's dresses, and make herself merry with her own unceremoniousness and Mrs. Coleridge's gravity. In all this, she took no liberty that she would not most readily have granted in return; she confided too unthinkingly in what she regarded as the natural privileges of friendship; and as little thought that she had been receiving or exacting a favour, as, under an exchange of their relative positions, she would have claimed to confer one. But Mrs. Coleridge viewed her freedoms with a far different eye: she felt herself no longer the entire mistress of her own house; she held a divided empire; and it barbed the arrow to her womanly feelings that Coleridge treated any sallies of resentment which might sometimes escape her as narrow-mindedness; whilst, on the other hand, her own female servant, and others in the same rank of life, began to drop expressions which alternately implied pity for her as an injured woman, or contempt for her as a very tame one.

The reader will easily apprehend the situation, and the unfortunate results which it boded to the harmony of a young married couple, without further illustration. Whether Coleridge would not, under any circumstances, have become indifferent to a wife not eminently capable of enlightened sympathy with his own ruling pursuits, I do not undertake to pronounce. My own impression is, that neither Coleridge nor Lord Byron could have failed, eventually, to quarrel with *any* wife, though a Pandora sent down from heaven to

bless him. But, doubtless, this consummation must
have been hastened by a situation which exposed Mrs.
Coleridge to an invidious comparison with a more intellectual person; as, on the other hand, it was most
unfortunate for Coleridge himself to be continually
compared with one so ideally correct and regular in his
habits as Mr. Southey. Thus was their domestic peace
prematurely soured: embarrassments of a pecuniary
nature would be likely to demand continual sacrifices;
no depth of affection existing, these would create disgust or dissension; and at length each would believe
that their union had originated in circumstances overruling their own deliberate choice.

The gloom, however, and the weight of dejection
which sat upon Coleridge's countenance and deportment at this time could not be accounted for by a disappointment (if such it were) to which time must,
long ago, have reconciled him. Mrs. Coleridge, if not
turning to him the more amiable aspects of her character, was at any rate a respectable partner. And the
season of youth was now passed. They had been married about ten years; had had four children, of whom
three survived; and the interests of a father were now
replacing those of a husband. Yet never had I beheld
so profound an expression of cheerless despondency.
And the restless activity of Coleridge's mind, in chasing abstract truths, and burying himself in the dark
places of human speculation, seemed to me, in a great
measure, an attempt to escape out of his own personal
wretchedness. I was right. In this instance, at least, I
had hit the mark; and Coleridge bore witness himself
at an after period to the truth of my divination by some
impressive verses. At dinner, when a very numerous
party had assembled, he knew that he was expected to
talk, and exerted himself to meet the expectation. But
he was evidently struggling with gloomy thoughts that

prompted him to silence, and perhaps to solitude: he talked with effort, and passively resigned himself to the repeated misrepresentations of several amongst his hearers. The subject chiefly discussed was Arthur Young, not for his Rural Economy, but for his Politics. It must be to this period of Coleridge's life that Wordsworth refers in those exquisite "Lines written in my pocket copy of *The Castle of Indolence.*" The passage which I mean comes after a description of Coleridge's countenance, and begins in some such terms as these:

A piteous sight it was to see this man,
When he came back to us, a wither'd flow'r, &c.

Withered he was, indeed, and to all appearance blighted. At night he entered into a spontaneous explanation of this unhappy overclouding of his life, on occasion of my saying accidentally that a toothache had obliged me to take a few drops of laudanum. At what time or on what motive he had commenced the use of opium, he did not say; but the peculiar emphasis of horror with which he warned me against forming a habit of the same kind impressed upon my mind a feeling that he never hoped to liberate himself from the bondage. My belief is that he never *did.* About ten o'clock at night I took leave of him; and, feeling that I could not easily go to sleep after the excitement of the day, and fresh from the sad spectacle of powers so majestic already besieged by decay, I determined to return to Bristol through the coolness of the night. The roads, though, in fact, a section of the great highway between seaports so turbulent as Bristol and Plymouth, were as quiet as garden-walks. Once only I passed through the expiring fires of a village fair or wake: that interruption excepted, through the whole stretch

of forty miles from Bridgewater to the Hotwells, I
saw no living creature but a surly dog, who followed
me for a mile along a park-wall, and a man, who was
moving about in the half-way town of Cross. The turn-
pike-gates were all opened by a mechanical contrivance
from a bedroom window; I seemed to myself in solitary
possession of the whole sleeping country. The summer
night was divinely calm; no sound, except once or
twice the cry of a child as I was passing the windows
of cottages, ever broke upon the utter silence; and all
things conspired to throw back my thoughts upon the
extraordinary man whom I had just quitted.

The fine saying of Addison is familiar to most readers—that Babylon in ruins is not so affecting a spectacle, or so solemn, as a human mind overthrown by
lunacy. How much more awful, then, when a mind so
regal as that of Coleridge is overthrown, or threatened
with overthrow, not by a visitation of Providence, but
by the treachery of its own will, and by the conspiracy,
as it were, of himself against himself! Was it possible
that this ruin had been caused or hurried forward by
the dismal degradations of pecuniary difficulties? That
was worth inquiring. I will here mention briefly that
I *did* inquire two days after; and, in consequence of
what I heard, I contrived that a particular service
should be rendered to Mr. Coleridge, a week after,
through the hands of Mr. Cottle of Bristol, which
might have the effect of liberating his mind from
anxiety for a year or two, and thus rendering his great
powers disposable to their natural uses. That service
was accepted by Coleridge.[1] To save him any feelings
of distress, all names were concealed; but, in a letter
written by him about fifteen years after that time, I
found that he had become aware of all the circumstances, perhaps through some indiscretion of Mr.

[1] A gift of £300.—ED.

Cottle's. A more important question I never ascertained, viz. whether this service had the effect of seriously lightening his mind. For some succeeding years, he did certainly appear to me released from that load of despondency which oppressed him on my first introduction. Grave, indeed, he continued to be, and at times absorbed in gloom; nor did I ever see him in a state of perfectly natural cheerfulness. But, as he strove in vain, for many years, to wean himself from his captivity to opium, a healthy state of spirits could not be much expected. Perhaps, indeed, where the liver and other organs had, for so large a period in life, been subject to a continual morbid stimulation, it might be impossible for the system ever to recover a natural action. Torpor, I suppose, must result from continued artificial excitement; and, perhaps, upon a scale of corresponding duration. Life, in such a case, may not offer a field of sufficient extent for unthreading the fatal links that have been wound about the machinery of health, and have crippled its natural play.

Meantime—to resume the thread of my wandering narrative—on this serene summer night of 1807, as I moved slowly along, with my eyes continually settling upon the northern constellations, which, like all the fixed stars, by their immeasurable and almost spiritual remoteness from human affairs, naturally throw the thoughts upon the perishableness of our earthly troubles, in contrast with their own utter peace and solemnity—I reverted, at intervals, to all I had ever heard of Coleridge, and strove to weave it into some continuous sketch of his life. I hardly remember how much I then knew; I know but little now: that little I will here jot down upon paper.

Samuel Taylor Coleridge was the son of a learned clergyman—the vicar of Ottery St. Mary, in the south-

ern quarter of Devonshire.[1] It is painful to mention
that he was almost an object of persecution to his
mother; why, I could never learn. His father was described to me, by Coleridge himself, as a sort of Parson
Adams, being distinguished by his erudition, his inex-
perience of the world, and his guileless simplicity. I
once purchased in London, and, I suppose, still possess,
two elementary books on the Latin language by this
reverend gentleman; one of them, as I found, making
somewhat higher pretensions than a common school
grammar.[2] In particular, an attempt is made to reform
the theory of the cases; and it gives a pleasant specimen
of the rustic scholar's *naïveté*, that he seriously proposes to banish such vexatious terms as the *accusative;*
and, by way of simplifying the matter to tender minds,
that we should call it, in all time to come, the "*quale-
quare-quidditive*" case, upon what incomprehensible
principle I never could fathom. He used regularly to
delight his village flock, on Sundays, with Hebrew quo-
tations in his sermons, which he always introduced as
the "immediate language of the Holy Ghost." This
proved unfortunate to his successor: he also was a
learned man, and his parishioners admitted it, but generally with a sigh for past times, and a sorrowful complaint that he was still far below Parson Coleridge—
for that *he* never gave them any "immediate language
of the Holy Ghost." I presume that, like the reverend
gentleman so pleasantly sketched in *St. Ronan's Well*,
Mr. Coleridge, who resembled that person in his oriental learning, in his absence of mind, and in his simplicity, must also have resembled him in shortsightedness, of which his son used to relate this ludicrous
instance. Dining in a large party, one day, the modest

---

[1] He was born on the 21st October, 1772.—ED.

[2] *A Critical Latin Grammar*, 1772, and *Sententiæ Excerptæ,*
explaining the Rules of Grammar, 1777.—ED.

divine was suddenly shocked by perceiving some part, as he conceived, of his own snowy shirt emerging from a part of his habiliments, which we will suppose to have been his waistcoat. It was *not* that; but for decorum we will so call it. The stray portion of his own supposed tunic was admonished of its errors by a forcible thrust-back into its proper home; but still another *limbus* persisted to emerge, or seemed to persist, and still another, until the learned gentleman absolutely perspired with the labour of re-establishing order. And, after all, he saw with anguish that some arrears of the snowy indecorum still remained to reduce into obedience. To this remnant of rebellion he was proceeding to apply himself—strangely confounded, however, at the obstinacy of the insurrection—when, the mistress of the house rising to lead away the ladies from the table, and all parties naturally rising with her, it became suddenly apparent to every eye that the worthy Orientalist had been most laboriously stowing away into the capacious receptacles of his own habiliments —under the delusion that it was his own shirt—the snowy folds of a lady's gown, belonging to his next neighbour; and so voluminously that a very small portion of it, indeed, remained for the lady's own use; the natural consequence of which was, of course, that the lady appeared inextricably yoked to the learned theologian, and could not in any way effect her release, until after certain operations upon the vicar's dress, and a continued refunding and rolling out of snowy mazes upon snowy mazes, in quantities which at length proved too much for the gravity of the company. Inextinguishable laughter arose from all parties, except the erring and unhappy doctor, who, in dire perplexity, continued still refunding with all his might—perspiring and refunding—until he had paid up the last arrears of his long debt, and thus put an end to a case of distress more memorable to himself and his parishioners than any "*quale-quare-quidditive*" case that probably had ever perplexed his learning.

In his childish days, and when he had become an orphan, Coleridge was removed to the heart of London, and placed on the great foundation of Christ's Hospital.[1] He there found himself associated, as a schoolfellow, with several boys destined to distinction in after life; particularly the brilliant Leigh Hunt, and more closely with one who, if not endowed with powers equally large and comprehensive as his own, had, however, genius not less original or exquisite—viz. the inimitable Charles Lamb. But, in learning, Coleridge out-stripped all competitors, and rose to be the captain of the school. It is, indeed, a memorable fact to be recorded of a boy, that, before completing his fifteenth year, he had translated the Greek Hymns of Synesius into English Anacreontic verse. This was not a school task, but a labour of love and choice. Before leaving school, Coleridge had an opportunity of reading the sonnets of Bowles, which so powerfully impressed his poetic sensibility that he made forty transcripts of them with his own pen, by way of presents to youthful friends. From Christ's Hospital, by the privilege of his station at school, he was transferred to Jesus College, Cambridge. What accident, or imprudence, carried him away from Cambridge before he had completed the usual period of study, I never heard. He had certainly won some distinction as a scholar, having obtained the prize for a Greek ode in Sapphic metre, of which the sentiments (as he observes himself) were better than the Greek. Porson was accustomed, meanly enough, to ridicule the Greek *lexis* of this ode; which was to break a fly upon the wheel. The ode was clever enough for a boy; but to such skill in Greek as could

[1] When he was ten years old.—ED.

have enabled him to compose with critical accuracy Coleridge never made pretensions.

The incidents of Coleridge's life about this period, and some account of a heavy disappointment in love, which probably it was that carried him away from Cambridge, are to be found embodied (with what modifications I know not) in the novel of *Edmund Oliver*, written by Charles Lloyd. It is well known that, in a frenzy of unhappy feeling at the rejection he met with from the lady of his choice, Coleridge enlisted as a private into a dragoon regiment. He fell off his horse on several occasions, but perhaps not more than raw recruits are apt to do when first put under the riding-master. But Coleridge was naturally ill framed for a good horseman. He is also represented in *Edmund Oliver* as having found peculiar difficulty or annoyance in grooming his horse. But the most romantic incident in that scene of his life was in the circumstances of his discharge. It is said (but I vouch for no part of the story) that Coleridge, as a private, mounted guard at the door of a room in which his officers were giving a ball. Two of them had a dispute upon some Greek word or passage when close to Coleridge's station. He interposed his authentic decision of the case. The officers stared as though one of their own horses had sung "Rule Britannia"; questioned him; heard his story; pitied his misfortune; and finally subscribed to purchase his discharge. So the story has been told; and also otherwise. Not very long after this, Coleridge became acquainted with the two celebrated Wedgwoods of Etruria, both of whom, admiring his fine powers, subscribed to send him into North Germany, where, at the University of Göttingen, he completed his education according to his own scheme. The most celebrated professor whose lectures he attended was the far-famed Blumenbach, of whom he continued to speak through

life with almost filial reverence. Returning to England, he attended Mr. Thomas Wedgwood, as a friend,
throughout the afflicting and anomalous illness which
brought him to the grave. It was supposed by medical
men that the cause of Mr. Wedgwood's continued misery was a stricture of the colon. The external symptoms were torpor and morbid irritability, together with
everlasting restlessness. By way of some relief to this
latter symptom, Mr. Wedgwood purchased a travelling
carriage, and wandered up and down England, taking
Coleridge as his companion. And, as a desperate attempt to rouse and irritate the decaying sensibility of
his system, I have been assured, by a surviving friend,
that Mr. Wedgwood at one time opened a butcher's
shop, conceiving that the affronts and disputes to which
such a situation would expose him might act beneficially upon his increasing torpor. This strange expedient [1] served only to express the anguish which had
now mastered his nature; it was soon abandoned; and
this accomplished but miserable man at length sank
under his sufferings. What made the case more memorable was the combination of worldly prosperity which
forced into strong relief and fiery contrast this curse
written in the flesh. He was rich, he was young, he
was popular, distinguished for his scientific attainments, publicly honoured for patriotic services, and
had before him, when he first fell ill, every prospect of
a career even nationally splendid.

[1] Which, however, his brother denied as a pure fable. On
reading this account, he wrote to me, and in very courteous
terms assured me that I had been misinformed. I now retain
the story simply as a version, partially erroneous, no doubt, of
perhaps some true anecdote that may have escaped the surviving Mr. Wedgwood's knowledge; my reason for thinking thus
being that the same anecdote essentially, but varied in the circumstances, has reached me at different periods from parties
having no connexion whatsoever.

By the death of Mr. Wedgwood, Coleridge succeeded to a regular annuity of £75, which that gentleman had bequeathed to him. The other Mr. Wedgwood granted him an equal allowance. Now came his marriage, his connexion with politics and political journals, his residence in various parts of Somersetshire, and his consequent introduction to Mr. Wordsworth. In his politics, Mr. Coleridge was most sincere and most enthusiastic. No man hailed with profounder sympathy the French Revolution; and, though he saw cause to withdraw his regard from many of the democratic zealots in this country, and even from the revolutionary interest as it was subsequently conducted, he continued to worship the original revolutionary cause in a pure Miltonic spirit.

Somewhere about this time, Coleridge attempted, under Sheridan's countenance, to bring a tragedy upon the stage of Drury Lane; but his prospect of success, as I once heard or read, was suddenly marred by Mr. Sheridan's inability to sacrifice what he thought a good jest. One scene presented a cave with streams of water weeping down the sides; and the first words were, in a sort of mimicry of the sound, "Drip, drip, drip!" Upon which Sheridan repeated aloud to the assembled green-room, expressly convoked for the purpose of hearing the play read, "Drip, drip, drip!—why, God bless me, there's nothing here but *dripping!*" and so arose a chorus of laughter amongst the actors fatal for the moment to the probationary play.

About the latter end of the century, Coleridge visited North Germany again, in company with Mr. and Miss Wordsworth. Their tour was chiefly confined to the Hartz Forest and its neighbourhood. But the incident most worthy of remembrance in their excursion was a visit made to Klopstock; either at Hamburg, or, perhaps, at the Danish town of Altona, on the same river

Elbe; for Klopstock was a pensioner of the Danish
king. An anonymous writer, who attacked Coleridge
most truculently in an early number of "Blackwood,"
and with an *acharnement* that must astonish the neutral reader, has made the mistake of supposing Coleridge to have been the chief speaker, who did not speak
at all. The case was this: Klopstock could not speak
English, though everybody remembers the pretty
broken English of his second wife. Neither Coleridge
nor Wordsworth, on the other hand, was able to *speak*
German with any fluency. French, therefore, was the
only medium of free communication; that being pretty
equally familiar to Wordsworth and to Klopstock. But
Coleridge found so much difficulty even in *reading*
French that, wherever (as in the case of Leibnitz's *The-
odicée*) there was a choice between an original written
in French and a translation, though it might be a very
faulty one, in German, he always preferred the latter.
Hence it happened that Wordsworth, on behalf of the
English party, was the sole supporter of the dialogue.
The anonymous critic says another thing, which certainly has an air of truth—viz. that Klopstock plays a
very secondary *rôle* in the interview (or words to that
effect). But how was this to be avoided in reporting the
case, supposing the fact to have been such? Now, the
plain truth is that Wordsworth, upon his own ground,
was an incomparable talker; whereas "Klubstick" (as
Coleridge used to call him) was always a feeble and
slovenly one, because a loose and incoherent thinker.
Besides, he was now old and decaying. Nor at any time,
nor in any accomplishment, could Klopstock have
shone, unless in the respectable art of skating. *There*
he had a real advantage. The author of *The Messiah*,
I have authority for saying, skated with the ease and
grace of a regular artist; whereas the poet of *The Excursion* sprawled upon the ice like a cow dancing a

cotillon. Wordsworth did the very opposite of that with which he was taxed; for, happening to look down at Klopstock's swollen legs, and recollecting his age, he felt touched by a sort of filial pity for his helplessness. And he came to the conclusion that it would not seem becoming in a young and as yet obscure author to report too consciously the real superiority which he found it easy to maintain in such a colloquy.

About the close of the first revolutionary war it must have been, or in the brief interval of peace, that Coleridge resorted to the English Lakes as a place of residence. Wordsworth had a natural connexion with that region, by birth, breeding, and family alliances. Wordsworth must have attracted Coleridge to the Lakes; and Coleridge, through his affinity to Southey, eventually attracted *him*. Southey, as is known to all who take an interest in the Lake colony, married a sister of Mrs. Coleridge's; and, as a singular eccentricity in the circumstances of that marriage, I may mention that, on his wedding-day, and from the very portico of the church, Southey left his bride to embark for Lisbon. His uncle, Dr. Herbert, was chaplain to the English factory in that city; and it was to benefit by the facilities in that way opened to him for seeing Portugal that Southey now went abroad. He extended his tour to Spain; and the result of his notices was communicated to the world in a volume of travels. By such accidents of personal or family connexion as I have mentioned was the Lake colony gathered; and the critics of the day, unaware of the real facts, supposed them to have assembled under common views in literature—particularly with regard to the true functions of poetry, and the true theory of poetic diction. Under this original blunder, laughable it is to mention that they went on to *find* in their writings all the agreements and common characteristics which their blunder had presumed; and they incorporated the whole community under the name of the *Lake School*. Yet Wordsworth and Southey never had one principle in common; their hostility was even flagrant. Indeed, Southey troubled himself little about abstract principles in anything; and, so far from agreeing with Wordsworth to the extent of setting up a separate school in poetry, he told me himself (August 1812) that he highly disapproved both of Mr. Wordsworth's theories and of his practice. It is very true that one man may sympathize with another, or even follow his leading, unconscious that he does so; or he may go so far as, in the very act of virtual imitation, to deem himself in opposition; but this sort of blind agreement could hardly be supposed of two men so discerning and so self-examining as Wordsworth and Southey. And, in fact, a philosophic investigation of the difficult questions connected with this whole slang about schools, Lake schools, &c., would show that Southey has not, nor ever had, any *peculiarities* in common with Wordsworth, beyond that of exchanging the old prescriptive diction of poetry, introduced between the periods of Milton and Cowper, for the simpler and profounder forms of daily life in some instances, and of the Bible in others. The bold and uniform practice of Wordsworth was here adopted, on perfectly independent views, by Southey. In this respect, however, Cowper had already begun the reform; and his influence, concurring with the now larger influence of Wordsworth, has operated so extensively as to make their own original differences at this day less perceptible.

By the way, the word *colony* reminds me that I have omitted to mention in its proper place some scheme for migrating to America which had been entertained by Coleridge and Southey about the year 1794–95, under the learned name of *Pantisocracy*. So far as I ever heard, it differed little, except in its Grecian name, from any other scheme for mitigating the privations of a wilderness by settling in a cluster of families, bound together by congenial tastes and uniform principles, rather than in self-depending, insulated households. Steadily pursued, it might, after all, have been a fortunate plan for Coleridge. "Soliciting my food from daily toil," a line in which Coleridge alludes to the scheme, implies a condition of life that would have upheld Coleridge's health and happiness somewhat better than the habits of luxurious city life as now constituted in Europe. But, returning to the Lakes, and to the Lake colony of poets: So little were Southey and Wordsworth connected by any personal intercourse in those days, and so little disposed to be connected, that, whilst the latter had a cottage in Grasmere, Southey pitched his tent at Greta Hall, on a little eminence rising immediately from the river Greta and the town of Keswick. Grasmere is in Westmorland; Keswick in Cumberland; and they are thirteen good miles apart. Coleridge and his family were domiciliated in Greta Hall; sharing that house, a tolerably large one, on some principle of amicable division, with Mr. Southey. But Coleridge personally was more often to be found at Grasmere—which presented the threefold attractions of loveliness so complete as to eclipse even the scenery of Derwentwater; a pastoral state of society, free from the deformities of a little town like Keswick; and, finally, for Samuel Taylor Coleridge, the society of Wordsworth.

At this time, when Coleridge first settled at the Lakes, or not long after, a romantic and somewhat tragical affair drew the eyes of all England, and, for many years, continued to draw the steps of tourists, to one of the most secluded Cumberland valleys, so little visited previously that it might be described almost as

an undiscovered chamber of that romantic district.
Coleridge was brought into a closer connexion with
this affair than merely by the general relation of neighbourhood; for an article of his in a morning paper, I
believe, unintentionally furnished the original clue for
unmasking the base impostor who figured as the central actor in this tale. The tale was at that time drama-
tized, and scenically represented by some of the minor
theatres in London, as noticed by Wordsworth in *The
Prelude*. But other generations have arisen since that
time, who must naturally be unacquainted with the circumstances; and on their account I will here recall
them: One day in the Lake season there drove up to
the Royal Oak, the principal inn at Keswick, a handsome and well-appointed travelling carriage, containing one gentleman of somewhat dashing exterior. The
stranger was a picturesque-hunter, but not of that order who fly round the ordinary tour with the velocity
of lovers posting to Gretna, or of criminals running
from the police; his purpose was to domiciliate himself
in this beautiful scenery, and to see it at his leisure.
From Keswick, as his head-quarters, he made excursions in every direction amongst the neighbouring valleys; meeting generally a good deal of respect and attention, partly on account of his handsome equipage,
and still more from his visiting cards, which designated him as "The Hon. Augustus Hope." Under this
name, he gave himself out for a brother of Lord Hope-
toun's. Some persons had discernment enough to doubt
of this; for the man's breeding and deportment, though
showy, had an under-tone of vulgarity about it; and
Coleridge assured me that he was grossly ungrammat-
ical in his ordinary conversation. However, one fact,
soon dispersed by the people of a little rustic post-office,
laid asleep all demurs; he not only received letters addressed to him under this assumed name—*that* might

be through collusion with accomplices—but he himself
continually *franked* letters by that name. Now, this
being a capital offence, being not only a forgery, but
(as a forgery on the Post-Office) sure to be prosecuted,
nobody presumed to question his pretensions any
longer; and, henceforward, he went to all places with
the consideration attached to an earl's brother. All
doors flew open at his approach: boats, boatmen, nets,
and the most unlimited sporting privileges, were placed
at the disposal of the "Honourable" gentleman: and
the hospitality of the district was put on its mettle, in
offering a suitable reception to the patrician Scotsman.
It could be no blame to a shepherd girl, bred in the
sternest solitude which England has to show, that she
should fall into a snare which many of her betters had
not escaped. Nine miles from Keswick, by the nearest
bridle-road through Newlands, but fourteen or fifteen
by any route which the honourable gentleman's trav-
elling-carriage could traverse, lies the Lake of Buttermere. Its margin, which is overhung by some of the
loftiest and steepest of the Cumbrian mountains, exhibits on either side few traces of human neighbourhood; the level area, where the hills recede enough to
allow of any, is of a wild pastoral character, or almost
savage; the waters of the lake are deep and sullen; and
the barrier mountains, by excluding the sun for much
of his daily course, strengthen the gloomy impressions.
At the foot of this lake (that is, at the end where its
waters issue) lie a few unornamented fields, through
which rolls a little brook-like river, connecting it with
the larger lake of Crummock; and at the edge of this
miniature domain, upon the roadside, stands a cluster
of cottages, so small and few that in the richer tracts of
England they would scarcely be complimented with
the name of hamlet. One of these, and I believe the
principal, belonged to an independent proprietor,

called, in the local dialect, a *"Statesman"* [1]; and more, perhaps, for the sake of attracting a little society than with much view to pecuniary profit at that era, this cottage offered the accommodations of an inn to the traveller and his horse. Rare, however, must have been the mounted traveller in those days, unless visiting Buttermere for itself, and as a *terminus ad quem;* since the road led to no further habitations of man, with the exception of some four or five pastoral cabins, equally humble, in Gatesgarthdale.

Hither, however, in an evil hour for the peace of this little brotherhood of shepherds, came the cruel spoiler from Keswick. His errand was, to witness or to share in the char-fishing; for in Derwentwater (the Lake of Keswick) no char is found, which breeds only in the deep waters, such as Windermere, Crummock, Buttermere, and Coniston—never in the shallow ones. But, whatever had been his first object, *that* was speedily forgotten in one more deeply interesting. The daughter of the house, a fine young woman of eighteen, acted as waiter. [2] In a situation so solitary, the stranger had unlimited facilities for enjoying her company, and recommending himself to her favour. Doubts about his pretensions never arose in so simple a place as this; they were overruled before they could well have arisen by the opinion now general in Kes-

---

[1] *i.e.*—A 'Statesman elliptically for an Estatesman—a native dalesman possessing and personally cultivating a patrimonial landed estate.

[2] *"Waiter"*: Since this was first written, social changes in London, by introducing females very extensively into the office (once monopolized by men) of attending the visitors at the tables of eating-houses, have introduced a corresponding new word—viz., *waitress;* which word, twenty-five years back, would have been simply ludicrous; but now is become as indispensable to precision of language as the words traitress, heiress, inheritrix, &c.

wick, that he really was what he pretended to be: and thus, with little demur, except in the shape of a few natural words of parting anger from a defeated or rejected rustic admirer, the young woman gave her hand in marriage to the showy and unprincipled stranger. I know not whether the marriage was, or could have been, celebrated in the little mountain chapel of Buttermere. From this sanctuary it was—from beneath the maternal shadow, if not from the very altar,[1] of this lonely chapel—that the heartless villain carried off the flower of the mountains. Between this place and Keswick they continued to move backwards and forwards, until at length, with the startling of a thunder-clap to the affrighted mountaineers, the bubble burst: officers of justice appeared: the stranger was easily intercepted from flight, and, upon a capital charge, was borne away to Carlisle. At the ensuing assizes he was tried for forgery on the prosecution of the Post-Office, found guilty, left for execution, and executed accordingly. On the day of his condemnation, Wordsworth and Coleridge passed through Carlisle, and endeavoured to obtain an interview with him. Wordsworth succeeded; but, for some unknown reason, the prisoner steadily refused to see Coleridge; a caprice which could not be penetrated. It is true that he had, during his whole residence at Keswick, avoided Coleridge with a solicitude which had revived the original suspicions against him in some quarters, after they had generally gone to sleep. But for this his motive had then been sufficient: he was of a Devonshire family, and naturally feared the eye, or the inquisitive examination

[1] My doubt is founded upon the varying tenure of these secluded chapels as to privileges of marrying or burying. The mere name of chapel, though, of course, in regular connexion with some mother church, does not of itself imply whether it has or has not the power to solemnize a marriage.

of one who bore a name immemorially associated with the southern part of that county.

Coleridge, however, had been transplanted so immaturely from his native region that few people in England knew less of its family connexions. That, perhaps, was unknown to this malefactor; but, at any rate, he knew that all motive was now at an end for disguise of any sort; so that his reserve, in this particular, had now become unintelligible. However, if not him, Coleridge saw and examined his very interesting papers. These were chiefly letters from women whom he had injured, pretty much in the same way, and by the same impostures, as he had so recently practised in Cumberland; and, as Coleridge assured me, were in part the most agonizing appeals that he had ever read to human justice and pity. The man's real name was, I think, Hatfield. And amongst the papers were two separate correspondences, of some length, with two young women, apparently of superior condition in life (one the daughter of an English clergyman), whom this villain had deluded by marriage, and, after some cohabitation, abandoned—one of them with a family of young children. Great was the emotion of Coleridge when he recurred to his remembrance of these letters, and bitter, almost vindictive, was the indignation with which he spoke of Hatfield. Coleridge said often, in looking back upon that frightful exposure of human guilt and misery, that the man who, when pursued by these heartrending apostrophes, and with this litany of anguish sounding in his ears, from despairing women and from famishing children, could yet find it possible to enjoy the calm pleasures of a Lake tourist, and deliberately to hunt for the picturesque, must have been a fiend of that order which fortunately does not often emerge amongst men. It is painful to remember that, in those days, amongst the multitudes who ended their

career in the same ignominious way, and the majority
for offences connected with the forgery of bank notes,
there must have been a considerable number who perished from the very opposite cause—viz., because they
felt, too passionately and profoundly for prudence, the
claims of those who looked up to them for support. One
common scaffold confounds the most flinty hearts and
the tenderest. However, in this instance, it was in some
measure the heartless part of Hatfield's conduct which
drew upon him his ruin: for the Cumberland jury
honestly declared their unwillingness to hang him for
having forged a frank; and both they, and those who
refused to aid his escape when first apprehended, were
reconciled to this harshness entirely by what they
heard of his conduct to their injured young fellow-
countrywoman.

It is an instance of Coleridge's carelessness that he,
who had as little of fixed ill-nature in his temper as
any person whom I have ever known, managed, in reporting this story at the time of its occurrence, to get
himself hooked into a personal quarrel, which hung
over his head unsettled for nine or ten years. A Liverpool merchant, who was then meditating a house in
the Vale of Grasmere, and perhaps might have incurred Coleridge's anger by thus disturbing, with inappropriate intrusions, this loveliest of all English
landscapes, had connected himself a good deal with
Hatfield during his Keswick masquerade; and was said
even to have carried his regard to that villain so far as
to have christened one of his own children by the
names of "Augustus Hope." With these and other circumstances, expressing the extent of the infatuation
amongst the swindler's dupes, Coleridge made the public merry. Naturally, the Liverpool merchant was not
amongst those who admired the facetiousness of Coleridge on this occasion, but swore vengeance whenever

they should meet. They never *did* meet, until ten years had gone by; and then, oddly enough, it was in the Liverpool man's own house—in that very nuisance of a house which had, I suppose, first armed Coleridge's wrath against him. This house, by time and accident, in no very wonderful way, had passed into the hands of Wordsworth as tenant. Coleridge, as was still less wonderful, had become the visitor of Wordsworth on returning from Malta; and the Liverpool merchant, as was also natural, either seeking his rent, or on the general errand of a friendly visit, calling upon Wordsworth, met Coleridge in the hall. Now came the hour for settling old accounts. I was present, and can report the case. Both looked grave, and coloured a little. But ten years work wonders: an armistice of that duration heals many a wound; and Samuel Taylor Coleridge, requesting his enemy's company in the garden, entered upon a long metaphysical dissertation, bordering upon what you might call *philosophical rigmarole*, and rather puzzling to answer. It seemed to be an expansion, by Thomas Aquinas, of that parody upon a well-known passage in Shenstone, where the writer says:

> *He kick'd me down-stairs with such a sweet grace*
> *That I thought he was handing me up.*

And, in the upshot, this conclusion *eventuated* (to speak Yankeeishly), that purely on principles of good neighbourhood and universal philanthropy could Coleridge have meditated or executed the insult offered in the *Morning Post*. The Liverpool merchant rubbed his forehead, and seemed a little perplexed; but he was a most good-natured man; and he was eminently a gentleman. At length, considering, perhaps, how very like Duns Scotus, or Albertus Magnus, Coleridge had shown himself in this luminous explanation, he might begin to reflect that, had any one of those distinguished men offered a similar affront, it would have been impossible to resent it; for who could think of kicking the "Doctor Seraphicus," or would it tell to any man's advantage in history that he had caned Thomas Aquinas? On these principles, therefore, without saying one word, Liverpoliensis held out his hand, and a lasting reconciliation followed.

Not very long, I believe, after this affair of Hatfield, Coleridge went to Malta. His inducement to such a step must have been merely a desire to see the most interesting regions of the Mediterranean under the shelter and advantageous introduction of an official station. It was, however, an unfortunate chapter of his life: for, being necessarily thrown a good deal upon his own resources in the narrow society of a garrison, he there confirmed and cherished, if he did not there form, his habit of taking opium in large quantities. I am the last person in the world to press conclusions harshly or uncandidly against Coleridge; but I believe it to be notorious that he first began the use of opium, not as a relief from any bodily pains or nervous irritations (since his constitution was strong and excellent), but as a source of luxurious sensations. It is a great misfortune, at least it is a great peril, to have tasted the enchanted cup of youthful rapture incident to the poetic temperament. That fountain of high-wrought sensibility once unlocked experimentally, it is rare to see a submission afterwards to the insipidities of daily life. Coleridge, to speak in the words of Cervantes, wanted better bread than was made of wheat; and, when youthful blood no longer sustained the riot of his animal spirits, he endeavoured to excite them by artificial stimulants.

At Malta he became acquainted with Commodore

Decatur and other Americans of distinction; and this brought him afterwards into connexion with Allston, the American artist. Of Sir Alexander Ball, one of Lord Nelson's captains in the battle of the Nile, and Governor of Malta, he spoke and wrote uniformly in a lavish style of panegyric, for which plainer men found it difficult to see the slightest ground. It was, indeed, Coleridge's infirmity to project his own mind, and his own very peculiar ideas, nay, even his own expressions and illustrative metaphors, upon other men, and to contemplate these reflex images from himself as so many characters having an absolute ground in some separate object. "Ball and Bell"—"Bell and Ball," [1]

---

[1] *"Ball and Bell"—"Bell and Ball"*: viz., Sir Alexander Ball, Governor of Malta, and Dr. Andrew Bell, the importer into England from Madras of that machinery for facilitating popular education which was afterwards fraudulently appropriated by Joseph Lancaster. The Bishop of Durham (Shute Barrington) gave to Dr. Bell, in reward of his Madras services, the princely Mastership of Sherborne Hospital. The doctor saved in this post £125,000, and with this money founded Trinity College, Glenalmond, in Perthshire. Most men have their enemies and calumniators: Dr. Bell had *his*, who happened rather indecorously to be his wife—from whom he was legally separated, or (as in Scotch law it is called) *divorced*; not, of course, divorced *à vinculo matrimonii* (which only amounts to a divorce in the English sense—such a divorce as enables the parties to contract another marriage), but simply divorced *à mensâ et thoro*. This legal separation, however, did not prevent the lady from persecuting the unhappy doctor with everlasting letters, indorsed outside with records of her enmity and spite. Sometimes she addressed her epistles thus: "To that supreme of rogues, who looks the hang-dog that he is, Doctor (such a doctor!) Andrew Bell." Or again: "To the ape of apes, and the knave of knaves, who is recorded to have once paid a debt—but a small one, you may be sure, it was that he selected for this wonderful experiment—in fact, it was 4½ d. Had it been on the other side of 6d., he must have died before he could have achieved so dreadful a sacrifice." Many others, most ingeniously varied in the style of abuse, I

were two of these pet subjects; he had a "craze" about each of them; and to each he ascribed thoughts and words to which, had they been put upon the rack, they never would have confessed.

From Malta, on his return homewards, he went to Rome and Naples. One of the cardinals, he tells us, warned him, by the Pope's wish, of some plot, set on foot by Bonaparte, for seizing him as an anti-Gallican writer. This statement was ridiculed by the anonymous assailant in *Blackwood* as the very consummation of moonstruck vanity; and it is there compared to John Dennis's frenzy in retreating from the sea-coast, under the belief that Louis XIV had commissioned emissaries to land on the English shore and make a dash at his person. But, after all, the thing is not so entirely improbable. For it is certain that some orator of the Opposition (Charles Fox, as Coleridge asserts) had

have heard rehearsed by Coleridge, Southey, Lloyd, &c.; and one, in particular, addressed to the doctor, when spending a summer at the cottage of Robert Newton, an old soldier, in Grasmere, presented on the back two separate adjurations: one specially addressed to Robert himself, pathetically urging him to look sharply after the rent of his lodgings; and the other more generally addressed to the unfortunate person, as yet undisclosed to the British public (and in this case turning out to be myself) who might be incautious enough to pay the postage at Ambleside. "Don't grant him an hour's credit," she urged upon the person unknown, "if I had any regard to my family." "*Cash down!*" she wrote twice over. Why the doctor submitted to these annoyances, nobody knew. Some said it was mere indolence; but others held it to be a cunning compromise with her inexorable malice. The letters were certainly open to the "public" eye; but meantime the "public" was a very narrow one; the clerks in the post-office had little time for digesting such amenities of conjugal affection; and the chance bearer of the letters to the doctor would naturally solve the mystery by supposing an *extra* portion of madness in the writer, rather than an *extra* portion of knavery in the reverend receiver.

pointed out all the principal writers in the *Morning Post* to Napoleon's vengeance, by describing the war as a war "of that journal's creation." And, as to the insinuation that Napoleon was above throwing his regards upon a simple writer of political essays, *that* is not only abundantly confuted by many scores of established cases, but also is specially put down by a case circumstantially recorded in the Second Tour to Paris by the celebrated John Scott of Aberdeen. It there appears that, on no other ground whatever than that of his connexion with the London newspaper press, some friend of Mr. Scott's had been courted most assiduously by Napoleon during the *Hundred Days*. Assuredly Coleridge deserved, beyond all other men that ever were connected with the daily press, to be regarded with distinction. Worlds of fine thinking lie buried in that vast abyss, never to be disentombed or restored to human admiration. Like the sea, it has swallowed treasures without end, that no diving-bell will bring up again. But nowhere, throughout its shoreless magazines of wealth, does there lie such a bed of pearls confounded with the rubbish and "purgamenta" of ages, as in the political papers of Coleridge. No more *appreciable* monument could be raised to the memory of Coleridge than a republication of his essays in the *Morning Post*, and afterwards in the *Courier*. And here, by the way, it may be mentioned that the sagacity of Coleridge, as applied to the signs of the times, is illustrated by this fact, that distinctly and solemnly he foretold the restoration of the Bourbons, at a period when most people viewed such an event as the most romantic of visions, and not less chimerical than that "march upon Paris" of Lord Hawkesbury's which for so many years supplied a theme of laughter to the Whigs.

Why Coleridge left Malta, is as difficult to explain

upon any principles of ordinary business, as why he
had ever gone thither. The post of secretary, if it imposed any official attendance of a regular kind, or any
official correspondence, must have been but poorly
filled by *him;* and Sir Alexander Ball, if I have collected his character justly, was not likely to accept the
gorgeous philosophy of Coleridge as an indemnification for irregular performance of his public duties.
Perhaps, therefore, though on the best terms of mutual
regard, mutually they might be pleased to part. Part
they did, at any rate, and poor Coleridge was sea-sick
the whole of his homeward (as he had been through
the whole of his outward) voyage.

It was not long after this event that my own introduction to Coleridge occurred. At that time some negotiation was pending between him and the Royal Institution, which ended in their engaging him to deliver
a course of lectures on Poetry and the Fine Arts during the ensuing winter. For this series (twelve or sixteen, I think) he received a sum of one hundred guineas. And, considering the slightness of the pains
which he bestowed upon them, he was well remuner-
ated. I fear that they did not increase his reputation;
for never did any man treat his audience with less respect, or his task with less careful attention. I was in
London for part of the time, and can report the circumstances, having made a point of attending duly at
the appointed hours. Coleridge was at that time living
uncomfortably enough at the *Courier* office, in the
Strand. In such a situation, annoyed by the sound of
feet passing his chamber-door continually to the print-
ing-rooms of this great establishment, and with no
gentle ministrations of female hands to sustain his
cheerfulness, naturally enough his spirits flagged; and
he took more than ordinary doses of opium. I called

upon him daily, and pitied his forlorn condition. There was no bell in the room; which for many months answered the double purpose of bedroom and sitting-room. Consequently, I often saw him, picturesquely enveloped in nightcaps, surmounted by handkerchiefs indorsed upon handkerchiefs, shouting from the attics of the *Courier* office, down three or four flights of stairs, to a certain "Mrs. Brainbridge," his sole attendant, whose dwelling was in the subterranean regions of the house. There did I often see the philosopher, with the most lugubrious of faces, invoking with all his might this uncouth name of "Brainbridge," each syllable of which he intonated with long-drawn emphasis, in order to overpower the hostile hubbub coming downwards from the creaking press, and the roar from the Strand, which entered at all the front windows. "Mistress Brainbridge! I say, Mistress Brainbridge!" was the perpetual cry, until I expected to hear the Strand, and distant Fleet Street, take up the echo of "Brainbridge!" Thus unhappily situated, he sank more than ever under the dominion of opium; so that, at two o'clock, when he should have been in attendance at the Royal Institution, he was too often unable to rise from bed. Then came dismissals of audience after audience, with pleas of illness; and on many of his lecture days I have seen all Albemarle Street closed by a "lock" of carriages, filled with women of distinction, until the servants of the Institution or their own footmen advanced to the carriage-doors with the intelligence that Mr. Coleridge had been suddenly taken ill. This plea, which at first had been received with expressions of concern, repeated too often, began to rouse disgust. Many in anger, and some in real uncertainty whether it would not be trouble thrown away, ceased to attend. And we that were more constant too often found reason to be disappointed with the quality of his lecture. His appearance was generally that of a person struggling with pain and overmastering illness. His lips were baked with feverish heat, and often black in colour; and, in spite of the water which he continued drinking through the whole course of his lecture, he often seemed to labour under an almost paralytic inability to raise the upper jaw from the lower. In such a state, it is clear that nothing could save the lecture itself from reflecting his own feebleness and exhaustion, except the advantage of having been precomposed in some happier mood. But that never happened: most unfortunately he relied upon his extempore ability to carry him through. Now, had he been in spirits, or had he gathered animation, and kindled by his own motion, no written lecture could have been more effectual than one of his unpremeditated colloquial harangues. But either he was depressed originally below the point from which any re-ascent was possible, or else this reaction was intercepted by continual disgust from looking back upon his own ill-success; for, assuredly, he never once recovered that free and eloquent movement of thought which he could command at any time in a private company. The passages he read, moreover, in illustrating his doctrines, were generally unhappily chosen, because chosen at haphazard, from the difficulty of finding at a moment's summons those passages which his purpose required. Nor do I remember any that produced much effect, except two or three, which I myself put ready marked into his hands, among the Metrical Romances edited by Ritson.

Generally speaking, the selections were as injudicious and as inappropriate as they were ill delivered; for, amongst Coleridge's accomplishments, good reading was not one; he had neither voice (so, at least, *I* thought) nor management of voice. This defect is unfortunate in a public lecturer; for it is inconceivable how much weight and effectual pathos can be communicated by sonorous depth and melodious cadences of the human voice to sentiments the most trivial; nor, on the other hand, how the grandest are emasculated by a style of reading which fails in distributing the lights and shadows of a musical intonation. However, this defect chiefly concerned the immediate impression; the most afflicting to a friend of Coleridge's was the entire absence of his own peculiar and majestic intellect; no heart, no soul, was in anything he said; no strength of feeling in recalling universal truths; no power of originality or compass of moral relations in his novelties: all was a poor faint reflection from jewels once scattered in the highway by himself in the prodigality of his early opulence—a mendicant dependence on the alms dropped from his own overflowing treasury of happier times.

The next opportunity I had of seeing Coleridge was at the Lakes, in the winter of 1809, and up to the autumn of the following year. During this period it was that he carried on the original publication of *The Friend;* and for much the greater part of the time I saw him daily. He lived as a visitor in the house occupied by Mr. Wordsworth. This house (Allan Bank by name) was in Grasmere; and in another part of the same vale, at a distance of barely one mile, I myself had a cottage, and a considerable library. Many of my books being German, Coleridge borrowed them in great numbers. Having a general licence from me to use them as he would, he was in the habit of accumulating them so largely at Allan Bank (the name of Mr. Wordsworth's house) that sometimes as many as five hundred were absent at once: which I mention in order to notice a practice of Coleridge's, indicating his very scrupulous honour in what regarded the rights of ownership. Literary people are not always so strict in respecting property of this description; and I know more than one celebrated man who professes as a maxim that he holds it no duty of honour to restore a borrowed book; not to speak of many less celebrated persons, who, without openly professing such a principle, do however, in fact, exhibit a lax morality in such cases. The more honourable it was to poor Coleridge, who had means so trifling of buying books for himself, that, to prevent my flocks from mixing and being confounded with the flocks already folded at Allan Bank (his own and Wordsworth's), or rather that they *might* mix without danger, he duly inscribed my name in the blank leaves of every volume; a fact which became rather painfully made known to me; for, as he had chosen to dub me *Esquire*, many years after this it cost myself and a female friend some weeks of labour to hunt out these multitudinous memorials and to erase this heraldic addition; which else had the appearance to a stranger of having been conferred by myself.

The Friend, in its original publication, was, as a pecuniary speculation, the least judicious, both for its objects and its means, I have ever known. It was printed at Penrith, a town in Cumberland, on the outer verge of the Lake district, and precisely twenty-eight miles removed from Coleridge's abode. This distance, enough of itself, in all conscience, was at least trebled in effect by the interposition of Kirkstone, a mountain which is scaled by a carriage ascent of three miles long, and so steep in parts that, without four horses, no solitary traveller can persuade the neighbouring innkeepers to carry him. Another road, by way of Keswick, is subject to its own separate difficulties. And thus, in any practical sense, for ease, for certainty, and for dispatch, Liverpool, ninety-five miles distant, was virtually nearer. Dublin even, or Cork, was more eligible.

Yet, in this town, so situated as I have stated, by way
of purchasing such intolerable difficulties at the highest price, Coleridge was advised, and actually persuaded, to set up a printer, to buy, to lay in a stock of
paper, types, &c., instead of resorting to some printer
already established in Kendal, a large and opulent
town not more than eighteen miles distant, and connected by a daily post, whereas between himself and
Penrith there was no post at all. Building his mechanical arrangements upon this utter "upside-down" inversion of all common sense, it is not surprising (as
"madness ruled the hour") that in all other circumstances of plan or execution the work moved by principles of downright crazy disregard to all that a judicious counsel would have suggested. The subjects were
chosen obstinately in defiance of the popular taste;
they were treated in a style studiously disfigured by
German modes of thinking, and by a German termi-
nology; no attempt was made to win or conciliate public taste; and the plans adopted for obtaining payment
were of a nature to insure a speedy bankruptcy to the
concern. Coleridge had a list—nobody could ever say
upon whose authority gathered together—of subscribers. He tells us himself that many of these renounced
the work from an early period; and some (as Lord
Corke) rebuked him for his presumption in sending it
unordered, but (as Coleridge asserts) neither returned
the copies nor remitted the price. And even those who
were conscientious enough to do this could not remit
four or five shillings for as many numbers without
putting Coleridge to an expense of treble postage at
the least. This he complains of bitterly in his *Biographia Literaria*, forgetting evidently that the evil
was due exclusively to his own defective arrangements.
People necessarily sent their subscriptions through
such channels as were open to them, or such as were

pointed out by Coleridge himself. It is also utterly
unworthy of Coleridge to have taxed, as he does, many
of his subscribers (or really, for anything that appears,
the whole body) with neglecting to pay at all. Probably not one neglected. And some ladies, to my knowledge, scrupulously anxious about transmitting their
subscriptions, paid three times over. Managed as the
reader will collect from these indications, the work
was going down-hill from the first. It never gained
any accessions of new subscribers; from what source,
then, was the continual dropping off of names to be
supplied? The printer became a bankrupt: Coleridge
was as much in arrear with his articles as with his lectures at the Royal Institution. *That* he was from the
very first; but now he was disgusted and desponding;
and with No. 28 or 29 the work came to a final stop.
Some years after, it was re-cast and re-published. But,
in fact, this re-cast was altogether and absolutely a
new work. The sole contributors to the original work
had been, first of all, Wordsworth, who gave a very
valuable paper on the principles concerned in the composition of Epitaphs; and, secondly, Professor Wilson,
who, in conjunction with Mr. (now Dr.) [Alexander]
Blair, an early friend, then visiting Mr. W. on Windermere, wrote the letter signed "Mathetes," the reply
to which came from Wordsworth.

At the Lakes, and summoned abroad by scenery so
exquisite—living, too, in the bosom of a family endeared to him by long friendship and by sympathy the
closest with all his propensities and tastes—Coleridge
(it may be thought) could not sequester himself so
profoundly as at the *Courier* Office within his own
shell, or shut himself out so completely from that large
dominion of eye and ear amongst the hills, the fields,
and the woods, which once he had exercised so delightfully to himself, and with a participation so immortal,

through his exquisite poems, to all generations. He was not now reduced to depend upon "Mrs. Brainbridge"——— (Mistress Brain—Brain—Brainbridge, I say——Oh heavens! *is* there, *can* there, *was* there, *will* there ever at any future period be, an undeniable use in saying and in pressing upon the attention of the Strand and Fleet Street at their earliest convenience the painful subject of Mistress Brain—Brain—Brainbridge, I say—— Do you hear, Mrs. Brain—Brain— Brainbridge——? Brain or Bain, it matters little— Bran or Brain, it's all one, I conceive) —here, on the contrary, he looked out from his study windows upon the sublime hills of *Seat Sandal* and *Arthur's Chair* and upon pastoral cottages at their feet; and all around him he heard hourly the murmurings of happy life, the sound of female voices, and the innocent laughter of children. But apparently he was not happy; opium, was it, or what was it, that poisoned all natural pleasure at its sources? He burrowed continually deeper into scholastic subtleties and metaphysical abstractions; and, like that class described by Seneca in the luxurious Rome of *his* days, he lived chiefly by candlelight. At two or four o'clock in the afternoon he would make his first appearance. Through the silence of the night, when all other lights had disappeared in the quiet cottages of Grasmere, *his* lamp might be seen invariably by the belated traveller, as he descended the long steep from Dunmailraise; and at seven or eight o'clock in the morning, when man was going forth to his labour, this insulated son of reverie was retiring to bed.

In the autumn of 1810, Coleridge left the Lakes; and, so far as I am aware, for ever. I once, indeed, heard a rumour of his having passed through with some party of tourists—some reason struck me at the

time for believing it untrue—but, at all events, he
never returned to them as a resident. What might be
his reason for this eternal self-banishment from scenes
which he so well understood in all their shifting forms
of beauty, I can only guess. Perhaps it was the very
opposite reason to that which is most obvious: not, possibly, because he had become indifferent to their attractions, but because his undecaying sensibility to
their commanding power had become associated with
too afflicting remembrances, and flashes of personal
recollections, suddenly restored and illuminated—recollections which will

> *Sometimes leap*
> *From hiding-places ten years deep,*

and bring into collision the present with some long-
forgotten past, in a form too trying and too painful for
endurance.

The immediate occasion of his departure from the
Lakes, in the autumn of 1810, was the favourable opportunity then presented to him of migrating in a
pleasant way. Mr. Basil Montagu, the Chancery barrister, happened at that time to be returning to London, with Mrs. Montagu, from a visit to the Lakes, or
to Wordsworth. His travelling carriage was roomy
enough to allow of his offering Coleridge a seat in it;
and his admiration of Coleridge was just then fervent
enough to prompt a friendly wish for that sort of close
connexion (viz. by domestication as a guest under Mr.
Basil Montagu's roof) which is the most trying to
friendship, and which in this instance led to a perpetual rupture of it. The domestic habits of eccentric
men of genius, much more those of a man so irreclaim-
ably irregular as Coleridge, can hardly be supposed to
promise very auspiciously for any connexion so close

as this. A very extensive house and household, together with the unlimited licence of action which belongs to the *ménage* of some great Dons amongst the nobility, could alone have made Coleridge an inmate perfectly desirable. Probably many little jealousies and offences had been mutually suppressed; but the particular spark which at length fell amongst the combustible materials already prepared, and thus produced the final explosion, took the following shape: Mr. Montagu had published a book against the use of wine and intoxicating liquors of every sort. Not out of parsimony or under any suspicion of inhospitality, but in mere self-consistency and obedience to his own conscientious scruples, Mr. Montagu would not countenance the use of wine at his own table. Such being the law of the castle, and that law well known to Coleridge, he, nevertheless, thought fit to ask to dinner Colonel (then Captain) Pasley, of the Engineers. Now, where or in what land abides that

Captain, or Colonel, or Knight-in-arms,

to whom wine in the analysis of dinner is a neutral or indifferent element? Wine, therefore, as it was not of a nature to be omitted, Coleridge took care to furnish at his own private cost. And so far, again, all was right. But why must Coleridge give his dinner to the captain in Mr. Montagu's house? There lay the affront; and, doubtless, it was a very inconsiderate action on the part of Coleridge. I report the case simply as it was then generally borne upon the breath, not of scandal, but of jest and merriment. The result, however, was no jest; for bitter words ensued—words that festered in the remembrance; and a rupture between the parties followed, which no reconciliation has ever healed.

Meantime, on reviewing this story, as generally adopted by the learned in literary scandal, one demur rises up. Dr. Parr, a lisping Whig pedant, without personal dignity or conspicuous power of mind, was a frequent and privileged inmate at Mr. Montagu's. Him now—this Parr—there was no conceivable motive for enduring; that point is satisfactorily settled by the pompous inanities of his works. Yet, on the other hand, his habits were in their own nature far less endurable than Samuel Taylor Coleridge's; for the monster smoked—and how? How did the "Birmingham Doctor" [1] smoke? Not as you, or I, or other civilized people smoke, with a gentle cigar—but with the very coarsest tobacco. And those who know how that abomination lodges and nestles in the draperies of window-curtains will guess the horror and detestation in which the old Whig's memory is held by all enlightened women. Surely, in a house where the Doctor had any toleration at all, Samuel Taylor Coleridge might have enjoyed an unlimited toleration.

From Mr. Montagu's Coleridge passed, by favour of what introduction I never heard, into a family as amiable in manners and as benign in disposition as I remember to have ever met with. On this excellent

[1] *"Birmingham Doctor"*: This was a *sobriquet* imposed on Dr. Parr by *The Pursuits of Literature*, that most popular of satires at the end of the eighteenth and opening of the nineteenth centuries. The name had a mixed reference to the Doctor's personal connexion with Warwickshire, but chiefly to the Doctor's spurious and windy imitation of Dr. Johnson. He was viewed as the Birmingham (or mock) Dr. Johnson. Why the word *Birmingham* has come for the last sixty or seventy years to indicate in every class of articles the spurious in opposition to the genuine, I suppose to have arisen from the Birmingham habit of reproducing all sorts of London or Paris trinkets, *bijouterie*, &c., in cheaper materials and with inferior workmanship.

family I look back with threefold affection, on account of their goodness to Coleridge, and because they were then unfortunate, and because their union has long since been dissolved by death. The family was composed of three members: of Mr. [John Morgan], once a lawyer, who had, however, ceased to practise; of Mrs. [Morgan], his wife, a blooming young woman, distinguished for her fine person; and a young lady, her unmarried sister. Here, for some years, I used to visit Coleridge; and, doubtless, as far as situation merely, and the most delicate attentions from the most amiable women, *could* make a man happy, he must have been so at this time; for both the ladies treated him as an elder brother, or as a father. At length, however, the cloud of misfortune, which had long settled upon the prospects of this excellent family, thickened; and I found, upon one of my visits to London, that they had given up their house in Berners Street, and had retired to a cottage in Wiltshire. Coleridge had accompanied them; and there I visited them myself, and, as it eventually proved, for the last time. Some time after this, I heard from Coleridge, with the deepest sorrow, that poor [Morgan] had been thrown into prison, and had sunk under the pressure of his misfortunes. The gentle ladies of his family had retired to remote friends; and I saw them no more, though often vainly making inquiries about them.

Coleridge, during this part of his London life, I saw constantly—generally once a day, during my own stay in London; and sometimes we were jointly engaged to dinner parties. In particular, I remember one party at which we met Lady Hamilton—Lord Nelson's Lady Hamilton—the beautiful, the accomplished, the enchantress! Coleridge admired her, as who would not have done, prodigiously; and she, in her turn, was fascinated with Coleridge. He was unusually effective

in his display; and she, by way of expressing her acknowledgements appropriately, performed a scene in
Lady Macbeth—how splendidly, I cannot better express than by saying that all of us who then witnessed
her performance were familiar with Mrs. Siddons's
matchless execution of that scene, and yet, with such a
model filling our imaginations, we could not but acknowledge the possibility of another, and a different
perfection, without a trace of imitation, equally original, and equally astonishing. The word "magnificent"
is, in this day, most lavishly abused: daily I hear or
read in the newspapers of magnificent objects, as
though scattered more thickly than blackberries; but
for my part I have seen few objects really deserving
that epithet. Lady Hamilton was one of them. She had
Medea's beauty, and Medea's power of enchantment.
But let not the reader too credulously suppose her the
unprincipled woman she has been described. I know of
no sound reason for supposing the connexion between
Lord Nelson and her to have been other than perfectly
virtuous. Her public services, I am sure, were most
eminent—for *that* we have indisputable authority;
and equally sure I am that they were requited with
rank ingratitude.

After the household of the poor [Morgan's] had
been dissolved, I know not whither Coleridge went
immediately: for I did not visit London until some
years had elapsed. In 1823–24 I first understood that
he had taken up his residence as a guest with Mr. Gill-
man, a surgeon, in Highgate. He had then probably
resided for some time at that gentleman's: there he
continued to reside on the same terms, I believe, of
affectionate friendship with the members of Mr. Gill-
man's family as had made life endurable to him in the
time of the [Morgans]; and there he died in July of
the present year. If, generally speaking, poor Cole-

ridge had but a small share of earthly prosperity, in one respect at least he was eminently favoured by Providence: beyond all men who ever perhaps have lived, he found means to engage a constant succession of most faithful friends; and he levied the services of sisters, brothers, daughters, sons, from the hands of strangers—attracted to him by no possible impulses but those of reverence for his intellect, and love for his gracious nature. How, says Wordsworth—

—— *How can* he *expect that others should*
Sow for him, *reap for* him, *and at his call*
Love him, who for himself will take no thought at all?

How can he, indeed? It is most unreasonable to do so: yet this expectation, if Coleridge ought not to have entertained, at all events he realized. Fast as one friend dropped off, another, and another, succeeded: perpetual relays were laid along his path in life, of judicious and zealous supporters, who comforted his days, and smoothed the pillow for his declining age, even when it was beyond all human power to take away the thorns which stuffed it.

And what *were* those thorns?—and whence derived? That is a question on which I ought to decline speaking, unless I could speak fully. Not, however, to make any mystery of what requires none, the reader will understand that *originally* his sufferings, and the death within him of all hope—the palsy, as it were, of that which is the life of life, and the heart within the heart—came from opium. But two things I must add —one to explain Coleridge's case, and the other to bring it within the indulgent allowance of equitable judges: *First*, the sufferings from morbid derangements, originally produced by opium, had very possibly lost that simple character, and had themselves reacted in producing secondary states of disease and irritation, not any longer dependent upon the opium, so as to disappear with its disuse: hence, a more than mortal discouragement to accomplish this disuse, when the pains of self-sacrifice were balanced by no gleams of restorative feeling. Yet, *secondly*, Coleridge did make prodigious efforts to deliver himself from this thraldom; and he went so far at one time in Bristol, to my knowledge, as to hire a man for the express purpose, and armed with the power of resolutely interposing between himself and the door of any druggist's shop. It is true that an authority derived only from Coleridge's will could not be valid against Coleridge's own counter-determination: he could resume as easily as he could delegate the power. But the scheme did not entirely fail; a man shrinks from exposing to another that infirmity of will which he might else have but a feeble motive for disguising to himself; and the delegated man, the external conscience, as it were, of Coleridge, though destined—in the final resort, if matters came to absolute rupture, and to an obstinate duel, as it were, between himself and his principal—in that extremity to give way, yet might have long protracted the struggle before coming to that sort of *dignus vindice nodus:* and in fact, I know, upon absolute proof, that, before reaching that crisis, the man showed fight, and, faithful to his trust, and comprehending the reasons for it, declared that, if he must yield, he would "know the reason why."

Opium, therefore, subject to the explanation I have made, was certainly the original source of Coleridge's morbid feelings, of his debility, and of his remorse. His pecuniary embarrassments pressed as lightly as could well be expected upon him. I have mentioned the annuity of £150 made to him by the two Wedgwoods. One half, I believe, could not be withdrawn, having been left by a regular testamentary bequest. But the other moiety, coming from the surviving brother, was withdrawn on the plea of commercial losses, somewhere, I think, about 1815. That would have been a heavy blow to Coleridge; and assuredly the generosity is not very conspicuous of having ever suffered an allowance of that nature to be left to the mercy of accident. Either it ought not to have been granted in that shape—viz. as an *annual* allowance, giving ground for expecting its periodical recurrence—or it ought not to have been withdrawn. However, this blow was broken to Coleridge by the bounty of George IV, who placed Coleridge's name in the list of twelve to whom he granted an annuity of 100 guineas per annum. This he enjoyed so long as that Prince reigned. But at length came a heavier blow than that from Mr. Wedgwood: a new King arose, who knew not Joseph. Yet surely *he* was not a King who could so easily resolve to turn adrift twelve men of letters, many of them most accomplished men, for the sake of appropriating a sum no larger to himself than 1200 guineas—no less to some of them than the total freight of their earthly hopes?—No matter: let the deed have been from whose hand it might, it was done εἴργασται, it was perpetrated, as saith the Medea of Euripides; and it will be mentioned hereafter, "more than either once or twice." It fell with weight, and with effect upon the latter days of Coleridge; it took from him as much heart and hope as at his years, and with his unworldly prospects, remained for man to blight: and, if it did not utterly crush him, the reason was—because for himself he had never needed much, and was now continually drawing near to that haven in which, for himself, he would need nothing; secondly, because his children were now independent of his aid; and, finally, because in this land there are men to be found always of minds large enough to comprehend the claims of genius, and with hearts, by good luck, more generous, by infinite degrees, than the hearts of Princes.

Coleridge, as I now understand, was somewhere about sixty-two years of age when he died. This, however, I take upon the report of the public newspapers; for I do not, of my own knowledge, know anything accurately upon that point.

WILLIAM WORDSWORTH

(First published in *Tait's Magazine*, 1839)

IN 1807 it was, at the beginning of winter, that I first saw William Wordsworth. I have already mentioned that I had introduced myself to his notice by letter as early as the spring of 1803. To this hour it has continued, I believe, a mystery to Wordsworth why it was that I suffered an interval of four and a half years to slip away before availing myself of the standing invitation with which I had been honoured to the poet's house. Very probably he accounted for this delay by supposing that the new-born liberty of an Oxford life, with its multiplied enjoyments, acting upon a boy just emancipated from the restraints of a school, and, in one hour, elevated into what we Oxonians so proudly and so exclusively denominate "a man," [1] might have tempted me into pursuits alien from the pure intellectual passions which had so powerfully mastered my youthful heart some years before.

[1] At the Universities of Oxford and Cambridge, where the town is viewed as a mere ministerial appendage to the numerous colleges—the civic Oxford, for instance, existing for the sake of the academic Oxford, and not *vice versâ*—it has naturally happened that the students honour with the name of "*a man*" him only who wears a cap and gown.

Extinguished such a passion could not be; nor could he think so, if remembering the fervour with which I had expressed it, the sort of "nympholepsy" which had seized upon me, and which, in some imperfect way, I had avowed with reference to the very lakes and mountains amongst which the scenery of this most original poetry had chiefly grown up and moved. The very names of the ancient hills—Fairfield, Seat Sandal, Helvellyn, Blencathara, Glaramara; the names of the sequestered glens—such as Borrowdale, Martindale, Mardale, Wasdale, and Ennerdale; but, above all, the shy pastoral recesses, not garishly in the world's eye, like Windermere or Derwentwater, but lurking half unknown to the traveller of that day—Grasmere, for instance, the lovely abode of the poet himself, solitary, and yet sowed, as it were, with a thin diffusion of humble dwellings—here a scattering, and there a clustering, as in the starry heavens—sufficient to afford, at every turn and angle, human remembrances and memorials of time-honoured affections, or of passions (as the "Churchyard amongst the Mountains" will amply demonstrate) not wanting even in scenic and tragical interest: these were so many local spells upon me, equally poetic and elevating with the Miltonic names of Valdarno and Vallombrosa.

Deep are the voices which seem to call, deep is the lesson which would be taught, even to the most thoughtless of men:

> *Could field, or grove, or any spot of earth,*
> *Show to his eye an image of the pangs*
> *Which it hath witnessed; render back an echo*
> *Of the sad steps by which it hath been trod.*[1]

[1] See the divine passage (in the Sixth Book of *The Excursion*) beginning—

> *Ah, what a lesson to a thoughtless man, &c.*

Meantime, my delay was due to anything rather than to waning interest. On the contrary, the real cause of my delay was the too great profundity, and the increasing profundity, of my interest in this regeneration of our national poetry, and the increasing awe, in due proportion to the decaying thoughtlessness of boyhood, which possessed me for the character of its author. So far from neglecting Wordsworth, it is a fact that twice I had undertaken a long journey expressly for the purpose of paying my respects to Wordsworth; twice I came so far as the little rustic inn (then the sole inn of the neighbourhood) at Church Coniston; and on neither occasion could I summon confidence enough to present myself before him. It was not that I had any want of proper boldness for facing the most numerous company of a mixed or ordinary character: reserved, indeed, I was, perhaps even shy—from the character of my mind, so profoundly meditative, and the character of my life, so profoundly sequestered— but still, from counteracting causes, I was not deficient in a reasonable self-confidence towards the world generally. But the very image of Wordsworth, as I prefigured it to my own planet-struck eye, crushed my faculties as before Elijah or St. Paul. Twice, as I have said, did I advance as far as the Lake of Coniston; which is about eight miles from the church of Grasmere, and once I absolutely went forwards from Coniston to the very gorge of Hammerscar, from which the whole Vale of Grasmere suddenly breaks upon the view in a style of almost theatrical surprise, with its lovely valley stretching before the eye in the distance, the lake lying immediately below, with its solemn ark-like island of four and a half acres in size seemingly floating on its surface, and its exquisite outline on the opposite shore, revealing all its little bays and wild sylvan margin, feathered to the edge with wild flowers and ferns. In one quarter, a little wood, stretching for about half a mile towards the outlet of the lake; more directly in opposition to the spectator, a few green fields; and beyond them, just two bowshots from the water, a little white cottage gleaming from the midst of trees, with a vast and seemingly never-ending series of ascents rising above it to the height of more than three thousand feet. That little cottage was Wordsworth's from the time of his marriage, and earlier; in fact, from the beginning of the century to the year 1808. Afterwards, for many a year, it was mine. Catching one hasty glimpse of this loveliest of landscapes, I retreated like a guilty thing, for fear I might be surprised by Wordsworth, and then returned faint-heartedly to Coniston, and so to Oxford, *re infectâ.*

This was in 1806. And thus far, from mere excess of nervous distrust in my own powers for sustaining a conversation with Wordsworth, I had for nearly five years shrunk from a meeting for which, beyond all things under heaven, I longed. In early youth I laboured under a peculiar embarrassment and penury of words, when I sought to convey my thoughts adequately upon interesting subjects: neither was it words only that I wanted; but I could not unravel, I could not even make perfectly conscious to myself, the subsidiary thoughts into which one leading thought often radiates; or, at least, I could not do this with anything like the rapidity requisite for conversation. I laboured like a sibyl instinct with the burden of prophetic woe, as often as I found myself dealing with any topic in which the understanding combined with deep feelings to suggest mixed and tangled thoughts: and thus partly—partly also from my invincible habit of reverie—at that era of my life, I had a most distinguished talent "*pour le silence.*" Wordsworth, from something of the same causes, suffered (by his own report to myself) at the same age from pretty much the same infirmity. And yet, in more advanced years—probably about twenty-eight or thirty—both of us acquired a remarkable fluency in the art of unfolding our thoughts colloquially. However, at that period my deficiencies were what I have described. And, after all, though I had no absolute cause for anticipating contempt, I was so far right in my fears, that since that time I have had occasion to perceive a worldly tone of sentiment in Wordsworth, not less than in Mrs. Hannah More and other literary people, by which they were led to set a higher value upon a limited respect from a person high in the world's esteem than upon the most lavish spirit of devotion from an obscure quarter. Now, in that point, *my* feelings are far otherwise.

Meantime, the world went on; events kept moving; and, amongst them, in the course of 1807, occurred the event of Coleridge's return to England from his official station in the Governor's family at Malta. At Bridgewater, as I have already recorded, in the summer of 1807, I was introduced to him. Several weeks after he came with his family to the Bristol Hot-Wells, at which, by accident, I was then visiting. On calling upon him, I found that he had been engaged by the Royal Institution to lecture at their theatre in Albemarle Street during the coming winter of 1807–8, and, consequently, was embarrassed about the mode of conveying his family to Keswick. Upon this, I offered my services to escort them in a post-chaise. This offer was cheerfully accepted; and at the latter end of October we set forwards—Mrs. Coleridge, viz., with her two sons—Hartley, aged nine, Derwent, about seven—her

beautiful little daughter,[1] about five, and, finally, myself. Going by the direct route through Gloucester,
Bridgenorth, &c., on the third day we reached Liverpool, where I took up my quarters at a hotel, whilst
Mrs. Coleridge paid a visit of a few days to a very
interesting family, who had become friends of Southey
during his visit to Portugal.

Leaving Liverpool, after about a week's delay, we
pursued our journey northwards. We had slept on the
first day at Lancaster. Consequently, at the rate of
motion which then prevailed throughout England—
which, however, was rarely equalled on that western
road, where all things were in arrear by comparison
with the eastern and southern roads of the kingdom—
we found ourselves, about three o'clock in the afternoon, at Ambleside, fourteen miles to the north-west
of Kendal, and thirty-six from Lancaster. There, for
the last time, we stopped to change horses; and about
four o'clock we found ourselves on the summit of the
White Moss, a hill which rises between the second and
third milestones on the stage from Ambleside to Keswick, and which then retarded the traveller's advance
by a full fifteen minutes, but is now evaded by a lower
line of road. In ascending this hill, from weariness of
moving so slowly, I, with the two Coleridges, had
alighted; and, as we all chose to refresh ourselves by
running down the hill into Grasmere, we had left the

[1] That most accomplished, and to Coleridge most pious
daughter, whose recent death afflicted so very many who knew
her only by her writings. She had married her cousin, Mr.
Serjeant Coleridge, and in that way retained her illustrious
maiden name as a wife. At seventeen, when last I saw her, she
was the most perfect of all pensive, nun-like, intellectual beauties that I have seen in real breathing life. The upper parts of
her face were verily divine. See, for an artist's opinion, the
Life of that admirable man Collins, by his son.

chaise behind us, and had even lost the sound of the wheels at times, when all at once we came, at an abrupt turn of the road, in sight of a white cottage, with two yew-trees breaking the glare of its white walls. A sudden shock seized me on recognizing this cottage, of which, in the previous year, I had gained a momentary glimpse from Hammerscar, on the opposite side of the lake. I paused, and felt my old panic returning upon me; but just then, as if to take away all doubt upon the subject, I saw Hartley Coleridge, who had gained upon me considerably, suddenly turn in at a garden gate; this motion to the right at once confirmed me in my belief that here at last we had reached our port; that this little cottage was tenanted by that man whom, of all the men from the beginning of time, I most fervently desired to see; that in less than a minute I should meet Wordsworth face to face. Coleridge was of opinion that, if a man were really and *consciously* to see an apparition, in such circumstances death would be the inevitable result; and, if so, the wish which we hear so commonly expressed for such experience is as thoughtless as that of Semele in the Grecian Mythology, so natural in a female, that her lover should visit her *en grand costume*—presumptuous ambition, that unexpectedly wrought its own ruinous chastisement! Judged by Coleridge's test, my situation could not have been so terrific as *his* who anticipates a ghost; for, certainly, I survived this meeting; but at that instant it seemed pretty much the same to my own feelings.

Never before or since can I reproach myself with having trembled at the approaching presence of any creature that is born of woman, excepting only, for once or twice in my life, woman herself. Now, however, I *did* tremble; and I forgot, what in no other circumstances I could have forgotten, to stop for the

coming up of the chaise, that I might be ready to hand
Mrs. Coleridge out. Had Charlemagne and all his
peerage been behind me, or Cæsar and his equipage, or
Death on his pale horse, I should have forgotten them
at that moment of intense expectation, and of eyes
fascinated to what lay before me, or what might in a
moment appear. Through the little gate I pressed forward; ten steps beyond it lay the principal door of the
house. To this, no longer clearly conscious of my own
feelings, I passed on rapidly; I heard a step, a voice,
and, like a flash of lightning, I saw the figure emerge
of a tallish man, who held out his hand, and saluted
me with most cordial expressions of welcome. The
chaise, however, drawing up to the gate at that moment, he (and there needed no Roman nomenclator to
tell me that this *he* was Wordsworth) felt himself
summoned to advance and receive Mrs. Coleridge. I,
therefore, stunned almost with the actual accomplishment of a catastrophe so long anticipated and so long
postponed, mechanically went forward into the house.
A little semi-vestibule between two doors prefaced the
entrance into what might be considered the principal
room of the cottage. It was an oblong square, not
above eight and a half feet high, sixteen feet long, and
twelve broad; very prettily wainscoted from the floor
to the ceiling with dark polished oak, slightly embel-
lished with carving. One window there was—a perfect
and unpretending cottage window, with little diamond
panes, embowered at almost every season of the year
with roses, and in the summer and autumn with a profusion of jasmine and other fragrant shrubs. From the
exuberant luxuriance of the vegetation around it, and
from the dark hue of the wainscoting, this window,
though tolerably large, did not furnish a very powerful light to one who entered from the open air. However, I saw sufficiently to be aware of two ladies just

entering the room, through a doorway opening upon a
little staircase. The foremost, a tallish young woman,
with the most winning expression of benignity upon
her features, advanced to me, presenting her hand with
so frank an air that all embarrassment must have fled
in a moment before the native goodness of her manner.
This was Mrs. Wordsworth, cousin of the poet, and,
for the last five years or more, his wife. She was now
mother of two children, a son and a daughter; and she
furnished a remarkable proof how possible it is for a
woman neither handsome nor even comely according
to the rigour of criticism—nay, generally pronounced
very plain—to exercise all the practical fascination of
beauty, through the mere compensatory charms of
sweetness all but angelic, of simplicity the most entire,
womanly self-respect and purity of heart speaking
through all her looks, acts, and movements. *Words*, I
was going to have added; but her words were few. In
reality, she talked so little that Mr. Slave-Trade Clarkson used to allege against her that she could only say
"*God bless you!*" Certainly, her intellect was not of
an active order; but, in a quiescent, reposing, meditative way, she appeared always to have a genial enjoyment from her own thoughts; and it would have been
strange, indeed, if she, who enjoyed such eminent advantages of training, from the daily society of her
husband and his sister, failed to acquire some power of
judging for herself, and putting forth some functions
of activity. But undoubtedly that was not her element:
to feel and to enjoy in a luxurious repose of mind—
there was her *forte* and her peculiar privilege; and
how much better this was adapted to her husband's
taste, how much more adapted to uphold the comfort
of his daily life, than a blue-stocking loquacity, or even
a legitimate talent for discussion, may be inferred
from his verses, beginning:

> *She was a phantom of delight,*
> *When first she gleam'd upon my sight.*

Once for all,[1] these exquisite lines were dedicated to
Mrs. Wordsworth; were understood to describe her—
to have been prompted by the feminine graces of her
character; hers they are, and will remain for ever. To
these, therefore, I may refer the reader for an idea of
what was most important in the partner and second
self of the poet. And I will add to this abstract of her
moral portrait these few concluding traits of her appearance in a physical sense. Her figure was tolerably
good. In complexion she was fair, and there was something peculiarly pleasing even in this accident of the
skin, for it was accompanied by an animated expression of health, a blessing which, in fact, she possessed
uninterruptedly. Her eyes, the reader may already
know, were

> *Like stars of twilight fair;*
> *Like twilight, too, her dark brown hair;*
> *But all things else about her drawn*
> *From May-time and the cheerful dawn.*

Yet strange it is to tell that, in these eyes of vesper
gentleness, there was a considerable obliquity of vision; and much beyond that slight obliquity which is
often supposed to be an attractive foible in the countenance: this *ought* to have been displeasing or repulsive; yet, in fact, it was not. Indeed all faults, had
they been ten times more and greater, would have been
neutralized by that supreme expression of her features

[1] *Once for all*, I say—on recollecting that Coleridge's verses
to *Sara* were made transferable to any Sara who reigned at the
time. At least three Saras appropriated them; all three long
since in the grave.

to the unity of which every lineament in the fixed parts, and every undulation in the moving parts, of her countenance, concurred, viz. a sunny benignity—a radiant graciousness—such as in this world I never saw surpassed.

Immediately behind her moved a lady, shorter, slighter, and perhaps, in all other respects, as different from her in personal characteristics as could have been wished for the most effective contrast. "Her face was of Egyptian brown"; rarely, in a woman of English birth, had I seen a more determinate gipsy tan. Her eyes were not soft, as Mrs. Wordsworth's, nor were they fierce or bold; but they were wild and startling, and hurried in their motion. Her manner was warm and even ardent; her sensibility seemed constitutionally deep; and some subtle fire of impassioned intellect apparently burned within her, which, being alternately pushed forward into a conspicuous expression by the irrepressible instincts of her temperament, and then immediately checked, in obedience to the decorum of her sex and age, and her maidenly condition, gave to her whole demeanour, and to her conversation, an air of embarrassment, and even of self-conflict, that was almost distressing to witness. Even her very utterance and enunciation often suffered, in point of clearness and steadiness, from the agitation of her excessive organic sensibility. At times, the self-counteraction and self-baffling of her feelings caused her even to stammer, and so determinately to stammer that a stranger who should have seen her and quitted her in that state of feeling would have certainly set her down for one plagued with that infirmity of speech as distressingly as Charles Lamb himself. This was Miss Wordsworth, the only sister of the poet—his "Dorothy"; who naturally owed so much to the lifelong intercourse with her great brother in his most solitary

and sequestered years; but, on the other hand, to whom
he has acknowledged obligations of the profoundest
nature; and, in particular, this mighty one, through
which we also, the admirers and the worshippers of
this great poet, are become equally her debtors—that,
whereas the intellect of Wordsworth was, by its original tendency, too stern, too austere, too much enamoured of an ascetic harsh sublimity, she it was—the
lady who paced by his side continually through sylvan
and mountain tracks, in Highland glens, and in the
dim recesses of German charcoal-burners—that first
couched his eye to the sense of beauty, humanized him
by the gentler charities, and engrafted, with her delicate female touch, those graces upon the ruder growths
of his nature which have since clothed the forest of his
genius with a foliage corresponding in loveliness and
beauty to the strength of its boughs and the massiness
of its trunks. The greatest deductions from Miss
Wordsworth's attractions, and from the exceeding interest which surrounded her in right of her character,
of her history, and of the relation which she fulfilled
towards her brother, were the glancing quickness of
her motions, and other circumstances in her deportment (such as her stooping attitude when walking),
which gave an ungraceful, and even an unsexual character to her appearance when out-of-doors. She did not
cultivate the graces which preside over the person and
its carriage. But, on the other hand, she was a person
of very remarkable endowments intellectually; and, in
addition to the other great services which she rendered
to her brother, this I may mention, as greater than all
the rest, and it was one which equally operated to the
benefit of every casual companion in a walk—viz. the
exceeding sympathy, always ready and always profound, by which she made all that one could tell her,
all that one could describe, all that one could quote

from a foreign author, reverberate, as it were, *à plusieurs reprises*, to one's own feelings, by the manifest impression it made upon *hers*. The pulses of light are not more quick or more inevitable in their flow and undulation, than were the answering and echoing movements of her sympathizing attention. Her knowledge of literature was irregular, and thoroughly unsystematic. She was content to be ignorant of many things; but what she knew and had really mastered lay where it could not be disturbed——in the temple of her own most fervid heart.

Such were the two ladies who, with himself and two children, and at that time one servant, composed the poet's household. They were both, I believe, about twenty-eight years old; and, if the reader inquires about the single point which I have left untouched in their portraiture——viz. the style of their manners——I may say that it was, in *some* points, naturally of a plain household simplicity, but every way pleasing, unaffected, and (as respects Mrs. Wordsworth) even dignified. Few persons had seen so little as this lady of the world. She had seen nothing of high life, for she had seen little of any. Consequently, she was unacquainted with the conventional modes of behaviour, prescribed in particular situations by high breeding. But, as these modes are little more than the product of dispassionate good sense, applied to the circumstances of the case, it is surprising how few deficiencies are perceptible, even to the most vigilant eye——or, at least, essential deficiencies——in the general demeanour of any unaffected young woman, acting habitually under a sense of sexual dignity and natural courtesy. Miss Wordsworth had seen more of life, and even of good company; for she had lived, when quite a girl, under the protection of Dr. Cookson, a near relative, canon of Windsor, and a personal favourite of the Royal

Family, especially of George III. Consequently, she ought to have been the more polished of the two; and yet, from greater natural aptitudes for refinement of manner in her sister-in-law, and partly, perhaps, from her more quiet and subdued manner, Mrs. Wordsworth would have been pronounced very much the more lady-like person.

From the interest which attaches to anybody so nearly connected as these two ladies with a great poet, I have allowed myself a larger latitude than else might have been justifiable in describing them. I now go on with my narrative:

I was ushered up a little flight of stairs, fourteen in all, to a little drawing-room, or whatever the reader chooses to call it. Wordsworth himself has described the fireplace of this room as his

Half-kitchen and half-parlour fire.

It was not fully seven feet six inches high, and, in other respects, pretty nearly of the same dimensions as the rustic hall below. There was, however, in a small recess, a library of perhaps three hundred volumes, which seemed to consecrate the room as the poet's study and composing room; and such occasionally it was. But far oftener he both studied, as I found, and composed, on the high road. I had not been two minutes at the fireside, when in came Wordsworth, returning from his friendly attentions to the travellers below, who, it seemed, had been over-persuaded by hospitable solicitations to stay for this night in Grasmere, and to make out the remaining thirteen miles of their road to Keswick on the following day. Wordsworth entered. And *"what-like"*—to use a Westmorland as well as a Scottish expression—*"what-like"* was Wordsworth? A reviewer in *Tait's Magazine*, noticing some recent col-

lection of literary portraits, gives it as his opinion that
Charles Lamb's head was the finest among them. This
remark may have been justified by the engraved portraits; but, certainly, the critic would have cancelled
it, had he seen the original heads—at least, had he
seen them in youth or in maturity; for Charles Lamb
bore age with less disadvantage to the intellectual expression of his appearance than Wordsworth, in whom
a sanguine complexion had, of late years, usurped upon
the original bronze-tint; and this change of hue, and
change in the quality of skin, had been made fourfold
more conspicuous, and more unfavourable in its general effect, by the harsh contrast of grizzled hair which
had displaced the original brown. No change in personal appearance ever can have been so unfortunate;
for, generally speaking, whatever other disadvantages
old age may bring along with it, one effect, at least in
male subjects, has a compensating tendency—that it
removes any tone of vigour too harsh, and mitigates
the expression of power too unsubdued. But, in Wordsworth, the effect of the change has been to substitute
an air of animal vigour, or, at least, hardiness, as if
derived from constant exposure to the wind and
weather, for the fine sombre complexion which he
once wore, resembling that of a Venetian senator or a
Spanish monk.

Here, however, in describing the personal appearance of Wordsworth, I go back, of course, to the point
of time at which I am speaking. He was, upon the
whole, not a well-made man. His legs were pointedly
condemned by all female connoisseurs in legs; not
that they were bad in any way which *would* force itself upon your notice—there was no absolute deformity about them; and undoubtedly they had been serviceable legs beyond the average standard of human
requisition; for I calculate, upon good data, that with

these identical legs Wordsworth must have traversed a
distance of 175,000 to 180,000 English miles—a mode
of exertion which, to him, stood in the stead of alcohol
and all other stimulants whatsoever to the animal spirits; to which, indeed, he was indebted for a life of
unclouded happiness, and we for much of what is most
excellent in his writings. But, useful as they have
proved themselves, the Wordsworthian legs were certainly not ornamental; and it was really a pity, as I
agreed with a lady in thinking, that he had not another pair for evening dress parties—when no boots
lend their friendly aid to mask our imperfections from
the eyes of female rigorists—those *elegantes forma-
rum spectatrices*. A sculptor would certainly have disapproved of their contour. But the worst part of Wordsworth's person was the bust; there was a narrowness
and a droop about the shoulders which became striking, and had an effect of meanness, when brought into
close juxtaposition with a figure of a more statuesque
build. Once on a summer evening, walking in the Vale
of Langdale with Wordsworth, his sister, and Mr.
J——, a native Westmorland clergyman, I remember that Miss Wordsworth was positively mortified by
the peculiar illustration which settled upon this defective conformation. Mr. J——, a fine towering figure,
six feet high, massy and columnar in his proportions,
happened to be walking, a little in advance, with
Wordsworth; Miss Wordsworth and myself being in
the rear; and from the nature of the conversation
which then prevailed in our front rank, something or
other about money, devises, buying and selling, we of
the rear-guard thought it requisite to preserve this arrangement for a space of three miles or more; during
which time, at intervals, Miss Wordsworth would exclaim, in a tone of vexation, "Is it possible—can that
be William? How very mean he looks!" And she did

not conceal a mortification that seemed really painful, until I, for my part, could not forbear laughing outright at the serious interest which she carried into this trifle. She was, however, right, as regarded the mere visual judgement. Wordsworth's figure, with all its defects, was brought into powerful relief by one which had been cast in a more square and massy mould; and in such a case it impressed a spectator with a sense of absolute meanness, more especially when viewed from behind and not counteracted by his countenance; and yet Wordsworth was of a good height (five feet ten), and not a slender man; on the contrary, by the side of Southey, his limbs looked thick, almost in a disproportionate degree. But the total effect of Wordsworth's person was always worst in a state of motion. Meantime, his face—that was one which would have made amends for greater defects of figure. Many such, and finer, I have seen amongst the portraits of Titian, and, in a later period amongst those of Vandyke, from the great era of Charles I, as also from the court of Elizabeth and of Charles II, but none which has more impressed me in my own time.

Haydon, in his great picture of "Christ's Entry into Jerusalem," has introduced Wordsworth in the character of a disciple attending his Divine Master, and Voltaire in the character of a sneering Jewish elder. This fact is well known; and, as the picture itself is tolerably well known to the public eye, there are multitudes now living who will have seen a very impressive likeness of Wordsworth—some consciously, some not suspecting it. There will, however, always be many who have *not* seen any portrait at all of Wordsworth; and therefore I will describe its general outline and effect. It was a face of the long order, often falsely classed as oval: but a greater mistake is made by many people in supposing the long face which prevailed so

remarkably in the Elizabethan and Carolinian periods
to have become extinct in our own.

The face of Sir Walter Scott, as Irving, the pulpit
orator, once remarked to me, was the indigenous face
of the Border: the mouth, which was bad, and the
entire lower part of the face, are seen repeated in thousands of working-men; or, as Irving chose to illustrate
his position, "in thousands of Border horse-jockeys."
In like manner, Wordsworth's face was, if not absolutely the indigenous face of the Lake district, at any
rate a variety of that face, a modification of that original type. The head was well filled out; and there, to
begin with, was a great advantage over the head of
Charles Lamb, which was absolutely truncated in the
posterior region—sawn off, as it were, by no timid
sawyer. The forehead was not remarkably lofty—and,
by the way, some artists, in their ardour for realizing
their phrenological preconceptions, not suffering nature to surrender quietly and by slow degrees her real
alphabet of signs and hieroglyphic characters, but
forcing her language prematurely into conformity
with their own crude speculations, have given to Sir
Walter Scott a pile of forehead which is unpleasing
and cataphysical, in fact, a caricature of anything that
is ever seen in nature, and would (if real) be esteemed
a deformity; in one instance—that which was introduced in some annual or other—the forehead makes
about two-thirds of the entire face. Wordsworth's forehead is also liable to caricature misrepresentations in
these days of phrenology: but, whatever it may appear
to be in any man's fanciful portrait, the real living
forehead, as I have been in the habit of seeing it for
more than five-and-twenty years, is not remarkable
for its height; but it *is*, perhaps, remarkable for its
breadth and expansive development. Neither are the
eyes of Wordsworth "large," as is erroneously stated

somewhere in *Peter's Letters;* on the contrary they
are (I think) rather small; but *that* does not interfere
with their effect, which at times is fine, and suitable to
his intellectual character. At times, I say, for the depth
and subtlety of eyes, even their colouring (as to condensation or dilation), varies exceedingly with the
state of the stomach; and, if young ladies were aware
of the magical transformations which can be wrought
in the depth and sweetness of the eye by a few weeks'
walking exercise, I fancy we should see their habits in
this point altered greatly for the better. I have seen
Wordsworth's eyes oftentimes affected powerfully in
this respect; his eyes are not, under any circumstances,
bright, lustrous, or piercing; but, after a long day's
toil in walking, I have seen them assume an appearance the most solemn and spiritual that it is possible
for the human eye to wear. The light which resides in
them is at no time a superficial light; but, under favourable accidents, it is a light which seems to come
from unfathomed depths: in fact, it is more truly entitled to be held "the light that never was on land or
sea," a light radiating from some far spiritual world,
than any the most idealizing that ever yet a painter's
hand created. The nose, a little arched, is large; which,
by the way (according to a natural phrenology, existing centuries ago amongst some of the lowest amongst
the human species), has always been accounted an
unequivocal expression of animal appetites organically
strong. And that expressed the simple truth: Wordsworth's intellectual passions were fervent and strong:
but they rested upon a basis of preternatural animal
sensibility diffused through *all* the animal passions
(or appetites) ; and something of that will be found to
hold of all poets who have been great by original force
and power, not (as Virgil) by means of fine management and exquisite artifice of composition applied to

their conceptions. The mouth, and the whole circum-
jacencies of the mouth, composed the strongest feature
in Wordsworth's face; there was nothing specially to
be noticed that I know of in the mere outline of the
lips; but the swell and protrusion of the parts above
and around the mouth are both noticeable in themselves, and also because they remind me of a very interesting fact which I discovered about three years
after this my first visit to Wordsworth.

Being a great collector of everything relating to
Milton, I had naturally possessed myself, whilst yet
very young, of Richardson the painter's thick octavo
volume of notes on the *Paradise Lost*. It happened,
however, that my copy, in consequence of that mania
for portrait collecting which has stripped so many
English classics of their engraved portraits, wanted
the portrait of Milton. Subsequently I ascertained that
it ought to have had a very good likeness of the great
poet; and I never rested until I procured a copy of the
book which had not suffered in this respect by the fatal
admiration of the amateur. The particular copy offered to me was one which had been priced unusually
high, on account of the unusually fine specimen which
it contained of the engraved portrait. This, for a particular reason, I was exceedingly anxious to see; and
the reason was—that, according to an anecdote reported by Richardson himself, this portrait, of all that
were shown to her, was the only one acknowledged by
Milton's last surviving daughter to be a strong likeness of her father. And her involuntary gestures concurred with her deliberate words—for, on seeing all
the rest, she was silent and inanimate; but the very
instant she beheld that crayon drawing from which is
derived the engraved head in Richardson's book, she
burst out into a rapture of passionate recognition;
exclaiming—"That is my father! that is my dear

father!" Naturally, therefore, after such a testimony, so much stronger than any other person in the world could offer to the authentic value of this portrait, I was eager to see it.

Judge of my astonishment when, in this portrait of Milton, I saw a likeness nearly perfect of Wordsworth, better by much than any which I have since seen of those expressly painted for himself. The likeness is tolerably preserved in that by Carruthers, in which one of the little Rydal waterfalls, &c., composes a background; yet this is much inferior, as a mere portrait of Wordsworth, to the Richardson head of Milton; and this, I believe, is the last which represents Wordsworth in the vigour of his power. The rest, which I have not seen, may be better as works of art (for anything I know to the contrary), but they must labour under the great disadvantage of presenting the features when "defeatured," in the degree and the way I have described, by the peculiar ravages of old age, as it affects this family; for it is noticed of the Wordsworths, by those who are familiar with their peculiarities, that in their very blood and constitutional differences lie hidden causes that are able, in some mysterious way,

> *Those shocks of passion to prepare*
> *That kill the bloom before its time,*
> *And blanch, without the owner's crime,*
> *The most resplendent hair.*

Some people, it is notorious, live faster by much than others; the oil is burned out sooner in one constitution than another: and the cause of this may be various; but in the Wordsworths one part of the cause is, no doubt, the secret fire of a temperament too fervid; the self-consuming energies of the brain, that gnaw at the heart and life-strings for ever. In that account which *The Excursion* presents to us of an imaginary Scotsman who, to still the tumult of his heart, when visiting the cataracts of a mountainous region, obliges himself to study the laws of light and colour as they affect the rainbow of the stormy waters, vainly attempting to mitigate the fever which consumed him by entangling his mind in profound speculations; raising a cross-fire of artillery from the subtilizing intellect, under the vain conceit that in this way he could silence the mighty battery of his impassioned heart: there we read a picture of Wordsworth and his own youth. In Miss Wordsworth every thoughtful observer might read the same self-consuming style of thought. And the effect upon each was so powerful for the promotion of a premature old age, and of a premature expression of old age, that strangers invariably supposed them fifteen to twenty years older than they were. And I remember Wordsworth once laughingly reporting to me, on returning from a short journey in 1809, a little personal anecdote, which sufficiently showed what was the spontaneous impression upon that subject of casual strangers, whose feelings were not confused by previous knowledge of the truth. He was travelling by a stage-coach, and seated outside, amongst a good half-dozen of fellow-passengers. One of these, an elderly man, who confessed to having passed the grand climacterical year (9 multiplied into 7) of 63, though he did not say precisely by how many years, said to Wordsworth, upon some anticipations which they had been mutually discussing of changes likely to result from enclosures, &c., then going on or projecting—"Ay, ay, another dozen of years will show us strange sights; but you and I can hardly expect to see them."—"How so?" said Wordsworth. "How so, my friend? How old do you take me to be?"—"Oh, I beg pardon," said the other; "I meant no offence—but what?" looking at Wordsworth more attentively—"you'll never see threescore, I'm of opinion"; meaning to say that Wordsworth *had* seen it already. And, to show that he was not singular in so thinking, he appealed to all the other passengers; and the motion passed (*nem. con.*) that Wordsworth was rather over than under sixty. Upon this he told them the literal truth—that he had not yet accomplished his thirty-ninth year. "God bless me!" said the climacterical man; "so then, after all, you'll have a chance to see your childer get up like, and get settled! Only to think of that!" And so closed the conversation, leaving to Wordsworth an undeniable record of his own prematurely expressed old age in this unaffected astonishment, amongst a whole party of plain men, that he could really belong to a generation of the forward-looking, who live by hope; and might reasonably expect to see a child of seven years old matured into a man. And yet, as Wordsworth lived into his eighty-second year, it is plain that the premature expression of decay does not argue any real decay.

Returning to the question of portraits, I would observe that this Richardson engraving of Milton has the advantage of presenting, not only by far the best likeness of Wordsworth, but of Wordsworth in the prime of his powers—a point essential in the case of one so liable to premature decay. It may be supposed that I took an early opportunity of carrying the book down to Grasmere, and calling for the opinions of Wordsworth's family upon this most remarkable coincidence. Not one member of that family but was as much impressed as myself with the accuracy of the likeness. All the peculiarities even were retained—a drooping appearance of the eyelids, that remarkable swell which I have noticed about the mouth, the way in which the hair lay upon the forehead. In two points only there was a deviation from the rigorous truth of Wordsworth's features—the face was a little too short and too broad, and the eyes were too large. There was also a wreath of laurel about the head, which (as Wordsworth remarked) disturbed the natural expression of the whole picture; else, and with these few allowances, he also admitted that the resemblance was, *for that period of his life*, perfect, or as nearly so as art could accomplish.

I have gone into so large and circumstantial a review of my recollections on this point as would have been trifling and tedious in excess, had these recollections related to a less important man; but I have a certain knowledge that the least of them will possess a lasting and a growing interest in connexion with William Wordsworth. How peculiar, how different from the interest which we grant to the ideas of a great philosopher, a great mathematician, or a great reformer, is that burning interest which settles on the great poets who have made themselves necessary to the human heart; who have first brought into consciousness, and have clothed in words, those grand catholic feelings that belong to the grand catholic situations of life through all its stages; who have clothed them in such words that human wit despairs of bettering them! Mighty were the powers, solemn and serene is the memory, of Archimedes; and Apollonius shines like "the starry Galileo" in the firmament of human genius; yet how frosty is the feeling associated with these names by comparison with that which, upon every sunny lawn, by the side of every ancient forest, even in the farthest depths of Canada, many a young innocent girl, perhaps at this very moment—looking now with fear to the dark recesses of the infinite forest, and now with love to the pages of the infinite poet, until the fear is absorbed and forgotten in the love—cherishes in her heart for the name and person of Shakespeare!

The English language is travelling fast towards the fulfilment of its destiny. Through the influence of the dreadful Republic that within the thirty last years has run through all the stages of infancy into the first stage of maturity, and through the English colonies—African, Canadian, Indian, Australian—the English language (and, therefore, the English literature) is running forward towards its ultimate mission of eating up, like Aaron's rod, all other languages. Even the German and the Spanish will inevitably sink before it; perhaps within 100 or 150 years. In the recesses of California, in the vast solitudes of Australia, "The Churchyard amongst the Mountains," from Wordsworth's *Excursion,* and many a scene of his shorter poems, will be read, even as now Shakespeare is read amongst the forests of Canada. All which relates to the writer of these poems will then bear a value of the same kind as that which attaches to our personal memorials (unhappily so slender) of Shakespeare.

Let me now attempt to trace, in a brief outline, the chief incidents in the life of William Wordsworth, which are interesting, not only in virtue of their illustrious subject, but also as exhibiting a most remarkable (almost a providential) arrangement of circumstances, all tending to one result—that of insulating from worldly cares, and carrying onward from childhood to the grave, in a state of serene happiness, one who was unfitted for daily toil, and, at all events, who could not, under such demands upon his time and anxieties, have prosecuted those genial labours in which all mankind have an interest.

William Wordsworth was born [in 1770] at Cockermouth, a small town of Cumberland, lying about a dozen miles to the north-west of Keswick, on the high road from that town to Whitehaven.

William passed his infancy on the very margin of the Lake district, just six miles, in fact, beyond the rocky screen of Whinlatter, and within one hour's ride of Bassenthwaite Water. To those who live in the tame scenery of Cockermouth, the blue mountains in the distance, the sublime peaks of Borrowdale and of Buttermere, raise aloft a signal, as it were, of a new country, a country of romance and mystery, to which the thoughts are habitually turning. Children are fascinated and haunted with vague temptations, when standing on the frontiers of such a foreign land; and so was Wordsworth fascinated, so haunted. Fortunate for Wordsworth that, at an early age, he was transferred to a quiet nook of this lovely district. At the little town of Hawkshead, seated on the north-west angle of Esthwaite Water, a grammar-school (which, in English usage, means a school for classical literature) was founded, in Queen Elizabeth's reign, by Archbishop Sandys, who belonged to the very ancient family of that name still seated in the neighbourhood. Here it was that Wordsworth passed his life, from the age of nine until the time arrived for his removal to college.

I do not conceive that Wordsworth *could* have been an amiable boy; he was austere and unsocial, I have reason to think, in his habits; not generous; and not self-denying. I am pretty certain that no consideration would ever have induced Wordsworth to burden himself with a lady's reticule, parasol, shawl, or anything exacting trouble and attention. Mighty must be the danger which would induce him to lead her horse by the bridle. Nor would he, without some demur, stop to offer her his hand over a stile. Freedom—unlimited, careless, insolent freedom—unoccupied possession of

his own arms—absolute control over his own legs and
motions—these have always been so essential to his
comfort, that, in any case where they were likely to become questionable, he would have declined to make one
of the party. Meantime, we are not to suppose that
Wordsworth the boy expressly sought for solitary
scenes of nature amongst woods and mountains with a
direct conscious anticipation of imaginative pleasure,
and loving them with a pure, disinterested love, on
their own separate account. These are feelings beyond
boyish nature, or, at all events, beyond boyish nature
trained amidst the selfishness of social intercourse.
Wordsworth, like his companions, haunted the hills
and the vales for the sake of angling, snaring birds,
swimming, and sometimes of hunting, according to the
Westmorland fashion (or the Irish fashion in Gal-
way), on foot; for riding to the chase is quite impossible, from the precipitous nature of the ground. It was
in the course of these pursuits, by an indirect effect
growing gradually upon him, that Wordsworth became a passionate lover of nature, at the time when the
growth of his intellectual faculties made it possible
that he should combine those thoughtful passions with
the experience of the eye and the ear.

Meanwhile, how prospered the classical studies
which formed the main business of Wordsworth at
Hawkshead? Not, in all probability, very well; for,
though Wordsworth finally became a very sufficient
master of the Latin language, and read certain favourite authors, especially Horace, with a critical nicety,
and with a feeling for the felicities of his composition,
I have reason to think that little of this skill had been
obtained at Hawkshead. As to Greek, that is a language which Wordsworth never had energy enough to
cultivate with effect.

From Hawkshead, and, I believe, after he had en-

tered his eighteenth year (a time which is tolerably
early on the English plan), probably at the latter end
of the year 1787, Wordsworth entered at St. John's
College, Cambridge. St. John's ranks as the second college in Cambridge—the second as to numbers, and influence, and general consideration; in the estimation
of the Johnians as the first, or at least as co-equal in all
things with Trinity; from which, at any rate, the general reader will collect that no such absolute supremacy
is accorded to any society in Cambridge as in Oxford
is accorded necessarily to Christ Church. The advantages of a large college are considerable, both to the
idle man, who wishes to lurk unnoticed in the crowd,
and to the brilliant man, whose vanity could not be
gratified by pre-eminence amongst a few. Wordsworth,
though not idle as regarded his own pursuits, was so as
regarded the pursuits of the place. With respect to
them he felt—to use his own words—that his hour was
not come; and that his doom for the present was a
happy obscurity, which left him, unvexed by the torments of competition, to the genial enjoyment of life
in its most genial hours.

It will excite some astonishment when I mention
that, on coming to Cambridge, Wordsworth actually
assumed the beau, or, in modern slang, the "dandy."
He dressed in silk stockings, had his hair powdered, and
in all things plumed himself on his gentlemanly habits. To those who remember the slovenly dress of his
middle and philosophic life, this will furnish matter for
a smile.

Stranger still it is to tell that, for the first time in
his life, Wordsworth became inebriated at Cambridge.
It is but fair to add that the first time was also the last
time. But perhaps the strangest part of the story is the
occasion of this drunkenness; which was in celebration
of his first visit to the very rooms at Christ College

once occupied by Milton—intoxication by way of homage to the most temperate of men; and this homage offered by one who has turned out himself to the full as temperate! Every man, meantime, who is not a churl, must grant a privilege and charter of large enthusiasm to such an occasion. And an older man than Wordsworth (at that era not fully nineteen), and a man even without a poet's blood in his veins, might have leave to forget his sobriety in such circumstances. Besides which, after all, I have heard from Wordsworth's own lips that he was not too far gone to attend chapel decorously during the very acme of his elevation.

The rooms which Wordsworth occupied at St. John's were singularly circumstanced; mementoes of what is highest and what is lowest in human things solicited the eye and the ear all day long. If the occupant approached the outdoors prospect, in one direction, there was visible, through the great windows in the adjacent chapel of Trinity, the statue of Newton "with his silent face and prism," memorials of the abstracting intellect, serene and absolute, emancipated from fleshly bonds. On the other hand, immediately below, stood the college kitchen; and, in that region, "from noon to dewy eve," resounded the shrill voice of scolding from the female ministers of the head cook, never suffering the mind to forget one of the meanest amongst human necessities. Wordsworth, however, as one who passed much of his time in social gaiety, was less in the way of this annoyance than a profounder student would have been. Probably he studied little beyond French and Italian during his Cambridge life; not, however, at any time forgetting (as I had so much reason to complain, when speaking of my Oxonian contemporaries) the literature of his own country. It is true that he took the regular degree of A.B., and in the regular course;

but this was won in those days by a mere nominal examination, unless where the mathematical attainments of the student prompted his ambition to contest the splendid distinction of Senior Wrangler. This, in common with all other honours of the University, is won in our days with far severer effort than in that age of relaxed discipline; but at no period could it have been won, let the malicious say what they will, without an amount of mathematical skill very much beyond what has ever been exacted of its *alumni* by any other European University. Wordsworth was a profound admirer of the sublimer mathematics; at least of the higher geometry. The secret of this admiration for geometry lay in the antagonism between this world of bodiless abstraction and the world of passion. And here I may mention appropriately, and I hope without any breach of confidence, that, in a great philosophic poem of Wordsworth's, which is still in MS., and will remain in MS. until after his death, there is, at the opening of one of the books, a dream, which reaches the very *ne plus ultra* of sublimity, in my opinion, expressly framed to illustrate the eternity, and the independence of all social modes or fashions of existence, conceded to these two hemispheres, as it were, that compose the total world of human power—mathematics on the one hand, poetry on the other.

During one of his long Cambridge vacations, stretching from June to November, he went over to Switzerland and Savoy, for a pedestrian excursion amongst the Alps; taking with him for his travelling companion a certain Mr. J——, of whom (excepting that he is once apostrophized in a sonnet, written at Calais in the year 1802) I never happened to hear him speak: whence I presume to infer that Mr. J—— owed this flattering distinction, not so much to any intellectual graces of his society, as, perhaps, to his powers of administering "punishment" (in the language of the "fancy") to restive and mutinous landlords; for such were abroad in those days—people who presented huge reckonings with one hand, and with the other a huge cudgel, by way of opening the traveller's eyes to the propriety of settling them without demur, and without discount. I do not positively know this to have been the case; but I have heard Wordsworth speak of the ruffian landlords who played upon his youth in the Grisons; and, however well qualified to fight his own battles, he might find, amongst such savage mountaineers, two combatants better than one.

Wordsworth's route, on this occasion, lay at first through Austrian Flanders, then (1788, I think) on the fret for an insurrectionary war against the capricious innovations of the imperial coxcomb, Joseph II. He passed through the camps then forming, and thence ascended the Rhine to Switzerland; crossed the Great St. Bernard, visited the Lake of Como, and other interesting scenes in the north of Italy, where, by the way, the tourists were benighted in a forest—having, in some way or other, been misled by the Italian clocks and their peculiar fashion of striking round to twenty-four o'clock. On his return, Wordsworth published a quarto pamphlet of verses, describing, with very considerable effect and brilliancy, the grand scenery amongst which he had been moving.[1]

After his return from this Swiss excursion, Wordsworth took up his parting residence at Cambridge, and prepared for a final adieu to academic pursuits and academic society.

It was about this period that the French Revolution broke out; and the reader who would understand its

[1] *Descriptive Sketches during a Pedestrian Tour on the Italian, Swiss, and Savoyard Alps.* London, 1793.

appalling effects—its convulsing, revolutionary effects upon Wordsworth's heart and soul—should consult the history of the Solitary, as given by himself in *The Excursion;* for that picture is undoubtedly a leaf from the personal experience of Wordsworth:

From that dejection I was roused—but how?

Mighty was the transformation which it wrought in the whole economy of his thoughts; miraculous almost was the expansion which it gave to his human sympathies; chiefly in this it showed its effects—in throwing the thoughts inwards into grand meditations upon man, his final destiny, his ultimate capacities of elevation; and, secondly, in giving to the whole system of the thoughts and feelings a firmer tone, and a sense of the awful *realities* which surround the mind; by comparison with which the previous literary tastes seemed (even where they were fine and elegant, as in Collins or Gray, unless where they had the self-sufficing reality of religion, as in Cowper) fanciful and trivial. In all lands this result was accomplished, and at the same time: Germany, above all, found her new literature the mere creation and rebound of this great moral tempest; and, in Germany or England alike, the poetry was so entirely regenerated, thrown into moulds of thought and of feeling so new, that the poets everywhere felt themselves to be putting away childish things, and now first, among those of their own century, entering upon the dignity and the sincere thinking of mature manhood.

Wordsworth, it is well known to all who know anything of his history, felt himself so fascinated by the gorgeous festival era of the Revolution—that era when the sleeping snakes which afterwards stung the national felicity were yet covered with flowers—that he

went over to Paris, and spent about one entire year between that city, Orleans, and Blois. There, in fact, he
continued to reside almost too long. He had been sufficiently connected with public men to have drawn upon
himself some notice from those who afterwards composed the Committee of Public Safety. And, as an Englishman, when that partiality began to droop which at
an earlier period had protected the English name, he
became an object of gloomy suspicion with those even
who would have grieved that he should fall a victim to
undistinguishing popular violence. Already *for* England, and in her behalf, he was thought to be that spy
which (as Coleridge tells us in his *Biographia Literaria*) afterwards he was accounted by Mr. Pitt's emissaries, in the worst of services *against* her.

Homewards fled all the English from a land which
now was fast making ready the shambles for its noblest citizens. Thither also came Wordsworth; and
there he spent his time for a year and more chiefly in
London, overwhelmed with shame and despondency
for the disgrace and scandal brought upon Liberty by
the atrocities committed in that holy name. Upon this
subject he dwells with deep emotion in the poem on his
own life; and he records the awful triumph for retribution accomplished which possessed him when crossing the sands of the great Bay of Morecambe from
Lancaster to Ulverstone, and hearing from a horseman
who passed him, in reply to the question—*Was there
any news?*—"Yes, that Robespierre had perished." Immediately a passion seized him, a transport of almost
epileptic fervour, prompting him, as he stood alone
upon this perilous [1] waste of sands, to shout aloud an-

[1] That tract of the lake country which stretches southwards
from Hawkshead and the lakes of Esthwaite, Windermere, and
Coniston, to the little town of Ulverstone (which may be regarded as the metropolis of the little romantic English Cala-

thems of thanksgiving for the great vindication of eternal justice. Still, though justice was done upon one great traitor to the cause, the cause itself was overcast with clouds too heavily to find support and employment for the hopes of a poet who had believed in a golden era ready to open upon the prospects of human nature. It gratified and solaced his heart that the indignation of mankind should have wreaked itself upon the chief monsters that had outraged their nature and their hopes; but for the present he found it necessary to comfort his disappointment by turning away from politics to studies less capable of deceiving his expectations.

From this period, therefore—that is, from the year 1794–95—we may date the commencement of Wordsworth's entire self-dedication to poetry as the study and main business of his life. Somewhere about this period also (though, according to my remembrance of what Miss Wordsworth once told me, I think one year or so later) his sister joined him; and they began [1] to keep house together: once at Race Down, in Dorsetshire; once at Clevedon, on the coast of Somersetshire; then amongst the Quantock Hills, in the same county,

bria called Furness), is divided from the main part of Lancashire by the estuary of Morecambe. The sea retires with the ebb tide to a vast distance, leaving the sands passable through a few hours for horses and carriages. But, partly from the daily variation in these hours, partly from the intricacy of the pathless track which must be pursued, and partly from the galloping pace at which the returning tide comes in, many fatal accidents are continually occurring—sometimes to the too venturous traveller who has slighted the aid of guides—sometimes to the guides themselves, when baffled and perplexed by mists. Gray the poet mentions one of the latter class as having then recently occurred, under affecting circumstances. Local tradition records a long list of such cases.

[1] I do not, on consideration, know when they might begin to keep house together: but, by a passage in *The Prelude*, they must have made a tour together as early as 1787.

or in that neighbourhood; particularly at Alfoxton, a
beautiful country-house, with a grove and shrubbery
attached, belonging to Mr. St. Aubyn, a minor, and
let (I believe) on the terms of keeping the house in
repair. Whilst resident at this last place it was, as I
have generally understood, and in the year 1797 or
1798, that Wordsworth first became acquainted with
Coleridge; though possibly in the year I am wrong;
for it occurs to me that, in a poem of Coleridge's, dated
in 1796, there is an allusion to a young writer of the
name of Wordsworth as one who had something austere in his style, but otherwise was more original than
any other poet of the age; and it is probable that this
knowledge of the poetry would be subsequent to a personal knowledge of the author, considering the little
circulation which any poetry of a Wordsworthian
stamp would be likely to attain at that time.

It was at Alfoxton that Miss Mary Hutchinson
visited her cousins the Wordsworths, and there, or previously in the north of England, at Stockton-upon-
Tees and Darlington, that the attachment began between Miss Mary Hutchinson and Wordsworth which
terminated in their marriage about the beginning of
the present century. The marriage took place in the
north; somewhere, I believe, in Yorkshire; and, immediately after the ceremony, Wordsworth brought
his bride to Grasmere; in which most lovely of English valleys he had previously obtained, upon a lease of
seven or eight years, the cottage in which I found him
living at my first visit to him in November 1807. I
have heard that there was a paragraph inserted on this
occasion in the *Morning Post* or *Courier*—and I have
an indistinct remembrance of having once seen it myself—which described this event of the poet's marriage in the most ludicrous terms of silly pastoral sen-
timentality; the cottage being described as "the abode

of content and all the virtues," the vale itself in the
same puerile slang, and the whole event in the style of
allegorical trifling about the Muses, &c. The masculine and severe taste of Wordsworth made him peculiarly open to annoyance from such absurd trifling;
and, unless his sense of the ludicrous overpowered his
graver feelings, he must have been much displeased
with the paragraph. But, after all, I have understood
that the whole affair was an unseasonable jest of Coleridge's or Lamb's.

To us who, in after years, were Wordsworth's
friends, or, at least, intimate acquaintances—viz., to
Professor Wilson and myself—the most interesting circumstance in this marriage, the one which perplexed
us exceedingly, was the very possibility that it should
ever have been brought to bear. For we could not conceive of Wordsworth as submitting his faculties to the
humilities and devotion of courtship. That self-surrender—that prostration of mind by which a man is too
happy and proud to express the profundity of his service to the woman of his heart—it seemed a mere impossibility that ever Wordsworth should be brought
to feel for a single instant; and what he did not sincerely feel, assuredly he was not the person to profess.
Wordsworth, I take it upon myself to say, had not the
feelings within him which make this total devotion to
a woman possible. There never lived a woman whom
he would not have lectured and admonished under circumstances that should have seemed to require it; nor
would he have conversed with her in any mood whatever without wearing an air of mild condescension to
her understanding. To lie at her feet, to make her his
idol, to worship her very caprices, and to adore the
most unreasonable of her frowns—these things were
impossible to Wordsworth; and, being so, never could
he, in any emphatic sense, have been a lover.

A lover, I repeat, in any passionate sense of the word, Wordsworth could not have been. And, moreover, it is remarkable that a woman who could dispense with that sort of homage in her suitor is not of a nature to inspire such a passion. That same meekness which reconciles her to the tone of superiority and freedom in the manner of her suitor, and which may afterwards in a wife become a sweet domestic grace, strips her of that too charming irritation, captivating at once and tormenting, which lurks in feminine pride. If there be an enchantress's spell yet surviving in this age of ours, it is the haughty grace of maidenly pride—the womanly sense of dignity, even when most in excess, and expressed in the language of scorn—which tortures a man and lacerates his heart, at the same time that it pierces him with admiration:

> Oh, *what a world of scorn looks beautiful*
> *In the contempt and anger of her lip!*

And she who spares a man the agitations of this thraldom robs him no less of its divinest transports. Wordsworth, however, who never could have laid aside his own nature sufficiently to have played *his* part in such an impassioned courtship, by suiting himself to this high sexual pride with the humility of a lover, quite as little could have enjoyed the spectacle of such a pride, or have viewed it in any degree as an attraction: it would to him have been a pure vexation. Looking down even upon the lady of his heart, as upon the rest of the world, from the eminence of his own intellectual superiority—viewing her, in fact, as a child—he would be much more disposed to regard any airs of feminine disdain she might assume as the impertinence of girlish levity than as the caprice of womanly pride; and much I fear that, in any case of dispute, he would have

called even his mistress, "Child! child!" and perhaps
even (but this I do not say with the same certainty)
might have bid her hold her tongue.

If, however, no lover, in a proper sense—though,
from many exquisite passages, one might conceive that
at some time of his life he was, as especially from the
inimitable stanzas beginning:

> *When she I loved was strong and gay,*
> *And like a rose in June,*

or perhaps (but less powerfully so, because here the
passion, though profound, is less the *peculiar* passion
of love) from the impassioned lamentation for "the
pretty Barbara," beginning:

> *'Tis said that some have died for love:*
> *And here and there, amidst unhallow'd ground*
> *In the cold north, &c.,*

yet, if no lover, or (which some of us have sometimes
thought) a lover disappointed at some earlier period,
by the death of her he loved, or by some other fatal
event (for he always preserved a mysterious silence on
the subject of that "Lucy," repeatedly alluded to or
apostrophized in his poems) ; at all events he made
what for him turned out a happy marriage. Few people have lived on such terms of entire harmony and affection as he lived with the woman of his final choice.
Indeed, the sweetness, almost unexampled, of temper,
which shed so sunny a radiance over Mrs. Wordsworth's manners, sustained by the happy life she led,
the purity of her conscience, and the uniformity of her
good health, made it impossible for anybody to have
quarrelled with *her;* and whatever fits of ill-temper
Wordsworth might have—for, with all his philosophy,

he had such fits—met with no fuel to support them,
except in the more irritable temperament of his sister.
She was all fire, and an ardour which, like that of the
first Lord Shaftesbury,

O'er-informed its tenement of clay;

and, as this ardour looked out in every gleam of her
wild eyes (those "wild eyes" so finely noticed in the
"Tintern Abbey"), as it spoke in every word of her
self-baffled utterance, as it gave a trembling movement
to her very person and demeanour—easily enough it
might happen that any apprehension of an unkind
word should with her kindle a dispute. It might have
happened; and yet, to the great honour of both, having
such impassioned temperaments, rarely it did happen;
and this was the more remarkable, as I have been assured that both were, in childhood, irritable or even ill-
tempered, and they were constantly together; for Miss
Wordsworth was always ready to walk out—wet or
dry, storm or sunshine, night or day; whilst Mrs.
Wordsworth was completely dedicated to her maternal
duties, and rarely left the house, unless when the
weather was tolerable, or, at least, only for short rambles. I should not have noticed this trait in Wordsworth's occasional manners, had it been gathered from
domestic or confidential opportunities. But, on the contrary, the first two occasions on which, after months'
domestic intercourse with Wordsworth, I became
aware of his possible ill-humour and peevishness, were
so public, that others, and those strangers, must have
been equally made parties to the scene. This scene occurred in Kendal.

Having brought down the history of Wordsworth to
the time of his marriage, I am reminded by that event

to mention the singular good fortune, in all points of
worldly prosperity, which has accompanied him
through life. His marriage—the capital event of life
—was fortunate, and inaugurated a long succession of
other prosperities. He has himself described, in his
"Leech-Gatherer," the fears that at one time, or at
least in some occasional moments of his life, haunted
him, lest at some period or other he might be reserved
for poverty. "Cold, pain, and hunger, and all fleshly
ills," occurred to his boding apprehension, and
"mighty poets in their misery dead."

> *He thought of Chatterton, the marvellous boy,*
> *The sleepless soul that perished in its pride;*
> *Of him who walked in glory and in joy*
> *Following his plough along the mountain-side.*

And, at starting on his career of life, certainly no man
had plainer reasons for anticipating the worst evils that
have ever persecuted poets, excepting only two reasons
which might warrant him in hoping better; and these
two were—his great prudence, and the temperance of
his daily life. He could not be betrayed into foolish
engagements; he could not be betrayed into expensive
habits. Profusion and extravagance had no hold over
him, by any one passion or taste. He was not luxurious
in anything; was not vain or even careful of external
appearances (not, at least, since he had left Cambridge,
and visited a mighty nation in civil convulsions) ; was
not even in the article of books expensive. Very few
books sufficed him; he was careless habitually of all the
current literature, or indeed of any literature that
could not be considered as enshrining the very ideal,
capital, and elementary grandeur of the human intellect. In this extreme limitation of his literary sensibilities he was as much assisted by that accident of his

own intellectual condition—viz. extreme, intense, unparalleled *onesidedness* (*einseitigkeit*)—as by any peculiar sanity of feeling. Thousands of books that have
given rapturous delight to millions of ingenuous minds
for Wordsworth were absolutely a dead letter—closed
and sealed up from his sensibilities and his powers of
appreciation, not less than colours from a blind man's
eye. Even the few books which his peculiar mind had
made indispensable to him were not in such a sense indispensable as they would have been to a man of more
sedentary habits. He lived in the open air, and the
enormity of pleasure which both he and his sister drew
from the common appearances of nature and their
everlasting variety—variety so infinite that, if no one
leaf of a tree or shrub ever exactly resembled another
in all its filaments and their arrangement, still less did
any one day ever repeat another in all its pleasurable
elements. This pleasure was to him in the stead of
many libraries:

> *One impulse, from a vernal wood,*
> *Could teach him more of Man,*
> *Of moral evil and of good,*
> *Than all the sages can.*

And he, we may be sure, who could draw,

> *Even from the meanest flower that blows,*
> *Thoughts that do often lie too deep for tears—*

to whom the mere daisy, the pansy, the primrose, could
furnish pleasures—not the puerile ones which his most
puerile and worldly insulters imagined, but pleasures
drawn from depths of reverie and meditative tenderness far beyond all power of *their* hearts to conceive:
that man would hardly need any large variety of

books. In fact, there were only two provinces of literature in which Wordsworth could be looked upon as decently well read—Poetry and Ancient History. Nor
do I believe that he would much have lamented, on his
own account, if all books had perished, excepting the
entire body of English Poetry, and, perhaps, *Plutarch's
Lives*.[1]

With these simple or rather austere tastes, Wordsworth (it might seem) had little reason to fear poverty,
supposing him in possession of any moderate income;
but meantime he had none. About the time when he
left college, I have good grounds for believing that his
whole regular income was precisely $= 0$. Some fragments must have survived from the funds devoted to
his education; and with these, no doubt, he supported
the expenses of his Continental tours, and his year's
residence in France. But, at length, "cold, pain, and
hunger, and all fleshly ills," must have stared him in
the face pretty earnestly. And hope of longer evading
an unpleasant destiny of daily toil, in some form or
other, there seemed absolutely none. "For," as he himself expostulates with himself:

For how can he *expect that others should
Sow for him, build for* him, *and, at his call
Love him, who for himself will take no thought at all?*

In this dilemma, he had all but resolved, as Miss
Wordsworth once told me, to take pupils; and perhaps
that, though odious enough, was the sole resource he
had; for Wordsworth never acquired any popular tal-

---

[1] I do not mean to insinuate that Wordsworth was at all in
the dark about the inaccuracy and want of authentic weight
attaching to Plutarch as a historian; but his business with
Plutarch was not for purposes of research: he was satisfied
with his fine moral effects.

ent of writing for the current press; and, at that period
of his life, he was gloomily unfitted for bending to such
a yoke. In this crisis of his fate it was that Wordsworth,
for once, and once only, became a martyr to some nervous affection. *That* raised pity; but I could not forbear smiling at the remedy, or palliation, which his
few friends adopted. Every night they played at cards
with him, as the best mode of beguiling his sense of
distress, whatever that might be: *cards*, which, in any
part of the thirty-and-one years since *I* have known
Wordsworth, could have had as little power to interest
him, or to cheat him of sorrow, as marbles or a top.
However, so it was; for my information could not be
questioned: it came from Miss Wordsworth.

The crisis, as I have said, had arrived for determining the future colour of his life. Memorable it is, that
exactly in those critical moments when some decisive
step had first become necessary, there happened the
first instance of Wordsworth's good luck; and equally
memorable that, at measured intervals throughout the
long sequel of his life since then, a regular succession
of similar but superior windfalls have fallen in, to sustain his expenditure, in exact concurrence with the
growing claims upon his purse. A more fortunate man,
I believe, does not exist than Wordsworth. The aid
which now dropped from heaven, as it were, to enable
him to range at will in paths of his own choosing, and

> *Finally array*
> *His temples with the Muses' diadem,*

came in the shape of a bequest from Raisley Calvert, a
young man of good family in Cumberland, who died
about this time of pulmonary consumption. A very remarkable young man he must have been, this Raisley
Calvert, to have discerned, at this early period, that fu-

ture superiority in Wordsworth which so few people
suspected. He was the brother of a Cumberland gentleman, whom slightly I know; a generous man,
doubtless; for he made no sort of objections (though
legally, I have heard, he might) to his brother's farewell memorial of regard; a good man to all his dependants, as I have generally understood, in the neighbourhood of Windy Brow, his mansion, near Keswick; and,
as Southey always said (who must know better than I
could do), a man of strong natural endowments; else,
as his talk was of oxen, I might have made the mistake
of supposing him to be, in heart and soul, what he was
in profession—a mere farming country gentleman,
whose ambition was chiefly directed to the turning up
of mighty turnips. The sum left by Raisley Calvert
was £900; and it was laid out in an annuity. This was
the basis of Wordsworth's prosperity in life; and upon
this he has built up, by a series of accessions, in which
each step, taken separately for itself, seems perfectly
natural, whilst the total result has undoubtedly something wonderful about it, the present goodly edifice of
his fortunes. Next in the series came the present Lord
Lonsdale's repayment of his predecessor's debt. Upon
that, probably, it was that Wordsworth felt himself entitled to marry. Then, I believe, came some fortune
with Miss Hutchinson; then—that is, fourthly—some
worthy uncle of the same lady was pleased to betake
himself to a better world, leaving to various nieces,
and especially to Mrs. Wordsworth, something or other
—I forget what, but it was expressed by thousands of
pounds. At this moment, Wordsworth's family had begun to increase; and the worthy old uncle, like everybody else in Wordsworth's case, finding his property
very clearly "wanted," and, as people would tell him,
"bespoke," felt how very indelicate it would look for
him to stay any longer in this world; and so off he

moved. But Wordsworth's family, and the wants of
that family, still continued to increase; and the next
person—viz., the fifth—who stood in the way, and
must, therefore, have considered himself rapidly growing into a nuisance, was the stamp-distributor for the
county of Westmorland. About March 1814, I think it
was, that his very comfortable situation was wanted.
Probably it took a month for the news to reach him;
because in April, and not before, feeling that he had
received a proper notice to quit, he, good man (this
stamp-distributor), like all the rest, distributed himself and his office into two different places—the latter
falling, of course, into the hands of Wordsworth.

This office, which it was Wordsworth's pleasure to
speak of as "a little one," yielded, I believe, somewhere
about £500 a year. Gradually, even *that*, with all former sources of income, became insufficient; which
ought not to surprise anybody; for a son at Oxford, as
a gentleman commoner, would spend, at the least,
£300 per annum; and there were other children. Still,
it is wrong to say that it *had* become insufficient; as
usual, it had not come to that; but, on the first symptoms arising that it soon *would* come to that, somebody, of course, had notice to consider himself a sort of
nuisance-elect—in this case, it was the distributor of
stamps for the county of Cumberland. His district was
absurdly large; and what so reasonable as that he
should submit to a Polish partition of his profits—no,
not Polish; for, on reflection, such a partition neither
was nor could be attempted with regard to an actual
incumbent. But then, since people had such consideration for him as not to remodel the office so long as he
lived, on the other hand, the least he could do for "people" in return—so as to show his sense of this consideration—was not to trespass on so much goodness
longer than necessary. Accordingly, here, as in all

cases before, the *Deus ex machinâ* who invariably interfered when any *nodus* arose in Wordsworth's affairs, such as could be considered *vindice dignus*,
caused the distributor to begone into a region where no
stamps are wanted, about the very month, or so, when
an additional £400 per annum became desirable. This,
or perhaps more, was understood to have been added,
by the new arrangement, to the Westmorland distribu-
torship; the small towns of Keswick and Cockermouth,
together with the important one of Whitehaven, being
severed, under this remodelling, from their old dependency on Cumberland (to which geographically they
belonged), and transferred to the small territory of
rocky Westmorland, the sum total of whose inhabitants was at that time not much above 50,000; of
which number, one-third, or nearly so, was collected
into the only important town of Kendal; but, of the
other two-thirds, a larger proportion was a simple agricultural or pastoral population than anywhere else in
England. In Westmorland, therefore, it may be supposed that the stamp demand could not have been so
great, not perhaps by three-quarters, as in Cumberland; which, besides having a population at least three
times as large, had more and larger towns. The result
of this new distribution was something that approached to an equalization of the districts—giving to
each, as was said, in round terms, a thousand a year.

Thus I have traced Wordsworth's ascent through its
several steps and stages, to what, for his moderate desires and habits so philosophic, may be fairly considered opulence. And it must rejoice every man who
joins in the public homage *now* rendered to his powers
(and what man is to be found that, more or less, does
not?) to hear, with respect to one so lavishly endowed
by nature, that he has not been neglected by fortune;
that he has never had the finer edge of his sensibilities

dulled by the sad anxieties, the degrading fears, the
miserable dependencies of debt; that he has been
blessed with competency even when poorest; has had
hope and cheerful prospects in reversion through every
stage of his life; that at all times he has been liberated
from *reasonable* anxieties about the final interests of
his children; that at all times he has been blessed with
leisure, the very amplest that ever man enjoyed, for intellectual pursuits the most delightful; yes, that, even
as regards those delicate and coy pursuits, he has possessed, in combination, all the conditions for their
most perfect culture—the leisure, the ease, the solitude, the society, the domestic peace, the local scenery
—Paradise for his eye, in Miltonic beauty, lying outside his windows, Paradise for his heart, in the perpetual happiness of his own fireside; and, finally, when
increasing years might be supposed to demand something more of modern luxuries, and expanding intercourse with society something more of refined elegancies, that his means, still keeping pace in almost
arithmetical ratio with his wants, had shed the graces
of art upon the failing powers of nature, had stripped
infirmity of discomfort, and (so far as the necessities of
things will allow) had placed the final stages of life, by
means of many compensations, by universal praise, by
plaudits reverberated from senates, benedictions wherever his poems have penetrated, honour, troops of
friends—in short, by all that miraculous prosperity
can do to evade the primal decrees of nature, had
placed the final stages upon a level with the first.

But now, reverting to the subject of Wordsworth's
prosperity, I have numbered up six separate stages of
good luck—six instances of pecuniary showers empty-
ing themselves into his very bosom, at the very moments when they *began* to be needed, on the first symptoms that they might be wanted—accesses of fortune

stationed upon his road like repeating frigates, connecting, to all appearance, some preconcerted line of operations, and, amidst the tumults of chance, wearing as much the air of purpose and design as if they supported a human plan. I have come down to the sixth case. Whether there were any seventh, I do not know: but confident I feel that, had a seventh been required by circumstances, a seventh would have happened. So true it is that still, as Wordsworth needed a place or a fortune, the holder of that place or fortune was immediately served with a summons to surrender it: so certainly was this impressed upon my belief, as one of the blind necessities making up the prosperity and fixed destiny of Wordsworth, that, for myself, had I happened to know of any peculiar adaptation in an estate or office of mine to an existing need of Wordsworth's, forthwith, and with the speed of a man running for his life, I would have laid it down at his feet. "Take it," I should have said; "take it, or in three weeks I shall be a dead man."

Well, let me pause: I think the reader is likely by this time to have a slight notion of *my* notion of Wordsworth's inevitable prosperity, and the sort of *lien* that he had upon the incomes of other men who happened to stand in his way. The same prosperity attended the other branches of the family, with the single exception of John, the brother who perished in the *Abergavenny*: and even he was prosperous up to the moment of his fatal accident. As to Miss Wordsworth, who will, by some people, be classed amongst the non-prosperous, I rank her amongst the most fortunate of women; or, at least, if regard be had to that period of life which is most capable of happiness. Her fortune, after its repayment by Lord Lonsdale, was, much of it, confided, with a sisterly affection, to the use of her brother John; and part of it, I have heard, perished in his ship. How much, I never felt myself entitled to ask; but certainly a part was on that occasion understood to have been lost irretrievably. Either it was that only a partial insurance had been effected; or else the nature of the accident, being in home waters (off the coast of Dorsetshire), might, by the nature of the contract, have taken the case out of the benefit of the policy. This loss, however, had it even been total, for a single sister amongst a family of flourishing brothers, could not be of any lasting importance. A much larger number of voices would proclaim her to have been unfortunate in life because she made no marriage connexion; and certainly, the insipid as well as unfeeling ridicule which descends so plentifully upon those women who, perhaps from strength of character, have refused to make such a connexion where it promised little of elevated happiness, *does* make the state of singleness somewhat of a trial to the patience of many; and to many the vexation of this trial has proved a snare for beguiling them of their honourable resolutions. Meantime, as the opportunities are rare in which all the conditions concur for happy marriage connexions, how important it is that the dignity of high-minded women should be upheld by society in the honourable election they make of a self-dependent virgin seclusion, by preference to a heartless marriage! Such women, as Mrs. Trollope justly remarks, fill a place in society which in their default would *not* be filled, and are available for duties requiring a tenderness and a punctuality that could not be looked for from women preoccupied with household or maternal claims. If there were no regular fund (so to speak) of women free from conjugal and maternal duties, upon what body could we draw for our "sisters of mercy," &c.? In another point Mrs. Trollope is probably right: few women live unmarried from necessity. Miss Wordsworth had several offers; amongst them, to my knowledge, one from Hazlitt; all of them she rejected decisively. And she did right. A happier life, by far, was hers in youth, coming as near as difference of scenery and difference of relations would permit to that which was promised to Ruth—the Ruth of her brother's creation [1] —by the youth who came from Georgia's shore; for, though not upon American savannah, or Canadian lakes,

> With all their fairy crowds
> Of islands, that together lie
> As quietly as spots of sky
> Amongst the evening clouds,

yet, amongst the loveliest scenes of sylvan England, and (at intervals) of sylvan Germany—amongst lakes, too, far better fitted to give the *sense* of their own character than the vast inland *seas* of America, and amongst mountains more romantic than many of the chief ranges in that country—her time fleeted away like some golden age, or like the life of primeval man; and she, like Ruth, was for years allowed

> To run, though not a bride,
> A sylvan huntress, by the side

[1] "*The Ruth of her brother's creation*": So I express it; because so much in the development of the story and situations necessarily belongs to the poet. Else, for the mere outline of the story, it was founded upon fact. Wordsworth himself told me, in general terms, that the case which suggested the poem was that of an American lady, whose husband forsook her at the very place of embarkation from England, under circumstances and under expectations, upon her part, very much the same as those of Ruth. I am afraid, however, that the husband was an attorney; which is intolerable; *nisi prius* cannot be harmonized with the dream-like fairyland of Georgia.

of him to whom she, like Ruth, had dedicated her days, and to whose children, afterwards, she dedicated a love like that of mothers. Dear Miss Wordsworth! How noble a creature did she seem when I first knew her!— and when, on the very first night which I passed in her brother's company, he read to me, in illustration of something he was saying, a passage from Fairfax's *Tasso*, ending pretty nearly with these words,

Amidst the broad fields and the endless wood,
The lofty lady kept her maidenhood,

I thought that, possibly, he had his sister in his thoughts. Yet "lofty" was hardly the right word. Miss Wordsworth was too ardent and fiery a creature to maintain the reserve essential to dignity; and dignity was the last thing one thought of in the presence of one so natural, so fervent in her feelings, and so embarrassed in their utterance—sometimes, also, in the attempt to check them. It must not, however, be supposed that there was any silliness or weakness of enthusiasm about her. She was under the continual restraint of severe good sense, though liberated from that false shame which, in so many persons, accompanies all expressions of natural emotion; and she had too long enjoyed the ennobling conversation of her brother, and his admirable comments on the poets, which they read in common, to fail in any essential point of logic or propriety of thought. Accordingly, her letters, though the most careless and unelaborate —nay, the most hurried that can be imagined—are models of good sense and just feeling. In short, beyond any person I have known in this world, Miss Wordsworth was the creature of impulse; but, as a woman most thoroughly virtuous and well-principled, as one who could not fail to be kept right by her own excellent heart, and as an intellectual creature from her cradle, with much of her illustrious brother's peculiarity of mind—finally, as one who had been, in effect, educated and trained by that very brother—she won the sympathy and the respectful regard of every man worthy to approach her. Properly, and in a spirit of prophecy, was she named *Dorothy;* in its Greek meaning,[1] *gift of God*, well did this name prefigure the relation in which she stood to Wordsworth, the mission with which she was charged—to wait upon him as the tenderest and most faithful of domestics; to love him as a sister; to sympathize with him as a confidante; to counsel him; to cheer him and sustain him by the natural expression of her feelings—so quick, so ardent, so unaffected—upon the probable effect of whatever thoughts or images he might conceive; finally, and above all other ministrations, to ingraft, by her sexual sense of beauty, upon his masculine austerity that delicacy and those graces which else (according to the grateful acknowledgements of his own maturest retrospect) it never could have had:

> *The blessing of my later years*
> *Was with me when I was a boy:*
> *She gave me hopes, she gave me fears,*
> *A heart the fountain of sweet tears,*

> *And love, and thought, and joy.*

[1] Of course, therefore, it is essentially the same name as *Theodora*, the same elements being only differently arranged. Yet how opposite is the impression upon the mind! and chiefly, I suppose, from the too prominent emblazonment of this name in the person of Justinian's scandalous wife; though, for my own part, I am far from believing all the infamous stories which we read about her.

And elsewhere he describes her, in a philosophic poem, still in MS., as one who planted flowers and blossoms with her feminine hand upon what might else have been an arid rock—massy, indeed, and grand, but repulsive from the severity of its features. I may sum up in one brief abstract the amount of Miss Wordsworth's character, as a companion, by saying, that she was the very wildest (in the sense of the most natural) person I have ever known; and also the truest, most inevitable, and at the same time the quickest and readiest in her sympathy with either joy or sorrow, with laughter or with tears, with the realities of life or the larger realities of the poets!

Meantime, amidst all this fascinating furniture of her mind, won from nature, from solitude, from enlightened companionship, Miss Wordsworth was as thoroughly deficient (some would say painfully deficient—I say charmingly deficient) in ordinary female accomplishments as "Cousin Mary" in dear Miss Mitford's delightful sketch. Of French, she might have barely enough to read a plain modern page of narrative; Italian, I question whether any; German, just enough to insult the German literati, by showing how little she had found them or their writings necessary to her heart. The *Luise* of Voss, the *Hermann und Dorothea* of Goethe she had begun to translate, as young ladies do *Télémaque;* but, like them, had chiefly cultivated the first two pages [1]; with the third she had a

[1] Viz., "Calypso ne savoit se consoler du départ," &c. For how long a period (viz., nearly two centuries) has Calypso been inconsolable in the morning studies of young ladies! As Fénelon's most dreary romance always opened at one or other of these three earliest and dreary pages, naturally to my sympathetic fancy the poor unhappy goddess seemed to be eternally aground on this Goodwin Sand of inconsolability. It is amongst the standing hypocrisies of the world, that most people affect a reverence for this book, which nobody reads.

slender acquaintance, and with the fourth she meditated an intimacy at some future day. Music, in her
solitary and out-of-doors life, she could have little reason for cultivating; nor is it possible that any woman
can draw the enormous energy requisite for this attainment, upon a *modern* scale of perfection, out of
any other principle than that of vanity (at least of
great value for social applause) or else of deep musical
sensibility; neither of which belonged to Miss Wordsworth's constitution of mind. But, as everybody agrees
in our days to think this accomplishment of no value
whatever, and, in fact, *unproduceable*, unless existing
in an exquisite state of culture, no complaint could be
made on that score, nor any surprise felt. But the case
in which the irregularity of Miss Wordsworth's education *did* astonish one was in that part which respected
her literary knowledge. In whatever she read, or neglected to read, she had obeyed the single impulse of her
own heart; where that led her, *there* she followed:
where that was mute or indifferent, not a thought had
she to bestow upon a writer's high reputation, or the
call for some acquaintance with his works to meet the
demands of society. And thus the strange anomaly
arose, of a woman deeply acquainted with some great
authors, whose works lie pretty much out of the fashionable beat; able, moreover, in her own person, to
produce brilliant effects; able on some subjects to write
delightfully, and with the impress of originality upon
all she uttered; and yet ignorant of great classical
works in her own mother tongue, and careless of literary history in a degree which at once exiled her from
the rank and privileges of *bluestockingism*.

The reader may, perhaps, have objected silently to
the illustration drawn from Miss Mitford, that "Cousin Mary" does not effect her fascinations out of pure
negations. Such negations, from the mere startling ef-

fect of their oddity in this present age, might fall in
with the general current of her attractions; but Cousin
Mary's undoubtedly lay in the *positive* witcheries of a
manner and a character transcending, by force of irresistible nature (as in a similar case recorded by Wordsworth in *The Excursion*) all the pomp of nature and
art united as seen in ordinary creatures. Now, in Miss
Wordsworth, there were certainly no "Cousin Mary"
fascinations of manner and deportment, that snatch a
grace beyond the reach of art: *there* she was, indeed,
painfully deficient; for hurry mars and defeats even
the most ordinary expression of the feminine character
—viz. its gentleness: abruptness and trepidation leave
often a joint impression of what seems for an instant
both rudeness and ungracefulness: and the least painful impression was that of unsexual awkwardness. But
the point in which Miss Wordsworth made the most
ample amends for all that she wanted of more customary accomplishments, was this very originality and
native freshness of intellect, which settled with so be-
witching an effect upon some of her writings, and
upon many a sudden remark or ejaculation, extorted
by something or other that struck her eye, in the
clouds, or in colouring, or in accidents of light and
shade, of form or combination of form. To talk of her
"writings" is too pompous an expression, or at least far
beyond any pretensions that she ever made for herself.
Of poetry she has written little indeed; and that little
not, in my opinion, of much merit. The verses published by her brother, and beginning, "Which way
does the wind come?", meant only as nursery lines, are
certainly wild and pretty; but the other specimen is
likely to strike most readers as feeble and trivial in the
sentiment. Meantime, the book which is in very deed a
monument to her power of catching and expressing all
the hidden beauties of natural scenery, with a felicity

of diction, a truth and strength, that far transcend Gil-
pin, or professional writers on those subjects, is her
record of a *first* tour in Scotland, made about the year
1802. This MS. book (unless my recollection of it,
from a period now gone by for thirty years, has deceived me greatly) is absolutely unique in its class;
and, though it never could be very popular, from the
minuteness of its details, intelligible only to the eye,
and the luxuriation of its descriptions, yet I believe no
person has ever been favoured with a sight of it that
has not yearned for its publication. Its own extraordinary merit, apart from the interest which *now* invests
the name of Wordsworth, could not fail to procure
purchasers for one edition on its first appearance.[1]

Coleridge was of the party at first; but afterwards,
under some attack of rheumatism, found or thought it
necessary to leave them. Melancholy it would be at this
time, thirty-six years and more from the era of that
tour, to read it under the afflicting remembrances of all
which has been suffered in the interval by two at least
out of the three who composed the travelling party; for
I fear that Miss Wordsworth has suffered not much
less than Coleridge, and, in any general expression of
it, from the same cause, viz. an excess of pleasurable
excitement and luxurious sensibility, sustained in
youth by a constitutional glow from animal causes, but
drooping as soon as that was withdrawn. It is painful
to point a moral from any story connected with those
whom one loves or has loved; painful to look for one
moment towards any "improvement" of such a case,
especially where there is no reason to tax the parties
with any criminal contribution to their own sufferings, except through that relaxation of the will and its

---

[1] *Recollections of a Tour made in Scotland, A.D. 1803*, by
Dorothy Wordsworth. Edited by J. C. Shairp, LL.D., 1874.
—ED.

potential energies through which most of us, at some time or other—I myself too deeply and sorrowfully—stand accountable to our own consciences. Not, therefore, with any intention of speaking in a monitorial or censorial character, do I here notice a defect in Miss Wordsworth's self-education of something that might have mitigated the sort of suffering which, more or less, ever since the period of her too genial, too radiant youth, I suppose her to have struggled with. I have mentioned the narrow basis on which her literary interests had been made to rest—the exclusive character of her reading, and the utter want of pretension, and of all that looks like *bluestockingism*, in the style of her habitual conversation and mode of dealing with literature. Now, to me it appears, upon reflection, that it would have been far better had Miss Wordsworth condescended a little to the ordinary mode of pursuing literature; better for her own happiness if she *had* been a bluestocking; or, at least, if she had been, in good earnest, a writer for the press, with the pleasant cares and solicitudes of one who has some little ventures, as it were, on that vast ocean.

We all know with how womanly and serene a temper literature has been pursued by Joanna Baillie, by Miss Mitford, and other women of admirable genius—with how absolutely no sacrifice or loss of feminine dignity they have cultivated the profession of authorship; and, if we could hear their report, I have no doubt that the little cares of correcting proofs, and the forward-looking solicitudes connected with the mere business arrangements of new publications, would be numbered amongst the minor pleasures of life; whilst the more elevated cares connected with the intellectual business of such projects must inevitably have done much to solace the troubles which, as human beings, they cannot but have experienced, and even to scatter

flowers upon their path. Mrs. Johnstone of Edinburgh
has pursued the profession of literature—the noblest
of professions, and the only one open to both sexes alike
—with even more assiduity, and as a *daily* occupation;
and, I have every reason to believe, with as much benefit to her own happiness as to the instruction and
amusement of her readers; for the petty cares of authorship are agreeable, and its serious cares are ennobling. More especially is such an occupation useful
to a woman without children, and without any *pros-
pective* resources—resources in objects that involve
hopes growing and unfulfilled. It is too much to expect
of any woman (or man either) that her mind should
support itself in a pleasurable activity, under the
drooping energies of life, by resting on the past or on
the present; some interest in reversion, some subject of
hope from day to day, must be called in to reinforce
the animal fountains of good spirits. Had that been
opened for Miss Wordsworth, I am satisfied that she
would have passed a more cheerful middle-age, and
would not, at any period, have yielded to that nervous
depression (or is it, perhaps, nervous irritation?)
which, I grieve to hear, has clouded her latter days.
Nephews and nieces, whilst young and innocent, are as
good almost as sons and daughters to a fervid and loving heart that has carried them in her arms from the
hour they were born. But, after a nephew has grown
into a huge hulk of a man, six feet high, and as stout as
a bullock; after he has come to have children of his
own, lives at a distance, and finds occasion to talk much
of oxen and turnips—no offence to him!—he ceases to
be an object of any very profound sentiment. There is
nothing in such a subject to rouse the flagging pulses of
the heart, and to sustain a fervid spirit, to whom, at the
very best, human life offers little of an adequate or sufficing interest, unless when idealized by the magic of

the mighty poets. Farewell, Miss Wordsworth! farewell, impassioned Dorothy! I have not seen you for many a day—shall, too probably, never see you again; but shall attend your steps with tender interest so long as I hear of you living: so will Professor Wilson; and, from two hearts at least, that knew and admired you in your fervid prime, it may sometimes cheer the gloom of your depression to be assured of never-failing remembrance, full of love and respectful pity.

WILLIAM WORDSWORTH AND ROBERT SOUTHEY
(First published in *Tait's Magazine*, July, 1839)

THAT night—the first of my personal intercourse with Wordsworth—the first in which I saw him face to face—was (it is little, indeed, to say) memorable: it was marked by a change even in the physical condition of my nervous system. Long disappointment —hope for ever baffled (and why should it be less painful because *self*-baffled?)—vexation and self-blame, almost self-contempt, at my own want of courage to face the man whom of all since the Flood I most yearned to behold—these feelings had impressed upon my nervous sensibilities a character of irritation —agitation—restlessness—eternal self-dissatisfaction —which were gradually gathering into a distinct, well-defined type, that would, but for youth—almighty youth, and the spirit of youth—have shaped itself into some nervous complaint, wearing symptoms *sui generis* (for most nervous complaints, in minds that are at all eccentric, will be *sui generis*) ; and, perhaps, finally, have been immortalized in some medical journal as the anomalous malady of an interesting young gentleman, aged twenty-two, who was supposed to have studied too severely, and to have per-

plexed his brain with German metaphysics. To this result things tended; but, in one hour, all passed away. It
was gone, never to return. The spiritual being whom
I had anticipated—for, like Eloisa,

> *My fancy framed him of the angelic kind,*
> *Some emanation of the all-beauteous mind—*

this ideal creature had at length been seen—seen "in
the flesh"—seen with fleshly eyes; and now, though he
did not cease for years to wear something of the glory
and the *aureola* which, in Popish legends, invests the
heads of superhuman beings, yet it was no longer as a
being to be feared: it was as Raphael, the "affable"
angel, who conversed on the terms of man with man,
that I now regarded him.

It was four o'clock, perhaps, when we arrived. At
that hour in November the daylight soon declined;
and, in an hour and a half, we were all collected about
the tea-table. This, with the Wordsworths, under the
simple rustic system of habits which they cherished
then, and for twenty years after, was the most delightful meal in the day; just as dinner is in great cities, and
for the same reason—because it was prolonged into a
meal of leisure and conversation.

That night, after hearing conversation superior by
much, in its tone and subject, to any which I had ever
heard before—one exception only being made in favour of Coleridge, whose style differed from Wordsworth's in this, that, being far more agile and more
comprehensive, consequently more showy and surprising, it was less impressive and weighty; for Wordsworth's was slow in its movement, solemn, majestic.
After a luxury so rare as this, I found myself, about
eleven at night, in a pretty bedroom, about fourteen
feet by twelve. Much I feared that this might turn out

the best room in the house; and it illustrates the hospitality of my new friends to mention that it was. Early in the morning, I was awoke by a little voice, issuing from a little cottage bed in an opposite corner, soliloquizing in a low tone. I soon recognized the words—"Suffered under Pontius Pilate; was crucified, dead, and buried"; and the voice I easily conjectured to be that of the eldest amongst Wordsworth's children, a son, and at that time about three years old. He was a remarkably fine boy in strength and size, promising (which has in fact been realized) a much more powerful person, physically, than that of his father. Miss Wordsworth I found making breakfast in the little sitting-room. No urn was there; no glittering breakfast service; a kettle boiled upon the fire, and everything was in harmony with these unpretending arrangements. I, the son of a merchant, and naturally, therefore, in the midst of luxurious (though not ostentatious) display from my childhood, had never seen so humble a *ménage:* and, contrasting the dignity of the man with this honourable poverty, and this courageous avowal of it, his utter absence of all effort to disguise the simple truth of the case, I felt my admiration increase to the uttermost by all I saw. This, thought I to myself, is, indeed, in his own words—

Plain living, and high thinking.

This is indeed to reserve the humility and the parsimonies of life for its bodily enjoyments, and to apply its lavishness and its luxury to its enjoyments of the intellect. So might Milton have lived; so Marvell. Throughout the day—which was rainy—the same style of modest hospitality prevailed. Wordsworth and his sister—myself being of the party—walked out in spite of the rain, and made the circuit of the two lakes,

Grasmere and its dependency Rydal—a walk of about
six miles. On the third day, Mrs. Coleridge having now
pursued her journey northward to Keswick, and having, at her departure, invited me, in her own name as
well as Southey's, to come and see them, Wordsworth
proposed that we should go thither in company, but
not by the direct route—a distance of only thirteen
miles: this we were to take in our road homeward; our
outward-bound journey was to be by way of Ulleswater—a circuit of forty-three miles.

On the third morning after my arrival in Grasmere,
I found the whole family, except the two children,
prepared for the expedition across the mountains. I
had heard of no horses, and took it for granted that we
were to walk; however, at the moment of starting, a
cart—the common farmers' cart of the country—
made its appearance; and the driver was a bonny
young woman of the vale. Such a vehicle I had never
in my life seen used for such a purpose; but what was
good enough for the Wordsworths was good enough
for me; and, accordingly, we were all carted along to
the little town, or large village, of Ambleside—three
and a half miles distant. Our style of travelling occasioned no astonishment; on the contrary, we met
a smiling salutation wherever we appeared—Miss
Wordsworth being, as I observed, the person most familiarly known of our party, and the one who took
upon herself the whole expenses of the flying colloquies exchanged with stragglers on the road. What
struck me with most astonishment, however, was the
liberal manner of our fair driver, who made no scruple of taking a leap, with the reins in her hand, and
seating herself dexterously upon the shafts (or, in
Westmorland phrase, the *trams*) of the cart. From
Ambleside—and without one foot of intervening flat
ground—begins to rise the famous ascent of Kirk-

stone; after which, for three long miles, all riding in a cart drawn by one horse becomes impossible. The ascent is computed at three miles, but is, probably, a little more. In some parts it is almost frightfully steep; for the road, being only the original mountain track of shepherds, gradually widened and improved from age to age (especially since the era of tourists began), is carried over ground which no engineer, even in alpine countries, would have viewed as practicable.

The pass, at the summit of this ascent, is nothing to be compared in sublimity with the pass under Great Gavil from Wastdalehead; but it is solemn, and profoundly impressive. At a height so awful as this, it may be easily supposed that all human dwellings have been long left behind: no sound of human life, no bells of churches or chapels ever ascend so far. And, as is noticed in Wordsworth's fine stanzas upon this memorable pass, the only sound that, even in noonday, disturbs the sleep of the weary pedestrian, is that of the bee murmuring amongst the mountain flowers—a sound as ancient

As man's imperial front, and woman's roseate bloom.

This way, and (which, to the sentiment of the case, is an important point) this way *of necessity* and *inevitably*, passed the Roman legions; for it is a mathematic impossibility that any other route could be found for an army nearer to the eastward of this pass than by way of Kendal and Shap; nearer to the westward, than by way of Legbesthwaite and St. John's Vale (and so by Threlkeld to Penrith). Now, these two roads are exactly twenty-five miles apart; and, since a Roman cohort was stationed at Ambleside (*Amboglane*), it is pretty evident that this cohort would not correspond with the more northerly stations by either of these remote routes—having immediately before it this direct though difficult pass to Kirkstone. On the solitary area of tableland which you find at the summit—though, Heaven knows, you might almost cover it with a drawing-room carpet, so suddenly does the mountain take to its old trick of precipitous descent, on both sides alike—there are only two objects to remind you of man and his workmanship. One is a guide-post—always a picturesque and interesting object, because it expresses a wild country and a labyrinth of roads, and often made much more interesting (as in this case) by the lichens which cover it, and which record the generations of men to whom it has done its office; as also by the crucifix form, which inevitably recalls, in all mountainous regions, the crosses of Catholic lands, raised to the memory of wayfaring men who have perished by the hand of the assassin. The other memorial of man is even more interesting— Amongst the fragments of rock which lie in the confusion of a ruin on each side of the road, one there is which exceeds the rest in height, and which, in shape, presents a very close resemblance to a church. This lies to the left of the road as you are going from Ambleside; and from its name, Churchstone (Kirkstone), is derived the name of the pass, and from the pass the name of the mountain. The guide-post—which was really the work of man—tells those going southwards (for to those who go northwards it is useless, since, in that direction, there is no choice of roads) that the left hand track conducts you to Troutbeck, and Bowness, and Kendal, the right hand to Ambleside, and Hawkshead, and Ulverstone. The church—which is but a phantom of man's handiwork—might, however, really be mistaken for such, were it not that the rude and almost inaccessible state of the adjacent ground proclaims the truth. As to size, *that* is remarkably difficult to estimate

upon wild heaths or mountain solitudes, where there
are no leadings through gradations of distance, nor
any artificial standards, from which height or breadth
can be properly deduced. This mimic church, however,
has a peculiarly fine effect in this wild situation, which
leaves so far below the tumults of this world: the phantom church, by suggesting the phantom and evanescent
image of a congregation, where never congregation
met; of the pealing organ, where never sound was
heard except of wild natural notes, or else of the wind
rushing through these mighty gates of everlasting rock
—in this way, the fanciful image that accompanies the
traveller on his road, for half a mile or more, serves to
bring out the antagonist feeling of intense and awful
solitude, which is the natural and presiding sentiment
—the *religio loci*—that broods for ever over the romantic pass.

Having walked up Kirkstone, we ascended our cart
again; then rapidly descended to Brothers' Water—a
lake which lies immediately below; and, about three
miles further, through endless woods and under the
shade of mighty fells, immediate dependencies and
processes of the still more mighty Helvellyn, we approached the vale of Patterdale, when, by moonlight,
we reached the inn. Here we found horses—by whom
furnished I never asked nor heard; perhaps I owe somebody for a horse to this day. All I remember is—that
through those most romantic woods and rocks of Sty-
barren—through those silent glens of Glencoin and
Glenridding—through that most romantic of parks
then belonging to the Duke of Norfolk, viz. Gobarrow
Park—we saw alternately, for four miles, the most
grotesque and the most awful spectacles—

Abbey windows
And Moorish temples of the Hindoos,

all fantastic, all as unreal and shadowy as the moonlight which created them; whilst, at every angle of the
road, broad gleams came upwards of Ulleswater,
stretching for nine miles northward, but, fortunately
for its effect, broken into three watery chambers of almost equal length, and rarely visible at once. At the
foot of the lake, in a house called Ewsmere, we passed
the night, having accomplished about twenty-two
miles only in our day's walking and riding.

The next day Wordsworth and I, leaving at Ewsmere the rest of our party, spent the morning in roaming through the woods of Lowther, and, towards evening, we dined together at Emont Bridge, one mile
short of Penrith. Afterwards, we walked into Penrith.
There Wordsworth left me in excellent quarters—the
house of Captain Wordsworth, from which the family
happened to be absent. Whither he himself adjourned,
I know not, nor on what business; however, it occupied
him throughout the next day; and, therefore, I employed myself in sauntering along the road, about
seventeen miles, to Keswick. There I had been directed
to ask for Greta Hall, which, with some little difficulty,
I found; for it stands out of the town a few hundred
yards, upon a little eminence overhanging the river
Greta. It was about seven o'clock when I reached
Southey's door; for I had stopped to dine at a little public house in Threlkeld, and had walked slowly for the
last two hours in the dark. The arrival of a stranger
occasioned a little sensation in the house; and, by the
time the front door could be opened, I saw Mrs. Coleridge, and a gentleman whom I could not doubt to be
Southey, standing, very hospitably, to greet my entrance. Southey was, in person, somewhat taller than
Wordsworth, being about five feet eleven in height, or
a trifle more, whilst Wordsworth was about five feet
ten; and, partly from having slender limbs, partly

from being more symmetrically formed about the shoulders than Wordsworth, he struck one as a better and lighter figure, to the effect of which his dress contributed; for he wore pretty constantly a short jacket and pantaloons, and had much the air of a Tyrolese mountaineer.

On the next day arrived Wordsworth. I could read at once, in the manner of the two authors, that they were not on particularly friendly, or rather, I should say, confidential terms. It seemed to me as if both had silently said—"We are too much men of sense to quarrel because we do not happen particularly to like each other's writings: we are neighbours, or what pass for such in the country. Let us show each other the courtesies which are becoming to men of letters; and, for any closer connexion, our distance of thirteen miles may be always sufficient to keep us from *that*." In after life, it is true—fifteen years, perhaps, from this time— many circumstances combined to bring Southey and Wordsworth into more intimate terms of friendship: agreement in politics, sorrows which had happened to both alike in their domestic relations, and the sort of tolerance for different opinions in literature, or, indeed, in anything else, which advancing years and experience are sure to bring with them. But at this period, Southey and Wordsworth entertained a mutual esteem, but did not cordially like each other. Indeed, it would have been odd if they had. Wordsworth lived in the open air: Southey in his library, which Coleridge used to call his wife. Southey had particularly elegant habits (Wordsworth called them finical) in the use of books. Wordsworth, on the other hand, was so negligent, and so self-indulgent in the same case, that, as Southey, laughing, expressed it to me some years afterwards, when I was staying at Greta Hall on a visit— "To introduce Wordsworth into one's library is like

letting a bear into a tulip garden." What I mean by
self-indulgent is this: generally it happens that new
books baffle and mock one's curiosity by their uncut
leaves; and the trial is pretty much the same as when,
in some town where you are utterly unknown, you
meet the postman at a distance from your inn, with
some letter for yourself from a dear, dear friend in
foreign regions, without money to pay the postage.
How is it with you, dear reader, in such a case? Are
you not tempted (*I am* grievously) to snatch the letter
from his tantalizing hand, spite of the roar which you
anticipate of "Stop thief!" and make off as fast as you
can for some solitary street in the suburbs, where you
may instantly effect an entrance upon your new estate
before the purchase money is paid down? Such were
Wordsworth's feelings in regard to new books; of
which the first exemplification I had was early in my
acquaintance with him, and on occasion of a book
which (if any could) justified the too summary style
of his advances in rifling its charms. On a level with
the eye, when sitting at the tea-table in my little cottage at Grasmere, stood the collective works of Edmund Burke. The book was to me an eye-sore and an
ear-sore for many a year, in consequence of the cacoph-
onous title lettered by the bookseller upon the back
—*Burke's Works*. I have heard it said, by the way, that
Donne's intolerable defect of ear grew out of his own
baptismal name, when harnessed to his own surname—
John Donne. No man, it was said, who had listened to
this hideous jingle from childish years, could fail to
have his genius for discord, and the abominable in
sound, improved to the utmost. Not less dreadful than
John Donne was *Burke's Works;* which, however, on
the old principle, that every day's work is no day's
work, continued to annoy me for twenty-one years.
Wordsworth took down the volume; unfortunately it

was uncut; fortunately, and by a special Providence
as to him, it seemed, tea was proceeding at the time.
Dry toast required butter; butter required knives; and
knives then lay on the table; but sad it was for the virgin purity of Mr. Burke's as yet unsunned pages, that
every knife bore upon its blade testimonies of the service it had rendered. Did *that* stop Wordsworth? Did
that cause him to call for another knife? Not at all; he

Look'd at the knife that caus'd his pain:
And look'd and sigh'd, and look'd and sigh'd again;

and then, after this momentary tribute to regret, he
tore his way into the heart of the volume with this
knife, that left its greasy honours behind it upon every
page: and are they not there to this day? This personal
experience first brought me acquainted with Wordsworth's habits in that particular especially, with his
intense impatience for one minute's delay which would
have brought a remedy; and yet the reader may believe
that it is no affectation in me to say that fifty such cases
could have given me but little pain, when I explain
that whatever could be made good by money, at that
time, I did not regard. Had the book been an old black-
letter book, having a value from its rarity, I should
have been disturbed in an indescribable degree; but
simply with reference to the utter impossibility of reproducing that mode of value. As to the Burke, it was
a common book; I had bought the book, with many
others, at the sale of Sir Cecil Wray's library, for about
two-thirds of the selling price: I could easily replace
it; and I mention the case at all, only to illustrate the
excess of Wordsworth's outrages on books, which made
him, in Southey's eyes, a mere monster; for Southey's
beautiful library was his estate; and this difference of
habits would alone have sufficed to alienate him from
Wordsworth. And so I argued in other cases of the

same nature. Meantime, had Wordsworth done as
Coleridge did, how cheerfully should I have acquiesced
in his destruction (such as it was, in a pecuniary sense)
of books, as the very highest obligation he could confer. Coleridge often spoiled a book; but, in the course
of doing this, he enriched that book with so many and
so valuable notes, tossing about him, with such lavish
profusion, from such a cornucopia of discursive reading, and such a fusing intellect, commentaries so
many-angled and so many-coloured that I have envied
many a man whose luck has placed him in the way of
such injuries; and that man must have been a churl
(though, God knows! too often this churl *has* existed)
who could have found in his heart to complain. But
Wordsworth rarely, indeed, wrote on the margin of
books; and, when he did, nothing could less illustrate
his intellectual superiority. The comments were such
as might have been made by anybody. Once, I remember, before I had ever seen Wordsworth—probably a
year before—I met a person who had once enjoyed the
signal honour of travelling with him to London. It was
in a stage-coach. But the person in question well knew
who it was that had been his *compagnon de voyage*.
Immediately he was glorified in my eyes. "And," said
I, to this glorified gentleman (who, *par parenthése*,
was also a donkey), "now, as you travelled nearly
three hundred miles in the company of Mr. Wordsworth, consequently (for this was in 1805) during two
nights and two days, doubtless you must have heard
many profound remarks that would inevitably fall
from his lips." Nay, Coleridge had also been of the
party; and, if Wordsworth *solus* could have been dull,
was it within human possibilities that these *gemini*
should have been so? "Was it possible?" I said; and
perhaps my donkey, who looked like one that had been
immoderately threatened, at last took courage; his eye

brightened; and he intimated that he *did* remember something that Wordsworth had said—an "observe," as the Scotch call it.

"Ay, indeed; and what was it now? What did the great man say?"

"Why, sir, in fact, and to make a long story short, on coming near to London, we breakfasted at Baldock —you know Baldock? It's in Hertfordshire. Well, now, sir, would you believe it, though we were quite in regular time, the breakfast was precisely good for nothing?"

"And Wordsworth?"

"He observed——"

"What did he observe?"

"That the buttered toast looked, for all the world, as if it had been soaked in hot water."

Ye heavens! *"buttered toast!"* And was it *this* I waited for? Now, thought I, had Henry Mackenzie been breakfasting with Wordsworth at Baldock (and, strange enough! in years to come I *did* breakfast with Henry Mackenzie, for the solitary time I ever met him, and at Wordsworth's house in Rydal), he would have carried off one sole reminiscence from the meeting— namely, a confirmation of his creed, that we English are all dedicated, from our very cradle, to the luxuries of the palate, and peculiarly to this.[1] *Proh pudor!* Yet, in sad sincerity, Wordsworth's pencil-notices in books were quite as disappointing. In *Roderick Random*, for

[1] It is not known to the English, but it is a fact which I can vouch for, from my six or seven years' residence in Scotland [written in 1839], that the Scotch, one and all, believe it to be an inalienable characteristic of an Englishman to be fond of good eating. What indignation have I, and how many a time, had occasion to feel and utter on this subject? But of this at some other time. Meantime, the Man of Feeling had this creed in excess; and, in some paper (of *The Mirror* or *The Lounger*), he describes an English tourist in Scotland by saying—"I

example, I found a note upon a certain luscious description, to the effect that "such things should be left to the imagination of the reader—not expressed." In another place, that it was "improper"; and, in a third, that "the principle laid down was doubtful," or, as Sir Roger de Coverley observes, "that much might be said on both sides." All this, however, indicates nothing more than that different men require to be roused by different stimulants. Wordsworth, in his marginal notes, thought of nothing but delivering himself of a strong feeling, with which he wished to challenge the reader's sympathy. Coleridge imagined an audience before him; and, however doubtful that consummation might seem, I am satisfied that he never wrote a line for which he did not feel the momentary inspiration of sympathy and applause, under the confidence, that, sooner or later, all which he had committed to the chance margins of books would converge and assemble in some common reservoir of reception. Bread scattered upon the water will be gathered after many days. This, perhaps, was the consolation that supported him; and the prospect that, for a time, his Arethusa of truth would flow underground, did not, perhaps, disturb, but rather cheered and elevated, the sublime old somnambulist.[1] Meantime, Wordsworth's habits of using books

would not wish to be thought national; yet, in mere reverence for truth, I am bound to say, and to declare to all the world (let who will be offended), that the first innkeeper in Scotland under whose roof we met with genuine buttered toast was an Englishman."

[1] Meantime, if it did not disturb *him*, it ought to disturb *us*, his immediate successors, who are at once the most likely to retrieve these *losses* by direct efforts, and the least likely to benefit by any casual or indirect retrievals, such as will be produced by time. Surely a subscription should be set on foot to recover all books enriched by his marginal notes. I would subscribe; and I know others who would largely.

—which, I am satisfied, would, in those days, alone have kept him at a distance from most men with fine libraries—were not vulgar; not the habits of those who turn over the page by means of a wet finger (though even this abomination I have seen perpetrated by a Cambridge tutor and fellow of a college; but then he had been bred up as a ploughman, and the son of a ploughman) : no; but his habits were more properly barbarous and licentious, and in the spirit of audacity belonging *de jure* to no man but him who could plead an income of four or five hundred thousand per annum, and to whom the Bodleian or the Vatican would be a three years' purchase. Gross, meantime, was his delusion upon this subject. Himself he regarded as the golden mean between the too little and the too much of care for books; and, as it happened that every one of his friends far exceeded him in this point, curiously felicitous was the explanation which he gave of this superfluous care, so as to bring it within the natural operation of some known fact in the man's peculiar situation. Southey (he was by nature something of an old bachelor) had his house filled with pretty articles —*bijouterie*, and so forth; and, naturally, he wished his books to be kept up to the same level—burnished and bright for show. Sir George Beaumont—this peculiarly elegant and accomplished man—was an old and most affectionate friend of Wordsworth's. Sir George Beaumont never had any children; if he had been so blessed, they, by familiarizing him with the spectacle of books ill used—stained, torn, mutilated, &c.—would have lowered the standard of his requisitions. The short solution of the whole case was—and it illustrated the nature of his education—he had never lived in a regular family at a time when habits are moulded. From boyhood to manhood he had been *sui juris*.

Returning to Southey and Greta Hall, both the house and the master may deserve a few words more of description. For the master, I have already sketched his person; and his face I profess myself unable to describe accurately. His hair was black, and yet his complexion was fair; his eyes I believe to be hazel and large; but I will not vouch for that fact: his nose aquiline; and he has a remarkable habit of looking up into the air, as if looking at abstractions. The expression of his face was that of a very acute and aspiring man. So far, it was even noble, as it conveyed a feeling of a serene and gentle pride, habitually familiar with elevating subjects of contemplation. And yet it was impossible that this pride could have been offensive to anybody, chastened as it was by the most unaffected modesty; and this modesty made evident and prominent by the constant expression of reverence for the great men of the age (when he happened to esteem them such), and for all the great patriarchs of our literature. The point in which Southey's manner failed the most in conciliating regard was in all which related to the external expressions of friendliness. No man could be more sincerely hospitable—no man more essentially disposed to give up even his time (the possession which he most valued) to the service of his friends. But there was an air of reserve and distance about him—the reserve of a lofty, self-respecting mind, but, perhaps, a little too freezing —in his treatment of all persons who were not among the *corps* of his ancient fireside friends. Still, even towards the veriest strangers, it is but justice to notice his extreme courtesy in sacrificing his literary employments for the day, whatever they might be, to the duty (for such he made it) of doing the honours of the lake and the adjacent mountains.

Southey was at that time (1807), and has continued ever since, the most industrious of all literary men on

record. A certain task he prescribed to himself every
morning before breakfast. This could not be a very
long one, for he breakfasted at nine, or soon after, and
never rose before eight, though he went to bed duly at
half-past ten; but, as I have many times heard him say,
less than nine hours' sleep he found insufficient. From
breakfast to a latish dinner (about half after five or
six) was his main period of literary toil. After dinner,
according to the accident of having or not having visitors in the house, he sat over his wine, or he retired to
his library again, from which, about eight, he was
summoned to tea. But, generally speaking, he closed
his *literary* toils at dinner; the whole of the hours after
that meal being dedicated to his correspondence. This,
it may be supposed, was unusually large, to occupy so
much of his time, for his letters rarely extended to any
length. At that period, the post, by way of Penrith,
reached Keswick about six or seven in the evening. And
so pointedly regular was Southey in all his habits that,
short as the time was, all letters were answered on the
same evening which brought them. At tea, he read the
London papers. It was perfectly astonishing to men of
less methodical habits to find how much he got through
of elaborate business by his unvarying system of arrangement in the distribution of his time. We often
hear it said, in accounts of pattern ladies and gentlemen (what Coleridge used contemptuously to style
goody people), that they found time for everything;
that business never interrupted pleasure; that labours
of love and charity never stood in the way of courtesy
and personal enjoyment. This is easy to say—easy to
put down as one feature of an imaginary portrait: but
I must say that in actual life I have seen few such cases.
Southey, however, *did* find time for everything. It
moved the sneers of some people, that even his poetry
was composed according to a predetermined rule; that

so many lines should be produced, by contract, as it were, before breakfast; so many at such another definite interval. And I acknowledge that so far I went along with the sneerers as to marvel exceedingly how that *could* be possible. But, if *a priori* one laughed and expected to see verses corresponding to this mechanic rule of construction, *a posteriori* one was bound to judge of the verses as one found them. Supposing them good, they were entitled to honour, no matter for the previous reasons which made it possible that they would *not* be good. And generally, however undoubtedly they *ought* to have been bad, the world has pronounced them good. In fact, they *are* good; and the sole objection to them is, that they are too intensely *objective*—too much reflect the mind, as spreading itself out upon external things—too little exhibit the mind as introverting itself upon its own thoughts and feelings. This, however, is an objection which only seems to limit the range of the poetry—and all poetry *is* limited in its range: none comprehends more than a section of the human power.

Meantime, the prose of Southey was that by which he lived. The *Quarterly Review* it was by which, as he expressed it to myself in 1810, he "*made the pot boil.*" About the same time, possibly as early as 1808 (for I think that I remember in that Journal an account of the Battle of Vimiera), Southey was engaged by an Edinburgh publisher (Constable, was it not?) to write the entire historical part of the *Edinburgh Annual Register*, at a salary of £400 per annum. Afterwards, the publisher, who was intensely national, and, doubtless, never from the first cordially relished the notion of importing English aid into a city teeming with briefless barristers and variety of talent, threw out a hint that perhaps he might reduce the salary to £300. Just about this time I happened to see Southey, who said laughingly—"If the man of Edinburgh does this, I shall *strike* for an advance of wages." I presume that he *did* strike, and, like many other "operatives," without effect. Those who work for lower wages during a strike are called *snobs*, the men who stand out being *nobs*. Southey became a resolute nob; but some snob was found in Edinburgh, some youthful advocate, who accepted £300 per annum, and thenceforward Southey lost this part of his income.

Of Southey, meantime, I had learned, upon this brief and hurried visit, so much in confirmation or in extension of my tolerably just preconceptions with regard to his character and manners, as left me not a very great deal to add, and nothing at all to alter, through the many years which followed of occasional intercourse with his family, and domestic knowledge of his habits. A man of more serene and even temper could not be imagined; nor more uniformly cheerful in his tone of spirits; nor more unaffectedly polite and courteous in his demeanour to strangers; nor more hospitable in his own wrong—I mean by the painful sacrifices which hospitality entailed upon him of time so exceedingly precious that, during his winter and spring months of solitude, or whenever he was left absolute master of its distribution, every half hour in the day had its peculiar duty. In the still "weightier matters of the law," in cases that involved appeals to conscience and high moral principle, I believe Southey to be as exemplary a man as can ever have lived. Were it to his own instant ruin, I am satisfied that he would do justice and fulfil his duty under any possible difficulties, and through the very strongest temptations to do otherwise. For honour the most delicate, for integrity the firmest, and for generosity within the limits of prudence, Southey cannot well have a superior; and

in the lesser moralities—those which govern the daily
habits, and transpire through the manners—he is certainly a better man—that is (with reference to the
minor principle concerned), a more *amiable* man—
than Wordsworth. He is less capable, for instance, of
usurping an undue share of the conversation; he is
more uniformly disposed to be charitable in his transient colloquial judgements upon doubtful actions of
his neighbours; more gentle and winning in his condescensions to inferior knowledge or powers of mind;
more willing to suppose it possible that he himself may
have fallen into an error; more tolerant of avowed indifference towards his own writings (though, by the
way, I shall have something to offer in justification of
Wordsworth, upon this charge); and, finally, if the
reader will pardon a violent instance of anti-climax,
much more ready to volunteer his assistance in carrying a lady's reticule or parasol.

As a more *amiable* man (taking that word partly in
the French sense, partly also in the loftier English
sense), it might be imagined that Southey would be a
more eligible companion than Wordsworth. But this is
not so; and chiefly for three reasons which more than
counterbalance Southey's greater amiability: *first*, because the natural reserve of Southey, which I have
mentioned before, makes it peculiarly difficult to place
yourself on terms of intimacy with him; *secondly*, because the range of his conversation is more limited than
that of Wordsworth—dealing less with life and the
interests of life—more exclusively with books; *thirdly*,
because the style of his conversation is less flowing and
diffusive—less expansive—more apt to clothe itself in
a keen, sparkling, aphoristic form—consequently
much sooner and more frequently coming to an abrupt
close. A sententious, epigrammatic form of delivering
opinions has a certain effect of *clenching* a subject,

which makes it difficult to pursue it without a corresponding smartness of expression, and something of
the same antithetic point and equilibration of clauses.
Not that the reader is to suppose in Southey a showy
master of rhetoric and colloquial sword-play, seeking
to strike and to dazzle by his brilliant hits or adroit
evasions. The very opposite is the truth. He seeks, indeed, to be effective, not for the sake of display, but as
the readiest means of retreating from display, and the
necessity for display: feeling that his station in literature and his laurelled honours make him a mark for
the curiosity and interest of the company—that a
standing appeal is constantly turning to him for his
opinion—a latent call always going on for his voice on
the question of the moment—he is anxious to comply
with this requisition at as slight a cost as may be of
thought and time. His heart is continually reverting
to his wife, viz. his library; and, that he may waste as
little effort as possible upon his conversational exercises—that the little he wishes to say may appear preg-
nant with much meaning—he finds it advantageous,
and, moreover, the style of his mind naturally prompts
him, to adopt a trenchant, pungent, aculeated form of
terse, glittering, stenographic sentences—sayings
which have the air of laying down the law without any
locus penitentiæ or privilege of appeal, but are not
meant to do so; in short, aiming at brevity for the company as well as for himself, by cutting off all opening
for discussion and desultory talk through the sudden
winding up that belongs to a sententious aphorism.
The hearer feels that "the record is closed"; and he has
a sense of this result as having been accomplished by
something like an oracular laying down of the law *ex
cathedra:* but this is an indirect collateral impression
from Southey's manner, and far from the one he medi-
tates or wishes. An oracular manner he does certainly

affect in certain dilemmas of a languishing or loitering conversation; not the peremptoriness, meantime, not the imperiousness of the oracle is what he seeks for, but its brevity, its dispatch, its conclusiveness.

Finally, as a fourth reason why Southey is less fitted for a genial companion than Wordsworth, his spirits have been, of late years, in a lower key than those of the latter. The tone of Southey's animal spirits was never at any time raised beyond the standard of an ordinary sympathy; there was in him no tumult, no agitation of passion; his organic and constitutional sensibilities were healthy, sound, perhaps strong—but not profound, not excessive. Cheerful he was, and animated at all times; but he levied no tributes on the spirits or the feelings beyond what all people could furnish. One reason why his bodily temperament never, like that of Wordsworth, threw him into a state of tumultuous excitement which required intense and elaborate conversation to work off the excessive fervour, was, that, over and above his far less fervid constitution of mind and body, Southey rarely took any exercise; he led a life as sedentary, except for the occasional excursions in summer (extorted from his sense of kindness and hospitality), as that of a city tailor. And it was surprising to many people, who did not know by experience the prodigious effect upon the mere bodily health of regular and congenial mental labour, that Southey should be able to maintain health so regular, and cheerfulness so uniformly serene. Cheerful, however, he was, in those early years of my acquaintance with him; but it was manifest to a thoughtful observer that his golden equanimity was bound up in a threefold chain—in a conscience clear of all offence, in the recurring enjoyments from his honourable industry, and in the gratification of his parental affections. If any one cord should give way, there (it seemed) would be an end to Southey's tranquillity. He had a son at that time, Herbert [1] Southey, a child in petticoats when I first knew him, very interesting even then, but annually putting forth fresh blossoms of unusual promise, that made even indifferent people fear for the safety of one so finely organized, so delicate in his sensibilities, and so prematurely accomplished. As to his father, it became evident that he lived almost in the light of young Herbert's smiles, and that the very pulses of his heart played in unison to the sound of his son's laughter. There was in his manner towards this child, and towards this only, something that marked an excess of delirious doting, perfectly unlike the ordinary chastened movements of Southey's affections; and something also which indicated a vague fear about him; a premature unhappiness, as if already the inaudible tread of calamity could be perceived, as if already he had lost him; which, for the latter years of the boy's life, seemed to poison the blessing of his presence.

A stronger evidence I cannot give of Southey's trem-

[1] Why he was called Herbert, if my young readers inquire, I must reply, that I do not precisely know; because I know of reasons too many by half why he might have been so called. Derwent Coleridge, the second son of Samuel Taylor Coleridge, and first cousin of Herbert Southey, was so called from the Lake of Keswick, commonly styled Derwentwater, which gave the title of Earl to the noble, and the noble-minded, though erring, family of the Radcliffes, who gave up, like heroes and martyrs, their lives and the finest estates in England for one who was incapable of appreciating the service. One of the islands on this lake is dedicated to St. Herbert, and this *might* have given a name to Southey's first-born child. But it is more probable that he derived this name from Dr. Herbert, uncle to the laureate.

bling apprehensiveness about this child than that the
only rude thing I ever knew him to do, the only dis-
courteous thing, was done on his account. A party of
us, chiefly composed of Southey's family and his visitors, were in a sailboat upon the lake. Herbert was one
of this party; and at that time not above five or six
years old. In landing upon one of the islands, most of
the gentlemen were occupied in assisting the ladies
over the thwarts of the boat; and one gentleman,
merely a stranger, observing this, good-naturedly took
up Herbert in his arms, and was stepping with him
most carefully from thwart to thwart, when Southey,
in a perfect frenzy of anxiety for his boy, his "moon"
as he used to call him (I suppose from some pun of his
own, or some mistake of the child's upon the equivocal
word *sun*), rushed forward, and tore him out of the
arms of the stranger without one word of apology; nor,
in fact, under the engrossing panic of the moment, lest
an unsteady movement along with the rocking and undulating of the boat should throw his little boy over-
board into the somewhat stormy waters of the lake,
did Southey become aware of his own exceedingly dis-
courteous action: fear for his boy quelled his very
power of perception. *That* the stranger, on reflection,
understood; a race of emotions travelled over his countenance. I saw the whole, a silent observer from the
shore. First a hasty blush of resentment mingled with
astonishment: then a good-natured smile of indulgence
to the *naïveté* of the paternal feeling as displaying itself in the act, and the accompanying gestures of frenzied impatience; finally, a considerate, grave expression of acquiescence in the whole act; but with a
pitying look towards father and son, as too probably
destined under such agony of affection to trials perhaps insupportable. If I interpreted aright the stran-

ger's feelings, he did not read their destinies amiss.
Herbert became, with his growing years, a child of
more and more hope; but, therefore, the object of more
and more fearful solicitude. He read, and read; and he
became at last

A very learned youth—

to borrow a line from his uncle's beautiful poem on the
wild boy who fell into a heresy whilst living under the
patronage of a Spanish grandee, and finally escaped
from a probable martyrdom by sailing up a great
American river, wide as any sea, after which he was
never heard of again. The learned youth of the river
Greta had an earlier and more sorrowful close to his
career. Possibly from want of exercise, combined with
inordinate exercise of the cerebral organs, a disease
gradually developed itself in the heart. It was not a
mere disorder in the functions, it was a disease in the
structure of the organ, and admitted of no permanent
relief, consequently of no final hope. He died [at the
age of ten]; and with him died for ever the golden
hopes, the radiant felicity, and the internal serenity, of
the unhappy father. It was from Southey himself,
speaking without external signs of agitation, calmly,
dispassionately, almost coldly, but with the coldness
of a settled despondency, that I heard, whilst accompanying him through Grasmere on his road homewards to Keswick from some visit he had been paying
to Wordsworth at Rydal Mount, his settled feelings
and convictions as connected with that loss. For *him*,
in this world, he said, happiness there could be none;
for his tenderest affections, the very deepest by many
degrees which he had ever known, were now buried in
the grave with his youthful and too brilliant Herbert!

SOUTHEY, WORDSWORTH, AND COLERIDGE

(First published in *Tait's Magazine*, August, 1839)

A CIRCUMSTANCE which, as much as anything, expounded to every eye the characteristic distinctions between Wordsworth and Southey, and would not suffer a stranger to forget it for a moment, was the insignificant place and consideration allowed to the small book-collection of the former, contrasted with the splendid library of the latter. The two or three hundred volumes of Wordsworth occupied a little, homely, painted book-case, fixed into one of two shallow recesses, formed on each side of the fireplace by the projection of the chimney in the little sitting-room up stairs which he had already described as his half kitchen and half parlour. They were ill bound, or not bound at all—in boards, sometimes in tatters; many were imperfect as to the number of volumes, mutilated as to the number of pages; sometimes, where it seemed worth while, the defects being supplied by manuscript; sometimes not: in short, everything showed that the books were for use, and not for show; and their limited amount showed that their possessor must have independent sources of enjoyment to fill up the major part of his time. In reality, when the weather was tolerable, I believe that Wordsworth rarely resorted to his books (unless, perhaps, to some little pocket edition of a poet which accompanied him in his rambles) except in the evenings, or after he had tired himself by walking. On the other hand, Southey's collection occupied a separate room, the largest, and every way the most agreeable in the house; and this room was styled, and not ostentatiously (for it really mer

ited that name), the Library. The house itself, Greta
Hall, stood upon a little eminence (as I have before
mentioned), overhanging the river Greta. There was
nothing remarkable in its internal arrangements. In
all respects it was a very plain, unadorned family
dwelling: large enough, by a little contrivance, to ac-
commodate two, or, in some sense, three families, viz.
Mr. Southey and *his* family, Mr. Coleridge and *his*,
together with Mrs. Lovell, who, when her son was
with her, might be said to compose a third. Mrs. Coleridge, Mrs. Southey, and Mrs. Lovell were sisters; all
having come originally from Bristol; and, as the different sets of children in this one house had each three
several aunts, all the ladies, by turns, assuming that relation twice over, it was one of Southey's many amusing jests, to call the hill on which Greta Hall was
placed the *ant-hill*.

In the morning, the two families might live apart:
but they met at dinner, and in a common drawing-
room; and Southey's library, in both senses of the
word, was placed at the service of all the ladies alike.
However, they did not intrude upon him, except in
cases where they wished for a larger reception room, or
a more interesting place for suggesting the topics of
conversation. Interesting this room was, indeed, and in
a degree not often rivalled. The library—the collection of books, I mean, which formed the most conspicuous part of its furniture within—was in all senses a
good one. The books were chiefly English, Spanish,
and Portuguese; well selected, being the great cardinal
classics of the three literatures; fine copies, and decorated externally with a reasonable elegance, so as to
make them in harmony with the other embellishments
of the room. This effect was aided by the horizontal
arrangement upon brackets of many rare manuscripts
—Spanish or Portuguese. Made thus gay within, this

room stood in little need of attractions from without.
Yet, even upon the gloomiest day of winter, the landscape from the different windows was too permanently
commanding in its grandeur, too essentially independent of the seasons or the pomp of woods, to fail in fascinating the gaze of the coldest and dullest of spectators.
The lake of Derwentwater in one direction, with its
lovely islands—a lake about ten miles in circuit, and
shaped pretty much like a boy's kite; the lake of Bas-
sinthwaite in another; the mountains of Newlands, arranging themselves like pavilions; the gorgeous confusion of Borrowdale just revealing its sublime chaos
through the narrow vista of its gorge: all these objects
lay in different angles to the front; whilst the sullen
rear, not fully visible on this side of the house, was
closed for many a league by the vast and towering
masses of Skiddaw and Blencathara—mountains which
are rather to be considered as frontier barriers, and
chains of hilly ground, cutting the county of Cumberland into great chambers and different climates, than
as insulated eminences, so vast is the area which they
occupy; though there *are* also such separate and insulated heights, and nearly amongst the highest in the
country. Southey's lot had therefore fallen, locally
considered, into a goodly heritage. This grand pano-
rama of mountain scenery, so varied, so expansive, and
yet having the delightful feeling about it of a deep seclusion and dell-like sequestration from the world—a
feeling which, in the midst of so expansive an area
spread out below his windows, could not have been sustained by any barriers less elevated than Glaramara,
Skiddaw, or (which could be also descried) "the
mighty Helvellyn and Catchedicam"—this congregation of hill and lake, so wide, and yet so prison-like in
its separation from all beyond it, lay for ever under the
eyes of Southey. His position locally, and, in some re-

spects, intellectually, reminded one of Gibbon: but with great advantage in the comparison to Southey. The little town of Keswick and its adjacent lake bore something of the same relation to mighty London that Geneva and its lake may be thought to bear towards brilliant Paris. Southey, like Gibbon, was a miscellaneous scholar; he, like Gibbon, of vast historical research; he, like Gibbon, signally industrious, and patient, and elaborate in collecting the materials for his historical works. Like Gibbon, he had dedicated a life of competent ease, in a pecuniary sense, to literature; like Gibbon, he had gathered to the shores of a beautiful lake, remote from great capitals, a large, or, at least, sufficient library (in each case, I believe, the library ranged, as to numerical amount, between seven and ten thousand); and, like Gibbon, he was the most accomplished *littérateur* amongst the erudite scholars of his time, and the most of an erudite scholar amongst the accomplished *littérateurs*. After all these points of agreement known, it remains as a pure advantage on the side of Southey—a mere *lucro ponatur*—that he was a poet; and, by all men's confession, a respectable poet, brilliant in his descriptive powers, and fascinating in his narration, however much he might want of

The vision and the faculty divine.

It is remarkable amongst the series of parallelisms that have been or might be pursued between two men, that both had the honour of retreating from a parliamentary life; Gibbon, after some silent and inert experience of that warfare; Southey, with a prudent foresight of the ruin to his health and literary usefulness, won from the experience of his nearest friends.

I took leave of Southey in 1807, at the descent into the vale of Legbesthwaite, as I have already noticed.

One year afterwards, I became a permanent resident in his neighbourhood; and, although, on various accounts, my intercourse with him was at no time very strict, partly from the very uncongenial constitution of my own mind, and the different direction of my studies, partly from my reluctance to levy any tax on time so precious and so fully employed, I was yet on such terms for the next ten or eleven years that I might, in a qualified sense, call myself his friend.

Yes! there were long years through which Southey might respect me, I *him*. But the years came—for I have lived too long, reader, in relation to many things! and the report of me would have been better, or more uniform at least, had I died some twenty years ago— the years came in which circumstances made me an Opium-Eater; years through which a shadow as of sad eclipse sate and rested upon my faculties; years through which I was careless of all but those who lived within *my* inner circle, within "my heart of hearts"; years—ah! heavenly years!—through which I lived, beloved, *with* thee, *to* thee, *for* thee, *by* thee! Ah! happy, happy years! in which I was a mere football of reproach, but in which every wind and sounding hurricane of wrath or contempt flew by like chasing enemies past some defying gates of adamant, and left me too blessed in thy smiles—angel of life!—to heed the curses or the mocking which sometimes I heard raving outside of our impregnable Eden. What any man said of me in those days, what he thought, did I ask? did I care? Then it was, or nearly then, that I ceased to see, ceased to hear of Southey; as much abstracted from all which concerned the world outside, and from the Southeys, or even the Coleridges, in its van, as though I had lived with the darlings of my heart in the centre of Canadian forests, and all men else in the centre of Hindostan.

There were (and perhaps more justly I might say there *are*) two notions currently received about Southey, one of which is altogether erroneous, and the other true only in a limited sense. The first is the belief that he belonged to what is known as the Lake school in poetry; with respect to which all that I need say in this place is involved in his own declaration frankly made to myself in Easedale, during the summer of 1812: that he considered Wordsworth's theory of poetic diction, and still more his principles as to the selection of subjects, and as to what constituted a poetic treatment, as founded on error. There is certainly some community of phraseology between Southey and the other Lakers, naturally arising out of their joint reverence for Scriptural language: this was a field in which they met in common: else it shows but little discernment and power of valuing the essences of things, to have classed Southey in the same school with Wordsworth and Coleridge. The other popular notion about Southey which I conceive to be expressed with much too little limitation regards his style. He has been praised, and justly, for his plain, manly, unaffected English, until the parrot echoers of other men's judgements, who adopt all they relish with undistinguishing blindness, have begun to hold him up as a great master of his own language, and a classical model of fine composition. Now, if the error were only in the degree, it would not be worth while to notice it; but the truth is, that Southey's defects in this particular power are as striking as his characteristic graces. Let a subject arise—and almost in any path there is a ready possibility that it should—in which a higher tone is required, of splendid declamation, or of impassionate fervour, and Southey's style will immediately betray its want of the loftier qualities as flagrantly as it now asserts its powers in that unpretending form which is best suited to his level character of writing and his humbler choice of themes. It is to mistake the character of Southey's mind, which is elevated but not sustained by the higher modes of enthusiasm, to think otherwise. Were a magnificent dedication required, moving with a stately and measured solemnity, and putting forward some majestic pretensions, arising out of a long and laborious life; were a pleading required against some capital abuse of the earth—war, slavery, oppression in its thousand forms; were a *Defensio pro Populo Anglicano* required; Southey's is not the mind, and, by a necessary consequence, Southey's is not the style, for carrying such purposes into full and memorable effect. His style is *therefore* good, because it has been suited to his themes; and those themes have hitherto been either narrative, which usually imposes a modest diction, and a modest structure of sentences, or argumentative in that class which is too overburthened with details, with replies, with interruption, and every mode of discontinuity, to allow a thought of eloquence, or of the periodic style which a perfect eloquence instinctively seeks.

I here close my separate notice of the Lake Poets— meaning those three who were originally so denominated—three men upon whom posterity, in every age, will look back with interest as profound as, perhaps, belongs to any other names of our era; for it happens, not unfrequently, that the *personal* interest in the author is not in the direct ratio of that which belongs to his works: and the character of an author better qualified to command a vast popularity for the creations of his pen is oftentimes more of a universal character, less peculiar, less fitted to stimulate the curiosity, or to sustain the sympathy of the intellectual, than the profounder and more ascetic solemnity of a Wordsworth, or the prodigal and magnificent eccentricities of a

Coleridge. With respect to both of these gifted men, some interesting notices still remain in arrear; but these will more properly come forward in their natural places, as they happen to arise in after years in connexion with my own memoirs.

THE SARACEN'S HEAD

(First published in *Tait's Magazine*, December, 1839)

MY FIRST visit to the Wordsworths had been made in November, 1807; but, on that occasion, from the necessity of saving the Michaelmas Term at Oxford, for which I had barely left myself time, I stayed only one week. On the last day, I witnessed a scene, the first and the last of its kind that ever I *did* witness, almost too trivial to mention, except for the sake of showing what things occur in the realities of experience which a novelist could not venture to imagine. Wordsworth and his sister were under an engagement of some standing to dine on that day with a literary lady about four miles distant; and, as the southern mail, which I was to catch at a distance of eighteen miles, would not pass that point until long after midnight, Miss Wordsworth proposed that, rather than pass my time at an inn, I should join the dinner party; a proposal rather more suitable to her own fervent and hospitable temper than to the habits of our hostess, who must (from what I came to know of her in after years) have looked upon me as an intruder. Something *had* reached Miss Wordsworth of her penurious *ménage*, but nothing that approached the truth. I was presented to the lady, whom we found a perfect *bas bleu* of a very commonplace order, but having some other accomplishments beyond her slender acquaintance with literature. Our party consisted of six—our hostess, who might be about fifty years of age; a pretty timid young woman, who was there in the character of a humble friend; some stranger or other; the Wordsworths, and myself. The dinner was the very humblest and simplest I had ever seen—in that there was nothing to offend—I did not then know that the lady was very rich —but also it was flagrantly insufficient in quantity. Dinner, however, proceeded; when, without any removals, in came a kind of second course, in the shape of a solitary pheasant. This, in a cold manner, she asked me to try; but we, in our humility, declined for the present; and also in mere good-nature, not wishing to expose too palpably the insufficiency of her dinner. May I die the death of a traitor, if she did not proceed, without further question to any one of us (and, as to the poor young companion, no form of even invitation was conceded to her), and, in the eyes of us all, eat up the whole bird, from alpha to omega. Upon my honour, I thought to myself, this is a scene I would not have missed. It is well to know the possibilities of human nature. Could she have a bet depending on the issue, and would she explain all to us as soon as she had won her wager? Alas! no explanation ever came, except, indeed, that afterwards her character, put *en evidence* upon a score of occasions, too satisfactorily explained everything. No; it was, as Mr. Coleridge expresses it, a psychological curiosity—a hollow thing—and only once matched in all the course of my reading, in or out of romances; but that once, I grieve to say it, was by a king, and a sort of hero.

The Duchess of Marlborough it is who reports the shocking anecdote of William III, that actually Princess Anne, his future wife, durst not take any of the green peas brought to the dinner table, when that vegetable happened to be as yet scarce and premature.

There was a gentleman! And such a lady had we for our hostess. However, we all observed a suitable gravity; but afterwards, when we left the house, the remembrance affected us differently. Miss Wordsworth laughed with undissembled glee; but Wordsworth thought it too grave a matter for laughing—he was thoroughly disgusted, and said repeatedly, "A person cannot be honest, positively not honest, who is capable of such an act." The lady is dead, and I shall not mention her name: she lived only to gratify her selfish propensities; and two little anecdotes may show the outrageous character of her meanness. I was now on the debtor side of her dinner account, and, therefore, in a future year she readily accepted an invitation to come and dine with me at my cottage. But, on a subsequent occasion, when I was to have a few literary people at dinner, whom I knew that she greatly wished to meet, she positively replied thus—"No; I have already come with my young lady to dine with you; that puts me on the wrong side by one; now, if I were to come again, as I cannot leave Miss —— behind, I shall then be on the wrong side by three; and that is more than I could find opportunities to repay before I go up to London for the winter." "Very well," I said; "give me 3s. and *that* will settle the account." She laughed, but positively persisted in not coming until after dinner, notwithstanding she had to drive a distance of ten miles.

The other anecdote is worse. She was exceedingly careful of her health; and not thinking it healthy to drive about in a close carriage—which, besides, could not have suited the narrow mountain tracks, to which her sketching habits attracted her—she shut up her town carriage for the summer, and jobbed some little open car. Being a very large woman, and, moreover, a masculine woman, with a bronzed complexion, and always choosing to wear, at night, a turban, round hair

that was as black as that of the "Moors of Malabar,"
she presented an exact likeness of a Saracen's Head, as
painted over inn-doors; whilst the timid and delicate
young lady by her side looked like "dejected Pity" at
the side of "Revenge" when assuming the war-de-
nouncing trumpet. Some Oxonians and Cantabs, who,
at different times, were in the habit of meeting this
oddly assorted party in all nooks of the country, used
to move the question, whether the poor horse or the
young lady had the worst of it? At length the matter
was decided: the horse was fast going off this sublunary stage; and the Saracen's Head was told as much,
and with this little addition—that his death was owing
inter alia to starvation. Her answer was remarkable:
"But, my dear madam, that is his master's fault; I pay
so much a-day—he is to keep the horse." That might
be, but still the horse was dying, and dying in the way
stated. The Saracen's Head persisted in using him under those circumstances—such was her "bond"—and
in a short time the horse actually died. Yes, the horse
died—and died of starvation—or at least of an illness
caused originally by starvation: for so said, not merely
the whole population of the little neighbouring town,
but also the surgeon. Not long after, however, the lady,
the Saracen's Head, died herself; but I fear *not* of starvation; for, though something like it did prevail at her
table, she prudently reserved it all for her guests; in
fact, I never heard of such vigilant care, and so much
laudable exertion, applied to the promotion of health:
yet all failed, and, in a degree which confounded people's speculations upon the subject—for she did not
live much beyond sixty; whereas everybody supposed
that the management of her physical system entitled
her to outwear a century. Perhaps the prayers of horses
might avail to order it otherwise.

But the singular thing about this lady's mixed and

contradictory character was, that in London and Bath, where her peculiar habits of life were naturally less accurately known, she maintained the reputation of one who united the accomplishments of literature and art with a remarkable depth of sensibility, and a most amiable readiness to enter into the distresses of her friends by sympathy the most cordial and consolation the most delicate. And certainly there was one fact, even in her Westmorland life, that *did* lend some countenance to the southern picture of her amiableness: and this lay in the cheerfulness with which she gave up her time (*time*, but not much of her redundant money) to the promotion of the charitable schemes set on foot by the neighbouring ladies; sometimes for the education of poor children, sometimes for the visiting of the sick, &c., &c. I have heard several of those ladies express their gratitude for her exertions, and declare that she was about their best member. But their horror was undisguised when the weekly committee came, by rotation, to hold its sittings at her little villa; for, as the business occupied them frequently from eleven o'clock in the forenoon to a late dinner hour, and as many of them had a fifteen or twenty miles' drive, they needed some refreshments: but these were, of course, a "great idea" at the Saracen's Head; since, according to the epigram which illustrates the maxim of Tacitus that *omne ignotum pro magnifico*, and, applying it to the case of a miser's horse, terminates by saying, "What vast ideas must he have of oats!"—upon the same principle these poor ladies, on those fatal committee days, never failed to form most exaggerated ideas of bread, butter, and wine. And at length some, more intrepid than the rest, began to carry biscuits in their muffs, and, with the conscious tremors of school girls (profiting by the absence of the mistress but momentarily expecting detection), they employed some casual absence

of their unhostly hostess in distributing and eating
their hidden "viaticum." However, it must be acknowledged, that time and exertion, and the sacrifice
of more selfish pleasure during the penance at the
school, were, after all, real indications of kindness to
her fellow-creatures; and, as I wish to part in peace
even with the Saracen's Head, I have reserved this anecdote to the last: for it is painful to have lived on
terms of good nature, and exchanging civilities, with
any human being of whom one can report absolutely
no good thing; and I sympathize heartily with that indulgent person of whom it is somewhere recorded that,
upon an occasion when the death of a man happened
to be mentioned who was unanimously pronounced a
wretch without one good quality, "*monstrum nullâ
virtute redemptum*," he ventured, however, at last, in
a deprecatory tone to say—"Well, he did *whistle* beautifully, at any rate."

Talking of "whistling" reminds me to return from
my digression; for on that night, the 12th of November, 1807, and the last of my visits to the Wordsworths,
I took leave of them in the inn at Ambleside about ten
at night; and the post-chaise in which I crossed the
country to catch the mail was driven by a postilion who
whistled so delightfully that, for the first time in my
life, I became aware of the prodigious powers which
are lodged potentially in so despised a function of the
vocal organs. For the whole of the long ascent up Orrest Head, which obliged him to walk his horses for a
full half-mile, he made the woods of Windermere ring
with the canorous sweetness of his half flute, half clarionet music; but, in fact, the subtle melody of the effect
placed it in power far beyond either flute or clarionet.
A year or two afterwards, I heard a fellow-servant of
this same postilion's, a black, play with equal superi-

ority of effect upon the jew's harp; making that, which in most hands is a mere monotonous jarring, a dull reverberating vibration, into a delightful lyre of no inconsiderable compass.

That night, as I was passing under the grounds of Elleray, then belonging to a Westmorland "statesman," a thought struck me, that I was now traversing a road with which, as yet, I was scarcely at all acquainted, but which, in years to come, might perhaps be as familiar to my eye as the rooms of my own house; and possibly that I might traverse them in company with faces as yet not even seen by me, but in those future years dearer than any which I had yet known. In this prophetic glimpse there was nothing very marvellous; for what could be more natural than that I should come to reside in the neighbourhood of the Wordsworths, and that this might lead to my forming connexions in a country which I should consequently come to know so well? I did not, however, anticipate so definitely and circumstantially as all this; but generally I had a dim presentiment that here, on this very road, I should often pass, and in company that, now not even conjecturally delineated or drawn out of the utter darkness in which they were as yet reposing, would hereafter plant memories in my heart, the last that will fade from it in the hour of death. Here, afterwards, at this very spot, or a little above it, but on this very estate, which from local peculiarities of ground, and of sudden angles, was peculiarly *kenspeck*, *i.e.* easy of recognition, and could have been challenged and identified at any distance of years; here afterwards lived Professor Wilson, the only very intimate male friend I have had; here, too, it was, my M[argaret], that, in long years afterwards, through many a score of nights—nights often dark as Erebus, and amidst thunders and lightnings the most sublime—we descended at twelve, one, and two o'clock at night, speeding from Kendal to our distant home, twenty miles away. Thou wert at present a child not nine years old, nor had I seen thy face, nor heard thy name. But within nine years from that same night thou wert seated by my side—and, thenceforwards, through a period of four-teen years, how often did we two descend, hand locked in hand, and thinking of things to come, at a pace of hurricane; whilst all the sleeping woods about us re-echoed the uproar of trampling hoofs and groaning wheels. Duly as we mounted the crest of Orrest Head, mechanically and of themselves almost, and spontane-ously, without need of voice or spur, according to Westmorland usage, the horses flew off into a gallop, like the pace of a swallow.[1] It was a railroad pace that we ever maintained; objects were descried far ahead in one moment, and in the next were crowding into the rear. Three miles and a half did this storm-flight con-tinue, for so long the descent lasted. Then, for many a mile, over undulating ground, did we alternately creep and fly, until again a long precipitous move-ment, again a storm-gallop, that hardly suffered the feet to touch the ground, gave warning that we drew near to that beloved cottage; warning to us—warning to them:

[1] It may be supposed, not literally, for the swallow (or at least that species called the swift) has been known to fly at the rate of 300 miles an hour. Very probably, however, this pace was not deduced from an entire hour's performance, but esti-mated by proportion from a flight of one or two minutes. An interesting anecdote is told by the gentleman (I believe the Rev. E. Stanley) who described in *Blackwood's Magazine* the opening of the earliest English railway, viz. that a bird (snipe was it, or field-fare, or plover?) ran, or rather flew, a race with the engine for three or four miles, until, finding itself likely to be beaten, it then suddenly wheeled away into the moors.

The silence that is here
Is of the grave, and of austere
But happy feelings of the dead.

Sometimes the nights were bright with cloudless moonlight, and of that awful breathless quiet which often
broods over vales that are peculiarly landlocked, and
which is, or seems to be, so much more expressive of a
solemn hush and a Sabbath-like rest from the labours
of nature than I remember to have experienced in flat
countries:

It is not quiet—is not peace—
But something deeper far than these.

And on such nights it was no sentimental refinement,
but a sincere and hearty feeling, that, in wheeling past
the village churchyard of Stavely, something like an
outrage seemed offered to the sanctity of its graves by
the uproar of our career. Sometimes the nights were
of that pitchy darkness which is more palpable and unfathomable wherever hills intercept the gleaming of
light which otherwise is usually seen to linger about
the horizon in the northern quarter; and then arose in
perfection that striking effect when the glare of lamps
searches for one moment every dark recess of the thickets, forces them into sudden, almost daylight, revelation, only to leave them within the twinkling of the
eye in darkness more profound; making them, like the
snow-flakes falling upon a cataract, "one moment
bright, then gone for ever." But, dark or moonlight
alike, in every instance throughout so long a course of
years, the road was entirely our own for the whole
twenty miles. After nine o'clock not many people are
abroad, after ten absolutely none, upon the roads of
Westmorland; a circumstance which gives a peculiar
solemnity to a traveller's route amongst these quiet

valleys upon a summer evening of latter May, of June, or early July; since, in a latitude so much higher than that of London, broad daylight prevails to an hour long after nine. Nowhere is the holiness of vesper hours more deeply felt.

And now, in 1839, from all these flying journeys and their stinging remembrances, hardly a wreck survives of what composed their living equipage: the men who chiefly drove in those days (for I have ascertained it) are gone; the horses are gone; darkness rests upon all, except myself. I, woe is me! am the solitary survivor from scenes that now seem to me as fugitive as the flying lights from our lamps as they shot into the forest recesses. God forbid that on such a theme I should seem to affect sentimentalism! It is from overmastering recollections that I look back on those distant days; and chiefly I have suffered myself to give way before the impulse that haunts me of reverting to those bitter, bitter thoughts, in order to notice one singular waywardness or caprice (as it might seem) incident to the situation, which, I doubt not, besieges many more people than myself: it is, that I find a more poignant suffering, a pang more searching, in going back, not to those enjoyments themselves, and the days when they were within my power, but to times anterior, when as yet they did not exist; nay, when some who were chiefly concerned in them as parties had not even been born. No night, I might almost say, of my whole life, remains so profoundly, painfully, and pathetically imprinted on my remembrance as this very one, on which I tried prelusively, as it were, that same road in solitude, and lulled by the sweet carollings of the postilion, which, *after* an interval of ten years, and *through* a period of more than equal duration, it was destined that I should so often traverse in circumstances of happiness too radiant, that for me are burned out for ever.

Ay, reader, all this may sound foolishness to you, that perhaps never had a heartache, or that may have all your blessings to come. But now let me return to my narrative. After about twelve months' interval, and therefore again in November, but November of the year 1808, I repeated my visit to Wordsworth, and upon a longer scale. I found him removed from his cottage to a house of considerable size, about three-quarters of a mile distant, called Allan Bank. This house had been very recently erected, at an expense of about £1500, by a gentleman from Liverpool, a merchant, and also a lawyer in some department or other. It was not yet completely finished; and an odd accident was reported to me as having befallen it in its earliest stage. The walls had been finished, and this event was to be celebrated at the village inn with an *ovation*, previously to the *triumph* that would follow on the roof-raising. The workmen had all housed themselves at the *Red Lion*, and were beginning their carouse, when up rode a traveller, who brought them the unseasonable news, that, whilst riding along the vale, he had beheld the downfall of the whole building. Out the men rushed, hoping that this might be a hoax; but too surely they found his report true, and their own festival premature. A little malice mingled unavoidably with the laughter of the Dalesmen; for it happened that the Liverpool gentleman had offered a sort of insult to the native artists, by bringing down both masons and carpenters from his own town; an unwise plan, for they were necessarily unacquainted with many points of local skill; and it was to some ignorance in their mode of laying the stones that the accident was due. The house had one or two capital defects —it was cold, damp, and, to all appearance, incurably smoky. Upon this latter defect, by the way, Wordsworth founded a claim, not for diminution of rent, but absolutely for entire immunity from any rent at all. It was truly comical to hear him argue the point with the Liverpool proprietor, Mr. C. He went on dilating on the hardship of living in such a house; of the injury, or suffering, at least, sustained by the eyes; until, at last, he had drawn a picture of himself as a very ill-used man; and I seriously expected to hear him sum up by demanding a round sum for damages. Mr. C. was a very good-natured man, calm, and gentlemanlike in his manners. He had also a considerable respect for Wordsworth, derived, it may be supposed, not from his writings, but from the authority (which many more besides him could not resist) of his conversation. However, he looked grave and perplexed. Nor do I know how the matter ended; but I mention it as an illustration of Wordsworth's keen spirit of business. Whilst foolish people supposed him a mere honeyed sentimentalist, speaking only in zephyrs and bucolics, he was in fact a somewhat hard pursuer of what he thought fair advantages.

In the February which followed, I left Allan Bank; but, upon Miss Wordsworth's happening to volunteer the task of furnishing for my use the cottage so recently occupied by her brother's family, I took it upon a seven years' lease. And thus it happened—this I mean was the mode of it (for, at any rate, I should have settled somewhere in the country)—that I became a resident in Grasmere.

DOVE COTTAGE

(First published in *Tait's Magazine*, January, 1840)

I N FEBRUARY, as I have said, of 1809, I quitted Allan Bank; and, from that time until the depth of summer, Miss Wordsworth was employed in the task she had volunteered, of renewing and furnishing the lit-

tle cottage in which I was to succeed the illustrious tenant who had, in my mind, hallowed the rooms by a
seven years' occupation, during, perhaps, the happiest
period of his life—the early years of his marriage, and
of his first acquaintance with parental affections. Cottage, immortal in my remembrance! as well it might
be; for this cottage I retained through just seven-and-
twenty years: this was the scene of struggle the most
tempestuous and bitter within my own mind: this the
scene of my despondency and unhappiness: this the
scene of my happiness—a happiness which justified the
faith of man's *earthly* lot, as, upon the whole, a dowry
from heaven. It was, in its exterior, not so much a picturesque cottage—for its outline and proportions, its
windows and its chimneys, were not sufficiently
marked and effective for the picturesque—as it was
lovely: one gable end was, indeed, most gorgeously apparelled in ivy, and so far picturesque; but the principal side, or what might be called front, as it presented
itself to the road, and was most illuminated by windows, was embossed—nay, it might be said, smothered
—in roses of different species, amongst which the moss
and the damask prevailed. These, together with as
much jessamine and honeysuckle as could find room to
flourish, were not only in themselves a most interesting garniture for a humble cottage wall, but they also
performed the acceptable service of breaking the unpleasant glare that would else have wounded the eye
from the whitewash; a glare which, having been renewed amongst the general preparations against my
coming to inhabit the house, could not be sufficiently
subdued in tone for the artist's eye until the storm of
several winters had weather-stained and tamed down
its brilliancy. The Westmorland cottages, as a class,
have long been celebrated for their picturesque forms,
and very justly so: in no part of the world are cottages

to be found more strikingly interesting to the eye by
their general outlines, by the sheltered porches of their
entrances, by their exquisite chimneys, by their rustic
windows, and by the distribution of the parts. These
parts are on a larger scale, both as to number and size,
than a stranger would expect to find as dependencies
and out-houses attached to dwelling-houses so modest;
chiefly from the necessity of making provision both in
fuel for themselves, and in hay, straw, and brackens
for the cattle against the long winter. But, in praising
the Westmorland dwellings, it must be understood
that only those of the native Dalesmen are contemplated; for, as to those raised by the alien intruders—
"the lakers," or "foreigners" as they are sometimes
called by the old indigenous possessors of the soil—
these, being designed to exhibit "a taste" and an eye
for the picturesque, are pretty often mere models of
deformity, as vulgar and as silly as it is well possible
for any object to be in a case where, after all, the work-
man, and obedience to custom, and the necessities of
the ground, &c., will often step in to compel the architects into common sense and propriety. The main defect in Scottish scenery, the eyesore that disfigures so
many charming combinations of landscape, is the offensive style of the rural architecture; but still, even
where it is worst, the *mode* of its offence is not by affectation and conceit, and preposterous attempts at
realizing sublime, Gothic, or castellated effects in little
gingerbread ornaments, and "tobacco pipes," and
make-believe parapets, and towers like kitchen or hot-
house flues; but in the hard undisguised pursuit of
mere coarse uses and needs of life.

Too often, the rustic mansion, that should speak of
decent poverty and seclusion, peaceful and comfortable, wears the most repulsive air of town confinement
and squalid indigence; the house being built of sub-

stantial stone, three storeys high, or even four, the
roof of massy slate; and everything strong which respects the future outlay of the proprietor—everything
frail which respects the comfort of the inhabitants:
windows broken and stuffed up with rags or old hats;
steps and door encrusted with dirt; and the whole tarnished with smoke. Poverty—how different the face it
wears looking with meagre staring eyes from such a
city dwelling as this, and when it peeps out, with rosy
cheeks, from amongst clustering roses and woodbines,
at a little lattice, from a little one-storey cottage! Are,
then, the main characteristics of the Westmorland
dwelling-houses imputable to superior taste? By no
means. Spite of all that I have heard Mr. Wordsworth
and others say in maintaining that opinion, I, for my
part, do and must hold, that the Dalesmen produce
none of the happy effects which frequently arise in
their domestic architecture under any search after
beautiful forms, a search which they despise with a
sort of Vandal dignity; no, nor with any sense or consciousness of their success. How then? Is it accident—
mere casual good luck—that has brought forth, for instance, so many exquisite forms of chimneys? Not so;
but it is this: it is good sense, on the one hand, bending
and conforming to the dictates or even the suggestions
of the climate, and the local circumstances of rocks,
water, currents of air, &c.; and, on the other hand,
wealth sufficient to arm the builder with all suitable
means for giving effect to his purpose, and to evade the
necessity of make-shifts. But the radical ground of the
interest attached to Westmorland cottage architecture
lies in its submission to the determining agencies of
the surrounding circumstances; such of them, I mean,
as are permanent, and have been gathered from long
experience. The porch, for instance, which does so
much to take away from a house the character of a

rude box, pierced with holes for air, light, and ingress, has evidently been dictated by the sudden rushes of wind through the mountain "ghylls," which make some kind of protection necessary to the ordinary door; and this reason has been strengthened, in cases of houses near to a road, by the hospitable wish to provide a sheltered seat for the wayfarer; most of these porches being furnished with one in each of the two recesses, to the right and to the left.

The long winter, again, as I have already said, and the artificial prolongation of the winter by the necessity of keeping the sheep long upon the low grounds, creates a call for large out-houses; and these, for the sake of warmth, are usually placed at right angles to the house; which has the effect of making a much larger system of parts than would else arise. But perhaps the main feature which gives character to the pile of building, is the roof, and, above all, the chimneys.

It is probable and many houses of the Elizabethan era confirm it, that a better taste prevailed, in this point, amongst our ancestors, both Scottish and English; that this elder fashion travelled, together with many other usages, from the richer parts of Scotland to the Borders, and thence to the vales of Westmorland; where they have continued to prevail, from their affectionate adhesion to all patriarchal customs. Some, undoubtedly, of these Westmorland forms have been dictated by the necessities of the weather, and the systematic energies of human skill, from age to age, applied to the very difficult task of training smoke into obedience, under the peculiar difficulties presented by the sites of Westmorland houses. These are chosen, generally speaking, with the same good sense and regard to domestic comfort, as the primary consideration (without, however, disdainfully slighting the sentiment, whatever it were, of peace, of seclusion, of

gaiety, of solemnity, the special "religio loci") , which
seems to have guided the choice of those who founded
religious houses.

And here, again, by the way, appears a marked difference between the Dalesmen and the intrusive gentry—not creditable to the latter. The native Dalesman,
well aware of the fury with which the wind often
gathers and eddies about any eminence, however trifling its elevation, never thinks of planting his house
there: whereas the stranger, singly solicitous about the
prospect or the range of lake which his gilt saloons are
to command, chooses his site too often upon points better fitted for a temple of Eolus than a human dwelling-
place; and he belts his house with balconies and veran-
das that a mountain gale often tears away in mockery.
The Dalesman, wherever his choice is not circum-
scribed, selects a sheltered spot (a *wray*,[1] for instance) ,
which protects him from the wind altogether, upon one
or two quarters, and on all quarters from its tornado
violence: he takes good care, at the same time, to be
within a few feet of a mountain beck: a caution so little heeded by some of the villa founders that absolutely, in a country surcharged with water, they have
sometimes found themselves driven, by sheer necessity,
to the after-thought of sinking a well. The very best
situation, however, in other respects, may be bad in
one, and sometimes find its very advantages, and the
beetling crags which protect its rear, obstructions the
most permanent to the ascent of smoke; and it is in the
contest with these natural baffling repellents of the
smoke, and in the variety of artifices for modifying its
vertical, or for accomplishing its lateral escape, that
have arisen the large and graceful variety of chimney

---

[1] *Wraie* is the old Danish or Icelandic word for *angel*. Hence
the many "wrays" in the Lake district.

models. My cottage, wanting this primary feature of elegance in the constituents of Westmorland cottage architecture, and wanting also another very interesting feature of the elder architecture, annually becoming more and more rare—viz. the outside gallery (which is sometimes merely of wood, but is much more striking when provided for in the original construction of the house, and completely *enfoncé* in the masonry)—could not rank high amongst the picturesque houses of the country; those, at least, which are such by virtue of their architectural form. It was, however, very irregular in its outline to the rear, by the aid of one little projecting room, and also of a stable and little barn, in immediate contact with the dwelling-house. It had, besides, the great advantage of a varying height: two sides being about fifteen or sixteen feet high from the exposure of both storeys; whereas the other two, being swathed about by a little orchard that rose rapidly and unequally towards the vast mountain range in the rear, exposed only the upper storey; and, consequently, on those side the elevation rarely rose beyond seven or eight feet. All these accidents of irregular form and outline gave to the house some little pretensions to a picturesque character; whilst its "separable accidents" (as the logicians say), its bowery roses and jessamine, clothed it in loveliness —its associations with Wordsworth crowned it, to my mind, with historical dignity—and, finally, my own twenty-seven years' off-and-on connexion with it have, by ties personal and indestructible, endeared it to my heart so unspeakably beyond all other houses, that even now I rarely dream through four nights running that I do not find myself (and others besides) in some one of those rooms, and, most probably, the last cloudy delirium of approaching death will re-install me in some chamber of that same humble cottage. "What a tale," says Foster, the eloquent essayist—"what a tale could be told by many a room, were the walls endowed with memory and speech!" or, in the more impassioned expressions of Wordsworth—

Ah! what a lesson to a thoughtless man
————————if any gladsome field of earth
Could render back the sighs to which it hath responded,
Or echo the sad steps by which it hath been trod!

And equally affecting it would be, if such a field or such a house could render up the echoes of joy, of festal music, of jubilant laughter—the innocent mirth of infants, or the gaiety, not less innocent, of youthful mothers—equally affecting would be such a reverberation of forgotten household happiness with the re-echoing records of sighs and groans. And few indeed are the houses that, within a period no longer than from the beginning of the century to 1835 (so long was it either mine or Wordsworth's) have crowded such ample materials for those echoes, whether sorrowful or joyous.

My cottage was ready in the summer; but I was playing truant amongst the valleys of Somersetshire; and, meantime, different families, throughout the summer, borrowed the cottage of the Wordsworths as my friends. They consisted chiefly of ladies; and some, by the delicacy of their attentions to the flowers, &c., gave me reason to consider their visit during my absence as a real honour; others—such is the difference of people in this world—left the rudest memorials of their careless habits impressed upon house, furniture, garden, &c. In November, at last, I, the long-expected, made my appearance. Some little sensation did really and naturally attend my coming, for most of the draperies belonging to beds, curtains, &c., had been sewed by the young women of that or the adjoining vales. This had caused me to be talked of. Many had seen me on my visit to the Wordsworths. Miss Wordsworth had introduced the curious to a knowledge of my age, name, prospects, and all the rest of what can be interesting to know. Even the old people of the vale were a little excited by the accounts (somewhat exaggerated, perhaps) of the never ending books that continued to arrive in packing-cases for several months in succession. Nothing in these vales so much fixes the attention and respect of the people as the reputation of being a "far learn'd" man. So far, therefore, I had already bespoke the favourable opinion of the Dalesmen. And a separate kind of interest arose amongst mothers and daughters, in the knowledge that I should necessarily want what—in a sense somewhat different from the general one—is called a "housekeeper"; that is, not an upper servant to superintend others, but one who could undertake, in her own person, all the duties of the house. It is not discreditable to these worthy people that several of the richest and most respectable families were anxious to secure the place for a daughter. Had I been a dissipated young man, I have good reason to know that there would have been no canvassing at all for the situation. But partly my books spoke for the character of my pursuits with these simple-minded people—partly the introduction of the Wordsworths guaranteed the safety of such a service. Even then, had I persisted in my original intention of bringing a manservant, no respectable young woman would have accepted the place. As it was, and it being understood that I had renounced this intention, many, in a gentle, diffident way, applied for the place, or their parents on their behalf. And I mention the fact, because it illustrates one feature in the manners of this primitive and peculiar people, the Dalesmen of Westmorland. However wealthy, they do not think it degrading to permit even the eldest daughter to go out a few years to service. The object is not to gain a sum of money in wages, but that sort of household experience which is supposed to be unattainable upon a suitable scale out of a gentleman's family. So far was this carried, that, amongst the offers made to myself, was one from a young woman whose family was amongst the very oldest in the country, and who was at that time under an engagement of marriage to the very richest young man in the vale. She and her future husband had a reasonable prospect of possessing ten thousand pounds in land; and yet neither her own family nor her husband's objected to her seeking such a place as I could offer. Her character and manners, I ought to add, were so truly excellent, and won respect so inevitably from everybody, that nobody could wonder at the honourable confidence reposed in her by her manly and spirited young lover. The issue of the matter, as respected my service, was, why I do not know, that Miss Wordsworth did not accept of her: and she fulfilled her purpose in another family, a very grave and respectable one, in Kendal. She stayed about a couple of years, returned, and married the young man to whom she had engaged herself, and is now the prosperous mother of a fine handsome family; and she together with her mother-in-law are the two leading matrons of the vale.

It was on a November night, about ten o'clock, that I first found myself installed in a house of my own— this cottage, so memorable from its past tenant to all men, so memorable to myself from all which has since passed in connexion with it.

THE DEATH OF LITTLE KATE WORDSWORTH
(First published in *Tait's Magazine*, August, 1840)

THUS, I have sketched the condition of the Lake District, as to society of an intellectual order, at the time (viz. the winter of 1808–9) when I became a personal resident in that district; and, indeed, from this era, through a period of about twenty years in succession, I may describe my domicile as being amongst the lakes and mountains of Westmorland. It is true, I often made excursions to London, Bath, and its neighbourhood, or northwards to Edinburgh, and, perhaps, on an average, passed one-fourth part of each year at a distance from this district; but here only it was that henceforwards I had a house and small establishment. The house, for a very long course of years, was that same cottage in Grasmere, embowered in roses and jessamine, which I have already described as a spot hallowed to the admirers of Mr. Wordsworth by his seven years' occupation of its pretty chambers and its rocky orchard: a little domain, which he has himself apostrophized as the "lowest stair in that magnificent temple" forming the north-eastern boundary of Grasmere. The little orchard is rightly called "the lowest stair"; for within itself all is ascending ground; hardly enough of flat area on which to pitch a pavilion, and even that scanty surface an inclined plane; whilst the rest of the valley, into which you step immediately from the garden gate, is (according to the characteristic beauty of the northern English valleys, as first noticed by Mr. Wordsworth himself) "flat as the floor of a temple."

In sketching the state of the literary society gathered or gathering about the English lakes, at the time of my settling amongst them, I have of course authorized the reader to suppose that I personally mixed freely amongst the whole; else I should have had neither the means for describing that society with truth, nor any motive for attempting it. Meantime, the direct object of my own residence at the lakes was the society of Mr. Wordsworth. And it will be a natural inference that, if I mingled on familiar or friendly terms with this society, *a fortiori* would Mr. Wordsworth do so, as belonging to the lake district by birth, and as having been, in some instances, my own introducer to members of this community. But it was not so; and never was a grosser blunder committed than by Lord Byron when, in a letter to Mr. Hogg (from which an extract is given in some volume of Mr. Lockhart's *Life of Sir Walter Scott*), he speaks of Wordsworth, Southey, &c., in connexion with Sir Walter, as all alike injured by mixing only with little adoring coteries, which each severally was supposed to have gathered about himself as a centre. Now, had this really been the case, I know not how the objects of such a partial or exclusive admiration could have been injured by it in any sense with which the public were concerned. A writer may——and of that there are many instances——write the worse for meeting nobody of sympathy with himself; no admiration sufficient to convince him that he has written powerfully: that misfortune, when it occurs, may injure a writer, or may cause him to cease cultivating his genius. But no man was ever injured by the strong reflection of his own power in love and admiration; not as a writer, I mean: though it is very true, from the great variety of modes in which praise, or the indirect flattery of silent homage, acts upon different minds, that some men may be injured as social companions: vanity, and, still more, egotism——the habit of making self the central point of reference in every treatment of every subject——may

certainly be cherished by the idolatry of a private circle, continually ascending; but arrogance and gloomy
anti-social pride are qualties much more likely to be
favoured by sympathy withheld, and the unjust denial
of a man's pretensions. This, however, need not be discussed with any reference to Mr. Wordsworth; for he
had no such admiring circle: no applauding coterie
ever gathered about him. Wordsworth was not a man
to be openly flattered; his pride repelled that kind of
homage, or any homage that offered itself with the air
of conferring honour; and repelled it in a tone of lofti-
ness or arrogance that never failed to kindle the pride
of the baffled flatterer. Nothing in the way of applause
could give Wordsworth any pleasure, unless it were
the spontaneous and half-unconscious utterance of delight in some passage—the implicit applause of love,
half afraid to express itself; or else the deliberate praise
of rational examination, study, and comparison, applied to his writings: these were the only modes of
admiration which could recommend themselves to
Wordsworth. But, had it been otherwise, there was another mistake in what Lord Byron said: The neighbouring people, in every degree, "gentle and simple,"
literary or half-educated, who had heard of Wordsworth, agreed in despising him. Never had poet or
prophet less honour in his own country. Of the gentry,
very few knew anything about Wordsworth. Grasmere
was a vale little visited at that time, except for an
hour's admiration. The case is now [1840] altered;
and partly by a new road, which, having pierced the
valley by a line carried along the water's edge, at a
most preposterous cost, and with a large arrear of debt
for the next generation, saves the labour of surmounting a laborious hill. The case is now altered no less for
the intellect of the age; and Rydal Mount is now one
of the most honoured abodes in the island. But, at that

time, Grasmere did not differ more from the Grasmere
of today than Wordsworth from the Wordsworth of
1809–20. I repeat that he was little known, even as a
resident in the country; and, as a poet, strange it would
have been had the little town of Ambleside undertaken
to judge for itself, and against a tribunal which had
for a time subdued the very temper of the age. Lord
Byron might have been sure that nowhere would the
contempt for Mr. Wordsworth be rifer than exactly
amongst those who had a local reason for curiosity
about the man, and who, of course, adopting the tone
of the presiding journals, adopted them with a personality of feeling unknown elsewhere.

Except, therefore, with the Lloyds, or occasionally
with Thomas Wilkinson the Quaker, or very rarely
with Southey, Wordsworth had no intercourse at all
beyond the limits of Grasmere: and in that valley I
was myself, for some years, his sole visiting friend; as,
on the other hand, my sole visitors as regarded that
vale, were himself and his family.

Among that family, and standing fourth in the
series of his children, was a little girl, whose life, short
as it was, and whose death, obscure and little heard of
as it was amongst all the rest of the world, connected
themselves with the records of my own life by ties of
passion so profound, by a grief so frantic, and so memorable through the injurious effects which it produced of a physical kind, that, had I left untouched
every other chapter of my own experience, I should
certainly have left behind some memorandum of this,
as having a permanent interest in the psychological
history of human nature. Luckily the facts are not
without a parallel, and in well authenticated medical
books; else I should have scrupled (as what man does
not scruple who values, above all things, the reputation for veracity?) to throw the whole stress of credi-

bility on my own unattached narration. But all experienced physicians know well that cases similar to mine, though not common, occur at intervals in every large community.

When I first settled in Grasmere, Catherine Wordsworth was in her infancy, but, even at that age, noticed me more than any other person, excepting, of course, her mother. She had for an attendant a young girl, perhaps thirteen years old—Sarah, one of the orphan children left by the unfortunate couple, George and Sarah Green, whose tragical end in a snow-storm I have already narrated. This Sarah Green was as far removed in character as could be imagined from that elder sister who had won so much admiration in her childish days, by her premature display of energy and household virtues. She was lazy, luxurious, and sensual: one, in fact, of those nurses who, in their anxiety to gossip about young men, leave their infant or youthful charges to the protection of chance. It was, however, not in her out-of-door ramblings, but at home, that the accident occurred which determined the fortunes of little Catherine. Mr. Coleridge was at that time a visitor to the Wordsworths at Allan Bank, that house in Grasmere to which Wordsworth had removed upon quitting his cottage. One day about noon, when, perhaps, he was coming down to breakfast, Mr. Coleridge passed Sarah Green, playing after her indolent fashion with the child; and between them lay a number of carrots. He warned the girl that raw carrots were an indigestible substance for the stomach of an infant. This warning was neglected: little Catherine ate—it was never known how many; and, in a short time, was seized with strong convulsions. I saw her in this state about two P.M. No medical aid was to be had nearer than Ambleside; about six miles distant. However, all proper measures were taken; and, by sunset, she had so far recovered as to be pronounced out of danger. Her left side, however, left arm, and left leg, from that time forward, were in a disabled state: not what could be called paralysed, but suffering a sort of atony or imperfect distribution of vital power.

Catherine was not above three years old when she died; so that there could not have been much room for the expansion of her understanding, or the unfolding of her real character. But there was room enough in her short life, and too much, for love the most frantic to settle upon her. The whole vale of Grasmere is not large enough to allow of any great distances between house and house; and, as it happened that little Kate Wordsworth returned my love, she in a manner lived with me at my solitary cottage; as often as I could entice her from home, walked with me, slept with me, and was my sole companion. That I was not singular in ascribing some witchery to the nature and manners of this innocent child, you may gather from the following most beautiful lines extracted from a sketch [1] towards her portraiture, drawn by her father (with whom, however, she was noways a favourite):

[1] It is entitled "Characteristics of a Child Three Years Old"; and is dated at the foot 1811, which must be an oversight, for she was not so old until the following year. I may as well add the first six lines, though I had a reason for beginning the extract where it does, in order to fix the attention upon the special circumstance which had so much fascinated myself, of her all-sufficiency to herself, and the way in which she "filled the air with gladness and involuntary songs." The other lines are these:

> Loving she is and tractable, though wild;
> And Innocence hath privilege in her
> To dignify arch looks and laughing eyes;
> And feats of cunning; and the pretty round
> Of trespasses, affected to provoke
> Mock-chastisement and partnership in play.

And, as a faggot sparkles on the hearth,
Not less if unattended and alone
Than when both young and old sit gathered round
And take delight in its activity;
Even so this happy creature of herself
Was all sufficient: solitude to her
Was blithe society, who filled the air
With gladness and involuntary songs.
Light were her sallies as the tripping fawn's,
Forth-startled from the form where she lay couch'd;
Unthought of, unexpected, as the stir
Of the soft breeze ruffling the meadow-flowers,
Or from before it chasing wantonly
The many coloured images impressed
Upon the bosom of a placid lake.

It was this radiant spirit of joyousness, making solitude for her blithe society, and filling from morning to night the air "with gladness and involuntary songs," this it was which so fascinated my heart that I became blindly, dotingly, in a servile degree, devoted to this one affection. In the spring of 1812, I went up to London; and, early in June, by a letter from Miss Wordsworth, her aunt, I learned the terrific news (for such to me it was) that she had died suddenly. She had gone to bed in good health about sunset on June 4th; was found speechless a little before midnight; and died in the early dawn, just as the first gleams of morning began to appear above Seat Sandel and Fairfield, the mightiest of the Grasmere barriers, about an hour, perhaps, before sunrise.

Never, perhaps, from the foundations of those mighty hills, was there so fierce a convulsion of grief as mastered my faculties on receiving that heart-shattering news. Over and above my excess of love for her, I had always viewed her as an impersonation of the

dawn and the spirit of infancy; and this abstraction
seated in her person, together with the visionary sort
of connexion which, even in her parting hours, she assumed with the summer sun, by timing her immersion
into the cloud of death with the rising and setting of
that fountain of life—these combined impressions
recoiled so violently into a contrast or polar antithesis
to the image of death that each exalted and brightened
the other. I returned hastily to Grasmere; stretched
myself every night, for more than two months running, upon her grave; in fact, often passed the night
upon her grave; not (as may readily be supposed) in
any parade of grief; on the contrary, in that quiet valley of simple shepherds, I was secure enough from observation until morning light began to return; but in
mere intensity of sick, frantic yearning after neighbourhood to the darling of my heart. Many readers
will have seen in Sir Walter Scott's *Demonology*, and
in Dr. Abercrombie's *Inquiries Concerning the Intellectual Powers*, some remarkable illustrations of the
creative faculties awakened in the eye or other organs
by peculiar states of passion; and it is worthy of a place
amongst cases of that nature that, in many solitary
fields, at a considerable elevation above the level of the
valleys—fields which, in the local dialect, are called
"intacks"—my eye was haunted at times, in broad
noonday (oftener, however, in the afternoon), with a
facility, but at times also with a necessity, for weaving, out of a few simple elements, a perfect picture of
little Kate in the attitude and onward motion of walking. I resorted constantly to these "intacks," as places
where I was little liable to disturbance; and usually I
saw her at the opposite side of the field, which might
sometimes be at a distance of a quarter of a mile, generally not so much. Always almost she carried a basket
on her head; and usually the first hint upon which the

figure arose commenced in wild plants, such as tall ferns, or the purple flowers of the foxglove; but, whatever might be the colours or the forms, uniformly the same little full-formed figure arose, uniformly dressed in the little blue bed-gown and black skirt of Westmorland, and uniformly with the air of advancing motion. Through part of June, July, and part of August, in fact throughout the summer, this frenzy of grief continued. It was reasonably to be expected that nature would avenge such senseless self-surrender to passion; for, in fact, so far from making an effort to resist it, I clung to it as a luxury (which, in the midst of suffering, it really was in part). All at once, on a day at the latter end of August, in one instant of time, I was seized with some nervous sensation that, for a moment, caused sickness. A glass of brandy removed the sickness; but I felt, to my horror, a sting as it were, of some stationary torment left behind—a torment absolutely indescribable, but under which I felt assured that life could not be borne. It is useless and impossible to describe what followed: with no apparent illness discoverable to any medical eye—looking, indeed, better than usual for three months and upwards, I was under the possession of some internal nervous malady, that made each respiration which I drew an act of separate anguish. I travelled southwards immediately to Liverpool, to Birmingham, to Bristol, to Bath, for medical advice; and finally rested—in a gloomy state of despair, rather because I saw no use in further change than that I looked for any change in this place more than others—at Clifton, near Bristol. Here it was, at length, in the course of November, that, in one hour, my malady began to leave me: it was not quite so abrupt, however, in its departure, as in its first development: a peculiar sensation arose from the knee downwards, about midnight: it went forwards through a space of about five hours, and then stopped, leaving me perfectly free from every trace of the awful malady which had possessed me, but so much debilitated as with difficulty to stand or walk. Going down soon after this, to Ilfracombe, in Devonshire, where there were hot sea baths, I found it easy enough to restore my shattered strength. But the remarkable fact in this catastrophe of my illness is that all grief for little Kate Wordsworth, nay, all remembrance of her, had, with my malady, vanished from my mind. The traces of her innocent features were utterly washed away from my heart: she might have been dead for a thousand years, so entirely abolished was the last lingering image of her face or figure. The little memorials of her which her mother had given to me, as, in particular, a pair of her red morocco shoes, won not a sigh from me as I looked at them: even her little grassy grave, white with snow, when I returned to Grasmere in January, 1813, was looked at almost with indifference; except, indeed, as now become a memorial to me of that dire internal physical convulsion thence arising by which I had been shaken and wrenched; and, in short, a case more entirely realizing the old Pagan superstition of a nympholepsy in the first place, and, secondly, of a Lethe or river of oblivion, and the possibility, by one draught from this potent stream, of applying an everlasting ablution to all the soils and stains of human anguish, I do not suppose the psychological history of man affords.

GRADUAL ESTRANGEMENT FROM WORDSWORTH
(First published in *Tait's Magazine*, October, 1840)

LONDON, however, great as were its attractions, did but rarely draw me away from Westmorland. There I found more and more a shelter and an anchor for my own wishes. Originally, as I have mentioned, the motive which drew me to this county, in combination with its own exceeding beauty, had been the society of Wordsworth. But in this I committed a great oversight. Men of extraordinary genius and force of mind are far better as objects for distant admiration than as daily companions—not that I would insinuate anything to the disadvantage of Mr. Wordsworth. What I have to say in the way of complaint shall be said openly and frankly: this is but fair; for insinuations or covert accusations always leave room for misconstruction and for large exaggeration. Mr. Wordsworth is not only a man of principle and integrity, according to the severest standard of such a character, but he is even a man, in many respects, of amiable manners. Still there are traits of character about him, and modes of expressing them in his manners, which make a familiar or neighbourly intercourse with him painful and mortifying. Pride, in its most exalted form, he was entitled to feel; but something there was, in the occasional expression of this pride, which was difficult to bear. Upon ground where he was really strong, Wordsworth was not arrogant. In a question of criticism, he was open to any man's suggestions. But there *were* fields of thought or of observation which he seemed to think locked up and sacred to himself; and any alien entrance upon those fields he treated almost as intrusions and usurpations. One of these, and which naturally occurred the most frequently, was the whole theory of picturesque beauty, as presented to our notice at every minute by the bold mountainous scenery amongst which we lived, and as it happened to be modified by the seasons of the year, by the time of day, or by the accidents of light and shade. Now, Wordsworth and his sister really had, as I have before acknowl-

edged, a peculiar depth of organic sensibility to the
effects of form and colour; and to *them* I was willing
to concede a vote, such as in ancient Rome was called
"a prerogative vote," upon such questions. But, not
content with this, Wordsworth virtually claimed the
same precedency for all who were connected with himself, though merely by affinity, and therefore standing
under no colourable presumption (as blood relations
might have done) of inheriting the same constitutional
gifts of organization. To everybody standing out of
this sacred and privileged pale Wordsworth behaved
with absolute insult in cases of this nature: he did not
even appear to listen; but, as if what they said on such
a theme must be childish prattle, turned away with an
air of perfect indifference; began talking, perhaps,
with another person on another subject; or, at all
events, never noticed what we said by an apology for
an answer. I, very early in our connexion, having observed this inhuman arrogance, took care never afterwards to lay myself under the possibility of such an
insult. Systematically I avoided saying anything, however suddenly tempted into any expression of my feelings, upon the natural appearances whether in the sky
or on the earth. Thus I evaded one cause of quarrel;
and so far Wordsworth was not aware of the irritation
and disgust which he had founded in the minds of his
friends. But there were other manifestations of the
same ungenial and exclusive pride, even still more offensive and of wider application.

With other men, upon finding or thinking one's self
ill-used, all one had to do was to make an explanation;
and, with any reasonable grounds of complaint, or any
reasonable temper to manage, one was tolerably sure
of redress. Not so with Wordsworth. He had learned
from Mrs. C—— a vulgar phrase for all attempts at
reciprocal explanations—he called them contemptu-

ously "*fending and proving.*" And you might lay your
account with being met *in limine*, and further progress
barred, by a declaration to this effect—"Mr. X. Y. Z.,
I will have nothing to do with fending and proving."
This amounted, in other words, to saying that he conceived himself to be liberated from those obligations
of justice and courtesy by which other men are bound.
Now, I knew myself well enough to be assured that,
under such treatment, I should feel too much indignation and disgust to persevere in courting the acquaintance of a man who thus avowed his contempt for the
laws of equal dealing. Redress I knew that I should
never get; and, accordingly, I reasoned thus: "I have
been ill-used to a certain extent; but do I think *that* a
sufficient reason for giving up all my intimacy with a
man like Wordsworth? If I do *not*, let me make no
complaint; for, inevitably, if I *do* make complaint, that
will be the result. For, though I am able to bear the
particular wrong I now complain of, yet I feel that
even from Wordsworth I could not tolerate an open
and contemptuous refusal of justice. The result, then,
if I pursue this matter, will be to rob me of Wordsworth's acquaintance. Reparation, already necessary
to my feelings, will then become necessary to my honour: I shall fail to obtain it; and then it will become
my *duty* to renounce his acquaintance. I will, therefore, rest contentedly where I am."

What then were the cases of injustice which I had to
complain of? Such they were as between two men could
hardly have arisen; but, wherever there are women—
unless the terms on which the parties stand are most
free and familiar, so that, fast as clouds arise of misunderstanding, explanations may have full leave to
move concurrently, and nothing be left for either side
to muse upon as wrong, or meditated insult—I hold it
next to impossible that occasions should not arise in

which both parties will suspect some undervaluing, or some failure in kindness or respect. I, to give one example, had, for the controller of my domestic *ménage,* a foolish, selfish, and ignorant old maid. Naturally, she ought to have been no enemy to the Wordsworths, for she had once lived as a servant with them; and, for my service, she had been engaged, at high wages, by Miss Wordsworth herself. These motives to a special regard for the W.'s were not weighty enough to overrule her selfishness. Having unlimited power in all which regarded the pecuniary arrangements of my house, she became a person of some consideration and some power amongst her little sphere. In my absence, she took upon herself the absolute command of everything; and I could easily perceive, by different anecdotes which reached me, that she was jealous of any abridgement to her own supreme discretion, such as might naturally arise through any exercise of the friendly rights claimed in my absence by those friends who conceived themselves to have the freedom of my house, and the right to use its accommodations in any honourable way prompted by their own convenience. To my selfish housekeeper this was a dangerous privilege; for, if it had brought no other evil with it, inevitably it would sometimes lay a restraint upon her gadding propensity, and detain her at home during months when otherwise my great distance gave her the amplest privilege of absence. In shaping remedies for this evil, which, from natural cowardice, she found it difficult to oppose in her own person, she had a ready resource in charging upon myself the measures which she found convenient. "*Master* (which was her technical designation for myself) thinks thus," or "Master left such and such directions." These were obvious fictions for a woman so selfish and mean. Any real friend of mine ought to have read, in the very situation which this woman held—

in her obvious interest, connected with her temper—a
sufficient commentary upon the real state of things. A
man more careless than myself of the petty interests
concerned in such a case could not exist. And it may be
supposed with what disgust and what reasonable indignation I heard of opinions uttered upon my character
by those who called themselves my friends; opinions
shaped to meet, not any conduct which I had ever held,
or which it could be pretended that I had countenanced, but to meet the false imputations of an interested woman, who was by those imputations doing to
me a far deeper injury than to those whom she merely
shut out from a momentary accommodation.

But why not, upon discovering such forgeries and
misrepresentations, openly and loudly denounce them
for what they were? I answer that, when a man is too
injuriously wounded by the words of his *soi-disant*
friends, oftentimes a strong movement of pride makes
it painful for him to degrade himself by explanations
or justifications. Besides that, when once a false idea
has prepossessed the minds of your friends, justification
oftentimes becomes impossible. My servant, in such a
case, would have worn the air of one who had offended
me, not by a base falsehood, but by an imprudence in
betraying too much of the truth; and, doubtless, when
my back was turned, she would insinuate that her own
interest had obliged her to put up with my disavowal
of what she had done; but that, in literal truth, she had
even fallen short of my directions. Others, again,
would think that, though no specific directions might
have been given to her, possibly she had collected my
sincere wishes from words of complaint dropped casually upon former occasions. Thus, in short, partly I
disdained, partly I found it impossible, to exonerate
myself from those most false imputations; and I sate
down half-contentedly under accusations which, in

every solemnity of truth, applied less justly to myself
than to any one person I knew amongst the whole circle of my acquaintance. The result was that ever after
I hated the name of the woman at whose hands I had
sustained this wrong, so far as such a woman could be
thought worthy of hatred, and that I began to despise
a little some of those who had been silly and undiscern-
ing enough to accredit such representations; and one
of them especially, who, though liberally endowed
with sunshiny temper and sweetness of disposition, was
perhaps a person weak intellectually beyond the ordinary standards of female weakness.

Hence began the waning of my friendship with the
Wordsworths. But, in reality, never after the first year
or so from my first introduction had I felt much possibility of drawing the bonds of friendship tight with
a man of Wordsworth's nature. He seemed to me too
much like his own Pedlar in *The Excursion*, a man so
diffused amongst innumerable objects of equal attraction that he had no cells left in his heart for strong individual attachments. I was not singular in this feeling.
Professor Wilson had become estranged from him:
Coleridge, one of his earliest friends, had become estranged: no one person could be deemed fervently his
friend. And, with respect to Coleridge, he certainly had
strong reasons to be estranged; and equally certain it
is that he held a profound sense of those reasons for
some years. He told me himself; and this was his peculiar inference from the case, and what he made its
moral—that married people rarely retain much capacity of friendship. Their thoughts, and cares, and
anxieties, are all so much engrossed by those who naturally and rightly sit nearest to their hearts that other
friends—chosen, perhaps, originally for intellectual
qualities chiefly, and seen only at casual intervals—
must, by mere human necessity, come to droop **and**

fade in their remembrance. I see no absolute necessity for this; nor have I felt it since my own experience of the situation supposed by Coleridge has enabled me to judge. But, at all events, poor Coleridge had found it true in his own case. The rupture between him and Wordsworth, which rather healed itself by lapse of time and the burning dim of fierce recollections, than by any formal reconciliation of pardon exchanged between the parties, arose thus: An old acquaintance of Coleridge's, happening to visit the Lakes, proposed to carry Coleridge with him to London on his return. This gentleman's wife, a lady of some distinction as to person and intellectual accomplishments, had an equal pleasure in Coleridge's society. They had a place disposable in their travelling carriage; and thus all things tallied towards the general purpose. Meantime, Wordsworth, irritated with what he viewed as excessive vanity in this gentleman (for his plan of taking Coleridge to London and making him an inmate in his house had originated in a higher purpose of weaning Coleridge from opium), ridiculed the whole scheme pointedly, as a visionary and Quixotic enterprise, such as no man of worldly experience could ever seriously countenance. The dispute—for it took that shape—tempted or drove Wordsworth into supporting his own views of Coleridge's absolute incorrigibility by all the anecdotes he could gather together illustrative of the utter and irredeemable slavery which had mastered the poor opium-martyr's will. And, most assuredly, he drew such a picture of Coleridge, and of his sensual effeminacy, as ought not to have proceeded from the hands of a friend. Notwithstanding all this, the purpose held amongst the three contracting parties: they went southwards; and, for a time, the plan was still farther realized of making Coleridge not merely a travelling companion, but also an inmate of their house. This plan, however, fell through, in consequence of incompatible habits. And, in the feud which followed, this gentleman and his wife upbraided Coleridge with the opinions held of him by his own oldest and most valued friend, William Wordsworth; and, perhaps as much to defend themselves as to annoy Coleridge, they repeated many of the arguments used by Wordsworth, and of the anecdotes by which he supported them; anecdotes which, unfortunately, vouched for their own authenticity, and were self-attested, since none but Wordsworth could have known them.

I have mentioned the kind of wrongs which first caused my personal feelings to grow colder towards the Wordsworths; and there were, afterwards, others added to these, of a nature still more irritating, because they related to more delicate topics. And, again and again, I was provoked to wonder that persons, of whom some commanded respect and attention simply as the near connexions of a great man, should so far forget the tenure on which their influence rested as to arrogate a tone of authority upon their own merits. Meantime, however much my personal feelings had altered gradually towards Wordsworth—and more, I think, in connexion with his pride than through any or all other causes acting jointly (insomuch that I used to say, Never describe Wordsworth as equal in pride to Lucifer: no; but, if you have occasion to write a life of Lucifer, set down that by possibility, in respect to pride, he might be some type of Wordsworth)—still, I say, my intellectual homage to Wordsworth had not been shaken. Even this, however, in a course of years, had gradually been modified. It is impossible to imagine the perplexity of mind which possessed me when I heard Wordsworth ridicule many books which I had been accustomed to admire profoundly. For some years, so equally ineradicable was either influence—my recollection, on the one hand, of the books despised, and of their power over my feelings; on the other, my blind and unquestioning veneration for Wordsworth—that I was placed in a strange sort of contradictory life; feeling that things were and were not at the same instant; believing and not believing in the same breath. And not until I had read much in German critics of what they were the first to notice—viz. the accident of *einseitigkeit*, or *one-sidedness*, as a peculiarity not unfrequently besetting the strongest minds—did I slowly come to the discovery that Wordsworth, beyond all men, perhaps, that have ever lived (and very likely as one condition towards the possibility of his own exceeding originality) , was *einseitig* in extremity. This one-sidedness shows itself most conspicuously in his dislikings; but occasionally even in his likings. Cotton, for instance, whom, in one of his critical disquisitions, he praises so extravagantly for his fancy, has never found an admirer except in himself. And this mistake to be made in a field of such enormous opulence as is that of fancy!

Perhaps, to the public, it may illustrate Wordsworth's one-sidedness more strikingly if I should mention my firm persuasion that he has never read one page of Sir Walter Scott's novels. Of this I am satisfied; though it is true that, latterly, feeling more indulgently to the public favourites as the public has come to appreciate himself more justly, he has spoken of these tales in a tone of assumed enthusiasm.[1] One of Mrs. Radcliffe's romances, viz. *The Italian*, he had by some strange accident, read—read, but only to laugh at it; whilst, on the other hand, the novels of Smollett, Fielding, and Le Sage—so disgusting by their moral scenery and the whole state of vicious society in which

[1] "Yarrow Revisited."

they keep the reader moving: these, and merely for the
ability of the execution, he read and remembered with
extreme delight.

Without going over any other examples, it may well
be understood that, by these striking instances of defective sympathy in Wordsworth with the universal feelings of his age, my intellectual, as well as my personal,
regard for him, would be likely to suffer. In fact, I
learned gradually that he was not only liable to human
error, but that, in some points, and those of large extent, he was frailer and more infirm than most of his
fellow-men. I viewed this defect, it is very true, as
being the condition and the price, as it were, or ransom, of his own extraordinary power and originality;
but still it raised a curtain which had hitherto sustained my idolatry. I viewed him now as a *mixed* creature, made up of special infirmity and special strength.
And, finally, I now viewed him as no longer capable
of an equal friendship.

With this revolution in my feelings, why did I not
now leave Westmorland? I will say: Other attractions
had arisen; different in kind; equally potent in degree.
These stepped in to enchain me precisely as my previous chains were unlinking themselves and leaving me
in freedom.

MRS. SIDDONS AND HANNAH MORE

(First published in *Tait's Magazine*, August, 1840)

FROM the Lakes, as I have mentioned before, I went
annually southwards—chiefly to Somersetshire or
to London, and more rarely to Edinburgh. In my Somersetshire visits, I never failed to see Mrs. Hannah
More. My own relative's house, in fact, standing
within one mile of Barley Wood, I seldom suffered a

week to pass without calling to pay my respects. There was a stronger motive to this than simply what arose from Mrs. H. More's company, or even from that of her sisters (one or two of whom were more entertaining, because more filled with animal spirits and less thoughtful, than Mrs. Hannah); for it rarely happened that one called within the privileged calling hours—which, with these rural ladies, ranged between twelve and four o'clock—but one met some person interesting by rank, station, political or literary eminence.

Here, accordingly, it was that, during one of my last visits to Somersetshire, either in 1813 or 1814, I met Mrs. Siddons, whom I had often seen upon the stage, but never before in private society. She had come into this part of the country chiefly, I should imagine, with a view to the medical advice at the Bristol Hot Wells and Clifton; for it happened that one of her daughters —a fine interesting young woman—was suffering under pulmonary consumption—that scourge of the British youth; of which malady, I believe, she ultimately died. From the Hot Wells, Mrs. Siddons had been persuaded to honour with her company a certain Dr. Wh——, whose splendid villa of Mendip Lodge stood about two miles from Barley Wood.

This villa, by the way, was a show place, in which a vast deal of money had been sunk upon two follies equally unproductive of pleasure to the beholder and of anything approaching a pecuniary compensation to the owner. The villa, with its embellishments, was supposed to have cost at least sixty thousand pounds; of which one-half had been absorbed, partly by a contest with the natural obstacles of the situation, and partly by the frailest of all ornaments—vast china jars, vases, and other "knick-knackery" baubles, which held their very existence by so frail a tenure as the carefulness of a housemaid, and which, at all events, if they should survive the accidents of life, never are known to reproduce to the possessor one-tenth part of what they have cost. Out of doors there were terraces of a mile long, one rising above another, and carried, by mere artifice of mechanic skill, along the perpendicular face of a lofty rock. Had they, when finished, any particular beauty? Not at all. Considered as a pleasure ground, they formed a far less delightful landscape, and a far less alluring haunt to rambling steps, than most of the uncostly shrubberies which were seen below, in unpretending situations, and upon the ordinary level of the vale. What a record of human imbecility! For all his pains and his expense in forming this costly "folly," his reward was daily anxiety, and one solitary *bon mot* which he used to record of some man who, on being asked by the Rev. Doctor what he thought of his place, replied that "he thought the Devil had tempted him up to an exceedingly high place." No part of the grounds, nor the house itself, was at all the better because originally it had been, beyond measure, difficult to form it: so difficult that, according to Dr. Johnson's witty remark on another occasion, there was good reason for wishing that it had been impossible. The owner, whom I knew, most certainly never enjoyed a happy day in this costly creation; which, after all, displayed but little taste, though a gorgeous array of finery. The show part of the house was itself a monument to the barrenness of invention in him who planned it; consisting, as it did, of one long suite of rooms in a straight line, without variety, without obvious parts, and therefore without symmetry or proportions. This long vista was so managed that, by means of folding-doors, the whole could be seen at a glance, whilst its extent was magnified by a vast mirror at the further end. The Doctor was a querulous old man, enormously tall and enormously bilious; so that he had a spectral appearance when pacing through the false gaieties of his glittering villa. He was a man of letters, and had known Dr. Johnson, whom he admired prodigiously; and had himself been, in earlier days, the author of a poem now forgotten. He belonged, at one period, to the coterie of Miss Seward, Dr. Darwin, Day, Mr. Edgeworth, &c.; consequently he might have been an agreeable companion, having so much anecdote at his command: but his extreme biliousness made him irritable in a painful degree and impatient of contradiction—impatient even of dissent in the most moderate shape. The latter stage of his life is worth recording, as a melancholy comment upon the blindness of human foresight, and in some degree also as a lesson on the disappointments which follow any departure from high principle, and the deception which seldom fails to lie in ambush for the deceiver. I had one day taken the liberty to ask him why, and with what ultimate purpose, he, who did not like trouble and anxiety, had embarrassed himself with the planning and construction of a villa that manifestly embittered his days? "That is, my young friend," replied the doctor, "speaking plainly, you mean to express your wonder that I, so old a man (for he was then not far from seventy), should spend my time in creating a show-box. Well now, I will tell you: precisely because I *am* old. I am naturally of a gloomy turn; and it has always struck me that we English, who are constitutionally haunted by melancholy, are too apt to encourage it by the gloomy air of the mansions we inhabit. Your fortunate age, my friend, can dispense with such aids: ours requires continual influxes of pleasure through the senses, in order to cheat the stealthy advances of old age, and to beguile us of our sadness. Gaiety, the *riant* style in everything, that is what we old men need. And I, who do not love the pains of creating, love the creation; and, in fact, require it as part of my artillery against time." Such was the amount of his explanation: and now, in a few words, for his subsequent history.

Finding himself involved in difficulties by the expenses of this villa, going on concurrently with a large London establishment, he looked out for a good marriage (being a widower) as the sole means within his reach for clearing off his embarrassments without proportionable curtailment of his expenses. It happened, unhappily for both parties, that he fell in with a widow lady, who was cruising about the world with precisely the same views, and in precisely the same difficulties. Each (or the friends of each) held out a false flag, magnifying their incomes respectively, and sinking the embarrassments. Mutually deceived, they married: and one change immediately introduced at the splendid villa was the occupation of an entire wing by a lunatic brother of the lady's; the care of whom, with a large allowance, had been committed to her by the Court of Chancery. This, of itself, shed a gloom over the place which defeated the primary purpose of the doctor (as explained by himself) in erecting it. Windows barred, maniacal howls, gloomy attendants from a lunatic hospital ranging about: these were sad disturbances to the doctor's rose-leaf system of life. This, however, if it were a nuisance, brought along with it some *solatium*, as the lawyers express it, in the shape of the Chancery allowance. But next came the load of debts for which there was no *solatium*, and which turned out to be the only sort of possession with which the lady was well endowed. The disconsolate doctor— an old man, and a clergyman of the Establishment— could not resort to such redress as a layman might have adopted: he was obliged to give up all his establishments; his gay villa was offered to Queen Caroline, who would, perhaps, have bought it, but that *her* final troubles in this world were also besetting her about that very time. For the present, therefore, the villa was shut up, and "left alone with its glory." The reverend and aged proprietor, now ten times more bilious and more querulous than ever, shipped himself off for France; and there, in one of the southern provinces— so far, therefore, as climate was concerned, realizing his vision of gaiety, but for all else the most melancholy of exiles—sick of the world and of himself, hating to live, yet more intensely hating to die, in a short time the unhappy old man breathed his last, in a common lodging house, gloomy and vulgar, and in all things the very antithesis to that splendid abode which he had planned for the consolation of his melancholy, and for the gay beguilement of old age.

At this gentleman's villa Mrs. Siddons had been paying a visit; for the doctor was a worshipper, in a servile degree, of all things which flourished in the sunshine of the world's applause. To have been the idolized favourite of nations, to have been an honoured and even a privileged [1] guest at Windsor, that was enough for him; and he did his utmost to do the honours of his neighbourhood, not less to glorify himself in the eye of the country, who was fortunate enough to have such a guest, than to show his respect for the distinguished visitor. Mrs. Siddons felt herself flattered by the worthy doctor's splendid hospitalities; for that they were really splendid may be judged by this fact,

[1] A *privileged* guest at Windsor. Mrs. Siddons used to mention that, when she was invited to Windsor Castle for the purpose of reading before the Queen and her royal daughters, on her first visit she was ready to sink from weariness under the effort of standing for so long a time; but on some subsequent visit I have understood that she was allowed to sit, probably on the suggestion of one of the younger ladies.

communicated to me by Hannah More, viz. that the
Bishop of London (Porteus), when on a visit to Barley Wood, being much pressed by the doctor to visit
him, had at length accepted a dinner invitation. Mrs.
Hannah More was, of course, included in the invitation, but had found it impossible to attend, from ill
health; and the next morning, at breakfast, the bishop
had assured her that, in all his London experience, in
that city of magnificent dinners beyond all other cities
of the earth, and amongst the princes of the land, he
had never witnessed an entertainment so perfect in its
appointments.

Gratified as she was, however, by her host's homage, as expressed in his splendid style of entertaining,
Mrs. Siddons was evidently more happy in her residence at Barley Wood. The style of conversation
pleased her. It was religious: but Mrs. Siddons was
herself religious; and at that moment, when waiting
with anxiety upon a daughter whose languor seemed
but too ominous in her maternal eyes, she was more
than usually open to religious impressions, and predisposed to religious topics. Certain I am, however, from
what I then observed, that Mrs. Siddons, in common
with many women of rank who were on the list of the
Barley Wood visitors, did not apprehend, in their full
sense and severity, the peculiar principles of Hannah
More. This lady, excellent as she was, and incapable of
practising any studied deceit, had, however, an instinct of worldly wisdom, which taught her to refrain
from shocking ears polite with too harsh or too broad
an exposure of all which she believed. This, at least, if
it were any duty of hers, she considered, perhaps, as already fulfilled by her writings; and, moreover, the
very tone of good breeding which she had derived from
the good company she had kept made her feel the im-

propriety of lecturing her visitors even when she must
have thought them in error. Mrs. Siddons obviously
thought Hannah More a person who differed from the
world chiefly by applying a greater energy, and sincerity, and zeal, to a system of religious truth equally
known to all. Repentance, for instance—all people
hold that to be a duty; and Mrs. Hannah More differed from them only by holding it to be a duty of all
hours, a duty for youth not less than for age. But how
much would she have been shocked to hear that Mrs.
Hannah More held all repentance, however indispensable, yet in itself, and though followed by the sincer-
est efforts at reformation of life, to be utterly unavailing as any operative part of the means by which man
gains acceptance with God. To rely upon repentance,
or upon anything that man can do for himself, that
Mrs. Hannah More considered as the mortal taint, as
the πρῶτον ψεῦδος, in the worldly theories of the
Christian scheme; and I have heard the two ladies—
Mrs. More and Mrs. Siddons, I mean—talking by the
hour together, as completely at cross purposes as it is
possible to imagine. Everything in fact of what was
special in the creed adopted by Mrs. Hannah More, by
Wilberforce, and many others known as Evangelical
Christians, is always capable, in lax conversation, of
being translated into a vague general sense, which
completely obscures the true limitations of the meaning.

Mrs. Hannah More, however, was too polished a
woman to allow of any sectarian movement being impressed upon the conversation; consequently, she soon
directed it to literature, upon which Mrs. Siddons was
very amusing, from her recollections of Dr. Johnson,
whose fine-turned compliment to herself (so much in
the spirit of those unique compliments addressed to
eminent people by Louis XIV) had for ever planted

the Doctor's memory in her heart.[1] She spoke also of
Garrick and of Mrs. Garrick; but not, I think, with so
much respect and affection as Mrs. Hannah More, who
had, in her youthful days, received the most friendly
attentions from both, though coming forward at that
time in no higher character than as the author of
Percy, the most insipid of tragedies.

Mrs. Siddons was prevailed on to read passages from
both Shakespeare and Milton. The dramatic readings
were delightful; in fact, they were almost stage rehearsals, accompanied with appropriate gesticulation.
One was the great somnambulist scene in *Macbeth*,
which was the *ne plus ultra* in the whole range of Mrs.
Siddons's scenical exhibitions, and can never be forgotten by any man who once had the happiness to witness that immortal performance of the divine artist.
Another, given at the request of a Dutch lady residing
in the neighbourhood of Barley Wood, was the scene
from *King John* of the Lady Constance, beginning—
"Gone to be married! gone to swear a peace!" &c. The
last, and truly superb for the musical intonation of the
cadences, was that inimitable apology or pleading of
Christian charity for Cardinal Wolsey, addressed to
his bitterest enemy, Queen Catherine. All these, in
different degrees and different ways, were exquisite.
But the readings from Milton were not to my taste.
And, some weeks after, when, at Mrs. Hannah More's
request, I had read to her some of Lord Byron's most
popular works, I got her to acknowledge, in then
speaking upon the subject of reading, that perhaps the

---

[1] Boswell describes her visit to Dr. Johnson thus: "When
Mrs. Siddons came into the room, there happened to be no
chair ready for her, which he observing, said with a smile,
'Madam, you who so often occasion a want of seats to other
people will the more easily excuse the want of one yourself.'"
—ED.

style of Mrs. Siddons's reading had been too much determined to the dramatic cast of emphasis, and the pointed expression of character and situation which must always belong to a speaker bearing a part in a dialogue, to admit of her assuming the tone of a rapt poetic inspiration.

Meantime, whatever she did—whether it were in display of her own matchless talents, but always at the earnest request of the company or of her hostess, or whether it were in gentle acquiescent attention to the display made by others, or whether it were as one member of a general party taking her part occasionally for the amusement of the rest and contributing to the general fund of social pleasure—nothing could exceed the amiable, kind, and unassuming deportment of Mrs. Siddons. She had retired from the stage,[1] and no longer regarded herself as a public character. But so much the stronger did she seem to think the claims of her friends upon anything she could do for their amusement.

Meantime, amongst the many pleasurable impressions which Mrs. Siddons's presence never failed to make, there was one which was positively painful and humiliating: it was the degradation which it inflicted upon other women. One day there was a large dinner party at Barley Wood: Mrs. Siddons was present; and I remarked to a gentleman who sat next to me—a remark which he heartily confirmed—that, upon rising to let the ladies leave us, Mrs. Siddons, by the mere necessity of her regal deportment, dwarfed the whole

[1] I saw her, however, myself upon the stage twice after this meeting at Barley Wood. It was at Edinburgh; and the parts were those of Lady Macbeth and Lady Randolph. But she then performed only as an expression of kindness to her grandchildren. Professor Wilson and myself saw her on the occasion from the stage-box, with a delight embittered by the certainty that we saw her for the last time.

party, and made them look ridiculous; though Mrs. H. More, and others of the ladies present, were otherwise really women of very pleasing appearance. One final remark is forced upon me by my recollections of Mrs. Jordan, and of her most unhappy end: it is this; and strange enough it seems—that the child of laughter and comic mirth, whose laugh itself thrilled the heart with pleasure, and who created gaiety of the noblest order for one entire generation of her countrymen, died prematurely, and in exile, and in affliction which really killed her by its own stings. If ever woman died of a broken heart, of tenderness bereaved, and of hope deferred, that woman was Mrs. Jordan. On the other hand, this sad votary of Melpomene, the queen of the tragic stage, died full of years and honours, in the bosom of her admiring country, in the centre of idolizing friends, and happy in all things except this, that some of those whom she most loved on earth had gone before her. Strange contrariety of lots for the two transcendent daughters of the comic and tragic muses. For my own part, I shall always regard my recollections of Mrs. Siddons as those in which chiefly I have an advantage over the coming generation; nay, perhaps over all generations; for many centuries may revolve without producing such another transcendent creature.

RECOLLECTIONS OF HANNAH MORE

(First published in *Tait's Magazine*, December, 1833)

I KNEW the late Mrs. Hannah More tolerably well, perhaps as well as it was possible that any man *should* know her who had not won her confidence by enrolling himself amongst her admirers. In these last

words I mean no offence: for I respect her memory,
and I respect the feelings of the many and excellent
friends who survive her. But it cannot reasonably offend the warmest of Mrs. More's friends if I say that
she, in common with most other female writers, required some homage—expected, in fact, to have some
court paid to her, before she would divest herself of
that reserve which clings more or less to all thoughtful people in England. There was nothing to complain
of in this; on the contrary, it is not easy to think well
of a woman who has so little self-respect as to extend
her confidence to one who has taken no pains to win
it, nor manifested by any signs that he would value it
if offered. For my part, I had no title to any peculiar
or confidential mark of Mrs. More's regard. I had
shown no disposition to conciliate her friendship; I
had never paid her a compliment; I had expressed no
interest in her works; I had not so much as appeared to
know that she was an author; and, even when calling
upon her to acquit myself of those customary attentions which were challenged by her sex, age, and
station in society, I had never travelled one hair's-
breadth beyond the line of distant and frigid polite-
ness. Indeed, on looking back from this distance of
time, I am afraid that I must even have appeared
churlish in my too punctilious care to have it understood how little I participated in the blind feelings of
admiration which congregated so many strangers in
her house. I am far from defending my own conduct.
I now begin to fear that it was almost atrocious. I
ought to have allowed a great deal more weight than I
did to her many excellent qualities; and with respect to
some of her opinions which disgusted me I might certainly have considered that they arose naturally from
the constitution of her own mind, and from the sort of
company which she had always kept; and, at all

events, I ought to have exercised, in behalf of so amiable a woman, and a woman so clever as she certainly was, a little more of that catholic toleration which one learns in passing through this world, and which she possibly, on her part, might sometimes feel called on to exercise towards myself. But I was young in those days. I had strong opinions; I had profound feelings; and the subjects which to me appeared important above all others were exactly those on which Mrs. H. More knew absolutely nothing at all, and some of which she affected to despise. Indeed, considering Mrs. More's early history, it must have been surprising if she had formed any opinions at all upon subjects which do not enter the range of ordinary conversation. Whatever opinions she had, I am fully persuaded, were pure, mirror-like reflections from the conversation of the people with whom she associated in her youth; and her own ability was shown chiefly in illustrating their tendencies, or delivering their substance in a graceful manner. But I am anticipating.

The occasion which drew me within Mrs. H. More's circle was this: In the year 1808, or 1809, a lady [1] with whose family I maintained a very intimate acquaintance had then recently begun to build a villa in the beautiful valley of Wrington; and in this valley, not above a mile and a half from my friend's rising house, stood the pretty cottage of Mrs. H. More and her sisters. She had previously occupied a house detached from the hills on either side, and not far, I think, from the centre of the vale. This place was called by the somewhat vulgar and sentimental name of *Cowslip Green*. But her present dwelling, standing under the shelter of the hills, bore the incoherent one of *Barley Wood*.

What had been the course of her previous life I

[1] De Quincey's own mother.—ED.

know only in the most general outline. Originally, I
have understood, she and her sisters conducted a board-
ing-school for young ladies in Bristol. There can be no
doubt that it was well managed; for all the sisters, five
in number when I first knew them, were in different
ways women of some talent. The ample fortune which
they were supposed to have made must have been
founded on the success of their school, though doubtless increased afterwards by Mrs. H. More's literary
emoluments. But it was not as an author that Mrs. H.
More had originally forced her way either to fortune
or to notoriety. She was one of those persons who owed
her reputation *partly*, it is true, to literary talent, and
that talent such that, cultivated and directed as it afterwards was, and allied with religious principles of peculiar strictness, it *might* have found its own road to
distinction, but which, in fact, was not, nor could be,
from circumstances of position, exposed to that severe
trial. From her earliest efforts to her latest, Mrs. H.
More was never suffered to swim alone, but was held
above water by such powerful hands as made it impossible that she should sink. I know not how soon in her
career, but certainly whilst yet considered a young
woman, she had been introduced to the domestic society of the Duchess of Beaufort, and of Mrs. Montagu,
so famous at one period for her Essay on Shakespeare
(against the cavils and laughable mistranslations of
Voltaire), for her literary parties, and for her generous patronage of the London chimney-sweepers.

Beginning life, then, in her character of author, under such patronage, we can easily understand how very
little merit would suffice—less indeed by a great deal
than she really had—to push the young and agreeable
Miss Hannah More into a vast deal of notoriety. Not
merely noticed, but caressed, by two potent leaders of
society in London, she could not fail of commanding

at once a pretty extensive popularity. It is true that
forced reputations usually decline faster even than
they have risen. And there can be no doubt that some
such reaction will operate powerfully upon the posthumous fame of Mrs. More; and I counsel every man
who has funded money in her works to sell now—for
assuredly five years will bring them down to a heavy
discount. But in her lifetime it was scarcely possible
that any revolution of that nature could affect her; for
the same artificial forces which had originally been
put in motion to elevate her unduly were continually
at work to sustain their own creation. And, very naturally, they acted with increasing advantages at every
step, and with accelerated power. For Mrs. More was
prudent and vigilant in the management of her interest. An old friend she never lost, except by death; and
she was continually strengthening her influence by
new friends in the same sphere of life. Her letters and
attentions she planted judiciously; nor did she ever
forget to be pointedly encouraging in her manners, or
to make her society and her house as agreeable as possible, to the rising generation of noble families. Her
epistolary correspondence was extensive; and there,
again, the learned in such branches of petty politics
know well the refinements of art by which adroit tac-
ticians vary and mask the modes of winning a powerful person to their aid, by giving him a motive for
reading passages from their letters, or for appealing to
their opinions, and thus eventually for giving currency to their names, and sustaining their authority.
One letter, we may suppose, expresses some forcible
opinions upon a great question, or an eminent person,
just at that moment occupying the public mind.
Everybody is eager to deliver his opinion upon it; and
it secures an attentive audience to say—"I will tell
you what Mrs. Hannah More says about it." Even

people not particularly under the influence of her name are apt to listen, under the belief that they will at least hear a natural and unbiased judgement, as from one who is a mere looker-on, living in retirement, and not warped, it may be presumed, by any disturbing forces of partisanship. Then another letter accompanies the present of a new work, just fresh from the press; and this perhaps contains thanks for valuable hints which, doubtless, really *had* been given, but only are prodigiously over-rated in value. A third letter, again, is not directly addressed to the person at whom it is mainly levelled: to this person is sent, circuitously, a message; which form of address makes it possible to say far more complimentary things than could decently be said to his face, with this farther advantage to his vanity, that a message, being communicated at the next rencontre, which is probably at a party, ensures to the flattering expressions something like a *publication*.

But all this, it will be said, is absolutely intrigue, or manœuvring chicanery; and can I mean to tax Mrs. Hannah More with anything so mean and worldly minded as this? *Intrigue* is an ugly word. What I mean to describe, and in a certain degree to charge upon Mrs. More, is not liable to any harsher name than that of *finessing*. It is that sort of diplomacy which, practised for public ends, and upon a broader scale, would be held strictly honourable, and looks mean only because it is practised for a somewhat selfish, and, by comparison, a trivial purpose—that of sustaining a name, or a certain amount of notoriety, by furnishing people of eminent stations with motives for talking about one's self, and by engaging their kind feelings in one's behalf. After all, I contend that the fault lies in the *degré*. Had Mrs. More dedicated extraordinary pains and much of her time to these artifices, or had she employed a very complex and elaborate machinery

for the purpose, in that case she would have stood open
to deep moral censure. As it was, and considering what
powerful *conductors* there had arisen latterly for calling off public attention from herself—considering
what perilous rivals she had in Bonaparte, in Lord
Byron, in Mr. Canning, and a thousand other over-
stimulating themes, all tending to reduce less agitating names and memorials to one common level of in-
sipidity—Mrs. More was warranted in sustaining so
much talk about herself in the London influential cir-
cles as might just serve to apprise people that she belonged to the living generation. Otherwise, as Mrs.
Hannah More had known Dr. Johnson, and as that
fact happened to have been well advertised by Boswell,
many people were apt to think of her as "the late Mrs.
Hannah More," who had been buried perhaps with all
her works before the French Revolution. But, apart
from this excuse, and supposing that she really had
been under no prudential obligation for refreshing the
world's remembrance of herself, I must confess that
even flattery the most direct has always appeared to
me a far more venial offence, and meriting far more
indulgence than it usually receives except from its objects. This much at least I can say with truth—that, in
every case of flattery which it has ever happened to me
personally to witness, nine-tenths of it, to say the least,
have been pure overflowings of courtesy, or perhaps of
benignity. And the true principle at work, after all,
was pure goodness of heart, or (at the very least) courtesy seeking to deliver itself of a debt by acknowledging those claims to which the public voice seemed to
give the right of challenging acknowledgement. These
opinions of mine with regard to flattery make it less
offensive to avow an overruling belief that Mrs. More's
reputation as an author had first commenced in a reciprocal intercourse of flattery, and that in some de-

gree it was kept alive by means of the same quality. And, therefore, when it is said to me, "Do you mean to tax Mrs. More with worldly mindedness?" I answer, "Certainly I do: in spite of her sincere piety, and her earnest wish to attain a higher standard of religious practice, I believe her to have been, in some considerable degree, though not immoderately, a woman of worldly mind; that is, involuntarily laying too much stress on rank, public honours, and, above all, on public opinion; and, what is more, I believe her to have been conscious of this infirmity, and to have struggled meritoriously against it, as against 'the sin which did too easily beset her.' "

However, to revert to her early life, I suppose that nobody at this time of day will think her early efforts in literature adequate of themselves to account for her early reputation. The way in which her position amongst people of rank was made to assist her is not exactly understood, even when it is made known as a fact. People will object that no countenance from the aristocracy could avail to warp or disturb either the public or the critical appreciation of her works. But the way in which a large body of fashionable supporters can be made to assist an author is this: A woman of rank goes about canvassing for subscribers or for purchasers, as the case may be: "An interesting young friend of mine," she says, "has written a sweet little thing called *Bas Bleu;* and positively I must have your name down on my list of patronizers to her genius." Now, with as much influence as belonged either to Mrs. Montagu or to the Duchess of Beaufort, it was easy to collect names enough to carry off three or four impressions. Then mark what follows. The fact, the naked fact, without comment or explanation, that three or four editions of a book have been carried off in three or four days, being reported in every newspaper,

travels with the speed of light all over the kingdom.
People in the provinces are naturally anxious to see
what is reported to have made so deep an impression on
the metropolis; and very often, doubtless, they create
for themselves all that they have been taught to expect.
I myself, within my own narrow experience, have
known many instances where a book was bought (as,
in particular, Mrs. More's *Cœlebs*) for no other reason
than because some startling amount of editions had already been sold in London; and this I have known
done by people who, had they happened to be in the secret, and to have been aware that the first three editions, which operated, by their rapid sale, as the *decoy
editions* to the public, had been really bought almost
exclusively by distinguished friends of the author,
prepared for months before its appearance to expect
the book, and who had in fact bespoke their copies,
would undoubtedly have allowed no weight at all to
the startling phenomenon of the sudden sale.

Such was the whole amount of Hannah More's history as known to myself, except as to one incident, perhaps to herself the most interesting in her life. This
was her marriage disappointment. What were the exact circumstances under which it took place I have
never been able to ascertain. . . . However, there certainly *was* some story of a delicate nature (in the belief of Mrs. More's best friends). And I have received
the following as the true fact from a clergyman of
great respectability, and a fervent friend of Mrs. H.
More's: The morning was fixed for the marriage; Mrs.
More's friends were all in attendance, and, after
breakfasting together, had actually proceeded to the
church where, by appointment, they were to meet the
bridegroom. They actually waited above an hour in
the porch, looking out for his arrival, and as yet with
no suspicion of his dishonourable intentions. At length

a single horseman was seen approaching; he advanced
to the steps, dismounted, and presented to Miss More a
letter, in which the gentleman pleaded simply, as a
reason for receding from his engagements, that he
could not bring his mind, at the hour of crisis, to so solemn and so irrevocable a contract. He offered, however, to make such reparation as could be made, in a
pecuniary sense, to Miss More; but this intention, if
he really had it at the time, would, no doubt, have died
away as soon as the immediate difficulty was overcome.
The friends of Miss More, aware of that, pressed him
vigorously, and would grant no delay. The sequel was
that, rather than stand a prosecution, he settled on
Miss More a handsome provision—my informant believes, not less, but rather more, than £400 per annum
for life.

I now return to my own personal acquaintance
with Mrs. H. More. My first introduction to her was
under the following circumstances: In the year 1809,
I had come down to Westhay (the villa of my friend
Mrs. ———[1]) on a visit of some months. The time of
year might be May, or early in June; and the particular morning was one of peculiar splendour. Sitting by
accident at a window of my dressing-room, which
looked out upon the approach to the house, I observed
a plain-looking carriage coming up the grounds, at the
rate of about four miles an hour. In those days the eye
was familiar enough with the image of languid motion under all possible varieties; even the Bristol mail,
the swiftest in the kingdom, did not then perform
much above seven miles an hour. But a pace so *very*
cautious indicated the presence of ladies, probably of
old ladies; and a sudden recollection that it was yet

[1] His mother.—ED.

scarcely twelve o'clock argued that the party must be a
privileged one; how else venture to present itself on a
morning call at an hour so antediluvian? Antediluvian, indeed, were all things inside and outside the
equipage. "Castor and Pollux!" exclaimed a young
Oxonian of the Westhay family, "what a set out!";
yet, at least, it wore an air of harmony in its self-consistency. The horses were manifestly pets, sleek and
dull, crammed up to the throats, and apparently
worked at the rate of thirty miles a month. The coachman seemed, after *his* kind, a pet also; consequently,
sleek and dull, crammed up to the throat, and worked
on the same severe scale. He wore a look of demure
solemnity, which it was his intention to pass off for the
expression of exceeding religious devotion. Unfortunately, it conveyed rather an opposite impression of
exceeding knavery; and, a knave he was, of the first
water—a *fourbe fourbissime*, in the language of Mo-
lière, or *rascal rascalissimus*, as I had afterwards occasion to know. The carriage itself had the air of being
also a pet. It was hung low, was sad-coloured, roomy
and considerate in its dimensions, allowing ample
scope and verge enough for the most Dutch proportions, and seemed so well furnished with cushions, or
squabs, to speak technically, and those squabs, again,
so luxuriously plump and downy, that one could not
figure to one's self for such a carriage any harsher destiny than that of carrying forth some podagrous bishop
upon his gentle matutinal airings in seasons when all
the zephyrs were abroad. Bishop, however, it was not,
but the friend of bishops, whom it now conveyed. We
had continued speculating upon its probable contents
as the lazy equipage moved towards the house; and at
last my young Oxonian friend, exclaiming suddenly to
me, "By the powers, it is Holy Hannah coming to look

at your premises," shot downwards to present his arm
to the ladies in executing the very difficult manœuvre
of alighting.

Imagine, then, at length, the portly carriage solemnly anchored alongside the main entrance of the
house, the carriage door opened, and the steps duly unfolded to the very last, which grazed the surface of the
ground, in preparation for discharging its jolly freightage of dames. Jolly they were, in every acceptation of
that word; ample and roomy as their carriage; and absolutely noisy in their expressions of gaiety and good
humour. Such, at least, was the description of the two
sisters who on that morning accompanied Mrs. Hannah More, but not of Mrs. Hannah herself: she was
neither large in person nor joyous in her manner. Her
deportment was lady-like and pleasing; but marked
with thoughtfulness, and sometimes, perhaps, with a
shade of sadness; or, to express both traits by a single
word, at least of pensiveness. People who are consciously the objects of much notice and curiosity wherever they appear rarely obtain so complete a mastery
over their feelings as to disembarrass themselves entirely of that constraint and awkward reserve which
accompany such a situation when continually forced
upon the consciousness. Certainly, for a woman who
had mixed so largely in the world, Mrs. H. More
seemed to have made as small advances toward such a
state of callous self-possession as any one person whom
it has been my fortune to know. She had even a tremor
in her manner, and at times, upon first presenting herself, a *mauvaise honte*, which almost amounted to agitation. But I am anticipating. The visit, as it appeared,
really was to myself, none being due at that time to
the family whom I was visiting. In saying this, I arrogate no particular importance beyond what Mrs.
More's courtesy allowed to every scholar; and such I

was reputed. My fame had been somewhat increased also, as I am ashamed to say, by a report current at that time which imputed to me, most untruly, some shape or other—I know not exactly what—of infidel philosophy.

My curiosity was, at any rate, sufficiently strong to have carried me down to the drawing-room; and, as it appeared that the visit was really to myself, it became my duty to descend. Of course, I did not keep the ladies waiting; and I had presented myself before they —so leisurely in their movements—had completed the process of seating themselves. All eyes directed me to the lion, or rather lioness, of the occasion. The lady of the house did me the favour to present me in form to her favourable notice. She received me with most gracious and winning smiles; and I took my seat upon a sofa by her side. I had previously seen almost everybody in England who enjoyed any great reputation for conversational talent; and I expected little in that way which could dazzle *me* from Mrs. H. More. In justice, I must say, that I found no more than I expected. Madame de Staël I had seen, but that was all. *Virgilium vidi tantum.* I could, through more channels than one, have commanded an introduction; but this my pride prevented me from seeking. Backed by no book of my own composition, I should have appeared to her a mere boy, and could not have interested her vanity in making a display before one so obscure. She, however, when she chose, or when she was adequately excited, could really perform with effect and execution; and, at times, she executed *bravuras,* or passages of colloquial effect, which electrified all who heard. Mrs. H. More was the most opposite creature in the world. She was modest, feminine, and, by nature, retiring. Her manners, which were those of a well-bred woman, accustomed to good society, and therefore free from all bustle, hurry, and excitement, supported the natural expression of her mind. It was only by a most unnatural and transient effort that she ever attempted to shine. On the other hand, to the eye, she was a far more pleasing woman than the masculine De Staël. That most pretending of God's women was a hideous-looking creature, with a huge structure of bones about the shoulders, fitter for a Mammoth or a Megatherium than a reasonable woman. Her chest, especially when viewed *en profile* was, as a London wit remarked, like a chest of drawers. And her black hair, floating in masses about her temples, her fierce eyes, and her impassioned gestures, gave her, when declaiming, the air of a Pythoness upon her tripod, or of some dark sibyl thirsting for the blood of Œdipus. Add whiskers and mustachios, and, without a doubt, she would have frightened and put to flight the advanced posts of an army. But Mrs. H. More was soft, delicate, and agreeable; and, in youth, must have been pretty. Her eyes only were too bright for absolute repose of countenance; else hers would have been nearly quiescent. Her sisters were, if not more interesting, at least more entertaining; especially Mrs. Sally, who had exuberant spirits, mirth, and good nature: and Mrs. Patty, who was distinguished for humour, or at least drollery; and from her pen had proceeded many of the most lively amongst the Repository Tracts.

The times in which I had thus become acquainted with Mrs. H. More were times of profound political interest—I may truly say, describing my own feelings, times of awful agitation. A power had arisen in France which, going on through stages of transmigration from one horrid birth to another, was at length settled, as might seem, in its final development, having obtained an organization more potent than ever this world had seen for evil, and for the propagation of evil.

Until the era of the Consulate, the French Revolution
had passed through many forms—all bad, and some
weak. . . . Under circumstances like these, and at a crisis so appalling, those who felt the interest appropriate
to the times had leisure for no other interest; and the
first question which arose with regard to any person on
whom much attention was fixed concerned the nature
and quality of their views upon foreign politics. Accordingly, my own first impulse, as regarded Mrs. H.
More, was to apply some mete-wand to the state of her
sentiments upon all that regarded Napoleon Bonaparte.
I knew that she was loyal, and well-affected to the
Government—that she was an Antigallican—that she
was an Antijacobin. Yet, having said this, I have said
all that does credit to her political firmness or sagacity; for, in other respects, she was deeply enslaved to
the meanest superstitions of the day. There was at that
time, and ever since the year 1796 there had been, a
most ridiculous prostration of the English mind to the
prestige of French generalship. This was an abject and
pitiable superstition; and often had I occasion to combat it in conversation, without finding a single ally,
until the triumphs of the Peninsular War, beginning
to dawn in 1808, first gave me some vantage-ground.
With Mrs. H. More I argued in the same key, but absolutely without effect. "I grant," she would often
say, "everything you can urge for British courage;
but——" and then came the old story of courage
matched against the magic of talent, &c.; the whole
amount of which was this, when put into plainer language, as I repeatedly told her—that we British were
in effect a race of brainless bull-dogs, with animal
courage enough and to spare, but without sense or sagacity to guide it; whilst the French had credit, not
merely for all the talent, but absolutely for a sort of
magic, and of supernatural art, by which effects were

produced beyond the reach of ordinary tactics to explain. Those days were the days of my fervid youth. I was then *calidus juventa, Consule Planco;* at which period of life a man's patience is not his most shining virtue. And very often, I confess, absolutely I shivered with wrath when I heard, by insinuation, such disparagement offered to the mighty nation amongst whom I gloried to have been born.

Contrasting the mighty object thus insulted with the trivial insulter (a blue-stocking manufacturer of sentiment), I acknowledge that I gradually became more careless of Mrs. H. More's acquaintance than I had even originally been, and still more insensible of any merit which she possessed. However, I determined that she should not mistake me for a mere John Bull, fierce upon his imagined superiority without knowing anything of the grounds which sustain it. Not enduring to talk much with her upon such a theme, I threw into what I meant for my parting colloquies some hits which, I was well assured, she could not parry; and I was truly delighted to see that I stung her beyond all power of dissembling. . . .

Here, then, at the very outset of my intimacy with Mrs. H. More, was laid a solid foundation for mutual dislike. We began our acquaintance with no great love; and, to use Mr. Slender's account of his progress with fair Mistress Ann Page, "it pleased God to decrease it upon further acquaintance." But, upon the very second visit which I paid her, another indication was drawn forth of Mrs. More's intellect, which sealed my disgust. Having called at Barley Wood in the morning, I had received an invitation to spend the evening there—an invitation which I willingly accepted, as two or three of the sisters were conspicuous for their high spirits and amiable temper, always ready to amuse and to be amused; besides which, one might generally rely upon meeting some agreeable society from the neighbouring families of the vale. On such occasions it was usual to go early; for the ladies dined at four o'clock, and were glad to see their friends as soon as possible after five. On this particular occasion I remember that I found a large party of young ladies assembled on the lawn. In the course of the evening some conversation had arisen in which one of the company had built some argument upon, or drawn some illustrations from, poetry. Upon this Mrs. Hannah More, with the air of one who is delivering some brilliant *propos*, had taken upon herself to say, "Poetry! oh! as to poetry, I forswore *that*, and I think everybody else should forswear it, together with pink ribbons"; meaning, I suppose, in youth. Mr. Wordsworth has remarked, as one feature of a luxurious and feeble condition of society in an intellectual sense, that the grandest functions of the human mind are degraded into the mere ministers of stimulation or of trivial ornament, and that people talk of a "taste" for poetry as they would of a taste for Frontiniac or for rope-dancing. I, however, had learned to think higher by far, and with mysterious reverence, of the genial art: I had learned to view it as the science of human passion in all its fluxes and refluxes—in its wondrous depths below depths, and its starry altitudes that ascended to the gates of heaven. Mrs. H. More would talk learnedly in her books upon the dignity of human nature: she could not do otherwise; for, though she delighted also to talk of its degradation and corruption, yet, unless originally and indefeasibly it possessed some unspeakable grandeur, how or with what propriety could its restoration have become the subject of a mysterious scheme in the councils of Heaven? Such, however, was her inconsistency that the very art which kept the golden keys for unlocking the whole economy of the human heart—that world of hopes and fears, of heights and shadowy depths, of laughter and of tears—was dismissed to her *chiffonier*, or rag depot, together with old filigree, paste pearls, and obsolete bracelets. I burned to speak in reply. But I had this infirmity— that, whenever I spoke (if it were but a word) upon a theme which challenged any peculiar depth of sympathy from its importance, inevitably my voice trembled. This effect, which I could not dissemble, made a pause and a "sensation" in the conversation, by too pointedly arresting the attention of the company; which was not in the right key of well-bred society. It made something too like a *scene*. On this account I was silent. But, just at the moment when it seemed certain that Mrs. H. More was to bear off her pretty remark, neither "noted" nor "protested," forth stepped a young lady, "severe in youthful beauty," and, with a modest but yet not a timid air, put in this unanswerable demurrer—"Really, Mrs. Hannah More, I could never presume so far as to look upon anything in the light of a trifle which Milton had not disdained to spend his life in cultivating. Surely I ought not to rank the *Paradise Lost* with pink ribbons?" Here was a *duplie* (in the lawyers' phrase) to which it was vain for Mrs. More to attempt a *triplie*. This was a smasher; and I could have kissed the lovely girl, if I durst, for so seasonable a service. As to Mrs. Hannah More, I am sorry to say that she took the reproof with no very charitable expression of eye; she was silent *per force;* for what *could* she have said? But her eye said for her as plainly as possible—"You are a very impertinent young woman!" However, Milton *v.* the Author of the *Search after Happiness* was a case admitting of no reply.

* * *

I have often wondered at the shallowness of the soil which could be supposed capable of receiving much

culture or much manuring from instructions so slight,
and so unsustained even by extensive reading, as Mrs.
Hannah More's. The whole stream of her illustrations
was naturally derived from History; and yet on how
narrow a basis reposed her acquaintance with that prodigious body of records, and in the choice of her reading how little had she shown of research or of desire to
visit the fountain-heads! One day I happened, in conversation with her, to mention Coligni, the well-
known Protestant leader in the times of Charles IX.
To my great surprise, she seemed perplexed, and quite
at fault. "Coligni," I repeated, "the Admiral: he, you
know, who became substantially the head of the Protestants after the assassination of Condé": and then, seeing that she still looked confused, I added, "the very
chief of those who suffered at Paris in the St. Bartholomew butchery." "Oh! yes," she replied, "the conspiracy of St. Bartholomew; I remember: that was a shocking affair." But, though she remembered the name and
designation of this great event, it was evident that she
had no remembrance at all of the great persons who
had figured in it, whether as actors or as sufferers. . . .
At length Mrs. H. More began to complain that all
history would unsettle its foundations, and nothing be
left to rely upon, if such a spirit of scrutiny were encouraged. But this was no better objection to the justice of such a course than it would be in a magistrate
to allege that some great criminal investigation must
be stifled as likely to involve too many or too distinguished persons in its consequences. On the whole,
however, I ascertained that she was neither well-read
in History (the only distinct branch of knowledge, excepting theology, which she professed), nor willing to
encounter the pains of steadily supplying her deficiencies. Often, indeed, I had occasion to remember
the cynical remark of Swift—that, after all, as respects

mere learning, the most accomplished woman is hardly
on a level with a schoolboy. In quoting this saying, I
have restricted it so as to offer no offence to the female
sex intellectually considered. Swift probably meant to
undervalue women generally. Now, I am well aware
that they have their peculiar province. But that province does not extend to *learning*, technically so called.
No woman ever was or will be a *polyhistor*, like Salmasius, for example; nor a philosopher; nor in fact
anything whatsoever, called by what name you like,
which demands either of these two combinations which
follow—1, great powers of combination, that is, of
massing or grouping under large comprehensive principles; or, 2, severe logic.[1]

The reason that Mrs. H. More had so slender an acquaintance with History was, in fact, that she had no
philosophical principles; none of any sort; and from
the very name and offices of all such knowledge she retreated with horror. Hence it was, and not from want
of reading, that she knew little or nothing of the true
steps by which Europe had attained her present state
of civilization. There is no way for retaining the mere
facts of history, and the prodigious succession of similar events, unless by attaching them as illustrations to
previous theories of the forces, powers, and agencies
then operating and moulding the course both of things
and persons without any distinct consciousness on the
part of those who forward the general process. Hannah
More had no such theories—no general principles, I
mean, of any kind, unless in theology; and upon that
subject only, clothed in the wisdom of others, she did
occasionally talk wisely.

She was, in fact, to sum up her pretensions, an

[1] Hence, by the way, *i.e.* from this last postulate, the difficulty that a woman should be a Political Economist—that is,
in a rigid sense.

agreeable, an amiable, and a clever woman, who had
been a little spoiled by flattery, and had been pushed
forward by feeble-minded women of rank to assume a
station of authority which did not naturally belong to
her, and which was never manifested without seeming
particularly unbecoming as associated with those retiring qualities of modesty and reserve which did really
cling to her inmost nature. As a writer, how eminently
artificial she was, notwithstanding some imaginary
admiration which she always professed for simplicity,
is evident from the very structure of her sentences;
which are all turned as in a lathe, and are so entirely
dependent for their effect upon antithesis, or direct
contraposition in the words, even where there is little
or none in the thoughts, that once a great poet, opening one of her works and reading a paragraph, made
this remark to me—"These feeble thinkers dare not
trust a single thought to its native powers: so afraid
are they of seeming dull, and so conscious of no innate
right to challenge or support attention, that each particular sentence is polished into a sparkling and independent whole; so that, open the book where you will,
all has an exterior brilliancy, and will bear being detached without any injury to its effect, having no sort
of natural cohesion with the context, or dependency
upon what goes before." Her *Cœlebs*, again, showed in
another way her artificial way of thinking; for, assuredly, her natural delicacy would have made her revolt from the grossness implied in the whole plan of
that novel, and expressed in its very title, *Cœlebs in
Search of a Wife*. Such a search would, in real life,
cover any man with ridicule, and the woman on whom
his preference settled with shame. But, with all these
ineradicable disadvantages, Mrs. More's works have
their value. The very dilution of their thoughts rec-
ommends them, and adapts them to those who would

shrink from severer or profounder speculations, and who seek, in all they read, to see their own ordinary sentiments reflected. Still, even thus, Mrs. H. More is not destined to any long existence. The species, the class, of such writers, it is true, will always be in demand; but the individual perishes, because each successive generation looks for specific adaptation to itself, for illustrations drawn from the objects moving upon its own peculiar field of experience, and possessing that sort of interest which is always attached preeminently to a living writer.

CHARLES LAMB [I]

(First published in *Tait's Magazine*, 1838)

AMONGST the earliest literary acquaintances I made was that with the inimitable Charles Lamb: inimitable, I say, but the word is too limited in its meaning; for, as is said of Milton in that well-known life of him attached to all common editions of the *Paradise Lost* (Fenton's, I think), "in both senses he was above imitation." Yes; it was as impossible to the moral nature of Charles Lamb that he should imitate another as, in an intellectual sense, it was impossible that any other should successfully imitate him. To write with patience even, not to say genially, for Charles Lamb it was a very necessity of his constitution that he should write from his own wayward nature; and that nature was so peculiar that no other man, the ablest at mimicry, could counterfeit its voice. But let me not anticipate; for these were opinions about Lamb which I had not when I first knew him, nor could have had by any reasonable title. "Elia," be it observed, the exquisite "Elia," was then unborn; Lamb had as yet published

nothing to the world which proclaimed him in his
proper character of a most original man of genius [1]: at
best, he could have been thought no more than a man
of talent—and of talent moving in a narrow path, with
a power rather of mimicking the quaint and the fantastic than any large grasp over catholic beauty. And,
therefore, it need not offend the most doting admirer
of Lamb as he is *now* known to us, a brilliant star for
ever fixed in the firmament of English Literature, that
I acknowledge myself to have sought his acquaintance
rather under the reflex honour he had enjoyed of being
known as Coleridge's friend than for any which he yet
held directly and separately in his own person. My
earliest advances towards this acquaintance had an in-
auspicious aspect; and it may be worth while reporting
the circumstances, for they were characteristic of
Charles Lamb; and the immediate result was—that
we parted, not perhaps (as Lamb says of his philosophic friend R. and the Parisians) "with mutual contempt," but at least with coolness; and, on my part,
with something that might have even turned to dis-

---

[1] *"Man of genius"* . . . *"man of talent"*: I have, in another
place, laid down what I conceive to be the true ground of distinction between *genius* and *talent*; which lies mainly in this
—that genius is intellectual power impregnated with the *moral*
nature, and expresses a synthesis of the active in man with his
original organic capacity of pleasure and pain. Hence the very
word *genius*, because the *genial* nature in its whole organization is expressed and involved in it. Hence, also, arises the
reason that genius is always peculiar and individual; one man's
genius never exactly repeats another man's. But talent is the
same in all men; and that which is effected by talent can
never serve to identify or indicate its author. Hence, too, that,
although talent is the object of respect, it never conciliates
love; you love a man of talent perhaps *in concreto*, but not
talent; whereas genius, even for itself, is idolized. I am the
more proud of this distinction since I have seen the utter failure of Mr. Coleridge, judging from his attempt in his *Table-
Talk*.

gust—founded, however, entirely on my utter misapprehension of Lamb's character and his manners—had it not been for the winning goodness of Miss Lamb, before which all resentment must have melted in a moment.

It was either late in 1804 or early in 1805, according to my present computations, that I had obtained from a literary friend a letter of introduction to Mr. Lamb. All that I knew of his works was his play of *John Woodvil*, which I had bought in Oxford, and perhaps *I* only had bought throughout that great University, at the time of my matriculation there, about the Christmas of 1803.

I had requested the letter of introduction to him rather with a view to some further knowledge of Coleridge (who was then absent from England) than from any special interest about Lamb himself. However, I felt the extreme discourtesy of approaching a man and asking for his time and civility under such an avowal: and the letter, therefore, as I believe, or as I requested, represented me in the light of an admirer. I hope it did; for that character might have some excuse for what followed, and heal the unpleasant impression likely to be left by a sort of *fracas* which occurred at my first meeting with Lamb. This was so characteristic of Lamb that I have often laughed at it since I came to know what *was* characteristic of Lamb.

But first let me describe my brief introductory call upon him at the India House. I had been told that he was never to be found at home except in the evenings; and to have called then would have been, in a manner, forcing myself upon his hospitalities, and at a moment when he might have confidential friends about him; besides that, he was sometimes tempted away to the theatres. I went, therefore, to the India House; made inquiries amongst the servants; and, after some trouble (for *that* was early in his Leadenhall Street career, and possibly he was not much known), I was shown into a small room, or else a small section of a large one (thirty-four years affects one's remembrance of some circumstances), in which was a very lofty writing-desk, separated by a still higher railing from that part of the floor on which the profane—the laity, like myself—were allowed to approach the *clerus*, or clerkly rulers of the room. Within the railing sat, to the best of my remembrances, six quill-driving gentlemen; not gentlemen whose duty or profession it was merely to drive the quill, but who were then driving it—*gens de plume*, such *in esse*, as well as *in posse*—in act as well as habit; for, as if they supposed me a spy sent by some superior power to report upon the situation of affairs as surprised by me, they were all too profoundly immersed in their oriental studies to have any sense of my presence. Consequently, I was reduced to a necessity of announcing myself and my errand. I walked, therefore, into one of the two open doorways of the railing, and stood closely by the high stool of him who occupied the first place within the little aisle. I touched his arm, by way of recalling him from his lofty Leadenhall speculations to this sublunary world; and, presenting my letter, asked if that gentleman (pointing to the address) were really a citizen of the present room; for I had been repeatedly misled, by the directions given me, into wrong rooms. The gentleman smiled; it was a smile not to be forgotten. This was Lamb. And here occurred a *very*, *very* little incident—one of those which pass so fugitively that they are gone and hurrying away into Lethe almost before your attention can have arrested them; but it was an incident which, to me, who happened to notice it, served to express the courtesy and delicate consideration of Lamb's manners. The seat upon which he sat was a very high

one; so absurdly high, by the way, that I can imagine
no possible use or sense in such an altitude, unless it
were to restrain the occupant from playing truant at
the fire by opposing Alpine difficulties to his descent.

Whatever might be the original purpose of this aspiring seat, one serious dilemma arose from it, and this
it was which gave the occasion to Lamb's act of courtesy. Somewhere there is an anecdote, meant to illustrate the ultra-obsequiousness of the man—either I
have heard of it in connexion with some actual man
known to myself, or it is told in a book of some historical coxcomb—that, being on horseback, and meeting
some person or other whom it seemed advisable to flat-
ter, he actually dismounted, in order to pay his court
by a more ceremonious bow. In Russia, as we all know,
this was, at one time, upon meeting any of the Imperial family, an act of legal necessity: and there, accordingly, but there only, it would have worn no ludicrous aspect. Now, in this situation of Lamb's, the act
of descending from his throne, a very elaborate process,
with steps and stages analogous to those on horseback
—of slipping your right foot out of the stirrup, throwing your leg over the crupper, &c.—was, to all intents
and purposes, the same thing as dismounting from a
great elephant of a horse. Therefore it both was, and
was felt to be by Lamb, supremely ludicrous. On the
other hand, to have sate still and stately upon this
aerial station, to have bowed condescendingly from
this altitude, would have been—not ludicrous indeed;
performed by a very superb person, and supported by
a very superb bow, it might have been vastly fine, and
even terrifying to many young gentlemen under sixteen; but it would have had an air of ungentlemanly
assumption. Between these extremes, therefore, Lamb
had to choose; between appearing ridiculous himself
for a moment, by going through a ridiculous evolu-

tion which no man could execute with grace; or, on the
other hand, appearing lofty and assuming, in a degree which his truly humble nature (for he was the
humblest of men in the pretensions which he put forward for himself) must have shrunk from with horror. Nobody who knew Lamb can doubt how the problem was solved: he began to dismount instantly; and,
as it happened that the very first *round* of his descent
obliged him to turn his back upon me as if for a sudden
purpose of flight, he had an excuse for laughing; which
he did heartily——saying, at the same time, something
to this effect: that I must not judge from first appearances; that he should revolve upon me; that he was not
going to fly; and other facetiæ, which challenged a
general laugh from the clerical brotherhood.

When he had reached the basis of terra firma on
which I was standing, naturally, as a mode of thank-
ing him for his courtesy, I presented my hand; which,
in a general case, I should certainly not have done; for
I cherished, in an ultra-English degree, the English
custom (a wise custom) of bowing in frigid silence on
a first introduction to a stranger; but, to a man of literary talent, and one who had just practised so much
kindness in my favour at so probable a hazard to himself of being laughed at for his pains, I could not maintain that frosty reserve. Lamb took my hand; did not
absolutely reject it: but rather repelled my advance by
his manner. This, however, long afterwards I found,
was only a habit derived from his too great sensitiveness to the variety of people's feelings, which run
through a gamut so infinite of degrees and modes as
to make it unsafe for any man who respects himself to
be too hasty in his allowances of familiarity. Lamb
had, as he was entitled to have, a high self-respect;
and me he probably suspected (as a young Oxonian)
of some aristocratic tendencies. The letter of introduc-

tion, containing (I imagine) no matters of business, was speedily run through; and I instantly received an invitation to spend the evening with him. Lamb was not one of those who catch at the chance of escaping from a bore by fixing some distant day, when accidents (in duplicate proportion, perhaps, to the number of intervening days) may have carried you away from the place: he sought to benefit by no luck of that kind; for he was, with his limited income—and I say it deliberately—positively the most hospitable man I have known in this world. That night, the same night, I was to come and spend the evening with him. I had gone to the India House with the express purpose of accepting whatever invitation he should give me; and, therefore, I accepted this, took my leave, and left Lamb in the act of resuming his aerial position.

I was to come so early as to drink tea with Lamb; and the hour was seven. He lived in the Temple; and I, who was not then, as afterwards I became, a student and member of "the Honourable Society of the Middle Temple," did not know much of the localities. However, I found out his abode, not greatly beyond my time: nobody had been asked to meet me—which a little surprised me, but I was glad of it; for, besides Lamb, there was present his sister, Miss Lamb, of whom, and whose talents and sweetness of disposition, I had heard. I turned the conversation, upon the first opening which offered, to the subject of Coleridge; and many of my questions were answered satisfactorily, because seriously, by Miss Lamb. But Lamb took a pleasure in baffling me, or in throwing ridicule upon the subject. Out of this grew the matter of our affray. We were speaking of "The Ancient Mariner." Now, to explain what followed, and a little to excuse myself, I must beg the reader to understand that I was under twenty years of age, and that my admiration for Cole-

ridge (as, in perhaps a still greater degree, for Wordsworth) was literally in no respect short of a religious
feeling: it had, indeed, all the sanctity of religion, and
all the tenderness of a human veneration. Then, also,
to imagine the strength which it would derive from
circumstances that do not exist now, but did then, let
the reader further suppose a case—not such as he may
have known since that era about Sir Walter Scotts and
Lord Byrons, where every man you could possibly fall
foul of, early or late, night or day, summer or winter,
was in perfect readiness to feel and express his sympathy with the admirer—but when no man, beyond
one or two in each ten thousand, had so much as heard
of either Coleridge or Wordsworth, and that one, or
those two, knew them only to scorn them, trample on
them, spit upon them. Men so abject in public estimation, I maintain, as that Coleridge and that Wordsworth, had not existed before, have not existed since,
will not exist again. We have heard in old times of
donkeys insulting effete or dying lions by kicking
them; but in the case of Coleridge and Wordsworth it
was effete donkeys that kicked living lions. They, Coleridge and Wordsworth, were the Pariahs of literature
in those days: as much scorned wherever they were
known; but escaping that scorn only because they were
as little known as Pariahs, and even more obscure.

Well, after this bravura, by way of conveying my
sense of the real position then occupied by these two authors—a position which thirty and odd years have altered, by a revolution more astonishing and total than
ever before happened in literature or in life—let the
reader figure to himself the sensitive horror with which
a young person, carrying his devotion about with him,
of necessity, as the profoundest of secrets, like a primitive Christian amongst a nation of Pagans, or a Roman
Catholic convert amongst the bloody idolaters of Japan

—in Oxford, above all places, hoping for no sympathy, and feeling a daily grief, almost a shame, in harbouring this devotion to that which, nevertheless, had done more for the expansion and sustenance of his own inner mind than all literature besides—let the reader figure, I say, to himself, the shock with which such a person must recoil from hearing the very friend and associate of these authors utter what seemed at that time a burning ridicule of all which belonged to them—their books, their thoughts, their places, their persons. This had gone on for some time before we came upon the ground of "The Ancient Mariner"; I had been grieved, perplexed, astonished; and how else could I have felt reasonably, knowing nothing of Lamb's propensity to mystify a stranger; he, on the other hand, knowing nothing of the depth of my feelings on these subjects, and that they were not so much mere literary preferences as something that went deeper than life or household affections? At length, when he had given utterance to some ferocious canon of judgement, which seemed to question the entire value of the poem, I said, perspiring (I dare say) in this detestable crisis—"But, Mr. Lamb, good heavens! how is it possible you can allow yourself in such opinions? What instance could you bring from the poem that would bear you out in these insinuations?"

"Instances!" said Lamb: "oh, I'll instance you, if you come to that. Instance, indeed! Pray, what do you say to this—

> *The many men so beautiful,*
> *And they all dead did lie?*

So beautiful, indeed! Beautiful! Just think of such a gang of Wapping vagabonds, all covered with pitch, and chewing tobacco; and the old gentleman himself—what do you call him?—the bright-eyed fellow?"

What more might follow I never heard; for, at this point, in a perfect rapture of horror, I raised my hands —both hands—to both ears; and, without stopping to think or to apologize, I endeavoured to restore equanimity to my disturbed sensibilities by shutting out all further knowledge of Lamb's impieties. At length he seemed to have finished; so I, on my part, thought I might venture to take off the embargo: and in fact he *had* ceased; but no sooner did he find me restored to my hearing than he said with a most sarcastic smile— which he could assume upon occasion—"If you please, sir, we'll say grace before we begin." I know not whether Lamb were really piqued or not at the mode by which I had expressed my disturbance: Miss Lamb certainly was not; her goodness led her to pardon me, and to treat me—in whatever light she might really view my almost involuntary rudeness—as the party who had suffered wrong; and, for the rest of the evening, she was so pointedly kind and conciliatory in her manner that I felt greatly ashamed of my boyish failure in self-command. Yet, after all, Lamb necessarily appeared so much worse, in my eyes, as a traitor is worse than an open enemy.

Lamb, after this one visit—not knowing at that time any particular reason for continuing to seek his acquaintance—I did not trouble with my calls for some years. At length, however, about the year 1808, and for the six or seven following years, in my evening visits to Coleridge, I used to meet him again; not often, but sufficiently to correct altogether the very false impression I had received of his character and manners. I have elsewhere described him as a "Diogenes with the heart of a St. John." And, by ascribing to Lamb any sort of resemblance to Diogenes, I had a view only to his plain speaking in the first place—his unequalled freedom from every mode of hypocrisy or affectation;

and, secondly, to his talent for saying keen, pointed things, sudden flashes, or revelations of hidden truths, in a short condensed form of words. In fact, the very foundation of Lamb's peculiar character was laid in his absolute abhorrence of all affectation. This showed itself in self-disparagement of every kind; never the mock disparagement which is self-praise in an indirect form, as when people accuse themselves of all the virtues by professing an inability to pay proper attention to prudence or economy—or uncontrollable disposition to be rash and inconsiderate on behalf of a weaker party when suffering apparent wrong. But Lamb's confessions of error, of infirmity, were never at any time acts of mock humility, meant to involve oblique compliment in the rebound. Thus, he honestly and frankly confessed his blank insensibility to music.

> *King David's harp, that made the madness flee*
> *From Saul, had been but a Jew's harp to me,*

is his plain, unvarnished admission, in verses admirable for their wit and their elegance: nor did he attempt to break the force of this unfortunate truth by claiming—which, perhaps, he might have claimed—a compensatory superiority in the endowments of his eye. It happened to him, as I believe it has often done to others—to Pope, perhaps, but certainly to Wordsworth—that the imperfect structure or imperfect development of the ear, denying any profound sensibility to the highest modes of impassioned music, has been balanced by a more than usual sensibility to some modes of visual beauty. Lamb sought his pleasures—not, as by this time all the world knows, in external nature, for which it was his pleasure to profess not merely an indifference, but even a horror which it de-

lighted him to exaggerate with a kind of playful malice to those whom he was hoaxing—but in the works
of the great painters: and for these I have good reason
to think that both he and his sister had a peculiarly
deep sensibility, and, after long practice, a fine and
matured taste. Here, then, was both a gift and an attainment which Lamb might have fairly pleaded in the
way of a set-off to his acknowledged defects of ear. But
Lamb was too really and sincerely humble ever to
think of nursing and tending his own character in any
man's estimation, or of attempting to blunt the effect
of his own honest avowals of imperfection by dexterously playing off before your eyes some counterbalanc-
ing accomplishment. He was, in fact, as I have said
before, the most humble and unpretending of human
beings, the most thoroughly sincere, the most impatient of either simulation or dissimulation, and the one
who threw himself the most unreservedly for your
good opinion upon the plain natural expression of his
real qualities, as nature had forced them, without artifice, or design, or disguise, more than you find in the
most childlike of children.

There was a notion prevalent about Lamb, which I
can affirm to have been a most erroneous one: it was—
that any flagrant act of wickedness formed a recommendation to his favour.

"Ah!" said one man to me, when asking a letter of
introduction from him—"ah! that I could but recommend you as a man that had robbed the mail, or the
King's exchequer—which would be better. In that case,
I need not add a word; you would take rank instantly
amongst the privileged friends of Lamb, without a
word from me."

Now, as to "*the King's Exchequer*," I cannot say.
A man who should have placed himself in relation with

Falstaff by obeying his commands [1] at a distance of four centuries (like the traveller who demanded of the turnpikeman—"How do you like your eggs dressed?" and, ten years after, on passing the same gate, received the monosyllabic reply—*poached*), that man might have presented irresistible claims to Lamb's affection. Shakespeare, or anything connected with Shakespeare, might have proved too much for his Roman virtue. But, putting aside any case so impossible as this, I can affirm that—so far from this being the truth, or approaching the truth—a rule the very opposite governed Lamb's conduct. So far from welcoming wicked, profligate, or dissolute people by preference, if they happened to be clever—he bore with numerous dull people, stupid people, asinine people, for no other reason upon earth than because he knew them, or believed them, to have been ill-used or oppressed by some clever but dissolute man. That was enough. Sufficient it was that they had been the objects of injustice, calumny, persecution, or wrong in any shape—and, without further question, they had "their place allowed" at Lamb's fireside. I knew some eminent instances of what I am now saying. And I used to think to myself, Were this feature of Lamb's character made known, and the natural results followed, what would he do? Refuse anybody, reject anybody, tell him to begone, he could not, no more than he could have danced upon his mother's grave. He would have received all who presented themselves with any rational pretensions, and would finally have gone to prison rather than reject anybody. I do not say this rhetorically. I knew Lamb; and I know certain cases in which he was concerned—cases which it is difficult to publish with any regard to the feelings of persons now living, but which

[1] "Rob me thy father's exchequer."—Falstaff, in *Henry IV*, *Part First*.

(if published in all their circumstances) would show him to be the very noblest of human beings. He was a man, in a sense more eminent than would be conceivable by many people, *princely*—nothing short of that —in his beneficence. Many liberal people I have known in this world—many who were charitable in the widest sense—many munificent people; but never any one upon whom, for bounty, for indulgence and forgiveness, for charitable construction of doubtful or mixed actions, and for regal munificence, you might have thrown yourself with so absolute a reliance as upon this comparatively poor Charles Lamb. Considered as a man of genius, he was not in the very first rank, simply because his range was a contracted one: within that range, he was perfect; of the peculiar powers which he possessed he has left to the world as exquisite a specimen as this planet is likely to exhibit. But, as a *moral* being, in the total compass of his relations to this world's duties, in the largeness and diffusiveness of his charity, in the graciousness of his condescension to inferior intellects, I am disposed, after a deliberate review of my own entire experience, to pronounce him the best man, the nearest in his approaches to an ideal standard of excellence, that I have known or read of. In the mingled purity—a childlike purity—and the benignity of his nature, I again express my own deep feeling of the truth, when I say that he recalled to my mind the image and character of St. John the Evangelist—of him who was at once the beloved apostle, and also, more peculiarly, the apostle of love. Well and truly, therefore, did the poet [1] say, in his beautiful lines upon this man's grave and memory—

[1] One feature there was in Lamb's charity which is but too frequently found wanting amongst the most liberal and large-hearted of the charitable, and especially where the natural temper is melancholy or desponding—one, moreover, which,

Oh, he was good, if e'er a good man lived!

Perhaps the foundation for the false notion I have mentioned about Lamb's predilections was to be found in his carelessness for those social proscriptions which have sometimes occurred in our stormy times with respect to writers, male and female, who set the dominant notions, or the prevailing feelings of men— (feelings with regard to sexual proprieties, to social distinctions, to the sanctity of property, to the sanctity of religious formulæ, &c. &c.) —at open defiance. Take, for example, Thelwall at one time, Holcroft, Godwin, Mrs. Wollstonecraft, Dr. Priestley, Hazlitt; all of whom were, more or less, in a backward or inverse sense, *tabooed*—that is, consecrated to public hatred and scorn. With respect to all these persons, feeling that the public alienation had gone too far, or had begun originally upon false grounds, Lamb threw his heart and his doors wide open. Politics—what cared he for politics? Religion—in the sense of theological dogmas—what cared he for religion? For religion in its

beyond any other aspect of charity, wears a winning grace— one, finally, which is indistinctly pointed out as a *duty* in our scriptural code of ethics: the habit of *hoping* cheerfully and kindly on behalf of those who were otherwise objects of moral blame. Lamb, if anybody, plagued as he was by a constitutional taint of morbid melancholy, might have been privileged to fail in this duty; but he did not. His goodness, making it too painful to him to cherish as *final* conclusions any opinions with regard to any individual which seemed to shut him out from the sympathy or the brotherly feeling of the just and good, overpowered the acuteness of his discernment; and, where it was quite impossible to find matter of approbation in the past or the present conduct, he would turn to the future for encouraging views of amendment, and would insist upon regarding what was past as the accidental irregularity, the anomaly, the exception, warranting no inferences with regard to what remained; and (whenever that was possible) would charge it all upon unfortunate circumstances.

moral aspects, and its relations to the heart of man, no
human being ever cared more. With respect to politics,
some of his friends could have wished him to hate men
when they grew *anti-national*, and in that case only;
but he would not. He persisted in liking men who made
an idol of Napoleon, who sighed over the dread name
of Waterloo, and frowned upon Trafalgar. *There* I
thought him wrong; but in that, as one of my guardians used to say of me, he "followed his own devil";
though, after all, I believe he took a secret, silent pleasure in the grandeur of his country, and would have
suffered in her suffering—would have been humiliated
in her humiliation—more than he altogether acknowledged to himself; in fact, his carelessness grew out of
the depth of his security. He could well afford to be
free of anxiety in a case like this; for the solicitudes of
jealous affection, the tremulous and apprehensive love,
as "of a mother or a child" (which painful mood of
love Wordsworth professes for his country, but only in
a wayward fit of passion), could scarcely be thought
applicable, even in the worst days of Napoleon, to a
national grandeur and power which seem as little liable
to chance or change, as essentially unapproachable by
any serious impeachment, as the principle of gravitation or the composition of the air. Why, therefore,
should *he* trouble himself more about the nice momentary oscillations of the national fortunes in war or
council, more than about adjusting his balance so as
not to disturb the equilibrium of the earth?

There was another trait of character about Charles
Lamb, which might have countenanced the common
notion that he looked indulgently upon dissolute men,
or men notorious for some criminal escapade. This was
his thorough hatred of all hypocrisy, and his *practical*
display of that hatred on all possible occasions. Even in
a point so foreign, as it might seem, from this subject

as his style, though chiefly founded upon his intellectual differences and his peculiar taste, the prevailing
tone of it was in part influenced (or at least sustained)
by his disgust for all which transcended the naked simplicity of truth. This is a deep subject, with as many
faces, or *facets* (to speak the language of jewellers), as
a rosecut diamond; and far be it from me to say one
word in praise of those—people of how narrow a sensibility!—who imagine that a simple (that is, according to many tastes, an unelevated and *unrhythmical*)
style—take, for instance, an Addisonian or a Swiftian
style—is *unconditionally* good. Not so: all depends
upon the subject; and there is a style transcending
these and all other modes of simplicity by infinite degrees, and in the same proportion impossible to most
men: the rhythmical—the continuous—what in
French is called the *soutenu;* which to humbler styles
stands in the relation of an organ to a shepherd's pipe.
This also finds its justification in its subject; and the
subject which *can* justify it must be of a corresponding
quality—loftier, and, therefore, rare.

If, then, in style—so indirect an expression as *that*
must be considered of his nature and moral feelings—
how much more in their direct and conscious expressions was Lamb impatient of hypocrisy! Hypocrisy
may be considered as the heroic form of affectation.
Now, the very basis of Lamb's character was laid in
downright horror of affectation. If he found himself
by accident using a rather fine word, notwithstanding
it might be the most forcible in that place (the word
arrest, suppose, in certain situations, for the word
catch), he would, if it were allowed to stand, make
merry with his own grandiloquence at the moment;
and, in after moments, he would continually ridicule
that class of words, by others carried to an extreme of
pedantry—the word *"arride,"* for instance, used in the

sense of *pleasing*, or *winning the approbation*—just as
Charles Fox, another patron of simplicity, or, at least,
of humility in style, was accustomed to use the word
"*vilipend*," as a standing way of sarcastically recalling
to the reader's mind the Latinizing writers of English.
Hence—that is, from this intense sincerity and truth
of character—Lamb would allow himself to say things
that shocked the feelings of the company—shocked
sometimes in the sense of startling or electrifying, as
by something that was odd; but also sometimes shocked
with the sense of what was revolting, as by a Swiftian
laying bare of naked shivering human nature. Such
exposures of masquerading vanity, such surgical prob-
ings and vexings of the secret feelings, I have seen almost truculently pursued by Lamb. He seemed angry
and fierce in such cases only; but the anger was for the
affectation and insincerity, which he could not endure,
unless where they covered some shame or timidity,
never where they were masks for attacking an individual. The case of insincerity, above all others, which
moved his bile was where, out of some pretended homage to public decorum, an individual was run down on
account of any moral infirmities, such as we all have,
or have had, or at least so easily and naturally may
have had that nobody knows whether we have them or
not. In such a case, and in this only almost, Lamb
could be savage in his manner. I remember one instance, where many of the leading authors of our age
were assembled—Coleridge, Wordsworth, Southey,
&c. Lamb was amongst them; and, when —— was denounced as a man careless in the education of his children, and generally reputed to lead a licentious life—
"Pretty fellows *we* are," said Lamb, "to abuse him on
that last score, when every one of us, I suppose, on
going out this night into the Strand, will make up to
the first pretty girl he sees." Some laughed; some

looked grim; some looked grand; but Wordsworth, smiling, and yet with solemnity, said—"I hope, I trust, Mr. Lamb, you are mistaken, or, at least, you do not include us all in this sweeping judgement?" "Oh, as to that," said Lamb, "who knows? There's no telling: sad Josephs are some of us in this very room." Upon which everybody laughed, and Lamb amongst them; but he had been indignant and sincere in this rebuke of the hypocritical sacrifice to decorum. He manifested a fervour of feeling in such cases; not of anger primarily to the assailant—*that* was but a reaction; his fervour was a movement of intense and conscientious justice towards the person assailed, as in one who felt that he himself, if not by the very same trespasses, had erred and was liable to err; that he also was a brother in human infirmity, and a debtor to the frailty of all flesh, though not possibly by the same overt acts or habits.

In reviewing the life of Lamb it is almost inevitable that, to a reader not specially acquainted with its events beyond what Sergeant Talfourd has judged it proper to communicate, many things will appear strange and unexplained. In a copy of the Sergeant's work now lying before me, which had been borrowed for my use from a distinguished literary lady, I find a pencil mark of interrogation attached to the word "*chequered*," by which, at p. 334, Vol. Two, Lamb's life is characterized. This is a natural expression of surprise, under the suppressions which have been here practised; suppressions dictated alike by delicacy for what is too closely personal, and by reverential pity for what is too afflicting. Still it will be asked by those who read attentively, In what sense was Lamb's life *chequered?*

This mysterious affliction of Lamb's life, making that a "chequered" one which else had been of a character too absolutely tranquil and monotonous—or ruffled, at least, only by *internal* irritations—was of a nature to revolve upon him at intervals. A poem of Wordsworth, one written at the very least thirty-two years ago, and having no reference at all to the Lambs —may furnish all the light which can be needed. The poet is speaking of a woman on the Borders, whose appearance and peculiar situation, in relation to a disabled husband, had caught his attention; and the expression of her eye is thus noticed:

> *I looked and scanned her o'er and o'er;*
> *The more I looked, I wondered more;*
> *When suddenly I seemed t' espy*
> *A trouble in her strong black eye—*
> *A remnant of uneasy light,*
> *A flash of something over-bright.*

Now, if the reader will ask himself what cause, apt to recur in some cases, would be likely to leave these morbid appearances in the eye, this *uneasy light,* and these flashes that were *over-bright*—he will then apprehend, in silence and reverential sympathy, what was that huge and steadfast affliction that besieged, through life, the heart of Charles Lamb.

If the reader will further understand that this affliction was not, as the heaviest afflictions oftentimes become, a mere remembrance echoing from past times— possibly "a long since cancelled woe"—but that it was a two-headed snake, looking behind and before, and gnawing at his heart by the double pangs of memory, and of anxiety, gloomy and fearful, watching for the future; and, finally, that the object of this anxiety, who might at any moment be torn from his fireside, to return after an interval of mutual suffering (not to be measured, or even guessed at, but in the councils of God), was that Madonna-like lady who to him re-

newed the case described with such pathetic tenderness
by the Homeric Andromache—being, in fact, his "all
the world"; fulfilling at once all offices of tenderness
and duty; and making up to him, in her single character of sister, all that he had lost of maternal kindness,
all that for *her* sake he had forborne to seek of affections conjugal or filial—weighing these accumulated
circumstances of calamity, the feeling reader will be
ready to admit that Lamb's cup of earthly sorrow was
full enough to excuse many more than he could be
taxed with of those half-crazy eccentricities in which
a constant load of secret affliction (such, I mean, as
must not be explained to the world) is apt to discharge
itself. Hence it might be in part—but some have supposed from a similar, though weaker, taint of the same
constitutional malady—that Lamb himself discovered
symptoms of irregular feeling or thinking, not such
as could have been alarming in a general or neutral
case, but in a subject known to be affected by these
hereditary predispositions *were* alarming, both to his
friends (those of them, at least, who had known the
circumstances), and, with far heavier reason, to himself. This also is therefore to be added to his afflictions
—not merely the fear constantly impending that his
fireside (as I said before) might be rendered desolate,
and *that* by a sudden blow, as well as for an indefinite
duration; but also the fear (not equally strong, but
equally impending for ever) that he himself, and all
his splendid faculties, might, as by a flash of lightning,
be swallowed up "in darkness infinite."

Such was the condition of Charles Lamb, and such
the temper that in part grew out of it—angelically benign, but also, in a morbid degree, melancholy—when
I renewed my acquaintance with him in 1808–14; a
period during which I learned to appreciate him better.
. . . And reason there was that I should. For in that

year 1814 occurred a trial of Lamb's hold upon his
friends' regard which was a test case—a test for each
side—since not every man could have mastered this offence, and far less could every man have merited that a
man *should* master it. This was the year which closed
the great war of wars by its first frail close—the capture of Paris by the Allies. And of these Allies all who
had any personal weight or interest (the Austrian Emperor, who was, however, expected at one time, is no
exception, for *his* weight was not personal but political)—all, I say, visited London and Oxford. I was at
London during that glad tumultuous season. I witnessed the fervent joy—the triumph, too noble, too religious, to be boastful—the rapture of that great era.

At this memorable season [Lamb's] wayward nature
showed itself more conspicuously than ever. One might
have thought that, if he manifested no sympathy in a
direct shape with the primary cause of the public emotion, still he would have sympathized, in a secondary
way, with the delirious joy which every street, every
alley, then manifested, to the ear as well as to the eye.
But no! Still, like Diogenes, he threw upon us all a
scoffing air, as of one who stands upon a pedestal of
eternity, looking down upon those who share in the
transitory feelings of their own age. How he felt in
the following year, when the mighty drama was consummated by Waterloo, I cannot say, for I was not
then in London: I guess, however, that he would have
manifested pretty much the same cynical contempt for
us children of the time that he did in all former cases.

Not until 1821, and again in 1823, did I come to
know Charles Lamb thoroughly. Politics, national enthusiasm, had then gone to sleep. I had come up to
London in a case connected with my own private interest. In the same spirit of frankness that I have shown
on other occasions in these personal sketches, I shall

here not scruple to mention that certain pecuniary embarrassments had rendered it necessary that I should extricate myself by literary toils. I was ill at that time, and for years after——ill from the effects of opium upon the liver; and one primary indication of any illness felt in that organ is peculiar depression of spirits. Hence arose a singular effect of reciprocal action, in maintaining a state of dejection. From the original physical depression caused by the derangement of the liver arose a sympathetic depression of the mind, disposing me to believe that I never *could* extricate myself; and from this belief arose, by reaction, a thousand-fold increase of the physical depression. I began to view my unhappy London life——a life of literary toils, odious to my heart——as a permanent state of exile from my Westmorland home. My three eldest children, at that time in the most interesting stages of childhood and infancy, were in Westmorland; and so powerful was my feeling (derived merely from a deranged liver) of some long, never-ending separation from my family, that at length, in pure weakness of mind, I was obliged to relinquish my daily walks in Hyde Park and Kensington Gardens, from the misery of seeing children in multitudes, that too forcibly recalled my own. The picture of Fox-ghyll, my Westmorland abode, and the solitary fells about it, upon which those were roaming whom I could not see, was for ever before my eyes. And it must be remembered that distance——the mere amount of distance——has much to do in such a case. You are equally divided from those you love, it is very true, by one hundred miles. But that, being a space which in England we often traverse in eight or ten hours, even without the benefit of railroads, has come to seem nothing at all. Fox-ghyll, on the other hand, was two hundred and eighty miles distant; and, from the obstacles at the latter end of the journey (cross-

roads and interruptions of all public communications),
it seemed twice as long.

Meantime, it is very true that the labours I had to
face would not, even to myself, in a state of good bodily
health, have appeared alarming. *Myself*, I say—for,
in any state of health, I do not write with rapidity.
Under the influence of opium, however, when it
reaches its maximum in diseasing the liver and derang-
ing the digestive functions, all exertion whatever is revolting in excess; intellectual exertion, above all, is
connected habitually, when performed under opium
influence, with a sense of disgust the most profound
for the subject (no matter what) which detains the
thoughts; all that morning freshness of animal spirits
which, under ordinary circumstances, consumes, as it
were, and swallows up the interval between one's self
and one's distant object (consumes, that is, in the same
sense as Virgil describes a high-blooded horse, on the
fret for starting, as traversing the ground with his eye,
and devouring the distance in fancy before it is approached): all that dewy freshness is exhaled and
burnt off by the parching effects of opium on the animal economy. You feel like one of Swift's *Strulbrugs*,
prematurely exhausted of life; and molehills are inevitably exaggerated by the feelings into mountains.
Not that it was molehills exactly which I had then to
surmount—they were moderate hills; but that made it
all the worse in the result, since my judgement could
not altogether refuse to go along with my feelings. I
was, besides, and had been for some time, engaged in
the task of unthreading the labyrinth by which I had
reached, unawares, my present state of slavery to
opium. I was descending the mighty ladder, stretching
to the clouds as it seemed, by which I had imperceptibly attained my giddy altitude—that point from
which it had seemed equally impossible to go forward

or backward. To wean myself from opium I had resolved inexorably; and finally I accomplished my vow. But the transition state was the worst state of all to support. All the pains of martyrdom were there: all the ravages in the economy of the great central organ, the stomach, which had been wrought by opium; the sickening disgust which attended each separate respiration; and the rooted depravation of the appetite and the digestion—all these must be weathered for months upon months, and without the stimulus (however false and treacherous) which, for some part of each day, the old doses of laudanum would have supplied. These doses were to be continually diminished; and, under this difficult dilemma: if, as some people advised, the diminution were made by so trifling a quantity as to be imperceptible—in that case, the duration of the process was interminable and hopeless. Thirty years would not have sufficed to carry it through. On the other hand, if twenty-five to fifty drops were withdrawn on each day (that is, from one to two grains of opium), inevitably within three, four, or five days, the deduction began to tell grievously; and the effect was to restore the craving for opium more keenly than ever. There was the collision of both evils—that from the laudanum, and that from the want of laudanum. The last was a state of distress perpetually increasing; the other was one which did not sensibly diminish—no, not for a long period of months. Irregular motions, impressed by a potent agent upon the blood or other processes of life, are slow to subside; they maintain themselves long after the exciting cause has been partially or even wholly withdrawn; and, in my case, they did not perfectly subside into the motion of tranquil health for several years.

From all this it will be easy to understand the *fact*—though, after all, impossible, without a similar experi-

ence, to understand the *amount*—of my suffering and
despondency in the daily task upon which circumstances had thrown me at this period—the task of writing and producing something for the journals *invita
Minerva*. Over and above the principal operation of my
suffering state, as felt in the enormous difficulty with
which it loaded every act of exertion, there was another secondary effect which always followed as a reaction from the first. And that this was no accident or
peculiarity attached to my individual temperament,
I may presume from the circumstance that Mr. Coleridge experienced the very same sensations, in the same
situation, throughout his literary life, and has often
noticed it to me with surprise and vexation. The sensation was that of powerful disgust with any subject
upon which he had occupied his thoughts, or had exerted his powers of composition for any length of time,
and an equal disgust with the result of his exertions—
powerful abhorrence I may call it, absolute loathing,
of all that he had produced.

Reverting to my own case, which was pretty nearly
the same as his, there was, however, this difference—
that, at times, when I had slept at more regular hours
for several nights consecutively, and had armed myself by a sudden increase of the opium for a few days
running, I recovered, at times, a remarkable glow of
jovial spirits. In some such artificial respites it was
from my usual state of distress, and purchased at a
heavy price of subsequent suffering, that I wrote the
greater part of the *Opium Confessions* in the autumn
of 1821. The introductory part (*i.e.* the narrative
part) written for the double purpose of creating an interest in what followed, and of making it intelligible,
since, without this narration, the dreams (which were
the real object of the whole work) would have had no
meaning, but would have been mere incoherencies—

this narrative part was written with singular rapidity. The rest might be said to have occupied an unusual length of time; since, though the mere penmanship might have been performed within moderate limits (and in fact under some pressure from the printer), the dreams had been composed slowly, and by separate efforts of thought, at wide intervals of time, according to the accidental prevalence, at any particular time, of the separate elements of such dream in my own real dream-experience. These circumstances I mention to account for my having written anything in a happy or genial state of mind, when I was in a general state so opposite, by my own description, to everything like enjoyment. That description, as a *general* one, states most truly the unhappy condition, and the somewhat extraordinary condition of feeling, to which opium had brought me. I, like Mr. Coleridge, could not endure what I had written for some time after I had written it. I also shrank from treating any subject which I had much considered; but more, I believe, as recoiling from the intricacy and the elaborateness which had been made known to me in the course of considering it, and on account of the difficulty or the toilsomeness which might be fairly presumed from the mere fact that I *had* long considered it, or could have found it necessary to do so, than from any blind mechanical feeling inevitably associated (as in Coleridge it was) with a second survey of the same subject.

One other effect there was from the opium, and I believe it had some place in Coleridge's list of morbid affections caused by opium, and of disturbances extended even to the intellect—which was, that the judgement was for a time grievously impaired, sometimes even totally abolished, as applied to anything which I had recently written. Fresh from the labour of composition, I believe, indeed, that almost every man, unless he has had a very long and close experience in the practice of writing, finds himself a little dazzled and bewildered in computing the effect, as it will appear to neutral eyes, of what he has produced. This result from the hurry and effort of composition doubtless we all experience, or at some time *have* experienced. But the incapacitation which I speak of here, as due to opium, is of another kind and another degree. It is mere childish helplessness, or senile paralysis, of the judgement, which distresses the man in attempting to grasp the upshot and the total effect (the *tout ensemble*) of what he has himself so recently produced. There is the same imbecility in attempting to hold things steadily together, and to bring them under a comprehensive or unifying act of the judging faculty, as there is in the efforts of a drunken man to follow a chain of reasoning. Opium is said to have some *specific* effect of debilitation upon the memory [1]; that is, not merely the general one which might be supposed to accompany its morbid effects upon the bodily system, but some other, more direct, subtle, and exclusive; and this, of whatever nature, may possibly extend to the faculty of judging.

Such, however, over and above the more known and more obvious ill effects upon the spirits and the health, were some of the stronger and more subtle effects of opium in disturbing the intellectual system, as well as the animal, the functions of the will also no less than

[1] The *technical* memory, or that which depends upon purely arbitrary links of connexion, and therefore more upon a *nisus* or separate activity of the mind—that memory, for instance, which recalls names—is undoubtedly affected, and most powerfully, by opium. On the other hand, the *logical* memory, or that which recalls facts that are connected by fixed relations, and where, A being given, B must go before or after—historical memory, for instance—is not much, if at all, affected by opium.

those of the intellect, from which both Coleridge and
myself were suffering at the period to which I now refer (1821–25) : evils which found their fullest exemplification in the very act upon which circumstances
had now thrown me as the *sine qua non* of my extrica-
tion from difficulties—viz. the act of literary composition. This necessity, the fact of its being my one sole
resource for the present, and the established experience
which I now had of the peculiar embarrassments and
counteracting forces which I should find in opium, but
still more in the train of consequences left behind by
past opium—strongly co-operated with the mere physical despondency arising out of the liver. And this state
of partial unhappiness, amongst other outward indications, expressed itself by one mark, which some people
are apt greatly to misapprehend, as if it were some result of a sentimental turn of feeling—I mean perpetual
sighs. But medical men must very well know that a
certain state of the liver, *mechanically*, and without
any co-operation of the will, expresses itself in sighs.
I was much too firm-minded, and too reasonable, to
murmur or complain. I certainly suffered deeply, as
one who finds himself a banished man from all that he
loves, and who had not the consolations of hope, but
feared too profoundly that all my efforts—efforts poisoned so sadly by opium—might be unavailing for the
end. But still I endured in silence. The mechanical
sighs, however, revealed, or seemed to reveal, what was
present in my thoughts. Lamb doubtless remarked
them; he knew the general outline of my situation;
and, after this, he set himself, with all the kindness of
a brother, Miss Lamb with the kindness of a sister, to
relieve my gloom by the closest attentions. They absolutely persecuted me with hospitalities; and, as it was
by their fireside that I felt most cheered, and sometimes elevated into hope, it may be supposed that I did

not neglect to avail myself of the golden hours thus benignantly interposed amongst my hours of solitude, despondency, and labour but partially effectual.

* * *

With respect to Lamb's personal habits, much has been said of his intemperance; and his biographer [1] justly remarks that a false impression prevails upon this subject. In eating he was peculiarly temperate; and, with respect to drinking, though his own admirable wit (as in that delightful letter to Mr. Carey where he describes himself, when confided to the care of some youthful protector, as "an old reprobate Telemachus consigned to the guidance of a wise young Mentor") —though, I say, his own admirable wit has held up too bright a torch to the illumination of his own infirmities, so that no efforts of pious friendship could now avail to disguise the truth, yet it must not be forgotten—first, That we are not to imagine Lamb's frailty in this respect habitual or deliberate—he made many powerful resistances to temptation; secondly, he often succeeded for long seasons in practising entire abstinence; thirdly, when he *did* yield to the mingled temptation of wine, social pleasure, and the expansion of his own brotherly heart, that prompted him to entire sympathy with those around him (and it cannot be denied that for any one man to preserve an absolute sobriety amongst a jovial company wears too much the churlish air of playing the spy upon the privileged extravagances of festive mirth) —whenever this *did* happen, Lamb, never, to my knowledge, passed the bounds of an agreeable elevation. He was joyous, radiant with wit and frolic, mounting with the sudden motion of a rocket into the highest heaven of outrageous fun and absurdity; then bursting into a fiery shower of puns,

[1] T. N. Talfourd.—Ed.

chasing syllables with the agility of a squirrel bounding amongst the trees, or a cat pursuing its own tail; but, in the midst of all this stormy gaiety, he never said or did anything that could by possibility wound or annoy. The most noticeable feature in his intoxication was the suddenness with which it ascended to its meridian. Half a dozen glasses of wine taken during dinner —for everybody was encouraged, by his sunshiny kindness, to ask *him* to take wine—these, with perhaps one or two after dinner, sufficed to complete his inebriation to the crisis of sleep; after awaking from which, so far as I know, he seldom recommenced drinking. This sudden consummation of the effects was not, perhaps, owing to a weaker (as Sergeant Talfourd supposes), but rather to a more delicate and irritable, system than is generally found amongst men. The sensibility of his organization was so exquisite that effects which travel by separate stages with most other men in him fled along the nerves with the velocity of light. He had great merit in his frequent trials of abstinence; for the day lost its most golden zest when he had not the genial evening on which to fasten his anticipations. True, his mornings were physically more comfortable upon this system; but then, unfortunately, that mode of pleasure was all reaped and exhausted in the act of enjoyment, whilst the greater pleasure of anticipation, *that* (as he complained himself) was wanting unavoidably, because the morning unhappily comes at the wrong end of the day; so that you may indeed look back to it as something which you have lost through the other hours of the day, but you can never look forward to it as something which is coming.

Finally, without attempting, in this place, any elaborate analysis of Lamb's merits (which would be no easy task), one word or two may be said generally

about the position he is entitled to hold in our literature, and, comparatively, in European literature. In
the literature of every nation, we are naturally disposed to place in the highest rank those who have produced some great and colossal work—a *Paradise Lost*,
a *Hamlet*, a *Novum Organum*—which presupposes an
effort of intellect, a comprehensive grasp, and a sustaining power, for its original conception, corresponding in grandeur to that effort, different in kind, which
must preside in its execution. But, after this highest
class, in which the power to conceive and the power to
execute are upon the same scale of grandeur, there
comes a second, in which brilliant powers of execution,
applied to conceptions of a very inferior range, are allowed to establish a classical rank. Every literature
possesses, besides its great national gallery, a cabinet
of minor pieces, not less perfect in their polish, possibly more so. In reality, the characteristic of this class
is elaborate perfection—the point of inferiority is not
in the finishing, but in the compass and power of the
original creation, which (however exquisite in its
class) moves within a smaller sphere. To this class belong, for example, *The Rape of the Lock*, that finished
jewel of English literature; *The Dunciad* (a still more
exquisite gem) ; *The Vicar of Wakefield* (in its earlier
part) ; in German, the *Luise* of Voss; in French—
what? Omitting some others that might be named
above all others, the *Fables* of La Fontaine. He is the
pet and darling, as it were, of the French Literature.
Now, I affirm that Charles Lamb occupies a corresponding station to his own literature. I am not speaking (it will be observed) of kinds, but of degrees in
literary merit; and Lamb I hold to be, as with respect
to English literature, that which La Fontaine is with
respect to French. For, though there may be little resemblance otherwise, in this they agree, that both were

wayward and eccentric humorists; both confined their
efforts to short flights; and both, according to the
standards of their several countries, were, occasionally, and, in a lower key, poets.

We need not, indeed, wonder at the profounder feeling, and the more intense, as well as consistent, originality of Lamb, when we contrast his character, disposition, life, and general demeanour, as I have here
endeavoured to sketch them, with what we know of La
Fontaine, viewed under the same aspects. Not only was
La Fontaine a vicious and heartless man, but it may
be said of him, with perfect truth, that his whole life
was a lie, and a piece of hollow masquerading. By some
accident, he had gained the character of an absent
man; and, for the sake of sustaining this distinction,
with the poor result of making sport for his circle, he
committed extravagances which argue equal defect of
good sense and sincere feeling in him who was the actor
and in those who accredited them. A man who could
seriously affect not to recognize his own son, and to put
questions about him as about a stranger, must have
been thoroughly wanting in truth of character. And
we may be assured that no depth of feeling in any walk
of literature or poetry ever grew upon the basis of radical affectation. The very substratum of Lamb's character, as I have said before, lay in the most intense hostility to affectation. This, however, touches the *quality*
of their social merits; and at present I am merely concerned with the *degree;* having selected La Fontaine
as that one amongst the French classics who best expresses by analogy the true position and relative rank
which the voice of posterity will assign to Charles
Lamb in the literature of his own country. His works
—I again utter my conviction—will be received as
amongst the most elaborately finished gems of literature; as cabinet specimens which express the utmost

delicacy, purity, and tenderness of the national intellect, together with the rarest felicity of finish and expression, although it may be the province of other
modes of literature to exhibit the highest models in the
grandeur and more impassioned forms of intellectual
power. Such is my own intimate conviction; and, accordingly, I reckon it amongst the rarest accidents of
good fortune which have gilded my literary experience,
that, although residing too often at a vast distance from
the metropolis to benefit by my opportunities so much
as I desired, yet, by cultivating those which fell naturally in my way at various periods, but, most of all, at
that period when I may consider my judgement to have
been maturest, I reaped so much delight from that intercourse, and so far improved it into a fraternal familiarity, as to warrant me in assuming the honourable distinction of having been a friend of Charles
Lamb.

CHARLES LAMB [II]

(First published in *The North British Review*, November, 1848,
as a review of T. N. Talfourd's *Final Memorials of Charles
Lamb*)

IT SOUNDS paradoxical, but is not so in a bad sense, to
say that in every literature of large compass some
authors will be found to rest much of the interest which
surrounds them on their essential *non*-popularity.
They are good for the very reason that they are not in
conformity to the current taste. They interest because
to the world they are *not* interesting. They attract by
means of their repulsion. Not as though it could separately furnish a reason for loving a book that the majority of men had found it repulsive. *Prima facie*, it
must suggest some presumption *against* a book that it
has failed to gain public attention. To have roused

hostility, indeed, to have kindled a feud against its own principles or its temper, may happen to be a good sign. *That* argues power. Hatred may be promising. The deepest revolutions of mind sometimes begin in hatred. But simply to have left a reader unimpressed is in itself a neutral result, from which the inference is doubtful. Yet even *that*, even simple failure to impress, may happen at times to be a result from positive powers in a writer, from special originalities, such as rarely reflect themselves in the mirror of the ordinary understanding. It seems little to be perceived how much the great scriptural [1] idea of the *worldly* and the *unworldly* is found to emerge in literature as well as in life. In reality, the very same combinations of moral qualities, infinitely varied, which compose the harsh physiognomy of what we call worldliness in the living groups of life, must unavoidably present themselves in books. A library divides into sections of worldly and unworldly, even as a crowd of men divides into that same majority and minority. The world has an instinct for recognizing its own, and recoils from certain qualities when exemplified in books, with the same disgust or defective sympathy as would have governed it in real life. From qualities, for instance, of childlike simplicity, of shy profundity, or of inspired self-communion, the world does and must turn away its face towards grosser, bolder, more determined, or more intelligible expressions of character and intellect; and not otherwise in literature, nor at all less in literature, than it does in the realities of life.

[1] *"Scriptural"* we call it, because this element of thought, so indispensable to a profound philosophy of morals, is not simply *more* used in Scripture than elsewhere, but is so exclusively significant or intelligible amidst the correlative ideas of Scripture as to be absolutely insusceptible of translation into classical Greek or classical Latin.

Charles Lamb, if any ever *was*, is amongst the class here contemplated; he, if any ever *has*, ranks amongst writers whose works are destined to be for ever unpopular, and yet for ever interesting; interesting, moreover, by means of those very qualities which guarantee their non-popularity. The same qualities which will be found forbidding to the world and the thoughtless, which will be found insipid to many even amongst robust and powerful minds, are exactly those which will continue to command a select audience in every generation. The prose essays, under the signature of *Elia*, form the most delightful section amongst Lamb's works. They traverse a peculiar field of observation, sequestered from general interest; and they are composed in a spirit too delicate and unobtrusive to catch the ear of the noisy crowd, clamouring for strong sensations. But this retiring delicacy itself, the pensiveness chequered by gleams of the fanciful, and the humour that is touched with cross lights of pathos, together with the picturesque quaintness of the objects casually described, whether men, or things, or usages, and, in the rear of all this, the constant recurrence to ancient recollections and to decaying forms of household life, as things retiring before the tumult of new and revolutionary generations——these traits in combination communicate to the papers a grace and strength of originality which nothing in any literature approaches, whether for degree or kind of excellence, except the most felicitous papers of Addison, such as those on Sir Roger de Coverley, and some others in the same vein of composition. They resemble Addison's papers also in the diction; which is natural and idiomatic, even to carelessness. They are equally faithful to the truth of nature; and in this only they differ remarkably——that the sketches of Elia reflect the stamp and impress of the writer's own character, whereas in all those of Addison the personal peculiarities of the delineator (though known to the reader from the beginning through the account of the club) are nearly quiescent. Now and then they are recalled into a momentary notice, but they do not act, or at all modify his pictures of Sir Roger or Will Wimble. *They* are slightly and amiably eccentric; but the Spectator himself, in describing them, takes the station of an ordinary observer.

Everywhere, indeed, in the writings of Lamb, and not merely in his *Elia*, the character of the writer co-operates in an under-current to the effect of the thing written. To understand, in the fullest sense, either the gaiety or the tenderness of a particular passage, you must have some insight into the particular bias of the writer's mind, whether native and original, or impressed gradually by the accidents of situation; whether simply developed out of predispositions by the action of life, or violently scorched into the constitution by some fierce fever of calamity. There is in modern literature a whole class of writers, though not a large one, standing within the same category: some marked originality of character in the writer becomes a co-efficient with what he says to a common result; you must sympathize with this *personality* in the author before you can appreciate the most significant parts of his views. In most books the writer figures as a mere abstraction, without sex or age or local station, whom the reader banishes from his thoughts. What is written seems to proceed from a blank intellect, not from a man clothed with fleshly peculiarities and differences. These peculiarities and differences neither do, nor (generally speaking) *could* intermingle with the texture of the thoughts, so as to modify their force or their direction. In such books—and they form the vast majority—there is nothing to be found or to be looked for beyond the direct objective. (*Sit venia verbo!*) But, in a small section of books, the objective in the thought becomes confluent with the subjective in the thinker—the two forces unite for a joint product; and, fully to enjoy the product, or fully to apprehend either element, both must be known. It is singular, and worth inquiring into, for the reason that the Greek and Roman literature had no such books. Timon of Athens, or Diogenes, one may conceive qualified for this mode of authorship, had journalism existed to rouse them in those days; their "articles" would no doubt have been fearfully caustic. But, as *they* failed to produce anything, and Lucian in an after age is scarcely characteristic enough for the purpose, perhaps we may pronounce Rabelais and Montaigne the earliest of writers in the class described. In the century following *theirs* came Sir Thomas Browne, and immediately after *him* La Fontaine. Then came Swift, Sterne, with others less distinguished: in Germany, Hippel, the friend of Kant, Harmann the obscure, and the greatest of the whole body—John Paul Richter. But nowhere could illustrations be found more interesting—shy, delicate, evanescent—shy as lightning, delicate and evanescent as the coloured pencillings on a frosty night from the northern lights—than in the better parts of Lamb.

To appreciate Lamb, therefore, it is requisite that his character and temperament should be understood in their coyest and most wayward features. A capital defect it would be if these could not be gathered silently from Lamb's works themselves. It would be a fatal mode of dependency upon an alien and separable accident if they needed an external commentary. But they do *not*. The syllables lurk up and down the writings of Lamb which decipher his eccentric nature. His character lies there dispersed in anagram; and to any

attentive reader the regathering and restoration of the
total word from its scattered parts is inevitable without
an effort. Still it is always a satisfaction, in knowing a
result, to know also its *why* and *how;* and in so far as
every character is likely to be modified by the particular experience, sad or joyous, through which the life
has travelled, it is a good contribution towards the
knowledge of that resulting character as a whole to
have a sketch of that particular experience. What trials
did it impose? What energies did it task? What temptations did it unfold? These calls upon the moral powers,
which in music so stormy many a life is doomed to
hear, how were they faced? The character in a capital
degree moulds oftentimes the life, but the life *always*
in a subordinate degree moulds the character. And, the
character being in this case of Lamb so much of a key
to the writings, it becomes important that the life
should be traced, however briefly, as a key to the character.

That is *one* reason for detaining the reader with
some slight record of Lamb's career. Such a record by
preference and of right belongs to a case where the
intellectual display, which is the sole ground of any
public interest at all in the man, has been intensely modified by the *humanities* and moral *personalities* distinguishing the subject. We read a Physiology, and need
no information as to the life and conversation of its author; a meditative poem becomes far better understood
by the light of such information; but a work of genial
and at the same time eccentric sentiment, wandering
upon untrodden paths, is barely intelligible without it.
There is a good reason for arresting judgement on the
writer, that the court may receive evidence on the life
of the man. But there is another reason, and, in any
other place, a better; which reason lies in the extraordinary value of the life considered separately for itself.

Logically, it is not allowable to say that *here;* and, considering the principal purpose of this paper, any possible *independent* value of the life must rank as a better reason for reporting it—since, in a case where the original object is professedly to estimate the writings of a man, whatever promises to further that object must, merely by that tendency, have, in relation to that place, a momentary advantage which it would lose if valued upon a more abstract scale. Liberated from this casual office of throwing light upon a book— raised to its grander station of a solemn deposition to the moral capacities of man in conflict with calamity —viewed as a return made into the chanceries of heaven upon an issue directed from that court to try the amount of power lodged in a poor desolate pair of human creatures for facing the very anarchy of storms —this obscure life of the two Lambs, brother and sister (for the two lives were one life), rises into a grandeur that is not paralleled once in a generation.

Rich, indeed, in moral instruction was the life of Charles Lamb; and perhaps in one chief result it offers to the thoughtful observer a lesson of consolation that is awful, and of hope that ought to be immortal, viz. in the record which it furnishes that by meekness of submission, and by earnest conflict with evil in the spirit of cheerfulness, it is possible ultimately to disarm or to blunt the very heaviest of curses—even the curse of lunacy. Had it been whispered, in hours of infancy, to Lamb, by the angel who stood by his cradle—"Thou, and the sister that walks by ten years before thee, shall be through life, each to each, the solitary fountain of comfort; and, except it be from this fountain of mutual love, except it be as brother and sister, ye shall not taste the cup of peace on earth!"—here, if there was sorrow in reversion, there was also consolation.

But what funeral swamps would have instantly in-

gulfed this consolation, had some meddling fiend prolonged the revelation, and, holding up the curtain from
the sad future a little longer, had said scornfully—
"Peace on earth! Peace for you two, Charles and Mary
Lamb! What peace is possible under the curse which
even now is gathering against your heads? Is there
peace on earth for the lunatic—peace for the parenti-
cide—peace for the girl that, without warning, and
without time granted for a penitential cry to Heaven,
sends her mother to the last audit?" And then, without
treachery, speaking bare truth, this prophet of woe
might have added—"Thou also, thyself, Charles
Lamb, thou in thy proper person, shalt enter the skirts
of this dreadful hail-storm; even thou shalt taste the
secrets of lunacy, and enter as a captive its house of
bondage [1]; whilst over thy sister the accursed scorpion
shall hang suspended through life, like Death hanging
over the beds of hospitals, striking at times, but more
often threatening to strike; or withdrawing its instant
menaces only to lay bare her mind more bitterly to the
persecutions of a haunted memory!" Considering the
nature of the calamity, in the first place; considering,
in the second place, its life-long duration; and, in the
last place, considering the quality of the resistance by
which it was met, and under what circumstances of
humble resources in money or friends: we have come
to the deliberate judgement that the whole range of
history scarcely presents a more affecting spectacle of
perpetual sorrow, humiliation, or conflict, and that
was supported to the end (that is, through forty years)
with more resignation, or with more absolute victory.

Charles Lamb was born in February of the year
1775. His immediate descent was humble; for his
father, though on one particular occasion civilly de-

---

[1] Lamb was himself confined for six weeks at one period of
his life in a lunatic asylum.

scribed as a "scrivener," was in reality a domestic servant to Mr. Salt—a bencher (and, therefore, a barrister
of some standing) in the Inner Temple. John Lamb,
the father, belonged by birth to Lincoln; from which
city, being transferred to London whilst yet a boy, he
entered the service of Mr. Salt without delay, and apparently from this period, throughout his life, continued in this good man's household to support the honourable relation of a Roman client to his *patronus*,
much more than that of a mercenary servant to a transient and capricious master. The terms on which Mr.
S. seems to have lived with the family of the Lambs
argue a kindness and a liberality of nature on both
sides. John Lamb recommended himself as an attendant by the versatility of his accomplishments; and Mr.
Salt, being a widower without children—which means,
in effect, an old bachelor—naturally valued that en-
cyclopædic range of dexterity which made his house
independent of external aid for every mode of service.
To kill one's own mutton is but an operose way of arriving at a dinner, and often a more costly way;
whereas to combine one's own carpenter, locksmith,
hairdresser, groom, &c., all in one man's person—to
have a Robinson Crusoe, up to all emergencies of life,
always in waiting—is a luxury of the highest class for
one who values his ease.

A consultation is held more freely with a man familiar to one's eye, and more profitably with a man
aware of one's peculiar habits. And another advantage
from such an arrangement is, that one gets any little
alteration or repair executed on the spot. To hear is to
obey, and by an inversion of Pope's rule—

One always is, *and never* to be, *blest.*

People of one sole accomplishment, like the *homo*

unius libri, are usually within that narrow circle disagreeably perfect, and, therefore, apt to be arrogant. People who can do all things usually do every one of them ill; and, living in a constant effort to deny this too palpable fact, they become irritably vain. But Mr. Lamb the elder seems to have been bent on perfection. He did all things; he did them all well; and yet was neither gloomily arrogant, nor testily vain. And, being conscious apparently that all mechanic excellencies tend to illiberal results, unless counteracted by perpetual sacrifices to the graces, he went so far as to cultivate poetry; he even printed his poems; and, were we possessed of a copy (which we are *not*, nor probably is the Vatican), it would give us pleasure at this point to digress for a moment, and to cut them up, purely on considerations of respect to the author's memory. It is hardly to be supposed that they did not really merit castigation; and we should best show the sincerity of our respect for Mr. Lamb senior, in all those cases where we *could* conscientiously profess respect, by an unlimited application of the knout in the cases where we could *not*.

The whole family of the Lambs seems to have won from Mr. Salt the consideration which is granted to humble friends, and from acquaintances nearer to their own standing to have won a tenderness of esteem such as is granted to decayed gentry. Yet, naturally, the social rank of the parents, as people still living, must have operated disadvantageously for the children. It is hard, even for the practised philosopher, to distinguish aristocratic graces of manner, and capacities of delicate feeling, in people whose very hearth and dress bear witness to the servile humility of their station. Yet such distinctions, as wild gifts of nature, timidly and half unconsciously asserted themselves in the unpretending Lambs. Already in *their* favour there existed a silent privilege analogous to the famous one of Lord Kinsale. He, by special grant from the crown, is allowed, when standing before the king, to forget that he is not himself a king: the bearer of that peerage, through all generations, has the privilege of wearing his hat in the royal presence. By a general though tacit concession of the same nature, the rising generation of the Lambs, John and Charles, the two sons, and Mary Lamb, the only daughter, were permitted to forget that their grandmother had been a housekeeper for sixty years, and that their father had worn a livery. Charles Lamb, individually, was so entirely humble, and so careless of social distinctions, that he has taken pleasure in recurring to these very facts in the family records amongst the most genial of his Elia recollections. He only continued to remember, without shame, and with a peculiar tenderness, these badges of plebeian rank, when everybody else, amongst the few survivors that could have known of their existence, had long dismissed them from their thoughts.

Probably through Mr. Salt's interest it was that Charles Lamb, in the autumn of 1782, when he wanted something more than four months of completing his eighth year, received a presentation to the magnificent school of Christ's Hospital.

Here Lamb remained until his fifteenth year; which year threw him on the world, and brought him alongside the golden dawn of the French Revolution. Here he learned a little elementary Greek, and of Latin more than a little; for his Latin notes to Mr. Cary (of Dante celebrity), though brief, are sufficient to reveal a true sense of what is graceful and idiomatic in Latinity. *We* say this, who have studied that subject more than most men. It is not that Lamb would have found it an easy task to compose a long paper in Latin—nobody *can* find it easy to do what he has no motive for habitually practising; but a single sentence of Latin wearing the secret countersign of the "sweet Roman hand" ascertains sufficiently that, in reading Latin classics, a man feels and comprehends their peculiar force or beauty. That is enough. It is requisite to a man's expansion of mind that he should make acquaintance with a literature so radically differing from all modern literature as is the Latin. It is *not* requisite that he should practise Latin composition. Here, therefore, Lamb obtained in sufficient perfection one priceless accomplishment, which even singly throws a graceful air of liberality over all the rest of a man's attainments: having rarely any pecuniary value, it challenges the more attention to its intellectual value. Here also Lamb commenced the friendships of his life; and of all which he formed he lost none. Here it was, as the consummation and crown of his advantages from the time-honoured hospital, that he came to know "Poor S. T. C." [1] τὸν θαυμάσιωτατον.

Until 1796, it is probable that he lost sight of Coleridge, who was then occupied with Cambridge, having been transferred thither as a privileged "Grecian" from Christ's Hospital. That year, 1796, was a year of change and fearful calamity for Charles Lamb. On that year revolved the wheels of his after life. During the three years succeeding to his school days, he had held a clerkship in the South Sea House. In 1795, he was transferred to the India House. As a junior clerk, he could not receive more than a slender salary; but even this was important to the support of his parents and sister. They lived together in lodgings near Hol-

---

[1] *"Poor S. T. C."*: The affecting expression by which Coleridge indicates himself in the few lines written during his last illness for an inscription upon his own grave; lines ill constructed in point of diction and compression, but otherwise speaking from the depths of his heart.

born; and in the spring of 1796 Miss Lamb (having
previously shown signs of lunacy at intervals), in a
sudden paroxysm of her disease, seized a knife from
the dinner table, and stabbed her mother, who died upon
the spot. A coroner's inquest easily ascertained the nature of a case which was transparent in all its circumstances, and never for a moment indecisive as regarded
the medical symptoms. The poor young lady was transferred to the establishment for lunatics at Hoxton. She
soon recovered, we believe; but her relapses were as
sudden as her recoveries, and she continued through
life to revisit, for periods of uncertain seclusion, that
house of woe. This calamity of his fireside, followed
soon after by the death of his father, who had for some
time been in a state of imbecility, determined the future
destiny of Lamb. Apprehending, with the perfect grief
of perfect love, that his sister's fate was sealed for life—
viewing her as his own greatest benefactress, which she
really *had* been through her advantage by ten years of
age—yielding with impassioned readiness to the depth
of his fraternal affection what at any rate he would
have yielded to the sanctities of duty as interpreted by
his own conscience—he resolved for ever to resign all
thoughts of marriage with a young lady whom he
loved, for ever to abandon all ambitious prospects that
might have tempted him into uncertainties, humbly to
content himself with the *certainties* of his Indian clerkship, to dedicate himself for the future to the care of
his desolate and prostrate sister, and to leave the rest to
God. These sacrifices he made in no hurry or tumult,
but deliberately, and in religious tranquillity. These
sacrifices were accepted in heaven; and even on this
earth they *had* their reward. She, for whom he gave up
all, in turn gave up all for *him*. She devoted herself to
his comfort. Many times she returned to the lunatic establishment, but many times she was restored to illu-

minate the household hearth for *him;* and, of the happiness which for forty years and more he had, no hour seemed true that was not derived from *her.* Henceforward, therefore, until he was emancipated by the noble generosity of the East India Directors, Lamb's time, for nine-and-twenty years, was given to the India House.

"*O fortunati nimium, sua si bona nôrint,*" is applicable to more people than "*agricolæ.*" Clerks of the India House are as blind to their own advantages as the blindest of ploughmen. Lamb was summoned, it is true, through the larger and more genial section of his life, to the drudgery of a copying clerk—making confidential entries into mighty folios, on the subject of calicoes and muslins. By this means, whether he would or not, he became gradually the author of a great "serial" work, in a frightful number of volumes, on as dry a department of literature as the children of the great desert could have suggested. Nobody, he must have felt, was ever likely to study this great work of his, not even Dr. Dryasdust. He had written in vain; which is not pleasant to know. There would be no second edition called for by a discerning public in Leadenhall Street; not a chance of *that.* And consequently the *opera omnia* of Lamb, drawn up in a hideous battalion, at the cost of labour so enormous, would be known only to certain families of spiders in one generation, and of rats in the next. Such a labour of Sisyphus—the rolling up a ponderous stone to the summit of a hill only that it might roll back again by the gravitation of its own dulness—seems a bad employment for a man of genius in his meridian energies. And yet, perhaps not. Perhaps the collective wisdom of Europe could not have devised for Lamb a more favourable condition of toil than this very India House clerkship. His works (his Leadenhall Street works) were certainly not read;

popular they *could* not be, for they were not read by
anybody; but then, to balance *that*, they were not reviewed. His folios were of that order which (in Cowper's words) "not even critics criticize." Is *that* nothing? Is it no happiness to escape the hands of merciless
reviewers? Many of us escape being *read;* the worshipful reviewer does not find time to read a line of us; but
we do not for that reason escape being criticized,
"shown up," and martyred. The list of *errata*, again,
committed by Lamb was probably of a magnitude to
alarm any possible compositor; and yet these *errata*
will never be known to mankind. They are dead and
buried. They have been cut off prematurely, and, for
any effect upon their generation, might as well never
have existed. Then the returns, in a pecuniary sense,
from these folios—how important were *they!* It is not
common, certainly, to write folios; but neither is it
common to draw a steady income of from £300 to
£400 per annum from volumes of any size. This will
be admitted; but would it not have been better to draw
the income without the toil? Doubtless it would always be more agreeable to have the rose without the
thorn. But in the case before us, taken with all its circumstances, we deny that the toil is truly typified as a
thorn; so far from being a thorn in Lamb's daily life,
on the contrary, it was a second rose ingrafted upon
the original rose of the income, that he had to earn it
by a moderate but continued exertion. Holidays, in a
national establishment so great as the India House,
and in our too fervid period, naturally could not be
frequent; yet all great English corporations are gracious masters, and indulgences of this nature could be
obtained on a special application. Not to count upon
these accidents of favour, we find that the regular toil
of those in Lamb's situation began at ten in the morning, and ended as the clock struck four in the after-

noon. Six hours composed the daily contribution of labour—that is, precisely one-fourth part of the total
day. But, as Sunday was exempted, the rigorous expression of the quota was one-fourth of six-sevenths,
which makes only six twenty-eighths and not six
twenty-fourths of the total time. Less toil than this
would hardly have availed to deepen the sense of value
in that large part of the time still remaining disposs-
able. Had there been any resumption whatever of labour in the evening, though but for half an hour, that
one encroachment upon the broad continuous area of
the eighteen free hours would have killed the tranquillity of the whole day, by *sowing* it (so to speak)
with intermitting anxieties—anxieties that, like tides,
would still be rising and falling. Whereas now, at the
early hour of four, when daylight is yet lingering in
the air, even at the dead of winter, in the latitude of
London, and when the *enjoying* section of the day is
barely commencing, everything is left which a man
would care to retain. A mere *dilettante* or amateur student, having no mercenary interest concerned, would,
upon a refinement of luxury—would, upon choice—
give up so much time to study, were it only to sharpen
the value of what remained for pleasure. And thus the
only difference between the scheme of the India House
distributing his time for Lamb, and the scheme of a
wise voluptuary distributing his time for himself, lay,
not in the *amount* of time deducted from enjoyment,
but in the particular mode of appropriating that deduction. An *intellectual* appropriation of the time, though
casually fatiguing, must have pleasures of its own;
pleasures denied to a task so mechanic and so monotonous as that of reiterating endless records of sales oi
consignments not *essentially* varying from each other.
True, it is pleasanter to pursue an intellectual study

than to make entries in a ledger. But even an intellectual toil is toil; few people can support it for more than
six hours in a day. And the only question, therefore,
after all, is, at what period of the day a man would
prefer taking this pleasure of study. Now, upon that
point, as regards the case of Lamb, there is no opening
for doubt. He, amongst his *Popular Fallacies*, humor-
ously illustrates the necessity of evening and artificial
lights to the prosperity of studies. After exposing, with
the perfection of fun, the savage unsociality of those
elder ancestors who lived (if life it was) before lamp-
light was invented—showing that "jokes came in
with candles," since "what repartees *could* have
passed" when people were "grumbling at one another
in the dark," and "when you must have felt about for
a smile, and handled a neighbour's cheek to be sure
that he understood it?"—he goes on to say, "This accounts for the seriousness of the elder poetry," viz. because they had no candle-light. Even eating he objects
to as a very imperfect thing in the dark; you are not
convinced that a dish tastes as it should do by the
promise of its name, if you dine in the twilight without candles. Seeing is believing. "The senses absolutely give and take reciprocally." The sight guarantees the taste. For instance, "Can you tell pork from
veal in the dark, or distinguish Sherries from pure
Malaga?"

To all enjoyments whatsoever candles are indispensable as an adjunct; but, as to *reading*, "there is," says
Lamb, "absolutely no such thing but by a candle. We
have tried the affectation of a book at noon-day in
gardens, but it was labour thrown away. It is a mockery, all that is reported of the influential Phœbus. No
true poem ever owed its birth to the sun's light. The
mild internal light, that reveals the fine shapings of

poetry, like fires on the domestic hearth, goes out in the sunshine. Milton's morning hymn in Paradise, we would hold a good wager, was penned at midnight; and Taylor's rich description of a sunrise smells decidedly of the taper." This view of evening and candle-light, as involved in the full delight of literature, may seem no more than a pleasant extravaganza; and no doubt it is in the nature of such gaieties to travel a little into exaggeration; but substantially it is certain that Lamb's sincere feelings pointed habitually in the direction here indicated. His literary studies, whether taking the colour of tasks or diversions, courted the aid of evening, which, by means of physical weariness, produces a more luxurious state of repose than belongs to the labour hours of day; they courted the aid of lamp-light, which, as Lord Bacon remarked, gives a gorgeousness to human pomps and pleasures, such as would be vainly sought from the homeliness of daylight. The hours, therefore, which were withdrawn from his own control by the India House happened to be exactly that part of the day which Lamb least valued, and could least have turned to account.

* * *

Anxious that our readers should see Lamb from as many angles as possible, we have obtained from an old friend of his a memorial—slight, but such as the circumstances allowed—of an evening spent with Charles and Mary Lamb, in the winter of 1821–22. The record is of the most unambitious character; it pretends to nothing, as the reader will see, not so much as to a pun —which it really required some singularity of luck to have missed from Charles Lamb, who often continued to fire puns, as minute guns, all through the evening. But, the more unpretending this record is, the more appropriate it becomes by that very fact to the memory of *him* who, amongst all authors, was the humblest and least pretending. We have often thought that the famous epitaph written for his own grave by Piron, the cynical author of *La Métromanie*, might have come from Lamb, were it not for one objection: Lamb's benign heart would have recoiled from a sarcasm, however effective, inscribed upon a grave-stone; or from a jest, however playful, that tended to a vindictive sneer amongst his own farewell words. We once translated this Piron epitaph into a kind of rambling Drayton couplet; and the only point needing explanation is that, from the accident of scientific men, Fellows of the Royal Society, being usually very solemn men, with an extra chance, therefore, for being, or for seeming, dull men in conversation, naturally it arose that some wit among our great-grandfathers translated F.R.S. into a short-hand expression for a Fellow Remarkably Stupid; to which version of the three letters our English epitaph alludes. The French original of Piron is this:

> *Ci git Piron; qui ne fut rien;*
> *Pas même académicien.*

The bitter arrow of the second line was feathered to hit the French Académie, who had declined to elect him a member. The English version is this:

Here lies Piron; who was—nothing; or, if that could be, was less:
How!—nothing? Yes, nothing; not so much as F.R.S.

But now to our friend's memorandum [1]:

[1] "Our friend's memorandum" was, of course, actually written by De Quincey himself.—ED.

October 6, 1848.

MY DEAR X: You ask me for some memorial, however trivial, of any dinner party, supper party, water party, no matter what, that I can circumstantially recall to recollection, by any features whatever, puns or repartees, wisdom or wit, connecting it with Charles Lamb. I grieve to say that my meetings of *any* sort with Lamb were few, though spread through a score of years. That sounds odd for one that loved Lamb so entirely, and so much venerated his character. But the reason was that I so seldom visited London, and Lamb so seldom quitted it. Somewhere about 1810 and 1812 I must have met Lamb repeatedly at the *Courier* Office in the Strand; that is, at Coleridge's, to whom, as an intimate friend, Mr. Daniel Stewart (a proprietor of the paper) gave up for a time the use of some rooms in the office. Thither, in the London season (May especially and June), resorted Lamb, Godwin, Sir H. Davy, and, once or twice, Wordsworth, who visited Sir George Beaumont's Leicestershire residence of Coleorton early in the spring, and then travelled up to Grosvenor Square with Sir George and Lady Beaumont, "*spectatum veniens, veniens spectetur ut ipse.*"

But in these miscellaneous gatherings Lamb said little, except when an opening arose for a pun. And how effectual that sort of small shot was from *him*, I need not say to anybody who remembers his infirmity of stammering, and his dexterous management of it for purposes of light and shade. He was often able to train the roll of stammers into settling upon the words immediately preceding the effective one; by which means the key-note of the jest or sarcasm, benefiting by the sudden liberation of his embargoed voice, was delivered with the force of a pistol shot. That stammer was worth an annuity to him as an ally of his wit.

Firing under cover of that advantage, he did triple
execution: for, in the first place, the distressing sympathy of the hearers with *his* distress of utterance won
for him unavoidably the silence of deep attention; and
then, whilst he had us all hoaxed into this attitude of
mute suspense by an appearance of distress that he
perhaps did not really feel, down came a plunging
shot into the very thick of us, with ten times the effect it would else have had. If his stammering, however, often did him true "yeoman's service," sometimes
it led him into scrapes. Coleridge told me of a ludicrous embarrassment which it caused him at Hastings.
Lamb had been medically advised to a course of sea-
bathing; and, accordingly, at the door of his bathing-
machine, whilst he stood shivering with cold, two
stout fellows laid hold of him, one at each shoulder,
like heraldic supporters. They waited for the word of
command from their principal, who began the following oration to them: "Hear me, men! Take notice of
this—I am to be dipped. But—" What more he would
have said is unknown to land or sea: for, having
reached the word dipped, he commenced such a rolling
fire of Di—di—di—di that, when at length he descended *à plomb* upon the full word *dipped*, the two
men, tired of the long suspense, became satisfied that
they reached what lawyers call the "operative clause"
of the sentence; and, both exclaiming, "Oh yes, sir,
we're quite aware of *that*," down they plunged him
into the sea. On emerging, Lamb sobbed so much from
the cold that he found no voice suitable to his indignation; from necessity he seemed tranquil; and, again
addressing the men, who stood respectfully listening,
he began thus: "Men! is it possible to obtain your
attention?" "Oh, surely, sir, by all means." "Then
listen: once more I tell you, I am to be di—di—di—,"
and then, with a burst of indignation, "dipped, I tell

you." "Oh, decidedly, sir," rejoined the men, "decidedly," and down the stammerer went for the second
time. Petrified with cold and wrath, for a third time
Lamb made a feeble attempt at explanation—"Grant
me pa—pa—patience; is it mum—um—murder you
me—me—mean? Again and a—ga—ga—gain, I tell
you, I am to be di—di—di—dipped," now speaking
furiously, with the voice of an injured man. "Oh, yes,
sir," the men replied, "we know that, we fully understood it," and for the third time down went Lamb into
the sea. "O limbs of Satan!" he said, on coming up for
the third time; "it's now too late; I tell you that I
am—no that I *was*—by medical direction—to be di—
di—di—dipped only *once*."

Since the rencontres with Lamb at Coleridge's I had
met him once or twice at literary dinner-parties. One
of these occurred at the house of Messrs. Taylor and
Hessey, the publishers. I myself was suffering too
much from illness at the time to take any pleasure in
what passed, or to notice it with any vigilance of attention. Lamb, I remember, as usual, was full of
gaiety; and, as usual, he rose too rapidly to the zenith
of his gaiety; for he shot upwards like a rocket, and, as
usual, people said he was "tipsy." To me, Lamb never
seemed intoxicated, but at most joyously elevated. He
never talked nonsense—which is a great point gained;
nor polemically—which is a greater, for it is a dreadful thing to find a drunken man bent upon converting
one's self; nor sentimentally—which is greatest of all.
You can stand a man's fraternizing with you; or, if he
swears an eternal friendship only once in an hour, you
do not think of calling the police; but once in every
three minutes is too much. Lamb did none of these
things; he was always rational, quiet, and gentlemanly
in his habits. Nothing memorable, I am sure, passed
upon this occasion, which was in November of 1821;

and yet the dinner was memorable by means of one fact not discovered until some years later.

Amongst the company, all literary men, sat a murderer—such he proved to be upon later discoveries, but even then looking prospectively towards that object— and a murderer of a freezing class, cool, calculating, wholesale in his operations, and moving all along under the advantages of unsuspecting confidence and domestic opportunities. This was Mr. Wainewright, who was subsequently brought to trial, but not for any of his murders, and transported for life. The story has been told both by Judge Talfourd, and previously by Sir Edward B. Lytton. Both have been much blamed for the use made of this extraordinary case; but I know not why. In itself it is a most remarkable case, for more reasons than one. It is remarkable for the appalling revelation which it makes of power spread through the hands of people not liable to suspicion, for purposes the most dreadful. It is remarkable also by the contrast which existed in this case between the murderer's dandy appearance and the terrific purposes with which he was always dallying. He was a contributor to a journal in which I also had written several papers.[1] This formed a shadowy link between us; and, ill as I was, I looked more attentively at *him* than at anybody else. Yet there were several men of wit and genius present—amongst whom Lamb (as I have said) and Thomas Hood, Hamilton Reynolds and Allan Cunningham. But *them* I already knew, whereas Mr. W. I now saw for the first time and the last. What interested me about *him* was this: the papers which had been pointed out to me as his (signed *Janus Weathercock* or else *Vinkbooms*) were written in a spirit of coxcombry that did not so much disgust as

[1] The *London Magazine.*—ED.

amuse. The writer could not conceal the ostentatious pleasure which he took in the luxurious fittings-up of his rooms, in the fancied splendour of his *bijouterie*, &c. Yet it was easy for a man of any experience to read two facts in all this idle *étalage:* one being that his finery was but of a second-rate order; the other, that he was a *parvenu*, not at home even amongst his second-rate splendour. So far there was nothing to distinguish Mr. W.'s papers from the papers of other triflers. But in this point there *was*, viz. that in his judgements upon the great Italian masters of painting, Da Vinci, Titian, &c., there seemed a tone of sincerity and of native sensibility, as in one who spoke for himself, and was not merely a copier from books. This it was that interested me; as also his reviews of the chief Italian engravers, Morghen, Volpato, &c.; not for the manner, which overflowed with levities and impertinence, but for the substance of his judgements in those cases where I happened to have had an opportunity of judging for myself. Here arose also a claim upon Lamb's attention: for Lamb and his sister, having no sensibility for music, had the deepest for painting. Accordingly, Lamb paid him a great deal of attention, and continued to speak of him for years with an interest that seemed disproportioned to his pretensions. This might be owing in part to an indirect compliment to Miss Lamb in one of W.'s papers; else his appearance would rather have repelled Lamb; it was commonplace, and better suited to express the dandyism which overspread the surface of his manner than the unaffected sensibility which apparently lay in his nature. Dandy or not, however, this man, on account of the schism in his papers—so much amiable puppyism on one side, so much deep feeling on the other (feeling, applied to some of the grandest objects that earth has to show) —did really move a trifle of interest in me, on a day when I hated the face of man and woman. Yet again, if I had known this man for the murderer that even then he was, what sudden loss of interest, what sudden growth of another interest, would have changed the face of the scene! Trivial creature, that didst carry thy dreadful eye kindling with perpetual treasons—dreadful creature, that didst carry thy trivial eye mantling with eternal levity—over the sleeping surfaces of confiding household life—oh, what a revolution for man wouldst thou have founded, had thy deep wickedness prospered! What *was* that wickedness? Here is its outline; but his murders were more than were ever made known judicially.

At this time (October 1848 [1]) the whole British island is appalled by a new chapter in the history of poisoning. Locusta in ancient Rome, Madame Brinvilliers in Paris, were people of original genius: not in any new artifice of toxicology; but in profiting by domestic openings for murder, unsuspected through their very atrocity. Such an opening was made some years ago by those who saw the possibility of founding purses for parents upon the murder of their children. This was done upon a larger scale than had been suspected, and upon a plausible pretence. To bury a corpse is costly; but, of a hundred children, only a few, in the ordinary course of mortality, will die within a given time. Five shillings apiece will produce £25 annually, and *that* will bury a considerable number. On this principle arose Infant Burial Societies. For a few shillings annually, a parent could secure a funeral for every child. If the child died, a few guineas fell

---

[1] This was written ten years ago; and doubtless I had ground sufficient for what I then said. At present [1858], however, I have entirely forgotten the particular case alluded to, unless (as rather I believe) it was a case of infant funerals with a view to the insurance-money.

due to the parent, and the funeral was accomplished without cost of *his*. But on this arose the suggestion —Why not execute an insurance of this nature twenty times over? One single insurance pays for the funeral —the other nineteen are so much clear gain, a *lucro ponatur*, for the parents. Yes; but on the supposition that the child dies! Twenty are no better than one, unless they are gathered into the garner. Now, if the child died naturally, all was right; but how if the child did *not* die? Why, clearly this—the child that *can* die, and won't die, may be made to die. There are many ways of doing that; and it is shocking to know that, according to recent discoveries, poison is comparatively a very merciful mode of murder. Six years ago a dreadful communication was made to the public by a medical man, viz. that three thousand children were annually burned to death under circumstances showing too clearly that they had been left by their mothers with the means and the temptations to set themselves on fire in their absence. But more shocking, because more lingering, are the deaths by artificial appliances of wet, cold, hunger, bad diet, and disturbed sleep, to the frail constitutions of children. By that machinery it is, and not by poison, that the majority qualify themselves for claiming the funeral allowances. Here, however, there occur to any man, on reflection, two eventual restraints on the extension of this domestic curse: First, as there is no pretext for wanting more than one funeral on account of one child, any insurances beyond one are in themselves a ground of suspicion. Now, if any plan were devised for securing the *publication* of such insurances, the suspicions would travel as fast as the grounds for them. Secondly, it occurs that eventually the evil checks itself, since a society established on the ordinary rates of mortality would be ruined when a murderous stim-

ulation was applied to that rate too extensively. Still
it is certain that, for a season, this atrocity *has* prospered in manufacturing districts for some years, and
more recently, as judicial investigations have shown,
in one agricultural district of Essex.

Now, Mr. W.'s scheme of murder was, in its outline, the very same, but not applied to the narrow purpose of obtaining burials from a public fund. He persuaded, for instance, two beautiful young ladies,
visitors in his family, and nearly related to his wife, to
insure their lives for a short period of two years. This
insurance was repeated in several different offices, until a sum of £18,000 had been secured in the event of
their deaths within the two years. Mr. W. took care
that they *should* die, and very suddenly, within that
period. I never saw either of the young women myself;
but I have been assured that one of them at least was
memorably distinguished by her personal attractions.
In the middle of the day which Mr. Wainewright had
fixed for their murder, he framed a pretence for drawing his wife out of doors upon a very long walk. His
fear was that *she* might have penetration enough to
notice and report the agonizing spasms caused by the
poison, whereas two young servant girls, totally inexperienced, were easily persuaded to believe it a case of
cholera. On returning, after a three hours' walk, Mr.
and Mrs. W. found the two young ladies dead. Having
previously secured from his victims an assignment to
himself of their claim, he endeavoured to make this assignment available. But the offices, which had vainly
endeavoured to extract from the young ladies any satisfactory account of the reasons for this limited insurance, had their suspicions at last strongly roused. One
office had recently experienced a case of the same nature, in which also the young lady had been poisoned
by the man in whose behalf she had effected the insur-

ance; all the offices declined to pay; actions at law arose; in the course of the investigation which followed, Mr. W.'s character was fully exposed. Finally, in the midst of the embarrassments which ensued, he committed forgery, and was transported.

From this Mr. W., some few days afterwards, I received an invitation to a dinner party, expressed in terms that were obligingly earnest. He mentioned the names of his principal guests, and amongst them rested most upon those of Lamb and Sir David Wilkie. From an accident, I was unable to attend, and greatly regretted it. Sir David one might rarely happen to see, except at a crowded party. But, as regarded Lamb, I was sure to see him or to hear of him again in some way or other within a short time. This opportunity, in fact, offered itself within a month through the kindness of the Lambs themselves. They had heard of my being in solitary lodgings, and insisted on my coming to dine with them; which more than once I did in the winter of 1821–22.

The mere reception by the Lambs was so full of goodness and hospitable feeling that it kindled animation in the most cheerless or torpid of invalids. I cannot imagine that any *memorabilia* occurred during the visit; but I will use the time that would else be lost upon the settling of that point in putting down any triviality that occurs to my recollection.

There were no strangers; Charles Lamb, his sister, and myself made up the party. Even this was done in kindness. They knew that I should have been oppressed by an effort such as must be made in the society of strangers; and they placed me by their own fireside, where I could say as much or as little as I pleased.

We dined about five o'clock; and it was one of the hospitalities inevitable to the Lambs that any game which they might receive from rural friends in the course of the week was reserved for the day of a friend's dining with them.

In regard to wine, Lamb and myself had the same habit—perhaps it rose to the dignity of a principle—viz. to take a great deal *during* dinner, none *after* it. Consequently, as Miss Lamb (who drank only water) retired almost with the dinner itself, nothing remained for men of our principles, the rigour of which we had illustrated by taking rather too much of old port before the cloth was drawn, except talking; amœbean colloquy, or, in Dr. Johnson's phrase, a dialogue of "brisk reciprocation." But this was impossible; over Lamb, at this period of his life, there passed regularly, after taking wine, a brief eclipse of sleep. It descended upon him as softly as a shadow. In a gross person, laden with superfluous flesh, and sleeping heavily, this would have been disagreeable; but in Lamb, thin even to meagreness, spare and wiry as an Arab of the desert, or as Thomas Aquinas wasted by scholastic vigils, the affection of sleep seemed rather a network of aerial gossamer than of earthly cobweb—more like a golden haze falling upon him gently from the heavens than a cloud exhaling upwards from the flesh. Motionless in his chair as a bust, breathing so gently as scarcely to seem certainly alive, he presented the image of repose midway between life and death, like the repose of sculpture; and, to one who knew his history, a repose affectingly contrasting with the calamities and internal storms of his life. I have heard more persons than I can now distinctly recall observe of Lamb, when sleeping, that his countenance in that state assumed an expression almost seraphic, from its intellectual beauty of outline, its child-like simplicity, and its benignity. It could not be called a transfiguration that sleep had worked in his face; for the features wore essentially the same expression when waking; but sleep spiritual-

ized that expression, exalted it, and almost harmonized
it. Much of the change lay in that last process. The
eyes it was that disturbed the unity of effect in Lamb's
waking face. They gave a restlessness to the character
of his intellect, shifting, like northern lights, through
every mode of combination with fantastic playfulness,
and sometimes by fiery gleams obliterating for the moment that pure light of benignity which was the predominant reading on his features. Some people have
supposed that Lamb had Jewish blood in his veins,
which seemed to account for his gleaming eyes. It
might be so; but this notion found little countenance
in Lamb's own way of treating the gloomy mediæval
traditions propagated throughout Europe about the
Jews, and their secret enmity to Christian races. Lamb,
indeed, might not be more serious than Shakespeare is
supposed to have been in his Shylock; yet he spoke at
times as from a station of wilful bigotry, and seemed
(whether laughingly or not) to sympathize with the
barbarous Christian superstitions upon the pretended
bloody practices of the Jews, and of the early Jewish
physicians. Being himself a Lincoln man, he treated
Sir Hugh of Lincoln,[1] the young child that suffered
death by secret assassination in the Jewish quarter
rather than suppress his daily anthems to the Virgin,
as a true historical personage on the rolls of martyrdom; careless that this fable, like that of the apprentice
murdered out of jealousy by his master the architect,
had destroyed its own authority by ubiquitous diffusion. All over Europe the same legend of the murdered
apprentice and the martyred child reappears under different names—so that in effect the verification of the
tale is none at all, because it is unanimous; is too nar-

[1] The story which furnishes a basis to the fine ballad in
Percy's *Reliques*, and to the Canterbury Tale of Chaucer's
Lady Abbess.

row, because it is too impossibly broad. Lamb, however, though it was often hard to say whether he were
not secretly laughing, swore to the truth of all these
old fables, and treated the liberalities of the present
generation on such points as mere fantastic and effeminate affectations—which, no doubt, they often are as
regards the sincerity of those who profess them. The
bigotry which it pleased his fancy to assume he used
like a sword against the Jew, as the official weapon of
the Christian, upon the same principle that a Capulet
would have drawn upon a Montague, without conceiving it any duty of *his* to rip up the grounds of so ancient a quarrel; it was a feud handed down to him by
his ancestors, and it was *their* business to see that originally it had been an honest feud. I cannot yet believe
that Lamb, if seriously aware of any family intercon-
nexion with Jewish blood, would, even in jest, have
held that one-sided language. More probable it is that
the fiery eye recorded not any alliance with Jewish
blood, but that disastrous alliance with insanity which
tainted his own life, and laid desolate his sister's.

The mercurialities of Lamb were infinite, and always uttered in a spirit of absolute recklessness for the
quality or the prosperity of the sally. It seemed to liberate his spirits from some burthen of blackest melancholy which oppressed it, when he had thrown off a
jest: he would not stop one instant to improve it; nor
did he care the value of a straw whether it were good
enough to be remembered, or so mediocre as to extort
high moral indignation from a collector who refused
to receive into his collection of jests and puns any that
were not felicitously good or revoltingly bad.

After tea, Lamb read to me a number of beautiful
compositions, which he had himself taken the trouble
to copy out into a blank paper folio, from unsuccessful
authors. Neglected people in every class won the sym-

pathy of Lamb. One of the poems, I remember, was a
very beautiful sonnet from a volume recently published by Lord Thurlow—which, and Lamb's just remarks upon which, I could almost repeat *verbatim* at
this moment, nearly twenty-seven years later, if your
limits would allow me. But these, you tell me, allow of
no such thing; at the utmost they allow only twelve
lines more. Now all the world knows that the sonnet itself would require fourteen lines; but take fourteen
from twelve and there remains very little, I fear; besides which, I am afraid two of my twelve are already
exhausted. This forces me to interrupt my account of
Lamb's reading, or reporting the very accident that
did interrupt it in fact; since that no less characteris-
tically expressed Lamb's peculiar spirit of kindness
(always quickening itself towards the ill-used or the
downtrodden) than it had previously expressed itself
in his choice of obscure readings. Two ladies came in,
one of whom at least had sunk in the scale of worldly
consideration. They were ladies who would not have
found much recreation in literary discussions—elderly, and habitually depressed. On *their* account,
Lamb proposed whist; and in that kind effort to amuse
them—which naturally drew forth some momentary
gaieties from himself, but not of a kind to impress
themselves on the recollection—the evening terminated.

Of Lamb's writings, some were confessedly failures,
and some were so memorably beautiful as to be unique
in their class. The character of Lamb it is, and the life-
struggle of Lamb, that must fix the attention of many,
even amongst those wanting in sensibility to his intellectual merits. This character and this struggle, as we
have already observed, impress many traces of themselves upon Lamb's writings. Even in that view, there-

fore, they have a ministerial value; but separately, for themselves, they have an independent value of the highest order. Upon this point we gladly adopt the eloquent words of Sergeant Talfourd:

The sweetness of Lamb's character, breathed through his writings, was felt even by strangers; but its heroic aspect was unguessed even by many of his friends. Let them now consider it, and ask if the annals of self-sacrifice can show anything in human action and endurance more lovely than its self-devotion exhibits? It was not merely that he saw, through the ensanguined cloud of misfortune which had fallen upon his family, the unstained excellence of his sister, whose madness had caused it; that he was ready to take her to his own home with reverential affection, and cherish her through life, and gave up, for her sake, all meaner and more selfish love, and all the hopes which youth blends with the passion which disturbs and ennobles it; not even that he did all this cheerfully, without pluming himself upon his brotherly nobleness as a virtue, or seeking to repay himself (as some uneasy martyrs do) by small instalments of long repining; but that he carried the spirit of the hour in which he first knew and took his course to his last. So far from thinking that his sacrifice of youth and love to his sister gave him a licence to follow his own caprice at the expense of her feelings, even in the lightest matters, he always wrote and spoke of her as his wiser self, his generous benefactress, of whose protecting care he was scarcely worthy.

It must be remembered also (which the Sergeant does not overlook) that Lamb's efforts for the becoming support of his sister lasted through a period of forty years. Twelve years before his death, the munifi-

cence of the India House, by granting him a liberal
retiring allowance, had placed his own support under
shelter from accidents of any kind. But this died with
himself; and he could not venture to suppose that, in
the event of his own death, the India House would
grant to his sister the same allowance as by custom is
granted to a wife. This, however, they did; but Lamb,
not venturing to calculate upon such nobility of patronage, had applied himself through life to the saving
of a provision for his sister under any accident to himself. And this he did with a persevering prudence but
little known in the literary class, amongst a continued
tenor of generosities, often so princely as to be scarcely
known in any class.

Charles Lamb is gone. His life was a continued
struggle in the service of love the purest, and within a
sphere visited by little of contemporary applause. Even
his intellectual displays won but a narrow sympathy at
any time, and in his earlier period were saluted with
positive derision and contumely on the few occasions
when they were not oppressed by entire neglect. But
slowly all things right themselves. All merit which is
founded in truth, and is strong enough, reaches by
sweet exhalations in the end a higher sensory; reaches
higher organs of discernment, lodged in a selecter audience. But the original obtuseness or vulgarity of feeling that thwarted all just estimation of Lamb in life
will continue to thwart its popular diffusion. There
are even some that continue to regard him with the old
hostility, and the old unmitigated scorn. And we,
therefore, standing by the side of Lamb's grave, seemed
to hear, on one side (but in abated tones), strains of
the ancient malice—"This man, that thought himself
to be somebody, is dead, is buried, is forgotten!" and,
on the other side, seemed to hear ascending as with the

solemnity of a saintly requiem—"This man, that thought himself to be nobody, is dead, is buried; his life has been searched; and his memory is hallowed for ever!"

PART THREE

CONFESSIONS OF
AN ENGLISH OPIUM-EATER
and
SUSPIRIA DE PROFUNDIS

PREFACE
TO THE ORIGINAL EDITION OF 1822

TO THE READER

I HERE *present you, courteous reader, with the record of a remarkable period of my life: according to my application of it, I trust that it will prove not merely an interesting record, but, in a considerable degree, useful and instructive. In* that *hope it is that I have drawn it up; and* that *must be my apology for breaking through that delicate and honourable reserve which, for the most part, restrains us from the public exposure of our own errors and infirmities. Nothing indeed, is more revolting to English feelings than the spectacle of a human being obtruding on our notice his moral ulcers, or scars, and tearing away that "decent drapery" which time, or indulgence to human frailty, may have drawn over them: accordingly, the greater part of* our *confessions (that is, spontaneous and extra-judicial confessions) proceed from demireps, adventurers, or swindlers; and, for any such acts of gratuitous self-humiliation from those who can be supposed in sympathy with the decent and self-respecting part of society, we must look to French literature, or to that part of the German which is tainted with the spurious and defective sensibility of the French. All this I feel so forcibly, and so nervously am I alive to reproach of this tendency, that I have for many months hesitated about the propriety of allowing this, or any part of my narrative, to come before the public eye until after my*

*death (when, for many reasons, the whole will be pub-
lished): and it is not without an anxious review of the
reasons for and against this step that I have, at last,
concluded on taking it.*

*Guilt and misery shrink, by a natural instinct, from
public notice: they court privacy and solitude; and,
even in their choice of a grave, will sometimes sequester themselves from the general population of the
churchyard, as if declining to claim fellowship with
the great family of man, and wishing (in the affecting
language of Mr. Wordsworth)*

———humbly to express
A penitential loneliness.

*It is well, upon the whole, and for the interest of us all,
that it should be so; nor would I willingly, in my own
person, manifest a disregard of such salutary feelings;
nor in act or word do anything to weaken them. But,
on the one hand, as my self-accusation does not amount
to a confession of guilt, so, on the other, it is possible
that, if it did, the benefit resulting to others, from the
record of an experience purchased at so heavy a price,
might compensate, by a vast overbalance, for any violence done to the feelings I have noticed, and justify a
breach of the general rule. Infirmity and misery do
not, of necessity, imply guilt. They approach, or recede from, the shades of that dark alliance, in proportion to the probable motives and prospects of the of-
fender, and the palliations, known or secret, of the
offence; in proportion as the temptations to it were potent from the first, and the resistance to it, in act or in
effort, was earnest to the last. For my own part, without breach of truth or modesty, I may affirm that my
life has been, on the whole, the life of a philosopher:
from my birth I was made an intellectual creature;*

and intellectual in the highest sense my pursuits and pleasures have been, even from my school-boy days. If opium-eating be a sensual pleasure, and if I am bound to confess that I have indulged in it to an excess, not yet recorded [1] *of any other man, it is no less true that I have struggled against this fascinating enthralment with a religious zeal, and have at length accomplished what I never yet heard attributed to any other man— have untwisted, almost to its final links, the accursed chain which fettered me. Such a self-conquest may reasonably be set off in counterbalance to any kind or degree of self-indulgence. Not to insist that, in my case, the self-conquest was unquestionable, the self-indulgence open to doubts of casuistry, according as that name shall be extended to acts aiming at the bare relief of pain, or shall be restricted to such as aim at the excitement of positive pleasure.*

Guilt, therefore, I do not acknowledge; and, if I did, it is possible that I might still resolve on the present act of confession, in consideration of the service which I may thereby render to the whole class of Opium-Eaters. But who are they? Reader, I am sorry to say, a very numerous class indeed. Of this I became convinced, some years ago, by computing, at that time, the number of those in one small class of English society (the class of men distinguished for talents, or of eminent station) who were known to me, directly or indirectly, as Opium-Eaters: such, for instance, as the eloquent and benevolent [William Wilberforce]; the late Dean of [Carlisle, Dr. Isaac Milner]; Lord [Erskine]; Mr. ——, the philosopher; a late under-secretary of state [Mr. Addington] (who described to me the sensation which first drove him to the use of opium in the very

[1] "Not yet *recorded*," I say; for there is one celebrated man of the present day who, if all be true which is reported of him, has greatly exceeded me in quantity.

same words as the Dean of [Carlisle], viz. "that he felt as though rats were gnawing and abrading the coats of his stomach"); Mr. [Coleridge]; and many others, hardly less known, whom it would be tedious to mention. Now, if one class, comparatively so limited, could furnish so many scores of cases (and that within the knowledge of one single inquirer), it was a natural inference that the entire population of England would furnish a proportionable number. The soundness of this inference, however, I doubted, until some facts became known to me, which satisfied me that it was not incorrect. I will mention two. 1. Three respectable London druggists, in widely remote quarters of London, from whom I happened lately to be purchasing small quantities of opium, assured me that the number of amateur Opium-Eaters (as I may term them) was, at this time, immense; and that the difficulty of distinguishing these persons, to whom habit had rendered opium necessary, from such as were purchasing it with a view to suicide, occasioned them daily trouble and disputes. This evidence respected London only. But, 2 (which will possibly surprise the reader more), some years ago, on passing through Manchester, I was informed by several cotton manufacturers that their work-people were rapidly getting into the practice of opium-eating; so much so, that on a Saturday afternoon the counters of the druggists were strewed with pills of one, two, or three grains, in preparation for the known demand of the evening. The immediate occasion of this practice was the lowness of wages, which, at that time, would not allow them to indulge in ale or spirits; and, wages rising, it may be thought that this practice would cease: but, as I do not readily believe that any man, having once tasted the divine luxuries of opium, will afterwards descend to the gross and mortal enjoyments of alcohol, I take it for granted

That those eat now who never ate before,
And those who always ate now eat the more.

*Indeed, the fascinating powers of opium are ad-
mitted even by medical writers, who are its greatest
enemies: thus, for instance, Awsiter, apothecary to
Greenwich Hospital, in his* Essay on the Effects of
Opium *(published in the year 1763), when attempting
to explain why Mead had not been sufficiently explicit
on the properties, counter-agents, &c., of this drug, expresses himself in the following mysterious terms*
(φωνᾶντα συνετοῖσι): "*Perhaps he thought the subject of too delicate a nature to be made common; and,
as many people might then indiscriminately use it, it
would take from that necessary fear and caution which
should prevent their experiencing the extensive power
of this drug;* for there are many properties in it, if universally known, that would habituate the use, and
make it more in request with us than the Turks them-
themselves; *the result of which knowledge*," he adds,
"*must prove a general misfortune.*" *In the necessity of
this conclusion I do not altogether concur; but upon
that point I shall have occasion to speak at the close of
my* Confessions, *where I shall present the reader with
the* moral *of my narrative.*

WHEN *it had been settled that, in the general series of these republications, the* Confessions of an English Opium-Eater *should occupy the Fifth Volume, I resolved to avail myself most carefully of the opening thus made for a revision of the entire work. By accident, a considerable part of the* Confessions *(all, in short, except the Dreams) had originally been written hastily; and, from various causes, had never received any strict revision, or virtually, so much as an ordinary verbal correction. But a great deal more was wanted than this. The main narrative should naturally have moved through a succession of secondary incidents; and, with leisure for recalling these, it might have been greatly inspirited. Wanting all opportunity for such advantages, this narrative had been needlessly impoverished. And thus it had happened that not so properly correction and retrenchment were called for as integration of what had been left imperfect, or amplification of what, from the first, had been insufficiently expanded.*

With these views, it would not have been difficult (though toilsome) to re-cast the little work in a better mould; and the result might, in all reason, count upon the approbation at least of its own former readers. Compared with its own former self, the book must certainly tend, by its very principle of change, whatever should be the execution *of that change, to become better: and in my own opinion, after all drawbacks and allowances for the faulty exemplification of a good principle, it is better. This should be a matter of mere logical or inferential necessity; since, in pure addition to everything previously approved, there would now be a clear surplus of extra matter—all that might be good in the old work, and a great deal beside that was new. Meantime this improvement has been won at a price of labour and suffering that, if they could be truly stated, would seem incredible. A nervous malady, of very peculiar character, which has attacked me intermittingly for the last eleven years, came on in May last, almost concurrently with the commencement of this revision; and so obstinately has this malady pursued its noiseless, and what I may call subterraneous, siege, since none of the symptoms are externally manifested, that, although pretty nearly dedicating myself to this one solitary labour, and not intermitting or relaxing it for a single day, I have yet spent, within a very few days, six calendar months upon the re-cast of this one small volume.*

The consequences have been distressing to all concerned. The press has groaned under the chronic visitation; the compositors shudder at the sight of my handwriting, though not objectionable on the score of legibility; and I have much reason to fear that, on days when the pressure of my complaint has been heaviest, I may have so far given way to it as to have suffered greatly in clearness of critical vision. Sometimes I may have overlooked blunders, mis-statements, or repetitions, implicit or even express. But more often I may have failed to appreciate the true effects from faulty management of style and its colourings. Sometimes, for instance, a heavy or too intricate arrangement of sentences may have defeated the tendency of what, un-

der its natural presentation, would have been affecting; or it is possible enough that, by unseasonable levity at other times, I may have repelled the sympathy of my readers—all or some. Endless are the openings for such kinds of mistake—that is, of mistakes not fully seen as such. But, even in a case of unequivocal mistake, seen and acknowledged, yet, when it is open to remedy only through a sudden and energetic act then or never—the press being for twenty minutes, suppose, free to receive an alteration, but beyond that time closed and sealed inexorably: such being supposed the circumstances, the humane reader will allow for the infirmity which even wilfully and consciously surrenders itself to the error, acquiescing in it deliberately rather than face the cruel exertion of correcting it most elaborately at a moment of sickening misery, and with the prevision that the main correction must draw after it half-a-dozen others for the sake of decent consistency. I am not speaking under any present consciousness of such a case existing against myself: I believe there is none such. But I choose to suppose an extreme case of even conscious error, in order that venial cases of oversight may, under shelter of such an outside licence, find toleration from a liberal critic. To fight up against the wearing siege of an abiding sickness imposes a fiery combat. I attempt no description of this combat, knowing the unintelligibility and the repulsiveness of all attempts to communicate the incommunicable. But the generous reader will not, for that forbearance on my part, the less readily show his indulgence, if a case should (unexpectedly to myself) arise for claiming it.

I have thus made the reader acquainted with one out of two cross currents that tended to thwart my efforts for improving this little work. There was, meantime, another, less open to remedy from my own uttermost

*efforts. All along I had relied upon a crowning grace,
which I had reserved for the final pages of this volume,
in a succession of some twenty or twenty-five dreams
and noon-day visions, which had arisen under the latter stages of opium influence. These have disappeared:
some under circumstances which allow me a reasonable prospect of recovering them; some unaccountably;
and some dishonourably. Five or six, I believe, were
burned in a sudden conflagration which arose from the
spark of a candle falling unobserved amongst a very
large pile of papers in a bedroom, when I was alone
and reading. Falling not on, but* amongst *and* within
*the papers, the fire would soon have been ahead of con-
flict; and, by communicating with the slight wood-
work and draperies of the bed, it would have immediately enveloped the laths of a ceiling overhead, and
thus the house, far from fire-engines, would have been
burned down in half-an-hour. My attention was first
drawn by a sudden light upon my book: and the whole
difference between a total destruction of the premises
and a trivial loss (from books charred) of five guineas
was due to a large Spanish cloak. This, thrown over,
and then drawn down tightly, by the aid of one sole
person, somewhat agitated, but retaining her presence
of mind, effectually extinguished the fire. Amongst
the papers burned partially, but not so burned as to be
absolutely irretrievable, was the "Daughter of Lebanon"; and this I have printed, and have intentionally
placed it at the end, as appropriately closing a record in
which the case of poor Ann the Outcast formed not
only the most memorable and the most suggestively
pathetic incident, but also* that *which, more than any
other, coloured—or (more truly I should say) shaped,
moulded and remoulded, composed and decomposed—
the great body of opium dreams. The search after the
lost features of Ann, which I spoke of as pursued in*

the crowds of London, was in a more proper sense pursued through many a year in dreams. The general idea of a search and a chase reproduced itself in many shapes. The person, the rank, the age, the scenical position, all varied themselves for ever; but the same leading traits more or less faintly remained of a lost Pariah woman, and of some shadowy malice which withdrew her, or attempted to withdraw her, from restoration and from hope. Such is the explanation which I offer why that particular addition which some of my friends had been authorized to look for has not in the main been given, *nor for the present* could *be given; and, secondly, why that part which* is *given has been placed in the conspicuous situation (as a closing passage) which it now occupies.*

NOVEMBER, 1856.

CONFESSIONS
OF AN ENGLISH OPIUM-EATER

(First published in *The London Magazine*, 1821; in book form in 1822. This is the revised and enlarged version of 1856)

PART I

INTRODUCTORY NARRATION

I HAVE often been asked how it was, and through what series of steps, that I became an Opium-Eater. Was it gradually, tentatively, mistrustingly, as one goes down a shelving beach into a deepening sea, and with a knowledge from the first of the dangers lying on that path; half-courting those dangers, in fact, whilst seeming to defy them? Or was it, secondly, in pure ignorance of such dangers, under the misleadings of mercenary fraud? since oftentimes lozenges for the relief of pulmonary affections found their efficacy upon the opium which they contain—upon this, and this only, though clamorously disavowing so suspicious an alliance—and under such treacherous disguises multitudes are seduced into a dependency which they had not foreseen upon a drug which they had not known; not known even by name or by sight: and thus the case is not rare that the chain of abject slavery is first detected when it has inextricably wound itself about the constitutional system. Thirdly, and lastly, was it (*Yes*, by passionate anticipation, I answer, before the question is finished)—was it on a sudden, overmastering

impulse derived from bodily anguish? Loudly I repeat,
Yes; loudly and indignantly—as in answer to a wilful
calumny. Simply as an anodyne it was, under the mere
coercion of pain the severest, that I first resorted to
opium; and precisely that same torment it is, or some
variety of that torment, which drives most people to
make acquaintance with that same insidious remedy.
Such was the fact; such by accident. Meantime, without blame it might have been otherwise. If in early
days I had fully understood the subtle powers lodged
in this mighty drug (when judiciously regulated),
(1) to tranquillize all irritations of the nervous system; (2) to stimulate the capacities of enjoyment; and
(3) under any call for extraordinary exertion (such as
all men meet at times) to sustain through twenty-
four consecutive hours the else drooping animal energies—most certainly, knowing or suspecting all this, I
should have inaugurated my opium career in the character of one seeking *extra* power and enjoyment, rather
than of one shrinking from *extra* torment. And why
not? If *that* argued any fault, is it not a fault that most
of us commit every day with regard to alcohol? Are we
entitled to use *that* only as a medicine? Is wine unlaw-
ful, except as an anodyne? I hope not: else I shall be
obliged to counterfeit and to plead some anomalous *tic*
in my little finger; and thus gradually, as in any Ovid-
ian metamorphosis, I, that am at present a truth-lov-
ing man, shall change by daily inches into a dissem-
bler. No: the whole race of man proclaim it lawful to
drink wine without pleading a medical certificate as a
qualification. That same licence extends itself therefore to the use of opium; what a man may lawfully
seek in wine surely he may lawfully find in opium; and
much more so in those many cases (of which mine
happens to be one) where opium deranges the animal
economy less by a great deal than an equivalent quan-

tity of alcohol. Coleridge, therefore, was doubly in error when he allowed himself to aim most unfriendly
blows at my supposed voluptuousness in the use of
opium; in error as to a principle, and in error as to a
fact. A letter of his, which I will hope that he did not
design to have published, but which, however, *has*
been published, points the attention of his correspondent to a broad distinction separating my case as an
Opium-Eater from his own. He, it seems, had fallen
excusably (because unavoidably) into this habit of
eating opium——as the one sole therapeutic resource
available against his particular malady; but I, wretch
that I am, being so notoriously charmed by fairies
against pain, must have resorted to opium in the abominable character of an adventurous voluptuary, angling in all streams for variety of pleasures. Coleridge
is wrong to the whole extent of what was possible;
wrong in his fact, wrong in his doctrine; in his little
fact, and his big doctrine. I did not do the thing which
he charges upon me; and, if I *had* done it, this would
not convict me as a citizen of Sybaris or Daphne. There
never was a distinction more groundless and visionary
than that which it has pleased him to draw between my
motives and his own; nor could Coleridge have possibly owed this mis-statement to any false information;
since no man surely, on a question of my own private
experience, could have pretended to be better informed
than myself. Or, if there really is such a person, perhaps he will not think it too much trouble to re-write
these *Confessions* from first to last, correcting their
innumerable faults; and, as it happens that some parts
of the unpublished sections for the present are missing,
would he kindly restore them——brightening the colours that may have faded, rekindling the inspiration
that may have drooped; filling up all those chasms
which else are likely to remain as permanent disfigu-

rations of my little work? Meantime the reader who
takes any interest in such a question will find that I
myself (upon such a theme not simply the best, but
surely the sole authority) have, without a shadow of
variation, always given a different account of the matter. Most truly I have told the reader that not any
search after pleasure, but mere extremity of pain from
rheumatic toothache—this and nothing else it was
that first drove me into the use of opium. Coleridge's
bodily affliction was simple rheumatism. Mine, which
intermittingly raged for ten years, was rheumatism in
the face combined with toothache. This I had inherited
from my father; or inherited (I should rather say)
from my own desperate ignorance; since a trifling dose
of colocynth, or of any similar medicine, taken three
times a-week, would more certainly than opium have
delivered me from that terrific curse.[1] In this ignorance, however, which misled me into making war
upon toothache when ripened and manifesting itself in
effects of pain, rather than upon its germs and gathering causes, I did but follow the rest of the world. To
intercept the evil whilst yet in elementary stages of
formation was the true policy; whereas I in my blindness sought only for some mitigation to the evil when
already formed, and past all reach of interception. In

---

[1] *"That terrific curse"*: Two things blunt the general sense
of horror which would else connect itself with toothache: viz.,
first, its enormous diffusion; hardly a household in Europe
being clear of it, each in turn having some one chamber intermittingly echoing the groans extorted by this cruel torture.
There—viz. in its ubiquity—lies one cause of its slight valuation. A second cause is found in its immunity from danger.
This latter ground of undervaluation is noticed in a saying
ascribed (but on what authority I know not) to Sir Philip
Sidney—viz. that, supposing toothache liable in ever so small
a proportion of its cases to a fatal issue, it would be generally
ranked as the most dreadful amongst human maladies; whereas
the certainty that it will in no extremity lead to death, and the

this stage of the suffering, formed and perfect, I was thrown passively upon chance advice, and therefore, by a natural consequence, upon opium—that being the one sole anodyne that is almost notoriously such, and which in that great function is universally appreciated.

Coleridge, therefore, and myself, as regards our baptismal initiation into the use of that mighty drug, occupy the very same position. We are embarked in the self-same boat; nor is it within the compass even of angelic hair-splitting to show that the dark shadow thrown by our several trespasses in this field, mine and his, had by so much as a pin's point any assignable difference. Trespass against trespass (if any trespass there were) —shadow against shadow (if any shadow were really thrown by this trespass over the snowy disk of pure ascetic morality) —in any case, that act in either of us would read into the same meaning, would count up as a debt into the same value, would measure as a delinquency into the same burden of responsibility. And vainly, indeed, does Coleridge attempt to differentiate two cases which ran into absolute identity, differing only as rheumatism differs from toothache. Amongst the admirers of Coleridge, I at all times stood in the foremost rank; and the more was

knowledge that in the very midst of its storms sudden changes may be looked for bringing long halcyon calms, have an unfair effect in lowering the appreciation of this malady considered as a trial of fortitude and patience. No stronger expression of its intensity and scorching fierceness can be imagined than this fact—that, within my private knowledge, two persons who had suffered alike under toothache and cancer have pronounced the former to be, on the scale of torture, by many degrees the worse. In both, there are *at times* what surgeons call "lancinating" pangs—keen, glancing, arrowy radiations of anguish; and upon these the basis of comparison was rested— paroxysm against paroxysm—with the result that I have stated.

my astonishment at being summoned so often to witness his carelessness in the management of controversial questions, and his demoniac inaccuracy in the
statement of facts. The more also was my sense of
Coleridge's wanton injustice in relation to myself individually. Coleridge's gross mis-statement of facts, in
regard to our several opium experiences, had its origin,
sometimes in flighty reading, sometimes in partial and
incoherent reading, sometimes in subsequent forgetfulness; and any one of these lax habits (it will occur
to the reader) is a venial infirmity. Certainly it is; but
surely *not* venial when it is allowed to operate disadvantageously upon the character for self-control of a
brother, who had never spoken of *him* but in the spirit
of enthusiastic admiration; of that admiration which
his exquisite works so amply challenge. Imagine the
case that I really *had* done something wrong, still it
would have been ungenerous——me it would have saddened, I confess, to see Coleridge rushing forward
with a public denunciation of my fault: "Know all
men by these presents that I, S. T. C., *a noticeable
man with large grey eyes*,[1] am a licensed Opium-
Eater, whereas this other man is a buccaneer, a pirate,
a flibustier, and can have none but a forged licence in
his disreputable pocket. In the name of Virtue, arrest
him!" But the truth is, that inaccuracy as to facts and
citations from books was in Coleridge a mere necessity
of nature. Not three days ago, in reading a short comment of the late Archdeacon Hare (*Guesses at Truth*)
upon a bold speculation of Coleridge's (utterly baseless) with respect to the machinery of Etonian Latin
verses, I found my old feelings upon this subject refreshed by an instance that is irresistibly comic, since
everything that Coleridge had relied upon as a cita-

[1] See Wordsworth's exquisite picture of S. T. C. and himself
as occasional denizens in the "Castle of Indolence."

tion from a book in support of his own hypothesis turns out to be a pure fabrication of his own dreams; though, doubtless (which indeed it is that constitutes the characteristic interest of the case), without a suspicion on his part of his own furious romancing. The archdeacon's good-natured smile upon that Etonian case naturally reminded me of the case now before us, with regard to the history of our separate careers as Opium-Eaters. Upon which case I need say no more, as by this time the reader is aware that Coleridge's entire statement upon that subject is perfect moonshine, and, like the sculptured imagery of the pendulous lamp in "Christabel,"

> *All carvèd from the carver's brain.*

This case, therefore, might now be counted on as disposed of; and what sport it could yield might reasonably be thought exhausted. Meantime, on consideration, another and much deeper oversight of Coleridge's becomes apparent; and, as this connects itself with an aspect of the case that furnishes the foundation to the whole of these ensuing *Confessions*, it cannot altogether be neglected. Any attentive reader, after a few moments' reflection, will perceive that, whatever may have been the casual *occasion* of mine or Coleridge's opium-eating, this could not have been the permanent *ground* of opium-eating; because neither rheumatism nor toothache is any *abiding* affection of the system. Both are intermitting maladies, and not at all capable of accounting for a *permanent* habit of opium-eating. Some months are requisite to found *that*. Making allowance for constitutional differences, I should say that *in less than 120 days* no habit of opium-eating could be formed strong enough to call for any extraordinary self-conquest in renouncing it, and even sud-

denly renouncing it. On Saturday you are an Opium-
Eater, on Sunday no longer such. What then was
it, after all, that made Coleridge a slave to opium, and
a slave that could not break his chain? He fancies, in
his headlong carelessness, that he has accounted for
this habit and this slavery; and in the meantime he has
accounted for nothing at all about which any question
has arisen. Rheumatism, he says, drove him to opium.
Very well; but with proper medical treatment the
rheumatism would soon have ceased; or even without
medical treatment, under the ordinary oscillations of
natural causes. And when the pain ceased, then the
opium should have ceased. Why did it not? Because
Coleridge had come to taste the genial pleasure of
opium; and thus the very impeachment which he fancied himself in some mysterious way to have evaded
recoils upon him in undiminished force. The rheumatic attack would have retired before the habit could
have had time to form itself. Or suppose that I under-
rate the strength of the possible habit—this tells
equally in *my* favour; and Coleridge was not entitled
to forget in *my* case a plea remembered in his own. It
is really memorable in the annals of human self-decep-
tions that Coleridge could have held such language in
the face of such facts. I, boasting not at all of my
self-conquests, and owning no moral argument against
the free use of opium, nevertheless on mere *prudential* motives break through the vassalage more than
once, and by efforts which I have recorded as modes
of transcendent suffering. Coleridge, professing to
believe (without reason assigned) that opium-eating
is criminal, and in some mysterious sense more criminal than wine-drinking or porter-drinking—having,
therefore, the strongest *moral* motive for abstaining
from it—yet suffers himself to fall into a captivity to
this same wicked opium, deadlier than was ever heard

of, and under no coercion whatever that he has anywhere explained to us. A slave he was to this potent
drug not less abject than Caliban to Prospero—his detested and yet despotic master. Like Caliban, he frets
his very heart-strings against the rivets of his chain.
Still, at intervals through the gloomy vigils of his
prison, you hear muttered growls of impotent muti-
neering swelling upon the breeze:

> *Irasque leonum*
> *Vincla recusantum——*

recusantum, it is true, still refusing yet still accepting,
protesting for ever against the fierce, overmastering
curb-chain, yet for ever submitting to receive it into
the mouth. It is notorious that in Bristol (to *that* I can
speak myself, but probably in many other places) he
went so far as to hire men—porters, hackney-coach-
men, and others—to oppose by force his entrance into
any druggist's shop. But, as the authority for stopping
him was derived simply from himself, naturally these
poor men found themselves in a metaphysical fix, not
provided for even by Thomas Aquinas or by the prince
of Jesuitical casuists. And in this excruciating dilemma would occur such scenes as the following:

"Oh, sir," would plead the suppliant porter—suppliant, yet semi-imperative (for equally if he *did*, and
if he did *not*, show fight, the poor man's daily 5s.
seemed endangered)—"really you must not; consider,
sir, your wife and——"

TRANSCENDENTAL PHILOSOPHER: "Wife! what
wife? I have no wife." [1]

PORTER: "But, really now, you must not, sir. Didn't
you say no longer ago than yesterday——"

TRANSCEND. PHILOS.: "Pooh, pooh! yesterday is a
long time ago. Are you aware, my man, that people

[1] *Vide Othello.*

are known to have dropped down dead for timely want of opium?"

PORTER: "Ay, but you tell't me not to hearken——"

TRANSCEND. PHILOS.: "Oh, nonsense! An emergency, a shocking emergency, has arisen—quite unlooked for. No matter what I told you in times long past. That which I *now* tell you is—that, if you don't remove that arm of yours from the doorway of this most respectable druggist, I shall have a good ground of action against you for assault and battery."

Am I the man to reproach Coleridge with this vassalage to opium? Heaven forbid! Having groaned myself under that yoke, I pity, and blame him not. But, undeniably, such a vassalage must have been created wilfully and consciously by his own craving after genial stimulation; a thing which I do not blame, but Coleridge *did*. For my own part, duly as the torment relaxed in relief of which I had resorted to opium, I laid aside the opium, not under any meritorious effort of self-conquest; nothing of that sort do I pretend to; but simply on a prudential instinct warning me not to trifle with an engine so awful of consolation and support, nor to waste upon a momentary uneasiness what might eventually prove, in the midst of all-shattering hurricanes, the great elixir of resurrection. What was it that did in reality make me an Opium-Eater? That affection which finally drove me into the *habitual* use of opium, what was it? Pain was it? No, but misery. Casual overcasting of sunshine was it? No, but blank desolation. Gloom was it that might have departed? No, but settled and abiding darkness—

> *Total eclipse,*
> *Without all hope of day!* [1]

[1] *Samson Agonistes.*

Yet whence derived? Caused by what? Caused, as I might truly plead, by youthful distresses in London, were it not that these distresses were due, in their ultimate origin, to my own unpardonable folly; and to that folly I trace many ruins. Oh, spirit of merciful interpretation, angel of forgiveness to youth and its aberrations, that hearkenest for ever as if to some sweet choir of far-off female intercessions! will ye, choir that intercede—wilt thou, angel that forgivest —join together, and charm away that mighty phantom, born amidst the gathering mists of remorse, which strides after me in pursuit from forgotten days —towering for ever into proportions more and more colossal, overhanging and overshadowing my head as if close behind, yet dating its nativity from hours that are fled by more than half-a-century? Oh heavens! that it should be possible for a child not seventeen years old, by a momentary blindness, by listening to a false, false whisper from his own bewildered heart, by one erring step, by a motion this way or that, to change the currents of his destiny, to poison the fountains of his peace, and in the twinkling of an eye to lay the foundations of a life-long repentance! Yet, alas! I must abide by the realities of the case. And one thing is clear, that, amidst such bitter self-reproaches as are now extorted from me by the anguish of my recollections, it cannot be with any purpose of weaving plausible excuses, or of evading blame, that I trace the origin of my confirmed opium-eating to a necessity growing out of my early sufferings in the streets of London. Because, though true it is that the re-agency of these London sufferings did in after years *enforce* the use of opium, equally it is true that the sufferings themselves grew out of my own folly. What really calls for excuse is not the recourse to opium, when opium had become the one sole remedy available for the malady, but those follies which had themselves produced that malady.

I, for my part, after I had become a regular Opium-Eater, and from mismanagement had fallen into miserable excesses in the use of opium, did nevertheless, four several times, contend successfully against the dominion of this drug; did four several times renounce it; renounced it for long intervals; and finally resumed it upon the warrant of my enlightened and deliberate judgement, as being of two evils by very much the least. In this I acknowledge nothing that calls for excuse. I repeat again and again that not the application of opium, with its deep tranquillizing powers to the mitigation of evils, bequeathed by my London hardships, is what reasonably calls for sorrow, but that extravagance of childish folly which precipitated me into scenes naturally producing such hardships.

These scenes I am now called upon to retrace. Possibly they are sufficiently interesting to merit, even on their own account, some short record; but at present, and at this point, they have become indispensable as a key to the proper understanding of all which follows. For in these incidents of my early life is found the entire substratum, together with the secret and underlying motive,[1] of those pompous dreams and dream-sceneries which were in reality the true objects—first and last—contemplated in these *Confessions*.

My father died when I was in my seventh year, leaving six children, including myself (viz. four sons and two daughters), to the care of four guardians, and

---

[1] "*Motive*": The word *motive* is here used in the sense attached by artists and connoisseurs to the technical word *motivo*, applied to pictures, or to the separate movements in a musical theme.

of our mother, who was invested with the legal authority of a guardian.

Some months after my eleventh birth-day, Greenhay was sold, and my mother's establishment—both children and servants—was translated to Bath: only that for a few months I and one brother were still left under the care of Mr. Samuel H.; so far, that is, as regarded our education. Else, as regarded the luxurious comforts of a thoroughly English home, we became the guests, by special invitation, of a young married couple in Manchester—viz. Mr. and Mrs. [Kelsall]. This incident, though otherwise without results, I look back upon with feelings inexpressibly profound, as a jewelly parenthesis of pathetic happiness—such as emerges but once in any man's life. Mr. [Kelsall] was a young and rising American merchant; by which I mean that he was an Englishman who exported to the United States. He had married about three years previously a pretty and amiable young woman—well educated, and endowed with singular compass of intellect. But the distinguishing feature in this household was the spirit of love which, under the benign superintendence of the mistress, diffused itself through all its members.

When I left the [Kelsalls'] I left Manchester; and during the next three years I was sent to two very different schools: first, to a public one—viz. the Bath Grammar School, then and since famous for its excellence; secondly, to a private school in Wiltshire. At the end of the three years, I found myself once again in Manchester.

On a day, therefore, it was in the closing autumn (or rather in the opening winter) of 1800 that my first introduction took place to the Manchester Grammar School. The school-room showed already in its

ample proportions some hint of its pretensions as an
endowed school, or school of that class which I believe
peculiar to England. To this limited extent had the
architectural sense of power been timidly and parsimoniously invoked. Beyond that, nothing had been
attempted; and the dreary expanse of whitewashed
walls, that at so small a cost might have been embel-
lished by plaster-of-Paris friezes and large medallions,
illustrating to the eye of the youthful student the most
memorable glorifications of literature—these were
bare as the walls of a poor-house or a lazaretto.

Puritanically bald and odious in my eyes, was the
hall up which my guardian and myself paced solemnly
—though not Miltonically "riding up to the Soldan's
chair," yet, in fact, within a more limited kingdom,
advancing to the chair of a more absolute despot.
This potentate was the head-master, or *archididascalus*, of the Manchester Grammar School; and that
school was variously distinguished. It was (1) ancient,
having in fact been founded by a bishop of Exeter in
an early part of the sixteenth century, so as to be now,
in 1856, more than 330 years old; (2) it was rich, and
was annually growing richer; and (3) it was dignified by a beneficial relation to the magnificent University of Oxford.

The head-master at that time was Mr. Charles
Lawson. In former editions of this work I created him
a doctor; my object being to evade too close an approach to the realities of the case, and consequently to
personalities, which (though indifferent to myself)
would have been in some cases displeasing to others. A
doctor, however, Mr. Lawson was not; nor in the account of law a clergyman. Yet most people, governed
unconsciously by the associations surrounding their
composite idea of a dignified schoolmaster, invested
him with the clerical character. And in reality he *had*

taken deacon's orders in the Church of England. But not the less he held himself to be a layman, and was addressed as such by all his correspondents of rank, who might be supposed best to understand the technical rules of English etiquette. Etiquette in such cases cannot entirely detach itself from law. Now, in English law, as was shown in Horne Tooke's case, the rule is, *Once a clergyman, and always a clergyman*. The sacred character with which ordination clothes a man is indelible. But, on the other hand, who *is* a clergyman? Not he that has taken simply the initial orders of a deacon—so at least I have heard—but he that has taken the second and full orders of a priest. If otherwise, then there was a great mistake current amongst Mr. Lawson's friends in addressing him as an esquire.

Squire or not a squire, however, parson or not a parson—whether sacred or profane—Mr. Lawson was in some degree interesting by his position and his recluse habits. Life was over with him, for its hopes and for its trials. Or at most one trial yet awaited him; which was—to fight with a painful malady, and fighting to die. He still had his dying to do: he was in arrear as to *that*: else all was finished. It struck me (but, with such limited means for judging, I might easily be wrong) that his understanding was of a narrow order. But that did not disturb the interest which surrounded him now in his old age (probably seventy-five, or more), nor make any drawback from the desire I had to spell backwards and re-compose the text of his life. What had been his fortunes in this world? Had they travelled upwards or downwards? What triumphs had he enjoyed in the sweet and solemn cloisters of Oxford? What mortifications in the harsh world outside? Two only had survived in the malicious traditions of "his friends." He was a Jacobite (as were so many amongst my dear Lancastrian compatriots);

had drunk the Pretender's health, and had drunk it in company with that Dr. Byrom who had graced the *symposium* by the famous equivocating *impromptu* [1] to the health of that prince. Mr. Lawson had therefore been obliged to witness the final prostration of his political party. That was his earliest mortification. His second, about seven years later, was that he had been jilted, and with circumstances (at least so I heard) of cruel scorn. Was it that *he* had interpreted in a sense too flattering for himself ambiguous expressions of favour in the lady? or that she in cruel caprice had disowned the hopes which she had authorized? However this might be, half-a-century of soothing and reconciling years had cicatrized the wounds of Mr. Lawson's heart. The lady of 1752, if living in 1800, must be furiously wrinkled. And a strange metaphysical question arises: Whether, when the object of an impassioned love has herself faded into a shadow, the fiery passion itself can still survive as an abstraction, still mourn over its wrongs, still clamour for redress. I have heard of such cases. In Wordsworth's poem of "Ruth" (which was founded, as I happen to know, upon facts) it is recorded as an affecting incident that, some months after the first frenzy of her disturbed mind had given way to medical treatment, and had lapsed into a gentler form of lunacy, she was dismissed from confinement; and, upon finding herself uncontrolled among the pastoral scenes where she played

[1] *"Equivocating impromptu"*: The party had gathered in a tumultuary way; so that some Capulets had mingled with the Montagues, one of whom called upon Dr. Byrom to drink *The King, God bless him! and Confusion to the Pretender!* Upon which the doctor sang out—

> God bless the king, of church and state defender;
> God bless (no harm in blessing) the Pretender!
> But who Pretender is, and who the King—
> God bless us all! that's quite another thing.

away her childhood, she gradually fell back to the
original habits of her life whilst yet undisturbed by
sorrow. Something similar had happened to Mr. Lawson; and some time after his first shock, amongst other
means for effacing that deep-grooved impression, he
had laboured to replace himself, as much as was possible, in the situation of a college student. In this
effort he was assisted considerably by the singular
arrangement of the house attached to his official station. For an English house it was altogether an oddity,
being, in fact, built upon a Roman plan. All the rooms
on both storeys had their windows looking down upon
a little central court. This court was a quadrangular,
but so limited in its dimensions that by a Roman it
would have been regarded as the *impluvium:* for Mr.
Lawson, however, with a little exertion of fancy, it
transmuted itself into a college quadrangle. Here,
therefore, were held the daily "callings-over," at
which every student was obliged to answer upon being
named. And thus the unhappy man, renewing continually the fancy that he was still standing in an
Oxford quadrangle, perhaps cheated himself into the
belief that all had been a dream which concerned the
caprices of the lady, and the lady herself a phantom.
College usages also which served to strengthen this
fanciful *alibi*—such, for instance, as the having two
plates arranged before him at dinner (one for the animal, the other for the vegetable, food) —were reproduced in Millgate. One sole luxury also, somewhat
costly, which, like most young men of easy income, he
had allowed himself at Oxford, was now retained long
after it had become practically useless. This was a
hunter for himself, and another for his groom, which
he continued to keep, in spite of the increasing war-
taxes, many a year after he had almost ceased to ride.
Once in three or four months he would have the horses

saddled and brought out. Then, with considerable effort, he swung himself into the saddle, moved off at a quiet amble, and in about fifteen or twenty minutes might be seen returning from an excursion of two miles, under the imagination that he had laid in a stock of exercise sufficient for another period of a hundred days.

Meantime Mr. Lawson had sought his main consolation in the great classics of elder days. His senior *alumni* were always working their way through some great scenic poet that had shaken the stage of Athens; and more than one of his classes, never ending, still beginning, were daily solacing him with the gaieties of Horace, in his Epistles or in his Satires. The Horation jests indeed to *him* never grew old. On coming to the *plagosus Orbilius,* or any other sally of pleasantry, he still threw himself back in his arm-chair, as he *had* done through fifty years, with what seemed heart-shaking bursts of sympathetic merriment. Mr. Lawson, indeed, could afford to be sincerely mirthful over the word *plagosus.* There are gloomy tyrants, exulting in the discipline of fear, to whom and to whose pupils this word must call up remembrances too degrading for any but affected mirth. Allusions that are too fearfully personal cease to be subjects of playfulness. Sycophancy only it is that laughs; and the artificial merriment is but the language of shrinking and grovelling deprecation.

Different, indeed, was the condition of the Manchester Grammar School. It was honourable both to the masters and the upper boys, through whom only such a result was possible, that in that school, during my knowledge of it (viz. during the closing year of the eighteenth century and the two opening years of the nineteenth), all punishments that appealed to the sense of bodily pain had fallen into disuse; and this at

a period long before any public agitation had begun to
stir in that direction. How then was discipline maintained? It was maintained through the self-discipline
of the senior boys, and through the efficacy of their
example, combined with their system of rules. Noble
are the impulses of opening manhood where they are
not utterly ignoble: at that period, I mean, when the
poetic sense begins to blossom, and when boys are first
made sensible of the paradise that lurks in female
smiles. Had the school been entirely a day-school, too
probable it is that the vulgar brawling tendencies of
boys left to themselves would have prevailed. But it
happened that the elder section of the school—those on
the brink of manhood, and by incalculable degrees the
more scholar-like section, all who read, meditated, or
began to kindle into the love of literature—were
boarders in Mr. Lawson's house. The students, therefore, of the house carried an overwhelming influence
into the school. They were bound together by links of
brotherhood; whereas the day-scholars were disconnected. Over and above this, it happened luckily that
there was no playground, not the smallest, attached to
the school; that is, none was attached to the *upper* or
grammar school. But there was also, and resting on
the same liberal endowment, a *lower* school, where the
whole machinery of teaching was applied to the lowest mechanical accomplishments of reading and writing. The hall in which this servile business was conducted ran under the upper school; it was, therefore, I
presume, a subterraneous duplicate of the upper hall.
And, since the upper rose only by two or three feet
above the level of the neighbouring streets, the lower
school should naturally have been at a great depth
below these streets. In that case it would be a dark
crypt, such as we see under some cathedrals; and it
would have argued a singular want of thoughtfulness

in the founder to have laid one part of his establishment under an original curse of darkness. As the access
to this plebeian school lay downwards through long
flights of steps, I never found surplus energy enough
for investigating the problem. But, as the ground broke
away precipitously at that point into lower levels, I
presume, upon consideration, that the subterranean
crypt will be found open on one side to visitations
from sun and moon. So that, for this base mechanic
school there may, after all, have been a playground.
But for ours in the upper air, I repeat, there was none;
not so much as would have bleached a lady's pocket-
handkerchief; and this one defect carried along with it
unforeseen advantages.

Lord Bacon it is who notices the subtle policy which
may lurk in the mere external figure of a table. A
square table, having an undeniable head and foot, two
polar extremities of what is highest and lowest, a
perihelion and an aphelion, together with equatorial
sides, opens at a glance a large career to ambition;
whilst a circular table sternly represses all such aspiring dreams, and so does a triangular table. Yet, if the
triangle should be right-angled, then the Lucifer
seated at the right angle might argue that he *sub-
tended* all the tenants of the hypothenuse; being,
therefore, as much nobler than they as Atlas was
nobler than the globe which he carried. It was, by the
way, some arrangement of this nature which constituted the original feature of distinction in John o'
Groat's house, and not at all (as most people suppose)
the high northern latitude of this house. John, it seems,
finished the feuds for precedency, not by legislating
this way or that, but by cutting away the possibility
of such feuds through the assistance of a round table.
The same principle must have guided King Arthur
amongst his knights, Charlemagne amongst his pala-

dins, and sailors in their effectual distribution of the
peril attached to a mutinous remonstrance by the admirable device of a "round-robin." Even two little
girls, as Harrington remarks in his *Oceana*, have
oftentimes hit upon an expedient, through pure
mother-wit, more effectual than all the schools of philosophy could have suggested, for insuring the impartial division of an orange; which expedient is that
either of the two shall divide, but then that the other
shall have the right of choice. You divide, and I
choose. Such is the formula; and an angel could not
devise a more absolute guarantee for the equity of the
division than by thus forcing the divider to become the
inheritor of any possible disadvantages that he may
have succeeded in creating by his own act of division.
In all these cases one seemingly trivial precaution
opens, in the next stage, into a world of irresistible
consequences.

And, in our case, an effect not less disproportionate
followed out of that one accident, apparently so slight,
that we had no playground. We of the seniority, who,
by thoughtfulness, and the conscious dignity of dealing largely with literature, were already indisposed to
boyish sports, found, through the defect of a playground, that our choice and our pride were also our
necessity. Even the proudest of us benefited by that
coercion; for many would else have sold their privilege of pride for an hour's amusement, and have become, at least, occasional conformists. A day more
than usually fine, a trial of skill more than usually
irritating to the sense of special superiority, would
have seduced most of us in the end into the surrender
of our exclusiveness. Indiscriminate familiarity would
have followed as an uncontrollable result; since to
mingle with others in common acts of business may
leave the sense of reserve undisturbed: but all reserve

gives way before a common intercourse in pleasure. As it was, what with our confederation through house-membership, what with our reciprocal sympathies in the problems suggested by books, we had become a club of boys (amongst whom might be four or five that were even young men, counting eighteen or nineteen years) altogether as thoughtful and as self-respecting as can often exist even amongst adults. Even the subterraneous school contributed something to our self-esteem. It formed a subordinate section of our own establishment, that kept before our eyes, by force of contrast, the dignity inherent in our own constitution. Its object was to master humble accomplishments that were within the reach of *mechanic* efforts: everything mechanic is limited; whereas we felt that *our* object, even if our name of *grammar* school presented that object in what seemed too limited a shape, was substantially noble, and tended towards the infinite. But in no long time I came to see that, as to the *name*, we were all of us under a mistake. Being asked what a *grammar* school indicates, what it professes to teach, there is scarcely any man who would not reply, "Teach? why, it teaches grammar: what else?" But this is a mistake: as I have elsewhere explained, *grammatica* in this combination does not mean grammar (though grammar also obeys the movements of a most subtle philosophy), but *literature*.

Having thus sketched the characteristic points distinguishing the school and the presiding master (for of masters, senior and junior, there were four in this upper school), I return to my own inaugural examination. On this day, memorable to myself, as furnishing the starting-point for so long a series of days, saddened by haughty obstinacy on one side, made effective by folly on the other, no sooner had my guardian retired than Mr. Lawson produced from his desk a

volume of the *Spectator*, and instructed me to throw
into as good Latin as I could some paper of Steele's—
not the whole, but perhaps a third part. No better exercise could have been devised for testing the extent of
my skill as a Latinist. And here I ought to make an
explanation. In the previous edition of these *Confessions*, writing sometimes too rapidly, and with little
precision in cases of little importance, I conveyed an
impression which I had not designed with regard to
the true nature of my pretensions as a Grecian; and
something of the same correction will apply to that
narrower accomplishment which was the subject of
my present examination. Neither in Greek nor in
Latin was my *knowledge* very extensive; my age made
that impossible; and especially because in those days
there were no decent guides through the thorny jun-
gles of the Latin language, far less of the Greek. When
I mention that the *Port Royal* Greek Grammar translated by Dr. Nugent was about the best key extant in
English to the innumerable perplexities of Greek diction, and that, for the *res metrica*, Morell's valuable
Thesaurus, having then never been reprinted, was
rarely to be seen, the reader will conclude that a
schoolboy's *knowledge* of Greek could not be other
than slender. Slender indeed was mine. Yet stop! *what*
was slender? Simply my *knowledge* of Greek; for that
knowledge stretches by tendency to the infinite; but
not therefore my *command* of Greek. The *knowledge*
of Greek must always hold some gross proportion to
the time spent upon it—probably, therefore, to the age
of the student; but the *command* over a language, the
power of adapting it plastically to the expression of
your own thoughts, is almost exclusively a gift of nature, and has very little connexion with time. Universally I contend that the faculty of clothing the
thoughts in a Greek dress is a function of natural sen-

sibility, in a great degree disconnected from the extent
or the accuracy of the writer's grammatical skill in
Greek.

These explanations are too long. The reader will
understand, as their sum, that what I needed in such a
case was, not so much a critical familiarity with the
syntax of the language, or a *copia verborum*, as great
agility in reviewing the relations of one idea to another, so as to present modern and unclassical objects
under such aspects as might suggest periphrases in
substitution for direct names, where names could not
be had, and everywhere to colour my translation with
as rich a display of idiomatic forms as the circumstances of the case would allow. I succeeded, and beyond my expectation. For once—being the first time
that he had been known to do such a thing, but also
the very last—Mr. Lawson did absolutely pay me a
compliment. And with another compliment more than
verbal he crowned his gracious condescensions—viz.
with my provisional instalment in his highest class;
not the highest at that moment, since there was one
other class above us; but this other was on the wing
for Oxford within some few weeks; which change being accomplished, we (viz. I and two others) immediately moved up into the supreme place.

Two or three days after this examination—viz. on
the Sunday following—I transferred myself to head-
quarters at Mr. Lawson's house. About nine o'clock in
the evening, I was conducted by a servant up a short
flight of stairs, through a series of gloomy and unfur-
nished little rooms, having small windows but no
doors, to the common room (as in Oxford it would
technically be called) of the senior boys. Everything
had combined to depress me. To leave the society of
accomplished women—*that* was already a signal privation. The season besides was rainy, which in itself is a

sure source of depression; and the forlorn aspect of the rooms completed my dejection. But the scene changed as the door was thrown open: faces kindling with animation became visible; and from a company of boys, numbering sixteen or eighteen, scattered about the room, two or three, whose age entitled them to the rank of leaders, came forward to receive me with a courtesy which I had not looked for. The grave kindness and the absolute sincerity of their manner impressed me most favourably. I had lived familiarly with boys gathered from all quarters of the island at the Bath Grammar School: and for some time (when visiting Lord Altamont at Eton) with boys of the highest aristocratic pretensions. At Bath and at Eton, though not equally, there prevailed a tone of higher polish; and in the air, speech, deportment of the majority could be traced at once a premature knowledge of the world. They had indeed the advantage over my new friends in graceful self-possession; but, on the other hand, the best of them suffered by comparison with these Manchester boys in the qualities of visible self-restraint and of self-respect. At Eton high rank was distributed pretty liberally; but in the Manchester school the parents of many boys were artisans, or of that rank; some even had sisters that were menial servants; and those who stood higher by pretensions of birth and gentle blood were, at the most, the sons of rural gentry or of clergymen.

*　*　*

I acknowledge, with deep self-reproach, that every possible indulgence was allowed to me which the circumstances of the establishment made possible. I had, for example, a private room allowed, in which I not only studied, but also slept at night. The room being airy and cheerful, I found nothing disagreeable in this double use of it. Naturally, however, this means of retirement tended to sequester me from my companions: for, whilst liking the society of some amongst them, I also had a deadly liking (perhaps a morbid liking) for solitude. To make my present solitude the more fascinating, my mother sent me five guineas *extra*, for the purchase of an admission to the Manchester Library; a library which I should not at present think *very* extensive, but which, however, benefited in its composition, as also in its administration, by the good sense and intelligence of some amongst its original committees. These two luxuries were truly and indeed such: but a third, from which I had anticipated even greater pleasure, turned out a total failure; and for a reason which it may be useful to mention, by way of caution to others. This was a pianoforte, together with the sum required for regular lessons from a music-master. But the first discovery I made was that practice through eight or even ten hours a-day was indispensable towards any great proficiency on this instrument. Another discovery finished my disenchantment: it was this. For the particular purpose which I had in view, it became clear that no mastery of the instrument, not even that of Thalberg, would be available. Too soon I became aware that to the deep voluptuous enjoyment of music absolute *passiveness* in the hearer is indispensable. Gain what skill you please, nevertheless activity, vigilance, anxiety must always accompany an elaborate effort of musical execution: and so far is that from being reconcilable with the entrancement and lull essential to the true fruition of music, that, even if you should suppose a vast piece of mechanism capable of executing a whole oratorio, but requiring, at intervals, a co-operating impulse from the foot of the auditor, even *that*, even so much as an occasional touch of the foot, would utterly undermine all your pleasure. A single psychological discovery, therefore, caused my musical anticipations to evanesce. Consequently, one of my luxuries burst like a bubble at an early stage. In this state of things, when the instrument had turned out a bubble, it followed naturally that the music-master should find himself to be a bubble. But he was so thoroughly good-natured and agreeable that I could not reconcile myself to such a catastrophe. Meantime, though accommodating within certain limits, this music-master was yet a conscientious man, and a man of honourable pride. On finding, therefore, that I was not seriously making any effort to improve, he shook hands with me one fine day, and took his leave for ever. Unless it were to point a moral and adorn a tale, the piano had then become useless. It was too big to hang upon willows, and willows there were none in that neighbourhood. But it remained for months as a lumbering monument of labour misapplied, of bubbles that had burst, and of musical visions that, under psychological tests, had foundered for ever.

Yes, certainly, this particular luxury—one out of three—had proved a bubble; too surely this had foundered; but not, therefore, the other two. The quiet study, lifted by two storeys above the vapours of earth, and liable to no unseasonable intrusion; the Manchester Library, so judiciously and symmetrically mounted in all its most attractive departments—no class disproportioned to the rest: these were no bubbles; these had not foundered. Oh, wherefore, then, was it—through what inexplicable growth of evil in myself or in others —that now in the summer of 1802, when peace was brooding over all the land, peace succeeding to a bloody seven years' war, but peace which already gave signs of breaking into a far bloodier war, some dark sympathizing movement within my own heart, as if echoing and repeating in mimicry the political menaces of the earth, swept with storm-clouds across that otherwise serene and radiant dawn which should have heralded my approaching entrance into life? *Inexplicable* I have allowed myself to call this fatal error in my life, because such it *must* appear to others; since, even to myself, so often as I fail to realize the case by reproducing a reflex impression in kind, and in degree, of the suffering before which my better angel gave way— yes, even to myself this collapse of my resisting energies seems inexplicable. Yet again, in simple truth, now that it becomes possible, through changes worked by time, to tell the *whole* truth (and not, as in former editions, only a part of it), there really was no absolute mystery at all. But this case, in common with many others, exemplifies to my mind the mere impossibility of making full and frank *Confessions*, whilst many of the persons concerned in the incidents are themselves surviving, or (which is worse still), if themselves dead and buried, are yet vicariously surviving in the persons of near and loving kinsmen. Rather than inflict mortifications upon people so circumstanced, any kindhearted man will choose to mutilate his narrative; will suppress facts, and will mystify explanations. For instance, at this point in my record, it has become my right, perhaps I might say my duty, to call a particular medical man of the penultimate generation a blockhead; nay, doubtfully, to call him a criminal blockhead. But could I do this without deep compunction, so long as sons and daughters of his were still living, from whom I, when a boy, had received most hospitable attentions? Often, on the very same day which brought home to my suffering convictions the atrocious ignorance of papa, I was benefiting by the courtesies of the daughters, and by the scientific accomplishments of the son. Not the less

this man, at that particular moment when a crisis of
gloom was gathering over my path, became effectually
my evil genius. Not that singly perhaps he could have
worked any durable amount of mischief: but he, as a
co-operator unconsciously with others, sealed and ratified that sentence of stormy sorrow then hanging over
my head. Three separate persons, in fact, made themselves unintentional accomplices in that ruin (a ruin
reaching me even at this day by its shadows) which
threw me out a homeless vagrant upon the earth before
I had accomplished my seventeenth year. Of these
three persons, foremost came myself, through my wilful despair and resolute adjuration of all *secondary*
hope: since, after all, some mitigation was possible,
supposing that perfect relief might *not* be possible.
Secondly, came that medical ruffian through whose
brutal ignorance it happened that my malady had not
been arrested before reaching an advanced stage.
Thirdly, came Mr. Lawson, through whose growing
infirmities it had arisen that this malady ever reached
its very earliest stage. Strange it was, but not the less a
fact, that Mr. Lawson was gradually becoming a curse
to all who fell under his influence, through pure zeal-
otry of conscientiousness. Being a worse man, he
would have carried far deeper blessings into his circle.
If he could have reconciled himself to an imperfect
discharge of his duties, he would not have betrayed his
insufficiency for those duties. But this he would not
hear of. He persisted in travelling over the appointed
course to the last inch: and the consequences told most
painfully upon the comfort of all around him. By the
old traditionary usages of the school, going in at seven
A.M., we ought to have been dismissed for breakfast
and a full hour's repose at nine. This hour of rest was
in strict justice a *debt* to the students—liable to no
discount either through the caprice or the tardiness of

the supreme master. Yet such were the gradual encroachments upon this hour that at length the bells of
the collegiate church—which, by an ancient usage,
rang every morning from half-past nine to ten, and
through varying modifications of musical key and
rhythmus that marked the advancing stages of the
half-hour—regularly announced to us, on issuing
from the school-room, that the bread and milk which
composed our simple breakfast must be dispatched at
a pace fitter for the fowls of the air than students of
Grecian philosophy. But was no compensatory encroachment for our benefit allowed upon the next hour
from ten to eleven? Not for so much as the fraction of
a second. Inexorably as the bells, by stopping, announced the hour of ten, was Mr. Lawson to be seen
ascending the steps of the school; and he that suffered
most by this rigorous exaction of duties could not allege that Mr. Lawson suffered less. If he required
others to pay, he also paid up to the last farthing. The
same derangement took place, with the same refusal
to benefit by any indemnification, at what *should*
have been the two-hours' pause for dinner. Only for
some mysterious reason, resting possibly upon the
family arrangements of the day-scholars—which, if
once violated, might have provoked a rebellion of
fathers and mothers—he still adhered faithfully to
five o'clock P.M. as the closing hour of the day's
labours.

Here then stood arrayed the whole machinery of
mischief in good working order; and through six
months or more, allowing for one short respite of four
weeks, this machinery had been operating with effect.
Mr. Lawson, to begin, had (without meaning it, or so
much as perceiving it) barred up all avenues from
morning to night through which any bodily exercise
could be obtained. Two or three chance intervals of

five minutes each, and even these not consecutively arranged, composed the whole available fund of leisure out of which any stroll into the country could have been attempted. But in a great city like Manchester the very suburbs had hardly been reached before that little fraction of time was exhausted. Very soon after Mr. Lawson's increasing infirmities had begun to tell severely in the contraction of our spare time, the change showed itself powerfully in my drooping health. Gradually the liver became affected: and connected with that affection arose, what often accompanies such ailments, profound melancholy. In such circumstances, indeed under any the slightest disturbance of my health, I had authority from my guardians to call for medical advice: but I was not left to my own discretion in selecting the adviser. This person was not a physician, who would of course have expected the ordinary fee of a guinea for every visit; nor a surgeon; but simply an apothecary. In any case of serious illness a physician would have been called in. But a less costly style of advice was reasonably held to be sufficient in any illness which left the patient strength sufficient to walk about. Certainly it ought to have been sufficient here: for no case could possibly be simpler. Three doses of calomel or blue pill, which unhappily I did not then know, would no doubt have re-established me in a week. But far better, as acting always upon me with a magical celerity and a magical certainty, would have been the authoritative prescription (privately notified to Mr. Lawson) of seventy miles' walking in each week. Unhappily my professional adviser was a comatose old gentleman, rich beyond all his needs, careless of his own practice, and standing under that painful necessity (according to the custom then regulating medical practice, which prohibited fees to apothecaries) of seeking his remunera-

tion in excessive deluges of medicine. Me, however, out
of pure idleness, he forbore to plague with any *variety*
of medicines. With sublime simplicity he confined himself to one horrid mixture, that must have suggested
itself to him when prescribing for a tiger. In ordinary
circumstances, and with plenty of exercise, no creature could be healthier than myself. But my organization was perilously frail. And to fight simultaneously with such a malady and such a medicine seemed
really too much. The proverb tells us that three "flit-
tings" are as bad as a fire. Very possibly. And I should
think that, in the same spirit of reasonable equation,
three such tiger-drenches must be equal to one apo-
plectic fit, or even to the tiger himself. Having taken
two of them, which struck me as quite enough for one
life, I declined to comply with the injunction of the
label pasted upon each several phial—viz. *Repetatur
haustus* [1]; and, instead of doing any such dangerous
thing, called upon Mr. —— (the apothecary), begging to know if his art had not amongst its reputed
infinity of resources any less abominable, and less
shattering to a delicate system than this. "None whatever," he replied. Exceedingly kind he was; insisted
on my drinking tea with his really amiable daughters; but continued at intervals to repeat "None whatever—none whatever"; then, as if rousing himself to
an effort, he sang out loudly "None whatever," which
in this final utterance he toned down syllabically into
"what*ever—ever—ver—er.*" The whole wit of man,
it seems, had exhausted itself upon the preparation of
that one infernal mixture.

Now then we three—Mr. Lawson, the somnolent
apothecary, and myself—had amongst us accomplished a climax of perplexity. Mr. Lawson, by mere
dint of conscientiousness, had made health for me im-

[1] "Let the draught be repeated."

possible. The apothecary had subscribed *his* little contribution, by ratifying and trebling the ruinous effects of this sedentariness. And for myself, as last in the series, it now remained to clench the operation by my own little contribution, all that I really had to offer—viz. absolute despair. Those who have ever suffered from a profound derangement of the liver may happen to know that of human despondencies through all their infinite gamut none is more deadly. Hope died within me. I could not look for medical relief, so deep being my own ignorance, so equally deep being that of my official counsellor. I could not expect that Mr. Lawson would modify his system—his instincts of duty being so strong, his incapacity to face that duty so steadily increasing. "It comes then to this," thought I, "that in myself only there lurks any arrear of help": as always for every man the ultimate reliance should be on himself. But this *self* of mine seemed absolutely bankrupt; bankrupt of counsel or device—of effort in the way of action, or of suggestion in the way of plan. I had for two months been pursuing with one of my guardians what I meant for a negotiation upon this subject; the main object being to obtain some considerable abbreviation of my school residence. But *negotiation* was a self-flattering name for such a correspondence, since there never had been from the beginning the slightest leaning on my guardian's part towards the shadow or pretence of a compromise. What compromise, indeed, was possible where neither party could concede a *part*, however small: the *whole* must be conceded, or nothing: since no *mezzo termine* was conceivable. In reality, when my eyes first glanced upon that disagreeable truth—that no opening offered for *reciprocal* concession, that the concession must all be on one side—naturally it struck me that no guardian could be expected to do *that*. At the same moment it also struck me that my guardian had all along never for a moment been arguing with a view to any *practical* result, but simply in the hope that he might win over my assent to the reasonableness of what, reasonable or not, was settled immovably. These sudden discoveries, flashing upon me simultaneously, were quite sufficient to put a summary close to the correspondence. And I saw also, which strangely had escaped me till this general revelation of disappointments, that any individual guardian—even if he *had* been disposed to concession—was but one after all amongst five. Well: this amongst the general blackness really brought a gleam of comfort. If the whole object on which I had spent so much excellent paper and midnight tallow (I am ashamed to use so vile a word, and yet truth forbids me to say *oil*) , if this would have been so nearly worthless when gained, then it became a kind of pleasure to have lost it. All considerations united now in urging me to waste no more of either rhetoric, tallow, or logic, upon my impassive granite block of a guardian. Indeed, I suspected, on reviewing his last communication, that he had just reached the last inch of his patience, or (in nautical diction) had "paid out" the entire cable by which he swung; so that, if I, acting on the apothecary's precedent of "*repetatur haustus,*" had endeavoured to administer another bolus or draught of expostulation, he would have followed my course as to the tiger-drench, in applying his potential *No* to any such audacious attempt. To my guardian, meantime, I owe this justice—that, over and above the absence on my side of any arguments wearing even a colourable strength (for to him the suffering from biliousness must have been a mere word) , he had the following weighty consideration to offer, "which even this foolish boy" (to himself he would say) "will think material some three years ahead." My patrimonial income, at the moment of my father's death, like that of all my brothers (then three), was exactly £150 per annum.[1] Now, according to the current belief, or boldly, one might say, according to the avowed traditional maxim throughout England, such an income was too little for an under-graduate, keeping his four terms annually at Oxford or Cambridge. Too little— by how much? By £50: the adequate income being set down as just £200. Consequently the precise sum by which my income was supposed (falsely supposed, as subsequently my own experience convinced me) to fall short of the income needed for Oxford, was that very sum which the funds of the Manchester Grammar School allocated to every student resident for a period of three years; and allocated not merely through a corresponding period of three years, but of seven years. Strong should have been the reasons that could neutralize such overwhelming pleadings of just and honourable prudence for submitting to the further residence required. O reader, urge not the crying arguments that spoke so tumultuously against me. Too sorrowfully I feel them. Out of thirty-six months' residence required, I had actually completed nineteen —*i.e.* the better half. Still, on the other hand, it is true that my sufferings were almost insupportable; and, but for the blind unconscious conspiracy of two persons, these sufferings would either (1) never have existed, or (2) would have been instantly relieved. In a great city like Manchester lay, probably, a ship-load

[1] "£150 *per annum*": Why in a long minority of more than fourteen years this was not improved, I never could learn. Nobody was open to any suspicion of positive embezzlement: and yet this case must be added to the other cases of passive neglects and negative injuries which so extensively disfigure the representative picture of guardianship all over Christendom.

of that same mercury which, by one fragment, not so large as an acorn, would have changed the colour of a human life, or would have intercepted the heavy funeral knell—heavy, though it may be partially muffled—of his own fierce self-reproaches.

But now, at last, came over me, from the mere excess of bodily suffering and mental disappointments, a frantic and rapturous re-agency. In the United States the case is well known, and many times has been described by travellers, of that furious instinct which, under a secret call for saline variations of diet, drives all the tribes of buffaloes for thousands of miles to the common centre of the "Salt-licks." Under such a compulsion does the locust, under such a compulsion does the lemming, traverse its mysterious path. They are deaf to danger, deaf to the cry of battle, deaf to the trumpets of death. Let the sea cross their path, let armies with artillery bar the road, even these terrific powers can arrest only by destroying; and the most frightful abysses, up to the very last menace of engulfment, up to the very instant of absorption, have no power to alter or retard the line of their inexorable advance.

Such an instinct it was, such a rapturous command —even so potent, and alas! even so blind—that, under the whirl of tumultuous indignation and of new-born hope, suddenly transfigured my whole being. In the twinkling of an eye, I came to an adamantine resolution—not as if issuing from any act or any choice of my own, but as if passively received from some dark oracular legislation external to myself. That I would elope from Manchester—this was the resolution. *Abscond* would have been the word, if I had meditated anything criminal. But whence came the indignation, and the hope? The indignation arose naturally against my three tormentors (guardian, Archididascalus, and the professor of tigrology) ; for those who *do* substantially co-operate to one result, however little designing it, unavoidably the mind unifies as a hostile confederacy. But the hope—how shall I explain *that?* Was it the first-born of the resolution, or was the resolution the first-born of the hope? Indivisibly they went together, like thunder and lightning; or each interchangeably ran before and after the other. Under that transcendent rapture which the prospect of sudden liberation let loose, all that natural anxiety which should otherwise have interlinked itself with my anticipations was actually drowned in the blaze of joy, as the light of the planet Mercury is lost and confounded on sinking too far within the blaze of the solar beams. Practically I felt no care at all stretching beyond two or three weeks. Not as being heedless and improvident; my tendencies lay generally in the other direction. No; the cause lurked in what Wordsworth, when describing the festal state of France during the happy morning-tide of her First Revolution (1788–1790), calls *"the senselessness of joy"*: this it was, joy —headlong—frantic—irreflective—and (as Wordsworth truly calls it), for that very reason, *sublime* [1] —which swallowed up all capacities of rankling care or heart-corroding doubt. I was, I had been long, a captive: I was in a house of bondage: one fulminating word—*Let there be freedom*—spoken from some hidden recess in my own will, had as by an earthquake rent asunder my prison gates. At any minute I could walk out. Already I trod by anticipation the sweet pastoral hills, already I breathed gales of the everlasting mountains, that to my feelings blew from the garden

[1] *The senselessness of joy was then sublime.* Wordsworth at Calais in 1802 (see his sonnets), looking back through thirteen years to the great era of social resurrection, in 1788-89, from a sleep of ten centuries.

of Paradise; and in that vestibule of an earthly heaven
it was no more possible for me to see vividly or in any
lingering detail the thorny cares which might hereafter multiply around me than amongst the roses of
June, and on the loveliest of June mornings, I could
gather depression from the glooms of the last December.

To go was settled. But *when* and *whither? When*
could have but one answer; for on more reasons than
one I needed summer weather, and as much of it as
possible. Besides that, when August came, it would
bring along with it my own birth-day: now, one codi-
cil in my general vow of freedom had been that my
seventeenth birth-day should not find me at school.
Still I needed some trifle of preparation. Especially I
needed a little money. I wrote, therefore, to the only
confidential friend that I had—viz. Lady Carbery.
Originally, as early friends of my mother's, both she
and Lord Carbery had distinguished me at Bath and
elsewhere, for some years, by flattering attentions;
and, for the last three years in particular, Lady Carbery, a young woman some ten years older than myself, and who was as remarkable for her intellectual
pretensions as she was for her beauty and her benevolence, had maintained a correspondence with me upon
questions of literature. She thought too highly of my
powers and attainments, and everywhere spoke of me
with an enthusiasm that, if I had been five or six years
older, and had possessed any personal advantages,
might have raised smiles at her expense. To her I now
wrote, requesting the loan of five guineas. A whole
week passed without any answer. This perplexed and
made me uneasy: for her ladyship was rich by a vast
fortune removed entirely from her husband's control;
and, as I felt assured, would have cheerfully sent me
twenty times the sum asked, unless her sagacity had

suggested some suspicion (which seemed impossible) of the real purpose, which I contemplated in the employment of the five guineas. Could I incautiously have said anything in my own letter tending that way? Certainly not; then why—— But at that moment my speculations were cut short by a letter bearing a coroneted seal. It was from Lady Carbery, of course, and enclosed ten guineas instead of five. Slow in those days were the mails; besides which, Lady Carbery happened to be down at the seaside, whither my letter had been sent after her. Now, then, including my own pocket-money, I possessed a dozen guineas; which seemed sufficient for my immediate purpose; and all ulterior emergencies, as the reader understands, I trampled under foot. This sum, however, spent at inns on the most economic footing, could not have held out for much above a calendar month; and, as to the plan of selecting secondary inns, these are not always cheaper; but the main objection is that in the solitary stations amongst the mountains (Cambrian no less than Cumbrian) there is often no choice to be found: the high-priced inn is the only one. Even this dozen of guineas it became necessary to diminish by three. The age of "vails" and perquisites to three or four servants at any gentleman's house where you dined—this age, it is true, had passed away by thirty years perhaps. But that flagrant abuse had no connexion at all with the English custom of distributing money amongst that part of the domestics whose daily labours may have been increased by a visitor's residence in the family for some considerable space of time. This custom (almost peculiar, I believe, to the English gentry) is honourable and just. I personally had been trained by my mother, who detested sordid habits, to look upon it as ignominious in a gentleman to leave a household without acknowledging the obliging services of those

who cannot openly remind him of their claims. On
this occasion, mere necessity compelled me to overlook
the housekeeper: for to her I could not have offered
less than two or three guineas; and, as she was a fixture, I reflected that I might send it at some future
period. To three inferior servants I found that I ought
not to give less than one guinea each: so much, therefore, I left in the hands of G——, the most honourable and upright of boys; since to have given it myself
would have been prematurely to publish my purpose.
These three guineas deducted, I still had nine, or
thereabouts. And now all things were settled, except
one: the *when* was settled, and the *how;* but not the
whither. That was still *sub judice.*

My plan originally had been to travel northwards
—viz. to the region of the English Lakes. That little
mountainous district, lying stretched like a pavilion
between four well-known points—viz. the small towns
of Ulverstone and Penrith as its two poles, south and
north; between Kendal, again, on the east, and Egremont on the west—measuring on the one diameter
about forty miles, and on the other perhaps thirty-five
—had for me a secret fascination, subtle, sweet, fantastic, and even from my seventh or eighth year spir-
itually strong. The southern section of that district,
about eighteen or twenty miles long, which bears the
name of Furness, figures in the eccentric geography of
English law as a section of Lancashire, though separated from that county by the estuary of Morecambe
Bay: and therefore, as Lancashire happened to be my
own native county, I had from childhood, on the
strength of this mere legal fiction, cherished as a mystic privilege, slender as a filament of air, some fraction of denizenship in the fairy little domain of the
English Lakes. The major part of these lakes lies in
Westmorland and Cumberland: but the sweet repos-

ing little water of Esthwaite, with its few emerald
fields, and the grander one of Coniston, with the sublime cluster of mountain groups, and the little network of quiet dells lurking about its head [1] all the way
back to Grasmere, lie in or near the upper chamber of
Furness; and all these, together with the ruins of the
once glorious abbey, had been brought out not many
years before into sunny splendour by the great enchantress of that generation—Anne Radcliffe. But
more even than Anne Radcliffe had the landscape
painters, so many and so various, contributed to the
glorification of the English lake district; drawing out
and impressing upon the heart the sanctity of repose
in its shy recesses—its alpine grandeurs in such passes
as those of Wastdalehead, Langdalehead, Borrowdale, Kirkstone, Hawsdale, &c., together with the monastic peace which seems to brood over its peculiar

[1] "*Its head*": That end of a lake which receives the rivulets
and brooks feeding its waters is locally called its *head;* and, in
continuation of the same constructive image, the counter terminus, which discharges its surplus water, is called its *foot.*
By the way, as a suggestion from this obvious distinction, I
may remark that in all cases the very existence of a head and
a foot to any sheet of water defeats the malice of Lord Byron's
sneer against the lake poets, in calling them by the contemptuous designation of "*pond* poets"; a variation which some part
of the public readily caught up as a natural reverberation of
that spitefulness, so petty and apparently so groundless, which
notoriously Lord Byron cherished against Wordsworth steadily, and more fitfully against Southey. The effect of transforming a living image—an image of restless motion—into an
image of foul stagnation was tangibly apprehensible. But what
was it that contradistinguished the "*vivi lacus*" of Virgil from
rotting ponds mantled with verdant slime? To have, or *not* to
have, a head and a foot (*i.e.*, a principle of perpetual change)
is at the very heart of this distinction; and to substitute for
lake a term which ignores and negatives the very differential
principle that constitutes a lake—viz., its current and its
eternal mobility—is to offer an insult in which the insulted
party has no interest or concern.

form of pastoral life, so much nobler (as Wordsworth notices) in its stern simplicity and continual conflict with danger hidden in the vast draperies of mist overshadowing the hills, and amongst the armies of snow and hail arrayed by fierce northern winters, than the effeminate shepherd's life in the classical Arcadia, or in the flowery pastures of Sicily.

Amongst these attractions that drew me so strongly to the Lakes, there had also by that time arisen in this lovely region the deep deep magnet (as to me *only* in all this world it then was) of William Wordsworth. Inevitably this close connexion of the poetry which most of all had moved me with the particular region and scenery that most of all had fastened upon my affections, and led captive my imagination, was calculated, under ordinary circumstances, to impress upon my fluctuating deliberations a summary and decisive bias. But the very depth of the impressions which had been made upon me, either as regarded the poetry or the scenery, was too solemn and (unaffectedly I may say it) too spiritual, to clothe itself in any hasty or chance movement as at all adequately expressing its strength, or reflecting its hallowed character. If you, reader, were a devout Mahometan, throwing gazes of mystical awe daily towards Mecca, or were a Christian devotee looking with the same rapt adoration to St. Peter's at Rome, or to El Kodah, the Holy City of Jerusalem (so called even amongst the Arabs, who hate both Christian and Jew)—how painfully would it jar upon your sensibilities if some friend, sweeping past you upon a high road, with a train (according to the circumstances) of dromedaries or of wheel carriages, should suddenly pull up, and say, "Come, old fellow, jump up alongside of me; I'm off for the Red Sea, and here's a spare dromedary," or "Off for Rome, and here's a well-cushioned barouche." Seasonable

and convenient it might happen that the invitation
were; but still it would shock you that a journey
which, with or without your consent, could not *but* assume the character eventually of a saintly pilgrimage,
should arise and take its initial movement upon a casual summons, or upon a vulgar opening of momentary convenience. In the present case, under no circumstances should I have dreamed of presenting
myself to Wordsworth. The principle of "veneration"
(to speak phrenologically) was by many degrees too
strong in me for any such overture on my part. Hardly
could I have found the courage to meet and to answer
such an overture coming from *him*. I could not even
tolerate the prospect (as a bare possibility) of Wordsworth's hearing my name first of all associated with
some case of pecuniary embarrassment. And, apart
from all *that*, it vulgarized the whole "interest" (no
other term can I find to express the case collectively)
—the whole "interest" of poetry and the enchanted
land—equally it vulgarized person and thing, the
vineyard and the vintage, the gardens and the ladies,
of the Hesperides, together with all their golden fruit-
age, if I should rush upon them in a hurried and
thoughtless state of excitement. I remembered the
fine caution on this subject involved in a tradition preserved by Pausanias. Those (he tells us) who visited
by night the great field of Marathon (where at certain times phantom cavalry careered, flying and pursuing) in a temper of vulgar sight-seeking, and under
no higher impulse than the degrading one of curiosity, were met and punished severely in the dark, by
the same sort of people, I presume, as those who handled Falstaff so roughly in the venerable shades of
Windsor: whilst loyal visitors, who came bringing a
true and filial sympathy with the grand deeds of their
Athenian ancestors, who came as children of the same

hearth, met with the most gracious acceptance, and fulfilled all the purposes of a pilgrimage or sacred mission. Under my present circumstances, I saw that the very motives of love and honour, which would have inclined the scale so powerfully in favour of the northern lakes, were exactly those which drew most heavily in the other direction—the circumstances being what they were as to hurry and perplexity. And just at that moment suddenly unveiled itself another powerful motive against taking the northern direction—viz. consideration for my mother—which made my heart recoil from giving her too great a shock; and in what other way could it be mitigated than by my personal presence in a case of emergency? For such a purpose North Wales would be the best haven to make for, since the road thither from my present home lay through Chester—where at that time my mother had fixed her residence.

If I had hesitated (and hesitate I did very sincerely) about such a mode of expressing the consideration due to my mother, it was not from any want of decision in my feeling, but really because I feared to be taunted with this act of tenderness, as arguing an exaggerated estimate of my own importance in my mother's eyes. To be capable of causing any alarming shock, must I not suppose myself an object of special interest? No: I did not agree to that inference. But no matter. Better to stand ten thousand sneers than one abiding pang, such as time could not abolish, of bitter self-reproach. So I resolved to face this taunt without flinching, and to steer a course for St. John's Priory— my mother's residence near Chester. At the very instant of coming to this resolution, a singular accident occurred to confirm it. On the very day before my rash journey commenced, I received through the post-office a letter bearing this address in a foreign hand·

writing—*A Monsieur Monsieur de Quincy, Chester.*
This iteration of the *Monsieur*, as a courteous French
fashion for effecting something equivalent to our own
Esquire, was to me at that time an unintelligible novelty. The best way to explain it was to read the letter;
which, to the extent of *mon possible*, I did, but vainly
attempted to decipher. So much, however, I spelled
out as satisfied me that the letter could not have been
meant for myself. The post-mark was, I think, *Hamburg:* but the date within was from some place **in**
Normandy; and eventually it came out that the person addressed was a poor emigrant, some relative of
Quatremére de Quincy,[1] who had come to Chester,
probably as a teacher of French, and now in 1802
found his return to France made easy by the brief and
hollow peace of Amiens. Such an obscure person was
naturally unknown to any English post-office; and the
letter had been forwarded to myself, as the oldest male
member of a family at that time necessarily well
known in Chester.

I was astonished to find myself translated by a
touch of the pen not only into a *Monsieur*, but even
into a self-multiplied *Monsieur;* or, speaking alge-
braically, into the square of Monsieur; having a
chance at some future day of being perhaps cubed into
Monsieur. From the letter, as I had hastily torn it
open, out dropped a draft upon Smith, Payne, and
Smith for somewhere about forty guineas. At this

[1] "*De Quincy*": The family of De Quincey, or Quincy, or
Quincie (spelt of course, like all proper names, under the
anarchy prevailing as to orthography until the last one hundred and fifty years, in every possible form open to human
caprice), was originally Norwegian. Early in the eleventh century this family emigrated from Norway to the South; and
since then it has thrown off three separate swarms—French,
English, and Anglo-American—each of which writes the name
with its own slight variations.

stage of the revelations opening upon me, it might be
fancied that the interest of the case thickened: since
undoubtedly, if this windfall could be seriously meant
for myself, *and no mistake,* never descended upon the
head of man, in the outset of a perilous adventure, aid
more seasonable, nay, more melodramatically critical.
But alas! my eye is quick to value the logic of evil
chances. Prophet of evil I ever am to myself: forced
for ever into sorrowful auguries that I have no power
to hide from my own heart, no, not through one
night's solitary dreams. In a moment I saw too plainly
that I was not Monsieur. I might be *Monsieur,* but
not *Monsieur to the second power.* Who indeed could
be *my* debtor to the amount of forty guineas? If there
really *was* such a person, why had he been so many
years in liquidating his debt? How shameful to suffer
me to enter upon my seventeenth year before he made
known his debt, or even his amiable existence. Doubtless, in strict morals, this dreadful procrastination
could not be justified. Still, as the man was apparently
testifying his penitence, and in the most practical form
(viz. payment), I felt perfectly willing to grant him
absolution for past sins, and a general release from all
arrears, if any should remain, through all coming
generations. But alas! the mere seasonableness of the
remittance floored my hopes. A five-guinea debtor
might have been a conceivable being: such a debtor
might exist in the flesh: *him* I could believe in; but
further my faith would not go; and, if the money
were, after all, *bonâ fide* meant for myself, clearly it
must come from the Fiend: in which case it became
an open question whether I ought to take it. At this
stage the case had become a Sphinx's riddle; and the
solution, if any, must be sought in the letter. But, as to
the letter, O heaven and earth! if the Sphinx of old
conducted her intercourse with Oedipus by way of let-

ter, and propounded her wicked questions through the
post-office of Thebes, it strikes me that she needed
only to have used French penmanship in order to baffle that fatal decipherer of riddles for ever and ever.
At Bath, where the French emigrants mustered in
great strength (six thousand, I have heard) during
the three closing years of the last century, I, through
my mother's acquaintance with several leading families amongst them, had gained a large experience of
French calligraphy. From this experience I had learned
that the French aristocracy still persisted (*did* persist
at that period, 1797–1800) in a traditional contempt
for all accomplishments of that class as clerkly and
plebeian, fitted only (as Shakespeare says, when
recording similar prejudices amongst his own countrymen) to do "yeoman's service." One and all, they delegated the care of their spelling to *valets and femmes-
de-chambre;* sometimes even those persons who
scoured their blankets and counterpanes scoured their
spelling—that is to say, their week-day spelling; but,
as to their Sunday spelling, that superfine spelling
which they reserved for their efforts in literature, this
was consigned to the care of compositors. Letters written by the royal family of France in 1792–93 still survive, in the memoirs of Cléry and others amongst their
most faithful servants, which display the utmost excess of ignorance as to grammar and orthography.
Then, as to the penmanship, all seemed to write the
same hand, and with the same piece of most ancient
wood, or venerable skewer; all alike scratching out
stiff perpendicular letters, as if executed (I should
say) with a pair of snuffers. I do not speak thus in any
spirit of derision. Such accomplishments were *wilfully* neglected, and even ambitiously, as if in open
proclamation of scorn for the arts by which humbler
people oftentimes got their bread. And a man of rank

would no more conceive himself dishonoured by any deficiencies in the snobbish accomplishments of penmanship, grammar, or correct orthography, than a gentleman amongst ourselves by inexpertness in the mystery of cleaning shoes, or of polishing furniture. The result, however, from this systematic and ostentatious neglect of calligraphy is oftentimes most perplexing to all who are called upon to decipher their MSS. It happens, indeed, that the product of this carelessness thus far differs: always it is coarse and inelegant, but sometimes (say in 1-20th of the cases) it becomes specially legible. Far otherwise was the case before me. Being greatly hurried on this my farewell day, I could not make out two consecutive sentences. Unfortunately, one-half of a sentence sufficed to show that the enclosure belonged to some needy Frenchman living in a country not his own, and struggling probably with the ordinary evils of such a condition— friendlessness and exile. Before the letter came into my hands, it had already suffered some days' delay. When I noticed this, I found my sympathy with the poor stranger naturally quickened. Already, and unavoidably, he had been suffering from the vexation of a letter delayed; but henceforth, and continually more so, he must be suffering from the anxieties of a letter gone astray. Throughout this farewell day I was unable to carve out any opportunity for going up to the Manchester post-office; and, without a distinct explanation in my own person, exonerating myself, on the written acknowledgement of the post-office, from all farther responsibility, I was most reluctant to give up the letter. It is true that the necessity of committing a forgery (which crime in those days was punished inexorably with death) before the money could have been fraudulently appropriated would, *if made known to the public*, have acquitted any casual

holder of the letter from all suspicion of dishonest intentions. But the danger was that, during the suspense
and progress of the case whilst awaiting its final settlement, ugly rumours should arise and cling to one's
name amongst the many that would hear only a fragmentary version of the whole affair.

At length all was ready. Midsummer, like an army
with banners, was moving through the heavens; already the longest day had passed; those arrangements,
few and imperfect, through which I attempted some
partial evasion of disagreeable contingencies likely to
arise, had been finished: what more remained for me
to do of things that I was able to do? None; and yet,
though now at last free to move off, I lingered; lingered as under some sense of dim perplexity, or even
of even of relenting love for the very captivity itself
which I was making so violent an effort to abjure, but
more intelligibly for all the external objects, living or
inanimate, by which that captivity had been surrounded and gladdened. What I was hastening to desert, nevertheless I grieved to desert; and, but for the
foreign letter, I might have long continued to loiter
and procrastinate. That, however, through various
and urgent motives which it suggested, quickened my
movements; and the same hour which brought this
letter into my hands witnessed my resolution (uttered
audibly to myself in my study) that early on the next
day I would take my departure. A day, therefore, had
at length arrived, had somewhat suddenly arrived,
which would be the last, the very last, on which I
should make my appearance in the school.

It is a just and a feeling remark of Dr. Johnson's
that we never do anything consciously for the last
time (of things, that is to say, which we have been
long in the habit of doing) without sadness of heart.
The secret sense of a farewell or testamentary act I

carried along with me into every word or deed of this
memorable day. Agent or patient, singly or one of a
crowd, I heard for ever some sullen echo of valediction in every change, casual or periodic, that varied
the revolving hours from morning to night. Most of
all I felt this valedictory sound as a pathetic appeal
when the closing hour of five P.M. brought with it the
solemn evening service of the English Church—read
by Mr. Lawson; read now, as always, under a reverential stillness of the entire school. Already in itself,
without the solemnity of prayers, the decaying light
of the dying day suggests a mood of pensive and sympathetic sadness. And, if the changes in the light are
less impressively made known so early as five o'clock
in the depth of summer-tide, not the less we are sensible of being as near to the hours of repose, and to the
secret dangers of the night, as if the season were mid-
winter. Even thus far there was something that oftentimes had profoundly impressed me in this evening
liturgy, and its special prayer against the perils of
darkness. But greatly was that effect deepened by the
symbolic treatment which this liturgy gives to this
darkness and to these perils.

Prayers had finished. The school had dissolved itself. Six o'clock came, seven, eight. By three hours
nearer stood the dying day to its departure. By three
hours nearer, therefore, stood we to that darkness
which our English liturgy calls into such symbolic
grandeur, as hiding beneath its shadowy mantle all
perils that besiege our human infirmity. But in summer, in the immediate suburbs of midsummer, the
vast scale of the heavenly movements is read in their
slowness. Time becomes the expounder of Space. And
now, though eight o'clock had struck, the sun was still
lingering above the horizon: the light, broad and

gaudy, having still two hours of travel to face before it would assume that tender fading hue prelusive to the twilight. Now came the last official ceremony of the day: the students were all mustered; and the names of all were challenged according to the order of precedency. My name, as usual, came first.[1] Stepping forward, I passed Mr. Lawson, and bowed to him, looking earnestly in his face, and saying to myself, "He is old and infirm, and in this world I shall not see him again." I was right; I never *did* see him again, nor ever shall. He looked at me complacently; smiled placidly; returned my salutation (not knowing it to be my valediction) ; and we parted for ever. Intellectually, I might not have seen cause to reverence him in any emphatic sense. But very sincerely I respected him as a conscientious man, faithful to his duties, and as, even in his latter ineffectual struggle with these duties, inflicting more suffering upon himself than upon others; finally, I respected him as a sound and accu-

---

[1] *"First"*: Within the school I should *not* have been first: for in the trinity which composed the head class there was no absolute or meritorious precedency, but simply a precedency of chance. Our dignity, as leaders of the school, raised us above all petty competitions; yet, as it was unavoidable to stand in some order, this was regulated by seniority. I, therefore, as junior amongst the three, was *tertius inter pares*. But my two seniors happened to be day-scholars: so that, in Mr. Lawson's house, I rose into the supreme place. *There*, I was *princeps senatûs*. Such trivial circumstantialities I notice, as checks upon all openings to inaccuracy, great or small. It would vitiate the interest which any reader might otherwise take in this narrative, if for one moment it were supposed that any feature of the case were varnished or distorted. From the very first, I had been faithful to the most rigorous law of accuracy—even in absolute trifles. But I became even more jealous over myself, after an Irish critic, specially brilliant as a wit and as a scholar, but also specially malicious, had attempted to impeach the accuracy of my narrative, in its London section, upon alleged internal grounds.

rate (though not brilliant) scholar. Personally I owed
him much gratitude; for he had been uniformly kind
to me, and had allowed me such indulgences as lay in
his power; and I grieved at the thought of the mortification I should inflict upon him.

The morning came which was to launch me into
the world; that morning from which, and from its
consequences, my whole succeeding life has, in many
important points, taken its colouring. At half after
three I rose, and gazed with deep emotion at the ancient collegiate church, "dressed in earliest light,"
and beginning to crimson with the deep lustre of a
cloudless July morning. I was firm and immovable
in my purpose, but yet agitated by anticipation of uncertain danger and troubles. To this agitation the deep
peace of the morning presented an affecting contrast,
and in some degree a medicine. The silence was more
profound than that of midnight: and to me the silence
of a summer morning is more touching than all other
silence, because, the light being broad and strong as
that of noonday at other seasons of the year, it seems
to differ from perfect day chiefly because man is not
yet abroad, and thus the peace of nature, and of the
innocent creatures of God, seems to be secure and deep
only so long as the presence of man, and his unquiet
spirit, are not there to trouble its sanctity. I dressed
myself, took my hat and gloves, and lingered a little
in the room. For nearly a year and a-half this room
had been my "pensive citadel": here I had read and
studied through all the hours of night; and, though
true it was that, for the latter part of this time, I had
lost my gaiety and peace of mind during the strife
and fever of contention with my guardian, yet, on the
other hand, as a boy passionately fond of books, and
dedicated to intellectual pursuits, I could not fail to

have enjoyed many happy hours in the midst of general dejection.

Happy hours? Yes; and was it certain that ever again I should enjoy hours *as* happy? At this point it is not impossible that, left to my own final impressions, I might have receded from my plan. But it seemed to me, as too often happens in such cases, that no retreat was now open. The confidence which unavoidably I had reposed in a groom of Mr. Lawson's made it dangerous. The effect of this distracted view was, not to alter my plan, but to throw despondency for one sad half-hour over the whole prospect before me. In that condition, with my eyes open, I dreamed. Suddenly a sort of trance, a frost as of some death-like revelation, wrapped round me; and I found renewed within me a hateful remembrance derived from a moment that I had long left behind. Two years before, when I wanted about as much of my fifteenth birth-day as now of my seventeenth, I happened to be in London for part of a single day, with a friend of my own age. Naturally, amongst some eight or ten great spectacles which challenged our earnest attention, St. Paul's Cathedral had been one. This we had visited, and consequently the Whispering Gallery.[1] More than by all beside I had been impressed by this: and some half-hour later, as we were standing beneath the dome, and I should imagine pretty nearly on the very spot where rather more than five years subsequently Lord Nelson was buried—a spot from which we saw, pompously floating to and fro in the upper spaces of a great aisle run-

[1] To those who have never visited the Whispering Gallery, nor have read any account of it amongst other acoustic phenomena described in scientific treatises, it may be proper to mention, as the distinguishing feature of the case, that a word or a question, uttered at one end of the gallery in the gentlest of whispers, is reverberated at the other end in peals of thunder.

ning westwards from ourselves, many flags captured
from France, Spain, and Holland—I, having my previous impressions of awe deepened by these solemn
trophies of chance and change amongst mighty nations, had suddenly been surprised by a dream as profound as at present, in which a thought that often had
persecuted me figured triumphantly. This thought
turned upon the fatality that must often attend an evil
choice. As an oracle of fear I remembered that great
Roman warning, *Nescit vox missa reverti* (that a word
once uttered is irrevocable), a freezing arrest upon the
motions of hope too sanguine that haunted me in many
shapes. Long before that fifteenth year of mine, I had
noticed, as a worm lying at the heart of life and fretting its security, the fact that innumerable acts of
choice change countenance and are variously ap-
praised at varying stages of life—shift with the shifting hours. Already, at fifteen, I had become deeply
ashamed of judgements which I had once pronounced,
of idle hopes that I had once encouraged, false admirations or contempts with which once I had sympathized. And, as to acts which I surveyed with any
doubts at all, I never felt sure that after some succession of years I might not feel withering doubts about
them, both as to principle and as to inevitable results.

This sentiment of nervous recoil from any word or
deed that could not be recalled had been suddenly re-
awakened on that London morning by the impressive
experience of the Whispering Gallery. At the earlier
end of the gallery had stood my friend, breathing in
the softest of whispers a solemn but not acceptable
truth. At the further end, after running along the
walls of the gallery, that solemn truth reached me as
a deafening menace in tempestuous uproars. And
now, in these last lingering moments, when I dreamed
ominously with open eyes in my Manchester study,

once again that London menace broke angrily upon me as out of a thick cloud with redoubled strength; a voice, too late for warning, seemed audibly to say, "Once leave this house, and a Rubicon is placed between thee and all possibility of return. Thou wilt not say that what thou doest is altogether approved in thy secret heart. Even now thy conscience speaks against it in sullen whispers; but at the other end of thy long life-gallery that same conscience will speak to thee in volleying thunders."

A sudden step upon the stairs broke up my dream, and recalled me to myself. Dangerous hours were now drawing near, and I prepared for a hasty farewell.

I shed tears as I looked round on the chair, hearth, writing-table, and other familiar objects, knowing too certainly that I looked upon them for the last time. Whilst I write this, it is nineteen [1] years ago; and yet, at this moment, I see, as if it were but yesterday, the lineaments and expressions of the object on which I fixed my parting gaze. It was the picture of a lovely lady, which hung over the mantelpiece; the eyes and mouth of which were so beautiful, and the whole countenance so radiant with divine tranquillity, that I had a thousand times laid down my pen, or my book, to gather consolation from it, as a devotee from his patron saint.[2] Whilst I was yet gazing upon it, the

[1] Written in August, 1821.

[2] The housekeeper was in the habit of telling me that the lady had *lived* (meaning, perhaps, had been *born*) two centuries ago; that date would better agree with the tradition that the portrait was a copy from Vandyke. All that she knew further about the lady was that either to the grammar school, or to that particular college at Oxford with which the school was connected, or else to that particular college at Oxford with which Mr. Lawson personally was connected, or else, fourthly, to Mr. Lawson himself as a private individual, the unknown lady had been a special benefactress. She was also a special benefactress to me, through eighteen months, by means of her

deep tones of the old church clock proclaimed that it was six o'clock. I went up to the picture, kissed it, then gently walked out, and closed the door for ever.

So blended and intertwisted in this life are occasions of laughter and of tears that I cannot yet recall without smiling an incident which occurred at that time, and which had nearly put a stop to the immediate execution of my plan. I had a trunk of immense weight; for, besides my clothes, it contained nearly all my library. The difficulty was to get this removed to a carrier's, my room being at an aerial elevation in the house; and (what was worse) the staircase which communicated with this angle of the building was accessible only by a gallery, which passed the head-master's chamber-door. I was a favourite with all the servants; and, knowing that any of them would screen me, and act confidentially, I communicated my embarrassment to a groom of the head-master's. The groom declared his readiness to do anything I wished; and, when the time arrived, went up-stairs to bring the trunk down. This I feared was beyond the strength of any one man: however, the groom was a man "of Atlantean shoulders," and had a back as spacious as Salisbury Plain. Accordingly he persisted in bringing down the trunk alone, whilst I stood waiting at the foot of the last flight, in great anxiety for the event. For some time I heard him descending with steps slow and steady; but, unfortunately, from his trepidation, as he drew near the dangerous quarter, within a few

sweet Madonna countenance. And in some degree it serves to spiritualize and to hallow this service that of her who unconsciously rendered it I know neither the name, nor the exact rank or age, nor the place where she lived and died. She was parted from me by perhaps two centuries; I from her by the gulf of eternity.

steps of the gallery, his foot slipped; and the mighty
burden, falling from his shoulders, gained such increase of impetus at each step of the descent, that, on
reaching the bottom, it trundled, or rather leaped,
right across, with the noise of twenty devils, against
the very bedroom-door of the Archididascalus. My
first thought suggested that all was lost, and that my
sole chance for effecting a retreat was to sacrifice my
baggage. However, on reflection, I determined to
abide the issue. The groom, meantime, was in the utmost alarm, both on his own account and mine: but,
in spite of this, so irresistibly had the sense of the ludicrous, in this unhappy *contretemps*, taken possession
of his fancy that he sang out a long, loud, and canorous
peal of laughter, that might have wakened the Seven
Sleepers. At the sound of this resonant merriment,
within the very ears of insulted authority, I could not
forbear joining in it; subdued to this, not so much by
the comic wilfulness of the trunk, trundling down
from step to step with accelerated pace and multiplying uproar, like the λαᾶς ἀναιδής [1] (the contumacious
stone) of Sisyphus, as by the effect it had upon the
groom. We both expected, as a matter of course, that
Mr. Lawson would sally out of his room; for, in general, if but a mouse stirred, he sprang out like a mastiff from his kennel. Strange to say, however, on this
occasion, when the noise of laughter had subsided, no
sound, or rustling even, was to be heard in the bedroom. Mr. Lawson had a painful complaint, which,
oftentimes keeping him awake, made his sleep, when
it *did* come, peculiarly deep. Gathering courage from
the silence, the groom hoisted his burden again, and
accomplished the remainder of his descent without accident. I waited until I saw the trunk placed on a

[1] "Αὖτις ἔπειτα πεδόνδε κυλίνδετο λαᾶς ἀναιδής."—*Hom. Odyss.*

wheel-barrow, and on its road to the carrier's: then, "with Providence my guide," or, more truly it might be said, with my own headstrong folly for law and impulse, I set off on foot; carrying a small parcel with some articles of dress under my arm, a favourite English poet in one pocket, and an odd volume, containing about one-half of Canter's *Euripides*, in the other.

On leaving Manchester, by a south-western route, towards Chester and Wales, the first town that I reached (to the best of my remembrance) was Altrincham—colloquially called *Awtrigem*. When a child of three years old, and suffering from the whooping-cough, I had been carried for change of air to different places on the Lancashire coast; and, in order to benefit by as large a compass as possible of varying atmospheres, I and my nurse had been made to rest for the first night of our tour at this cheerful little town of Altrincham. On the next morning, which ushered in a most dazzling day of July, I rose earlier than my nurse fully approved: but in no long time she found it advisable to follow my example; and, after putting me through my morning's drill of ablutions and the Lord's-prayer, no sooner had she fully arranged my petticoats than she lifted me up in her arms, threw open the window, and let me suddenly look down upon the gayest scene I had ever beheld—viz. the little market-place of Altrincham at eight o'clock in the morning. It happened to be the market-day; and I, who till then had never consciously been in any town whatever, was equally astonished and delighted with the novel gaiety of the scene. Fruits, such as can be had in July, and flowers were scattered about in profusion: even the stalls of the butchers, from their brilliant cleanliness, appeared attractive: and the bonny young women of Altrincham were all tripping about in caps and aprons coquettishly dis-

posed. The general hilarity of the scene at this early
hour, with the low murmurings of pleasurable conversation and laughter, that rose up like a fountain to the
open window, left so profound an impression upon me
that I never lost it. All this occurred, as I have said,
about eight o'clock on a superb July morning. Exactly
at that time of the morning, on exactly such another
heavenly day of July, did I, leaving Manchester at six
A.M., naturally enough find myself in the centre of the
Altrincham market-place. Nothing had altered. There
were the very same fruits and flowers; the same bonny
young women tripping up and down in the same (no,
not the same) coquettish bonnets; everything was apparently the same: perhaps the window of my bedroom
was still open, only my nurse and I were not looking
out; for alas! on recollection, fourteen years precisely
had passed since then. Breakfast time, however, is always a cheerful stage of the day; if a man can forget
his cares at any season, it is then; and after a walk of
seven miles it is doubly so. I felt it at the time, and
have stopped, therefore, to notice it, as a singular coincidence, that twice, and by the merest accident, I should
find myself, precisely as the clocks on a July morning
were all striking eight, drawing inspiration of pleasurable feelings from the genial sights and sounds in the
little market-place of Altrincham. There I breakfasted; and already by the two hours' exercise I felt
myself half restored to health. After an hour's rest, I
started again upon my journey: all my gloom and
despondency were already retiring to the rear; and, as
I left Altrincham, I said to myself, "All places, it
seems, are not Whispering Galleries."

The distance between Manchester and Chester *was*
about forty miles. What it *is* under railway changes I
know not. This I planned to walk in two days: for,
though the whole might have been performed in one, I

saw no use in exhausting myself; and my walking powers were rusty from long disuse. I wished to bisect the journey; and, as nearly as I could expect—*i.e.* within two or three miles—such a bisection was attained in a clean roadside inn, of the class so commonly found in England. A kind, motherly landlady, easy in her circumstances, having no motive for rapacity, and looking for her livelihood much less to her inn than to her farm, guaranteed to me a safe and profound night's rest. On the following morning there remained not quite eighteen miles between myself and venerable Chester. Before I reached it, so mighty now (as ever before and since) had become the benefit from the air and the exercise that oftentimes I felt inebriated and crazy with ebullient spirits. But for the accursed letter, which sometimes

> *Came over me,*
> *As doth the raven o'er the infected house,*

I should have too much forgot my gravity under this newborn health. For two hours before reaching Chester, from the accident of the south-west course which the road itself pursued, I saw held up aloft before my eyes that matchless spectacle,

> *New, and yet as old*
> *As the foundations of the heavens and earth,*

an elaborate and pompous sunset hanging over the mountains of North Wales. The clouds passed slowly through several arrangements, and in the last of these I read the very scene which six months before I had read in a most exquisite poem of Wordsworth's, extracted entire into a London newspaper (I think the *St. James's Chronicle*). It was a Canadian lake,

With all its fairy crowds
Of islands that together lie
As quietly as spots of sky
Amongst the evening clouds.

The scene in the poem ("Ruth"), that had been originally mimicked by the poet from the sky, was here
re-mimicked and rehearsed to the life, as it seemed, by
the sky from the poet. Was I then, in July, 1802, really
quoting from Wordsworth? Yes, reader; and I only in
all Europe. In 1799 I had become acquainted with
"We are Seven" at Bath. In the winter of 1801–2 I
had read the whole of "Ruth"; early in 1803 I had
written to Wordsworth. In May of 1803 I had received
a very long answer from Wordsworth.

The next morning after reaching Chester, my first
thought on rising was directed to the vexatious letter
in my custody. The odious responsibility, thrust upon
me in connexion with this letter, was now becoming
every hour more irritating, because every hour more
embarrassing to the freedom of my own movements,
since it must by this time have drawn the post-office
into the ranks of my pursuers. Indignant I was that
this letter should have the power of making myself an
accomplice in causing anxiety, perhaps even calamity,
to the poor emigrant—a man doubly liable to unjust
suspicion; first, as by his profession presumably poor,
and, secondly, as an alien. Indignant I was that this
most filthy of letters should also have the power of
forcing me into all sorts of indirect and cowardly
movements at inns; for beyond all things it seemed to
me important that I should not be arrested, or even for
a moment challenged, as the wrongful holder of an
important letter, before I had testified, by my own
spontaneous transfer of it, that I had not dallied with

any idea of converting it to my own benefit. In some way I must contrive to restore the letter. But was it not then the simplest of all courses to take my hat before sitting down to breakfast, present myself at the post-office, tender my explanation, and then (like Christian in Bunyan's allegory) to lay down my soul-wearying burden at the feet of those who could sign my certificate of absolution? Was not *that* simple? Was not *that* easy? Oh yes, beyond a doubt. And, if a favourite fawn should be carried off by a lion, would it not be a very simple and easy course to walk after the robber, follow him into his den, and reason with the wretch on the indelicacy of his conduct? In my particular circumstances, the post-office was in relation to myself simply a lion's den. Two separate parties, I felt satisfied, must by this time be in chase of me; and the two chasers would be confluent at the post-office. Beyond all other objects which I had to keep in view, paramount was that of fencing against my own re-capture. Anxious I was on behalf of the poor foreigner; but it did not strike me that to this anxiety I was bound to sacrifice myself. Now, if I went to the post-office, I felt sure that nothing else would be the result; and afterwards it turned out that in this anticipation I had been right. For it struck me that the nature of the enclosure in the French letter—viz. the fact that without a forgery it was not negotiable—could not be known certainly to anybody but myself. Doubts upon that point must have quickened the anxieties of all connected with myself, or connected with the case. More urgent consequently would have been the applications of "Monsieur Monsieur" to the post-office; and consequently of the post-office to the Priory; and consequently more easily suggested and concerted between the post-office and the Priory would be all the arrangements for stopping me, in the

event of my taking the route of Chester—in which
case it was natural to suppose that I might *personally*
return the letter to the official authorities. Of course,
none of these measures was certainly known to myself;
but I guessed at them as reasonable probabilities; and
it was evident that the fifty and odd hours since my
elopement from Manchester had allowed ample time
for concerting all the requisite preparations. As a last
resource, in default of any better occurring, it is likely
enough that my anxiety would have tempted me into
this mode of surrendering my abominable trust, which
by this time I regarded with such eyes of burning malice as Sindbad must have directed at intervals towards
the venerable ruffian that sat astride upon his shoulders. But things had not yet come to Sindbad's state of
desperation; so, immediately after breakfast, I took my
hat, determining to review the case and adopt some final decision in the open air. For I have always found it
easier to think over a matter of perplexity whilst walking in wide open spaces, under the broad eye of the natural heavens, than whilst shut up in a room. But at the
very door of the inn I was suddenly brought to a pause
by the recollection that some of the servants from the
Priory were sure on every forenoon to be at times in the
streets. The streets, however, could be evaded by shaping a course along the city walls; which I did, and descended into some obscure lane that brought me gradually to the banks of the river Dee. In the infancy of its
course amongst the Denbighshire mountains, this river
(famous in our pre-Norman history for the earliest parade of English monarchy) is wild and picturesque;
and even below my mother's Priory it wears a character of interest. But, a mile or so nearer to its mouth,
when leaving Chester for Parkgate, it becomes miserably tame; and the several reaches of the river take the

appearance of formal canals. On the right bank [1] of the river runs an artificial mound, called the Cop. It was, I believe, originally a Danish work; and certainly its name is Danish (*i.e.* Icelandic, or old Danish), and the same from which is derived our architectural word *coping*.

Upon this bank I was walking, and throwing my gaze along the formal vista presented by the river. Some trifle of anxiety might mingle with this gaze at the first, lest perhaps Philistines might be abroad; for it was just possible that I had been watched. But I have generally found that, if you are in quest of some certain escape from Philistines of whatsoever class—sheriff-officers, bores, no matter what—the surest refuge is to be found amongst hedgerows and fields, amongst cows and sheep: in fact, cows are amongst the gentlest of breathing creatures; none show more passionate tenderness to their young when deprived of them; and, in short, I am not ashamed to profess a deep love for these quiet creatures. On the present occasion there were many cows grazing in the fields below the Cop: but all along the Cop itself I could descry no person whatever answering to the idea of a Philistine: in fact, there was

[1] "*Right bank*": But which bank *is* right, and which left, under circumstances of position varying by possibility without end? This is a reasonable demur; but yet it argues an inexperienced reader. For always the position of the spectator is conventionally fixed. In military tactics, in philosophic geography, in history, &c., the uniform assumption is that you are standing with your back to the source of the river, and your eyes travelling along with its current. That bank of the river which under these circumstances lies upon your right is the right bank *absolutely*, and not *relatively* only (as would be the case if a room, and not a river, were concerned). Hence it follows that the Middlesex side of the Thames is always the left bank, and the Surrey side always the right bank, no matter whether you are moving from London to Oxford, or reversely from Oxford to London.

nobody at all, except one woman, apparently middle-aged (meaning by *that* from thirty-five to forty-five), neatly dressed, though perhaps in rustic fashion, and by no possibility belonging to any class of my enemies; for already I was near enough to see so much. This woman might be a quarter-of-a-mile distant, and was steadily advancing towards me—face to face. Soon, therefore, I was beginning to read the character of her features pretty distinctly; and her countenance naturally served as a mirror to echo and reverberate my own feelings, consequently my own horror (horror without exaggeration it was), at a sudden uproar of tumultuous sounds rising clamorously ahead. *Ahead* I mean in relation to myself, but to *her* the sound was from the rear.

Our situation was briefly this. Nearly half-a-mile behind the station of the woman, that reach of the river along which we two were moving came to an abrupt close; so that the next reach, making nearly a right-angled turn, lay entirely out of view. From this unseen reach it was that the angry clamour, so passionate and so mysterious, arose: and I, for *my* part, having never heard such a fierce battling outcry, nor even heard *of* such a cry, either in books or on the stage, in prose or verse, could not so much as whisper a guess to myself upon its probable cause. Only this I felt, that blind, unorganized nature it must be—and nothing in human or in brutal wrath—that could utter itself by such an anarchy of sea-like uproars. What was it? Where was it? Whence was it? Earthquake was it? convulsion of the steadfast earth? or was it the breaking loose from ancient chains of some deep morass like that of Solway? More probable it seemed that the ἄνω ποτάμων of Euripides (the flowing backwards of rivers to their fountains) now, at last, after ages of expectation, had been suddenly realized. Not long I needed to speculate;

for within half-a-minute, perhaps, from the first arrest of our attention, the proximate cause of this mystery declared itself to our eyes, although the remote cause (the hidden cause of that visible cause) was still as dark as before. Round that right-angled turn which I have mentioned as wheeling into the next succeeding reach of the river, suddenly as with the trampling of cavalry—but all dressing accurately—and the water at the outer angle sweeping so much faster than that at the inner angle as to keep the front of advance rigorously in line, violently careered round into our own placid watery vista a huge charging block of waters, filling the whole channel of the river, and coming down upon us at the rate of forty miles an hour. Well was it for us, myself and that respectable rustic woman, us the Deucalion and Pyrrha of this perilous moment, sole survivors apparently of the deluge (since by accident there was at that particular moment on that particular Cop nothing else to survive) , that by means of this Cop, and of ancient Danish hands (possibly not yet paid for their work) , we *could* survive. In fact, this watery breastwork, a perpendicular wall of water carrying itself as true as if controlled by a mason's plumb-line, rode forward at such a pace that obviously the fleetest horse or dromedary would have had no chance of escape. Many a decent railway even, among railways since born its rivals, would not have had above the third of a chance. Naturally, I had too short a time for observing much or accurately; and universally I am a poor hand at observing; else I should say that this riding block of crystal waters did not gallop, but went at a long trot; yes, long trot—that most frightful of paces in a tiger, in a buffalo, or in a rebellion of waters. Even a ghost, I feel convinced, would appal me more if coming up at a long diabolical trot than at a canter or gallop.

The first impulse to both of us was derived from cowardice; cowardice the most abject and selfish. Such is man, though a Deucalion elect; such is woman, though a decent Pyrrha. Both of us ran like hares; neither did I, Deucalion, think of poor Pyrrha at all for the first sixty seconds. Yet, on the other hand, why *should* I? It struck me seriously that St. George's Channel (and, if so, beyond a doubt, the Atlantic Ocean) had broke loose, and was, doubtless, playing the same insufferable gambols upon all rivers along a seaboard of six to seven thousand miles; in which case, as all the race of woman must be doomed, how romantic a speculation it was for me, sole relic of literature, to think specially of one poor Pyrrha, probably very illiterate, whom I had never yet spoken to! That idea pulled me up. *Not spoken to her?* Then I *would* speak to her; and the more so because the sound of the pursuing river told me that flight was useless. And, besides, if any reporter or subeditor of some Chester chronicle should, at this moment, with his glass be sweeping the Cop, and discover me flying under these unchivalrous circumstances, he might gibbet me to all eternity. Halting, therefore (and really I had not run above eighty or a hundred steps), I waited for my solitary co-tenant of the Cop. She was a little blown by running, and could not easily speak; besides which, at the very moment of her coming up, the preternatural column of waters, running in the very opposite direction to the natural current of the river, came up with us, ran by with the ferocious uproar of a hurricane, sent up the sides of the Cop a salute of waters, as if hypocritically pretending to kiss our feet, but secretly understood by all parties as a vain treachery for pulling us down into the flying deluge; whilst all along both banks the mighty refluent wash was heard as it rode along, leaving memorials, by sight and by sound, of its victorious power. But my female associate in this terrific drama, what said she, on coming up with me? Or what said I? For, by accident, I it was that spoke first; notwithstanding the fact, notorious and undeniable, that *I had never been introduced to her*. Here, however, be it understood, as a case now solemnly adjudicated and set at rest, that, in the midst of any great natural convulsion—earthquake, suppose, waterspout, tornado, or eruption of Vesuvius—it shall and may be lawful in all time coming (any usage or tradition to the contrary notwithstanding) for two English people to communicate with each other, although, by affidavit made before two justices of the peace, it shall have been proved that no previous introduction had been possible: in all other cases the old statute of non-intercourse holds good. Meantime, the present case, in default of more circumstantial evidence, might be regarded, if not as an earthquake, yet as ranking amongst the first-fruits or blossoms of an earthquake. So I spoke without scruple. All my freezing English reserve gave way under this boiling sense of having been so recently running for life: and then, again, suppose the water column should come back—riding *along with* the current, and no longer riding *against* it—in that case, we and all the County Palatine might soon have to run for our lives. Under such threatenings of common peril, surely the παρρησία, or unlimited licence of speech, ought spontaneously to proclaim itself without waiting for sanction.

So I asked her the meaning of this horrible tumult in the waters: how did she read the mystery? Her answer was, that, though she had never before seen such a thing, yet from her grandmother she had often heard of it; and, if she had run before it, *that* was because *I* ran; and a little, perhaps, because the noise frightened her. What was it, then? I asked. "It was," she said, "*The Bore;* and it was an affection to which only some few rivers here and there were liable; and the Dee was one of these." So ignorant was I that, until that moment, I had never heard of such a nervous affection in rivers. Subsequently I found that, amongst English rivers, the neighbouring river Severn, a far more important stream, suffered at spring-tides the same kind of hysterics, and perhaps some few other rivers in this British Island; but amongst Indian rivers only the Ganges.

At last, when *The Bore* had been discussed to the full extent of our united ignorance, I went off to the subject of that other curse, far more afflicting than any conceivable bore—viz. the foreign letter in my pocket. *The Bore* had certainly alarmed us for ninety or a hundred seconds, but the letter would poison my very existence, like the bottle-imp, until I could transfer it to some person truly qualified to receive it. Might not my fair friend on the Cop be marked out by Fate as "the coming woman" born to deliver me from this pocket curse? It is true that she displayed a rustic simplicity somewhat resembling that of Audrey in *As You Like It. Her*, in fact, not at all more than Audrey had the gods been pleased to make "poetical." But, for my particular mission, *that* might be amongst her best qualifications. At any rate, I was wearied in spirit under my load of responsibility: personally to liberate myself by visiting the post-office too surely I felt as the ruin of my enterprise in its very outset. Some agent *must* be employed; and where could one be found promising by looks, words, manners, more trustworthiness than this agent, sent by accident? The case almost explained itself. She readily understood how the resemblance of a name had thrown the letter into my possession; and that the simple remedy was to restore it to the right owner through the right channel, which channel was the never-enough-to-be-esteemed General post-office at that time pitching its tents and bivouacking nightly

in Lombard Street, but for this special case legally represented by the Chester head-office: a service of no risk
to *her*, for which, on the contrary, all parties would
thank her. I, to begin, begged to put *my* thanks into
the shape of half-a-crown: but, as some natural doubts
arose with respect to her precise station in life (for she
might be a farmer's wife, and not a servant), I thought
it advisable to postulate the existence of some youthful
daughter: to which mythological person I begged to
address my offering, when incarnated in the shape of a
doll.

I therefore, Deucalion that was or had been provi-
sionally through a brief interval of panic, took leave of
my Pyrrha, sole partner in the perils and anxieties
of that astounding Bore, dismissing her—Thessalian
Pyrrha—not to any Thessalian vales of Tempe, but—
O ye powers of moral anachronism!—to the Chester
post-office; and warning her on no account to be prematurely wheedled out of her secret. Her position,
diplomatically speaking, was better (as I made her understand) than that of the post-office: she having something in her gift—viz. an appointment to forty guineas; whereas in the counter-gift of the proud post-office
was nothing; neither for instant fruition nor in far-off
reversion. Her, in fact, one might regard as a Pandora,
carrying a box with something better than hope at the
bottom; for hope too often betrays; but a draft upon
Smith, Payne, and Smith, which never betrays, and for
a sum which, on the authority of Goldsmith, makes an
English clergyman "passing rich" through a whole
twelvemonth, entitled her to look scornfully upon
every second person that she met.

In about two hours the partner of my solitary kingdom upon the Cop re-appeared, with the welcome assurance that Chester had survived the Bore, that all was
right, and that anything which ever *had* been looking

crooked was now made straight as the path of an arrow. She had given "my love" (so she said) to the post-office; had been thanked by more than either one or two amongst the men of letters who figured in the equipage of that establishment; and had been assured that, long before daylight departed, one large cornucopia of justice and felicity would be emptied out upon the heads of all parties in the drama. I myself, not the least afflicted person on the roll, was already released—suddenly released, and fully—from the iniquitous load of responsibility thrust upon me; the poor emigrant was released from his conflict with fears that were uncertain, and creditors too certain; the post-office was released from the scandal and embarrassment of a gross irregularity, that might eventually have brought the postmaster-general down upon their haunches; and the household at the Priory were released from all anxieties, great and small, sound and visionary, on the question of my fancied felony.

In those anxieties one person there was that never had condescended to participate. This was my eldest sister Mary—just eleven months senior to myself. She was among the gentlest of girls, and yet from the very first she had testified the most incredulous disdain of all who fancied *her* brother capable of any thought so base as that of meditating a wrong to a needy exile. At present, after exchanging a few parting words, and a few final or farewell farewells with my faithful female [1] agent, further business I had none to detain me in Chester, except what concerned this particular sister.

[1] Some people are irritated, or even fancy themselves insulted, by overt acts of alliteration, as many people are by puns. On their account let me say that, although there are here eight separate f's in less than half a sentence, this is to be held as pure accident. In fact, at one time there were nine f's in the original cast of the sentence, until I, in pity of the affronted people, substituted *female agent* for *female friend.*

My business with *her* was not to thank her for the resolute justice which she had done me, since as yet I could
not know of that service, but simply to see her, to learn
the domestic news of the Priory, and, according to the
possibilities of the case, to concert with her some plan
of regular correspondence. Meantime it happened that
a maternal uncle, a military man on the Bengal establishment, who had come to England on a three-years'
leave of absence (according to the custom in those
days), was at this time a visitor at the Priory. My
mother's establishment of servants was usually limited
to five persons—all, except one, elderly and torpid. But
my uncle, who had brought to England some beautiful
Arab and Persian horses, found it necessary to gather
about his stables an extra body of men and boys. These
were all alert and active; so that, when I reconnoitred
the windows of the Priory in the dusk, hoping in some
way to attract my sister's attention, I not only failed in
that object, seeing no lights in any room which could
naturally have been occupied by her, but I also found
myself growing into an object of special attention to
certain unknown servants, who, having no doubt received instructions to look out for me, easily inferred
from my anxious movements that I must be the person
"wanted." Uneasy at all the novel appearances of
things, I went away, and returned, after an hour's interval, armed with a note to my sister, requesting her
to watch for an opportunity of coming out for a few
minutes under the shadows of the little ruins in the
Priory garden, where I meantime would be waiting.
This note I gave to a stranger, whose costume showed
him to be a groom, begging him to give it to the young
lady whose address it bore. He answered, in a respectful tone, that he would do so; but he could not sincerely have meant it, since (as I soon learned) it was
impossible. In fact, not one minute had I waited, when

in glided amongst the ruins—not my fair sister, but my bronzed Bengal uncle!

A Bengal tiger would not more have startled me. Now, to a dead certainty, I said, here comes a fatal barrier to the prosecution of my scheme. I was mistaken. Between my mother and my uncle there existed the very deepest affection; for they regarded each other as sole reliques of a household once living together in memorable harmony. But in many features of character no human beings could stand off from each other in more lively repulsion. And this was seen on the present occasion. My dear excellent mother, from the eternal quiet of her decorous household, looked upon every violent or irregular movement, and therefore upon mine at present, much as she would have done upon the opening of the seventh seal in the Revelations. But my uncle was thoroughly a man of the world; and, what told even more powerfully on my behalf in this instance, he was a man of even morbid activity. It was so exquisitely natural in his eyes that any rational person should prefer moving about amongst the breezy mountains of Wales to a slavish routine of study amongst books grim with dust and masters too probably still more dusty, that he seemed disposed to regard my conduct as an extraordinary act of virtue. On his advice, it was decided that there could be no hope in any contest with my main wishes, and that I should be left to pursue my original purpose of walking amongst the Welsh mountains; provided I chose to do so upon the slender allowance of a guinea a-week. My uncle, whose Indian munificence ran riot upon all occasions, would gladly have had a far larger allowance made to me, and would himself have clandestinely given me anything I asked. But I myself, from general ignorance (in which accomplishment I excelled), judged this to be sufficient; and at this point my mother, hitherto passively aquiescent in my uncle's proposals, interfered with a decisive rigour that in my own heart I could not disapprove. Any larger allowance, most reasonably she urged, what was it but to "make proclamation to my two younger brothers that rebellion bore a premium, and that mutiny was the ready road to ease and comfort?" My conscience smote me at these words: I felt something like an electric shock on this sudden reference, so utterly unexpected, to my brothers; for, to say the truth, I never once admitted them to my thoughts in forecasting the eventual consequences that might possibly unroll themselves from my own headstrong act. Here now, within three days, rang like a solemn knell, reverberating from the sounding-board within my awakened conscience, one of those many self-reproaches so dimly masked, but not circumstantially prefigured, by the secret thought under the dome of St. Paul's Cathedral about its dread Whispering Gallery. In this particular instance I know that the evil consequences from my own example never did take effect. But, at the moment of my mother's sorrowful suggestion, the fear that they *might* take effect thrilled me with remorse.

Saddened by these reflections, I was still more saddened by the chilling manner of my mother. If I could presume to descry a fault in my mother, it was that she turned the chilling aspects of her high-toned character too exclusively upon those whom, in any degree, she knew or supposed to be promoters of evil. Sometimes her austerity might seem even unjust. But at present the whole artillery of her displeasure seemed to be unmasked, and *justly* unmasked, against a moral aberration that offered for itself no excuse that was obvious in one moment, that was legible at one glance, that could utter itself in one word. My mother was predisposed to think ill of all causes that required many

words: I, predisposed to subtleties of all sorts and degrees, had naturally become acquainted with cases that
could not unrobe their apparellings down to that degree of simplicity. If in this world there is one misery
having no relief, it is the pressure on the heart from
the *Incommunicable*. And, if another Sphinx should
arise to propose another enigma to man—saying, What
burden is that which only is insupportable by human
fortitude? I should answer at once—*It is the burden of
the Incommunicable*. At this moment, sitting in the
same room of the Priory with my mother, knowing
how reasonable she was—how patient of explanations
—how candid—how open to pity—not the less I sank
away in a hopelessness that was immeasurable from
all effort at explanation. She and I were contemplating
the very same act; but she from one centre, I from another. Certain I was that, if through one half-minute
she could realize in one deadly experience the suffering
with which I had fought through more than three
months, the amount of physical anguish, the desolation of all genial life, she would have uttered a rapturous absolution of that which else must always seem to
her a mere explosion of wilful insubordination. "In
this brief experience," she would exclaim, "I read the
record of your acquittal; in this fiery torment I acknowledge the gladiatorial resistance." Such in the
case supposed would have been her revised verdict. But
this case was exquisitely impossible. Nothing which
offered itself to my rhetoric gave any but the feeblest
and most childish reflection of my past sufferings. Just
so helpless did I feel, disarmed into just the same languishing impotence to face (or make an effort at facing) the difficulty before me, as most of us have felt in
the dreams of our childhood when lying down without
a struggle before some all-conquering lion. I felt that
the situation was one without hope; a solitary word,

which I attempted to mould upon my lips, died away into a sigh; and passively I acquiesced in the apparent confession spread through all the appearances—that in reality I had no palliation to produce.

One alternative, in the offer made to me, was that I had permission to stay at the Priory. The Priory, or the mountainous region of Wales, was offered freely to my choice. Either of the two offered an attractive abode. The Priory, it may be fancied, was clogged with the liability to fresh and intermitting reproaches. But this was not so. I knew my mother sufficiently to be assured that, once having expressed her sorrowful condemnation of my act, having made it impossible for me to misunderstand her views, she was ready to extend her wonted hospitality to me, and (as regarded all practical matters) her wonted kindness; but not that sort of kindness which could make me forget that I stood under the deepest shadows of her displeasure, or could leave me for a moment free to converse at my ease upon any and every subject. A man that is talking on simple toleration, and, as it were, under permanent protest, cannot feel himself morally at his ease, unless very obtuse and coarse in his sensibilities.

Mine, under any situation approaching to the present, were so far from being obtuse that they were morbidly and extravagantly acute. I had erred: that I knew, and did not disguise from myself. Indeed, the rapture of anguish with which I had recurred involuntarily to my experience of the Whispering Gallery, and the symbolic meaning which I had given to that experience, manifested indirectly my deep sense of error, through the dim misgiving which attended it that in some mysterious way the sense and the consequences of this error would magnify themselves at every stage of life, in proportion as they were viewed retrospectively from greater and greater distances. I had, besides, through the casual allusion to my brothers, suddenly become painfully aware of another and separate failure in the filial obligations resting on myself. Any mother who is a widow has especial claims on the co-operation of her eldest son in all means of giving a beneficial bias to the thoughts and purposes of the younger children: and, if *any* mother, then by a title how special could my own mother invoke such co-operation, who had on *her* part satisfied all the claims made upon her maternal character by self-sacrifices as varied as privately I knew them to be exemplary. Whilst yet comparatively young, not more than thirty-six, she had sternly refused all countenance, on at least two separate occasions, to distinguished proposals of marriage, out of pure regard to the memory of my father, and to the interests of his children. Could I fail to read, in such ostentatious exemplifications of maternal goodness, a summons to a corresponding earnestness on my part in lightening, as much as possible, the burden of her responsibilities? Alas! too certainly, as regarded *that* duty, I felt my own failure: one opportunity had been signally lost. And yet, on the other hand, I also felt that more might be pleaded on my behalf than could by possibility be apparent to a neutral bystander. But this, to be pleaded effectually, needed to be said—not by myself, but by a disinterested advocate: and no such advocate was at hand. In blind distress of mind, conscience-stricken and heart-stricken, I stretched out my arms, seeking for my one sole auxiliary; that was my eldest sister Mary; for my younger sister Jane was a mere infant. Blindly and mechanically, I stretched out my arms as if to arrest her attention; and, giving utterance to my labouring thoughts, I was beginning to speak, when all at once I became sensible that Mary was not there. I had heard a step behind me, and supposed it hers: since the

groom's ready acceptance of my letter to her had preoccupied me with the belief that I should see her in a
few moments. But she was far away, on a mission of
anxious, sisterly love.

Immediately after my elopement, an express had
been sent off to the Priory from Manchester; this express, well mounted, had not spent more than four
hours on the road. He must have passed me on my first
day's walk; and, within an hour after *his* arrival, came
a communication from the post-office, explaining the
nature and value of the letter that had been so vexa-
tiously thrust into my hands. Alarm spread through
the Priory: for it must be confessed that the coincidence of my elopement with this certified delivery of
the letter to myself gave but too reasonable grounds for
connecting the two incidents. I was grateful to dear
Mary for resisting such strong plausibilities against
me; and yet I could not feel entitled to complain of
those who had *not* resisted. The probability seemed
that I must have violated the laws to some extent,
either by forgery or by fraudulent appropriation. In
either case, the most eligible course seemed to be my
instant expatriation. France (this being the year of
peace) or Holland would offer the best asylum until
the affair should be settled; and, as there could be no
anxieties in any quarter as to the main thing concerned
in the issue—viz. the money—in any case there was no
reason to fear a vindictive pursuit, even on the worst
assumption as regarded the offence. An elderly gentleman, long connected with the family, and in many
cases an agent for the guardians, at this moment offered his services as counsellor and protector to my
sister Mary. Two hours therefore from the arrival of
the Manchester express (who, starting about 11 A.M.,
had reached Chester at 3 P.M.), all the requisite steps
having been concerted with one of the Chester banks

for getting letters of credit, &c., a carriage-and-four was at the Priory gate, into which stepped my sister Mary, with one female attendant and her friendly escort. And thus, the same day on which I had made my exit from Mr. Lawson's saw the chase after me commencing. Sunset saw the pursuers crossing the Mersey, and trotting into Liverpool. Thence to Ormskirk, thirteen miles, and thence to *proud Preston*, about twenty more. Within a trifle, these three stages make fifty miles; and so much did my chasers, that pursued when no man fled, accomplish before sleeping. On the next day, long and long before the time when I, in my humble pedestrian character, reached Chester, my sister's party had reached Ambleside—distant about ninety-two miles from Liverpool; consequently somewhere about a hundred and seven miles from the Priory. This chasing party, with good reason, supposed themselves to be on my traces ever after reaching "proud Preston," which is the point of confluence for the Liverpool and Manchester roads northwards. For I myself, having originally planned my route for the English Lakes, purposely suffered some indications of that plan to remain behind me, in the hope of thus giving a false direction to any pursuit that might be attempted.

The further course of this chase was disagreeably made known to me about four years later, on attaining my majority, by a "little account" of about £150 against my little patrimonial fortune. Of all the letters from the Priory (which, however, from natural oversight were not thought of until the day after my own arrival at the Priory—*i.e.*, the third day after my sister's departure), not one caught them: which was unfortunate. For the journey to and from the Lakes, together with a circuit of more than one hundred and fifty miles amongst the Lakes, would at any rate have run up to nearly four hundred miles. But it happened that my pursuers, not having time to sift such intelligence as they received, were misled into an excursus of full two hundred miles more, by chasing an imaginary *"me"* to the caves, thence to Bolton Abbey, thence nearly to York. Altogether, the journey amounted to above six hundred miles, all performed with four horses. Now, at that time the cost of four horses— which in the cheapest hay and corn seasons was three shillings a-mile, and in dear seasons four—was three and sixpence a-mile; to which it was usual to compute an average addition of one shilling a-mile for gates, postilions, ostlers; so that the total amount, with the natural expenses of the three travellers at the inns, ran up to five shillings a-mile. Consequently, five shillings being the quarter of a pound, six hundred miles cost the quarter of £600. The only item in this long account which consoled me to the amount of a solitary smile for all this money thrown away was an item in a bill at Patterdale (head of Ulleswater) —

To an echo, first quality £0 10 0
To do.,   second quality 0   5 0

It seems the price of echoes varied, reasonably enough, with the amount of gunpowder consumed. But at Low-wood, on Windermere, half-crown echoes might be had by those base snobs who would put up with a vile Brummagem substitute for "the genuine article."

Trivial, meantime, as regarded any permanent consequences, would have been this casual inroad upon my patrimony. Had I waited until my sister returned home, which I might have been sure could only have been delayed through the imperfectly concerted system of correspondence, all would have prospered. From

her I should have received the cordiality and the genial
sympathy which I needed; I could have quietly pursued my studies; and my Oxford matriculation would
have followed as a matter of course. But, unhappily,
having for so long a time been seriously shaken in
health, any interruption of my wild open-air system
of life instantly threw me back into nervous derangements. Past all doubt it had now become that the *al
fresco* life, to which I had looked with so much hopefulness for a sure and rapid restoration to health, was
even more potent than I had supposed it. Literally irresistible it seemed in re-organizing the system of my
languishing powers. Impatient, therefore, under the
absence of my sister, and agitated every hour so long as
my home wanted its central charm in some household
countenance, some σύντροφον ὄμμα, beaming with perfect sympathy, I resolved to avail myself of those wild
mountainous and sylvan attractions which at present
lay nearest to me. Those parts, indeed, of Flintshire, or
even of Denbighshire, which lay near to Chester, were
not in any very eminent sense attractive. The vale of
Gressford, for instance, within the Flintshire border,
and yet not more than seven miles distant, offered a
lovely little seclusion; and to this I had a privileged
access; and at first I tried it; but it was a dressed and
ornamented pleasure-ground: and two ladies of some
distinction, nearly related to each other, and old
friends of my mother, were in a manner the ladies
paramount within the ring fence of this Arcadian vale.
But this did not offer what I wanted. Everything was
elegant, polished, quiet, throughout the lawns and
groves of this verdant retreat: no rudeness was allowed
here; even the little brooks were trained to "behave
themselves"; and the two villas of the reigning ladies
(Mrs. Warrington and Mrs. Parry) showed the perfection of good taste. For both ladies had cultivated a

taste for painting, and I believe some executive power.
Here my introductions were rather too favourable;
since they forced me into society. From Gressford,
however, the character of the scene, considered as a
daily residence, very soon repelled me, however otherwise fascinating by the accomplishments of its two
possessors. Just two-and-twenty miles from Chester,
meantime, lay a far grander scene, the fine vale of
Llangollen in the centre of Denbighshire. Here, also,
the presiding residents were two ladies, whose romantic retirement from the world at an early age had attracted for many years a general interest to their
persons, habits, and opinions. These ladies were Irish
—Miss Ponsonby, and Lady Eleanor Butler, a sister of
Lord Ormond. I had twice been formally presented to
them by persons of a rank to stamp a value upon this
introduction. But, naturally, though high-bred courtesy concealed any such open expressions of feeling,
they must have felt a very slight interest in myself or
my opinions.[1] I grieve to say that my own feelings
were not more ardent towards *them*. Nevertheless, I
presented myself at their cottage as often as I passed
through Llangollen; and was always courteously re-

[1] It is worthy of notice that, when I, in this year 1802, and
again in after years, endeavoured to impress them favourably
with regard to Wordsworth as a poet (that subject having not
been introduced by myself, but by one of the ladies, who happened to have a Cambridge friend intimate with the man, and
perhaps with his works), neither of them was disposed to look
with any interest or hopefulness upon his pretensions. But, at
a period long subsequent to this, when the House of Commons
had rung with applause on Sergeant Talfourd's mention of his
name, and when all American tourists of any distinction
flocked annually to Rydal Mount, Wordsworth's own poems
bear witness that a great revolution had been worked at
Llangollen. I mention this anecdote, because I have good reason to think that a large proportion of the "conversions" in
the case of Wordsworth took place under the same influence.

ceived when they happened to be in the country. However, as it was not ladies that I was seeking in Wales, I now pushed on to Carnarvonshire; and for some weeks took a very miniature suite of rooms—viz. one room and a closet—at Bangor.

My landlady had been a lady's-maid, or a nurse, or something of that sort, in the Bishop of Bangor's family; and had but lately married away from that family, or (to use her own expression) had "settled." In a little town like Bangor, barely to have lived in the Bishop's family conferred some distinction; and my good landlady had rather more than her share of the pride natural to that glorious advantage. What "my lord" said, and what "my lord" did, how useful he was in Parliament, and how indispensable at Oxford, formed the daily burden of her talk. All this I bore very well; for it cost no great effort to make allowance for the garrulity of an old servant; and luckily nothing in our daily routine of life brought us often into each other's company. Sometimes, however, we met; and of necessity, on such occasions, I must have appeared in her eyes very inadequately impressed with the Bishop's importance, and with the grandeur of having lived in a palace; and, perhaps, to punish me for my indifference, or it might, after all, be mere accident, she one day repeated to me a conversation in which I was indirectly a party concerned. She had been to the palace; and, dinner being over, she had been summoned into the dining-room. In giving an account of her household economy, she happened to mention that she had let what she styled somewhat magnificently her "apartments." The good Bishop (it seemed) had thence taken occasion to caution her as to her selection of inmates; "for," said he, "you must recollect, Betty, that Bangor is in the high road to the Head" (*the Head* was the common colloquial expression for Holyhead), "so that multitudes of Irish swindlers, running away from their debts into England, and of English swindlers, running away from their debts to the Isle of Man, are likely to take this place in their route." Such advice was certainly not without reasonable grounds, but rather fitted to be stored up for Mrs. Betty's private meditations than specially reported to me. What followed was worse:

"O my lord," answered my landlady (according to her own representation of the matter), "I really don't think that this young gentleman is a swindler; because——"

"You don't *think* me a swindler?" said I, interrupting her, in a tumult of indignation; "for the future I shall spare you the trouble of thinking about it." And without delay I prepared for my departure.

Some concessions the good woman seemed disposed to make; but a harsh and contemptuous expression, which I fear that I applied to the learned dignitary himself, roused *her* indignation in turn; and reconciliation then became impossible. I was, indeed, greatly irritated at the Bishop's having suggested any grounds of suspicion, however remotely, against a person whom he had never seen; and I thought of letting him know my mind in Greek; which, at the same time that it would furnish some presumption in behalf of my respectability, might also (I hoped) compel the Bishop to answer in the same language; and in that case I doubted not to make good my superiority, as a versatile wielder of arms rarely managed with effect, against all the terrors of his lordship's wig.

I was wrong if I said anything in my anger that was disparaging or sceptical as to the Bishop's intellectual pretensions; which were not only very sound, but very appropriate to the particular stations which he filled. For the Bishop of Bangor (at that time Dr. Cleaver) was also the head of Brasenose, Oxford—which college was indebted to him for its leadership at that era in scholarship and discipline. In this academic character I learned afterwards that he might be called almost a reformer —a wise, temperate, and successful reformer; and, as a scholar, I saw many years later that he had received the laudatory notice of Porson. But, on the other hand, the Bishop was not altogether without blame in unchaining his local influence, were it only by hint or insinuation, against a defenceless stranger. For so great a man, in so small a town as Bangor, was really as much of an autocrat as a post-captain on the quarterdeck of his own vessel. A "sea-lawyer" in such a case must contrive to pocket his wrongs, until he finds himself and the captain on shore. Yet, after all, my scheme was not altogether so absurd; and the anger, in which perhaps it might begin, all melted away in the fun which would have accompanied its execution. It will strike the reader that my plan of retaliation must have failed by arming against me the official pride of the Bishop. Any man, it will be thought, occupying so dignified a place in public life—a lord of Parliament, holder of a prize in the episcopal lottery (for Bangor was worth six thousand a-year), a leading Don at Oxford—in short, a splendid pluralist, armed with diocesan thunder and lightning—would never stoop from his Jovian altitude to notice any communication whatever from a boy. But it would make all the difference in the world that this communication by the supposition was to be in Greek. Mere curiosity in such a case would compel the Bishop to read it. And then, shockingly irregular as such a course would be, a fatal temptation would arise to the hazardous experiment of answering it in Greek. It would not be pleasant to shrink from the sort of silent challenge thrown out by such an eccentric form of epistle, when worded in the tone of respect due to the Bishop's age and spiritual office. And certainly the degradation would be conspicuously less in replying even to a boy, if armed with that sort of accomplishment. But was not the Bishop a learned man, well qualified to answer, whose reading must naturally be greater by a score of times than mine? I had heard so; and I was told also, but long after, that he had written well and learnedly (*but not in Greek*) on the Arundel marbles; even to attempt which, in our days, when the forestalling labours of two centuries have so much narrowed the field open to original sagacity, argues an erudition far from common. But I have already given it as my opinion that there is no proportion held between a man's general knowledge of Greek and the special art of writing Greek; that is, using it as a vehicle for ordinary and familiar intercourse. This advantage, not necessarily or usually belonging to the most exquisite Greek scholarship, I myself wielded with a preternatural address for varying the forms of expression, and for bringing the most refractory ideas within the harness of Grecian phraseology. Had the Bishop yielded to the temptation of replying, then I figured to myself the inevitable result—the episcopal hulk lying motionless on the water like a huge three-decker, not able to return a gun, whilst I, as a light agile frigate, should have sailed round and round him, and raked him at pleasure as opportunity offered. He could have had no opening for his erudition (as, for instance, upon the Arundel marbles), without too flagrantly recalling the cosmogony man in the *Vicar of Wakefield*, with his ἄναρχον ἄρα καὶ ἀτελεύταιον τὸ πᾶν. Once falling into the snare of replying at all, his lordship would not be at liberty either to break off the correspondence abruptly, or to continue it without damage to his episcopal pomp. My anger, meantime, sudden and fiery, as under a sense of real injury, had not been malicious; and it was already propitiated beforehand by the mere fun and comic effect of the picture which I thus prefigured as arising between us. In no case could I have found pleasure in causing any mortifications to the Bishop—mortifications which the Methodists (by this time swarming in Carnarvonshire) would exultingly have diffused. In the end I should probably have confined myself to a grave and temperate remonstrance, simply stating the distressing consequences which were likely to result to me from the too unguarded insinuations of his lordship.

But these consequences travelled fast upon the traces of those insinuations; and already, upon the very day when my foolish landlady (more, perhaps, in thoughtlessness than with any purpose of mischief) had repeated the Bishop's words in what seemed to me so insulting a tone, and so entirely without provocation (since there never had been the smallest irregularity in our little weekly settlements), one of those consequences was that I became houseless. For I disdained to profit by the shelter of a house from which truth and courtesy seemed alike banished. And from that one consequence naturally enough flowed others; for, having, at any rate, to seek a new home, I left Bangor at once, and rambled away to Carnarvon—distant about two-and-a-half hours' smart walking. At Carnarvon I found no lodging that altogether suited my purposes— hired lodgings being then thinly sown in North Wales; and for some time, therefore, having a small reserve of guineas, I lived very much at inns.

This change of abode naturally drew my thoughts away from the Bishop. And thus gradually all my thoughts of expostulation faded away. This I am disposed to regard as an unfortunate solution of the affair, which otherwise would probably have taken the following course: The Bishop, as I afterwards heard

when resident myself at Oxford and personally acquainted with men of Brasenose (to which college, indeed, subsequently, my own youngest brother belonged), was a reasonable and even amiable man. On
receiving, therefore, my Greek remonstrance, he was
sure as a scholar to have taken some interest in the
writer; and he was too equitable to have neglected any
statement, Greek or not Greek, which reflected, with
some apparent justice, upon his own conduct as not
sufficiently considerate. He would, therefore, almost
certainly have replied to me in courteous terms; re-
gretting the accident which had made me houseless;
but reminding me that all communications made to a
dependent within a man's own gates, and never meant
as grounds of action, but simply as cautions—general
and not special—are in law and usage held to be privileged communications, and equally whether written
or spoken. The insulting use made of this caution he
would have treated as due simply to the woman's
coarseness, but in part, perhaps, as due to a cause which
has much to do with the harsh and uncivil expressions
of uneducated people—viz., their very limited command of language. They use phrases much stronger
than naturally belong to their thoughts and meaning,
simply because the narrowness of their vocabulary
oftentimes suggests to their embarrassed choice no
variation of expression wearing a character less offensive. To such a letter I should have made a suitable reply; and, thenceforward, it is probable that, until the
Michaelmas term drew the Bishop's family away to
Oxford, I should have found my abode in Bangor, or
its neighbourhood, much improved as regards the command of books. That advantage would have been fugitive. But other and remoter advantages might have
been more serious. It happened that the college to
which the Manchester Grammar School would have

consigned me as a privileged *alumnus* was that very college over which the Bishop presided. I have no reason to think that the Bishop would have had power to retrieve for me any part of the privileges which by my elopement I had wilfully forfeited: but he would have had it abundantly in his power to place the ordinary college advantages of Fellowships, &c., within my reach: whereas afterwards, going under erroneous counsel to a college disconnected from my own county and my own schools, I never enjoyed those ordinary opportunities of advancement, and consequently of literary leisure, which the English universities open to almost every man who qualifies himself duly to obtain them. All this, however, was thrown into the world of dreams and fable by my hasty movement to Carnarvon, and that region which Pennant first distinguished by the name of Snowdonia.

There were already, even in those days of 1802, numerous inns, erected at reasonable distances from each other, for the accommodation of tourists: and no sort of disgrace attached in Wales, as too generally upon the great roads of England, to the pedestrian style of travelling. Indeed, the majority of those whom I met as fellow-tourists in the quiet little cottage-parlours of the Welsh posting-houses were pedestrian travellers. All the way from Shrewsbury through Llangollen, Llanrwst,[1] Conway, Bangor, then turning to the left at right angles through Carnarvon, and so on to Dolgelly (the chief town of Merionethshire), Tan-y-Bwlch, Harlech, Barmouth, and through the sweet solitudes of Cardiganshire, or turning back sharply towards the English border through the gorgeous wood scenery of Montgomeryshire—everywhere,

---

[1] *"Llanrwst"*: This is an alarming word for the eye; one vowel to what the English eye counts as seven consonants: but it is easily pronounced as *Tlanroost*.

at intermitting distances of twelve to sixteen miles, I
found the most comfortable inns. One feature indeed
of repose in all this chain of solitary resting-houses—
viz. the fact that none of them rose above two storeys
in height—was due to the modest scale on which the
travelling system of the Principality had moulded itself in correspondence to the calls of England, which
then (but be it remembered this *then* was in 1802, a
year of peace) threw a very small proportion of her
vast migratory population annually into this sequestered channel. No huge Babylonian centres of commerce towered into the clouds on these sweet sylvan
routes: no hurricanes of haste, or fever-stricken armies
of horses and flying chariots, tormented the echoes in
these mountain recesses. And it has often struck me
that a world-wearied man, who sought for the peace of
monasteries separated from their gloomy captivity—
peace and silence such as theirs, combined with the
large liberty of nature—could not do better than revolve amongst these modest inns in the five northern
Welsh counties of Denbigh, Montgomery, Carnarvon,
Merioneth, and Cardigan. Sleeping, for instance, and
breakfasting at Carnarvon; then, by an easy nine-mile
walk, going forwards to dinner at Bangor, thence to
Aber—nine miles; or to Llanberris; and so on for ever,
accomplishing seventy to ninety or one hundred miles
in a week. This, upon actual experiment, and for week
after week, I found the most delightful of lives. Here
was the eternal motion of winds and rivers, or of the
Wandering Jew liberated from the persecution which
compelled him to move and turned his breezy freedom
into a killing captivity. Happier life I cannot imagine
than this vagrancy, if the weather were but tolerable,
through endless successions of changing beauty, and
towards evening a courteous welcome in a pretty rustic
home—that, having all the luxuries of a fine hotel (in

particular some luxuries [1] that are almost sacred to alpine regions), was at the same time liberated from the inevitable accompaniments of such hotels in great cities or at great travelling stations—viz. the tumult and uproar.

Life on this model was but too delightful; and to myself especially, that am never thoroughly in health unless when having pedestrian exercise to the extent of fifteen miles at the most, and eight to ten miles at the least. Living thus, a man earned his daily enjoyment. But what did it cost? About half-a-guinea a-day: whilst my boyish allowance was not a third of this. The flagrant health, health boiling over in fiery rapture, which ran along, side by side, with exercise on this scale, whilst all the while from morning to night I was inhaling mountain air, soon passed into a hateful scourge. Perquisites to servants and a bed would have absorbed the whole of my weekly guinea. My policy therefore was, if the autumnal air were warm enough, to save this expense of a bed and the chambermaid by sleeping amongst ferns or furze upon a hillside; and perhaps, with a cloak of sufficient *weight* as well as compass, or an Arab's burnoose, this would have been no great hardship. But then in the daytime what an oppressive burden to carry! So perhaps it was as well that I had no cloak at all. I did, however, for some weeks try the plan of carrying a canvas tent manufactured by myself, and not larger than an ordinary umbrella: but to pitch this securely I found difficult; and on windy nights it became a troublesome companion. As winter drew near, this bivouacking system became too dangerous to attempt. Still one may bivouack decently, barring rain and wind, up to the end of Octo-

[1] But a luxury of another class, and quite peculiar to Wales, was in those days (I hope in these) the Welsh harp, in attendance at every inn.

ber. And I counted, on the whole, that in a fortnight I spent nine nights abroad. There are, as perhaps the reader knows by experience, no jaguars in Wales—nor pumas—nor anacondas—nor (generally speaking) any Thugs. What I feared most, but perhaps only through ignorance of zoology, was lest, whilst my sleeping face was upturned to the stars, some one of the many Brahminical-looking cows on the Cambrian hills, one or other, might poach her foot into the centre of my face. I do not suppose any fixed hostility of that nature to English faces in Welsh cows: but everywhere I observe in the feminine mind something of beautiful caprice, a floral exuberance of that charming wilfulness which characterizes our dear human sisters, I fear, through all worlds. Against Thugs I had Juvenal's licence to be careless in the emptiness of my pockets (*cantabit vacuus coram latrone viator*). But I fear that Juvenal's licence will not always hold water. There are people bent upon cudgelling one who will persist in excusing one's having nothing but a bad shilling in one's purse, without reading in that Juvenalian *vacuitas* any privilege or licence of exemption from the general fate of travellers that intrude upon the solitude of robbers.

Dr. Johnson, upon some occasion which I have forgotten, is represented by his biographers as accounting for an undeserving person's success in these terms: "Why, I suppose that *his* nonsense suited *their* nonsense." Can *that* be the humiliating solution of my own colloquial success at this time in Carnarvonshire inns? Do not suggest such a thought, most courteous reader. No matter: won in whatsoever way, success *is* success; and even nonsense, if it is to be victorious nonsense—victorious over the fatal habit of yawning in those who listen, and in some cases over the habit of disputing—must involve a deeper art or more effective secret of power than is easily attained. Nonsense, in fact, is a very difficult thing. Not every seventh son of a seventh son (to use Milton's words) is equal to the task of keeping and maintaining a company of decent men in orthodox nonsense for a matter of two hours. Come from what fountain it may, all talk that succeeds to the extent of raising a wish to meet the talker again must contain *salt;* must be seasoned with some flavouring element pungent enough to neutralize the natural tendencies of all mixed conversation, not vigilantly tended, to lose itself in insipidities and platitudes. Above all things, I shunned, as I would shun a pestilence, Coleridge's capital error, which through life he practised, of keeping the audience in a state of passiveness. Unjust this was to others, but most of all to himself. This eternal stream of talk which never for one instant intermitted, and allowed no momentary opportunity of reaction to the persecuted and baited auditor, was absolute ruin to the interests of the talker himself. Always passive, always acted upon, never allowed to react, into what state did the poor afflicted listener—he that played the *rôle* of listener—collapse? He returned home in the exhausted condition of one that has been drawn up just before death from the bottom of a well occupied by foul gases; and, of course, hours before he had reached that perilous point of depression, he had lost all power of distinguishing, understanding, or connecting. I, for my part, without needing to think of the unamiable arrogance involved in such a habit, simply on principles of deadliest selfishness, should have avoided thus incapacitating my hearer from doing any justice to the rhetoric or the argument with which I might address him.

Some great advantages I had for colloquial purposes, and for engaging the attention of people wiser than myself. Ignorant I was in a degree past all imagination of daily life—even as it exists in England. But, on the other hand, having the advantage of a prodigious memory, and the far greater advantage of a logical instinct for feeling in a moment the secret analogies or parallelisms that connected things else apparently remote, I enjoyed these two peculiar gifts for conversation: first, an inexhaustible fertility of topics, and therefore of resources for illustrating or for varying any subject that chance or purpose suggested; secondly, a prematurely awakened sense of *art* applied to conversation. I had learned the use of vigilance in evading with civility the approach of wearisome discussions, and in impressing, quietly and oftentimes imperceptibly, a new movement upon dialogues that loitered painfully, or see-sawed unprofitably. That it was one function of art to hide and mask itself (*artis est artem celare*), this I well knew. Neither was there much art required. The chief demand was for new facts, or new views, or for views newly coloured impressing novelty upon old facts. To throw in a little of the mysterious every now and then was useful, even with those that by temperament were averse to the mysterious; pointed epigrammatic sayings and jests—even somewhat worn —were useful; a seasonable quotation in verse was always effective; and illustrative anecdotes diffused a grace over the whole movement of the dialogue. It would have been coxcombry to practise any elaborate or any conspicuous art: few and simple were any artifices that I ever employed; but, being hidden and seasonable, they were often effective. And the whole result was that I became exceedingly popular within my narrow circle of friends. This circle was necessarily a fluctuating one, since it was mainly composed of tourists that happened to linger for a few weeks in or near Snowdonia, making their headquarters at Bethgellert or Carnarvon, or at the utmost roaming no farther than the foot of Cader Idris.

Amongst these fugitive members of our society, I recollect with especial pleasure Mr. De Haren, an accomplished young German, who held, or *had* held, the commission of lieutenant in our British navy, but now, in an interval of peace, was seeking to extend his knowledge of England, and also of the English language; though in *that*, as regarded the fullest command of it colloquially, he had little indeed to learn. From him it was that I obtained my first lessons in German and my first acquaintance with German literature. Paul Richter I then first heard of, together with Hippel, a humorist admired by Kant, and Hamann, also classed as a humorist, but a nondescript writer, singularly obscure, whom I have never since seen in the hands of any Englishman, except once of Sir William Hamilton. With all these writers Mr. De Haren had the means of making me usefully acquainted in the small portable library which filled one of his trunks.

But the most stationary members of this semi-literary circle were Welshmen; two of them lawyers, one a clergyman. This last had been regularly educated at Oxford—as a member of Jesus (the Welsh college)—and was a man of extensive information. The lawyers had not enjoyed the same advantages, but they had read diligently, and were interesting companions. Wales, as is pretty well known, breeds a population somewhat litigious. I do not think the worse of them for *that*. The martial Butlers and the heroic Talbots of the fifteenth century, having no regular opening for their warlike fury in the seventeenth century, took to quarrelling with each other; and no letters are more bitter than those which to this day sur-

vive from the hostile correspondence of the brother
Talbots contemporary with the last days of Shakespeare. One channel being closed against their martial
propensities, naturally they opened such others as circumstances made available. This temper, widely spread
amongst the lower classes of the Welsh, made it a necessity that the lawyers should itinerate on market-
days through all the principal towns in their districts.
In those towns continually I met them; and continually
we renewed our literary friendship.

Meantime alternately I sailed upon the high-priced
and the low-priced tack. So exceedingly cheap were
provisions at that period, when the war taxation of Mr.
Pitt was partially intermitting, that it was easy beyond
measure upon any three weeks' expenditure, by living
with cottagers, to save two guineas out of the three.
Mr. De Haren assured me that even in an inn, and not
in a poor man's cottage (but an unpretending rustic
inn, where the mistress of the house took upon herself
the functions of every possible servant in turn—cook,
waiter, chambermaid, boots, ostler), he had passed a
day or two; and for what he considered a really elegant
dinner, as regarded everything except the table equipage (that being rude and coarse), he had paid only
sixpence. This very inn, about ten or twelve miles
south of Dolgelly, I myself visited some time later; and
I found Mr. De Haren's account in all points confirmed: the sole drawback upon the comfort of the
visitor being that the fuel was chiefly of green wood,
and with a chimney that smoked. I suffered so much
under this kind of smoke, which irritates and inflames
the eyes more than any other, that on the following
day reluctantly I took leave of that obliging pluralist
the landlady, and really felt myself blushing on settling the bill, until I bethought me of the green wood,
which, upon the whole, seemed to balance the account.

I could not then, nor can I now, account for these preposterously low prices; which same prices, strange to say, ruled (as Wordsworth and his sister often assured me) among the same kind of scenery—*i.e.* amongst the English Lakes—at the very same time. To account for it, as people often do, by alleging the want of markets for agricultural produce, is crazy political economy; since the remedy for paucity of markets, and consequent failure of competition, is, certainly not to sell at losing rates, but to forbear producing, and consequently not to sell at all.[1]

[1] Thirteen years later—viz. in the year of Waterloo—happening to walk through the whole Principality from south to north, beginning at Cardiff and ending at Bangor, I turned aside about twenty-five miles to inquire after the health of my excellent hostess, that determined pluralist and intense antipole of all possible sinecurists. I found her cleaning a pair of boots and spurs, and purposing (I rather think) to enter next upon the elegant office of greasing a horse's heels. In that design, however, she was thwarted for the present by myself and another tourist, who claimed her services in three or four other characters previously. I inquired after the chimney—was it still smoking? She seemed surprised that it had ever been suspected of anything criminal; so, as it was not a season for fires, I said no more. But I saw plenty of green wood, and but a small proportion of peats. I fear, therefore, that this, the state-room of the whole concern, still poisons the peace of the unhappy tourists. One personal indemnification, meantime, I must mention which this little guilty room made to me on that same night for all the tears it had caused me to shed. It happened that there was a public dance held at this inn on this very night. I therefore retired early to my bedroom, having had so long a walk, and not wishing to annoy the company, or the excellent landlady, who had, I daresay, to play the fiddle to the dancers. The noise and uproar were almost insupportable; so that I could not sleep at all. At three o'clock all became silent, the company having departed in a body. Suddenly from the little parlour, separated from my bedroom overhead by the slightest and most pervious of ceilings, arose with the rising dawn the very sweetest of female voices perhaps that ever I had heard, although for many years an *habitué* of the

So cheap in fact were all provisions which one had any chance of meeting with in a labouring man's house that I found it difficult under such a roof to spend sixpence a-day. Tea or coffee there was none: and I did not at that period very much care for either. Milk, with bread (coarse, but more agreeable by much than the insipid *whitey-grey* bread of towns), potatoes if one wished, and also a little goat's, or kid's flesh— these composed the cottager's choice of viands; not luxurious, but palatable enough to a person who took much exercise. And, if one wished, fresh-water fish could be had cheap enough; especially trout of the very finest quality. In these circumstances, I never found it easy to spend even five shillings (no, not three shillings, unless whortleberries or fish had been bought) in one week. And thus it was easy enough to create funds for my periodical transmigrations back into the character of gentleman-tourist. Even the half of five shillings I could not always find means to spend: for in some families, raised above dependence upon daily wages, when I performed any services in the way of letter-writing, I found it impossible at times to force any money at all upon them. Once, in particular, near the small lake of Talyllyn (so written, I believe, but pronounced Taltlyn), in a sequestered part of Merionethshire, I was entertained for upwards of three days by a family of young people, with an affectionate and fraternal kindness that left an impression upon my

opera. She was a stranger; a visitor from some distance; and (I was told in the morning) a Methodist. What she sang, or at least sang last, were the beautiful verses of Shirley, ending—

> Only the actions of the just
> Smell sweet, and blossom in the dust.

This incident caused me to forget and forgive the wicked little chimney.

heart not yet impaired. The family consisted, at that time, of four sisters and three brothers, all grown up, and remarkable for elegance and delicacy of manners. So much beauty, or so much native good breeding and refinement, I do not remember to have seen before or since in any cottage, except once or twice in Westmorland and Devonshire. They spoke English; an accomplishment not often met with in so many members of one Welsh family, especially in villages remote from the high road. Here I wrote, on my first introduction, a letter about prize-money for one of the brothers, who had served on board an English man-of-war; and, more privately, two letters to sweethearts for two of the sisters. They were both interesting in appearance; and one of uncommon loveliness. In the midst of their confusion and blushes, whilst dictating, or rather giving me general instructions, it did not require any great penetration to discover that they wished their letters to be as kind as was consistent with proper maidenly reserve. I contrived so to temper my expressions as to reconcile the gratification of both feelings; and they were as much pleased with the way in which I had given expression to their thoughts as (in their simplicity) they were astonished at my having so readily discovered them. The reception one meets with from the women of a family generally determines the tenor of one's whole entertainment. In this case I had discharged my confidential duties as secretary so much to the general satisfaction, perhaps also amusing them with my conversation, that I was pressed to stay; and pressed with a cordiality which I had little inclination to resist. I slept unavoidably with the brothers, the only unoccupied bed standing in the chamber of the young women: but in all other points they treated me with a respect not usually paid to purses as light as mine; making it evident that my scholarship and courteous demeanour were considered sufficient arguments of gentle blood. Thus I lived with them for three days, and great part of a fourth; and, from the undiminished kindness which they continued to show me, I believe that I might have stayed with them up to this time, if their power had corresponded with their wishes. On the last morning, however, I perceived upon their countenances, as they sat at breakfast, the approach of some unpleasant communication; and soon after one of the brothers explained to me that, on the day before my arrival, their parents had gone to an annual meeting of Methodists, held at Carnarvon, and in the course of that day were expected to return; "and, if they should not be so civil as they ought to be," he begged, on the part of all the young people, that I would not take it amiss. The parents returned with churlish faces, and *"Dym Sasse-nach"* (*no English*) in answer to all my addresses. I saw how matters stood; and so, taking an affectionate leave of my kind and interesting young hosts, I went my way. For, though they spoke warmly to their parents on my behalf, and often excused the manner of the old people by saying that it was "only their way," yet I easily understood that my talent for writing love-letters would do as little to recommend me with two sexagenarian Welsh Methodists as my Greek Sapphics or Alcaics; and what had been hospitality, when offered with the gracious courtesy of my young friends, would become charity, when connected with the harsh demeanour of their parents.

About this time—just when it was becoming daily more difficult to eke out the weekly funds for high-priced inns by the bivouacking system—as if some overmastering fiend, some instinct of migration, sorrowful but irresistible, were driving me forth to wander like the unhappy Io of the Grecian mythus, some oestrus of hidden persecution that bade me fly when no man pursued—not in false hope, for my hopes whispered but a doubtful chance—not in reasonable fear, for all was sweet pastoral quiet and autumnal beauty around me—suddenly I took a fierce resolution to sacrifice my weekly allowance, to slip my anchor, and to throw myself in desperation upon London. Not to make the case more frantic than it really was, let the reader remember what it was that I found grievous in my present position, and upon what possibilities it was that I relied for bettering it. With a more extended knowledge of life than I at that time had, it would not have been so hopeless a speculation for a boy having my accomplishments to launch himself on the boundless ocean of London. I possessed attainments that bore a money value. For instance, as a "*Reader*" to the Press in the field of Greek re-publications, I might perhaps have earned a livelihood. But these chances, which I really had, never occurred to me in the light of useful resources; or, to speak the truth, they were unknown to me: and those which I chiefly relied on were most unlikely to prove available.

But what, meantime, was it that I complained of in the life that I was at present living? It was this: the dilemma proposed to my choice was that, if I *would*—positively *would*—have society, I must live at inns. But, if I reconciled myself to a quiet stationary abode in some village or hamlet, in that case for *me*, so transcendently careless about diet, my weekly guinea would have procured all that I wanted, and in some houses the advantage, quite indispensable to my comfort, of a private sitting-room. Yet even here the expense was most needlessly enhanced by the aristocratic luxuriousness of our English system, which presumes it impossible for a gentleman to sleep in his sitting-room. On this footing, however, I might perhaps have commanded clean and comfortable accommodations in some respectable families, to whom my noiseless habits, and my respectful courtesy to women, would have recommended me as a desirable inmate. But the deadly drawback on this scheme was the utter want of access to books, or (generally speaking) to any intellectual intercourse. I languished all the day through, and all the week through—with nothing whatever, not so much as the county newspaper once in seven days to relieve my mortal ennui.

I have told the reader how inexplicably cheap was the life in poor men's cottages. But this did not affect the prices at the first-class hotels, where only I had any chance of meeting society. Those, and chiefly on the plea that the season was so brief, charged London prices. To meet such prices, it would no longer be possible, as winter came on, to raise one-half the funds by passing half the time in a less costly mode. There was an end of any feasible plan for interleaving days of hardship with days of ease and intellectual luxury. Meantime, whilst this perplexity was resounding in one ear, in the other were continually echoing the kind offers of my Welsh friends, especially the two lawyers, to furnish me with any money which I might think necessary for my visit to London. Twelve guineas, at length, I mentioned as probably enough. This they lent me on the spot. And now, all at once, I was—ready for London.

My farewell to the Principality was in the same unassuming character of pedestrian tourist as that in which I had entered it. *Impedimenta* of any kind—that is, the encumbrances of horse or baggage—I had none even to the last. Where I pleased, and *when* I pleased, I could call a halt. My last halt of any duration was at Oswestry. Mere accident carried me thither, and accident very naturally in so small a town threw me across the path of the very warmest amongst my Welsh friends, who, as it turned out, resided there. He, by mere coercion of kindness, detained me for several days; for denial he would not take. Being as yet unmarried, he could not vivify the other attractions of his most hospitable abode by the reinforcement of female society. His own, however, coming recommended as it did by the graces of a youthful frankness and a kindling intellect, was all-sufficient for the beguiling of the longest day. This Welsh friend was one of many whom I have crossed in life, chained by early accident or by domestic necessity to the calls of a professional service, whilst all the while his whole nature, wild and refractory, ran headlong into intellectual channels that could not be trained into reconciliation with his hourly duties.

His library was already large, and as select as under the ordinary chances of provincial book-collection could be reasonably expected. For generally one-half, at the least, of a young man's library in a provincial town may be characterized as a mere dropping or deposition from local accidents, a casual windfall of fruits stripped and strewed by the rough storms of bankruptcy. In many cases, again, such a provincial library will represent simply that part of the heavy baggage which many a family, on removing to some distant quarter, has shrunk from the cost of transporting— books being amongst the heaviest of household goods. Sometimes also, though more rarely, it happens that —an ancient family, dying out, having unavoidably left to executors the duty of selling every chattel attached to its ancient habits of life—suddenly with meteoric glare there emerges from its hiding-place of centuries some great jewel of literature, a First Folio of the 1623 Shakespeare, an uncastrated *Decamerone*, or other dazzling κειμήλιον. And thus it is that a large provincial library, though naturally and peacefully ac-

cumulated, yet sometimes shows mute evidence of convulsions and household tragedies; speaks is if by
records of storms, and through dim mementoes of half-
forgotten shipwrecks. Real shipwrecks present often
such incoherent libraries on the floors of the hungry
sea. Magnificent is the library that sleeps unvexed by
criticism at the bottom of the ocean, Indian or Atlantic, from the mere annual contributions and keepsakes,
the never-ending *Forget-me-nots*, of mighty English
Indiamen. The Halsewell, with its sad parting between
the captain and his daughters, the Grosvenor, the Win-
terton, the Abergavenny, and scores of vessels on the
same scale, with populations varying by births, deaths,
and marriages, populations large as cities, and rich as
gold mines, capable of factions and rebellions, all and
each have liberally patronized, by the gift of many
Large-Paper copies, that vast submarine Bodleian,
which stands in far less risk from fire than the insolent
Bodleian of the upper world.

This private Oswestry library wore something of the
same wild tumultuary aspect, fantastic and disordi-
nate, but was not for that reason the less attractive;
everything was there that you never expected to meet
anywhere, but certainly not to meet in company; so
that, what between the library and the mercurial conversation of its proprietor, elated by the rare advantage
of fraternal sympathy, I was in danger of finding attractions strong enough to lay me asleep over the proprieties of the case, or even to set me a-dreaming over
imaginary cases. In fact, I had some excuse for doing
so; since I knew very imperfectly the common routine
of my friend's life; and, from *his* lofty Castilian sense
of the obligations imposed by the great goddess Hospitality, I never should have been suffered to guess at the
extent in which I was now gradually and unconsciously
coming daily into collision with the regular calls upon

his time. To ride off, under mask of "business," upon a circuit of a week, would, in *his* eyes, have been *virtually*, as regards the result—meanly and evasively, as regards the mode—to turn me out of his house. He would sooner have died. But in the meantime an accident, which revealed to me the true state of things, or at least revealed a suspicion of it, all at once armed my sense of delicacy against any further lingering. Suddenly and peremptorily I announced my departure— *that*, and the mode of it. For a long time he fought with unaffected zeal against my purpose, as nowise essential to his own free action. But at last, seeing that I was in earnest, he forbore to oppose my plan, contenting himself with guiding and improving its details. My plan had been to walk over the border into England, as far as Shrewsbury (distant from Oswestry, I think, about eighteen miles), and there to ascend any of the heavy stages which would convey me cheaply to Birmingham—the grand focus to which all the routes of England in its main central area converge. Any such plan moved on the assumption that rain would be falling steadily and heavily—a reasonable assumption at the close of November. But, in the possible event of fair weather lasting over four or five days, what should prevent me from traversing the whole distance on foot? It is true that the aristocratic scowl of the landlord might be looked for as a customary salutation at the close of each day's journey; but, unless at solitary posting-houses, this criminal fact of having advanced by base pedestrian methods, known only to patriarchs of older days and to modern *"tramps"* (so they are called in solemn acts of Parliament), is easily expiated and cleansed by distributing your dust, should you fortunately have any to show, amongst the streets that you have invaded as a stranger. Happily the scandal of pedestrianism is in one respect more hopefully situated than that of scrofula or leprosy; it is not in any case written in your face. The man who is guilty of pedestrianism, on entering any town whatever, by the simple artifice of diving into the crowds of those untainted by that guilt, will emerge, for all practical purposes, washed and rebaptized. The landlord, indeed, of any one inn knows that you did not reach *him* on horseback, or in a carriage; but you may have been visiting for weeks at the house of some distinguished citizen, whom it might be dangerous to offend; and you may even be favourably known at some other inn. Else, as a general imputation, undoubtedly pedestrianism, in the estimate of English landlords, carries with it the most awful shadow and shibboleth of the pariah. My Welsh friend knew this, and strongly urged me to take advantage of the public carriages, both on that motive and others. A journey of a hundred and eighty miles, as a pedestrian, would cost me nine or ten days; for which extent the mere amount of expenses at inns would more than defray the fare of the dearest carriage. To this there was no sound reply, except that corresponding expenses would arise, at any rate, on these nine or ten days, wherever I might be—in London, or on the road. However, as it seemed ungracious to offer too obstinate a resistance to suggestions prompted so entirely by consideration for my own comfort, I submitted to my friend's plan in all its details; one being that I should go by the Holyhead Mail, and not by any of the heavy coaches. This stipulation pointed to a novel feature in the machinery of travelling just then emerging. The light coaches charged almost mail prices. But the heavy coaches were at that time beginning to assume a new and dreadful form. Locomotion was so prodigiously on the increase that, in order to meet its demands, the old form of coach (carrying at most six insides) was exchanging itself, on all great roads, for a long, boatlike vehicle, very much resembling our modern detestable *omnibus*, but without our modern improvements. This carriage was called a *"long coach,"* and the passengers, twelve or fourteen insides, sat along the sides; and, as ventilation was little regarded in those days—the very existence of an atmosphere being usually ignored—it followed that the horrors of Governor Holwell's black cage at Calcutta were every night repeated, in smaller proportions, upon every great English road. It was finally agreed that I should leave Oswestry on foot, simply with a view to the best enjoyment of the lovely weather; but that, as the mail passed through Oswestry, my friend should secure a place for me the whole way to London, so as to shut out competitors.

The day on which I left Oswestry (convoyed for nearly five miles by my warmhearted friend) was a day of golden sunshine amongst the closing days of November. As truly as Jessica's moonlight (*Merchant of Venice*), this golden sunshine might be said to *sleep* upon the woods and the fields; so awful was the universal silence, so profound the death-like stillness. It was a day belonging to a brief and pathetic season of farewell summer resurrection, which, under one name or other, is known almost everywhere. In North America it is called the "Indian Summer." In North Germany and Midland Germany it is called the "Old Wives' Summer," and more rarely the "Girls' Summer." It is that last brief resurrection of summer in its most brilliant memorials, a resurrection that has no root in the past nor steady hold upon the future, like the lambent and fitful gleams from an expiring lamp, mimicking what is called the "lightning before death" in sick patients, when close upon their end. There is the feeling of a conflict that has been going on between the lingering powers of summer and the strengthening powers of winter, not unlike that which moves by an-

tagonist forces in some deadly inflammation hurrying forwards through fierce struggles into the final
repose of mortification. For a time the equilibrium has
been maintained between the hostile forces; but at last
the antagonism is overthrown; the victory is accomplished for the powers that fight on the side of death;
simultaneously with the conflict, the pain of conflict
has departed: and thenceforward the gentle process of
collapsing life, no longer fretted by countermovements,
slips away with holy peace into the noiseless deeps of
the Infinite. So sweet, so ghostly, in its soft, golden
smiles, silent as a dream, and quiet as the dying trance
of a saint, faded through all its stages this departing
day, along the whole length of which I bade farewell
for many a year to Wales, and farewell to summer. In
the very aspect and the sepulchral stillness of the motionless day, as solemnly it wore away through morning, noontide, afternoon, to meet the darkness that was
hurrying to swallow up its beauty, I had a fantastic
feeling as though I read the very language of resignation when bending before some irresistible agency. And
at intervals I heard—in how different a key!—the
raving, the everlasting uproar, of that dreadful metropolis which at every step was coming nearer, and
beckoning (as it seemed) to myself for purposes as dim,
for issues as incalculable, as the path of cannon-shots
fired at random and in darkness.

It was not late, but it was at least two hours after
nightfall, when I reached Shrewsbury. Was I not liable
to the suspicion of pedestrianism? Certainly I was:
but, even if my criminality had been more unequivocally attested than it could be under the circumstances, still there is a *locus penitentiæ* in such a case.
Surely a man may repent of *any* crime; and therefore
of pedestrianism. I might have erred, and a court of
pié poudré (dusty foot) might have found the evi-

dences of my crime on my shoes. Yet secretly I might
be forming good resolutions to do so no more. Certainly
it looked like this, when I announced myself as a passenger "booked" for that night's mail. This character
at once installed me as rightfully a guest of the inn,
however profligate a life I might have previously led
as a pedestrian. Accordingly I was received with special courtesy; and it so happened that I was received
with something even like pomp. Four wax-lights carried before me by obedient mutes, these were but ordinary honours, meant (as old experience had instructed
me) for the first engineering step towards effecting a
lodgement upon the stranger's purse. In fact the wax-
lights are used by innkeepers, both abroad and at home,
to "try the range of their guns." If the stranger submits quietly, as a good anti-pedestrian ought surely to
do, and fires no counter gun by way of protest, then he
is recognized at once as passively within range, and
amenable to orders. I have always looked upon this fine
of five or seven shillings (for wax that you do not absolutely need) as a sort of inaugural *honorarium*, entrance-money—what in jails used to be known as *smart*
money—proclaiming me to be a man *comme il faut;*
and no toll in this world of tolls do I pay so cheerfully.
This, meantime, as I have said, was too customary a
form to confer much distinction. The wax-lights, to
use the magnificent Grecian phrase ἐπομπεύε, moved
pompously before me, as the holy—holy fire, the inextinguishable fire and its golden hearth, moved before
Cæsar *semper* Augustus, when he made his official or
ceremonial *avatars*. Yet still this moved along the ordinary channels of glorification: it rolled along ancient
grooves: I might say, indeed, like one of the twelve
Cæsars when dying, *Ut puto, Deus fio* (It's my private
opinion that at this very moment I am turning into a
god) ; but still the metamorphosis was not complete.

That was accomplished when I stepped into the sumptuous room allotted to me. It was a ball-room [1] of noble proportions—lighted, if I chose to issue orders, by three gorgeous chandeliers, not basely wrapped up in paper, but sparkling through all their thickets of crystal branches, and flashing back the soft rays of my tall waxen lights. There were, moreover, two orchestras, which money would have filled within thirty minutes. And, upon the whole, one thing only was wanting— viz. a throne—for the completion of my *apotheosis*.

It might be seven P.M. when first I entered upon my kingdom. About three hours later I rose from my chair, and with considerable interest looked out into the night. For nearly two hours I had heard fierce winds arising; and the whole atmosphere had, by this time, become one vast laboratory of hostile movements in all directions. Such a chaos, such a distracting wilderness of dim sights, and of those awful "sounds that live in darkness" (Wordsworth's *Excursion*), never had I consciously witnessed. Rightly, and by a true instinct, had I made my farewell adieus to summer. All through the day, Wales and her grand mountain ranges—Penmaenmawr, Snowdon, Cader Idris—had divided my thoughts with London. But now rose London—sole, dark, infinite—brooding over the whole capacities of my heart. Other object, other thought, I could not admit. Long before midnight the whole household (with the exception of a solitary waiter) had retired to rest. Two hours, at least, were left to me, after twelve o'clock had struck, for heart-shaking reflections. More than ever I stood upon the brink of a precipice; and the local

[1] "*It was a ball-room*": The explanation of the case was simply that the hotel was under some extensive process of purification, adornment, and, I believe, extension: and, under the accident of being myself on that particular night the sole visitor of the house, I slipped unavoidably into the honours of a semi-regal reception.

circumstances around me deepened and intensified these reflections, impressed upon them solemnity and terror, sometimes even horror. It is all but inconceivable to men of unyielding and callous sensibilities how profoundly others find their reveries modified and overruled by the external characters of the immediate scene around them. Many a suicide that hung dubiously in the balances has been ratified, and carried into summary effect, through the forlorn, soul-revolting aspect of a crazy, dilapidated home. Oftentimes, without extravagance, the whole difference between a mind that spurns life and the same mind reconciled to life turns upon the outside features of that particular domestic scenery which hourly besieges the eyes. I, in this Shrewsbury hotel, naturally contemplated a group of objects tending to far different results. And yet in some respects they agreed.

The unusual dimensions of the rooms, especially their towering height, brought up continually and obstinately, through natural links of associated feelings or images, the mighty vision of London waiting for me afar off. An altitude of nineteen or twenty feet showed itself unavoidably upon an exaggerated scale in some of the smaller side-rooms, meant probably for cards or for refreshments. This single feature of the rooms—their unusual altitude, and the echoing hollowness which had become the exponent of that altitude—this one terrific feature (for terrific it was in the effect), together with crowding and evanescent images of the flying feet that so often had spread gladness through these halls on the wings of youth and hope at seasons when every room rang with music: all this, rising in tumultuous vision, whilst the dead hours of night were stealing along—all around me, household and town, sleeping—and whilst against the windows more and more the storm outside was raving, and to all appearance endlessly growing—threw me into the deadliest condition of nervous emotion under contradictory forces, high over which predominated horror recoiling from that unfathomed abyss in London into which I was now so wilfully precipitating myself. Often I looked out and examined the night. Wild it was beyond all description, and dark as "the inside of a wolf's throat." But at intervals, when the wind, shifting continually, swept in such a direction as to clear away the vast curtain of vapour, the stars shone out, though with a light unusually dim and distant. Still, as I turned inwards to the echoing chambers, or outwards to the wild, wild night, I saw London expanding her visionary gates to receive me, like some dreadful mouth of Acheron (*Acherontis avari*). Thou also, Whispering Gallery! once again in those moments of conscious and wilful desolation didst to my ear utter monitorial sighs. For once again I was preparing to utter an irrevocable word, to enter upon one of those fatally tortuous paths of which the windings can never be unlinked.

Such thoughts, and visions without number corresponding to them, were moving across the *camera obscura* of my fermenting fancy, when suddenly I heard a sound of wheels; which, however, soon died off into some remote quarter. I guessed at the truth—viz. that it was the Holyhead Mail [1] wheeling off on its

---

[1] The Holyhead Mail, depending in its earliest stages upon winds and waters (though not upon tides), could not realize the same exquisite accuracy as mails that moved exclusively upon land. Sixty miles of watery transit between Dublin and Holyhead were performed with miraculous precision. The packets were intrusted by the General post-office to none but post-captains, who had commanded frigates. And the salaries were so high as to make these commands confessedly prizes in nautical life, and objects of keen competition. No evil, therefore, which care, foresight, and professional skill could remedy, was suffered to exist. Yet, after all, baffling winds would

primary duty of delivering its bags at the post-office. In a few minutes it was announced as having changed horses; and off I was to London.

All the mails in the kingdom, with one solitary exception (that of Liverpool), in those days, were so arranged as to reach London early in the morning. Between the hours of four and six A.M., one after the other, according to their station upon the roll, all the mails from the N[orth], the E[ast], the W[est], the S[outh]—whence, according to some curious etymologists, comes the magical word *NEWS*—drove up successively to the post-office, and rendered up their heart-shaking budgets; none earlier than four o'clock, none later than six. I am speaking of days when all things moved slowly. The condition of the roads was then such that, in order to face it, a corresponding build of coaches hyperbolically massive was rendered necessary: the mails were upon principle made so strong as to be the heaviest of all carriages known to the wit or the experience of man; and, from these joint evils of ponderous coaches and roads that were quagmires, it was impossible for even the picked breed of English coach-horses, all bone and blood, to carry forward their huge tonnage at a greater rate than six-and-a-half miles an hour. Consequently, it cost eight-and-twenty massy hours for us, leaving Shrewsbury at two o'clock in the dead of night, to reach the General post-office, and faithfully to deposit upon the threshing-floors of Lombard Street all that weight of love and hatred which Ireland had found herself able to muster through

now and then (especially in three or four weeks *after* the equinox) make it impossible for the very ablest man, under the total defect of steam resources, to keep his time. Six hours, I believe, were allowed by the Post-office for the sixty miles; but at times this must have proved a very inadequate allowance

twenty-four hours in the great depôt of Dublin, by
way of donation to England.

* * *

On reflection, I have done myself some injustice.
Not altogether without a plan had I been from the
first; and in coming along I had matured it. My success in such a plan would turn upon my chance of borrowing on personal security. £200, without counting
any interest upon it, would subdivide into four sums of
£50. Now, what interval was it that divided me from
my majority? Simply an interval of four years. London, I knew or believed, was the dearest of all cities for
three items of expenditure: (1) servants' wages; (2)
lodgings; (3) dairy produce. In other things, London
was often cheaper than most towns. Now, in a London
street, having no pretensions beyond those of decent
respectability, it has always been possible for the last
half-century to obtain two furnished rooms at a weekly
cost of half-a-guinea. This sum (or say £25) deducted
would leave me annually about the same sum for my
other expenses. Too certainly I knew that this would
suffice. If, therefore, I could obtain the £200, my plan
was to withdraw from the knowledge of all my connexions until I should become *mei juris* by course of law.
In such a case, it is true that I must have waived all
the advantages, fancied or real, small or great, from
residence at a university. But, as in fact I never drew
the slightest advantage or emolument from any university, my scheme when realized would have landed
me in the same point which finally I attained by its
failure. The plan was simple enough, but it rested on
the assumption that I could melt the obduracy of
money-lenders. On this point I had both hopes and
fears. But more irritating than either was the *delay*

which eventually I came to recognize as an essential element in the policy of all money-lenders: in that way only can they raise up such claims on behalf of their law-agents as may be fitted for sustaining their zeal.

I lost no time in opening the business which had brought me to London. By ten A.M., an hour when all men of business are presumed to be at their posts, personally or by proxy, I presented myself at the money-lender's office. My name was already known there: for I had, by letters from Wales, containing very plain and very accurate statements of my position in life and my pecuniary expectations (some of which statements it afterwards appeared that he had personally investigated and verified), endeavoured to win his favourable attention.

The money-lender, as it turned out, had one fixed rule of action. He never granted a personal interview to any man; no, not to the most beloved of his clients. One and all—myself, therefore, among the crowd—he referred for information, and for the means of prosecuting any kind of negotiation, to an attorney, who called himself, on most days of the week, by the name of Brunell, but occasionally (might it perhaps be on *red-letter* days?) by the more common name of Brown. Mr. Brunell-Brown, or Brown-Brunell, had located his hearth (if ever he had possessed one); and his household gods (when they were not in the custody of the sheriff), in Greek Street, Soho. The house was not in itself, supposing that its face had been washed now and then, at all disrespectable. But it wore an unhappy countenance of gloom and unsocial fretfulness, due in reality to the long neglect of painting, cleansing, and in some instances of repairing. There were, however, no fractured panes of glass in the windows; and the deep silence which invested the house, not only from the absence of all visitors, but also of those common household functionaries, bakers, butchers, beer-carriers, sufficiently accounted for the desolation, by suggesting an excuse not strictly true—viz. that it might be tenantless. The house already had tenants through the day, though of a noiseless order, and was destined soon to increase them.

Mr. Brown-Brunell, after reconnoitring me through a narrow side-window (such as is often attached to front-doors in London), admitted me cheerfully, and conducted me, as an honoured guest, to his private *officina diplomatum* at the back of the house. From the expression of his face, but much more from the contradictory and self-counteracting play of his features, you gathered in a moment that he was a man who had much to conceal, and much, perhaps, that he would gladly forget. His eye expressed wariness against surprise, and passed in a moment into irrepressible glances of suspicion and alarm. No smile that ever his face naturally assumed but was pulled short up by some freezing counteraction, or was chased by some close-following expression of sadness. One feature there was of relenting goodness and nobleness in Mr. Brunell's character, to which it was that subsequently I myself was most profoundly indebted for an asylum that saved my life. He had the deepest, the most liberal, and unaffected love of knowledge, but, above all, of that specific knowledge which we call literature. His own stormy (and no doubt oftentimes disgraceful) career in life, that had entangled him in perpetual feuds with his fellow-men, he ascribed, with bitter imprecations, to the sudden interruption of his studies consequent upon his father's violent death, and to the necessity which threw him, at a boyish age, upon a professional life in the lower branches of law—threw him, therefore, upon daily temptations, by surrounding him with opportu-

nities for taking advantages not strictly honourable,
before he had formed any fixed principles at all. From
the very first, Mr. Brunell had entered zealously into
such conversations with myself as either gave openings
for reviving his own delightful remembrances of classic authors, or brought up sometimes doubts for solution, sometimes perplexities and cases of intricate construction for illustration and disentanglement.

Hunger-bitten as the house and the household genius seemed, wearing the legend of *Famine* upon every
mantelpiece and "coigne of vantage," and vehemently
protesting, as it must have done through all its echoes,
against the introduction of supernumerary mouths,
nevertheless there was (and, I suppose, of necessity) a
clerk, who bore the name of Pyment, or Pyemont, then
first of all, then last of all, made known to me as a
possible surname. Mr. Pyment had no *alias*—or not to
my knowledge, except, indeed, in the vituperative vocabulary of Mr. Brunell; in which most variegated
nomenclature he bore many scores of opprobrious
names, having no reference whatever to any real habits
of the man, good or bad. At two rooms' distance, Mr.
Brunell always assumed a minute and circumstantial
knowledge of what Pyment was doing then, and what
he was going to do next. All which Pyment gave himself little trouble to answer, unless it happened (as now
and then it did) that he could do so with ludicrous effect. What made the necessity for Pyment was the continual call for "an appearance" to be put in at some of
the subordinate courts in Westminster—courts of conscience, sheriff courts, &c. But it happens often that he
who is most indispensable, and gets through most work
at one hour, becomes a useless burden at another; as the
hardest working reaper seems, in the eyes of an igno-
ramus, on a wet, wintry day, to be a luxurious idler. Of
these ups and downs in Pyment's working life Mr.

Brunell made a most cynical use; making out that Pyment not only did nothing, but also that he created much work for the afflicted Brunell. However, it happened occasionally that the truth vindicated itself, by making a call upon Pyment's physics—aggressive or defensive—that needed an instant attention. "Pyment, I say; this way, Pyment—you're wanted, Pyment." In fact, both were big, hulking men, and had need to be so; for sometimes, whether with good reason or none, clients at the end of a losing suit, or of a suit nominally gained, but unexpectedly laden with heavy expenses, became refractory, showed fight, and gave Pyment reason for saying that at least on this day he had earned his salary by serving an ejectment on a client whom on any other plan it might have been hard to settle with.

But I am anticipating. I go back, therefore, for a few explanatory words, to the day of my arrival in London. How beneficial to me would a little candour have been at that early period! If (which was the simple truth, known to all parties but myself) I had been told that nothing would be brought to a close in less than six months, even assuming the ultimate adoption of my proposals, I should from the first have dismissed all hopes of this nature, as being unsuited to the practicabilities of my situation. It will be seen further on that there was a real and sincere intention of advancing the money wanted. But it was then too late. And universally I believe myself entitled to say that even honourable lawyers will not in a case of this nature move at a faster pace: they will all alike loiter upon varied allegations through six months; and for this reason— that any shorter period, they fancy, will hardly seem to justify, in the eyes of their client, the sum which they find themselves entitled to charge for their trouble and their preliminary correspondence. How much better for both sides, and more honourable, as more frank and free from disguises, that the client should say, "Raise this sum" (of, suppose, £400) "in three weeks —which can be done, if it can be done in three years; and here is a *bonus* of £100. Delay for two months, and I decline the whole transaction." Treated with that sort of openness, how much bodily suffering of an extreme order, and how much of the sickness from hope deferred, should I have escaped! Whereas, under the system (pursued with me as with all clients) of continually refreshing my hopes with new delusions, whiling me on with pretended preparation of deeds, and extorting from me, out of every little remittance I received from old family friends casually met in London, as much as possible for the purchase of imaginary stamps, the result was that I myself was brought to the brink of destruction through pure inanition; whilst, on the other hand, those concerned in these deceptions gained nothing that might not have been gained honourably and rightfully under a system of plain dealing.

As it was, subject to these eternal deceptions, I continued for seven or eight weeks to live most parsimoniously in lodgings. These lodgings, though barely decent in my eyes, ran away with at least two-thirds of my remaining guineas. At length, whilst it was yet possible to reserve a solitary half-guinea towards the more urgent interest of finding daily food, I gave up my rooms, and, stating exactly the circumstances in which I stood, requested permission of Mr. Brunell to make use of his large house as a nightly asylum from the open air. Parliament had not then made it a crime, next door to a felony, for a man to sleep out-of-doors (as some twenty years later was done by our benign legislators) ; as yet *that* was no crime. By the law I came to know sin, and, looking back to the Cambrian hills from distant years, discovered to my surprise what a parliamentary wretch I had been in elder days, when

I slept amongst cows on the open hill-sides. Lawful as
yet this was; but not, therefore, less full of misery.
Naturally, then, I was delighted when Mr. Brunell not
only most readily assented to my request, but begged
of me to come that very night, and turn the house to
account as fully as I possibly could. The cheerfulness
of such a concession brought with it one drawback. I
now regretted that I had not, at a much earlier period,
applied for this liberty; since I might thus have saved
a considerable fund of guineas, applicable, of course, to
all urgent necessities, but at this particular moment to
one of clamorous urgency—viz. the purchase of blankets. O ancient women, daughters of toil and suffering,
amongst all the hardships and bitter inheritances of
flesh that ye are called upon to face, not one—not even
hunger—seems in my eyes comparable to that of
nightly cold. To seek a refuge from cold in bed, and
then, from the thin, gauzy texture of the miserable,
worn-out blankets, "not to sleep a wink," as Wordsworth records of poor old women in Dorsetshire, where
coals, from local causes, were at the very dearest—what
a terrific enemy was *that* for poor old grandmothers to
face in fight! How feelingly I learned at this time, as
heretofore I had learned of the wild hill-sides in Wales,
what an unspeakable blessing is that of warmth! A
more killing curse there does not exist for man or woman than that bitter combat between the weariness that
prompts sleep and the keen, searching cold that forces
you from the first access of sleep to start up horror-
stricken, and to seek warmth vainly in renewed exercise, though long since fainting under fatigue. However, even without blankets, it was a fine thing to have
an asylum from the open air, and to be assured of this
asylum as long as I was likely to want it.

Towards nightfall I went down to Greek Street, and
found, on taking possession of my new quarters, that

the house already contained one single inmate—a poor,
friendless child, apparently ten years old; but she
seemed hunger-bitten; and sufferings of that sort often
make children look older than they are. From this forlorn child I learned that she had slept and lived there
alone for some time before I came; and great joy the
poor creature expressed when she found that I was in
future to be her companion through the hours of darkness. The house could hardly be called large—that is,
it was not large on each separate storey; but, having
four storeys in all, it was large enough to impress vividly the sense of its echoing loneliness; and, from the
want of furniture, the noise of the rats made a prodigious uproar on the staircase and hall; so that, amidst
the real fleshly ills of cold and hunger, the forsaken
child had found leisure to suffer still more from the
self-created one of ghosts. Against these enemies I
could promise her protection; human companionship
was in itself protection; but of other and more needful
aid I had, alas! little to offer. We lay upon the floor,
with a bundle of law-papers for a pillow, but with no
other covering than a large horseman's cloak; afterwards, however, we discovered in a garret an old sofa-
cover, a small piece of rug, and some fragments of other
articles, which added a little to our comfort. The poor
child crept close to me for warmth, and for security
against her ghostly enemies. When I was not more than
usually ill, I took her into my arms, so that, in general,
she was tolerably warm, and often slept when I could
not; for, during the last two months of my sufferings, I
slept much in the daytime, and was apt to fall into
transient dozings at all hours. But my sleep distressed
me more than my watching; for, besides the tumultu-
ousness of my dreams (which were only not so awful
as those which I shall have hereafter to describe as produced by opium), my sleep was never more than what

is called *dog-sleep;* so that I could hear myself moaning; and very often I was awakened suddenly by my own voice. About this time, a hideous sensation began to haunt me as soon as I fell into a slumber, which has since returned upon me, at different periods of my life —viz. a sort of twitching (I knew not where, but apparently about the region of the stomach), which compelled me violently to throw out my feet for the sake of relieving it. This sensation coming on as soon as I began to sleep, and the effort to relieve it constantly awaking me, at length I slept only from exhaustion; and, through increasing weakness (as I said before), I was constantly falling asleep and constantly awaking. Too generally the very attainment of any deep repose seemed as if mechanically linked to some fatal necessity of self-interruption. It was as though a cup were gradually filled by the sleepy overflow of some natural fountain, the fulness of the cup expressing symbolically the completeness of the rest: but then, in the next stage of the process, it seemed as though the rush and torrent-like babbling of the redundant waters, when running over from every part of the cup, interrupted the slumber which in their earlier stage of silent gathering they had so naturally produced. Such and so regular in its swell and its collapse—in its tardy growth and its violent dispersion—did this endless alternation of stealthy sleep and stormy awaking travel through stages as natural as the increments of twilight, or the kindlings of the dawn: no rest that was not a prologue to terror; no sweet tremulous pulses of restoration that did not suddenly explode through rolling clamours of fiery disruption.

Meantime, the master of the house sometimes came in upon us suddenly, and very early; sometimes not till ten o'clock; sometimes not at all. He was in constant fear of arrest. Improving on the plan of Cromwell, every night he slept in a different quarter of London; and I observed that he never failed to examine, through a private window, the appearance of those who knocked at the door, before he would allow it to be opened. He breakfasted alone; indeed, his tea equipage would hardly have admitted of his hazarding an invitation to a second person, any more than the quantity of esculent *material*, which, for the most part, was little more than a roll, or a few biscuits, purchased on his road from the place where he had slept. Or, if he *had* asked a party, as I once learnedly observed to him, the several members of it must have *stood* in the relation to each other (not *sat* in any relation whatever) of succession, and not of co-existence; in the relation of parts of time, and not of the parts of space. During his breakfast, I generally contrived a reason for lounging in; and, with an air of as much indifference as I could assume, took up such fragments as might chance to remain; sometimes, indeed, none at all remained. In doing this, I committed no robbery, except upon Mr. Brunell himself, who was thus obliged, now and then, to send out at noon for an extra biscuit; but he, through channels subsequently explained, was repaid a thousand-fold; and, as to the poor child, *she* was never admitted into his study (if I may give that name to his chief depository of parchments, law-writings, &c.); that room was to her the Bluebeard room of the house, being regularly locked on his departure to dinner, about six o'clock, which usually was his final departure for the day. Whether this child were an illegitimate daughter of Mr. Brunell, or only a servant, I could not ascertain; she did not herself know; but certainly she was treated altogether as a menial servant. No sooner did Mr. Brunell make his appearance than she went below-stairs, brushed his shoes, coat, &c.; and, except when she was summoned to run upon some errand, she

never emerged from the dismal Tartarus of the kitch-
ens to the upper air until my welcome knock towards
nightfall called up her little trembling footsteps to the
front-door. Of her life during the daytime, however, I
knew little but what I gathered from her own account
at night; for, as soon as the hours of business commenced, I saw that my absence would be acceptable;
and, in general, therefore, I went off and sat in the
parks or elsewhere until the approach of twilight.

But who, and what, meantime, was the master of the
house himself? Reader, he was one of those anomalous
practitioners in lower departments of the law who, on
prudential reasons, or from necessity, deny themselves
all indulgence in the luxury of too delicate a conscience. In many walks of life a conscience is a more
expensive encumbrance than a wife or a carriage; and,
as people talk of "laying down" their carriages, so I
suppose my friend Mr. Brunell had "laid down" his
conscience for a time; meaning, doubtless, to resume it
as soon as he could afford it. He was an advertising attorney, who continually notified to the public, through
the morning papers, that he undertook to raise loans
for approved parties in what would generally be regarded as desperate cases—viz. where there was nothing better than *personal* security to offer. But, as he
took good care to ascertain that there were ample funds
in reversion to be counted on, or near connexions that
would not suffer the family name to be dishonoured,
and as he insured the borrower's life over a sufficient
period, the risk was not great; and even of this the
whole rested upon the actual money-lender, who stood
aloof in the background, and never revealed himself to
clients in his proper person, transacting all affairs
through his proxies learned in the law—Mr. Brunell
or others. The inner economy of such a man's daily life
would present a monstrous picture. Even with my lim-

ited opportunities for observing what went on, I saw scenes of intrigue and complex chicanery at which I sometimes smile to this day, and at which I smiled then in spite of my misery. My situation, however, at that time, gave me little experience, in my own person, of any qualities in Mr. Brunell's character but such as did him honour; and of his whole strange composition I ought to forget everything, but that towards me he was obliging, and, to the extent of his power, generous.

That power was not, indeed, very extensive. However, in common with the rats, I sat rent free; and, as Dr. Johnson has recorded that he never but once in his life had as much wall-fruit as he wished, so let me be grateful that, on that single occasion, I had as large a choice of rooms, or even of apartments, in a London mansion—viz., as I am now at liberty to add, at the north-west corner of Greek Street, being the house on that side the street nearest to Soho Square—as I could possibly desire. Except the Bluebeard room, which the poor child believed to be permanently haunted, and which, besides, was locked, all others, from the attics to the cellars, were at our service. "The world was all before us," and we pitched our tent for the night in any spot we might fancy.

This house I have described as roomy and respectable. It stands in a conspicuous situation, and in a well-known part of London. Many of my readers will have passed it, I doubt not, within a few hours of reading this. For myself, I never fail to visit it when accident draws me to London. About ten o'clock this very night (August 15, 1821, being my birthday), I turned aside from my evening walk along Oxford Street, in order to take a glance at it. It is now in the occupation of some family, apparently respectable. The windows are no longer coated by a paste composed of ancient soot and superannuated rain; and the whole exterior no longer wears an aspect of gloom. By the lights in the front drawing-room, I observed a domestic party, assembled, perhaps, at tea, and apparently cheerful and gay— marvellous contrast, in my eyes, to the darkness, cold, silence, and desolation, of that same house nineteen years ago, when its nightly occupants were one famishing scholar and a poor, neglected child. Her, by the bye, in after years, I vainly endeavoured to trace. Apart from her situation, she was not what would be called an interesting child. She was neither pretty, nor quick in understanding, nor remarkably pleasing in manners. But, thank God! even in those years I needed not the embellishments of elegant accessories to conciliate my affections. Plain human nature, in its humblest and most homely apparel, was enough for me; and I loved the child because she was my partner in wretchedness. If she is now living, she is probably a mother, with children of her own; but, as I have said, I could never trace her.

This I regret; but another person there was, at that time, whom I have since sought to trace with far deeper earnestness, and with far deeper sorrow at my failure. This person was a young woman, and one of that unhappy class who belong to the outcasts and pariahs of our female population. I feel no shame, nor have any reason to feel it, in avowing that I was then on familiar and friendly terms with many women in that unfortunate condition. Smile not, reader too carelessly facile! Frown not, reader too unseasonably austere! Little call was there here either for smiles or frowns. A penniless schoolboy could not be supposed to stand within the range of such temptations; besides that, according to the ancient Latin proverb, *"sine Cerere et Baccho,"* &c. These unhappy women, to me, were simply sisters in calamity; and sisters amongst whom, in as large measure as amongst any other equal number of persons commanding more of the world's respect, were to be found humanity, disinterested generosity, courage that would not falter in defence of the helpless, and fidelity that would have scorned to take bribes for betraying. But the truth is that at no time of my life have I been a person to hold myself polluted by the touch or approach of any creature that wore a human shape. I cannot suppose, I will not believe, that any creatures wearing the form of man or woman are so absolutely rejected and reprobate outcasts that merely to talk with them inflicts pollution. On the contrary, from my very earliest youth, it has been my pride to converse familiarly, *more Socratico*, with all human beings—man, woman, and child—that chance might fling in my way; for a philosopher should not see with the eyes of the poor limitary creature calling himself a man of the world, filled with narrow and self-regarding prejudices of birth and education, but should look upon himself as a catholic creature, and as standing in an equal relation to high and low, to educated and uneducated, to the guilty and the innocent. Being myself, at that time, of necessity a peripatetic, or a walker of the streets, I naturally fell in more frequently with those female peripatetics who are technically called street-walkers. Some of these women had occasionally taken my part against watchmen who wished to drive me off the steps of houses where I was sitting; others had protected me against more serious aggressions. But one amongst them—the one on whose account I have at all introduced this subject—yet no! let me not class thee, O noble-minded Ann ——, with that order of women; let me find, if it be possible, some gentler name to designate the condition of her to whose bounty and compassion—ministering to my necessities when all the world stood aloof from me—I owe it that I am at this time alive. For many weeks I had walked, at nights, with this poor friendless girl up and down Oxford Street, or had rested with her on steps and under the shelter of porticos.

She could not be so old as myself: she told me, indeed, that she had not completed her sixteenth year. By such questions as my interest about her prompted, I had gradually drawn forth her simple history. Hers was a case of ordinary occurrence (as I have since had reason to think), and one in which, if London beneficence had better adapted its arrangements to meet it, the power of the law might oftener be interposed to protect and to avenge. But the stream of London charity flows in a channel which, though deep and mighty, is yet noiseless and underground—not obvious or readily accessible to poor, houseless wanderers; and it cannot be denied that the outside air and framework of society in London, as in all vast capitals, is unavoidably harsh, cruel, and repulsive. In any case, however, I saw that part of her injuries might have been redressed; and I urged her often and earnestly to lay her complaint before a magistrate. Friendless as she was, I assured her that she would meet with immediate attention; and that English justice, which was no respecter of persons, would speedily and amply avenge her on the brutal ruffian who had plundered her little property. She promised me often that she would; but she delayed taking the steps I pointed out, from time to time; for she was timid and dejected to a degree which showed how deeply sorrow had taken hold of her young heart; and perhaps she thought justly that the most upright judge and the most righteous tribunals could do nothing to repair her heaviest wrongs. Something, however, would perhaps have been done; for it had been settled between us at length (but, unhappily, on the very last time but one that I was ever to see her) that in a day or two I, accompanied by her, should state her case to a magistrate. This little service it was destined, however, that I should never realize.

Meantime, that which she rendered to me, and which was greater than I could ever have repaid her, was this: One night, when we were pacing slowly along Oxford Street, and after a day when I had felt unusually ill and faint, I requested her to turn off with me into Soho Square. Thither we went; and we sat down on the steps of a house, which to this hour I never pass without a pang of grief, and an inner act of homage to the spirit of that unhappy girl, in memory of the noble act which she there performed. Suddenly, as we sat, I grew much worse. I had been leaning my head against her bosom, and all at once I sank from her arms, and fell backwards on the steps. From the sensations I then had, I felt an inner conviction of the liveliest kind that, without some powerful and reviving stimulus, I should either have died on the spot, or should, at least, have sunk to a point of exhaustion from which all re-ascent, under my friendless circumstances, would soon have become hopeless. Then it was, at this crisis of my fate, that my poor orphan companion, who had herself met with little but injuries in this world, stretched out a saving hand to me. Uttering a cry of terror, but without a moment's delay, she ran off into Oxford Street, and, in less time than could be imagined, returned to me with a glass of port-wine and spices, that acted upon my empty stomach (which at that time would have rejected all solid food) with an instantaneous power of restoration; and for this glass the generous girl, without a murmur, paid out of her own humble purse, at a time, be it remembered, when she had scarcely wherewithal to purchase the bare necessaries of life, and when she could have no reason to expect that I should ever be able to reimburse her. O youthful benefactress! how often in succeeding years, standing in solitary places, and thinking of thee with grief of heart and perfect love—how often have I wished that, as in ancient times the curse of a father was believed to have a supernatural power, and to pursue its object with a fatal necessity of self-fulfilment, even so the benediction of a heart oppressed with gratitude might have a like prerogative; might have power given it from above to chase, to haunt, to waylay, to pursue thee into the central darkness of a London brothel, or (if it were possible) even into the darkness of the grave, there to awaken thee with an authentic message of peace and forgiveness, and of final reconciliation!

Some feelings, though not deeper or more passionate, are more tender than others; and often when I walk, at this time, in Oxford Street by dreamy lamp-light, and hear those airs played on a common street-organ which years ago solaced me and my dear youthful companion, I shed tears, and muse with myself at the mysterious dispensation which so suddenly and so critically separated us for ever. How it happened, the reader will understand from what remains of this introductory narration.

Soon after the period of the last incident I have recorded, I met in Albemarle Street a gentleman of his late Majesty's household. This gentleman had received hospitalities, on different occasions, from my family; and he challenged me upon the strength of my family likeness. I did not attempt any disguise, but answered his questions ingenuously; and, on his pledging his word of honour that he would not betray me to my guardians, I gave him my real address in Greek Street. The next day I received from him a ten-pound banknote. The letter enclosing it was delivered, with other letters of business, to the attorney; but, though his look and manner informed me that he suspected its contents, he gave it up to me honourably, and without demur.

This present, from the particular service to which much of it was applied, leads me naturally to speak again of the original purpose which had allured me up to London, and which I had been without intermission prosecuting through Mr. Brunell from the first day of my arrival in London.

In so mighty a world as London, it will surprise my readers that I should not have found some means of staving off the last extremities of penury; and it will strike them that two resources, at least, must have been open to me: viz. either to seek assistance from the friends of my family, or to turn my youthful accomplishments, such as they were, into some channel of pecuniary emolument. As to the first course, I may observe, generally, that what I dreaded beyond all other evils was the chance of being reclaimed by my guardians; not doubting that whatever power the law gave them would have been enforced against me to the utmost; that is, to the extremity of forcibly restoring me to the school which I had quitted—a restoration which, as it would, in my eyes, have been a dishonour even if submitted to voluntarily, could not fail, when extorted from me in contempt and defiance of my own known wishes and earnest resistance, to have proved a humiliation worse to me than death, and which would, indeed, have terminated in death. I was, therefore, shy enough of applying for assistance even in those quarters where I was sure of receiving it, if at any risk of furnishing my guardians with a clue for tracing me. My father's friends, no doubt, had been many, and were scattered all over the kingdom; but, as to London in particular, though a large section of these friends would certainly be found there, yet (as full ten years had passed since his death) I knew very few of them

even by name; and, never having seen London before
—except once, in my fifteenth year, for a few hours—
I knew not the address of even those few. To this mode
of gaining help, therefore, in part the difficulty, but
much more the danger which I have mentioned, habitually indisposed me. In regard to the other mode—that
of turning any talents or knowledge that I might possess to a lucrative use—I now feel half inclined to join
my reader in wondering that I should have overlooked
it. As a corrector of Greek proofs (if in no other way),
I might surely have gained enough for my slender
wants. Such an office as this I could have discharged
with an exemplary and punctual accuracy that would
soon have gained me the confidence of my employers.
And there was this great preliminary advantage in
giving such a direction to my efforts, that the intellectual dignity and elegance associated with all ministerial services about the press would have saved my
pride and self-respect from mortification. In an extreme case, such as mine had now become, I should not
have absolutely disdained the humble station of
"devil." A subaltern situation in a service inherently
honourable is better than a much higher situation in a
service pointing to ultimate objects that are mean or
ignoble. I am, indeed, not sure that I could adequately
have discharged the functions of this office. To the perfection of the diabolic character I fear that patience is
one of the indispensable graces; more, perhaps, than I
should be found on trial to possess for dancing attendance upon crotchety authors, superstitiously fastidious
in matters of punctuation. But why talk of my qualifications? Qualified or not, where could I obtain such an
office? For it must not be forgotten that even a diabolic
appointment requires interest. Towards *that* I must
first of all have an introduction to some respectable
publisher; and this I had no means of obtaining. To

say the truth, however, it had never once occurred to me to think of literary labours as a source of profit. No mode sufficiently speedy of obtaining money had ever suggested itself but that of borrowing it on the strength of my future claims and expectations. This mode I sought by every avenue to compass; and amongst other persons I applied to a Jew named D——.[1]

[1] At this period (autumn of 1856), when thirty-five years have elapsed since the first publication of these memoirs, reasons of delicacy can no longer claim respect for concealing the Jew's name, or at least the name which he adopted in his dealings with the Gentiles. I say, therefore, without scruple, that the name was Dell: and some years later it was one of the names that came before the House of Commons in connexion with something or other (I have long since forgotten *what*) growing out of the parliamentary movement against the Duke of York, in reference to Mrs. Clark, &c. Like all the other Jews with whom I have had negotiations, he was frank and honourable in his mode of conducting business. What he promised he performed; and, if his terms were high, as naturally they could not *but* be, to cover his risks, he avowed them from the first.

To this same Mr. Dell, by the way, some eighteen months afterwards, I applied again on the same business; and, dating at that time from a respectable college, I was fortunate enough to win his serious attention to my proposals. My necessities had not arisen from any extravagance or youthful levities (these my habits forbade), but simply from the vindictive malice of my guardian, who, when he found himself no longer able to prevent me from going to the university, had, as a parting token of his regard, refused to sign an order for granting me a shilling beyond the allowance made to me at school —viz. £100 per annum. Upon this sum it was, in my time (*i.e.* in the first decennium of this century), barely possible to have lived at college; and not possible to a man who, though above the affectation of ostentatious disregard for money, and without any expensive tastes, confided, nevertheless, rather too much in servants, and did not delight in the petty details of minute economy. I soon, therefore, became embarrassed: in a movement of impatience, instead of candidly avowing my condition to my mother, or to some one of the guardians, more than one of whom would have advanced me the £250 wanted

To this Jew, and to other advertising money-lenders, I had introduced myself, with an account of my expectations; which account they had little difficulty in ascertaining to be correct. The person there mentioned as the second son of —— was found to have all the claims (or more than all) that I had stated: but one question still remained, which the faces of the Jews pretty significantly suggested—was I that person? This doubt had never occurred to me as a possible one; I had rather feared, whenever my Jewish friends scrutinized me keenly, that I might be too well known to be that person, and that some scheme might be passing in their minds for entrapping me and selling me to my guardians. It was strange to me to find my own self, *materialiter* considered (so I expressed it, for I doted on logical accuracy of distinction), suspected of counterfeiting my own self, *formaliter* considered. However, to satisfy their scruples, I took the only course in my power. Whilst I was in Wales, I had received various letters from young friends; these I produced, for I carried them constantly in my pocket. Most of these letters were from the Earl of Altamont, who was at that time, and had been for some years back, amongst my confidential friends. These were dated from Eton. I had

(not in his legal character of guardian, but as a private friend), I was so foolish as to engage in a voluminous negotiation with the Jew, and was put in possession of the sum I asked for, on the "regular" terms of paying seventeen and a-half per cent by way of annuity on all the money furnished; Israel, on his part, graciously resuming no more than about ninety guineas of the said money, on account of an attorney's bill (for what services, to whom rendered, and when—whether at the siege of Jerusalem, or at the building of the Second Temple —I have not yet discovered). How many perches this bill measured I really forget; but I still keep it in a cabinet of natural curiosities.

also some from the Marquis of Sligo, his father; who, though absorbed in agricultural pursuits, yet having been an Etonian himself, and as good a scholar as a nobleman needs to be, still retained an affection for classical studies and for youthful scholars. He had, accordingly, from the time that I was fifteen, corresponded with me—sometimes upon the great improvements which he had made, or was meditating, in the counties of Mayo and Sligo, since I had been there; sometimes upon the merits of a Latin poet; at other times, suggesting subjects on which he fancied that I could write verses myself, or breathe poetic inspiration into the mind of my once familiar companion, his son.

On reading the letters, one of my Jewish friends agreed to furnish two or three hundred pounds on my personal security, provided I could persuade the young earl—who was, by the way, not older than myself—to guarantee the payment on our joint coming of age; the Jew's final object being, as I now suppose, not the trifling profit he could expect to make by me, but the prospect of establishing a connexion with my noble friend, whose great expectations were well known to him. In pursuance of this proposal on the part of the Jew, about eight or nine days after I had received the £10, I prepared to visit Eton. Nearly three guineas of the money I had given to my money-lending friend in the background; or, more accurately, I had given that sum to Mr. Brunell, *alias* Brown, as representing Mr. Dell, the Jew; and a smaller sum I had given directly to himself, on his own separate account. What he alleged in excuse for thus draining my purse at so critical a moment was that stamps must be bought, in order that the writings might be prepared whilst I was away from London. I thought in my heart that he was lying, but I did not wish to give him any excuse for charging his own delays upon me. About fifteen shillings I had employed in re-establishing (though in a very humble way) my dress. Of the remainder, I gave one-quarter (something more than a guinea) to Ann, meaning, on my return, to have divided with her whatever might remain.

These arrangements made, soon after six o'clock, on a dark winter evening, I set off, accompanied by Ann, towards Piccadilly; for it was my intention to go down as far as the turn to Salt Hill and Slough on the Bath or Bristol mail. Our course lay through a part of the town which has now totally disappeared, so that I can no longer retrace its ancient boundaries—having been replaced by Regent Street and its adjacencies. *Swallow Street* is all that I remember of the names superseded by this large revolutionary usurpation. Having time enough before us, however, we bore away to the left, until we came into Golden Square. There, near the corner of Sherrard Street, we sat down, not wishing to part in the tumult and blaze of Piccadilly. I had told Ann of my plans some time before, and now I assured her again that she should share in my good fortune, if I met with any, and that I would never forsake her, as soon as I had power to protect her. This I fully intended, as much from inclination as from a sense of duty; for, setting aside gratitude (which in any case must have made me her debtor for life), I loved her as affectionately as if she had been my sister; and at this moment with sevenfold tenderness, from pity at witnessing her extreme dejection. I had apparently most reason for dejection, because I was leaving the saviour of my life; yet I, considering the shock my health had received, was cheerful and full of hope. She, on the contrary, who was parting with one who had had little means of serving her, except by kindness and brotherly treatment, was overcome by sorrow, so that, when I kissed her at our final farewell, she put her arms about my neck, and wept, without speaking a word. I hoped to return in a week, at furthest, and I agreed with her that, on the fifth night from that, and every night afterwards, she should wait for me, at six o'clock, near the bottom of Great Titchfield Street; which had formerly been our customary haven of rendezvous, to prevent our missing each other in the great Mediterranean of Oxford Street. This, and other measures of precaution, I took; one, only, I forgot. She had either never told me, or (as a matter of no great interest) I had forgotten, her surname. It is a general practice, indeed, with girls of humble rank in her unhappy condition, not (as novel-reading women of higher pretensions) to style themselves *Miss Douglas*, *Miss Montague*, &c., but simply by their Christian names, *Mary*, *Jane*, *Frances*, &c. Her surname, as the surest means of tracing her, I ought now to have inquired; but the truth is, having no reason to think that our meeting again could, in consequence of a short interruption, be more difficult or uncertain than it had been for so many weeks, I scarcely for a moment adverted to it as necessary, or placed it amongst my memoranda against this parting interview; and, my final anxieties being spent in comforting her with hopes, and in pressing upon her the necessity of getting some medicine for a violent cough with which she was troubled, I wholly forgot this precaution until it was too late to recall her.

When I reached the Gloucester Coffee-house in Piccadilly, at which, in those days, all the western mails stopped for a few minutes in going out of London, it was already a quarter-of-an-hour past eight o'clock; the Bristol Mail was on the point of going off, and I mounted on the outside. The fine fluent motion [1] of this mail soon laid me asleep. It is somewhat remarkable that the first easy or refreshing sleep which I had enjoyed for some months was on the outside of a mail-coach—a bed which, at this day, I find rather an uneasy one. Connected with this sleep was a little incident which served, as hundreds of others did at that time, to convince me how easily a man who has never been in any great distress may pass through life without knowing in his own person, and experimentally testing, the possible goodness of the human heart, or, as unwillingly I add, its possible churlishness. So thick a curtain of *manners* is drawn over the features and expression of men's natures that, to the ordinary observer, the two extremities, and the infinite field of varieties which lie between them, are all confounded under one neutral disguise. The case was this: For the first four or five miles out of London, I annoyed my fellow-passenger on the roof by occasionally falling against him when the coach gave a lurch; and, indeed, if the road had been less smooth and level than it was, I should have fallen off from weakness. Of this annoyance he complained heavily; as, perhaps, in the same circumstances, most people would. He expressed his complaint, however, more morosely than the occasion seemed to warrant; and, if I had parted with him at that moment, I should have thought of him as a surly and almost brutal fellow. Still I was conscious that I had given him some cause for complaint; and therefore I apologized, assuring him that I would do what I could to avoid falling

---

[1] The Bristol Mail was at that time the best appointed in the kingdom—owing that advantage, first of all, to an unusually good road—and this advantage it shared with the Bath Mail (their route being exactly the same for a hundred and five miles); but, secondly, it had the separate advantage of an *extra* sum for expenses subscribed by the Bristol merchants.

asleep for the future; and, at the same time, in as few
words as possible, I explained to him that I was ill,
and in a weak state from long suffering, and that I
could not afford to take an inside place. The man's
manner changed upon hearing this explanation in an
instant: and, when I next woke for a minute, from
the noise and lights of Hounslow (for, in spite of my
efforts, I had again fallen asleep within two minutes),
I found that he had put his arm round me to protect
me from falling off; and for the rest of my journey he
behaved to me with the gentleness of a woman. And
this was the more kind, as he could not have known
that I was not going the whole way to Bath or Bristol.
Unfortunately, indeed, I *did* go further than I intended; for so genial and refreshing was my sleep, being in the open air, that, upon the sudden pulling up
of the mail (possibly at a post-office), I found that we
had reached some place six or seven miles to the west
of Salt Hill. Here I alighted; and, during the half-
minute that the mail stopped, I was entreated by my
friendly companion (who, from the transient glimpse
I had of him under the glaring lights of Piccadilly,
might be a respectable upper servant) to go to bed
without delay. This, under the feeling that some consideration was due to one who had done me so seasonable a service, I promised, though with no intention of
doing so; and, in fact, I immediately moved forward
on foot.

It must then have been nearly eleven; but so slowly
did I creep along that I heard a clock in a cottage strike
four as I was on the point of turning down the road
from Slough to Eton. The air and the sleep had both
refreshed me; but I was weary, nevertheless. I remember a thought (obvious enough, and pointedly expressed by a Roman poet) which gave me some consolation, at that moment, under my poverty. There had

been, some weeks before, a murder committed on Hounslow Heath, which at that time was really a heath, entirely unenclosed, and exhibiting a sea-like expanse in all directions, except one. I cannot be mistaken when I say that the name of the murdered person was *Steele*, and that he was the owner of a lavender plantation in that neighbourhood.[1] Every step of my regress (for I now walked with my face towards London) was bringing me nearer to the heath; and it naturally occurred to me that I and the accursed murderer, if he were that night abroad, might, at every instant, be unconsciously approaching each other through the darkness; in which case, said I, supposing myself—instead of being little better than an outcast,

Lord of my learning, and no land beside—

like my friend Lord Altamont, heir, by general repute, to £30,000 per annum, what a panic should I be under at this moment about my throat! Indeed, it was not likely that Lord Altamont should ever be in my situation; but, nevertheless, the spirit of the remark

[1] Two men, Holloway and Haggerty, were long afterwards convicted, upon very questionable evidence, as the perpetrators of this murder. The main testimony against them was that of a Newgate turnkey, who had imperfectly overheard a conversation between the two men. The current impression was that of great dissatisfaction with the evidence; and this impression was strengthened by the pamphlet of an acute lawyer, exposing the unsoundness and incoherency of the statements relied upon by the court. They were executed, however, in the teeth of all opposition. And, as it happened that an enormous wreck of life occurred at the execution (not fewer, I believe, than sixty persons having been trampled under foot by the unusual pressure of some brewers' draymen forcing their way with linked arms to the space below the drop), this tragedy was regarded for many years by a section of the London mob as a providential judgement upon the passive metropolis.

remains true, that vast power and possessions make a man shamefully afraid of dying; and I am convinced that many of the most intrepid adventurers who, being poor, enjoy the full use of their natural energies, would, if at the very instant of going into action news were brought to them that they had unexpectedly succeeded to an estate in England of £50,000 a-year, feel their dislike to bullets furiously sharpened,[1] and their efforts at self-possession proportionably difficult. So true it is, in the language of a wise man, whose own experience had made him acquainted equally with good and evil fortune, that riches are better fitted

> *To slacken virtue, and abate her edge,*
> *Than prompt her to do aught merit praise.*
> *—Paradise Regained*

I dally with my subject, because, to myself, the remembrance of these times is profoundly interesting. But my reader shall not have any further cause to complain; for now I hasten to its close. In the road between Slough and Eton I fell asleep; and, just as the morning began to dawn, I was awakened by the voice of a man standing over me, and apparently studying my *physics*, whilst to me—upon so sudden an introduction to him in so suspicious a situation—his *morals* naturally suggested a more interesting subject of inquiry. I know not what he was. He was an ill-looking fellow, but not, therefore, of necessity, an ill-meaning fellow; or, if he were, I suppose he thought that no per-

[1] It will be objected that many men, of the highest rank and wealth, have, notwithstanding, in our own day, as well as throughout our history, been amongst the foremost in courting danger on the field of battle. True; but this is not the case supposed. Long familiarity with power and with wealth has, to them, deadened their effect and attractions.

son sleeping out-of-doors in winter could be worth robbing. In which conclusion, however, as it regarded myself, I have the honour to assure him, supposing him ever to find himself amongst my readers, that he was entirely mistaken. I was not sorry at his disturbance, as it roused me to pass through Eton before people were generally astir. The night had been heavy and misty; but towards the morning it had changed to a slight frost, and the trees were now covered with rime.

I slipped through Eton unobserved; washed myself, and as far as possible adjusted my dress, at a little public-house in Windsor; and, about eight o'clock, went down towards the precincts of the college, near which were congregated the houses of the "Dames." On my road I met some junior boys, of whom I made inquiries. An Etonian is always a gentleman; and, in spite of my shabby habiliments, they answered me civilly. My friend Lord Altamont was gone to Jesus College, Cambridge. "*Ibi omnis effusus labor!*" I had, however, other friends at Eton; but it is not to all who wear that name in prosperity that a man is willing to present himself in distress. On recollecting myself, however, I asked for the Earl of Desart,[1] to whom (though my acquaintance with him was not so intimate as with some others) I should not have shrunk from presenting myself under any circumstances. He was still at Eton, though, I believe, on the wing for Cambridge. I called, was received kindly, and asked to breakfast.

[1] I had known Lord Desart, the eldest son of a very large family, some years earlier, when bearing the title of Lord Castlecuffe. Cuffe was the family name; and I believe that they traced their descent from a person of some historic interest—viz. that Cuffe who was secretary to the unhappy Earl of Essex during his treasonable *émeute* against the government of Queen Elizabeth

Lord Desart placed before me a magnificent breakfast. It was really such; but in my eyes it seemed trebly magnificent from being the first regular meal, the first "good man's table," that I had sat down to for months. Strange to say, I could scarcely eat anything. On the day when I first received my ten-pound bank-note, I had gone to a baker's shop and bought a couple of rolls; this very shop I had some weeks before surveyed with an eagerness of desire which it was humiliating to recollect. I remembered the story (which, however, I now believed to be a falsehood) about Otway,[1] and feared that there might be danger in eating too rapidly. But there was no cause for alarm; my appetite was utterly gone, and I nauseated food of every kind. This effect, from eating what approached to a meal, I continued to feel for weeks. On the present occasion, at Lord Desart's table, I found myself not at all better than usual; and, in the midst of luxuries, appetite I had none. I had, however, unfortunately, at all times a craving for wine: I explained my situation, therefore, to Lord Desart, and gave him a short account of my late sufferings; with which he expressed deep sympathy, and called for wine. This gave me instantaneous relief and immoderate pleasure; and on all occasions, when I had an opportunity, I never failed to drink wine. Obvious it is, however, that this indulgence in wine would continue to strengthen my malady, for the tone of my stomach was apparently quite sunk; but, by a better regimen, it might sooner, and, perhaps, effectually, have been restored.

I hope that it was not from this love of wine that I lingered in the neighbourhood of my Eton friends; I persuaded myself *then* that it was from reluctance to

[1] Thomas Otway, the dramatist, is supposed to have choked to death on a morsel of bread which someone gave him when he was starving.—ED.

ask Lord Desart, on whom I was conscious of having no sufficient claims, the particular service in quest of which I had come to Eton. I was, however, unwilling to lose my journey, and—I asked it. Lord Desart, whose good-nature was unbounded, and which, in regard to myself, had been measured rather by his compassion, perhaps, for my condition, and his knowledge of my intimacy with several of his relatives, than by an over-rigorous inquiry into the extent of my own direct claims, faltered, nevertheless, at this request. He acknowledged that he did not like to have any dealings with money-lenders, and feared lest such a transaction might come to the ears of his connexions. Moreover, he doubted whether *his* signature, whose expectations were so much more bounded than those of his cousin, would avail with my unchristian friends. Still he did not wish, apparently, to mortify me by a refusal peremptory and absolute; for, after a little consideration, he promised, under certain conditions, which he pointed out, to give his security. Lord Desart was at this time not above eighteen years of age; but I have often doubted, on recollecting since the good sense and prudence which on this occasion he mingled with so much urbanity of manner (which in him wore the grace of youthful sincerity), whether any statesman, the oldest and the most accomplished in diplomacy, could have acquitted himself better under the same circumstances.

Re-comforted by this promise, which was not quite equal to the best, but far above the worst that I had anticipated, I returned in a Windsor coach to London three days after I had quitted it. And now I come to the end of my story. The Jews did not approve of Lord Desart's conditions, or so they said. Whether they would in the end have acceded to them, and were only seeking time for making further inquiries, I know

not; but many delays were made—time passed on—
the small fragment of my bank-note had just melted
away, and before any conclusion could have been put
to the business I must have relapsed into my former
state of wretchedness. Suddenly, at this crisis, an
opening was made, almost by accident, for reconciliation with my guardians. I quitted London in haste,
and returned to the Priory; after some time, I proceeded to Oxford; and it was not until many months
had passed away that I had it in my power again to revisit the ground which had become so interesting to
me, and to this day remains so, as the chief scene of
my youthful sufferings.

Meantime, what had become of Ann? Where was
she? Whither had she gone? According to our agreement, I sought her daily, and waited for her every
night, so long as I stayed in London, at the corner of
Titchfield Street; and during the last days of my stay
in London I put into activity every means of tracing
her that my knowledge of London suggested, and the
limited extent of my power made possible. The street
where she had lodged I knew, but not the house; and
I remembered, at last, some account which she had
given of ill-treatment from her landlord, which made
it probable that she had quitted those lodgings before
we parted. She had few acquaintance; most people,
besides, thought that the earnestness of my inquiries
arose from motives which moved their laughter or
their slight regard; and others, thinking that I was in
chase of a girl who had robbed me of some trifles, were
naturally and excusably indisposed to give me any
clue to her, if indeed they had any to give. Finally, as
my despairing resource, on the day I left London I put
into the hands of the only person who (I was sure)
must know Ann by sight, from having been in company with us once or twice, an address to the Priory.

All was in vain. To this hour I have never heard a syllable about her. This, amongst such troubles as most men meet with in this life, has been my heaviest affliction. If she lived, doubtless we must have been sometimes in search of each other, at the very same moment, through the mighty labyrinths of London; perhaps even within a few feet of each other—a barrier no wider, in a London street, often amounting in the end to a separation for eternity! During some years I hoped that she *did* live; and I suppose that, in the literal and unrhetorical use of the word *myriad*, I must, on my different visits to London, have looked into many myriads of female faces, in the hope of meeting Ann. I should know her again amongst a thousand, and if seen but for a moment. Handsome she was not; but she had a sweet expression of countenance, and a peculiarly graceful carriage of the head. I sought her, I have said, in hope. So it was for years; but now I should fear to see her; and her cough, which grieved me when I parted with her, is now my consolation. Now I wish to see her no longer, but think of her, more gladly, as one long since laid in the grave —in the grave, I would hope, of a Magdalen; taken away before injuries and cruelty had blotted out and transfigured her ingenuous nature, or the brutalities of ruffians had completed the ruin they had begun.

* * *

So then, Oxford Street, stony-hearted stepmother, thou that listenest to the sighs of orphans, and drinkest the tears of children, at length I was dismissed from thee! The time was come that I no more should pace in anguish thy never-ending terraces, no more should wake and dream in captivity to the pangs of hunger. Successors too many to myself and Ann have, doubtless, since then trodden in our footsteps, inheritors of our calamities. Other orphans than Ann have sighed; tears have been shed by other children; and thou, Oxford Street, hast since those days echoed to the groans of innumerable hearts. For myself, however, the storm which I had outlived seemed to have been the pledge of a long fair weather; the premature sufferings which I had paid down to have been accepted as a ransom for many years to come, as a price of long immunity from sorrow; and, if again I walked in London, a solitary and contemplative man (as oftentimes I did), I walked for the most part in serenity and peace of mind. And, although it is true that the calamities of my novitiate in London had struck root so deeply in my bodily constitution that afterwards they shot up and flourished afresh, and grew into a noxious umbrage that has overshadowed and darkened my latter years, yet these second assaults of suffering were met with a fortitude more confirmed, with the resources of a maturer intellect, and with alleviations, how deep! from sympathizing affection.

Thus, however, with whatsoever alleviations, years far asunder were bound together by subtle links of suffering derived from a common root. And herein I notice the shortsightedness of human desires—that oftentimes, on moonlight nights, during my first mournful abode in London, my consolation was (if such it could be thought) to gaze from Oxford Street up every avenue in succession which pierces northwards through the heart of Marylebone to the fields and the woods; for *that*, said I, travelling with my eyes up the long vistas which lay part in light and part in shade—"*that* is the road to the north, and, therefore, to Grasmere" (upon which, though as yet unknown to me, I had a presentiment that I should fix my choice for a residence); "and, if I had the wings of a dove, *that* way I would fly for rest." Thus I said, and thus I wished in my blindness; yet, even in that very northern region it was, in that very valley to which my erroneous wishes pointed, that this second birth of my sufferings began, and that they again threatened to besiege the citadel of life and hope. There it was that for years I was persecuted by visions as ugly, and by phantoms as ghastly, as ever haunted the couch of Orestes; and in this unhappier than he—that sleep, which comes to all as a respite and a restoration, and to him especially as a blessed balm for his wounded heart and his haunted brain, visited me as my bitterest scourge. Thus blind was I in my desires. And yet, if a veil interposes between the dim-sightedness of man and his future calamities, the same veil hides from him their alleviations; and a grief which had not been feared is met by consolations which had not been hoped. I, therefore, who participated, as it were, in the troubles of Orestes (excepting only in his agitated conscience), participated no less in all his supports; my Eumenides, like his, were at my bed-feet, and stared in upon me through the curtains; but, watching by my pillow, or defrauding herself of sleep to bear me company through the heavy watches of the night, sat my Electra; for thou, beloved M[argaret], dear companion of my later years, thou wast my Electra, and neither in nobility of mind nor in long-suffering affection wouldst permit that a Grecian sister should excel an English wife. For thou thoughtest not much to stoop to humble offices of kindness, and to servile ministrations of tenderest affection; to wipe away for years the unwholesome dews upon the forehead, or to refresh the lips when parched and baked with fever; nor even when thy own peaceful slumbers had by long sympathy become infected with the spectacle of my dread contest with phantoms and shadowy

enemies that oftentimes bade me "sleep no more"—
not even then didst thou utter a complaint or any murmur, nor withdraw thy angelic smiles, nor shrink
from thy service of love, more than Electra did of old.
For she, too, though she was a Grecian woman, and
the daughter of the king of men,[1] yet wept sometimes,
and hid her face [2] in her robe.

But these troubles are past, and thou wilt read these
records of a period so dolorous to us both as the legend
of some hideous dream that can return no more.
Meantime I am again in London, and again I pace the
terraces of Oxford Street by night; and oftentimes—
when I am oppressed by anxieties that demand all my
philosophy and the comfort of thy presence to support,
and yet remember that I am separated from thee by
three hundred miles and the length of three dreary
months—I look up the streets that run northward
from Oxford Street, upon moonlight nights, and recollect my youthful ejaculation of anguish; but then,
remembering that thou art sitting alone in that same
valley, and mistress of that very house to which my
heart turned in its blindness nineteen years ago, I
think that, though blind indeed, and scattered to the
winds of late, the promptings of my heart may yet
have had reference to a remoter time, and may be justified if read in another meaning; and, if I could al-

[1] Agamemnon—ἄναξ ἀνδρῶν.

[2] Ὄμμα θεῖς᾽ εἰς πέπλον. The scholar will know that
throughout this passage I refer to the early scenes of the
Orestes—one of the most beautiful exhibitions of the domestic affections which even the dramas of Euripides can furnish. To the unlearned reader it may be necessary to say that
the situation at the opening of the drama is that of a brother
attended only by his sister during the demoniacal possession
of a suffering conscience (or, in the mythology of the play,
haunted by the Furies), under circumstances of immediate
danger from enemies, and of desertion or cold regard from
nominal friends.

low myself to descend again to the impotent wishes of childhood, I should again say to myself, as I look to the north, "Oh, that I had the wings of a dove!" and with how just a confidence in thy good and gracious nature might I add the other half of my early ejacu- lation—"and *that* way I would fly for comfort!"

PART II

THE PLEASURES OF OPIUM

IT IS very long since I first took opium; *so* long that, if it had been a trifling incident in my life, I might have forgotten its date: but cardinal events are not to be forgotten; and, from circumstances connected with it, I remember that this inauguration into the use of opium must be referred to the spring or to the autumn of 1804; during which seasons I was in London, hav- ing come thither for the first time since my entrance at Oxford. And this event arose in the following way: From an early age I had been accustomed to wash my head in cold water at least once a day. Being suddenly seized with toothache, I attributed it to some relaxa- tion caused by a casual intermission of that practice, jumped out of bed, plunged my head into a basin of cold water, and with hair thus wetted went to sleep. The next morning, as I need hardly say, I awoke with excruciating rheumatic pains of the head and face, from which I had hardly any respite for about twenty days. On the twenty-first day I think it was, and on a Sunday, that I went out into the streets; rather to run away, if possible, from my torments, than with any distinct purpose of relief. By accident, I met a col- lege acquaintance, who recommended opium. Opium! dread agent of unimaginable pleasure and pain! I had

heard of it as I had heard of manna or of ambrosia,
but no further. How unmeaning a sound was opium
at that time! what solemn chords does it now strike
upon my heart! what heartquaking vibrations of sad
and happy remembrances! Reverting for a moment to
these, I feel a mystic importance attached to the minutest circumstances connected with the place, and the
time, and the man (if man he was), that first laid open
to me the paradise of Opium-Eaters. It was a Sunday
afternoon, wet and cheerless; and a duller spectacle
this earth of ours has not to show than a rainy Sunday
in London. My road homewards lay through Oxford
Street; and near "the *stately* Pantheon" (as Mr.
Wordsworth has obligingly called it [1]) I saw a druggist's shop. The druggist (unconscious minister of
celestial pleasures!), as if in sympathy with the rainy
Sunday, looked dull and stupid, just as any mortal
druggist might be expected to look on a rainy London
Sunday; and, when I asked for the tincture of opium,
he gave it to me as any other man might do; and,
furthermore, out of my shilling returned to me what
seemed to be real copper halfpence, taken out of a
real wooden drawer. Nevertheless, and notwithstanding all such indications of humanity, he has ever since
figured in my mind as a beatific vision of an immortal
druggist, sent down to earth on a special mission to
myself. And it confirms me in this way of considering
him that, when I next came up to London, I sought
him near the stately Pantheon, and found him not;
and thus to me, who knew not his name (if, indeed, he
had one), he seemed rather to have vanished from Oxford Street than to have flitted into any other locality,

[1] *"Stately"*: It is but fair to say that Wordsworth meant to
speak of the *interior*, which could very little be inferred from
the mean, undistinguished outside, as seen presenting itself
endways in Oxford Street.

or (which some abominable man suggested) to have absconded from the rent. The reader may choose to think of him as, possibly, no more than a sublunary druggist; it may be so, but my faith is better. I believe him to have evanesced.[1] So unwillingly would I connect any mortal remembrances with that hour, and place, and creature that first brought me acquainted with the celestial drug.

Arrived at my lodgings, it may be supposed that I lost not a moment in taking the quantity prescribed. I was necessarily ignorant of the whole art and mystery of opium-taking; and what I took I took under every disadvantage. But I took it; and in an hour, O heavens! what a revulsion! what a resurrection, from its lowest depths, of the inner spirit! what an apocalypse of the world within me! That my pains had vanished was now a trifle in my eyes; this negative effect was swallowed up in the immensity of those positive effects which had opened before me, in the abyss of divine enjoyment thus suddenly revealed. Here was a panacea, a φάρμακον νηπενθές for all human woes; here was the secret of happiness, about which philosophers had disputed for so many ages, at once discovered; happiness might now be bought for a penny, and carried in the waistcoat-pocket; portable ecstasies might be had corked up in a pint-bottle; and peace of mind could be sent down by the mail.

---

[1] "*Evanesced*": This way of going off from the stage of life appears to have been well known in the seventeenth century, but at that time to have been considered a peculiar privilege of royalty, and by no means open to the use of druggists. For, about the year 1686, a poet of rather ominous name (and who, apparently, did justice to his name) —viz. Mr. Flatman—in speaking of the death of Charles II, expresses his surprise that any prince should commit so vulgar an act as dying; because, says he,

Kings should disdain to die, and only disappear.

And, first, one word with respect to its bodily effects; for upon all that has been hitherto written on the subject of opium, whether by travellers in Turkey (who may plead their privilege of lying as an old immemorial right), or by professors of medicine writing *ex cathedra*, I have but one emphatic criticism to pronounce—Nonsense! I remember once, in passing a book-stall, to have caught these words from a page of some satiric author—"By this time I became convinced that the London newspapers spoke truth at least twice a-week—viz. on Tuesday and Saturday [1] —and might safely be depended upon for—the list of bankrupts." In like manner, I do by no means deny that some truths have been delivered to the world in regard to opium: thus, it has been repeatedly affirmed by the learned that opium is a tawny brown in colour —and this, take notice, I grant; secondly, that it is rather dear—which also I grant, for in my time East India opium has been three guineas a-pound, and Turkey eight; and, thirdly, that, if you eat a good deal of it, most probably you must do what is disagreeable to any man of regular habits—viz. die.[2] These weighty propositions are, all and singular, true; I cannot gainsay them; and truth ever was, and will be,

---

[1] *"Tuesday and Saturday"*: viz. the two days on which the *Gazette* is (or used to be) published.

[2] Of this, however, the learned appear latterly to have doubted; for, in a pirated edition of Buchan's *Domestic Medicine*, which I once saw in the hands of a farmer's wife, who was studying it for the benefit of her health, the doctor was made to caution his readers against taking more than "twenty-five *ounces*" of laudanum at one dose. The true reading had doubtless been twenty-five *drops* or minims, which in a gross equation is held equivalent to one grain of average opium; but opium itself—crude opium—varies enormously in purity and strength; consequently the tincture prepared from it. And most of the medical connoisseurs whom I have known boiled their opium, so as to cleanse it from gross impurities.

commendable. But in these three theorems I believe
we have exhausted the stock of knowledge as yet accumulated by man on the subject of opium. And therefore, worthy doctors, as there seems to be room for
further discoveries, stand aside, and allow me to come
forward and lecture on this matter.

First, then, it is not so much affirmed as taken for
granted by all who ever mention opium, formally or
incidentally, that it does or can produce intoxication.
Now, reader, assure yourself, *meo periculo*, that no
quantity of opium ever did, or could, intoxicate. As to
the tincture of opium (commonly called laudanum),
that might certainly intoxicate, if a man could bear
to take enough of it; but why? Because it contains so
much proof spirits of wine, and not because it contains so much opium. But crude opium, I affirm peremptorily, is incapable of producing any state of body
at all resembling that which is produced by alcohol;
and not in *degree* only incapable, but even in *kind;* it
is not in the quantity of its effects merely, but in the
quality, that it differs altogether. The pleasure given
by wine is always rapidly mounting, and tending to a
crisis, after which as rapidly it declines; that from
opium, when once generated, is stationary for eight or
ten hours: the first, to borrow a technical distinction
from medicine, is a case of acute, the second of
chronic, pleasure; the one is a flickering flame, the
other a steady and equable glow. But the main distinction lies in this——that, whereas wine disorders the
mental faculties, opium, on the contrary (if taken in
a proper manner), introduces amongst them the most
exquisite order, legislation, and harmony. Wine robs
a man of his self-possession; opium sustains and rein-
forces it. Wine unsettles the judgement, and gives a
preternatural brightness and a vivid exaltation to the
contempts and the admirations, to the loves and the

hatreds, of the drinker; opium, on the contrary, communicates serenity and equipoise to all the faculties,
active or passive; and, with respect to the temper and
moral feelings in general, it gives simply that sort of
vital warmth which is approved by the judgement,
and which would probably always accompany a bodily
constitution of primeval or antediluvian health. Thus,
for instance, opium, like wine, gives an expansion to
the heart and the benevolent affections; but, then,
with this remarkable difference, that, in the sudden
development of kindheartedness which accompanies
inebriation, there is always more or less of a maudlin
and a transitory character, which exposes it to the contempt of the bystander. Men shake hands, swear eternal friendship, and shed tears—no mortal knows why;
and the animal nature is clearly uppermost. But the
expansion of the benigner feelings incident to opium
is no febrile access, no fugitive paroxysm; it is a
healthy restoration to that state which the mind would
naturally recover upon the removal of any deep-
seated irritation from pain that had disturbed and
quarrelled with the impulses of a heart originally just
and good. True it is that even wine up to a certain
point, and with certain men, rather tends to exalt and
to steady the intellect; I myself, who have never been
a great wine-drinker, used to find that half-a-dozen
glasses of wine advantageously affected the faculties,
brightened and intensified the consciousness, and gave
to the mind a feeling of being *ponderibus librata
suis;* and certainly it is most absurdly said, in popular
language, of any man, that he is *disguised* in liquor;
for, on the contrary, most men are disguised by sobriety, and exceedingly disguised; and it is when they
are drinking that men display themselves in their true
complexion of character; which surely is not disguising themselves. But still, wine constantly leads a man

to the brink of absurdity and extravagance; and, beyond a certain point, it is sure to volatilize and to disperse the intellectual energies; whereas opium always seems to compose what had been agitated, and to concentrate what had been distracted. In short, to sum up all in one word, a man who is inebriated, or tending to inebriation, is, and feels that he is, in a condition which calls up into supremacy the merely human, too often the brutal, part of his nature; but the Opium-Eater (I speak of him simply *as* such, and assume that he is in a normal state of health) feels that the diviner part of his nature is paramount——that is, the moral affections are in a state of cloudless serenity, and high over all the great light of the majestic intellect.

This is the doctrine of the true church on the subject of opium: of which church I acknowledge myself to be the Pope (consequently infallible), and self-appointed *legate a latere* to all degrees of latitude and longitude. But then it is to be recollected that I speak from the ground of a large and profound personal experience, whereas most of the unscientifio[1] authors

[1] Amongst the great herd of travellers, &c., who show sufficiently by their thoughtlessness that they never held any intercourse with opium, I must caution my readers specially against the brilliant author of *Anastasius* [Thomas Hope, 1770–1831]. This gentleman, whose wit would lead one to presume him an Opium-Eater, has made it impossible to consider him in that character, from the grievous misrepresentation which he has given of its effects at pages 215-217 of Vol. I. Upon consideration, it must appear such to the author himself; for, waiving the errors I have insisted on in the text, which (and others) are adopted in the fullest manner, he will himself admit that an old gentleman, "with a snow-white beard," who eats "ample doses of opium," and is yet able to deliver what is meant and received as very weighty counsel on the bad effects of that practice, is but an indifferent evidence that opium either kills people prematurely, or sends them into a madhouse. But, for my part, I see into this old gentleman and his

who have at all treated of opium, and even of those who have written professionally on the *materia medica*, make it evident, by the horror they express of it, that their experimental knowledge of its action is none at all.

Two tendencies I will mention as diagnostic, or characteristic and inseparable marks of ordinary alcoholic intoxication, but which no excess in the use of opium ever develops. One is the loss of self-command, in relation to all one's acts and purposes, which steals gradually (though with varying degrees of speed) over *all* persons indiscriminately when indulging in wine or distilled liquors beyond a certain limit. The tongue and other organs become unmanageable: the intoxicated man speaks inarticulately; and, with regard to certain words, makes efforts ludicrously earnest, yet oftentimes unavailing, to utter them. The eyes are bewildered, and see double; grasping too little, and too much. The hand aims awry. The legs stumble, and lose their power of *concurrent* action. To this result *all* people tend, though by varying rates of acceleration. Secondly, as another characteristic, it may be noticed that in alcoholic intoxication the movement is always along a kind of arch; the drinker rises through continual ascents to a summit or *apex*, from which he descends through corresponding steps of declension. There is a crowning point in the movement upwards, which once attained cannot be renewed: and it is the blind, unconscious, but always

motives: the fact is, he was enamoured of "the little golden receptacle of the pernicious drug" which Anastasius carried about him; and no way of obtaining it so safe and so feasible occurred as that of frightening its owner out of his wits. This commentary throws a new light upon the case, and greatly improves it as a story; for the old gentleman's speech, as a lecture on pharmacy, is absurd; but, considered as a hoax on Anastasius, it reads excellently.

unsuccessful effort of the obstinate drinker to restore
this supreme altitude of enjoyment which tempts him
into excesses that become dangerous. After reaching
this *acme* of genial pleasure, it is a mere necessity of
the case to sink through corresponding stages of collapse. Some people have maintained, in my hearing,
that they had been drunk upon green tea; and a medical student in London, for whose knowledge in his profession I have reason to feel great respect, assured me,
the other day, that a patient, in recovering from an
illness, had got drunk on a beef-steak. All turns, in
fact, upon a rigorous definition of intoxication.

Having dwelt so much on this first and leading
error in respect to opium, I shall notice briefly a second and a third; which are, that the elevation of spirits
produced by opium is necessarily followed by a pro-
portionate depression, and that the natural and even
immediate consequence of opium is torpor and stagnation, animal as well as mental. The first of these
errors I shall content myself with simply denying;
assuring my reader that, for ten years during which
I took opium not regularly but intermittingly, the
day succeeding to that on which I allowed myself this
luxury was always a day of unusually good spirits.

With respect to the torpor supposed to follow, or
rather (if we were to credit the numerous pictures of
Turkish Opium-Eaters) to accompany, the practice
of opium-eating, I deny that also. Certainly, opium is
classed under the head of narcotics, and some such effect it may produce in the end; but the primary effects
of opium are always, and in the highest degree, to excite and stimulate the system. This first stage of its
action always lasted with me, during my novitiate,
for upwards of eight hours; so that it must be the fault
of the Opium-Eater himself if he does not so time his
exhibition of the dose as that the whole weight of its

narcotic influence may descend upon his sleep. Turkish Opium-Eaters, it seems, are absurd enough to sit,
like so many equestrian statues, on logs of wood as
stupid as themselves. But, that the reader may judge
of the degree in which opium is likely to stupefy the
faculties of an Englishman, I shall (by way of treating the question illustratively, rather than argumen-
tatively) describe the way in which I myself often
passed an opium evening in London during the period
between 1804 and 1812. It will be seen that at least
opium did not move me to seek solitude, and much less
to seek inactivity, or the torpid state of self-involution
ascribed to the Turks. I give this account at the risk
of being pronounced a crazy enthusiast or visionary;
but I regard that little. I must desire my reader to bear
in mind that I was a hard student, and at severe studies for all the rest of my time; and certainly I had a
right occasionally to relaxations as well as other
people.

The late Duke of Norfolk used to say, "Next Monday, wind and weather permitting, I purpose to be
drunk"; and in like manner I used to fix beforehand
how often within a given time, when, and with what
accessory circumstances of festal joy, I would commit
a debauch of opium. This was seldom more than once
in three weeks; for at that time I could not have ventured to call every day (as afterwards I did) for "*a
glass of laudanum negus, warm, and without sugar.*"
No; once in three weeks sufficed; and the time selected
was either a Tuesday or a Saturday night; my reason
for which was this: Tuesday and Saturday were for
many years the regular nights of performance at the
King's Theatre (or Opera House); and there it was
in those times that Grassini sang; and her voice (the
richest of *contraltos*) was delightful to me beyond all
that I had ever heard. Yes; or have since heard; or

ever shall hear. I know not what may be the state of
the opera-house now, having never been within its
walls for seven or eight years; but at that time it was
by much the most pleasant place of resort in London
for passing an evening.[1] Half-a-guinea admitted you
to the pit, under the troublesome condition, however,
of being *en grande tenue*. But to the gallery five shillings admitted you; and that gallery was subject to far
less annoyance than the pit of most theatres. The orchestra was distinguished by its sweet and melodious
grandeur from all English orchestras; the composition
of which, I confess, is not acceptable to my ear, from
the predominance of the clangorous instruments, and
in some instances from the tyranny of the violin.
Thrilling was the pleasure with which almost always
I heard this angelic Grassini. Shivering with expectation I sat, when the time drew near for her golden
epiphany; shivering I rose from my seat, incapable
of rest, when that heavenly and harp-like voice sang
its own victorious welcome in its prelusive *threttánelo*
—*threttánelo* [2] (ϑρεττάνελω—ϑρεττάνελω) . The cho-

[1] I trust that my reader has not been so inattentive to the
windings of my narrative as to fancy me speaking here of the
Brown-Brunell and Pyment period. Naturally I had no money
disposable at that period for the opera. I am speaking here of
years stretching far beyond those boyish scenes—interludes in
my Oxford life, or long after Oxford.

[2] "*Threttánelo—threttánelo*": The beautiful representative
echo by which Aristophanes expresses the sound of the Grecian
phorminx, or of some other instrument, which conjecturally
has been shown most to resemble our modern European harp.
In the case of ancient Hebrew instruments used in the temple
service, random and idle must be all the guesses through the
Greek Septuagint or the Latin Vulgate to identify any one of
them. But as to Grecian instruments the case is different;
always there is a remote chance of digging up some marble
sculpture of orchestral appurtenances and properties.

ruses were divine to hear; and, when Grassini [1] appeared in some interlude, as she often did, and poured forth her passionate soul as Andromache at the tomb of Hector, &c., I question whether any Turk, of all that ever entered the paradise of Opium-Eaters, can have had half the pleasure I had. But, indeed, I honour the barbarians too much by supposing them capable of any pleasures approaching to the intellectual ones of an Englishman. For music is an intellectual or a sensual pleasure, according to the temperament of him who hears it. And, by the bye, with the exception of the fine extravaganza on that subject in *Twelfth Night*, I do not recollect more than one thing said adequately on the subject of music in all literature. It is a passage in the *Religio Medici* [2] of Sir T. Browne, and, though chiefly remarkable for its sublimity, has also a philosophic value, inasmuch as it points to the true theory of musical effects.

The mistake of most people is, to suppose that it is by the ear they communicate with music, and therefore that they are purely passive as to its effects. But this is not so; it is by the reaction of the mind upon the notices of the ear (the *matter* coming by the senses,

[1] Yet all things change: this same Grassini, whom once I adored, afterwards, when gorged with English gold, went off to Paris; and, when I heard on what terms she lived with a man so unmagnanimous as Napoleon, I came to hate her. Did I complain of any man's hating England, or teaching a woman to hate her benefactress? Not at all; but simply of his adopting at second-hand the malice of a jealous nation, with which originally he could have had no sincere sympathy. Hate us, if you please; but not sycophantishly, by way of paying court to others.

[2] I have not the book at this moment to consult; but I think the passage begins, "And even that tavern music, which makes one man merry, another mad, in me strikes a deep fit of devotion," &c.

the *form* from the mind) that the pleasure is constructed; and therefore it is that people of equally good ear differ so much in this point from one another. Now opium, by greatly increasing the activity of the mind, generally increases, of necessity, that particular mode of its activity by which we are able to construct out of the raw material of organic sound an elaborate intellectual pleasure. "But," says a friend, "a succession of musical sounds is to me like a collection of Arabic characters: I can attach no ideas to them." Ideas! my dear friend! there is no occasion for them; all that class of ideas which can be available in such a case has a language of representative feelings. But this is a subject foreign to my present purposes; it is sufficient to say that a chorus, &c., of elaborate harmony displayed before me, as in a piece of arras-work, the whole of my past life—not as if recalled by an act of memory, but as if present and incarnated in the music; no longer painful to dwell upon, but the detail of its incidents removed, or blended in some hazy abstraction, and its passions exalted, spiritualized, and sublimed. All this was to be had for five shillings— that being the price of admission to the gallery; or, if a man preferred the high-bred society of the pit, even this might be had for half-a-guinea; or, in fact, for half-a-crown less, by purchasing beforehand a ticket at the music shops. And, over and above the music of the stage and the orchestra, I had all around me, in the intervals of the performance, the music of the Italian language talked by Italian women—for the gallery was usually crowded with Italians—and I listened with a pleasure such as that with which Weld, the traveller, lay and listened, in Canada, to the sweet laughter of Indian women; for, the less you understand of a language, the more sensible you are to the melody or harshness of its sounds. For such a purpose, therefore, it was an advantage to me that in those days I was a poor Italian scholar, reading it but little, and not speaking it at all, nor understanding a tenth part of what I heard spoken.

These were my opera pleasures; but another pleasure I had, which, as it could be had only on a Saturday night, occasionally struggled with my love of the opera; for, in those years, Tuesday and Saturday were the regular opera nights. On this subject I am afraid I shall be rather obscure, but, I can assure the reader, not at all more so than Marinus in his *Life of Proclus*, or many other biographers and autobiographers of fair reputation. This pleasure, I have said, was to be had only on a Saturday night. What, then, was Saturday night to me more than any other night? I had no labours that I rested from; no wages to receive; what needed I to care for Saturday night, more than as it was a summons to hear Grassini? True, most logical reader; what thou sayest is, and ever will be, unanswerable. And yet so it was that, whereas different men throw their feelings into different channels, and most men are apt to show their interest in the concerns of the poor chiefly by sympathy with their distresses and sorrows, I at that time was disposed to express mine by sympathizing with their pleasures. The pains of poverty I had lately seen too much of—more than I wished to remember; but the pleasures of the poor, their hopes, their consolations of spirit, and their restings from toil, can never become oppressive to contemplate. Now, Saturday night is the season for the chief regular and periodic return of rest to the poor, and to all that live by bodily labour; in this point the most hostile sects unite, and acknowledge a common link of brotherhood: almost all Christendom rests from its labours. It is a rest introductory to another rest, and divided by a whole day and two nights from the renewal of toil. On this account I feel always on a Saturday night as though I also were released from some yoke of bondage, had some wages to receive, and some luxury of repose to enjoy. For the sake, therefore, of witnessing, upon as large a scale as possible, a spectacle with which my sympathy was so entire, I used often, on Saturday nights, after I had taken opium, to wander forth, without much regarding the direction or the distance, to all the markets, and other parts of London, whither the poor resort on a Saturday night for laying out their wages. Many a family party, consisting of a man, his wife, and sometimes one or two of their children, have I listened to, as they stood consulting on their ways and means, or the strength of their exchequer, or the price of household articles. Gradually I became familiar with their wishes, their difficulties, and their opinions. Sometimes there might be heard murmurs of discontent; but far oftener expressions on the countenance, or uttered in words, of patience, of hope, and of reconciliation to their lot. Generally speaking, the impression left upon my mind was that the poor are practically more philosophic than the rich; that they show a more ready and cheerful submission to what they consider as irremediable evils or irreparable losses. Whenever I saw occasion, or could do it without appearing to be intrusive, I joined their parties, and gave my opinion upon the matter in discussion, which, if not always judicious, was always received indulgently. If wages were a little higher, or were expected to be so—if the quartern loaf were a little lower, or it was reported that onions and butter were falling—I was glad; yet, if the contrary were true, I drew from opium some means of consolation. For opium (like the bee, that extracts its materials indiscriminately from roses and from the soot [1] of chimneys) can overrule all feelings into a compliance with the master-key. Some of these rambles led me to great distances; for an Opium-Eater is too happy to observe the motion of time. And sometimes, in my attempts to steer homewards, upon nautical principles, by fixing my eye on the pole-star, and seeking ambitiously for a north-west passage, instead of circumnavigating all the capes and headlands I had doubled in my outward voyage, I came suddenly upon such knotty problems of alleys, alleys without soundings, such enigmatical entries, and such sphinx's riddles of streets without obvious outlets or thoroughfares, as must baffle the audacity of porters, and confound the intellects of hackney coachmen. I could almost have believed, at times, that I must be the first discoverer of some of these *terræ incognitæ*, and doubted whether they had yet been laid down in the modern charts of London. Positively, in one line of communication to the south of Holborn for foot-passengers (known, I doubt not, to many of my London readers), the road lay through a man's kitchen; and, as it was a small kitchen, you needed to steer cautiously, or else you might run foul of the dripping-pan. For all this, however, I paid a heavy price in distant years, when the human face tyrannized over my dreams, and the perplexities of my steps in London came back and haunted my sleep with the feeling of perplexities, moral or intellectual, that brought con-

---

[1] *"Soot"*: In the large capacious chimneys of the rustic cottages throughout the Lake district you can see up the entire cavity from the seat which you occupy, as an honoured visitor, in the chimney corner. There I used often to hear (though not to see) bees. Their murmuring was audible, though their bodily forms were too small to be visible at that altitude. On inquiry, I found that soot (chiefly from wood and peats) was useful in some stage of their wax or honey manufacture.

fusion to the reason, that brought anguish and remorse to the conscience.

Thus I have shown, or tried to show, that opium
does not of necessity produce inactivity or torpor; but
that, on the contrary, it often led me into markets and
theatres. Yet, in candour, I will admit that markets
and theatres are not the appropriate haunts of the
Opium-Eater, when in the divinest state incident to his
enjoyment. In that state crowds become an oppression
to him; music, even, too sensual and gross. He naturally seeks solitude and silence, as indispensable conditions of those trances, or profoundest reveries, which
are the crown and consummation of what opium can
do for human nature. I, whose disease it was to medi-
tate too much and to observe too little, and who, upon
my first entrance at college, was nearly falling into
a deep melancholy, from brooding too much on the
sufferings which I had witnessed in London, was sufficiently aware of these tendencies in my own thoughts
to do all I could to counteract them. I was, indeed,
like a person who, according to the old Pagan legend,
had entered the cave of Trophonius; and the remedies
I sought were to force myself into society, and to keep
my understanding in continual activity upon subtleties of philosophic speculation. But for these remedies, I should certainly have become hypochondria-
cally melancholy. In after years, however, when my
cheerfulness was more fully re-established, I yielded
to my natural inclination for a solitary life. At that
time I often fell into such reveries after taking opium;
and many a time it has happened to me on a summer
night—when I have been seated at an open window,
from which I could overlook the sea at a mile below
me, and could at the same time command a view of
some great town standing on a different radius of my
circular prospect, but at nearly the same distance—

that from sunset to sunrise, all through the hours of night, I have continued motionless, as if frozen, without consciousness of myself as of an object anywise distinct from the multiform scene which I contemplated from above. Such a scene in all its elements was not unfrequently realized for me on the gentle eminence of Everton. Obliquely to the left lay the many-languaged town of Liverpool; obliquely to the right, the multitudinous sea. The scene itself was somewhat typical of what took place in such a reverie. The town of Liverpool represented the earth, with its sorrows and its graves left behind, yet not out of sight, nor wholly forgotten. The ocean, in everlasting but gentle agitation, yet brooded over by dove-like calm, might not unfitly typify the mind, and the mood which then swayed it. For it seemed to me as if then first I stood at a distance aloof from the uproar of life; as if the tumult, the fever, and the strife, were suspended; a respite were granted from the secret burdens of the heart—some sabbath of repose, some resting from human labours. Here were the hopes which blossom in the paths of life, reconciled with the peace which is in the grave; motions of the intellect as unwearied as the heavens, yet for all anxieties a halcyon calm; tranquillity that seemed no product of inertia, but as if resulting from mighty and equal antagonisms; infinite activities, infinite repose.

O just, subtle, and all-conquering opium! that, to the hearts of rich and poor alike, for the wounds that will never heal, and for the pangs of grief that "tempt the spirit to rebel," bringest an assuaging balm—eloquent opium! that with thy potent rhetoric stealest away the purposes of wrath, pleadest effectually for relenting pity, and through one night's heavenly sleep callest back to the guilty man the visions of his infancy, and hands washed pure from blood—O just

and righteous opium! that to the chancery of dreams
summonest, for the triumphs of despairing innocence,
false witnesses, and confoundest perjury, and dost
reverse the sentences of unrighteous judges—thou
buildest upon the bosom of darkness, out of the fantastic imagery of the brain, cities and temples, beyond
the art of Phidias and Praxiteles, beyond the splendours of Babylon and Hekatómpylos [1]; and, "from the
anarchy of dreaming sleep," callest into sunny light
the faces of long-buried beauties, and the blessed
household countenances, cleansed from the "dishon-
ours of the grave." Thou only givest these gifts to
man; and thou hast the keys of Paradise, O just, subtle, and mighty opium!

* * *

Courteous, and I hope indulgent, reader, having accompanied me thus far, now let me request you to
move onwards for about eight years; that is to say,
from 1804 (when I said that my acquaintance with
opium began) to 1812. The years of academic life are
now over and gone—almost forgotten; the student's
cap no longer presses my temples; if my cap exists at
all, it presses those of some youthful scholar, I trust,
as happy as myself, and as passionate a lover of knowledge. My gown is, by this time, I dare to say, in the
same condition with many thousands of excellent
books in the Bodleian—viz. diligently perused by certain studious moths and worms; or departed, however
(which is all that I know of its fate), to that great
reservoir of *somewhere*, to which all the tea-cups, tea-

---

[1] *i.e.*, the *hundred-gated* (from ἑκατόν, *hekaton*, a hundred,
and πύλη, *pyle*, a gate). This epithet of hundred-gated was
applied to the Egyptian Thebes in contradistinction to the
ἑπτάπυλος (*heptápylos*, or *seven-gated*) which designated the
Grecian Thebes, within one day's journey of Athens.

caddies, tea-pots, tea-kettles, &c., have departed, which occasional resemblances in the present generation of tea-cups, &c., remind me of having once possessed, but of whose departure and final fate I, in common with most gownsmen of either university, could give but an obscure and conjectural history. The persecutions of the chapel bell, sounding its unwelcome summons to matins, interrupts my slumbers no longer; the porter who rang it is dead, and has ceased to disturb anybody; and I, with many others who suffered much from his tintinnabulous propensities, have now agreed to overlook his errors, and have forgiven him. Even with the bell I am now in charity; it rings, I suppose, as formerly, thrice a-day, and cruelly annoys, I doubt not, many worthy gentlemen, and disturbs their peace of mind; but, as to me, in this year 1812, I regard its treacherous voice no longer (treacherous I call it, for, by some refinement of malice, it spoke in as sweet and silvery tones as if it had been inviting one to a party) ; its tones have no longer, indeed, power to reach me, let the wind sit as favourably as the malice of the bell itself could wish; for I am two hundred and fifty miles away from it, and buried in the depth of mountains.

And what am I doing amongst the mountains? Taking opium. Yes; but what else? Why, reader, in 1812, the year we are now arrived at, as well as for some years previous, I have been chiefly studying German metaphysics, in the writings of Kant, Fichte, Schelling, &c. And how, and in what manner, do I live? in short, what class or description of men do I belong to? I am at this period—viz. in 1812—living in a cottage; and with a single female servant (*honi soit qui mal y pense*), who, amongst my neighbours, passes by the name of my "housekeeper." And, as a scholar and a man of learned education, I may presume to class myself as an unworthy member of that indefinite body

called *gentlemen*. Partly on the ground I have assigned—partly because, from having no visible calling
or business, it is rightly judged that I must be living
on my private fortune—I am so classed by my neighbours; and, by the courtesy of modern England, I am
usually addressed on letters, &c., *Esquire*, though having, I fear, in the rigorous construction of heralds,
antique or antic, dressed like the knaves of spades or
diamonds, but slender pretensions to that distinguished
honour—yes, in popular estimation, I am X. Y. Z.,
Esquire, but not Justice of the Peace, nor Custos Ro-
tulorum. Am I married? Not yet. And I still take
opium? On Saturday nights. And, perhaps, have taken
it unblushingly ever since "the rainy Sunday," and
"the stately Pantheon," and "the beatific druggist" of
1804? Even so. And how do I find my health after all
this opium-eating? in short, how do I do? Why, pretty
well, I thank you, reader. In fact, if I dared to say the
real and simple truth (though, in order to satisfy the
theories of some medical men, I ought to be ill), I was
never better in my life than in the spring of 1812; and
I hope sincerely that the quantity of claret, port, or
"London particular Madeira," which, in all probability, you, good reader, have taken, and design to
take, for every term of eight years during your natural life, may as little disorder your health as mine was
disordered by all the opium I had taken (though in
quantity such that I might well have bathed and
swum in it) for the eight years between 1804 and 1812.
Hence you may see again the danger of taking any
medical advice from Anastasius; in divinity, for anything I know, he may be a safe counsellor, but not in
medicine. No; it is far better to consult Dr. Buchan,
as I did; for I never forgot that worthy man's excellent suggestion, and I was "particularly careful not to
take above five-and-twenty ounces of laudanum." To

this moderation and temperate use of the article I may ascribe it, I suppose, that as yet at least (that is, in 1812) I am ignorant and unsuspicious of the avenging terrors which opium has in store for those who abuse its long-suffering. At the same time, as yet I had been only a *dilettante* eater of opium; even eight years' practice, with the single precaution of allowing sufficient intervals between every indulgence, has not been sufficient to make opium necessary to me as an article of daily diet.

But now comes a different era. Move on, then, if you please, reader, to 1813. In the summer of the year we have just quitted I had suffered much in bodily health from distress of mind connected with a melancholy event. This event, being nowise related to the subject now before me, further than through the bodily illness which it produced, I need not more particularly notice. Whether this illness of 1812 had any share in that of 1813, I know not; but so it was that, in the latter year, I was attacked by a most appalling irritation of the stomach, in all respects the same as that which had caused me so much suffering in youth, and accompanied by a revival of all the old dreams. Now, then, it was—viz. in the year 1813—that I became a regular and confirmed (no longer an intermitting) Opium-Eater. And here I find myself in a perplexing dilemma. Either, on the one hand, I must exhaust the reader's patience by such a detail of my malady, and of my struggles with it, as might suffice to establish the fact of my inability to wrestle any longer with irritation and constant suffering; or, on the other hand, by passing lightly over this critical part of my story, I must forgo the benefit of a stronger impression left on the mind of the reader, and must lay myself open to the misconstruction of having slipped, by the easy and gradual steps of self-indulging persons, from the first to the final stage of opium-eating (a misconstruction to which there will be a lurking predisposition in most readers from my previous acknowledgements). This is the dilemma, the first horn of which is not to be thought of. It remains, then, that I *postulate* so much as is necessary for my purpose. And let me take as full credit for this as if I had demonstrated it, good reader, at the expense of your patience and my own. Be not so ungenerous as to let me suffer in your good opinion through my own forbearance and regard for your comfort. No; believe all that I ask of you—viz. that I could resist no longer—believe it liberally, and as an act of grace, or else in mere prudence; for, if not, then in my next edition I will make you believe and tremble; and, *à force d'ennuyer*, by mere dint of pandiculation, vulgarly called yawning, I will terrify all readers of mine from ever again questioning any postulate that I shall think fit to make.

This, then, let me repeat: I postulate that, at the time I began to take opium daily, I could not have done otherwise. Whether, indeed, afterwards I might not have succeeded in breaking off the habit, even when it seemed to me that all efforts would be unavailing, and whether many of the innumerable efforts which I *did* make might not have been carried much further, and my gradual re-conquests of lost ground might not have been followed up much more energetically—these are questions which I must decline. Perhaps I might make out a case of palliation, but (shall I speak ingenuously?) I confess it, as a besetting infirmity of mine, that I am too much of an Eudæmonist; I hanker too much after a state of happiness, both for myself and others; I cannot face misery, whether my own or not, with an eye of sufficient firmness, and am little capable of encountering present pain for the sake of any reversionary benefit. On some other matters, I can agree with the gentlemen of The Porch [1] at Manchester in affecting the Stoic philosophy; but not in this. Here I take the liberty of an Eclectic philosopher, and I look out for some courteous and considerate sect that will condescend more to the infirm condition of an Opium-Eater—that are pleasant men and courteous, such as Chaucer describes, to hear confession or to give absolution, and will show some conscience in the penances they inflict, or the efforts of abstinence they exact from poor sinners like myself. An inhuman moralist I can no more endure, in my nervous state, than opium that has not been boiled. At any rate, he who summons me to send out a large freight of self-denial and mortification upon any cruising voyage of moral improvement must make it clear to my understanding that the concern is a hopeful one. At my time of life (six-and-thirty years of age), it cannot be supposed that I have much energy to spare; in fact, I find it all little enough for the intellectual labours I have on my hands; and, therefore, let no man expect to frighten me, by a few hard words, into embarking any part of it upon desperate adventures of morality.

Desperate or not, however, the issue of the struggle in 1813 was what I have mentioned; and from this date the reader is to consider me as a regular and confirmed Opium-Eater, of whom to ask whether on any particular day he had or had not taken opium would be to ask whether his lungs had performed respiration, or the heart fulfilled its functions. Now, then, reader, you understand what I am; and you are by this time

[1] A handsome news-room, of which I was very courteously made free, in passing through Manchester, by several gentlemen of that place, is called either *The Porch* or *The Portico*, which in Greek is the *Stoa;* from which I, a stranger in Manchester, inferred that the subscribers meant to profess themselves Stoics, or followers of Zeno. But I have been since assured that this is a mistake.

aware that no old gentleman, "with a snow-white beard," will have any chance of persuading me (like Anastasius) to surrender "the little golden receptacle of the pernicious drug." No; I give notice to all, whether moralists or surgeons, that, whatever be their pretensions and skill in their respective lines of practice, they must not hope for any countenance from me, if they think to begin by any savage proposition for a Lent or Ramadan of abstinence from opium. This being fully understood between us, we shall in future sail before the wind. Now, then, reader, from the year 1813, where all this time we have been sitting down and loitering, rise up, if you please; walk forward about three years more; draw up the curtain, and you shall see me in a new character.

If any man, poor or rich, were to say that he would tell us what had been the happiest day in his life, and the why and the wherefore, I suppose that we should all cry out, Hear him! hear him! As to the happiest day, that must be very difficult for any wise man to assign; because any event that could occupy so distinguished a place in a man's retrospect of life, or be entitled to have shed a special, separate, and supreme felicity on any one day, ought to be of such an enduring character as that (accidents apart) it should have continued to shed the same felicity, or one not distinguishably less, on very many years together. To the happiest *lustrum*, however, or even to the happiest *year*, a man may perhaps allowably point without discountenance from wisdom. This year, in *my* case, reader, was the one which we have now reached; though it stood, I confess, as a parenthesis between years of a gloomier character. It was a year of brilliant water (to speak after the manner of jewellers), set, as it were, and insulated, in the gloomy umbrage of opium. Strange as it may sound, I had a little before this time descended suddenly, and without any considerable effort, from three hundred and twenty grains of opium (that is, eight thousand drops of laudanum) per day, to forty grains, or one-eighth part. Instantaneously, and as if by magic, the cloud of profoundest melancholy which rested upon my brain, like some black vapours that I have seen roll away from the summit of a mountain, drew off in one week; passed away with its murky banners as simultaneously as a ship that has been stranded, and is floated off by a spring-tide,

> *That moveth altogether, if it move at all.*

Now, then, I was again happy: I now took only one thousand drops of laudanum per day—and what was that? A latter spring had come to close up the season of youth. My brain performed its functions as healthily as ever before. I read Kant again; and again I understood him, or fancied that I did. Again my feelings of pleasure expanded themselves to all around me; and, if any man from Oxford or Cambridge, or from neither, had been annouced to me in my unpretending cottage, I should have welcomed him with as sumptuous a reception as so poor a man could offer. Whatever else might be wanting to a wise man's happiness, of laudanum I would have given him as much as he wished, and in a silver-gilt, if not golden, cup. And, by the way, now that I speak of giving laudanum away, I remember about this time a little incident, which I mention because, trifling as it was, the reader will soon meet it again in my dreams, which it influenced more fearfully than could be imagined. One day a Malay knocked at my door. What business a Malay could have to transact amongst the recesses of English mountains is not my business to conjecture;

but possibly he was on his road to a seaport—viz.,
Whitehaven, Workington, &c.—about forty miles distant.[1]

The servant who opened the door to him was a
young girl, born and bred amongst the mountains,
who had never seen an Asiatic dress of any sort: his
turban, therefore, confounded her not a little; and, as
it turned out that *his* knowledge of English was exactly commensurate with *hers* of Malay, there seemed
to be an impassable gulf fixed between all communication of ideas, if either party had happened to possess
any. In this dilemma, the girl, recollecting the reputed
learning of her master (and, doubtless, giving me
credit for a knowledge of all the languages of the
earth, besides, perhaps, a few of the lunar ones), came
and gave me to understand that there was a sort of
demon below, whom she clearly imagined that my art
could exorcize from the house. The group which presented itself, arranged as it was by accident, though not
very elaborate, took hold of my fancy and my eye more
powerfully than any of the statuesque attitudes or

[1] Between the seafaring populations on the coast of Lancashire and the corresponding populations on the coast of Cumberland (such as Ravenglass, Whitehaven, Workington, Mary-
port, &c.) there was a slender current of interchange constantly
going on, and especially in the days of pressgangs—in part by
sea, but in part also by land. By the way, I may mention, as an
interesting fact which I discovered from an almanack and
itinerary, dated about the middle of Queen Elizabeth's reign
(say 1579), that the official route in *her* days for queen's messengers to the north of Ireland, and of course for travellers
generally, was not (as now) through Grasmere, and thence by
St. John's Vale, Threlkeld (for the short cut by Shoulthwaite
Moss was then unknown), Keswick, Cockermouth, and Whitehaven. Up to St. Oswald's Church, Gresmere (so it was then
spelled, in deference to its Danish original), the route lay as
at present. Thence it turned round the lake to the left, crossed
Hammerscar, up *Little* Langdale, across Wrynose to Egremont, and from Egremont to Whitehaven.

groups exhibited in the ballets at the opera-house, though so ostentatiously complex. In a cottage kitchen, but not looking so much like *that* as a rustic hall of entrance, being panelled on the wall with dark wood, that from age and rubbing resembled oak, stood the Malay, his turban and loose trousers of dingy white relieved upon the dark panelling; he had placed himself nearer to the girl than she seemed to relish, though her native spirit of mountain intrepidity contended with the feeling of simple awe which her countenance expressed as she gazed upon the tiger-cat before her. A more striking picture there could not be imagined than the beautiful English face of the girl,[1] and its exquisite bloom, together with her erect and independent attitude, contrasted with the sallow and bilious skin of the Malay, veneered with mahogany tints by climate and marine air, his small, fierce, restless eyes, thin lips, slavish gestures and adorations. Half-hidden by the ferocious-looking Malay, was a little child from a neighbouring cottage, who had crept in after him, and was now in the act of reverting its head and gazing upwards at the turban and the fiery eyes be-

---

[1] This girl, Barbara Lewthwaite, was already at that time a person of some poetic distinction, being (unconsciously to herself) the chief speaker in a little pastoral poem of Wordsworth's. That she was really beautiful, and not merely so described by me for the sake of improving the picturesque effect, the reader will judge from this line in the poem, written perhaps ten years earlier, when Barbara might be six years old—

'*Twas little Barbara Lewthwaite, a child of beauty rare!*

This, coming from William Wordsworth, both a fastidious judge and a truth-speaker of the severest literality, argues some real pretensions to beauty, or real at that time. But it is notorious that, in the anthologies of earth through all her zones, one flower beyond every other is liable to change, which flower is the countenance of woman.

neath it, whilst with one hand he caught at the dress of the lovely girl for protection.

My knowledge of the oriental tongues is not remarkably extensive, being, indeed, confined to two words—the Arabic word for barley, and the Turkish for opium (*madjoon*), which I have learned from Anastasius. And, as I had neither a Malay dictionary, nor even Adelung's *Mithridates*, which might have helped me to a few words, I addressed him in some lines from the Iliad; considering that, of such languages as I possessed, the Greek, in point of longitude, came geographically nearest to an oriental one. He worshipped me in a devout manner, and replied in what I suppose to have been Malay. In this way I saved my reputation as a linguist with my neighbours; for the Malay had no means of betraying the secret. He lay down upon the floor for about an hour, and then pursued his journey. On his departure, I presented him, *inter alia*, with a piece of opium. To him, as a native of the East, I could have no doubt that opium was not less familiar than his daily bread; and the expression of his face convinced me that it was. Nevertheless, I was struck with some little consternation when I saw him suddenly raise his hand to his mouth, and bolt the whole, divided into three pieces, at one mouthful. The quantity was enough to kill some half-dozen dragoons, together with their horses, supposing neither bipeds nor quadrupeds to be regularly trained Opium-Eaters. I felt some alarm for the poor creature; but what could be done? I had given him the opium in pure compassion for his solitary life, since, if he had travelled on foot from London, it must be nearly three weeks since he could have exchanged a thought with any human being. Ought I to have violated the laws of hospitality by having him seized and drenched with an emetic, thus frightening him into a

notion that we were going to sacrifice him to some
English idol? No: there was clearly no help for it.
The mischief, if any, was done. He took his leave, and
for some days I felt anxious; but, as I never heard of
any Malay, or of any man in a turban, being found
dead on any part of the very slenderly peopled road
between Grasmere and Whitehaven, I became satisfied that he was familiar with opium,[1] and that I must
doubtless have done him the service I designed, by giving him one night of respite from the pains of wandering.

This incident I have digressed to mention, because
this Malay (partly from the picturesque exhibition he
assisted to frame, partly from the anxiety I connected
with his image for some days) fastened afterwards
upon my fancy, and through *that* upon my dreams,
bringing with him other Malays worse than himself,
that ran "a-muck" [2] at me, and led me into a world
of nocturnal troubles. But, to quit this episode, and to
return to my intercalary year of happiness. I have already said that, on a subject so important to us all as
happiness, we should listen with pleasure to any man's
experience or experiments, even though he were but a
ploughboy, who cannot be supposed to have ploughed
very deep in such an intractable soil as that of human

---

[1] This, however, is not a necessary conclusion; the varieties
of effect produced by opium on different constitutions are infinite. A London magistrate (Harriott's *Struggles through
Life*, vol. iii. p. 391, third edition) has recorded that, on the
first occasion of his trying laudanum for the gout, he took
FORTY drops, the next night SIXTY, and on the fifth night
EIGHTY, without any effect whatever; and this at an advanced
age.

[2] See the common accounts, in any eastern traveller or voy-
ager, of the frantic excesses committed by Malays who have
taken opium, or are reduced to desperation by ill luck at
gambling.

pains and pleasures, or to have conducted his researches upon any very enlightened principles. But I, who have taken happiness, both in a solid and a liquid shape, both boiled and unboiled, both East Indian and Turkish——who have conducted my experiments upon this interesting subject with a sort of galvanic battery, and have, for the general benefit of the world, inoculated myself, as it were, with the poison of eight thousand drops of laudanum per day (and for the same reason as a French surgeon inoculated himself lately with a cancer, an English one twenty years ago with plague, and a third, who was also English, with hydrophobia), I, it will be admitted, must surely now know what happiness is, if anybody does. And therefore I will here lay down an analysis of happiness; and, as the most interesting mode of communicating it, I will give it, not didactically, but wrapped up and involved in a picture of one evening, as I spent every evening during the intercalary year when laudanum, though taken daily, was to me no more than the elixir of pleasure.

Let there be a cottage, standing in a valley,[1] eight-

---

[1] The cottage and the valley concerned in this description were not imaginary: the valley was the lovely one, *in those days*, of Grasmere; and the cottage was occupied for more than twenty years by myself, as immediate successor, in the year 1809, to Wordsworth. Looking to the limitation here laid down—viz. *in those days*—the reader will inquire in what way *Time* can have affected the beauty of Grasmere. Do the Westmorland valleys turn grey-headed? O reader! this is a painful memento for some of us! Thirty years ago, a gang of Vandals (nameless, I thank heaven, to me), for the sake of building a mail-coach road that never would be wanted, carried, at a cost of £3000 to the defrauded parish, a horrid causeway of sheer granite masonry, for three-quarters-of-a-mile, right through the loveliest succession of secret forest dells and shy recesses of the lake, margined by unrivalled ferns, amongst which was the *Osmunda regalis*. This sequestered angle of Grasmere is described by Wordsworth, as it unveiled itself on a September morning, in the exquisite poems on the "Naming of Places."

een miles from any town; no spacious valley, but about two miles long by three-quarters-of-a-mile in average width—the benefit of which provision is that all the families resident within its circuit will compose, as it were, one larger household, personally familiar to your eye, and more or less interesting to your affections. Let the mountains be real mountains, between three and four thousand feet high, and the cottage a real cottage, not (as a witty author has it) "a cottage with a double coach-house"; let it be, in fact (for I must abide by the actual scene), a white cottage, embowered with flowering shrubs, so chosen as to unfold a succession of flowers upon the walls, and clustering around the windows, through all the months of spring, summer, and autumn; beginning, in fact, with May roses, and ending with jasmine. Let it, however, *not* be spring, nor summer, nor autumn; but winter, in its sternest shape. This is a most important point in the science of happiness. And I am surprised to see people overlook it, as if it were actually a matter of congratulation that winter is going, or, if coming, is not likely to be a severe one. On the contrary, I put up a petition, annually, for as much snow, hail, frost, or storm of one kind or other, as the skies can possibly afford. Surely everybody is aware of the divine pleasures which attend a winter fireside—candles at four o'clock, warm hearth-rugs, tea, a fair tea-maker, shutters closed, curtains flowing in ample draperies on the floor, whilst the wind and rain are raging audibly without,

From this also—viz. this spot of ground, and this magnificent crest (the *Osmunda*)—was suggested that unique line, the finest independent line through all the records of verse,

> *Or lady of the lake,*
> *Sole-sitting by the shores of old romance.*

Rightly, therefore, did I introduce this limitation. The Grasmere before and after this outrage were two different vales.

And at the doors and windows seem to call,
As heaven and earth they would together mell;
Yet the least entrance find they none at all;
Whence sweeter grows our rest secure in massy hall.
—Castle of Indolence

All these are items in the description of a winter evening which must surely be familiar to everybody born in a high latitude. And it is evident that most of these delicacies cannot be ripened without weather stormy or inclement in some way or other. I am not *"particular"* whether it be snow, or black frost, or wind so strong that (as Mr. Anti-slavery Clarkson says) "you may lean your back against it like a post." I can put up even with rain, provided that it rains cats and dogs, or, as sailors say, "great guns and marline-spikes"; but something of the sort I must have; and, if I have it not, I think myself in a manner ill-used: for why am I called on to pay so heavily for winter in coals, candles, &c., if I am not to have the article good of its kind? No: a Canadian winter for my money, or a Russian one, where every man is but a co-proprietor with the north wind in the fee-simple of his own ears. Indeed, so great an epicure am I in this matter that I cannot relish a winter night fully if it be much past St. Thomas's Day, and have degenerated into disgusting tendencies towards vernal indications: in fact, it must be divided by a thick wall of dark nights from all return of light and sunshine. Start, therefore, at the first week of November: thence to the end of January, Christmas Eve being the meridian line, you may compute the period when happiness is in season—which, in my judgement, enters the room with the tea-tray. For tea, though ridiculed by those who are naturally coarse in their nervous sensibilities, or are become so from wine-drinking, and are not susceptible of influence from so refined a stimulant, will always be the favourite beverage of the intellectual; and, for my part, I would have joined Dr. Johnson in a *bellum internecinum* against Jonas Hanway, or any other impious person who should have presumed to disparage it. But here, to save myself the trouble of too much verbal description, I will introduce a painter, and give him directions for the rest of the picture. Painters do not like white cottages, unless a good deal weather-stained; but, as the reader now understands that it is a winter night, his services will not be required except for the *inside* of the house.

Paint me, then, a room seventeen feet by twelve, and not more than seven and a-half feet high. This, reader, is somewhat ambitiously styled, in my family, the drawing-room; but, being contrived "a double debt to pay," it is also, and more justly, termed the library; for it happens that books are the only article of property in which I am richer than my neighbours. Of these I have about five thousand, collected gradually since my eighteenth year. Therefore, painter, put as many as you can into this room. Make it populous with books; and, furthermore, paint me a good fire; and furniture plain and modest, befitting the unpretending cottage of a scholar. And near the fire paint me a tea-table; and (as it is clear that no creature can come to see one on such a stormy night) place only two cups and saucers on the tea-tray; and, if you know how to paint such a thing, symbolically or otherwise, paint me an eternal teapot—eternal *a parte ante*, and *a parte post;* for I usually drink tea from eight o'clock at night to four in the morning. And, as it is very unpleasant to make tea, or to pour it out for one's self, paint me a lovely young woman sitting at the table. Paint her arms like Aurora's, and her smiles like Hebe's; but no, dear M[argaret]! not even in jest let me insinuate that

thy power to illuminate my cottage rests upon a tenure
so perishable as mere personal beauty, or that the
witchcraft of angelic smiles lies within the empire of
any earthly pencil. Pass, then, my good painter, to
something more within its power; and the next article
brought forward should naturally be myself—a picture of the Opium-Eater, with his "little golden receptacle of the pernicious drug" lying beside him on
the table. As to the opium, I have no objection to see a
picture of *that;* you may paint it, if you choose; but I
apprise you that no "little" receptacle would, even in
1816, answer *my* purpose, who was at a distance from
the "stately Pantheon" and all druggists (mortal or
otherwise). No: you may as well paint the real receptacle, which was not of gold, but of glass, and as much
like a sublunary wine-decanter as possible. In fact,
one day, by a series of happily conceived experiments,
I discovered that it *was* a decanter. Into this you may
put a quart of ruby-coloured laudanum; that, and a
book of German metaphysics placed by its side, will
sufficiently attest my being in the neighbourhood; but,
as to myself, there I demur. I admit that, naturally, I
ought to occupy the foreground of the picture; that,
being the hero of the piece, or (if you choose) the
criminal at the bar, my body should be had into court.
This seems reasonable; but why should I confess on
this point to a painter? or why confess it at all? If the
public (into whose private ear I am confidentially
whispering my Confessions, and not into any painter's) should chance to have framed some agreeable picture for itself of the Opium-Eater's exterior—should
have ascribed to him, romantically, an elegant person
or a handsome face—why should I barbarously tear
from it so pleasing a delusion?—pleasing both to the
public and to me. No: paint me, if at all, according to
your own fancy; and, since a painter's fancy should

teem with beautiful creations, I cannot fail, in that way, to be a gainer.

And now, reader, we have run through all the ten categories of my condition, as it stood about 1816–17, up to the middle of which latter year I judge myself to have been a happy man; and the elements of that happiness I have endeavoured to place before you, in the above sketch of the interior of a scholar's library, in a cottage among the mountains, on a stormy winter evening, rain driving vindictively and with malice aforethought against the windows, and darkness such that you cannot see your own hand when held up against the sky.

But now farewell, a long farewell, to happiness, winter or summer! farewell to smiles and laughter! farewell to peace of mind, to tranquil dreams, and to the blessed consolations of sleep! For more than three years and a-half I am summoned away from these. Here opens upon me an Iliad of woes: for I now enter upon—

PART III

THE PAINS OF OPIUM

As when some great painter dips
His pencil in the gloom of earthquake and eclipse.
SHELLEY'S *Revolt of Islam*

READER, who have thus far accompanied me, I must request your attention, before we go farther, to a few explanatory notes.

I. You are already aware, I hope—else you must have a low opinion of my logic—that the opium miseries, which are now on the point of pressing forward to the front of this narrative, connect themselves with

my early hardships in London (and therefore more remotely with those in Wales) by natural links of affilia-
tion—that is, the early series of sufferings was the
parent of the later. Otherwise, these *Confessions* would
break up into two disconnected sections: first, a record
of boyish calamities; secondly, a record (totally independent) of sufferings consequent upon excesses in
opium. And the two sections would have no link whatever to connect them, except the slight one of having
both happened to the same person. But a little attention will show the strictness of the inter-connexion.
The boyish sufferings, whether in Wales or London,
pressing upon an organ peculiarly weak in my bodily
system—viz. the stomach—caused that subsequent
distress and irritability of the stomach which drove me
to the use of opium as the sole remedy potent enough
to control it. Here already there is exposed a sufficient
causal connexion between the two several sections of
my experience. The opium would probably never have
been promoted into the dignity of a daily and a life-
long resource, had it not proved itself to be the one sole
agent equal to the task of tranquillizing the miseries
left behind by the youthful privations. Thus far the
nexus, as between cause and effect, is sufficiently established between the one experience and the other—
between the boyish records and the records of mature
life. There needed no other *nexus* to justify the unity
of the entire *Confessions*. But, though not wanted,
nevertheless it happens that there *is* another and a distinct link connecting the two separate records. The
main phenomenon by which opium expressed itself
permanently, and the sole phenomenon that was com-
municable, lay in the dreams (and in the peculiar
dream-scenery) which followed the opium excesses.
But naturally these dreams, and this dream-scenery,
drew their outlines and materials—their great lights

and shadows—from those profound revelations which had been ploughed so deeply into the heart, from those *encaustic* records which in the mighty furnaces of London life had been burned into the undying memory by the fierce action of misery. And thus in reality the early experiences of erring childhood not only led to the secondary experiences of opium, but also determined the particular form and pressure of the chief phenomena in those secondary experiences. Here is the briefest possible abstract of the total case: The final object of the whole record lay in the dreams. For the sake of those the entire narrative arose. But what caused the dreams? Opium used in unexampled excess. But what caused this excess in the use of opium? Simply the early sufferings; these, and these only, through the derangements which they left behind in the animal economy. On this mode of viewing the case, moving regressively from the end to the beginning, it will be seen that there is one uninterrupted bond of unity running through the entire succession of experiences, first and last: the dreams were an inheritance from the opium; the opium was an inheritance from the boyish follies.

II. You will think, perhaps, that I am too confidential and communicative of my own private history. It may be so. But my way of writing is rather to think aloud, and follow my own humours, than much to inquire who is listening to me; for, if once I stop to consider what is proper to be said, I shall soon come to doubt whether any part at all is proper. The fact is, I imagine myself writing at a distance of twenty—thirty—fifty years ahead of this present moment, either for the satisfaction of the few who may then retain any interest in myself, or of the many (a number that is sure to be continually growing) who will take an inextinguishable interest in the mysterious

powers of opium. For opium *is* mysterious; mysterious
to the extent, at times, of apparent self-contradiction;
and *so* mysterious that my own long experience in its
use—sometimes even in its abuse—did but mislead me
into conclusions ever more and more remote from what
I now suppose to be the truth. Fifty-and-two years'
experience of opium, as a magical resource under *all*
modes of bodily suffering, I may now claim to have
had—allowing only for some periods of four or six
months, during which, by unexampled efforts of self-
conquest, I had accomplished a determined abstinence
from opium.[1] These parentheses being subtracted, as

[1] With what final result I have much difficulty in saying.
Invariably, after such victories, I returned, upon deliberate
choice (after weighing all the consequences on this side and on
that), to the daily use of opium, but with silent changes, many
and great (worked apparently by these reiterated struggles),
in the opium-eating habits. Amongst other changes was this,
that the quantity required gradually fell by an enormous proportion. According to the modern slang phrase, I had in the
meridian stage of my opium career used "*fabulous*" quantities. Stating the quantities—not in solid opium, but in the
tincture (known to everybody as *laudanum*)—my daily ration
was eight thousand drops. If you write down that amount in
the ordinary way as 8000, you see at a glance that you may
read it into eight quantities of a thousand, or into eight hundred quantities of ten, or lastly, into eighty quantities of one
hundred. Now, a single quantity of one hundred will about fill
a very old-fashioned obsolete tea-spoon, of that order which
you find still lingering amongst the respectable poor. Eighty
such quantities, therefore, would have filled eighty of such
antediluvian spoons—that is, it would have been the common
hospital dose for three hundred and twenty adult patients.
But the ordinary tea-spoon of this present nineteenth century
is nearly as capacious as the dessert-spoon of our ancestors.
Which I have heard accounted for thus: Throughout the
eighteenth century, when first tea became known to the working population, the tea-drinkers were almost exclusively
women; men, even in educated classes, very often persisting
(down to the French Revolution) in treating such a beverage
as an idle and effeminate indulgence. This obstinate twist in

also, and secondly, some off-and-on fits of tentative
and intermitting dalliance with opium in the opening
of my career——these deductions allowed for, I may
describe myself as experimentally acquainted with
opium for something more than half-a-century. What,
then, is my final report upon its good and evil results?
In particular, upon these two capital tendencies of habitual opium-eating under the popular misconceptions: viz. its supposed necessity of continually clamouring for increasing quantities; secondly, its supposed
corresponding declension in power and efficacy. Upon
these ugly scandals what is my most deliberate award?
At the age of forty, the reader is aware that, under our
ancestral proverb, every man is a fool or a physician.
Apparently our excellent ancestors, aiming undeniably at alliteration, spelled *physician* with an *f*. And
why not? A man's physic might be undeniable, although his spelling should be open to some slight improvements. But I presume that the proverb meant to
exact from any man only so much medical skill as
should undertake the responsibility of his own individual health. It is my duty, it seems, thus far to be a
physician——to guarantee, so far as human foresight
can guarantee, my own corporeal sanity. And this, trying the case by ordinary practical tests, I have accomplished. And I add solemnly that without opium most
certainly I could not have accomplished such a result.
Thirty-five years ago, beyond all doubt, I should have
been in my grave. And, as to the two popular dilem-

masculine habits it was that secretly controlled the manufacture of tea-spoons. Up to Waterloo, tea-spoons were adjusted
chiefly to the calibre of female mouths. Since then, greatly to
the benefit of the national health, the grosser and browner sex
have universally fallen into the effeminate habit of tea-drink-
ing; and the capacity of tea-spoons has naturally conformed to
the new order of cormorant mouths that have alighted by
myriads upon the tea-trays of these later generations.

mas: that either you must renounce opium, or else in-
definitely augment the daily ration; and, secondly,
that, even submitting to such a postulate, you must
content yourself, under any scale of doses, with an effect continually decaying—in fact, that you must ultimately descend into the despairing condition of the
martyr to dram-drinking—at this point I make a resolute stand, in blank denial of the whole doctrine. Originally, when first entering upon my opium career, I
did so with great anxiety: and before my eyes floated
for ever the analogies—dim, or *not* dim, according to
my spirits at the moment—of the poor, perishing
brandy-drinker, often on the brink of *delirium tremens!* Opium I pursued under a harsh necessity, as an
unknown, shadowy power, leading I knew not whither,
and a power that might suddenly change countenance
upon this unknown road. Habitually I lived under such
an impression of awe as we have all felt from stories
of fawns, or seeming fawns, that have run before some
mounted hunter for many a league, until they have
tempted him far into the mazes of a boundless forest,
and at that point, where all regress had become lost and
impossible, either suddenly vanished, leaving the man
utterly bewildered, or assumed some more fearful
shape. A part of the evil which I feared actually unfolded itself; but all was due to my own ignorance, to
neglect of cautionary measures, or to gross mismanagement of my health in points where I well knew the
risks, but grievously underrated their urgency and
pressure. I was temperate: that solitary advantage I
had; but I sank under the lulling seductions of opium
into total sedentariness, and *that* whilst holding firmly
the belief that powerful exercise was omnipotent
against all modes of debility or obscure nervous irritations. The account of my depression, and almost of my
helplessness, in the next memorandum (No. III), is

faithful as a description to the real case. But, in ascribing that case to opium, as any transcendent and
overmastering agency, I was thoroughly wrong.
Twenty days of exercise, twenty times twenty miles
of walking, at the ordinary pace of three and a-half
miles an hour, or perhaps half that amount, would
have sent me up as buoyantly as a balloon into regions
of natural and healthy excitement, where dejection is
an impossible phenomenon. O heavens! how man
abuses or neglects his natural resources! Yes, the
thoughtful reader is disposed to say; but very possibly
distinguishing between such *natural* resources and
opium as a resource that is *not* natural, but highly artificial, or even absolutely unnatural. I think otherwise. Upon the basis of my really vast, perhaps unequalled, experience (let me add of my *tentative*
experience, varying its trials in every conceivable mode
so as to meet the question at issue under every angle),
I advance these three following propositions, all of
them unsuspected by the popular mind, and the last of
them (as cannot much longer fail to be discovered)
bearing a national value—I mean, as meeting our
English hereditary complaint—

1. With respect to the morbid growth upon the
Opium-Eater of his peculiar habit, when once rooted
in the system, and throwing out *tentacula* like a cancer, it is out of my power to deliver any such oracular
judgement upon the case—*i.e.* upon the apparent danger of such a course, and by what stages it might be
expected to travel towards its final consummation—as
naturally I should wish to do. Being an oracle, it is
my wish to behave myself like an oracle, and not to
evade any decent man's questions in the way that
Apollo too often did at Delphi. But, in this particular
instance before me, the accident of my own individual
seamanship in presence of this storm interfered with

the natural evolution of the problem in its extreme form of danger. I had become too uneasy under the consciousness of that intensely artificial condition into which I had imperceptibly lapsed through unprecedented quantities of opium; the shadows of eclipse were too dark and lurid not to rouse and alarm me into a spasmodic effort for reconquering the ground which I had lost. Such an effort I made: every step by which I had gone astray did I patiently unthread. And thus I fought off the natural and spontaneous catastrophe, whatever *that* might be, which mighty Nature would else have let loose for redressing the wrongs offered to herself. But what followed? In six or eight months more, upon fresh movements arising of insupportable nervous irritation, I fleeted back into the same opium lull. To and fro, up and down, did I tilt upon those mountainous seas, for year after year. "See-saw,[1] like Margery Daw, that sold her bed and lay on straw." Even so did I, led astray, perhaps, by the classical example of Miss Daw, see-saw for year after year, out and in, of manœuvres the most intricate, dances the most elaborate, receding or approaching, round my great central sun of opium. Sometimes I ran perilously close into my perihelion; sometimes I became frightened, and wheeled off into a vast cometary aphelion, where for six months "opium" was a word unknown. How nature stood all these see-sawings is quite a mystery to me: I must have led her a sad life in those days. Nervous irritation forced me, at times, upon frightful excesses; but terror from anomalous

[1] *"See-saw,"* &c.: O dear reader, surely you don't want an oracle to tell you that this is a good old nursery lyric, which through four centuries has stood the criticism, stood the anger against Daw's enemies, stood the pity for Daw herself, so infamously reduced to straw, of children through eighty generations, reckoning five years to each nursery succession.

symptoms sooner or later forced me back. This terror was strengthened by the vague hypotheses current at that period about spontaneous combustion. Might I not myself take leave of the literary world in that fashion? According to the popular fancy, there were two modes of this spontaneity, and really very little to choose between them. Upon one variety of this explosion, a man blew up in the dark, without match or candle near him, leaving nothing behind him but some bones, of no use to anybody, and which were supposed to be *his* only because nobody else ever applied for them. It was fancied that some volcanic agency—an unknown deposition—accumulated from some vast redundancy of brandy, furnished the self-exploding principle. But this startled the faith of most people; and a more plausible scheme suggested itself, which depended upon the concurrence of a lucifer-match. Without an incendiary, a man could not take fire. We sometimes see the hands of inveterate dram-drinkers throw off an atmosphere of intoxicating vapours, strong enough to lay flies into a state of sleep or *coma;* and on the same principle it was supposed that the breath might be so loaded with spirituous particles as to catch fire from a match applied to a pipe when held between the lips. If so, then what should hinder the "devouring element" (as newspapers call fire) from spreading through the throat to the cavity of the chest? in which case, not being insured, the man would naturally become a total loss. Opium, however, it will occur to the reader, is not alcohol. That is true. But it might, for anything that was known experimentally, be ultimately worse. Coleridge, the only person known to the public as having dallied systematically and for many years with opium, could not be looked to for any candid report of its history and progress; besides that, Coleridge was under a permanent

craze of having nearly accomplished his own liberation from opium; and thus he had come to have an
extra reason for self-delusion. Finding myself, therefore, walking on a solitary path of bad repute, leading
whither no man's experience could tell me, I became
proportionably cautious; and, if nature had any plot
for making an example of me, I was resolved to balk
her. Thus it was that I never followed out the seductions of opium to their final extremity. But, nevertheless, in evading that extremity, I stumbled upon as
great a discovery as if I had *not* evaded it. After the
first or second self-conquest in this conflict—although
finding it impossible to persist through more than a
few months in the abstinence from opium—I remarked, however, that the domineering tyranny of its
exactions was at length steadily declining. Quantities
noticeably less had now become sufficient: and, after
the fourth of these victories, won with continually de-
creasing efforts, I found that not only had the daily
dose (upon relapsing) suffered a self-limitation to an
enormous extent, but also that, upon any attempt obstinately to renew the old doses, there arose a new
symptom—viz. an irritation on the surface of the skin
—which soon became insupportable, and tended to
distraction. In about four years, without any further
efforts, my daily ration had fallen *spontaneously* from
a varying quantity of eight, ten, or twelve thousand
drops of laudanum to about three hundred. I describe
the drug as *laudanum,* because another change ran
along collaterally with this supreme change—viz.
that the solid opium began to require a length of time,
continually increasing, to expand its effects sensibly,
oftentimes not less than four hours; whereas the tincture manifested its presence instantaneously.

Thus, then, I had reached a position from which
authoritatively it might be pronounced, as a result of

long, anxious, and vigilant experience, that, on the assumption of earnest (even though intermitting) efforts towards recurrent abstinences on the part of the Opium-Eater, the practice of indulging to the very greatest excess in this narcotic tends to a natural (almost an inevitable) euthanasy. Many years ago, when briefly touching on this subject, I announced (as a fact even *then* made known to me) that no instance of abstinence, though it were but of three days' continuance, ever perishes. Ten grains, deducted from a daily ration of five hundred, will tell through a series of many weeks, and will be found again modifying the final result, even at the close of the year's reckoning. At this day, after a half-century of oscillating experience, and after no efforts or trying acts of self-denial beyond those severe ones attached to the several processes (five or six in all) of reconquering my freedom from the yoke of opium, I find myself pretty nearly at the same station which I occupied at that vast distance of time. It is recorded of Lord Nelson that, even after the Nile and Copenhagen, he still paid the penalty, on the first days of resuming his naval life, which is generally exacted by nature from the youngest little middy or the rawest griffin—viz. seasickness. And this happens to a considerable proportion of sailors: they do not recover their sea-legs till some days after getting afloat. The very same thing happens to veteran Opium-Eaters, when first, after long intermissions, resuming too abruptly their ancient familiarities with opium. It is a fact, which I mention as indicating the enormous revolutions passed through, that, within these five years, I have turned pale, and felt warnings, pointing towards such an uneasiness, after taking not more than twenty grains of opium. At present, and for some years, I have been habitually content with five or six grains daily, instead of three hundred and twenty to four hundred grains. Let me wind up this retrospect with saying that the powers of opium, as an anodyne, but still more as a tranquillizer of nervous and anomalous sensations, have not in the smallest degree decayed, and that, if it has casually unveiled its early power of exacting slight penalties from any trivial inattention to accurate proportions, it has more than commensurately renewed its ancient privilege of lulling irritation and of supporting preternatural calls for exertion.

My first proposition, therefore, amounts to this—that the process of weaning one's self from the deep bondage of opium, by many people viewed with despairing eyes, is not only a possible achievement, and one which grows easier in every stage of its progress, but is and promoted by nature in secret ways that could not, without some experience, have been suspected. This, however, is but a sorry commendation of any resource making great pretensions, that, by a process confessedly trying to human firmness, it can ultimately be thrown aside. Certainly little would be gained by the negative service of cancelling a drawback upon any agency whatever, until it were shown that this drawback has availed to disturb and neutralize great positive blessings lying within the gift of that agency. What are the advantages connected with opium that can merit any such name as blessings?

2. Briefly let me say, in the *second* proposition, that, if the reader had, in any South American forest, seen growing rankly some great febrifuge (such as the Jesuits' bark), he would probably have noticed it with slight regard. To understand its value, he must first have suffered from intermittent fever. Bark might strike him as an unnatural stimulant; but, when he came to see that tertian or quartan fever was also

an unnatural pressure upon human energies, he would begin to guess that two counter unnaturals may terminate in one most natural and salubrious result. Nervous irritation is the secret desolator of human life; and for this there is probably no adequate controlling power but that of opium, taken daily, under steady regulation.

3. But even more momentous is the burden of my *third* proposition. Are you aware, reader, what it is that constitutes the scourge (physically speaking) of Great Britain and Ireland? All readers who direct any part of their attention to medical subjects must know that it is pulmonary consumption. If you walk through a forest at certain seasons, you will see what is called a *blaze* of white paint upon a certain *élite* of the trees marked out by the forester as ripe for the axe. Such a blaze, if the shadowy world could reveal its futurities, would be seen everywhere distributing its secret badges of cognizance amongst our youthful men and women. Of those that, in the expression of Pericles, constitute the vernal section of our population, what a multitudinous crowd would be seen to wear upon their foreheads the same sad ghastly blaze, or some equivalent symbol of dedication to an early grave. How appalling in its amount is this annual slaughter amongst those that should by birthright be specially the children of hope, and levied impartially from *every* rank of society! Is the income-tax or the poor-rate, faithful as each is to its regulating tidetables, paid by *any* class with as much punctuality as this premature *florilegium*, this gathering and rendering up of blighted blossoms, by *all* classes? Then comes the startling question—that pierces the breaking hearts of so many thousand afflicted relatives—Is there no remedy? Is there no palliation of the evil? Waste not a thought upon the idle question whether

he that speaks is armed with this form or that form of authorization and sanction! Think within yourself how infinite would be the scorn of any poor sorrow-stricken mother, if she—standing over the coffin of her daughter—could believe or could imagine that any vestige of ceremonial scruples, or of fool-born superstitions, or the terror of a word, or old traditional prejudice, had been allowed to neutralize one chance in a thousand for her daughter—had by possibility (but, as I could tell her, had sometimes to a certainty) stepped between patients and deliverance from the grave, sure and perfect! "What matter," she would cry out, indignantly, "who it is that says the thing, so long as the thing itself is true?" It is the potent and faithful *word* that is wanted, in perfect slight of the organ through which it is uttered. Let me premise this notorious fact, that all consumption, though latent in the constitution, and indicated often to the eye in bodily conformation, does not therefore manifest itself as a disease, until some form of "cold," or bronchitis, some familiar affection of the chest or of the lungs, arises to furnish a starting-point for the morbid development.[1] Now the one fatal blunder lies in suffering that development to occur; and the one counter-working secret for pre-arrestment of this evil

[1] Here is a parallel case, equally fatal where it occurs, but happily moving within a far narrower circle. About fifty years ago, Sir Everard Home, a surgeon of the highest class, mentioned as a dreadful caution that, within his own experience, many an indolent tumour in the face, not unfrequently the most trifling pimple, which for thirty or more years had caused no uneasiness whatever, suddenly might chance to receive the slightest possible wound from a razor in the act of shaving. What followed? Once disturbed, the trivial excrescence became an open cancer. Is the parallel catastrophe in the pulmonary system, when pushed forward into development, at all less likely to hide its importance from uninstructed eyes? Yet, on the other hand, it is a thousand times more likely to happen.

lies in steadily, by whatever means, keeping up and
promoting the insensible perspiration. In that one
simple art of controlling a constant function of the
animal economy lies a magician's talisman for defeat-
ing the forces leagued against the great organs of respiration. Pulmonary affections, if not *previously* suffered to develop themselves, cannot live under the
hourly counter-working of this magical force. Consequently, the one question in arrear is, what potent
drug is that which possesses this power, a power
like that of "Amram's son," for evoking salubrious
streams, welling forth benignly from systems else
parched and arid as rocks in the wilderness? There is
none that I know of answering the need but opium.
The powers of that great agent I first learned dimly to
guess at from a remark made to me by a lady in London: then, and for some time previously, she had been
hospitably entertaining Coleridge, whom, indeed, she
tended with the anxiety of a daughter. Consequently,
she was familiarly acquainted with his opium habits;
and, on my asking, in reply to some remark of hers,
how she could be so sure as her words implied that
Coleridge was just then likely to be incapacitated for
writing (or, indeed, for any literary *exertion*), she
said, "Oh, I know it well by the glistening of his
cheeks." Coleridge's face, as is well known to his acquaintances, exposed a large surface of cheek; too
large for the intellectual expression of his features
generally, had not the final effect been redeemed by
what Wordsworth styled his "godlike forehead." The
result was that no possible face so broadly betrayed
and published any effects whatever, especially these
lustrous effects from excesses in opium. For some years
I failed to consider reflectively, or else, reflecting, I
failed to decipher, this resplendent acreage of cheek.
But at last, either *proprio marte*, or prompted by some

medical hint, I came to understand that the glistening face, glorious from afar like the old Pagan face of the demigod Æsculapius, simply reported the gathering accumulations of insensible perspiration. In the very hour, a memorable hour, of making that discovery, I made another. My own history, medically speaking, involved a mystery. At the commencement of my opium career, I had myself been pronounced repeatedly a martyr elect to pulmonary consumption. And, although, in the common decencies of humanity, this opinion upon my prospects had always been accompanied with some formal words of encouragement— as, for instance, that constitutions, after all, varied by endless differences—that nobody could fix limits to the powers of medicine, or, in default of medicine, to the healing resources of nature herself—yet, without something like a miracle in my favour, I was instructed to regard myself as a condemned subject. That was the upshot of these agreeable communications; alarming enough; and they were rendered more so by these three facts: First, the opinions were pronounced by the highest authorities in Christendom—viz. the physicians at Clifton and the Bristol Hotwells, who saw more of pulmonary disorders in one twelvemonth than the rest of the profession through all Europe in a century; for the disease, it must be remembered, was almost peculiar as a national scourge to Britain, interlinked with the local accidents of the climate and its restless changes; so that only in England could it be studied, and even there only in perfection at these Bristolian adjacencies—the reason being that all opulent patients resorted to the Devonshire watering-places, where the balmy temperature of the air and prevailing winds allowed the myrtle and other greenhouse shrubs to stand out-of-doors all winter through, and naturally on the road to Devonshire all patients alike touched at Clifton. There I was myself continually resident. Many, therefore, and of supreme authority, were the prophets of evil that announced to me my doom. Secondly, they were countenanced by the ugly fact that I out of eight children was the one who most closely inherited the bodily conformation of a father who had died of consumption at the early age of thirty-nine. Thirdly, I offered at the first glance, to a medical eye, every symptom of *phthisis* broadly and conspicuously developed. The hectic colours on the face, the nocturnal perspirations, the growing embarrassment of the respiration, and other expressions of gathering feebleness under any attempts at taking exercise—all these symptoms were steadily accumulating between the age of twenty-two and twenty-four. What was it that first arrested them? Simply the use, continually becoming more regular, of opium. Nobody recommended this drug to me; on the contrary, under that ignorant horror which everywhere invested opium, I saw too clearly that any avowed use of it would expose me to a rabid persecution.[1] Under the sincere and unaffected hope of saving me from destruction, I should have been hunted into the grave within six months. I kept my own counsel; said nothing; awakened no suspicions; persevered more and more determinately in the

[1] *"Rabid persecution"*: I do not mean that, in the circumstances of my individual position, any opening could have arisen to an opposition more than verbal; since it would have been easy for me at all times to withdraw myself by hundreds of leagues from controversies upon the case. But the reasons for concealment were not the less urgent. For it would have been painful to find myself reduced to the dilemma of either practising habitual and complex dissimulation, or, on the other hand, of throwing myself headlong into that fiery vortex of hotheaded ignorance upon the very name of opium which to this hour (though with less of rancorous bigotry) makes it hazardous to avow any daily use of so potent a drug.

use of opium; and finally effected so absolute a conquest over all pulmonary symptoms as could not have
failed to fix upon me the astonishment of Clifton, had
not the sense of wonder been broken by the lingering
time consumed in the several stages of the malady,
and still more effectually by my own personal with-
drawal from Clifton and its neighbourhoods.

Finally arose what will inevitably turn out a more
decisive chapter in such a record. I had always fixed
my eyes and my expectations upon a revolution in the
social history of opium which could not (as I assured
myself) by accident or by art be materially deferred.
The great social machinery of life-insurance, supposing no other agency to be brought into play, how
would *that* affect the great medicinal interests of
opium? I knew that insurance offices, and the ablest
actuaries of such offices, were not less ignorant upon
the real merits of the opium question, and (which was
worse) not less profoundly *prejudiced*, or less fanatical in their prejudices, than the rest of society. But,
then, there were interests, growing continually, which
would very soon force them into relaxing these prejudices. It would be alleged, at first, that opium-eating
increased the risk of a life-insurance. Waiving the
question whether it really *did* increase that risk, in
any case that increase of risk, like other risks, could
be valued, and *must* be valued. New habits were arising in society: that I well knew. And the old machin-
eries for insuring life interests, under these or any
other shifting conditions, would be obliged to adapt
themselves to changing circumstances. If the old offices should be weak enough to persist in their misdi-
rected obstinacy, new ones would arise. Meantime the
history of this question moved through the following
aspects: Sixteen and seventeen years ago, the offices all
looked with horror upon Opium-Eaters. Thus far, all

men must have disapproved the principles of their policy. Habitual brandy-drinkers met with no repulse.
And yet alcohol leads into daily dangers—for instance, that of *delirium tremens*. But no man ever
heard of opium leading into *delirium tremens*. In the
one case, there are well-ascertained and notorious dangers besetting the path; but, in the other, supposing
any corresponding dangers to exist, they have yet to
be discovered. However, the offices would not look at
us who came forward avowing ourselves to be Opium-
Eaters. Myself in particular they regarded, I believe,
as the abomination of desolation. And fourteen offices
in succession, within a few months, repulsed me as a
candidate for insurance on that solitary ground of
having owned myself to be an Opium-Eater. The insurance was of very little consequence to myself,
though involving some interest to others. And I contented myself with saying, "Ten years hence, gentlemen, you will have come to understand your own interests better." In less than *seven* years I received a
letter from Mr. Tait, surgeon to the Police Force in
Edinburgh, reporting a direct investigation officially
pursued by him under private instructions received
from two or more insurance offices. I knew, at the beginning of these seven years, or had strong reasons for
believing, that the habit of opium-eating was spreading extensively, and through classes of society widely
disconnected. This diffusion would, beyond a doubt, as
one of its earliest consequences, coerce the insurance
offices into a strict revision of their old blind policy. Accordingly it had already done so; and the earliest fruits of this revolution were now before me in the
proof-sheets so obligingly transmitted by Mr. Tait.
His object, as I understood it, in sending these proofs
to myself, was simply to collect such additional notices, suggestions, or sceptical queries, as might rea-

sonably be anticipated from any reflective opium experience so extensive as my own. Most unhappily, this
gentleman, during the course of our brief correspondence, was suddenly attacked by typhus fever; and, after
a short illness, to my own exceeding regret, he died.
On all accounts I had reason for sorrow. Knowing
him only through his very interesting correspondence with myself, I had learned to form high expectations from Mr. Tait's philosophic spirit and his determined hostility to traditional cant. He had recorded,
in the communications made to myself, with great
minuteness and anxiety for rigour of accuracy, the
cases of more than ninety patients. And he had shown
himself inexorably deaf to all attempts at confounding evils specially belonging to opium as a stimulant,
as a narcotic, or as a poison, with those which belong
to opium merely as a cause of constipation or other ordinary irregularities in the animal economy. Most
people of sedentary habits, but amongst such people
notoriously those who think much, need some slight
means of stimulating the watchwork of the animal
system into action. Neglect of such means will of
course derange the health. But in such derangements
there is no special impeachment of opium: many
thousands of agents terminate in the same or more obstinate derangements, unless vigilantly counteracted.
The paramount mission of Mr. Tait, under his instructions from insurance offices, as I interpreted his
own account of this mission, was to report firmly and
decisively upon the tendencies of opium in relation to
the lengthening or shortening of life. At that point
where his proof-sheets were interrupted by the fatal
attack of fever, he had not entirely finished his record
of cases; so that his final judgement or summing up
had not commenced. It was, however, evident to me in
what channel this final judgement would have flowed.

To a certainty, he would have authorized his clients (the insurance offices) to dismiss all anxiety as to the life-abridging tendencies of opium. But he would have pointed their jealousy in another direction—viz. this, that in some proportion of cases there may always be a reasonable ground for suspecting, not the opium as separately in itself any cause of mischief, but the opium as a conjectural indication of some secret distress or irritation that had fastened upon the system, and had in that way sought relief; cases, in short, which the use of opium had not caused, but which, on the contrary, had caused the use of opium—opium having been called in to redress or to relieve the affection. In all such circumstances, the insurance office is entitled to call for a frank disclosure of the ailment; but not, as hitherto, entitled to assume the opium as itself an ailment. It may very easily have happened that simply the genial restoration derived from opium, its power of qualifying a man suddenly to face (that is, upon an hour's warning to face) some twelve hours' unusual exertion—qualifying him both as to spirits and as to strength; or again, simply the general purpose of seeking relief from ennui, or *tædium vitæ* —any one of these motives may satisfactorily account for the applicant's having resorted to opium. He might reply to the office in Professor Wilson's word,[1] "Gentlemen, I am a *Hedonist;* and, if you *must* know why I take opium, that's the reason why." But still, upon every admission from a candidate that he took opium, it would be a prudent question and a just question on the part of the office, to ask *"why,"* and in what circumstances the practice had originated. If in any lo-

[1] From the Greek word for *voluptuous pleasure*—viz. *Hedone* ('Ηδονή)—Professor Wilson coined the English word *Hedonist*, which he sometimes applied in playful reproach to myself and others.

cal uneasiness, then would arise a natural right on the part of the office to press for a surgical examination. But, apart from such special cases, it was evident that this acute and experienced surgeon saw no reason whatever in the simple practice of opium-eating for hesitating upon a life-insurance proposal, or for exacting a higher rate of premium.

Here I pause. The reader will infer, from what I have now said, that all passages, written at an earlier period under cloudy and uncorrected views of the evil agencies presumable in opium, stand retracted; although, shrinking from the labour of altering an error diffused so widely under my own early misconceptions of the truth, I have suffered them to remain as they were. My general views upon the powers and natural tendencies of opium were all supported and strengthened by this fortunate advantage of a professional correspondence. My special doctrine I now repeat at this point of valediction, and in a rememberable form. Lord Bacon said once, too boldly and hazardously, that he who discovers the secret of making myrrh soluble by human blood has discovered the secret of immortal life. I propose a more modest form of magic——that he who discovers the secret of stimulating and keeping up unintermittingly the insensible perspiration has discovered the secret of intercepting pulmonary consumption. In my medical character, I here take leave of the reader, and fall back into the current of my regular narrative.

III. My studies have now been long interrupted. I cannot read to myself with any pleasure, hardly with a moment's endurance. Yet I sometimes read aloud for the pleasure of others; because reading is an accomplishment of mine, and, in the slang use of the word *accomplishment* as a superficial and ornamental attainment, almost the only one I possess; and formerly, if I had any vanity at all connected with any endowment or attainment of mine, it was with this; for I had observed that no accomplishment is more rare. Actors are the worst readers of all. John Kemble is not effective as a reader, though he has the great advantage of mature scholarship; and his sister, the immortal Siddons, with all her superiority to him in voice, reads even less effectively. She reads nothing well but dramatic works. In the *Paradise Lost*, which I heard her attempt at Barley Wood, her failure was distressing; almost as distressing as the sycophantic applause of the surrounding company—all lost, of course, in nearly speechless admiration. Neither Coleridge nor Southey is a good reader of verse. Southey is admirable almost in all things, but not in this. Both he and Coleridge read as if crying, or at least wailing lugubriously. People in general either read poetry without any passion at all, or else overstep the modesty of nature. Of late, if I have felt moved by anything in books, it has been by the grand lamentations of *Samson Agonistes*, or the great harmonies of the Satanic speeches in *Paradise Regained*, when read aloud by myself. We are far from towns; but a young lady sometimes comes and drinks tea with us; at her request and M[argaret]'s, I now and then read Wordsworth's poems to them. (Wordsworth, by the bye, is the only poet I ever met who could read his own verses; often, indeed, he reads admirably.)

For nearly two years I believe that I read nothing and studied nothing. Analytic studies are continuous studies, and not to be pursued by fits and starts, or fragmentary efforts. All these were become insupportable to me; I shrank from them with a sense of powerless and infantine feebleness that gave me an anguish the greater from remembering the time when I grappled with them to my own hourly delight; and for this further reason, because I had devoted the labour of my whole life, had dedicated my intellect, blossoms and fruits, to the slow and elaborate toil of constructing one single work, to which I had presumed to give the title of an unfinished work of Spinosa's—viz. *De Emendatione Humani Intellectûs*. This was now lying locked up as by frost, like any Spanish bridge or aqueduct begun upon too great a scale for the resources of the architect; and, instead of surviving me, as a monument of wishes at least, and aspirations, and long labours, dedicated to the exaltation of human nature in that way in which God had best fitted me to promote so great an object, it was likely to stand a memorial to my children of hopes defeated, of baffled efforts, of materials uselessly accumulated, of foundations laid that were never to support a superstructure, of the grief and the ruin of the architect. In this state of imbecility, I had, for amusement, turned my attention to political economy. My understanding, which formerly had been as active and restless as a panther, could not, I suppose (so long as I lived at all), sink into utter lethargy; and political economy offers this advantage to a person in my state—that, though it is eminently an organic science (no part, that is to say, but what acts on the whole, as the whole again reacts on and through each part), yet still the several parts may be detached and contemplated singly. Great as was the prostration of my powers at this time, yet I could not forget my knowledge; and my understanding had been far too many years intimate with severe thinkers, with logic, and the great masters of knowledge, not to be aware of a great call made by political economy at this crisis for a new law and a transcendent legislator. Suddenly, in 1818, a friend in Edinburgh sent me down Mr. Ricardo's book; and, recur-

ring to my own prophetic anticipation of some coming
legislator for this science, I said, before I had finished
the first chapter, "Thou art the man!" Wonder and curiosity were emotions that had long been dead in me.
Yet I wondered once more—wondered at myself that
could once again be stimulated to the effort of reading; and much more I wondered at the book. Had this
profound work been really written during the tumultuous hurry of the nineteenth century? Could it be
that an Englishman, and he not in academic bowers,
but oppressed by mercantile and senatorial cares, had
accomplished what all the universities of Europe, and
a century of thought, had failed even to advance by
one hair's-breadth? Previous writers had been crushed
and overlaid by the enormous weights of facts, details,
and exceptions; Mr. Ricardo had deduced, *a priori*,
from the understanding itself, laws which first shot
arrowy light into the dark chaos of materials, and had
thus constructed what hitherto was but a collection of
tentative discussions into a science of regular proportions, now first standing upon an eternal basis.

Thus did one simple work of a profound understanding avail to give me a pleasure and an activity
which I had not known for years; it roused me even to
write, or, at least, to dictate what M[argaret] wrote
for me. It seemed to me that some important truths
had escaped even "the inevitable eye" of Mr. Ricardo;
and, as these were, for the most part, of such a nature
that I could express or illustrate them briefly and elegantly by algebraic symbols, the whole would hardly
have reached the bulk of a pamphlet. With M[ar-
garet] for my amanuensis, even at this time, incapable as I was of all general exertion, I drew up,
therefore, my *Prolegomena to all Future Systems of
Political Economy*.

This exertion, however, was but a momentary flash,

as the sequel showed. Arrangements were made at a provincial press, about eighteen miles distant, for printing it. An additional compositor was retained for some days on this account. The work was even twice advertised; and I was, in a manner, pledged to the fulfilment of my intention. But I had a preface to write, and a dedication, which I wished to make impressive, to Mr. Ricardo. I found myself quite unable to accomplish all this. The arrangements were countermanded, the compositor dismissed, and my *Prolegomena* rested peacefully by the side of its elder and more dignified brother.

In thus describing and illustrating my intellectual torpor, I use terms that apply, more or less, to every part of the years during which I was under the Circean spells of opium. But for misery and suffering, I might, indeed, be said to have existed in a dormant state. I seldom could prevail on myself to write a letter; an answer of a few words to any that I received, was the utmost that I could accomplish; and often *that* not until the letter had lain for weeks, or even months, on my writing-table. Without the aid of M[argaret], my whole domestic economy, whatever became of political economy, must have gone into irretrievable confusion. I shall not afterwards allude to this part of the case; it is one, however, which the Opium-Eater will find, in the end, most oppressive and tormenting, from the sense of incapacity and feebleness, from the direct embarrassments incident to the neglect or procrastination of each day's appropriate labours, and from the remorse which must often exasperate the stings of these evils to a conscientious mind. The Opium-Eater loses none of his moral sensibilities or aspirations; he wishes and longs as earnestly as ever to realize what he believes possible, and feels to be exacted by duty; but his intellectual apprehension of what is possible infinitely outruns his power, not of execution only, but even of proposing or willing. He lies under a world's weight of incubus and nightmare; he lies in sight of all that he would fain perform, just as a man forcibly confined to his bed by the mortal languor of paralysis, who is compelled to witness injury or outrage offered to some object of his tenderest love—he would lay down his life if he might but rise and walk; but he is powerless as an infant, and cannot so much as make an effort to move.

But from this I now pass to what is the main subject of these latter *Confessions*—to the history and journal of what took place in my dreams; for these were the immediate and proximate cause of shadowy terrors that settled and brooded over my whole waking life.

The first notice I had of any important change going on in this part of my physical economy was from the re-awaking of a state of eye oftentimes incident to childhood. I know not whether my reader is aware that many children have a power of painting, as it were, upon the darkness all sorts of phantoms: in some that power is simply a mechanic affection of the eye; others have a voluntary or semi-voluntary power to dismiss or summon such phantoms; or, as a child once said to me, when I questioned him on this matter, "I can tell them to go, and they go; but sometimes they come when I don't tell them to come." He had by one-half as unlimited a command over apparitions as a Roman centurion over his soldiers. In the middle of 1817 this faculty became increasingly distressing to me: at night, when I lay awake in bed, vast processions moved along continually in mournful pomp; friezes of never-ending stories, that to my feelings were as sad and solemn as stories drawn from times before Œdipus or Priam, before Tyre, before Memphis. And, concurrently with this, a corresponding change took place in my dreams; a theatre seemed suddenly opened and lighted up within my brain, which presented nightly spectacles of more than earthly splendour. And the four following facts may be mentioned, as noticeable at this time:

1. That, as the creative state of the eye increased, a sympathy seemed to arise between the waking and the dreaming states of the brain in one point—that whatsoever I happened to call up and to trace by a voluntary act upon the darkness was very apt to transfer itself to my dreams; and at length I feared to exercise this faculty; for, as Midas turned all things to gold that yet baffled his hopes and defrauded his human desires, so whatsoever things capable of being visually represented I did but think of in the darkness immediately shaped themselves into phantoms for the eye; and, by a process apparently no less inevitable, when thus once traced in faint and visionary colours, like writings in sympathetic ink, they were drawn out, by the fierce chemistry of my dreams, into insufferable splendour that fretted my heart.

2. This and all other changes in my dreams were accompanied by deep-seated anxiety and funereal melancholy, such as are wholly incommunicable by words. I seemed every night to descend—not metaphorically, but literally to descend—into chasms and sunless abysses, depths below depths, from which it seemed hopeless that I could ever re-ascend. Nor did I, by waking, feel that I *had* re-ascended. Why should I dwell upon this? For indeed the state of gloom which attended these gorgeous spectacles, amounting at last to utter darkness, as of some suicidal despondency, cannot be approached by words.

3. The sense of space, and in the end the sense of time, were both powerfully affected. Buildings, land-

scapes, &c., were exhibited in proportions so vast as
the bodily eye is not fitted to receive. Space swelled,
and was amplified to an extent of unutterable and self-
repeating infinity. This disturbed me very much less
than the vast expansion of time. Sometimes I seemed
to have lived for seventy or a hundred years in one
night; nay, sometimes had feelings representative of a
duration far beyond the limits of any human experience.

4. The minutest incidents of childhood, or forgotten scenes of later years, were often revived. I could
not be said to recollect them; for, if I had been told of
them when waking, I should not have been able to
acknowledge them as parts of my past experience. But,
placed as they were before me in dreams like intui-
tions, and clothed in all their evanescent circumstances
and accompanying feelings, I *recognized* them instantaneously. I was once told by a near relative of mine
that, having in her childhood fallen into a river, and
being on the very verge of death but for the assistance
which reached her at the last critical moment, she saw
in a moment her whole life, clothed in its forgotten
incidents, arrayed before her as in a mirror, not successively, but simultaneously; and she had a faculty
developed as suddenly for comprehending the whole
and every part. This, from some opium experiences, I
can believe; I have, indeed, seen the same thing asserted twice in modern books, and accompanied by a
remark which probably is true—viz. that the dread
book of account which the Scriptures speak of is, in
fact, the mind itself of each individual. Of this, at
least, I feel assured, that there is no such thing as ultimate *forgetting;* traces once impressed upon the memory are indestructible; a thousand accidents may and
will interpose a veil between our present consciousness
and the secret inscriptions on the mind. Accidents of

the same sort will also rend away this veil. But alike, whether veiled or unveiled, the inscription remains for ever; just as the stars seem to withdraw before the common light of day, whereas, in fact, we all know that it is the light which is drawn over them as a veil, and that they are waiting to be revealed whenever the obscuring daylight itself shall have withdrawn.

Having noticed these four facts as memorably distinguishing my dreams from those of health, I shall now cite a few illustrative cases; and shall then cite such others as I remember, in any order that may give them most effect as pictures to the reader.

I had been in youth, and ever since, for occasional amusement, a great reader of Livy, whom I confess that I prefer, both for style and matter, to any other of the Roman historians; and I had often felt as solemn and appalling sounds, emphatically representative of Roman majesty, the two words so often occurring in Livy, *Consul Romanus;* especially when the consul is introduced in his military character. I mean to say that the words *king, sultan, regent,* &c., or any other titles of those who embody in their own persons the collective majesty of a great people, had less power over my reverential feelings. I had also, though no great reader of History, made myself critically familiar with one period of English history—viz. the period of the Parliamentary War—having been attracted by the moral grandeur of some who figured in that day, and by the interesting memoirs which survive those unquiet times. Both these parts of my lighter reading, having furnished me often with matter of reflection, now furnished me with matter for my dreams. Often I used to see, after painting upon the blank darkness a sort of rehearsal whilst waking, a crowd of ladies, and perhaps a festival and dances. And I heard it said, or I said to myself, "These are English ladies from the unhappy times of Charles I. These are the wives and daughters of those who met in peace, and sat at the same tables, and were allied by marriage or by blood; and yet, after a certain day in August 1642, never smiled upon each other again, nor met but in the field of battle; and at Marston Moor, at Newbury, or at Naseby, cut asunder all ties of love by the cruel sabre, and washed away in blood the memory of ancient friendship." The ladies danced, and looked as lovely as at the court of George IV. Yet even in my dream I knew that they had been in the grave for nearly two centuries. This pageant would suddenly dissolve; and, at a clapping of hands, would be heard the heart-shaking sound of *Consul Romanus;* and immediately came "sweeping by," in gorgeous paludaments, Paullus or Marius, girt around by a company of centurions, with the crimson tunic [1] hoisted on a spear, and followed by the *alalagmos* [2] of the Roman legions.

Many years ago, when I was looking over Piranesi's *Antiquities of Rome,* Coleridge, then standing by, described to me a set of plates from that artist, called his "Dreams," and which record the scenery of his own visions during the delirium of a fever. Some of these (I describe only from memory of Coleridge's account) represented vast Gothic halls; on the floor of which stood mighty engines and machinery, wheels, cables, catapults, &c., expressive of enormous power put forth, or resistance overcome. Creeping along the sides of the walls, you perceived a staircase; and upon this, groping his way upwards, was Piranesi himself. Follow the stairs a little farther, and you perceive them

---

[1] *"The crimson tunic":* The signal which announced a day of battle.

[2] *"Alalagmos":* A word expressing collectively the gathering of the Roman war-cries—*Alála, Alála!*

reaching an abrupt termination, without any balustrade, and allowing no step onwards to him who should reach the extremity, except into the depths below. Whatever is to become of poor Piranesi, at least you suppose that his labours must now in some way terminate. But raise your eyes, and behold a second flight of stairs still higher, on which again Piranesi is perceived, by this time standing on the very brink of the abyss. Once again elevate your eye, and a still more aerial flight of stairs is descried; and there, again, is the delirous Piranesi, busy on his aspiring labours: and so on, until the unfinished stairs and the hopeless Piranesi both are lost in the upper gloom of the hall. With the same power of endless growth and self-reproduction did my architecture proceed in dreams. In the early stage of the malady, the splendours of my dreams were indeed chiefly architectural; and I beheld such pomp of cities and palaces as never yet was beheld by the waking eye, unless in the clouds. From a great modern poet [1] I cite the part of a passage which describes, as an

---

[1] *"From a great modern poet"*: What poet? It was Wordsworth; and why did I not formally name him? This throws a light backwards upon the strange history of Wordsworth's reputation. The year in which I wrote and published these *Confessions* was 1821; and at that time the name of Wordsworth, though beginning to emerge from the dark cloud of scorn and contumely which had hitherto overshadowed it, was yet most imperfectly established. Not until ten years later was his greatness cheerfully and generally acknowledged. I, therefore, as the very earliest (without one exception) of all who came forward, in the beginning of his career, to honour and welcome him, shrank with disgust from making any sentence of mine the occasion for an explosion of vulgar malice against him. But the grandeur of the passage here cited inevitably spoke for itself; and he that would have been most scornful on hearing the name of the poet coupled with this epithet of "great" could not but find his malice intercepted, and himself cheated into cordial admiration, by the splendour of the verses.

appearance actually beheld in the clouds, what in many
of its circumstances I saw frequently in sleep:

> *The appearance, instantaneously disclosed,*
> *Was of a mighty city—boldly say*
> *A wilderness of building, sinking far*
> *And self-withdrawn into a wondrous depth,*
> *Far sinking into splendour without end!*
> *Fabric it seemed of diamond and of gold,*
> *With alabaster domes and silver spires,*
> *And blazing terrace upon terrace, high*
> *Uplifted; here, serene pavilions bright,*
> *In avenues disposed; there, towers begirt*
> *With battlements that on their restless fronts*
> *Bore stars—illumination of all gems!*
> *By earthly nature had the effect been wrought*
> *Upon the dark materials of the storm*
> *Now pacified; on them, and on the coves,*
> *And mountain steeps and summits, whereunto*
> *The vapours had receded, taking there*
> *Their station under a cerulean sky.*

The sublime circumstance—"that on their *restless*
fronts bore stars"—might have been copied from my
own architectural dreams, so often did it occur. We
hear it reported of Dryden, and in later times of Fu-
seli, that they ate raw meat for the sake of obtaining
splendid dreams: how much better, for such a purpose,
to have eaten opium, which yet I do not remember
that any poet is recorded to have done, except the
dramatist Shadwell; and in ancient days, Homer is, I
think, rightly reputed to have known the virtues of
opium as a φάρμακον νηπενθές—*i.e.* as an anodyne.

   To my architecture succeeded dreams of lakes and
silvery expanses of water: these haunted me so much
that I feared lest some dropsical state or tendency of

the brain might thus be making itself (to use a metaphysical word) *objective*,[1] and that the sentient organ might be projecting itself as its own object. For two months I suffered greatly in my head—a part of my bodily structure which had hitherto been so clear from all touch or taint of weakness (physically, I mean) that I used to say of it, as the last Lord Orford said of his stomach, that it seemed likely to survive the rest of my person. Till now I had never felt a headache even, or any the slightest pain, except rheumatic pains caused by my own folly.

The waters gradually changed their character— from translucent lakes, shining like mirrors, they became seas and oceans. And now came a tremendous change, which, unfolding itself slowly like a scroll, through many months, promised an abiding torment; and, in fact, it never left me, though recurring more or less intermittingly. Hitherto the human face had often mixed in my dreams, but not despotically, nor with any special power of tormenting. But now that affection which I have called the tyranny of the human face began to unfold itself. Perhaps some part of my London life (the searching for Ann amongst fluctuating crowds) might be answerable for this. Be that as it may, now it was that upon the rocking waters of the ocean the human face began to reveal itself; the sea appeared paved with innumerable faces, upturned to the heavens; faces, imploring, wrathful, despairing; faces that surged upwards by thousands, by myriads, by generations: infinite was my agitation; my mind

---

[1] *"Objective"*: This word, so nearly unintelligible in 1821, so intensely scholastic, and, consequently, when surrounded by familiar and vernacular words, so apparently pedantic, yet, on the other hand, so indispensable to accurate thinking, and to *wide* thinking, has since 1821 become too common to need any apology.

tossed, as it seemed, upon the billowy ocean, and wel-
tered upon the weltering waves.

May 1818. The Malay has been a fearful enemy for
months. Every night, through his means, I have been
transported into Asiatic scenery. I know not whether
others share in my feelings on this point; but I have
often thought that, if I were compelled to forgo England, and to live in China, among Chinese manners
and modes of life and scenery, I should go mad. The
causes of my horror lie deep, and some of them must
be common to others. Southern Asia, in general, is the
seat of awful images and associations. As the cradle of
the human race, if on no other ground, it would have
a dim, reverential feeling connected with it. But there
are other reasons. No man can pretend that the wild,
barbarous, and capricious superstitions of Africa, or
of savage tribes elsewhere, affect him in the way that
he is affected by the ancient, monumental, cruel, and
elaborate religions of Hindostan. The mere antiquity
of Asiatic things, of their institutions, histories—
above all, of their mythologies, &c.—is so impressive
that to me the vast age of the race and name over-
powers the sense of youth in the individual. A young
Chinese seems to me an antediluvian man renewed.
Even Englishmen, though not bred in any knowledge of such institutions, cannot but shudder at the
mystic sublimity of *castes* that have flowed apart, and
refused to mix, through such immemorial tracts of
time; nor can any man fail to be awed by the sanctity
of the Ganges, or by the very name of the Euphrates.
It contributes much to these feelings that South-
eastern Asia is, and has been for thousands of years,
the part of the earth most swarming with human life,
the great *officina gentium*. Man is a weed in those regions. The vast empires, also, into which the enormous
population of Asia has always been cast, give a further

sublimity to the feelings associated with all oriental names or images. In China, over and above what it has in common with the rest of Southern Asia, I am terrified by the modes of life, by the manners, by the barrier of utter abhorrence placed between myself and *them*, by counter-sympathies deeper than I can analyse. I could sooner live with lunatics, with vermin, with crocodiles or snakes. All this, and much more than I can say, the reader must enter into before he can comprehend the unimaginable horror which these dreams of oriental imagery and mythological tortures impressed upon me. Under the connecting feeling of tropical heat and vertical sunlights, I brought together all creatures, birds, beasts, reptiles, all trees and plants, usages and appearances, that are found in all tropical regions, and assembled them together in China or Hindostan. From kindred feelings, I soon brought Egypt and her gods under the same law. I was stared at, hooted at, grinned at, chattered at, by monkeys, by paroquets, by cockatoos. I ran into pagodas, and was fixed for centuries at the summit, or in secret rooms; I was the idol; I was the priest; I was worshipped; I was sacrificed. I fled from the wrath of Brama through all the forests of Asia; Vishnu hated me; Siva lay in wait for me. I came suddenly upon Isis and Osiris: I had done a deed, they said, which the ibis and the crocodile trembled at. Thousands of years I lived and was buried in stone coffins, with mummies and sphinxes, in narrow chambers at the heart of eternal pyramids. I was kissed, with cancerous kisses, by crocodiles, and was laid, confounded with all unutterable abortions, amongst reeds and Nilotic mud.

Some slight abstraction I thus attempt of my oriental dreams, which filled me always with such amazement at the monstrous scenery that horror seemed absorbed for a while in sheer astonishment. Sooner or

later came a reflux of feeling that swallowed up the
astonishment, and left me, not so much in terror, as
in hatred and abomination of what I saw. Over every
form, and threat, and punishment, and dim sightless
incarceration, brooded a killing sense of eternity and
infinity. Into these dreams only it was, with one or two
slight exceptions, that any circumstances of physical
horror entered. All before had been moral and spiritual
terrors. But here the main agents were ugly birds, or
snakes, or crocodiles, especially the last. The cursed
crocodile became to me the object of more horror than
all the rest. I was compelled to live with him; and (as
was always the case in my dreams) for centuries.
Sometimes I escaped, and found myself in Chinese
houses. All the feet of the tables, sofas, &c., soon became instinct with life: the abominable head of the
crocodile, and his leering eyes, looked out at me, multiplied into ten thousand repetitions; and I stood loathing and fascinated. So often did this hideous reptile
haunt my dreams that many times the very same dream
was broken up in the very same way: I heard gentle
voices speaking to me (I hear everything when I am
sleeping), and instantly I awoke; it was broad noon,
and my children were standing, hand in hand, at my
bedside, come to show me their coloured shoes, or new
frocks, or to let me see them dressed for going out. No
experience was so awful to me, and at the same time
so pathetic, as this abrupt translation from the darkness of the infinite to the gaudy summer air of highest noon, and from the unutterable abortions of mis-
created gigantic vermin to the sight of infancy and
innocent *human* natures.

June 1819. I have had occasion to remark, at various periods of my life, that the deaths of those whom
we love, and, indeed, the contemplation of death generally, is (*cæteris paribus*) more affecting in summer

than in any other season of the year. And the reasons
are these three, I think: first, that the visible heavens
in summer appear far higher, more distant, and (if
such a solecism may be excused) more infinite; the
clouds by which chiefly the eye expounds the distance
of the blue pavilion stretched over our heads are in
summer more voluminous, more massed, and are accumulated in far grander and more towering piles;
secondly, the light and the appearances of the declining and the setting sun are much more fitted to be types
and characters of the infinite; and, thirdly (which is
the main reason), the exuberant and riotous prodigality of life naturally forces the mind more powerfully upon the antagonist thought of death, and the
wintry sterility of the grave. For it may be observed
generally that, wherever two thoughts stand related
to each other by a law of antagonism, and exist, as it
were, by mutual repulsion, they are apt to suggest
each other. On these accounts it is that I find it impossible to banish the thought of death when I am
walking alone in the endless days of summer; and any
particular death, if not actually more affecting, at
least haunts my mind more obstinately and besieg-
ingly, in that season. Perhaps this cause, and a slight
incident which I omit, might have been the immediate
occasions of the following dream, to which, however,
a predisposition must always have existed in my mind;
but, having been once roused, it never left me, and split
into a thousand fantastic variations, which often suddenly re-combined, locked back into startling unity,
and restored the original dream.

I thought that it was a Sunday morning in May;
that it was Easter Sunday, and as yet very early in the
morning. I was standing, as it seemed to me, at the
door of my own cottage. Right before me lay the very
scene which could really be commanded from that sit-

uation, but exalted, as was usual, and solemnized by
the power of dreams. There were the same mountains,
and the same lovely valley at their feet; but the mountains were raised to more than Alpine height, and there
was interspace far larger between them of savannahs
and forest lawns; the hedges were rich with white
roses; and no living creature was to be seen, excepting
that in the green churchyard there were cattle tran-
quilly reposing upon the verdant graves, and particularly round about the grave of a child whom I had once
tenderly loved, just as I had really beheld them, a little
before sunrise, in the same summer when that child
died. I gazed upon the well-known scene, and I said
to myself, "It yet wants much of sunrise; and it is
Easter Sunday; and that is the day on which they cele-
brate the first-fruits of Resurrection. I will walk
abroad; old griefs shall be forgotten today: for the air
is cool and still, and the hills are high, and stretch
away to heaven; and the churchyard is as verdant as
the forest lawns, and the forest lawns are as quiet as
the churchyard; and with the dew I can wash the fever
from my forehead; and then I shall be unhappy no
longer." I turned, as if to open my garden gate, and
immediately I saw upon the left a scene far different;
but which yet the power of dreams had reconciled into
harmony. The scene was an oriental one; and there
also it was Easter Sunday, and very early in the morning. And at a vast distance were visible, as a stain
upon the horizon, the domes and cupolas of a great
city—an image or faint abstraction, caught perhaps
in childhood from some picture of Jerusalem. And not
a bow-shot from me, upon a stone, shaded by Judean
palms, there sat a woman; and I looked, and it was—
Ann! She fixed her eyes upon me earnestly; and I said
to her at length, "So, then, I have found you at last."
I waited; but she answered me not a word. Her face

was the same as when I saw it last; the same, and yet, again, how different! Seventeen years ago, when the lamp-light of mighty London fell upon her face, as for the last time I kissed her lips (lips, Ann, that to me were not polluted!), her eyes were streaming with tears. The tears were now no longer seen. Sometimes she seemed altered; yet again sometimes *not* altered; and hardly older. Her looks were tranquil, but with unusual solemnity of expression, and I now gazed upon her with some awe. Suddenly her countenance grew dim; and, turning to the mountains, I perceived vapours rolling between us; in a moment all had vanished; thick darkness came on; and in the twinkling of an eye I was far away from mountains, and by lamp-light in London, walking again with Ann—just as we had walked, when both children, eighteen years before, along the endless terraces of Oxford Street.

Then suddenly would come a dream of far different character—a tumultuous dream—commencing with a music such as now I often heard in sleep—music of preparation and of awakening suspense. The undulations of fast-gathering tumults were like the opening of the Coronation Anthem; and, like *that*, gave the feeling of a multitudinous movement, of infinite cavalcades filing off, and the tread of innumerable armies. The morning was come of a mighty day—a day of crisis and of ultimate hope for human nature, then suffering mysterious eclipse, and labouring in some dread extremity. Somewhere, but I knew not where —somehow, but I knew not how—by some beings, but I knew not by whom—a battle, a strife, an agony, was travelling through all its stages—was evolving itself, like the catastrophe of some mighty drama, with which my sympathy was the more insupportable from deepening confusion as to its local scene, its cause, its nature, and its undecipherable issue. I (as

is usual in dreams where, of necessity, we make ourselves central to every movement) had the power,
and yet had not the power, to decide it. I had the
power, if I could raise myself to will it; and yet again
had not the power, for the weight of twenty Atlantics
was upon me, or the oppression of inexpiable guilt.
"Deeper than ever plummet sounded," I lay inactive.
Then, like a chorus, the passion deepened. Some
greater interest was at stake, some mightier cause,
than ever yet the sword had pleaded, or trumpet had
proclaimed. Then came sudden alarms; hurryings to
and fro; trepidations of innumerable fugitives, I knew
not whether from the good cause or the bad; darkness
and lights; tempest and human faces; and at last, with
the sense that all was lost, female forms, and the features that were worth all the world to me; and but a
moment allowed—and clasped hands, with heart-
breaking partings, and then—everlasting farewells!
and, with a sigh such as the caves of hell sighed when
the incestuous mother uttered the abhorred name of
Death, the sound was reverberated—everlasting farewells! and again, and yet again reverberated—everlasting farewells!

And I awoke in struggles, and cried aloud, "I will
sleep no more!"

Now, at last, I had become awestruck at the approach of sleep, under the condition of visions so afflicting, and so intensely life-like as those which persecuted my phantom-haunted brain. More and more
also I felt violent palpitations in some internal region,
such as are commonly, but erroneously, called palpitations of the heart—being, as I suppose, referable
exclusively to derangements in the stomach. These
were evidently increasing rapidly in frequency and in
strength. Naturally, therefore, on considering how
important my life had become to others besides my-

self, I became alarmed; and I paused seasonably; but with a difficulty that is past all description. Either way it seemed as though death had, in military language, "thrown himself astride of my path." Nothing short of mortal anguish, in a physical sense, it seemed, to wean myself from opium; yet, on the other hand, death through overwhelming nervous terrors—death by brain-fever or by lunacy—seemed too certainly to besiege the alternative course. Fortunately I had still so much of firmness left as to face that choice, which, with most of instant suffering, showed in the far distance a possibility of final escape.

This possibility was realized: I *did* accomplish my escape. And the issue of that particular stage in my opium experiences (for such it was—simply a provisional stage, that paved the way subsequently for many milder stages, to which gradually my constitutional system accommodated itself) was, pretty nearly in the following words, communicated to my readers in the earliest edition of these *Confessions:*

I triumphed. But infer not, reader, from this word *"triumphed,"* a condition of joy or exaltation. Think of me as of one, even when four months had passed, still agitated, writhing, throbbing, palpitating, shattered; and much, perhaps, in the situation of him who has been racked, as I collect the torments of that state from the affecting account of them left by a most innocent sufferer in the time of James I.[1] Meantime, I derived no benefit from any medicine whatever, except ammoniated tincture of valerian. The moral of

---

[1] William Lithgow. His book *(Travels, &c.)* is tedious and not well written; but the account of his own sufferings on the rack at Malaga, and subsequently, is overpoweringly affecting. Less circumstantial, but the same in tendency, is the report of the results from torture published in 1830 by Juan Van Halen.

the narrative is addressed to the Opium-Eater; and therefore, of necessity, limited in its application. If he is taught to fear and tremble, enough has been effected. But he may say that the issue of my case is at least a proof that opium, after an eighteen years' use, and an eight years' abuse, of its powers, may still be renounced; and that he may chance to bring to the task greater energy than I did, or that, with a stronger constitution, he may obtain the same results with less. This may be true; I would not presume to measure the efforts of other men by my own. Heartily I wish him more resolution; heartily I wish him an equal success. Nevertheless, I had motives external to myself which he may unfortunately want; and these supplied me with conscientious supports, such as merely selfish interests might fail in supplying to a mind debilitated by opium.

Lord Bacon conjectures that it may be as painful to be born as to die.[1] That seems probable; and, during the whole period of diminishing the opium, I had the torments of a man passing out of one mode of existence into another, and liable to the mixed or the alternate pains of birth and death. The issue was not death, but a sort of physical regeneration; and I may add that ever since, at intervals, I have had a restoration of more than youthful spirits.

One memorial of my former condition nevertheless remains: my dreams are not calm; the dread swell and

[1] In all former editions I had ascribed this sentiment to Jeremy Taylor. On a close search, however, wishing to verify the quotation, it appeared that I had been mistaken. Something very like it occurs more than once in the bishop's voluminous writings: but the exact passage moving in my mind had evidently been this which follows, from Lord Bacon's "Essay on Death": "It is as natural to die as to be born; and to a little infant perhaps the one is as painful as the other."

agitation of the storm have not wholly subsided; the legions that encamped in them are drawing off, but not departed; my sleep is still tumultuous; and, like the gates of Paradise to our first parents when looking back from afar, it is still (in the tremendous line of Milton) —

With dreadful faces thronged and fiery arms.

SUSPIRIA DE PROFUNDIS
Being a Sequel to
the *Confessions of an English Opium-Eater*

THE DAUGHTER OF LEBANON

(First published in the Collective Edition of De Quincey's
works, 1856, as an appendage to the *Confessions*)

DAMASCUS, first-born of cities, *Om el Denia*,[1]
mother of generations, that wast before Abraham, that wast before the Pyramids! what sounds are
those that, from a postern gate, looking eastwards
over secret paths that wind away to the far distant
desert, break the solemn silence of an oriental night?
Whose voice is that which calls upon the spearmen,
keeping watch for ever in the turret surmounting the
gate, to receive him back into his Syrian home? Thou
knowest him, Damascus, and hast known him in seasons of trouble as one learned in the afflictions of man;
wise alike to take counsel for the suffering spirit or
for the suffering body. The voice that breaks upon the
night is the voice of a great evangelist—one of the
four; and he is also a great physician. This do the
watchmen at the gate thankfully acknowledge, and
joyfully they give him entrance. His sandals are
white with dust; for he has been roaming for weeks

[1] "*Om el Denia*": Mother of the World is the Arabic title of
Damascus. That it was before Abraham—*i.e.*, already an old
establishment much more than a thousand years before the
siege of Troy, and than two thousand years before our Christian era—may be inferred from Gen. xv. 2; and, by the general
consent of all eastern races, Damascus is accredited as taking
precedence in age of all cities to the west of the Indus.

beyond the desert, under the guidance of Arabs, on missions of hopeful benignity to Palmyra [1]; and in spirit he is weary of all things, except faithfulness to God, and burning love to man.

Eastern cities are asleep betimes; and sounds few or none fretted the quiet of all around him, as the evangelist paced onward to the market-place; but there another scene awaited him. On the right hand, in an upper chamber, with lattices widely expanded, sat a festal company of youths, revelling under a noonday blaze of light from cressets and from bright tripods that burned fragrant woods—all joining in choral songs, all crowned with odorous wreaths from Daphne and the banks of the Orontes. Them the evangelist heeded not; but far away upon the left, close upon a sheltered nook, lighted up by a solitary vase of iron fretwork filled with cedar boughs, and hoisted high upon a spear, behold there sat a woman of loveliness so transcendent that, when suddenly revealed, as now, out of deepest darkness, she appalled men as a mockery, or a birth of the air. Was she born of woman? Was it perhaps the angel—so the evangelist argued with himself—that met him in the desert after sunset, and strengthened him by secret talk? The evangelist went up, and touched her forehead; and, when he found that she was indeed human, and guessed, from the station which she had chosen, that that she waited for some one amongst this dissolute crew as her companion, he groaned heavily in spirit, and said, half to himself, but half to her, "Wert thou, poor ruined flower, adorned so divinely at thy birth —glorified in such excess that not Solomon in all his pomp—no, nor even the lilies of the field—can ap-

[1] Palmyra had not yet reached its meridian splendour of Grecian development, as afterwards near the age of Aurelian; but it was already a noble city.

proach thy gifts—only that thou shouldest grieve the
Holy Spirit of God?" The woman trembled exceedingly, and said, "Rabbi, what should I do? For behold! all men forsake me." The Evangelist mused a
little, and then secretly to himself he said, "Now will
I search this woman's heart—whether in very truth it
inclineth itself to God, and hath strayed only before
fiery compulsion." Turning therefore to the woman,
the Prophet [1] said, "Listen: I am the messenger of
Him whom thou hast not known; of Him that made
Lebanon and the cedars of Lebanon; that made the
sea, and the heavens, and the host of the stars; that
made the light; that made the darkness; that blew the
spirit of life into the nostrils of man. His messenger
I am: and from Him all power is given me to bind and
to loose, to build and to pull down. Ask, therefore,
whatsoever thou wilt—great or small—and through
me thou shalt receive it from God. But, my child, ask
not amiss. For God is able out of thy own evil asking
to weave snares for thy footing. And oftentimes to
the lambs whom He loves he gives by seeming to refuse; gives in some better sense, or" (and his voice
swelled into the power of anthems) "in some far happier world. Now, therefore, my daughter, be wise on
thy own behalf; and say what it is that I shall ask for

---

[1] *"The Prophet"*: Though a Prophet was not *therefore* and
in virtue of that character an evangelist, yet every evangelist
was necessarily in the scriptural sense a Prophet. For let it be
remembered that a Prophet did not mean a *Pre*dicter, or *Fore*-
shower of events, except derivatively and inferentially. What
was a Prophet in the uniform scriptural sense? He was a man
who drew aside the curtain from the secret counsels of Heaven.
He declared, or made public, the previously hidden truths of
God: and, because future events might chance to involve divine truth, therefore a revealer of future events might happen
so far to be a Prophet. Yet still small was that part of a
Prophet's functions which concerned the foreshowing of
events; and not necessarily *any* part.

thee from God." But the Daughter of Lebanon needed
not his caution; for immediately, dropping on one
knee to God's ambassador, whilst the full radiance
from the cedar torch fell upon the glory of a penitential eye, she raised her clasped hands in supplication,
and said, in answer to the evangelist asking for a
second time what gift he should call down upon her
from Heaven, "Lord, that thou wouldest put me back
into my father's house." And the evangelist, because
he was human, dropped a tear as he stooped to kiss her
forehead, saying, "Daughter, thy prayer is heard in
heaven; and I tell thee that the day-light shall not
come and go for thirty times, not for the thirtieth time
shall the sun drop behind Lebanon, before I will put
thee back into thy father's house."

Thus the lovely lady came into the guardianship of
the evangelist. She sought not to varnish her history,
or to palliate her own transgressions. In so far as she
had offended at all, her case was that of millions in
every generation. Her father was a prince in Lebanon,
proud, unforgiving, austere. The wrongs done to his
daughter by her dishonourable lover, because done
under favour of opportunities created by her confidence in his integrity, her father persisted in resent-
ing as wrongs done by this injured daughter herself;
and, refusing to her all protection, drove her, whilst
yet confessedly innocent, into criminal compliances
under sudden necessities of seeking daily bread from
her own uninstructed efforts. Great was the wrong she
suffered both from father and lover; great was the
retribution. She lost a churlish father and a wicked
lover; she gained an apostolic guardian. She lost a
princely station in Lebanon; she gained an early heritage in heaven. For this heritage is hers within thirty
days, if she will not defeat it herself. And, whilst the
stealthy motion of time travelled towards this thir-

tieth day, behold! a burning fever desolated Damascus, which also laid its arrest upon the Daughter of Lebanon, yet gently, and so that hardly for an hour did it withdraw her from the heavenly teachings of the evangelist. And thus daily the doubt was strengthened —would the holy apostle suddenly touch her with his hand, and say, "Woman, be thou whole!" or would he present her on the thirtieth day as a pure bride to Christ? But perfect freedom belongs to Christian service, and she only must make the election.

Up rose the sun on the thirtieth morning in all his pomp, but suddenly was darkened by driving storms. Not until noon was the heavenly orb again revealed; then the glorious light was again unmasked, and again the Syrian valleys rejoiced. This was the hour already appointed for the baptism of the new Christian daughter. Heaven and earth shed gratulation on the happy festival; and, when all was finished, under an awning raised above the level roof of her dwelling-house, the regenerate Daughter of Lebanon, looking over the rose-gardens of Damascus, with amplest prospect of her native hills, lay in blissful trance, making proclamation, by her white baptismal robes, of recovered innocence and of reconciliation with God. And, when the sun was declining to the west, the evangelist, who had sat from noon by the bedside of his spiritual daughter, rose solemnly, and said, "Lady of Lebanon, the day is already come, and the hour is coming, in which my covenant must be fulfilled with thee. Wilt thou, therefore, being now wiser in thy thoughts, suffer God thy new Father to give by seeming to refuse; to give in some better sense, or in some far happier world?" But the Daughter of Lebanon sorrowed at these words; she yearned after her native hills; not for themselves, but because there it was that she had left that sweet twin-born sister with whom from infant days hand-

in-hand she had wandered amongst the everlasting
cedars. And again the evangelist sat down by her bedside; whilst she by intervals communed with him, and
by intervals slept gently under the oppression of her
fever. But, as evening drew nearer, and it wanted now
but a brief space to the going down of the sun, once
again, and with deeper solemnity, the evangelist rose
to his feet, and said, "O daughter! this is the thirtieth
day, and the sun is drawing near to his rest; brief,
therefore, is the time within which I must fulfil the
word that God spoke to thee by me." Then, because
light clouds of delirium were playing about her brain,
he raised his pastoral staff, and, pointing it to her temples, rebuked the clouds, and bade that no more they
should trouble her vision, or stand between her and
the forests of Lebanon. And the delirious clouds parted
asunder, breaking away to the right and to the left.
But upon the forests of Lebanon there hung a mighty
mass of overshadowing vapours, bequeathed by the
morning's storm. And a second time the evangelist
raised his pastoral staff, and, pointing it to the gloomy
vapours, rebuked them, and bade that no more they
should stand between his daughter and her father's
house. And immediately the dark vapours broke away
from Lebanon to the right and to the left; and the
farewell radiance of the sun lighted up all the paths
that ran between the everlasting cedars and her
father's palace. But vainly the lady of Lebanon
searched every path with her eyes for memorials of her
sister. And the evangelist, pitying her sorrow, turned
away her eyes to the clear blue sky, which the departing vapours had exposed. And he showed her the peace
which was there. And then he said, "O daughter! this
also is but a mask." And immediately for the third
time he raised his pastoral staff, and, pointing it to the
fair blue sky, he rebuked it, and bade that no more it

should stand between her and the vision of God. Immediately the blue sky parted to the right and to the left, laying bare the infinite revelations that can be made visible only to dying eyes. And the Daughter of Lebanon said to the evangelist, "O father! what armies are these that I see mustering within the infinite chasm?" And the evangelist replied, "These are the armies of Christ, and they are mustering to receive some dear human blossom, some first-fruits of Christian faith, that shall rise this night to Christ from Damascus." Suddenly, as thus the child of Lebanon gazed upon the mighty vision, she saw bending forward from the heavenly host, as if in gratulation to herself, the one countenance for which she hungered and thirsted. The twin-sister, that should have waited for her in Lebanon, had died of grief, and was waiting for her in Paradise. Immediately in rapture she soared upwards from her couch; immediately in weakness she fell back; and, being caught by the evangelist, she flung her arms around his neck; whilst he breathed into her ear his final whisper, "Wilt thou now suffer that God should give by seeming to refuse?"—"Oh yes—yes—yes," was the fervent answer from the Daughter of Lebanon. Immediately the evangelist gave the signal to the heavens, and the heavens gave the signal to the sun; and in one minute after the Daughter of Lebanon had fallen back a marble corpse amongst her white baptismal robes; the solar orb dropped behind Lebanon; and the evangelist, with eyes glorified by mortal and immortal tears, rendered thanks to God that had thus accomplished the word which he spoke through himself to the Magdalen of Lebanon—that not for the thirtieth time should the sun go down behind her native hills before he had put her back into her Father's house.

DREAMING

(First published in *Blackwood's Magazine*, March, 1845)

IN 1821, as a contribution to a periodical work—in 1822, as a separate volume—appeared the *Confessions of an English Opium-Eater*. The object of that work was to reveal something of the grandeur which belongs *potentially* to human dreams. Whatever may be the number of those in whom this faculty of dreaming splendidly can be supposed to lurk, there are not, perhaps, very many in whom it is developed. He whose talk is of oxen will probably dream of oxen; and the condition of human life which yokes so vast a majority to a daily experience incompatible with much elevation of thought oftentimes neutralizes the tone of grandeur in the reproductive faculty of dreaming, even for those whose minds are populous with solemn imagery. Habitually to dream magnificently, a man must have a constitutional determination to reverie. This in the first place; and even this, where it exists strongly, is too much liable to disturbance from the gathering agitation of our present English life. Already, what by the procession through fifty years of mighty revolutions amongst the kingdoms of the earth, what by the continual development of vast physical agencies—steam in all its applications, light getting under harness as a slave for man, powers from heaven descending upon education and accelerations of the press, powers from hell (as it might seem, but these also celestial) coming round upon artillery and the forces of destruction—the eye of the calmest observer is troubled; the brain is haunted as if by some jealousy of ghostly beings moving amongst us; and it becomes too evident that, unless this colossal pace of advance can be retarded (a thing not to be expected), or, which is happily more probable, can be met by counter-forces of corresponding magnitude—forces in the direction of religion or profound philosophy that shall radiate centrifugally against this storm of life so perilously centripetal towards the vortex of the merely human—left to itself, the natural tendency of so chaotic a tumult must be to evil; for some minds to lunacy, for others a reagency of fleshly torpor. How much this fierce condition of eternal hurry upon an arena too exclusively human in its interests is likely to defeat the grandeur which is latent in all men, may be seen in the ordinary effect from living too constantly in varied company. The word *dissipation,* in one of its uses, expresses that effect; the action of thought and feeling is consciously dissipated and squandered. To reconcentrate them into meditative habits, a necessity is felt by all observing persons for sometimes retiring from crowds. No man ever will unfold the capacities of his own intellect who does not at least checker his life with solitude. How much solitude, so much power. Or, if not true in that rigour of expression, to this formula undoubtedly it is that the wise rule of life must approximate.

Among the powers in man which suffer by this too intense life of the *social* instincts, none suffers more than the power of dreaming. Let no man think this a trifle. The machinery for dreaming planted in the human brain was not planted for nothing. That faculty, in alliance with the mystery of darkness, is the one great tube through which man communicates with the shadowy. And the dreaming organ, in connexion with the heart, the eye, and the ear, composes the magnificent apparatus which forces the infinite into the chambers of a human brain, and throws dark reflections from eternities below all life upon the mirrors of that mysterious *camera obscura*—the sleeping mind.

But, if this faculty suffers from the decay of solitude, which is becoming a visionary idea in England, on the other hand it is certain that some merely physical agencies can and do assist the faculty of dreaming almost preternaturally. Amongst these is intense exercise—to some extent at least, for some persons; but beyond all others is opium: which indeed seems to possess a *specific* power in that direction; not merely for exalting the colours of dream-scenery, but for deepening its shadows, and, above all, for strengthening the sense of its fearful *realities*.

The *Opium Confessions* were written with some slight secondary purpose of exposing this specific power of opium upon the faculty of dreaming, but much more with the purpose of displaying the faculty itself; and the outline of the work travelled in this course—Supposing a reader acquainted with the true object of the *Confessions* as here stated—namely, the revelation of dreaming—to have put this question:

"But how came you to dream more splendidly than others?"

The answer would have been—

"Because (*prœmissis prœmittendis*) I took excessive quantities of opium."

Secondly, suppose him to say, "But how came you to take opium in this excess?"

The answer to *that* would be, "Because some early events in my life had left a weakness in one organ which required (or seemed to require) that stimulant."

Then, because the opium dreams could not always have been understood without a knowledge of these events, it became necessary to relate them. Now, these two questions and answers exhibit the *law* of the work

—that is, the principle which determined its form—
but precisely in the inverse or regressive order. The
work itself opened with the narration of my early adventures. These, in the natural order of succession, led
to the opium as a resource for healing their consequences; and the opium as naturally led to the dreams.
But, in the synthetic order of presenting the facts,
what stood last in the succession of development stood
first in the order of my purposes.

At the close of this little work, the reader was instructed to believe, and *truly* instructed, that I had
mastered the tyranny of opium. The fact is that *twice*
I mastered it, and by efforts even more prodigious in
the second of these cases than in the first. But one error
I committed in both. I did not connect with the abstinence from opium, so trying to the fortitude under
any circumstances, that enormity of exercise which
(as I have since learned) is the one sole resource for
making it endurable. I overlooked, in those days, the
one *sine qua non* for making the triumph permanent.
Twice I sank, twice I rose again. A third time I sank;
partly from the cause mentioned (the oversight as to
exercise), partly from other causes, on which it avails
not now to trouble the reader. I could moralize, if I
chose; and perhaps *he* will moralize, whether I choose
it or not. But, in the meantime, neither of us is acquainted properly with the circumstances of the case:
I, from natural bias of judgement, not altogether acquainted; and he (with his permission) not at all.

During this third prostration before the dark idol,
and after some years, new and monstrous phenomena
began slowly to arise. For a time, these were neglected
as accidents, or palliated by such remedies as I knew
of. But, when I could no longer conceal from myself
that these dreadful symptoms were moving forward
for ever, by a pace steadily, solemnly, and equably in-

creasing, I endeavoured, with some feeling of panic, for a third time to retrace my steps. But I had not reversed my motions for many weeks before I became profoundly aware that this was impossible. Or, in the imagery of my dreams, which translated everything into their own language, I saw, through vast avenues of gloom, those towering gates of ingress which hitherto had always seemed to stand open now at last barred against my retreat, and hung with funeral crape. I, upon seeing those awful gates closed and hung with draperies of woe, as for a death already past, spoke not, nor started, nor groaned. One profound sigh ascended from my heart, and I was silent for days.

* * *

In the *Opium Confessions* I touched a little upon the extraordinary power connected with opium (after long use) of amplifying the dimensions of time. Space, also, it amplifies by degrees that are sometimes terrific. But time it is upon which the exalting and multiplying power of opium chiefly spends its operation. Time becomes infinitely elastic, stretching out to such immeasurable and vanishing termini that it seems ridiculous to compute the sense of it, on waking, by expressions commensurate to human life. As in starry fields one computes by diameters of the Earth's orbit, or of Jupiter's, so, in valuing the *virtual* time lived during some dreams, the measurement by generations is ridiculous—by millennia is ridiculous; by æons, I should say, if æons were more determinate, would be also ridiculous.

* * *

Here pause, reader! Imagine yourself seated in some cloud-scaling swing, oscillating under the impulse of lunatic hands; for the strength of lunacy may belong

to human dreams, the fearful caprice of lunacy, and
the malice of lunacy, whilst the *victim* of those dreams
may be all the more certainly removed from lunacy;
even as a bridge gathers cohesion and strength from
the increasing resistance into which it is forced by increasing pressure. Seated in such a swing, fast as you
reach the lowest point of depression, may you rely on
racing up to a starry altitude of corresponding ascent.
Ups and downs you will see, heights and depths, in our
fiery course together, such as will sometimes tempt
you to look shyly and suspiciously at me, your guide,
and the ruler of the oscillations. Here, at the point
where I have called a halt, the reader has reached the
lowest depths in my nursery afflictions. From that
point according to the principles of *art* which govern
the movement of these *Confessions*, I had meant to
launch him upwards through the whole arch of ascending visions which seemed requisite to balance the
sweep downwards, so recently described in his course.
But accidents of the press have made it impossible to
accomplish this purpose. There is reason to regret that
the advantages of position which were essential to the
full effect of passages planned for the equipoise and
mutual resistance have thus been lost. Meantime, upon
the principle of the mariner who rigs a *jury*-mast in
default of his regular spars, I find my resource in a
sort of "jury" peroration, not sufficient in the way of
a balance by its *proportions*, but sufficient to indicate
the *quality* of the balance which I had contemplated.
He who has *really* read the preceding parts of these
present *Confessions* will be aware that a stricter scrutiny of the past, such as was natural after the whole
economy of the dreaming faculty had been convulsed
beyond all precedents on record, led me to the conviction that not one agency, but two agencies had co-
operated to the tremendous result. The nursery experi-

ence had been the ally and the natural coefficient of
the opium. For that reason it was that the nursery experience has been narrated. Logically it bears the very
same relation to the convulsions of the dreaming faculty as the opium. The idealizing tendency existed in
the dream-theatre of my childhood; but the preternatural strength of its action and colouring was first developed after the confluence of the *two* causes. The
reader must suppose me at Oxford; twelve years and
a half are gone by; I am in the glory of youthful happiness: but I have now first tampered with opium;
and now first the agitations of my childhood reopened
in strength; now first they swept in upon the brain
with power and the grandeur of recovered life under
the separate and the concurring inspirations of opium.

THE PALIMPSEST OF THE HUMAN BRAIN

(First published in *Blackwood's Magazine*, March, 1845)

YOU know perhaps, masculine reader, better than I
can tell you, what is a *Palimpsest*. Possibly you
have one in your own library. But yet, for the sake of
others who may *not* know, or may have forgotten, suffer me to explain it here, lest any female reader who
honours these papers with her notice should tax me
with explaining it once too seldom; which would be
worse to bear than a simultaneous complaint from
twelve proud men that I had explained it three times
too often. You, therefore, fair reader, understand that
for *your* accommodation exclusively I explain the
meaning of this word. It is Greek; and our sex enjoys
the office and privilege of standing counsel to yours in
all questions of Greek. We are, under favour, perpetual

and hereditary dragomans to you. So that if, by accident, you know the meaning of a Greek word, yet by
courtesy to us, your counsel learned in that matter,
you will always seem *not* to know it.

A palimpsest, then, is a membrane or roll cleansed
of its manuscript by reiterated successions.

What was the reason that the Greeks and the Romans had not the advantage of printed books? The
answer will be, from ninety-nine persons in a hundred
—Because the mystery of printing was not then discovered. But this is altogether a mistake. The secret
of printing must have been discovered many thousands
of times before it was used, or *could* be used. The inventive powers of man are divine; and also his stupidity is divine, as Cowper so playfully illustrates in
the slow development of the *sofa* through successive
generations of immortal dulness. It took centuries of
blockheads to raise a joint stool into a chair; and it required something like a miracle of genius, in the estimate of elder generations, to reveal the possibility of
lengthening a chair into a *chaise-longue*, or a sofa.
Yes, these were inventions that cost mighty throes of
intellectual power. But still, as respects printing, and
admirable as is the stupidity of man, it was really not
quite equal to the task of evading an object which
stared him in the face with so broad a gaze. It did not
require an Athenian intellect to read the main secret
of printing in many scores of processes which the ordinary uses of life were *daily* repeating. To say nothing
of analogous artifices amongst various mechanic artisans, all that is essential in printing must have been
known to every nation that struck coins and medals.
Not, therefore, any want of a printing art—that is,
of an art for multiplying impressions—but the want
of a cheap material for *receiving* such impressions,
was the obstacle to an introduction of printed books

even as early as Pisistratus. The ancients *did* apply printing to records of silver and gold; to marble, and many other substances cheaper than gold or silver, they did *not*, since each monument required a *separate* effort of inscription. Simply this defect it was of a cheap material for receiving impresses which froze in its very fountains the early resources of printing.

Some twenty years ago this view of the case was luminously expounded by Dr. Whately, and with the merit, I believe, of having first suggested it. Since then, this theory has received indirect confirmation. Now, out of that original scarcity affecting all materials proper for durable books, which continued up to times comparatively modern, grew the opening for palimpsests. Naturally, when once a roll of parchment or of vellum had done its office, by propagating through a series of generations what once had possessed an interest for *them*, but which, under changes of opinion or of taste, had faded to their feelings or had become obsolete for their undertakings, the whole *membrana* or vellum skin, the twofold product of human skill and costly material, and the costly freight of thought which it carried, drooped in value concurrently—supposing that each were inalienably associated to the other. Once it had been the impress of a human mind which stamped its value upon the vellum; the vellum, though costly, had contributed but a secondary element of value to the total result. At length, however, this relation between the vehicle and its freight has gradually been undermined. The vellum, from having been the setting of the jewel, has risen at length to be the jewel itself; and the burden of thought, from having given the chief value to the vellum, has now become the chief obstacle to its value; nay, has totally extinguished its value, unless it can

be dissociated from the connexion. Yet, if this unlinking *can* be effected, then, fast as the inscription upon
the membrane is sinking into rubbish, the membrane
itself is reviving in its separate importance; and, from
bearing a ministerial value, the vellum has come at last
to absorb the whole value.

Hence the importance for our ancestors that the separation *should* be effected. Hence it arose in the Middle Ages as a considerable object for chemistry to discharge the writing from the roll, and thus to make it
available for a new succession of thoughts. The soil, if
cleansed from what once had been hot-house plants,
but now were held to be weeds, would be ready to receive a fresh and more appropriate crop. In that object
the monkish chemists succeeded; but after a fashion
which seems almost incredible—incredible not as regards the extent of their success, but as regards the
delicacy of restraints under which it moved—so
equally adjusted was their success to the immediate
interests of that period, and to the reversionary objects
of our own. They did the thing; but not so radically as
to prevent us, their posterity, from *un*doing it. They
expelled the writing sufficiently to leave a field for the
new manuscript, and yet not sufficiently to make the
traces of the elder manuscript irrecoverable for us. Could
magic, could Hermes Trismegistus, have done more?
What would you think, fair reader, of a problem such
as this: to write a book which should be sense for your
own generation, nonsense for the next; should revive
into sense for the next after that, but again become
nonsense for the fourth; and so on by alternate successions sinking into night or blazing into day, like the
Sicilian river Arethusa and the English river Mole, or
like the undulating motions of a flattened stone which
children cause to skim the breast of a river, now diving

below the water, now grazing its surface, sinking heavily into darkness, rising buoyantly into light, through a long vista of alternations? Such a problem, you say, is impossible. But really it is a problem not harder apparently than to bid a generation kill, so that a subsequent generation may call back into life; bury, so that posterity may command to rise again. Yet *that* was what the rude chemistry of past ages effected when coming into combination with the reaction from the more refined chemistry of our own. Had *they* been better chemists, had *we* been worse, the mixed result —namely, that, dying for *them*, the flower should revive for *us*—could not have been effected. They did the thing proposed to them: they did it effectually, for they founded upon it all that was wanted: and yet ineffectually, since we unravelled their work, effacing all above which they had superscribed, restoring all below which they had effaced.

Here, for instance, is a parchment which contained some Grecian tragedy—the *Agamemnon* of Æschylus, or the *Phœnissæ* of Euripides. This had possessed a value almost inappreciable in the eyes of accomplished scholars, continually growing rarer through generations. But four centuries are gone by since the destruction of the Western Empire. Christianity, with towering grandeurs of another class, has founded a different empire; and some bigoted, yet perhaps holy monk has washed away (as he persuades himself) the heathen's tragedy, replacing it with a monastic legend; which legend is disfigured with fables in its incidents, and yet in a higher sense is true, because interwoven with Christian morals, and with the sublimest of Christian revelations. Three, four, five, centuries more find man still devout as ever; but the language has become obsolete; and even for Christian devotion

a new era has arisen, throwing it into the channel of
crusading zeal or of chivalrous enthusiasm. The *membrana* is wanted now for a knightly romance—for *My
Cid* or *Cœur de Lion,* for *Sir Tristram* or *Lybœus Dis-
conus.* In this way, by means of the imperfect chemistry known to the medieval period, the same roll has
served as a conservatory for three separate generations
of flowers and fruits, all perfectly different, and yet
all specially adapted to the wants of the successive possessors. The Greek tragedy, the monkish legend, the
knightly romance, each has ruled its own period. One
harvest after another has been gathered into the garners of man through ages far apart. And the same
hydraulic machinery has distributed, through the
same marble fountains, water, milk, or wine, according to the habits and training of the generations that
came to quench their thirst.

Such were the achicvements of rude monastic chemistry. But the more elaborate chemistry of our own
days has reversed all these motions of our simple ancestors, with results in every stage that to *them* would
have realized the most fantastic amongst the promises
of thaumaturgy. Insolent vaunt of Paracelsus, that
he would restore the original rose or violet out of the
ashes settling from its combustion—*that* is now rivalled in this modern achievement. The traces of each
successive handwriting, regularly effaced, as had been
imagined, have, in the inverse order, been regularly
called back: the footsteps of the game pursued, wolf
or stag, in each several chase, have been unlinked, and
hunted back through all their doubles; and, as the
chorus of the Athenian stage unwove through the an-
tistrophe every step that had been mystically woven
through the strophe, so, by our modern conjurations
of science, secrets of ages remote from each other have

been exorcized [1] from the accumulated shadows of centuries. Chemistry, a witch as potent as the Erichtho of Lucan (*Pharsalia*, lib. vi or vii), has extorted by her torments, from the dust and ashes of forgotten centuries, the secrets of a life extinct for the general eye, but still glowing in the embers. Even the fable of the Phœnix, that secular bird who propagated his solitary existence, and his solitary births, along the line of centuries, through eternal relays of funeral mists, is but a type of what we have done with palimpsests. We have backed upon each phœnix in the long *regressus*, and forced him to expose his ancestral phœnix, sleeping in the ashes below his own ashes. Our good old forefathers would have been aghast at our sorceries; and, if they speculated on the propriety of burning Dr. Faustus, *us* they would have burned by acclamation. Trial there would have been none; and they could not otherwise have satisfied their horror of the brazen profligacy marking our modern magic than by ploughing up the houses of all who had been parties to it, and sowing the ground with salt.

Fancy not, reader, that this tumult of images, illustrative or allusive, moves under any impulse or purpose of mirth. It is but the coruscation of a restless understanding, often made ten times more so by irritation of the nerves, such as you will first learn to comprehend (its *how* and its *why*) some stage or two ahead. The image, the memorial, the record, which for me is derived from a palimpsest as to one great fact in our human being, and which immediately I will show you, is but too repellent of laughter; or, even if

---

[1] Some readers may be apt to suppose, from all English experience, that the word *exorcize* means properly banishment to the shades. Not so. Citation *from* the shades, or sometimes the torturing coercion of mystic adjurations, is more truly the primary sense.

laughter *had* been possible, it would have been such laughter as oftentimes is thrown off from the fields of ocean,[1] laughter that hides, or that seems to evade, mustering tumult; foam-bells that weave garlands of phosphoric radiance for one moment round the eddies of gleaming abysses; mimicries of earthborn flowers that for the eye raise phantoms of gaiety, as oftentimes for the ear they raise the echoes of fugitive laughter, mixing with the ravings and choir-voices of an angry sea.

What else than a natural and mighty palimpsest is the human brain? Such a palimpsest is my brain; such a palimpsest, oh reader! is yours. Everlasting layers of ideas, images, feelings, have fallen upon your brain softly as light. Each succession has seemed to bury all that went before. And yet, in reality, not one has been extinguished. And, if in the vellum palimpsest, lying amongst the other *diplomata* of human archives or libraries, there is anything fantastic or which moves to laughter, as oftentimes there is in the grotesque collisions of those successive themes, having no natural connexion, which by pure accident have consecutively occupied the roll, yet, in our own heaven-created palimpsest, the deep memorial palimpsest of the brain, there are not and cannot be such incoherencies. The fleeting accidents of a man's life, and its external shows, may indeed be irrelate and incongruous; but the organizing principles which fuse into

---

[1] Many readers will recall, though, at the moment of writing, my own thoughts did *not* recall, the well-known passage in the *Prometheus*—

ποντιων τε κυματων
Ανηριθμον γελασμα.

"O multitudinous laughter of the ocean billows!" It is not clear whether Æschylus contemplated the laughter as addressing the ear or the eye.

harmony, and gather about fixed predetermined centres, whatever heterogeneous elements life may have accumulated from without, will not permit the grandeur of human unity greatly to be violated, or its ultimate repose to be troubled, in the retrospect from dying moments, or from other great convulsions.

Such a convulsion is the struggle of gradual suffocation, as in drowning; and in the original *Opium Confessions* I mentioned a case of that nature communicated to me by a lady from her own childish experience. The lady was then still living, though of unusually great age; and I may mention that amongst her faults never was numbered any levity of principle, or carelessness of the most scrupulous veracity, but, on the contrary, such faults as arise from austerity, too harsh, perhaps, and gloomy, indulgent neither to others nor herself. And, at the time of relating this incident, when already very old, she had become religious to asceticism. According to my present belief, she had completed her ninth year when, playing by the side of a solitary brook, she fell into one of its deepest pools. Eventually, but after what lapse of time nobody ever knew, she was saved from death by a farmer, who, riding in some distant lane, had seen her rise to the surface; but not until she had descended within the abyss of death and looked into its secrets, as far, perhaps, as ever human eye *can* have looked that had permission to return. At a certain stage of this descent, a blow seemed to strike her; phosphoric radiance sprang forth from her eyeballs; and immediately a mighty theatre expanded within her brain. In a moment, in the twinkling of an eye, every act, every design of her past life, lived again, arraying themselves not as a succession, but as parts of a coexistence. Such a light fell upon the whole path of her life backwards into the shades of infancy as the light, perhaps, which wrapt the destined Apostle on his road to Damascus. Yet that light blinded for a season; but hers poured celestial vision upon the brain, so that her consciousness became omnipresent at one moment to every feature in the infinite review.

This anecdote was treated sceptically at the time by some critics. But, besides that it has since been confirmed by other experiences essentially the same, reported by other parties in the same circumstances, who had never heard of each other, the true point for astonishment is not the *simultaneity* of arrangement under which the past events of life, though in fact successive, had formed their dread line of revelation. This was but a secondary phenomenon; the deeper lay in the resurrection itself, and the possibility of resurrection for what had so long slept in the dust. A pall, deep as oblivion, had been thrown by life over every trace of these experiences; and yet suddenly, at a silent command, at the signal of a blazing rocket sent up from the brain, the pall draws up, and the whole depths of the theatre are exposed. Here was the greater mystery. Now, this mystery is liable to no doubt; for it is repeated, and ten thousand times repeated, by opium, for those who are its martyrs.

Yes, reader, countless are the mysterious handwritings of grief or joy which have inscribed themselves successively upon the palimpsest of your brain; and, like the annual leaves of aboriginal forests, or the undissolving snows on the Himalayas, or light falling upon light, the endless strata have covered up each other in forgetfulness. But by the hour of death, but by fever, but by the searchings of opium, all these can revive in strength. They are not dead, but sleeping. In the illustration imagined by myself from the case of some individual palimpsest, the Grecian tragedy had seemed to be displaced, but was *not* displaced, by the monkish legend; and the monkish legend had seemed to be displaced, but was *not* displaced, by the knightly romance. In some potent convulsion of the system, all wheels back into its earliest elementary stage. The bewildering romance, light tarnished with darkness, the semi-fabulous legend, truth celestial mixed with human falsehoods, these fade even of themselves as life advances. The romance has perished that the young man adored; the legend has gone that deluded the boy; but the deep, deep tragedies of infancy, as when the child's hands were unlinked for ever from his mother's neck, or his lips for ever from his sister's kisses, these remain lurking below all, and these lurk to the last.

VISION OF LIFE

(First published in *Blackwood's Magazine*, July, 1845)

UPON me, as upon others scattered thinly by tens and twenties over every thousand years, fell too powerfully and too early the vision of life. The horror of life mixed itself already in earliest youth with the heavenly sweetness of life; that grief which one in a hundred has sensibility enough to gather from the sad retrospect of life in its closing stage for *me* shed its dews as a prelibation upon the fountains of life whilst yet sparkling to the morning sun. I saw from afar and from before what I was to see from behind. Is this the description of an early youth passed in the shades of gloom? No; but of a youth passed in the divinest happiness. And, if the reader has (which so few have) the passion without which there is no reading of the legend and superscription upon man's brow, if he is not (as most are) deafer than the grave to every *deep* note that sighs upwards from the Delphic caves of human life, he will know that the rapture of life

(or anything which by approach can merit that name)
does not arise, unless as perfect music arises, music of
Mozart or Beethoven, by the confluence of the mighty
and terrific discords with the subtle concords. Not by
contrast, or as reciprocal foils, do these elements act—
which is the feeble conception of many—but by union.
They are the sexual forces in music: "male and female
created he them"; and these mighty antagonists do not
put forth their hostilities by repulsion, but by deepest
attraction.

As "in today already walks tomorrow," so in the
past experience of a youthful life may be seen dimly
the future. The collisions with alien interests or hostile views of a child, boy, or very young man, so insulated as each of these is sure to be—those aspects of
opposition which such a person *can* occupy—are
limited by the exceedingly few and trivial lines of connexion along which he is able to radiate any essential
influence whatever upon the fortunes or happiness of
others. Circumstances may magnify his importance
for the moment; but, after all, any cable which he
carries out upon other vessels is easily slipped upon a
feud arising. Far otherwise is the state of relations
connecting an adult or responsible man with the cir-
cles around him as life advances. The network of these
relations is a thousand times more intricate, the jarring of these intricate relations a thousand times more
frequent, and the vibrations a thousand times harsher
which these jarrings diffuse. This truth is felt beforehand, misgivingly and in troubled vision, by a
young man who stands upon the threshold of manhood. One earliest instinct of fear and horror would
darken his spirit if it could be revealed to itself and
self-questioned at the moment of birth: a second instinct of the same nature would again pollute that
tremulous mirror if the moment were as punctually

marked as physical birth is marked which dismisses
him finally upon the tides of absolute self-control. A
dark ocean would seem the total expanse of life from
the first; but far darker and more appalling would
seem that inferior and second chamber of the ocean
which called him away for ever from the direct ac-
countability of others. Dreadful would be the morning
which should say, "Be thou a human child incarnate";
but more dreadful the morning which should say,
"Bear thou henceforth the sceptre of thy self-domin-
ion through life, and the passion of life!" Yes, dreadful would be both; but without a basis of the dreadful
there is no perfect rapture. It is in part through the
sorrow of life, growing out of dark events, that this
basis of awe and solemn darkness slowly accumulates.
That I have illustrated. But, as life expands, it is more
through the *strife* which besets us, strife from conflict-
ing opinions, positions, passions, interests, that the
funereal ground settles and deposits itself which sends
upward the dark lustrous brilliancy through the jewel
of life, else revealing a pale and superficial glitter.
Either the human being must suffer and struggle, as
the price of a more searching vision, or his gaze must
be shallow and without intellectual revelation.

SAVANNAH-LA-MAR

(First published in *Blackwood's Magazine*, June, 1845)

GOD smote Savannah-la-mar, and in one night, by
earthquake, removed her, with all her towers
standing and population sleeping, from the steadfast
foundations of the shore to the coral floors of ocean.
And God said, "Pompeii did I bury and conceal from
men through seventeen centuries: this city I will bury,

but not conceal. She shall be a monument to men of my mysterious anger, set in azure light through generations to come; for I will enshrine her in a crystal dome of my tropic seas." This city, therefore, like a mighty galleon with all her apparel mounted, streamers flying, and tackling perfect, seems floating along the noiseless depths of ocean; and oftentimes in glassy calms, through the translucid atmosphere of water that now stretches like an air-woven awning above the silent encampment, mariners from every clime look down into her courts and terraces, count her gates, and number the spires of her churches. She is one ample cemetery, and *has* been for many a year; but, in the mighty calms that brood for weeks over tropic latitudes, she fascinates the eye with a *Fata-Morgana* revelation, as of human life still subsisting in submarine asylums sacred from the storms that torment our upper air.

Thither, lured by the loveliness of cerulean depths, by the peace of human dwellings privileged from molestation, by the gleam of marble altars sleeping in everlasting sanctity, oftentimes in dreams did I and the Dark Interpreter cleave the watery veil that divided us from her streets. We looked into the belfries, where the pendulous bells were waiting in vain for the summons which should awaken their marriage peals; together we touched the mighty organ-keys, that sang no *jubilates* for the ear of heaven, that sang no requiems for the ear of human sorrow; together we searched the silent nurseries, where the children were all asleep, and *had* been asleep through five generations. "They are waiting for the heavenly dawn," whispered the Interpreter to himself: "and, when *that* comes, the bells and the organs will utter a *jubilate* repeated by the echoes of Paradise." Then, turning to me, he said, "This is sad, this is piteous; but less would not have sufficed for the purpose of God. Look here. Put into a Roman clepsydra one hundred drops of water; let these run out as the sands in an hour-glass, every drop measuring the hundredth part of a second, so that each shall represent but the three-hundred-and-sixty-thousandth part of an hour. Now, count the drops as they race along; and, when the fiftieth of the hundred is passing, behold! forty-nine are not, because already they have perished, and fifty are not, because they are yet to come. You see, therefore, how narrow, how incalculably narrow, is the true and actual present. Of that time which we call the present, hardly a hundredth part but belongs either to a past which has fled, or to a future which is still on the wing. It has perished, or it is not born. It was, or it is not. Yet even this approximation to the truth is *infinitely* false. For again subdivide that solitary drop, which only was found to represent the present, into a lower series of similar fractions, and the actual present which you arrest measures now but the thirty-six-millionth of an hour; and so by infinite declensions the true and very present, in which only we live and enjoy, will vanish into a mote of a mote, distinguishable only by a heavenly vision. Therefore the present, which only man possesses, offers less capacity for his footing than the slenderest film that ever spider twisted from her womb. Therefore, also, even this incalculable shadow from the narrowest pencil of moonlight is more transitory than geometry can measure, or thought of angel can overtake. The time which *is* contracts into a mathematic point; and even that point perishes a thousand times before we can utter its birth. All is finite in the present; and even that finite is infinite in its velocity of flight towards death. But in God there is nothing finite; but in God there is nothing transitory; but in God there *can* be nothing that tends to death. There-

fore it follows that for God there can be no present.
The future is the present of God, and to the future it
is that he sacrifices the human present. Therefore it is
that he works by earthquake. Therefore it is that he
works by grief. O, deep is the ploughing of earthquake! O, deep"— (and his voice swelled like a *sanctus* rising from the choir of a cathedral) —"O, deep is
the ploughing of grief! But oftentimes less would not
suffice for the agriculture of God. Upon a night of
earthquake he builds a thousand years of pleasant habitations for man. Upon the sorrow of an infant he
raises oftentimes from human intellects glorious vintages that could not else have been. Less than these
fierce ploughshares would not have stirred the stub-
born soil. The one is needed for Earth, our planet, for
Earth itself as the dwelling-place of man; but the other
is needed yet oftener for God's mightiest instrument,
yes" (and he looked solemnly at myself), "is needed
for the mysterious children of the Earth!"

LEVANA AND OUR LADIES OF SORROW [1]

(First printed in *Blackwood's Magazine*, June, 1845)

OFTENTIMES at Oxford I saw Levana in my dreams.
I knew her by her Roman symbols. Who is
Levana? Reader, that do not pretend to have leisure
for very much scholarship, you will not be angry with

[1] To "Levana and Our Ladies of Sorrow" as printed in
Blackwood's, De Quincey added this note: The reader who
wishes at all to understand the course of these Confessions
ought not to pass over this dream-legend. There is no great
wonder that a vision which occupied my waking thoughts in
those years should reappear in my dreams. It was, in fact, a
legend recurring in sleep, most of which I had myself silently
written or sculptured in my daylight reveries. But its impor-

me for telling you. Levana was the Roman goddess that performed for the new-born infant the earliest office of ennobling kindness—typical, by its mode, of that grandeur which belongs to man everywhere, and of that benignity in powers invisible which even in Pagan worlds sometimes descends to sustain it. At the very moment of birth, just as the infant tasted for the first time the atmosphere of our troubled planet, it was laid on the ground. *That* might bear different interpretations. But immediately, lest so grand a creature should grovel there for more than one instant, either the paternal hand, as proxy for the goddess Levana, or some near kinsman, as proxy for the father, raised it upright, bade it look erect as the king of all this world, and presented its forehead to the stars, saying, perhaps, in his heart, "Behold what is greater than yourselves!" This symbolic act represented the function of Levana. And that mysterious lady, who never revealed her face (except to me in dreams), but always acted by delegation, had her name from the Latin verb (as still it is the Italian verb) *levare*, to raise aloft.

This is the explanation of Levana. And hence it has arisen that some people have understood by Levana the tutelary power that controls the education of the nursery. She, that would not suffer at his birth even a prefigurative or mimic degradation for her awful ward, far less could be supposed to suffer the real degradation attaching to the non-development of his powers. She therefore watches over human education. Now, the

tance to the present *Confessions* is this—that it rehearses or prefigures their course. This FIRST Part belongs to Madonna. The THIRD belongs to the "Mater Suspiriorum," and will be entitled *The Pariah Worlds*. The FOURTH, which terminates the work, belongs to the "Mater Tenebrarum," and will be entitled *The Kingdom of Darkness*. As to the SECOND, it is an interpolation requisite to the effect of the others, and will be explained in its proper place.

word *edŭco,* with the penultimate short, was derived
(by a process often exemplified in the crystallization
of languages) from the word *edūco,* with the penultimate long. Whatsoever *educes,* or develops, *educates.*
By the education of Levana, therefore, is meant, not
the poor machinery that moves by spelling-books and
grammars, but by that mighty system of central forces
hidden in the deep bosom of human life, which by passion, by strife, by temptation, by the energies of resistance, works for ever upon children, resting not day
or night, any more than the mighty wheel of day and
night themselves, whose moments, like restless spokes,
are glimmering [1] for ever as they revolve.

If, then, *these* are the ministries by which Levana
works, how profoundly must she reverence the agencies
of grief! But you, reader, think that children generally are not liable to grief such as mine. There are two
senses in the word *generally*—the sense of Euclid,
where it means *universally* (or in the whole extent of
the *genus*), and a foolish sense of this world, where it
means *usually.* Now, I am far from saying that children universally are capable of grief like mine. But
there are more than you ever heard of who die of grief

[1] As I have never allowed myself to covet any man's ox nor
his ass, nor anything that is his, still less would it become a
philosopher to covet other people's images or metaphors. Here,
therefore, I restore to Mr. Wordsworth this fine image of the
revolving wheel and the glimmering spokes, as applied by him
to the flying successions of day and night. I borrowed it for
one moment in order to point my own sentence; which being
done, the reader is witness that I now pay it back instantly by
a note made for that sole purpose. On the same principle I
often borrow their seals from young ladies, when closing my
letters, because there is sure to be some tender sentiment upon
them about "memory," or "hope," or "roses," or "reunion,"
and my correspondent must be a sad brute who is not touched
by the eloquence of the seal, even if his taste is so bad that he
remains deaf to mine.

in this island of ours. I will tell you a common case. The rules of Eton require that a boy on the *foundation* should be there twelve years: he is superannuated at eighteen; consequently he must come at six. Children torn away from mothers and sisters at that age not unfrequently die. I speak of what I know. The complaint is not entered by the registrar as grief; but *that* it is. Grief of that sort, and at that age, has killed more than ever have been counted amongst its martyrs.

Therefore it is that Levana often communes with the powers that shake man's heart; therefore it is that she dotes upon grief. "These ladies," said I softly to myself, on seeing the ministers with whom Levana was conversing, "these are the Sorrows; and they are three in number: as the *Graces* are three, who dress man's life with beauty; the *Parcæ* are three, who weave the dark arras of man's life in their mysterious loom always with colours sad in part, sometimes angry with tragic crimson and black; the *Furies* are three, who visit with retributions called from the other side of the grave offences that walk upon this; and once even the *Muses* were but three, who fit the harp, the trumpet, or the lute, to the great burdens of man's impassioned creations. These are the Sorrows; all three of whom I know." The last words I say now; but in Oxford I said, "one of whom I know, and the others too surely I *shall* know." For already, in my fervent youth, I saw (dimly relieved upon the dark background of my dreams) the imperfect lineaments of the awful Sisters.

These Sisters—by what name shall we call them? If I say simply "The Sorrows," there will be a chance of mistaking the term; it might be understood of individual sorrow—separate cases of sorrow—whereas I want a term expressing the mighty abstractions that incarnate themselves in all individual sufferings of man's heart, and I wish to have these abstractions pre-

sented as impersonations, that is, as clothed with
human attributes of life, and with functions pointing
to flesh. Let us call them, therefore, *Our Ladies of
Sorrow*.

I know them thoroughly, and have walked in all
their kingdoms. Three sisters they are, of one mysterious household; and their paths are wide apart; but of
their dominion there is no end. Them I saw often conversing with Levana, and sometimes about myself. Do
they talk, then? O no! Mighty phantoms like these
disdain the infirmities of language. They may utter
voices through the organs of man when they dwell in
human hearts, but amongst themselves is no voice nor
sound; eternal silence reigns in *their* kingdoms. They
spoke not as they talked with Levana; they whispered
not; they sang not; though oftentimes methought they
might have sung: for I upon earth had heard their
mysteries oftentimes deciphered by harp and timbrel,
by dulcimer and organ. Like God, whose servants they
are, they utter their pleasure not by sounds that perish,
or by words that go astray, but by signs in heaven, by
changes on earth, by pulses in secret rivers, heraldries
painted on darkness, and hieroglyphics written on the
tablets of the brain. *They* wheeled in mazes; *I* spelled
the steps. *They* telegraphed from afar; *I* read the signals. *They* conspired together; and on the mirrors of
darkness *my* eye traced the plots. *Theirs* were the symbols; *mine* are the words.

What is it the Sisters are? What is it that they do?
Let me describe their form and their presence, if form
it were that still fluctuated in its outline, or presence
it were that for ever advanced to the front or for ever
receded amongst shades.

The eldest of the three is named *Mater Lachrymarum*, Our Lady of Tears. She it is that night and
day raves and moans, calling for vanished faces. She

stood in Rama, where a voice was heard of lamentation—Rachel weeping for her children, and refusing
to be comforted. She it was that stood in Bethlehem on
the night when Herod's sword swept its nurseries of
Innocents, and the little feet were stiffened for ever
which, heard at times as they trotted along floors overhead, woke pulses of love in household hearts that were
not unmarked in heaven. Her eyes are sweet and subtle,
wild and sleepy, by turns; oftentimes rising to the
clouds, oftentimes challenging the heavens. She wears
a diadem round her head. And I knew by childish
memories that she could go abroad upon the winds,
when she heard the sobbing of litanies, or the thundering of organs, and when she beheld the mustering
of summer clouds. This Sister, the elder, it is that carries keys more than papal at her girdle, which open
every cottage and every palace. She, to my knowledge,
sat all last summer by the bedside of the blind beggar,
him that so often and so gladly I talked with, whose
pious daughter, eight years old, with the sunny countenance, resisted the temptations of play and village
mirth, to travel all day long on dusty roads with her
afflicted father. For this did God send her a great reward. In the spring time of the year, and whilst yet
her own spring was budding, He recalled her to himself. But her blind father mourns for ever over *her*:
still he dreams at midnight that the little guiding hand
is locked within his own; and still he wakens to a darkness that is *now* within a second and a deeper darkness.
This *Mater Lachrymarum* also has been sitting all this
winter of 1844–5 within the bedchamber of the Czar,
bringing before his eyes a daughter (not less pious)
that vanished to God not less suddenly, and left behind
her a darkness not less profound. By the power of the
keys it is that Our Lady of Tears glides, a ghostly intruder, into the chambers of sleepless men, sleepless

women, sleepless children, from Ganges to the Nile, from Nile to Mississippi. And her, because she is the first-born of her house, and has the widest empire, let us honour with the title of "Madonna."

The second Sister is called *Mater Suspiriorum*, Our Lady of Sighs. She never scales the clouds, nor walks abroad upon the winds. She wears no diadem. And her eyes, if they were ever seen, would be neither sweet nor subtle; no man could read their story; they would be found filled with perishing dreams, and with wrecks of forgotten delirium. But she raises not her eyes; her head, on which sits a dilapidated turban, droops for ever, for ever fastens on the dust. She weeps not. She groans not. But she sighs inaudibly at intervals. Her sister, Madonna, is oftentimes stormy and frantic, raging in the highest against heaven, and demanding back her darlings. But Our Lady of Sighs never clamours, never defies, dreams not of rebellious aspirations. She is humble to abjectness. Hers is the meekness that belongs to the hopeless. Murmur she may, but it is in her sleep. Whisper she may, but it is to herself in the twilight. Mutter she does at times, but it is in solitary places that are desolate as she is desolate, in ruined cities, and when the sun has gone down to his rest. This Sister is the visitor of the Pariah, of the Jew, of the bondsman to the oar in the Mediterranean galleys; of the English criminal in Norfolk Island, blotted out from the books of remembrance in sweet far-off England; of the baffled penitent reverting his eyes for ever upon a solitary grave, which to him seems the altar overthrown of some past and bloody sacrifice, on which altar no oblations can now be availing, whether towards pardon that he might implore, or towards reparation that he might attempt. Every slave that at noonday looks up to the tropical sun with timid reproach, as he points with one hand to the earth, our

general mother, but for *him* a stepmother, as he points
with the other hand to the Bible, our general teacher,
but against *him* sealed and sequestered [1]; every woman
sitting in darkness, without love to shelter her head,
or hope to illumine her solitude, because the heaven-
born instincts kindling in her nature germs of holy
affections, which God implanted in her womanly
bosom, having been stifled by social necessities, now
burn sullenly to waste, like sepulchral lamps amongst
the ancients; every nun defrauded of her unreturning
May-time by wicked kinsman, whom God will judge;
every captive in every dungeon; all that are betrayed,
and all that are rejected; outcasts by traditionary law,
and children of *hereditary* disgrace: all these walk
with Our Lady of Sighs. She also carries a key; but she
needs it little. For her kingdom is chiefly amongst the
tents of Shem, and the houseless vagrant of every
clime. Yet in the very highest ranks of man she finds
chapels of her own; and even in glorious England
there are some that, to the world, carry their heads as
proudly as the reindeer, who yet secretly have received
her mark upon their foreheads.

But the third Sister, who is also the youngest——!
Hush! whisper whilst we talk of *her!* Her kingdom is
not large, or else no flesh should live; but within that
kingdom all power is hers. Her head, turreted like that
of Cybele, rises almost beyond the reach of sight. She
droops not; and her eyes, rising so high, *might* be
hidden by distance. But, being what they are, they
cannot be hidden: through the treble veil of crape

---

[1] This, the reader will be aware, applies chiefly to the cotton and tobacco States of North America; but not to them
only: on which account I have not scrupled to figure the sun
which looks down upon slavery as *tropical*—no matter if
strictly within the tropics, or simply so near to them as to produce a similar climate.

which she wears the fierce light of a blazing misery, that rests not for matins or for vespers, for noon of day or noon of night, for ebbing or for flowing tide, may be read from the very ground. She is the defier of God. She also is the mother of lunacies, and the suggestress of suicides. Deep lie the roots of her power; but narrow is the nation that she rules. For she can approach only those in whom a profound nature has been upheaved by central convulsions; in whom the heart trembles and the brain rocks under conspiracies of tempest from without and tempest from within. Madonna moves with uncertain steps, fast or slow, but still with tragic grace. Our Lady of Sighs creeps timidly and stealthily. But this youngest Sister moves with incalculable motions, bounding, and with tiger's leaps. She carries no key; for, though coming rarely amongst men, she storms all doors at which she is permitted to enter at all. And *her* name is *Mater Tenebrarum*— Our Lady of Darkness.

These were the *Semnai Theai* or Sublime Goddesses,[1] these were the *Eumenides* or Gracious Ladies (so called by antiquity in shuddering propitiation), of my Oxford dreams. Madonna spoke. She spoke by her mysterious hand. Touching my head, she beckoned to Our Lady of Sighs; and *what* she spoke, translated out of the signs which (except in dreams) no man reads, was this:

"Lo! here is he whom in childhood I dedicated to my altars. This is he that once I made my darling. Him I led astray, him I beguiled; and from heaven I stole away his young heart to mine. Through me did he become idolatrous; and through me it was, by languish-

---

[1] "*Sublime Goddesses*": The word σεμνός is really rendered *venerable* in dictionaries—not a very flattering epithet for females. But I am disposed to think that it comes nearest to our idea of the *sublime*—as near as a Greek word *could* come.

ing desires, that he worshipped the worm, and prayed
to the wormy grave. Holy was the grave to him; lovely
was its darkness; saintly its corruption. Him, this
young idolater, I have seasoned for thee, dear gentle
Sister of Sighs! Do thou take him now to *thy* heart, and
season him for our dreadful sister. And thou," turning
to the *Mater Tenebrarum*, she said, "wicked sister, that
temptest and hatest, do thou take him from *her*. See
that thy sceptre lie heavy on his head. Suffer not woman and her tenderness to sit near him in his darkness.
Banish the frailties of hope; wither the relenting of
love; scorch the fountains of tears; curse him as only
thou canst curse. So shall he be accomplished in the
furnace; so shall he see the things that ought *not* to be
seen, sights that are abominable, and secrets that are
unutterable. So shall he read elder truths, sad truths,
grand truths, fearful truths. So shall he rise again
before he dies. And so shall our commission be accomplished which from God we had—to plague his heart
until we had unfolded the capacities of his spirit."

WHO IS THIS WOMAN THAT BECKONETH AND WARN-
ETH ME FROM THE PLACE WHERE SHE IS, AND IN
WHOSE EYES IS WOEFUL REMEMBRANCE? I GUESS
WHO SHE IS

(First published in *The Posthumous Works of
Thomas De Quincey*, Vol. I, 1891)

IN MY dreams were often prefigurements of my future,
as I could not but read the signs. What man has not
some time in dewy morn, or sequestered eve, or in the
still night-watches, when deep sleep falleth on other
men but visiteth not his weary eyelids—what man, I
say, has not some time hushed his spirit and questioned

with himself whether some things seen or obscurely felt, were not anticipated as by mystic foretaste in some far halcyon time, post-natal or ante-natal he knew not; only assuredly he knew that for him past and present and future merged in one awful moment of lightning revelation. O spirit that dwelleth in man, how subtle are *thy* revelations, how deep, how delirious the raptures thou canst inspire; how poignant the stings with which thou canst pierce the heart; how sweet the honey with which thou assuagest the wound; how dark the despairs and accusings that lie behind thy curtains, and leap upon us like lightning from the cloud, with the sense as of some heavenly blazoning, and oftentimes carry us beyond ourselves!

It is a sweet morning in June, and the fragrance of the roses is wafted towards me as I move—for I am walking in a lawny meadow, still wet with dew—and a wavering mist lies over the distance. Suddenly it seems to lift, and out of the dewy dimness emerges a cottage, embowered with roses and clustering clematis; and the hills, in which it is set like a gem, are tree-clad, and rise billowy behind it, and to the right and to the left are glistening expanses of water. Over the cottage there hangs a halo, as if clouds had but parted there. From the door of that cottage emerges a figure, the countenance full of the trepidation of some dread woe feared or remembered. With waving arm and tearful uplifted face the figure first beckons me onward, and then, when I have advanced some yards, frowning, warns me away. As I still continue to advance, despite the warning, darkness falls: figure, cottage, hills, trees, and halo fade and disappear; and all that remains to me is the look on the face of her that beckoned and warned me away. I read that glance as by the inspiration of a moment. We had been together; together we had entered some troubled gulf; struggled together, suffered together. Was it as lovers torn asunder by calamity? Was it as combatants forced by bitter necessity into bitter feud, when we only, in all the world, yearned for peace together? Oh, what a searching glance was that which she cast on me! as if she, being now in the spiritual world, abstracted from flesh, remembered things that I could not remember. Oh, how I shuddered as the sweet sunny eyes in the sweet sunny morning of June—the month that was my "angelical"; half spring, yet with summer dress, that to me was very "angelical"—seemed reproachfully to challenge in me recollections of things passed thousands of years ago (old indeed, yet that were made new again for us, because now first it was that we met again). Oh, heavens! it came over me as doth the raven over the infected house, as from a bed of violets sweeps the saintly odour of corruption. What a glimpse was thus revealed! glory in despair, as of that gorgeous vegetation that hid the sterilities of the grave in the tropics of that summer long ago; of that heavenly beauty which slept side by side within my sister's coffin in the month of June; of those saintly swells that rose from an infinite distance—I know not whether to or from my sister. Could this be a memorial of that nature? Are the nearer and more distant stages of life thus dimly connected, and the connexion hidden, but suddenly revealed for a moment?

This lady, for years appeared to me in dreams; in that, considering the electric character of my dreams, and that they were far less like a lake reflecting the heavens than like the pencil of some mighty artist—Da Vinci or Michael Angelo—that cannot copy in simplicity, but comments in freedom, while reflecting in fidelity, there was nothing to surprise. But a change in this appearance was remarkable. Oftentimes, after eight years had passed, she appeared in summer dawn at a window. It was a window that opened on a balcony. This feature only gave a distinction, a refinement, to the aspect of the cottage—else all was simplicity. Spirit of Peace, dove-like dawn that slept upon the cottage, ye were not broken by any participation in my grief and despair! For ever the vision of that cottage was renewed. Did I roam in the depths of sweet pastoral solitudes in the West, with the tinkling of sheep-bells in my ears, a rounded hillock, seen vaguely, would shape itself into a cottage; and at the door my monitory, regretful Hebe would appear. Did I wander by the sea-shore, one gently swelling wave in the vast heaving plain of waters would suddenly transform itself into a cottage, and I, by some involuntary inward impulse, would in fancy advance toward it.

Ah, reader, you will think this which I am going to say too near, too holy, for recital. But not so. The deeper a woe touches me in heart, so much the more am I urged to recite it. The world disappears: I see only the grand reliques of a world—memorials of a love that has departed, has been—the record of a sorrow that is, and has its greyness converted into verdure —monuments of a wrath that has been reconciled, of a wrong that has been atoned for—convulsions of a storm that has gone by. What I am going to say is the most like a superstitious thing that I ever shall say. And I have reason to think that every man who is not a villain once in his life must be superstitious. It is a tribute which he pays to human frailty, which tribute if he will not pay, which frailty if he will not share, then also he shall not have any of its strength.

The face of this monitory Hebe haunted me for some years in a way that I must faintly attempt to explain. It is little to say that it was the sweetest face, with the most peculiar expression of sweetness, that I had ever seen: that was much, but that was earthly.

There was something more terrific, believe me, than this; yet that was not the word: terror looks to the future; and this perhaps did, but not primarily. Chiefly it looked at some unknown past, and was for that reason awful; yes, awful—that was the word.

Thus, on any of those heavenly sunny mornings, that now are buried in an endless grave, did I, transported by no human means, enter that cottage, and descend to that breakfast-room, my earliest salute was to her, that ever, as the look of pictures do, with her eyes pursued me round the room, and oftentimes with a subtle checking of grief, as if great sorrow had been or would be hers. And it was, too, in the sweet May-time. Oh yes; she was but as if she had been—as if it were her original . . . chosen to have been the aurora of a heavenly clime; and then suddenly she was as one of whom, for some thousand years, Paradise had received no report; then, again, as if she entered the gates of Paradise not less innocent; and, again, as if she could not enter; and some blame—but I knew not what blame—was mine; and now she looked as though broken with a woe that no man could read, as she sought to travel back to her early joy—yet no longer a joy that is sublime in innocency, but a joy from which sprung abysses of memories polluted into anguish, till her tears seemed to be suffused with drops of blood. All around was peace and the deep silence of untroubled solitude; only in the lovely lady was a sign of horror, that had slept, under deep ages of frost, in her heart, and now rose, as with the rushing of wings, to her face. Could it be supposed that one life—so pitiful a thing —was what moved her care? Oh no; it was, or it seemed, as if this poor wreck of a life happened to be that one which determined the fate of some thousand others. Nothing less; nothing so abject as one poor fifty years—nothing less than a century of centuries could have stirred the horror that rose to her lovely lips, as once more she waved me away from the cottage.

Oh, reader, five years after, I saw that sweet face in reality—saw it in the flesh; saw that pomp of woman-hood; saw that cottage; saw a thousand times that lovely domicile that heard the cooing of the solitary dove in the solitary morning; saw the grave of child-hood and the shadows of graves that lay, like creatures asleep, in the sunshine; saw, also, the horror, somehow realized as a shadowy reflection from myself, which warned me off from that cottage, and which still rings through the dreams of five-and-twenty years.

THE DARK INTERPRETER

(First published in *The Posthumous Works of Thomas De Quincey*, Vol. I, 1891)

Oh, eternity with outstretched wings, that broodest over the secret truths in whose roots lie the mysteries of man—his whence, his whither—have I searched thee, and struck a right key on thy dreadful organ!

SUFFERING is a mightier agency in the hands of na-ture, as a Demiurgus creating the intellect, than most people are aware of.

The truth I heard often in sleep from the lips of the Dark Interpreter. Who is he? He is a shadow, reader, but a shadow with whom you must suffer me to make you acquainted. You need not be afraid of him, for when I explain his nature and origin you will see that he is essentially inoffensive; or if sometimes he men-aces with his countenance, that is but seldom: and then, as his features in those moods shift as rapidly as clouds in a gale of wind, you may always look for the terrific aspects to vanish as fast as they have gathered. As to his origin—what it is, I know exactly, but cannot without a little circuit of preparation make *you* understand. Perhaps you are aware of that power in the eye of many children by which in darkness they project a vast theatre of phantasmagorical figures moving forwards or backwards between their bed-curtains and the chamber walls. In some children this power is semi-voluntary—they can control or perhaps suspend the shows; but in others it is altogether automatic. I myself, at the date of my last confessions, had seen in this way more processions—generally solemn, mournful, belonging to eternity, but also at times glad, triumphal pomps, that seemed to enter the gates of Time —than all the religions of paganism, fierce or gay, ever witnessed. Now, there is in the dark places of the human spirit—in grief, in fear, in vindictive wrath— a power of self-projection not unlike to this. Thirty years ago, it may be, a man called Symons committed several murders in a sudden epilepsy of planet-struck fury. According to my recollection, this case happened at Hoddesdon, which is in Middlesex. "Revenge is sweet!" was his hellish motto on that occasion, and that motto itself records the abysses which a human will can open. Revenge is *not* sweet, unless by the mighty charm of a charity that seeketh not her own it has become benignant. And what he had to revenge was woman's scorn. He had been a plain farm-servant; and, in fact, he was executed, as such men often are, on a proper point of professional respect to their calling, in a smock-frock, or blouse, to render so ugly a clash of syllables. His young mistress was every way and by much his superior, as well in prospects as in education. But the man, by nature arrogant, and little acquainted with the world, presumptuously raised his eyes to one of his young mistresses. Great was the scorn with which she repulsed his audacity, and her sisters participated in her disdain. Upon this affront he brooded night and day; and, after the term of his service was over, and he, in effect, forgotten by the family, one day he suddenly descended amongst the women of the family like an Avatar of vengeance. Right and left he threw out his murderous knife without distinction of person, leaving the room and the passage floating in blood.

The final result of this carnage was not so terrific as it threatened to be. Some, I think, recovered; but, also, one, who *did* not recover, was unhappily a stranger to the whole cause of his fury. Now, this murderer always maintained, in conversation with the prison chaplain, that, as he rushed on in his hellish career, he perceived distinctly a dark figure on his right hand, keeping pace with himself. Upon *that* the superstitious, of course, supposed that some fiend had revealed himself, and associated his superfluous presence with the dark atrocity. Symons was not a philosopher, but my opinion is, that he was too much so to tolerate that hypothesis, since, if there was one man in all Europe that needed no tempter to evil on that evening, it was precisely Mr. Symons, as nobody knew better than Mr. Symons himself. I had not the benefit of his acquaintance, or I would have explained it to him. The fact is, in point of awe a fiend would be a poor, trivial *bagatelle* compared to the shadowy projections, *umbras* and *penumbras*, which the unsearchable depths of man's nature is capable, under adequate excitement, of throwing off, and even into stationary forms. I shall have occasion to notice this point again. There are creative agencies in every part of human nature, of which the thousandth part could never be revealed in one life.

* * *

You have heard, reader, in the vision which describes Our Ladies of Sorrow, particularly in the dark admonition of Madonna, to her wicked sister that hateth and tempteth, what root of dark uses may lie in moral convulsions; not the uses hypocritically vaunted by theatrical devotion which affronts the majesty of God, that ever and in all things loves Truth—prefers sincerity that is erring to piety that cants. Rebellion which is the sin of witch-craft is more pardonable in His sight than speechifying resignation, listening with complacency to its own self-conquests. Show always as much neighbourhood as thou canst to grief that abases itself, which will cost thee but little effort if thine own grief hath been great. But God, who sees thy efforts in secret, will slowly strengthen those efforts, and make that to be a real deed, bearing tranquillity for thyself, which at first was but a feeble wish breathing homage to *Him*.

In after-life, from twenty to twenty-four, on looking back to those struggles of my childhood, I used to wonder exceedingly that a child could be exposed to struggles on such a scale. But two views unfolded upon me as my experience widened, which took away that wonder. The first was the vast scale upon which the sufferings of children are found everywhere expanded in the realities of life. The generation of infants which you see is but part of those who belong to it; were born in it; and make, the world over, not one half of it. The missing half, more than an equal number to those of any age that are now living, have perished by every kind of torments. Three thousand children per annum —that is, three hundred thousand per century; that is (omitting Sundays), about ten every day—pass to heaven through flames [1] in this very island of Great Britain. And of those who survive to reach maturity what multitudes have fought with fierce pangs of hunger, cold, and nakedness! When I came to know all this, then reverting my eye to *my* struggle, I said oftentimes it was nothing! Secondly, in watching the infancy of my own children, I made another discovery —it is well known to mothers, to nurses, and also to philosophers—that the tears and lamentations of infants during the year or so when they have no *other* language of complaint run through a gamut that is as inexhaustible as the Cremona of Paganini. An ear but moderately learned in that language cannot be deceived as to the rate and *modulus* of the suffering which it indicates. A fretful or peevish cry cannot by any efforts make itself impassioned. The cry of impatience, of hunger, of irritation, of reproach, of alarm, are all different—different as a chorus of Beethoven from a chorus of Mozart. But if ever you saw an infant suffering for an hour, as sometimes the healthiest does, under some attack of the stomach, which has the tiger-grasp of the Oriental cholera, then you will hear moans that address to their mothers an anguish of supplication for aid such as might storm the heart of Moloch. Once hearing it, you will not forget it. Now, it was a constant remark of mine, after any storm of that nature (occurring, suppose, once in two months), that always on the following day, when a long, long sleep had chased away the darkness, and the memory of the darkness from the little creature's brain, a sensible expansion had taken place in the intellectual faculties of

[1] Three thousand children are annually burnt to death in the nations of England and Scotland, chiefly through the carelessness of parents. I shudder to add another and darker cause, which is a deep disgrace to the present age.

attention, observation, and animation. It renewed the
case of our great modern poet, who, on listening to the
raving of the midnight storm, and the crashing which
it was making in the mighty woods, reminded himself
that all this hell of trouble

Tells also of bright calms that shall succeed.

Pain driven to agony, or grief driven to frenzy, is essential to the ventilation of profound natures. A sea
which is deeper than any that Count Massigli [1] measured cannot be searched and torn up from its sleeping
depths without a levanter or a monsoon. A nature
which is profound in excess, but also introverted and
abstracted in excess, so as to be in peril of wasting itself in interminable reverie, cannot be awakened sometimes without afflictions that go to the very foundations, heaving, stirring, yet finally harmonizing; and
it is in such cases that the Dark Interpreter does his
work, revealing the worlds of pain and agony and woe
possible to man—possible even to the innocent spirit of
a child.

[1] Count Massigli (an Austrian officer in the imperial service) about sixty years ago fathomed and attempted to
fathom many parts of the Mediterranean and the Atlantic. If I remember rightly, he found the bottom within less than an English
mile.

PART FOUR

ESSAYS

THE ENGLISH MAIL-COACH

(First published in *Blackwood's Magazine* in 1849)

I. THE GLORY OF MOTION

SOME twenty or more years before I matriculated at Oxford, Mr. Palmer, at that time M.P. for Bath, had accomplished two things, very hard to do on our little planet, the Earth, however cheap they may be held by eccentric people in comets: he had invented mail-coaches, and he had married the daughter of a duke. He was, therefore, just twice as great a man as Galileo, who did certainly invent (or, which is the same thing,[1] discover) the satellites of Jupiter, those very next things extant to mail-coaches in the two capital pretensions of speed and keeping time, but, on the other hand, who did *not* marry the daughter of a duke.

These mail-coaches, as organized by Mr. Palmer, are entitled to a circumstantial notice from myself, having had so large a share in developing the anarchies of my subsequent dreams: an agency which they accomplished, first, through velocity at that time unprecedented—for they first revealed the glory of motion; secondly, through grand effects for the eye between lamp-light and the darkness upon solitary roads; thirdly, through animal beauty and power so

---

[1] "*The same thing*": Thus, in the calendar of the Church Festivals, the discovery of the true cross (by Helen, the mother of Constantine) is recorded (and, one might think, with the express consciousness of sarcasm) as the *Invention* of the Cross.

913

often displayed in the class of horses selected for this mail service; fourthly, through the conscious presence of a central intellect, that, in the midst of vast distances [1]—of storms, of darkness, of danger—overruled all obstacles into one steady co-operation to a national result. For my own feeling, this post-office service spoke as by some mighty orchestra, where a thousand instruments, all disregarding each other, and so far in danger of discord, yet all obedient as slaves to the supreme *baton* of some great leader, terminate in a perfection of harmony like that of heart, brain, and lungs in a healthy animal organization. But, finally, that particular element in this whole combination which most impressed myself, and through which it is that to this hour Mr. Palmer's mail-coach system tyrannizes over my dreams by terror and terrific beauty, lay in the awful *political* mission which at that time it fulfilled. The mail-coach it was that distributed over the face of the land, like the opening of apocalyptic vials, the heart-shaking news of Trafalgar, of Salamanca, of Vittoria, of Waterloo.

The mail-coach, as the national organ for publishing these mighty events, thus diffusively influential, became itself a spiritualized and glorified object to an impassioned heart; and naturally, in the Oxford of that day, *all* hearts were impassioned, as being all (or nearly all) in *early* manhood. In most universities there is one single college; in Oxford there were five-and-twenty, all of which were peopled by young men, the *élite* of their own generation; not boys, but men: none under eighteen. In some of these many colleges

---

[1] "*Vast distances*": One case was familiar to mail-coach travellers where two mails in opposite directions, north and south, starting at the same minute from points six hundred miles apart, met almost constantly at a particular bridge which bisected the total distance.

the custom permitted the student to keep what are
called "short terms"; that is, the four terms of Michaelmas, Lent, Easter, and Act, were kept by a residence, in the aggregate, of ninety-one days, or thirteen weeks. Under this interrupted residence, it was
possible that a student might have a reason for going
down to his home four times in the year. This made
eight journeys to and fro. But, as these homes lay dispersed through all the shires of the island, and most
of us disdained all coaches except His Majesty's mail,
no city out of London could pretend to so extensive a
connexion with Mr. Palmer's establishment as Oxford. Three mails, at the least, I remember as passing
every day through Oxford, and benefiting by my personal patronage—viz. the Worcester, the Gloucester,
and the Holyhead mail. Naturally, therefore, it became a point of some interest with us, whose journeys
revolved every six weeks on an average, to look a little
into the executive details of the system. With some of
these Mr. Palmer had no concern; they rested upon
by-laws enacted by posting-houses for their own benefit, and upon other by-laws, equally stern, enacted
by the inside passengers for the illustration of their
own haughty exclusiveness. These last were of a nature to rouse our scorn; from which the transition
was not very long to systematic mutiny. Up to this
time, say 1804, or 1805 (the year of Trafalgar), it
had been the fixed assumption of the four inside people (as an old tradition of all public carriages derived
from the reign of Charles II) that they, the illustrious
quaternion, constituted a porcelain variety of the human race, whose dignity would have been compromised by exchanging one word of civility with the
three miserable delf-ware outsides. Even to have
kicked an outsider might have been held to attaint the
foot concerned in that operation, so that, perhaps, it

would have required an act of Parliament to restore its purity of blood. What words, then, could express the horror, and the sense of treason, in that case, which *had* happened, where all three outsides (the trinity of Pariahs) made a vain attempt to sit down at the same breakfast-table or dinner-table with the consecrated four? I myself witnessed such an attempt; and on that occasion a benevolent old gentleman endeavoured to soothe his three holy associates, by suggesting that, if the outsides were indicted for this criminal attempt at the next assizes, the court would regard it as a case of lunacy or *delirium tremens* rather than of treason. England owes much of her grandeur to the depth of the aristocratic element in her social composition, when pulling against her strong democracy. I am not the man to laugh at it. But sometimes, undoubtedly, it expressed itself in comic shapes. The course taken with the infatuated outsiders, in the particular attempt which I have noticed, was that the waiter, beckoning them away from the privileged *salle-à-manger*, sang out, "This way, my good men," and then enticed these good men away to the kitchen. But that plan had not always answered. Sometimes, though rarely, cases occurred where the intruders, being stronger than usual, or more vicious than usual, resolutely refused to budge, and so far carried their point as to have a separate table arranged for themselves in a corner of the general room. Yet, if an Indian screen could be found ample enough to plant them out from the very eyes of the high table, or *dais*, it then became possible to assume as a fiction of law that the three delf fellows, after all, were not present. They could be ignored by the porcelain men, under the maxim that objects not appearing and objects not existing are governed by the same logical construction.

Such being, at that time, the usage of mail-coaches,

what was to be done by us of young Oxford? We, the most aristocratic of people, who were addicted to the practice of looking down superciliously even upon the insides themselves as often very questionable characters—were we, by voluntarily going outside, to court indignities? If our dress and bearing sheltered us generally from the suspicion of being "raff" (the name at that period for "snobs" [1]), we really *were* such constructively by the place we assumed. If we did not submit to the deep shadow of eclipse, we entered at least the skirts of its penumbra. And the analogy of theatres was valid against us—where no man can complain of the annoyances incident to the pit or gallery, having his instant remedy in paying the higher price of the boxes. But the soundness of this analogy we disputed. In the case of the theatre, it cannot be pretended that the inferior situations have any separate attractions, unless the pit may be supposed to have an advantage for the purposes of the critic or the dramatic reporter. But the critic or reporter is a rarity. For most people, the sole benefit is in the price. Now, on the contrary, the outside of the mail had its own incommunicable advantages. These we could not forgo. The higher price we would willingly have paid, but not the price connected with the condition of riding inside; which condition we pronounced insufferable. The air, the freedom of prospect, the proximity to the horses, the elevation of seat: these were what we required; but, above all, the certain anticipation of purchasing occasional opportunities of driving.

[1] "*Snobs*," and its antithesis, "*nobs*," arose among the internal factions of shoemakers perhaps ten years later. Possibly enough, the terms may have existed much earlier; but they were then first made known, picturesquely and effectively, by a trial at some assizes which happened to fix the public attention.

Such was the difficulty which pressed us; and under the coercion of this difficulty we instituted a searching inquiry into the true quality and valuation of the different apartments about the mail. We conducted this inquiry on metaphysical principles; and it was ascertained satisfactorily that the roof of the coach, which by some weak men had been called the attics, and by some the garrets, was in reality the drawing-room; in which drawing-room the box was the chief ottoman or sofa; whilst it appeared that the *inside*, which had been traditionally regarded as the only room tenantable by gentlemen, was, in fact, the coal-cellar in disguise.

Great wits jump. The very same idea had not long before struck the celestial intellect of China. Amongst the presents carried out by our first embassy to that country was a state-coach. It had been specially selected as a personal gift by George III; but the exact mode of using it was an intense mystery to Pekin. The ambassador, indeed (Lord Macartney), had made some imperfect explanations upon this point; but, as His Excellency communicated these in a diplomatic whisper at the very moment of his departure, the celestial intellect was very feebly illuminated, and it became necessary to call a cabinet council on the grand state question, "Where was the Emperor to sit?" The hammer-cloth happened to be unusually gorgeous; and, partly on that consideration, but partly also because the box offered the most elevated seat, was nearest to the moon, and undeniably went foremost, it was resolved by acclamation that the box was the imperial throne, and, for the scoundrel who drove —he might sit where he could find a perch. The horses, therefore, being harnessed, solemnly His Imperial Majesty ascended his new English throne under a flourish of trumpets, having the first lord of the treasury on his right hand, and the chief jester on his left. Pekin gloried in the spectacle; and in the whole flowery people, constructively present by representation, there was but one discontented person, and *that* was the coachman. This mutinous individual audaciously shouted, "Where am *I* to sit?" But the privy council, incensed by his disloyalty, unanimously opened the door, and kicked him into the inside. He had all the inside places to himself; but such is the rapacity of ambition that he was still dissatisfied. "I say," he cried out in an extempore petition addressed to the Emperor through the window—"I say, how am I to catch hold of the reins?"—"Anyhow," was the imperial answer; "don't trouble *me*, man, in my glory. How catch the reins? Why, through the windows, through the keyholes—*any*how." Finally this contumacious coachman lengthened the check-strings into a sort of jury-reins communicating with the horses; with these he drove as steadily as Pekin had any right to expect. The Emperor returned after the briefest of circuits; he descended in great pomp from his throne, with the severest resolution never to remount it. A public thanksgiving was ordered for His Majesty's happy escape from the disease of broken neck; and the state-coach was dedicated thenceforward as a votive offering to the god Fo Fo—whom the learned more accurately called Fi Fi.

A revolution of this same Chinese character did young Oxford of that era effect in the constitution of mail-coach society. It was a perfect French Revolution; and we had good reason to say, *ça ira*. In fact, it soon became *too* popular. The "public"—a well-known character, particularly disagreeable, though slightly respectable, and notorious for affecting the chief seats in synagogues—had at first loudly opposed this revolution; but, when the opposition showed itself

to be ineffectual, our disagreeable friend went into it
with headlong zeal. At first it was a sort of race between us; and, as the public is usually from thirty to
fifty years old, naturally we of young Oxford, that
averaged about twenty, had the advantage. Then the
public took to bribing, giving fees to horse-keepers,
&c., who hired out their persons as warming-pans on
the box-seat. *That*, you know, was shocking to all
moral sensibilities. Come to bribery, said we, and
there is an end to all morality—Aristotle's, Zeno's,
Cicero's, or anybody's. And, besides, of what use was
it? For *we* bribed also. And, as our bribes, to those of
the public, were as five shillings to sixpence, here
again young Oxford had the advantage. But the contest was ruinous to the principles of the stables connected with the mails. This whole corporation was
constantly bribed, rebribed, and often sur-rebribed; a
mail-coach yard was like the hustings in a contested
election; and a horse-keeper, ostler, or helper, was
held by the philosophical at that time to be the most
corrupt character in the nation.

There was an impression upon the public mind, natural enough from the continually augmenting velocity of the mail, but quite erroneous, that an outside
seat on this class of carriages was a post of danger. On
the contrary, I maintained that, if a man had become
nervous from some gipsy prediction in his childhood,
allocating to a particular moon now approaching some
unknown danger, and he should inquire earnestly,
"Whither can I fly for shelter? Is a prison the safest
retreat? or a lunatic hospital? or the British Museum?"
I should have replied, "Oh no; I'll tell you what to do.
Take lodgings for the next forty days on the box of His
Majesty's mail. Nobody can touch you there. If it is
by bills at ninety days after date that you are made
unhappy—if noters and protestors are the sort of

wretches whose astrological shadows darken the house of life—then note you what I vehemently protest: viz. that, no matter though the sheriff and under-sheriff in every county should be running after you with his *posse*, touch a hair of your head he cannot whilst you keep house and have your legal domicile on the box of the mail. It is felony to stop the mail; even the sheriff cannot do that. And an *extra* touch of the whip to the leaders (no great matter if it grazes the sheriff) at any time guarantees your safety." In fact, a bedroom in a quiet house seems a safe enough retreat; yet it is liable to its own notorious nuisances —to robbers by night, to rats, to fire. But the mail laughs at these terrors. To robbers, the answer is packed up and ready for delivery in the barrel of the guard's blunderbuss. Rats again! there *are* none about mail-coaches, any more than snakes in Von Troil's *Iceland* [1]; except, indeed, now and then a parliamentary rat, who always hides his shame in what I have shown to be the "coal-cellar." And, as to fire, I never knew but one in a mail-coach; which was in the Exeter mail, and caused by an obstinate sailor bound to Devonport. Jack, making light of the law and the lawgiver that had set their faces against his offence, insisted on taking up a forbidden seat [2] in the rear of

[1] *"Von Troil's Iceland":* The allusion is to a well-known chapter in Von Troil's work, entitled, "Concerning the Snakes of Iceland." The entire chapter consists of these six words: *"There are no snakes in Iceland."*

[2] *"Forbidden seat":* The very sternest code of rules was enforced upon the mails by the Post-office. Throughout England, only three outsides were allowed, of whom one was to sit on the box, and the other two immediately behind the box; none, under any pretext, to come near the guard; an indispensable caution; since else, under the guise of a passenger, a robber might by any one of a thousand advantages—which sometimes are created, but always are favoured, by the animation of frank social intercourse—have disarmed the guard. Beyond the Scot-

the roof, from which he could exchange his own yarns
with those of the guard. No greater offence was then
known to mail-coaches; it was treason, it was *læsa
majestas*, it was by tendency arson; and the ashes of
Jack's pipe, falling amongst the straw of the hinder
boot, containing the mail-bags, raised a flame which
(aided by the wind of our motion) threatened a revolution in the republic of letters. Yet even this left the
sanctity of the box unviolated. In dignified repose, the
coachman and myself sat on, resting with benign com-
posure upon our knowledge that the fire would have
to burn its way through four inside passengers before
it could reach ourselves. I remarked to the coachman,
with a quotation from Virgil's *Æneid* really too hack-
neyed—

> *Jam proximus ardet*
> *Ucalegon.*

But, recollecting that the Virgilian part of the coachman's education might have been neglected, I interpreted so far as to say that perhaps at that moment
the flames were catching hold of our worthy brother
and inside passenger, Ucalegon. The coachman made
no answer, which is my own way when a stranger
addresses me either in Syriac or in Coptic; but by his

tish border, the regulation was so far relaxed as to allow of
four outsides, but not relaxed at all as to the mode of placing
them. One, as before, was seated on the box, and the other three
on the front of the roof, with a determinate and ample separation from the little insulated chair of the guard. This relaxation was conceded by way of compensating to Scotland her
disadvantages in point of population. England, by the superior
density of her population, might always count upon a large
fund of profits in the fractional trips of chance passengers riding for short distances of two or three stages. In Scotland this
chance counted for much less. And therefore, to make good the
deficiency, Scotland was allowed a compensatory profit upon
one *extra* passenger.

faint sceptical smile he seemed to insinuate that he knew better, for that Ucalegon, as it happened, was not in the way-bill, and therefore could not have been booked.

No dignity is perfect which does not at some point ally itself with the mysterious. The connexion of the mail with the state and the executive government—a connexion obvious, but yet not strictly defined—gave to the whole mail establishment an official grandeur which did us service on the roads, and invested us with seasonable terrors. Not the less impressive were those terrors because their legal limits were imperfectly ascertained. Look at those turnpike gates: with what deferential hurry, with what an obedient start, they fly open at our approach! Look at that long line of carts and carters ahead, audaciously usurping the very crest of the road. Ah! traitors, they do not hear us as yet; but, as soon as the dreadful blast of our horn reaches them with proclamation of our approach, see with what frenzy of trepidation they fly to their horses' heads, and deprecate our wrath by the precipitation of their crane-neck quarterings. Treason they feel to be their crime; each individual carter feels himself under the ban of confiscation and attainder; his blood is attainted through six generations; and nothing is wanting but the headsman and his axe, the block and the sawdust, to close up the vista of his horrors. What! shall it be within benefit of clergy to delay the king's message on the high road?—to interrupt the great respirations, ebb and flood, *systole* and *diastole*, of the national intercourse?—to endanger the safety of tidings running day and night between all nations and languages? Or can it be fancied, amongst the weakest of men, that the bodies of the criminals will be given up to their widows for Christian burial? Now, the doubts which were raised as to our powers did more to wrap them in terror, by wrapping them in uncertainty, than could have been effected by the sharpest definitions of the law from the Quarter Sessions. We, on our parts (we, the collective mail, I mean), did our utmost to exalt the idea of our privileges by the insolence with which we wielded them. Whether this insolence rested upon law that gave it a sanction, or upon conscious power that haughtily dispensed with that sanction, equally it spoke from a potential station; and the agent, in each particular insolence of the moment, was viewed reverentially, as one having authority.

Sometimes after breakfast His Majesty's mail would become frisky; and, in its difficult wheelings amongst the intricacies of early markets, it would upset an apple-cart, a cart loaded with eggs, &c. Huge was the affliction and dismay, awful was the smash. I, as far as possible, endeavoured in such a case to represent the conscience and moral sensibilities of the mail; and, when wildernesses of eggs were lying poached under our horses' hoofs, then would I stretch forth my hands in sorrow, saying (in words too celebrated at that time, from the false echoes [1] of Marengo), "Ah! wherefore have we not time to weep over you?"—which was evidently impossible, since, in fact, we had not time to laugh over them. Tied to post-office allowance in some cases of fifty minutes for eleven miles, could the royal mail pretend to undertake the offices of sympathy and condolence? Could it be expected to provide tears for the accidents of the road? If even it seemed to trample

[1] "*False echoes*": Yes, false! for the words ascribed to Napoleon, as breathed to the memory of Desaix, never were uttered at all. They stand in the same category of theatrical fictions as the cry of the foundering line-of-battle ship *Vengeur*, as the vaunt of General Cambronne at Waterloo, "*La Garde meurt, mais ne se rend pas*," or as the repartees of Talleyrand.

on humanity, it did so, I felt, in discharge of its own more peremptory duties.

Upholding the morality of the mail, *a fortiori* I upheld its rights; as a matter of duty, I stretched to the uttermost its privilege of imperial precedency, and astonished weak minds by the feudal powers which I hinted to be lurking constructively in the charters of this proud establishment. Once I remember being on the box of the Holyhead mail, between Shrewsbury and Oswestry, when a tawdry thing from Birmingham, some "Tallyho" or "Highflyer," all flaunting with green and gold, came up alongside of us. What a contrast to our royal simplicity of form and colour in this plebeian wretch! The single ornament on our dark ground of chocolate colour was the mighty shield of the imperial arms, but emblazoned in proportions as modest as a signet-ring bears to a seal of office. Even this was displayed only on a single panel, whispering, rather than proclaiming, our relations to the mighty state; whilst the beast from Birmingham, our green-and-gold friend from false, fleeting, perjured Brummagem, had as much writing and painting on its sprawling flanks as would have puzzled a decipherer from the tombs of Luxor. For some time this Birmingham machine ran along by our side—a piece of familiarity that already of itself seemed to me sufficiently jacobinical. But all at once a movement of the horses announced a desperate intention of leaving us behind. "Do you see *that?*" I said to the coachman. "I see," was his short answer. He was wide awake, yet he waited longer than seemed prudent; for the horses of our audacious opponent had a disagreeable air of freshness and power. But his motive was loyal; his wish was that the Birmingham conceit should be full-blown before he froze it. When *that* seemed right, he unloosed, or, to speak by a stronger word, he *sprang*, his known resources: he slipped our royal horses like cheetahs, or hunting-leopards, after the affrighted game. How they could retain such a reserve of fiery power after the work they had accomplished seemed hard to explain. But on our side, besides the physical superiority, was a tower of moral strength, namely the king's name, "which they upon the adverse faction wanted." Passing them without an effort, as it seemed, we threw them into the rear with so lengthening an interval between us as proved in itself the bitterest mockery of their presumption; whilst our guard blew back a shattering blast of triumph that was really too painfully full of derision.

I mention this little incident for its connexion with what followed. A Welsh rustic, sitting behind me, asked if I had not felt my heart burn within me during the progress of the race? I said, with philosophic calmness, *No;* because we were not racing with a mail, so that no glory could be gained. In fact, it was sufficiently mortifying that such a Birmingham thing should dare to challenge us. The Welshman replied that he didn't see *that;* for that a cat might look at a king, and a Brummagem coach might lawfully race the Holyhead mail. "*Race* us, if you like," I replied, "though even *that* has an air of sedition; but not *beat* us. This would have been treason; and for its own sake I am glad that the 'Tallyho' was disappointed." So dissatisfied did the Welshman seem with this opinion that at last I was obliged to tell him a very fine story from one of our elder dramatists: viz. that once, in some far oriental kingdom, when the sultan of all the land, with his princes, ladies, and chief omrahs, were flying their falcons, a hawk suddenly flew at a majestic eagle, and, in defiance of the eagle's natural advantages, in contempt also of the eagle's traditional royalty, and before the whole assembled field of astonished spectators from Agra and Lahore, killed the eagle on the spot. Amazement seized the sultan at the unequal contest, and burning admiration for its unparalleled result. He commanded that the hawk should be brought before him; he caressed the bird with enthusiasm; and he ordered that, for the commemoration of his matchless courage, a diadem of gold and rubies should be solemnly placed on the hawk's head, but then that, immediately after this solemn coronation, the bird should be led off to execution, as the most valiant indeed of traitors, but not the less a traitor, as having dared to rise rebelliously against his liege lord and anointed sovereign, the eagle. "Now," said I to the Welshman, "to you and me, as men of refined sensibilities, how painful it would have been that this poor Brummagem brute, the 'Tallyho,' in the impossible case of a victory over us, should have been crowned with Birmingham tinsel, with paste diamonds and Roman pearls, and then led off to instant execution." The Welshman doubted if that could be warranted by law. And, when I hinted at the sixth of Edward Longshanks, chap. 18, for regulating the precedency of coaches, as being probably the statute relied on for the capital punishment of such offences, he replied drily that, if the attempt to pass a mail really were treasonable, it was a pity that the "Tallyho" appeared to have so imperfect an acquaintance with law.

The modern modes of travelling cannot compare with the old mail-coach system in grandeur and power. They boast of more velocity—not, however, as a consciousness, but as a fact of our lifeless knowledge, resting upon *alien* evidence: as, for instance, because somebody *says* that we have gone fifty miles in the hour, though we are far from feeling it as a personal experience; or upon the evidence of a result, as that actually we find ourselves in York four hours after leaving London. Apart from such an assertion, or such a result, I myself am little aware of the pace. But, seated on the old mail-coach, we needed no evidence out of ourselves to indicate the velocity. On this system the word was not *magna loquimur*, as upon railways, but *vivimus*. Yes, "magna *vivimus*"; we do not make verbal ostentation of our grandeurs, we realize our grandeurs in act, and in the very experience of life. The vital experience of the glad animal sensibilities made doubts impossible on the question of our speed; we heard our speed, we saw it, we felt it as a thrilling; and this speed was not the product of blind insensate agencies, that had no sympathy to give, but was incarnated in the fiery eyeballs of the noblest amongst brutes, in his dilated nostril, spasmodic muscles, and thunder-beating hoofs. The sensibility of the horse, uttering itself in the maniac light of his eye, might be the last vibration of such a movement; the glory of Salamanca might be the first. But the intervening links that connected them, that spread the earthquake of battle into the eyeball of the horse, were the heart of man and its electric thrillings—kindling in the rapture of the fiery strife, and then propagating its own tumults by contagious shouts and gestures to the heart of his servant the horse. But now, on the new system of travelling, iron tubes and boilers have disconnected man's heart from the ministers of his locomotion. Nile nor Trafalgar has power to raise an extra bubble in a steam-kettle. The galvanic cycle is broken up for ever; man's imperial nature no longer sends itself forward through the electric sensibility of the horse; the interagencies are gone in the mode of communication between the horse and his master out of which grew so many aspects of sublimity under accidents of mists that hid, or sudden blazes that revealed, of mobs that

agitated, or midnight solitudes that awed. Tidings
fitted to convulse all nations must henceforwards
travel by culinary process; and the trumpet that once
announced from afar the laurelled mail, heart-shaking
when heard screaming on the wind and proclaiming
itself through the darkness to every village or solitary
house on its route, has now given way for ever to the
pot-wallopings of the boiler. Thus have perished multiform openings for public expressions of interest,
scenical yet natural, in great national tidings, for
revelations of faces and groups that could not offer
themselves amongst the fluctuating mobs of a railway
station. The gatherings of gazers about a laurelled mail
had one centre, and acknowledged one sole interest.
But the crowds attending at a railway station have as
little unity as running water, and own as many centres as there are separate carriages in the train.

How else, for example, than as a constant watcher
for the dawn, and for the London mail that in summer
months entered about daybreak amongst the lawny
thickets of Marlborough forest, couldest thou, sweet
Fanny of the Bath Road, have become the glorified inmate of my dreams? Yet Fanny, as the loveliest young
woman for face and person that perhaps in my whole
life I have beheld, merited the station which even now,
from a distance of forty years, she holds in my dreams;
yes, though by links of natural association she brings
along with her a troop of dreadful creatures, fabulous
and not fabulous, that are more abominable to the
heart than Fanny and the dawn are delightful.

Miss Fanny of the Bath Road, strictly speaking, lived
at a mile's distance from that road, but came so continually to meet the mail that I on my frequent transits
rarely missed her, and naturally connected her image
with the great thoroughfare where only I had ever
seen her. Why she came so punctually I do not exactly

know; but I believe with some burden of commissions,
to be executed in Bath, which had gathered to her own
residence as a central rendezvous for converging them.
The mail-coachman who drove the Bath mail and wore
the royal livery [1] happened to be Fanny's grandfather.
A good man he was, that loved his beautiful grand-
daughter, and, loving her wisely, was vigilant over
her deportment in any case where young Oxford might
happen to be concerned. Did my vanity then suggest
that I myself, individually, could fall within the line
of his terrors? Certainly not, as regarded any physical
pretensions that I could plead; for Fanny (as a chance
passenger from her own neighbourhood once told me)
counted in her train a hundred and ninety-nine professed admirers, if not open aspirants to her favour;
and probably not one of the whole brigade but excelled
myself in personal advantages. Ulysses even, with the
unfair advantage of his accursed bow, could hardly
have undertaken that amount of suitors. So the danger
might have seemed slight—only that woman is universally aristocratic; it is amongst her nobilities of
heart that she *is* so. Now, the aristocratic distinctions
in my favour might easily with Miss Fanny have compensated my physical deficiencies. Did I then make
love to Fanny? Why, yes; about as much love as one
could make whilst the mail was changing horses—a
process which, ten years later, did not occupy above

[1] *"Wore the royal livery"*: The general impression was that
the royal livery belonged of right to the mail-coachmen as
their professional dress. But that was an error. To the guard
it *did* belong, I believe, and was obviously essential as an official warrant, and as a means of instant identification for his
person, in the discharge of his important public duties. But
the coachman, and especially if his place in the series did not
connect him immediately with London and the General Post-
office, obtained the scarlet coat only as an honorary distinction
after long (or, if not long, trying and special) service.

eighty seconds; but *then*—viz. about Waterloo—it occupied five times eighty. Now, four hundred seconds
offer a field quite ample enough for whispering into a
young woman's ear a great deal of truth, and (by way
of parenthesis) some trifle of falsehood. Grandpapa
did right, therefore, to watch me. And yet, as happens
too often to the grandpapas of earth in a contest with
the admirers of granddaughters, how vainly would he
have watched me had I meditated any evil whispers to
Fanny! She, it is my belief, would have protected herself against any man's evil suggestions. But he, as the
result showed, could not have intercepted the opportunities for such suggestions. Yet, why not? Was he
not active? Was he not blooming? Blooming he was
as Fanny herself.

Say, all our praises why should lords——

Stop, that's not the line.

Say, all our roses why should girls engross?

The coachman showed rosy blossoms on his face deeper
even than his granddaughter's—*his* being drawn from
the ale-cask, Fanny's from the fountains of the dawn.
But, in spite of his blooming face, some infirmities he
had; and one particularly in which he too much resembled a crocodile. This lay in a monstrous inaptitude for turning round. The crocodile, I presume, owes
that inaptitude to the absurd *length* of his back; but in
our grandpapa it arose rather from the absurd *breadth*
of his back, combined, possibly, with some growing
stiffness in his legs. Now, upon this crocodile infirmity
of his I planted a human advantage for tendering my
homage to Miss Fanny. In defiance of all his honourable vigilance, no sooner had he presented to us his

mighty Jovian back (what a field for displaying to mankind his royal scarlet!), whilst inspecting professionally the buckles, the straps, and the silvery turrets [1] of his harness, than I raised Miss Fanny's hand to my lips, and, by the mixed tenderness and respectfulness of my manner, caused her easily to understand how happy it would make me to rank upon her list as No. 10 or 12: in which case a few casualties amongst her lovers (and, observe, they *hanged* liberally in those days) might have promoted me speedily to the top of the tree; as, on the other hand, with how much loyalty of submission I acquiesced by anticipation in her award, supposing that she should plant me in the very rearward of her favour, as No. 199 + 1. Most truly I loved this beautiful and ingenuous girl; and, had it not been for the Bath mail, timing all courtships by post-office allowance, heaven only knows what might have come of it. People talk of being over head and ears in love; now, the mail was the cause that I sank only over ears in love, which, you know, still left a trifle of brain to overlook the whole conduct of the affair.

Ah, reader! when I look back upon those days, it seems to me that all things change—all things perish. "Perish the roses and the palms of kings": perish even the crowns and trophies of Waterloo: thunder and lightning are not the thunder and lightning which I remember. Roses are degenerating. The Fannies of our island—though this I say with reluctance—are not

---

[1] *"Turrets"*: As one who loves and venerates Chaucer for his unrivalled merits of tenderness, of picturesque characterization, and of narrative skill, I noticed with great pleasure that the word *torrettes* is used by him to designate the little devices through which the reins are made to pass. This same word, in the same exact sense, I heard uniformly used by many scores of illustrious mail-coachmen to whose confidential friendship I had the honour of being admitted in my younger days.

visibly improving; and the Bath Road is notoriously superannuated. Crocodiles, you will say, are stationary. Mr. Waterton tells me that the crocodile does *not* change—that a cayman, in fact, or an alligator, is just as good for riding upon as he was in the time of the Pharaohs. *That* may be; but the reason is that the crocodile does not live fast—he is a slow coach. I believe it is generally understood among naturalists that the crocodile is a blockhead. It is my own impression that the Pharaohs were also blockheads. Now, as the Pharaohs and the crocodile domineered over Egyptian society, this accounts for a singular mistake that prevailed through innumerable generations on the Nile. The crocodile made the ridiculous blunder of supposing man to be meant chiefly for his own eating. Man, taking a different view of the subject, naturally met that mistake by another: he viewed the crocodile as a thing sometimes to worship, but always to run away from. And this continued till Mr. Waterton [1] changed the relations between the animals. The mode of escaping from the reptile he showed to be not by running away, but by leaping on its back booted and spurred. The two animals had misunderstood each other. The use of the crocodile has now been cleared up—viz. to be ridden; and the final cause of man is that he may improve

[1] "*Mr. Waterton*": Had the reader lived through the last generation, he would not need to be told that, some thirty or thirty-five years back, Mr. Waterton, a distinguished country gentleman of ancient family in Northumberland, publicly mounted and rode in top-boots a savage old crocodile, that was restive and very impertinent, but all to no purpose. The crocodile jibbed and tried to kick, but vainly. He was no more able to throw the squire than Sindbad was to throw the old scoundrel who used his back without paying for it, until he discovered a mode (slightly immoral, perhaps, though some think not) of murdering the old fraudulent jockey, and so circuitously of unhorsing him.

the health of the crocodile by riding him a-foxhunting before breakfast. And it is pretty certain that any crocodile who has been regularly hunted through the season, and is master of the weight he carries, will take a six-barred gate now as well as ever he would have done in the infancy of the pyramids.

Perhaps, therefore, the crocodile does *not* change, but all things else *do;* even the shadow of the pyramids grows less. And often the restoration in vision of Fanny and the Bath Road makes me too pathetically sensible of that truth. Out of the darkness, if I happen to call up the image of Fanny from thirty-five years back, arises suddenly a rose in June; or, if I think for an instant of a rose in June, up rises the heavenly face of Fanny. One after the other, like the antiphonies in a choral service, rises Fanny and the rose in June, then back again the rose in June and Fanny. Then come both together, as in a chorus; roses and Fannies, Fannies and roses, without end—thick as blossoms in paradise. Then comes a venerable crocodile, in a royal livery of scarlet and gold, or in a coat with sixteen capes; and the crocodile is driving four-in-hand from the box of the Bath mail. And suddenly we upon the mail are pulled up by a mighty dial, sculptured with the hours, and with the dreadful legend of TOO LATE. Then all at once we are arrived in Marlborough forest, amongst the lovely households of the roe-deer: these retire into the dewy thickets; the thickets are rich with roses; the roses call up (as ever) the sweet countenance of Fanny, who, being the granddaughter of a crocodile, awakens a dreadful host of wild semi-legendary animals—griffins, dragons, basilisks, sphinxes—till at length the whole vision of fighting images crowds into one towering armorial shield, a vast emblazonry of human charities and human loveliness that have perished, but quartered heraldically with unutterable horrors of

monstrous and demoniac natures; whilst over all rises,
as a surmounting crest, one fair female hand, with the
fore-finger pointing, in sweet, sorrowful admonition,
upwards to heaven, and having power (which, without experience, I never could have believed) to awaken
the pathos that kills, in the very bosom of the horrors
that madden, the grief that gnaws at the heart, together with the monstrous creations of darkness that
shock the belief, and make dizzy the reason, of man.
This is the peculiarity that I wish the reader to notice,
as having first been made known to me for a possibility
by this early vision of Fanny on the Bath Road. The
peculiarity consisted in the confluence of two different keys, though apparently repelling each other, into
the music and governing principles of the same dream;
horror, such as possesses the maniac, and yet, by momentary transitions, grief, such as may be supposed
to possess the dying mother when leaving her infant
children to the mercies of the cruel. Usually, and perhaps always, in an unshaken nervous system, these two
modes of misery exclude each other—here first they
met in horrid reconciliation. There was always a separate peculiarity in the quality of the horror. This was
afterwards developed into far more revolting complexities of misery and incomprehensible darkness; and
perhaps I am wrong in ascribing any value as a *causa-
tive* agency to this particular case on the Bath Road—
possibly it furnished merely an *occasion* that accidentally introduced a mode of horrors certain, at any
rate, to have grown up, with or without the Bath Road,
from more advanced stages of the nervous derangement. Yet, as the cubs of tigers or leopards, when domesticated, have been observed to suffer a sudden development of their latent ferocity under too eager an
appeal to their playfulness—the gaieties of sport in
them being too closely connected with the fiery bright-

ness of their murderous instincts—so I have remarked that the caprices, the gay arabesques, and the lively floral luxuriations of dreams, betray a shocking tendency to pass into finer maniacal splendours. That gaiety, for instance (for such at first it was), in the dreaming faculty, by which one principal point of resemblance to a crocodile in the mail-coachman was soon made to clothe him with the form of a crocodile, and yet was blended with accessory circumstances derived from his *human* functions, passed rapidly into a further development, no longer gay or playful, but terrific, the most terrific that besieges dreams—viz. the horrid inoculation upon each other of incompatible natures. This horror has always been secretly felt by man; it was felt even under pagan forms of religion, which offered a very feeble, and also a very limited, gamut for giving expression to the human capacities of sublimity or of horror. We read it in the fearful composition of the sphinx. The dragon, again, is the snake inoculated upon the scorpion. The basilisk unites the mysterious malice of the evil eye, unintentional on the part of the unhappy agent, with the intentional venom of some other malignant natures. But these horrid complexities of evil agency are but *objectively* horrid; they inflict the horror suitable to their compound nature; but there is no insinuation that they *feel* that horror. Heraldry is so full of these fantastic creatures that, in some zoologies, we find a separate chapter or a supplement dedicated to what is denominated heraldic zoology. And why not? For these hideous creatures, however visionary, have a real traditionary ground in medieval belief—sincere and partly reasonable, though adulterating with mendacity, blundering, credulity, and intense superstition. But the dream-horror which I speak of is far more frightful. The dreamer finds housed within himself—occupying, as it were, some separate chamber in his brain—holding, perhaps, from that station a secret and detestable commerce with his own heart—some horrid alien nature. What if it were his own nature repeated—still, if the duality were distinctly perceptible, even that— even this mere numerical double of his own consciousness—might be a curse too mighty to be sustained. But how if the alien nature contradicts his own, fights with it, perplexes and confounds it? How, again, if not one alien nature, but two, but three, but four, but five, are introduced within what once he thought the inviolable sanctuary of himself? These, however, are horrors from the kingdom of anarchy and darkness, which, by their very intensity, challenge the sanctity of concealment, and gloomily retire from exposition. Yet it was necessary to mention them, because the first introduction to such appearances (whether causal or merely casual) lay in the heraldic monsters, which monsters were themselves introduced (though playfully) by the transfigured coachman of the Bath mail.

* |* *

Going Down with Victory

But the grandest chapter of our experience within the whole mail-coach service was on those occasions when we went down from London with the news of victory. A period of about ten years stretched from Trafalgar to Waterloo; the second and third years of which period (1806 and 1807) were comparatively sterile; but the other nine (from 1805 to 1815 inclusively) furnished a long succession of victories, the least of which, in such a contest of Titans, had an inappreciable value of position: partly for its absolute interference with the plans of our enemy, but still

more from its keeping alive through central Europe
the sense of a deep-seated vulnerability in France.
Even to tease the coasts of our enemy, to mortify them
by continual blockades, to insult them by capturing if
it were but a baubling schooner under the eyes of their
arrogant armies, repeated from time to time a sullen
proclamation of power lodged in one quarter to which
the hopes of Christendom turned in secret. How much
more loudly must this proclamation have spoken in the
audacity of having bearded the *élite* of their troops,
and having beaten them in pitched battles! Five years
of life it was worth paying down for the privilege of
an outside place on a mail-coach when carrying down
the first tidings of any such event. And it is to be noted
that, from our insular situation, and the multitude of
our frigates disposable for the rapid transmission of
intelligence, rarely did any unauthorized rumour steal
away a prelibation from the first aroma of the regular
dispatches. The government news was generally the
earliest news.

From eight P.M. to fifteen or twenty minutes later
imagine the mails assembled on parade in Lombard
Street; where, at that time,[1] and not in St. Martin's-
le-Grand, was seated the General Post-office. In what
exact strength we mustered I do not remember; but,
from the length of each separate *attelage*, we filled
the street, though a long one, and though we were
drawn up in double file. On *any* night the spectacle
was beautiful. The absolute perfection of all the appointments about the carriages and the harness, their
strength, their brilliant cleanliness, their beautiful
simplicity—but, more than all, the royal magnificence
of the horses—were what might first have fixed the
attention. Every carriage on every morning in the

[1] "*At that time*": I speak of the era previous to Waterloo.

year was taken down to an official inspector for examination: wheels, axles, linchpins, pole, glasses, lamps, were all critically probed and tested. Every part of every carriage had been cleaned, every horse had been groomed, with as much rigour as if they belonged to a private gentleman; and that part of the spectacle offered itself always. But the night before us is a night of victory; and, behold! to the ordinary display what a heart-shaking addition!—horses, men, carriages, all are dressed in laurels and flowers, oak-leaves and ribbons. The guards, as being officially his Majesty's servants, and of the coachmen such as are within the privilege of the post-office, wear the royal liveries of course; and, as it is summer (for all the *land* victories were naturally won in summer), they wear, on this fine evening, these liveries exposed to view, without any covering of upper coats. Such a costume, and the elaborate arrangement of the laurels in their hats, dilate their hearts, by giving to them openly a personal connexion with the great news in which already they have the general interest of patriotism. That great national sentiment surmounts and quells all sense of ordinary distinctions. Those passengers who happen to be gentlemen are now hardly to be distinguished as such except by dress; for the usual reserve of their manner in speaking to the attendants has on this night melted away. One heart, one pride, one glory, connects every man by the transcendent bond of his national blood. The spectators, who are numerous beyond precedent, express their sympathy with these fervent feelings by continual hurrahs. Every moment are shouted aloud by the post-office servants, and summoned to draw up, the great ancestral names of cities known to history through a thousand years—Lincoln, Winchester, Portsmouth, Gloucester, Oxford, Bristol, Manchester, York, Newcastle, Edinburgh, Glasgow, Perth, Stir-

ling, Aberdeen——expressing the grandeur of the empire by the antiquity of its towns, and the grandeur
of the mail establishment by the diffusive radiation
of its separate missions. Every moment you hear the
thunder of lids locked down upon the mail-bags. That
sound to each individual mail is the signal for drawing off; which process is the finest part of the entire
spectacle. Then come the horses into play. Horses!
can these be horses that bound off with the action and
gestures of leopards? What stir!——what sea-like fer-
ment!——what a thundering of wheels!——what a trampling of hoofs!——what a sounding of trumpets!——what
farewell cheers——what redoubling peals of brotherly
congratulation, connecting the name of the particular
mail——"Liverpool for ever!"——with the name of the
particular victory——"Badajoz for ever!" or "Salamanca for ever!" The half-slumbering consciousness
that all night long, and all the next day——perhaps for
even a longer period——many of these mails, like fire
racing along a train of gunpowder, will be kindling
at every instant new successions of burning joy, has an
obscure effect of multiplying the victory itself, by multiplying to the imagination into infinity the stages of
its progressive diffusion. A fiery arrow seems to be let
loose, which from that moment is destined to travel,
without intermission, westwards for three hundred [1]

[1] "*Three hundred*": Of necessity, this scale of measurement,
to an American, if he happens to be a thoughtless man, must
sound ludicrous. Accordingly, I remember a case in which an
American writer indulges himself in the luxury of a little fib-
bing, by ascribing to an Englishman a pompous account of the
Thames, constructed entirely upon American ideas of grandeur, and concluding in something like these terms: "And, sir,
arriving at London, this mighty father of rivers attains a
breadth of at least two furlongs, having, in its winding course,
traversed the astonishing distance of one hundred and seventy
miles." And this the candid American thinks it fair to contrast

miles—northwards for six hundred; and the sympathy
of our Lombard Street friends at parting is exalted a
hundredfold by a sort of visionary sympathy with the
yet slumbering sympathies which in so vast a succession we are going to awake.

Liberated from the embarrassments of the city, and
issuing into the broad uncrowded avenues of the northern suburbs, we soon begin to enter upon our natural
pace of ten miles an hour. In the broad light of the
summer evening, the sun, perhaps, only just at the
point of setting, we are seen from every storey of
every house. Heads of every age crowd to the windows; young and old understand the language of our
victorious symbols; and rolling volleys of sympathiz-

with the scale of the Mississippi. Now, it is hardly worth while
to answer a pure fiction gravely; else one might say that no
Englishman out of Bedlam ever thought of looking in an island
for the rivers of a continent, nor, consequently, could have
thought of looking for the peculiar grandeur of the Thames in
the length of its course, or in the extent of soil which it drains.
Yet, if he *had* been so absurd, the American might have recollected that a river, not to be compared with the Thames even
as to volume of water—viz. the Tiber—has contrived to make
itself heard of in this world for twenty-five centuries to an extent not reached as yet by any river, however corpulent, of his
own land. The glory of the Thames is measured by the destiny
of the population to which it ministers, by the commerce which
it supports, by the grandeur of the empire in which, though
far from the largest, it is the most influential stream. Upon
some such scale, and not by a transfer of Columbian standards,
is the course of our English mails to be valued. The American
may fancy the effect of his own valuations to our English ears
by supposing the case of a Siberian glorifying his country in
these terms: "These wretches, sir, in France and England,
cannot march half a mile in any direction without finding a
house where food can be had and lodging; whereas such is the
noble desolation of our magnificent country that in many a
direction for a thousand miles I will engage that a dog shall
not find shelter from a snow-storm, nor a wren find an apology
for breakfast."

ing cheers run along us, behind us, and before us. The
beggar, rearing himself against the wall, forgets his
lameness—real or assumed—thinks not of his whin-
ing trade, but stands erect, with bold exulting smiles,
as we pass him. The victory has healed him, and says,
Be thou whole! Women and children, from garrets
alike and cellars, through infinite London, look down
or look up with loving eyes upon our gay ribbons and
our martial laurels; sometimes kiss their hands; sometimes hang out, as signals of affection, pocket-hand-
kerchiefs, aprons, dusters, anything that, by catching
the summer breezes, will express an aerial jubilation.
On the London side of Barnet, to which we draw near
within a few minutes after nine, observe that private
carriage which is approaching us. The weather being
so warm, the glasses are all down; and one may read,
as on the stage of a theatre, everything that goes on
within. It contains three ladies—one likely to be
"mamma," and two of seventeen or eighteen, who are
probably her daughters. What lovely animation, what
beautiful unpremeditated pantomime, explaining to us
every syllable that passes, in these ingenuous girls! By
the sudden start and raising of the hands on first dis-
covering our laurelled equipage, by the sudden movement and appeal to the elder lady from both of them,
and by the heightened colour on their animated countenances, we can almost hear them saying, "See, see!
Look at their laurels! Oh, mamma! there has been a
great battle in Spain; and it has been a great victory."
In a moment we are on the point of passing them. We
passengers—I on the box, and the two on the roof behind me—raise our hats to the ladies; the coachman
makes his professional salute with the whip; the guard
even, though punctilious on the matter of his dignity
as an officer under the crown, touches his hat. The
ladies move to us, in return, with a winning gracious-

ness of gesture; all smile on each side in a way that nobody could misunderstand, and that nothing short of a grand national sympathy could so instantaneously prompt. Will these ladies say that we are nothing to *them?* Oh no; they will not say *that*. They cannot deny —they do not deny—that for this night they are our sisters; gentle or simple, scholar or illiterate servant, for twelve hours to come, we on the outside have the honour to be their brothers. Those poor women, again, who stop to gaze upon us with delight at the entrance of Barnet, and seem, by their air of weariness, to be returning from labour—do you mean to say that they are washerwomen and charwomen? Oh, my poor friend, you are quite mistaken. I assure you they stand in a far higher rank; for this one night they feel themselves by birthright to be daughters of England, and answer to no humbler title.

Every joy, however, even rapturous joy—such is the sad law of earth—may carry with it grief, or fear of grief, to some. Three miles beyond Barnet, we see approaching us another private carriage, nearly repeating the circumstances of the former case. Here, also, the glasses are all down; here, also, is an elderly lady seated; but the two daughters are missing; for the single young person sitting by the lady's side seems to be an attendant—so I judge from her dress, and her air of respectful reserve. The lady is in mourning; and her countenance expresses sorrow. At first she does not look up; so that I believe she is not aware of our approach, until she hears the measured beating of our horses' hoofs. Then she raises her eyes to settle them painfully on our triumphal equipage. Our decorations explain the case to her at once; but she beholds them with apparent anxiety, or even with terror. Some time before this, I, finding it difficult to hit a flying mark when embarrassed by the coachman's person and reins intervening, had given to the guard a *Courier* evening paper, containing the gazette, for the next carriage that might pass. Accordingly he tossed it in, so folded that the huge capitals expressing some such legend as GLORIOUS VICTORY might catch the eye at once. To see the paper, however, at all, interpreted as it was by our ensigns of triumph, explained everything; and, if the guard were right in thinking the lady to have received it with a gesture of horror, it could not be doubtful that she had suffered some deep personal affliction in connexion with this Spanish war.

Here, now, was the case of one who, having formerly suffered, might, erroneously perhaps, be distressing herself with anticipations of another similar suffering. That same night, and hardly three hours later, occurred the reverse case. A poor woman, who too probably would find herself, in a day or two, to have suffered the heaviest of afflictions by the battle, blindly allowed herself to express an exultation so unmeasured in the news and its details as gave to her the appearance which amongst Celtic Highlanders is called *fey*. This was at some little town where we changed horses an hour or two after midnight. Some fair or wake had kept the people up out of their beds, and had occasioned a partial illumination of the stalls and booths, presenting an unusual but very impressive effect. We saw many lights moving about as we drew near; and perhaps the most striking scene on the whole route was our reception at this place. The flashing of torches and the beautiful radiance of blue lights (technically, Bengal lights) upon the heads of our horses; the fine effect of such a showery and ghostly illumination falling upon our flowers and glittering laurels [1]; whilst

---

[1] *"Glittering laurels":* I must observe that the colour of *green* suffers almost a spiritual change and exaltation under the effect of Bengal lights.

all around ourselves, that formed a centre of light, the darkness gathered on the rear and flanks in massy blackness: these optical splendours, together with the prodigious enthusiasm of the people, composed a picture at once scenical and affecting, theatrical and holy. As we stayed for three or four minutes, I alighted; and immediately from a dismantled stall in the street, where no doubt she had been presiding through the earlier part of the night, advanced eagerly a middle-aged woman. The sight of my newspaper it was that had drawn her attention upon myself. The victory which we were carrying down to the provinces on *this* occasion was the imperfect one of Talavera—imperfect for its results, such was the virtual treachery of the Spanish general, Cuesta, but not imperfect in its ever-memorable herosim.

I told her the main outline of the battle. The agitation of her enthusiasm had been so conspicuous when listening, and when first applying for information, that I could not but ask her if she had not some relative in the Peninsular army. Oh yes; her only son was there. In what regiment? He was a trooper in the 23d Dragoons. My heart sank within me as she made that answer. This sublime regiment, which an Englishman should never mention without raising his hat to their memory, had made the most memorable and effective charge recorded in military annals. They leaped their horses—*over* a trench where they could; *into* it, and with the result of death or mutilation, when they could *not*. What proportion cleared the trench is nowhere stated. Those who *did* closed up and went down upon the enemy with such divinity of fervour (I use the word *divinity* by design: the inspiration of God must have prompted this movement to those whom even then He was calling to His presence) that two results followed. As regarded the enemy, this 23d Dragoons, not,

I believe, originally three hundred and fifty strong, paralysed a French column six thousand strong, then ascended the hill, and fixed the gaze of the whole French army. As regarded themselves, the 23d were supposed at first to have been barely not annihilated; but eventually, I believe, about one in four survived. And this, then, was the regiment—a regiment already for some hours glorified and hallowed to the ear of all London, as lying stretched, by a large majority, upon one bloody aceldama—in which the young trooper served whose mother was now talking in a spirit of such joyous enthusiasm. Did I tell her the truth? Had I the heart to break up her dreams? No. Tomorrow, said I to myself—tomorrow, or the next day, will publish the worst. For one night more wherefore should she not sleep in peace? After tomorrow the chances are too many that peace will forsake her pillow. This brief respite, then, let her owe to *my* gift and *my* forbearance. But, if I told her not of the bloody price that had been paid, not therefore was I silent on the contributions from her son's regiment to that day's service and glory. I showed her not the funeral banners under which the noble regiment was sleeping. I lifted not the overshadowing laurels from the bloody trench in which horse and rider lay mangled together. But I told her how these dear children of England, officers and privates, had leaped their horses over all obstacles as gaily as hunters to the morning's chase. I told her how they rode their horses into the mists of death—saying to myself, but not saying to *her*, "and laid down their young lives for thee, O mother England! as willingly—poured out their noble blood as cheerfully—as ever, after a long day's sport, when infants, they had rested their wearied heads upon their mother's knees, or had sunk to sleep in her arms." Strange it is, yet true, that she seemed to have no fears for her son's safety, even after this knowledge that the 23d Dragoons had been memorably engaged; but so much was she enraptured by the knowledge that *his* regiment, and therefore that *he*, had rendered conspicuous service in the dreadful conflict—a service which had actually made them, within the last twelve hours, the foremost topic of conversation in London—so absolutely was fear swallowed up in joy—that, in the mere simplicity of her fervent nature, the poor woman threw her arms round my neck, as she thought of her son, and gave to *me* the kiss which secretly was meant for *him*.

II. THE VISION OF SUDDEN DEATH

What is to be taken as the predominant opinion of man, reflective and philosophic, upon SUDDEN DEATH? It is remarkable that in different conditions of society sudden death has been variously regarded as the consummation of an earthly career most fervently to be desired, or, again, as that consummation which is with most horror to be deprecated. Cæsar the Dictator, at his last dinner-party (*cœna*), on the very evening before his assassination, when the minutes of his earthly career were numbered, being asked what death, in *his* judgement, might be pronounced the most eligible, replied, "That which should be most sudden." On the other hand, the divine Litany of our English Church, when breathing forth supplications, as if in some representative character, for the whole human race prostrate before God, places such a death in the very van of horrors: "From lightning and tempest; from plague, pestilence, and famine; from battle and murder, and from SUDDEN DEATH—*Good Lord, deliver us.*" Sudden death is here made to crown the climax in a grand ascent of calamities; it is ranked among the last of curses; and yet by the noblest of Romans it was ranked as the first of blessings. In that difference most readers will see little more than the essential difference between Christianity and Paganism. But this, on consideration, I doubt. The Christian Church may be right in its estimate of sudden death; and it is a natural feeling, though after all it may also be an infirm one, to wish for a quiet dismissal from life, as that which *seems* most reconcilable with meditation, with penitential retrospects, and with the humilities of farewell prayer. There does not, however, occur to me any direct scriptural warrant for this earnest petition of the English Litany, unless under a special construction of the word "sudden." It seems a petition indulged rather and conceded to human infirmity than exacted from human piety. It is not so much a doctrine built upon the eternities of the Christian system as a plausible opinion built upon special varieties of physical temperament. Let that, however, be as it may, two remarks suggest themselves as prudent restraints upon a doctrine which else *may* wander, and *has* wandered, into an uncharitable superstition. The first is this: that many people are likely to exaggerate the horror of a sudden death from the disposition to lay a false stress upon words or acts simply because by an accident they have become *final* words or acts. If a man dies, for instance, by some sudden death when he happens to be intoxicated, such a death is falsely regarded with peculiar horror; as though the intoxication were suddenly exalted into a blasphemy. But *that* is unphilosophic. The man was, or he was not, *habitually* a drunkard. If not, if his intoxication were a solitary accident, there can be no reason for allowing special emphasis to this act simply because through misfortune it became his final act. Nor, on the other hand, if

it were no accident, but one of his *habitual* transgressions, will it be the more habitual or the more a transgression because some sudden calamity, surprising
him, has caused this habitual transgression to be also
a final one. Could the man have had any reason even
dimly to foresee his own sudden death, there would
have been a new feature in his act of intemperance—
a feature of presumption and irreverence, as in one
that, having known himself drawing near to the presence of God, should have suited his demeanour to an
expectation so awful. But this is no part of the case
supposed. And the only new element in the man's act
is not any element of special immorality, but simply
of special misfortune.

The other remark has reference to the meaning of
the word *sudden*. Very possibly Cæsar and the Christian Church do not differ in the way supposed—that
is, do not differ by any difference of doctrine as
between Pagan and Christian views of the moral temper appropriate to death; but perhaps they are contemplating different cases. Both contemplate a violent death, a Βιαθανατος—death that is βιαιος, or, in
other words, death that is brought about, not by internal and spontaneous change, but by active force having its origin from without. In this meaning the two
authorities agree. Thus far they are in harmony. But
the difference is that the Roman by the word "sudden" means *unlingering*, whereas the Christian Litany
by "sudden death" means a death *without warning*,
consequently without any available summons to religious preparation. The poor mutineer who kneels
down to gather into his heart the bullets from twelve
firelocks of his pitying comrades dies by a most sudden death in Cæsar's sense; one shock, one mighty
spasm, one (possibly *not* one) groan, and all is over.
But, in the sense of the Litany, the mutineer's death is

far from sudden: his offence originally, his imprisonment, his trial, the interval between his sentence and its execution, having all furnished him with separate warnings of his fate—having all summoned him to meet it with solemn preparation.

Here at once, in this sharp verbal distinction, we comprehend the faithful earnestness with which a holy Christian Church pleads on behalf of her poor departing children that God would vouchsafe to them the last great privilege and distinction possible on a death-bed, viz. the opportunity of untroubled preparation for facing this mighty trial. Sudden death, as a mere variety in the modes of dying where death in some shape is inevitable, proposes a question of choice which, equally in the Roman and the Christian sense, will be variously answered according to each man's variety of temperament. Meantime, one aspect of sudden death there is, one modification, upon which no doubt can arise, that of all martyrdoms it is the most agitating—viz. where it surprises a man under circumstances which offer (or which seem to offer) some hurrying, flying, inappreciably minute chance of evading it. Sudden as the danger which it affronts must be any effort by which such an evasion can be accomplished. Even *that*, even the sickening necessity for hurrying in extremity where all hurry seems destined to be vain, even that anguish is liable to a hideous exasperation in one particular case: viz. where the appeal is made not exclusively to the instinct of self-preservation, but to the conscience, on behalf of some other life besides your own, accidentally thrown upon *your* protection. To fail, to collapse in a service merely your own, might seem comparatively venial; though, in fact, it is far from venial. But to fail in a case where Providence has suddenly thrown into your hands the final interests of another—a fellow-creature shuddering between the gates of life and death: this, to a man of apprehensive conscience, would mingle the misery of an atrocious criminality with the misery of a bloody calamity. You are called upon, by the case supposed, possibly to die, but to die at the very moment when, by any even partial failure or effeminate collapse of your energies, you will be self-denounced as a murderer. You had but the twinkling of an eye for your effort, and that effort might have been unavailing; but to have risen to the level of such an effort would have rescued you, though not from dying, yet from dying as a traitor to your final and farewell duty.

The situation here contemplated exposes a dreadful ulcer, lurking far down in the depths of human nature. It is not that men generally are summoned to face such awful trials. But potentially, and in shadowy outline, such a trial is moving subterraneously in perhaps all men's natures. Upon the secret mirror of our dreams such a trial is darkly projected, perhaps, to every one of us. That dream, so familiar to childhood, of meeting a lion, and, through languishing prostration in hope and the energies of hope, that constant sequel of lying down before the lion, publishes the secret frailty of human nature—reveals its deep-seated falsehood to itself—records its abysmal treachery. Perhaps not one of us escapes that dream; perhaps, as by some sorrowful doom of man, that dream repeats for every one of us, through every generation, the original temptation in Eden. Every one of us, in this dream, has a bait offered to the infirm places of his own individual will; once again a snare is presented for tempting him into captivity to a luxury of ruin; once again, as in aboriginal Paradise, the man falls by his own choice; again, by infinite iteration, the ancient earth groans to Heaven, through her secret caves, over the weakness of her child. "Nature, from her seat, sighing through all her works," again "gives signs of woe that all is lost"; and again the counter-sigh is repeated to the sorrowing heavens for the endless rebellion against God. It is not without probability that in the world of dreams every one of us ratifies for himself the original transgression. In dreams, perhaps under some secret conflict of the midnight sleeper, lighted up to the consciousness at the time, but darkened to the memory as soon as all is finished, each several child of our mysterious race completes for himself the treason of the aboriginal fall.

The incident, so memorable in itself by its features of horror, and so scenical by its grouping for the eye, which furnished the text for this reverie upon *Sudden Death*, occurred to myself in the dead of night, as a solitary spectator, when seated on the box of the Manchester and Glasgow mail, in the second or third summer after Waterloo. I find it necessary to relate the circumstances, because they are such as could not have occurred unless under a singular combination of accidents. In those days, the oblique and lateral communications with many rural post-offices were so arranged, either through necessity or through defect of system, as to make it requisite for the main northwestern mail (*i.e.* the *down* mail) on reaching Manchester to halt for a number of hours; how many, I do not remember; six or seven, I think; but the result was that, in the ordinary course, the mail recommenced its journey northwards about midnight. Wearied with the long detention at a gloomy hotel, I walked out about eleven o'clock at night for the sake of fresh air; meaning to fall in with the mail and resume my seat at the post-office. The night, however, being yet dark, as the moon had scarcely risen, and the streets being at that hour empty, so as to offer no opportunities for asking the road, I lost my way, and did not reach the post-office until it was considerably past midnight; but, to my great relief (as it was important for me to be in Westmorland by the morning), I saw in the huge saucer eyes of the mail, blazing through the gloom, an evidence that my chance was not yet lost. Past the time it was; but, by some rare accident, the mail was not even yet ready to start. I ascended to my seat on the box, where my cloak was still lying as it had lain at the Bridgewater Arms. I had left it there in imitation of a nautical discoverer, who leaves a bit of bunting on the shore of his discovery, by way of warning off the ground the whole human race, and notifying to the Christian and the heathen worlds, with his best compliments, that he has hoisted his pocket-handkerchief once and for ever upon that virgin soil: thenceforward claiming the *jus dominii* to the top of the atmosphere above it, and also the right of driving shafts to the centre of the earth below it; so that all people found after this warning either aloft in upper chambers of the atmosphere, or groping in subterraneous shafts, or squatting audaciously on the surface of the soil, will be treated as trespassers—kicked, that is to say, or decapitated, as circumstances may suggest, by their very faithful servant, the owner of the said pocket-handkerchief. In the present case, it is probable that my cloak might not have been respected, and the *jus gentium* might have been cruelly violated in my person—for, in the dark, people commit deeds of darkness, gas being a great ally of morality; but it so happened that on this night there was no other outside passenger; and thus the crime, which else was but too probable, missed fire for want of a criminal.

Having mounted the box, I took a small quantity of laudanum, having already travelled two hundred and fifty miles—viz. from a point seventy miles beyond London. In the taking of laudanum there was nothing extraordinary. But by accident it drew upon me the special attention of my assessor on the box, the coachman. And in *that* also there was nothing extraordinary. But by accident, and with great delight, it drew my own attention to the fact that this coachman was a monster in point of bulk, and that he had but one eye. In fact, he had been foretold by Virgil as

> *Monstrum horrendum, informe, ingens,*
> *cui lumen ademptum.*

He answered to the conditions in every one of the items: 1, a monster he was; 2, dreadful; 3, shapeless; 4, huge; 5, who had lost an eye. But why should *that* delight me? Had he been one of the Calendars in the *Arabian Nights*, and had paid down his eye as the price of his criminal curiosity, what right had *I* to exult in his misfortune? I did *not* exult; I delighted in no man's punishment, though it were even merited. But these personal distinctions (Nos. 1, 2, 3, 4, 5) identified in an instant an old friend of mine whom I had known in the south for some years as the most masterly of mail-coachmen. He was the man in all Europe that could (if *any* could) have driven six-in-hand full gallop over *Al Sirat*—that dreadful bridge of Mahomet, with no side battlements, and of *extra* room not enough for a razor's edge—leading right across the bottomless gulf. I used to call him *Cyclops Mastigophorus*, Cyclops the Whip-bearer, until I observed that his skill made whips useless, except to fetch off an impertinent fly from a leader's head; upon which I changed his Grecian name to *Cyclops Diphrélates* (Cyclops the Charioteer). I, and others known to me, studied under him the diphrelatic art. Excuse, reader, a word too elegant to be pedantic. And also take this remark from me as a *gage d'amitié*—that no word ever was or *can* be pedantic which, by supporting a distinction, supports the accuracy of logic, or which fills up a chasm for the understanding.

As a pupil, though I paid extra fees, it is to be lamented that I did not stand high in his esteem. It showed his dogged honesty (though, observe, not his discernment) that he could not see my merits. Let us excuse his absurdity in this particular by remembering his want of an eye. Doubtless *that* made him blind to my merits. In the art of conversation, however, he admitted that I had the whip-hand of him. On this present occasion great joy was at our meeting. But what was Cyclops doing here? Had the medical men recommended northern air, or how? I collected, from such explanations as he volunteered, that he had an interest at stake in some suit-at-law now pending at Lancaster; so that probably he had got himself transferred to this station for the purpose of connecting with his professional pursuits an instant readiness for the calls of his lawsuit.

Meantime, what are we stopping for? Surely we have now waited long enough. Oh, this procrastinating mail, and this procrastinating post-office! Can't they take a lesson upon that subject from *me?* Some people have called *me* procrastinating. Yet you are witness, reader, that I was here kept waiting for the post-office. Will the post-office lay its hand on its heart, in its moments of sobriety, and assert that ever it waited for me? What are they about? The guard tells me that there is a large extra accumulation of foreign mails this night, owing to irregularities caused by war, by wind, by weather, in the packet service, which as yet does not benefit at all by steam. For an *extra* hour, it seems, the post-office has been engaged in threshing out the pure wheaten correspondence of Glasgow, and winnowing it from the chaff of all baser intermediate towns. But at last all is finished. Sound your horn, guard! Manchester, good-bye! we've lost an hour by your criminal conduct at the post-office: which, however, though I do not mean to part with a serviceable ground of complaint, and one which really *is* such for the horses, to me secretly is an advantage, since it compels us to look sharply for this lost hour amongst the next eight or nine, and to recover it (if we can) at the rate of one mile extra per hour. Off we are at last, and at eleven miles an hour; and for the moment I detect no changes in the energy or in the skill of Cyclops.

From Manchester to Kendal, which virtually (though not in law) is the capital of Westmorland, there were at this time seven stages of eleven miles each. The first five of these, counting from Manchester, terminate in Lancaster; which is therefore fifty-five miles north of Manchester, and the same distance exactly from Liverpool. The first three stages terminate in Preston (called, by way of distinction from other towns of that name, *Proud* Preston); at which place it is that the separate roads from Liverpool and from Manchester to the north become confluent.[1] Within these first three stages lay the foundation, the progress, and termination of our night's adventure. During the first stage, I found out that Cyclops was mortal: he was liable to the shocking affection of sleep

---

[1] *"Confluent"*: Suppose a capital Y (the Pythagorean letter): Lancaster is at the foot of this letter; Liverpool at the top of the *right* branch; Manchester at the top of the *left;* Proud Preston at the centre, where the two branches unite. It is thirty-three miles along either of the two branches; it is twenty-two miles along the stem—viz. from Preston in the middle to Lancaster at the root. There's a lesson in geography for the reader!

—a thing which previously I had never suspected. If a man indulges in the vicious habit of sleeping, all the skill in aurigation of Apollo himself, with the horses of Aurora to execute his notions, avails him nothing. "Oh, Cyclops!" I exclaimed, "that art mortal. My friend, thou snorest." Through the first eleven miles, however, this infirmity—which I grieve to say that he shared with the whole Pagan Pantheon—betrayed itself only by brief snatches. On waking up, he made an apology for himself which, instead of mending matters, laid open a gloomy vista of coming disasters. The summer assizes, he reminded me, were now going on at Lancaster: in consequence of which for three nights and three days he had not lain down in a bed. During the day he was waiting for his own summons as a witness on the trial in which he was interested, or else, lest he should be missing at the critical moment, was drinking with the other witnesses under the pastoral surveillance of the attorneys. During the night, or that part of it which at sea would form the middle watch, he was driving. This explanation certainly accounted for his drowsiness, but in a way which made it much more alarming; since now, after several days' resistance to this infirmity, at length he was steadily giving way. Throughout the second stage he grew more and more drowsy. In the second mile of the third stage he surrendered himself finally and without a struggle to his perilous temptation. All his past resistance had but deepened the weight of this final oppression. Seven atmospheres of sleep rested upon him; and, to consummate the case, our worthy guard, after singing "Love amongst the Roses" for perhaps thirty times, without invitation and without applause, had in revenge moodily resigned himself to slumber —not so deep, doubtless, as the coachman's, but deep enough for mischief. And thus at last, about ten miles from Preston, it came about that I found myself left in charge of His Majesty's London and Glasgow mail, then running at the least twelve miles an hour.

What made this negligence less criminal than else it must have been thought was the condition of the roads at night during the assizes. At that time, all the law business of populous Liverpool, and also of populous Manchester, with its vast cincture of populous rural districts, was called up by ancient usage to the tribunal of Lilliputian Lancaster. To break up this old traditional usage required, 1, a conflict with powerful established interests, 2, a large system of new arrangements, and 3, a new parliamentary statute. But as yet this change was merely in contemplation As things were at present, twice in the year [1] so vast a body of business rolled northwards from the southern quarter of the county that for a fortnight at least it occupied the severe exertions of two judges in its dispatch. The consequence of this was that every horse available for such a service, along the whole line of road, was exhausted in carrying down the multitudes of people who were parties to the different suits. By sunset, therefore, it usually happened that, through utter exhaustion amongst men and horses, the road sank into profound silence. Except the exhaustion in the vast adjacent county of York from a contested election, no such silence succeeding to no such fiery uproar was ever witnessed in England.

On this occasion the usual silence and solitude prevailed along the road. Not a hoof nor a wheel was to be heard. And, to strengthen this false luxurious confidence in the noiseless roads, it happened also that the night was one of peculiar solemnity and peace. For

[1] "*Twice in the year*": There were at that time only two assizes even in the most populous counties—viz. the Lent Assizes and the Summer Assizes.

my own part, though slightly alive to the possibilities
of peril, I had so far yielded to the influence of the
mighty calm as to sink into a profound reverie. The
month was August; in the middle of which lay my
own birthday—a festival to every thoughtful man
suggesting solemn and often sigh-born [1] thoughts.
The county was my own native county—upon which,
in its southern section, more than upon any equal area
known to man past or present, had descended the original curse of labour in its heaviest form, not master-
ing the bodies only of men, as of slaves, or criminals
in mines, but working through the fiery will. Upon no
equal space of earth was, or ever had been, the same
energy of human power put forth daily. At this particular season also of the assizes, that dreadful hurricane of flight and pursuit, as it might have seemed to
a stranger, which swept to and from Lancaster all day
long, hunting the county up and down, and regularly
subsiding back into silence about sunset, could not fail
(when united with this permanent distinction of Lancashire as the very metropolis and citadel of labour)
to point the thoughts pathetically upon that counter-
vision of rest, of saintly repose from strife and sorrow,
towards which, as to their secret haven, the profounder
aspirations of man's heart are in solitude continually
travelling. Obliquely upon our left we were nearing
the sea; which also must, under the present circumstances, be repeating the general state of halcyon repose. The sea, the atmosphere, the light, bore each an
orchestral part in this universal lull. Moonlight and
the first timid tremblings of the dawn were by this
time blending; and the blendings were brought into a
still more exquisite state of unity by a slight silvery

[1] "*Sigh-born*": I owe the suggestion of this word to an obscure remembrance of a beautiful phrase in Giraldus Cam-
brensis—viz. *suspiriosæ cogitationes.*

mist, motionless and dreamy, that covered the woods and fields, but with a veil of equable transparency. Except the feet of our own horses—which, running on a sandy margin of the road, made but little disturbance—there was no sound abroad. In the clouds and on the earth prevailed the same majestic peace; and, in spite of all that the villain of a schoolmaster has done for the ruin of our sublimer thoughts, which are the thoughts of our infancy, we still believe in no such nonsense as a limited atmosphere. Whatever we may swear with our false feigning lips, in our faithful hearts we still believe, and must for ever believe, in fields of air traversing the total gulf between earth and the central heavens. Still, in the confidence of children that tread without fear *every* chamber in their father's house, and to whom no door is closed, we, in that Sabbatic vision which sometimes is revealed for an hour upon nights like this, ascend with easy steps from the sorrow-stricken fields of earth upwards to the sandals of God.

Suddenly, from thoughts like these I was awakened to a sullen sound, as of some motion on the distant road. It stole upon the air for a moment; I listened in awe; but then it died away. Once roused, however, I could not but observe with alarm the quickened motion of our horses. Ten years' experience had made my eye learned in the valuing of motion; and I saw that we were now running thirteen miles an hour. I pretend to no presence of mind. On the contrary, my fear is that I am miserably and shamefully deficient in that quality as regards action. The palsy of doubt and distraction hangs like some guilty weight of dark unfathomed remembrances upon my energies when the signal is flying for *action*. But, on the other hand, this accursed gift I have, as regards *thought*, that in

the first step towards the possibility of a misfortune I
see its total evolution; in the radix of the series I see
too certainly and too instantly its entire expansion; in
the first syllable of the dreadful sentence I read already the last. It was not that I feared for ourselves.
Us our bulk and impetus charmed against peril in any
collision. And I had ridden through too many hundreds of perils that were frightful to approach, that
were matter of laughter to look back upon, the first
face of which was horror, the parting face a jest—for
any anxiety to rest upon *our* interests. The mail was
not built, I felt assured, nor bespoke, that could betray *me* who trusted to its protection. But any carriage that we could meet would be frail and light in
comparison of ourselves. And I remarked this ominous accident of our situation—we were on the wrong
side of the road. But then, it may be said, the other
party, if other there was, might also be on the wrong
side; and two wrongs might make a right. *That* was
not likely. The same motive which had drawn *us* to
the right-hand side of the road—viz. the luxury of
the soft beaten sand as contrasted with the paved centre—would prove attractive to others. The two adverse carriages would therefore, to a certainty, be
travelling on the same side; and from this side, as not
being ours in law, the crossing over to the other would,
of course, be looked for from *us*.[1] Our lamps, still
lighted, would give the impression of vigilance on our
part. And every creature that met us would rely upon

[1] It is true that, according to the law of the case as established by legal precedents, all carriages were required to give
way before royal equipages, and therefore before the mail as
one of them. But this only increased the danger, as being a
regulation very imperfectly made known, very unequally enforced, and therefore often embarrassing the movements on
both sides.

us for quartering.[1] All this, and if the separate links of the anticipation had been a thousand times more, I saw, not discursively, or by effort, or by succession, but by one flash of horrid simultaneous intuition.

Under this steady though rapid anticipation of the evil which *might* be gathering ahead, ah! what a sullen mystery of fear, what a sigh of woe, was that which stole upon the air, as again the far-off sound of a wheel was heard! A whisper it was—a whisper from, perhaps, four miles off—secretly announcing a ruin that, being foreseen, was not the less inevitable; that, being known, was not therefore healed. What could be done—who was it that could do it—to check the storm-flight of these maniacal horses? Could I not seize the reins from the grasp of the slumbering coachman? You, reader, think that it would have been in *your* power to do so. And I quarrel not with your estimate of yourself. But, from the way in which the coachman's hand was viced between his upper and lower thigh, this was impossible. Easy was it? See, then, that bronze equestrian statue. The cruel rider has kept the bit in his horse's mouth for two centuries. Unbridle him for a minute, if you please, and wash his mouth with water. Easy was it? Unhorse me, then, that imperial rider; knock me those marble feet from those marble stirrups of Charlemagne.

The sounds ahead strengthened, and were now too clearly the sounds of wheels. Who and what could it be? Was it industry in a taxed cart? Was it youthful gaiety in a gig? Was it sorrow that loitered, or joy that raced? For as yet the snatches of sound were too intermitting, from distance, to decipher the character of the motion. Whoever were the travellers, something

---

[1] "*Quartering*": This is the technical word, and, I presume, derived from the French *cartayer*, to evade a rut or any obstacle.

must be done to warn them. Upon the other party rests the active responsibility, but upon *us*—and, woe is me! that *us* was reduced to my frail opium-shattered self—rests the responsibility of warning. Yet, how should this be accomplished? Might I not sound the guard's horn? Already, on the first thought, I was making my way over the roof to the guard's seat. But this, from the accident which I have mentioned, of the foreign mails being piled upon the roof, was a difficult and even dangerous attempt to one cramped by nearly three hundred miles of outside travelling. And, fortunately, before I had lost much time in the attempt, our frantic horses swept round an angle of the road which opened upon us that final stage where the collision must be accomplished and the catastrophe sealed. All was apparently finished. The court was sitting; the case was heard; the judge had finished; and only the verdict was yet in arrear.

Before us lay an avenue straight as an arrow, six hundred yards, perhaps, in length; and the umbrageous trees, which rose in a regular line from either side, meeting high overhead, gave to it the character of a cathedral aisle. These trees lent a deeper solemnity to the early light; but there was still light enough to perceive, at the farther end of this Gothic aisle, a a frail reedy gig, in which were seated a young man, and by his side a young lady. Ah, young sir! what are you about? If it is requisite that you should whisper your communications to this young lady—though really I see nobody, at an hour and on a road so solitary, likely to overhear you—is it therefore requisite that you should carry your lips forward to hers? The little carriage is creeping on at one mile an hour; and the parties within it, being thus tenderly engaged, are naturally bending down their heads. Between them and eternity, to all human calculation, there is but a

minute and a-half. Oh heavens! what is it that I shall
do? Speaking or acting, what help can I offer? Strange
it is, and to a mere auditor of the tale might seem
laughable, that I should need a suggestion from the
Iliad to prompt the sole resource that remained. Yet so
it was. Suddenly I remembered the shout of Achilles,
and its effect. But could I pretend to shout like the son
of Peleus, aided by Pallas? No: but then I needed not
the shout that should alarm all Asia militant; such a
shout would suffice as might carry terror into the
hearts of two thoughtless young people and one gig-
horse. I shouted—and the young man heard me not.
A second time I shouted—and now he heard me, for
now he raised his head.

Here, then, all had been done that, by me, *could* be
done; more on *my* part was not possible. Mine had
been the first step; the second was for the young man;
the third was for God. If, said I, this stranger is a
brave man, and if indeed he loves the young girl at
his side—or, loving her not, if he feels the obligation,
pressing upon every man worthy to be called a man,
of doing his utmost for a woman confided to his protection—he will at least make some effort to save her.
If *that* fails, he will not perish the more, or by a death
more cruel, for having made it; and he will die as a
brave man should, with his face to the danger, and
with his arm about the woman that he sought in vain
to save. But, if he makes no effort, shrinking without
a struggle from his duty, he himself will not the less
certainly perish for this baseness of poltroonery. He
will die no less: and why not? Wherefore should we
grieve that there is one craven less in the world? No;
let him perish, without a pitying thought of ours
wasted upon him; and, in that case, all our grief will
be reserved for the fate of the helpless girl who now,
upon the least shadow of failure in *him*, must by the

fiercest of translations—must without time for a prayer—must within seventy seconds—stand before the judgement-seat of God.

But craven he was not: sudden had been the call upon him, and sudden was his answer to the call. He saw, he heard, he comprehended, the ruin that was coming down: already its gloomy shadow darkened above him; and already he was measuring his strength to deal with it. Ah! what a vulgar thing does courage seem when we see nations buying it and selling it for a shilling a-day: ah! what a sublime thing does courage seem when some fearful summons on the great deeps of life carries a man, as if running before a hurricane, up to the giddy crest of some tumultuous crisis from which lie two courses, and a voice says to him audibly, "One way lies hope; take the other, and mourn for ever!" How grand a triumph if, even then, amidst the raving of all around him, and the frenzy of the danger, the man is able to confront his situation —is able to retire for a moment into solitude with God, and to seek his counsel from *Him!*

For seven seconds, it might be, of his seventy, the stranger settled his countenance steadfastly upon us, as if to search and value every element in the conflict before him. For five seconds more of his seventy he sat immovably, like one that mused on some great purpose. For five more, perhaps, he sat with eyes upraised, like one that prayed in sorrow, under some extremity of doubt, for light that should guide him to the better choice. Then suddenly he rose; stood upright; and, by a powerful strain upon the reins, raising his horse's fore-feet from the ground, he slewed him round on the pivot of his hind-legs, so as to plant the little equipage in a position nearly at right angles to ours. Thus far his condition was not improved; except as a first step had been taken towards the possibility of a second.

If no more were done, nothing was done; for the little carriage still occupied the very centre of our path, though in an altered direction. Yet even now it may not be too late: fifteen of the seventy seconds may still be unexhausted; and one almighty bound may avail to clear the ground. Hurry, then, hurry! for the flying moments—*they* hurry. Oh, hurry, hurry, my brave young man! for the cruel hoofs of our horses—*they* also hurry! Fast are the flying moments, faster are the hoofs of our horses. But fear not for *him*, if human energy can suffice; faithful was he that drove to his terrific duty; faithful was the horse to *his* command. One blow, one impulse given with voice and hand, by the stranger, one rush from the horse, one bound as if in the act of rising to a fence, landed the docile creature's fore-feet upon the crown or arching centre of the road. The larger half of the little equipage had then cleared our over-towering shadow: *that* was evident even to my own agitated sight. But it mattered little that one wreck should float off in safety if upon the wreck that perished were embarked the human freightage. The rear part of the carriage—was *that* certainly beyond the line of absolute ruin? What power could answer the question? Glance of eye, thought of man, wing of angel, which of these had speed enough to sweep between the question and the answer, and divide the one from the other? Light does not tread upon the steps of light more indivisibly than did our all-conquering arrival upon the escaping efforts of the gig. *That* must the young man have felt too plainly. His back was now turned to us; not by sight could he any longer communicate with the peril; but, by the dreadful rattle of our harness, too truly had his ear been instructed that all was finished as regarded any effort of *his*. Already in resignation he had rested from his struggle; and perhaps in his heart he was whispering, "Father, which art in heaven, do Thou finish

above what I on earth have attempted." Faster than
ever mill-race we ran past them in our inexorable
flight. Oh, raving of hurricanes that must have
sounded in their young ears at the moment of our
transit! Even in that moment the thunder of collision
spoke aloud. Either with the swingle-bar, or with the
haunch of our near leader, we had struck the off-wheel
of the little gig; which stood rather obliquely, and not
quite so far advanced as to be accurately parallel with
the near-wheel. The blow, from the fury of our passage, resounded terrifically. I rose in horror, to gaze
upon the ruins we might have caused. From my elevated station I looked down, and looked back upon the
scene; which in a moment told its own tale, and wrote
all its records on my heart for ever.

Here was the map of the passion that now had finished. The horse was planted immovably, with his fore-
feet upon the paved crest of the central road. He of
the whole party might be supposed untouched by the
passion of death. The little cany carriage—partly, perhaps, from the violent torsion of the wheels in its recent movement, partly from the thundering blow we
had given to it—as if it sympathized with human horror, was all alive with tremblings and shiverings. The
young man trembled not, nor shivered. He sat like a
rock. But *his* was the steadiness of agitation frozen
into rest by horror. As yet he dared not to look round;
for he knew that, if anything remained to do, by him
it could no longer be done. And as yet he knew not for
certain if their safety were accomplished. But the
lady——

But the lady——! Oh, heavens! will that spectacle
ever depart from my dreams, as she rose and sank upon
her seat, sank and rose, threw up her arms wildly to
heaven, clutched at some visionary object in the air,
fainting, praying, raving, despairing? Figure to yourself, reader, the elements of the case; suffer me to re-

call before your mind the circumstances of that unparalleled situation. From the silence and deep peace of this saintly summer night—from the pathetic blending of this sweet moonlight, dawnlight, dreamlight—from the manly tenderness of this flattering, whispering, murmuring love—suddenly as from the woods and fields—suddenly as from the chambers of the air opening in revelation—suddenly as from the ground yawning at her feet, leaped upon her, with the flashing of cataracts, Death the crowned phantom, with all the equipage of his terrors, and the tiger roar of his voice.

The moments were numbered; the strife was finished; the vision was closed. In the twinkling of an eye, our flying horses had carried us to the termination of the umbrageous aisle; at the right angles we wheeled into our former direction; the turn of the road carried the scene out of my eyes in an instant, and swept it into my dreams for ever.

III. DREAM-FUGUE FOUNDED ON THE PRECEDING THEME OF SUDDEN DEATH

> *Whence the sound*
> *Of instruments, that made melodious chime,*
> *Was heard, of harp and organ; and who moved*
> *Their stops and chords was seen; his volant touch*
> *Instinct through all proportions, low and high,*
> *Fled and pursued transverse the resonant fugue.*
> PARADISE LOST, Bk. XI.

Tumultuosissimamente

Passion of sudden death! that once in youth I read and interpreted by the shadows of thy averted signs! [1]

[1] *"Averted signs"*: I read the course and changes of the lady's agony in the succession of her involuntary gestures; but it must be remembered that I read all this from the rear, never once catching the lady's full face, and even her profile imperfectly.

—rapture of panic taking the shape (which amongst tombs in churches I have seen) of woman bursting her sepulchral bonds—of woman's Ionic form bending forward from the ruins of her grave with arching foot, with eyes upraised, with clasped adoring hands—waiting, watching, trembling, praying for the trumpet's call to rise from dust for ever! Ah, vision too fearful of shuddering humanity on the brink of almighty abysses!—vision that didst start back, that didst reel away, like a shrivelling scroll from before the wrath of fire racing on the wings of the wind! Epilepsy so brief of horror, wherefore is it that thou canst not die? Passing so suddenly into darkness, wherefore is it that still thou sheddest thy sad funeral blights upon the gorgeous mosaics of dreams? Fragment of music too passionate, heard once, and heard no more, what aileth thee, that thy deep rolling chords come up at intervals through all the worlds of sleep, and after forty years have lost no element of horror?

I

Lo, it is summer—almighty summer! The everlasting gates of life and summer are thrown open wide; and on the ocean, tranquil and verdant as a savannah, the unknown lady from the dreadful vision and I myself are floating—she upon a fairy pinnace, and I upon an English three-decker. Both of us are wooing gales of festal happiness within the domain of our common country, within that ancient watery park, within the pathless chase of ocean, where England takes her pleasure as a huntress through winter and summer, from the rising to the setting sun. Ah, what a wilderness of floral beauty was hidden, or was suddenly revealed, upon the tropic islands through which the pinnace moved! And upon her deck what a bevy

of human flowers: young women how lovely, young
men how noble, that were dancing together, and
slowly drifting towards *us* amidst music and incense,
amidst blossoms from forests and gorgeous corymbı
from vintages, amidst natural carolling, and the echoes
of sweet girlish laughter. Slowly the pinnace nears us,
gaily she hails us, and silently she disappears beneath
the shadow of our mighty bows. But then, as at some
signal from heaven, the music, and the carols, and the
sweet echoing of girlish laughter—all are hushed.
What evil has smitten the pinnace, meeting or overtaking her? Did ruin to our friends couch within our
own dreadful shadow? Was our shadow the shadow of
death? I looked over the bow for an answer, and, behold! the pinnace was dismantled; the revel and the
revellers were found no more; the glory of the vintage
was dust; and the forests with their beauty were left
without a witness upon the seas. "But where," and I
turned to our crew—"where are the lovely women that
danced beneath the awning of flowers and clustering
corymbi? Whither have fled the noble young men that
danced with *them?*" Answer there was none. But suddenly the man at the mast-head, whose countenance
darkened with alarm, cried out, "Sail on the weather
beam! Down she comes upon us: in seventy seconds she
also will founder."

II

I looked to the weather side, and the summer had
departed. The sea was rocking, and shaken with gathering wrath. Upon its surface sat mighty mists, which
grouped themselves into arches and long cathedral
aisles. Down one of these, with the fiery pace of a
quarrel from a cross-bow, ran a frigate right athwart
our course. "Are they mad?" some voice exclaimed

.rom our deck. "Do they woo their ruin?" But in a moment, as she was close upon us, some impulse of a heady current or local vortex gave a wheeling bias to her course, and off she forged without a shock. As she ran past us, high aloft amongst the shrouds stood the lady of the pinnace. The deeps opened ahead in malice to receive her, towering surges of foam ran after her, the billows were fierce to catch her. But far away she was borne into desert spaces of the sea: whilst still by sight I followed her, as she ran before the howling gale, chased by angry sea-birds and by maddening billows; still I saw her, as at the moment when she ran past us, standing amongst the shrouds, with her white draperies streaming before the wind. There she stood, with hair dishevelled, one hand clutched amongst the tackling—rising, sinking, fluttering, trembling, praying; there for leagues I saw her as she stood, raising at intervals one hand to heaven, amidst the fiery crests of the pursuing waves and the raving of the storm; until at last, upon a sound from afar of malicious laughter and mockery, all was hidden for ever in driving showers; and afterwards, but when I know not, nor how.

III

Sweet funeral bells from some incalculable distance, wailing over the dead that die before the dawn, awakened me as I slept in a boat moored to some familiar shore. The morning twilight even then was breaking; and, by the dusky revelations which it spread, I saw a girl, adorned with a garland of white roses about her head for some great festival, running along the solitary strand in extremity of haste. Her running was the running of panic; and often she looked back as to some dreadful enemy in the rear. But, when I leaped ashore, and followed on her steps to warn her of a peril in front, alas! from me she fled as from another peril, and vainly I shouted to her of quicksands that lay ahead. Faster and faster she ran; round a promontory of rocks she wheeled out of sight; in an instant I also wheeled round it, but only to see the treacherous sands gathering above her head. Already her person was buried; only the fair young head and the diadem of white roses around it were still visible to the pitying heavens; and, last of all, was visible one white marble arm. I saw by the early twilight this fair young head, as it was sinking down to darkness—saw this marble arm, as it rose above her head and her treacherous grave, tossing, faltering, rising, clutching, as at some false deceiving hand stretched out from the clouds— saw this marble arm uttering her dying hope, and then uttering her dying despair. The head, the diadem, the arm—these all had sunk; at last over these also the cruel quicksand had closed; and no memorial of the fair young girl remained on earth, except my own solitary tears, and the funeral bells from the desert seas, that, rising again more softly, sang a requiem over the grave of the buried child, and over her blighted dawn.

I sat, and wept in secret the tears that men have ever given to the memory of those that died before the dawn, and by the treachery of earth, our mother. But suddenly the tears and funeral bells were hushed by a shout as of many nations, and by a roar as from some great king's artillery, advancing rapidly along the valleys, and heard afar by echoes from the mountains. "Hush!" I said, as I bent my ear earthwards to listen—"hush!—this either is the very anarchy of strife, or else"—and then I listened more profoundly, and whispered as I raised my head—"or else, oh heavens! it is *victory* that is final, victory that swallows up all strife."

IV

Immediately, in trance, I was carried over land and sea to some distant kingdom, and placed upon a triumphal car, amongst companions crowned with laurel. The darkness of gathering midnight, brooding over all the land, hid from us the mighty crowds that were weaving restlessly about ourselves as a centre: we heard them, but saw them not. Tidings had arrived, within an hour, of a grandeur that measured itself against centuries; too full of pathos they were, too full of joy, to utter themselves by other language than by tears, by restless anthems, and *Te Deums* reverberated from the choirs and orchestras of earth. These tidings we that sat upon the laurelled car had it for our privilege to publish amongst all nations. And already, by signs audible through the darkness, by snortings and tramplings, our angry horses, that knew no fear of fleshly weariness, upbraided us with delay. Wherefore *was* it that we delayed? We waited for a secret word, that should bear witness to the hope of nations as now accomplished for ever. At midnight the secret word arrived; which word was—*Waterloo and Recovered Christendom!* The dreadful word shone by its own light; before us it went; high above our leaders' heads it rode, and spread a golden light over the paths which we traversed. Every city, at the presence of the secret word, threw open its gates. The rivers were conscious as we crossed. All the forests, as we ran along their margins, shivered in homage to the secret word. And the darkness comprehended it.

Two hours after midnight we approached a mighty Minster. Its gates, which rose to the clouds, were closed. But, when the dreadful word that rode before us reached them with its golden light, silently they moved back upon their hinges; and at a flying gallop our equipage entered the grand aisle of the cathedral. Headlong was our pace; and at every altar, in the little chapels and oratories to the right hand and left of our course, the lamps, dying or sickening, kindled anew in sympathy with the secret word that was flying past. Forty leagues we might have run in the cathedral, and as yet no strength of morning light had reached us, when before us we saw the aerial galleries of organ and choir. Every pinnacle of the fretwork, every station of advantage amongst the traceries, was crested by white-robed choristers that sang deliverance; that wept no more tears, as once their fathers had wept; but at intervals that sang together to the generations, saying,

Chant the deliverer's praise in every tongue,

and receiving answers from afar,

Such as once in heaven and earth were sung.

And of their chanting was no end; of our headlong pace was neither pause nor slackening.

Thus as we ran like torrents—thus as we swept with bridal rapture over the Campo Santo [1] of the cathedral

---

[1] *"Campo Santo":* It is probable that most of my readers will be acquainted with the history of the Campo Santo (or cemetery) at Pisa, composed of earth brought from Jerusalem from a bed of sanctity, as the highest prize which the noble piety of crusaders could ask or imagine. To readers who are unacquainted with England, or who (being English) are yet unacquainted with the cathedral cities of England, it may be right to mention that the graves within-side the cathedrals often form a flat pavement over which carriages and horses *might* run; and perhaps a boyish remembrance of one particular cathedral, across which I had seen passengers walk and burdens carried, as about two centuries back they were through the middle of St. Paul's in London, may have assisted my dream.

graves—suddenly we became aware of a vast necropolis rising upon the far-off horizon—a city of sepulchres, built within the saintly cathedral for the warrior dead that rested from their feuds on earth. Of purple granite was the necropolis; yet, in the first minute, it lay like a purple stain upon the horizon, so mighty was the distance. In the second minute it trembled through many changes, growing into terraces and towers of wondrous altitude, so mighty was the pace. In the third minute already, with our dreadful gallop, we were entering its suburbs. Vast sarcophagi rose on every side, having towers and turrets that, upon the limits of the central aisle, strode forward with haughty intrusion, that ran back with mighty shadows into answering recesses. Every sarcophagus showed many bas-reliefs—bas-reliefs of battles and of battle-fields; battles from forgotten ages, battles from yesterday; battle-fields that, long since, nature had healed and reconciled to herself with the sweet oblivion of flowers; battle-fields that were yet angry and crimson with carnage. Where the terraces ran, there did *we* run; where the towers curved, there did *we* curve. With the flight of swallows our horses swept round every angle. Like rivers in flood wheeling round headlands, like hurricanes that ride into the secrets of forests, faster than ever light unwove the mazes of darkness, our flying equipage carried earthly passions, kindled warrior instincts, amongst the dust that lay around us— dust oftentimes of our noble fathers that had slept in God from Crécy to Trafalgar. And now had we reached the last sarcophagus, now were we abreast of the last bas-relief, already had we recovered the arrow-like flight of the illimitable central aisle, when coming up this aisle to meet us we beheld afar off a female child, that rode in a carriage as frail as flowers. The mists which went before her hid the fawns that drew her, but could not hide the shells and tropic flowers with which she played—but could not hide the lovely smiles by which she uttered her trust in the mighty cathedral, and in the cherubim that looked down upon her from the mighty shafts of its pillars. Face to face she was meeting us; face to face she rode, as if danger there were none. "Oh, baby!" I exclaimed, "shalt thou be the ransom for Waterloo? Must we, that carry tidings of great joy to every people, be messengers of ruin to thee!" In horror I rose at the thought; but then also, in horror at the thought, rose one that was sculptured on a bas-relief—a Dying Trumpeter. Solemnly from the field of battle he rose to his feet; and, unslinging his stony trumpet, carried it, in his dying anguish, to his stony lips—sounding once, and yet once again; proclamation that, in *thy* ears, oh baby! spoke from the battlements of death. Immediately deep shadows fell between us, and aboriginal silence. The choir had ceased to sing. The hoofs of our horses, the dreadful rattle of our harness, the groaning of our wheels, alarmed the graves no more. By horror the bas-relief had been unlocked unto life. By horror we, that were so full of life, we men and our horses, with their fiery fore-legs rising in mid air to their everlasting gallop, were frozen to a bas-relief. Then a third time the trumpet sounded; the seals were taken off all pulses; life, and the frenzy of life, tore into their channels again; again the choir burst forth in sunny grandeur, as from the muffling of storms and darkness; again the thunderings of our horses carried temptation into the graves. One cry burst from our lips, as the clouds, drawing off from the aisle, showed it empty before us—"Whither has the infant fled?—is the young child caught up to God?" Lo! afar off, in a vast recess, rose three mighty windows to the clouds; and on a level with their summits, at height insuperable to man,

rose an altar of purest alabaster. On its eastern face
was trembling a crimson glory. A glory was it from the
reddening dawn that now streamed *through* the windows? Was it from the crimson robes of the martyrs
painted *on* the windows? Was it from the bloody bas-
reliefs of earth? There, suddenly, within that crimson
radiance, rose the apparition of a woman's head, and
then of a woman's figure. The child it was—grown up
to woman's height. Clinging to the horns of the altar,
voiceless she stood—sinking, rising, raving, despairing; and behind the volume of incense that, night and
day, streamed upwards from the altar, dimly was seen
the fiery font, and the shadow of that dreadful being
who should have baptized her with the baptism of
death. But by her side was kneeling her better angel,
that hid his face with wings; that wept and pleaded for
her; that prayed when *she* could *not;* that fought with
Heaven by tears for *her* deliverance; which also, as he
raised his immortal countenance from his wings, I saw,
by the glory in his eye, that from Heaven he had won
at last.

V

Then was completed the passion of the mighty
fugue. The golden tubes of the organ, which as yet had
but muttered at intervals—gleaming amongst clouds
and surges of incense—threw up, as from fountains
unfathomable, columns of heart-shattering music.
Choir and anti-choir were filling fast with unknown
voices. Thou also, Dying Trumpeter, with thy love
that was victorious, and thy anguish that was finishing, didst enter the tumult; trumpet and echo—farewell love, and farewell anguish—rang through the
dreadful *sanctus.* Oh, darkness of the grave! that from
the crimson altar and from the fiery font wert visited

and searched by the effulgence in the angel's eyes—
were these indeed thy children? Pomps of life, that,
from the burials of centuries, rose again to the voice of
perfect joy, did ye indeed mingle with the festivals of
Death? Lo! as I looked back for seventy leagues
through the mighty cathedral, I saw the quick and the
dead that sang together to God, together that sang to
the generations of man. All the hosts of jubilation, like
armies that ride in pursuit, moved with one step. Us,
that, with laurelled heads, were passing from the cathedral, they overtook, and, as with a garment, they
wrapped us round with thunders greater than our own.
As brothers we moved together; to the dawn that advanced, to the stars that fled; rendering thanks to God
in the highest—that, having hid His face through one
generation behind thick clouds of War, once again
was ascending, from the Campo Santo of Waterloo was
ascending, in the visions of Peace; rendering thanks
for thee, young girl! whom having overshadowed with
His ineffable passion of death, suddenly did God relent, suffered thy angel to turn aside His arm, and even
in thee, sister unknown! shown to me for a moment
only to be hidden for ever, found an occasion to glorify
His goodness. A thousand times, amongst the phantoms of sleep, have I seen thee entering the gates of the
golden dawn, with the secret word riding before thee,
with the armies of the grave behind thee, seen thee
sinking, rising, raving, despairing; a thousand times
in the worlds of sleep have seen thee followed by God's
angel through storms, through desert seas, through the
darkness of quicksands, through dreams and the dreadful revelations that are in dreams; only that at the last,
with one sling of His victorious arm, He might snatch
thee back from ruin, and might emblazon in thy deliverance the endless resurrections of His love!

The English Mail-Coach. This little paper, according to my original intention, formed part of the *Suspiria de Profundis;* from which, for a momentary purpose, I did not scruple to detach it, and to publish it
apart, as sufficiently intelligible even when dislocated
from its place in a larger whole. To my surprise, however, one or two critics, not carelessly in conversation,
but deliberately in print, professed their inability to
apprehend the meaning of the whole, or to follow the
links of the connexion between its several parts. I am
myself as little able to understand where the difficulty
lies, or to detect any lurking obscurity, as these critics
found themselves to unravel my logic. Possibly I may
not be an indifferent and neutral judge in such a case.
I will therefore sketch a brief abstract of the little
paper according to my original design, and then leave
the reader to judge how far this design is kept in sight
through the actual execution.

Thirty-seven years ago, or rather more, accident
made me, in the dead of night, and of a night memorably solemn, the solitary witness of an appalling
scene, which threatened instant death in a shape the
most terrific to two young people whom I had no means
of assisting, except in so far as I was able to give them
a most hurried warning of their danger; but even *that*
not until they stood within the very shadow of the
catastrophe, being divided from the most frightful of
deaths by scarcely more, if more at all, than seventy
seconds.

Such was the scene, such in its outline, from which
the whole of this paper radiates as a natural expansion.
This scene is circumstantially narrated in Section the
Second, entitled "The Vision of Sudden Death."

But a movement of horror, and of spontaneous recoil

from this dreadful scene, naturally carried the whole
of that scene, raised and idealized, into my dreams, and
very soon into a rolling succession of dreams. The actual scene, as looked down upon from the box of the
mail, was transformed into a dream, as tumultuous
and changing as a musical fugue. This troubled dream
is circumstantially reported in Section the Third, entitled "Dream-Fugue on the theme of Sudden Death."
What I had beheld from my seat upon the mail—the
scenical strife of action and passion, of anguish and
fear, as I had there witnessed them moving in ghostly
silence—this duel between life and death narrowing
itself to a point of such exquisite evanescence as the
collision neared: all these elements of the scene
blended, under the law of association, with the previous and permanent features of distinction investing
the mail itself; which features at that time lay—first,
in velocity unprecedented, secondly, in the power and
beauty of the horses, thirdly, in the official connexion
with the government of a great nation, and, fourthly,
in the function, almost a consecrated function, of publishing and diffusing through the land the great political events, and especially the great battles, during
a conflict of unparalleled grandeur. These honorary
distinctions are all described circumstantially in the
First or Introductory Section ("The Glory of Motion"). The three first were distinctions maintained
at all times; but the fourth and grandest belonged exclusively to the war with Napoleon; and this it was
which most naturally introduced Waterloo into the
dream. Waterloo, I understand, was the particular
feature of the "Dream-Fugue" which my censors were
least able to account for. Yet surely Waterloo, which,
in common with every other great battle, it had been
our special privilege to publish over all the land, most
naturally entered the dream under the licence of our

privilege. If not—if there be anything amiss—let the
Dream be responsible. The Dream is a law to itself;
and as well quarrel with a rainbow for showing, or for
not showing, a secondary arch. So far as I know, every
element in the shifting movements of the Dream derived itself either primarily from the incidents of the
actual scene, or from secondary features associated
with the mail. For example, the cathedral aisle derived
itself from the mimic combination of features which
grouped themselves together at the point of approaching collision—viz. an arrow-like section of the road,
six hundred yards long, under the solemn lights described, with lofty trees meeting overhead in arches.
The guard's horn, again—a humble instrument in itself—was yet glorified as the organ of publication for
so many great national events. And the incident of
the Dying Trumpeter, who rises from a marble bas-
relief, and carries a marble trumpet to his marble lips
for the purpose of warning the female infant, was
doubtless secretly suggested by my own imperfect effort to seize the guard's horn, and to blow a warning
blast. But the Dream knows best; and the Dream, I
say again, is the responsible party.

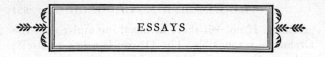

ON MURDER
CONSIDERED AS ONE OF THE FINE ARTS

FIRST PAPER

(First published in *Blackwood's Magazine* in February, 1827)

I. ADVERTISEMENT OF A MAN MORBIDLY VIRTUOUS

Most of us who read books have probably heard of a Society for the Promotion of Vice, of the Hell-Fire Club founded in the last century by Sir Francis Dashwood, &c. At Brighton I think it was that a Society was formed for the Suppression of Virtue. That society was itself suppressed; but I am sorry to say that another exists in London, of a character still more atrocious. In tendency, it may be denominated a Society for the Encouragement of Murder; but, according to their own delicate εὐφημισμος, it is styled, the Society of Connoisseurs in Murder. They profess to be curious in homicide, amateurs and dilettanti in the various modes of carnage, and, in short, Murder-Fanciers. Every fresh atrocity of that class which the police annals of Europe bring up, they meet and criticize as they would a picture, statue, or other work of art. But I need not trouble myself with any attempt to describe the spirit of their proceedings, as the reader will collect *that* much better from one of the Monthly Lectures read before the society last year. This has fallen into my hands accidentally, in spite of all the vigilance exercised to keep their transactions from the public eye. The publication of it will alarm them; and my purpose is that it should.

982

II. THE LECTURE

GENTLEMEN: I have had the honour to be appointed by your committee to the trying task of reading the Williams Lecture on Murder Considered as One of the Fine Arts—a task which might be easy enough three or four centuries ago, when the art was little understood, and few great models had been exhibited; but in this age, when masterpieces of excellence have been executed by professional men, it must be evident that in the style of criticism applied to them the public will look for something of a corresponding improvement. Practice and theory must advance *pari passu.* People begin to see that something more goes to the composition of a fine murder than two blockheads to kill and be killed, a knife, a purse, and a dark lane. Design, gentlemen, grouping, light and shade, poetry, sentiment, are now deemed indispensable to attempts of this nature. Mr. Williams has exalted the ideal of murder to all of us,[1] and to me, therefore, in particular, has deepened the arduousness of my task. Like Æschylus or Milton in poetry, like Michael Angelo in painting, he has carried his art to a point of colossal sublimity, and, as Mr. Wordsworth observes, has in a manner "created the taste by which he is to be enjoyed." To sketch the history of the art, and to examine its principles critically, now remains as a duty for the connoisseur, and for judges of quite another stamp from his Majesty's Judges of Assize.

Before I begin, let me say a word or two to certain prigs, who affect to speak of our society as if it were in some degree immoral in its tendency. Immoral!

---

[1] The Williams and the M'Kean murders are described in full by De Quincey in the *Postscript.*—ED.

God bless my soul, gentlemen! what is it that people mean? I am for morality, and always shall be, and for virtue, and all that; and I do affirm, and always shall (let what will come of it), that murder is an improper line of conduct, highly improper; and I do not stick to assert that any man who deals in murder must have very incorrect ways of thinking, and truly inaccurate principles; and, so far from aiding and abetting him by pointing out his victim's hiding-place, as a great moralist of Germany declared it to be every good man's duty to do,[1] I would subscribe one shilling and six-pence to have him apprehended—which is more by eighteen-pence than the most eminent moralists have hitherto subscribed for that purpose. But what then? Everything in this world has two handles. Murder, for instance, may be laid hold of by its moral handle (as it generally is in the pulpit and at the Old Bailey), and *that*, I confess, is its weak side; or it may also be treated *aesthetically*, as the Germans call it—that is, in rela-tion to good taste.

To illustrate this, I will urge the authority of three eminent persons: viz. S. T. Coleridge, Aristotle, and Mr. Howship the surgeon.

To begin with S. T. C.: One night, many years ago, I was drinking tea with him in Berners Street (which, by the way, for a short street, has been uncommonly fruitful in men of genius). Others were there besides myself; and, amidst some carnal considerations of tea

[1] Kant—who carried his demands of unconditional veracity to so extravagant a length as to affirm that, if a man were to see an innocent person escape from a murderer, it would be his duty, on being questioned by the murderer, to tell the truth, and to point out the retreat of the innocent person, under any certainty of causing murder. Lest this doctrine should be sup-posed to have escaped him in any heat of dispute, on being taxed with it by a celebrated French writer, he solemnly re-affirmed it, with his reasons.

and toast, we were all imbibing a dissertation on Plotinus from the Attic lips of S. T. C. Suddenly a cry arose of *"Fire—fire!"* upon which all of us, master and disciples, Plato and οἱ περι τον Πλατωνα, rushed out, eager for the spectacle. The fire was in Oxford Street, at a pianoforte-maker's; and, as it promised to be a conflagration of merit, I was sorry that my engagements forced me away from Mr. Coleridge's party before matters had come to a crisis. Some days after, meeting with my Platonic host, I reminded him of the case, and begged to know how that very promising exhibition had terminated. "Oh, sir," said he, "it turned out so ill that we damned it unanimously." Now, does any man suppose that Mr. Coleridge—who, for all he is too fat to be a person of active virtue, is undoubtedly a worthy Christian—that is good S. T. C., I say, was an incendiary, or capable of wishing any ill to the poor man and his pianofortes (many of them, doubtless, with the additional keys)? On the contrary, I know him to be that sort of man that I durst stake my life upon it he would have worked an engine in a case of necessity, although rather of the fattest for such fiery trials of his virtue. But how stood the case? Virtue was in no request. On the arrival of the fire engines, morality had devolved wholly on the insurance office. This being the case, he had a right to gratify his taste. He had left his tea. Was he to have nothing in return?

I contend that the most virtuous man, under the premises stated, was entitled to make a luxury of the fire, and to hiss it, as he would any other performance that raised expectations in the public mind which afterwards it disappointed. Again, to cite another great authority, what says the Stagirite? He (in the Fifth Book, I think it is, of his *Metaphysics*) describes what he calls κλεπτὴν τέλειον—*i.e. a perfect thief;* and, as to Mr. Howship, in a work of his on Indigestion he makes no scruple to talk with admiration of a certain ulcer which he had seen, and which he styles "a beautiful ulcer." Now, will any man pretend that, abstractly considered, a thief could appear to Aristotle a perfect character, or that Mr. Howship could be enamoured of an ulcer? Aristotle, it is well known, was himself so very moral a character that, not content with writing his *Nicomachean Ethics* in one volume octavo, he also wrote another system, called *Magna Moralia*, or Big Ethics. Now, it is impossible that a man who composes any ethics at all, big or little, should admire a thief *per se;* and, as to Mr. Howship, it is well known that he makes war upon all ulcers, and, without suffering himself to be seduced by their charms, endeavours to banish them from the county of Middlesex. But the truth is that, however objectionable *per se*, yet, relatively to others of their class, both a thief and an ulcer may have infinite degrees of merit. They are both imperfections, it is true; but, to be imperfect being their essence, the very greatness of their imperfection becomes their perfection. *Spartam nactus es, hanc exorna.* A thief like Autolycus or the once famous George Barrington, and a grim phagedænic ulcer, superbly defined, and running regularly through all its natural stages, may no less justly be regarded as ideals after *their* kind than the most faultless moss-rose amongst flowers, in its progress from bud to "bright consummate flower," or, amongst human flowers, the most magnificent young female, apparelled in the pomp of womanhood. And thus not only the ideal of an inkstand may be imagined, as Mr. Coleridge illustrated in his celebrated correspondence with Mr. Blackwood —in which, by the way, there is not so much, because an inkstand is a laudable sort of thing, and a valuable member of society—but even imperfection itself may have its ideal or perfect state.

Really, gentlemen, I beg pardon for so much philosophy at one time; and now let me apply it. When a murder is in the paulo-post-futurum tense—not done, not even (according to modern purism) *being* done, but only going to be done—and a rumour of it comes to our ears, by all means let us treat it morally. But suppose it over and done, and that you can say of it, Τετέλεσται, It is finished, or (in that adamantine molossus of *Medea*) Εἴργασται, Done it is, it is a *fait accompli*; suppose the poor murdered man to be out of his pain, and the rascal that did it off like a shot nobody knows whither; suppose, lastly, that we have done our best, by putting out our legs, to trip up the fellow in his flight, but all to no purpose—"*abiit, evasit, excessit, erupit*," &c.—why, then, I say, what's the use of any more virtue? Enough has been given to morality; now comes the turn of Taste and the Fine Arts. A sad thing it was, no doubt, very sad; but *we* can't mend it. Therefore let us make the best of a bad matter; and, as it is impossible to hammer anything out of it for moral purpose, let us treat it aesthetically, and see if it will turn to account in that way. Such is the logic of a sensible man; and what follows? We dry up our tears, and have the satisfaction, perhaps, to discover that a transaction which, morally considered, was shocking, and without a leg to stand upon, when tried by principles of Taste, turns out to be a very meritorious performance. Thus all the world is pleased; the old proverb is justified, that it is an ill wind which blows nobody good; the amateur, from looking bilious and sulky by too close an attention to virtue, begins to pick up his crumbs; and general hilarity prevails.

The first murder is familiar to you all. As the inventor of murder, and the father of the art, Cain must have been a man of first-rate genius. All the Cains

were men of genius. Tubal Cain invented tubes, I
think, or some such thing. But, whatever might be the
originality and genius of the artist, every art was then
in its infancy; and the works turned out from each
several *studio* must be criticized with a recollection of
that fact. Even Tubal's work would probably be little
approved at this day in Sheffield; and therefore of Cain
(Cain senior, I mean) it is no disparagement to say
that his performance was but so-so. Milton, however,
is supposed to have thought differently. By his way
of relating the case, it should seem to have been rather
a pet murder with him, for he retouches it with an
apparent anxiety for its picturesque effect:

> *Whereat he inly raged, and, as they talked,*
> *Smote him into the midriff with a stone*
> *That beat out life: he fell, and, deadly pale,*
> *Groaned out his soul*, with gushing blood effused.
> Paradise Lost, *Bk. XI.*

Upon this Richardson, the painter, who had an eye for
effect, remarks as follows in his *Notes on Paradise Lost*,
p. 497: "It has been thought," says he, "that Cain
beat (as the common saying is) the breath out of his
brother's body with a great stone: Milton gives in to
this, with the addition, however, of a large wound."
In this place it was a judicious addition; for the rudeness of the weapon, unless raised and enriched by a
warm, sanguinary colouring, has too much of the
naked air of the savage school; as if the deed were perpetrated by a Polypheme, without science, premedita-
tion, or anything but a mutton-bone. However, I am
chiefly pleased with the improvement, as it implies that
Milton was an amateur. As to Shakespeare, there never
was a better; witness his description of the murdered
Duncan, Banquo, &c.; and above all witness his incom-

parable miniature, in *Henry VI*, of the murdered Gloucester.

The foundation of the art having been once laid, it is pitiable to see how it slumbered without improvement for ages. In fact, I shall now be obliged to leap over all murders, sacred and profane, as utterly unworthy of notice until long after the Christian era. Greece, even in the age of Pericles, produced no murder, or at least none is recorded, of the slightest merit; and Rome had too little originality of genius in any of the arts to succeed where her model failed her.[1] In fact, the Latin language sinks under the very idea of murder. "The man was murdered"—how will this sound in Latin? *Interfectus est, interemptus est*—which simply expresses a homicide; and hence the Christian Latinity of the middle ages was obliged to introduce a new word, such as the feebleness of classic conceptions never ascended to. *Murdratus est*, says the sublimer dialect of Gothic ages. Meantime, the Jewish school of murder kept alive whatever was yet known in the art, and gradually transferred it to the Western World. Indeed, the Jewish school was always respect-

---

[1] At the time of writing this [1827] I held the common opinion upon that subject. Mere inconsideration it was that led to so erroneous a judgement. Since then, on closer reflection, I have seen ample reason to retract it: satisfied I now [1854] am that the Romans, in every art which allowed to them any parity of advantages, had merits as racy, native, and characteristic, as the best of the Greeks. Elsewhere I shall plead this cause circumstantially, with the hope of converting the reader. In the meantime, I was anxious to lodge my protest against this ancient error—an error which commenced in the timeserving sycophancy of Virgil the court-poet. With the base purpose of gratifying Augustus in his vindictive spite against Cicero, and by way of introducing, therefore, the little clause *orabunt causas melius* as applying to all Athenian against all Roman orators, Virgil did not scruple to sacrifice by wholesale the just pretensions of his compatriots collectively.

able, even in its medieval stages, as the case of Hugh of Lincoln shows, which was honoured with the approbation of Chaucer, on occasion of another performance from the same school, which, in his Canterbury Tales, he puts into the mouth of the Lady Abbess.

Recurring, however, for one moment, to classical antiquity, I cannot but think that Catiline, Clodius, and some of that coterie, would have made first-rate artists; and it is on all accounts to be regretted that the priggism of Cicero robbed his country of the only chance she had for distinction in this line. As the *subject* of a murder, no person could have answered better than himself. Lord! how he would have howled with panic, if he had heard Cethegus under his bed. It would have been truly diverting to have listened to him; and satisfied I am, gentlemen, that he would have preferred the *utile* of creeping into a closet, or even into a *cloaca,* to the *honestum* of facing the bold artist.

To come now to the Dark Ages— (by which we that speak with precision mean, *par excellence*, the tenth century as a meridian line, and the two centuries immediately before and after, full midnight being from A.D. 888 to A.D. 1111)—those ages ought naturally to be favourable to the art of murder, as they were to church architecture, to stained glass, &c.; and, accordingly, about the latter end of this period, there arose a great character in our art—I mean the Old Man of the Mountains. He was a shining light indeed, and I need not tell you that the very word "assassin" is deduced from him.[1] So keen an amateur was he that on

[1] The name "Old Man of the Mountains" does not designate any individual person, but was the title—in Arabic *Sheikh-al-jebal*, "Prince of the Mountain"—of a series of chiefs who presided from 1090 to 1258 over a community or military order of fanatical Mohammedan sectaries, called *The Assassins*, distributed through Persia and Syria, but with certain mountain-ranges for their headquarters. But, though there is

one occasion, when his own life was attempted by a
favourite assassin, he was so much pleased with the
talent shown that, notwithstanding the failure of the
artist, he created him a duke upon the spot, with remainder to the female line, and settled a pension on
him for three lives. Assassination is a branch of the art
which demands a separate notice; and it is possible that
I may devote an entire lecture to it. Meantime, I shall
only observe how odd it is that this branch of the art
has flourished by intermitting fits. It never rains but
it pours. Our own age can boast of some fine specimens,
such, for instance, as Bellingham's affair with the
prime minister Perceval, the Duc de Berri's case at the
Parisian Opera House, the Maréchal Brune's case at
Avignon; and about two and a half centuries ago, there
was a most brilliant constellation of murders in this
class. I need hardly say that I allude especially to those
seven splendid works: the assassinations of William I.
of Orange; of the three French Henries, viz. of Henri,
Duke of Guise, that had a fancy for the throne of
France, of Henri III, last prince of the line of Valois,
who then occupied that throne, and finally of Henri
IV, his brother-in-law, who succeeded to that throne
as first prince in the line of Bourbon: not eighteen
years later came the fifth on the roll, viz. that of our
Duke of Buckingham (which you will find excellently
described in the letters published by Sir Henry Ellis, of

no doubt that the words *assassin* and *assassination*, as terms
for secret murder, and especially for secret murder by stab-
bing, are a recollection of the reputed habits of this old Persian
and Syrian community, the original etymology of the word
Assassins itself, as the name of the community, is not so certain. Skeat sets it down as simply the Arabic *hashishin*,
"hashish-drinkers," from the fact or on the supposition that
the agents of the Old Man of the Mountains, when they were
detached on their murderous errands, went forth nerved for
the task by the intoxication of *hashish*, or Indian hemp.

the British Museum), sixthly of Gustavus Adolphus, and seventhly of Wallenstein. What a glorious Pleiad of Murders! And it increases one's admiration that this bright constellation of artistic displays, comprehending 3 Majesties, 3 Serene Highnesses, and 1 Excellency, all lay within so narrow a field of time as between A.D. 1588 and 1635. The King of Sweden's assassination, by the bye, is doubted by many writers, Harte amongst others; but they are wrong. He *was* murdered; and I consider his murder unique in its excellence; for he was murdered at noon-day, and on the field of battle—a feature of original conception which occurs in no other work of art that I remember. To conceive the idea of a secret murder on private account as enclosed within a little parenthesis on a vast stage of public battle-carnage is like Hamlet's subtle device of a tragedy within a tragedy. Indeed, all of these assassinations may be studied with profit by the advanced connoisseur. They are all of them *exemplaria*, model murders, pattern murders, of which one may say

Nocturna versate manu, versate diurna—

especially *nocturna*.

In these assassinations of princes and statesmen there is nothing to excite our wonder. Important changes often depend on their deaths; and, from the eminence on which they stand, they are peculiarly exposed to the aim of every artist who happens to be possessed by the craving for scenical effect. But there is another class of assassinations, which has prevailed from an early period of the seventeenth century, that really *does* surprise me: I mean the assassination of philosophers. For, gentlemen, it is a fact that every philosopher of eminence for the two last centuries has

either been murdered, or at the least been very near it
—insomuch that, if a man calls himself a philosopher
and never had his life attempted, rest assured there is
nothing in him; and against Locke's Philosophy in
particular I think it an unanswerable objection (if we
needed any) that, although he carried his throat about
with him in this world for seventy-two years, no man
ever condescended to cut it. As these cases of philosophers are not much known, and are generally good
and well composed in their circumstances, I shall here
read an excursus on that subject, chiefly by way of
showing my own learning.

The first great philosopher of the seventeenth century (if we except Bacon and Galileo) was Descartes;
and, if ever one could say of a man that he was all *but*
murdered—murdered within an inch—one must say it
of him. The case was this, as reported by Baillet in his
Vie de M. Descartes, tom. i. pp. 102-3: In the year
1621, when Descartes might be about twenty-six years
old, he was touring about as usual (for he was as restless as a hyena) ; and, coming to the Elbe, either at
Gluckstadt or at Hamburg, he took shipping for East
Friesland. What he could want in East Friesland no
man has ever discovered; and perhaps he took this into
consideration himself: for, on reaching Emden, he
resolved to sail instantly for *West* Friesland; and,
being very impatient of delay, he hired a bark, with a
few mariners to navigate it. No sooner had he got out
to sea than he made a pleasing discovery, viz. that he
had shut himself up in a den of murderers. His crew,
says M. Baillet, he soon found out to be *"des scélérats"*
—not *amateurs*, gentlemen, as we are, but professional
men, the height of whose ambition at that moment was
to cut his individual throat. But the story is too pleasing to be abridged; I shall give it, therefore, accurately
from the French of his biographer: "M. Descartes had

no company but that of his servant, with whom he was
conversing in French. The sailors, who took him for a
foreign merchant, rather than a cavalier, concluded
that he must have money about him. Accordingly, they
came to a resolution by no means advantageous to his
purse. There is this difference, however, between sea-
robbers and the robbers in forests, that the latter may
without hazard spare the lives of their victims, whereas
the others cannot put a passenger on shore in such a
case without running the risk of being apprehended.
The crew of M. Descartes arranged their measures
with a view to evade any danger of that sort. They observed that he was a stranger from a distance, without
acquaintance in the country, and that nobody would
take any trouble to inquire about him, in case he should
never come to hand (*quand il viendroit à manquer*)."
Think, gentlemen, of these Friesland dogs discussing
a philosopher as if he were a puncheon of rum consigned to some shipbroker. "His temper, they remarked, was very mild and patient; and, judging from
the gentleness of his deportment, and the courtesy with
which he treated themselves, that he could be nothing
more than some green young man, without station or
root in the world, they concluded that they should have
all the easier task in disposing of his life. They made
no scruple to discuss the whole matter in his presence,
as not supposing that he understood any other language than that in which he conversed with his servant; and the amount of their deliberation was—to
murder him, then to throw him into the sea, and to
divide his spoils."

Excuse my laughing, gentlemen; but the fact is I
always *do* laugh when I think of this case—two things
about it seem so droll. One is the horrid panic or
"funk" (as the men of Eton call it) in which Descartes

must have found himself upon hearing this regular drama sketched for his own death, funeral, succession and administration to his effects. But another thing which seems to me still more funny about this affair is that, if these Friezland hounds had been "game," we should have no Cartesian philosophy; and how we could have done without *that*, considering the world of books it has produced, I leave to any respectable trunk-maker to declare.

However, to go on: spite of his enormous funk, Descartes showed fight, and by that means awed these Anti-Cartesian rascals. "Finding," says M. Baillet, "that the matter was no joke, M. Descartes leaped upon his feet in a trice, assumed a stern countenance that these cravens had never looked for, and, addressing them in their own language, threatened to run them through on the spot if they dared to give him any insult." Certainly, gentlemen, this would have been an honour far above the merits of such inconsiderable rascals—to be spitted like larks upon a Cartesian sword; and therefore I am glad M. Descartes did not rob the gallows by executing his threat, especially as he could not possibly have brought his vessel to port after he had murdered his crew; so that he must have continued to cruise for ever in the Zuyder Zee, and would probably have been mistaken by sailors for the *Flying Dutchman* homeward bound. "The spirit which M. Descartes manifested," says his biographer, "had the effect of magic on these wretches. The suddenness of their consternation struck their minds with a confusion which blinded them to their advantage, and they conveyed him to his destination as peaceably as he could desire."

Possibly, gentlemen, you may fancy that, on the model of Cæsar's address to his poor ferryman—"*Cæsarem vehis et fortunas ejus*"—M. Descartes needed only to have said, "Dogs, you cannot cut my throat, for you carry Descartes and his philosophy," and might safely have defied them to do their worst. A German emperor had the same notion when, being cautioned to keep out of the way of a cannonading, he replied, "Tut! man. Did you ever hear of a cannon-ball that killed an emperor?" [1] As to an emperor I cannot say, but a less thing has sufficed to smash a philosopher; and the next great philosopher of Europe undoubtedly *was* murdered. This was Spinoza.

I know very well the common opinion about him is that he died in his bed. Perhaps he did, but he was murdered for all that; and this I shall prove by a book published at Brussels in the year 1731, entitled *La Vie de Spinoza*, par M. Jean Colerus, with many additions from a MS. life by one of his friends. Spinoza died on the 21st of February, 1677, being then little more than forty-four years old. This, of itself, looks suspicious; and M. Jean admits that a certain expression in the MS. life of him would warrant the conclusion *"que sa mort n'a pas été tout-à-fait naturelle."* Living in a damp country, and a sailor's country, like Holland, he may be thought to have indulged a good deal in grog, especially in punch, which was then newly discovered. Undoubtedly he might have done so; but the fact is that he did not. M. Jean calls him *"extrêmement sobre en son boire et en son manger."* And, though some wild stories were afloat about his using the juice of mandragora (p. 140) and opium (p. 144), yet neither of these articles is found in his druggist's bill. Living,

---

[1] This same argument has been employed at least once too often. Some centuries back a dauphin of France, when admonished of his risk from small-pox, made the same demand as the emperor—"Had any gentleman heard of a dauphin killed by small-pox?" No; not any gentleman *had* heard of such a case. And yet, for all that, this dauphin died of that same small-pox.

therefore, with such sobriety, how was it possible that he should die a natural death at forty-four? Hear his biographer's account: "Sunday morning, the 21st of February, before it was church time, Spinoza came downstairs, and conversed with the master and mistress of the house." At this time, therefore, perhaps ten o'clock on Sunday morning, you see that Spinoza was alive, and pretty well. But it seems "he had summoned from Amsterdam a certain physician, whom," says the biographer, "I shall not otherwise point out to notice than by these two letters, L. M." This L. M. had directed the people of the house to purchase "an ancient cock," and to have him boiled forthwith, in order that Spinoza might take some broth about noon; which in fact he did, and ate some of the *old cock* with a good appetite, after the landlord and his wife had returned from church.

"In the afternoon, L. M. stayed alone with Spinoza, the people of the house having returned to church; on coming out from which, they learned, with much surprise, that Spinoza had died about three o'clock, in the presence of L. M., who took his departure for Amsterdam that same evening, by the night-boat, without paying the least attention to the deceased"——and probably without paying very much attention to the payment of his own little account. "No doubt, he was the readier to dispense with these duties as he had possessed himself of a ducatoon, and a small quantity of silver, together with a silver-hafted knife, and had absconded with his pillage." Here you see, gentlemen, the murder is plain, and the manner of it. It was L. M. who murdered Spinoza for his money. Poor Spinoza was an invalid, meagre and weak: as no blood was observed, L. M. no doubt threw him down, and smothered him with pillows——the poor man being already half suffocated by his infernal dinner. After masticating that "ancient cock," which I take to mean a cock of the preceding century, in what condition could the poor invalid find himself for a stand-up fight with L. M.?

Hobbes—but why, or on what principle, I never could understand—was not murdered. This was a capital oversight of the professional men in the seventeenth century; because in every light he was a fine subject for murder, except, indeed, that he was lean and skinny; for I can prove that he had money, and (what was very funny) he had no right to make the least resistance; since, according to himself, irresistible power creates the very highest species of right, so that it is rebellion of the blackest dye to refuse to be murdered when a competent force appears to murder you. However, gentlemen, though he was not murdered, I am happy to assure you that (by his own account) he was three times very near being murdered—which is consolatory. The first time was in the spring of 1640, when he pretends to have circulated a little MS. on the King's behalf against the Parliament. He never could produce this MS., by the bye; but he says that, "had not His Majesty dissolved the Parliament" (in May), "it had brought him into danger of his life." Dissolving the Parliament, however, was of no use; for in November of the same year the Long Parliament assembled, and Hobbes, a second time fearing he should be murdered, ran away to France. In France, Hobbes managed to take care of his throat pretty well for ten years; but at the end of that time, by way of paying court to Cromwell, he published his *Leviathan*. The old coward now began to "funk" horribly for the third time; he fancied the swords of the Cavaliers were constantly at his throat, recollecting how they had served the Parliament ambassadors at the Hague and Madrid. *"Tum,"* says he, in his dog-Latin life of himself—

Tum venit in mentem mihi Dorislaus et Ascham;
Tanquam proscripto terror ubique aderat.[1]

And, accordingly, he ran home to England. Now, certainly, it is very true that a man deserved a cudgelling for writing *Leviathan*, and two or three cudgellings for writing a pentameter ending so villainously as *"terror ubique aderat"!* But no man ever thought him worthy of anything beyond cudgelling. And, in fact, the whole story is a bounce of his own. For, in a most abusive letter which he wrote "to a learned person" (meaning Wallis the mathematician), he gives quite another account of the matter, and says (p. 8), he ran home "because he would not trust his safety with the French clergy"; insinuating that he was likely to be murdered for his religion; which would have been a high joke indeed—Tom's being brought to the stake for religion!

The seventeenth and eighteenth centuries, together with so much of the nineteenth as we have yet seen, jointly compose the Augustan age of Murder. The finest work of the seventeenth century is, unquestionably, the murder of Sir Edmundbury Godfrey, which has my entire approbation. In the grand feature of *mystery*, which in some shape or other ought to colour every judicious attempt at murder, it is excellent; for the mystery is not yet dispersed. The attempt to fasten the murder upon the Papists, which would injure it as much as some well-known Correggios have been in-

---

[1] "Then there came into my mind Dorislaus and Ascham; fear attended me everywhere as one proscribed."

jured by the professional picture-cleaners, or would
even ruin it by translating it into the spurious class of
mere political or partisan murders, thoroughly wanting in the murderous *animus*, I exhort the society to
discountenance.

It must be observed that the quantity of murder
was not great in Sir Edmundbury's century, at least
amongst our own artists; which, perhaps, is attribut-
able to the want of enlightened patronage. *Sint Mœ-
cenates, non deerunt, Flacce, Marones.* Consulting
Grant's *Observations on the Bills of Mortality* (4th
edition, Oxford, 1665), I find that, out of 229,250
who died in London during one period of twenty years
in the seventeenth century, not more than eighty-six
were murdered; that is, about four and three-tenths
per annum. A small number this, gentlemen, to found
an academy upon; and, certainly, where the quantity
is so small, we have a right to expect that the quality
should be first-rate. Perhaps it was; yet still I am of
opinion that the best artist in this century was not
equal to the best in that which followed. For instance,
however praiseworthy the case of Sir Edmundbury
Godfrey may be (and nobody can be more sensible of
its merits than I am), still I cannot consent to place it
on a level with that of Mrs. Ruscombe of Bristol,
either as to originality of design, or boldness and
breadth of style. This good lady's murder took place
early in the reign of George III—a reign which was
notoriously favourable to the arts generally. She lived
in College Green, with a single maid-servant, neither
of them having any pretension to the notice of History but what they derived from the great artist whose
workmanship I am recording. One fine morning,
when all Bristol was alive and in motion, some suspicion arising, the neighbours forced an entrance into
the house, and found Mrs. Ruscombe murdered in her

bedroom, and the servant murdered on the stairs: this was at noon; and, not more than two hours before, both mistress and servant had been seen alive. To the best of my remembrance, this was in 1764; upwards of sixty years, therefore, have now elapsed, and yet the artist is still undiscovered. The suspicions of posterity have settled upon two pretenders—a baker and a chimney-sweeper. But posterity is wrong; no unpractised artist could have conceived so bold an idea as that of a noonday murder in the heart of a great city. It was no obscure baker, gentlemen, or anonymous chimney-sweeper, be assured, that executed this work. I know who it was. (*Here there was a general buzz, which at length broke out into open applause; upon which the lecturer blushed, and went on with much earnestness.*) For heaven's sake, gentlemen, do not mistake me; it was not *I* that did it. I have not the vanity to think myself equal to any such achievement; be assured that you greatly overrate my poor talents; Mrs. Ruscombe's affair was far beyond my slender abilities. But I came to know who the artist was from a celebrated surgeon who assisted at his dissection. This gentleman had a private museum in the way of his profession, one corner of which was occupied by a cast from a man of remarkably fine proportions.

"That," said the surgeon, "is a cast from the celebrated Lancashire highwayman who concealed his profession for some time from his neighbours by drawing woollen stockings over his horse's legs, and in that way muffling the clatter which he must else have made in riding up a flagged alley that led to his stable. At the time of his execution for highway robbery I was studying under Cruickshank; and the man's figure was so uncommonly fine that no money or exertion was spared to get into possession of him with the least possible delay. By the connivance of the under-sheriff, he was cut down within the legal time, and instantly put into a chaise-and-four; so that, when he reached Cruickshank's, he was positively not dead. Mr. ———, a young student at that time, had the honour of giving him the *coup de grâce*, and finishing the sentence of the law."

This remarkable anecdote, which seemed to imply that all the gentlemen in the dissecting-room were amateurs of our class, struck me a good deal; and I was repeating it one day to a Lancashire lady, who thereupon informed me that she had herself lived in the neighbourhood of that highwayman, and well remembered two circumstances which combined, in the opinion of all his neighbours, to fix upon him the credit of Mrs. Ruscombe's affair. One was the fact of his absence for a whole fortnight at the period of that murder; the other, that within a very little time after the neighbourhood of this highwayman was deluged with dollars: now Mrs. Ruscombe was known to have hoarded about two thousand of that coin.

But, whilst I thus eulogize the Ruscombian case, let me not be supposed to overlook the many other specimens of extraordinary merit spread over the face of this century. Such cases, indeed, as that of Miss Bland, or of Captain Donnellan and Sir Theophilus Boughton, shall never have any countenance from me. Fie on these dealers in poison, say I: can they not keep to the old honest way of cutting throats, without introducing such abominable innovations from Italy? I consider all these poisoning cases, compared with the legitimate style, as no better than waxwork by the side of sculpture, or a lithographic print by the side of a fine Volpato. But, dismissing these, there remain many excellent works of art in a pure style, such as nobody need be ashamed to own; and this every candid connoisseur will admit. *Candid*, observe, I say; for

great allowances must be made in these cases; no artist
can ever be sure of carrying through his own fine preconception. Awkward disturbances will arise; people
will not submit to have their throats cut quietly; they
will run, they will kick, they will bite; and, whilst the
portrait-painter often has to complain of too much
torpor in his subject, the artist in our line is generally
embarrassed by too much animation. At the same
time, however disagreeable to the artist, this tendency
in murder to excite and irritate the subject is certainly
one of its advantages to the world in general which we
ought not to overlook, since it favours the development of latent talent. Jeremy Taylor notices with admiration the extraordinary leaps which people will
take under the influence of fear. There was a striking
instance of this in the recent case of the M'Keans: the
boy cleared a height such as he will never clear again
to his dying day. Talents also of the most brilliant description for thumping, and, indeed, for all the gym-
nastic exercises, have sometimes been developed by
the panic which accompanies our artists—talents else
buried and hid under a bushel, to the possessors, as
much as to their friends. I remember an interesting illustration of this fact in a case of which I learned in
Germany.

Riding one day in the neighbourhood of Munich, I
overtook a distinguished amateur of our society, whose
name, for obvious reasons, I shall conceal. This gentleman informed me that, finding himself wearied
with the frigid pleasures (such he esteemed them) of
mere amateurship, he had quitted England for the
Continent—meaning to practise a little professionally. For this purpose he resorted to Germany, conceiving the police in that part of Europe to be more
heavy and drowsy than elsewhere. His *début* as a
practitioner took place at Mannheim; and, knowing

me to be a brother amateur, he freely communicated
the whole of his maiden adventure. "Opposite to my
lodging," said he, "lived a baker: he was somewhat of
a miser, and lived quite alone. Whether it were his
great expanse of chalky face, or what else, I know not,
but the fact was, I 'fancied' him, and resolved to commence business upon his throat; which, by the way,
he always carried bare—a fashion which is very irritating to my desires. Precisely at eight o'clock in the
evening, I observed that he regularly shut up his windows. One night I watched him when thus engaged—
bolted in after him—locked the door—and, addressing him with great suavity, acquainted him with the
nature of my errand; at the same time advising him to
make no resistance, which would be mutually unpleasant. So saying, I drew out my tools, and was proceeding to operate. But at this spectacle the baker,
who seemed to have been struck by catalepsy at my
first announcement, awoke into tremendous agitation.
'I will *not* be murdered!' he shrieked aloud; 'what for
will I' (meaning *shall* I) 'lose my precious throat?'—
'What for?' said I; 'if for no other reason, for this—
that you put alum into your bread. But no matter;
alum or no alum (for I was resolved to forestall any
argument on that point), know that I am a virtuoso in
the art of murder—am desirous of improving myself
in its details—and am enamoured of your vast surface
of throat, to which I am determined to be a customer.'
—'Is it so?' said he; 'but I'll find you a customer in
another line'; and, so saying, he threw himself into a
boxing attitude. The very idea of his boxing struck
me as ludicrous. It is true, a London baker had distinguished himself in the ring, and became known to
fame under the title of The Master of the Rolls; but
he was young and unspoiled; whereas this man was a

monstrous feather-bed in person, fifty years old, and
totally out of condition. Spite of all this, however, and
contending against *me*, who am a master in the art, he
made so desperate a defence that many times I feared
he might turn the tables upon me, and that I, an amateur, might be murdered by a rascally baker. What a
situation! Minds of sensibility will sympathize with
my anxiety. How severe it was you may understand
by this, that for the first thirteen rounds the baker
positively had the advantage. Round the fourteenth, I
received a blow on the right eye, which closed it up; in
the end, I believe, this was my salvation; for the anger
it roused in me was so great that in the next, and every
one of the three following rounds, I floored the baker.

"Round nineteenth. The baker came up piping,
and manifestly the worse for wear. His geometrical
exploits in the four last rounds had done him no good.
However, he showed some skill in stopping a message
which I was sending to his cadaverous mug; in delivering which my foot slipped, and I went down.

"Round twentieth. Surveying the baker, I became
ashamed of having been so much bothered by a shapeless mass of dough; and I went in fiercely, and administered some severe punishment. A rally took place—
both went down—baker undermost—ten to three on
amateur.

"Round twenty-first. The baker jumped up with
surprising agility; indeed, he managed his pins capitally, and fought wonderfully, considering that he
was drenched in perspiration; but the shine was now
taken out of him, and his game was the mere effect of
panic. It was now clear that he could not last much
longer. In the course of this round we tried the weaving system, in which I had greatly the advantage, and
hit him repeatedly on the conk. My reason for this was

that his conk was covered with carbuncles, and I thought I should vex him by taking such liberties with his conk—which in fact I did.

"The three next rounds, the master of the rolls staggered about like a cow on the ice. Seeing how matters stood, in round twenty-fourth I whispered something into his ear which sent him down like a shot. It was nothing more than my private opinion of the value of his throat at an annuity office. This little confidential whisper affected him greatly; the very perspiration was frozen on his face, and for the next two rounds I had it all my own way. And, when I called *time* for the twenty-seventh round, he lay like a log on the floor."

After which, said I to the amateur, "It may be presumed that you accomplished your purpose."—"You are right," said he mildly; "I did; and a great satisfaction, you know, it was to my mind, for by this means I killed two birds with one stone"; meaning that he had both thumped the baker and murdered him. Now, for the life of me, I could not see *that;* for, on the contrary, to my mind it appeared that he had taken two stones to kill one bird, having been obliged to take the conceit out of him first with his fist, and then with his tools. But no matter for his logic. The moral of his story was good, for it showed what an astonishing stimulus to latent talent is contained in any reasonable prospect of being murdered. A pursy, unwieldy, half-cataleptic baker of Mannheim had absolutely fought seven-and-twenty rounds with an accomplished English boxer, merely upon this inspiration; so greatly was natural genius exalted and sublimed by the genial presence of his murderer.

Really, gentlemen, when one hears of such things as these, it becomes a duty, perhaps, a little to soften that extreme asperity with which most men speak of murder. To hear people talk, you would suppose that all the disadvantages and inconveniences were on the side of being murdered, and that there were none at all in *not* being murdered. But considerate men think otherwise. "Certainly," says Jeremy Taylor, "it is a less temporal evil to fall by the rudeness of 'a sword than the violence of a fever: and the axe'" (to which he might have added the ship-carpenter's mallet and the crowbar) "a much less affliction than a strangury." Very true; the bishop talks like a wise man and an amateur, as I am sure he was; and another great philosopher, Marcus Aurelius, was equally above the vulgar prejudices on this subject. He declares it to be one of "the noblest functions of reason to know whether it is time to walk out of the world or not" (Book III, Collers's Translation). No sort of knowledge being rarer than this, surely *that* man must be a most philanthropic character who undertakes to instruct people in this branch of knowledge gratis, and at no little hazard to himself. All this, however, I throw out only in the way of speculation to future moralists; declaring in the meantime my own private conviction that very few men commit murder upon philanthropic or patriotic principles, and repeating what I have already said once at least—that, as to the majority of murderers, they are very incorrect characters.

With respect to the Williams murders, the sublimest and most entire in their excellence that ever were committed, I shall not allow myself to speak incidentally. Nothing less than an entire lecture, or even an entire course of lectures, would suffice to expound their merits. But one curious fact connected with his case I shall mention, because it seems to imply that the blaze of his genius absolutely dazzled the eye of criminal justice. You all remember, I doubt not, that

the instruments with which he executed his first great
work (the murder of the Marrs) were a ship-carpenter's mallet and a knife. Now, the mallet belonged to
an old Swede, one John Peterson, and bore his initials.
This instrument Williams left behind him in Marr's
house, and it fell into the hands of the magistrates.
But, gentlemen, it is a fact that the publication of this
circumstance of the initials led immediately to the apprehension of Williams, and, if made earlier, would
have prevented his second great work (the murder of
the Williamsons), which took place precisely twelve
days after. Yet the magistrates kept back this fact from
the public for the entire twelve days, and until that
second work was accomplished. That finished, they
published it, apparently feeling that Williams had
now done enough for his fame, and that his glory was
at length placed beyond the reach of accident.

But it is now time that I should say a few words
about the principles of murder, not with a view to
regulate your practice, but your judgement. As to old
women, and the mob of newspaper readers, they are
pleased with anything, provided it is bloody enough.
But the mind of sensibility requires something more.
First, then, let us speak of the kind of person who is
adapted to the purpose of the murderer; *secondly*, of
the place where; *thirdly*, of the time when, and other
little circumstances.

As to the person, I suppose it is evident that he
ought to be a good man, because, if he were not, he
might himself, by possibility, be contemplating murder at the very time; and such "diamond-cut-dia-
mond" tussles, though pleasant enough where nothing better is stirring, are really not what a critic can
allow himself to call murders. I could mention some
people (I name no names) who have been murdered

by other people in a dark lane; and so far all seemed
correct enough; but, on looking further into the matter, the public have become aware that the murdered
party was himself, at the moment, planning to rob his
murderer, at the least, and possibly to murder him, if
he had been strong enough. Whenever that is the case,
or may be thought to be the case, farewell to all the
genuine effects of the art. For the final purpose of
murder, considered as a fine art, is precisely the same
as that of tragedy in Aristotle's account of it; viz. "to
cleanse the heart by means of pity and terror." Now,
terror there may be, but how can there be any pity for
one tiger destroyed by another tiger?

It is also evident that the person selected ought not
to be a public character. For instance, no judicious
artist would have attempted to murder Abraham Newland.[1] For the case was this: everybody read so much
about Abraham Newland, and so few people ever saw
him, that to the general belief he was a mere abstract
idea. And I remember that once, when I happened to
mention that I had dined at a coffee-house in company with Abraham Newland, everybody looked
scornfully at me, as though I had pretended to have
played at billiards with Prester John, or to have had
an affair of honour with the Pope. And, by the way,
the Pope would be a very improper person to murder;
for he has such a virtual ubiquity as the father of
Christendom, and, like the cuckoo, is so often heard

[1] Abraham Newland [chief cashier of the Bank of England]
is now utterly forgotten. But, when this was written [1827],
his name had not ceased to ring in British ears, as the most
familiar and most significant that perhaps has ever existed. It
was the name which appeared on the face of all Bank of England notes, great or small; and had been, for more than a
quarter of a century (especially through the whole career of
the French Revolution), a shorthand expression for paper
money in its safest form.

but never seen, that I suspect most people regard *him* also as an abstract idea. Where, indeed, a public man is in the habit of giving dinners, "with every delicacy of the season," the case is very different: every person is satisfied that *he* is no abstract idea; and, therefore, there can be no impropriety in murdering him; only that his murder will fall into the class of assassinations, which I have not yet treated.

Thirdly. The subject chosen ought to be in good health; for it is absolutely barbarous to murder a sick person, who is usually quite unable to bear it. On this principle, no tailor ought to be chosen who is above twenty-five, for after that age he is sure to be dyspeptic. Or, at least, if a man will hunt in that warren, he will of course think it his duty, on the old established equation, to murder some multiple of 9—say 18, 27, or 36. And here, in this benign attention to the comfort of sick people, you will observe the usual effect of a fine art to soften and refine the feelings. The world in general, gentlemen, are very bloody-minded; and all they want in a murder is a copious effusion of blood; gaudy display in this point is enough for *them*. But the enlightened connoisseur is more refined in his taste; and from our art, as from all the other liberal arts when thoroughly mastered, the result is, to humanize the heart; so true is it that

> *Ingenuas didicisse fideliter artes*
> *Emollit mores, nec sinit esse feros.*

A philosophic friend, well known for his philanthropy and general benignity, suggests that the subject chosen ought also to have a family of young children wholly dependent on his exertions, by way of deepening the pathos. And, undoubtedly, this is a judicious caution. Yet I would not insist too keenly on such a condition. Severe good taste unquestionably suggests it; but still, where the man was otherwise unobjectionable in point of morals and health, I would not look with too curious a jealousy to a restriction which might have the effect of narrowing the artist's sphere.

So much for the person. As to the time, the place, and the tools, I have many things to say which at present I have no room for. The good sense of the practitioner has usually directed him to night and privacy. Yet there have not been wanting cases where this rule was departed from with excellent effect. In respect to time, Mrs. Ruscombe's case is a beautiful exception which I have already noticed; and in respect both to time and place there is a fine exception in the annals of Edinburgh (year 1805), familiar to every child in Edinburgh, but which has unaccountably been defrauded of its due portion of fame amongst English amateurs. The case I mean is that of a porter to one of the banks, who was murdered whilst carrying a bag of money, in broad daylight, on turning out of the High Street, one of the most public streets in Europe; and the murderer is to this hour undiscovered.

> *Sed fugit interea, fugit irreparabile tempus,*
> *Singula dum capti circumvectamur amore.*

And now, gentlemen, in conclusion, let me again solemnly disclaim all pretensions on my own part to the character of a professional man. I never attempted any murder in my life, except in the year 1801— upon the body of a tom-cat; and *that* turned out differently from my intention. My purpose, I own, was downright murder. *"Semper ego auditor tantum?"* said I, *"nunquamne reponam?"* And I went downstairs in search of Tom at one o'clock on a dark night, with the *animus*, and no doubt with the fiendish looks, of a murderer. But, when I found him, he was in the act of plundering the pantry of bread and other things. Now this gave a new turn to the affair; for, the time being one of general scarcity, when even Christians were reduced to the use of potato-bread, rice-bread, and all sorts of things, it was downright treason in a tom-cat to be wasting good wheaten-bread in the way he was doing. It instantly became a patriotic duty to put him to death; and, as I raised aloft and shook the glittering steel, I fancied myself rising, like Brutus, effulgent from a crowd of patriots, and, as I stabbed him, I

> *Called aloud on Tully's name,*
> *And bade the father of his country hail!*

Since then, what wandering thoughts I may have had of attempting the life of an ancient ewe, of a superannuated hen, and such "small deer," are locked up in the secrets of my own breast; but for the higher departments of the art I confess myself to be utterly unfit. My ambition does not rise so high. No, gentlemen: in the words of Horace,

> *Fungar vice cotis, acutum*
> *Reddere quæ ferrum valet, exsors ipsa secandi.*

SECOND PAPER

(First published in *Blackwood's Magazine*, November, 1839)

A GOOD many years ago, the reader may remember that I came forward in the character of a *dilettante* in murder. Perhaps *dilettante* is too strong a word. *Connoisseur* is better suited to the scruples and infirmity of public taste. I suppose there is no harm in *that*, at least. A man is not bound to put his eyes, ears, and understanding into his breeches pocket when he meets with a murder. If he is not in a downright coma-tose state, I suppose he must see that one murder is better or worse than another, in point of good taste. Murders have their little differences and shades of merit, as well as statues, pictures, oratorios, cameos, intaglios, or what not. You may be angry with the man for talking too much, or too publicly (as to the too much, that I deny—a man can never cultivate his taste too highly) ; but you must allow him to think, at any rate. Well, would you believe it? all my neigh-bours came to hear of that little aesthetic essay which I had published; and, unfortunately, hearing at the very same time of a club that I was connected with, and a dinner at which I presided—both tending to the same little object as the essay, viz. the diffusion of a just taste among Her Majesty's subjects [1]—they got up the most barbarous calumnies against me. In par-ticular, they said that I, or that the club (which comes to the same thing) , had offered bounties on well-con-ducted homicides—with a scale of drawbacks, in case of any one defect or flaw, according to a table issued to private friends. Now, let me tell the whole truth about the dinner and the club, and it will be seen how malicious the world is. But, first, confidentially, allow me to say what my real principles are upon the matter in question.

As to murder, I never committed one in my life.

---

[1] *Her* Majesty: In the lecture, having occasion to refer to the reigning sovereign, I said "*His* Majesty"; for at that time [1827] George IV was on the throne; but between the lecture and this supplement had occurred the accession of our present Queen.

It's a well-known thing amongst all my friends. I can get a paper to certify as much, signed by lots of people. Indeed, if you come to that, I doubt whether many people could produce as strong a certificate. Mine would be as big as a breakfast tablecloth. There is indeed one member of the club who pretends to say he caught me once making too free with his throat on a club night, after everybody else had retired. But, observe, he shuffles in his story according to his state of civilization. When not far gone, he contents himself with saying that he caught me ogling his throat, and that I was melancholy for some weeks after, and that my voice sounded in a way expressing, to the nice ear of a connoisseur, *the sense of opportunities lost;* but the club all know that he is a disappointed man himself, and that he speaks querulously at times about the fatal neglect of a man's coming abroad without his tools. Besides, all this is an affair between two amateurs, and everybody makes allowances for little asperities and fibs in such a case. "But," say you, "if no murderer, you may have encouraged, or even have bespoken, a murder." No, upon my honour—no. And that was the very point I wished to argue for your satisfaction. The truth is, I am a very particular man in everything relating to murder; and perhaps I carry my delicacy too far. The Stagirite most justly, and possibly with a view to my case, placed virtue in the τὸ μέσον, or middle point between two extremes. A golden mean is certainly what every man should aim at. But it is easier talking than doing; and, my infirmity being notoriously too much milkiness of heart, I find it difficult to maintain that steady equatorial line between the two poles of too much murder on the one hand and too little on the other. I am too soft; and people get excused through me—nay, go through life without an attempt made upon them—that ought *not* to be excused. I believe, if I had the management of things, there would hardly be a murder from year's end to year's end. I'm for virtue, and goodness, and all that sort of thing. And two instances I'll give you to what an extremity I carry my virtue. The first may seem a trifle; but not if you knew my nephew, who was certainly born to be hanged, and would have been so long ago, but for my restraining voice. He is horribly ambitious, and thinks himself a man of cultivated taste in most branches of murder, whereas, in fact, he has not one idea on the subject but such as he has stolen from me. This is so well known that the club has twice blackballed him, though every indulgence was shown to him as my relative. People came to me and said—"Now really, President, we would do much to serve a relative of yours. But still, what can be said? You know yourself that he'll disgrace us. If we were to elect him, why, the next thing we should hear of would be some vile butcherly murder, by way of justifying our choice. And what sort of a concern would it be? You know, as well as we do, that it would be a disgraceful affair, more worthy of the shambles than of an artist's *atelier*. He would fall upon some great big man, some huge farmer returning drunk from a fair. There would be plenty of blood, and *that* he would expect us to take in lieu of taste, finish, scenical grouping. Then, again, how would he tool? Why, most probably with a cleaver and a couple of paving stones: so that the whole *coup d'œil* would remind you rather of some hideous Ogre or Cyclops than of the delicate operator of the nineteenth century." The picture was drawn with the hand of truth; *that* I could not but allow, and, as to personal feelings in the matter, I dismissed them from the first. The next morning I spoke to my nephew: I was delicately situated, as you see, but I determined that no consideration should induce me to flinch from my duty. "John," said I, "you seem to me to have taken an erroneous view of life and its duties. Pushed on by ambition, you are dreaming rather of what it might be glorious to attempt than what it would be possible for you to accomplish. Believe me, it is not necessary to a man's respectability that he should commit a murder. Many a man has passed through life most respectably without attempting any species of homicide—good, bad, or indifferent. It is your first duty to ask yourself, *quid valeant humeri, quid ferre recusent?* We cannot all be brilliant men in this life. And it is for your interest to be contented rather with a humble station well filled than to shock everybody with failures, the more conspicuous by contrast with the ostentation of their promises." John made no answer; he looked very sulky at the moment, and I am in high hopes that I have saved a near relative from making a fool of himself by attempting what is as much beyond his capacity as an epic poem. Others, however, tell me that he is meditating a revenge upon me and the whole club. But, let this be as it may, *liberavi animam meam;* and, as you see, have run some risk with a wish to diminish the amount of homicide.

A man came to me as a candidate for the place of my servant, just then vacant. He had the reputation of having dabbled a little in our art; some said, not without merit. What startled me, however, was, that he supposed this art to be part of his regular duties in my service, and talked of having it considered in his wages. Now, that was a thing I would not allow; so I said at once, "Richard (or James, as the case might be), you misunderstand my character. If a man will and must practise this difficult (and, allow me to add, dangerous) branch of art—if he has an overruling genius for it—why, in that case, all I say is that he

might as well pursue his studies whilst living in my
service as in another's. And also I may observe that it
can do no harm either to himself or to the subject on
whom he operates that he should be guided by men of
more taste than himself. Genius may do much, but
long study of the art must always entitle a man to offer advice. So far I will go—general principles I will
suggest. But, as to any particular case, once for all I
will have nothing to do with it. Never tell me of any
special work of art you are meditating—I set my face
against it *in toto*. For, if once a man indulges himself
in murder, very soon he comes to think little of robbing, and from robbing he comes next to drinking
and Sabbath-breaking, and from that to incivility and
procrastination. Once begin upon this downward path,
you never know where you are to stop. Many a man
dated his ruin from some murder or other that perhaps he thought little of at the time. *Principiis obsta*
—that's my rule." Such was my speech, and I have
always acted up to it; so, if that is not being virtuous,
I should be glad to know what is.

But now about the dinner and the club. The club
was not particularly of my creation; it arose—pretty
much as other similar associations for the propagation
of truth and the communication of new ideas—rather
from the necessities of things than upon any one man's
suggestion. As to the dinner, if any man more than
another could be held responsible for that, it was a
member known amongst us by the name of *Toad-in-
the-hole*. He was so called from his gloomy misan-
thropical disposition, which led him into constant
disparagements of all modern murders as vicious abortions, belonging to no authentic school of art. The finest performances of our own age he snarled at cyni-
cally; and at length this querulous humour grew upon
him so much, and he became so notorious as a *lauda-*

tor temporis acti, that few people cared to seek his society. This made him still more fierce and truculent.
He went about muttering and growling; wherever you
met him, he was soliloquizing, and saying "Despicable
pretender—without grouping—without two ideas
upon handling—without—"; and there you lost him.
At length existence seemed to be painful to him; he
rarely spoke; he seemed conversing with phantoms
in the air; his housekeeper informed us that his reading was nearly confined to *God's Revenge upon Murder* by Reynolds, and a more ancient book of the same
title, noticed by Sir Walter Scott in his *Fortunes of
Nigel*. Sometimes, perhaps, he might read in the *Newgate Calendar* down to the year 1788; but he never
looked into a book more recent. In fact, he had a theory with regard to the French Revolution, as having
been the great cause of degeneration in murder.

"Very soon, sir," he used to say, "men will have
lost the art of killing poultry: the very rudiments of
the art will have perished!"

In the year 1811 he retired from general society.
Toad-in-the-hole was no more seen in any public resort. We missed him from his wonted haunts: "Nor up
the lawn, nor at the wood was he." By the side of the
main conduit his listless length at noontide he would
stretch, and pore upon the filth that muddled by.
"Even dogs," this pensive moralist would say, "are
not what they were, sir—not what they should be. I
remember in my grandfather's time that some dogs
had an idea of murder. I have known a mastiff, sir,
that lay in ambush for a rival—yes, sir, and finally
murdered him, with pleasing circumstances of good
taste. I also was on intimate terms of acquaintance
with a tom-cat that was an assassin. But now—";
and then, the subject growing too painful, he dashed

his hand to his forehead, and went off abruptly in a homeward direction towards his favourite conduit; where he was seen by an amateur in such a state that he thought it dangerous to address him. Soon after Toad shut himself entirely up; it was understood that he had resigned himself to melancholy; and at length the prevailing notion was that Toad-in-the-hole had hanged himself.

The world was wrong *there*, as it had been on some other questions. Toad-in-the-hole might be sleeping, but dead he was not; and of that we soon had ocular proof. One morning in 1812, an amateur surprised us with the news that he had seen Toad-in-the-hole brushing with hasty steps the dews away, to meet the postman by the conduit side. Even that was something: how much more, to hear that he had shaved his beard—had laid aside his sad-coloured clothes, and was adorned like a bridegroom of ancient days. What could be the meaning of all this? Was Toad-in-the-hole mad? or how? Soon after the secret was explained: in more than a figurative sense "the murder was out." For in came the London morning papers, by which it appeared that, but three days before, a murder the most superb of the century by many degrees had occurred in the heart of London. I need hardly say that this was the great exterminating *chef-d'œuvre* of Williams at Mr. Marr's, No. 29 Ratcliffe Highway. That was the *début* of the artist; at least for anything the public knew. What occurred at Mr. Williamson's twelve nights afterwards—the second work turned out from the same chisel—some people pronounced even superior. But Toad-in-the-hole always "reclaimed," he was even angry, at such comparisons. "This vulgar *goût de comparaison*, as La Bruyère calls it," he would often remark, "will be our ruin;

each work has its own separate characteristics—each in and for itself is incomparable. One, perhaps, might suggest the Iliad—the other the Odyssey: but what do you get by such comparisons? Neither ever was or will be surpassed; and, when you've talked for hours, you must still come back to that." Vain, however, as all criticism might be, he often said that volumes might be written on each case for itself; and he even proposed to publish a quarto on the subject.

Meantime, how had Toad-in-the-hole happened to hear of this great work of art so early in the morning? He had received an account by express, dispatched by a correspondent in London who watched the progress of art on *Toad's* behalf, with a general commission to send off a special express, at whatever cost, in the event of any estimable works appearing. The express arrived in the night-time; Toad-in-the-hole was then gone to bed; he had been muttering and grumbling for hours; but of course he was called up. On reading the account, he threw his arms round the express, declared him his brother and his preserver, and expressed his regret at not having it in his power to knight him. We, amateurs, having heard that he was abroad, and therefore had *not* hanged himself, made sure of soon seeing him amongst us. Accordingly he soon arrived; seized every man's hand as he passed him—wrung it almost frantically, and kept ejaculating, "Why, now, here's something like a murder!— this is the real thing—this is genuine—this is what you can approve, can recommend to a friend: this— says every man, on reflection—this is the thing that ought to be! Such works are enough to make us all young." And in fact the general opinion is that Toad-in-the-hole would have died but for this regeneration of art, which he called a second age of Leo the Tenth; and it was our duty, he said, solemnly to commemorate it. At present, and *en attendant*, he proposed that the club should meet and dine together. A dinner, therefore, was given by the club; to which all amateurs were invited from a distance of one hundred miles.

Of this dinner there are ample shorthand notes amongst the archives of the club. But they are not "extended," to speak diplomatically; and the reporter who only could give the whole report *in extenso* is missing—I believe, murdered. Meantime, in years long after that day, and on an occasion perhaps equally interesting, viz. the turning up of Thugs and Thuggism, another dinner was given. Of this I myself kept notes, for fear of another accident to the shorthand reporter. And I here subjoin them.

Toad-in-the-hole, I must mention, was present at this dinner. In fact, it was one of its sentimental incidents. Being as old as the valleys at the dinner of 1812, naturally he was as old as the hills at the Thug dinner of 1838. He had taken to wearing his beard again; why, or with what view, it passes my persimmon to tell you. But so it was. And his appearance was most benign and venerable. Nothing could equal the angelic radiance of his smile as he inquired after the unfortunate reporter (whom, as a piece of private scandal, I should tell you that he was himself supposed to have murdered in a rapture of creative art). The answer was, with roars of laughter, from the under-sheriff of our county—*"Non est inventus."* Toad-in-the-hole laughed outrageously at this: in fact, we all thought he was choking; and, at the earnest request of the company, a musical composer furnished a most beautiful glee upon the occasion, which was sung five times after dinner, with universal applause and inextinguishable laughter, the words being these (and the chorus so contrived, as most beautifully to mimic the peculiar laughter of Toad-in-the-hole) :

Et interrogatum est a Toad-in-the-hole—Ubi est ille
*   reporter?*
Et responsum est cum cachinno—Non est inventus.

CHORUS

Deinde iteratum est ab omnibus, cum cachinnatione
*   undulante, trepidante*—Non est inventus.

—Toad-in-the-hole, I ought to mention, about nine years before, when an express from Edinburgh brought him the earliest intelligence of the Burke-and-Hare revolution in the art, went mad upon the spot, and, instead of a pension to the express for even one life, or a knighthood, endeavoured to Burke *him;* in consequence of which he was put into a strait-waistcoat. And that was the reason we had no dinner then. But now all of us were alive and kicking, strait-waistcoaters and others; in fact, not one absentee was reported upon the entire roll. There were also many foreign amateurs present.

Dinner being over, and the cloth drawn, there was a general call made for the new glee of *Non est inventus;* but, as this would have interfered with the requisite gravity of the company during the earlier toasts, I overruled the call. After the national toasts had been given, the first official toast of the day was *The Old Man of the Mountains*—drunk in solemn silence.

Toad-in-the-hole returned thanks in a neat speech. He likened himself to the Old Man of the Mountains in a few brief allusions that made the company yell with laughter; and he concluded with giving the health of

Mr. von Hammer, with many thanks to him for his learned History of the Old Man and his subjects the Assassins.

Upon this I rose and said that doubtless most of the company were aware of the distinguished place assigned by Orientalists to the very learned Turkish scholar, Von Hammer the Austrian; that he had made the profoundest researches into our art, as connected with those early and eminent artists, the Syrian assassins in the period of the Crusaders; that his work had been for several years deposited, as a rare treasure of art, in the library of the club. Even the author's name, gentlemen, pointed him out as the historian of our art—Von Hammer—

"Yes, yes," interrupted Toad-in-the-hole, "Von Hammer—he's the man for a *malleus hæreticorum*. You all know what consideration Williams bestowed on the hammer, or the ship-carpenter's mallet, which is the same thing. Gentlemen, I give you another great hammer—Charles the Hammer, the Marteau, or, in Old French, the Martel: he hammered the Saracens till they were all as dead as doornails."

"*Charles the Hammer*, with all the honours."

But the explosion of Toad-in-the-hole, together with the uproarious cheers for the grandpapa of Charlemagne, had now made the company unmanageable. The orchestra was again challenged with shouts the stormiest for the new glee. I foresaw a tempestuous evening; and I ordered myself to be strengthened with three waiters on each side—the vice-president with as many. Symptoms of unruly enthusiasm were beginning to show out; and I own that I myself was considerably excited as the orchestra opened with its storm of music and the impassioned glee began—"*Et inter-*

rogatum est a Toad-in-the-hole—Ubi est ille Reporter?" And the frenzy of the passion became absolutely convulsing as the full chorus fell in—*"Et iteratum est ab omnibus—Non est inventus."*

The next toast was—*The Jewish Sicarii.*

Upon which I made the following explanation to the company: "Gentlemen, I am sure it will interest you all to hear that the Assassins, ancient as they were, had a race of predecessors in the very same country. All over Syria, but particularly in Palestine, during the early years of the Emperor Nero, there was a band of murderers, who prosecuted their studies in a very novel manner. They did not practise in the night-time, or in lonely places; but, justly considering that great crowds are in themselves a sort of darkness by means of the dense pressure, and the impossibility of finding out who it was that gave the blow, they mingled with mobs everywhere; particularly at the great paschal feast in Jerusalem; where they actually had the audacity, as Josephus assures us, to press into the temple —and whom should they choose for operating upon but Jonathan himself, the Pontifex Maximus? They murdered him, gentlemen, as beautifully as if they had had him alone on a moonless night in a dark lane. And, when it was asked who was the murderer, and where he was——"

"Why, then, it was answered," interrupted Toad-in-the-hole, " '*Non est inventus.*' " And then, in spite of all I could do or say, the orchestra opened, and the whole company began—*"Et interrogatum est a Toad-in-the-hole—Ubi est ille Sicarius? Et responsum est ab omnibus—Non est inventus."*

When the tempestuous chorus had subsided, I began again: "Gentlemen, you will find a very circumstantial account of the Sicarii in at least three different parts of Josephus: once in Book XX, sec. v, c. viii, of his *Antiquities;* once in Book I. of his *Wars:* but in sec. x of the chapter first cited you will find a particular description of their tooling. This is what he says: 'They tooled with small scimitars not much different from the Persian *acinacæ*, but more curved, and for all the world most like the Roman semi-lunar *sicæ.*' It is perfectly magnificent, gentlemen, to hear the sequel of their history. Perhaps the only case on record where a regular army of murderers was assembled, a *justus exercitus*, was in the case of these *Sicarii.* They mustered in such strength in the wilderness that Festus himself was obliged to march against them with the Roman legionary force. A pitched battle ensued; and this army of amateurs was all cut to pieces in the desert. Heavens, gentlemen, what a sublime picture! The Roman legions—the wilderness—Jerusalem in the distance—an army of murderers in the foreground!"

The next toast was—"To the further improvement of Tooling, and thanks to the Committee for their services."

Mr. L., on behalf of the Committee who had reported on that subject, returned thanks. He made an interesting extract from the report, by which it appeared how very much stress had been laid formerly on the mode of tooling by the Fathers, both Greek and Latin. In confirmation of this pleasing fact, he made a very striking statement in reference to the earliest work of antediluvian art. Father Mersenne, that learned French Roman Catholic, in page one thousand four hundred and thirty-one of his operose Commentary on Genesis, mentions, on the authority of several rabbis, that the quarrel of Cain with Abel was about a young woman; that, according to various accounts, Cain had tooled with his teeth (*Abelem fuisse* morsibus *dilaceratum a Cain*) ; according to many others, with the jawbone of an ass—which is the tooling adopted by most painters. But it is pleasing to the mind of sensibility to know that, as science expanded, sounder views were adopted. One author contends for a pitchfork, St. Chrysostom for a sword, Irenæus for a scythe, and Prudentius, the Christian poet of the fourth century, for a hedging-bill. This last writer delivers his opinion thus:

> *Frater, probatæ sanctitatis æmulus,*
> *Germana curvo colla frangit sarculo:*

i.e. his brother, jealous of his attested sanctity, fractures his fraternal throat with a curved hedging-bill. "All which is respectfully submitted by your Committee, not so much as decisive of the question (for it is not), but in order to impress upon the youthful mind the importance which has ever been attached to the quality of the tooling by such men as Chrysostom and Irenæus."

"Irenæus be hanged!" said Toad-in-the-hole, who now rose impatiently to give the next toast: "Our Irish friends; wishing them a speedy revolution in their mode of tooling, as well as in everything else connected with the art!

"Gentlemen, I'll tell you the plain truth. Every day of the year when we take up a paper we read the opening of a murder. We say, This is good, this is charming, this is excellent! But, behold you! scarcely have we read a little farther before the word Tipperary or Ballina-something betrays the Irish manufacture. Instantly we loathe it; we call to the waiter; we say, 'Waiter, take away this paper; send it out of the house; it is absolutely a scandal in the nostrils of all just taste.' I appeal to every man whether, on finding a murder (otherwise perhaps promising enough) to be Irish, he does not feel himself as much insulted as when, Madeira being ordered, he finds it to be Cape, or when, taking up what he takes to be a mushroom, it turns out what children call a toad-stool? Tithes, politics, something wrong in principle, vitiate every Irish murder. Gentlemen, this must be reformed, or Ireland will not be a land to live in; at least, if we do live there, we must import all our murders, that's clear." Toad-in-the-hole sat down, growling with suppressed wrath; and the uproarious "Hear, hear!" clamorously expressed the general concurrence.

The next toast was—"The sublime epoch of Burkism and Harism!"

This was drunk with enthusiasm; and one of the members who spoke to the question made a very curious communication to the company: "Gentlemen, we fancy Burkism to be a pure invention of our own times; and in fact no Pancirollus has ever enumerated this branch of art when writing *de rebus deperditis*. Still, I have ascertained that the essential principle of this variety in the art *was* known to the ancients; although, like the art of painting upon glass, of making the myrrhine cups, &c., it was lost in the dark ages for want of encouragement. In the famous collection of Greek epigrams made by Planudes is one upon a very fascinating case of Burkism: it is a perfect little gem of art. The epigram itself I cannot lay my hand upon at this moment; but the following is an abstract of it by Salmasius, as I find it in his notes on Vopiscus: '*Est et elegans epigramma Lucilii, ubi medicus et pollinctor de compacto sic egerunt ut medicus ægros omnes curæ suæ commissos occideret.*' This was the basis of the contract, you see—that on the one part the doctor, for himself and his assigns, doth undertake and contract duly and truly to murder all the patients committed to his charge: but why? There lies the beauty of the case—'*Et ut pollinctori amico suo traderet pollingen-*

dos.' The *pollinctor*, you are aware, was a person whose business it was to dress and prepare dead bodies for burial. The original ground of the transaction appears to have been sentimental: 'He was my friend,' says the murderous doctor—'he was dear to me'—in speaking of the pollinctor. But the law, gentlemen, is stern and harsh: the law will not hear of these tender motives: to sustain a contract of this nature in law, it is essential that a 'consideration' should be given. Now, what *was* the consideration? For thus far all is on the side of the pollinctor: he will be well paid for his services; but meantime the generous, the noble-minded doctor gets nothing. What *was* the equivalent, again I ask, which the law would insist on the doctor's taking, in order to establish that 'consideration' without which the contract had no force? You shall hear: *'Et ut pollinctor vicissim* τελαμῶνας *quos furabatar de pollinctione mortuorum medico mitteret donis ad alliganda vulnera eorum quos curabat'; i.e.* and that reciprocally the pollinctor should transmit to the physician, as free gifts for the binding up of wounds in those whom he treated medically, the belts or trusses (τελαμῶνας) which he had succeeded in purloining in the course of his functions about the corpses.

"Now the case is clear: the whole went on a principle of reciprocity which would have kept up the trade for ever. The doctor was also a surgeon: he could not murder *all* his patients: some of the patients must be retained intact. For these he wanted linen bandages. But, unhappily, the Romans wore woollen; on which account it was that they bathed so often. Meantime, there *was* linen to be had in Rome; but it was monstrously dear; and the τελαμῶνες, or linen swathing bandages, in which superstition obliged them to bind up corpses, would answer capitally for the surgeon. The doctor, therefore, contracts to furnish his friend with a constant succession of corpses—provided, and be it understood always, that his said friend, in return, should supply him with one-half of the articles he would receive from the friends of the parties murdered or to be murdered. The doctor invariably recommended his invaluable friend the pollinctor (whom let us call the undertaker) ; the undertaker, with equal regard to the sacred rights of friendship, uniformly recommended the doctor. Like Pylades and Orestes, they were models of a perfect friendship: in their lives they were lovely; and on the gallows, it is to be hoped, they were not divided.

"Gentlemen, it makes me laugh horribly when I think of those two friends drawing and re-drawing on each other: 'Pollinctor in account with Doctor, debtor by sixteen corpses: creditor by forty-five bandages, two of which damaged.' Their names unfortunately are lost; but I conceive they must have been Quintus Burkius and Publius Harius. By the way, gentlemen, has anybody heard lately of Hare? I understand he is comfortably settled in Ireland, considerably to the west, and does a little business now and then; but, as he observes with a sigh, only as a retailer—nothing like the fine thriving wholesale concern so carelessly blown up at Edinburgh. 'You see what comes of neglecting business'—is the chief moral, the ἐπιμύθιον, as Æsop would say, which Hare draws from his past experience."

At length came the toast of the day—*Thugdom in all its branches*.

The speeches *attempted* at this crisis of the dinner were past all counting. But the applause was so furious, the music so stormy, and the crashing of glasses so incessant, from the general resolution never again to drink an inferior toast from the same glass, that I am unequal to the task of reporting. Besides which,

Toad-in-the-hole now became ungovernable. He kept firing pistols in every direction; sent his servant for a blunderbuss, and talked of loading with ball-cartridge. We conceived that his former madness had returned at the mention of Burke and Hare; or that, being again weary of life, he had resolved to go off in a general massacre. This we could not think of allowing; it became indispensable, therefore, to kick him out; which we did with universal consent, the whole company lending their toes *uno pede*, as I may say, though pitying his grey hairs and his angelic smile. During the operation the orchestra poured in their old chorus. The universal company sang, and (what surprised us most of all) Toad-in-the-hole joined us furiously in singing—

Et interrogatum est ab omnibus—Ubi est ille Toad-in-the Hole?
Et responsum est ab omnibus—Non est inventus.

POSTSCRIPT

(First published in the *Collective Edition*, Vol. IV, 1854)

AN ACCOUNT OF THE WILLIAMS AND M'KEAN MURDERS

NEVER, throughout the annals of universal Christendom, has there indeed been any act of one solitary insulated individual armed with power so appalling over the hearts of men as that exterminating murder by which, during the winter of 1811–12, John Williams, in one hour, smote two houses with emptiness, exterminated all but two entire households, and asserted his own supremacy above all the children of Cain. It would be absolutely impossible adequately to describe the frenzy of feelings which, throughout the next fortnight, mastered the popular heart—the mere delirium of indignant horror in some, the mere delirum of panic in others. For twelve succeeding days, under some groundless notion that the unknown murderer had quitted London, the panic which had convulsed the mighty metropolis diffused itself all over the island. I was myself at that time nearly three hundred miles from London; but there, and everywhere, the panic was indescribable. One lady, my next neighbour, whom personally I knew, living at the moment, during the absence of her husband, with a few servants in a very solitary house, never rested until she had placed eighteen doors (so she told me, and, indeed, satisfied me by ocular proof), each secured by ponderous bolts, and bars, and chains, between her own bedroom and any intruder of human build. To reach her, even in her drawing-room, was like going as a flag of truce into a beleaguered fortress; at every sixth step one was stopped by a sort of portcullis. The panic was not confined to the rich; women in the humblest ranks more than once died upon the spot from the shock attending some suspicious attempts at intrusion upon the part of vagrants meditating probably nothing worse than a robbery, but whom the poor women, misled by the London newspapers, had fancied to be the dreadful London murderer. Meantime this solitary artist, that rested in the centre of London, self-supported by his own conscious grandeur, as a domestic Attila, or "Scourge of God"—this man that walked in darkness, and relied upon murder (as afterwards transpired) for bread, for clothes, for promotion in life—was silently preparing an effectual answer to the public journals; and on the twelfth day after his inaugural murder he advertised his presence in London, and published to all men the absurdity of ascribing to *him* any ruralizing propensities, by striking a second blow and accomplishing a second family extermination. Somewhat lightened was the *provincial* panic by this proof that the murderer had not condescended to sneak into the country, or to abandon for a moment, under any motive of caution or fear, the great metropolitan *castra stativa* of gigantic crime seated for ever on the Thames. In fact, the great artist disdained a provincial reputation; and he must have felt, as a case of ludicrous disproportion, the contrast between a country town or village, on the one hand, and, on the other, a work more lasting than brass—a κτημα ἐς αει—a murder such in quality as any murder that *he* would condescend to own for a work turned out from his own *studio*.

Coleridge, whom I saw some months after these terrific murders, told me that, for *his* part, though at the time resident in London, he had not shared in the prevailing panic; *him* they affected only as a philosopher, and threw him into a profound reverie upon the tremendous power which is laid open in a moment to any man who can reconcile himself to the abjuration of all conscientious restraints, if at the same time thoroughly without fear. Not sharing in the public panic, however, Coleridge did not consider that panic at all unreasonable; for, as he said most truly, in that vast metropolis there are many thousands of households composed exclusively of women and children; many other thousands there are who necessarily confide their safety, in the long evenings, to the discretion of a young servant girl; and, if she suffers herself to be beguiled by the pretence of a message from her mother, sister, or sweetheart, into opening the door, there, in one second of time, goes to wreck the security of the house. However, at that time, and for many months afterwards, the practice of steadily putting the chain upon the door before it was opened prevailed generally, and for a long time served as a record of that deep impression left upon London by Mr. Williams. Southey, I may add, entered deeply into the public feeling on this occasion, and said to me, within a week or two of the first murder, that it was a private event of that order which rose to the dignity of a national event.

Yet, first of all, one word as to the local scene of the murders. Ratcliffe Highway is a public thoroughfare in a most chaotic quarter of eastern or nautical London; and at this time (viz. in 1812), when no adequate police existed except the *detective* police of Bow Street —admirable for its own peculiar purposes, but utterly incommensurate to the general service of the capital —it was a most dangerous quarter. Every third man at the least might be set down as a foreigner. Lascars, Chinese, Moors, Negroes, were met at every step. And, apart from the manifold ruffianism shrouded impenetrably under the mixed hats and turbans of men whose past was untraceable to any European eye, it is well known that the navy (especially, in time of war, the commercial navy) of Christendom is the sure receptacle of all the murderers and ruffians whose crimes have given them a motive for withdrawing themselves for a season from the public eye. It is true that few of this class are qualified to act as "able" seamen; but at all times, and especially during war, only a small proportion (or *nucleus*) of each ship's company consists of such men—the large majority being mere untutored landsmen. John Williams, however, who had been occasionally rated as a seaman on board of various Indiamen, &c., was probably a very accomplished seaman. Pretty generally, in fact, he was a ready and adroit man, fertile in resources under all sudden difficulties, and most flexibly adapting himself to all varieties of social life. Williams was a man of middle stature (five feet seven and a half to five feet eight inches high), slenderly built, rather thin, but wiry,

tolerably muscular, and clear of all superfluous flesh.
A lady who saw him under examination (I think at
the Thames Police Office) assured me that his hair was
of the most extraordinary and vivid colour—viz. bright
yellow, something between an orange and a lemon
colour. Williams had been in India; chiefly in Bengal
and Madras, but he had also been upon the Indus. Now,
it is notorious that in the Punjab horses of a high
caste are often painted—crimson, blue, green, purple;
and it struck me that Williams might, for some casual
purpose of disguise, have taken a hint from this practice of Sind and Lahore, so that the colour might not
have been natural. In other respects his appearance
was natural enough, and—judging by a plaster cast
of him which I purchased in London—I should say
mean as regarded his facial structure. One fact, however, was striking, and fell in with the impression of
his natural tiger character—that his face wore at all
times a bloodless ghastly pallor. "You might imagine,"
said my informant, "that in his veins circulated not
red life-blood, such as could kindle into the blush of
shame, of wrath, of pity—but a green sap that welled
from no human heart." His eyes seemed frozen and
glazed, as if their light were all converged upon some
victim lurking in the far background. So far his appearance might have repelled; but, on the other hand,
the concurrent testimony of many witnesses, and also
the silent testimony of facts, showed that the oiliness
and snaky insinuation of his demeanour counteracted
the repulsiveness of his ghastly face, and amongst inexperienced young women won for him a very favourable reception. In particular, one gentle-mannered
girl, whom Williams had undoubtedly designed to
murder, gave in evidence that once, when sitting alone
with her, he had said, "Now, Miss R., supposing that
I should appear about midnight at your bedside armed

with a carving knife, what would you say?" To which the confiding girl had replied, "Oh, Mr. Williams, if it was anybody else, I should be frightened. But, as soon as I heard *your* voice, I should be tranquil." Poor girl! had this outline sketch of Mr. Williams been filled in and realized, she would have seen something in the corpselike face, and heard something in the sinister voice, that would have unsettled her tranquillity for ever. But nothing short of such dreadful experiences could avail to unmask Mr. John Williams.

Into this perilous region it was that, on a Saturday night in December, Mr. Williams, whom we must suppose to have long since made his *coup d'essai*, forced his way through the crowded streets, bound on business. To say was to do. And this night he had said to himself secretly that he would execute a design which he had already sketched, and which, when finished, was destined on the following day to strike consternation into "all that mighty heart" of London, from centre to circumference. It was afterwards remembered that he had quitted his lodgings on this dark errand about eleven o'clock P.M.: not that he meant to begin so soon; but he needed to reconnoitre. He carried his tools closely buttoned up under his loose roomy coat. It was in harmony with the general subtlety of his character, and his polished hatred of brutality, that by universal agreement his manners were distinguished for exquisite suavity; the tiger's heart was masked by the most insinuating and snaky refinement. All his acquaintances afterwards described his dissimulation as so ready and so perfect that, if, in making his way through the streets, always so crowded on Saturday night in neighbourhoods so poor, he had accidentally jostled any person, he would (as they were all satisfied) have stopped to offer the most gentlemanly apologies: with his devilish heart brooding over the most hellish of purposes, he would yet have paused to express a benign hope that the huge mallet buttoned up under his elegant surtout, with a view to the little business that awaited him about ninety minutes further on, had not inflicted any pain on the stranger with whom he had come into collision. Titian, I believe, but certainly Rubens, and perhaps Vandyke, made it a rule never to practise their art but in full dress— point-ruffles, bag-wig, and diamond-hilted sword; and Mr. Williams, there is reason to believe, when he went out for a grand compound massacre (in another sense, one might have applied to it the Oxford phrase of *going out as Grand Compounder*), always assumed black silk stockings and pumps; nor would he on any account have degraded his position as an artist by wearing a morning gown. In his second great performance, it was particularly noticed and recorded, by the one sole trembling man who under killing agonies of fear was compelled (as the reader will find) from a secret stand to become the solitary spectator of his atrocities, that Mr. Williams wore a long blue frock, of the very finest cloth, and richly lined with silk. Amongst the anecdotes which circulated about him, it was also said at the time that Mr. Williams employed the first of dentists and also the first of chiropodists. On no account would he patronize any second-rate skill. And, beyond a doubt, in that perilous little branch of business which was practised by himself he might be regarded as the most aristocratic and fastidious of artists.

But who meantime was the victim to whose abode he was hurrying? For surely he never could be so indiscreet as to be sailing about on a roving cruise in search of some chance person to murder? Oh no; he had suited himself with a victim some time before, viz. an old and very intimate friend. For he seems to have laid it down as a maxim that the best person to murder was

a friend, and, in default of a friend, which is an article one cannot always command, an acquaintance: because, in either case, on first approaching his subject,
suspicion would be disarmed, whereas a stranger might
take alarm, and find in the very countenance of his
murderer elect a warning summons to place himself on
guard. However, in the present case, his destined victim was supposed to unite both characters: originally
he had been a friend; but subsequently, on good cause
arising, he had become an enemy. Or more probably,
as others said, the feelings had long since languished
which gave life to either relation of friendship or of
enmity. Marr was the name of that unhappy man who
(whether in the character of friend or enemy) had
been selected for the subject of this present Saturday
night's performance. And the story current at that
time about the connexion between Williams and Marr
—having (whether true or not true) never been con-
tradicted upon authority—was that they sailed in the
same Indiaman to Calcutta, and that they had quarrelled when at sea. But another version of the story
said—No: they had quarrelled after returning from
sea; and the subject of their quarrel was Mrs. Marr,
a very pretty young woman, for whose favour they
had been rival candidates, and at one time with most
bitter enmity towards each other. Some circumstances
give a colour of probability to this story. Otherwise it
has sometimes happened, on occasion of a murder not
sufficiently accounted for, that, from pure goodness of
heart intolerant of a mere sordid motive for a striking
murder, some person has forged, and the public has
accredited, a story representing the murderer as having moved under some loftier excitement: and in this
case the public, too much shocked at the idea of Williams having on the single motive of gain consummated so complex a tragedy, welcomed the tale which

represented him as governed by deadly malice, growing out of the more impassioned and noble rivalry for
the favour of a woman. The case remains in some degree doubtful; but, certainly, the probability is that
Mrs. Marr had been the true cause, the *causa teterrima*, of the feud between the men. Meantime the minutes are numbered, the sands of the hour-glass are running out, that measure the duration of this feud upon
earth. This night it shall cease. Tomorrow is the day
which in England they call Sunday, which in Scotland they call by the Judaic name of "Sabbath." To
both nations, under different names, the day has the
same functions; to both it is a day of rest. For thee
also, Marr, it shall be a day of rest; so is it written;
thou, too, young Marr, shalt find rest—thou, and thy
household, and the stranger that is within thy gates.
But that rest must be in the world which lies beyond
the grave. On this side the grave ye have all slept your
final sleep.

The night was one of exceeding darkness; and in
this humble quarter of London, whatever the night
happened to be, light or dark, quiet or stormy, all shops
were kept open on Saturday nights until twelve o'clock
at the least, and many for half an hour longer. There
was no rigorous and pedantic Jewish superstition about
the exact limits of Sunday. At the very worst, the Sunday stretched over from one o'clock A.M. of one day
up to eight o'clock A.M. of the next, making a clear
circuit of thirty-one hours. This, surely, was long
enough. Marr, on this particular Saturday night,
would be content if it were even shorter, provided it
would come more quickly; for he has been toiling
through sixteen hours behind his counter. Marr's position in life was this—He kept a little hosier's shop,
and had invested in his stock and the fittings of his shop

about £180. Like all men engaged in trade, he suffered some anxieties. He was a new beginner; but already bad debts had alarmed him, and bills were coming to maturity that were not likely to be met by commensurate sales. Yet, constitutionally, he was a sanguine hoper. At this time he was a stout, fresh-coloured young man of twenty-seven; in some slight degree uneasy from his commercial prospects; but still cheerful, and anticipating— (how vainly!) —that for this night, and the next night, at least, he will rest his wearied head and his cares upon the faithful bosom of his sweet, lovely young wife. The household of Marr, consisting of five persons, is as follows: First, there is himself, who, if he should happen to be ruined in a limited commercial sense, has energy enough to jump up again, like a pyramid of fire, and soar high above ruin many times repeated. Yes, poor Marr, so it might be if thou wert left to thy native energies unmolested; but even now there stands on the other side of the street one born of hell who puts his peremptory negative on all these flattering prospects. Second in the list of this household stands his pretty and amiable wife; who is happy after the fashion of youthful wives, for she is only twenty-two, and anxious (if at all) only on account of her darling infant. For, thirdly, there is in a cradle, not quite nine feet below the street, viz. in a warm, cosy kitchen, and rocked at intervals by the young mother, a baby eight months old. Nineteen months have Marr and herself been married; and this is their first-born child. Grieve not for this child, that it must keep the deep rest of Sunday in some other world; for wherefore should an orphan, steeped to the lips in poverty when once bereaved of father and mother, linger upon an alien and a murderous earth? Fourthly, there is a stoutish boy, an apprentice, say thirteen years old, a Devonshire boy, with handsome features, such as most Devonshire youths have [1]; satisfied with his place; not overworked; treated kindly, and aware that he was treated kindly, by his master and mistress. Fifthly, and lastly, bringing up the rear of this quiet household, is a servant girl, a grown-up young woman; and she, being particularly kind-hearted, occupied (as often happens in families of humble pretensions as to rank) a sort of sisterly place in her relation to her mistress. Mary, the female servant, felt a sincere and unaffected respect for a mistress whom she saw so steadily occupied with her domestic duties, and who, though so young, and invested with some slight authority, never exerted it capriciously, or even showed it at all conspicuously. According to the testimony of all the neighbours, she treated her mistress with a shade of unobtrusive respect on the one hand, and yet was eager to relieve her, whenever that was possible, from the weight of her maternal duties, with the cheerful voluntary service of a sister.

To this young woman it was that, suddenly, within three or four minutes of midnight, Marr called aloud from the head of the stairs—directing her to go out and purchase some oysters for the family supper. Upon what slender accidents hang oftentimes solemn lifelong results! Marr, occupied in the concerns of his shop, Mrs. Marr, occupied with some little ailment and restlessness of her baby, had both forgotten the affair of supper; the time was now narrowing every moment as regarded any variety of choice; and oysters were perhaps ordered as the likeliest article to be had at all after

[1] An artist told me in this year, 1812, that, having accidentally seen a native Devonshire regiment (either volunteers or militia), nine hundred strong, marching past a station at which he had posted himself, he did not observe a dozen men that would not have been described in common parlance as "good-looking."

twelve o'clock should have struck. And yet upon this trivial circumstance depended Mary's life. Had she been sent abroad for supper at the ordinary time of ten or eleven o'clock, it is almost certain that she, the solitary member of the household who escaped from the exterminating tragedy, would *not* have escaped; too surely she would have shared the general fate. It had now become necessary to be quick. Hastily, therefore, receiving money from Marr, with a basket in her hand, but unbonneted, Mary tripped out of the shop. It became afterwards, on recollection, a heart-chilling remembrance to herself that, precisely as she emerged from the shop-door, she noticed, on the opposite side of the street, by the light of the lamps, a man's figure; stationary at the instant, but in the next instant slowly moving. This was Williams, as a little incident, either just before or just after (at present it is impossible to say which), sufficiently proved. Now, when one considers the inevitable hurry and trepidation of Mary under the circumstances stated, time barely sufficing for any chance of executing her errand, it becomes evident that she must have connected some deep feeling of mysterious uneasiness with the movements of this unknown man; else, assuredly, she would not have found her attention disposable for such a case. Thus far she herself threw some little light upon what it might be that, semi-consciously, was then passing through her mind: she said that, notwithstanding the darkness, which would not permit her to trace the man's features, or to ascertain the exact direction of his eyes, it yet struck her that, from his carriage when in motion, and from the apparent inclination of his person, he must be looking at No. 29. The little incident which I have alluded to as confirming Mary's belief was that, at some period not very far from midnight, the watchman had specially noticed this

stranger; he had observed him continually peeping into
the window of Marr's shop, and had thought this act,
connected with the man's appearance, so suspicious
that he stepped into Marr's shop and communicated
what he had seen. This fact he afterwards stated before
the magistrates; and he added that subsequently, viz.
a few minutes after twelve (eight or ten minutes, probably, after the departure of Mary), he (the watchman), when re-entering upon his ordinary half-hourly
beat, was requested by Marr to assist him in closing the
shutters. Here they had a final communication with
each other; and the watchman mentioned to Marr that
the mysterious stranger had now apparently taken
himself off; for that he had not been visible since the
first communication made to Marr by the watchman.
There is little doubt that Williams had observed the
watchman's visit to Marr, and had thus had his attention seasonably drawn to the indiscretion of his own
demeanour; so that the warning, given unavailingly
to Marr, had been turned to account by Williams.
There can be still less doubt that the bloodhound had
commenced his work within one minute of the watchman's assisting Marr to put up his shutters; and on
the following consideration: That which prevented
Williams from commencing even earlier was the exposure of the shop's whole interior to the gaze of street
passengers. It was indispensable that the shutters
should be accurately closed before Williams could
safely get to work. But, as soon as ever this preliminary
precaution had been completed, once having secured
that concealment from the public eye, it then became
of still greater importance not to lose a moment by
delay than previously it had been not to hazard anything by precipitance. For all depended upon going in
before Marr should have locked the door. On any other
mode of effecting an entrance (as, for instance, by

waiting for the return of Mary, and making his entrance simultaneously with her) it will be seen that Williams must have forfeited that particular advantage which mute facts, when read into their true construction, will soon show the reader that he must have employed. Williams waited, of necessity, for the sound of the watchman's retreating steps; waited, perhaps, for thirty seconds; but, when that danger was past, the next danger was lest Marr should lock the door: one turn of the key, and the murderer would have been locked out. In, therefore, he bolted, and by a dexterous movement of his left hand, no doubt, turned the key, without letting Marr perceive this fatal stratagem. It is really wonderful and most interesting to pursue the successive steps of this monster, and to notice the absolute certainty with which the silent hieroglyphics of the case betray to us the whole process and movements of the bloody drama, not less surely and fully than if we had been ourselves hidden in Marr's shop, or had looked down from the heavens of mercy upon this hell-kite that knew not what mercy meant. That he had concealed from Marr his trick, secret and rapid, upon the lock, is evident; because else Marr would instantly have taken the alarm, especially after what the watchman had communicated. But it will soon be seen that Marr had *not* been alarmed. In reality, towards the full success of Williams it was important, in the last degree, to intercept and forestall any yell or shout of agony from Marr. Such an outcry, and in a situation so slenderly fenced off from the street, viz. by walls the very thinnest, makes itself heard outside pretty nearly as well as if it were uttered in the street. Such an outcry it was indispensable to stifle. It *was* stifled; and the reader will soon understand *how*. Meantime, at this point, let us leave the murderer alone with his victims. For fifty minutes let him work his pleasure.

The front-door, as we know, is now fastened against all help. Help there is none. Let us, therefore, in vision, attach ourselves to Mary; and, when all is over, let us come back with *her*, again raise the curtain, and read the dreadful record of all that has passed in her absence.

The poor girl, uneasy in her mind to an extent that she could but half understand, roamed up and down in search of an oyster shop; and, finding none that was still open within any circuit that her ordinary experience had made her acquainted with, she fancied it best to try the chances of some remoter district. Lights she saw gleaming or twinkling at a distance, that still tempted her onwards; and thus, amongst unknown streets poorly lighted,[1] and on a night of peculiar darkness, and in a region of London where ferocious tumults were continually turning her out of what seemed to be the direct course, naturally she got bewildered. The purpose with which she started had by this time become hopeless. Nothing remained for her now but to retrace her steps. But this was difficult; for she was afraid to ask directions from chance passengers whose appearance the darkness prevented her from reconnoitring. At length by his lantern she recognized a watchman; through him she was guided into the right road; and in ten minutes more she found herself back at the door of No. 29, in Ratcliffe Highway. But by this time she felt satisfied that she must have been absent for fifty or sixty minutes; indeed, she had heard, at a distance, the cry of *past one o'clock*, which, com-

---

[1] I do not remember, chronologically, the history of gas-lights. But in London, long after Mr. Winsor [a German] had shown the value of gas-lighting, and its applicability to street purposes, various districts were prevented, for many years, from resorting to the new system, in consequence of old contracts with oil-dealers, subsisting through long terms of years.

mencing a few seconds after one, lasted intermittingly
for ten or thirteen minutes.

In the tumult of agonizing thoughts that very soon
surprised her, naturally it became hard for her to recall distinctly the whole succession of doubts, and jealousies, and shadowy misgivings that soon opened upon
her. But, so far as could be collected, she had not in the
first moment of reaching home noticed anything decisively alarming. In very many cities bells are the main
instruments for communicating between the street
and the interior of houses; but in London knockers
prevail. At Marr's there was both a knocker and a bell.
Mary rang, and at the same time very gently knocked.
She had no fear of disturbing her master or mistress;
them she made sure of finding still up. Her anxiety
was for the baby, who, being disturbed, might again
rob her mistress of a night's rest. And she well knew
that, with three people all anxiously awaiting her return, and by this time, perhaps, seriously uneasy at her
delay, the least audible whisper from herself would in
a moment bring one of them to the door. Yet how is
this? To her astonishment—but with the astonishment came creeping over her an icy horror—no stir
nor murmur was heard ascending from the kitchen.
At this moment came back upon her, with shuddering
anguish, the indistinct image of the stranger in the
loose dark coat whom she had seen stealing along under
the shadowy lamp-light, and too certainly watching
her master's motions: keenly she now reproached herself that, under whatever stress of hurry, she had not
acquainted Mr. Marr with the suspicious appearances.
Poor girl! she did not then know that, if this communication could have availed to put Marr upon his guard,
it had reached him from another quarter; so that her
own omission, which had in reality arisen under her
hurry to execute her master's commission, could not

be charged with any bad consequences. But all such reflections this way or that were swallowed up at this point in overmastering panic. That her double summons *could* have been unnoticed—this solitary fact in one moment made a revelation of horror. One person might have fallen asleep, but two—but three—*that* was a mere impossibility. And, even supposing all three together with the baby locked in sleep, still how unaccountable was this utter—utter silence! Most naturally at this moment something like hysterical horror overshadowed the poor girl, and now at last she rang the bell with the violence that belongs to sickening terror. This done, she paused: self-command enough she still retained, though fast and fast it was slipping away from her, to bethink herself that, if any overwhelming accident *had* compelled both Marr and his apprentice-boy to leave the house in order to summon surgical aid from opposite quarters—a thing barely supposable—still, even in that case Mrs. Marr and her infant would be left, and some murmuring reply, under any extremity, would be elicited from the poor mother. To pause, therefore, to impose stern silence upon herself, so as to leave room for the possible answer to this final appeal, became a duty of spasmodic effort. Listen, therefore, poor trembling heart; listen, and for twenty seconds be still as death! Still as death she was; and during that dreadful stillness, when she hushed her breath that she might listen, occurred an incident of killing fear, that to her dying day would never cease to renew its echoes in her ear. She, Mary, the poor trembling girl, checking and overruling herself by a final effort, that she might leave full opening for her dear young mistress's answer to her own last frantic appeal, heard at last and most distinctly a sound within the house. Yes, now beyond a doubt there is coming an answer to her summons. What was it?

On the stairs—not the stairs that led downwards to the kitchen, but the stairs that led upwards to the single storey of bedchambers above—was heard a creaking sound. Next was heard most distinctly a footfall: one, two, three, four, five stairs were slowly and distinctly descended. Then the dreadful footsteps were heard advancing along the little narrow passage to the door. The steps—oh heavens! *whose* steps?—have paused at the door. The very breathing can be heard of that dreadful being who has silenced all breathing except his own in the house. There is but a door between him and Mary. What is he doing on the other side of the door? A cautious step, a stealthy step it was that came down the stairs, then paced along the little narrow passage—narrow as a coffin—till at last the step pauses at the door. How hard the fellow breathes! He, the solitary murderer, is on one side the door; Mary is on the other side. Now, suppose that he should suddenly open the door, and that incautiously in the dark Mary should rush in, and find herself in the arms of the murderer. Thus far the case is a possible one—that to a certainty, had this little trick been tried immediately upon Mary's return, it would have succeeded; had the door been opened suddenly upon her first tingle-tingle, headlong she would have tumbled in, and perished. But now Mary is upon her guard. The unknown murderer and she have both their lips upon the door, listening, breathing hard; but luckily they are on different sides of the door; and upon the least indication of unlocking or unlatching she would have recoiled into the asylum of general darkness.

What was the murderer's meaning in coming along the passage to the front-door? The meaning was this: Separately, as an individual, Mary was worth nothing at all to him. But, considered as a member of a household, she had this value, viz. that she, if caught and murdered, perfected and rounded the desolation of the house. The case being reported, as reported it would be all over Christendom, led the imagination captive. The whole covey of victims was thus netted; the household ruin was thus full and orbicular; and in that proportion the tendency of men and women, flutter as they might, would be helplessly and hopelessly to sink into the all-conquering hands of the mighty murdered. He had but to say "My testimonials are dated from No. 29 Ratcliffe Highway," and the poor vanquished imagination sank powerless before the fascinating rattlesnake eye of the murderer. There is not a doubt that the motive of the murderer for standing on the inner side of Marr's front-door whilst Mary stood on the outside was a hope that, if he quietly opened the door, whisperingly counterfeiting Marr's voice, and saying, What made you stay so long? possibly she might have been inveigled. He was wrong; the time was past for that; Mary was now maniacally awake; she began now to ring the bell and to ply the knocker with unintermitting violence. And the natural consequence was that the next-door neighbour, who had recently gone to bed and instantly fallen asleep, was roused; and by the incessant violence of the ringing and the knocking, which now obeyed a delirious and uncontrollable impulse in Mary, he became sensible that some very dreadful event must be at the root of so clamorous an uproar. To rise, to throw up the sash, to demand angrily the cause of this unseasonable tumult, was the work of a moment. The poor girl remained sufficiently mistress of herself rapidly to explain the circumstance of her own absence for an hour, her belief that Mr. and Mrs. Marr's family had all been murdered in the interval, and that at this very moment the murderer was in the house.

The person to whom she addressed this statement

was a pawnbroker; and a thoroughly brave man he
must have been; for it was a perilous undertaking,
merely as a trial of physical strength, singly to face a
mysterious assassin, who had apparently signalized his
prowess by a triumph so comprehensive. But, again,
for the imagination it required an effort of self-conquest to rush headlong into the presence of one invested with a cloud of mystery, whose nation, age,
motives, were all alike unknown. Rarely on any field
of battle has a soldier been called upon to face so complex a danger. For, if the entire family of his neighbour Marr had been exterminated—were this indeed
true—such a scale of bloodshed would seem to argue
that there must have been two persons as the perpetrators; or, if one singly had accomplished such a ruin, in
that case how colossal must have been his audacity!
probably, also, his skill and animal power! Moreover,
the unknown enemy (whether single or double)
would, doubtless, be elaborately armed. Yet, under all
these disadvantages, did this fearless man rush at once
to the field of butchery in his neighbour's house. Waiting only to draw on his trousers, and to arm himself
with the kitchen poker, he went down into his own little back-yard. On this mode of approach, he would have
a chance of intercepting the murderer; whereas from
the front there would be no such chance, and there
would also be considerable delay in the process of
breaking open the door. A brick wall, 9 or 10 feet high,
divided his own back premises from those of Marr.
Over this he vaulted; and, at the moment when he was
recalling himself to the necessity of going back for a
candle, he suddenly perceived a feeble ray of light already glimmering on some part of Marr's premises.
Marr's back-door stood wide open. Probably the murderer had passed through it one half-minute before.
Rapidly the brave man passed onwards to the shop, and

there beheld the carnage of the night stretched out on
the floor, and the narrow premises so floated with gore
that it was hardly possible to escape the pollution of
blood in picking out a path to the front-door. In the
lock of the door still remained the key which had given
to the unknown murderer so fatal an advantage over
his victims. By this time the heart-shaking news involved in the outcries of Mary (to whom it occurred
that by possibility some one out of so many victims
might still be within the reach of medical aid, but that
all would depend upon speed) had availed, even at that
late hour, to gather a small mob about the house. The
pawnbroker threw open the door. One or two watchmen headed the crowd; but the soul-harrowing spectacle checked them, and impressed sudden silence upon
their voices, previously so loud. The tragic drama read
aloud its own history, and the succession of its several
steps—few and summary. The murderer was as yet
altogether unknown; not even suspected. But there
were reasons for thinking that he must have been a
person familiarly known to Marr. He had entered the
shop by opening the door after it had been closed by
Marr. But it was justly argued that, after the caution
conveyed to Marr by the watchman, the appearance
of any stranger in the shop at that hour, and in so dangerous a neighbourhood, and entering by so irregular
and suspicious a course (*i.e.* walking in after the door
had been closed, and after the closing of the shutters
had cut off all open communication with the street),
would naturally have roused Marr to an attitude of
vigilance and self-defence. Any indication, therefore,
that Marr had *not* been so roused would argue to a
certainty that *something* had occurred to neutralize
this alarm, and fatally to disarm the prudent jealousies
of Marr. But this "something" could only have lain in
one simple fact, viz. that the person of the murderer

was familiarly known to Marr as that of an ordinary and unsuspected acquaintance.

This being presupposed as the key to all the rest, the whole course and evolution of the subsequent drama becomes clear as daylight: The murderer, it is evident, had opened gently, and again closed behind him with equal gentleness, the street-door. He had then advanced to the little counter, all the while exchanging the ordinary salutation of an old acquaintance with the unsuspecting Marr. Having reached the counter, he would then ask Marr for a pair of unbleached cotton socks. In a shop so small as Marr's there could be no great latitude of choice for disposing of the different commodities. The arrangement of these had no doubt become familiar to the murderer; and he had already ascertained that, in order to reach down the particular parcel wanted at present, Marr would find it requisite to face round to the rear, and at the same moment to raise his eyes and his hands to a level eighteen inches above his own head. This movement placed him in the most disadvantageous possible position with regard to the murderer; who now, at the instant when Marr's hands and eyes were embarrassed, and the back of his head fully exposed, suddenly from below his large surtout had unslung a heavy ship-carpenter's mallet, and with one solitary blow had so thoroughly stunned his victim as to leave him incapable of resistance. The whole position of Marr told its own tale. He had collapsed naturally behind the counter, with his hands so occupied as to confirm the whole outline of the affair as I have here suggested it. Probable enough it is that the very first blow, the first indication of treachery that reached Marr, would also be the last blow as regarded the abolition of consciousness. The murderer's plan and *rationale* of murder started systematically from this infliction of apoplexy, or at least of a stunning sufficient to insure a long loss of consciousness. This opening step placed the murderer at his ease. But still, as returning sense might constantly have led to the fullest exposures, it was his settled practice, by way of consummation, to cut the throat. To one invariable type all the murders on this occasion conformed: the skull was first shattered; this step secured the murderer from instant retaliation; and then, by way of locking up all into eternal silence, uniformly the throat was cut. The rest of the circumstances, as self-revealed, were these: The fall of Marr might, probably enough, cause a dull confused sound of a scuffle, and the more so as it could not now be confounded with any street uproar—the shop-door being shut. It is more probable, however, that the signal for the alarm passing down to the kitchen would arise when the murderer proceeded to cut Marr's throat. The very confined situation behind the counter would render it impossible, under the critical hurry of the case, to expose the throat broadly; the horrid scene would proceed by partial and interrupted cuts; deep groans would arise; and then would come the rush upstairs. Against this, as the only dangerous stage in the transaction, the murderer would have specially prepared. Mrs. Marr and the apprentice-boy, both young and active, would make, of course, for the street-door; had Mary been at home, and three persons at once had combined to distract the purposes of the murderer, it is barely possible that one of them would have succeeded in reaching the street. But the dreadful swing of the heavy mallet intercepted both the boy and his mistress before they could reach the door. Each of them lay stretched out on the centre of the shop floor; and the very moment that this disabling was accomplished the accursed hound was down upon their throats with his razor. The fact is that, in the mere blindness of pity for poor Marr on hearing his groans, Mrs. Marr had lost sight of her obvious policy: she and the boy ought to have made for the back-door; the alarm would thus have been given in the open air; which, of itself, was a great point; and several means of distracting the murderer's attention offered upon that course which the extreme limitation of the shop denied to them upon the other.

Vain would be all attempts to convey the horror which thrilled the gathering spectators of this piteous tragedy. It was known to the crowd that one person had, by some accident, escaped the general massacre; but she was now speechless, and probably delirious; so that, in compassion for her pitiable situation, one female neighbour had carried her away, and put her to bed. Hence it had happened, for a longer space of time than could else have been possible, that no person present was sufficiently acquainted with the Marrs to be aware of the little infant; for the bold pawnbroker had gone off to make a communication to the coroner, and another neighbour to lodge some evidence which he thought urgent at a neighbouring police-office. Suddenly some person appeared amongst the crowd who was aware that the murdered parents had a young infant; this would be found either below-stairs, or in one of the bedrooms above. Immediately a stream of people poured down into the kitchen, where at once they saw the cradle—but with the bedclothes in a state of indescribable confusion. On disentangling these, pools of blood became visible; and the next ominous sign was that the hood of the cradle had been smashed to pieces. It became evident that the wretch had found himself doubly embarrassed—first, by the arched hood at the head of the cradle, which accordingly he had beat into a ruin with his mallet, and, secondly, by the gathering of the blankets and pillows about the baby's

head. The free play of his blows had thus been baffled.
And he had therefore finished the scene by applying
his razor to the throat of the little innocent; after
which, with no apparent purpose, as though he had
become confused by the spectacle of his own atrocities,
he had busied himself in piling the clothes elaborately
over the child's corpse. This incident undeniably gave
the character of a vindictive proceeding to the whole
affair, and so far confirmed the current rumour that
the quarrel between Williams and Marr had originated in rivalship. One writer, indeed, alleged that the
murderer might have found it necessary for his own
safety to extinguish the crying of the child; but it was
justly replied that a child only eight months old could
not have cried under any sense of the tragedy proceeding, but simply in its ordinary way for the absence of
its mother; and such a cry, even if audible at all out of
the house, must have been precisely what the neighbours were hearing constantly, so that it could have
drawn no special attention, nor suggested any reasonable alarm to the murderer. No one incident, indeed,
throughout the whole tissue of atrocities, so much en-
venomed the popular fury against the unknown ruffian as this useless butchery of the infant.

Naturally, on the Sunday morning that dawned
four or five hours later, the case was too full of horror
not to diffuse itself in all directions; but I have no reason to think that it crept into any one of the numerous
Sunday papers. In the regular course, any ordinary occurrence, not occurring or not transpiring until 15
minutes after 1 A.M. on a Sunday morning, would first
reach the public ear through the Monday editions of
the Sunday papers, and the regular morning papers of
the Monday. But, if such were the course pursued on
this occasion, never can there have been a more signal
oversight. For it is certain that to have met the public

demand for details on the Sunday, which might so easily have been done by cancelling a couple of dull columns, and substituting a circumstantial narrative, for which the pawnbroker and the watchman could have furnished the materials, would have made a small fortune. By proper handbills dispersed through all quarters of the infinite metropolis, 250,000 extra copies might have been sold—that is, by any journal that should have collected *exclusive* materials, meeting the public excitement, everywhere stirred to the centre by flying rumours, and everywhere burning for ampler information. On the Sunday se'ennight (Sunday the *octave* from the event) took place the funeral of the Marrs: in the first coffin was placed Marr; in the second Mrs. Marr, and the baby in her arms; in the third the apprentice-boy. They were buried side by side; and 30,000 labouring people followed the funeral procession, with horror and grief written in their countenances.

As yet no whisper was astir that indicated, even conjecturally, the hideous author of those ruins—this patron of gravediggers. Had as much been known on this Sunday of the funeral concerning that person as became known universally six days later, the people would have gone right from the churchyard to the murderer's lodgings, and (brooking no delay) would have torn him limb from limb. As yet, however, in mere default of any object on whom reasonable suspicion could settle, the public wrath was compelled to suspend itself. Else, far indeed from showing any tendency to subside, the public emotion strengthened every day conspicuously, as the reverberation of the shock began to travel back from the provinces to the capital. On every great road in the kingdom continual arrests were made of vagrants and "trampers" who could give no satisfactory account of themselves, or whose appearance in any respect answered to the imperfect description of Williams furnished by the watchman.

With this mighty tide of pity and indignation pointing backwards to the dreadful past there mingled also in the thoughts of reflecting persons an under-current of fearful expectation for the immediate future. "The earthquake," to quote a fragment from a striking passage in Wordsworth—

The earthquake is not satisfied at once.

All perils, specially malignant, are recurrent. A murderer who is such by passion and by a wolfish craving for bloodshed as a mode of unnatural luxury cannot relapse into *inertia*. Such a man, even more than the Alpine chamois-hunter, comes to crave the dangers and the hairbreadth escapes of his trade, as a condiment for seasoning the insipid monotonies of daily life. But, apart from the hellish instincts that might too surely be relied on for renewed atrocities, it was clear that the murderer of the Marrs, wheresoever lurking, must be a needy man, and a needy man of that class least likely to seek or to find resources in honourable modes of industry; for which, equally by haughty disgust and by disuse of the appropriate habits, men of violence are specially disqualified. Were it, therefore, merely for a livelihood, the murderer, whom all hearts were yearning to decipher, might be expected to make his resurrection on some stage of horror, after a reasonable interval. Even in the Marr murder, granting that it had been governed chiefly by cruel and vindictive impulses, it was still clear that the desire of booty had co-operated with such feelings. Equally clear it was that this desire must have been disappointed: excepting the trivial sum reserved by Marr for the week's expenditures, the murderer found, doubtless, little or nothing that he could turn to account. Two guineas, perhaps, would be the outside of what he had obtained in the way of booty. A week or so would see the end of that. The conviction, therefore, of all people was that in a month or two, when the fever of excitement might a little have cooled down, or have been superseded by other topics of fresher interest, so that the new-born vigilance of household life would have had time to re-lax, some new murder, equally appalling, might be counted upon.

Such was the public expectation. Let the reader then figure to himself the pure frenzy of horror when in this hush of expectation, looking, indeed, and waiting for the unknown arm to strike once more, but not believ-ing that any audacity could be equal to such an attempt as yet—whilst all eyes were watching—suddenly, on the twelfth night from the Marr murder, a second case of the same mysterious nature, a murder on the same exterminating plan, was perpetrated in the very same neighbourhood. It was on the Thursday next but one succeeding to the Marr murder that this second atroc-ity took place; and many people thought at the time that in its dramatic features of thrilling interest this second case even went beyond the first. The family which suffered in this instance was that of a Mr. Wil-liamson; and the house was situated, if not absolutely in Ratcliffe Highway, at any rate immediately round the corner of some secondary street, running at right angles to this public thoroughfare. Mr. Williamson was a well-known and respectable man, long settled in that district; he was supposed to be rich; and, more with a view to the employment furnished by such a calling than with much anxiety for further accumula-tions, he kept a sort of tavern which, in this respect, might be considered on an old patriarchal footing—

that, although people of considerable property resorted
to the house in the evenings, no kind of anxious separation was maintained between them and the other
visitors from the class of artisans or common labourers.
Anybody who conducted himself with propriety was
free to take a seat and call for any liquor that he might
prefer. And thus the society was pretty miscellaneous;
in part stationary, but in some proportion fluctuating.
The household consisted of the following five persons:
1, Mr. Williamson, its head, who was an old man above
seventy, and was well fitted for his situation, being
civil, and not at all morose, but at the same time firm
in maintaining order; 2, Mrs. Williamson, his wife,
about ten years younger than himself; 3, a little grand-
daughter, about nine years old; 4, a housemaid, who
was nearly forty years old; 5, a young journeyman,
aged about twenty-six, belonging to some manufacturing establishment (of what class I have forgotten;
neither do I remember of what nation he was). It was
the established rule at Mr. Williamson's that exactly
as the clock struck eleven all the company, without
favour or exception, moved off. That was one of the
customs by which, in so stormy a district, Mr. Williamson had found it possible to keep his house free
from brawls. On the present Thursday night everything had gone on as usual, except for one slight
shadow of suspicion, which had caught the attention of
more persons than one. Perhaps at a less agitating time
it would hardly have been noticed; but now, when the
first question and the last in all social meetings turned
upon the Marrs and their unknown murderer, it was
a circumstance naturally fitted to cause some uneasiness that a stranger, of sinister appearance, in a wide
surtout, had flitted in and out of the room at intervals
during the evening, had sometimes retired from the
light into obscure corners, and by more than one per-

son had been observed stealing into the private passages of the house. It was presumed in general that the
man must be known to Williamson. And, in some
slight degree, as an occasional customer of the house,
it is not impossible that he *was*. But afterwards this
repulsive stranger, with his cadaverous ghastliness,
extraordinary hair, and glazed eyes, showing himself
intermittingly through the hours from 8 to 11 P.M.,
revolved upon the memory of all who had steadily observed him with something of the same freezing effect
as belongs to the two assassins in *Macbeth* who present
themselves reeking from the murder of Banquo, and
gleaming dimly, with dreadful faces, from the misty
background, athwart the pomps of the regal banquet.

Meantime the clock struck eleven; the company
broke up; the door of entrance was nearly closed; and
at this moment of general dispersion the situation of
the five inmates left upon the premises was precisely
this: The three elders, viz. Williamson, his wife, and
his female servant, were all occupied on the ground-
floor. Williamson himself was drawing ale, porter, &c.,
for those neighbours in whose favour the house-door
had been left ajar until the hour of twelve should
strike; Mrs. Williamson and her servant were moving
to and fro between the back-kitchen and a little parlour; the little grand-daughter, whose sleeping-room
was on the *first* floor (which term in London means always the floor raised by one flight of stairs above the
level of the street), had been fast asleep since nine
o'clock; lastly, the journeyman artisan had retired to
rest for some time. He was a regular lodger in the
house; and his bedroom was on the second floor. For
some time he had been undressed, and had lain down
in bed. Being, as a working man, bound to habits of
early rising, he was naturally anxious to fall asleep as
soon as possible. But, on this particular night, his un-

easiness, arising from the recent murders at No. 29, rose to a paroxysm of nervous excitement which kept him awake. It is possible that from somebody he had heard of the suspicious-looking stranger or might even personally have observed him slinking about. But, were it otherwise, he was aware of several circumstances dangerously affecting this house: for instance, the ruffianism of this whole neighbourhood, and the disagreeable fact that the Marrs had lived within a few doors of this very house, which again argued that the murderer also lived at no great distance. These were matters of *general* alarm. But there were others peculiar to this house: in particular, the notoriety of Williamson's opulence—the belief, whether well or ill founded, that he accumulated in desks and drawers the money continually flowing into his hands; and, lastly, the danger so ostentatiously courted by that habit of leaving the house-door ajar through one entire hour— and that hour loaded with extra danger by the well-advertised assurance that no collision need be feared with chance convivial visitors, since all such people were banished at eleven. A regulation which had hitherto operated beneficially for the character and comfort of the house now, on the contrary, under altered circumstances, became a positive proclamation of exposure and defencelessness through one entire period of an hour. Williamson himself, it was said generally, being a large unwieldly man, past seventy, and signally inactive, ought, in prudence, to make the locking of his door coincident with the dismissal of his evening party.

Upon these and other grounds of alarm (particularly this, that Mrs. Williamson was reported to possess a considerable quantity of plate), the journeyman was musing painfully, and the time might be within twenty-eight or twenty-five minutes of twelve, when all at once, with a crash, proclaiming some hand of hideous violence, the house-door was suddenly shut and locked. Here, then, beyond all doubt, was the diabolic man, clothed in mystery, from No. 29 Ratcliffe Highway. Yes, that dreadful being, who for twelve days had employed all thoughts and all tongues, was now, too certainly, in this defenceless house, and would, in a few minutes, be face to face with every one of its inmates. A question still lingered in the public mind—whether at Marr's there might not have been *two* men at work. If so, there would be two at present; and one of the two would be immediately disposable for the upstairs work; since no danger could obviously be more immediately fatal to such an attack than any alarm given from an upper window to the passengers in the street. Through one half-minute the poor panic-stricken man sat up motionless in bed. But then he rose, his first movement being towards the door of his room. Not for any purpose of securing it against intrusion—too well he knew that there was no fastening of any sort—neither lock nor bolt; nor was there any such moveable furniture in the room as might have availed to barricade the door, even if time could be counted on for such an attempt. It was no effect of prudence, merely the fascination of killing fear it was, that drove him to open the door. One step brought him to the head of the stairs; he lowered his head over the balustrade in order to listen; and at that moment ascended from the little parlour this agonizing cry from the woman-servant, "Lord Jesus Christ! we shall all be murdered!" What a Medusa's head must have lurked in those dreadful bloodless features, and those glazed rigid eyes, that seemed rightfully belonging to a corpse, when one glance at them sufficed to proclaim a death-warrant.

Three separate death-struggles were by this time

over; and the poor petrified journeyman, quite unconscious of what he was doing, in blind, passive, self-
surrender to panic, absolutely descended both flights of
stairs. Infinite terror inspired him with the same impulse as might have been inspired by headlong courage.
In his shirt, and upon old decaying stairs, that at times
creaked under his feet, he continued to descend, until
he had reached the lowest step but four. The situation
was tremendous beyond any that is on record. A sneeze,
a cough, almost a breathing, and the young man would
be a corpse, without a chance or a struggle for his life.
The murderer was at that time in the little parlour—
the door of which parlour faced you in descending the
stairs; and this door stood ajar; indeed, much more
considerably open than what is understood by the term
"ajar." Of that quadrant, or 90 degrees, which the
door would describe in swinging so far open as to stand
at right angles to the lobby, or to itself in a closed position, 55 degrees at the least were exposed. Consequently, two out of three corpses were exposed to the
young man's gaze. Where was the third? And the murderer—where was he? As to the murderer, he was
walking rapidly backwards and forwards in the parlour, audible but not visible at first, being engaged
with something or other in that part of the room which
the door still concealed. What the something might be
the sound soon explained; he was applying keys tentatively to a cupboard, a closet, and a scrutoire, in the
hidden part of the room. Very soon, however, he came
into view; but, fortunately for the young man, at this
critical moment the murderer's purpose too entirely
absorbed him to allow of his throwing a glance to the
staircase, on which else the white figure of the journeyman, standing in motionless horror, would have been
detected in one instant, and seasoned for the grave in
the second. As to the third corpse, the missing corpse,

viz. Mr. Williamson's, *that* is in the cellar; and how its
local position can be accounted for remains as a separate question, much discussed at the time, but never
satisfactorily cleared up.

Meantime, that Williamson was dead became evident to the young man; since else he would have been
heard stirring or groaning. Three friends, therefore,
out of four whom the young man had parted with forty
minutes ago, were now extinguished; remained, therefore, 40 per cent (a large percentage for Williams to
leave) ; remained, in fact, himself and his pretty young
friend, the little grand-daughter, whose childish innocence was still slumbering, without fear for herself,
or grief for her aged grand-parents. If *they* are gone
for ever, happily one friend (for such he will prove
himself indeed, if from such a danger he can save this
child) is pretty near to her. But alas! he is still nearer
to a murderer. At this moment he is unnerved for any
exertion whatever; he has changed into a pillar of ice;
for the objects before him, separated by just thirteen
feet, are these: The housemaid had been caught by the
murderer on her knees; she was kneeling before the
fire-grate, which she had been polishing with black
lead. That part of her task was finished; and she had
passed on to another task—viz. the filling of the grate
with wood and coals, not for kindling at this moment,
but so as to have it ready for kindling on the next day.
The appearances all showed that she must have been
engaged in this labour at the very moment when the
murderer entered; and perhaps the succession of the
incidents arranged itself as follows: From the awful
ejaculation and loud outcry to Christ, as overheard by
the journeyman, it was clear that then first she had
been alarmed; yet this was at least one and a half or
even two minutes after the door-slamming. Consequently the alarm which had so fearfully and season-

ably alarmed the young man must, in some unaccountable way, have been misinterpreted by the two women. It was said, at the time, that Mrs. Williamson laboured under some dulness of hearing; and it was conjectured that the servant, having her ears filled with the noise of her own scrubbing, and her head half under the grate, might have confounded it with the street noises, or else might have imputed this violent closure to some mischievous boys. But, howsoever explained, the fact was evident that, until the words of appeal to Christ, the servant had noticed nothing suspicious, nothing which interrupted her labours. If so, it followed that neither had Mrs. Williamson noticed anything; for, in that case, she would have communicated her own alarm to the servant, since both were in the same small room. Apparently the course of things after the murderer had entered the room was this: Mrs. Williamson had probably not seen him, from the accident of standing with her back to the door. Her, therefore, before he was himself observed at all, he had stunned and prostrated by a shattering blow on the back of her head; this blow, inflicted by a crowbar, had smashed in the hinder part of the skull. She fell; and by the noise of her fall (for all was the work of a moment) had first roused the attention of the servant, who then uttered the cry which had reached the young man; but before she could repeat it the murderer had descended with his uplifted instrument upon *her* head, crushing the skull inwards upon the brain. Both the women were irrecoverably destroyed, so that further outrages were needless; and, moreover, the murderer was conscious of the imminent danger from delay; and yet, in spite of his hurry, so fully did he appreciate the fatal consequences to himself, if any of his victims should so far revive into consciousness as to make circumstantial depositions, that, by way of making this impossible, he had proceeded instantly to cut the throats of each. All this tallied with the appearances as now presenting themselves. Mrs. Williamson had fallen backwards with her head to the door; the servant, from her kneeling posture, had been incapable of rising, and had presented her head passively to blows; after which, the miscreant had but to bend her head backwards so as to expose her throat, and the murder was finished. It is remarkable that the young artisan, paralysed as he had been by fear, and evidently fascinated for a time so as to walk right towards the lion's mouth, yet found himself able to notice everything important.

The reader must suppose him at this point watching the murderer whilst hanging over the body of Mrs. Williamson, and whilst renewing his search for certain important keys. Doubtless it was an anxious situation for the murderer; for, unless he speedily found the keys wanted, all this hideous tragedy would end in nothing but a prodigious increase of the public horror, in tenfold precautions therefore, and redoubled obstacles interposed between himself and his future game. Nay, there was even a nearer interest at stake; his own immediate safety might, by a probable accident, be compromised. Most of those who came to the house for liquor were giddy girls or children, who, on finding this house closed, would go off carelessly to some other; but, let any thoughtful woman or man come to the door now, a full quarter of an hour before the established time of closing, in that case suspicion would arise too powerful to be checked. There would be a sudden alarm given; after which, mere luck would decide the event. For it is a remarkable fact, and one that illustrates the singular inconsistency of this villain—who, being often so superfluously subtle, was in other directions so reckless and improvident—that at this

very moment, standing amongst corpses that had deluged the little parlour with blood, Williams must have
been in considerable doubt whether he had any sure
means of egress. There were windows, he knew, to the
back; but upon what ground they opened he seems to
have had no certain information; and in a neighbourhood so dangerous the windows of the lower storey
would not improbably be nailed down; those in the
upper might be free, but then came the necessity of a
leap too formidable. From all this, however, the sole
practical inference was to hurry forward with the trial
of further keys, and to detect the hidden treasure. This
it was, this intense absorption in one overmastering
pursuit, that dulled the murderer's perceptions as to
all around him; otherwise he must have heard the
breathing of the young man, which to himself at times
became fearfully audible. As the murderer stood once
more over the body of Mrs. Williamson, and searched
her pockets more narrowly, he pulled out various clusters of keys, one of which, dropping, gave a harsh jin-
gling sound upon the floor. At this time it was that
the secret witness, from his secret stand, noticed the
fact of Williams's surtout being lined with silk of the
finest quality. One other fact he noticed, which eventually became more immediately important than many
stronger circumstances of incrimination: this was that
the shoes of the murderer, apparently new, and bought
probably with poor Marr's money, creaked as he
walked, harshly and frequently. With the new clusters
of keys, the murderer walked off to the hidden section
of the parlour. And here, at last, was suggested to the
journeyman the sudden opening for an escape. Some
minutes would be lost to a certainty in trying all these
keys, and subsequently in searching the drawers, supposing that the keys answered—or in violently forcing
them, supposing that they did *not*. He might thus

count upon a brief interval of leisure, whilst the rattling of the keys might obscure to the murderer the
creaking of the stairs under the reascending journeyman. His plan was now formed. On regaining his bedroom, he placed the bed against the door by way of a
transient retardation to the enemy, that might give
him a short warning, and, in the worst extremity,
might give him a chance for life by means of a desperate leap. This change made as quietly as was possible, he tore the sheets, pillowcases, and blankets into
broad ribbons, and, after plaiting them into ropes,
spliced the different lengths together. But at the very
first he descries this ugly addition to his labours. Where
shall he look for any staple, hook, bar, or other fixture,
from which his rope, when twisted, may safely depend? Measured from the window-*sill*—*i.e.* the lowest
part of the window architrave—there count but
twenty-two or twenty-three feet to the ground. Of this
length ten or twelve feet may be looked upon as cancelled, because to that extent he might drop without
danger. So much being deducted, there would remain,
say, a dozen feet of rope to prepare. But, unhappily,
there is no stout iron fixture anywhere about his window. The nearest, indeed the sole, fixture of that sort
is not near to the window at all; it is a spike fixed (for
no reason at all that is apparent) in the bed-tester.
Now, the bed being shifted, the spike is shifted; and its
distance from the window, having always been four
feet, is now seven. Seven entire feet, therefore, must
be added to that which would have sufficed if measured from the window. But courage! God, by the proverb of all nations in Christendom, helps those that help
themselves. This our young man thankfully acknowl-
edges; he reads already, in the very fact of any spike
at all being found where hitherto it has been useless,
an earnest of providential aid. Were it only for himself

that he worked, he could not feel himself meritoriously employed; but this is not so. In deep sincerity he is now agitated for the poor child, whom he knows and loves; every minute, he feels, brings ruin nearer to *her;* and, as he passed her door, his first thought had been to take her out of bed in his arms, and to carry her where she might share his chances. But, on consideration, he felt that this sudden awaking of her, and the impossibility of even whispering any explanation, would cause her to cry audibly; and the inevitable indiscretion of one would be fatal to the two. As the Alpine avalanches, when suspended above the traveller's head, oftentimes (we are told) come down through the stirring of the air by a simple whisper, precisely on such a tenure of a whisper was now suspended the murderous malice of the man below. No; there is but one way to save the child; towards *her* deliverance the first step is through his own. And he has made an excellent beginning; for the spike, which too fearfully he had expected to see torn away by any strain upon it from the half-carious wood, stands firmly when tried against the pressure of his own weight. He has rapidly fastened on to it three lengths of his new rope, measuring eleven feet. He plaits it roughly; so that only three feet have been lost in the intertwisting; he has spliced on a second length equal to the first; so that, already, sixteen feet are ready to throw out of the window; and thus, let the worst come to the worst, it will not be absolute ruin to swarm down the rope so far as it will reach, and then to drop boldly.

All this has been accomplished in about six minutes; and the hot contest between above and below is still steadily, but fervently, proceeding. Murderer is working hard in the parlour; journeyman is working hard in the bedroom. Miscreant is getting on famously downstairs; one batch of bank-notes he has already bagged, and is hard upon the scent of a second. He has also sprung a covey of golden coins. Sovereigns as yet were not; but guineas at this period fetched thirty shillings apiece; and he has worked his way into a little quarry of these. Murderer is almost joyous; and, if any creature is still living in this house, as shrewdly he suspects and very soon means to know, with that creature he would be happy, before cutting the creature's throat, to drink a glass of something. Instead of the glass, might he not make a present to the poor creature of his throat? Oh no! impossible! Throats are a sort of thing that he never makes presents of; business—business must be attended to. Really the two men, considered simply as men of business, are both meritorious. Like chorus and semi-chorus, strophe and anti-strophe, they work each against the other. Pull journeyman, pull murderer! Pull baker, pull devil! As regards the journeyman, he is now safe. To his sixteen feet, of which seven are neutralized by the distance of the bed, he has at last added six feet more; which will be short of reaching the ground by perhaps ten feet—a trifle which man or boy may drop without injury. All is safe, therefore, for him; which is more than one can be sure of for miscreant in the parlour.

Miscreant, however, takes it coolly enough: the reason being that, with all his cleverness, for once in his life miscreant has been overreached. The reader and I know, but miscreant does not in the least suspect, a little fact of some importance, viz. that just now through a space of full three minutes he has been overlooked and studied by one who (though reading in a dreadful book and suffering under mortal panic) took accurate notes of so much as his limited opportunities allowed him to see, and will assuredly report the creaking shoes and the silk-mounted surtout in quarters where such little facts will tell very little to his advantage. But, although it is true that Mr. Williams, unaware of the journeyman's having "assisted" at the examination of Mrs. Williamson's pockets, could not connect any anxiety with that person's subsequent proceedings, nor specially therefore with his having embarked in the rope-weaving line, assuredly he knew of reasons enough for not loitering. And yet he *did* loiter. Reading his acts by the light of such mute traces as he left behind him, the police became aware that latterly he must have loitered. And the reason which governed him is striking; because at once it records that murder was not pursued by him simply as a means to an end, but also as an end for itself. Mr. Williams had now been upon the premises for perhaps fifteen or twenty minutes; and in that space of time he had dispatched, in a style satisfactory to himself, a considerable amount of business. He had done, in commercial language, "a good stroke of business." Upon two floors, viz. the cellar-floor and the ground-floor, he has "accounted for" all the population. But there remained at least two floors more; and it now occurred to Mr. Williams that, although the landlord's somewhat chilling manner had shut him out from any familiar knowledge of the household arrangements, too probably on one or other of those floors there must be some throats. As to plunder, he has already bagged the whole. And it was next to impossible that any arrear, the most trivial, should still remain for a gleaner. But the throats—the throats—there it was that arrears and gleanings might perhaps be counted on. And thus it appeared that, in his wolfish thirst for blood, Mr. Williams put to hazard the whole fruits of his night's work, and his life into the bargain. At this moment, if the murderer knew all—could he see the open window above stairs ready for the descent of the journeyman, could he witness the life-and-death rapidity with which that journeyman is working, could he guess at the almighty uproar which within ninety seconds will be maddening the population of this populous district —no picture of a maniac in flight of panic or in pursuit of vengeance would adequately represent the agony of haste with which he would himself be hurrying to the street-door for final evasion. That mode of escape was still free. Even at this moment there yet remained time sufficient for a successful flight, and, therefore, for the following revolution in the romance of his own abominable life: He had in his pockets above a hundred pounds of booty—means, therefore, for a full disguise. This very night, if he will shave off his yellow hair, and blacken his eyebrows, buying, when morning light returns, a dark-coloured wig, and clothes such as may co-operate in personating the character of a grave professional man, he may elude all suspicions of impertinent policemen—may sail by any one of a hundred vessels bound for any port along the huge line of seaboard (stretching through 2400 miles) of the American United States; may enjoy fifty years for leisurely repentance; and may even die in the odour of sanctity. On the other hand, if he prefer active life, it is not impossible that, with *his* subtlety, hardihood, and unscrupulousness, in a land where the simple process of naturalization converts the alien at once into a child of the family, he might rise to the President's chair; might have a statue at his death; and afterwards a life in three volumes quarto, with no hint glancing towards No. 29 Ratcliffe Highway. But all depends on the next ninety seconds. Within that time there is a sharp turn to be taken; there is a wrong turn, and a right turn. Should his better angel guide him to the right one, all may yet go well as regards this world's prosperity. But behold! in two minutes from this point we shall see him take the wrong one; and then Nemesis will be at his heels with ruin perfect and sudden.

Meantime, if the murderer allows himself to loiter, the ropemaker overhead does *not*. Well he knows that the poor child's fate is on the edge of a razor; for all turns upon the alarm being raised before the murderer reaches her bedside.

And at this very moment, whilst desperate agitation is nearly paralysing his fingers, he hears the sullen stealthy step of the murderer creeping up through the darkness. It had been the expectation of the journey-man (founded on the clamorous uproar with which the street-door was slammed) that Williams, when disposable for his upstairs work, would come racing at a long jubilant gallop, and with a tiger roar; and perhaps, on his natural instincts, he would have done so. But this mode of approach, which was of dreadful effect when applied to a case of surprise, became dangerous in the case of people who might by this time have been placed fully upon their guard. The step which he had heard was on the staircase—but upon which stair? He fancied upon the lowest; and, in a movement so slow and cautious, even this might make all the difference; yet might it not have been the tenth, twelfth, or fourteenth stair? Never, perhaps, in this world did any man feel his own responsibility so cruelly loaded and strained as at this moment did the poor journeyman on behalf of the slumbering child. Lose but two seconds, through awkwardness or through the self-counteractions of panic, and for *her* the total difference arose between life and death. Still there is a hope; and nothing can so frightfully expound the hellish nature of him whose baleful shadow, to speak astrologically, at this moment darkens the house of life, as the simple expression of the ground on which this hope rested.

The journeyman felt sure that the murderer would not be satisfied to kill the poor child whilst unconscious. This would be to defeat his whole purpose in murdering her at all. To an epicure in murder such as Williams, it would be taking away the very sting of the enjoyment if the poor child should be suffered to drink off the bitter cup of death without fully apprehending the misery of the situation. But this luckily would require time: the double confusion of mind—first, from being roused up at so unusual an hour, and, secondly, from the horror of the occasion when explained to her —would at first produce fainting, or some mode of insensibility or distraction, such as must occupy a considerable time. The logic of the case, in short, all rested upon the *ultra* fiendishness of Williams. Were he likely to be content with the mere fact of the child's death, apart from the process and leisurely expansion of its mental agony—in that case there would be no hope. But, because our present murderer is fastidiously finical in his exactions—a sort of martinet in the scenical grouping and draping of the circumstances in his murders—therefore it is that hope becomes reasonable, since all such refinements of preparation demand time. Murders of mere necessity Williams was obliged to hurry: but in a murder of pure voluptuousness, entirely disinterested, where no hostile witness was to be removed, no extra booty to be gained, and no revenge to be gratified, it is clear that to hurry would be altogether to ruin. If this child, therefore, is to be saved, it will be on pure aesthetical considerations.[1]

[1] Let the reader who is disposed to regard as exaggerated or romantic the pure fiendishness imputed to Williams recollect that, except for the luxurious purpose of basking and revelling in the anguish of dying despair, he had no motive at all, small or great, for attempting the murder of this young girl. She had seen nothing, heard nothing—was fast asleep, and her door

But all considerations whatever are at this moment suddenly cut short. A second step is heard on the stairs, but still stealthy and cautious; a third—and then the child's doom seems fixed. But just at that moment all is ready. The window is wide open; the rope is swinging free; the journeyman has launched himself; and already he is in the first stage of his descent. Simply by the weight of his person he descended, and by the resistance of his hands he retarded the descent. The danger was that the rope should run too smoothly through his hands, and that by too rapid an acceleration of pace he should come violently to the ground. Happily he was able to resist the descending impetus; the knots of the splicings furnished a succession of retardations. But the rope proved shorter by four or five feet than he had calculated: ten or eleven feet from the ground he hung suspended in the air; speechless for the present through long-continued agitation, and not daring to drop boldly on the rough carriage pavement, lest he should fracture his legs. But the night was not dark, as it had been on occasion of the Marr murders. And yet, for purposes of criminal police, it was by accident worse than the darkest night that ever hid a murder or baffled a pursuit. London, from east to west, was covered with a deep pall (rising from the river) of universal fog. Hence it happened that for twenty or thirty seconds the young man hanging in the air was not observed. His white shirt at length attracted notice. Three or four people ran up, and received him in their arms, all anticipating some dreadful annunciation. To what house did he belong? Even *that* was not instantly apparent; but he pointed with

was closed; so that, as a witness against him, he knew that she was as useless as any one of the three corpses. And yet he *was* making preparations for her murder when the alarm in the street interrupted him.

his finger to Williamson's door, and said in a half-choking whisper—"*Marr's murderer, now at work!*"

All explained itself in a moment: the silent language of the fact made its own eloquent revelation. The mysterious exterminator of No. 29 Ratcliffe Highway had visited another house; and, behold! one man only had escaped through the air, and in his night-dress, to tell the tale. Superstitiously, there was something to check the pursuit of this unintelligible criminal. Morally, and in the interests of vindictive justice, there was everything to rouse, quicken, and sustain it.

Yes, Marr's murderer—the man of mystery—was again at work; at this moment perhaps extinguishing some lamp of life, and not at any remote place, but here—in the very house which the listeners to this dreadful announcement were actually touching. The chaos and blind uproar of the scene which followed, measured by the crowded reports in the journals of many subsequent days, and in one feature of that case, has never to my knowledge had its parallel; or, if a parallel, only in one case—what followed, I mean, on the acquittal of the seven bishops at Westminster in 1688. At present there was more than passionate enthusiasm. The frenzied movement of mixed horror and exultation—the ululation of vengeance which ascended instantaneously from the individual street, and then by a sublime sort of magnetic contagion from all the adjacent streets—can be adequately expressed only by a rapturous passage in Shelley:

The transport of a fierce and monstrous gladness
  Spread through the multitudinous streets, fast flying
Upon the wings of fear—From his dull madness
  The starveling waked, and died in joy: the dying,
  Among the corpses in stark agony lying,
  Just heard the happy tidings, and in hope

Closed their faint eyes: from house to house replying
  With loud acclaim, the living shook heaven's cope
And filled the startled earth with echoes.

There was something, indeed, half inexplicable in the instantaneous interpretation of the gathering shout according to its true meaning. In fact, the deadly roar of vengeance, and its sublime unity, *could* point in this district only to the one demon whose idea had brooded and tyrannized, for twelve days, over the general heart; every door, every window in the neighbourhood, flew open as if at a word of command; multitudes, without waiting for the regular means of egress, leaped down at once from the windows on the lower storey; sick men rose from their beds; in one instance, as if expressly to verify the image of Shelley (in v. 4, 5, 6, 7), a man whose death had been looked for through some days, and who actually *did* die on the following day, rose, armed himself with a sword, and descended in his shirt into the street. The chance was a good one, and the mob were made aware of it, for catching the wolfish dog in the high noon and carnival of his bloody revels—in the very centre of his own shambles. For a moment the mob was self-baffled by its own numbers and its own fury. But even that fury felt the call for self-control. It was evident that the massy street-door must be driven in, since there was no longer any living person to co-operate with their efforts from within, excepting only a female child. Crowbars dexterously applied in one minute threw the door out of hangings, and the people entered like a torrent. It may be guessed with what fret and irritation to their consuming fury a signal of pause and absolute silence was made by a person of local importance. In the hope of receiving some useful communication, the mob became silent. "Now, listen," said the

man of authority, "and we shall learn whether he is
above-stairs or below." Immediately a noise was heard
as if of someone forcing windows, and clearly the
sound came from a bedroom above. Yes, the fact was
apparent that the murderer was even yet in the house:
he had been caught in a trap. Not having made himself familiar with the details of Williamson's house,
to all appearance he had suddenly become a prisoner in
one of the upper rooms. Towards this the crowd now
rushed impetuously. The door, however, was found to
be slightly fastened; and, at the moment when this
was forced, a loud crash of the window, both glass and
frame, announced that the wretch had made his escape.
He had leaped down; and several persons in the crowd,
who burned with the general fury, leaped after him.
These persons had not troubled themselves about the
nature of the ground; but now, on making an examination of it with torches, they reported it to be an inclined plane, or embankment of clay, very wet and adhesive. The prints of the man's footsteps were deeply
impressed upon the clay, and therefore easily traced up
to the summit of the embankment; but it was perceived
at once that pursuit would be useless, from the density
of the mist. Two feet ahead of you a man was entirely
withdrawn from your power of identification; and, on
overtaking him, you could not venture to challenge
him as the same whom you had lost sight of. Never,
through the course of a whole century, could there be
a night expected more propitious to an escaping criminal: means of disguise Williams now had in excess;
and the dens were innumerable in the neighbourhood
of the river that could have sheltered him for years
from troublesome inquiries. But favours are thrown
away upon the reckless and the thankless. That night,
when the turning-point offered itself for his whole future career, Williams took the wrong turn; for, out of

mere indolence, he took the turn to his old lodgings—
that place which, in all England, he had just now the
most reason to shun.

Meantime the crowd had thoroughly searched the
premises of Williamson. The first inquiry was for the
young grand-daughter. Williams, it was evident, had
gone into her room; but in this room apparently it was
that the sudden uproar in the streets had surprised
him; after which his undivided attention had been directed to the windows, since through these only any
retreat had been left open to him. Even this retreat he
owed only to the fog, and to the hurry of the moment,
and to the difficulty of approaching the premises by
the rear. The little girl was naturally agitated by the
influx of strangers at that hour; but otherwise, through
the humane precautions of the neighbours, she was
preserved from all knowledge of the dreadful events
that had occurred whilst she herself was sleeping. Her
poor old grandfather was still missing, until the crowd
descended into the cellar; he was then found lying
prostrate on the cellar floor: apparently he had been
thrown down from the top of the cellar stairs, and with
so much violence that one leg was broken. After he had
been thus disabled, Williams had gone down to him,
and cut his throat. There was much discussion at the
time, in some of the public journals, upon the possibility of reconciling these incidents with other circumstantialities of the case, supposing that only one man
had been concerned in the affair. That there *was* only
one man concerned seems to be certain. One only was
seen or heard at Marr's; one only, and beyond all doubt
the same man, was seen by the young journeyman in
Mrs. Williamson's parlour; and one only was traced
by his footmarks on the clay embankment. Apparently
the course which he had pursued was this: He had
introduced himself to Williamson by ordering some

beer. This order would oblige the old man to go down into the cellar; Williams would wait until he had reached it, and would then "slam" and lock the street door in the violent way described. Williamson would come up in agitation upon hearing this violence. The murderer, aware that he would do so, met him, no doubt, at the head of the cellar stairs, and threw him down; after which he would go down to consummate the murder in his ordinary way. All this would occupy a minute, or a minute and a half; and in that way the interval would be accounted for that elapsed between the alarming sound of the street-door as heard by the journeyman and the lamentable outcry of the female servant. It is evident also that the reason why no cry whatsoever had been heard from the lips of Mrs. Williamson is due to the positions of the parties as I have sketched them. Coming behind Mrs. Williamson—unseen therefore, and from her deafness unheard—the murderer would inflict entire abolition of consciousness while she was yet unaware of his presence. But with the servant, who had unavoidably witnessed the attack upon her mistress, the murderer could not obtain the same fullness of advantage; and *she* therefore had time for making an agonizing ejaculation.

It has been mentioned that the murderer of the Marrs was not for nearly a fortnight so much as suspected—meaning that, previously to the Williamson murder, no vestige of any ground for suspicion in any direction whatever had occurred either to the general public or to the police. But there were two very limited exceptions to this state of absolute ignorance. Some of the magistrates had in their possession something which, when closely examined, offered a very probable means for tracing the criminal. But as yet they had *not* traced him. Until the Friday morning next after the destruction of the Williamsons, they had not published the important fact that upon the ship-carpenter's mallet (with which, as regarded the stunning or disabling process, the murders had been achieved) were inscribed the letters "J. P." This mallet had, by a strange oversight on the part of the murderer, been left behind in Marr's shop; and it is an interesting fact, therefore, that, had the villain been intercepted by the grave pawnbroker, he would have been met virtually disarmed. This public notification was made officially on the Friday, viz. on the thirteenth day after the first murder. And it was instantly followed (as will be seen) by a most important result. Meantime, within the secrecy of one single bedroom in all London, it is a fact that Williams had been whisperingly the object of very deep suspicion from the very first—that is, within that same hour which witnessed the Marr tragedy. And singular it is that the suspicion was due entirely to his own folly.

Williams lodged, in company with other men of various nations, at a public-house. In a large dormitory there were arranged five or six beds. These were occupied by artisans, generally of respectable character. One or two Englishmen there were, one or two Scotchmen, three or four Germans, and Williams, whose birthplace was not certainly known. On the fatal Saturday night, about half-past one o'clock, when Williams returned from his dreadful labours, he found the English and Scotch party asleep, but the Germans awake: one of them was sitting up with a lighted candle in his hands, and reading aloud to the other two. Upon this, Williams said, in an angry and very peremptory tone, "Oh, put that candle out; put it out directly: we shall all be burned in our beds." Had the British party in the room been awake, Mr. Williams would have roused a mutinous protest against this arrogant mandate. But Germans are generally mild and facile in their tempers; so the light was complaisantly extinguished. Yet, as there were no curtains, it struck the Germans that the danger was really none at all; for bedclothes, massed upon each other, will no more burn than the leaves of a closed book. Privately, therefore, the Germans drew an inference that Mr. Williams must have had some urgent motive for withdrawing his own person and dress from observation. What this motive might be the next day's news diffused all over London, and of course at this house, not two furlongs from Marr's shop, made awfully evident; and, as may well be supposed, the suspicion was communicated to the other members of the dormitory. All of them, however, were aware of the legal danger attaching, under English law, to insinuations against a man, even if true, which might not admit of proof. In reality, had Williams used the most obvious precautions, had he simply walked down to the Thames (not a stone's-throw distant) and flung two of his implements into the river, no conclusive proof could have been adduced against him. And he might have realized the scheme of Courvoisier (the murderer of Lord William Russell)—viz. have sought each separate month's support in a separate well-concerted murder. The party in the dormitory, meantime, were satisfied themselves, but waited for evidences that might satisfy others. No sooner, therefore, had the official notice been published as to the initials J. P. on the mallet than every man in the house recognized at once the well-known initials of an honest Norwegian ship-carpenter, John Petersen, who had worked in the English dockyards until the present year, but, having occasion to revisit his native land, had left his box of tools in the garrets of this inn. These garrets were now searched. Petersen's tool-chest was found, but wanting the mallet; and, on further examination, another overwhelming discovery was made. The surgeon who examined the corpses at Williamson's had given it as his opinion that the throats were not cut by means of a razor, but of some implement differently shaped. It was now remembered that Williams had recently borrowed a large French knife of peculiar construction; and, accordingly, from a heap of old lumber and rags, there was soon extricated a waistcoat, which the whole house could swear to as recently worn by Williams. In this waistcoat, and glued by gore to the lining of its pockets, was found the French knife. Next, it was matter of notoriety to everybody in the inn that Williams ordinarily wore at present a pair of creaking shoes, and a brown surtout lined with silk. Many other presumptions seemed scarcely called for. Williams was immediately apprehended, and briefly examined. This was on the Friday. On the Saturday morning (viz. fourteen days from the Marr murders) he was again brought up. The circumstantial evidence was overwhelming. Williams watched its course, but said very little. At the close, he was fully committed for trial at the next sessions; and it is needless to say that, on his road to prison, he was pursued by mobs so fierce that, under ordinary circumstances, there would have been small hope of escaping summary vengeance. But upon this occasion a powerful escort had been provided; so that he was safely lodged in jail. In this particular jail at this time the regulation was that at five o'clock P.M. all the prisoners on the criminal side should be finally locked up for the night, and without candles. For fourteen hours (that is, until seven o'clock on the next morning) they were left unvisited, and in total darkness. Time, therefore, Williams had for committing suicide. The means in other respects were small. One iron bar there was, meant (if I remember) for the suspension of a lamp; upon this he had hanged himself by his braces. At what hour was uncertain: some people fancied at midnight. And in that case, precisely at the hour when, fourteen days before, he had been spreading horror and desolation through the quiet family of poor Marr, now was he forced into drinking of the same cup, presented to his lips by the same accursed hands.

* * *

The case of the M'Keans, which has been specially alluded to, merits also a slight rehearsal for the dreadful picturesqueness of some two or three amongst its circumstances. The scene of this murder was at a rustic inn, some few miles (I think) from Manchester; and the advantageous situation of this inn it was out of which arose the twofold temptations of the case. Generally speaking, an inn argues, of course, a close cincture of neighbours, as the original motive for opening such an establishment. But in this case the house individually was solitary, so that no interruption was to be looked for from any persons living within reach of screams; and yet, on the other hand, the circumjacent vicinity was eminently populous; as one consequence of which, a benefit club had established its weekly rendezvous in this inn, and left the pecuniary accumulations in their club-room, under the custody of the landlord. This fund arose often to a considerable amount, fifty or seventy pounds, before it was transferred to the hands of a banker. Here, therefore, was a treasure worth some little risk, and a situation that promised next to none. These attractive circumstances had, by accident, become accurately known to one or both of the two M'Keans; and, unfortunately, at a moment of overwhelming misfortune to themselves. They were hawkers, and until lately had borne most respectable characters; but some mercantile crash had overtaken them with utter ruin, in which their joint capital had been swallowed up to the last shilling. This sudden prostration had made them desperate: their own little property had been swallowed up in a large *social* catastrophe, and society at large they looked upon as accountable to them for a robbery. In preying, therefore, upon society, they considered themselves as pursuing a wild natural justice of retaliation. The money aimed at did certainly assume the character of public money, being the product of many separate subscriptions. They forgot, however, that in the murderous acts which too certainly they meditated as preliminaries to the robbery they could plead no such imaginary social precedent. In dealing with a family that seemed almost helpless, if all went smoothly, they relied entirely upon their own bodily strength. They were stout young men, twenty-eight to thirty-two years old: somewhat undersized as to height; but squarely built, deep-chested, broad-shouldered, and so beautifully formed, as regarded the symmetry of their limbs and their articulations, that, after their execution, the bodies were privately exhibited by the surgeons of the Manchester Infirmary as objects of statuesque interest.

On the other hand, the household which they proposed to attack consisted of the following four persons: 1, the landlord, a stoutish farmer—but *him* they intended to disable by a trick then newly introduced amongst robbers, and termed *hocussing, i.e.* clandestinely drugging the liquor of the victim with laudanum; 2, the landlord's wife; 3, a young servant-woman; 4, a boy, twelve or fourteen years old. The danger was that out of four persons, scattered by possibility over a house which had two separate exits, one at least might escape, and, by better acquaintance with the adjacent paths, might succeed in giving an alarm to some of the houses a furlong distant. Their final resolution was—to be guided by circumstances as to the mode of conducting the affair; and yet, as it seemed essential to success that they should assume the air of strangers to each other, it was necessary that they should preconcert some general outline of their plan; since it would on this scheme be impossible, without awaking violent suspicions, to make any communications under the eyes of the family. This outline included, at the least, one murder: so much was settled; but otherwise their subsequent proceedings make it evident that they wished to have as little bloodshed as was consistent with their final object. On the appointed day they presented themselves separately at the rustic inn, and at different hours. One came as early as four o'clock in the afternoon; the other not until half-past seven. They saluted each other distantly and shyly; and, though occasionally exchanging a few words in the character of strangers, did not seem disposed to any familiar intercourse. With the landlord, however, on his return about eight o'clock from Manchester, one of the brothers entered into a lively conversation, invited him to take a tumbler of punch; and, at a moment when the landlord's absence from the room allowed it, poured into the punch a spoonful of laudanum. Some time after this the clock struck ten; upon which the elder M'Kean, professing to be weary, asked to be shown up to his bedroom: for each brother, immediately on arriving, had engaged a bed. On this, the poor servant-girl presented herself with a bed-candle to light him upstairs.

At this critical moment the family were distributed thus: The landlord, stupefied with the horrid narcotic which he had drunk, had retired to a private room adjoining the public room, for the purpose of reclining upon a sofa; and *he*, luckily for his own safety, was looked upon as entirely incapacitated for action. The landlady was occupied with her husband. And thus the younger M'Kean was left alone in the public room. He rose, therefore, softly, and placed himself at the foot of the stairs which his brother had just ascended, so as to be sure of intercepting any fugitive from the bedroom above. Into that room the elder M'Kean was ushered by the servant, who pointed to two beds—one of which was already half occupied by the boy, and the other empty: in these she intimated that the two strangers must dispose of themselves for the night, according to any arrangement that they might agree upon. Saying this, she presented him with the candle; which he in a moment placed upon the table, and, intercepting her retreat from the room, threw his arms around her neck with a gesture as though he meant to kiss her. This was evidently what she herself anticipated, and endeavoured to prevent. Her horror may be imagined when she felt the perfidious hand that clasped her neck armed with a razor, and violently cutting her throat. She was hardly able to utter one scream before she sank powerless upon the floor. This dreadful spectacle was witnessed by the boy; who was not asleep, but had presence of mind enough instantly to close his eyes. The murderer advanced hastily to the bed, and anxiously examined the expression of the boy's features: satisfied he was not, and he then placed his hand upon the boy's heart, in order to judge by its beatings whether he were agitated or not. This was a dreadful trial; and no doubt the counterfeit sleep would immediately have been detected, when suddenly a dreadful spectacle drew off the attention of the murderer. Solemnly, and in ghostly silence, uprose in her dying delirium the murdered girl; she stood upright, she walked steadily for a moment or two, she bent her steps towards the door. The murderer turned away to pursue her; and at that moment the boy, feeling that his one solitary chance was to fly whilst this scene was in progress, bounded out of bed. On the landing at the head of the stairs was one murderer; at the foot of the stairs was the other: who could believe that the boy had the shadow of a chance for escaping? And yet, in the most natural way, he surmounted all hindrances. In the boy's horror, he laid his left hand on the balustrade, and took a flying leap over it, which landed him at the bottom of the stairs, without having touched a single stair. He had thus effectually passed one of the murderers: the other, it is true, was still to be passed; and this would have been impossible but for a sudden accident. The landlady had been alarmed by the faint scream of the young woman; had hurried from her private room to the girl's assistance; but at the foot of the stairs had been intercepted by the younger brother, and was at this moment struggling with *him*. The confusion of this life-and-death conflict had allowed the boy to whirl past them. Luckily he took a turn into a kitchen out of which was a back-door, fastened by a single bolt that ran freely at a touch; and through this door he rushed into the open fields. But at this moment the elder brother was set free for pursuit by the death of the poor girl. There is no doubt that in her delirium the image moving through her thoughts was that of the club, which met once a-week. She fancied it no doubt sitting; and to this room, for help and for safety, she staggered along; she entered it, and within the doorway once more she dropped down and instantly expired. Her murderer, who had followed her closely, now saw himself set at liberty for the pursuit of the boy. At this critical moment all was at stake; unless the boy were caught the enterprise was ruined. He passed his brother, therefore, and the landlady, without pausing, and rushed through the open door into the fields. By a single second perhaps, he was too late. The boy was keenly aware that, if he continued in sight, he would have no chance of escaping from a powerful young man. He made, therefore, at once for a ditch; into which he tumbled headlong. Had the murderer ventured to make a leisurely examination of the nearest ditch, he would easily have found the boy—made so conspicuous by his white shirt. But he lost all heart, upon failing at once to arrest the boy's flight. And every succeeding second made his despair the greater. If the boy had really effected his escape to the neighbouring farm-houses, a party of men might be gathered within five minutes; and already it might have become difficult for himself and his brother, unacquainted with the field paths, to evade being intercepted. Nothing remained, therefore, but to summon his brother away. Thus it happened that the landlady, though mangled, escaped with life, and eventually recovered. The landlord owed his safety to the stupefying potion. And the baffled murderers had the misery of knowing that their dreadful crime had been altogether profitless. The road, indeed, was now open to the club-room; and, probably, forty seconds would have sufficed to carry off the box of treasure, which afterwards might have been burst open and pillaged at leisure. But the fear of intercepting enemies was too strongly upon them; and they fled rapidly by a road which carried them actually within six feet of the lurking boy.

That night they passed through Manchester. When daylight returned, they slept in a thicket twenty miles distant from the scene of their guilty attempt. On the second and third nights, they pursued their march on foot, resting again during the day. About sunrise on the fourth morning they were entering some village near Kirby Lonsdale, in Westmorland. They must have designedly quitted the direct line of route; for their object was Ayrshire, of which county they were natives, and the regular road would have led them through Shap, Penrith, Carlisle. Probably they were seeking to elude the persecution of the stagecoaches, which, for the last thirty hours, had been scattering at all the inns and road-side *cabarets* hand-bills describing their persons and dress. It happened (perhaps through design) that on this fourth morning they had separated, so as to enter the village ten minutes apart from each other. They were exhausted and footsore. In this condition it was easy to stop them. A blacksmith had silently reconnoitred them, and compared their appearance with the descriptions of the handbills. They were then easily overtaken, and separately arrested. Their trial and condemnation speedily followed at Lancaster; and in those days it followed, of course, that they were executed. Otherwise, their case fell so far within the sheltering limits of what would *now* be regarded as extenuating circumstances that, whilst a murder more or less was not to repel them from their object, very evidently they were anxious to economize the bloodshed as much as possible. Immeasurable, therefore, was the interval which divided them from the monster Williams.

They perished on the scaffold: Williams, as I have said, by his own hand; and, in obedience to the law as it then stood, he was buried in the centre of a *quadrivium*, or conflux of four roads (in this case four streets), with a stake driven through his heart. And over him drives for ever the uproar of unresting London!

ON THE KNOCKING AT THE GATE IN "MACBETH"

(First published in the *London Magazine*, October, 1823)

FROM my boyish days I had always felt a great perplexity on one point in *Macbeth*. It was this: The
knocking at the gate which succeeds to the murder of
Duncan produced to my feelings an effect for which I
never could account. The effect was that it reflected
back upon the murderer a peculiar awfulness and a
depth of solemnity; yet, however obstinately I endeavoured with my understanding to comprehend
this, for many years I never could see *why* it should
produce such an effect.

Here I pause for one moment, to exhort the reader
never to pay any attention to his understanding when
it stands in opposition to any other faculty of his mind.
The mere understanding, however useful and indispensable, is the meanest faculty in the human mind,
and the most to be distrusted; and yet the great majority of people trust to nothing else—which may do
for ordinary life, but not for philosophical purposes.
Of this out of ten thousand instances that I might produce I will cite one. Ask of any person whatsoever
who is not previously prepared for the demand by a
knowledge of the perspective to draw in the rudest
way the commonest appearance which depends upon
the laws of that science—as, for instance, to represent the effect of two walls standing at right angles to
each other, or the appearance of the houses on each
side of a street as seen by a person looking down the
street from one extremity. Now, in all cases, unless
the person has happened to observe in pictures how it

is that artists produce these effects, he will be utterly
unable to make the smallest approximation to it. Yet
why? For he has actually seen the effect every day of
his life. The reason is that he allows his understanding to overrule his eyes. His understanding, which
includes no intuitive knowledge of the laws of vision,
can furnish him with no reason why a line which is
known and can be proved to be a horizontal line should
not *appear* a horizontal line: a line that made any angle with the perpendicular less than a right angle
would seem to him to indicate that his houses were all
tumbling down together. Accordingly, he makes the
line of his houses a horizontal line, and fails, of course,
to produce the effect demanded. Here, then, is one instance out of many in which not only the understanding is allowed to overrule the eyes, but where the understanding is positively allowed to obliterate the
eyes, as it were; for not only does the man believe the
evidence of his understanding in opposition to that of
his eyes, but (what is monstrous) the idiot is not
aware that his eyes ever gave such evidence. He does
not know that he has seen (and therefore *quoad* his
consciousness has *not* seen) that which he *has* seen
every day of his life.

But to return from this digression. My understanding could furnish no reason why the knocking at the
gate in *Macbeth* should produce any effect, direct or
reflected. In fact, my understanding said positively
that it could *not* produce any effect. But I knew better; I felt that it did; and I waited and clung to the
problem until further knowledge should enable me to
solve it. At length, in 1812, Mr. Williams made his
début on the stage of Ratcliffe Highway, and executed those unparalleled murders which have procured for him such a brilliant and undying reputation. On which murders, by the way, I must observe

that in one respect they have had an ill effect, by making the connoisseur in murder very fastidious in his taste, and dissatisfied by anything that has been since done in that line. All other murders look pale by the deep crimson of his; and, as an amateur once said to me in a querulous tone, "There has been absolutely nothing *doing* since his time, or nothing that's worth speaking of." But this is wrong; for it is unreasonable to expect all men to be great artists, and born with the genius of Mr. Williams. Now, it will be remembered that in the first of these murders (that of the Marrs) the same incident (of a knocking at the door soon after the work of extermination was complete) did actually occur which the genius of Shakespeare has invented; and all good judges, and the most eminent dilettanti, acknowledged the felicity of Shakespeare's suggestion as soon as it was actually realized. Here, then, was a fresh proof that I was right in relying on my own feeling, in opposition to my understanding; and I again set myself to study the problem. At length I solved it to my own satisfaction; and my solution is this: Murder, in ordinary cases, where the sympathy is wholly directed to the case of the murdered person, is an incident of coarse and vulgar horror; and for this reason—that it flings the interest exclusively upon the natural but ignoble instinct by which we cleave to life: an instinct which, as being indispensable to the primal law of self-preservation, is the same in kind (though different in degree) amongst all living creatures. This instinct, therefore, because it annihilates all distinctions, and degrades the greatest of men to the level of "the poor beetle that we tread on," exhibits human nature in its most abject and humiliating attitude. Such an attitude would little suit the purposes of the poet. What then must he do? He must throw the interest on the murderer. Our sympathy must be with *him* (of course I mean a sympathy of comprehension, a sympathy by which we enter into his feelings, and are made to understand them—not a sympathy of pity or approbation).[1] In the murdered person, all strife of thought, all flux and reflux of passion and of purpose, are crushed by one overwhelming panic; the fear of instant death smites him "with its petrific mace." But in the murderer, such a murderer as a poet will condescend to, there must be raging some great storm of passion—jealousy, ambition, vengeance, hatred—which will create a hell within him; and into this hell we are to look.

In *Macbeth*, for the sake of gratifying his own enormous and teeming faculty of creation, Shakespeare has introduced two murderers: and, as usual in his hands, they are remarkably discriminated: but—though in Macbeth the strife of mind is greater than in his wife, the tiger spirit not so awake, and his feelings caught chiefly by contagion from her—yet, as both were finally involved in the guilt of murder, the murderous mind of necessity is finally to be presumed in both. This was to be expressed; and, on its own account, as well as to make it a more proportionable antagonist to the unoffending nature of their victim, "the gracious Duncan," and adequately to expound "the deep damnation of his taking off," this was to be expressed with peculiar energy. We were to be made

---

[1] It seems almost ludicrous to guard and explain my use of a word in a situation where it would naturally explain itself. But it has become necessary to do so, in consequence of the unscholarlike use of the word sympathy, at present so general, by which, instead of taking it in its proper sense, as the act of reproducing in our minds the feelings of another, whether for hatred, indignation, love, pity, or approbation, it is made a mere synonym of the word *pity*; and hence, instead of saying "sympathy *with* another," many writers adopt the monstrous barbarism of "sympathy *for* another."

to feel that the human nature—*i.e.* the divine nature of love and mercy, spread through the hearts of all creatures, and seldom utterly withdrawn from man—was gone, vanished, extinct, and that the fiendish nature had taken its place. And, as this effect is marvellously accomplished in the *dialogues* and *soliloquies* themselves, so it is finally consummated by the expedient under consideration; and it is to this that I now solicit the reader's attention. If the reader has ever witnessed a wife, daughter, or sister in a fainting fit, he may chance to have observed that the most affecting moment in such a spectacle is *that* in which a sigh and a stirring announce the recommencement of suspended life. Or, if the reader has ever been present in a vast metropolis on the day when some great national idol was carried in funeral pomp to his grave, and, chancing to walk near the course through which it passed, has felt powerfully, in the silence and desertion of the streets, and in the stagnation of ordinary business, the deep interest which at that moment was possessing the heart of man—if all at once he should hear the death-like stillness broken up by the sound of wheels rattling away from the scene, and making known that the transitory vision was dissolved, he will be aware that at no moment was his sense of the complete suspension and pause in ordinary human concerns so full and affecting as at that moment when the suspension ceases, and the goings-on of human life are suddenly resumed. All action in any direction is best expounded, measured, and made apprehensible, by reaction. Now, apply this to the case in *Macbeth.* Here, as I have said, the retiring of the human heart and the entrance of the fiendish heart was to be expressed and made sensible. Another world has stepped in; and the murderers are taken out of the region of human things, human purposes, human desires. They are transfigured: Lady Macbeth is "unsexed"; Macbeth has forgot that he was born of woman; both are conformed to the image of devils; and the world of devils is suddenly revealed. But how shall this be conveyed and made palpable? In order that a new world may step in, this world must for a time disappear. The murderers and the murder must be insulated—cut off by an immeasurable gulf from the ordinary tide and succession of human affairs—locked up and sequestered in some deep recess; we must be made sensible that the world of ordinary life is suddenly arrested, laid asleep, tranced, racked into a dread armistice; time must be annihilated, relation to things without abolished; and all must pass self-withdrawn into a deep syncope and suspension of earthly passion. Hence it is that, when the deed is done, when the work of darkness is perfect, then the world of darkness passes away like a pageantry in the clouds: the knocking at the gate is heard, and it makes known audibly that the reaction has commenced; the human has made its reflux upon the fiendish; the pulses of life are beginning to beat again; and the re-establishment of the goings-on of the world in which we live first makes us profoundly sensible of the awful parenthesis that had suspended them.

O mighty poet! Thy works are not as those of other men, simply and merely great works of art, but are also like the phenomena of nature, like the sun and the sea, the stars and the flowers, like frost and snow, rain and dew, hail-storm and thunder, which are to be studied with entire submission of our own faculties, and in the perfect faith that in them there can be no too much or too little, nothing useless or inert, but that, the farther we press in our discoveries, the more we shall see proofs of design and self-supporting arrangement where the careless eye had seen nothing but accident!

THE LITERATURE OF KNOWLEDGE
AND THE LITERATURE OF POWER

(First published in the *North British Review*, August, 1848,
as part of a critical essay on Pope)

EVERY great classic in our native language should
from time to time be reviewed anew; and especially if he belongs in any considerable extent to that
section of the literature which connects itself with
manners, and if his reputation originally, or his style
of composition, is likely to have been much influenced
by the transient fashions of his own age. The with-
drawal, for instance, from a dramatic poet, or a sati-
rist, of any false lustre which he has owed to his
momentary connexion with what we may call the *personalities* of a fleeting generation, or of any undue
shelter to his errors which may have gathered round
them from political bias, or from intellectual infirmities amongst his partisans, will sometimes seriously
modify, after a century or so, the fairest *original* appreciation of a fine writer. A window composed of
Claude Lorraine glasses spreads over the landscape
outside a disturbing effect, which not the most practised eye can evade. The *eidola theatri* affect us all.
No man escapes the contagion from his contemporary
bystanders.

As books multiply to an unmanageable excess, selection becomes more and more a necessity for readers,
and the power of selection more and more a desperate
problem for the busy part of readers. The possibility

of selecting wisely is becoming continually more hopeless as the necessity for selection is becoming continually more pressing. Exactly as the growing weight of
books overlays and stifles the power of comparison,
pari passu is the call for comparison the more clamorous; and thus arises a duty correspondingly more
urgent of searching and revising until everything spurious has been weeded out from amongst the Flora of
our highest literature, and until the waste of time for
those who have so little at their command is reduced
to a *minimum*. For, where the good cannot be read in
its twentieth part, the more requisite it is that no part
of the bad should steal an hour of the available time;
and it is not to be endured that people without a minute to spare should be obliged first of all to read a book
before they can ascertain whether in fact it is *worth*
reading. The public cannot read by proxy as regards
the good which it is to appropriate, but it *can* as regards the poison which it is to escape. And thus, as
literature expands, becoming continually more of a
household necessity, the duty resting upon critics
(who are the vicarious readers for the public) becomes continually more urgent—of reviewing all
works that may be supposed to have benefited too
much or too indiscriminately by the superstition of a
name. The *prægustatores* should have tasted of every
cup, and reported its quality, before the public call for
it; and, above all, they should have done this in all
cases of the higher literature—that is, of literature
properly so called.

What is it that we mean by *literature?* Popularly,
and amongst the thoughtless, it is held to include
everything that is printed in a book. Little logic is required to disturb *that* definition. The most thoughtless person is easily made aware that in the idea of *lit-*

erature one essential element is some relation to a general and common interest of man—so that what applies only to a local, or professional, or merely personal interest, even though presenting itself in the shape of a book, will not belong to literature. So far the definition is easily narrowed; and it is as easily expanded. For not only is much that takes a station in books not literature; but inversely, much that really *is* literature never reaches a station in books. The weekly sermons of Christendom, that vast pulpit literature which acts so extensively upon the popular mind—to warn, to uphold, to renew, to comfort, to alarm—does not attain the sanctuary of libraries in the ten-thousandth part of its extent. The drama again—as, for instance, the finest of Shakespeare's plays in England, and all leading Athenian plays in the noontide of the Attic stage—operated as a literature on the public mind, and were (according to the strictest letter of that term) *published* through the audiences that witnessed [1] their representation some time before they were published as things to be read; and they were published in this scenical mode of publication with much more effect than they could have had as books during ages of costly copying or of costly printing.

Books, therefore, do not suggest an idea coextensive and interchangeable with the idea of literature; since much literature, scenic, forensic, or didactic (as from lecturers and public orators), may never come into books, and much that *does* come into books may con-

---

[1] Charles I, for example, when Prince of Wales, and many others in his father's court, gained their known familiarity with Shakespeare not through the original quartos, so slenderly diffused, nor through the first folio of 1623, but through the court representations of his chief dramas at Whitehall.

nect itself with no literary interest.[1] But a far more important correction, applicable to the common vague idea of literature, is to be sought not so much in a better definition of literature as in a sharper distinction of the two functions which it fulfils. In that great social organ which, collectively, we call literature, there may be distinguished two separate offices that may blend and often *do* so, but capable, severally, of a severe insulation, and naturally fitted for reciprocal repulsion. There is, first, the Literature of *Knowledge;* and, secondly, the Literature of *Power*. The function of the first is—to *teach;* the function of the second is —to *move:* the first is a rudder; the second, an oar or a sail. The first speaks to the *mere* discursive understanding; the second speaks ultimately, it may happen, to the higher understanding or reason, but always *through* affections of pleasure and sympathy. Remotely, it may travel towards an object seated in what Lord Bacon calls *dry* light; but, proximately, it does and must operate—else it ceases to be a Literature of *Power*—on and through that *humid* light which clothes itself in the mists and glittering *iris* of human passions, desires, and genial emotions. Men have so little reflected on the higher functions of literature as to find it a paradox if one should describe it as a mean or subordinate purpose of books to give information. But this is a paradox only in the sense which makes it

---

[1] What are called *The Blue Books*—by which title are understood the folio Reports issued every session of Parliament by committees of the two Houses, and stitched into blue covers— though often sneered at by the ignorant as so much waste paper, will be acknowledged gratefully by those who have used them diligently as the main well-heads of all accurate information as to the Great Britain of this day. As an immense depository of faithful (*and not superannuated*) statistics, they are indispensable to the honest student. But no man would therefore class *The Blue Books* as literature.

honourable to be paradoxical. Whenever we talk in ordinary language of seeking information or gaining knowledge, we understand the words as connected with something of absolute novelty. But it is the grandeur of all truth which *can* occupy a very high place in human interests that it is never absolutely novel to the meanest of minds: it exists eternally by way of germ or latent principle in the lowest as in the highest, needing to be developed, but never to be planted. To be capable of transplantation is the immediate criterion of a truth that ranges on a lower scale. Besides which, there is a rarer thing than truth—namely, *power*, or deep sympathy with truth. What is the effect, for instance, upon society, of children? By the pity, by the tenderness, and by the peculiar modes of admiration, which connect themselves with the helplessness, with the innocence, and with the simplicity of children, not only are the primal affections strengthened and continually renewed, but the qualities which are dearest in the sight of heaven—the frailty, for instance, which appeals to forbearance, the innocence which symbolizes the heavenly, and the simplicity which is most alien from the worldly—are kept up in perpetual remembrance, and their ideals are continually refreshed. A purpose of the same nature is answered by the higher literature, viz. the Literature of Power. What do you learn from *Paradise Lost?* Nothing at all. What do you learn from a cookery-book? Something new, something that you did not know before, in every paragraph. But would you therefore put the wretched cookery-book on a higher level of estimation than the divine poem? What you owe to Milton is not any knowledge, of which a million separate items are still but a million of advancing steps on the same earthly level; what you owe is *power*—that is, exercise and expansion to your own latent capacity of sympathy with the infinite, where every pulse and each separate influx is a step upwards, a step ascending as upon a Jacob's ladder from earth to mysterious altitudes above the earth. *All* the steps of knowledge, from first to last, carry you further on the same plane, but could never raise you one foot above your ancient level of earth: whereas the very *first* step in power is a flight—is an ascending movement into another element where earth is forgotten.

Were it not that human sensibilities are ventilated and continually called out into exercise by the great phenomena of infancy, or of real life as it moves through chance and change, or of literature as it recombines these elements in the mimicries of poetry, romance, &c., it is certain that, like any animal power or muscular energy falling into disuse, all such sensibilities would gradually droop and dwindle. It is in relation to these great *moral* capacities of man that the Literature of Power, as contradistinguished from that of knowledge, lives and has its field of action. It is concerned with what is highest in man; for the Scriptures themselves never condescended to deal by suggestion or co-operation with the mere discursive understanding: when speaking of man in his intellectual capacity, the Scriptures speak not of the understanding, but of *"the understanding heart"*—making the heart, *i.e.* the great *intuitive* (or non-discursive) organ, to be the interchangeable formula for man in his highest state of capacity for the infinite. Tragedy, romance, fairy tale, or epopee, all alike restore to man's mind the ideals of justice, of hope, of truth, of mercy, of retribution, which else (left to the support of daily life in its realities) would languish for want of sufficient illustration. What is meant, for instance, by *poetic justice?*—It does not mean a justice that differs by its object from the ordinary justice of human jurisprudence; for then it must be confessedly a very bad kind of justice; but it means a justice that differs from common forensic justice by the degree in which it *attains* its object, a justice that is more omnipotent over its own ends, as dealing—not with the refractory elements of earthly life, but with the elements of its own creation, and with materials flexible to its own purest preconceptions. It is certain that, were it not for the Literature of Power, these ideals would often remain amongst us as mere arid notional forms; whereas, by the creative forces of man put forth in literature, they gain a vernal life of restoration, and germinate into vital activities. The commonest novel, by moving in alliance with human fears and hopes, with human instincts of wrong and right, sustains and quickens those affections. Calling them into action, it rescues them from torpor. And hence the pre-eminency over all authors that merely *teach* of the meanest that *moves*, or that teaches, if at all, indirectly *by* moving. The very highest work that has ever existed in the Literature of Knowledge is but a *provisional* work: a book upon trial and sufferance, and *quamdiu bene se gesserit*. Let its teaching be even partially revised, let it be but expanded—nay, even let its teaching be but placed in a better order—and instantly it is superseded. Whereas the feeblest works in the Literature of Power, surviving at all, survive as finished and unalterable amongst men. For instance, the *Principia* of Sir Isaac Newton was a book *militant* on earth from the first. In all stages of its progress it would have to fight for its existence: first, as regards absolute truth; secondly, when that combat was over, as regards its form or mode of presenting the truth. And as soon as a Laplace, or anybody else, builds higher upon the foundations laid by this book, effectually he throws it out of the sunshine into decay and darkness; by weapons won from this book he superannuates and destroys this book, so that soon the name of Newton remains as a mere *nominis umbra*, but his book, as a living power, has transmigrated into other forms. Now, on the contrary, the Iliad, the *Prometheus* of Æschylus, the *Othello* or *King Lear*, the *Hamlet* or *Macbeth*, and the *Paradise Lost*, are not militant, but triumphant for ever as long as the languages exist in which they speak or can be taught to speak. They never *can* transmigrate into new incarnations. To reproduce *these* in new forms, or variations, even if in some things they should be improved, would be to plagiarize. A good steam-engine is properly superseded by a better. But one lovely pastoral valley is not superseded by another, nor a statue of Praxiteles by a statue of Michael Angelo. These things are separated not by imparity, but by disparity. They are not thought of as unequal under the same standard, but as different in *kind*, and, if otherwise equal, as equal under a different standard. Human works of immortal beauty and works of nature in one respect stand on the same footing: they never absolutely repeat each other, never approach so near as not to differ; and they differ not as better and worse, or simply by more and less: they differ by undecipherable and incommunicable differences, that cannot be caught by mimicries, that cannot be reflected in the mirror of copies, that cannot become ponderable in the scales of vulgar comparison.

All works in this class, as opposed to those in the Literature of Knowledge, first, work by far deeper agencies, and, secondly, are more permanent; in the strictest sense they are κτηματα ἐς ἀει: and what evil they do, or what good they do, is commensurate with the national language, sometimes long after the nation has departed. At this hour, five hundred years since their creation, the tales of Chaucer, never equalled on

this earth for their tenderness, and for life of picturesqueness, are read familiarly by many in the charming language of their natal day, and by others in the
modernizations of Dryden, of Pope, and Wordsworth.
At this hour, one thousand eight hundred years since
their creation, the Pagan tales of Ovid, never equalled
on this earth for the gaiety of their movement and the
capricious graces of their narrative, are read by all
Christendom. This man's people and their monuments
are dust; but *he* is alive: he has survived them, as he
told us that he had it in his commission to do, by a
thousand years; "and *shall* a thousand more."

All the Literature of Knowledge builds only ground-
nests, that are swept away by floods, or confounded by
the plough; but the Literature of Power builds nests in
aerial altitudes of temples sacred from violation, or of
forests inaccessible to fraud. *This* is a great prerogative of the *power* literature; and it is a greater which
lies in the mode of its influence. The *knowledge* literature, like the fashion of this world, passeth away. An
encyclopædia is its abstract; and, in this respect, it
may be taken for its speaking symbol—that before
one generation has passed an encyclopædia is superannuated; for it speaks through the dead memory and
unimpassioned understanding, which have not the repose of higher faculties, but are continually enlarging
and varying their phylacteries. But all literature properly so called—literature χατ' ἐξοχην—for the very
same reason that it is so much more durable than the
Literature of Knowledge, is (and by the very same
proportion it is) more intense and electrically searching in its impressions. The directions in which the
tragedy of this planet has trained our human feelings
to play, and the combinations into which the poetry of
this planet has thrown our human passions of love
and hatred, of admiration and contempt, exercise a

power for bad or good over human life that cannot be contemplated, when stretching through many generations, without a sentiment allied to awe.[1] And of this let every one be assured—that he owes to the impassioned books which he has read many a thousand more of emotions than he can consciously trace back to them. Dim by their origination, these emotions yet arise in him, and mould him through life, like forgotten incidents of his childhood.

[1] The reason why the broad distinctions between the two literatures of power and knowledge so little fix the attention lies in the fact that a vast proportion of books—history, biography, travels, miscellaneous essays, &c.—lying in a middle zone, confound these distinctions by interblending them. All that we call "amusement" or "entertainment" is a diluted form of the power belonging to passion, and also a mixed form; and, where threads of direct *instruction* intermingle in the texture with these threads of *power*, this absorption of the duality into one representative *nuance* neutralizes the separate perception of either. Fused into a *tertium quid*, or neutral state, they disappear to the popular eye as the repelling forces which, in fact, they are.

JOAN OF ARC [1]

(First published in *Tait's Magazine*, March and August, 1847)

WHAT is to be thought of *her?* What is to be thought of the poor shepherd girl from the hills and forests of Lorraine, that—like the Hebrew shepherd boy from the hills and forests of Judea—rose suddenly out of the quiet, out of the safety, out of the religious inspiration, rooted in deep pastoral solitudes, to a station in the van of armies, and to the more perilous station at the right hand of kings? The Hebrew boy inaugurated his patriotic mission by an *act*, by a victorious *act*, such as no man could deny. But so did the girl of Lorraine, if we

---

[1] "*Arc*": Modern France, that should know a great deal better than myself, insists that the name is not D'Arc—*i.e.* of Arc—but *Darc*. Now it happens sometimes that, if a person whose position guarantees his access to the best information will content himself with gloomy dogmatism, striking the table with his fist, and saying in a terrific voice "It *is* so, and there's an end of it," one bows deferentially, and submits. But, if, unhappily for himself, won by this docility, he relents too amiably into reasons and arguments, probably one raises an insurrection against him that may never be crushed; for in the fields of logic one can skirmish, perhaps, as well as he. Had he confined himself to dogmatism, he would have intrenched his position in darkness, and have hidden his own vulnerable points. But, coming down to base reasons, he lets in light, and one sees where to plant the blows. Now, the worshipful reason of modern France for disturbing the old received spelling is that Jean Hordal, a descendant of *La Pucelle's* brother, spelled the name *Darc* in 1612. But what of that? It is notorious that what small matter of spelling Providence had thought fit to disburse amongst man in the seventeenth century was all monopolized by printers: now, M. Hordal was *not* a printer.

read her story as it was read by those who saw her nearest. Adverse armies bore witness to the boy as no pretender; but so they did to the gentle girl. Judged by the voices of all who saw them *from a station of good-will*, both were found true and loyal to any promises involved in their first acts. Enemies it was that made the difference between their subsequent fortunes. The boy rose to a splendour and a noonday prosperity, both personal and public, that rang through the records of his people, and became a by-word amongst his posterity for a thousand years, until the sceptre was departing from Judah. The poor, forsaken girl, on the contrary, drank not herself from that cup of rest which she had secured for France. She never sang together with the songs that rose in her native Domrémy as echoes to the departing steps of invaders. She mingled not in the festal dances at Vaucouleurs which celebrated in rapture the redemption of France. No! for her voice was then silent; no! for her feet were dust. Pure, innocent, noble-hearted girl! whom, from earliest youth, ever I believed in as full of truth and self-sacrifice, this was amongst the strongest pledges for *thy* truth, that never once—no, not for a moment of weakness—didst thou revel in the vision of coronets and honour from man. Coronets for thee! Oh no! Honours, if they come when all is over, are for those that share thy blood.[1] Daughter of Domrémy, when the gratitude of thy king shall awaken, thou wilt be sleeping the sleep of the dead. Call her, King of France, but she will not hear thee. Cite her by the apparitors to come and receive a robe of honour, but she will be found *en contumace*. When the thunders of universal France, as even yet may happen, shall proclaim the grandeur of the poor shepherd girl that gave up all for

---

[1] *"Those that share thy blood"*: A collateral relative of Joanna's was subsequently ennobled by the title of *Du Lys*.

her country, thy ear, young shepherd girl, will have been deaf for five centuries. To suffer and to do, that was thy portion in this life; that was thy destiny; and not for a moment was it hidden from thyself. Life, thou saidst, is short; and the sleep which is in the grave is long; let me use that life, so transitory, for the glory of those heavenly dreams destined to comfort the sleep which is so long! This pure creature—pure from every suspicion of even a visionary self-interest, even as she was pure in senses more obvious—never once did this holy child, as regarded herself, relax from her belief in the darkness that was travelling to meet her. She might not prefigure the very manner of her death; she saw not in vision, perhaps, the aerial altitude of the fiery scaffold, the spectators without end on every road pouring into Rouen as to a coronation, the surging smoke, the volleying flames, the hostile faces all around, the pitying eye that lurked but here and there, until nature and imperishable truth broke loose from artificial restraints—these might not be apparent through the mists of the hurrying future. But the voice that called her to death, *that* she heard for ever.

Great was the throne of France even in those days, and great was he that sat upon it: but well Joanna knew that not the throne, nor he that sat upon it, was for *her;* but, on the contrary, that she was for *them;* not she by them, but they by her, should rise from the dust. Gorgeous were the lilies of France, and for centuries had the privilege to spread their beauty over land and sea, until, in another century, the wrath of God and man combined to wither them; but well Joanna knew, early at Domrémy she had read that bitter truth, that the lilies of France would decorate no garland for *her.* Flower nor bud, bell nor blossom, would ever bloom for *her!*

I am not going to write the history of *La Pucelle:* to do this, or even circumstantially to report the history of her persecution and bitter death, of her struggle with false witnesses and with ensnaring judges, it would be necessary to have before us *all* the documents, and therefore the collection only now forthcoming in Paris.[1] But *my* purpose is narrower. There have been great thinkers, disdaining the careless judgements of contemporaries, who have thrown themselves boldly on the judgement of a far posterity, that should have had time to review, to ponder, to compare. There have been great actors on the stage of tragic humanity that might, with the same depth of confidence, have appealed from the levity of compatriot friends—too heartless for the sublime interest of their story, and too impatient for the labour of sifting its perplexities —to the magnanimity and justice of enemies. To this class belongs the Maid of Arc.

Joanna, as we in England should call her, but, according to her own statement, Jeanne D'Arc, was born at Domrémy, a village on the marches of Lorraine and Champagne, and dependent upon the town of Vaucouleurs. I have called her a Lorrainer, not simply because the word is prettier, but because Champagne too odiously reminds us English of what are for *us* imaginary wines—which, undoubtedly, *La Pucelle* tasted as rarely as we English: we English, because the Champagne of London is chiefly grown in Devonshire; *La Pucelle*, because the Champagne of Champagne never, by any chance, flowed into the fountain of Domrémy, from which only she drank.

These disputes, however, turn on refinements too nice. Domrémy stood upon the frontiers, and, like other frontiers, produced a *mixed* race, representing

[1] *"Only now forthcoming":* In 1847 *began* the publication (from official records) of Joanna's trial.

the *cis* and the *trans*. A river (it is true) formed the
boundary-line at this point—the river Meuse; and
that, in old days, might have divided the populations;
but in these days it did not: there were bridges, there
were ferries, and weddings crossed from the right bank
to the left. Here lay two great roads, not so much for
travellers that were few, as for armies that were too
many by half. These two roads, one of which was the
great high road between France and Germany, *de-
cussated* at this very point; which is a learned way of
saying that they formed a St. Andrew's Cross, or letter
X. I hope the compositor will choose a good large **X**
in which case the point of intersection, the *locus* of
conflux and intersection for these four diverging arms,
will finish the reader's geographical education, by
showing him to a hair's-breadth where it was that
Domrémy stood. These roads, so grandly situated, as
great trunk arteries between two mighty realms,[1]
and haunted for ever by wars or rumours of wars, de-
cussated (for anything I know to the contrary) absolutely under Joanna's bedroom window: one rolling
away to the right, past Monsieur D'Arc's old barn, and
the other unaccountably preferring to sweep round
that odious man's pig-sty to the left.

That great four-headed road was a perpetual memento to patriotic ardour. To say "This way lies the
road to Paris, and that other way to Aix-la-Chapelle;
this to Prague, that to Vienna," nourished the warfare
of the heart by daily ministrations of sense. The eye
that watched for the gleams of lance or helmet from
the hostile frontier, the ear that listened for the groaning of wheels, made the high-road itself, with its rela-

---

[1] And reminding one of that inscription, so justly admired
by Paul Richter, which a Russian Czarina placed on a guide-
post near Moscow: *This is the road that leads to Constanti-
nople.*

tions to centres so remote, into a manual of patriotic duty.

The situation, therefore, *locally*, of Joanna was full of profound suggestions to a heart that listened for the stealthy steps of change and fear that too surely were in motion. But, if the place were grand, the time, the burden of the time, was far more so. The air overhead in its upper chambers was *hurtling* with the obscure sound; was dark with sullen fermenting of storms that had been gathering for a hundred and thirty years. The battle of Agincourt in Joanna's childhood had re-opened the wounds of France. Crécy and Poictiers, those withering overthrows for the chivalry of France, had, before Agincourt occurred, been tranquillized by more than half-a-century; but this resurrection of their trumpet wails made the whole series of battles and endless skirmishes take their stations as parts in one drama. The graves that had closed sixty years ago seemed to fly open in sympathy with a sorrow that echoed their own. The monarchy of France laboured in extremity, rocked and reeled like a ship fighting with the darkness of monsoons. The madness of the poor king (Charles VI) falling in at such a crisis, like the case of women labouring in childbirth during the storming of a city, trebled the awfulness of the time. Even the wild story of the incident which had immediately occasioned the explosion of this madness—the case of a man unknown, gloomy, and perhaps maniacal himself, coming out of a forest at noonday, laying his hand upon the bridle of the king's horse, checking him for a moment to say, "Oh, king, thou art betrayed," and then vanishing, no man knew whither, as he had appeared for no man knew what—fell in with the universal prostration of mind that laid France on her knees, as before the slow unweaving of some ancient prophetic doom. The famines, the extraordinary diseases, the insurrections of the peasantry up and down Europe—these were chords struck from the same mysterious harp; but these were transitory chords. There had been others of deeper and more ominous sound. The termination of the Crusades, the destruction of the Templars, the Papal interdicts, the tragedies caused or suffered by the house of Anjou, and by the Emperor —these were full of a more permanent significance. But, since then, the colossal figure of feudalism was seen standing, as it were on tiptoe, at Crécy, for flight from earth: that was a revolution unparalleled; yet *that* was a trifle by comparison with the more fearful revolutions that were mining below the Church. By her own internal schisms, by the abominable spectacle of a double pope—so that no man, except through political bias, could even guess which was Heaven's vice-gerent, and which the creature of Hell—the Church was rehearsing, as in still earlier forms she had already rehearsed, those vast rents in her foundations which no man should ever heal.

These were the loftiest peaks of the cloudland in the skies that to the scientific gazer first caught the colours of the *new* morning in advance. But the whole vast range alike of sweeping glooms overhead dwelt upon all meditative minds, even upon those that could not distinguish the tendencies nor decipher the forms. It was, therefore, not her own age alone as affected by its immediate calamities that lay with such weight upon Joanna's mind, but her own age as one section in a vast mysterious drama, unweaving through a century back, and drawing nearer continually to some dreadful crisis. Cataracts and rapids were heard roaring ahead; and signs were seen far back, by help of old men's memories, which answered secretly to signs now coming forward on the eye, even as locks answer to keys. It was not wonderful that in such a haunted solitude, with such a haunted heart, Joanna should see angelic visions, and hear angelic voices. These voices whispered to her for ever the duty, self-imposed, of delivering France. Five years she listened to these monitory voices with internal struggles. At length she could resist no longer. Doubt gave way; and she left her home for ever in order to present herself at the dauphin's court.

The education of this poor girl was mean according to the present standard: was ineffably grand, according to a purer philosophic standard: and only not good for our age because for us it would be unattainable. She read nothing, for she could not read; but she had heard others read parts of the Roman martyrology. She wept in sympathy with the sad *Misereres* of the Romish Church; she rose to heaven with the glad triumphant *Te Deums* of Rome; she drew her comfort and her vital strength from the rites of the same Church. But, next after these spiritual advantages, she owed most to the advantages of her situation. The fountain of Domrémy was on the brink of a boundless forest; and it was haunted to that degree by fairies that the parish priest (*curé*) was obliged to read mass there once a-year, in order to keep them in any decent bounds. Fairies are important, even in a statistical view: certain weeds mark poverty in the soil; fairies mark its solitude. As surely as the wolf retires before cities does the fairy sequester herself from the haunts of the licensed victualler. A village is too much for her nervous delicacy: at most, she can tolerate a distant view of a hamlet. We may judge, therefore, by the uneasiness and extra trouble which they gave to the parson, in what strength the fairies mustered at Domrémy, and, by a satisfactory consequence, how thinly sown with men and women must have been that region even in its inhabited spots. But the forests of Domrémy—those were the glories of the land: for in them abode mysterious powers and ancient secrets that towered into tragic strength. "Abbeys there were, and abbey windows"—"like Moorish temples of the Hindoos"—that exercised even princely power both in Lorraine and in the German Diets. These had their sweet bells that pierced the forests for many a league at matins or vespers, and each its own dreamy legend. Few enough, and scattered enough, were these abbeys, so as in no degree to disturb the deep solitude of the region; yet many enough to spread a network or awning of Christian sanctity over what else might have seemed a heathen wilderness. This sort of religious talisman being secured, a man the most afraid of ghosts (like myself, suppose, or the reader) becomes armed into courage to wander for days in their sylvan recesses. The mountains of the Vosges, on the eastern frontier of France, have never attracted much notice from Europe, except in 1813-14 for a few brief months, when they fell within Napoleon's line of defence against the Allies. But they are interesting for this amongst other features, that they do not, like some loftier ranges, repel woods: the forests and the hills are on sociable terms. *Live and let live* is their motto. For this reason, in part, these tracts in Lorraine were a favourite hunting-ground with the Carlovingian princes. About six hundred years before Joanna's childhood, Charlemagne was known to have hunted there. That, of itself, was a grand incident in the traditions of a forest or a chase. In these vast forests, also, were to be found (if anywhere to be found) those mysterious fawns that tempted solitary hunters into visionary and perilous pursuits. Here was seen (if anywhere seen) that ancient stag who was already nine hundred years old, but possibly a hundred or two more, when met by Charlemagne; and the thing was put beyond doubt by the inscription upon his golden collar. I believe Charlemagne knighted the stag; and, if ever he is met again by a king, he ought to be made an earl, or, being upon the marches of France, a marquis. Observe, I don't absolutely vouch for all these things: my own opinion varies. On a fine breezy forenoon I am audaciously sceptical; but as twilight sets in my credulity grows steadily, till it becomes equal to anything that could be desired. And I have heard candid sportsmen declare that, outside of these very forests, they laughed loudly at all the dim tales connected with their haunted solitudes, but, on reaching a spot notoriously eighteen miles deep within them, they agreed with Sir Roger de Coverley that a good deal might be said on both sides.

Such traditions, or any others that (like the stag) connect distant generations with each other, are, for that cause, sublime; and the sense of the shadowy, connected with such appearances that reveal themselves or not according to circumstances, leaves a colouring of sanctity over ancient forests, even in those minds that utterly reject the legend as a fact.

But, apart from all distinct stories of that order, in any solitary frontier between two great empires—as here, for instance, or in the desert between Syria and the Euphrates—there is an inevitable tendency, in minds of any deep sensibility, to people the solitudes with phantom images of powers that were of old so vast. Joanna, therefore, in her quiet occupation of a shepherdess, would be led continually to brood over the political condition of her country by the traditions of the past no less than by the mementos of the local present.

It is not requisite for the honour of Joanna, nor is there in this place room, to pursue her brief career of *action*. That, though wonderful, forms the earthly part of her story: the spiritual part is the saintly passion of her imprisonment, trial, and execution. It is sufficient, as concerns *this* section of Joanna's life, to say that she fulfilled, to the height of her promises, the restoration of the prostrate throne. France had become a province of England, and for the ruin of both, if such a yoke could be maintained. Dreadful pecuniary exhaustion caused the English energy to droop; and that critical opening *La Pucelle* used with a corresponding felicity of audacity and suddenness (that were in themselves portentous) for introducing the wedge of French native resources, for rekindling the national pride, and for planting the dauphin once more upon his feet. When Joanna appeared, he had been on the point of giving up the struggle with the English, distressed as they were, and of flying to the south of France. She taught him to blush for such abject counsels. She liberated Orleans, that great city, so decisive by its fate for the issue of the war, and then beleaguered by the English with an elaborate application of engineering skill unprecedented in Europe. Entering the city after sunset on the 29th of April, she sang mass on Sunday, May 8, for the entire disappearance of the besieging force. On the 29th of June she fought and gained over the English the decisive battle of Patay; on the 9th of July she took Troyes by a *coup-de-main* from a mixed garrison of English and Burgundians; on the 15th of that month she carried the dauphin into Rheims; on Sunday the 17th she crowned him; and there she rested from her labour of triumph. All that was to be *done* she had now accomplished: what remained was—to *suffer*.

All this forward movement was her own: excepting one man, the whole Council was against her. Her enemies were all that drew power from earth. Her supporters were her own strong enthusiasms, and the headlong contagion by which she carried this sublime frenzy into the hearts of women, of soldiers, and of all who lived by labour. Henceforwards she was thwarted; and the worst error that she committed was to lend the sanction of her presence to counsels which she had ceased to approve. But she had now accomplished the capital objects which her own visions had dictated. These involved all the rest. Errors were now less important; and doubtless it had now become more difficult for herself to pronounce authentically what *were* errors. The noble girl had achieved, as by a rapture of motion, the capital end of clearing out a free space around her sovereign, giving him the power to move his arms with effect, and, secondly, the inappreciable end of winning for that sovereign what seemed to all France the heavenly ratification of his rights, by crowning him with the ancient solemnities. She had made it impossible for the English now to step before her. They were caught in an irretrievable blunder, owing partly to discord amongst the uncles of Henry VI, partly to a want of funds, but partly to the very impossibility which they believed to press with tenfold force upon any French attempt to forestall theirs. They laughed at such a thought; and, whilst they laughed, she *did* it. Henceforth the single redress for the English of this capital oversight, but which never *could* have redressed it effectually, was to vitiate and taint the coronation of Charles VII as the work of a witch. That policy, and not malice, was the moving principle in the subsequent prosecution of Joanna. Unless they unhinged the force of the first coronation in the popular mind by associating it with power given from hell, they felt that the sceptre of the invader was broken.

But she, the child that, at nineteen, had wrought wonders so great for France, was she not elated? Did she not lose, as men so often *have* lost, all sobriety of mind when standing upon the pinnacle of success so giddy? Let her enemies declare. During the progress of her movement, and in the centre of ferocious struggles, she had manifested the temper of her feelings by the pity which she had everywhere expressed for the suffering enemy. She forwarded to the English leaders a touching invitation to unite with the French, as brothers, in a common crusade against infidels—thus opening the road for a soldierly retreat. She interposed to protect the captive or the wounded; she mourned over the excesses of her countrymen; she threw herself off her horse to kneel by the dying English soldier, and to comfort him with such ministrations, physical or spiritual, as his situation allowed. "*Nolebat,*" says the evidence, "*uti ense suo, aut quemquam interficere.*" She sheltered the English that invoked her aid in her own quarters. She wept as she beheld, stretched on the field of battle, so many brave enemies that had died without confession. And, as regarded herself, her elation expressed itself thus: On the day when she had finished her work, she wept; for she knew that, when her *triumphal* task was done, her end must be approaching. Her aspirations pointed only to a place which seemed to her more than usually full of natural piety, as one in which it would give her pleasure to die. And she uttered, between smiles and tears, as a wish that inexpressibly fascinated her heart, and yet was half-fantastic, a broken prayer that God would return her to the solitudes from which he had drawn her, and suffer her to become a shepherdess once more. It was a natural prayer, because nature has laid a necessity upon every human heart to seek for rest and to shrink from torment. Yet, again, it was a half-fantastic prayer, because, from childhood upwards, visions that she had no power to mistrust, and the voices which sounded in her ear for ever, had long since persuaded her mind that for *her* no such prayer could be granted. Too well she felt that her mission must be worked out to the end, and that the end was now at hand. All went wrong from this time. She herself had created the *funds* out of which the French restoration should grow; but she was not suffered to witness their development, or their prosperous application. More than one military plan was entered upon which she did not approve. But she still continued to expose her person as before. Severe wounds had not taught her caution. And at length, in a sortie from Compiègne (whether through treacherous collusion on the part of her own friends is doubtful to this day), she was made prisoner by the Burgundians, and finally surrendered to the English.

Now came her trial. This trial, moving of course under English influence, was conducted in chief by the Bishop of Beauvais. He was a Frenchman, sold to English interests, and hoping, by favour of the English leaders, to reach the highest preferment. *Bishop that art, Archbishop that shalt be, Cardinal that mayest be*, were the words that sounded continually in his ear; and doubtless a whisper of visions still higher, of a triple crown, and feet upon the necks of kings, sometimes stole into his heart.

Never from the foundations of the earth was there such a trial as this, if it were laid open in all its beauty of defence, and all its hellishness of attack. Oh, child of France! shepherdess, peasant girl! trodden under foot by all around thee, how I honour thy flashing intellect, quick as God's lightning, and true as God's lightning to its mark, that ran before France and laggard Europe by many a century, confounding the malice of the ensnarer, and making dumb the oracles of falsehood! Is it not scandalous, is it not humiliating to civilization, that, even at this day, France exhibits the horrid spectacle of judges examining the prisoner against himself; seducing him, by fraud, into treacherous conclusions against his own head; using the terrors of their power for extorting confessions from the frailty of hope; nay (which is worse), using the blandishments of condescension and snaky kindness for thawing into compliances of gratitude those whom they had failed to freeze into terror? Wicked judges! barbarian jurisprudence!—that, sitting in your own conceit on the summits of social wisdom, have yet failed to learn the first principles of criminal justice— sit ye humbly and with docility at the feet of this girl from Domrémy, that tore your webs of cruelty into shreds and dust. "Would you examine me as a witness against myself?" was the question by which many times she defied their arts. Continually she showed that their interrogations were irrelevant to any business before the court, or that entered into the ridiculous charges against her. General questions were proposed to her on points of casuistical divinity; two-edged questions, which not one of themselves could have answered, without, on the one side, landing himself in heresy (as then interpreted), or, on the other, in some presumptuous expression of self-esteem. Next came a wretched Dominican, that pressed her with an objection, which, if applied to the Bible, would tax every one of its miracles with unsoundness. The monk had the excuse of never having read the Bible. Her answer to this, if there were room to place the whole in a clear light, was as shattering as it was rapid. Another thought to entrap her by asking what language the angelic visitors of her solitude had talked—as though heavenly counsels could want polyglot interpreters for every word, or that God needed language at all in whispering thoughts to a human heart. Then came a

worse devil, who asked her whether the Archangel
Michael had appeared naked. Not comprehending the
vile insinuation, Joanna, whose poverty suggested to
her simplicity that it might be the *costliness* of suitable
robes which caused the demur, asked them if they
fancied God, who clothed the flowers of the valleys,
unable to find raiment for his servants. The answer of
Joanna moves a smile of tenderness, but the disappointment of her judges makes one laugh exultingly. Others
succeeded by troops, who upbraided her with leaving
her father; as if that greater Father, whom she believed herself to have been serving, did not retain the
power of dispensing with his own rules, or had not
said that for a less cause than martyrdom man and
woman should leave both father and mother.

On Easter Sunday, when the trial had been long
proceeding, the poor girl fell so ill as to cause a belief
that she had been poisoned. It was not poison. Nobody
had any interest in hastening a death so certain.
Joanna had a twofold malady. She was visited by a
paroxysm of the complaint called *home-sickness*. The
cruel nature of her imprisonment, and its length, could
not but point her solitary thoughts, in darkness and in
chains (for chained she was), to Domrémy. And the
season, which was the most heavenly period of the
spring, added stings to this yearning. That was one of
her maladies—*nostalgia*, as medicine calls it; the other
was weariness and exhaustion from daily combats with
malice. She saw that everybody hated her, and thirsted
for her blood; nay, many kind-hearted creatures that
would have pitied her profoundly, as regarded all political charges, had their natural feelings warped by
the belief that she had dealings with fiendish powers.
She knew she was to die; that was *not* the misery: the
misery was that this consummation could not be
reached without so much intermediate strife, as if she

were contending for some chance (where chance was none) of happiness, or were dreaming for a moment of escaping the inevitable. Why, then, *did* she contend? Knowing that she would reap nothing from answering her persecutors, why did she not retire by silence from the superfluous contest? It was because her quick and eager loyalty to truth would not suffer her to see it darkened by frauds which *she* could expose, but others, even of candid listeners, perhaps, could not; it was through that imperishable grandeur of soul which taught her to submit meekly and without a struggle to her punishment, but taught her *not* to submit—no, not for a moment—to calumny as to facts, or to misconstruction as to motives. Besides, there were secretaries all around the court taking down her words. That was meant for no good to *her*. But the end does not always correspond to the meaning. And Joanna might say to herself, "These words that will be used against me tomorrow and the next day perhaps in some nobler generation may rise again for my justification." Yes, Joanna, they *are* rising even now in Paris, and for more than justification!

On the Wednesday after Trinity Sunday in 1431, being then about nineteen years of age, the Maid of Arc underwent her martyrdom. She was conducted before mid-day, guarded by eight hundred spearmen, to a platform of prodigious height, constructed of wooden billets supported by occasional walls of lath and plaster, and traversed by hollow spaces in every direction for the creation of air-currents.

The executioner had been directed to apply his torch from below. He did so. The fiery smoke rose upwards in billowing volumes. A Dominican monk was then standing almost at her side. Wrapped up in his sublime office, he saw not the danger, but still persisted in his prayers. Even then, when the last enemy was racing up the fiery stairs to seize her, even at that moment did this noblest of girls think only for *him*, the one friend that would not forsake her, and not for herself; bidding him with her last breath to care for his own preservation, but to leave *her* to God.

Bishop of Beauvais! thy victim died in fire upon a scaffold—thou upon a down bed. But, for the departing minutes of life, both are oftentimes alike. At the farewell crisis, when the gates of death are opening, and flesh is resting from its struggles, oftentimes the tortured and the torturer have the same truce from carnal torment; both sink together into sleep; together both sometimes kindle into dreams. When the mortal mists were gathering fast upon you two, bishop and shepherd girl—when the pavilions of life were closing up their shadowy curtains about you—let us try, through the gigantic glooms, to decipher the flying features of your separate visions.

The shepherd girl that had delivered France—she, from her dungeon, she, from her baiting at the stake, she, from her duel with fire, as she entered her last dream—saw Domrémy, saw the fountain of Domrémy, saw the pomp of forests in which her childhood had wandered. That Easter festival which man had denied to her languishing heart—that resurrection of spring-time, which the darkness of dungeons had intercepted from *her*, hungering after the glorious liberty of forests—were by God given back into her hands, as jewels that had been stolen from her by robbers. With those, perhaps (for the minutes of dreams can stretch into ages), was given back to her by God the bliss of childhood. By special privilege for *her* might be created, in this farewell dream, a second childhood, innocent as the first; but not, like *that*, sad with the gloom of a fearful mission in the rear. This mission had now been fulfilled. The storm was weathered; the skirts even of that mighty storm were drawing off. The blood that she was to reckon for had been exacted; the tears that she was to shed in secret had been paid to the last. The hatred to herself in all eyes had been faced steadily, had been suffered, had been survived. And in her last fight upon the scaffold she had triumphed gloriously; victoriously she had tasted the stings of death. For all, except this comfort from her farewell dream, she had died—died, amidst the tears of ten thousand enemies—died, amidst the drums and trumpets of armies—died, amidst peals redoubling upon peals, volleys upon volleys, from the saluting clarions of martyrs.

Bishop of Beauvais! because the guilt-burdened man is in dreams haunted and waylaid by the most frightful of his crimes, and because upon that fluctuating mirror—rising (like the mocking mirrors of *mirage* in Arabian deserts) from the fens of death—most of all are reflected the sweet countenances which the man has laid in ruins; therefore I know, bishop, that you also, entering your final dream, saw Domrémy. That fountain, of which the witnesses spoke so much, showed itself to your eyes in pure morning dews: but neither dews, nor the holy dawn, could cleanse away the bright spots of innocent blood upon its surface. By the fountain, bishop, you saw a woman seated, that hid her face. But, as *you* draw near, the woman raises her wasted features. Would Domrémy know them again for the features of her child? Ah, but *you* know them, bishop, well! Oh, mercy! what a groan was *that* which the servants, waiting outside the bishop's dream at his beside, heard from his labouring heart, as at this moment he turned away from the fountain and the woman, seeking rest in the forests afar off. Yet not *so* to escape the woman, whom once again he must behold before he dies. In the forests to which he prays for pity, will he find a respite? What a tumult, what a gathering of feet is there! In glades where only wild deer should run armies and nations are assembling; towering in the fluctuating crowd are phantoms that belong to departed hours. There is the great English Prince, Regent of France. There is my Lord of Winchester, the princely cardinal, that died and made no sign. There is the Bishop of Beauvais, clinging to the shelter of thickets. What building is that which hands so rapid are raising? Is it a martyr's scaffold? Will they burn the child of Domrémy a second time? No: it is a tribunal that rises to the clouds; and two nations stand around it, waiting for a trial. Shall my Lord of Beauvais sit again upon the judgement-seat, and again number the hours for the innocent? Ah no! he is the prisoner at the bar. Already all is waiting: the mighty audience is gathered, the Court is hurrying to their seats, the witnesses are arrayed, the trumpets are sounding, the judge is taking his place. Oh! but this is sudden. My lord, have you no counsel? "Counsel I have none: in heaven above, or on earth beneath, counsellor there is none now that would take a brief from *me:* all are silent." Is it, indeed, come to this? Alas! the time is short, the tumult is wondrous, the crowd stretches away into infinity; but yet I will search in it for somebody to take your brief: I know of somebody that will be your counsel. Who is this that cometh from Domrémy? Who is she in bloody coronation robes from Rheims? Who is she that cometh with blackened flesh from walking the furnaces of Rouen? This is she, the shepherd girl, counsellor that had none for herself, whom I choose, bishop, for yours. She it is, I engage, that shall take my lord's brief. She it is, bishop, that would plead for you: yes, bishop, SHE—when heaven and earth are silent.

REVOLT OF THE TARTARS

OR, FLIGHT OF THE KALMUCK KHAN AND HIS PEOPLE FROM THE
RUSSIAN TERRITORIES TO THE FRONTIERS OF CHINA

(First published in *Blackwood's Magazine*, July, 1837)

THERE is no great event in modern history, or, perhaps it may be said more broadly, none in all history from its earliest records, less generally known, or more striking to the imagination, than the flight eastwards of a principal Tartar nation across the boundless *steppes* of Asia in the latter half of the last century. The *terminus a quo* of this flight, and the *terminus ad quem,* are equally magnificent; the mightiest of Christian thrones being the one, the mightiest of Pagan the other. And the grandeur of these two terminal objects is harmoniously supported by the romantic circumstances of the flight. In the abruptness of its commencement, and the fierce velocity of its execution, we read the wild barbaric character of those who conducted the movement. In the unity of purpose connecting this myriad of wills, and in the blind but unerring aim at a mark so remote, there is something which recalls to the mind those almighty instincts that propel the migrations of the swallow and the lemming, or the life-withering marches of the locust. Then, again, in the gloomy vengeance of Russia and her vast artillery, which hung upon the rear and the skirts of the fugitive vassals, we are reminded of Miltonic images—such, for instance, as that of the solitary hand pursuing through desert spaces and through ancient chaos a rebellious host, and overtaking with volleying thunders those who believed themselves already within the security of darkness and of distance.

On the 21st of January 1761 the young Prince Ou-bacha assumed the sceptre of the Kalmucks upon the death of his father. Some part of the power attached to this dignity he had already wielded since his fourteenth year, in quality of Vice-Khan, by the express appointment and with the avowed support of the Russian Government. He was now about eighteen years of age, amiable in his personal character, and not without titles to respect in his public character as a sovereign prince.

At the outset of his reign, he met with a rival in popular favour—almost a competitor—in the person of Zebek-Dorchi, a prince with considerable pretensions to the throne, and perhaps, it might be said, with equal pretensions. Zebek-Dorchi was a direct descendant of the same royal house as himself, through a different branch. On public grounds, his claim stood, perhaps, on a footing equally good with that of Oubacha, whilst his personal qualities, even in those aspects which seemed to a philosophical observer most odious and repulsive, promised the most effectual aid to the dark purposes of an intriguer or a conspirator, and were generally fitted to win a popular support precisely in those points where Oubacha was most defective. He was much superior in external appearance to his rival on the throne, and so far better qualified to win the good opinion of a semi-barbarous people; whilst his dark intellectual qualities of Machiavellian dissimulation, profound hypocrisy, and perfidy which knew no touch of remorse, were admirably calculated to sustain any ground which he might win from the simple hearted people with whom he had to deal, and from the frank carelessness of his unconscious competitor.

At the very outset of his treacherous career, Zebek-Dorchi was sagacious enough to perceive that nothing could be gained by open declaration of hostility to the reigning prince: the choice had been a deliberate act on the part of Russia, and Elizabeth Petrovna was not the person to recall her own favours with levity, or upon slight grounds. Openly, therefore, to have declared his enmity towards his relative on the throne could have had no effect but that of arming suspicions against his own ulterior purposes in a quarter where it was most essential to his interest that, for the present, all suspicion should be hoodwinked. Accordingly, after much meditation, the course he took for opening his snares was this: He raised a rumour that his own life was in danger from the plots of several Saissang (that is, Kalmuck nobles), who were leagued together, under an oath, to assassinate him; and immediately after, assuming a well-counterfeited alarm, he fled to Tcherkask, followed by sixty-five tents. From this place he kept up a correspondence with the Imperial Court; and, by way of soliciting his cause more effectually, he soon repaired in person to St. Petersburg. Once admitted to personal conferences with the cabinet, he found no difficulty in winning over the Russian counsels to a concurrence with some of his political views, and thus covertly introducing the point of that wedge which was finally to accomplish his purposes.

Having thus completely blindfolded the Cabinet of Russia, Zebek-Dorchi proceeded in his new character to fulfil his political mission with the Khan of the Kalmucks. So artfully did he prepare the road for his favourable reception at the court of this prince that he was at once and universally welcomed as a benefactor. The first use which he made of his new functions about

the Khan's person was to attack the Court of Russia.
This was a dangerous step: but it was indispensable to
his further advance upon the gloomy path which he
had traced out for himself. A triple vengeance was
what he meditated: 1, upon the Russian Cabinet for
having undervalued his own pretensions to the throne;
2, upon his amiable rival for having supplanted him;
and, 3, upon all those of the nobility who had manifested their sense of his weakness by their neglect, or
their sense of his perfidious character by their suspicions. Here was a colossal outline of wickedness; and
by one in his situation, feeble (as it might seem) for
the accomplishment of its humblest parts, how was the
total edifice to be reared in its comprehensive grandeur? He, a worm as he was, could he venture to assail
the mighty behemoth of Muscovy, the potentate who
counted three hundred languages around the footsteps
of his throne, and from whose "lion ramp" recoiled
alike "baptized and infidel"—Christendom on the one
side, strong by her intellect and her organization, and
the "Barbaric East" on the other, with her unnumbered numbers? The match was a monstrous one; but
in its very monstrosity there lay this germ of encouragement, that it could not be suspected. The very
hopelessness of the scheme grounded his hope, and he
resolved to execute a vengeance which should involve,
as it were, in the unity of a well-laid tragic fable, all
whom he judged to be his enemies. That vengeance lay
in detaching from the Russian Empire the whole Kalmuck nation, and breaking up that system of intercourse which had thus far been beneficial to both. This
last was a consideration which moved him but little.
True it was, that Russia to the Kalmucks had secured
lands and extensive pasturage; true it was, that the
Kalmucks reciprocally to Russia had furnished a
powerful cavalry. But the latter loss would be part of

his triumph, and the former might be more than compensated in other climates under other sovereigns. Here was a scheme which, in its final accomplishment, would avenge him bitterly on the Czarina, and in the course of its accomplishment might furnish him with ample occasions for removing his other enemies. It may be readily supposed, indeed, that he who could deliberately raise his eyes to the Russian autocrat as an antagonist in single duel with himself was not likely to feel much anxiety about Kalmuck enemies of whatever rank. He took his resolution, therefore, sternly and irrevocably, to effect this astonishing translation of an ancient people across the pathless deserts of Central Asia, intersected continually by rapid rivers, rarely furnished with bridges, and of which the fords were known only to those who might think it for their interest to conceal them, through many nations inhospitable or hostile: frost and snow around them (from the necessity of commencing their flight in winter), famine in their front, and the sabre, or even the artillery of an offended and mighty empress, hanging upon their rear for thousands of miles. But what was to be their final mark—the port of shelter after so fearful a course of wandering? Two things were evident: it must be some power at a great distance from Russia, so as to make return even in that view hopeless; and it must be a power of sufficient rank to insure them protection from any hostile efforts on the part of the Czarina for reclaiming them, or for chastising their revolt. Both conditions were united obviously in the person of Kien Long, the reigning Emperor of China, who was further recommended to them by his respect for the head of their religion. To China, therefore, and, as their first rendezvous, to the shadow of the great Chinese Wall, it was settled by Zebek that they should direct their flight.

Next came the question of time—*when* should the
flight commence? and, finally, the more delicate question as to the choice of accomplices. To extend the
knowledge of the conspiracy too far was to insure its
betrayal to the Russian Government. Yet, at some
stage of the preparations, it was evident that a very
extensive confidence must be made, because in no other
way could the mass of the Kalmuck population be persuaded to furnish their families with the requisite
equipments for so long a migration. This critical step,
however, it was resolved to defer up to the latest possible moment, and, at all events, to make no general
communication on the subject until the time of departure should be definitely settled. This could only
be done by addressing themselves to the great head of
their religion, the Dalai-Lama of Tibet. Him they
easily persuaded to countenance their schemes: and
an oracle was delivered solemnly at Tibet, to the effect
that no ultimate prosperity would attend this great
exodus unless it were pursued through the years of the
tiger and the *hare*. Now, the Kalmuck custom is to distinguish their years by attaching to each a denomination taken from one of twelve animals, the exact order
of succession being absolutely fixed, so that the cycle
revolves of course through a period of a dozen years.
Consequently, if the approaching year of the *tiger* were
suffered to escape them, in that case the expedition
must be delayed for twelve years more; within which
period, even were no other unfavourable changes to
arise, it was pretty well foreseen that the Russian Government would take the most effectual means for bri-
dling their vagrant propensities by a ring-fence of forts
or military posts; to say nothing of the still readier
plan for securing their fidelity (a plan already talked
of in all quarters) by exacting a large body of hostages
selected from the families of the most influential no-

bles. On these cogent considerations, it was solemnly determined that this terrific experiment should be made in the next year of the *tiger,* which happened to fall upon the Christian year 1771. With respect to the month, there was, unhappily for the Kalmucks, even less latitude allowed to their choice than with respect to the year. It was absolutely necessary, or it was thought so, that the different divisions of the nation which pastured their flocks on both banks of the Volga should have the means of effecting an instantaneous junction; because the danger of being intercepted by flying columns of the imperial armies was precisely the greatest at the outset. Now, from the want of bridges, or sufficient river craft for transporting so vast a body of men, the sole means which could be depended upon (especially where so many women, children, and camels were concerned) was *ice:* and this, in a state of sufficient firmness, could not be absolutely counted upon before the month of January. Hence it happened that this astonishing exodus of a whole nation, before so much as a whisper of the design had begun to circulate amongst those whom it most interested, before it was even suspected that any man's wishes pointed in that direction, had been definitely appointed for January of the year 1771. And almost up to the Christmas of 1770 the poor simple Kalmuck herdsmen and their families were going nightly to their peaceful beds, without even dreaming that the *fiat* had already gone forth from their rulers which consigned those quiet abodes, together with the peace and comfort which reigned within them, to a withering desolation, now close at hand.

The time was now rapidly approaching for the mighty experiment. The day was drawing near on which the signal was to be given for raising the standard of revolt, and by a combined movement on both sides of the Volga for spreading the smoke of one vast

conflagration, that should wrap in a common blaze
their own huts and the stately cities of their enemies,
over the breadth and length of those great provinces
in which their flocks were dispersed. The year of the
tiger was now within one little month of its commencement; the fifth morning of that year was fixed
for the fatal day when the fortunes and happiness of a
whole nation were to be put upon the hazard of a
dicer's throw; and as yet that nation was in profound
ignorance of the whole plan. The Khan, such was the
kindness of his nature, could not bring himself to make
the revelation so urgently required. It was clear, however, that this could not be delayed; and Zebek-Dorchi
took the task willingly upon himself. But where or
how should this notification be made, so as to exclude
Russian hearers? After some deliberation, the following plan was adopted: Couriers, it was contrived,
should arrive in furious haste, one upon the heels of
another, reporting a sudden inroad of the Kirghises
and Bashkirs upon the Kalmuck lands, at a point distant about 120 miles. Thither all the Kalmuck families, according to immemorial custom, were required
to send a separate representative; and there accordingly, within three days, all appeared. The distance,
the solitary ground appointed for the rendezvous, the
rapidity of the march, all tended to make it almost certain that no Russian could be present. Zebek-Dorchi
then came forward. He did not waste many words upon
rhetoric. He unfurled an immense sheet of parchment,
visible from the uttermost distance at which any of this
vast crowd could stand; the total number amounted to
80,000; all saw, and many heard. They were told of
the oppressions of Russia; of her pride and haughty
disdain evidenced towards them by a thousand acts;
of her contempt for their religion; of her determination to reduce them to absolute slavery; of the pre-

liminary measures she had already taken by erecting
forts upon many of the great rivers in their neighbourhood; of the ulterior intentions she thus announced to
circumscribe their pastoral lands, until they would all
be obliged to renounce their flocks, and to collect in
towns like Sarepta, there to pursue mechanical and
servile trades of shoemaker, tailor, and weaver, such
as the free-born Tartar had always disdained. "Then,
again," said the subtle prince, "she increases her military levies upon our population every year; we pour
out our blood as young men in her defence, or more
often in support of her insolent aggressions; and, as
old men, we reap nothing from our sufferings, nor
benefit by our survivorship where so many are sacrificed." At this point of his harangue, Zebek produced
several papers (forged, as it is generally believed),
containing projects of the Russian court for a general
transfer of the eldest sons, taken *en masse* from the
greatest Kalmuck families, to the imperial court. "Now
let this be once accomplished," he argued, "and there
is an end of all useful resistance from that day forwards. Petitions we might make, or even remon-
strances; as men of words we might play a bold part;
but for deeds, for that sort of language by which our
ancestors were used to speak—holding us by such a
chain, Russia would make a jest of our wishes, knowing full well that we should not dare to make any
effectual movement."

Having thus sufficiently roused the angry passions
of his vast audience, and having alarmed their fears
by this pretended scheme against their first-born (an
artifice which was indispensable to his purpose, because it met beforehand *every* form of amendment to
his proposal coming from the more moderate nobles,
who would not otherwise have failed to insist upon trying the effect of bold addresses to the Empress before

resorting to any desperate extremity), Zebek-Dorchi
opened his scheme of revolt, and, if so, of instant revolt; since any preparations reported at St. Petersburg
would be a signal for the armies of Russia to cross into
such positions from all parts of Asia as would effectually intercept their march. It is remarkable, however,
that, with all his audacity and his reliance upon the
momentary excitement of the Kalmucks, the subtle
prince did not venture, at this stage of his seduction,
to make so startling a proposal as that of a flight to
China. All that he held out for the present was a rapid
march to the Temba or some other great river, which
they were to cross, and to take up a strong position on
the farther bank, from which, as from a post of conscious security, they could hold a bolder language to
the Czarina, and one which would have a better chance
of winning a favourable audience.

These things, in the irritated condition of the simple
Tartars, passed by acclamation; and all returned homewards to push forward with the most furious speed the
preparations for their awful undertaking. Rapid and
energetic these of necessity were; and in that degree
they became noticeable and manifest to the Russians
who happened to be intermingled with the different
hordes, either on commercial errands, or as agents officially from the Russian Government, some in a fi-
nancial, others in a diplomatic character.

Christmas arrived; and, a little before that time,
courier upon courier came dropping in, one upon the
very heels of another, to St. Petersburg, assuring the
Czarina that beyond all doubt the Kalmucks were in
the very crisis of departure.

Precisely on the 5th of January, the day so solemnly
appointed under religious sanctions by the Lama, the
Kalmucks on the east bank of the Volga were seen at
the earliest dawn of day assembling by troops and

squadrons, and in the tumultuous movement of some
great morning of battle. Tens of thousands continued
moving off the ground at every half-hour's interval.
Women and children, to the amount of two hundred
thousand and upwards, were placed upon waggons, or
upon camels, and drew off by masses of twenty thousand at once—placed under suitable escorts, and continually swelled in numbers by other outlying bodies
of the horde, who kept falling in at various distances
upon the first and second day's march. From sixty to
eighty thousand of those who were the best mounted
stayed behind the rest of the tribes, with purposes of
devastation and plunder more violent than prudence
justified, or the amiable character of the Khan could
be supposed to approve. But in this, as in other instances, he was completely overruled by the malignant
counsels of Zebek-Dorchi. The first tempest of the
desolating fury of the Tartars discharged itself upon
their own habitations. But this, as cutting off all infirm looking backward from the hardships of their
march, had been thought so necessary a measure by all
the chieftains that even Oubacha himself was the first
to authorize the act by his own example. He seized
a torch previously prepared with materials the most
durable as well as combustible, and steadily applied it
to the timbers of his own palace. Nothing was saved
from the general wreck except the portable part of the
domestic utensils, and that part of the wood-work
which could be applied to the manufacture of the long
Tartar lances. This chapter in their memorable day's
work being finished, and the whole of their villages
throughout a district of ten thousand square miles in
one simultaneous blaze, the Tartars waited for further
orders.

These, it was intended. should have taken a character of valedictory vengeance, and thus have left be-

hind to the Czarina a dreadful commentary upon the
main motives of their flight. It was the purposes of
Zebek-Dorchi that all the Russian towns, churches,
and buildings of every description, should be given up
to pillage and destruction, and such treatment applied
to the defenceless inhabitants as might naturally be
expected from a fierce people already infuriated by the
spectacle of their own outrages, and by the bloody retaliations which they must necessarily have provoked.
This part of the tragedy, however, was happily intercepted by a providential disappointment at the very
crisis of departure. It has been mentioned already that
the motive for selecting the depth of winter as the season of flight (which otherwise was obviously the very
worst possible) had been the impossibility of effecting
a junction sufficiently rapid with the tribes on the west
of the Volga, in the absence of bridges, unless by a
natural bridge of ice. For this one advantage, the Kalmuck leaders had consented to aggravate by a thou-
sandfold the calamities inevitable to a rapid flight over
boundless tracts of country, with women, children, and
herds of cattle—for this one single advantage; and
yet, after all, it was lost. The reason never has been explained satisfactorily, but the fact was such. Some have
said that the signals were not properly concerted for
marking the moment of absolute departure—that is,
for signifying whether the settled intention of the
Eastern Kalmucks might not have been suddenly interrupted by adverse intelligence. Others have supposed that the ice might not be equally strong on both
sides of the river, and might even be generally insecure
for the treading of heavy and heavily-laden animals
such as camels. But the prevailing notion is that some
accidental movements on the 3d and 4th of January
of Russian troops in the neighbourhood of the Western Kalmucks, though really having no reference to

them or their plans, had been construed into certain signs that all was discovered; and that the prudence of the Western chieftains, who, from situation, had never been exposed to those intrigues by which Zebek-Dorchi had practised upon the pride of the Eastern tribes, now stepped in to save their people from ruin. Be the cause what it might, it is certain that the Western Kalmucks were in some way prevented from forming the intended junction with their brethren of the opposite bank; and the result was that at least one hundred thousand of these Tartars were left behind in Russia. This accident it was which saved their Russian neighbours universally from the desolation which else awaited them. One general massacre and conflagration would assuredly have surprised them, to the utter extermination of their property, their houses, and themselves, had it not been for this disappointment. But the Eastern chieftains did not dare to put to hazard the safety of their brethren under the first impulse of the Czarina's vengeance for so dreadful a tragedy; for, as they were well aware of too many circumstances by which she might discover the concurrence of the Western people in the general scheme of revolt, they justly feared that she would thence infer their concurrence also in the bloody events which marked its outset.

Little did the Western Kalmucks guess what reasons they also had for gratitude on account of an interposition so unexpected, and which at the moment they so generally deplored. Could they but have witnessed the thousandth part of the sufferings which overtook their Eastern brethren in the first month of their sad flight, they would have blessed Heaven for their own narrow escape; and yet these sufferings of the first month were but a prelude or foretaste comparatively slight of those which afterwards succeeded.

For now began to unroll the most awful series of

calamities, and the most extensive, which is anywhere
recorded to have visited the sons and daughters of men.
It is possible that the sudden inroads of destroying nations, such as the Huns, or the Avars, or the Mongol
Tartars, may have inflicted misery as extensive; but
there the misery and the desolation would be sudden,
like the flight of volleying lightning. Those who were
spared at first would generally be spared to the end;
those who perished at all would perish at once. It is
possible that the French retreat from Moscow may
have made some nearer approach to this calamity in
duration, though still a feeble and miniature approach;
for the French sufferings did not commence in good
earnest until about one month from the time of leaving Moscow; and, though it is true that afterwards the
vials of wrath were emptied upon the devoted army
for six or seven weeks in succession, yet what is that
to this Kalmuck tragedy, which lasted for more than
as many months? But the main feature of horror by
which the Tartar march was distinguished from the
French lies in the accompaniment of women and children. There were both, it is true, with the French
army, but not so many as to bear any marked proportion to the total numbers concerned. The French, in
short, were merely an army—a host of professional
destroyers, whose regular trade was bloodshed, and
whose regular element was danger and suffering. But
the Tartars were a nation carrying along with them
more than two hundred and fifty thousand women and
children, utterly unequal, for the most part, to any
contest with the calamities before them.

The first point to be reached, before any hope of repose could be encouraged, was the river Jaik. This was
not above 300 miles from the main point of departure
on the Volga; and, if the march thither was to be a
forced one, and a severe one, it was alleged, on the

other hand, that the suffering would be the more brief
and transient; one summary exertion, not to be repeated, and all was achieved. Forced the march was,
and severe beyond example: there the forewarning
proved correct; but the promised rest proved a mere
phantom of the wilderness—a visionary rainbow,
which fled before their hope-sick eyes, across these interminable solitudes, for seven months of hardship
and calamity, without a pause. These sufferings, by
their very nature, and the circumstances under which
they arose, were (like the scenery of the steppes) somewhat monotonous in their colouring and external features; what variety, however, there was will be most
naturally exhibited by tracing historically the successive stages of the general misery, exactly as it unfolded itself under the double agency of weakness still
increasing from within and hostile pressure from without. Viewed in this manner, under the real order of
development, it is remarkable that these sufferings of
the Tartars, though under the moulding hands of accident, arrange themselves almost with a scenical propriety. They seem combined as with the skill of an
artist; the intensity of the misery advancing regularly
with the advances of the march, and the stages of the
calamity corresponding to the stages of the route; so
that, upon raising the curtain which veils the great
catastrophe, we behold one vast climax of anguish,
towering upwards by regular gradations, as if constructed artificially for picturesque effect—a result
which might not have been surprising had it been reasonable to anticipate the same rate of speed, and even
an accelerated rate, as prevailing through the later
stages of the expedition. But it seemed, on the contrary,
most reasonable to calculate upon a continual decre-
ment in the rate of motion according to the increasing
distance from the headquarters of the pursuing enemy

This calculation, however, was defeated by the extraordinary circumstance that the Russian armies did not begin to close in very fiercely upon the Kalmucks until after they had accomplished a distance of full 2000 miles: 1000 miles farther on the assaults became even more tumultuous and murderous: and already the great shadows of the Chinese Wall were dimly descried when the frenzy and *acharnement* of the pursuers, and the bloody desperation of the miserable fugitives, had reached its uttermost extremity. Let us briefly rehearse the main stages of the misery, and trace the ascending steps of the tragedy, according to the great divisions of the route marked out by the central rivers of Asia.

The first stage, we have already said, was from the Volga to the Jaik; the distance about 300 miles; the time allowed seven days. For the first week, therefore, the rate of marching averaged about 43 English miles a-day. The weather was cold, but bracing; and, at a more moderate pace, this part of the journey might have been accomplished without much distress by a people as hardy as the Kalmucks: as it was, the cattle suffered greatly from over-driving; milk began to fail even for the children; the sheep perished by wholesale; and the children themselves were saved only by the innumerable camels.

The Cossacks, who dwelt upon the banks of the Jaik, were the first among the subjects of Russia to come into collision with the Kalmucks. Great was their surprise at the suddenness of the irruption, and great also their consternation; for, according to their settled custom, by far the greater part of their number was absent during the winter months at the fisheries upon the Caspian. Some who were liable to surprise at the most exposed points fled in crowds to the fortress of Koulagina, which was immediately invested and summoned

by Oubacha. He had, however, in his train only a few
light pieces of artillery; and the Russian commandant
at Koulagina, being aware of the hurried circumstances in which the Khan was placed, and that he
stood upon the very edge, as it were, of a renewed
flight, felt encouraged by these considerations to a
more obstinate resistance than might else have been
advisable, with an enemy so little disposed to observe
the usages of civilized warfare. The period of his anxiety was not long: on the fifth day of the siege he
descried from the walls a succession of Tartar couriers,
mounted upon fleet Bactrian camels, crossing the vast
plains around the fortress at a furious pace, and riding
into the Kalmuck encampment at various points. Great
agitation appeared immediately to follow: orders were
soon after dispatched in all directions: and it became
speedily known that upon a distant flank of the Kalmuck movement a bloody and exterminating battle
had been fought the day before, in which one entire
tribe of the Khan's dependants, numbering not less
than 9000 fighting men, had perished to the last man.
This was the *ouloss*, or clan, called Feka-Zechorr, between whom and the Cossacks there was a feud of ancient standing. In selecting, therefore, the points of
attack, on occasion of the present hasty inroad, the
Cossack chiefs were naturally eager so to direct their
efforts as to combine with the service of the Empress
some gratification to their own party hatreds: more
especially as the present was likely to be their final
opportunity for revenge, if the Kalmuck evasion
should prosper. Having, therefore, concentrated as
large a body of Cossack cavalry as circumstances allowed, they attacked the hostile *ouloss* with a precipitation which denied to it all means for communicating
with Oubacha; for the necessity of commanding an

ample range of pasturage, to meet the necessities of their vast flocks and herds, had separated this *ouloss* from the Khan's head-quarters by an interval of 80 miles; and thus it was, and not from oversight, that it came to be thrown entirely upon its own resources. These had proved insufficient: retreat, from the exhausted state of their horses and camels, no less than from the prodigious encumbrances of their live stock, was absolutely out of the question: quarter was disdained on the one side, and would not have been granted on the other: and thus it had happened that the setting sun of that one day (the thirteenth from the first opening of the revolt) threw his parting rays upon the final agonies of an ancient *ouloss*, stretched upon a bloody field, who on that day's dawning had held and styled themselves an independent nation.

Universal consternation was diffused through the wide borders of the Khan's encampment by this disastrous intelligence; not so much on account of the numbers slain, or the total extinction of a powerful ally, as because the position of the Cossack force was likely to put to hazard the future advances of the Kalmucks, or at least to retard and hold them in check until the heavier columns of the Russian army should arrive upon their flanks. The siege of Koulagina was instantly raised; and that signal, so fatal to the happiness of the women and their children, once again resounded through the tents—the signal for flight, and this time for a flight more rapid than ever. About 150 miles ahead of their present position, there arose a tract of hilly country, forming a sort of margin to the vast sea-like expanse of champaign savannahs, steppes, and occasionally of sandy deserts, which stretched away on each side of this margin both eastwards and westwards. Pretty nearly in the centre of this hilly range lay a narrow defile, through which passed the nearest and the most practicable route to the river Torgau (the farther bank of which river offered the next great station of security for a general halt). It was the more essential to gain this pass before the Cossacks, inasmuch as not only would the delay in forcing the pass give time to the Russian pursuing columns for combining their attacks, and for bringing up their artillery, but also because (even if all enemies in pursuit were thrown out of the question) it was held by those best acquainted with the difficult and obscure geography of these pathless steppes—that the loss of this one narrow strait amongst the hills would have the effect of throwing them (as their only alternative in a case where so wide a sweep of pasturage was required) upon a circuit of at least 500 miles extra; besides that, after all, this circuitous route would carry them to the Torgau at a point ill fitted for the passage of their heavy baggage. The defile in the hills, therefore, it was resolved to gain; and yet, unless they moved upon it with the velocity of light cavalry, there was little chance but it would be found preoccupied by the Cossacks. They also, it is true, had suffered greatly in the bloody action with the defeated *ouloss;* but the excitement of victory, and the intense sympathy with their unexampled triumph, had again swelled their ranks, and would probably act with the force of a vortex to draw in their simple countrymen from the Caspian. The question, therefore, of pre-occupation was reduced to a race. The Cossacks were marching upon an oblique line not above 50 miles longer than that which led to the same point from the Kalmuck head-quarters before Koulagina; and therefore, without the most furious haste on the part of the Kalmucks, there was not a chance for them, burdened and "trashed" [1] as they were, to anticipate so agile a light cavalry as Cossacks in seizing this important pass.

Dreadful were the feelings of the poor women on hearing this exposition of the case. For they easily understood that too capital an interest (the *summa rerum*) was now at stake, to allow of any regard to minor interests, or what would be considered such in their present circumstances. The dreadful week already passed— their inauguration in misery—was yet fresh in their remembrance. The scars of suffering were impressed not only upon their memories, but upon their very persons and the persons of their children. And they knew that, where no speed had much chance of meeting the cravings of the chieftains, no test would be accepted, short of absolute exhaustion, that as much had been accomplished as could have been accomplished. Weseloff, the Russian captive, has recorded the silent wretchedness with which the women and elder boys assisted in drawing the tent-ropes. On the 5th of January all had been animation, and the joyousness of indefinite expectation; now, on the contrary, a brief but bitter experience had taught them to take an amended calculation of what it was that lay before them.

One whole day and far into the succeeding night had the renewed flight continued; the sufferings had been greater than before; for the cold had been more intense; and many perished out of the living creatures through every class, except only the camels—whose powers of endurance seemed equally adapted to cold

---

[1] *"Trashed":* This is an expressive word used by Beaumont and Fletcher in their *Bonduca,* &c., to describe the case of a person retarded and embarrassed in flight, or in pursuit, by some encumbrance. whether thing or person, too valuable to be left behind.

and to heat. The second morning, however, brought
an alleviation to the distress. Snow had begun to fall,
and, though not deep at present, it was easily foreseen
that it soon would be so; and that, as a halt would in
that case become unavoidable, no plan could be better
than that of staying where they were; especially as
the same cause would check the advance of the Cossacks. Here then was the last interval of comfort which
gleamed upon the unhappy nation during their whole
migration. For ten days the snow continued to fall
with little intermission. At the end of that time keen,
bright, frosty weather succeeded; the drifting had
ceased; in three days the smooth expanse became firm
enough to support the treading of the camels; and the
flight was recommenced. But during the halt much
domestic comfort had been enjoyed; and for the last
time universal plenty. The cows and oxen had perished
in such vast numbers on the previous marches that an
order was now issued to turn what remained to account
by slaughtering the whole, and salting whatever part
should be found to exceed the immediate consumption.
This measure led to a scene of general banqueting and
even of festivity amongst all who were not incapacitated for joyous emotions by distress of mind, by grief
for the unhappy experience of the few last days, and
by anxiety for the too gloomy future. Seventy thousand persons of all ages had already perished, exclusively of the many thousand allies who had ben cut
down by the Cossack sabre. And the losses in reversion
were likely to be many more. For rumours began now
to arrive from all quarters, by the mounted couriers
whom the Khan had dispatched to the rear and to each
flank as well as in advance, that large masses of the
imperial troops were converging from all parts of Central Asia to the fords of the river Torgau, as the most
convenient point for intercepting the flying tribes; and

it was by this time well known that a powerful division was close in their rear, and was retarded only by the numerous artillery which had been judged necessary to support their operations. New motives were thus daily arising for quickening the motions of the wretched Kalmucks, and for exhausting those who were already but too much exhausted.

It was not until the second day of February that the Khan's advanced guard came in sight of Ouchim, the defile among the hills of Mougaldchares, in which they anticipated so bloody an opposition from the Cossacks. A pretty large body of these light cavalry had, in fact, preoccupied the pass by some hours; but the Khan, having two great advantages—namely, a strong body of infantry, who had been conveyed by sections of five on about 200 camels, and some pieces of light artillery which he had not yet been forced to abandon—soon began to make a serious impression upon this unsupported detachment; and they would probably at any rate have retired; but at the very moment when they were making some dispositions in that view Zebek-Dorchi appeared upon the rear with a body of trained riflemen. These men had contrived to crawl unobserved over the cliffs which skirted the ravine, availing themselves of the dry beds of the summer torrents, and other inequalities of the ground, to conceal their movement. Disorder and trepidation ensued instantly in the Cossack files; the Khan, who had been waiting with the *élite* of his heavy cavalry, charged furiously upon them; total overthrow followed to the Cossacks, and a slaughter such as in some measure avenged the recent bloody extermination of their allies, the ancient *ouloss* of Feka-Zechorr. The slight horses of the Cossacks were unable to support the weight of heavy Polish dragoons and a body of trained *cameleers* (that is, cuirassiers mounted on camels) ; hardy they were, but not strong, nor a match for their antagonists in weight; and their extraordinary efforts through the last few days to gain their present position had greatly diminished their powers for effecting an escape. Very few, in fact, *did* escape; and the bloody day at Ouchim became as memorable amongst the Cossacks as that which, about twenty days before, had signalized the complete annihilation of the Feka-Zechorr.

The road was now open to the river Irgitch, and as yet even far beyond it to the Torgau; but how long this state of things would continue was every day more doubtful. Certain intelligence was now received that a large Russian army, well appointed in every arm, was advancing upon the Torgau, under the command of General Traubenberg. This officer was to be joined on his route by ten thousand Bashkirs, and pretty nearly the same amount of Kirghises—both hereditary enemies of the Kalmucks, both exasperated to a point of madness by the bloody trophies which Oubacha and Momotbacha had, in late years, won from such of their compatriots as served under the Sultan. The Czarina's yoke these wild nations bore with submissive patience, but not the hands by which it had been imposed; and, accordingly, catching with eagerness at the present occasion offered to their vengeance, they sent an assurance to the Czarina of their perfect obedience to her commands, and at the same time a message significantly declaring in what spirit they meant to execute them, viz. "that they would not trouble her Majesty with prisoners."

Here then arose, as before with the Cossacks, a race for the Kalmucks with the regular armies of Russia, and concurrently with nations as fierce and semi-humanized as themselves. The forces, and more especially the artillery, of Russia were far too overwhelm-

ing to bear the thought of a regular opposition in
pitched battles, even with a less dilapidated state of
their resources than they could reasonably expect at
the period of their arrival on the Torgau. In their
speed lay their only hope—in strength of foot, as before, and not in strength of arm. Onward, therefore,
the Kalmucks pressed, marking the lines of their wide-
extending march over the sad solitudes of the steppes
by a never-ending chain of corpses. The old and the
young, the sick man on his couch, the mother with her
baby—all were dropping fast. Such sights as these,
with the many rueful aggravations incident to the
helpless condition of infancy—of disease and of female
weakness abandoned to the wolves amidst a howling
wilderness, continued to track their course through a
space of full two thousand miles; for so much, at the
least, it was likely to prove, including the circuits to
which they were often compelled by rivers or hostile
tribes, from the point of starting on the Volga, until
they could reach their destined halting ground on the
east bank of the Torgau. For the first seven weeks of
this march their sufferings had been embittered by the
excessive severity of the cold; and every night—so
long as wood was to be had for fires, either from the
lading of the camels, or from the desperate sacrifice of
their baggage-waggons, or (as occasionally happened)
from the forests which skirted the banks of the many
rivers which crossed their path—no spectacle was more
frequent than that of a circle, composed of men, wom-
en, and children, gathered by hundreds round a central
fire, all dead and stiff at the return of morning light.
Myriads were left behind from pure exhaustion, of
whom none had a chance, under the combined evils
which beset them, of surviving through the next
twenty-four hours. Frost, however, and snow at length
ceased to persecute; the vast extent of the march at

length brought them into more genial latitudes, and the unusual duration of the march was gradually bringing them into more genial seasons of the year. Two thousand miles had at last been traversed; February, March, April, were gone; the balmy month of May had opened; vernal sights and sounds came from every side to comfort the heart-weary travellers; and at last, in the latter end of May, crossing the Torgau, they took up a position where they hoped to find liberty to repose themselves for many weeks in comfort as well as in security, and to draw such supplies from the fertile neighbourhood as might restore their shattered forces to a condition for executing, with less of wreck and ruin, the large remainder of the journey.

Yes; it was true that two thousand miles of wandering had been completed, but in a period of nearly five months, and with the terrific sacrifice of at least two hundred and fifty thousand souls, to say nothing of herds and flocks past all reckoning. These had all perished: ox, cow, horse, mule, ass, sheep, or goat, not one survived—only the camels. These arid and adust creatures, looking like the mummies of some antediluvian animals, without the affections or sensibilities of flesh and blood—these only still erected their speaking eyes to the eastern heavens, and had to all appearance come out from this long tempest of trial unscathed and hardly diminished. The Khan, knowing how much he was individually answerable for the misery which had been sustained, must have wept tears even more bitter than those of Xerxes when he threw his eyes over the myriads whom he had assembled: for the tears of Xerxes were unmingled with remorse. Whatever amends were in his power the Khan resolved to make, by sacrifices to the general good of all personal regards; and, accordingly, even at this point of their advance, he once more deliberately brought under review the whole question of the revolt. The question was formally debated before the Council whether, even at this point, they should untread their steps, and, throwing themselves upon the Czarina's mercy, return to their old allegiance. In that case, Oubacha professed himself willing to become the scapegoat for the general transgression. This, he argued, was no fantastic scheme, but even easy of accomplishment; for the unlimited and sacred power of the Khan, so well known to the Empress, made it absolutely iniquitous to attribute any separate responsibility to the people —upon the Khan rested the guilt, upon the Khan would descend the imperial vengeance. This proposal was applauded for its generosity, but was energetically opposed by Zebek-Dorchi. Were they to lose the whole journey of two thousand miles? Was their misery to perish without fruit? True it was that they had yet reached only the half-way house; but, in that respect, the motives were evenly balanced for retreat or for advance. Either way they would have pretty nearly the same distance to traverse, but with this difference —that, forwards, their route lay through lands comparatively fertile; backwards, through a blasted wilderness, rich only in memorials of their sorrow, and hideous to Kalmuck eyes by the trophies of their calamity. Besides, though the Empress might accept an excuse for the past, would she the less forbear to suspect for the future? The Czarina's *pardon* they might obtain, but could they ever hope to recover her *confidence?* Doubtless there would now be a standing presumption against them, an immortal ground of jealousy; and a jealous government would be but another name for a harsh one. Finally, whatever motives there ever had been for the revolt surely remained unimpaired by anything that had occurred. In reality, the revolt was, after all, no revolt, but (strictly speaking) a return to their old allegiance; since, not above one hundred and fifty years ago (viz. in the year 1616), their ancestors had revolted from the Emperor of China. They had now tried both governments; and for them China was the land of promise, and Russia the house of bondage.

Spite, however, of all that Zebek could say or do, the yearning of the people was strongly in behalf of the Khan's proposal; the pardon of their prince, they persuaded themselves, would be readily conceded by the Empress: and there is little doubt that they would at this time have thrown themselves gladly upon the imperial mercy; when suddenly all was defeated by the arrival of two envoys from Traubenberg. This general had reached the fortress of Orsk, after a very painful march, on the 12th of April; thence he set forwards towards Oriemburg; which he reached upon the 1st of June, having been joined on his route at various times during the month of May by the Kirghises and a corps of ten thousand Bashkirs. From Oriemburg he sent forward his official offers to the Khan, which were harsh and peremptory, holding out no specific stipulations as to pardon or impunity, and exacting unconditional submission as the preliminary price of any cessation from military operations. The personal character of Traubenberg, which was anything but energetic, and the condition of his army, disorganized in a great measure by the length and severity of the march, made it probable that, with a little time for negotiation, a more conciliatory tone would have been assumed. But, unhappily for all parties, sinister events occurred in the meantime, such as effectually put an end to every hope of the kind.

The two envoys sent forward by Traubenberg had reported to this officer that a distance of only ten days' march lay betwen his own head-quarters and those of the Khan. Upon this fact transpiring, the Kirghises, by their prince Nourali, and the Bashkirs, entreated the Russian general to advance without delay. Once having placed his cannon in position, so as to command the Kalmuck camp, the fate of the rebel Khan and his people would be in his own hands: and they would themselves form his advanced guard. Traubenberg, however (*why* has not been certainly explained), refused to march, grounding his refusal upon the condition of his army, and their absoute need of refreshment. Long and fierce was the altercation; but at length, seeing no chance of prevailing, and dreading above all other events the escape of their detested enemy, the ferocious Bashkirs went off in a body by forced marches. In six days they reached the Torgau, crossed by swimming their horses, and fell upon the Kalmucks, who were dispersed for many a league in search of food or provender for their camels. The first day's action was one vast succession of independent skirmishes, diffused over a field of thirty to forty miles in extent; one party often breaking up into three or four, and again (according to the accidents of ground) three or four blending into one; flight and pursuit, rescue and total overthrow, going on simultaneously, under all varieties of form, in all quarters of the plain. The Bashkirs had found themselves obliged, by the scattered state of the Kalmucks, to split up into innumerable sections; and thus, for some hours, it had been impossible for the most practised eye to collect the general tendency of the day's fortune. Both the Khan and Zebek-Dorchi were at one moment made prisoners, and more than once in imminent danger of being cut down; but at length Zebek succeeded in rallying a strong column of infantry, which, with the support of the camel-corps on each flank, compelled the Bashkirs to retreat. Clouds, however, of these wild

cavalry continued to arrive through the next two days
and nights, followed or accompanied by the Kirghises.
These being viewed as the advanced parties of Traubenberg's army, the Kalmuck chieftains saw no hope
of safety but in flight; and in this way it happened that
a retreat, which had so recently been brought to a
pause, was resumed at the very moment when the unhappy fugitives were anticipating a deep repose without further molestation the whole summer through.

* * *

It would be useless to pursue circumstantially
through the whole two thousand miles of suffering
which remained; for the character of that suffering
was even more monotonous than on the former half of
the flight, and also more severe. Its main elements were
excessive heat, with the accompaniments of famine and
thirst, but aggravated at every step by the murderous
attacks of their cruel enemies the Bashkirs and the
Kirghises.

These people, "more fell than anguish, hunger, or
the sea," stuck to the unhappy Kalmucks like a swarm
of enraged hornets. And very often, whilst *they* were
attacking them in the rear, their advanced parties and
flanks were attacked with almost equal fury by the
people of the country which they were traversing; and
with good reason, since the law of self-preservation
had now obliged the fugitive Tartars to plunder provisions, and to forage wherever they passed. In this
respect their condition was a constant oscillation of
wretchedness; for sometimes, pressed by grinding famine, they took a circuit of perhaps a hundred miles, in
order to strike into a land rich in the comforts of life;
but in such a land they were sure to find a crowded
population, of which every arm was raised in unre-

lenting hostility, with all the advantages of local
knowledge, and with constant preoccupation of all the
defensible positions, mountain passes, or bridges.
Sometimes, again, wearied out with this mode of suffering, they took a circuit of perhaps a hundred miles,
in order to strike into a land with few or no inhabitants. But in such a land they were sure to meet absolute starvation. Then, again, whether with or without
this plague of starvation, whether with or without this
plague of hostility in front, whatever might be the
"fierce varieties" of their misery in this respect, no
rest ever came to their unhappy rear; *post equitem
sedet atra cura;* it was a torment like the undying worm
of conscience. And, upon the whole, it presented a
spectacle altogether unprecedented in the history of
mankind. Private and personal malignity is not unfrequently immortal; but rare indeed is it to find the same
pertinacity of malice in a nation. And what embittered the interest was that the malice was reciprocal.
Thus far the parties met upon equal terms; but that
equality only sharpened the sense of their dire inequality as to other circumstances. The Bashkirs were
ready to fight "from morn to dewy eve." The Kalmucks, on the contrary, were always obliged to run.
Was it *from* their enemies as creatures whom they
feared? No; but *towards* their friends—towards that
final haven of China—as what was hourly implored
by the prayers of their wives, and the tears of their
children. But, though they fled unwillingly, too often
they fled in vain—being unwillingly recalled. There
lay the torment. Every day the Bashkirs fell upon
them; every day the same unprofitable battle was renewed; as a matter of course, the Kalmucks recalled
part of their advanced guard to fight them; every day
the battle raged for hours, and uniformly with the
same result. For no sooner did the Bashkirs find them-

selves too heavily pressed, and that the Kalmuck march
had been retarded by some hours, than they retired
into the boundless deserts, where all pursuit was hopeless. But, if the Kalmucks resolved to press forward,
regardless of their enemies, in that case their attacks
became so fierce and overwhelming that the general
safety seemed likely to be brought into question; nor
could any effectual remedy be applied to the case, even
for each separate day, except by a most embarrassing
halt, and by countermarches, that, to men in their circumstances, were almost worse than death. It will not
be surprising that the irritation of such a systematic
persecution, superadded to a previous and hereditary
hatred, and accompanied by the stinging consciousness
of utter impotence as regarded all effectual vengeance,
should gradually have inflamed the Kalmuck animos-
ity into the wildest expression of downright madness
and frenzy. Indeed, long before the frontiers of China
were approached, the hostility of both sides had assumed the appearance much more of a warfare
amongst wild beasts than amongst creatures acknowledging the restraints of reason or the claims of a common nature. The spectacle became too atrocious; it
was that of a host of lunatics pursued by a host of
fiends.

* * *

On a fine morning in early autumn of the year
1771, Kien Long, the Emperor of China, was pursuing
his amusements in a wild frontier district lying on the
outside of the Great Wall. For many hundred square
leagues the country was desolate of inhabitants, but
rich in woods of ancient growth, and overrun with
game of every description. In a central spot of this
solitary region the Emperor had built a gorgeous hunting lodge, to which he resorted annually for recreation

and relief from the cares of government. Led onwards
in pursuit of game, he had rambled to a distance of
200 miles or more from this lodge, followed at a little
distance by a sufficient military escort, and every night
pitching his tent in a different situation, until at
length he had arrived on the very margin of the vast
central deserts of Asia. Here he was standing by accident at an opening of his pavilion, enjoying the morning sunshine, when suddenly to the westwards there
arose a vast cloudy vapour, which by degrees expanded,
mounted, and seemed to be slowly diffusing itself over
the whole face of the heavens. By and by this vast sheet
of mist began to thicken towards the horizon, and to
roll forward in billowy volumes. The Emperor's suite
assembled from all quarters. The silver trumpets were
sounded in the rear, and from all the glades and forest
avenues began to trot forward towards the pavilion
the yagers—half cavalry, half huntsmen—who composed the imperial escort. Conjecture was on the stretch
to divine the cause of this phenomenon, and the interest continually increased, in proportion as simple curiosity gradually deepened into the anxiety of uncertain
danger. At first it had been imagined that some vast
troops of deer, or other wild animals of the chase, had
been disturbed in their forest haunts by the Emperor's
movements, or possibly by wild beasts prowling for
prey, and might be fetching a compass by way of re-
entering the forest grounds at some remoter points
secure from molestation. But this conjecture was dissipated by the slow increase of the cloud, and the
steadiness of its motion. In the course of two hours
the vast phenomenon had advanced to a point which
was judged to be within five miles of the spectators,
though all calculations of distance were difficult, and
often fallacious, when applied to the endless expanses
of the Tartar deserts. Through the next hour, during

which the gentle morning breeze had a little fresh-
ened, the dusty vapour had developed itself far and
wide into the appearance of huge aerial draperies,
hanging in mighty volumes from the sky to the earth;
and at particular points, where the eddies of the breeze
acted upon the pendulous skirts of these aerial curtains, rents were perceived, sometimes taking the form
of regular arches, portals, and windows, through which
began dimly to gleam the heads of camels "indorsed" [1]
with human beings—and at intervals the moving of
men and horses in tumultuous array—and then
through other openings or vistas at far distant points
the flashing of polished arms. But sometimes, as the
wind slackened or died away, all those openings, of
whatever form, in the cloudy pall would slowly close,
and for a time the whole pageant was shut up from
view; although the growing din, the clamours, shrieks,
and groans, ascending from infuriated myriads, reported, in a language not to be misunderstood, what
was going on behind the cloudy screen.

It was in fact the Kalmuck host, now in the last extremities of their exhaustion, and very fast approaching to that final stage of privation and killing misery,
beyond which few or none could have lived, but also,
happily for themselves, fast approaching (in a literal
sense) that final stage of their long pilgrimage at
which they would meet hospitality on a scale of royal
magnificence, and full protection from their enemies.
These enemies, however, as yet, were still hanging on
their rear as fiercely as ever, though this day was destined to be the last of their hideous persecution. The
Khan had, in fact, sent forward couriers with all the
requisite statements and petitions, addressed to the Emperor of China. These had been duly received, and

[1] *Camels "indorsed"*: "And elephants indorsed with towers."—Milton in *Paradise Regained* [iii. 329].

preparations made in consequence to welcome the Kalmucks with the most paternal benevolence. But, as these couriers had been dispatched from the Torgau at the moment of arrival thither, and before the advance of Traubenberg had made it necessary for the Khan to order a hasty renewal of the flight, the Emperor had not looked for their arrival on his frontiers until full three months after the present time. The Khan had indeed expressly notified his intention to pass the summer heats on the banks of the Torgau, and to recommence his retreat about the beginning of September. The subsequent change of plan, being unknown to Kien Long, left him for some time in doubt as to the true interpretation to be put upon this mighty apparition in the desert; but at length the savage clamours of hostile fury, and the clangour of weapons, unveiled to the Emperor the true nature of those unexpected calamities which had so prematurely precipitated the Kalmuck measures.

Apprehending the real state of affairs, the Emperor instantly perceived that the first act of his fatherly care for these erring children (as he esteemed them), now returning to their ancient obedience, must be— to deliver them from their pursuers. And this was less difficult than might have been supposed. Not many miles in the rear was a body of well-appointed cavalry, with a strong detachment of artillery, who always attended the Emperor's motions. These were hastily summoned. Meantime it occurred to the train of courtiers that some danger might arise to the Emperor's person from the proximity of a lawless enemy; and accordingly he was induced to retire a little to the rear. It soon appeared, however, to those who watched the vapoury shroud in the desert, that its motion was not such as would argue the direction of the march to be exactly upon the pavilion, but rather in a diagonal line, making an angle of full 45 degrees with that line in which the imperial *cortège* had been standing, and therefore with a distance continually increasing. Those who knew the country judged that the Kalmucks were making for a large fresh-water lake about seven or eight miles distant. They were right; and to that point the imperial cavalry was ordered up; and it was precisely in that spot, and about three hours after, and at noon-day on the 8th of September, that the great exodus of the Kalmuck Tartars was brought to a final close, and with a scene of such memorable and hellish fury as formed an appropriate winding up to an expedition in all its parts and details so awfully disastrous. The Emperor was not personally present, or at least he saw whatever he *did* see from too great a distance to discriminate its individual features; but he records in his written memorial the report made to him of this scene by some of his own officers.

The lake of Tengis, near the dreadful desert of Kobi, lay in a hollow amongst hills of a moderate height, ranging generally from two to three thousand feet high. About eleven o'clock in the forenoon, the Chinese cavalry reached the summit of a road which led through a cradle-like dip in the mountains right down upon the margin of the lake. From this pass, elevated about two thousand feet above the level of the water, they continued to descend, by a very winding and difficult road, for an hour and a half; and during the whole of this descent they were compelled to be inactive spectators of the fiendish spectacle below. The Kalmucks, reduced by this time from about six hundred thousand souls to two hundred and sixty thousand, and after enduring for so long a time the miseries I have previously described—outrageous heat, famine, and the destroying scimitar of the Kirghises and the Bashkirs—had for the last ten days been trav-

ersing a hideous desert, where no vestiges were seen
of vegetation, and no drop of water could be found.
Camels and men were already so overladen that it was
a mere impossibility that they should carry a tolerable
sufficiency for the passage of this frightful wilderness.
On the eighth day, the wretched daily allowance,
which had been continually diminishing, failed entirely; and thus, for two days of insupportable fatigue,
the horrors of thirst had been carried to the fiercest
extremity. Upon this last morning, at the sight of the
hills and the forest scenery, which announced to those
who acted as guides the neighbourhood of the lake of
Tengis, all the people rushed along with maddening
eagerness to the anticipated solace. The day grew hotter and hotter, the people more and more exhausted,
and gradually, in the general rush forwards to the
lake, all discipline and command were lost—all attempts to preserve a rearguard were neglected—the
wild Bashkirs rode in amongst the encumbered people,
and slaughtered them by wholesale, and almost without resistance. Screams and tumultuous shouts proclaimed the progress of the massacre; but none heeded
—none halted; all alike, pauper or noble, continued to
rush on with maniacal haste to the waters—all with
faces blackened by the heat preying upon the liver,
and with tongue drooping from the mouth. The cruel
Bashkir was affected by the same misery, and manifested the same symptoms of his misery as the wretched
Kalmuck; the murderer was oftentimes in the same
frantic misery as his murdered victim—many indeed
(an ordinary effect of thirst) in both nations had become lunatic, and in this state, whilst mere multitude
and condensation of bodies alone opposed any check
to the destroying scimitar and the trampling hoof, the
lake was reached; and into that the whole vast body of
enemies together rushed, and together continued to

rush, forgetful of all things at that moment but of one
almighty instinct. This absorption of the thoughts in
one maddening appetite lasted for a single half-hour;
but in the next arose the final scene of parting vengeance. Far and wide the waters of the solitary lake
were instantly dyed red with blood and gore: here rode
a party of savage Bashkirs, hewing off heads as fast as
the swathes fall before the mower's scythe; there stood
unarmed Kalmucks in a death-grapple with their detested foes, both up to the middle in water, and oftentimes both sinking together below the surface, from
weakness or from struggles, and perishing in each
other's arms. Did the Bashkirs at any point collect into
a cluster for the sake of giving impetus to the assault?
Thither were the camels driven in fiercely by those
who rode them, generally women or boys; and even
these quiet creatures were forced into a share in this
carnival of murder, by trampling down as many as
they could strike prostrate with the lash of their fore-
legs. Every moment the water grew more polluted; and
yet every moment fresh myriads came up to the lake
and rushed in, not able to resist their frantic thirst,
and swallowing large draughts of water, visibly con-
taminated with the blood of their slaughtered compatriots. Wheresoever the lake was shallow enough to
allow of men raising their heads above the water, there,
for scores of acres, were to be seen all forms of ghastly
fear, of agonizing struggle, of spasm, of death, and the
fear of death—revenge, and the lunacy of revenge—
until the neutral spectators, of whom there were not a
few, now descending the eastern side of the lake, at
length averted their eyes in horror. This horror, which
seemed incapable of further addition, was, however,
increased by an unexpected incident. The Bashkirs,
beginning to perceive here and there the approach of
the Chinese cavalry, felt it prudent—wheresoever they

were sufficiently at leisure from the passions of the murderous scene—to gather into bodies. This was noticed by the governor of a small Chinese fort, built upon an eminence above the lake; and immediately he threw in a broadside, which spread havoc amongst the Bashkir tribe. As often as the Bashkirs collected into "*globes*" and "*turms*," as their only means of meeting the long lines of descending Chinese cavalry—so often did the Chinese governor of the fort pour in his exterminating broadside; until at length the lake, at its lower end, became one vast seething cauldron of human bloodshed and carnage. The Chinese cavalry had reached the foot of the hills: the Bashkirs, attentive to *their* movements, had formed; skirmishes had been fought: and, with a quick sense that the contest was henceforwards rapidly becoming hopeless, the Bashkirs and Kirghises began to retire. The pursuit was not as vigorous as the Kalmuck hatred would have desired. But, at the same time, the very gloomiest hatred could not but find, in their own dreadful experience of the Asiatic deserts, and in the certainty that these wretched Bashkirs had to repeat that same experience a second time, for thousands of miles, as the price exacted by a retributory Providence for their vindictive cruelty—not the very gloomiest of the Kalmucks, or the least reflecting, but found in all this a retaliatory chastisement more complete and absolute than any which their swords and lances could have obtained, or human vengeance have devised.

* * *

Here ends the tale of the Kalmuck wanderings in the Desert; for any subsequent marches which awaited them were neither long nor painful. Every possible alleviation and refreshment for their exhausted bodies had been already provided by Kien Long with the most princely munificence; and lands of great fertility were immediately assigned to them in ample extent along the river Ily, not very far from the point at which they had first emerged from the wilderness of Kobi. Thus, after their memorable year of misery, the Kalmucks were replaced in territorial possessions, and in comfort equal perhaps, or even superior, to that which they had enjoyed in Russia, and with superior political advantages.

One word remains to be said upon the *personal* interests concerned in this great drama. The catastrophe in this respect was remarkable and complete. The Emperor informed himself accurately of all the particulars connected with the transaction—of all the rights and claims put forward—and of the way in which they would severally affect the interests of the Kalmuck people. The consequence was that he adopted the cause of Oubacha, and repressed the pretensions of Zebek-Dorchi, who, on his part, so deeply resented this discountenance to his ambitious projects that, in conjunction with other chiefs, he had the presumption even to weave nets of treason against the Emperor himself. Finally, Zebek-Dorchi was invited to the imperial lodge, together with all his accomplices; and, under the skilful management of the Chinese nobles in the Emperor's establishment, the murderous artifices of these Tartar chieftains were made to recoil upon themselves, and the whole of them perished by assassination at a great imperial banquet. For the Chinese morality is exactly of that kind which approves in everything the *lex talionis:*

> *Lex nec justior ulla est (as* they *think)*
> *Quam necis artifices arte perire sua.*

So perished Zebek-Dorchi, the author and originator of the great Tartar exodus. Oubacha, meantime, and his people, were gradually recovering from the effects of their misery, and repairing their losses. Peace and prosperity, under the gentle rule of a fatherly lord paramount, redawned upon the tribes: their household *lares*, after so harsh a translation to distant climes, found again a happy reinstatement in what had in fact been their primitive abodes: they found themselves settled in quiet sylvan scenes, rich in all the luxuries of life, and endowed with the perfect loveliness of Arcadian beauty. But from the hills of this favoured land, and even from the level grounds as they approached its western border, they still look out upon that fearful wilderness which once beheld a nation in agony—the utter extirpation of nearly half a million from amongst its numbers, and, for the remainder, a storm of misery so fierce that in the end (as happened also at Athens during the Peloponnesian War from a different form of misery) very many lost their memory; all records of their past life were wiped out as with a sponge— utterly erased and cancelled: and many others lost their reason; some in a gentle form of pensive melancholy, some in a more restless form of feverish delirium and nervous agitation, and others in the fixed forms of tempestuous mania, raving frenzy, or moping idiocy. Two great commemorative monuments arose in after years to mark the depth and permanence of the awe—the sacred and reverential grief with which all persons looked back upon the dread calamities attached to the year of the tiger—all who had either personally shared in those calamities, and had themselves drunk from that cup of sorrow, or who had effectually been made witnesses to their results and associated with their relief: two great monuments; one embodied in the religious solemnity, enjoined by the

Dalai Lama, called in the Tartar language a *Roman-ang*—that is, a national commemoration, with music the most rich and solemn, of all the souls who departed to the rest of Paradise from the afflictions of the Desert (this took place about six years after the arrival in China) ; secondly, another, more durable and more commensurate to the scale of the calamity and to the grandeur of this national exodus, in the mighty columns of granite and brass erected by the Emperor Kien Long near the banks of the Ily. These columns stand upon the very margin of the *steppes;* and they bear a short but emphatic inscription to the following effect:

By the Will of God,
Here, upon the Brink of these Deserts,
Which from this Point begin and stretch away
Pathless, treeless, waterless,
For thousands of miles, and along the margins of
many mighty Nations,
Rested from their labours and from great afflictions,
Under the shadow of the Chinese Wall,
And by the favour of KIEN LONG, *God's Lieutenant*
upon Earth,
The ancient Children of the Wilderness—the Torgote
Tartars—
Flying before the wrath of the Grecian Czar,
Wandering Sheep who had strayed away from the
Celestial Empire in the year 1616,
But are now mercifully gathered again, after infinite
sorrow,
Into the fold of their forgiving Shepherd.
Hallowed be the spot for ever,
and
Hallowed be the day—September 8, 1771!
AMEN.

A SHORT BIBLIOGRAPHY
OF WORKS PERTAINING TO
THOMAS DE QUINCEY

HORACE AINSWORTH EATON. *Thomas De Quincey*. New York and Oxford, 1936.

EDWARD SACKVILLE WEST. *Thomas De Quincey, His Life and Work*. London and New Haven, 1936.

WILLARD HALLAM BONNER. *De Quincey at Work*. Buffalo, 1936.

MALCOLM ELWIN. *Thomas De Quincey*. London, 1935.

HENRY S. SALT. *De Quincey*. London, 1904.

JAMES HOGG (Editor). *De Quincey and His Friends*. London, 1895.

DAVID MASSON. *Thomas De Quincey*. London, 1881.

A. H. JAPP (pseudonym H. A. PAGE). *Thomas De Quincey: His Life and Writings*. London, 1877.